Sixth Edition

SYLVAN BARNET
Tufts University

MORTON BERMAN
Boston University

WILLIAM BURTO
University of Lowell

HarperCollins*CollegePublishers*

Acquisitions Editor: Lisa Moore
Developmental Editor: Judith Leet
Project Coordination, Text and Cover Design: PC&F, Inc.
Cover Photo: The faithful Earl of Kent (Colin Blakely), disguised as Caius, apprehensively watches over the mad King Lear (Laurence Olivier) during the storm, in a 1983 television production of *King Lear.* Copyright © Granada Television.
Photo Researchers: Carol Parden/Rosemary Hunter
Production/Manufacturing: Michael Weinstein/Paula Keller
Compositor: PC&F, Inc.
Printer and Binder: R.R. Donnelley & Sons Company
Cover Printer: The Lehigh Press, Inc.

For permission to use copyrighted material, grateful acknowledgment is made to the copyright holders on pp. 805–806, which are hereby made part of this copyright page.

TYPES OF DRAMA: PLAYS AND ESSAYS, Sixth Edition

Library of Congress Cataloging-in-Publication Data

Types of drama : plays and essays / [compiled by] Sylvan Barnet, Morton Berman, William Burto, -- 6th ed.
p. cm.
ISBN 0-673-52181-8
1. Drama--Collections. 2. Drama--History and criticism. I. Barnet, Sylvan. II. Berman, Morton. III. Burto, William.
PN6112.T96 1992
808.2--dc20 92-9000
CIP

92 93 94 95 9 8 7 6 5 4 3 2 1

Contents

Preface

In this edition of *Types of Drama* we have added eleven plays: the anonymous *Second Shepherds' Play,* J. M. Barrie's *The Twelve-Pound Look,* Pirandello's *Six Characters in Search of an Author,* Brecht's *The Good Woman of Setzuan,* Synge's *Riders to the Sea,* O'Neill's *Desire under the Elms,* Gertrude Stein's *The Mother of Us All,* Luis Valdez's *Los Vendidos,* Wendy Wasserstein's *The Man in a Case,* Harvey Fierstein's *On Tidy Endings,* and Joyce Carol Oates's *Tone Clusters.* Two of these—the plays by Wasserstein and Valdez—are very short, and can be performed as part of a class hour. Another of these—Barrie's delightful *The Twelve-Pound Look*—is a little longer, but it is still short enough (like Susan Glaspell's *Trifles*) so that students can without a great expenditure of time stage a production in class.

For eleven of the plays we have also added material we call *Contexts.* With only two exceptions (Aristotle, whose *Poetics* we give along with Sophocles's *Oedipus the King,* and the composer Virgil Thomson, who set Stein's *The Mother of Us All* to music) the authors of the comments are the playwrights themselves, not critics. The comments range from preliminary notes, in which the authors are feeling their way, to essays, and, in the case of some contemporary authors, to interviews, in which the authors reflect upon their plays.

The book is divided into three parts. *Part One: Getting Started,* quickly introduces readers to the language of drama. It moves from an examination of a play of only a few lines to a brief discussion of "Plot, Character, Theme" and some advice on "How to Read a Play." Next, it gives two one-act plays, Susan Glaspell's *Trifles* and J. M. Barrie's comedy, *The Twelve-Pound Look,* each of which is followed by some questions that are intended to stimulate thinking about dramatic form. The section concludes with a discussion of tragedy, comedy, and tragicomedy.

Part Two: A Collection of Plays is a chronologically arranged anthology, from ancient Greek drama to modern plays. Each play is preceded by a short biographical note and an introduction. Because, as Hamlet said, "The play's the thing," we have kept our introductions short. They are not attempts to explicate the plays but they contain, we think, some useful and relevant points that will also be helpful with other plays. Thus, the commentary on *A Midsummer Night's Dream* includes a discussion of two traditions of comedy, "critical" comedy and "romantic" comedy, material that is also relevant to other plays in the book, including *The Misanthrope* and *Arms and the Man.* Similarly, the commentary on *The Glass Menagerie* goes beyond the play by discussing presentational theater, a topic relevant to almost all drama before Ibsen and to a fair amount of contemporary drama. But even those commentaries that are sharply focused on a given play do not seek to utter the last word. On the contrary, they seek to provide material that will stimulate discussion in class or that may be the topic of a writing assignment. The *Topics for Discussion and Writing* that follow each play are similarly designed. And, as we have already mentioned, eleven plays are followed by *Contexts.* One example is Arthur Miller's *Death of a Salesman,* which is accompanied by an essay by Miller ("Tragedy and the Common Man") and also by some of his remarks in an interview (here entitled "Willy Loman's Ideals"). The *illustrations* show the plays in performance; further, we have included illustrations of Greek and Elizabethan theaters in an effort to assist readers to imagine the play on an unfamiliar stage.

Part Three: Writing is devoted chiefly to writing about drama (it includes substantial advice on such matters as writing a review, finding a topic, organizing a comparison, providing documentation), but it also includes material on "Writing Drama" for classes in which students may be asked to write a scene or even a one-act play.

Two appendixes conclude the book, one an essay by Peter Arnott on "The Script and the Stage," and the other a glossary of more than two hundred dramatic terms. Though some of the definitions are brief, many are fairly long. Students and instructors have told us that the glossary can actually be read with interest, and that the definitions, far from perfunctory, are genuinely helpful.

Having briefly described the book, we want (before we turn to the pleasant job of acknowledging our debts) to offer a comment on the theater in the second half of the twentieth century. The 1950s saw the growth of the theater of the absurd; the mid 1960s in the United States saw the birth of a very different sort of drama, an affirmative drama that can be called the theater of commitment. Opposition to the war in Vietnam was one great source of commitment; a second source was the civil rights movement, which stimulated black dramatists to affirm black power. Inspired especially by the black power movement, other movements soon developed: gay theater, women's theater, Chicano theater, Asian-American theater, and Native American theater. The products of these movements are highly diverse, and it is too early to say that they constitute a substantial body of enduring works; many of the plays were frankly designed as a means of consciousness-raising. Still, one notices a new eloquence, not an attempt (necessarily doomed) to revive Shakespeare's poetry, but a prose more eloquent or more confident than, say, the language of Albee's characters. It seems clear that today's dramatists have a new faith in human beings, a faith not simply that people will endure but that they can talk meaningfully. Beckett's characters showed their strength in persistently waiting for Godot; the new theater's characters show their strength in asserting themselves, not as tragic heroes demanding that life make sense, and certainly not as comic figures making an amusing spectacle of themselves, but as men and women on the way to attaining the dignity that is rightfully theirs.

Acknowledgments

We have been fortunate in getting permission to print important modern plays and distinguished translations of older plays; we are grateful to the authors, translators, and publishers who have cooperated. In preparing the Sixth Edition, we are grateful for the help we received from: Joanne Altieri, University of Washington; David Boudreaux, Nicholls State University; Victor Cahn, Skidmore College; Douglas Cole, Northwestern University; Dorothy Cook, Central Connecticut State University; E. T. A. Davidson, State University of New York/Oneonta; Jeanne Fosket, El Paso Community College; Charlotte Goodman, Skidmore College; Virginia Hale, University of Hartford; Elsie Galbreath Haley, Metropolitan State College/Denver; Thomas Hatton, Southern Illinois University, Carbondale; JoAnn Holonbek, College of St. Catherine; Kathleen Klein, Southern Connecticut State University; Thomas Kranidas, State University of

New York/Stony Brook; Jayne Lewis, University of California at Los Angeles; Helen Lojek, Boise State University; Mary J. McCue, College of San Mateo; Don Moore, Louisiana State University; Lee Orchard, Northeast Missouri State University; Paige Price, University of Oregon; Bruce Robbins, Boise State University; Eric Rothstein, University of Wisconsin; Beverly Simpson, Ball State University; Jyotsna Singh, Southern Methodist University; Iris Smith, University of Kansas; and Charles Watson, Jr., Syracuse University.

We are also grateful to the many teachers who have given advice: Jacob H. Adler, Purdue University; Terry Browne, State University of New York, Geneseo; Leslie Phillips Butterworth, Holyoke Community College; Kenneth Campbell, Virginia Commonwealth University; Charles L. Darn, University of Pittsburgh at Johnstown; Cheryl Faraone, State University of New York, Geneseo; John C. Freeman, El Paso Community College; Catherine Gannon, California State University at San Bernardino; Russell Goldfarb, Western Michigan University; John Gronbeck-Tedesco, University of Kansas; JoAnn Holonbek, College of Saint Catherine; Richard L. Homan, Rider College; Grace McLaughlin, Portland Community College; John B. Pieters, University of Florida; George Ray, Washington and Lee University; Gail Salo, George Mason University; David K. Sauer, Spring Hill College; Myron Simon, University of California at Irvine; Keith Slocum, Montclair State College; Lucille Stelling, Normandale Community College; Edna M. Troiano, Charles County Community College; Robert L. Vales, Gannon University; and Bruce E. Woodruff, Baker University.

We also gladly acknowledge our debts to Jeanne Newlin of the Harvard Theatre Collection, and to Ren Draya, Arthur Friedman, Harry Ritchie, Laurence Senelick, Marcia Stubbs, and, at HarperCollins, Lisa Moore, Carol Parden, and Judith Leet.

We are again indebted to Virginia Creeden, who effectively handled the difficult job of obtaining permission for copyrighted material.

Sylvan Barnet
Morton Berman
William Burto

PART ONE

Getting Started

The Language of Drama

Although a play usually tells a story, "the medium of drama," as Ezra Pound observed, "is not words, but persons moving about on a stage using words." Another, even briefer, statement about the essence of drama holds that it consists of three boards, two actors, and a passion—that is, a *place* where *impersonators* engage in a *conflict.* It's not a bad idea to recall, from time to time, both of these statements when thinking about even the most sophisticated plays.

A play is written to be seen and to be heard. We go to *see* a play in a theater (*theater* is derived from a Greek word meaning "to watch"), but in the theater we also *hear* it, thus becoming an audience (*audience* is derived from a Latin word meaning "to hear".) Hamlet was speaking the ordinary language of his day when he said, "We'll hear a play tomorrow." When we read a play rather than see and hear it in a theater, we see it in the mind's eye (Hamlet's words), and we hear it in the mind's ear.

In reading a play it's not enough mentally to hear the lines. We must try to see the characters, costumed and moving within a specified setting; costumes, sets, and gestures are parts of the language of drama. When we are in the theater, our job is much easier, of course; we have only to pay attention to the performers. But when we are readers, we must do what we can to perform the play in the theater under our hat.

Let's look at a tiny example of early European drama—but first, a tiny bit of history. Although the ancient Greeks and Romans had developed drama to a high art, the early Christians opposed dramatic spectacles, partly because such spectacles included gladiatorial contests and naked dancing. After the Roman emperors made Christianity the official state religion, and after Rome was sacked by the Visigoths in 410 A.D., public acting was prohibited; and by the sixth century, drama had virtually disappeared from Europe, except for such rudimentary entertainments as puppet shows, minstrelsy, and acrobatics. Yet, amazingly, the drama was reborn within the church itself.

The New Testament reports that when women went to the tomb of the crucified Jesus in order to anoint the body, they found an angel, who told them that Jesus had risen from the tomb. Drawing on this narrative (chiefly Matthew 28.1–7 and Mark 16.1–8), the Church by the ninth century had developed an introductory text for the Mass on Easter Sunday morning, the anniversary of the Resurrection from the Dead of the Crucified Christ. The Latin words were chanted antiphonally, that is, with one voice or group of voices answering another. In translation the words go thus:

FIRST VOICE. Whom do you seek in the sepulchre?
SECOND VOICE. Jesus of Nazareth.
FIRST VOICE. He is not here; he is risen as predicted when it was prophesied that he would rise from the dead.
SECOND VOICE. Alleluia! The Lord is risen!
ALL VOICES. Come and see the place.

Now take the lines of the *First Voice,* and let them be sung by a priest representing an angel in the sepulcher—itself represented by the altar-table—and take the lines of the

Second Voice and let them be sung by three priests representing the three Marys who, according to tradition, visited the tomb in order to anoint the corpse. Exactly such a development took place in the tenth century. In a document of about 970, Ethelwold, Bishop of Winchester, England, provides dialogue and stage directions for a miniature play to be performed by priests. What follows is a translation of Ethelwold's Latin account of the work known by its first words, *Quem Quaeritis* ("Whom do you seek?").

ANONYMOUS *Quem Quaeritis*

While the third lesson is being chanted, let four brethren dress themselves. Let one of these, dressed in a white robe, enter as though to take part in the service, and let him go to the sepulcher without attracting attention and sit there quietly with a palm in his hand. While the third respond is chanted, let the remaining three follow, and let them all, dressed in copes, bearing in their hand incense containers and stepping delicately as if seeking something, approach the sepulcher.*

These things are done in imitation of the angel sitting on the tomb and the women with spices coming to anoint the body of Jesus. When, therefore, the seated one beholds the three approach him like wanderers who seek something, let him begin to sing in a sweet and moderate voice.

Whom do you seek in the sepulcher, O followers of Christ?

And when he has sung it to the end, let the three reply in unison:

Jesus of Nazareth who was crucified, O celestial one!

So he:

He is not here, He has risen as He foretold.
Go, announce that He is risen from the dead.

At the word of this bidding let those three turn to the choir and say:

Alleluia! The Lord is risen today,
The strong lion, Christ the Son of God! Unto God give thanks, eia!

This said, let the one, still sitting there and as if recalling them, say the anthem:

Come, and see the place where the Lord was laid,
Alleluia! Alleluia!

And saying this, let him rise, and lift the veil, and show them the place bare of the cross, but only the cloths laid there in which the cross was wrapped:

Go quickly, and tell the disciples that the Lord is risen.
Alleluia! Alleluia!

And when they have seen this, let them set down the incense containers which they bear in that same sepulcher, and take the cloth, and hold it up in the face of the clergy, and as if to demonstrate that the Lord has risen and is no longer wrapped therein, let them sing the anthem:

The Lord is risen from the sepulcher,
Who for us was hanged on the cross, alleluia!

and lay the cloth upon the altar. When the anthem is done, let the prior, sharing in their gladness

***copes** capelike garments

at the triumph of Our King, in that, having vanquished death, He rose again, begin the hymn "We praise you, Lord." And this begun, all the bells chime out together.

All the elements of a play are here: an **imitation** by actors (here, priests) of an **action.** By "action" we do not mean the physical movements of the characters, but a story, a happening, in this case a story of characters moving from doubt to joyful certainty. Normally the action of a play includes a conflict; here we might say that the conflict is between the uncertainty and presumably the sorrow of the women, and the knowledge and joy of the angel. We can say, too, that the angel wins the women over to his side.

The dialogue of course is essential, but notice that the imitation is aided by **scenery** ("the place bare of the cross"), **hand properties** (incense vessels, representing the spices that the women brought to the tomb, and also the angel's palm branch), **costumes** (a white garment for the priest who plays the angel, and copes—capelike garments—for the priests who play the women), and **gestures** ("stepping delicately as if seeking something"). Even **sound effects** are used: "All the bells chime out together."*

Plot, Character, Theme

Although **plot** is sometimes equated with the gist of the narrative—the story—it is sometimes reserved to denote the writer's *arrangement* of the happenings in the story. Thus, all plays about the assassination of Julius Caesar have pretty much the same story, but by beginning with a scene of workmen enjoying a holiday (and thereby introducing the motif of the fickleness of the mob), Shakespeare's *Julius Caesar* has a plot different from a play that omits such a scene.

Handbooks on the drama often suggest that a plot (arrangement of happenings) should have a **rising action,** a **climax,** and a **falling action.** This sort of plot can be diagramed as a pyramid, the tension rising through complications, or **crises,** to a **climax,** at which point the fate of the **protagonist** (chief character) is firmly established; the climax is the apex, and the tension allegedly slackens as we witness the **dénouement** (unknotting). Shakespeare sometimes used a pyramidal structure, placing his climax neatly in the middle of what seems to us to be the third of five acts.† Roughly the first half of *Julius Caesar* shows Brutus rising, reaching his height in 3.1 with the death of Caesar;

**Quem Quaeritis* is available on a videocassette, in *Early English Drama,* in the History of Drama series issued by Films for the Humanities and Sciences, Inc., Box 2053, Princeton, N.J. (telephone 1–800–257–5126)

†An **act** is a main division in a drama or opera. Act divisions probably stem from Roman theory and derive ultimately from the Greek practice of separating episodes in a play by choral interludes, but Greek (and probably Roman) plays were performed without interruption, for the choral interludes were part of the plays themselves. Elizabethan plays, too, may have been performed without breaks; the division of Elizabethan plays into five acts is usually the work of editors rather than of authors. Frequently an act division today (commonly indicated by lowering the curtain and turning up the houselights) denotes change in locale and lapse of time. A **scene** is a smaller unit, either (1) a division with no change of locale or abrupt shift of time, or (2) a division consisting of an actor or group of actors on the stage; according to the second definition, the departure or entrance of an actor changes the composition of the group and thus introduces a new scene. (In an entirely different sense, the scene is the locale where a work is set.)

but later in this scene he gives Marc Antony permission to speak at Caesar's funeral and thus he sets in motion his own fall, which occupies the second half of the play. In *Macbeth,* the protagonist attains his height in 3.1 ("Thou hast it now: King"), but he soon perceives that he is going downhill:

I am in blood
Stepped in so far, that, should I wade no more,
Returning were as tedious as go o'er.

Of course, no law demands such a structure, and a hunt for the pyramid usually causes the hunter to overlook all the crises but the middle one. William Butler Yeats once suggestively diagramed a good plot not as a pyramid but as a line moving diagonally upward, punctuated by several crises. Perhaps it is sufficient to say that a good plot has its moments of tension, but the location of these will vary with the play. They are the product of **conflict,** but not all conflict produces tension; there is conflict but little tension in a ball game when the score is 10–0 in the ninth inning with two out and none on base.

Regardless of how a plot is diagrammed, the **exposition** is the part that tells the audience what it has to know about the past, the **antecedent action.** That is, the exposition tells the audience what the present situation is. When the three Marys say they are seeking Jesus "who was crucified," they are offering exposition, filling us in on what has already happened. In later plays, when two gossiping servants tell each other that after a year away in Paris the young master is coming home tomorrow with a new wife, they are giving the audience the exposition by introducing characters and defining relationships.

The Elizabethans and the Greeks sometimes tossed out all pretense at dialogue and began with a **prologue,** like the one spoken by the Chorus at the outset of *Romeo and Juliet:*

Two households, both alike in dignity
In fair Verona, where we lay our scene.
From ancient grudge break to new mutiny,
Where civil blood makes civil hands unclean.
From forth the fatal loins of these two foes
A pair of star-crossed lovers take their life....

And in Tennessee Williams's *The Glass Menagerie,* Tom's first speech is a sort of prologue. However, the exposition also may extend far into the play, so that the audience keeps getting bits of information that clarify the present and build suspense about the future.

Character has two meanings: someone who appears in a play (for instance, Juliet), and second, the intellectual, emotional, and moral qualities that add up to a personality (as when we say that Juliet's character is more complex than Romeo's).

When dramatic characters speak, they are doing at least two things: they are revealing themselves (if they are speaking deceitfully to their hearers, they are revealing themselves as deceivers to us), and they are also *doing things to other characters,* evoking from these characters agreement, anger, amusement, or whatever. **Dialogue,** then, is a form of action; when characters speak, they are bombarding other characters, who in turn reply and further advance the plot, perhaps by heightening the conflict.

One character may be in conflict either with another character or with a group of characters. In Susan Glaspell's *Trifles,* for instance, there is at first a subdued conflict between Mrs. Peters and Mrs. Hale (Mrs. Peters is stronger on the idea of dutifully following the law than Mrs. Hale is), but later the two women join forces in a conflict with the men. Each woman is a **foil** to the other, that is, a contrasting figure, one who helps to set off or define another figure.

Finally, one may ask, What does a play add up to? What is the underlying **theme,** or meaning, of a play? Some critics, arguing that the concept of theme is meaningless, hold that any play gives us only an extremely detailed history of some imaginary people. But surely this view is desperate. Dramatists may begin by being fascinated by a particular character or by some particular happening (real or imagined), but as they work on their play they see to it that the characters and the plot add up to something. (A *plot* is what happens; a *theme* is what the happenings add up to.) *Quem Quaeritis,* for the believer, is about the conquest of death through the sacrifice of Jesus; *Trifles* is (at least in part) about a patriarchal society that foolishly underestimates the intelligence and resourcefulness of women. To the reply that the theme, when stated, is usually banal, we can counter that the plays present these ideas in such a way that they take on life and become a part of us. And surely we are in no danger of equating the play with the theme that we sense underlies it. We never believe that our rough statement of the theme is really the equivalent of the play itself. The play, we recognize, presents the theme with such detail that our statement of the theme is only a wedge that helps us to enter the play so we may more fully (in Henry James's words) "appropriate it."

In Brief: How to Read a Play

If as a reader you develop the following principles into habits, you will get far more out of a play than if you read it as though it were a novel consisting only of dialogue.

1. *Pay attention to the* ***list of characters,*** *and carefully read whatever* ***descriptions*** *the playwright has provided.* Early dramatists, such as Shakespeare, did not provide much in the way of description ("Othello, the Moor" or "Iago, a villain" is about as much as we find in Elizabethan texts), but later playwrights are often very forthcoming. Here, for instance, is Tennessee Williams introducing us to Amanda Wingfield in *The Glass Menagerie.* (We give only the beginning of his longish description.)

> *Amanda Wingfield,* the mother. A little woman of great but confused vitality clinging frantically to another time and place.

And here is Susan Glaspell introducing us to all of the characters in her one-act play, *Trifles:*

> . . . the Sheriff comes in followed by the County Attorney and Hale. The Sheriff and Hale are men in middle life, the County Attorney is a young man; all are much bundled up and go at once to the stove. They are followed by the two women—the Sheriff's wife [Mrs. Peters] first; she is a slight wiry woman, a thin nervous face. Mrs. Hale is larger and

would ordinarily be called more comfortable looking, but she is disturbed now and looks fearfully about as she enters. The women have come in slowly and stand close together near the door.

Glaspell's description of her characters is not nearly so explicit as Tennessee Williams's, but Glaspell does tell a reader a good deal. What do we know about the men? They differ in age, they are bundled up, and they "go at once to the stove." What do we know about the women? Mrs. Peters is slight, and she has a "nervous face"; Mrs. Hale is "larger" but she too is "disturbed." The women enter "slowly," and they "stand close together near the door." In short, the men, who take over the warmest part of the room, are more confident than the women, who nervously huddle together near the door. It's a man's world.

2. *Pay attention to* ***gestures*** *and* ***costumes*** *that are specified in stage directions or are implied by the dialogue.* We have just seen how Glaspell distinguishes between the men and the women by what they do—the men take over the warm part of the room, the women stand insecurely near the door. Most dramatists from the late nineteenth century to the present have been fairly generous with their stage directions, but when we read the works of earlier dramatists we often have to deduce the gestures from the speeches. For instance, although Shakespeare has an occasional direction such as "She takes a sword and runs at him," for the most part he is very sparing. We must, then, infer the gestures from the dialogue. Consider this exchange between the Earl of Gloucester and King Lear. Earlier in the play Lear has acted despotically; then he suffers so greatly that his mind becomes unhinged. Gloucester, finding the mad king, says,

O, let me kiss that hand.

Lear replies,

Let me wipe it first; it smells of mortality.

Surely when Gloucester speaks his line he reaches for Lear's hand (and probably he also kneels), and Lear withdraws his hand and wipes it on his tattered clothing. Exactly *how* Lear withdraws his hand—suddenly, or with some dignity—is not specified in the words. Nor is it specified whether Lear smells his hand when he says, "It smells of mortality." All readers will have to decide such matters for themselves, but we can probably agree that although the words are immensely moving, the gestures that accompany them (Gloucester's gestures of humility and Lear's unwillingness to accept those gestures) are also part of the "language" of the play.

In addition to thinking about gestures, don't forget the costumes that the characters wear. Costumes, of course, identify the characters as soldiers or farmers or whatever, and changes of costume can be especially symbolic. When we first meet King Lear, for instance, he is dressed as a king. (The text doesn't specify this, but since he is engaged in officially giving away kingdoms, he presumably wears his crown and his robe of office.) Later, driven to madness, he tears off his clothing, thus showing his realization that he is powerless; and still later, after his madness has somewhat abated, he appears dressed in fresh clothing, a sign that at least to some degree he is restored to civilization. Or consider Nora, in Ibsen's *A Doll's House.* In the first act she wears ordinary clothing, but in the middle of the second act she puts on "a long multi-colored shawl" when she frantically rehearses her Italian dance. The shawl of course is appropriate to the tarantella dance, but its multitude of colors also helps to express Nora's conflicting emotions, her near hysteria, expressed too in the fact that "her hair works loose and falls over her shoulders" but "she ignores it." In the middle of the third act, she is wearing her Italian costume, dressed for a masquerade—her life has been a masquerade—but later she returns in her "everyday dress." The pretense is over.

3. *Keep in mind the* ***kind of theater*** *for which the play was written.* The plays in this book were written for various kinds of theaters. Sophocles, author of *Antigone* and *King Oedipus,* wrote for the ancient Greek theater, essentially a space where performers acted in front of an audience seated on a hillside. (See the illustration on page 45.) This theater was open to the heavens, with a structure representing a palace or temple behind the actors, in itself a kind of image of a society governed by the laws of the state and the laws of the gods. Moreover, the chorus enters the playing space by marching down the side aisles, close to the audience, thus helping to unite the world of the audience with that of the players. On the other hand, the audience in most modern theaters sits in a darkened area, separated by a proscenium arch from the performers, and watches them move about in a boxlike setting. The box set of Ibsen's plays or of Glaspell's *Trifles*—a room with the front wall missing—is, it often seems, an appropriate image of the confined lives of the characters of the play.

4. *If the playwright describes the locale and the furnishings, try to* ***envision the set*** *clearly. Pay attention also to the* ***lighting.*** Glaspell, for instance, tells us a good deal about the set. We quote only the first part.

> The kitchen in the now abandoned farmhouse of John Wright, a gloomy kitchen, and left without having been put in order . . .

These details about a gloomy and disordered kitchen may seem to be mere realism—after all, the play has to take place somewhere—but it turns out that the disorder and, for that matter, the gloominess are extremely important. You'll have to read the play to find out why.

Another example of a setting that provides important information is Arthur Miller's, in *Death of a Salesman.* Again we quote only the beginning of the description.

> Before us is the Salesman's house. We are aware of towering, angular shapes behind it, surrounding it on all sides. Only the blue light of the sky falls upon the house and forestage; the surrounding area shows an angry glow of orange.

Here the lighting, especially the "angry glow of orange," is also a part of the language of the dramatist. Tennessee Williams uses lighting in a similar way in *The Glass Menagerie;* while two characters quarrel, the stage "is lit with a turgid smoky red glow." These examples of symbolic lighting are obvious, but what at first seems to be merely realistic lighting may also be symbolic. In *A Doll's House,* as Nora's terror grows in the second act, Ibsen tells us in a stage direction, "It begins to grow dark."

If we read older drama, we find that playwrights do not give us much help, but by paying attention to the words we can at least to some degree visualize the locale. For instance, in *King Lear* Shakespeare establishes the setting by giving Gloucester this line:

Alack, the night comes on, and the high winds
Do sorely ruffle. For many miles about
There's scarce a bush.

And, again, this locale says something about the impoverished people who move in it.

5. *Pay attention to whatever* ***sound effects*** *are specified in the play.* In *Death of a Salesman,* before the curtain goes up, "A melody is heard, played upon a flute. It is small and fine, telling of grass and trees and the horizon." Then the curtain rises, revealing the Salesman's house, with "towering, angular shapes behind it, surrounding it on all sides." Obviously the sound of the flute is meant to tell us of the world that the Salesman is shut off from. In *Quem Quaeritis,* the bells at the end help to communicate the joy and harmony of the action that the play sets forth.

A sound effect, however, need not be so evidently symbolic to be important in a play. In Glaspell's *Trifles,* for instance, almost at the very end of the play we hear the "sound of a knob turning in the other room." The sound has an electrifying effect on the audience, as it does on the two women on the stage, and it precedes a decisive action.

6. *Pay attention, at least on second reading, to* ***silences,*** *including pauses within speeches or between speeches.* Late in *Trifles* a stage direction tells us that "The women's eyes meet for an instant." We won't say what this exchange of looks indicates, but when you read the play you will see that the moment of silence is significant.

7. *Of course* ***dialogue*** *is the most persistent sound in a play. Pay attention to what the characters say, but keep in mind that (like real people) dramatic characters are not always to be trusted.* An obvious case is Shakespeare's Edmund in *King Lear,* an utterly unscrupulous villain who knows that he is a liar, but a character may be self-deceived, or, to put it a bit differently, characters may say what they honestly think but may not know what they are talking about.

SUSAN GLASPELL *Trifles*

Susan Glaspell (1882–1948) was born in Davenport, Iowa, and educated at Drake University in Des Moines. In 1903 she married George Cram Cook and, with Cook and other writers, actors, and artists, in 1915 founded the Provincetown Players, a group that remained vital until 1929. Glaspell wrote *Trifles* (1916) for the Provincetown Players, but she also wrote stories, novels, and a biography of her husband. In 1931 she won the Pulitzer Prize for *Alison's House,* a play about the family of a deceased poet who in some ways resembles Emily Dickinson.

Scene: The kitchen in the now abandoned farmhouse of John Wright, a gloomy kitchen, and left without having been put in order—unwashed pans under the sink, a loaf of bread outside the breadbox, a dish towel on the table—other signs of

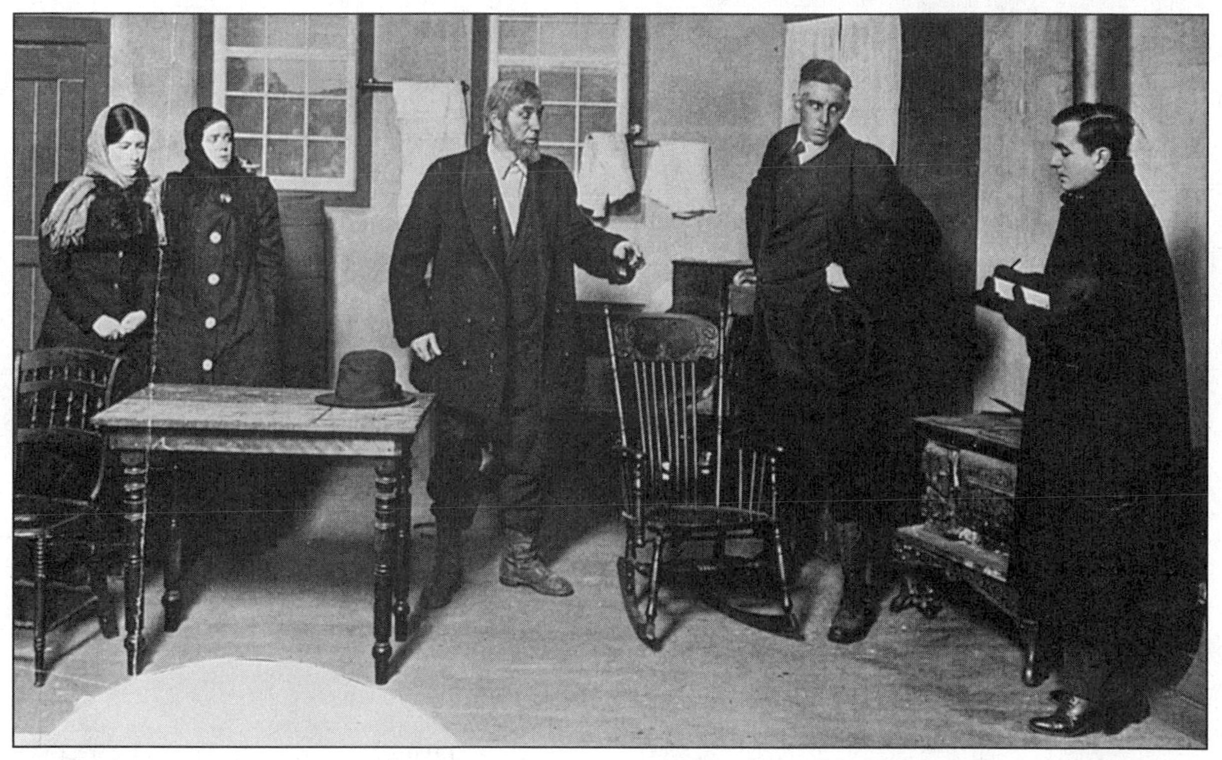

Marjorie Vonnegut, Elinor M. Cox, John King, Arthur F. Hole, and T. W. Gibson in a scene from *Trifles,* as published in *Theatre Magazine,* January 1917. (Photograph courtesy of The New York Public Library Billy Rose Theatre Collection.)

incompleted work. At the rear the outer door opens, and the Sheriff comes in, followed by the County Attorney and Hale. The Sheriff and Hale are men in middle life, the County Attorney is a young man; all are much bundled up and go at once to the stove. They are followed by the two women—the Sheriff's wife first; she is a slight wiry woman, a thin nervous face. Mrs. Hale is larger and would ordinarily be called more comfortable looking, but she is disturbed now and looks fearfully about as she enters. The women have come in slowly and stand close together near the door.

COUNTY ATTORNEY (*rubbing his hands*). This feels good. Come up to the fire, ladies.

MRS. PETERS (*after taking a step forward*). I'm not—cold.

SHERIFF (*unbuttoning his overcoat and stepping away from the stove as if to the beginning of official business*). Now, Mr. Hale, before we move things about, you explain to Mr. Henderson just what you saw when you came here yesterday morning.

COUNTY ATTORNEY. By the way, has anything been moved? Are things just as you left them yesterday?

SHERIFF (*looking about*). It's just the same. When it dropped below zero last night, I thought I'd better send Frank out this morning to make a fire for us—no use getting pneumonia with a big case on; but I told him not to touch anything except the stove—and you know Frank.

COUNTY ATTORNEY. Somebody should have been left here yesterday.

SHERIFF. Oh—yesterday. When I had to send Frank to Morris Center for that man who went crazy—I want you to know I had my hands full yesterday. I knew you could get back from Omaha by today, and as long as I went over everything here myself—

COUNTY ATTORNEY. Well, Mr. Hale, tell just what happened when you came here yesterday morning.

HALE. Harry and I had started to town with a load of potatoes. We came along the road from my place; and as I got here, I said, "I'm going to see if I can't get John Wright to go in with me on a party telephone!" I spoke to Wright about it once before, and he put me off, saying folks talked too much anyway, and all he asked was peace and quiet—I guess you know about how much he talked himself; but I thought maybe if I went to the house and talked about it before his wife, though I said to Harry that I didn't know as what his wife wanted made much difference to John—

COUNTY ATTORNEY. Let's talk about that later, Mr. Hale. I do want to talk about that, but tell now just what happened when you got to the house.

HALE. I didn't hear or see anything; I knocked at the door, and still it was all quiet inside. I knew they must be up, it was past eight o'clock. So I knocked again, and I thought I heard somebody say, "Come in." I wasn't sure, I'm not sure yet, but I opened the door—this door (*indicating the door by which the two women are still standing*), and there in that rocker—(*pointing to it*) sat Mrs. Wright. (*They all look at the rocker.*)

COUNTY ATTORNEY. What—was she doing?

HALE. She was rockin' back and forth. She had her apron in her hand and was kind of—pleating it.

COUNTY ATTORNEY. And how did she—look?

HALE. Well, she looked queer.

COUNTY ATTORNEY. How do you mean—queer?

HALE. Well, as if she didn't know what she was going to do next. And kind of done up.

COUNTY ATTORNEY. How did she seem to feel about your coming?

HALE. Why, I don't think she minded—one way or other. She didn't pay much attention. I said, "How do, Mrs. Wright, it's cold, ain't it?" And she said, "Is it?" —and went on kind of pleating at her apron. Well, I was surprised; she didn't ask me to come up to the stove, or to set down, but just sat there, not even looking at me, so I said, "I want to see John." And then she—laughed. I guess you would call it a laugh. I thought of Harry and the team outside, so I said a little sharp: "Can't I see John?" "No," she says, kind o' dull like. "Ain't he home?" says I. "Yes," says she, "he's home." "Then why can't I see him?" I asked her, out of patience. "'Cause he's dead," says she. *"Dead?"* says I. She just nodded her head, not getting a bit excited, but rockin' back and forth. "Why—where is he?" says I, not knowing what to say. She just pointed upstairs—like that (*himself pointing to the room above*). I got up, with the idea of going up there. I walked from there to here—then I says, "Why, what did he die of?" "He died of a rope around his neck," says she, and just went on pleatin' at her apron. Well, I went out and called Harry. I thought I might—need help. We went upstairs, and there he was lyin'—

COUNTY ATTORNEY. I think I'd rather have you go into that upstairs, where you can point it all out. Just go on now with the rest of the story.

HALE. Well, my first thought was to get that rope off. I looked . . . (*Stops, his face twitches.*) . . . but Harry, he went up to him, and he said, "No, he's dead all right, and we'd better not touch anything." So we went back downstairs. She was still sitting that same way. "Has anybody been notified?" I asked. "No," says she, unconcerned. "Who did this, Mrs. Wright?" said Harry. He said it businesslike—and she stopped pleatin' of her apron. "I don't know," she says. "You don't *know?*" says Harry. "No," says she, "Weren't you sleepin' in the bed with him?" says Harry. "Yes," says she, "but I was on the inside." "Somebody slipped a rope round his neck and strangled him, and you didn't wake up?" says Harry. "I didn't wake up," she said after him. We must 'a looked as if we didn't see how that could be, for after a minute she said, "I sleep sound." Harry was going to ask her more questions, but I said maybe we ought to let her tell her story first to the coroner, or the sheriff, so Harry went fast as he could to Rivers' place, where there's a telephone.

COUNTY ATTORNEY. And what did Mrs. Wright do when she knew that you had gone for the coroner?

HALE. She moved from that chair to this over here . . . (*Pointing to a small chair in the corner*) . . . and just sat there with her hands held together and looking down. I got a feeling that I ought to make some conversation, so I said I had come in to see if John wanted to put in a telephone, and at that she started to laugh, and then she stopped and looked at me—scared. (*The County Attorney, who has had his notebook out, makes a note.*) I dunno, maybe it wasn't scared. I wouldn't like to say it was. Soon Harry got back, and then Dr. Lloyd came, and you, Mr. Peters, and so I guess that's all I know that you don't.

COUNTY ATTORNEY (*looking around*). I guess we'll go upstairs first—and then out to the barn and around there. (*To the Sheriff.*) You're convinced that there was nothing important here—nothing that would point to any motive?

SHERIFF. Nothing here but kitchen things.

(*The County Attorney, after again looking around the kitchen, opens the door of a cupboard closet. He gets up on a chair and looks on a shelf. Pulls his hand away, sticky.*)

COUNTY ATTORNEY. Here's a nice mess.

(*The women draw nearer.*)

MRS. PETERS (*to the other woman*). Oh, her fruit; it did freeze. (*To the Lawyer.*) She worried about that when it turned so cold. She said the fir'd go out and her jars would break.

SHERIFF. Well, can you beat the women! Held for murder and worryin' about her preserves.

COUNTY ATTORNEY. I guess before we're through she may have something more serious than preserves to worry about.

HALE. Well, women are used to worrying over trifles.

(*The two women move a little closer together.*)

COUNTY ATTORNEY (*with the gallantry of a young politician*). And yet, for all their worries, what would we do without the ladies? (*The women do not unbend. He goes to the sink, takes a dipperful of water from the pail and, pouring it into a basin, washes his hands. Starts to wipe them on the roller towel, turns it for a cleaner place.*) Dirty towels! (*Kicks his foot against the pans under the sink.*) Not much of a housekeeper, would you say, ladies?

MRS. HALE (*stiffly*). There's a great deal of work to be done on a farm.

COUNTY ATTORNEY. To be sure. And yet . . . (*With a little bow to her*) . . . I know there are some Dickson county farmhouses which do not have such roller towels. (*He gives it a pull to expose its full length again.*)

MRS. HALE. Those towels get dirty awful quick. Men's hands aren't always as clean as they might be.

COUNTY ATTORNEY. Ah, loyal to your sex I see. But you and Mrs. Wright were neighbors. I suppose you were friends, too.

MRS. HALE (*shaking her head*). I've not seen much of her of late years. I've not been in this house—it's more than a year.

COUNTY ATTORNEY. And why was that? You didn't like her?

MRS. HALE. I liked her all well enough. Farmers' wives have their hands full, Mr. Henderson. And then—

COUNTY ATTORNEY. Yes—?

MRS. HALE (*looking about*). It never seemed a very cheerful place.

COUNTY ATTORNEY. No—it's not cheerful. I shouldn't say she had the homemaking instinct.

MRS. HALE. Well, I don't know as Wright had, either.

COUNTY ATTORNEY. You mean that they didn't get on very well?

MRS. HALE. No, I don't mean anything. But I don't think a place'd be any cheerfuler for John Wright's being in it.

COUNTY ATTORNEY. I'd like to talk more of that a little later. I want to get the lay of things upstairs now. (*He goes to the left, where three steps lead to a stair door.*)

SHERIFF. I suppose anything Mrs. Peters does'll be all right. She was to take in some clothes for her, you know, and a few little things. We left in such a hurry yesterday.

COUNTY ATTORNEY. Yes, but I would like to see what you take, Mrs. Peters, and keep an eye out for anything that might be of use to us.

MRS. PETERS. Yes, Mr. Henderson.

(*The women listen to the men's steps on the stairs, then look about the kitchen.*)

MRS. HALE. I'd hate to have men coming into my kitchen, snooping around and criticizing. (*She arranges the pans under sink which the Lawyer had shoved out of place.*)

MRS. PETERS. Of course it's no more than their duty.

MRS. HALE. Duty's all right, but I guess that deputy sheriff that came out to make the fire might have got a little of this on. (*Gives the roller towel a pull.*) Wish I'd thought of that sooner. Seems mean to talk about her for not having things slicked up when she had to come away in such a hurry.

MRS. PETERS (*who has gone to a small table in the left rear corner of the room, and lifted one end of a towel that covers a pan*). She had bread set. (*Stands still.*)

MRS. HALE (*eyes fixed on a loaf of bread beside the breadbox, which is on a low shelf at the other side of the room. Moves slowly toward it*). She was going to put this in there. (*Picks up loaf, then abruptly drops it. In a manner of returning to familiar things.*) It's a shame about her fruit. I wonder if it's all gone. (*Gets up on the chair and looks.*) I think there's some here that's all right, Mrs. Peters. Yes—here; (*Holding it toward the window.*) this is cherries, too. (*Looking again.*) I declare I believe that's the only one. (*Gets down, bottle in her hand. Goes to the sink and wipes it off on the outside.*) She'll feel awful bad after all her hard work in the hot weather. I remember the afternoon I put up my cherries last summer. (*She puts the bottle on the big kitchen table, center of the room, front table. With a sigh, is about to sit down in the rocking chair. Before she is seated realizes what chair it is; with a slow look at it, steps back. The chair, which she has touched, rocks back and forth.*)

MRS. PETERS. Well, I must get those things from the front room closet. (*She goes to the door at the right, but after looking into the other room steps back.*) You coming with me, Mrs. Hale? You could help me carry them. (*They go into the other room; reappear, Mrs. Peters carrying a dress and skirt, Mrs. Hale following with a pair of shoes.*)

MRS. PETERS. My, it's cold in there. (*She puts the cloth on the big table, and hurries to the stove.*)

MRS. HALE (*examining the skirt*). Wright was close. I think maybe that's why she kept so much to herself. She didn't even belong to the Ladies' Aid. I suppose she felt she couldn't do her part, and then you don't enjoy things when you feel shabby. She used to wear pretty clothes and be lively, when she was Minnie Foster, one of the town girls singing in the choir. But that—oh, that was thirty years ago. This all you was to take in?

MRS. PETERS. She said she wanted an apron. Funny thing to want, for there isn't much to get you dirty in jail, goodness knows. But I suppose just to make her feel more natural. She said they was in the top drawer in this cupboard. Yes, here. And then her little shawl that always hung behind the door. (*Opens stair door and looks.*) Yes, here it is. (*Quickly shuts door leading upstairs.*)

MRS. HALE (*abruptly moving toward her*). Mrs. Peters?

MRS. PETERS. Yes, Mrs. Hale?

MRS. HALE. Do you think she did it?

MRS. PETERS (*in a frightened voice*). Oh, I don't know.

MRS. HALE. Well, I don't think she did. Asking for an apron and her little shawl. Worrying about her fruit.

MRS. PETERS (*starts to speak, glances up, where footsteps are heard in the room above. In a low voice*). Mr. Peters says it looks bad for her. Mr. Henderson is awful sarcastic in speech, and he'll make fun of her sayin' she didn't wake up.

MRS. HALE. Well, I guess John Wright didn't wake when they was slipping that rope under his neck.

MRS. PETERS. No, it's strange. It must have been done awful crafty and still. They say it was such a—funny way to kill a man, rigging it all up like that.

MRS. HALE. That's just what Mr. Hale said. There was a gun in the house. He says that's what he can't understand.

MRS. PETERS. Mr. Henderson said coming out that what was needed for the case was a motive; something to show anger, or—sudden feeling.

MRS. HALE (*who is standing by the table*). Well, I don't see any signs of anger around here. (*She puts her hand on the dish towel which lies on the table, stands looking down at the table, one half of which is clean, the other half messy.*) It's wiped here. (*Makes a move as if to finish work, then turns and looks at loaf of bread outside the breadbox. Drops towel. In that voice of coming back to familiar things.*) Wonder how they are finding things upstairs? I hope she had it a little more red-up there. You know, it seems kind of *sneaking.* Locking her up in town and then coming out here and trying to get her own house to turn against her!

MRS. PETERS. But, Mrs. Hale, the law is the law.

MRS. HALE. I s'pose 'tis. (*Unbuttoning her coat.*) Better loosen up your things, Mrs. Peters. You won't feel them when you go out.

(*Mrs. Peters takes off her fur tippet, goes to hang it on hook at the back of room, stands looking at the under part of the small corner table.*)

MRS. PETERS. She was piecing a quilt. (*She brings the large sewing basket, and they look at the bright pieces.*)

MRS. HALE. It's log cabin pattern. Pretty, isn't it? I wonder if she was goin' to quilt or just knot it?

(*Footsteps have been heard coming down the stairs. The Sheriff enters, followed by Hale and the County Attorney.*)

SHERIFF. They wonder if she was going to quilt it or just knot it. (*The men laugh, the women look abashed.*)

COUNTY ATTORNEY (*rubbing his hands over the stove*). Frank's fire didn't do much up there, did it? Well, let's go out to the barn and get that cleared up. (*The men go outside.*)

MRS. HALE (*resentfully*). I don't know as there's anything so strange, our takin' up our time with little things while we're waiting for them to get the evidence. (*She sits down at the big table, smoothing out a block with decision.*) I don't see as it's anything to laugh about.

MRS. PETERS (*apologetically*). Of course they've got awful important things on their minds. (*Pulls up a chair and joins Mrs. Hale at the table.*)

MRS. HALE (*examining another block*). Mrs. Peters, look at this one. Here, this is the one she was working on, and look at the sewing! All the rest of it has been so nice and even. And look at this! It's all over the place! Why, it looks as if she didn't know what she was about! (*After she has said this, they look at each other, then started to glance back at the door. After an instant Mrs. Hale has pulled at a knot and ripped the sewing.*)

MRS. PETERS. Oh, what are you doing, Mrs. Hale?

MRS. HALE (*mildly*). Just pulling out a stitch or two that's not sewed very good. (*Threading a needle.*) Bad sewing always made me fidgety.

MRS. PETERS (*nervously*). I don't think we ought to touch things.

MRS. HALE. I'll just finish up this end. (*Suddenly stopping and leaning forward.*) Mrs. Peters?

MRS. PETERS. Yes, Mrs. Hale?

MRS. HALE. What do you suppose she was so nervous about?

MRS. PETERS. Oh—I don't know. I don't know as she was nervous. I sometimes sew awful queer when I'm just tired. (*Mrs. Hale starts to say something, looks at Mrs. Peters, then goes on sewing.*) Well, I must get these things wrapped up. They may be through sooner than we think. (*Putting apron and other things together.*) I wonder where I can find a piece of paper, and string.

MRS. HALE. In that cupboard, maybe.

MRS. PETERS (*looking in cupboard*). Why, here's a birdcage. (*Holds it up.*) Did she have a bird, Mrs. Hale?

MRS. HALE. Why, I don't know whether she did or not—I've not been here for so long. There was a man around last year selling canaries cheap, but I don't know as she took one; maybe she did. She used to sing real pretty herself.

MRS. PETERS (*glancing around*). Seems funny to think of a bird here. But she must have had one, or why should she have a cage? I wonder what happened to it?

MRS. HALE. I s'pose maybe the cat got it.

MRS. PETERS. No, she didn't have a cat. She's got that feeling some people have about cats—being afraid of them. My cat got in her room, and she was real upset and asked me to take it out.

MRS. HALE. My sister Bessie was like that. Queer, ain't it?

MRS. PETERS (*examining the cage*). Why, look at this door. It's broke. One hinge is pulled apart.

MRS.HALE (*looking, too*). Looks as if someone must have been rough with it.

MRS. PETERS. Why, yes. (*She brings the cage forward and puts it on the table.*)

MRS. HALE. I wish if they're going to find any evidence they'd be about it. I don't like this place.

MRS. PETERS. But I'm awful glad you came with me, Mrs. Hale. It would be lonesome for me sitting here alone.

MRS. HALE. It would, wouldn't it? (*Dropping her sewing.*) But I tell you what I do wish, Mrs. Peters. I wish I had come over sometimes when *she* was here. I—(*looking around the room.*)—wish I had.

MRS. PETERS. But of course you were awful busy, Mrs. Hale—your house and your children.

MRS. HALE. I could've come. I stayed away because it weren't cheerful—and that's why I ought to have come. I—I've never liked this place. Maybe because it's down in a hollow, and you don't see the road. I dunno what it is, but it's a lonesome place and always was. I wish I had come over to see Minnie Foster sometimes. I can see now—(*Shakes her head.*)

MRS. PETERS. Well, you mustn't reproach yourself, Mrs. Hale. Somehow we just don't see how it is with other folks until—something comes up.

MRS. HALE. Not having children makes less work—but it makes a quiet house, and Wright out to work all day, and no company when he did come in. Did you know John Wright, Mrs. Peters?

MRS. PETERS. Not to know him; I've seen him in town. They say he was a good man.

MRS. HALE. Yes—good; he didn't drink, and kept his word as well as most, I guess, and paid his debts. But he was a hard man, Mrs. Peters. Just to pass the time of day with him. (*Shivers.*) Like a raw wind that gets to the bone. (*Pauses, her eye falling on the cage.*) I should think she would 'a wanted a bird. But what do you suppose went with it?

MRS. PETERS. I don't know, unless it got sick and died. (*She reaches over and swings the broken door, swings it again; both women watch it.*)

MRS. HALE. You weren't raised round here, were you? (*Mrs. Peters shakes her head.*) You didn't know—her?

MRS. PETERS. Not till they brought her yesterday.

MRS. HALE. She—come to think of it, she was kind of like a bird herself—real sweet and pretty, but kind of timid and—fluttery. How—she—did—change. (*Silence; then as if struck by a happy thought and relieved to get back to everyday things.*) Tell you what, Mrs. Peters, why don't you take the quilt in with you? It might take up her mind.

MRS. PETERS. Why, I think that's a real nice idea, Mrs. Hale. There couldn't possible be any objection to it, could there? Now, just what would I take? I wonder if her patches are in here—and her things. (*They look in the sewing basket.*)

MRS. HALE. Here's some red. I expect this has got sewing things in it (*Brings out a fancy box.*) What a pretty box. Looks like something somebody would give you. Maybe her scissors are in here. (*Opens box. Suddenly puts her hand to her nose.*) Why—(*Mrs. Peters bends nearer; then turns her face away.*) There's something wrapped up in this piece of silk.

MRS. PETERS. Why, this isn't her scissors.

MRS. HALE (*lifting the silk*). Oh, Mrs. Peters—it's—(*Mrs. Peters bends closer*)

MRS. PETERS. It's the bird.

MRS. HALE (*jumping up*). But, Mrs. Peters—look at it. Its neck! Look at its neck! It's all—other side *to*.

MRS. PETERS. Somebody—wrung—its neck.

(*Their eyes meet. A look of growing comprehension of horror. Steps are heard outside. Mrs. Hale slips box under quilt pieces, and sinks into her chair. Enter Sheriff and County Attorney. Mrs. Peters rises.*)

COUNTY ATTORNEY (*as one turning from serious things to little pleasantries*). Well, ladies, have you decided whether she was going to quilt it or knot it?

MRS. PETERS. We think she was going to—knot it.

COUNTY ATTORNEY. Well, that's interesting, I'm sure. (*Seeing the birdcage.*) Has the bird flown?

MRS. HALE (*putting more quilt pieces over the box*). We think the—cat got it.

COUNTY ATTORNEY (*preoccupied*). Is there a cat?

(*Mrs. Hale glances in a quick covert way at Mrs. Peters.*)

MRS. PETERS. Well, not now. They're superstitious, you know. They, leave.

COUNTY ATTORNEY (*to Sheriff Peters, continuing an interrupted conversation*). No sign at all of anyone having come from the outside. Their own rope. Now let's go up again and go over it piece by piece. (*They start upstairs.*) It would have to have been someone who knew just the—

(*Mrs. Peters sits down. The two women sit there not looking at one another, but as if peering into something and at the same time holding back. When they talk now, it is the manner of feeling their way over strange ground, as if afraid of what they are saying, but as if they cannot help saying it.*)

MRS. HALE. She liked the bird. She was going to bury it in that pretty box.

MRS. PETERS (*in a whisper*). When I was a girl—my kitten—there was a boy took a hatchet, and before my eyes—and before I could get there— (*Covers her face an instant.*) If they hadn't held me back, I would have— (*Catches herself, looks upstairs where steps are heard, falters weakly.*)—hurt him.

MRS. HALE (*with a slow look around her*). I wonder how it would seem never to have had any children around. (*Pause.*) No, Wright wouldn't like the bird—a thing that sang. She used to sing. He killed that, too.

MRS. PETERS (*moving uneasily*). We don't know who killed the bird.

MRS. HALE. I knew John Wright.

MRS. PETERS. It was an awful thing was done in this house that night, Mrs. Hale. Killing a man while he slept, slipping a rope around his neck that choked the life out of him.

MRS. HALE. His neck. Choked the life out of him.

(*Her hand goes out and rests on the birdcage.*)

MRS. PETERS (*with a rising voice*). We don't know who killed him. We don't know.

MRS. HALE (*her own feeling not interrupted*). If there'd been years and years of nothing, then a bird to sing to you, it would be awful—still, after the bird was still.

MRS. PETERS (*something within her speaking*). I know what stillness is. When we homesteaded in Dakota, and my first baby died—after he was two years old, and me with no other then—

MRS. HALE (*moving*). How soon do you suppose they'll be through, looking for evidence?

MRS. PETERS. I know what stillness is. (*Pulling herself back.*) The law has got to punish crime, Mrs. Hale.

MRS. HALE (*not as if answering that*). I wish you'd seen Minnie Foster when she wore a white dress with blue ribbons and stood up there in the choir and sang. (*A look around the room.*) Oh, I *wish* I'd come over here once in a while! That was a crime! That was a crime! Who's going to punish that?

MRS. PETERS (*looking upstairs*). We mustn't—take on.

MRS. HALE. I might have known she needed help! I know how things can be—for women. I tell you, it's queer, Mrs. Peters. We live close together and we live far apart. We all go through the same things—it's all just a different kind of the same thing. (*Brushes her eyes, noticing the bottle of fruit, reaches out for it.*) If I was you, I wouldn't tell her her fruit was gone. To her it *ain't*. Tell her it's all right. Take this in to prove it to her. She—she may never know whether it was broke or not.

MRS. PETERS (*takes the bottle, looks about for something to wrap it in; takes petticoat from the clothes brought from the other room, very nervously begins winding this around the bottle. In a false voice*). My, it's a good thing the men couldn't hear us. Wouldn't they just laugh! Getting all stirred up over a little thing like a—dead canary. As if that could have anything to do with—with—wouldn't they *laugh!*

(*The men are heard coming downstairs.*)

MRS. HALE (*under her breath*). Maybe they would—maybe they wouldn't.

COUNTY ATTORNEY. No, Peters, it's all perfectly clear except a reason for doing it. But you know juries when it comes to women. If there was some definite thing. Something to show—something to make a story about—a thing that would connect up with this strange way of doing it.

(*The women's eyes meet for an instant. Enter Hale from outer door.*)

HALE. Well, I've got the team around. Pretty cold out there.

COUNTY ATTORNEY. I'm going to stay here awhile by myself. (*To the Sheriff.*) You can send Frank out for me, can't you? I want to go over everything. I'm not satisfied that we can't do better.

SHERIFF. Do you want to see what Mrs. Peters is going to take in? (*The Lawyer goes to the table, picks up the apron, laughs.*)

COUNTY ATTORNEY. Oh I guess they're not very dangerous things the ladies have picked up. (*Moves a few things about, disturbing the quilt pieces which cover the box. Steps back.*) No, Mrs. Peters doesn't need supervising. For that matter, a sheriff's wife is married to the law. Ever think of it that way, Mrs. Peters?

MRS. PETERS. Not—just that way.

SHERIFF (*chuckling*). Married to the law. (*Moves toward the other room.*) I just want you to come in here a minute, George. We ought to take a look at these windows.

COUNTY ATTORNEY (*scoffingly*). Oh, windows!

SHERIFF. We'll be right out, Mr. Hale.

(*Hale goes outside. The Sheriff follows the County Attorney into the other room. Then Mrs. Hale rises, hands tight together, looking intensely at Mrs. Peters, whose eyes take a slow turn, finally meeting Mrs. Hale's. A moment Mrs. Hale holds her, then her own eyes point the way to where the box is concealed. Suddenly Mrs. Peters throws back quilt pieces and tries to put the box in the bag she is wearing. It is too big. She opens box, starts to take the bird out, cannot touch it, goes to pieces, stands there helpless. Sound of a knob turning in the other room. Mrs. Hale snatches the box and puts it in the pocket of her big coat. Enter County Attorney and Sheriff.*)

COUNTY ATTORNEY (*facetiously*). Well, Henry, at least we found out that she was not going to quilt it. She was going to—what is it you call it, ladies?

MRS. HALE (*her hand against her pocket*). We call it—knot it, Mr. Henderson.

CURTAIN

TOPICS FOR DISCUSSION AND WRITING

1. Briefly describe the setting, indicating what it "says" and what atmosphere it evokes.
2. How would you characterize Mr. Henderson, the county attorney?
3. In what way or ways are Mrs. Peters and Mrs. Hale different from each other?
4. Several times the men "laugh" or "chuckle." In their contexts, what do these expressions of amusement convey?
5. On page 16, "*the women's eyes meet for an instant.*" What do you think this bit of action "says"? What do you understand by the exchange of glances?
6. On page 16, when Mrs. Peters tells of the boy who killed her cat, she says, "If they hadn't held me back, I would have— (*catches herself, looks upstairs where steps are heard, falters weakly.*)—hurt him." What do you think she was about to say before she faltered? Why do you suppose Glaspell included this speech about Mrs. Peters's girlhood?
7. On page 14, Mrs. Hale, looking at a quilt, wonders whether Mrs. Wright "was going to quilt it or just knot it." The men are amused by the women's concern with this topic, and the last line of the play returns to the issue. What do you make of this emphasis on the matter?
8. We never see Mrs. Wright on stage. Nevertheless, by the end of *Trifles* we know a great deal about her. Explain both what we know about her—physical characteristics, habits, interests, personality, life before her marriage and after—and *how* we know these things.
9. The title of the play is ironic—the "trifles" are important. What other ironies do you find in the play? (On irony, see Glossary.)
10. Do you think the play is immoral? Explain.

A Second Short Play for Study

In a moment we will give the text of a one-act play by J. M. Barrie, but first some rather indirect introductory comment may be useful.

In reading Susan Glaspell's *Trifles* you probably were chiefly occupied with the drama (even the melodrama), that is, with the exciting conflict and resolution; perhaps only on reflection did you concern yourself much with the ideas implicit in the play, for instance with the role that a male society attributes to women, or with the rightness or wrongness of Minnie's action.

"The material of the dramatist," Bernard Shaw once said, "is always some conflict of human feeling with circumstances." In much of the drama before the late nineteenth century, the "circumstances" were thought to be unchanging facts of life, for instance human passions, or fate, or divine will, rather than the particular conditions of a society. The Norwegian dramatist Henrik Ibsen (1823–1906) changed all that, partly by introducing what has come to be called "the problem play." In some of his plays, including *A Doll's House* and *Ghosts,* Ibsen turned his attention to human institutions that, it seemed, could be altered if we thought about them. In *A Doll's House,* for example, Nora forces her husband to sit down and talk about their relationship. Nora decides that she cannot continue to live with him, though she allows for the possibility that he may change and that they will be able to enter into a new relationship. The problem, then, might be stated something along these lines: Does marriage as it is now constituted corrupt the partners? If so, how should it be altered?

Today we can hardly imagine the furor that greeted productions of Ibsen's plays in the 1880s and 90s. For instance, many critics were outraged that Nora leaves her husband and especially that she leaves her children, and they took some satisfaction in the thought that she would be unable to provide for herself once she left her husband's roof. J. M. Barrie himself in 1891 wrote a short satiric play spoofing what was widely regarded as the gloominess of Ibsen's plays. In time the furor died down, but Ibsen had left his mark on the theater. Even Barrie, most of whose work is sentimental rather than bold, was influenced by Ibsen, as you will see when you read *The Twelve-Pound Look,* a short comedy. Barrie's play certainly does not have the weight or urgency of Ibsen's plays, but it could not have been written before Ibsen wrote.

Barrie called Ibsen "the dramatist I have always known to be the greatest of his age," and said Ibsen was "the mightiest craftsman that ever wrote." As you read and re-read *The Twelve-Pound Look,* you might spend some time thinking about Barrie's own craftsmanship.

Barrie's play is somewhat unusual in the fullness of the stage directions. He came to the drama only after he had achieved success as a novelist, and he was always careful to make the published texts of his plays highly readable. You may, in fact, feel that in his stage directions he goes too far in trying to engage the reader's good will.

J. M. BARRIE *The Twelve-Pound Look*

James Matthew Barrie (1860–1937) was born in Scotland, the son of humble weavers. After graduating from Edinburgh University he turned to journalism, settling in London, where he began to write novels. By 1888 he was fairly well known. In 1891 a novel, *The Little Minister,* established him as an important writer, and in the same year he saw his first play on the stage, but it was a failure. In the following year, however, he achieved fame as a playwright, with a comedy called *Walker.*

During his lifetime Barrie was equally esteemed as a novelist and a playwright. Today he is known chiefly for one play, *Peter Pan* (1904). (In the following play, "pound"

"The £12 Look" by J. M. Barrie, from *Collier's*, March 11, 1911.
(The Newberry Library, Chicago.)

refers to a British unit of money. In Barrie's day, 12 pounds would have been worth approximately $120–50 of today's American money.)

If quite convenient (as they say about cheques) you are to conceive that the scene is laid in your own house, and that Harry Sims is you. Perhaps the ornamentation of the house is a trifle ostentatious, but if you cavil at that we are willing to re-decorate: you don't get out of being Harry Sims on a mere matter of plush and dados. It pleases us to make him a city man, but (rather than lose you) he can be turned with a scrape of the pen into a K.C.,[2] fashionable doctor, Secretary of State, or what you will. We conceive him of a pleasant rotundity with a thick red neck, but we shall waive that point if you know him to be thin.

It is that day in your career when everything went wrong just when everything seemed to be superlatively right.

In Harry's case it was a woman who did the mischief. She came to him in his great hour and told him she did not admire him. Of course he turned her out of the house and was soon himself again, but it spoilt the morning for him. This is the subject of the play, and quite enough too.

Harry is to receive the honour of knighthood in a few days, and we discover him in the sumptuous "snuggery" of his home in Kensington (or is it Westminster?), rehearsing the ceremony with his wife. They have been at it all the morning, a pleasing occupation. Mrs. Sims (as we may call her for the last time, as it were, and strictly as a good-natured joke) is wearing her presentation gown, and personates the august one who is about to dub her Harry knight. She is seated regally. Her jewelled shoulders proclaim aloud her husband's generosity. She must be an extraordinarily proud and happy woman, yet she has a drawn face and shrinking ways as if there were some one near her of whom she is afraid. She claps her hands, as the signal to Harry. He enters bowing, and with a graceful swerve of the leg. He is only partly in costume, the sword and the real stockings not having arrived yet. With a gliding motion that is only delayed while one leg makes up on the other, he reaches his wife, and, going on one knee, raises her hand superbly to his lips. She taps him on the shoulder with a paper-knife and says huskily, "Rise, Sir Harry." He rises, bows, and glides about the room, going on his knees to various articles of furniture, and rising from each a knight. It is a radiant domestic scene, and Harry is as dignified as if he knew that royalty was rehearsing it at the other end.

SIR HARRY (*complacently*). Did that seem all right, eh?

LADY SIMS (*much relieved*). I think perfect.

SIR HARRY. But was it dignified?

LADY SIMS. Oh, very. And it will be still more so when you have the sword.

[2]**K.C.** King's Counsel, a high-ranking lawyer

SIR HARRY. The sword will lend it an air. There are really the five moments (*suiting the action to the word*)—the glide—the dip—the kiss—the tap—and you back out a knight. It's short, but it's a very beautiful ceremony. (*Kindly*) Anything you can suggest?

LADY SIMS. No—oh no. (*Nervously, seeing him pause to kiss the tassel of a cushion*) You don't think you have practised till you know what to do almost too well?

(*He has been in a blissful temper, but such niggling criticism would try any man.*)

SIR HARRY. I do not. Don't talk nonsense. Wait till your opinion is asked for.

LADY SIMS (*abashed*). I'm sorry, Harry. (*A perfect butler appears and presents a card.*) "The Flora Type-Writing Agency."

SIR HARRY. Ah, yes. I telephoned them to send some one. A woman, I suppose, Tombes?

TOMBES. Yes, Sir Harry.

SIR HARRY. Show her in here. (*He has very lately become a stickler for etiquette.*) And, Tombes, strictly speaking, you know, I am not Sir Harry till Thursday.

TOMBES. Beg pardon, sir, but it is such a satisfaction to us.

SIR HARRY (*good-naturedly*). Ah, they like it downstairs, do they?

TOMBES (*unbending*). Especially the females, Sir Harry.

SIR HARRY. Exactly. You can show her in, Tombes. (*The butler departs on his mighty task.*) You can tell the woman what she is wanted for, Emmy, while I change. (*He is too modest to boast about himself, and prefers to keep a wife in the house for that purpose.*) You can tell her the sort of things about me that will come better from you. (*Smiling happily*) You heard what Tombes said, "Especially the females." And he is right. Success! The women like it even better than the men. And rightly. For they share. *You* share, *Lady* Sims. Not a woman will see that gown without being sick with envy of it. I know them. Have all our lady friends in to see it. It will make them ill for a week.

(*These sentiments carry him off light-heartedly, and presently the disturbing element is shown in. She is a mere typist, dressed in uncommonly good taste, but at contemptibly small expense, and she is carrying her typewriter in a friendly way rather than as a badge of slavery, as of course it is. Her eye is clear; and in odd contrast to Lady Sims, she is self-reliant and serene.*)

KATE (*respectfully, but she should have waited to be spoken to*). Good morning, madam.

LADY SIMS (*in her nervous way, and scarcely noticing that the typist is a little too ready with her tongue*). Good morning. (*As a first impression she rather likes the woman, and the woman, though it is scarcely worth mentioning, rather likes her. Lady Sims has a maid for buttoning and unbuttoning her, and probably another for waiting on the maid, and she gazes with a little envy perhaps at a woman who does things for herself*). Is that the type-writing machine?

KATE (*who is getting it ready for use*). Yes (*not "Yes, madam," as it ought to be*). I suppose if I am to work here I may take this off. I get on better without it. (*She is referring to her hat.*)

LADY SIMS. Certainly. (*But the hat is already off.*) I ought to apologise for my gown. I am to be presented this week, and I was trying it on. (*Her tone is not really apologetic. She is rather clinging to the glory of her gown, wistfully, as if not absolutely certain, you know, that it is a glory.*)

KATE. It is beautiful, if I may presume to say so. (*She frankly admires it. She probably has a best, and a second best of her own: that sort of thing.*)

LADY SIMS (*with a flush of pride in the gown*). Yes, it is very beautiful. (*The beauty of it gives her courage.*) Sit down, please.

KATE (*the sort of woman who would have sat down in any case*). I suppose it is some copying you want done? I got no particulars. I was told to come to this address, but that was all.

LADY SIMS (*almost with the humility of a servant*). Oh, it is not work for me, it is for my husband, and what he needs is not exactly copying. (*Swelling, for she is proud of Harry*) He wants a number of letters answered—hundreds of them—letters and telegrams of congratulation.

KATE (*as if it were all in the day's work*). Yes?

LADY SIMS (*remembering that Harry expects every wife to do her duty*). My husband is a remarkable man. He is about to be knighted. (*Pause, but Kate does not fall to the floor.*) He is to be knighted for his services to— (*on reflection*) —for his services. (*She is conscious that she is not doing Harry justice.*) He can explain it so much better than I can.

KATE (*in her business-like way*). And I am to answer the congratulations?

LADY SIMS (*afraid that it will be a hard task*). Yes.

KATE (*blithely*). It is work I have had some experience of. (*She proceeds to type.*)

LADY SIMS. But you can't begin till you know what he wants to say.

KATE. Only a specimen letter. Won't it be the usual thing?

LADY SIMS (*to whom this is a new idea*). Is there a usual thing?

KATE. Oh yes.

(*She continues to type, and Lady Sims, half-mesmerised, gazes at her nimble fingers. The useless woman watches the useful one, and she sighs, she could not tell why.*)

LADY SIMS. How quickly you do it. It must be delightful to be able to do something, and to do it well.

KATE (*thankfully*). Yes, it is delightful.

LADY SIMS (*again remembering the source of all her greatness*). But, excuse me, I don't think that will be any use. My husband wants me to explain to you that his is an exceptional case. He did not try to get this honour in any way. It was a complete surprise to him—

KATE (*who is a practical Kate and no dealer in sarcasm*). That is what I have written.

LADY SIMS (*in whom sarcasm would meet a dead wall*). But how could you know?

KATE. I only guessed.

LADY SIMS. Is that the usual thing?

KATE. Oh yes.

LADY SIMS. They don't try to get it?

KATE. I don't know. That is what we are told to say in the letters.

(*To her at present the only important thing about the letters is that they are ten shillings the hundred.*)

LADY SIMS (*returning to surer ground*). I should explain that my husband is not a man who cares for honours. So long as he does his duty—

KATE. Yes, I have been putting that in.

LADY SIMS. Have you? But he particularly wants it to be known that he would have declined a title were it not—

KATE. I have got it here.

LADY SIMS. What have you got?

KATE (*reading*). "Indeed I would have asked to be allowed to decline had it not been that I want to please my wife."

LADY SIMS (*heavily*). But how could you know it was that?

KATE. Is it?

LADY SIMS (*who after all is the one with the right to ask questions*). Do they all accept it for that reason?

KATE. That is what we are told to say in the letters.

LADY SIMS (*thoughtlessly*). It is quite as if you knew my husband.

KATE. I assure you, I don't even know his name.

LADY SIMS (*suddenly showing that she knows him*). Oh, he wouldn't like that.

(*And it is here that Harry re-enters in his city garments, looking so gay, feeling so jolly that we bleed for him. However, the annoying Katherine is to get a shock also.*)

LADY SIMS. This is the lady, Harry.

SIR HARRY (*shooting his cuffs*). Yes, yes. Good morning, my dear.

(*Then they see each other, and their mouths open, but not

for words. After the first surprise Kate seems to find some humour in the situation, but Harry lowers like a thunder-cloud.)

LADY SIMS (*who has seen nothing*). I have been trying to explain to her—

SIR HARRY. Eh—what? (*He controls himself.*) Leave it to me, Emmy; I'll attend to her.

(*Lady Sims goes, with a dread fear that somehow she has vexed her lord, and then Harry attends to the intruder.*)

SIR HARRY (*with concentrated scorn*). You!

KATE (*as if agreeing with him*). Yes, it's funny.

SIR HARRY. The shamelessness of your daring to come here!

KATE. Believe me, it is not less a surprise to me than it is to you. I was sent here in the ordinary way of business. I was given only the number of the house. I was not told the name.

SIR HARRY (*withering her*). The ordinary way of business! This is what you have fallen to—a typist!

KATE (*unwithered*). Think of it!

SIR HARRY. After going through worse straits, I'll be bound.

KATE (*with some grim memories*). Much worse straits.

SIR HARRY (*alas, laughing coarsely*). My congratulations.

KATE. Thank you, Harry.

SIR HARRY (*who is annoyed, as any man would be, not to find her abject*). Eh? What was that you called me, madam?

KATE. Isn't it Harry? On my soul, I almost forget.

SIR HARRY. It isn't Harry to you. My name is Sims, if you please.

KATE. Yes, I had not forgotten that. It was my name, too, you see.

SIR HARRY (*in his best manner*). It was your name till you forfeited the right to bear it.

KATE. Exactly.

SIR HARRY (*gloating*). I was furious to find you here, but on second thoughts it pleases me. (*From the depths of his moral nature*) There is a salt justice in this.

KATE (*sympathetically*). Tell me?

SIR HARRY. Do you know what you were brought here to do?

KATE. I have just been learning. You have been made a knight, and I was summoned to answer the messages of congratulation.

SIR HARRY. That's it, that's it. You come on this day as my servant!

KATE. I, who might have been Lady Sims.

SIR HARRY. And you are her typist instead. And she has four men-servants. Oh, I am glad you saw her in her presentation gown.

KATE. I wonder if she would let me do her washing, Sir Harry?

(*Her want of taste disgusts him.*)

SIR HARRY (*with dignity*). You can go. The mere thought that only a few flights of stairs separates such as you from my innocent children—

(*He will never know why a new light has come into her face.*)

KATE (*slowly*). You have children?

SIR HARRY (*inflated*). Two.

(*He wonders why she is so long in answering.*)

KATE (*resorting to impertinence*). Such a nice number.

SIR HARRY (*with an extra turn of the screw*). Both boys.

KATE. Successful in everything. Are they like you, Sir Harry?

SIR HARRY (*expanding*). They are very like me.

KATE. That's nice.

(*Even on such a subject as this she can be ribald.*)

SIR HARRY. Will you please to go.

KATE. Heigho! What shall I say to my employer?

SIR HARRY. That is no affair of mine.

KATE. What will you say to Lady Sims?

SIR HARRY. I flatter myself that whatever I say, Lady Sims will accept without comment.

(*She smiles, heaven knows why, unless her next remark explains it.*)

KATE. Still the same Harry.

SIR HARRY. What do you mean?

KATE. Only that you have the old confidence in your profound knowledge of the sex.

SIR HARRY (*beginning to think as little of her intellect as of her morals*). I suppose I know my wife.

KATE (*hopelessly dense*). I suppose so. I was only remembering that you used to think you knew her in the days when I was the lady. (*He is merely wasting his time on her, and he indicates the door. She is not sufficiently the lady to retire worsted.*) Well, good-bye, Sir Harry. Won't you ring, and the four men-servants will show me out?

(*But he hesitates.*)

SIR HARRY (*in spite of himself*). As you are here, there is something I want to get out of you. (*Wishing he could ask it less eagerly*) Tell me, who was the man?

(*The strange woman—it is evident now that she has always been strange to him—smiles tolerantly.*)

KATE. You never found out?

SIR HARRY. I could never be sure.

KATE (*reflectively*). I thought that would worry you.

SIR HARRY (*sneering*). It's plain that he soon left you.

KATE. Very soon.

SIR HARRY. As I could have told you. (*But still she surveys him with the smile of the free. The badgered man has to entreat.*) Who was he? It was fourteen years ago, and cannot matter to any of us now. Kate, tell me who he was?

(*It is his first youthful moment, and perhaps because of that she does not wish to hurt him.*)

KATE (*shaking a motherly head*). Better not ask.

SIR HARRY. I do ask. Tell me.

KATE. It is kinder not to tell you.

SIR HARRY (*violently*). Then, by James, it was one of my own pals. Was it Bernard Roche? (*She shakes her head.*) It may have been some one who comes to my house still.

KATE. I think not. (*Reflecting*) Fourteen years! You found my letter that night when you went home?

SIR HARRY (*impatient*). Yes.

KATE. I propped it against the decanters. I thought you would be sure to see it there. It was a room not unlike this, and the furniture was arranged in the same attractive way. How it all comes back to me. Don't you see me, Harry, in hat and cloak, putting the letter there, taking a last look round, and then stealing out into the night to meet—

SIR HARRY. Whom?

KATE. Him. Hours pass, no sound in the room but the tick-tack of the clock, and then about midnight you return alone. You take—

SIR HARRY (*gruffly*). I wasn't alone.

KATE (*the picture spoilt*). No? oh. (*Plaintively*) Here have I all these years been conceiving it wrongly. (*She studies his face.*) I believe something interesting happened?

SIR HARRY (*growling*). Something confoundedly annoying.

KATE (*coaxing*). Do tell me.

SIR HARRY. We won't go into that. Who was the man? Surely a husband has a right to know with whom his wife bolted.

KATE (*who is detestably ready with her tongue*). Surely the wife has a right to know how he took it. (*The woman's love of bargaining comes to her aid.*) A fair exchange. You tell me what happened, and I will tell you who he was.

SIR HARRY. You will? Very well. (*It is the first point on which they have agreed, and, forgetting himself, he takes a place beside her on the fire-seat. He is thinking only of what he is to tell her, but she, woman-like, is conscious of their proximity.*)

KATE (*tastelessly*). Quite like old times. (*He moves away from her indignantly.*) Go on, Harry.

SIR HARRY (*who has a manful shrinking from saying anything that is to his disadvantage*). Well, as you know, I was dining at the club that night.

KATE. Yes.

SIR HARRY. Jack Lamb drove me home. Mabbett Green was with us, and I asked them to come in for a few minutes.

KATE. Jack Lamb, Mabbett Green? I think I remember them. Jack was in Parliament.

SIR HARRY. No, that was Mabbett. They came into the house with me and—(*with sudden horror*)—was it him?

KATE (*bewildered*). Who?

SIR HARRY. Mabbett?

KATE. What?

SIR HARRY. The man?

KATE. What man? (*Understanding*) Oh no. I thought you said he came into the house with you.

SIR HARRY. It might have been a blind.

KATE. Well, it wasn't. Go on.

SIR HARRY. They came in to finish a talk we had been having at the club.

KATE. An interesting talk, evidently.

SIR HARRY. The papers had been full that evening of the elopement of some countess woman with a fiddler. What was her name?

KATE. Does it matter?

SIR HARRY. No. (*Thus ends the countess.*) We had been discussing the thing and—(*he pulls a wry face*) —and I had been rather warm—

KATE (*with horrid relish*). I begin to see. You had been saying it served the husband right, that the man who could not look after his wife deserved to lose her. It was one of your favourite subjects. Oh, Harry, say it was that!

SIR HARRY (*sourly*). It may have been something like that.

KATE. And all the time the letter was there, waiting; and none of you knew except the clock. Harry, it is sweet of you to tell me. (*His face is not sweet. The illiterate woman has used the wrong adjective.*) I forget what I said precisely in the letter.

SIR HARRY (*pulverising her*). So do I. But I have it still.

KATE (*not pulverised*). Do let me see it again. (*She has observed his eye wandering to the desk.*)

SIR HARRY. You are welcome to it as a gift. (*The fateful letter, a poor little dead thing, is brought to light from a locked drawer.*)

KATE (*taking it*). Yes, this is it. Harry; how you did crumple it! (*She reads, not without curiosity.*) "Dear husband—I call you that for the last time—I am off. I am what you call making a bolt of it. I won't try to excuse myself nor to explain, for you would not accept the excuses nor understand the explanation. It will be a little shock to you, but only to your pride; what will astound you is that any woman could be such a fool as to leave such a man as you. I am taking nothing with me that belongs to you. May you be very happy.—Your ungrateful KATE. *P.S.*—You need not try to find out who he is. You will try, but you won't succeed." (*She folds the nasty little thing up.*) I may really have it for my very own?

SIR HARRY. You really may.

KATE (*impudently*). If you would care for a typed copy ——?

SIR HARRY (*in a voice with which he used to frighten his grandmother*). None of your sauce. (*Wincing*) I had to let them see it in the end.

KATE. I can picture Jack Lamb eating it.

SIR HARRY. A penniless parson's daughter.

KATE. That is all I was.

SIR HARRY. We searched for the two of you high and low.

KATE. Private detectives?

SIR HARRY. They couldn't get on the track of you.

KATE (*smiling*). No?

SIR HARRY. But at last the courts let me serve the papers by advertisement on a man unknown, and I got my freedom.

KATE. So I saw. It was the last I heard of you.

SIR HARRY (*each word a blow for her*). And I married again just as soon as ever I could.

KATE. They say that is always a compliment to the first wife.

SIR HARRY (*violently*). I showed them.

KATE. You soon let them see that if one woman was a fool, you still had the pick of the basket to choose from.

SIR HARRY. By James, I did.

KATE (*bringing him to earth again*). But still, you wondered who he was.

SIR HARRY. I suspected everybody—even my pals. I felt like jumping at their throats and crying, "It's you!"

KATE. You had been so admirable to me, an instinct told you that I was sure to choose another of the same.

SIR HARRY. I thought, it can't be money, so it must be looks. Some dolly face. (*He stares at her in perplexity.*) He must have had something wonderful about him to make you willing to give up all that you had with me.

KATE (*as if he was the stupid one*). Poor Harry!

SIR HARRY. And it couldn't have been going on for long, for I would have noticed the change in you.

KATE. Would you?

SIR HARRY. I knew you so well.

KATE. You amazing man.

SIR HARRY. So who was he? Out with it.

KATE. You are determined to know?

SIR HARRY. Your promise. You gave your word.

KATE. If I must—— (*She is the villain of the piece, but it must be conceded that in this matter she is reluctant to pain him.*) I am sorry I promised. (*Looking at him steadily*) There was no one, Harry; no one at all.

SIR HARRY (*rising*). If you think you can play with me——

KATE. I told you that you wouldn't like it.

SIR HARRY (*rasping*). It is unbelievable.

KATE. I suppose it is; but it is true.

SIR HARRY. Your letter itself gives you the lie.

KATE. That was intentional. I saw that if the truth were known you might have a difficulty in getting your freedom; and as I was getting mine it seemed fair that you should have yours also. So I wrote my good-bye in words that would be taken to mean what you thought they meant, and I knew the law would back you in your opinion. For the law, like you, Harry, has a profound understanding of women.

SIR HARRY (*trying to straighten himself*). I don't believe you yet.

KATE (*looking not unkindly into the soul of this man*). Perhaps that is the best way to take it. It is less unflattering than the truth. But you were the only one. (*Summing up her life*). You sufficed.

SIR HARRY. Then what mad impulse——

KATE. It was no impulse, Harry. I had thought it out for a year.

SIR HARRY (*dazed*). A year? One would think to hear you that I hadn't been a good husband to you.

KATE (*with a sad smile*). You were a good husband according to your lights.

SIR HARRY (*stoutly*). I think so.

KATE. And a moral man, and chatty, and quite the philanthropist.

SIR HARRY (*on sure ground*). All women envied you.

KATE. How you loved me to be envied.

SIR HARRY. I swaddled you in luxury.

KATE (*making her great revelation*). That was it.

SIR HARRY (*blankly*). What?

KATE (*who can be serene because it is all over*). How you beamed at me when I sat at the head of your fat dinners in my fat jewelry, surrounded by our fat friends.

SIR HARRY (*aggrieved*). They weren't so fat.

KATE (*a side issue*). All except those who were so thin. Have you ever noticed, Harry, that many jewels make women either incredibly fat or incredibly thin?

SIR HARRY (*shouting*). I have not. (*Is it worth while to argue with her any longer?*) We had all the most interesting society of the day. It wasn't only business men. There were politicians, painters, writers

KATE. Only the glorious, dazzling successes. Oh, the fat talk while we ate too much—about who had made a hit and who was slipping back, and what the noo house cost and the noo motor and the gold soup-plates, and who was to be the noo knight.

SIR HARRY (*who it will be observed is unanswerable from*

first to last). Was anybody getting on better than me, and consequently you?

KATE. Consequently me! Oh, Harry, you and your sublime religion.

SIR HARRY (*honest heart*). My religion? I never was one to talk about religion, but—

KATE. Pooh, Harry, you don't even know what your religion was and is and will be till the day of your expensive funeral. (*And here is the lesson that life has taught her.*) One's religion is whatever he is most interested in, and yours is Success.

SIR HARRY (*quoting from his morning paper*). Ambition—it is the last infirmity of noble minds.

KATE. Noble minds!

SIR HARRY (*at last grasping what she is talking about*). You are not saying that you left me because of my success?

KATE. Yes, that was it. (*And now she stands revealed to him.*) I couldn't endure it. If a failure had come now and then—but your success was suffocating me. (*She is rigid with emotion.*) The passionate craving I had to be done with it, to find myself among people who had not got on.

SIR HARRY (*with proper spirit*). There are plenty of them.

KATE. There were none in our set. When they began to go down-hill they rolled out of our sight.

SIR HARRY (*clinching it*). I tell you I am worth a quarter of a million.

KATE (*unabashed*). That is what you are worth to yourself. I'll tell you what you are worth to me: exactly twelve pounds. For I made up my mind that I could launch myself on the world alone if I first proved my mettle by earning twelve pounds; and as soon as I had earned it I left you.

SIR HARRY (*in the scales*). Twelve pounds!

KATE. That is your value to a woman. If she can't make it she has to stick to you.

SIR HARRY (*remembering perhaps a rectory garden*). You valued me at more than that when you married me.

KATE (*seeing it also*). Ah, I didn't know you then. If only you had been a man, Harry.

SIR HARRY. A man? What do you mean by a man?

KATE (*leaving the garden*). Haven't you heard of them? They are something fine; and every woman is loath to admit to herself that her husband is not one. When she marries, even though she has been a very trivial person, there is in her some vague stirring toward a worthy life, as well as a fear of her capacity for evil. She knows her chance lies in him. If there is something good in him, what is good in her finds it and they join forces against the baser parts. So I didn't give you up willingly, Harry. I invented all sorts of theories to explain you. Your hardness—I said it was a fine want of mawkishness. Your coarseness—I said it goes with strength. Your contempt for the weak—I called it virility. Your want of ideals was clear-sightedness. Your ignoble views of women—I tried to think them funny. Oh, I clung to you to save myself. But I had to let go; you had only the one quality, Harry, success; you had it so strong that it swallowed all the others.

SIR HARRY (*not to be diverted from the main issue*). How did you earn that twelve pounds?

KATE. It took me nearly six months; but I earned it fairly. (*She presses her hand on the typewriter as lovingly as many a woman has pressed a rose.*) I learned this. I hired it and taught myself. I got some work through a friend, and with my first twelve pounds I paid for my machine. Then I considered that I was free to go, and I went.

SIR HARRY. All this going on in my house while you were living in the lap of luxury! (*She nods.*) By God, you were determined.

KATE (*briefly*). By God, I was.

SIR HARRY (*staring*). How you must have hated me.

KATE (*smiling at the childish word*). Not a bit—after I saw that there was a way out. From that hour you amused me, Harry; I was even sorry for you, for I saw that you couldn't help yourself. Success is just a fatal gift.

SIR HARRY. Oh, thank you.

KATE (*thinking, dear friends in front, of you and me perhaps*). Yes, and some of your most successful friends knew it. One or two of them used to look very sad at times, as if they thought they might have come to something if they hadn't got on.

SIR HARRY (*who has a horror of sacrilege*). The battered crew you live among now—what are they but folk who have tried to succeed and failed?

KATE. That's it; they try, but they fail.

SIR HARRY. And always will fail.

KATE. Always. Poor souls—I say of them. Poor soul—they say of me. It keeps us human. That is why I never tire of them.

SIR HARRY (*comprehensively*). Bah! Kate, I tell you I'll be worth half a million yet.

KATE. I'm sure you will. You're getting stout, Harry.

SIR HARRY. No, I'm not.

KATE. What was the name of that fat old fellow who used to fall asleep at our dinner-parties?

SIR HARRY. If you mean Sir William Crackley——

KATE. That was the man. Sir William was to me a perfect picture of the grand success. He had got on so well that he was very, very stout, and when he sat on a chair it was thus (*her hands meeting in front of her*) —as if he were holding his success together. That is what you are working for, Harry. You will have that and the half million about the same time.

SIR HARRY (*who has surely been very patient*). Will you please to leave my house.

KATE (*putting on her gloves, soiled things*). But don't let us part in anger. How do you think I am looking, Harry, compared to the dull, inert thing that used to roll round in your padded carriages?

SIR HARRY (*in masterly fashion*). I forget what you were like. I'm very sure you never could have held a candle to the present Lady Sims.

KATE. That is a picture of her, is it not?

SIR HARRY (*seizing his chance again*). In her wedding-gown. Painted by an R.A.[3]

KATE (*wickedly*). A knight?

SIR HARRY (*deceived*). Yes.

KATE (*who likes Lady Sims: a piece of presumption on her part*). It is a very pretty face.

SIR HARRY (*with the pride of possession*). Acknowledged to be a beauty everywhere.

KATE. There is a merry look in the eyes, and character in the chin.

SIR HARRY (*like an auctioneer*). Noted for her wit.

KATE. All her life before her when that was painted. It is a *spirituelle* face too. (*Suddenly she turns on him with anger, for the first and only time in the play.*) Oh, Harry, you brute!

SIR HARRY (*staggered*). Eh? What?

KATE. That dear creature capable of becoming a noble wife and mother—she is the spiritless woman of no account that I saw here a few minutes ago. I forgive you for myself, for I escaped, but that poor lost soul, oh, Harry, Harry!

SIR HARRY (*waving her to the door*). I'll thank you—If ever there was a woman proud of her husband and happy in her married life, that woman is Lady Sims.

KATE. I wonder.

SIR HARRY. Then you needn't wonder.

KATE (*slowly*). If I was a husband—it is my advice to all of them—I would often watch my wife quietly to see whether the twelve-pound look was not coming into her eyes. Two boys, did you say, and both like you?

SIR HARRY. What is that to you?

KATE (*with glistening eyes*). I was only thinking that somewhere there are two little girls who, when they grow up—the, dear, pretty girls who are all meant for the men that don't get on! Well, good-bye, Sir Harry.

SIR HARRY (*showing a little human weakness, it is to be feared*). Say first that you're sorry.

KATE. For what?

SIR HARRY. That you left me. Say you regret it bitterly. You know you do. (*She smiles and shakes her head. He is pettish. He makes a terrible announcement.*) You have spoilt the day for me.

KATE (*to hearten him*). I am sorry for that; but it is only a pin-prick, Harry. I suppose it is a little jarring in the moment of your triumph to find that there is—one old friend—who does not think you a success; but you will soon forget it. Who cares what a typist thinks?

SIR HARRY (*heartened*). Nobody. A typist at eighteen shillings a week!

KATE (*proudly*). Not a bit of it, Harry. I double that.

SIR HARRY (*neatly*). Magnificent!

(*There is a timid knock at the door.*)

LADY SIMS. May I come in?

SIR HARRY (*rather appealingly*). It is Lady Sims.

KATE. I won't tell. She is afraid to come into her husband's room without knocking!

SIR HARRY. She is not. (*Uxoriously*) Come in, dearest. (*Dearest enters carrying the sword. She might have had the sense not to bring it in while this annoying person is here.*)

LADY SIMS (*thinking she has brought her welcome with her*). Harry, the sword has come.

SIR HARRY (*who will dote on it presently*). Oh, all right.

LADY SIMS. But I thought you were so eager to practise with it.

(*The person smiles at this. He wishes he had not looked to see if she was smiling.*)

SIR HARRY (*sharply*). Put it down.

(*Lady Sims flushes a little as she lays the sword aside.*)

KATE (*with her confounded courtesy*). It is a beautiful sword, if I may say so.

LADY SIMS (*helped*). Yes.

(*The person thinks she can put him in the wrong, does she? He'll show her.*)

SIR HARRY (*with one eye on Kate*). Emmy, the one thing your neck needs is more jewels.

LADY SIMS (*faltering*). More!

SIR HARRY. Some ropes of pearls. I'll see to it. It's a bagatelle to me. (*Kate conceals her chagrin, so she had better be shown the door. He rings.*) I won't detain you any longer, miss.

KATE. Thank you.

LADY SIMS. Going already? You have been very quick.

SIR HARRY. The person doesn't suit, Emmy.

LADY SIMS. I'm sorry.

KATE. So am I, madam, but it can't be helped. Good-bye, your ladyship—good-bye, Sir Harry. (*There is a suspicion of an impertinent curtsey, and she is escorted off the premises by Tombes. The air of the room is purified by her going. Sir Harry notices it at once.*)

LADY SIMS (*whose tendency is to say the wrong thing*). She seemed such a capable woman.

SIR HARRY (*on his hearth*). I don't like her style at all.

[3]**R.A.** member of the Royal Academy

LADY SIMS (*meekly*). Of course you know best. (*This is the right kind of woman.*)

SIR HARRY (*rather anxious for corroboration*). Lord, how she winced when I said I was to give you those ropes of pearls.

LADY SIMS. Did she? I didn't notice. I suppose so.

SIR HARRY (*frowning*). Suppose? Surely I know enough about women to know that.

LADY SIMS. Yes, oh yes.

SIR HARRY. (*Odd that so confident a man should ask this.*) Emmy, I know you well, don't I? I can read you like a book, eh?

LADY SIMS (*nervously*). Yes, Harry.

SIR HARRY (*jovially, but with an inquiring eye*). What a different existence yours is from that poor lonely wretch's.

LADY SIMS. Yes, but she has a very contented face.

SIR HARRY (*with a stamp of his foot*). All put on. What?

LADY SIMS (*timidly*). I didn't say anything.

SIR HARRY (*snapping*). One would think you envied her.

LADY SIMS. Envied? Oh no—but I thought she looked so alive. It was while she was working the machine.

SIR HARRY. Alive! That's no life. It is you that are alive. (*Curtly*) I'm busy, Emmy. (*He sits at his writing-table.*)

LADY SIMS (*dutifully*). I'm sorry; I'll go, Harry. (*Inconsequentially*) Are they very expensive?

SIR HARRY. What?

LADY SIMS. Those machines?

(*When she has gone the possible meaning of her question startles him. The curtain hides him from us, but we may be sure that he will soon be bland again. We have a comfortable feeling, you and I, that there is nothing of Harry Sims in us.*)

TOPICS FOR DISCUSSION AND WRITING

1. In the first line of his introductory remarks Barrie says, "Harry Sims is you." Now that you have read the play, what do you take Barrie to be getting at in this remark?
2. Look at the description of Mrs. Sims in Barrie's introduction, and explain it in the light of the entire play.
3. Barrie's introduction ends thus: "*It is a radiant domestic scene, and Harry is as dignified as if he knew that royalty was rehearsing it at the other end.*" Imagine the action—stage it in your mind. As you see it, is Harry "dignified" at this moment? Why, or why not?
4. Where do you hear the first note of conflict? What does the passage tell you about the two characters?
5. Before the arrival of the typist, Harry says, "Success! The women like it even better than the men." How much does Harry know about women? About himself?
6. If you found certain passages of dialogue especially amusing, try to account for why at least one of them pleases you.

Some Kinds of Drama

Tragedy and Comedy

Whimsical assertions that all of us are Platonists or Aristotelians, or liberals or conservatives ("Nature wisely does contrive / That every boy and every gal / That's born into the world alive / Is either a little Liberal / Or else a little Conservative"), reveal a tendency to divide things into two. Two is about right: Peace and war, man and woman, day and night, life and death. There may be middle cases; there is the cold war, and Edmund Burke suggested that no one can point to the precise moment that divides day from night—but Burke also suggested that everyone can make the useful distinction between day and night. The distinction between comedy and tragedy may not always be easy to make, but until the twentieth century it was usually clear enough.

Hamlet, which in Horatio's words is concerned with "woe or wonder," is a tragedy; *A Midsummer Night's Dream,* which in Puck's words is concerned with things that pleasingly "befall preposterously," is a comedy. The best plays of our century, however, are another thing, and discussion of these plays—somewhat desperately called tragicomedy—will be postponed until later in this chapter.

What befalls—preposterous or not—is the action of the play. The gestures on the stage are, of course, "actions," but they are not the action of the play in the sense of Aristotle's use of ***praxis,*** or "action" in *The Poetics,* a fragmentary treatise of the fourth century B.C. that remains the starting point for most discussions of drama. For Aristotle, drama is the imitation (i.e., representation, re-presentation, re-creation) by impersonators, of an action. In tragedy the action is serious and important, something that matters, done by people who count (e.g., King Oedipus's discovery that he has killed his father and married his mother); in comedy (for Aristotle), the action is done by unimportant laughable people who make mistakes that do not cause us pain. Commonly the tragic action is a man's perception of a great mistake he has made; he suffers intensely and perhaps dies, having exhausted all the possibilities of his life. (Female tragic heroes are rare.) The comic action often is the exposure of folly and the renewal rather than the exhaustion of human nature. Crabby parents, for example, find that they cannot keep young lovers apart, and so they join in the marriage festivities. Byron jocosely put the matter thus:

IMITATION OF AN ACTION

> All tragedies are finished by a death,
> All comedies are ended by a marriage.

All tragedies and all comedies do not in fact end thus, but the idea is right; tragedy has the solemnity, seriousness, and finality we often associate with death,[1] and comedy has the joy and fertility and suggestion of a new life we often associate with marriage.

This concept of *an action* (i.e., an underlying motif, not merely gestures) in tragedy and in comedy makes clear that comedy is not a mere matter of jokes or funny bits of business. It also makes clear what the Greek comic playwright Menander meant when he told a friend that he had composed a play, and now had only to write the dialogue: he had worked out the happenings that would embody the action, and there remained only the slighter task of providing the spirited words. The same idea is implicit in Ibsen's comment that the drafts of his plays differed "very much from each other in characterization, not in action." The action or happening dramatized in a tragedy or a comedy may be conceived of as a single course or train of events manifested on the stage by a diversity of activities. Think of such expressions as "the closing of the frontier," or "the revival of learning"; each might be said to denote an action, though such action is seen only in its innumerable manifestations.

[1] Shakespeare's tragedies all end with the death of the tragic hero, but a good many Greek tragedies do not. In *Oedipus the King* the hero remains alive, but he is blind and banished and seems to have exhausted the possibilities of his life. Some other Greek tragedies have what can reasonably be called a happy ending; i.e., some sort of joyful reconciliation. For example, in Sophocles's *Philoctetes,* the weapon which has been taken from the sick Philoctetes is returned to him, and Heracles, a messenger from Zeus, announces that Philoctetes will be healed. But these tragedies with happy endings, like those with unhappy endings, deal with "important" people, and they are about "serious" things. If there is finally joy, it is a solemn joy.

HAPPENINGS AND HAPPENINGS

Tragic playwrights take some happening, from history (for example, the assassination of Julius Caesar), or from fiction (Shakespeare derived Othello from an Italian short story), or from their own imagination, and they make or shape or arrange episodes that clarify the action. They make (in common terminology) a *plot* that embodies the action or spiritual content. Even when playwrights draw on history, they make their own plot because they select and rearrange the available historical facts. A reenactment of everything that Julius Caesar did during his last days or hours would not be a play with an action, for drama is not so much concerned with what in fact *happened* as with some sort of typical and coherent or unified thing that *happens,* a significant action. Sometimes, of course, history provides substantial material for drama, but even Shakespeare's *Julius Caesar* takes frequent liberties with the facts as Shakespeare knew them, and Shakespeare's source, the biographer Plutarch, doubtless had already assimilated the facts to a literary form. At most we can say that history provided Shakespeare with a man whose life lent itself well to an established literary form. Not every life does lend itself thus. We are told that Aeschylus, the earliest tragic playwright who has left us any complete plays, was killed when an eagle mistook his bald head for a rock and dropped a turtle on it to break the shell. Aeschylus's death was a great loss, but it did not have the unified significant action required of tragedy. By chance an eagle that had captured a turtle was near to Aeschylus, and Aeschylus by chance (or rather by his chemistry) was bald. There is no relation between these two circumstances; Aeschylus's death (allegedly) happened this way, and we can account for it, but the event has no intelligible unity. (A sentence from Vladimir Nabokov's *Pale Fire* comes to mind: If one is contemplating suicide, "jumping from a high bridge is not recommended even if you cannot swim, for wind and water abound in weird contingencies, and tragedy ought not to culminate in a record dive or a policeman's promotion.")

UNITY

In tragedy things cohere. The hero normally does some deed and suffers as a consequence. Actions have consequences in the moral world no less than in the materialistic world of the laboratory. The tragic playwright's solemn presentation of "the remorseless working of things," Alfred North Whitehead pointed out (in his *Science and the Modem World,* 1925), is "the vision possessed by science," and it cannot be accidental that the two great periods of tragic drama, fifth-century B.C. Athens and England around 1600, were periods of scientific inquiry.

THE TRAGIC HERO

This emphasis on causality means that the episodes are related, connected, and not merely contiguous. Generally the formula is to show the tragic hero moving toward committing some deed that will cause great unintended suffering, committing it, and then, by seeing the consequences, learning the true nature of his deed. The plot, that is, involves a credible character whose doings are related to his nature. For Aristotle, in the best sort of tragedy the tragic hero is an important person, almost preeminently virtuous, who makes some sort of great mistake that entails great suffering. Calamity does not descend upon him from above, does not happen *to* him, nor does he consciously will a destructive act; he merely makes a great mistake. The mistake is Aristotle's ***hamartia,*** sometimes translated as "error," sometimes as "flaw." Probably Aristotle did not mean by *hamartia* a trait, such as rashness or ambition, which the translation "flaw" implies, but simply meant an action based on a mental error, a sort of false step.

HAMARTIA

Oedipus, erroneously thinking that Polybus and Meropê are his parents, flees from them when he hears that he will kill his father and sleep with his mother. His action is commendable, but it happens to be a great mistake because it brings him to his real parents. Nevertheless, despite the scholarly elucidations of Aristotle, we can sometimes feel that the erring action proceeds from a particular kind of character, that a person with different traits would not have acted in the same way. The Oedipus that we see in the play, for example, is a self-assured quick-tempered man—almost a rash man, we might say—who might well have neglected to check the facts before he fled from Corinth. There are at least times, even when reading *Oedipus the King*, when one feels with George Meredith (1828–1909) that

> in tragic life, God wot,
> No villain need be! Passions spin the plot:
> We are betrayed by what is false within.

HYBRIS

From this it is only a short step to identifying *hamartia* with a flaw, and the flaw most often attributed to the tragic hero is ***hybris,*** a word that for the Greeks meant something like "bullying," "abuse of power," but in dramatic criticism usually is translated as "overweening pride." The tragic hero forgets that (in Montaigne's words) "on the loftiest throne in the world we are still sitting only on our own rear," and he believes his actions are infallible. King Lear, for example, banishes his daughter Cordelia with "Better thou / Hadst not been born than not t' have pleased me better." Macbeth, told that he will be king of Scotland, chooses to make the prophecy come true by murdering his guest, King Duncan; Brutus decides that Rome can be saved from tyranny only by killing Caesar, and he deludes himself into thinking he is not murdering Caesar but sacrificing Caesar for the welfare of Rome.

PERIPETEIA

We have talked of *hamartia* and *hybris* in tragedy; two more Greek words, ***peripeteia*** and ***anagnorisis,*** also common in discussions of tragedy, ought to be mentioned. A peripeteia (sometimes anglicized to *peripety* or translated as "reversal") occurs when the action takes a course not intended by the doer. Aristotle gives two examples: (1) the Messenger comes to cheer up Oedipus by freeing him from fears but the message heightens Oedipus' fears; (2) Danaus (in a lost play) prosecutes a man but is himself killed.

A few other examples may be useful: Oedipus flees from Corinth to avoid contact with his parents, but his flight brings him to them; Macbeth kills Duncan to gain the crown but his deed brings him fearful nights instead of joyful days; Lear, seeking a peaceful old age, puts himself in the hands of two daughters who maltreat him, and banishes the one daughter who later will comfort him. The Bible—especially the Hebrew Bible—is filled with such peripeties or ironic actions. For example, the Philistines brought Samson before them to entertain them, and he performed his most spectacular feat by destroying his audience. But the archetypal tragic story is that of Adam and Eve: aiming to be like gods, they lost their immortality and the earthly paradise, and brought death to themselves.

ANAGNORISIS

The other Greek word, ***anagnorisis,*** translated as "recognition" or "discovery" or "disclosure," seems to have meant for Aristotle a clearing up of some misunderstanding, such as the proper identification of someone or the revelation of some previously unknown fact. But later critics have given it a richer meaning and used it to describe the hero's perception of his or her true nature or true plight. In the narrow sense, it is an anagnorisis or "recognition" when King Lear learns that Regan and Goneril are ungrateful and cruel. In the wider sense, the anagnorisis is in his speech in 3.4, when he confesses his former ignorance and his neglect of his realm:

> Poor naked wretches, wheresoe'er you are,
> That bide the pelting of this pitiless storm,
> How shall your houseless heads and unfed sides,
> Your looped and windowed raggedness, defend you
> From seasons such as these? O, I have ta'en
> Too little care of this! Take physic, pomp;
> Expose thyself to feel what wretches feel,
> That thou mayst shake the superflux to them,
> And show the heavens more just.

Similarly Hamlet's "There is special providence in the fall of a sparrow," and Othello's "one that loved not wisely, but too well," may be called recognition scenes. Here is Macbeth's recognition that his purpose has been frustrated, that his deed has been ironic:

> My way of life
> Is fall'n into the sear, the yellow leaf
> And that which should accompany old age,
> As honor, love, obedience, troops of friends,
> I must not look to have.

THE SOCIAL WORLD OF COMEDY

"Troops of friends" abound in comedy. Where tragedy is primarily the dramatization of the single life that ripens and then can only rot, that reaches its fullest and then is destroyed, comedy is primarily the dramatization of the renewing of the self and of social relationships. Tragic heroes are isolated from society, partly by their different natures, and partly by their tragic acts; comedy suggests that selfhood is found not in assertion of individuality, but in joining in the fun, in becoming part of the flow of common humanity. Where tragedy suggests an incompatibility between the energy or surge of the individual life and the laws of life or the norms of society, comedy suggests that norms are valid and necessary. Tragic heroes do what they feel compelled to do; they assert themselves, and are intensely aware that they are special persons and not members of the crowd. But that their mistake always reveals that they are hybristic is not at all certain. The Greek tragic hero is commonly set against a chorus of ordinary mortals who caution him, wring their hands, and lament the hero's boldness, but these ordinary mortals are always aware that if they are law-abiding people, they are also less fully human beings than the hero. That they obey society's laws is not due to superior virtue, to the triumph of reason over will, to self-discipline; rather, their obedience is due to a lower vision, or to timidity, and indeed sometimes to a fear of what resides in their own breasts.

TRAGIC ISOLATION

Tragic heroes are, of course, in one way inferior to those about them; their actions cost them great suffering, and they are thus immobilized as the others are not. But their greatness remains indisputable; the anguish that at times paralyzes Hamlet also makes him greater than, say, Horatio and Laertes. In fact, tragic heroes are circumscribed, certainly after the deed, when they are necessarily subject to the consequences (Brutus kills Caesar and finds that he brings to Rome a turmoil that makes him flee from Rome and that ultimately makes him take his own life); even before doing the tragic deed, the heroes are circumscribed because their action proceeds from something, either from their personality or from their circumstances. Still, their action seems to them to be freely theirs, and indeed we feel that it is an action that lesser persons could not perform. This perception is almost a way of arguing that a tragic hero may err not so much from weakness as from strength. Why can Iago so easily deceive Othello? Not because Othello is an unthinking savage, or an unsophisticated foreigner, but because (as Iago admits) Othello is of a "loving noble nature," and, again,

TRAGIC VIRTUE

> The Moor is of *a free and open nature*
> *That thinks men honest* that but seem to be so;
> And will as tenderly be led by th' nose
> As asses are.

Why can Claudius see to it that Laertes murders Hamlet during a fencing match? Not because Hamlet is a poor fencer, or a coward, but because Hamlet

> *Most generous, and free from all contriving,*
> Will not peruse the foils.

TRAGIC JOY

This is not to say that tragic heroes are faultless, or that they are quite happy with themselves and with their action; but they do experience a kind of exultation even in their perception that disaster is upon them. If they grieve over their deeds, we sense a glory in their grief, for they find, like Captain Ahab, that in their topmost grief lies their topmost greatness. At last they see everything and know that nothing more can be experienced. They have lived their lives to the limits. Othello put it thus:

> Here is my journey's end, here is my butt,
> And very seamark of my utmost sail.

(In a comedy Shakespeare tells us that "journeys end in lovers meeting," that is, the end is a new beginning.)

In "Under Ben Bulben" William Butler Yeats (1865–1939) suggests the sense of completeness that the tragic hero experiences when, under the influence of a great passion, he exhausts his nature and seems to be not a man among men but a partner (rather than a subject) of fate:

> Know that when all words are said
> And a man is fighting mad,
> Something drops from eyes long blind,
> He completes his partial mind,
> For an instant stands at ease,
> Laughs aloud, his heart at peace.
> Even the wisest man grows tense
> With some sort of violence
> Before he can accomplish fate,
> Know his work or choose his mate.

Elsewhere Yeats put his distinction between the tragic hero and the world the hero is up against thus: "Some Frenchman[2] has said that farce is the struggle against a ridiculous object, comedy against a movable object, tragedy against an immovable; and because the will, or energy, is greatest in tragedy, tragedy is the more noble; but I add that 'will or energy is eternal delight,' and when its limit is reached it may become a pure, aimless joy, though the man, the shade, still mourns his lost object."

COMIC ASSERTION

What of the contexts and times when we find passionate self-assertion funny? Much depends on what is being asserted, and on what or who the antagonist is. King Lear against his tigerish daughters is a tragic figure, but a pedant against a dull schoolboy may be a comic one. The lament of the tragic hero is proportionate to the event, but the effort extended by the comic figure is absurdly disproportionate. Furthermore, as Henri Bergson (1859–1941) pointed out, the comic figure usually is a sort of mechanism, repeating his actions and catch phrases with clocklike regularity in contexts where they are inappropriate. He quotes Latin on every occasion, or he never travels without his pills, or she always wants to know how much something costs, or he is forever spying on his wife. Bergson, who suggested that the comic is "the mechanical encrusted on the living," illustrated his point by telling of the customs officers who bravely rescue the crew of a sinking vessel, and then ask, the moment the shore is reached, "Have you anything to declare?" The mechanical question, inappropriate in the situation, reveals that the officers value trivial regulations as much as they do life itself. In *The Circus* Charlie Chaplin is dusting things off; he comes upon the magician's bowl of goldfish, takes the fish out and wipes them, and then returns them to the bowl.

COMIC JOY

The comic world seems to be presided over by a genial, tolerant deity who enjoys the variety that crosses the stage. The sketchbooks of the Japanese artist Hokusai (1760– 1849) wonderfully reveal this comic delight in humanity. There are pages of fat men, pages of thin men (no less engagingly drawn), pages of men making funny faces, and there is a delightful drawing of a man holding a magnifying glass in front of his face so that his nose seems enormous. Comic playwrights give us something of this range of types and grotesques, and they give us also variety in language (e.g., puns, inverted clichés, malapropisms) and variety in episodes (much hiding behind screens, dressing in disguise). The characters, then, who insist on being themselves, who mechanically hold to a formula of language or of behavior, are laughably out of place in the world of varied people who live and let live. What comedy does not tolerate is intolerance; it regularly suggests that the intolerant—for example, the pedant and the ascetic—are fools and probably hypocrites. Here is the self-righteous Alceste, in Molière's *The Misanthrope:*

COMIC ISOLATION

> Some men I hate for being rogues: the others,
> I hate because they treat the rogues like brothers,
> And, lacking a virtuous scorn for what is vile,
> Receive the villain with a complaisant smile.
> Notice how tolerant people choose to be
> Toward that bold rascal who's at law with me.

[2]Yeats is rather freely summarizing Ferdinand Brunetière's *La Loi du théâtre.* A translation of Brunetière's treatise is available in *European Theories of the Drama,* ed. Barrett H. Clark.

Philinte genially replies,

> Let's have an end of rantings and of railings,
> And show some leniency toward human failings.
> This world requires a pliant rectitude;
> Too stern a virtue makes one stiff and rude.

Here is the puritanical Malvolio in *Twelfth Night,* trying to quiet down some tipsy but genial revelers:

> My masters, are you mad? Or what are you? Have you no wit, manners nor honesty, but to gabble like tinkers at this time of night? Do ye make an alehouse of my lady's house? . . . Is there not respect of place, persons, nor time in you?

He is aptly answered:

> Art any more than a steward? Dost thou think, because thou art virtuous, there shall be no more cakes and ale?

This suspicion of a "virtue" that is opposed to cakes and ale runs through the history of comedy.

In Shakespeare's *Love's Labor Lost,* the young noblemen who vow to devote themselves to study, and to forgo the company of women, are laughed at until they accept their bodies and admit interest in those of the ladies. The celebration of the human body, or at least the good-natured acceptance of it which is present in comedy, is well-put by the General in Anouilh's *The Waltz of the Toreadors:*

> You're in the ocean, splashing about, doing your damndest not to drown, in spite of whirlpools and cross currents. The main thing is to do the regulation breast-stroke and if you're not a clod, never to let the life-buoy ["the ideal"] out of sight. No one expects any more than that out of you. Now if you relieve yourself in the water now and then, that's your affair. The sea is big, and if the top half of your body still looks as though it's doing the breaststroke, nobody will say a word.

DETACHMENT AND ENGAGEMENT

One way of distinguishing between comedy and tragedy is summarized in Horace Walpole's aphorism "This world is a comedy to those that think, a tragedy to those that feel." Life seen thoughtfully, with considerable detachment, viewed from above, as it were, is an amusing pageant, and the comic writer gives us something of this view. With Puck we look at the antics in the forest, smile tolerantly, and say with a godlike perspective, "Lord, what fools these mortals be!" But in tragedy we are to a greater degree engaged; the tragic dramatist manages to make us in large measure identify ourselves with the hero, feel his plight as if it were our own, and value his feelings as he values them.[3] Yeats noticed this when he said that "character is continuously present in comedy alone," and that "tragedy must always be a drowning and breaking of the dykes that separate man from man. . . . It is upon these dykes comedy keeps house." And Yeats again: "Nor when the tragic reverie is at its height do we say, 'How well that

[3] Bergson's theory that a human being—an organism—is comical when it behaves mechanically requires, as Bergson said, a modification: feelings must be suppressed. A crippled man is not comic despite his mechanical limp, because we feel for him. Comedy requires, Bergson said, an "anesthesia of the heart."

man is realised, I should know him were I to meet him in the street,' for it is always ourselves that we see upon the [tragic] stage."

One consequence of this distinction between tragedy and comedy, between looking-at and feeling-with, is that the comic plot is usually more intricate than the tragic plot, and less plausible. The comic plot continues to trip up its characters, bringing them into numerous situations that allow them to display their folly over and again. The complex comic plot is often arbitrary, full of the workings of Fortune or Chance, and we delight at each new unexpected or unlikely happening. In tragedy, Fate (sometimes in the form that "character is destiny") or Necessity rules, there is the consistency and inevitability, the "remorseless working of things," that has already been mentioned. If Macbeth were struck dead by a falling roof tile while he dozed in the palace after a good meal, instead of dying on Macduff's sword, or if Brutus were to die by slipping in his bath, instead of dying on the very sword with which he killed Caesar, we would have arbitrary happenings that violate the spirit of everything that precedes. But the unexpected letters and the long-lost relatives that often turn up at the close of a comedy are thoroughly in the spirit of the comic vision, which devalues not only rigidly consistent character but rigidity of every sort, even of plot. Tragedy usually follows a straight course, comedy a delightfully twisted one.

TRAGIC FATE AND COMIC FORTUNE IN PLOTS

The rigid behavior of some of comedy's laughably serious characters (e.g., misers, jealous husbands, stern fathers) is paralleled in the rigid circumstances that often are sketched at the beginning of a comedy. In *A Midsummer Night's Dream* the Athenian law requires that a young woman marry the man of her father's choice, or be put to death, or live chastely in a nunnery. Gilbert and Sullivan, to draw on familiar material, afford plenty of examples of comedy's fondness for a cantankerous beginning: *The Mikado* opens with a chorus of Japanese noblemen whose code of etiquette makes them appear to be "worked by strings"; they live in a town where a law ordered that "all who flirted, leered or winked / Should forthwith be beheaded." (Comedy often begins with a society dominated by some harsh law.) Although this law has been suspended, another harsh decree is in effect: the pretty Yum-Yum is betrothed to her old guardian, Ko-Ko. We learn, too, that her appropriate wooer, Nanki-Poo, is a prince who has had to disguise himself as a humble wandering minstrel to escape his father's decree that he marry Katisha, an old and ugly lady of the court.

COMIC BEGINNINGS AND ENDINGS

After various doings in a comedy, a new—presumably natural, prosperous, fertile, and free—society is formed, usually centered around young lovers who are going to be married. Yum-Yum and Nanki-Poo finally contrive to get married, evading Katisha and Ko-Ko, who make the best of things by marrying each other. The whole business is satisfactorily explained to the Mikado, who affably accepts, and ruffled tempers are soothed:

> The threatened cloud has passed away,
> And brightly shines the dawning day;
> What though the night may come too soon,
> We've years and years of afternoon!
>
> Then let the throng
> Our joy advance,

With laughing song
　　And merry dance,
With joyous shout and ringing cheer,
Inaugurate our new career!

The first four lines are sung by the young lovers, the remaining six are sung by "All," the new, or renewed, society, free from unnatural law. *H.M.S. Pinafore* begins with lovers who cannot marry because of disparity in rank, but ends with appropriate shifts in rank so that there can be "three loving pairs on the same day united."

In comedy there is often not only an improbable turn in events but an improbable (but agreeable) change in character—or at least in rank; troublesome persons become enlightened, find their own better nature, and join in the fun, commonly a marriage-feast. Finding one's own nature is common in tragedy, too, but there self-knowledge is co-terminous with death or some death-like condition, such as blindness. *Oedipus the King* ends with a note of finality, even though Oedipus is alive at the end; the fact that twenty-five years later Sophocles decided to write a play showing Oedipus's apotheosis does not allow us to see the earlier play as less than complete. The chorus in *Oedipus the King* has the last word:

SELF-KNOWLEDGE

　　　　　　　　　This man was Oedipus.
That mighty King, who knew the riddle's mystery,
Whom all the city envied, Fortune's favorite.
Behold, in the event, the storm of his calamities,
And, being mortal, think on that last day of death,
Which all must see, and speak of no man's happiness
Till, without sorrow, he hath passed the goal of life.

Or consider the irreparable loss at the end of Shakespeare's tragedies: "This was the noblest Roman of them all"; "We that are young / Shall never see so much, nor live so long"; "The rest is silence." But comedy ends with a new beginning, a newly formed society, usually a wedding party; the tragic figure commonly awakens to the fact that he has made a big mistake and his life is over, but the comic figure commonly awakens to his better nature. He usually sheds his aberration and is restored to himself and to a renewed society. Alceste's refusal to change, at the end of *The Misanthrope,* helps to push that comedy toward the borderline between comedy and tragedy. Oedipus learns that his parents were not those whom he had supposed, and he learns that even the mighty Oedipus can be humbled. Othello comes to see himself as a man "that loved not wisely but too well," and, having reached his journey's end, he executes justice upon himself by killing himself. That is, at the end of the play he finds himself, but this finding of the self separates him forever from those around him, whereas the comic figure who finds himself usually does so by putting aside in some measure his individuality and by submitting himself to a partner or to the group.

Comedy and tragedy offer different visions and represent different psychological states. And they are equally useful. The tragic vision may have more prestige, but it is no small thing to make people laugh, to call attention amusingly to the follies and joys of life, and to help develop the sense of humor—and humility—that may be indispensable to survival in a world continually threatened by aggressive ideals that demand uncritical acceptance. Infants smile easily, and children laugh often, but growing up is often attended by a frightening seriousness. True, hostile laughter, the scarcely veiled aggressiveness that manifests itself in derision, remains an adult possession, but the laughter evoked by the best comedy is good-natured while it is critical, and it is in part directed at ourselves. We look at bumbling humanity and we recall Puck's words, "Lord, what fools these mortals be." This is not to say that the comic vision is cynical; rather, it attributes to folly what less generous visions attribute to ill will or to hopeless corruption, and when it laughs it forgives. Analyses of laughter are sometimes funny but more often they are tedious; still, they at least pay the comic spirit the compliment of recognizing it as worthy of our best efforts.

Tragicomedy

TRAGICOMEDY BEFORE 1900

The word *tragicomedy* is much newer than the words *tragedy* and *comedy;* it first appeared about 186 B.C., when Plautus spoke of *tragicocomoedia* in his *Amphitryon,* a Roman comedy in which gods assume mortal shapes in order to dupe a husband and seduce his wife. Mercury, in a joking prologue to the play, explains the author's dilemma:

> I'll make it a mixture, a tragicomedy. It wouldn't be right for me to make it all a comedy since kings and gods appear. Well, then, since there's a slave part too, I'll do as I said and make it a tragicomedy.

But the play is a traditional comedy, unalloyed with the solemnity, terror, and pity of tragedy. It shows laughable activities that finally turn out all right. It should be mentioned again, however, that although tragedy and comedy were clearly separated in the ancient world, not all ancient tragedies ended with death, or even ended unhappily. Aeschylus's trilogy, *The Oresteia,* ends with reconciliation and solemn joy (but it has been bought at the price of great suffering), and Sophocles's *Philoctetes* and Euripides's *Iphigeneia at Taurus* end with catastrophes averted. They were tragic for the Greeks because momentous issues were treated seriously, though we might say that the plots have a comic structure because they end happily.

In the Renaissance there was much fussing over the meanings of tragedy, comedy, and tragicomedy, but most theoreticians inclined to the view that tragedy dealt with noble figures engaged in serious actions, was written in a lofty style, and ended unhappily; comedy dealt with humbler figures engaged in trivial actions, was written in relatively common diction, and ended happily. Tragicomedy, whether defined as some mixture (e.g., high people in trivial actions) or as a play in which, to quote Sir Philip Sidney, the writer "thrust in the clown by head and shoulders to play a part in majestical matters," was for the most part scorned by academic critics as a mongrel. It was merely additive, bits of comedy added to a tragedy. At best the advocates for tragicomedy could argue that a play without the terror of tragedy and the absurdity of comedy can cover a good deal of life and can please a good many tastes. But this sort of play, unlike modern tragicomedy, is not so much a union of tragedy and comedy as an exclusion of both, lacking, for example, the awe we associate with tragedy and the fun we associate with comedy.

In the twentieth century the word and the form have become thoroughly respectable; indeed, it is now evident that most of the best plays of our century are best described not as tragedies or as comedies but as tragicomedies—distinctive fusions (not mere aggregations) of tragedy and comedy. For a start we can take William Hazlitt's statement that "man is the only animal that laughs and weeps; for he is the only animal that is struck with the difference between what things are, and what they ought to be." Another way of putting it is to say that human beings have an ideal of conduct, but circumstances and human limitations prevent them from fulfilling this ideal. This pursuit of the ideal thus can seem noble, or foolish, or a mixture of the two.

Most of the best playwrights of the twentieth century have adopted the more complicated mixed view. Comedy had customarily invoked a considerable degree of detachment; in Bergson's formula (1900), already quoted, comedy requires an anesthesia of the spectators' hearts as they watch folly on the stage. Tragedy, on the other hand, has customarily invoked a considerable degree of involvement or sympathy; in Walpole's formula, also already quoted, "The world is a comedy to those that think, a tragedy to those that feel." But tragicomedy shows us comic characters for whom we feel deep sympathy. Pirandello, in his essay *Umorismo* (1908), gives an interesting example of the phenomenon. Suppose, he says, we see an elderly woman with dyed hair and much too much makeup. We find her funny; but if we realize that she is trying to hold the attention of her husband, our sympathy is aroused. Our sense of her absurdity is not totally dissipated, but we feel for her and so our laughter is combined with pity.

DETACHMENT AND ENGAGEMENT AGAIN

THEATER OF THE ABSURD

In the third quarter of the twentieth century the theater that was most vital was not the Broadway musical, the earnest problem-play, or the well-made drawing-room comedy (although these continued to be written) but a fairly unified body of drama called the absurd, whose major writers are Beckett, Genet, Ionesco, Pinter, and Albee. Their theme is human anguish, but their techniques are those of comedy: improbable situations and unheroic characters who say funny things. These writers differ, of course, and differ from play to play, but they are all preoccupied with the loneliness of people in a world without the certainties afforded by God or by optimistic rationalism. This loneliness is heightened by a sense of impotence derived partly from an awareness of our inability to communicate in a society that has made language meaningless, and partly from an awareness of the precariousness of our existence in an atomic age.

Behind this vision are some two hundred years of thinking that have conspired to make it difficult to think of any person as a hero who confronts a mysterious cosmic order. Man, Ionesco says in *Notes and Counter Notes,* is "cut off from his religious and metaphysical roots." One of the milestones in the journey toward contemporary nihilism is the bourgeois drama of the middle of the eighteenth century, which sought to show the dignity of the common people but which, negatively put, undermined the concept of a tragic hero. Instead of showing a heroic yet universal figure, it showed ordinary people in relation to their society, thus paving the way for Arthur Miller's Willy Loman, who apparently would have been okay, as we all would be, if our economic system allowed for early retirement. Miller's play makes no claim for Willy's grandeur or for the glory of life; it claims only that he is an ordinary man at the end of his rope in a deficient society and that he is entitled to a fair deal.

DIMINUTION OF HUMAN BEINGS

Other landmarks on the road to our awareness of our littleness are, like bourgeois drama, developments in thinking that were believed by their builders to be landmarks on the road to our progressive conquest of fear. Among these we can name Darwin's *The Origin of Species* (1859), which, in the popular phrase, seemed to record progress "up from apes," but which, more closely read, reduced human beings to the product of "accidental variations" and left God out of the picture, substituting for a cosmic order a barbaric struggle for existence. (In the second edition, 1860, Darwin spoke of life as "breathed by the creator," but the creator was not Darwin's concern and he later abandoned all religious beliefs. Probably he retained his belief that the process of "natural selection works solely by and for the good of each being," but by 1889 his disciple Huxley saw it differently. Huxley said he knew of no study "so unutterably saddening as that of the evolution of humanity.") Karl Marx, studying the evolution of societies at about the same time, was attributing our sense of alienation to economic forces, thereby implying that we have no identity we can properly call our own. Moreover, Marxist thinking, like Darwinian thinking, suggested that human beings could not do anything of really great importance, nor could they be blamed for their misfortunes. At the end of the nineteenth century, and in the early twentieth century, Freud, also seeking to free us from tyranny, turned to the forces within our mind. Ironically, the effort to chart our unconscious drives and anarchic impulses in order to help us to know ourselves induced a profound distrust of the self: we can scarcely be confident of our behavior, for we know that apparently heroic behavior has unconscious unheroic motives rooted in the experiences of infancy. Tragic heroes are people with complexes, and religious codes are only wishful thinking.

DISSOLUTION OF CHARACTER AND PLOT

The result of such developments in thought seems to be that a "tragic sense" in the twentieth century commonly means a despairing or deeply uncertain view, something very different from what it meant in Greece and in Elizabethan England. This uncertainty is not merely about the cosmos but even about character or identity. In 1888, in the Preface to *Miss Julie,* August Strindberg called attention to the new sense of the instability of character:

> I have made the people in my play fairly "characterless." The middle-class conception of a fixed character was transferred to the stage, where the middle class has always ruled. A character there came to mean an actor who was always one and the same, always drunk, always comic or always melancholy, and who needed to be characterized only by some physical defect such as a club foot, a wooden leg, or a red nose, or by the repetition of some such phrase such as, "That's capital," or "Barkis is willin'." . . . Since the persons in my play are modern characters, living in a transitional era more hurried and hysterical than the previous one at least, I have depicted them as more unstable, as torn and divided, a mixture of the old and the new.

In 1902, in his preface to *A Dream Play,* he is more explicit: "Anything may happen, anything seems possible and probable. . . . The characters split, double, multiply, vanish, solidify, blur, clarify." Strindberg's view of the fluidity of character—the characterlessness of character, one might say—has continued and is apparent in almost all of Pirandello's work, in the underground film, and in much of the Theater of the Absurd. Ionesco, in *Fragments of a Journal,* says, "I often find it quite impossible to hold an opinion about a fact, a thing or a person. Since it's all a matter of interpretation, one has to choose a particular interpretation." In *Notes and Counter Notes* Ionesco said, "chance formed us," and that we would be different if we had different experiences; characteristically a few years later he said that he was no longer sure that he believed in chance.

Along with the sense of characterlessness, or at least of the mystery of character, there developed in the drama (and in the underground film and the novel) a sense of plotlessness, or fundamental untruthfulness of the traditional plot that moved by cause and effect. "Plots," Ionesco has said in *Conversations,* "are never interesting," and again he has said that a play should be able to stop at any point; it ends only because "the audience has to go home to bed. . . . It's true for real life. Why should it be different for art?" Ionesco has treated his own plots very casually, allowing directors to make "all the cuts needed" and suggesting that endings other than those he wrote are possibilities. After all, in a meaningless world one can hardly take a dramatic plot seriously. In Ionesco's *Victims of Duty* a character defends a new kind of irrational, anti-Aristotelian drama: "The theater of my dreams would be irrationalist. . . . The contemporary theater doesn't reflect the cultural tone of our period, it's not in harmony with the general drift of the other manifestations of the modern spirit. . . . We'll get rid of the principle of identity and unity of character. . . . Personality doesn't exist." A policeman-psychologist (a materialist who demands law and order) offers an old-fashioned view: "I don't believe in the absurd, everything hangs together, everything can be comprehended . . . thanks to the achievements of human thought and science," but he is murdered by the anti-Aristotelian.

Thus, Becket's *Waiting for Godot* ends—as the first act ended—without anything ending:

> VLADIMIR. Well? Shall we go?
> ESTRAGON. Yes, let's go.
>
> *They do not move.*
> *Curtain.*

To bring an action to a completion, as drama traditionally did, is to imply an orderly world of cause and effect, of beginnings and endings, but for the dramatists of the absurd, there is no such pattern. At best it is *Hamlet* as Tom Stoppard's Rosencrantz and Guildenstern see it: they are supposed to do a job they don't understand, and instead of a pattern or "order" they encounter only "Incidents! Incidents! Dear God, is it too much to expect a little sustained action?" Well, yes; it is too much to expect.

There can be no tragedy, because, as Ionesco explains in *Notes,* tragedy admits the existence of fate or destiny, which is to say it admits the existence of objective (however incomprehensible) laws ruling the universe, whereas the new comic perception of incongruity is that existence itself is absurd because there is no objective law. The new comic vision is far darker than the old tragic vision; it has nothing in it of what Yeats called "tragic joy." But what is our reaction to this joyless comedy? Let Ionesco, whose plays sometimes include meaningless babble, have the last word:

THE TRAGEDY OF COMEDY

> The fact of being astonishes us, in a world that now seems all illusion and pretense, in which all human behavior tells of absurdity and all history of absolute futility; all reality and all language appear to lose their articulation, to disintegrate and collapse, so what possible reaction is there left, when everything has ceased to matter, but laugh at it all.[4]

[4] *Notes and Counter Notes: Writings on the Theatre* (New York: Grove Press, 1964), p. 163.

PART TWO

A Collection of Plays

A NOTE ON *The Origins of Greek Drama and the Structure of Greek Tragedy*

THE ORIGINS

Although the ancient Greeks were fairly confident that they knew the origin and history of drama, modern scholars are less certain. The Greeks—notably Aristotle (384–322 B.C.)—said that both tragedy and comedy originated in improvisations; tragedy, according to Aristotle, originated in improvisations in choral poems honoring Dionysus (the god of fertility and wine), and comedy originated in improvisations in phallic songs. Around the middle of the sixth century B.C. a man named Thespis stepped out of the chorus and, singing in a different meter, became an impersonator who sang not *about* a god but *in the role of* a god. Thespis thus was the first actor, and by taking on an identity apart from the chorus, he and his successors made possible dialogue between a character and the chorus. Later the playwright Aeschylus (525–456 B.C.) added a second actor, thus increasing the dramatic (as opposed to the lyric and narrative) element, and still later Sophocles (c. 496–406 B.C.) added the third. The number of actors became fixed at three, so in ancient Greek drama there are never more than three speaking parts onstage at one time. However, since the actors could double in roles, there may be eight or even ten speaking parts in a play.

Unfortunately, there is little evidence to support the assertion that Greek tragedy originated in festivals honoring Dionysus. The chief evidence for the theory, aside from Aristotle's assertion (made some three centuries after the supposed fact), is that tragic plays from 534 B.C. were indeed performed at a festival called the Dionysia, honoring Dionysus. But, surprisingly, Dionysus figures importantly in only one Greek tragedy, which is puzzling if Greek tragedy really did originate in songs honoring him. The old view dies hard, however, and one still usually reads that tragedy originated in choral songs sung at fertility festivals honoring Dionysus, and that at some decisive moment Thespis impersonated him or some other god, and tragic drama was born.

A sort of corollary goes thus: Since Dionysus was god of the vine, the original songs were performed during revels in honor of the rebirth of the vine, which was seen as the rebirth of the year, the renewal of life after the death of the year in winter. The celebration of the renewal of the "year spirit" involved dramatizing the death of this divine power, and that's what Greek tragedy supposedly shows, though the "divine power" or "year spirit" came to be put into the forms of Greek heroes rather than of the god Dionysus. This is all pretty imaginative; skeptics have asked not only why Dionysus virtually disappears from the plays but also why these plays, supposedly rooted in festivals honoring the renewal of the year, end with death and lamentation rather than with renewal and joy. To the second objection, the answer is sometimes made that the plays do indeed include a suggestion of renewal; the hero comes to perceive his or her fate, and in recognizing it, and in magnificently singing about it, shows a sort of spiritual rebirth. Confronted with this answer, skeptics remain (justifiably) skeptical.

One other alleged connection with ritual should be mentioned. We know that Greek actors wore masks when they performed. Advocates of the ritual origin of Greek drama argue that the masks derived from masks that priests wore for two reasons: to impersonate the gods, and to disguise themselves lest the gods be displeased with them. Skeptics reply that the masks, with their bold, stylized features, were necessary in order to identify the characters to the audience in the vast theaters, since a Greek theater held some 15,000 people. That is, even a spectator at a great distance from the stage would immediately be able to know, upon seeing a character enter with a stereotyped mask, that this was a tragic king, or a young woman, or a messenger, or whatever. It is also argued that the mouths of the masks were designed to serve as megaphones, though in fact the acoustics in Greek theaters are so remarkably good that megaphones seem unnecessary.

THE STRUCTURE OF GREEK TRAGEDY

A tragedy commonly begins with a *prologue,* during which the exposition is given. Next comes the chorus's *ode* of entrance, sung while the chorus marches into the theater, through the side aisles and onto the orchestra. The ensuing *scene* is followed by a choral song. Usually there are four or five scenes, alternating with odes. Each of these choral odes has a *strophe* (lines presumably sung while the chorus dances in one direction) and an *antistrophe* (lines presumably sung while the chorus retraces its steps). Sometimes a third part, an *epode,* concludes an ode. (In addition to odes that are *stasima,* there can be odes within episodes; the fourth episode of *Antigone* contains an ode complete with *epode.*) After the last part of the last ode comes the epilogue or final scene.

The actors (all male) seem to have chanted much of the play. Perhaps the total result of combining speech with music and dancing was a sort of music-drama roughly akin to opera with some spoken dialogue, such as Mozart's *Magic Flute.*

For a brief additional remark about Dionysus, see the entry on him in the Glossary.

A NOTE ON *The Greek Theater*

The great age of the Greek drama was the fifth century B.C. The audience sat on wooden benches in tiers on a hillside (see photo, p. 45), looking down at a flat circular dancing place (the ***orchestra***), about eighty-five feet in diameter, in the middle of which was an altar to Dionysus; behind the dancing place was a playing area, which logic (but no concrete evidence) suggests may have been slightly elevated. Visible behind the playing area was the ***skene,*** a wooden "scene-building" introduced about 458 B.C. that served as a background (as in our word "scene"), as a place for actors to make entrances from and exits to, and as a dressing room where actors could change masks and costumes.

To speak of these elements in a little more detail: the seating area, which held as many as 15,000 people, was the ***theatron*** ("seeing-place"); fan-shaped or horseshoe-shaped, it swept around the orchestra in a segment a little greater than a semicircle. The chorus of singers and dancers, entering by an aisle (***parodos***) at each side of the *theatron,* danced in the orchestra. The front (i.e., the façade) of the *skene* (or perhaps a

The Greek theater of Epidaurus on the Peloponnesus east of Nauplia.
(Photograph: Frederick Ayer, Photo Researchers, Inc.)

temporary screen) and sometimes the playing area in front of it seem to have been called the ***proskenion.*** Though the *skene*'s façade perhaps suggested the front of a temple or a palace, there were further efforts at indicating locale: Sophocles is said to have invented scene painting (a painted cloth or screen in front of the *skene*?), and there are allusions to ***periaktoi,*** upright prisms bearing a different decoration on each side. Apparently when a new locality in the same town was to be indicated, the *periaktos* at the right was turned; when an entirely new locality was to be indicated, both *periaktoi* were turned. Other machines were the ***eccyclema,*** a platform that was rolled out of the *skene* to indicate a scene indoors, and the ***mechane,*** a crane from which a god could descend or by means of which a character could soar through the air. (See, in the glossary, ***deus ex machina.***)

Speaking a bit broadly, we can say that the Greek theater, open to the heavens, with its orchestra representing a city square and the *skene* representing a temple or palace, is itself a symbol of the ancient Athenian world view of a society that operates under divine and human law. Further, the diminutive size of the actors in the vast theater, and the background of trees and mountains, must also have conveyed a sense of the sublime natural world surrounding human passions.

Plays were put on chiefly during two holidays, the **Lenaea** (Feast of the Wine Press) in January, and the **Great** (or **City**) **Dionysia** in March or April. The Lenaea was chiefly associated with comedy, the Great Dionysia with tragedy. At the latter, on each of three mornings a tragic dramatist presented three tragedies and one **satyr-play.** The expense was born by a *choregos,* a rich citizen ordered by the state to assume the financial burden. Consult Margarete Bieber, *The History of the Greek and Roman Theater;* T. B. L. Webster, *Greek Theatre Production,* 2nd ed.; Graham Ley, *A Short Introduction to the Ancient Greek Theater;* and Peter Arnott, *The Ancient Greek and Roman Theatre.*

SOPHOCLES

Oedipus the King

Translated into English verse by H. D. F. Kitto

Sophocles (c. 496–406 B.C.), the son of a wealthy Athenian, is one of the three Greek tragic writers whose work survives. (The other two are Aeschylus and Euripides.) Of Sophocles's more than 120 plays, we have seven. The exact dates of most of Sophocles's plays are unknown. *Antigone* probably was written about 441 B.C.; *Oedipus the King,* which deals with earlier material concerning the House of Oedipus, was written later, about 430 B.C. Some twenty-five years later, when he was almost ninety, Sophocles wrote *Oedipus at Colonus,* dramatizing Oedipus's last deeds.

COMMENTARY

Classroom discussions of *Oedipus the King,* like discussions in books, are usually devoted to the problem of fate versus free will. Students (who ought to be filled with youthful confidence in the freedom of the will) generally argue that Oedipus is fated; instructors (who ought to be old enough to know that the inexplicable and unwilled often comes about) generally argue that Oedipus is free and of his own accord performed the actions that fulfilled the prophecy. Prophecy or prediction or foreknowledge, instructors patiently explain, is not the same as foreordination. The physician who says that the newborn babe will never develop mentally beyond the age of six is predicting, not ordaining or willing. So, the argument usually runs, the oracle who predicted that Oedipus would kill his father and marry his mother was not *causing* Oedipus to do these things but was simply, in his deep knowledge, announcing what a man like Oedipus would do. But that may be too sophisticated a reading, and a reading that derives from the much later European view of human beings as creatures who can shape their destiny. It is hard for us—especially if the tragedy we know best is Shakespeare's—to recognize the possibility of another sort of tragic drama that does not relate the individual's suffering to his or her own actions but that postulates some sort of Necessity that works within an individual.

Whatever the merits of these views, the spectators or readers undeniably already know, when they set out to see or read the play, that Oedipus must end wretchedly. The story is known to all, fixed in Sophocles's text, and Oedipus cannot extricate himself from it. Something along these lines was suggested in the middle of the fourth century B.C. when a Greek comic dramatist complained that the comic writer's task was harder than the tragic writer's: "Tragedy has the best of it since the stories are known beforehand to the spectators even before anyone speaks; so the poet only has to remind them. For if I merely say the name Oedipus, they all know the rest—his father Laius, mother Iocasta, daughters, who his sons are, what will happen to him, what he did."

In fact, it should be mentioned, the tragic writer's task was not quite so easy. First of all, we have Aristotle's statement that "even the known legends are known to only a few," and, second, we have evidence that the tragic writer could vary the details. In Homer's *Iliad* we read that Oedipus continued to rule even after his dreadful history was known, but Sophocles exiles him. And a fragment of Euripides indicates that his Oedipus was blinded by Laius's followers, whereas Sophocles's Oedipus blinds himself. These are details, but they are rather important ones. Probably the ancient Greeks knew the legends in a rough sort of way, as most of us know the Bible or some nuggets of Roman history. Robert Frost and Archibald MacLeish have both drawn from the Book of Job, but their works are enormously different. Writers who use Job can scarcely omit Job's great suffering, and they can assume that their audience will know that Job had a wife and some comforters, but they are free to go on from there.

Still, the main outline of Oedipus's life must have been fixed, and for us even the details are forever fixed in Sophocles's version. (We know that the Greeks wrote a dozen plays about Oedipus's discovery of his terrible actions, but only Sophocles's survives.) This means that as we read or watch it, each speech has for us a meaning somewhat different from the meaning it has for the speaker and the audience on the stage. Oedipus says he will hunt out the polluted man; we know, as he and the Thebans do not, that *he* is the hunted as well as the hunter. Oedipus says the killer of King Laius may well try to strike at him; we know that Oedipus will find himself out and will strike out his own eyes. A messenger from Corinth tries to allay Oedipus's fears, but he sets them going.

What we are talking about, of course, is tragic irony, or Sophoclean irony, in which words and deeds have a larger meaning for the spectator than for the dramatis personae. And surely it is in part because Sophocles so persistently uses this device of giving speeches a second, awesome significance that we feel the plot is a masterpiece of construction in which Oedipus is caught. If ever a man had confidence in his will, it was Oedipus, but if ever a man moved toward a predicted point, it was Oedipus. He had solved the riddle of the sphinx (by himself, without the aid of birds, he somewhat hybristically boasts), but he did not yet know himself. That knowledge was to come later, when he commendably pursued the quest for Laius's slayer and inevitably found himself. The thing is as inevitable as the history described in the sphinx's riddle, which in J. T. Sheppard's version goes thus:

> A thing there is whose voice is one;
> Whose feet are four and two and three.
> So mutable a thing is none
> That moves in earth or sky or sea.
> When on most feet this thing doth go,
> Its strength is weakest and its pace most slow.

This is the history of humanity, willy-nilly. In Sophocles's time people grew from crawling infancy, through erect adulthood, to bent old age supported by a stick, and so they do in our time, as the child's rhyme still claims:

> Walks on four feet,
> On two feet, on three,
> The more feet it walks on,
> The weaker it be.

There was scarcely an infant weaker than the maimed Oedipus; there was scarcely a man stronger than King Oedipus at his height; and there was scarcely a man more in need of a staff than the blind exile. However free each of his actions—and we can only feel that the figure whom we see on the stage is acting freely when he abuses Teiresias and Creon—Oedipus was by fate a human being, and thus the largest pattern of his life could be predicted easily enough.

SOPHOCLES *Oedipus the King*

List of Characters

OEDIPUS, *King of Thebes*
PRIEST OF ZEUS
CREON, *brother of Iocasta*
TEIRESIAS, *a Seer*
IOCASTA, *Queen of Thebes*
A CORINTHIAN SHEPHERD
A THEBAN SHEPHERD
A MESSENGER
CHORUS *of Theban citizens*
PRIESTS, ATTENDANTS, *etc.*

Scene: Thebes, before the royal palace.

OEDIPUS.
My children, latest brood of ancient Cadmus,
What purpose brings you here, a multitude
Bearing the boughs that mark the suppliant?
Why is our air so full of frankincense,
5 So full of hymns and prayers and lamentations?
This, children, was no matter to entrust
To others: therefore I myself am come
Whose fame is known to all—I, Oedipus.
—You, Sir, are pointed out by length of years
10 To be the spokesman: tell me, what is in
Your hearts? What fear? What sorrow? Count on all
That I can do, for I am not so hard
As not to pity such a supplication.

PRIEST.
Great King of Thebes, and sovereign Oedipus,
15 Look on us, who now stand before the altars—
Some young, still weak of wing; some bowed with age—
The priests, as I, of Zeus; and these, the best
Of our young men; and in the market-place,
And by Athena's temples and the shrine
20 Of fiery divination, there is kneeling,
Each with his suppliant branch, the rest of Thebes.
The city, as you see yourself, is now
Storm-tossed, and can no longer raise its head
Above the waves and angry surge of death.
The fruitful blossoms of the land are barren, 25
The herds upon our pastures, and our wives
In childbirth, barren. Last, and worst of all,
The withering god of fever swoops on us
To empty Cadmus' city and enrich
Dark Hades with our groans and lamentations. 30
No god we count you, that we bring our prayers,
I and these children, to your palace-door,
But wise above all other men to read
Life's riddles, and the hidden ways of Heaven;
For it was you who came and set us free 35
From the blood-tribute that the cruel Sphinx
Had laid upon our city; without our aid
Or our instruction but, as we believe,
With god as ally, you gave us back our life.
So now, most dear, most mighty Oedipus, 40
We all entreat you on our bended knees,
Come to our rescue, whether from the gods
Or from some man you can find means to save.
For I have noted, *that* man's counsel is
Of best effect, who has been tried in action. 45
Come, noble Oedipus! Come, save our city.
Be well advised; for that past service given
This city calls you Savior; of your kingship
Let not the record be that first we rose
From ruin, then to ruin fell again. 50
No, save our city, let it stand secure.
You brought us gladness and deliverance
Before; now do no less. You rule this land;
Better to rule it full of living men
Than rule a desert; citadel or ship 55
Without its company of men is nothing.

OEDIPUS.
My children, what you long for, that I know
Indeed, and pity you. I know how cruelly
You suffer; yet, though sick, not one of you
Suffers a sickness half as great as mine. 60

Laurence Olivier as Oedipus in the Old Vic production, 1945. (Photograph by John Vickers.)

Yours is a single pain; each man of you
Feels but his own. My heart is heavy with
The city's pain, my own, and yours together.
You come to me not as to one asleep
65 And needing to be wakened; many a tear
I have been shedding, every path of thought
Have I been pacing; and what remedy,
What single hope my anxious thought has found
That I have tried. Creon, Menoeceus' son,
70 My own wife's brother, I have sent to Delphi
To ask in Phoebus' house what act of mine,
What word of mine, may bring deliverance.
Now, as I count the days, it troubles me
What he is doing; his absence is prolonged
75 Beyond the proper time. But when he comes
Then write me down a villain, if I do
Not each particular that the god discloses.

PRIEST.
You give us hope. —And here is more, for they
Are signaling that Creon has returned.

OEDIPUS.
80 O Lord Apollo, even as Creon smiles,
Smile now on us, and let it be deliverance!

PRIEST.
The news is good; or he would not be wearing
That ample wreath of richly berried laurel.

OEDIPUS.
We soon shall know; my voice will reach so far:
85 Creon my lord, my kinsman, what response
Do you bring with you from the god of Delphi?

(*Enter Creon.*)

CREON.
Good news! Our sufferings, if they are guided right,
Can even yet turn to a happy issue.

OEDIPUS.
This only leaves my fear and confidence
90 In equal balance: what did Phoebus say?

CREON.
Is it your wish to hear it now in public,
Or in the palace? I am at your service.

OEDIPUS.
Let them all hear! Their sufferings distress
Me more than if my own life were at stake.

CREON.
95 Then I will tell you what Apollo said—
And it was very clear. There is pollution
Here in our midst, long-standing. This must we
Expel, nor let it grow past remedy.

OEDIPUS.
What has defiled us? and how are we to purge it?

CREON.
By banishing or killing one who murdered, 100
And so called down this pestilence upon us.

OEDIPUS.
Who is the man whose death the god denounces?

CREON.
Before the city passed into your care,
My lord, we had a king called Laius.

OEDIPUS.
So I have often heard. —I never saw him. 105

CREON.
His death, Apollo clearly charges us,
We must avenge upon his murderers.

OEDIPUS.
Where are they now? And where shall we disclose
The unseen traces of that ancient crime?

CREON.
The god said, Here. —A man who hunts with care 110
May often find what other men will miss.

OEDIPUS.
Where was he murdered? In the palace here?
Or in the country? Or was he abroad?

CREON.
He made a journey to consult the god,
He said—and never came back home again. 115

OEDIPUS.
But was there no report? no fellow traveler
Whose knowledge might have helped you in your search?

CREON.
All died, except one terror-stricken man,
And he could tell us nothing—next to nothing.

OEDIPUS.
And what was that? One thing might lead to much, 120
If only we could find one ray of light.

CREON.
He said they met with brigands—not with one,
But a whole company; they killed Laius.

OEDIPUS.
A brigand would not *dare*—unless perhaps
Conspirators in Thebes had bribed the man. 125

CREON.
There *was* conjecture; but disaster came
And we were leaderless, without our king.

OEDIPUS.
Disaster? With a king cut down like that
You did not seek the cause? Where was the hindrance?

CREON.
The Sphinx. *Her* riddle pressed us harder still; 130
For Laius—out of sight was out of mind.

OEDIPUS.
I will begin again; *I'll* find the truth.

The dead man's cause has found a true defender
In Phoebus, and in you. And I will join you
135 In seeking vengeance on behalf of Thebes
And Phoebus too; indeed, I must: if I
Remove this taint, it is not for a stranger,
But for myself: the man who murdered him
Might make the same attempt on me; and so,
140 Avenging him, I shall protect myself.—
Now you, my sons, without delay, arise,
Take up your suppliant branches. —Someone, go
And call the people here, for I will do
What can be done; and either, by the grace
145 Of God we shall be saved—or we shall fall.

PRIEST.
My children, we will go: the King has promised
All that we came to ask. —O Phoebus, thou
Hast given us an answer: give us too
Protection! grant remission of the plague!
(*Exeunt Creon, Priests, etc. Oedipus remains.*)

(*Enter the Chorus representing the citizens of Thebes.*)

STROPHE I

CHORUS.
Sweet is the voice of the god, that
150 (*mainly dactyls:* $\frac{4}{4}$)[1] sounds in the
Golden shrine of Delphi.
What message has it sent to Thebes? My trembling
Heart is torn with anguish.
Thou god of Healing, Phoebus Apollo,
155 How do I fear! What hast thou in mind
To bring upon us now? what is to be fulfilled
From days of old?
Tell me this, O Voice divine,
Thou child of golden Hope.

ANTISTROPHE I

160 First on the Daughter of Zeus I call for
Help, divine Athene;
And Artemis, whose throne is all the earth, whose
Shrine is in our city;
Apollo too, who shoots from afar:
Trinity of Powers, come to our defense! 165
If ever in the past, when ruin threatened us,
You stayed its course
And turned aside the flood of Death,
O then, protect us now!

STROPHE 2

(*agitated:* $\frac{3}{8}$) Past counting are the woes we suffer; 170
Affliction bears on all the city, and
Nowhere is any defense against destruction.
The holy soil can bring no increase,
Our women suffer and cry in childbirth
But do not bring forth living children. 175
The souls of those who perish, one by one,
Unceasingly, swift as raging fire,
Rise and take their flight to the dark realms of the dead.

ANTISTROPHE 2

Past counting, those of us who perish:
They lie upon the ground, unpitied, 180
Unburied, infecting the air with deadly pollution.
Young wives, and gray-haired mothers with them,
From every quarter approach the altars
And cry aloud in supplication.
The prayer for healing, the loud wail of lament, 185
Together are heard in dissonance:
O thou golden Daughter of Zeus, grant thy aid!

STROPHE 3

(*mainly iambic:* $\frac{3}{8}$)[2] The fierce god of War has laid aside
His spear; but yet his terrible cry
Rings in our ears; he spreads death and destruction. 190
Ye gods, drive him back to his distant home!
For what the light of day has spared,
That the darkness of night destroys.
Zeus our father! All power is thine:
The lightning-flash is thine: hurl upon him 195
Thy thunderbolt, and quell this god of War!

ANTISTROPHE 3

We pray, Lord Apollo: draw thy bow
In our defense. Thy quiver is full of
Arrows unerring: shoot! slay the destroyer!
And thou, radiant Artemis, lend thy aid! 200
Thou whose hair is bound in gold,

[1] Taking a hint from the French translators for the Budé series I have here and there added to the lyrical portions a quasi-musical indication of tempo or mood, on no authority except that of common sense. These may at least serve to remind the reader, if he needs reminding, that the lyrics were not recited; they were a fusion of intense poetry, music, and dancing. Of the music we know nothing; of the dance we can at least infer that its range extended from grave processional movements to the expression of great excitement, whether of joy or despair. [Kitto.] **dactyls** lines consisting of feet composed of two short syllables followed by one long syllable

[2] **iambic** referring to a metrical foot consisting of one short syllable followed by one long syllable

Bacchus, lord of the sacred dance,
Theban Bacchus! Come, show thyself!
Display thy blazing torch; drive from our midst
205 The savage god, abhorred by other gods!

OEDIPUS.
Would you have answer to these? prayers? Then hear
My words; give heed; your help may bring
Deliverance, and the end of all our troubles.
Here do I stand before you all, a stranger
210 Both to the deed and to the story. —What
Could I have done alone, without a clue?
But I was yet a foreigner; it was later
That I became a Theban among Thebans.
So now do I proclaim to all the city:
215 If any Theban knows by what man's hand
He perished, Laius, son of Labdacus,
Him I command to tell me all he can;
And if he is afraid, let him annul
Himself the charge he fears; no punishment
220 Shall fall on him, save only to depart
Unharmed from Thebes. Further, if any knows
The slayer to be a stranger from abroad,
Let him speak out; I will reward him, and
Besides, he will have all my gratitude.
225 But if you still keep silent, if any man
Fearing for self or friend shall disobey me,
This will I do—and listen to my words:
Whoever he may be, I do forbid
All in this realm, of which I am the King
230 And high authority, to shelter in their houses
Or speak to him, or let him be their partner
In prayers or sacrifices to the gods, or give
Him lustral water; I command you all
To drive him from your doors; for he it is
235 That brings this plague upon us, as the god
Of Delphi has but now declared to me.—
So stern an ally do I make myself
Both of the god and of our murdered king.—
And for the man that slew him, whether he
240 Slew him alone, or with a band of helpers,
I lay this curse upon him, that the wretch
In wretchedness and misery may live.
And more: if with my knowledge he be found
To share my hearth and home, then upon me
245 Descend that doom that I invoke on him.
This charge I lay upon you, to observe
All my commands: to aid myself, the god,
And this our land, so spurned of Heaven, so ravaged.
For such a taint we should not leave unpurged—
250 The death of such a man, and he your king—
Even if Heaven had not commanded us,
But we should search it out. Now, since 'tis I
That wear the crown that he had worn before me,
And have his Queen to wife, and common children
Were born to us, but that his own did perish, 255
And sudden death has carried him away—
Because of this, I will defend his cause
As if it were my father's; nothing I
Will leave undone to find the man who killed
The son of Labdacus, and offspring of 260
Polydorus, Cadmus, and of old Agenor.
On those that disobey, this is my curse:
May never field of theirs give increase, nor
Their wives have children; may our present plagues,
And worse, be ever theirs, for their destruction. 265
But for the others, all with whom my words
Find favour, this I pray: Justice and all
The gods be ever at your side to help you.

CHORUS-LEADER.
Your curse constrains me; therefore will I speak.
I did not kill him, neither can I tell 270
Who did. It is for Phoebus, since he laid
The task upon us, to declare the man.

OEDIPUS.
True; but to force the gods against their will—
That is a thing beyond all human power.

CHORUS-LEADER.
All I could say is but a second best. 275

OEDIPUS.
Though it were third best, do not hold it back.

CHORUS-LEADER.
I know of none that reads Apollo's mind
So surely as the lord Teiresias;
Consulting him you best might learn the truth.

OEDIPUS.
Not even this have I neglected: Creon 280
Advised me, and already I sent
Two messengers. —Strange he has not come.

CHORUS-LEADER.
There's nothing else but old and idle gossip.

OEDIPUS.
And what was that? I clutch at any straw.

CHORUS-LEADER.
They said that he was killed by travelers. 285

OEDIPUS.
So I have heard; but no one knows a witness.

CHORUS-LEADER.
But if he is not proof against *all* fear
He'll not keep silent when he hears your curse.

OEDIPUS.
And will they fear a curse, who dared to kill?

CHORUS-LEADER.
Here is the one to find him, for at last 290

They bring the prophet here. He is inspired.
The only man whose heart is filled with truth.

(*Enter Teiresias, led by a boy.*)

OEDIPUS.
Teiresias, by your art you read the signs
And secrets of the earth and of the sky;
295 Therefore you know, although you cannot see,
The plague that is besetting us; from this
No other man but you, my lord, can save us.
Phoebus has said—you may have heard already—
In answer to our question, that this plague
300 Will never cease unless we can discover
What men they were who murdered Laius,
And punish them with death or banishment.
Therefore give freely all that you have learned
From birds or other form of divination;
305 Save us; save me, the city, and yourself,
From the pollution that his bloodshed causes.
No finer task, than to give all one has
In helping others; we are in your hands.

TEIRESIAS.
Ah! what a burden knowledge is, when knowledge
310 Can be of no avail! I knew this well,
And yet forgot, or I should not have come.

OEDIPUS.
Why, what is this? Why are you so despondent?

TEIRESIAS.
Let me go home! It will be best for you,
And best for me, if you will let me go.

OEDIPUS.
315 But to withhold your knowledge! This is wrong,
Disloyal to the city of your birth.

TEIRESIAS.
I know that what you say will lead you on
To ruin; therefore, lest the same befall me too . . .

OEDIPUS.
No, by the gods! Say all you know, for we
320 Go down upon our knees, your suppliants.

TEIRESIAS.
Because *you* do *not* know! I never shall
Reveal my burden—I will not say *yours.*

OEDIPUS.
You know, and will not tell us? Do you wish
To ruin Thebes and to destroy us all?

TEIRESIAS.
325 *My* pain, and yours, will not be caused by me.
Why these vain questions?—for I will not speak.

OEDIPUS.
You villain!—for you would provoke a stone
To anger: you'll not speak, but show yourself
So hard of heart and so inflexible?

TEIRESIAS.
You heap the blame on me; but what is yours 330
You do not know—therefore *I* am the villain!

OEDIPUS.
And who would not be angry, finding that
You treat our people with such cold disdain?

TEIRESIAS.
The truth will come to light, without *my* help.

OEDIPUS.
If it is bound to come, you ought to speak it. 335

TEIRESIAS.
I'll say no more, and you, if so you choose,
May rage and bluster on without restraint.

OEDIPUS.
Restraint? Then I'll show none! I'll tell you all
That I can see in you: I do believe
This crime was planned and carried out by you, 340
All but the killing; and were you not blind
I'd say your hand alone had done that murder.

TEIRESIAS.
So? Then I tell you this: submit yourself
To that decree that you have made; from now
Address no word to these men or to me: 345
You are the man whose crimes pollute our city.

OEDIPUS.
What, does your impudence extend thus far?
And do you hope that it will go scot-free?

TEIRESIAS.
It will. I have a champion—the truth.

OEDIPUS.
Who taught you that? For it was not your art. 350

TEIRESIAS.
No; you! You made me speak, against my will.

OEDIPUS.
Speak what? Say it again, and say it clearly.

TEIRESIAS.
Was I not clear? Or are you tempting me?

OEDIPUS.
Not clear enough for me. Say it again.

TEIRESIAS.
You are yourself the murderer you seek. 355

OEDIPUS.
You'll not affront me twice and go unpunished!

TEIRESIAS.
Then shall I give you still more cause for rage?

OEDIPUS.
Say what you will; you'll say it to no purpose.

TEIRESIAS.
I know, *you* do not know, the hideous life
Of shame you lead with those most near to you. 360

OEDIPUS.
You'll pay most dearly for this insolence!

TEIRESIAS.
No, not if Truth is strong, and can prevail.
OEDIPUS.
It is—except in you; for you are blind
In eyes and ears and brains and everything.
TEIRESIAS.
365 You'll not forget these insults that you throw
At me, when all men throw the same at you.
OEDIPUS.
You live in darkness; you can do no harm
To me or any man who has his eyes.
TEIRESIAS.
No; *I* am not to bring you down, because
370 Apollo is enough; he'll see to it.
OEDIPUS.
Creon, or you? Which of you made this plot?
TEIRESIAS.
Creon's no enemy of yours; you are your own.
OEDIPUS.
O Wealth! O Royalty! whose commanding art
Outstrips all other arts in life's contentions!
375 How great a store of envy lies upon you,
If for this scepter, that the city gave
Freely to me, unasked—if now my friend,
The trusty Creon, burns to drive me hence
And steal it from me! So he has suborned
380 This crafty schemer here, this mountebank,
Whose purse alone has eyes, whose art is blind.—
Come, prophet, show your title! When the Sphinx
Chanted her music here, why did not *you*
Speak out and save the city? Yet such a question
385 Was one for augury, not for mother wit.
You were no prophet then; your birds, your voice
From Heaven, were dumb. But I, who came by chance,
I, knowing nothing, put the Sphinx to flight,
Thanks to my wit—no thanks to divination!
390 And now you try to drive me out; you hope
When Creon's king to bask in Creon's favor.
You'll expiate the curse? Ay, and repent it,
Both you and your accomplice. But that you
Seem old, I'd teach you what you gain by treason!
CHORUS-LEADER.
395 My lord, he spoke in anger; so I think,
Did you. What help in angry speeches? Come,
This is the task, how we can best discharge
The duty that the god has laid on us.
TEIRESIAS.
King though you are, I claim the privilege
400 Of equal answer. No, I have the right;
I am no slave of yours—I serve Apollo,
And therefore am not listed *Creon's* man.
Listen—since you have taunted me with blindness!
You have your sight, and yet you cannot see
Where, nor with whom, you live, nor in what horror. 405
Your parents—do you know them? or that you
Are enemy to your kin, alive or dead?
And that a father's and a mother's curse
Shall join to drive you headlong out of Thebes
And change the light that now you see to darkness? 410
Your cries of agony, where will they reach?
Where on Cithaeron will they not re-echo?
Where you have learned what meant the marriage-song
Which bore you to an evil haven here
After so fair a voyage? And you are blind 415
To other horrors, which shall make you one
With your own children. Therefore, heap your scorn
On Creon and on me, for no man living
Will meet a doom more terrible than yours.
OEDIPUS.
What? Am I to suffer words like this from him? 420
Ruin, damnation seize you! Off at once
Out of our sight! Go! Get you whence you came!
TEIRESIAS.
Had you not called me, I should not be here.
OEDIPUS.
And had I known that you would talk such folly,
I'd not have called you to a house of mine. 425
TEIRESIAS.
To you I seem a fool, but to your parents,
To those who did beget you, I was wise.
OEDIPUS.
Stop! Who were they? Who *were* my parents? Tell me!
TEIRESIAS.
This day will show your birth and your destruction.
OEDIPUS.
You are too fond of dark obscurities. 430
TEIRESIAS.
But do you not excel in reading riddles?
OEDIPUS.
I scorn your taunts; my skill has brought me glory.
TEIRESIAS.
And this success brought you to ruin too.
OEDIPUS.
I am content, if so I saved this city.
TEIRESIAS.
Then I will leave you. Come, boy, take my hand. 435
OEDIPUS.
Yes, let him take it. You are nothing but
Vexation here. Begone, and give me peace!
TEIRESIAS.
When I have had my say. No frown of yours
Shall frighten *me;* you cannot injure me.
Here is my message: that man whom you seek 440
With threats and proclamations for the death

Of Laius, he is living here; he's thought
To be a foreigner, but shall be found
Theban by birth—and little joy will this
445 Bring *him;* when, with his eyesight turned to blindness,
His wealth to beggary, on foreign soil
With staff in hand he'll tap his way along,
His children with him; and he will be known
Himself to be their father and their brother,
450 The husband of the mother who gave him birth,
Supplanter of his father, and his slayer.
—There! Go, and think on this; and if you find
That I'm deceived, say then—and not before—
That I am ignorant in divination.
(*Exeunt severally Teiresias and Oedipus.*)

STROPHE I

CHORUS.
455 The voice of god rang out in the holy cavern,
Denouncing one who has killed a King—the crime of crimes.
Who is the man? Let him begone in
Headlong flight, swift as a horse!
(*anapests*)[3] For the terrible god, like a warrior armed,
460 Stands ready to strike with a lightning-flash:
The Furies who punish crime, and never fail,
Are hot in their pursuit.

ANTISTROPHE I

The snow is white on the cliffs of high Parnassus.
It has flashed a message: Let every Theban join the hunt!
465 Lurking in caves among the mountains,
Deep in the woods—where is the man?
(*anapests*)[3] In wearisome flight, unresting, alone,
An outlaw, he shuns Apollo's shrine;
But ever the living menace of the god
470 Hovers around his head.

STROPHE 2

(*choriambics*)[4] Strange, disturbing, what the wise
Prophet has said. What can he mean?
Neither can I believe, nor can I disbelieve;
I do not know what to say.
475 I look here, and there; nothing can I find—
No strife, either now or in the past,
Between the kings of Thebes and Corinth.
A hand unknown struck down the King;
Though I would learn who it was dealt the blow,
That *he* is guilty whom all revere— 480
How can I believe this with no proof?

ANTISTROPHE 2

Zeus, Apollo—they have knowledge;
They understand the ways of life.
Prophets are men, like me; that they can understand
More than is revealed to me— 485
Of that, I can find nowhere certain proof
Though one man is wise, another foolish.
Until the charge is manifest
I will not credit his accusers.
I saw myself how the Sphinx challenged him: 490
He proved his wisdom; he saved our city;
Therefore how can I now condemn him?

(*Enter Creon*)

CREON.
They tell me, Sirs, that Oedipus the King
Has made against me such an accusation
That I will not endure. For if he thinks 495
That in this present trouble I have done
Or said a single thing to do him harm,
Then let me die, and not drag out my days
With such a name as that. For it is not
One injury this accusation does me; 500
It touches my whole life, if you, my friends,
And all the city are to call me traitor.

CHORUS-LEADER.
The accusation may perhaps have come
From heat of temper, not from sober judgment.

CREON.
What was it made him think contrivances 505
Of mine suborned the seer to tell his lies?

CHORUS-LEADER.
Those were his words; I do not know his reasons.

CREON.
Was he in earnest, master of himself,
When he attacked me with this accusation?

CHORUS-LEADER.
I do not closely scan what kings are doing.— 510
But here he comes in person from the palace.

(*Enter Oedipus.*)

OEDIPUS.
What, *you*? You dare come here? How can you find
The impudence to show yourself before
My house, when you are clearly proven
To have sought my life and tried to steal my crown? 515
Why, do you think me then a coward, or

[3]**anapests** metrical feet consisting of two short syllables followed by one long syllable
[4]**choriambics** metrical feet consisting of a trochee (a long syllable followed by a short syllable) and an iamb (a short syllable followed by a long syllable)

A fool, that you should try to lay this plot?
Or that I should not see what you were scheming,
And so fall unresisting, blindly, to you?
520 But you were mad, so to attempt the throne,
Poor and unaided; this is not encompassed
Without the strong support of friends and money!

CREON.
This you must do: now you have had your say
Hear my reply; then yourself shall judge.

OEDIPUS.
525 A ready tongue! But I am bad at listening—
To you. For I have found how much you hate me.

CREON.
One thing: first listen to what I have to say.

OEDIPUS.
One thing: do not pretend you're not a villain.

CREON.
If you believe it is a thing worth having,
530 Insensate stubbornness, then you are wrong.

OEDIPUS.
If you believe that one can harm a kinsman
Without retaliation, you are wrong.

CREON.
With this I have no quarrel; but explain
What injury you say that I have done you.

OEDIPUS.
535 Did you advise, or did you not, that I
Should send a man for that most reverend prophet?

CREON.
I did, and I am still of that advice.

OEDIPUS.
How long a time is it since Laius . . .

CREON.
Since Laius did *what?* How can I say?

OEDIPUS.
540 Was seen no more, but met a violent death?

CREON.
It would be many years now past and gone.

OEDIPUS.
And had this prophet learned his art already?

CREON.
Yes, his repute was great—as it is now.

OEDIPUS.
Did he make any mention then of me?

CREON.
545 He never spoke of you within my hearing.

OEDIPUS.
Touching the murder: did you make no search?

CREON.
No search? Of course we did; but we found nothing.

OEDIPUS.
And why did this wise prophet not speak *then*?

CREON.
Who knows? Where I know nothing I say nothing.

OEDIPUS.
This much you know—and you'll do well to answer: 550

CREON.
What is it? If I know, I'll tell you freely.

OEDIPUS.
That if he had not joined with you, he'd not
Have said that I was Laius' murderer.

CREON.
If he said this, I did not know. —But I
May rightly question you, as you have me. 555

OEDIPUS.
Ask what you will. You'll never prove *I* killed him.

CREON.
Why then: are you not married to my sister?

OEDIPUS.
I am indeed; it cannot be denied.

CREON.
You share with her the sovereignty of Thebes?

OEDIPUS.
She need but ask, and anything is hers. 560

CREON.
And am I not myself conjoined with you?

OEDIPUS.
You are; not rebel therefore, but a traitor!

CREON.
Not so, if you will reason with yourself,
As I with you. This first: would any man,
To gain no increase of authority, 565
Choose kingship, with its fears and sleepless nights?
Not I. What I desire, what every man
Desires, if he has wisdom, is to take
The substance, not the show, of royalty.
For now, through you, I have both power and ease, 570
But were I king, I'd be oppressed with cares.
Not so: while I have ample sovereignty
And rule in peace, why should I want the crown?
I am not yet so mad as to give up
All that which brings me honor and advantage. 575
Now, every man greets me, and I greet him;
Those who have need of you make much of me,
Since I can make or mar them. Why should I
Surrender this to load myself with that?
A man of sense was never yet a traitor; 580
I have no taste for that, nor could I force
Myself to aid another's treachery.
But you can test me: go to Delphi; ask
If I reported rightly what was said.
And further: if you find that I had dealings 585
With that diviner, you may take and kill me
Not with your single vote, but yours and mine,

But not on bare suspicion, unsupported.
How wrong it is, to use a random judgment
590 And think the false man true, the true man false!
To spurn a loyal friend, that is no better
Than to destroy the life to which we cling.
This you will learn in time, for Time alone
Reveals the upright man; a single day
595 Suffices to unmask the treacherous.

CHORUS-LEADER.
My lord, he speaks with caution, to avoid
Grave error. Hasty judgment is not sure.

OEDIPUS.
But when an enemy is quick to plot
And strike, I must be quick in answer too.
600 If I am slow, and wait, then I shall find
That he has gained his end, and I am lost.

CREON.
What do you wish? To drive me into exile?

OEDIPUS.
No, more than exile: I will have your life.[5]

CREON.
<When will it cease, this monstrous rage of yours?>

OEDIPUS.
605 When your example shows what comes of envy.

CREON.
Must you be stubborn? Cannot you believe me?

OEDIPUS.
<You speak to me as if I were a fool!>

CREON.
Because I know you're wrong.

OEDIPUS. Right, for myself!

CREON.
It is not right for me!

OEDIPUS. But you're a traitor.

[5]The next two verses, as they stand in the mss., are impossible. Editors are agreed on this, though no single remedy has found general acceptance. The mss. attribute v. 604 [Oedipus' next speech] to Creon, and v. 605 [Creon's next speech] to Oedipus. I can make no real sense of this: the only φθόνοσ, "envy," that is in question is the envy of his royal power that Oedipus is attributing to Creon; and the words ὑπείξων, "yield," "not to be stubborn," and πιστεύσων, "believe," must surely be used by Creon of Oedipus, not by Oedipus of Creon. Since a translator who hopes to be acted must give the actors something to say, preferably good sense, and cannot fob them off with a row of dots, I have reconstructed the passage by guesswork, putting my guesses within brackets. I have assumed that two verses were lost, one after v. 603 and one after v. 605, and that the wrong attribution of vv. 604 and 605 followed almost inevitably. [Kitto.]

CREON.
What if your charge is false?

OEDIPUS. I have to govern. 610

CREON.
Not govern badly!

OEDIPUS. Listen to him, Thebes!

CREON.
You're not the city! I am Theban too.

CHORUS-LEADER.
My lords, no more! Here comes the Queen, and not
Too soon, to join you. With her help, you must
Compose the bitter strife that now divides you. 615

(*Enter Iocasta.*)

IOCASTA.
You frantic men! What has aroused this wild
Dispute? Have you no shame, when such a plague
Afflicts us, to indulge in private quarrels?
Creon, go home, I pray. You, Oedipus,
Come in; do not make much of what is nothing. 620

CREON.
My sister: Oedipus, your husband here,
Has thought it right to punish me with one
Of two most awful dooms: exile, or death.

OEDIPUS.
I have: I have convicted him, Iocasta,
Of plotting secretly against my life. 625

CREON.
If I am guilty in a single point
Of such a crime, then may I die accursed.

IOCASTA.
O, by the gods, believe him, Oedipus!
Respect the oath that he has sworn, and have
Regard for me, and for these citizens. 630

(*In what follows, the parts given to the chorus are sung, the rest, presumably, spoken. The rhythm of the music and dance is either dochmiac,[6] five-time, or a combination of three- and five-time.*)

STROPHE

CHORUS.
My lord, I pray, give consent.
Yield to us; ponder well.

OEDIPUS.
What is it you would have me yield?

CHORUS.
Respect a man ripe in years, 635

[6]**dochmiac** usually, but not necessarily, a metrical foot consisting of three long and two short syllables

Bound by this mighty oath he has sworn.
OEDIPUS.
Your wish is clear?
CHORUS. It is.
OEDIPUS. Then tell it me.
CHORUS.
Not to repel, and drive out of our midst a friend,
Scorning a solemn curse, for uncertain cause.
OEDIPUS.
I tell you this: your prayer will mean for me
640 My banishment from Thebes, or else my death.
CHORUS.
No, no! by the Sun, the chief of gods,
Ruin and desolation and all evil come upon me
If I harbor thoughts such as these!
No; our land racked with plague breaks my heart.
Do not now deal a new wound on Thebes to crown
645 the old!
OEDIPUS.
Then let him be, though I must die twice over,
Or be dishonored, spurned and driven out.
It's your entreaty, and not his, that moves
My pity; he shall have my lasting hatred.
CREON.
650 You yield ungenerously; but when your wrath
Has cooled, how it will prick you! Natures such
As yours give most vexation to themselves.
OEDIPUS.
O, let me be! Get from my sight.
CREON. I go,
Misjudged by you—but these will judge me better
(*indicating Chorus*).

(*Exit Creon.*)

ANTISTROPHE

CHORUS.
655 My lady, why now delay?
Let the King go in with you.
IOCASTA.
When you have told me what has passed.
CHORUS.
Suspicion came. —Random words, undeserved,
Will provoke men to wrath.
IOCASTA.
It was from both?
CHORUS. It was.
660 IOCASTA. And what was said?
CHORUS.
It is enough for me, more than enough, when I
Think of our ills, that this should rest where it lies.
OEDIPUS.
You and your wise advice, blunting my wrath,
Frustrated me—and it has come to this!
CHORUS.
This, O my King, I said, and say again: 665
I should be mad, distraught,
I should be a fool, and worse,
If I sought to drive you away.
Thebes was near sinking; you brought her safe
Through the storm. Now again we pray that you may
save us. 670
IOCASTA.
In Heaven's name, my lord, I too must know
What was the reason for this blazing anger.
OEDIPUS.
There's none to whom I more defer; and so.
I'll tell you: Creon and his vile plot against me.
IOCASTA.
What has he done, that you are so incensed? 675
OEDIPUS.
He says that I am Laius' murderer.
IOCASTA.
From his own knowledge? Or has someone told him?
OEDIPUS.
No; that suspicion should not fall upon
Himself, he used a tool—a crafty prophet.
IOCASTA.
Why, have no fear of *that.* Listen to me, 680
And you will learn that the prophetic art
Touches our human fortunes not at all.
I soon can give you proof. —An oracle
Once came to Laius—from the god himself
I do not say, but from his ministers: 685
His fate it was, that should he have a son
By me, that son would take his father's life.
But he was killed—or so they said—by strangers,
By brigands, at a place where three ways meet.
As for the child, it was not three days old 690
When Laius fastened both its feet together
And had it cast over a precipice.
Therefore Apollo failed; for neither did
His son kill Laius, nor did Laius meet
The awful end he feared, killed by his son. 695
So much for what prophetic voices uttered.
Have no regard for them. The god will bring
To light himself whatever thing he chooses.
OEDIPUS.
Iocasta, terror seizes me, and shakes
My very soul, at one thing you have said. 700
IOCASTA.
Why so? What have I said to frighten you?
OEDIPUS.
I think I heard you say that Laius
Was murdered at a place where three ways meet?

IOCASTA.
So it was said—indeed, they say it still.
OEDIPUS.
705 Where is the place where this encounter happened?
IOCASTA.
They call the country Phokis, and a road
From Delphi joins a road from Daulia.
OEDIPUS.
Since that was done, how many years have passed?
IOCASTA.
It was proclaimed in Thebes a little time
710 Before the city offered you the crown.
OEDIPUS.
O Zeus, what fate hast thou ordained for me?
IOCASTA.
What is the fear that so oppresses you?
OEDIPUS.
One moment yet: tell me of Laius.
What age was he? and what was his appearance?
IOCASTA.
715 A tall man, and his hair was touched with white;
In figure he was not unlike yourself.
OEDIPUS.
O God! Did I, then, in my ignorance,
Proclaim that awful curse against myself?
IOCASTA.
What are you saying? How you frighten me!
OEDIPUS.
720 I greatly fear that prophet was not blind.
But yet one question; that will show me more.
IOCASTA.
For all my fear, I'll tell you what I can.
OEDIPUS.
Was he alone, or did he have with him
A royal bodyguard of men-at-arms?
IOCASTA.
725 The company in all were five; the King
Rode in a carriage, and there was a Herald.
OEDIPUS.
Ah God! How clear the picture is! . . . But who,
Iocasta, brought report of this to Thebes?
IOCASTA.
A slave, the only man that was not killed.
OEDIPUS.
730 And is he round about the palace now?
IOCASTA.
No, he is not. When he returned, and saw
You ruling in the place of the dead King,
He begged me, on his bended knees, to send him
Into the hills as shepherd, out of sight,
735 As far as could be from the city here.
I sent him, for he was a loyal slave;
He well deserved this favor—and much more.
OEDIPUS.
Could he be brought back here—at once—to see me?
IOCASTA.
He could; but why do you desire his coming?
OEDIPUS.
I fear I have already said, Iocasta, 740
More than enough; and therefore I will see him.
IOCASTA.
Then he shall come. But, as your wife, I ask you,
What is the terror that possesses you?
OEDIPUS.
And you shall know it, since my fears have grown
So great; for who is more to me than you, 745
That I should speak to *him* at such a moment?
My father, then, was Polybus of Corinth;
My mother, Merope. My station there
Was high as any man's—until a thing
Befell me that was strange indeed, though not 750
Deserving of the thought I gave to it.
A man said at a banquet—he was full
Of wine—that I was not my father's son.
It angered me; but I restrained myself
That day. The next I went and questioned both 755
My parents. They were much incensed with him
Who had let fall the insult. So, from them,
I had assurance. Yet the slander spread
And always chafed me. Therefore secretly,
My mother and my father unaware, 760
I went to Delphi. Phoebus would return
No answer to my question, but declared
A thing most horrible: he foretold that I
Should mate with my own mother, and beget
A brood that men would shudder to behold, 765
And that I was to be the murderer
Of my own father.
Therefore, back to Corinth
I never went—the stars alone have told me
Where Corinth lies—that I might never see
Cruel fulfillment of that oracle. 770
So journeying, I came to that same spot
Where, as you say, this King was killed. And now,
This is the truth, Iocasta: when I reached
The place where three ways meet, I met a herald,
And in a carriage drawn by colts was such 775
A man as you describe. By violence
The herald and the older man attempted
To push me off the road, I, in my rage,
Struck at the driver, who was hustling me.
The old man, when he saw me level with him, 780
Taking a double-goad, aimed at my head
A murderous blow. He paid for that, full measure.

Swiftly I hit him with my staff; he rolled
Out of his carriage, flat upon his back.
785 I killed them all. —But if, between this stranger
And Laius there was any bond of kinship,
Who could be in more desperate plight than I?
Who more accursèd in the eyes of Heaven?
For neither citizen nor stranger may
790 Receive me in his house, nor speak to me,
But he must bar the door. And it was none
But I invoked this curse on my own head!
And I pollute the bed of him I slew
With my own hands! Say, am I vile? Am I
795 Not all impure? Seeing I must be exiled,
And even in my exile must not go
And see my parents, nor set foot upon
My native land; or, if I do, I must
Marry my mother, and kill Polybus
800 My father, who engendered me and reared me.
If one should say it was a cruel god
Brought this upon me, would he not speak right?
No, no, you holy powers above! Let me
Not see that day! but rather let me pass
805 Beyond the sight of men, before I see
The stain of such pollution come upon me!

CHORUS-LEADER.
My lord, this frightens me. But you must hope,
Until we hear the tale from him that saw it.

OEDIPUS.
That is the only hope that's left to me;
810 We must await the coming of the shepherd.

IOCASTA.
What do you hope from him, when he is here?

OEDIPUS.
I'll tell you: if his story shall be found
The same as yours, then I am free of guilt.

IOCASTA.
But what have *I* said of especial note?

OEDIPUS.
815 You said that he reported it was brigands
Who killed the King. If he still speaks of "men,"
It was not I; a single man, and "men,"
Are not the same. But if he says it was
A traveler journeying alone, why then,
820 The burden of the guilt must fall on me.

IOCASTA.
But that is what he said, I do assure you!
He cannot take it back again! Not I
Alone, but the whole city heard him say it!
But even if he should revoke the tale
825 He told before, not even so, my lord,
Will he establish that the King was slain
According to the prophecy. For that was clear:
His son, and mine, should slay him. —He, poor thing,
Was killed himself, and never killed his father.
Therefore, so far as divination goes, 830
Or prophecy, I'll take no notice of it.

OEDIPUS.
And that is wise. —But send a man to bring
The shepherd: I would not have that neglected.

IOCASTA.
I'll send at once. —But come with me; for I
Would not do anything that could displease you. 835
(*Exeunt Oedipus and Iocasta.*)

STROPHE I

CHORUS.
I pray that I may pass my life
(*in a steady rhythm*) In reverent holiness of word and deed.
For there are laws enthroned above;
Heaven created them,
Olympus was their father. 840
And mortal men had no part in their birth;
Nor ever shall their power pass from sight
In dull forgetfulness;
A god moves in them; he grows not old.

ANTISTROPHE I

Pride makes the tyrant—pride of wealth 845
And power, too great for wisdom and restraint;
For Pride will climb the topmost height;
Then is the man cast down
To uttermost destruction.
There he finds no escape, no resource. 850
But high contention for the city's good
May the gods preserve.
For me—may the gods be my defense!

STROPHE 2

If there is one who walks in pride
Of word or deed, and has no fear of Justice, 855
No reverence for holy shrines—
May utter ruin fall on him!
So may his ill-starred pride be given its reward.
Those who seek dishonorable advantage
And lay violent hands on holy things 860
And do not shun impiety—
Who among these will secure himself from the wrath of
God?
If deeds like these are honored,
Why should I join in the sacred dance?

ANTISTROPHE 2

No longer shall Apollo's shrine, 865
The holy center of the Earth, receive my worship;

No, nor his seat at Abae, nor
The temple of Olympian Zeus,
If what the god foretold does not come to pass.
870 Mighty Zeus—if so I should address Thee—
O great Ruler of all things, look on this!
Now are thy oracles falling into contempt, and men
Deny Apollo's power.
Worship of the gods is passing away.

(*Enter Iocasta, attended by a girl carrying a wreath and incense.*)

IOCASTA.
875 My lords of Thebes, I have bethought myself
To approach the altars of the gods, and lay
These wreaths on them, and burn this frankincense.
For every kind of terror has laid hold
On Oedipus; his judgment is distracted.
880 He will not read the future by the past
But yields himself to any who speaks fear.
Since then no words of mine suffice to calm him
I turn to Thee Apollo—Thou art nearest—
Thy suppliant, with these votive offerings.
885 Grant us deliverance and peace, for now
Fear is on all, when we see Oedipus,
The helmsman of the ship, so terrified.

(*A reverent silence, while Iocasta lays the wreath at the altar and sets fire to the incense. The wreath will remain and the incense smoke during the rest of the play.*)
(*Enter a Shepherd from Corinth.*)

CORINTHIAN.
Might I inquire of you where I may find
The royal palace of King Oedipus?
890 Or, better, where himself is to be found?
CHORUS-LEADER.
There is the palace; himself, Sir, is within,
But here his wife and mother of his children.
CORINTHIAN.
Ever may happiness attend on her,
And hers, the wedded wife of such a man.
IOCASTA.
895 May you enjoy the same; your gentle words
Deserve no less. —Now, Sir, declare your purpose;
With what request, what message have you come?
CORINTHIAN.
With good news for your husband and his house.
IOCASTA.
What news is this? And who has sent you here?
CORINTHIAN.
900 I come from Corinth, and the news I bring
Will give you joy, though joy be crossed with grief.
IOCASTA.
What is this, with its two-fold influence?
CORINTHIAN.
The common talk in Corinth is that they
Will call on Oedipus to be their king.
IOCASTA.
What? Does old Polybus no longer reign? 905
CORINTHIAN.
Not now, for Death has laid him in his grave.
IOCASTA.
Go quickly to your master, girl; give him
The news. —You oracles, where are you now?
This is the man whom Oedipus so long
Has shunned, fearing to kill him; now he's dead, 910
And killed by Fortune, not by Oedipus.

(*Enter Oedipus, very nervous.*)

OEDIPUS.
My dear Iocasta, tell me, my dear wife,
Why have you sent to fetch me from the palace?
IOCASTA.
Listen to *him,* and as you hear, reflect
What has become of all those oracles. 915
OEDIPUS.
Who is this man?—What has he to tell me?
IOCASTA.
He is from Corinth, and he brings you news
About your father. Polybus is dead.
OEDIPUS.
What say you, sir? Tell me the news yourself.
CORINTHIAN.
If you would have me first report on this, 920
I tell you; death has carried him away.
OEDIPUS.
By treachery? Or did sickness come to him?
CORINTHIAN.
A small mischance will lay an old man low.
OEDIPUS.
Poor Polybus! He died, then, of a sickness?
CORINTHIAN.
That, and the measure of his many years. 925
OEDIPUS.
Ah me! Why then, Iocasta, should a man
Regard the Pythian house of oracles,
Or screaming birds, on whose authority
I was to slay my father? But he is dead;
The earth has covered him; and here am I, 930
My sword undrawn—unless perchance *my* loss
Has killed him; so might I be called his slayer.
But for those oracles about my father,

Those he has taken with him to the grave
935 Wherein he lies, and they are come to nothing.

IOCASTA.
Did I not say long since it would be so?

OEDIPUS.
You did; but I was led astray by fear.

IOCASTA.
So none of this deserves another thought.

OEDIPUS.
Yet how can I not fear my mother's bed?

IOCASTA.
940 Why should we fear, seeing that man is ruled
By chance, and there is room for no clear fore-
thought?
No; live at random, live as best one can.
So do not fear this marriage with your mother;
Many a man has suffered this before—
945 But only in his dreams. Whoever thinks
The least of this, he lives most comfortably.

OEDIPUS.
Your every word I do accept, if she
That bore me did not live; but as she does—
Despite your wisdom, how can I but tremble?

IOCASTA.
950 Yet there is comfort in your father's death.

OEDIPUS.
Great comfort, but still fear of her who lives.

CORINTHIAN.
And who is this who makes you so afraid?

OEDIPUS.
Merope, my man, the wife of Polybus.

CORINTHIAN.
And what in *her* gives cause of fear in *you*?

OEDIPUS.
955 There was an awful warning from the gods.

CORINTHIAN.
Can it be told, or must it be kept secret?

OEDIPUS.
No secret. Once Apollo said that I
Was doomed to lie with my own mother, and
Defile my own hands with my father's blood.
960 Wherefore has Corinth been, these many years,
My home no more. My fortunes have been fair.—
But it is good to see a parent's face.

CORINTHIAN.
It was for fear of *this* you fled the city?

OEDIPUS.
This, and the shedding of my father's blood.

CORINTHIAN.
965 Why then, my lord, since I am come in friendship,
I'll rid you here and now of that misgiving.

OEDIPUS.
Be sure, your recompense would be in keeping.

CORINTHIAN.
It was the chief cause of my coming here
That your return might bring me some advantage.

OEDIPUS.
Back to my parents I will never go. 970

CORINTHIAN.
My son, it is clear, you know not what you do . . .

OEDIPUS.
Not know? What is this? Tell me what you mean.

CORINTHIAN.
If for this reason you avoid your home.

OEDIPUS.
Fearing Apollo's oracle may come true.

CORINTHIAN.
And you incur pollution from your parents? 975

OEDIPUS.
That is the thought that makes me live in terror.

CORINTHIAN.
I tell you then, this fear of yours is idle.

OEDIPUS.
How? Am I not their child, and they my parents?

CORINTHIAN.
Because there's none of Polybus in you.

OEDIPUS.
How can you say so? Was he not my father? 980

CORINTHIAN.
I am your father just as much as he!

OEDIPUS.
A stranger equal to the father? How?

CORINTHIAN.
Neither did he beget you, nor did I.

OEDIPUS.
Then for what reason did he call me son?

CORINTHIAN.
He had you as a gift—from my own hands. 985

OEDIPUS.
And showed such love to me? Me, not his own?

CORINTHIAN.
Yes, his own childlessness so worked on him.

OEDIPUS.
You, when you gave me: had you bought, or found me?

CORINTHIAN.
I found you in the woods upon Cithaeron.

OEDIPUS.
Why were you traveling in that neighborhood? 990

CORINTHIAN.
I tended flocks of sheep upon the mountain.

OEDIPUS.
You were a shepherd, then, wandering for hire?

CORINTHIAN.
I was, my son; but that day, your preserver.
OEDIPUS.
How so? What ailed me when you took me up?
CORINTHIAN.
995 For that, your ankles might give evidence.
OEDIPUS.
Alas! why speak of this, my life-long trouble?
CORINTHIAN.
I loosed the fetters clamped upon your feet.
OEDIPUS.
A pretty gift to carry from the cradle!
CORINTHIAN.
It was for this they named you Oedipus.
OEDIPUS.
1000 Who did, my father or my mother? Tell me.
CORINTHIAN.
I cannot; he knows more, from whom I had you.
OEDIPUS.
It was another, not yourself, that found me?
CORINTHIAN.
Yes, you were given me by another shepherd.
OEDIPUS.
Who? Do you know him? Can you name the man?
CORINTHIAN.
1005 They said that he belonged to Laius.
OEDIPUS.
What—him who once was ruler here in Thebes?
CORINTHIAN.
Yes, he it was for whom this man was shepherd.
OEDIPUS.
And is he still alive, that I can see him?
CORINTHIAN (*turning to the Chorus*).
You that are native here would know that best.
OEDIPUS.
1010 Has any man of you now present here
Acquaintance with this shepherd, him he speaks of?
Has any seen him, here, or in the fields?
Speak; on this moment hangs discovery.
CHORUS-LEADER.
It is, I think, the man that you have sent for,
1015 The slave now in the country. But who should know
The truth of this more than Iocasta here?
OEDIPUS.
The man he speaks of: do you think, Iocasta,
He is the one I have already summoned?
IOCASTA.
What matters who he is? Pay no regard.—
1020 The tale is idle; it is best forgotten.
OEDIPUS.
It cannot be that I should have this clue
And then not find the secret of my birth.

IOCASTA.
In God's name stop, if you have any thought
For your own life! My ruin is enough.
OEDIPUS.
Be not dismayed; nothing can prove you base. 1025
Not though I find my mother thrice a slave.
IOCASTA.
O, I beseech you, do not! Seek no more!
OEDIPUS.
You cannot move me. I *will* know the truth.
IOCASTA.
I know that what I say is for the best.
OEDIPUS.
This "best" of yours! I have no patience with it. 1030
IOCASTA.
O may you never learn what man you are!
OEDIPUS.
Go, someone, bring the herdsman here to me,
And leave her to enjoy her pride of birth.
IOCASTA.
O man of doom! For by no other name
Can I address you now or evermore. 1035

(*Exit Iocasta.*)

CHORUS-LEADER.
The Queen has fled, my lord, as if before
Some driving storm of grief. I fear that from
Her silence may break forth some great disaster.
OEDIPUS.
Break forth what will! My birth, however humble,
I am resolved to find. But she, perhaps, 1040
Is proud, as women will be; is ashamed
Of my low birth. But I do rate myself
The child of Fortune, giver of all good,
And I shall not be put to shame, for I
Am born of Her; the Years who are my kinsmen 1045
Distinguished my estate, now high, now low;
So born, I could not make me someone else
And not do all to find my parentage.

STROPHE

CHORUS.
If I have power of prophecy,
(*animated rhythm*) If I have judgment wise and sure, 1050
Cithaeron
(I swear by Olympus),
Thou shalt be honored when the moon
Next is full, as mother and foster-nurse
And birthplace of Oedipus, with festival and dancing,
For thou hast given great blessings to our King. 1055
To Thee, Apollo, now we raise our cry:
O grant our prayer find favor in thy sight!

ANTISTROPHE

Who is thy mother, O my son?
Is she an ageless nymph among the mountains,
1060 That bore thee to Pan?
Or did Apollo father thee?
For dear to him are the pastures in the hills.
Or Hermes, who ruleth from the summit of Kyllene?
Or Dionysus on the mountain-tops,
1065 Did he receive thee from thy mother's arms,
A nymph who follows him on Helicon?

OEDIPUS.
If I, who never yet have met the man,
May risk conjecture, I think I see the herdsman
Whom we have long been seeking. In his age
1070 He well accords; and more, I recognize
Those who are with him as of my own household.
But as for knowing, you will have advantage
Of me, if you have seen the man before.

CHORUS-LEADER.
'Tis he, for certain—one of Laius's men,
1075 One of the shepherds whom he trusted most.

(*Enter the Theban Shepherd.*)

OEDIPUS.
You first I ask, you who have come from Corinth:
Is that the man you mean?

CORINTHIAN. That very man.

OEDIPUS.
Come here, my man; look at me; answer me
My questions. Were you ever Laius's man?

THEBAN.
1080 I was; his slave—born in the house, not bought.

OEDIPUS.
What was your charge, or what your way of life?

THEBAN.
Tending the sheep, the most part of my life.

OEDIPUS.
And to what regions did you most resort?

THEBAN.
Now it was Cithaeron, now the country round.

OEDIPUS.
1085 And was this man of your acquaintance there?

THEBAN.
In what employment? Which is the man you mean?

OEDIPUS.
Him yonder. Had you any dealings with him?

THEBAN.
Not such that I can quickly call to mind.

CORINTHIAN.
No wonder, Sir, but though he has forgotten
I can remind him. I am very sure, 1090
He knows the time when, round about Cithaeron,
He with a double flock, and I with one,
We spent together three whole summer seasons,
From spring until the rising of Arcturus.
Then, with the coming on of winter, I 1095
Drove my flocks home, he his, to Laius's folds.
Is this the truth? or am I telling lies?

THEBAN.
It is true, although it happened long ago.

CORINTHIAN.
Then tell me: do you recollect a baby
You gave me once to bring up for my own? 1100

THEBAN.
Why this? Why are you asking me this question?

CORINTHIAN.
My friend, *here* is the man who was that baby!

THEBAN.
O, devil take you! Cannot you keep silent?

OEDIPUS.
Here, Sir! This man needs no reproof from you.
Your tongue needs chastisement much more than his. 1105

THEBAN.
O best of masters, how am I offending?

OEDIPUS.
Not telling of the child of whom he speaks.

THEBAN.
He? He knows nothing. He is wasting time.

OEDIPUS (*threatening*).
If you'll not speak from pleasure, speak from pain.

THEBAN.
No, no, I pray! Not torture an old man! 1110

OEDIPUS.
Here, someone quickly! Twist this fellow's arms!

THEBAN.
Why, wretched man? What would you know besides?

OEDIPUS.
That child: you gave it him, the one he speaks of?

THEBAN.
I did. Ah God, would I have died instead!

OEDIPUS.
And die you shall, unless you speak the truth. 1115

THEBAN.
And if I do, then death is still more certain.

OEDIPUS.
This man, I think, is trying to delay me.

THEBAN.
Not I! I said I gave the child—just now.

OEDIPUS.
And got it—where? Your own? or someone else's?

THEBAN.
No, not my own. Someone had given it me. 1120

OEDIPUS.
Who? Which of these our citizens? From what house?
THEBAN.
No, I implore you, master! Do not ask!
OEDIPUS.
You die if I must question you again.
THEBAN.
Then, 'twas a child of one in Laius' house.
OEDIPUS.
1125 You mean a slave? Or someone of his kin?
THEBAN.
God! I am on the verge of saying it.
OEDIPUS.
And I of hearing it, but hear I must.
THEBAN.
His own, or so they said. But she within
Could tell you best—your wife—the truth of it.
OEDIPUS.
What, did she give you it?
1130 THEBAN. She did, my lord.
OEDIPUS.
With what intention?
THEBAN. That I should destroy it.
OEDIPUS.
Her own?—How could she?
THEBAN. Frightened by oracles.
OEDIPUS.
What oracles?
THEBAN. That it would kill its parents.
OEDIPUS.
Why did you let it go to this man here?
THEBAN.
1135 I pitied it, my lord. I thought to send
The child abroad, whence this man came. And he
Saved it, for utter doom. For if you are
The man he says, then you were born for ruin.
OEDIPUS.
Ah God! Ah God! This is the truth, at last!
1140 O Sun, let me behold thee this once more,
I who am proved accursed in my conception,
And in my marriage, and in him I slew.
(*Exeunt severally Oedipus, Corinthian, Theban.*)

STROPHE I

CHORUS.
Alas! you generations of men!
(*glyconics*)[7] Even while you live you are next to nothing!
Has any man won for himself 1145
More than the shadow of happiness,
A shadow that swiftly fades away?
Oedipus, now as I look on you,
See your ruin, how can I say that
Mortal man can be happy? 1150

ANTISTROPHE I

For who won greater prosperity?
Sovereignty and wealth beyond all desiring?
The crooked-clawed, riddling Sphinx,
Maiden and bird, you overcame;
You stood like a tower of strength to Thebes. 1155
So you received our crown, received the
Highest honors that we could give—
King in our mighty city.

STROPHE 2

Who more wretched, more afflicted now,
With cruel misery, with fell disaster, 1160
Your life in dust and ashes?
O noble Oedipus!
How could it be? to come again
A bridegroom of her who gave you birth!
How could such a monstrous thing 1165
Endure so long, unknown?

ANTISTROPHE 2

Time sees all, and Time, in your despite,
Disclosed and punished your unnatural marriage—
A child, and then a husband.
O son of Laius, 1170
Would I had never looked on you!
I mourn you as one who mourns the dead.
First you gave me back my life,
And now, that life is death.

(*Enter, from the palace, a Messenger.*)

MESSENGER.
My Lords, most honored citizens of Thebes, 1175
What deeds am I to tell of, you to see!
What heavy grief to bear, if still remains
Your native loyalty to our line of kings.
For not the Ister, no, or Phasis's flood
Could purify this house, such things it hides, 1180
Such others will it soon display to all,
Evils self-sought. Of all our sufferings
Those hurt the most that we ourselves inflict.
CHORUS-LEADER.
Sorrow enough—too much—in what was known
Already. What new sorrow do you bring? 1185

[7]**glyconics** metrical feet consisting of a spondee (two long syllables), a dactyl (two short syllables followed by one long syllable), and an amphimacer, or cretic (one long syllable followed by one short syllable followed by one long syllable)

MESSENGER.
Quickest for me to say and you to hear:
It is the Queen, Iocasta—she is dead.

CHORUS-LEADER.
Iocasta, dead? But how? What was the cause?

MESSENGER.
By her own hand. Of what has passed, the worst
1190 Cannot be yours: that was, to see it.
But you shall hear, so far as memory serves,
The cruel story. —In her agony
She ran across the courtyard, snatching at
Her hair with both her hands. She made her way
1195 Straight to her chamber; she barred fast the doors
And called on Laius, these long years dead,
Remembering their by-gone procreation.
"Through this did you meet death yourself, and leave
To me, the mother, child-bearing accursed
1200 To my own child." She cried aloud upon
The bed where she had borne a double brood,
Husband from husband, children from a child.
And thereupon she died, I know not how;
For, groaning, Oedipus burst in, and we,
1205 For watching him, saw not *her* agony
And how it ended. He, raging through the palace,
Came up to each man calling for a sword,
Calling for her whom he had called his wife,
Asking where was she who had borne them all,
1210 Himself and his own children. So he raved.
And then some deity showed him the way,
For it was none of us that stood around;
He cried aloud, as if to someone who
Was leading him; he leapt upon the doors,
1215 Burst from their sockets the yielding bars, and fell
Into the room; and there, hanged by the neck,
We saw his wife, held in a swinging cord.
He, when he saw it, groaned in misery
And loosed her body from the rope. When now
1220 She lay upon the ground, awful to see
Was that which followed: from her dress he tore
The golden brooches that she had been wearing,
Raised them, and with their points struck his own eyes,
Crying aloud that they should never see
1225 What he had suffered and what he had done,
But in the dark henceforth they should behold
Those whom they ought not; nor should recognize
Those whom he longed to see. To such refrain
He smote his eyeballs with the pins, not once,
1230 Nor twice; and as he smote them, blood ran down
His face, not dripping slowly, but there fell
Showers of black rain and blood-red hail together.
Not on his head alone, but on them both,
Husband and wife, this common storm has broken.
Their ancient happiness of early days 1235
Was happiness indeed; but now, today,
Death, ruin, lamentation, shame—of all
The ills there are, not one is wanting here.

CHORUS-LEADER.
Now is there intermission in his agony?

MESSENGER.
He shouts for someone to unbar the gates, 1240
And to display to Thebes the parricide,
His mother's—no, I cannot speak the words;
For, by the doom he uttered, he will cast
Himself beyond our borders, not remain
To be a curse at home. But he needs strength, 1245
And one to guide him; for these wounds are greater
Than he can bear—as you shall see; for look!
They draw the bolts. A sight you will behold
To move the pity even of any enemy.

(*The doors open, Oedipus slowly advances.*)

CHORUS.
O horrible, dreadful sight. More dreadful far 1250

(*These verses sung or chanted in a slow march-time.*)

Than any I have yet seen. What cruel frenzy
Came over you? What spirit with superhuman leap
Came to assist your grim destiny?
Ah, most unhappy man!
But no! I cannot bear even to look at you, 1255
Though there is much that I would ask and see and hear.
But I shudder at the very sight of you.

OEDIPUS (*sings in the dochmiac rhythm*).
Alas! alas! and woe for my misery!
Where are my steps taking me?
My random voice is lost in the air. 1260
O God! how hast thou crushed me!

CHORUS-LEADER (*spoken*).
Too terribly for us to hear or see.

OEDIPUS (*sings*).
O cloud of darkness abominable,
My enemy unspeakable,
In cruel onset insuperable. 1265
Alas! alas! Assailed at once by pain
Of pin-points and of memory of crimes.

CHORUS-LEADER.
In such tormenting pains you well may cry
A double grief and feel a double woe.

OEDIPUS (*sings*).
Ah, my friend! 1270
Still at my side? Still steadfast?
Still you can endure me?
Still care for me, a blind man?

(*Speaks.*) For it is you, my friend; I know 'tis you;
1275 Though all is darkness, yet I know your voice.

CHORUS-LEADER.

O, to destroy your sight! How could you bring
Yourself to do it? What god incited you?

OEDIPUS (*sings*).

It was Apollo, friends, Apollo.
He decreed that I should suffer what I suffer;
1280 But the hand that struck, alas! was my own,
And not another's.
For why should I have sight,
When sight of nothing could give me pleasure?

CHORUS.

It was even as you say.

OEDIPUS.

1285 What have I left, my friends, to see,
To cherish, whom to speak with, or
To listen to, with joy?
Lead me away at once, far from Thebes;
Lead me away, my friends!
1290 I have destroyed; I am accursed, and, what is more,
Hateful to Heaven, as no other.

CHORUS-LEADER (*speaks*).

Unhappy your intention, and unhappy
Your fate. O would that I had never known you!

OEDIPUS (*sings*).

Curses on him, whoever he was,
1295 Who took the savage fetters from my feet,
Snatched me from death, and saved me.
No thanks I owe him,
For had I died that day
Less ruin had I brought on me and mine.

CHORUS.

1300 That wish is my wish too.

OEDIPUS.

I had not then come and slain my father.
Nor then would men have called me
Husband of her that bore me.
Now am I God's enemy, child of the guilty,
1305 And she that bore me has borne too my children;
And if there is evil surpassing evil,
That has come to Oedipus.

CHORUS-LEADER.

How can I say that you have counseled well?
Far better to be dead than to be blind.

OEDIPUS.

1310 That what is done was not done for the best
Seek not to teach me: counsel me no more.
I know not how I could have gone to Hades
And with these eyes have looked upon my father
Or on my mother; such things have I done
1315 To them, death is no worthy punishment.
Or could I look for pleasure in the sight
Of my own children, born as they were born?
Never! No pleasure there, for eyes of mine,
Nor in this city, nor its battlements
Nor sacred images. From these—ah, miserable!— 1320
I, the most nobly born of any Theban
Am banned forever by my own decree
That the defiler should be driven forth,
The man accursed of Heaven and Laius's house.
Was I to find such taint in me, and then 1325
With level eyes to look *them* in the face?
Nay more: if for my ears I could have built
Some dam to stay the flood of sound, that I
Might lose both sight and hearing, and seal up
My wretched body—that I would have done. 1330
How good to dwell beyond the reach of pain!
Cithaeron! Why did you accept me? Why
Did you not take and kill me? Never then
Should I have come to dwell among the Thebans.
O Polybus! Corinth! and that ancient home 1335
I thought my father's—what a thing you nurtured!
How fair, how foul beneath! For I am found
Foul in myself and in my parentage.
O you three ways, that in a hidden glen
Do meet: you narrow branching roads within 1340
The forest—you, through my own hands, did drink
My father's blood, that was my own. —Ah! do you
Remember what you saw me do? And what
I did again in Thebes? You marriages!
You did beget me: then, having begotten, 1345
Bore the same crop again, and brought to light
Commingled blood of fathers, brothers, sons,
Brides, mothers, wives; all that there can be
Among the human kind most horrible!
But that which it is foul to do, it is 1350
Not fair to speak of. Quick as you can, I beg,
Banish me, hide me, slay me! Throw me forth
Into the sea, where I may sink from view.
I pray you, deign to touch one so afflicted,
And do not fear: there is no man alive 1355
Can bear this load of evil but myself.

CHORUS-LEADER.

To listen to your prayers, Creon is here,
For act or guidance opportune; for he,
In your defection, is our champion.

(*Enter Creon.*)

OEDIPUS.

Alas! alas! How can I speak to him? 1360
What word of credit find? In all my commerce
With him aforetime I am proven false.

CREON.

No exultation, Oedipus, and no reproach

Of injuries inflicted brings me here;
1365 But if the face of men moves not your shame,
Then reverence show to that all-nurturing fire.
The holy Sun, that he be not polluted
By such accursèd sight, which neither Earth
Nor rain from Heaven nor sunlight can endure.
1370 Take him within, and quickly: it is right
His kinsmen only should behold and hear
Evils that chiefly on his kinsmen fall.

OEDIPUS.
In Heaven's name—since you cheat my expectation,
So noble towards my baseness—grant me this:
1375 It is for you I ask it, not myself.

CREON.
What is this supplication that you make?

OEDIPUS.
Drive me at once beyond your bounds, where I
Shall be alone, and no one speak to me.

CREON.
I would have done it; but I first desired
1380 To ask the God what he would have me do.

OEDIPUS.
No, his command was given in full, to slay
Me, the polluter and the parricide.

CREON.
Those were his words; but in our present need
It would be wise to ask what we should do.

OEDIPUS.
1385 You will inquire for such a wretch as I?

CREON.
I will: for now *you* may believe the god.

OEDIPUS.
Yes; and on you I lay this charge and duty:
Give burial, as you will, to her who lies
Within—for she is yours, and this is proper:
1390 And, while I live, let not my father's city
Endure to have me as a citizen.
My home must be the mountains—on Cithaeron,
Which, while they lived, my parents chose to be
My tomb: they wished to slay me; now they shall.
1395 For this I know: sickness can never kill me,
Nor any other evil; I was not saved
That day from death. except for some strange doom,
My fate must take the course it will. —Now, for my sons,
Be not concerned for them: they can, being men,
1400 Fend for themselves, wherever they may be:
But my unhappy daughters, my two girls,
Whose chairs were always set beside my own
At table—they who shared in every dish
That was prepared for me—oh Creon! these
1405 Do I commend to you. And grant me this:
To take them in my arms, and weep for them.
My lord! most noble Creon! could I now
But hold them in my arms, then I should think
I had them, as I had when I could see them.
Ah! what is this? 1410
Ah Heaven! do I not hear my dear ones, sobbing?
Has Creon, in his pity, sent to me
My darling children? Has he? Is it true?

CREON.
It is; they have been always your delight;
So, knowing this, I had them brought to you. 1415

OEDIPUS.
Then Heaven reward you, and for this kind service
Protect you better than it protected me!
Where are you, children? Where? O come to me!
Come, let me clasp you with a brother's arms,
These hands, which helped your father's eyes, once bright, 1420
To look upon you as they see you now—
Your father who, not seeing, nor inquiring,
Gave you for mother her who bore himself.
See you I cannot; but I weep for you,
For the unhappiness that must be yours, 1425
And for the bitter life that you must lead.
What gathering of the citizens, what festivals,
Will you have part in? Your high celebrations
Will be to go back home, and sit in tears.
And when the time for marriage comes, what man 1430
Will stake upon the ruin and the shame
That *I* am to my parents and to you?
Nothing is wanting there: your father slew
His father, married her who gave him birth,
And then, from that same source whence he himself 1435
Had sprung, got you. —With these things they will taunt
you;
And who will take you then in marriage? —Nobody;
But you must waste, unwedded and unfruitful.
Ah, Creon! Since they have no parent now
But you—for both of us who gave them life 1440
Have perished—suffer them not to be cast out
Homeless and beggars; for they are your kin.
Have pity on them, for they are so young,
So desolate, except for you alone.
Say "Yes," good Creon! Let your hand confirm it. 1445
And now, my children, for my exhortation
You are too young; but you can pray that I
May live henceforward—where I should; and you
More happily than the father who begot you.

CREON.
Now make an end of tears, and go within. 1450

OEDIPUS.
Then I must go—against my will.

CREON.
There is a time for everything.

OEDIPUS.
You know what I would have you do?

CREON.
If you will tell me, I shall know.
OEDIPUS.
1455 Send me away, away from Thebes.
CREON.
The God, not I, must grant you this.
OEDIPUS.
The gods hate no man more than me!
CREON.
Then what you ask they soon will give.
OEDIPUS.
You promise this?
CREON. Ah no! When I
1460 Am ignorant, I do not speak.
OEDIPUS.
Then lead me in; I say no more.
CREON.
Release the children then, and come.
OEDIPUS.
What? Take these children from me? No!
CREON.
Seek not to have your way in all things:
Where you had your way before, 1465
Your mastery broke before the end.

(*There was no doubt a short concluding utterance from the Chorus. What stands in the mss. appears to be spurious.*)[8]

TOPICS FOR DISCUSSION AND WRITING

1. On the basis of the lines 1–149, characterize Oedipus. What additional traits are revealed in lines 205–491?
2. In your opinion, how fair is it to say that Oedipus is morally guilty? Does he argue that he is morally innocent because he did not intend to do immoral deeds? Can it be said that he is guilty of *hybris* but that *hybris* (see page 30) has nothing to do with his fall?
3. Oedipus says that he blinds himself in order not to look upon people he should not. What further reasons can be given? Why does he not (like Iocasta) commit suicide?
4. How fair is it to say that the play shows the contemptibleness of human efforts to act intelligently?
5. How fair is it to say that in *Oedipus* the gods are evil?
6. Are the choral odes lyrical interludes that serve to separate the scenes, or do they advance the dramatic action?
7. Matthew Arnold said that Sophocles saw life steadily and saw it whole. But in this play is Sophocles facing the facts of life, or, on the contrary, is he avoiding life as it usually is and presenting a series of unnatural and outrageous coincidences?
8. Can you describe your emotions at the end of the play? Do they include pity for Oedipus? Pity for all human beings, including yourself? Fear that you might be punished for some unintended transgression? Awe, engendered by a perception of the interrelatedness of things? Relief that the story is only a story? Exhilaration?

A CONTEXT FOR *OEDIPUS*

The Poetics

Aristotle

Translated by L. J. Potts

It is no exaggeration to say that the history of tragic criticism is a series of footnotes to Aristotle. In a fragmentary treatise usually called the *Poetics,* Aristotle (384–322 B.C.) raises almost all the points that have subsequently been argued, such as the nature of the hero, the emotional effect on the spectator, the coherence of the plot. Whether or not he gave the right answers, it has seemed for more than two thousand years that he asked the right questions.

[*Art Is Imitation*]

Let us talk of the art of poetry as a whole, and its different species with the particular force of each of them; how

[8]Few other scholars share Professor Kitto's suspicion that the concluding lines in the manuscript are spurious. The passage is translated thus by J. T. Sheppard:

CHORUS.
Look, ye who dwell in Thebes. This man was Oedipus.
That mighty King, who knew the riddle's mystery,
Whom all the city envied, Fortune's favorite.
Behold, in the event, the storm of his calamities,
And, being mortal, think on that last day of death,
Which all must see, and speak of no man's happiness
Till, without sorrow, he hath passed the goal of life.

[Eds.]

the fables must be put together if the poetry is to be well formed; also what are its elements and their different qualities; and all other matters pertaining to the subject.

To begin in the proper order, at the beginning. The making of epics and of tragedies, and also comedy, and the art of the dithyramb, and most flute and lyre art, all have this in common, that they are imitations. But they differ from one another in three respects: the different kinds of medium in which they imitate, the different objects they imitate, and the different manner in which they imitate (when it does differ).... When the imitators imitate the doings of people, the people in the imitation must be either high or low; the characters almost always follow this line exclusively, for all men differ in character according to their degree of goodness or badness. They must therefore be either above our norm, or below it, or normal; as, in painting, Polygnōtus depicted superior, Pauson inferior, and Dionysius normal, types. It is clear that each variant of imitation that I have mentioned will have these differences, and as the object imitated varies in this way so the works will differ. Even in the ballet, and in flute and lyre music, these dissimilarities can occur; and in the art that uses prose, or verse without music.... This is the difference that marks tragedy out from comedy; comedy is inclined to imitate persons below the level of our world, tragedy persons above it.

[*Origins of Poetry*]

There seem to be two causes that gave rise to poetry in general, and they are natural. The impulse to imitate is inherent in man from his childhood; he is distinguished among the animals by being the most imitative of them, and he takes the first steps of his education by imitating. Everyone's enjoyment of imitation is also inborn. What happens with works of art demonstrates this: though a thing itself is disagreeable to look at, we enjoy contemplating the most accurate representations of it—for instance, figures of the most despicable animals, or of human corpses. The reason for this lies in another fact: learning is a great pleasure, not only to philosophers but likewise to everyone else, however limited his gift for it may be. He enjoys looking at these representations, because in the act of studying them he is learning—identifying the object by an inference (for instance, recognizing who is the original of a portrait); since, if he happens not to have already seen the object depicted, it will not be the imitation as such that is giving him pleasure, but the finish of the workmanship, or the colouring, or some such other cause.

And just as imitation is natural to us, so also are music and rhythm (metres, clearly, are constituent parts of rhythms). Thus, from spontaneous beginnings, mankind developed poetry by a series of mostly minute changes out of these improvisations.

[*The Elements of Tragedy*]

Let us now discuss tragedy, having first picked up from what has been said the definition of its essence that has so far emerged. Tragedy, then, is an imitation of an action of high importance, complete and of some amplitude; in language enhanced by distinct and varying beauties; acted not narrated; by means of pity and fear effecting its purgation of these emotions. By the beauties enhancing the language I mean rhythm and melody; by "distinct and varying" I mean that some are produced by metre alone, and others at another time by melody.

Now since the imitating is done by actors, it would follow of necessity that one element in a tragedy must be the *Mise en scène.* Others are Melody and Language, for these are the media in which the imitating is done. By Language, I mean the component parts of the verse, whereas Melody has an entirely sensuous effect. Again, since the object imitated is an action, and doings are done by persons, whose individuality will be determined by their Character and their Thought (for these are the factors we have in mind when we define the quality of their doings), it follows that there are two natural causes of these doings, Thought and Character; and these causes determine the good or ill fortune of everyone. But the Fable is the imitation of the action; and by the Fable I mean the whole structure of the incidents. By Character I mean the factor that enables us to define the particular quality of the people involved in the doings; and Thought is shown in everything they say when they are demonstrating a fact or disclosing an opinion. There are therefore necessarily six elements in every tragedy, which give it its quality; and they are the Fable, Character, Language, Thought, the *Mise en scène,* and Melody. Two of these are the media in which the imitating is done, one is the manner of imitation, and three are its objects; there is no other element besides these. Numerous poets have turned these essential components to account; all of them are always present—the *Mise en scène,* Character, the Fable, Language, Melody, and Thought.

The chief of these is the plotting of the incidents; for tragedy is an imitation not of men but of doings, life, happiness; unhappiness is located in doings, and our end is a certain kind of doing, not a personal quality; it is their characters that give men their quality, but their doings that make them happy or the opposite. So it is not the purpose of the actors to imitate character, but they include character as a factor in the doings. Thus it is the incidents (that is to say the Fable) that are the end for which tragedy exists; and the end is more important than anything else. Also, without an action there could not be a tragedy, but without Character there could. (In fact, the tragedies of most of the moderns are non-moral, and there are many non-moral poets of all periods; this also applies to the paintings of Zeuxis, if he is compared with Polygnōtus, for whereas Polygnōtus is a good portrayer of character the painting of Zeuxis leaves it out.) Again, if any one strings together moral speeches with the language and thought well worked out, he will be doing what is the business of tragedy; but it will be done much better by a tragedy that handles these elements more weakly, but has a fable with the incidents connected by a plot. Further, the chief means by which tragedy moves us, Irony of events and Disclosure, are elements in the Fable. A pointer in the same direction is that beginners in the art of poetry are able to get the language and characterization right before they can plot their incidents, and so were almost all the earliest poets.

So the source and as it were soul of tragedy is the Fable; and Character comes next. For, to instance a parallel from the art of painting, the most beautiful colours splashed on anyhow would not be as pleasing as a recognizable picture in black and white. Tragedy is an imitation of an action, and it is chiefly for this reason that it imitates the persons involved.

Third comes Thought: that is, the ability to say what circumstances allow and what is appropriate to them. It is the part played by social morality and rhetoric in making the dialogue: the old poets made their characters talk like men of the world, whereas our contemporaries make them talk like public speakers. Character is what shows a man's disposition—the kind of things he chooses or rejects when his choice is not obvious. Accordingly those speeches where the speaker shows no preferences or aversions whatever are nonmoral. Thought, on the other hand, is shown in demonstrating a matter of fact or disclosing a significant opinion.

Fourth comes the Language. By Language I mean, as has already been said, words used semantically. It has the same force in verse as in prose.

Of the remaining elements, Melody is the chief of the enhancing beauties. The *Mise en scène* can excite emotion, but it is the crudest element and least akin to the art of poetry; for the force of tragedy exists even without stage and actors; besides, the fitting out of a *Mise en scène* belongs more to the wardrobe-master's art than to the poet's.

[*The Tragic Fable*]

So much for analysis. Now let us discuss in what sort of way the incidents should be plotted, since that is the first and chief consideration in tragedy. Our data are that tragedy is an imitation of a whole and complete action of some amplitude (a thing can be whole and yet quite lacking in amplitude). Now a whole is that which has a beginning, a middle, and an end. A beginning is that which does not itself necessarily follow anything else, but which leads naturally to another event or development; an end is the opposite, that which itself naturally (either of necessity or most commonly) follows something else, but nothing else comes after it; and a middle is that which itself follows something else and is followed by another thing. So, well-plotted fables must not begin or end casually, but must follow the pattern here described.

But, besides this, a picture, or any other composite object, if it is to be beautiful, must not only have its parts properly arranged, but be of an appropriate size; for beauty depends on size and structure. Accordingly, a minute picture cannot be beautiful (for when our vision has almost lost its sense of time it becomes confused); nor can an immense one (for we cannot take it all in together, and so our vision loses its unity and wholeness)—imagine a picture a thousand miles long! So, just as there is a proper size for bodies and pictures (a size that can be well surveyed), there is also a proper amplitude for fables (what can be kept well in one's mind). The length of the performance on the stage has nothing to do with art; if a hundred tragedies had to be produced, the length of the production would be settled by the clock, as the story goes that another kind of performance once was. But as to amplitude, the invariable rule dictated by the nature of the action is the fuller the more beautiful so long as the outline remains clear; and for a simple rule of size, the number of happenings that will make a chain of probability (or necessity) to change a given situation from misfortune to good fortune or from good fortune to misfortune is the minimum.

[*Unity*]

Unity in a fable does not mean, as some think, that it has one man for its subject. To any one man many things happen—an infinite number—and some of them do not make any sort of unity; and in the same way one man has many doings which cannot be made into a unit of action. . . . Accordingly, just as in the other imitative arts the object of each imitation is a unit, so, since the fable is an imitation of an action, that action must be a complete unit, and the events of which it is made up must be so plotted that if any of these elements is moved or removed the whole is altered and upset. For when a thing can be included or not included without making any noticeable difference, that thing is no part of the whole.

[*Probability*]

From what has been said it is also clear that it is not the poet's business to tell what has happened, but the kind of things that would happen—what is possible according to probability or necessity. The difference between the historian and the poet is not the difference between writing in verse or prose; the work of Herodotus could be put into verse, and it would be just as much a history in verse as it is in prose. The difference is that the one tells what has happened, and the other the kind of things that would happen. It follows therefore that poetry is more philosophical and of higher value than history; for poetry unifies more, whereas history aggregates. To unify is to make a man of a certain description say or do the things that suit him, probably or necessarily, in the circumstances (this is the point of the descriptive proper names in poetry); what Alcibiades did or what happened to him is an aggregation. In comedy this has now become clear. They first plot the fable on a base of probabilities, and then find imaginary names for the people—unlike the lampooners, whose work was an aggregation of personalities. But in tragedy they keep to the names of real people. This is because possibility depends on conviction; if a thing has not happened we are not yet convinced that it is possible, but if it has happened it is clearly possible, for it would not have happened if it were impossible. Even tragedies, however, sometimes have all their persons fictitious except for one or two known names; and sometimes they have not a single known name, as in the *Anthos* of Agathon, in which both the events and the names are equally fictitious, without in the least reducing the delight it gives. It is not, therefore, requisite at all costs to keep to the traditional fables from which our tragedies draw their subject-matter. It would be absurd to insist on that, since even the known legends are known only to a few, and yet the delight is shared by everyone. . . .

[*Simple and Complex Fables*]

The action imitated must contain incidents that evoke fear and pity, besides being a complete action; but this effect is accentuated when these incidents occur logically as well as unexpectedly, which will be more sensational than if they happen arbitrarily, by chance. Even when events are accidental the sensation is greater if they appear to have a purpose, as when the statue of Mitys at Argos killed the man who had caused his death, by falling on him at a public entertainment. Such things appear not to have happened blindly. Inevitably, therefore, plots of this sort are finer.

Some fables are simple, others complex: for the obvious reason that the original actions imitated by the fables are the one or the other. By a simple action I mean one that leads to the catastrophe in the way we have laid down, directly and singly, without Irony of events or Disclosure.

An action is complex when the catastrophe involves Disclosure, or Irony, or both. But these complications should develop out of the very structure of the fable, so that they fit what has gone before, either necessarily or probably. To happen after something is by no means the same as to happen because of it.

[*Irony*]

Irony is a reversal in the course of events, of the kind specified, and, as I say, in accordance with probability or necessity. Thus in the *Oedipus* the arrival of the messenger, which was expected to cheer Oedipus up by releasing him from his fear about his mother, did the opposite by showing him who he was; and in the *Lynceus* [Abas], who was awaiting sentence of death, was acquitted, whereas his prosecutor Dănaüs was killed, and all this arose out of what had happened previously.

A Disclosure, as the term indicates, is a change from ignorance to knowledge; if the people are marked out for good fortune it leads to affection, if for misfortune, to enmity. Disclosure produces its finest effect when it is connected with Irony, as the disclosure in the *Oedipus* is. There are indeed other sorts of Disclosure: the process I have described can even apply to inanimate objects of no significance, and mistakes about what a man has done or not done can be cleared up. But the sort I have specified is more a part of the fable and of the action than any other sort; for this coupling of Irony and Disclosure will carry with it pity or fear, which we have assumed to be the nature of the doings tragedy imitates; and further, such doings will constitute good or ill fortune. Assuming then that it is a disclosure of the identity of persons, it may be of one person only, to the other, when the former knows who the latter is; or sometimes both have to be disclosed—for instance, the sending of the letter led Orestes to the discovery of Iphigeneia, and there had to be another disclosure to make him known to her.

This then is the subject-matter of two elements in the Fable, Irony and Disclosure. A third element is the Crisis of feeling. Irony and Disclosure have been defined; the Crisis of feeling is a harmful or painful experience, such as deaths in public, violent pain, physical injuries, and everything of that sort.

[*The Tragic Pattern*]

Following the proper order, the next subject to discuss after this would be: What one should aim at and beware of in plotting fables; that is to say, What will produce the tragic effect. Since, then, tragedy, to be at its finest, requires a complex, not a simple, structure, and its structure should also imitate fearful and pitiful events (for that is the peculiarity of this sort of imitation), it is clear: first, that decent people must not be shown passing from good fortune to misfortune (for that is not fearful or pitiful but disgusting); again, vicious people must not be shown passing from misfortune to good fortune (for that is the most untragic situation possible—it has none of the requisites, it is neither humane, nor pitiful, nor fearful); nor again should an utterly evil man fall from good fortune into misfortune (for though a plot of that kind would be humane, it would not induce pity or fear—pity is induced by undeserved misfortune, and fear by the misfortunes of normal people, so that this situation will be neither pitiful nor fearful). So we are left with the man between these extremes: that is to say, the kind of man who neither is distinguished for excellence and virtue, nor comes to grief on account of baseness and vice, but on account of some error; a man of great reputation and prosperity, like Oedipus and Thyestes and conspicuous people of such families as theirs. So, to be well informed, a fable must be single rather than (as some say) double—there must be no change from misfortune to good fortune, but only the opposite, from good fortune to misfortune; the cause must not be vice, but a great error; and the man must be either of the type specified or better, rather than worse. This is borne out by the practice of poets; at first they picked a fable at random and made an inventory of its contents, but now the finest tragedies are plotted, and concern a few families—for example, the tragedies about Alcmeon, Oedipus, Orestes, Mĕlĕāger, Thyestes, Tēlĕphus, and any others whose lives were attended by terrible experiences or doings.

This is the plot that will produce the technically finest tragedy. Those critics are therefore wrong who censure Euripides on this very ground—because he does this in his tragedies, and many of them end in misfortune; for it is, as I have said, the right thing to do. This is clearly demonstrated on the stage in the competitions, where such plays, if they succeed, are the most tragic, and Euripides, even if he is inefficient in every other respect, still shows himself the most tragic of our poets. The next best plot, which is said by some people to be the best, is the tragedy with a double plot, like the *Odyssey,* ending in one way for the better people and in the opposite way for the worse. But it is the weakness of theatrical performances that gives priority to this kind; when poets write what the audience would like to happen, they are in leading strings. This is not the pleasure proper to tragedy, but rather to comedy, where the greatest enemies in the fable, say Orestes and Aegisthus, make friends and go off at the end, and nobody is killed by anybody.

[*The Tragic Emotions*]

The pity and fear can be brought about by the *Mise en scène;* but they can also come from the mere plotting of the incidents, which is preferable, and better poetry. For, without seeing anything, the fable ought to have been so plotted that if one heard the bare facts, the chain of circumstances would make one shudder and pity. That would happen to anyone who heard the fable of the *Oedipus.* To produce this effect by the *Mise en scène* is less artistic and puts one at the mercy of the technician; and those who use it not to frighten but merely to startle have lost touch with tragedy altogether. We should not try to get all sorts of pleasure from tragedy, but the particular tragic pleasure. And clearly, since this pleasure coming from pity and fear has to be produced by imitation, it is by his handling of the incidents that the poet must create it.

Let us, then, take next the kind of circumstances that seem terrible or lamentable. Now, doings of that kind must be between friends, or enemies, or neither. If an enemy injures an enemy, there is no pity either beforehand or at the time, except on account of the bare fact; nor is there if they are neutral; but when sufferings are engendered among the affections—for example, if murder is done or planned, or some similar outrage is committed, by brother on brother, or son on father, or mother on son, or son on mother—that is the thing to aim at.

Though it is not permissible to ruin the traditional fables—I mean, such as the killing of Clytemnestra by Orestes, or Erĭphȳle by Alcmeon—the poet should use his own invention to refine on what has been handed down to him. Let me explain more clearly what I mean by "refine." The action may take place, as the old poets used to make it, with the knowledge and understanding of the participants; this was how Euripides made Medea kill her children. Or they may do it, but in ignorance of the horror of the deed, and then afterwards discover the tie of affection, like the Oedipus of Sophocles; his act was outside the play, but there are examples where it is inside the tragedy itself—Alcmeon in the play by Astydămas, or Tēlĕgōnus in *The Wounded Odysseus.* Besides these, there is a third possibility: when a man is about to do some fatal act in ignorance, but is enlightened before he does it. These are the only possible alternatives. One must either act or not act, and either know or not know. Of these alternatives, to know, and to be about to act, and then not to act, is thoroughly bad—it is disgusting without being tragic, for there is no emotional crisis; accordingly poets only rarely create such situations, as in the *Antigone,* when Haemon fails to kill Creon. Next in order is to act; and if the deed is done in ignorance and its nature is disclosed afterwards, so much the better—there is no bad taste in it, and the revelation is overpowering. But the last is best; I mean, like Mĕrŏpe in the *Cresphontes,* intending to kill her son, but recognizing him and not killing him; and the brother and sister in the *Iphigeneia;* and in the *Helle,* the son recognizing his mother just as he was going to betray her.—This is the reason for what was mentioned earlier: that the subject-matter of our tragedies is drawn from a few families. In their search for matter they discovered this recipe in the fables, not by cunning but by luck. So they are driven to have recourse to those families where such emotional crises have occurred. . . .

[*Character*]

And in the characterization, as in the plotting of the incidents, the aim should always be either necessity or probability: so that they say or do such things as it is necessary or probable that they would, being what they are; and that for this to follow that is either necessary or probable. . . . As for extravagant incidents, there should be none in the story, or if there are they should be kept outside the tragedy, as is the one in the *Oedipus* of Sophocles.

Since tragedy is an imitation of people above the normal, we must be like good portrait-painters, who follow the original model closely, but refine on it; in the same way the poet, in imitating people whose character is choleric or phlegmatic, and so forth, must keep them as they are and at the same time make them attractive. So Homer made Achilles noble, as well as a pattern of obstinacy. . . .

[*Chorus*]

Treat the chorus as though it were one of the actors; it should be an organic part of the play and reinforce it, not as it is in Euripedes, but as in Sophocles. In their successors the songs belong no more to the fable than to that of any other tragedy. This has led to the insertion of borrowed lyrics, an innovation for which Agathon was responsible.

1984 production of *Antigone* at Cottesloe with Jane Lapotaire as Antigone. Directed by John Burgess and Peter Gill. (Photography by Donald Cooper © PHOTOSTAGE.)

SOPHOCLES

Antigone

Translated into English verse by H. D. F. Kitto

Sophocles (c. 495–06 B.C.), the son of a wealthy Athenian, is one of the three Greek tragic writers whose work survives. (The other two are Aeschylus and Euripides.) Of Sophocles's more than 120 plays, we have 7. The exact dates of most of his plays are unknown. *Antigone* was written about 441 B.C.; *Oedipus the King,* which deals with earlier material concerning the house of Oedipus, was written later, probably about 430 B.C.

COMMENTARY

The German philosopher Georg Wilhelm Friedrich Hegel, in the early nineteenth century, offered a view that makes a good starting point, although few have accepted it without qualification. For Hegel, the play is not a conflict of right against wrong; rather, it shows "a collision between the two highest moral powers," the rightful demands of the family versus those of the state. "The public law of the state and the instinctive family-love and duty towards a brother are here set in conflict." And elsewhere in Hegel: "Each of these two sides realizes only one of the moral powers . . . , and the meaning of eternal justice is shown in this, that both end in injustice because they are one-sided." Moreover, this conflict between ties of kinship and the claims of society reflects or is rooted in a conflict of divine law (the duty of the ruler to govern so as to preserve order, and of the citizen to obey). For Hegel, then, Sophocles's *Antigone* denies neither the claim of the family nor the claim of the state; what it denies is the absoluteness of either claim.

Few modern readers have agreed with Hegel that Creon and Antigone are equally right and equally wrong. Most readers find Antigone much more sympathetic than Creon. Suppose, then, we briefly make a case for Antigone. We can say, first of all, that she is right and Creon is wrong. (Even Creon's strongest defenders finally cannot say that Creon is right and Antigone is wrong.) She acts bravely, persisting in a course that she knows will bring her to suffering. And she does this not out of any hope of private gain. Moreover, she persists even though she sees that her course of action isolates her from everyone else—from her sister Ismene, and from the chorus of men (Creon's counselors).

What can be said against Antigone? Some readers have found her to be a bit too eager for martyrdom, a bit too headstrong, a bit too aware of her superiority to Ismene. There is, perhaps, also some validity to Hegel's comment that "the gods she reveres are the Gods of the Underworld, the instinctive powers of feeling, love, and blood, not the daylight gods of a free, self-conscious life of nation and people."

And what of Creon? The play itself, of course, refutes his early view that he is right in denying burial to Polyneices. And he is in many ways, even from the start, unattractive. One can note, for instance, his touchy male chauvinism, in such a passage as this:

> Now she would be the man, not I, if she
> Defeated me and did not pay for it. (Lines 474–75)

He soon comes to feel that the city is his personal property, so that his word is law, whether just or not. Can anything be said on his behalf? Perhaps at least this: First, he is new on the throne, and his inexperience apparently makes him suspicious, uneasy, and quick to act. Second, as ruler, he does indeed have the responsibility of maintaining order in a city that has recently undergone a civil war. Third, his refusal to allow Polyneices to be buried is not based on personal hatred of Polyneices; he believes (wrongly, it turns out, but perhaps understandably) that the gods cannot sympathize with a man who has come to burn their shrines. Fourth, perhaps it can be said in his behalf that the last third of the play arouses some sympathy (or at least pity) for him; although he repents, he is nevertheless terribly punished by the deaths of his son and his wife, and he must live with the knowledge that these deaths, as well as Antigone's, are his responsibility.

Much more, of course, can be said—must be said—about both Antigone and Creon; a reader of the play may well feel that not only can more be said but that less can be said, since several of the assertions just made about the two chief figures may strike some readers as scarcely relevant. For instance, one might say, "Yes, Creon is new on the throne, and, yes, he is ruling during a state of emergency, but that's of no importance since he is so clearly in the wrong." One might tentatively test this assertion by looking to see what the chorus has to say. To what degree does it support Creon, and to what degree does it support Antigone? But of course there is a problem here: the chorus is a character in the play, not simply Sophocles's spokesperson. Indeed, it is quite interesting to study this chorus of rather conventional male advisers to Creon. They give Antigone a little sympathy when she is led off to her death, but not until after they hear Teiresias (the seer) do they advise Creon to reverse his order. And, to take only one passage, we can notice that at the end of the first choral ode, celebrating civilization and the city, the chorus utters cautious words to the effect that the laws must be observed, and the "anarchic" person must be shunned. These words seem aimed at the rebel who has defied Creon, but at the end of the play the audience may well apply them not to Antigone but to Creon.

The more one reads the play and thinks about it, the more subtle it becomes. This is not to suggest that one cannot (perhaps) come out and say, for instance, "Antigone is the tragic hero, and Creon is clearly wrong"; but it is to suggest that as soon as one has come out and said such a thing, one realizes that there is more to be said. For instance, to continue with the position just taken, one wants to see and to say exactly why and how Creon is "wrong," and even while listing his faults one finds that he holds one's attention. And of course even those few who find Antigone a headstrong girl (readers familiar with *Oedipus the King* may think she has inherited her father's irritability), a bit too intent on martyrdom, must, on reading the play, admit that she compels our admiration. Scholarly books on ancient Greece rightly tell us that women played a severely limited role in Athenian society. Pericles, the Athenian statesman and general, probably summed up the average man's view when he said, "A woman's glory is not to show more weakness than is natural to her sex, and not to be talked about, for good or for evil, among men." The scholarly books on ancient Athens are probably right, in the main. Luckily, Sophocles didn't read them.

In 1849 Matthew Arnold published a splendid poem in which he said that Sophocles "saw life steadily, and saw it whole." But Arnold, no indiscriminate admirer of Sophocles's work, a few years later granted that the interests of the ancient writers were sometimes so remote from ours that "we can no longer sympathize. An action like the action of the *Antigone* of Sophocles, which turns upon the conflict between the heroine's duty to her brother's corpse and that to the laws of her country, is no longer one in which it is possible that we should feel a deep interest."

One might indeed think that a play that makes a fuss about ancient Greek burial rites could be of only remote interest to later readers, and yet Sophocles's *Antigone* has seemed highly relevant to later ages. Modern writers have sometimes shown this interest by rewriting the play, finding in the old story a new meaning. For instance, during World War II, when France was occupied by the Nazis, Jean Anouilh produced his own version of *Antigone* in which it was evident that Antigone stood for the French resistance and that Creon, efficient and ruthless, stood for the Nazis. But Sophocles's play itself—not merely the gist of his plot as reinterpreted by later playwrights—continues to hold our interest, too—although a few words about the plot may be helpful to begin our discussion.

Behind the story of Antigone is the story of her father, Oedipus (as told in Sophocles's *Oedipus the King;* see pp. 47–70), who unknowingly killed his own father and slept with his own mother. The curse on the house of Oedipus outlived him and descended to his children: His sons Polyneices and Eteocles quarreled and killed each other, and his daughter Antigone was put to death when she sought to confer on Polyneices the burial rites she felt were his due.

More precisely, after the fall of Oedipus his two sons inherited the rule of Thebes. They were to rule jointly, but they quarreled and Eteocles banished his brother Polyneices. Polyneices returned to Thebes, armed with allies, and in the ensuing conflict both brothers were killed. Creon, their maternal uncle (and Antigone's), thereupon set about ruling the city. One of his first acts was to order that Eteocles be given a state funeral but that Polyneices, who had come in arms against his own city and had thereby (in Creon's opinion) assaulted the gods of the city, be denied burial. For the Greeks, the denial of funeral rites—a fate reserved for the worst criminals—meant that the soul of the corpse could not enter the next world and be honored. Antigone defied her uncle's edict, gave the corpse a symbolic burial, was caught, and was sent to death. Creon ultimately relented, but his change of mind came too late: Antigone was dead, and so were Creon's wife and son.

This brief summary has done little to suggest that Matthew Arnold may have been mistaken when he said that a modern audience could not be much interested in *Antigone.* And yet even a single reading of the play will let a reader see that it is not simply about ancient rites. Nor is it about the workings of fate, for although the household curse is several times mentioned in the play, the tragic outcome does not seem to be arbitrarily imposed on the characters. But what, then, is the play about?

SOPHOCLES *Antigone*

List of Characters

ANTIGONE, *daughter of Oedipus and Iocasta*
ISMENE, *her sister*
CREON, *King of Thebes, brother of Iocasta*
HAEMON, *his son*
A GUARD
TEIRESIAS, *a Seer*
MESSENGER *or messengers*[1]
EURYDICE, *wife of Creon*
CHORUS *of Theban nobles*

Scene: Thebes, before the royal palace

Antigone and Ismene are the last members of a royal line that stretched back, through Oedipus and Laius, to Cadmus, who had founded the city by sowing the Dragon's teeth from which sprang its warrior-race.

(*Enter, from the palace, Antigone and Ismene.*)

ANTIGONE.
Ismene, my own sister, dear Ismene,
How many miseries our father caused!
And is there one of them that does not fall
On us while yet we live? Unhappiness,
5 Calamity, disgrace, dishonor—which
Of these have you and I not known? And now
Again: there is the order which they say
Brave Creon has proclaimed to all the city.
You understand? or do you not yet know
10 What outrage threatens one of those we love?

ISMENE.
Of them, Antigone, I have not heard
Good news or bad—nothing, since we two sisters
Were robbed of our two brothers on one day
When each destroyed the other. During the night
15 The enemy has fled: so much I know,
But nothing more, either for grief or joy.

ANTIGONE.
I knew it; therefore I have brought you here,
Outside the doors, to tell you secretly.

ISMENE.
What is it? Some dark shadow is upon you.

ANTIGONE.
Our brothers' burial. —Creon, has ordained 20
Honor for one, dishonor for the other.
Eteocles, they say, has been entombed
With every solemn rite and ceremony
To do him honor in the world below;
But as for Polyneices, Creon has ordered 25
That none shall bury him or mourn for him;
He must be left to lie unwept, unburied,
For hungry birds of prey to swoop and feast
On his poor body. So he has decreed,
Our noble Creon, to all the citizens: 30
To you, to me. To me! And he is coming
To make it public here, that no one may
Be left in ignorance; nor does he hold it
Of little moment: he who disobeys
In any detail shall be put to death 35
By public stoning in the streets of Thebes.
So it is now for you to show if you
Are worthy, or unworthy, of your birth.

ISMENE.
O my poor sister! If it has come to this
What can I do, either to help or hinder? 40

ANTIGONE.
Will you join hands with me and share my task?

ISMENE.
What dangerous enterprise have you in mind?

ANTIGONE.
Will you join me in taking up the body?

ISMENE.
What? Would you bury him, against the law?

ANTIGONE.
No one shall say *I* failed him! I will bury 45
My brother—and yours too, if you will not.

ISMENE.
You reckless girl! When Creon has forbidden?

ANTIGONE.
He has no right to keep me from my own!

ISMENE.
Think of our father, dear Antigone,
And how we saw him die, hated and scorned, 50
When his own hands had blinded his own eyes
Because of sins which he himself disclosed;
And how his mother-wife, two names in one,
Knotted a rope, and so destroyed herself.
And, last of all, upon a single day 55

[1] There is not the slightest indication in the text whether the messenger who brings the news of Eurydice's death is a man or a woman. Presumably Sophocles used the same man who had brought the news from the cavern, but it is a matter of complete indifference. [Kitto.]

Our brothers fought each other to the death
And shed upon the ground the blood that joined them.
Now you and I are left, alone; and think:
If we defy the King's prerogative
60 And break the law, our death will be more shameful
Even than theirs. Remember too that we
Are women, not made to fight with men. Since they
Who rule us now are stronger far than we,
In this and worse than this we must obey them.
65 Therefore, beseeching pardon from the dead,
Since what I do is done on hard compulsion,
I yield to those who have authority;
For useless meddling has no sense at all.

ANTIGONE.

I will not urge you. Even if you should wish
70 To give your help I would not take it now.
Your choice is made. But I shall bury him.
And if I have to die for this pure crime,
I am content, for I shall rest beside him;
His love will answer mine. I have to please
75 The dead far longer than I need to please
The living; with them, I have to dwell for ever.
But you, if so you choose, you may dishonor
The sacred laws that Heaven holds in honor.

ISMENE.

I do them no dishonor, but to act
80 Against the city's will I am too weak.

ANTIGONE.

Make that your pretext! I will go and heap
The earth upon the brother whom I love.

ISMENE.

You reckless girl! I tremble for your life.

ANTIGONE.

Look to yourself and do not fear for me.

ISMENE.

85 At least let no one hear of it, but keep
Your purpose secret, and so too will I.

ANTIGONE.

Go and denounce me! I shall hate you more
If you keep silent and do not proclaim it.

ISMENE.

Your heart is hot upon a wintry work!

ANTIGONE.

90 I know I please whom most I ought to please.

ISMENE.

But can you do it? It is impossible!

ANTIGONE.

When I can do no more, then I will stop.

ISMENE.

But why attempt a hopeless task at all?

ANTIGONE.

O stop, or I shall hate you! He will hate
You too, forever, justly. Let me be, 95
Me and my folly! I will face the danger
That so dismays you, for it cannot be
So dreadful as to die a coward's death.

ISMENE.

Then go and do it, if you must. It is
Blind folly—but those who love you love you dearly. 100

(*Exeunt severally.*)

FIRST ODE

STROPHE I

CHORUS.

Welcome, light of the Sun, the fairest
(*glyconics*)[2] Sun that ever has dawned upon
Thebes, the city of seven gates!
At last thou art arisen, great
Orb of shining day, pouring 105
Light across the gleaming water of Dirkê.
Thou hast turned into headlong flight,
Galloping faster and faster, the foe who
Bearing a snow-white shield in full
Panoply came from Argos. 110

(*anapests*)[3] He had come to destroy us, in Polyneices's
Fierce quarrel. *He* brought them against our land;
And like some eagle screaming his rage
From the sky he descended upon us,
With his armour about him, shining like snow, 115
With spear upon spear,
And with plumes that swayed on their helmets.

ANTISTROPHE I

(*glyconics*) Close he hovered above our houses,
Circling around our seven gates, with
Spears that thirsted to drink our blood. 120
He's gone! gone before ever his jaws
Snapped on our flesh, before he sated
Himself with our blood, before his blazing firebrand
Seized with its fire our city's towers.
Terrible clangor of arms repelled him, 125
Driving him back, for hard it is to
Strive with the sons of a Dragon.

(*anapests*) For the arrogant boast of an impious man
Zeus hateth exceedingly. So, when he saw

[2]**glyconics** metrical feet consisting of a spondee (two long syllables), a dactyl (two short syllables followed by one long syllable), and an amphimacer or cretic (one long syllable followed by one short syllable followed by one long syllable)
[3]**anapests** metrical feet consisting of two short syllables followed by one long syllable

130 This army advancing in swollen flood
In the pride of its gilded equipment,
He struck them down from the rampart's edge
With a fiery bolt
In the midst of their shout of "Triumph!"

STROPHE 2

(*more strongly marked rhythm*) Heavily down to the earth
135 did he fall, and lie there,
He who with torch in his hand and possessed with frenzy
Breathed forth bitterest hate
Like some fierce tempestuous wind.
So it fared then with him;
140 And of the rest, each met his own terrible doom,
Given by the great War-god, our deliverer.

(*anapests*) Seven foemen appointed to our seven gates
Each fell to a Theban, and Argive arms
Shall grace our Theban temple of Zeus:
145 Save two, those two of unnatural hate,
Two sons of one mother, two sons of one King;
They strove for the crown, and shared with the sword
Their estate, each slain by his brother.

ANTISTROPHE 2

Yet do we see in our midst, and acclaim with gladness,
150 Victory, glorious Victory, smiling, welcome.
Now, since danger is past,
Thoughts of war shall pass from our minds.
Come! let all thank the gods,
Dancing before temple and shrine all through the night,
155 Following Thee, Theban Dionysus.

CHORUS-LEADER.
But here comes Creon, the new king of Thebes,
In these new fortunes that the gods have given us.
What purpose is he furthering, that he
Has called this gathering of his Counsellors?

(*Enter Creon, attended.*)

CREON.
160 My lords: for what concerns the state, the gods
Who tossed it on the angry surge of strife
Have righted it again; and therefore you
By royal edict I have summoned here,
Chosen from all our number. I know well
165 How you revered the thrones of Laius;
And then, when Oedipus maintained our state,
And when he perished, round his sons you rallied,
Still firm and steadfast in your loyalty.
Since they have fallen by a double doom
170 Upon a single day, two brothers each
Killing the other with polluted sword,
I now possess the throne and royal power
By right of nearest kinship with the dead.
There is no art that teaches us to know
The temper, mind or spirit of any man 175
Until he has been proved by government
And lawgiving. A man who rules a state
And will not ever steer the wisest course,
But is afraid, and says not what he thinks,
That man is worthless; and if any holds 180
A friend of more account than his own city,
I scorn him; for if I should see destruction
Threatening the safety of my citizens,
I would not hold my peace, nor would I count
That man my friend who was my country's foe, 185
Zeus be my witness. For be sure of this:
It is the city that protects us all;
She bears us through the storm; only when she
Rides safe and sound can we make loyal friends.
This I believe, and thus will I maintain 190
Our city's greatness. —Now, conformably,
Of Oedipus's two sons I have proclaimed
This edict: he who in his country's cause
Fought gloriously and so laid down his life,
Shall be entombed and graced with every rite 195
That men can pay to those who die with honor;
But for his brother, him called Polyneices,
Who came from exile to lay waste his land,
To burn the temples of his native gods,
To drink his kindred blood, and to enslave 200
The rest, I have proclaimed to Thebes that none
Shall give him funeral honors or lament him,
But leave him there unburied, to be devoured
By dogs and birds, mangled most hideously.
Such is my will; never shall I allow 205
The villain to win more honor than the upright;
But any who show love to this our city
In life and death alike shall win my praise.

CHORUS-LEADER.
Such is your will, my lord; so you requite
Our city's champion and our city's foe. 210
You, being so sovereign, make what laws you will
Both for the dead and those of us who live.

CREON.
See then that you defend the law now made.

CHORUS-LEADER.
No, lay that burden on some younger men.

CREON.
I have appointed guards to watch the body. 215

CHORUS-LEADER.
What further charge, then, do you lay on us?

CREON.
Not to connive at those that disobey me.

CHORUS-LEADER.
None are so foolish as to long for death.
CREON.
Death is indeed the price, but love of gain
220 Has often lured a man to his destruction.

(*Enter a Guard.*)

GUARD.
My lord: I cannot say that I am come
All out of breath with running. More than once
I stopped and thought and turned round in my path
And started to go back. My mind had much
225 To say to me. One time it said "You fool!
Why do you go to certain punishment?"
Another time "What? Standing still, you wretch?
You'll smart for it, if Creon comes to hear
From someone else." And so I went along
230 Debating with myself not swift nor sure.
This way, a short road soon becomes a long one.
At last this was the verdict: I must come
And tell you. It may be worse than nothing; still,
I'll tell you. I can suffer nothing more
235 Than what is in my fate. There is my comfort!
CREON.
And what is this that makes you so despondent?
GUARD.
First for myself: I did not see it done,
I do not know who did it. Plainly then,
I cannot rightly come to any harm.
CREON.
240 You are a cautious fellow, building up
This barricade. You bring unpleasant news?
GUARD.
I do, and peril makes a man pause long.
CREON.
O, won't you tell your story and be gone?
GUARD.
Then, here it is. The body: someone has
245 Just buried it, and gone away. He sprinkled
Dry dust on it, with all the sacred rites.
CREON.
What? Buried it? What man has so defied me?
GUARD.
How can I tell? There was no mark of pickaxe,
No sign of digging; the earth was hard and dry
250 And undisturbed; no wagon had been there;
He who had done it left no trace at all.
So, when the first day-watchman showed it to us,
We were appalled. We could not see the body;
It was not buried but was thinly covered
255 With dust, as if by someone who had sought
To avoid a curse. Although we looked, we saw
No sign that any dog or bird had come
And torn the body. Angry accusations
Flew up between us; each man blamed another,
And in the end it would have come to blows, 260
For there was none to stop it. Each single man
Seemed guilty, yet proclaimed his ignorance
And could not be convicted. We were all
Ready to take hot iron in our hands,
To walk through fire, to swear by all the gods 265
We had not done it, nor had secret knowledge
Of any man who did it or contrived it.
We could not find a clue. Then one man spoke:
It made us hang our heads in terror, yet
No one could answer him, nor could we see 270
Much profit for ourselves if we should do it.
He said "We must report this thing to Creon;
We dare not hide it"; and his word prevailed.
I am the unlucky man who drew the prize
When we cast lots, and therefore I am come 275
Unwilling and, for certain, most unwelcome:
Nobody loves the bringer of bad news.
CHORUS-LEADER.
My lord, the thought has risen in my mind:
Do we not see in this the hand of God?
CREON.
Silence! or you will anger me. You are 280
An old man: must you be a fool as well?
Intolerable, that you suppose the gods
Should have a single thought for this dead body.
What? should they honor him with burial
As one who served them well, when he had come 285
To burn their pillared temples, to destroy
Their treasuries, to devastate their land
And overturn its laws? Or have you noticed
The gods prefer the vile? No, from the first
There was a muttering against my edict, 290
Wagging of heads in secret, restiveness
And discontent with my authority.
I know that some of these perverted others
And bribed them to this act. Of all vile things
Current on earth, none is so vile as money. 295
For money opens wide the city-gates
To ravishers, it drives the citizens
To exile, it perverts the honest mind
To shamefulness, it teaches men to practice
All forms of wickedness and impiety. 300
These criminals who sold themselves for money
Have bought with it their certain punishment;
For, as I reverence the throne of Zeus,
I tell you plainly, and confirm it with
My oath: unless you find, and bring before me, 305
The very author of this burial-rite

Mere death shall not suffice; you shall be hanged
Alive, until you have disclosed the crime,
That for the future you may ply your trade
310 More cleverly, and learn not every pocket
Is safely to be picked. Ill-gotten gains
More often lead to ruin than to safety.

GUARD.
May I reply? Or must I turn and go?

CREON.
Now, as before, your very voice offends me.

GUARD.
315 Is it your ears that feel it, or your mind?

CREON.
Why must you probe the seat of our displeasure?

GUARD.
The rebel hurts your mind: I but your ears.

CREON.
No more of this! You are a babbling fool!

GUARD.
If so, I cannot be the one who did it.

CREON.
320 Yes, but you did—selling your life for money!

GUARD.
It's bad, to judge at random, and judge wrong!

CREON.
You judge my judgment as you will—but bring
The man who did it, or you shall proclaim
What punishment is earned by crooked dealings.

GUARD.
325 God grant he may be found! But whether he
Be found or not—for this must lie with chance—
You will not see me coming *here* again.
Alive beyond my hope and expectation,
I thank the gods who have delivered me.
(*Exeunt severally Creon and Guard.*)

SECOND ODE

STROPHE 1

CHORUS.
330 Wonders are many, yet of all
(*glyconics*) Things is Man the most wonderful.
He can sail on the stormy sea
Though the tempest rage, and the loud
Waves roar around, as he makes his
335 Path amid the towering surge.

(*dactyls*)[4] Earth inexhaustible, ageless, he wearies, as
Backwards and forwards, from season to season, his
Ox-team drives along the ploughshare.

ANTISTROPHE 1

He can entrap the cheerful birds, 340
Setting a snare, and all the wild
Beasts of the earth he has learned to catch, and
Fish that teem in the deep sea, with
Nets knotted of stout cords; of
Such inventiveness is man. 345
Through his inventions he becomes lord
Even of the beasts of the mountain: the long-haired
Horse he subdues to the yoke on his neck, and the
Hill-bred bull, of strength untiring.

STROPHE 2

And speech he has learned, and thought 350
So swift, and the temper of mind
To dwell within cities, and not to lie bare
Amid the keen, biting frosts
Or cower beneath pelting rain;
Full of resource against all that comes to him 355
Is Man. Against Death alone
He is left with no defense.
But painful sickness he can cure
By his own skill.

ANTISTROPHE 2

Surpassing belief, the device and 360
Cunning that Man has attained,
And it bringeth him now to evil, now to good.
If he observe Law, and tread
The righteous path God ordained,
Honored is he; dishonored, the man whose reckless 365
heart
Shall make him join hands with sin:
May I not think like him,
Nor may such an impious man
Dwell in my house,

(*Enter Guard, with Antigone.*)

CHORUS-LEADER.
What evil spirit is abroad? I know 370
Her well: Antigone. But how can I
Believe it? Why, O you unlucky daughter
Of an unlucky father, what is this?
Can it be you, so mad and so defiant,
So disobedient to a King's decree? 375

GUARD.
Here is the one who did the deed, this girl;
We caught her burying him. —But where is Creon?

[4] **dactyls** metrical feet consisting of two short syllables followed by one long syllable

CHORUS-LEADER.
He comes, just as you need him, from the palace.

(*Enter Creon, attended.*)

CREON.
How? What occasion makes my coming timely?

GUARD.
380 Sir, against nothing should a man take oath,
For second thoughts belie him. Under your threats
That lashed me like a hailstorm, I'd have said
I would not quickly have come here again;
But joy that comes beyond our dearest hope
385 Surpasses all in magnitude. So I
Return, though I had sworn I never would,
Bringing this girl detected in the act
Of honoring the body. This time no lot
Was cast; the windfall is my very own.
390 And so, my lord, do as you please: take her
Yourself, examine her, cross-question her.
I claim the right of free and final quittance.

CREON.
Why do you bring this girl? Where was she taken?

GUARD.
In burying the body. That is all.

CREON.
395 You know what you are saying? Do you mean it?

GUARD.
I saw her giving burial to the corpse
You had forbidden. Is that plain and clear?

CREON.
How did you see and take her so red-handed?

GUARD.
It was like this. When we had reached the place,
400 Those dreadful threats of yours upon our heads,
We swept aside each grain of dust that hid
The clammy body, leaving it quite bare,
And sat down on a hill, to the windward side
That so we might avoid the smell of it.
405 We kept sharp look-out; each man roundly cursed
His neighbor, if he should neglect his duty.
So the time passed, until the blazing sun
Reached his mid-course and burned us with his heat.
Then, suddenly, a whirlwind came from heaven
410 And raised a storm of dust, which blotted out
The earth and sky; the air was filled with sand
And leaves ripped from the trees. We closed our eyes
And bore this visitation as we could.
At last it ended; then we saw the girl.
415 She raised a bitter cry, as will a bird
Returning to its nest and finding it
Despoiled, a cradle empty of its young.
So, when she saw the body bare, she raised
A cry of anguish mixed with imprecations
Laid upon those who did it; then at once 420
Brought handfuls of dry dust, and raised aloft
A shapely vase of bronze, and three times poured
The funeral libation for the dead.
We rushed upon her swiftly, seized our prey,
And charged her both with this offense and that. 425
She faced us calmly; she did not disown
The double crime. How glad I was—and yet
How sorry too; it is a painful thing
To bring a friend to ruin. Still, for me,
My own escape comes before everything. 430

CREON.
You there, who keep your eyes fixed on the ground,
Do you admit this, or do you deny it?

ANTIGONE.
No, I do not deny it. I admit it.

CREON (*to Guard*).
Then you may go; go where you like. You have
Been fully cleared of that grave accusation. (*Exit Guard.*) 435
You: tell me briefly—I want no long speech:
Did you not know that this had been forbidden?

ANTIGONE.
Of course I knew. There was a proclamation.

CREON.
And so you dared to disobey the law?

ANTIGONE.
It was not Zeus who published this decree, 440
Nor have the Powers who rule among the dead
Imposed such laws as this upon mankind;
Nor could I think that a decree of yours—
A man—could override the laws of Heaven
Unwritten and unchanging. Not of today 445
Or yesterday is their authority;
They are eternal; no man saw their birth.
Was I to stand before the gods' tribunal
For disobeying *them,* because I feared
A man? I knew that I should have to die, 450
Even without your edict; if I die
Before my time, why then, I count it gain;
To one who lives as I do, ringed about
With countless miseries, why, death is welcome.
For me to meet this doom is little grief; 455
But when my mother's son lay dead, had I
Neglected him and left him there unburied,
That would have caused me grief; this causes none.
And if you think it folly, then perhaps
I am accused of folly by the fool. 460

CHORUS-LEADER.
The daughter shows her father's temper—fierce,

Defiant; she will not yield to any storm.

CREON.
But it is those that are most obstinate
Suffer the greatest fall; the hardest iron,
465 Most fiercely tempered in the fire, that is
Most often snapped and splintered. I have seen
The wildest horses tamed, and only by
The tiny bit. There is no room for pride
In one who is a slave! This girl already
470 Had fully learned the art of insolence
When she transgressed the laws that I established;
And now to that she adds a second outrage—
To boast of what she did, and laugh at us.
Now she would be the man, not I, if she
475 Defeated me and did not pay for it.
But though she be my niece, or closer still
Than all our family, she shall not escape
The direst penalty; no, nor shall her sister:
I judge her guilty too; she played her part
480 In burying the body. Summon her.
Just now I saw her raving and distracted
Within the palace. So it often is:
Those who plan crime in secret are betrayed
Despite themselves; they show it in their faces.
485 But this is worst of all: to be convicted
And then to glorify the crime as virtue.

(*Exeunt some Guards.*)

ANTIGONE.
Would you do more than simply take and kill me?

CREON.
I will have nothing more, and nothing less.

ANTIGONE.
Then why delay? To me no word of yours
490 Is pleasing—God forbid it should be so!—
And everything in me displeases you.
Yet what could I have done to win renown
More glorious than giving burial
To my own brother? These men too would say it,
495 Except that terror cows them into silence.
A king has many a privilege: the greatest,
That he can say and do all that he will.

CREON.
You are the only one in Thebes to think it!

ANTIGONE.
These think as I do—but they dare not speak.

CREON.
500 Have you no shame, not to conform with others?

ANTIGONE.
To reverence a brother is no shame.

CREON.
Was he no brother, he who died for Thebes?

ANTIGONE.
One mother and one father gave them birth.

CREON.
Honoring the traitor, you dishonor *him.*

ANTIGONE.
He will not bear this testimony, in death. 505

CREON.
Yes! if the traitor fare the same as he.

ANTIGONE.
It was a brother, not a slave who died!

CREON.
He died attacking Thebes; the other saved us.

ANTIGONE.
Even so, the god of Death demands these rites.

CREON.
The good demand more honor than the wicked. 510

ANTIGONE.
Who knows? In death they may be reconciled.

CREON.
Death does not make an enemy a friend!

ANTIGONE.
Even so, I give both love, not share their hatred.

CREON.
Down then to Hell! Love there, if love you must.
While I am living, no woman shall have rule. 515

(*Enter Guards, with Ismene.*)

CHORUS-LEADER.
See where Ismene leaves the palace-gate,
In tears shed for her sister. On her brow
A cloud of grief has blotted out her sun,
And breaks in rain upon her comeliness.

CREON.
You, lurking like a serpent in my house, 520
Drinking my life-blood unawares; nor did
I know that I was cherishing two fiends,
Subverters of my throne: come, tell me this:
Do you confess you shared this burial,
Or will you swear you had no knowledge of it? 525

ISMENE.
I did it too, if she allows my claim;
I share the burden of this heavy charge.

ANTIGONE.
No! Justice will not suffer that; for you
Refused, and I gave you no part in it.

ISMENE.
But in your stormy voyage I am glad 530
To share the danger, traveling at your side.

ANTIGONE.
Whose was the deed the god of Death knows well;
I love not those who love in words alone.

ISMENE.
My sister, do not scorn me, nor refuse
535 That I may die with you, honoring the dead.
ANTIGONE.
You shall not die with me, nor claim as yours
What you rejected. My death will be enough.
ISMENE.
What life is left to me if I lose you?
ANTIGONE.
Ask Creon! It was Creon that you cared for.
ISMENE.
540 O why taunt me, when it does not help you?
ANTIGONE.
If I do taunt you, it is to my pain.
ISMENE.
Can I not help you, even at this late hour?
ANTIGONE.
Save your own life. I grudge not your escape.
ISMENE.
Alas! Can I not join you in your fate?
ANTIGONE.
545 You cannot: you chose life, and I chose death.
ISMENE.
But not without the warning that I gave you!
ANTIGONE.
Some thought *you* wise; the dead commended me.
ISMENE.
But my offense has been as great as yours.
ANTIGONE.
Be comforted; you live, but I have given
550 My life already, in service of the dead.
CREON.
Of these two girls, one has been driven frantic,
The other has been frantic since her birth.
ISMENE.
Not so, my lord; but when disaster comes
The reason that one has cannot stand firm.
CREON.
555 Yours did not, when you chose to partner crime!
ISMENE.
But what is life to me, without my sister?
CREON.
Say not "my sister": sister you have none.
ISMENE.
But she is Haemon's bride—and can you kill her?
CREON.
Is she the only woman he can bed with?
ISMENE.
560 The only one so joined in love with him.
CREON.
I hate a son to have an evil wife.
ANTIGONE.
O my dear Haemon! How your father wrongs you!
CREON.
I hear too much of you and of your marriage.
ISMENE.
He is your son; how can you take her from him?
CREON.
It is not I, but Death, that stops this wedding. 565
CHORUS-LEADER.
It is determined, then, that she must die?
CREON.
For you, and me, determined. (*To the Guards.*) Take them in
At once; no more delay. Henceforward let
Them stay at home, like women, not roam abroad.
Even the bold, you know, will seek escape 570
When they see death at last standing beside them.
(*Exeunt Antigone and Ismene into the palace, guarded. Creon remains.*)

THIRD ODE

STROPHE I

CHORUS.
Thrice happy are they who have never known disaster!
Once a house is shaken of Heaven, disaster
Never leaves it, from generation to generation.
'Tis even as the swelling sea 575
When the roaring wind from Thrace
Drives blustering over the water and makes it black:
It bears up from below
A thick, dark cloud of mud,
And groaning cliffs repel the smack of wind and angry breakers. 580

ANTISTROPHE I

I see, in the house of our kings, how ancient sorrows
Rise again; disaster is linked with disaster.
Woe again must each generation inherit. Some god
Besets them, nor will give release.
On the last of royal blood 585
There gleamed a shimmering light in the house of Oedipus.
But Death comes once again
With blood-stained axe, and hews
The sapling down; and Frenzy lends her aid, and vengeful Madness.

STROPHE 2

Thy power, Zeus, is almighty! No 590
Mortal insolence can oppose Thee!

Sleep, which conquers all else, cannot overcome Thee,
Nor can the never-wearied
Years, but throughout
595 Time Thou art strong and ageless,
In thy own Olympus
Ruling in radiant splendor.
For today, and in all past time,
And through all time to come,
600 This is the law: that in Man's
Life every success brings with it some disaster.

ANTISTROPHE 2

Hope springs high, and to many a man
Hope brings comfort and consolation;
Yet she is to some nothing but fond illusion:
605 Swiftly they come to ruin,
As when a man
Treads unawares on hot fire.
For it was a wise man
First made that ancient saying:
610 To the man whom God will ruin
One day shall evil seem
Good, in his twisted judgment
He comes in a short time to fell disaster.

CHORUS-LEADER.
See, here comes Haemon, last-born of your children,
615 Grieving, it may be, for Antigone.
CREON.
Soon we shall know, better than seers can tell us.

(*Enter Haemon.*)

My son:
You have not come in rage against your father
Because your bride must die? Or are you still
620 My loyal son, whatever I may do?
HAEMON.
Father, I am your son; may your wise judgment
Rule me, and may I always follow it.
No marriage shall be thought a greater prize
For me to win than your good government.
CREON.
625 So may you ever be resolved, my son,
In all things to be guided by your father.
It is for this men pray that they may have
Obedient children, that they may requite
Their father's enemy with enmity
630 And honor whom their father loves to honor.
One who begets unprofitable children
Makes trouble for himself and gives his foes
Nothing but laughter. Therefore do not let
Your pleasure in a woman overcome
Your judgment, knowing this, that if you have 635
An evil wife to share your house, you'll find
Cold comfort in your bed. What other wound
Can cut so deep as treachery at home?
So, think this girl your enemy; spit on her,
And let her find her husband down in Hell! 640
She is the only one that I have found
In all the city disobedient.
I will not make myself a liar. I
Have caught her; I will kill her. Let her sing
Her hymns to Sacred Kinship! If I breed 645
Rebellion in the house, then it is certain
There'll be no lack of rebels out of doors.
No man can rule a city uprightly
Who is not just in ruling his own household.
Never will I approve of one who breaks 650
And violates the law, or would dictate
To those who rule. Lawful authority
Must be obeyed in all things, great or small,
Just and unjust alike; and such a man
Would win my confidence both in command 655
And as a subject; standing at my side
In the storm of battle he would hold his ground,
Not leave me unprotected. But there is
No greater curse than disobedience.
This brings destruction on a city, this 660
Drives men from hearth and home, this brings about
A sudden panic in the battle-front.
Where all goes well, obedience is the cause.
So we must vindicate the law; we must not be
Defeated by a woman. Better far 665
Be overthrown, if need be, by a man
Than to be called the victim of a woman.
CHORUS-LEADER.
Unless the years have stolen away our wits,
All you say is said most prudently.
HAEMON.
Father, it is the gods who give us wisdom; 670
No gift of theirs more precious. I cannot say
That you are wrong, nor would I ever learn
That impudence, although perhaps another
Might fairly say it. But it falls to me,
Being your son, to note what others say, 675
Or do, or censure in you, for your glance
Intimidates the common citizen;
He will not say, before your face, what might
Displease you; I can listen freely, now
The city mourns this girl. "No other woman," 680
So they are saying, "so undeservedly
Has been condemned for such a glorious deed.
When her own brother had been slain in battle
She would not let his body lie unburied

685 To be devoured by dogs or birds of prey.
Is not this worthy of a crown of gold?"—
Such is the muttering that spreads everywhere.
Father, no greater treasure can I have
Than your prosperity; no son can find
690 A greater prize than his own father's fame,
No father than his son's. Therefore let not
This single thought possess you: only what
You say is right, and nothing else. The man
Who thinks that he alone is wise, that he
695 Is best in speech or counsel, such a man
Brought to the proof is found but emptiness.
There's no disgrace, even if one is wise,
In learning more, and knowing when to yield.
See how the trees that grow beside a torrent
700 Preserve their branches, if they bend; the others,
Those that resist, are torn out, root and branch.
So to the captain of a ship; let him
Refuse to shorten sail, despite the storm—
He'll end his voyage bottom uppermost.
705 No, let your anger cool, and be persuaded.
If one who is still young can speak with sense,
Then I would say that he does best who has
Most understanding; second best, the man
Who profits from the wisdom of another.

CHORUS-LEADER.
710 My lord, he has not spoken foolishly;
You each can learn some wisdom from the other.

CREON.
What? men of our age go to school again
And take a lesson from a very boy?

HAEMON.
If it is worth the taking. I am young,
715 But think what should be done, not of my age.

CREON.
What should be done! To honor disobedience!

HAEMON.
I would not have you honor criminals.

CREON.
And is this girl then not a criminal?

HAEMON.
The city with a single voice denies it.

CREON.
720 Must I give orders then by their permission?

HAEMON.
If youth is folly, this is childishness.

CREON.
Am I to rule for them, not for myself?

HAEMON.
That is not government, but tyranny.

CREON.
The king is lord and master of his city.

HAEMON.
Then you had better rule a desert island! 725

CREON.
This man, it seems, is the ally of the woman.

HAEMON.
If you're the woman, yes! I fight for you.

CREON.
Villain! Do you oppose your father's will?

HAEMON.
Only because you are opposing Justice.

CREON.
When I regard my own prerogative? 730

HAEMON.
Opposing God's, you disregard your own.

CREON.
Scoundrel, so to surrender to a woman!

HAEMON.
But not to anything that brings me shame.

CREON.
Your every word is in defense of her.

HAEMON.
And me, and you—and of the gods below. 735

CREON.
You shall not marry her this side the grave!

HAEMON.
So, she must die—and will not die alone.

CREON.
What? Threaten me? Are you so insolent?

HAEMON.
It is no threat, if I reply to folly.

CREON.
The fool would teach me sense! You'll pay for it. 740

HAEMON.
I'd call you mad, if you were not my father.

CREON.
I'll hear no chatter from a woman's plaything.

HAEMON.
Would you have all the talk, and hear no answer?

CREON.
So?
I swear to God, you shall not bandy words 745
With me and not repent it! Bring her out
That loathsome creature! I will have her killed
At once, before her bridegroom's very eyes.

HAEMON.
How can you think it? I will not see that,
Nor shall you ever see my face again. 750
Those friends of yours who can must tolerate
Your raging madness; I will not endure it.

(*Exit Haemon.*)

CHORUS-LEADER.
How angrily he went, my lord! The young,

When they are greatly hurt, grow desperate.
CREON.
755 Then let his pride and folly do their worst!
He shall not save these women from their doom.
CHORUS-LEADER.
Is it your purpose then to kill them both?
CREON.
Not her who had no part in it. —I thank you.
CHORUS-LEADER.
And for the other: how is she to die?
CREON.
760 I'll find a cave in some deserted spot,
And there I will imprison her alive
With so much food—no more—as will avert
Pollution and a curse upon the city.
There let her pray to Death, the only god
765 Whom she reveres, to rescue her from death,
Or learn at last, though it be late, that it
Is wanton folly to respect the dead.
(*Creon remains on the stage.*)

FOURTH ODE

STROPHE

CHORUS.
Invincible, implacable Love, O
Love, that makes havoc of all wealth;
770 That peacefully keeps his night-watch
On tender cheek of a maiden:
The Sea is no barrier, nor
Mountainous waste to Love's flight; for
No one can escape Love's domination,
775 Man, no, nor immortal god. Love's
Prey is possessed by madness.

ANTISTROPHE

By Love, the mind even of the just
Is bent awry; he becomes unjust.
So here: it is Love that stirred up
780 This quarrel of son with father.
The kindling light of Love in the soft
Eye of a bride conquers, for
Love sits on his throne, one of the great Powers;
Nought else can prevail against
785 Invincible Aphrodite.

(*Enter Antigone, under guard. From this point up to the end of the fifth ode everything is sung, except the two speeches in blank verse.*)

CHORUS.
I too, when I see this sight, cannot stay
(*anapests*) Within bounds; I cannot keep back my tears
Which rise like a flood. For behold, they bring
Antigone here, on the journey that all
Must make, to the silence of Hades. 790

COMMOS

STROPHE I

ANTIGONE.
Behold me, O lords of my native city!
(*glyconics*) Now do I make my last journey;
Now do I see the last
Sun that ever I shall behold.
Never another! Death, that lulls 795
All to sleep, takes me while I live
Down to the grim shore of Acheron.
No wedding day can be
Mine, no hymn will he raised to honor
Marriage of mine; for I 800
Go to espouse the bridegroom, Death.
CHORUS.
Yet a glorious death, and rich in fame
(*anapests*) Is yours; you go to the silent tomb
Not smitten with wasting sickness, nor
Repaying a debt to the sharp-edged sword; 805
But alone among mortals you go to the home
Of the dead while yet you are living.

ANTISTROPHE I

ANTIGONE.
They tell of how cruelly she did perish,
(*glyconics*) Niobe, Queen in Thebes;
For, as ivy grows on a tree, 810
Strangling it, so she slowly turned to
Stone on a Phrygian mountain-top.
Now the rain-storms wear her away—
So does the story run—and
Snow clings to her always: 815
Tears fall from her weeping eyes for
Ever and ever. Like to hers, the
Cruel death that now awaits me.
CHORUS.
But she was a goddess, and born of the gods;
(*anapests*) We are but mortals, of mortals born. 820
For a mortal to share in the doom of a god,
That brings her renown while yet she lives,
And a glory that long will outlive her.

STROPHE 2

ANTIGONE.
Alas, they laugh! O by the gods of Thebes, my
(*more passionate rhythm*) native city,
Mock me, if you must, when I am gone, not to my face! 825

O Thebes my city, O you lordly men of Thebes!
O water of Dirkê's stream! Holy soil where our chariots
run!
You, you do I call upon; you, you shall testify
How all unwept of friends, by what harsh decree,
They send me to the cavern that shall be my everlasting
830 grave.
Ah, cruel doom! to be banished from earth, nor welcomed
Among the dead, set apart, for ever!

CHORUS.
Too bold, too reckless, you affronted
(*more spirited*) Justice. Now that awful power
835 Takes terrible vengeance, O my child.
For some old sin you make atonement.

ANTISTROPHE 2

ANTIGONE.
My father's sin! There is the source of all my anguish.
Harsh fate that befell my father! Harsh fate that has held
Fast in its grip the whole renowned race of Labdacus!
O the blind madness of my father's and my mother's
840 marriage!
O cursed union of a son with his own mother!
From such as those I draw my own unhappy life;
And now I go to dwell with them, unwedded and
accursed.
O brother, through an evil marriage you were slain; and I
845 Live—but your dead hand destroys me.

CHORUS.
Such loyalty is a holy thing.
Yet none that holds authority
Can brook disobedience, O my child.
Your self-willed pride has been your ruin.

EPODE

ANTIGONE.
850 Unwept, unwedded and unbefriended,
Alone, pitilessly used,
Now they drag me to death.
Never again, O thou Sun in the heavens,
May I look on thy holy radiance!
855 Such is my fate, and no one laments it;
No friend is here to mourn me.

CREON.
Enough of this! If tears and lamentations
Could stave off death they would go on forever.
Take her away at once, and wall her up
860 Inside a cavern, as I have commanded,
And leave her there, alone, in solitude.
Her home shall be her tomb; there she may live
Or die, as she may choose: my hands are clean;
But she shall live no more among the living.

ANTIGONE.
O grave, my bridal-chamber, everlasting 865
Prison within a rock: now I must go
To join my own, those many who have died
And whom Persephone has welcomed home;
And now to me, the last of all, so young,
Death comes, so cruelly. And yet I go 870
In the sure hope that you will welcome me,
Father, and you, my mother; you, my brother.
For when you died it was my hands that washed
And dressed you, laid you in your graves, and poured
The last libations. Now, because to you, 875
Polyneices, I have given burial,
To me they give a recompense like this!
Yet what I did, the wise will all approve.
For had I lost a son, or lost a husband,
Never would I have ventured such an act 880
Against the city's will. And wherefore so?
My husband dead, I might have found another;
Another son from him, if I had lost
A son. But since my mother and my father
Have both gone to the grave, there can be none 885
Henceforth that I can ever call my brother.
It was for this I paid you such an honor,
Dear Polyneices, and in Creon's eyes
Thus wantonly and gravely have offended.
So with rude hands he drags me to my death. 890
No chanted wedding-hymn, no bridal-joy,
No tender care of children can be mine;
But like an outcast, and without a friend,
They take me to the cavernous home of death.
What ordinance of the gods have I transgressed? 895
Why should I look to Heaven any more
For help, or seek an ally among men?
If this is what the gods approve, why then,
When I am dead I shall discern my fault;
If theirs the sin, may they endure a doom 900
No worse than mine, so wantonly inflicted!

CHORUS.
Still from the same quarter the same wild winds
(*anapests*) Blow fiercely, and shake her stubborn soul.

CREON.
And therefore, for this, these men shall have
cause,
(*anapests*) Bitter cause, to lament their tardiness. 905

CHORUS.
I fear these words bring us closer yet
To the verge of death.

CREON.
I have nothing to say, no comfort to give:
The sentence is passed, and the end is here.

ANTIGONE.
910 O city of Thebes where my fathers dwelt,
O gods of our race,
Now at last their hands are upon me!
You princes of Thebes, O look upon me,
The last that remain of a line of kings!
915 How savagely impious men use me,
For keeping a law that is holy.
(Exit Antigone, under guard. Creon remains.)

FIFTH ODE

STROPHE I

CHORUS.
There was one in days of old who was imprisoned
(*slow three-time*) In a chamber like a grave, within a tower:
Fair Danaë, who in darkness was held, and never saw the pure daylight.
920 Yet she too, O my child, was of an ancient line,
Entrusted with divine seed that had come in shower of gold.
Mysterious, overmastering, is the power of Fate.
(*faster three-time*) From this, nor wealth nor force of arms
Nor strong encircling city-walls
925 Nor storm-tossed ship can give deliverance.

ANTISTROPHE I

Close bondage was ordained by Dionysus
For one who in a frenzy had denied
His godhead: in a cavern Lycurgus, for his sin, was imprisoned.
In such wise did his madness bear a bitter fruit,
930 Which withered in a dungeon. So he learned it was a god
He had ventured in his blindness to revile and taunt.
The sacred dances he had tried
To quell, and end the Bacchic rite,
Offending all the tuneful Muses.

STROPHE 2

(*fairly fast, becoming faster; three- and four-time mixed*)
935 There is a town by the rocks where a sea meets another sea,
Two black rocks by the Bosphorus, near the Thracian coast,
Salmŷdessus; and there a wife had been spurned,
Held close in bitter constraint.[5]
Then upon both her children

[5]These two verses are a paraphrase rather than a translation. It seemed better to give the audience something which it could follow rather than the mythological reference in the Greek, which it certainly would not. [Kitto.]

A blinding wound fell from her cruel rival: 940
With shuttle in hand she smote the open eyes with sharp
And blood-stained point, and brought to Phineus'
Two sons a darkness that cried for vengeance.

ANTISTROPHE 2

In bitter grief and despair they bewailed their unhappy lot,
Children born to a mother whose marriage proved accursed. 945
Yet she came of a race of ancient kings,
Her sire the offspring of gods.
Reared in a distant country,
Among her fierce, northern father's tempests,
She went, a Boread, swift as horses, over the lofty 950
Mountains. Yet not even she was
Safe against the long-lived Fates, my daughter.

(*Enter Teiresias, led by a boy.*)

TEIRESIAS.
My lords, I share my journey with this boy
Whose eyes must see for both; for so the blind
Must move abroad, with one to guide their steps. 955
CREON.
Why, what is this? Why are *you* here, Teiresias?
TEIRESIAS.
I will explain; you will do well to listen.
CREON.
Have I not always followed your good counsel?
TEIRESIAS.
You have; therefore we have been guided well.
CREON.
I have had much experience of your wisdom. 960
TEIRESIAS.
Then think: once more you tread the razor's edge.
CREON.
You make me tremble! What is it you mean?
TEIRESIAS.
What divination has revealed to me,
That I will tell you. To my ancient seat
Of augury I went, where all the birds 965
Foregather. There I sat, and heard a clamor
Strange and unusual—birds screaming in rage.
I knew that they were tearing at each other
With murderous claws: the beating of their wings
Meant nothing less than that; and I was frightened. 970
I made a blazing fire upon the altar
And offered sacrifice: it would not burn;
The melting fat oozed out upon the embers
And smoked and bubbled; high into the air
The bladder sported gall, and from the bones 975
The fatty meat slid off and left them bare.

Such omens, baffling, indistinct, I learned
From him who guides me, as I am guide to others.
Sickness has come upon us, and the cause
980 Is you: our altars and our sacred hearths
Are all polluted by the dogs and birds
That have been gorging on the fallen body
Of Polyneices. Therefore heaven will not
Accept from us our prayers, no fire will burn
985 Our offerings, nor will birds give out clear sounds,
For they are glutted with the blood of men.
Be warned, my son. No man alive is free
From error, but the wise and prudent man
When he has fallen into evil courses
990 Does not persist, but tries to find amendment.
It is the stubborn man who is the fool.
Yield to the dead, forbear to strike the fallen;
To slay the slain, is that a deed of valor?
Your good is what I seek; and that instruction
995 Is best that comes from wisdom, and brings profit.

CREON.
Sir, all of you, like bowmen at a target,
Let fly your shafts at me. Now they have turned
Even diviners on me! By that tribe
I am bought and sold and stowed away on board.
1000 Go, make your profits, drive your trade
In Lydian silver or in Indian gold,
But him you shall not bury in a tomb,
No, not though Zeus' own eagles eat the corpse
And bear the carrion to their master's throne:
1005 Not even so, for fear of that defilement,
Will I permit his burial—for well I know
That mortal man can not defile the gods.
But, old Teiresias, even the cleverest men
Fall shamefully when for a little money
1010 They use fair words to mask their villainy.

TEIRESIAS.
Does any man reflect, does any know . . .

CREON.
Know *what?* Why do you preach at me like this?

TEIRESIAS.
How much the greatest blessing is good counsel?

CREON.
As much, I think, as folly is his plague.

TEIRESIAS.
1015 Yet with this plague you are yourself infected.

CREON.
I will not bandy words with any prophet.

TEIRESIAS.
And yet you say my prophecies are dishonest!

CREON.
Prophets have always been too fond of gold.

TEIRESIAS.
And tyrants, of the shameful use of power.

CREON.
You know it is your King of whom you speak? 1020

TEIRESIAS.
King of the land I saved from mortal danger.

CREON.
A clever prophet—but an evil one.

TEIRESIAS.
You'll rouse me to awaken my dark secret.

CREON.
Awaken it, but do not speak for money.

TEIRESIAS.
And do you think that I am come to *that?* 1025

CREON.
You shall not buy and sell *my* policy.

TEIRESIAS.
Then I will tell you this: you will not live
Through many circuits of the racing sun
Before you give a child of your own body
To make amends for murder, death for death; 1030
Because you have thrust down within the earth
One who should walk upon it, and have lodged
A living soul dishonorably in a tomb;
And impiously have kept upon the earth
Unburied and unblest one who belongs 1035
Neither to you nor to the upper gods
But to the gods below, who are despoiled
By you. Therefore the gods arouse against you
Their sure avengers; they lie in your path
Even now to trap you and to make you pay 1040
Their price. —Now think: do I say *this* for money?
Not many hours will pass before your house
Rings loud with lamentation, men and women.
Hatred for you is moving in those cities
Whose mangled sons had funeral-rites from dogs 1045
Or from some bird of prey, whose wings have carried
The taint of dead men's flesh to their own homes,
Polluting hearth and altar.
These are the arrows that I launch at you,
Because you anger me. I shall not miss 1050
My aim, and you shall not escape their smart.
Boy, lead me home again, that he may vent
His rage upon some younger man, and learn
To moderate his violent tongue, and find
More understanding than he has today. 1055

(*Exit Teiresias.*)

CHORUS-LEADER.
And so, my lord, he leaves us, with a threat
Of doom. I have lived long, but I am sure
Of this: no single prophecy that he

Has made to Thebes has gone without fulfillment.

CREON.

1060 I know it too, and I am terrified.
To yield is very hard, but to resist
And meet disaster, that is harder still.

CHORUS-LEADER.

Creon, this is no time for wrong decision.

CREON.

What shall I do? Advise me; I will listen.

CHORUS-LEADER.

1065 Release Antigone from her rock-hewn dungeon,
And lay the unburied body in a tomb.

CREON.

Is this your counsel? You would have me yield?

CHORUS-LEADER.

I would, and quickly. The destroying hand
Of Heaven is quick to punish human error.

CREON.

1070 How hard it is! And yet one cannot fight
Against Necessity. —I will give way.

CHORUS-LEADER.

Go then and do it; leave it not to others.

CREON.

Just as I am I go. You men-at-arms,
You here, and those within: away at once
1075 Up to the hill, and take your implements.
Now that my resolution is reversed
I who imprisoned her will set her free.—
I fear it may be wiser to observe
Throughout one's life the laws that are established.

(*Exit Creon.*)

SIXTH ODE

STROPHE I

CHORUS.

1080 Thou Spirit whose names are many, Dionysus,
Born to Zeus the loud-thunderer,
Joy of thy Theban mother-nymph,
Lover of famous Italy:
King art thou in the crowded shrine
1085 Where Demeter has her abode, O
Bacchus! Here is thy mother's home,
Here is thine, by the smooth Is-
menûs's flood, here where the savage
Dragon's teeth had offspring.

ANTISTROPHE I

1090 Thou art seen by the nymphs amid the smoky torchlight,
Where, upon Parnassus' height,
They hold revels to honor Thee
Close to the spring of Castaly.
Thou art come from the ivy-clad
Slopes of Asian hills, and vineyards 1095
Hanging thick with clustering grapes.
Mystic voices chant: "O
Bacchus! O Bacchus!" in
The roads and ways of Thebê.

STROPHE 2

Here is thy chosen home, 1100
In Thebes above all lands,
With thy mother, bride of Zeus.
Wherefore, since a pollution holds
All our people fast in its grip,
O come with swift healing across the wall of high
Parnassus, 1105
Or over the rough Eurîpus.

ANTISTROPHE 2

Stars that move, breathing flame,
Honor Thee as they dance;
Voices cry to Thee in the night.
Son begotten of Zeus, appear! 1110
Come, Lord, with thy company,
Thy own nymphs, who with wild, nightlong dances praise
Thee,
Bountiful Dionysus!

(*Enter a Messenger.*)

MESSENGER.

You noblemen of Thebes, how insecure
Is human fortune! Chance will overthrow 1115
The great, and raise the lowly; nothing's firm,
Either for confidence or for despair;
No one can prophesy what lies in store.
An hour ago, how much I envied Creon!
He had saved Thebes, we had accorded him 1120
The sovereign power; he ruled our land
Supported by a noble prince, his son.
Now all is lost, and he who forfeits joy
Forfeits his life; he is a breathing corpse.
Heap treasures in your palace, if you will, 1125
And wear the pomp of royalty; but if
You have no happiness, I would not give
A straw for all of it, compared with joy.

CHORUS-LEADER.

What is this weight of heavy news you bring?

MESSENGER.

Death!—and the blood-guilt rests upon the living. 1130

CHORUS-LEADER.

Death? Who is dead? And who has killed him? Tell me.

MESSENGER.
Haemon is dead, and by no stranger's hand.
CHORUS-LEADER.
But by his father's? Or was it his own?
MESSENGER.
His own—inflamed with anger at his father.
CHORUS-LEADER.
1135 Yours was no idle prophecy, Teiresias!
MESSENGER.
That is my news. What next, remains with you.
CHORUS-LEADER.
But look! There is his wife, Eurydice;
She is coming from the palace. Has she heard
About her son, or is she here by chance?

(*Enter Eurydice.*)

EURYDICE.
1140 You citizens of Thebes, I overheard
When I was standing at the gates, for I
Had come to make an offering at the shrine
Of Pallas, and my hand was on the bar
That holds the gate, to draw it; then there fell
1145 Upon my ears a voice that spoke of death.
My terror took away my strength; I fell
Into my servants' arms and swooned away.
But tell it me once more; I can endure
To listen; I am no stranger to bad news.
MESSENGER.
1150 Dear lady, I was there, and I will tell
The truth; I will not keep it back from you.
Why should I gloze it over? You would hear
From someone else, and I should seem a liar.
The truth is always best.
I went with Creon
1155 Up to the hill where Polyneices' body
Still lay, unpitied, torn by animals.
We gave it holy washing, and we prayed
To Hecate and Pluto that they would
Restrain their anger and be merciful.
1160 And then we cut some branches, and we burned
What little had been left, and built a mound
Over his ashes of his native soil.
Then, to the cavern, to the home of death,
The bridal-chamber with its bed of stone.
1165 One of us heard a cry of lamentation
From that unhallowed place; he went to Creon
And told him. On the wind, as he came near,
Cries of despair were borne. He groaned aloud
In anguish: "O, and are my fears come true?
1170 Of all the journeys I have made, am I
To find this one the most calamitous?
It is my son's voice greets me. Hurry, men;
Run to the place, and when you reach the tomb
Creep in between the gaping stones and see
If it be Haemon there, or if the gods 1175
Are cheating me." Upon this desperate order
We ran and looked. Within the furthest chamber
We saw her hanging, dead; strips from her dress
Had served her for a rope. Haemon we saw
Embracing her dead body and lamenting 1180
His loss, his father's deed, and her destruction.
When Creon saw him he cried out in anguish,
Went in, and called to him: "My son! my son!
O why? What have you done? What brought you here?
What is this madness? O come out, my son, 1185
Come, I implore you!" Haemon glared at him
With anger in his eyes, spat in his face,
Said nothing, drew his double-hilted sword,
But missed his aim as Creon leapt aside.
Then in remorse he leaned upon the blade 1190
And drove it half its length into his body.
While yet the life was in him he embraced
The girl with failing arms, and breathing hard
Poured out his life-blood on to her white face.
So side by side they lie, and both are dead. 1195
Not in this world but in the world below
He wins his bride, and shows to all mankind
That folly is the worst of human evils.

(*Exit Eurydice.*)

CHORUS-LEADER.
What can we think of this? The Queen is gone
Without one word of good or evil omen. 1200
MESSENGER.
What can it mean? But yet we may sustain
The hope that she would not display her grief
In public, but will rouse the sad lament
For Haemon's death among her serving-women
Inside the palace. She has true discretion, 1205
And she would never do what is unseemly.
CHORUS-LEADER.
I cannot say, but wild lament would be
Less ominous than this unnatural silence.
MESSENGER.
It *is* unnatural; there may be danger.
I'll follow her; it may be she is hiding 1210
Some secret purpose in her passionate heart.

(*Exit Messenger, into the palace.*)

CHORUS.
Look, Creon draws near, and the burden he bears
(*anapests*) Gives witness to his misdeeds; the cause
Lies only in his blind error.

(*Enter Creon and the Guards, with the body of Haemon.*)[6]

STROPHE 1

CREON.
1215 Alas!
The wrongs I have done by ill-counselling!
Cruel and fraught with death.
You behold, men of Thebes,
The slayer, the slain; a father, a son.
1220 My own stubborn ways have borne bitter fruit.
My son! Dead, my son! So soon torn from me,
So young, so young!
The fault only mine, not yours, O my son.

CHORUS-LEADER.
Too late, too late you see the path of wisdom.

CREON.
1225 Alas!
A bitter lesson I have learned! The god
Coming with all his weight has borne down on me,
And smitten me with all his cruelty;
My joy overturned, trampled beneath his feet.
1230 What suffering besets the whole race of men!

(*Enter Messenger, from the palace.*)

MESSENGER.
My master, when you came you brought a burden
Of sorrow with you; now, within your house,
A second store of misery confronts you.

CREON.
Another sorrow come to crown my sorrow?

MESSENGER.
1235 The Queen, true mother of her son, is dead;
In grief she drove a blade into her heart.

ANTISTROPHE 1

CREON.
Alas!
Thou grim hand of death, greedy and unappeased,
Why so implacable?
1240 Voice of doom, you who bring
Such dire news of grief, O, can it be true?
What have you said, my son? O, you have slain the slain!
Tell me, can it be true? Is death crowning death?
My wife! my wife!

[6]From this point up to the final utterance of the chorus the dialogue is in strictly strophic form. Creon's lines, except those rendered in blank verse, are sung; they are in the strongly marked dochmiac rhythm. [Kitto.]

My son dead, and now my wife taken too! 1245

(*Eurydice's body is discovered.*)

CHORUS-LEADER.
But raise your eyes: there is her lifeless body.

CREON.
Alas!
Here is a sorrow that redoubles sorrow.
Where will it end? What else can Fate hold in store?
While yet I clasp my dead son in my arms 1250
Before me there lies another struck by death.
Alas cruel doom! the mother's and the son's.

MESSENGER.
She took a sharp-edged knife, stood by the altar,
And made lament for Megareus who was killed
Of old, and next for Haemon. Then at last, 1255
Invoking evil upon you, the slayer
Of both her sons, she closed her eyes in death.

STROPHE 2

CREON.
A curse, a thing of terror! O, is there none
Who unsheathe a sword to end all my woes
With one deadly thrust? My grief crushes me. 1260

MESSENGER.
She cursed you for the guilt of Haemon's death
And of the other son who died before.

CREON.
What did she do? How did she end her life?

MESSENGER.
She heard my bitter story; then she put
A dagger to her heart and drove it home. 1265

CREON.
The guilt falls on me alone; none but I
Have slain her; no other shares in the sin.
'Twas I dealt the blow. This is the truth, my friends.
Away, take me away, far from the sight of men!
My life now is death. Lead me away from here. 1270

CHORUS-LEADER.
That would he well, if anything is well.
Briefest is best when such disaster comes.

ANTISTROPHE 2

CREON.
O come, best of all the days I can see,
The last day of all, the day that brings death.
O come quickly! Come, thou night with no dawn! 1275

CHORUS-LEADER.
That's for the future; here and now are duties
That fall on those to whom they are allotted.

CREON.
I prayed for death; I wish for nothing else.
CHORUS-LEADER.
Then pray no more; from suffering that has been
1280 Decreed no man will ever find escape.
CREON.
Lead me away, a rash, a misguided man,
Whose blindness has killed a wife and a son.
O where can I look? What strength can I find?
On me has fallen a doom greater than I can bear.
(*Exeunt Creon and Guards into the palace.*)
CHORUS.
Of happiness, far the greatest part 1285
(*anapests*) Is wisdom, and reverence towards the gods.
Proud words of the arrogant man, in the end,
Meet punishment, great as his pride was great,
Till at last he is schooled in wisdom.

TOPICS FOR DISCUSSION AND WRITING

1. Would you use masks for some (or all) of the characters? If so, would they be masks that fully cover the face, Greek-style, or some sort of half-masks? (A full mask enlarges the face, and conceivably the mouthpiece can amplify the voice, but only an exceptionally large theater might require such help. Perhaps half-masks are enough if the aim is chiefly to distance the actors from the audience and from daily reality, and to force the actors to develop resources other than facial gestures. One director, arguing in favor of half-masks, has said that actors who wear even a half-mask learn to act not with the eyes but with the neck.)
2. How would you costume the players? Would you dress them as the Greeks might have? Why? One argument sometimes used by those who hold that modern productions of Greek drama should use classical costumes is that Greek drama *ought* to be remote and ritualistic. Evaluate this view. What sort of modern dress might be effective?
3. If you were directing a college production of *Antigone,* how large a chorus would you use? (Sophocles is said to have used a chorus of fifteen.) Would you have the chorus recite (or chant) the odes in unison, or would you assign lines to single speakers?
4. If you have read *Oedipus the King,* compare and contrast the Creon of *Antigone* with the Creon of *Oedipus.*
5. Although Sophocles called his play *Antigone,* many critics say that Creon is the real tragic hero, pointing out that Antigone is absent from the last third of the play. Evaluate this view.
6. In some Greek tragedies, fate plays a great role in bringing about the downfall of the tragic hero. Though there are references to the curse on the House of Oedipus in *Antigone,* do we feel that Antigone goes to her death as a result of the workings of fate? Do we feel that fate is responsible for Creon's fall? Are both Antigone and Creon the creators of their own tragedy?
7. Are the words *hamartia* and *hybris* (pages 29–30) relevant to Antigone? To Creon?
8. Why does Creon, contrary to the Chorus's advice (lines 1065–66), bury the body of Polyneices before he releases Antigone? Does his action show a zeal for piety as short-sighted as his earlier zeal for law? Is his action plausible, in view of the facts that Teiresias has dwelt on the wrong done to Polyneices and that Antigone has ritual food to sustain her? Or are we not to worry about Creon's motive?
9. A *foil* is a character who, by contrast, sets off or helps define another character. To what extent is Ismene a foil to Antigone? Is she entirely without courage?
10. What function does Eurydice serve? How deeply do we feel about her fate?

Patrick Hines in the Phoenix Theater production of *Lysistrata* in New York, 1959.
(Photograph: Joseph Abeles Studio.)

ARISTOPHANES

Lysistrata

English version by Dudley Fitts

Nothing of much interest is known about Aristophanes (c. 450 to c. 385 B.C.). An Athenian, he competed for about forty years in the annual festivals of comic drama to which three playwrights each contributed one play. His first play was produced in 427 B.C., his last extant play in 388 B.C., but he is known to have written two comedies after this date. Of the forty or so plays he wrote, eleven survive. *Lysistrata* was produced in 411 B.C.

COMMENTARY

Of the hundreds of ancient Greek comedies that were written, only eleven by Aristophanes and four by Menander (c. 342–299 B.C.) are extant, and three of Menander's four survive only in long fragments. Aristophanes seems to have written about forty plays, Menander more than twice as many. Hundreds of other men wrote comedies in ancient Greece, but they are mere names, or names attached to brief fragments. This means that when we talk about Greek comedy we are really talking about a fraction of Aristophanes's work, and an even smaller fraction of Menander's.

Greek comedy is customarily divided into three kinds: Old Comedy (486 B.C., when comedy was first given official recognition at the festival called the City Dionysia, to 404 B.C., the end of the Peloponnesian War, when Athens was humbled and freedom of speech was curtailed); Middle Comedy (404 B.C. to 336 B.C., the accession of Alexander, when Athens was no longer free); and New Comedy (336 B.C. to c. 250 B.C., the approximate date of the last fragments). Of Old Comedy, there are Aristophanes's plays; of Middle Comedy, there is *Plutus,* one of Aristophanes's last plays; of New Comedy, there are Menander's fragments and his recently discovered *Dyskolos* (*The Disagreeable Man*).

Old Comedy—*Lysistrata* is an example—is a curious combination of obscenity, farce, political allegory, satire, and lyricism. Puns, literary allusions, phallic jokes, and political jibes periodically give way to joyful song; Aristophanes seems to have been something of a combination of Joyce, Swift, and Shelley. Other comparisons may be helpful. Perhaps we can say that in their loosely connected episodes and their rapid shifts from lyricism and fantasy to mockery the plays are something like a Marx Brothers movie (Harpo's musical episodes juxtaposed with Groucho's irreverent wisecracks and outrageous ogling), though the plays are more explicitly political; and they are something like the rock musical *Hair,* which combined lyricism and politics with sex. The players of male roles wore large phalluses, and all the players wore masks, usually with grotesque expressions.

Normally Aristophanes's plays have the following structure:

1. *Prologos:* prologue or exposition. Someone has a bright idea and sets it forth either in monologue or dialogue. In *Lysistrata,* the prologue consists of lines 1–212, in which Lysistrata persuades the women to refrain from sex with their husbands and thus compel their husbands to give up the war.
2. *Parados:* entrance of the chorus. The twenty-four or so members of the chorus express their opinion of the idea. (The *koryphaios,* or leader of the chorus, perhaps sings some lines by himself.) *Lysistrata* is somewhat unusual in having two half-choruses (*hemichori*), one of Old Men and another of Old Women, each with its own leader. Probably each half-chorus had twelve members.
3. *Epeisodion:* episode or scene. In the first scene of *Lysistrata* the women defeat the Commissioner. (A scene in this position, that is, before the *parabasis,* is sometimes called the *agon,* or debate.)
4. *Parabasis:* usually an elaborate composition in which the leader of the chorus ordinarily sheds his dramatic character and addresses the audience on the poet's behalf, the other actors having briefly retired. The *parabasis* in *Lysistrata* is unusual: it is much shorter than those in Aristophanes's earlier plays, and the chorus does not speak directly for the playwright.
5. *Epeisodia:* episodes or scenes, sometimes briefly separated by choral songs. These episodes have to do with the working out of the original bright idea. In *Lysistrata* the first scene of this group (labeled Scene II because we have already had one scene before the *parabasis*) shows the women seeking to desert the cause, the second shows Myrrhine—loyal to the idea—tormenting her husband Kinesias, the third shows the Spartan herald discomfited by an erection, and the fourth shows the Spartan ambassadors similarly discomfited.
6. *Exodos:* final scene, customarily of reconciliation and rejoicing. There is often talk of a wedding and a feast. In this play a Spartan sings in praise not only of Sparta but also of Athens, and the chorus praises the deities worshipped in both states.

Perhaps all Old Comedy was rather like this, but it should be remembered that even Aristophanes's eleven plays do not all follow the pattern exactly. *Lysistrata,* for example, is unusual in having two hemichori and in having the chorus retain its identity during the parabasis. But *Lysistrata* (the accent is on the second syllable, and the name in effect means "Disbander-of-the-Army") is typical in its political concern, in its fantasy, in its bawdry, and in its revelry. It touches on serious, destructive themes, but it is joyous and extravagant, ending with a newly unified society. These points require some explanation.

First, Aristophanes's political concern. *Lysistrata* is the last of Aristophanes's three plays opposing the Peloponnesian War (the earlier two are *Acharnians* and *Peace*). This drawn-out war (431–404 B.C.), named for a peninsula forming the southern part of Greece, was fought between Athens (with some allies) and a confederacy headed by Sparta. Though enemies when the play was performed in 411 B.C., Athens and Sparta and other communities had been allies in 478 B.C. in order to defeat a common enemy, the Persians, but once the Persian threat was destroyed, Athens deprived most of its allies of their autonomy and, in effect, Athens ruled an empire.

Moreover, Athens tried to extend its empire. The war ultimately cost Athens its overseas empire and its leadership on the mainland. In 413 B.C. Athens had suffered an especially disastrous naval defeat; it had made something of a recovery by the time of

Lysistrata, but the cost in manpower and money was enormous. Yet Athens persisted in its dream of conquest and of colonizing.

To counter this fantastic idea Aristophanes holds up another fantastic idea: the women will end the war by a sex strike. Actually, this is not one fantastic idea but two, for the idea of a sex strike is no more fantastic (for Athenians of the fifth century B.C.) than the idea of women playing a role—not to speak of a decisive role—in national affairs. Lysistrata, reporting her husband's view, is reporting the view of every Athenian: "War's a man's affair." (He was quoting from Homer's *Iliad,* so the point was beyond dispute.) And so there is something wild in her suggestion that the women can save the Greek cities (her hope goes beyond Athens, to Sparta and the other combatants), and in her comparison of the state to a ball of tangled yarn:

COMMISSIONER.
All this is beside the point.
Will you be so kind
as to tell me how you mean to save Greece?
LYSISTRATA. Of course.
Nothing could be simpler.
COMMISSIONER. I assure you, I'm all ears.
LYSISTRATA.
Do you know anything about weaving?
Say the yarn gets tangled: we thread it
this way and that through the skein, up and down,
until it's free. And it's like that with war.
We'll send our envoys
up and down, this way and that, all over Greece,
until it's finished.
COMMISSIONER. Yarn? Thread? Skein?
Are you out of your mind? I tell you,
war is a serious business.
LYSISTRATA. So serious
that I'd like to go on talking about weaving.
COMMISSIONER.
All right. Go ahead.
LYSISTRATA. The first thing we have to do
is to wash our yarn, get the dirt out of it.
You see? Isn't there too much dirt here in Athens?
You must wash those men away.
Then our spoiled wool—
that's like your job-hunters, out for a life
of no work and big pay. Back to the basket,
citizens or not, allies or not,
or friendly immigrants.
And your colonies?
Hanks of wool lost in various places. Pull them
together, weave them into one great whole,
and our voters are clothed for ever.

To the Commissioner, this is utterly fantastic:

COMMISSIONER. It would take a woman
to reduce state questions to a matter of carding and weaving.

Such is the male view, and so these fantastic women, in order to exert influence, must resort to another fantastic idea, the sex strike, and here we encounter Aristophanes's famous bawdry. In fact the play's reputation for bawdry is grossly exaggerated. Until recently, when pornography was hard to get, *Lysistrata*—because it was literature—provided one of the few available texts that talked of erections and of female delight in sex, and Aubrey Beardsley's illustrations (1896) doubtless helped to establish the book's reputation as a sexual stimulus. But it is really pretty tame stuff compared to what is now readily available, and the play, for all its sexual jokes, is not really about sex but about peace, harmony, and union—union between husbands and wives, between all in Athens, and between Athens and the other Greeks-speaking communities.

One final point: the whole play, of course, not only is utterly improbable but also is utterly impossible: The women complain that they are sex-starved because the men are away at the war, but we soon find that the women will remedy this situation by withholding sex from the men—who, we thought, were away at war. How can one withhold sex from men who are supposedly not present? But Old Comedy never worried about such consistency.

A few words should be said about Middle Comedy and New Comedy. Middle Comedy is a convenient label to apply to the lost plays that must have marked the transition from Old Comedy to New Comedy—that is, to the surviving work of Menander. In New Comedy, written when Athens's political greatness was gone, and when political invective was impossible, the chorus has dwindled to musicians and dancers who perform intermittently, characters tend to be types (the young lover, the crabby old father, etc.), and the plot is regularly a young man's wooing of a maid. Fortune seems unfair and unpredictable, but in the end the virtuous are rewarded. The personal satire and obscenity of Old Comedy are gone, and in their place is a respectably conducted tale showing how, after humorous difficulties, the young man achieves his goal. The plot steadily moves toward the happy ending, which is far more integral than the more or less elusive allegoric (or metaphoric) union at the end of *Lysistrata.* It was New Comedy that influenced Rome (which could scarcely have imitated the political satire of Old Comedy), and through Rome modern Europe. Shakespeare, for example, whose comedies have been described as obstacle races to the altar, was a descendant of Menander though he knew nothing of Menander's work first-hand.

ARISTOPHANES *Lysistrata*

List of Characters

LYSISTRATA [*pronounced* Ly SIS tra ta]
KALONIKE [*pronounced* Ka lo NI ke]
MYRRHINE [*pronounced* MYR rhi nee]
LAMPITO [*pronounced* LAM pee toe]
CHORUS
COMMISSIONER
KINESIAS [*pronounced* ki NEE see as]
SPARTAN HERALD
SPARTAN AMBASSADOR
A SENTRY

Until the exodos, *the Chorus is divided into two hemichori: the first, of Old Men; the second, of Old Women. Each of these had its* Koryphaios *(i.e., leader). In the* exodos, *the hemichori return as Athenians and Spartans.*

The supernumeraries include the baby son of Kinesias;

Stratyllis, a member of the hemichorus of Old Women; various individual speakers, both Spartan and Athenian.

Scene: Athens. First, a public square; later, beneath the walls of the Akropolis; later, a courtyard within the Akropolis.

PROLOGUE

(*Athens; a public square; early morning; Lysistrata alone.*)

LYSISTRATA.
If someone had invited them to a festival—
of Bacchos, say; or to Pan's shrine, or to Aphrodite's°[1]
over at Kolias—, you couldn't get through the streets,
what with the drums and the dancing. But now,
not a woman in sight!
5 Except—oh, yes!

(*Enter Kalonike.*)

Here's one of my neighbors, at last. Good
morning, Kalonike.
KALONIKE. Good morning, Lysistrata. Darling,
don't frown so! You'll ruin your face!
LYSISTRATA. Never mind my face.
Kalonike,
10 the way we women behave! Really, I don't blame the men
for what they say about us.
KALONIKE. No; I imagine they're right.
LYSISTRATA.
For example: I call a meeting
to think out a most important matter—and what
happens?
The women all stay in bed!
KALONIKE. Oh, they'll be along.
It's hard to get away, you know: a husband, a cook,
15 a child . . . Home life can be *so* demanding!
LYSISTRATA.
What I have in mind is even more demanding.
KALONIKE.
Tell me: what is it?
LYSISTRATA. It's big.
KALONIKE. Goodness! *How* big?
LYSISTRATA.
Big enough for all of us.

[1]The degree sign (°) indicates a footnote, which is keyed to the text by the line number. Text references are printed in **boldface** type; the annotation follows in lightface type.
2 **Bacchos, Pan, Aphrodite** The first two are gods associated with wine; Aphrodite is the goddess of love.

KALONIKE. But we're not all here!
LYSISTRATA.
We would be, if *that's* what was up!
No, Kalonike, 20
this is something I've been turning over for nights,
long sleepless nights.
KALONIKE. It must be getting worn down, then,
if you've spent so much time on it.
LYSISTRATA. Worn down or not,
it comes to this: Only we women can save Greece!
KALONIKE.
Only we women? Poor Greece!
LYSISTRATA. Just the same, 25
it's up to us. First, we must liquidate
the Peloponnesians—
KALONIKE. Fun, fun!
LYSISTRATA. —and then the Boiotians.°
KALONIKE.
Oh! But not those heavenly eels!
LYSISTRATA. You needn't worry.
I'm not talking about eels.—But here's the point:
If we can get the women from those places— 30
all those Boiotians and Peloponnesians—
to join us women here, why, we can save
all Greece!
KALONIKE. But dearest Lysistrata!
How can women do a thing so austere, so
political? We belong at home. Our only armor's 35
our perfumes, our saffron dresses and
our pretty little shoes!
LYSISTRATA. Exactly. Those
transparent dresses, the saffron, the
perfume, those pretty shoes—
KALONIKE. Oh?
LYSISTRATA. Not a single man would lift
his spear—
KALONIKE. I'll send my dress to the dyer's tomorrow! 40
LYSISTRATA.
—or grab a shield—
KALONIKE. The sweetest little negligée—
LYSISTRATA.
—or haul out his sword.
KALONIKE. I know where I can buy
the dreamiest sandals!
LYSISTRATA. Well, so you see. Now shouldn't
the women have come?
KALONIKE. Come? They should have *flown!*
LYSISTRATA.
Athenians are always late.

27 **Boiotia** A country north of Attika, noted for the crudity of its inhabitants and the excellence of its seafood.

45 But imagine!
There's no one here from the South Shore, or from Salamis.
KALONIKE.
Things are hard over in Salamis, I swear.
They have to get going at dawn.
LYSISTRATA. And nobody from Acharnai.
I thought they'd be here hours ago.
KALONIKE. Well, you'll get
50 that awful Theagenes woman: she'll be
a sheet or so in the wind.
But look!
Someone at last! Can you see who they are?

(*Enter Myrrhine and other women.*)

LYSISTRATA.
They're from Anagyros.
KALONIKE. They certainly are.
You'd know them anywhere, by the scent.
MYRRHINE.
Sorry to be late, Lysistrata.
55 Oh come,
don't scowl so. Say something!
LYSISTRATA. My dear Myrrhine,
what is there to say? After all,
you've been pretty casual about the whole thing.
MYRRHINE. Couldn't find
my girdle in the dark, that's all.
But what *is*
"the whole thing"?
60 KALONIKE. No, we've got to wait
for those Boiotians and Peloponnesians.
LYSISTRATA.
That's more like it.—But, look!
Here's Lampito!

(*Enter Lampito with women from Sparta.*)

LYSISTRATA. Darling Lampito,
how pretty you are today! What a nice color!
65 Goodness, you look as though you could strangle a bull!
LAMPITO.
Ah think Ah could! It's the work-out
In the gym every day; and, of co'se that dance of ahs
where y' kick yo' own tail.
KALONIKE. What an adorable figure!
LAMPITO.
Lawdy, when y' touch me lahk that,
Ah feel lahk a heifer at the altar!
70 LYSISTRATA. And this young lady?
Where is she from?
LAMPITO. Boiotia. Social-Register type.
LYSISTRATA.
Ah. "Boiotia of the fertile plain."
KALONIKE. And if you look,
you'll find the fertile plain has just been mowed.
LYSISTRATA.
And this lady?
LAMPITO. Hagh, wahd, handsome. She comes from Korinth.
KALONIKE.
High and wide's the word for it.
LAMPITO. Which one of you 75
called this heah meeting, and why?
LYSISTRATA. I did.
LAMPITO. Well, then, tell us:
What's up?
MYRRHINE. Yes, darling, what *is* on your mind, after all?
LYSISTRATA.
I'll tell you.—But first, one little question.
MYRRHINE. Well?
LYSISTRATA.
It's your husbands. Fathers of your children. Doesn't it bother you
that they're always off with the Army? I'll stake my life, 80
not one of you has a man in the house this minute!
KALONIKE.
Mine's been in Thrace the last five months, keeping an eye
on that General.
MYRRHINE. Mine's been in Pylos for seven.
LAMPITO. And mahn,
whenever he gets a *dis*charge, he goes raht back
with that li'l ole shield of his, and enlists again! 85
LYSISTRATA.
And not the ghost of a lover to be found!
From the very day the war began—
those Milesians!
I could skin them alive!
—I've not seen so much, even,
as one of those leather consolation prizes.—
But there! What's important is: If I've found a way 90
to end the war, are you with me?
MYRRHINE. I should *say* so!
Even if I have to pawn my best dress and
drink up the proceeds.
KALONIKE. Me, too! Even if they split me
right up the middle, like a flounder.
LAMPITO. Ah'm shorely with you.
Ah'd crawl up Taygetos° on mah knees 95
if that'd bring peace.
LYSISTRATA. All right, then; here it is:
Women! Sisters!
If we really want our men to make peace,

95 **Taygetos** a mountain range

we must be ready to give up—
MYRRHINE. Give up what?
Quick, tell us!
LYSISTRATA. But *will* you?
100 MYRRHINE. We will, even if it kills us.
LYSISTRATA.
Then we must give up going to bed with our men.

(*Long silence.*)

Oh? So now you're sorry? Won't look at me?
Doubtful? Pale? All teary-eyed?
But come: be frank with me.
Will you do it, or not? Well? Will you do it?
MYRRHINE. I couldn't. No.
Let the war go on.
105 KALONIKE. Nor I. Let the war go on.
LYSISTRATA.
You, you little flounder,
ready to be split up the middle?
KALONIKE. Lysistrata, no!
I'd walk through the fire for you—you *know* I would! but don't
ask us to give up *that!* Why, there's nothing like it!
LYSISTRATA.
And you?
110 BOIOTIAN. No. I must say *I'd* rather walk through fire.
LYSISTRATA.
What an utterly perverted sex we women are!
No wonder poets write tragedies about us.
There's only one thing we can think of.
But you from Sparta:
If you stand by me, we may win yet! Will you?
It means so much!
115 LAMPITO. Ah sweah, it means *too* much!
By the Two Goddesses, it does! Asking a girl
to sleep—Heaven knows how long!—in a great big bed
with nobody there but herself! But Ah'll stay with you!
Peace comes first!
LYSISTRATA. Spoken like a true Spartan!
KALONIKE.
But if—
oh dear!
120 —if we give up what you tell us to,
will there *be* any peace?
LYSISTRATA. Why, mercy, of course there will!
We'll just sit snug in our very thinnest gowns,
perfumed and powdered from top to bottom, and those men
simply won't stand still! And when we say No,
125 they'll go out of their minds! And there's your peace.
You can take my word for it.
LAMPITO. Ah seem to remember
that Colonel Menelaos threw his sword away
when he saw Helen's breast all bare.
KALONIKE. But, goodness me!
What if they just get up and leave us?
LYSISTRATA. In that case
we'll have to fall back on ourselves, I suppose. 130
But they won't.
KALONIKE. I must say that's not much help. But
what if they drag us into the bedroom?
LYSISTRATA. Hang on to the door.
KALONIKE.
What if they slap us?
LYSISTRATA. If they do, you'd better give in.
But be sulky about it. Do I have to teach you how?
You know there's no fun for men when they have to force you. 135
There are millions of ways of getting them to see reason.
Don't you worry: a man
doesn't like it unless the girl co-operates.
KALONIKE.
I suppose so. Oh, all right. We'll go along.
LAMPITO.
Ah imagine us Spahtans can arrange a peace. But you 140
Athenians! Why, you're just war-mongerers!
LYSISTRATA. Leave that to me.
I know how to make them listen.
LAMPITO. Ah don't see how.
After all, they've got their boats; and there's lots of money
piled up in the Akropolis.°
LYSISTRATA. The Akropolis? Darling,
we're taking over the Akropolis today! 145
That's the older women's job. All the rest of us
are going to the Citadel to sacrifice—you understand me?
And once there, we're in for good!
LAMPITO. Whee! Up the rebels!
Ah can see you're a good strat*ee*gist.
LYSISTRATA. Well, then, Lampito,
what we have to do now is take a solemn oath. 150
LAMPITO.
Say it. We'll sweah.
LYSISTRATA. This is it.
—But where's our Inner Guard?
—Look, Guard: you see this shield?
Put it down here. Now bring me the victim's entrails.
KALONIKE.
But the oath?
LYSISTRATA. You remember how in Aischylos' *Seven*

144 **Akropolis** At the beginning of the war, Perikles stored emergency funds in the Akropolis, the citadel sacred to Athene.

155 they killed a sheep and swore on a shield? Well, then?

KALONIKE.

But I don't see how you can swear for peace on a shield.

LYSISTRATA.

What else do you suggest?

KALONIKE. Why not a white horse?

We could swear by that.

LYSISTRATA. And where will you get a white horse?

KALONIKE.

I never thought of that. *What* can we do?

LYSISTRATA. I have it!

160 Let's set this big black wine-bowl on the ground
and pour in a gallon or so of Thasian, and swear
not to add one drop of water.

LAMPITO. Ah lahk *that* oath!

LYSISTRATA.

Bring the bowl and the wine-jug.

KALONIKE. Oh, what a simply *huge* one!

LYSISTRATA.

Set it down. Girls, place your hands on the gift-offering.
165 O Goddess of Persuasion! And thou, O Loving-cup:
Look upon this our sacrifice, and
be gracious!

KALONIKE.

See the blood spill out. How red and pretty it is!

LAMPITO.

And Ah must say it smells good.

MYRRHINE. Let me swear first!

KALONIKE.

170 No, by Aphrodite, we'll match for it!

LYSISTRATA.

Lampito: all of you women: come, touch the bowl,
and repeat after me—remember, this is an oath—:
I WILL HAVE NOTHING TO DO WITH MY
HUSBAND OR MY LOVER

KALONIKE.

I will have nothing to do with my husband or my lover

LYSISTRATA.

THOUGH HE COME TO ME IN PITIABLE
175 CONDITION

KALONIKE.

Though he come to me in pitiable condition
(Oh Lysistrata! This is killing me!)

LYSISTRATA.

IN MY HOUSE I WILL BE UNTOUCHABLE

KALONIKE.

In my house I will be untouchable

LYSISTRATA.

180 IN MY THINNEST SAFFRON SILK

KALONIKE.

In my thinnest saffron silk

LYSISTRATA.

AND MAKE HIM LONG FOR ME.

KALONIKE.

And make him long for me.

LYSISTRATA.

I WILL NOT GIVE MYSELF

KALONIKE.

I will not give myself 185

LYSISTRATA.

AND IF HE CONSTRAINS ME

KALONIKE.

And if he constrains me

LYSISTRATA.

I WILL BE COLD AS ICE AND NEVER MOVE

KALONIKE.

I will be cold as ice and never move

LYSISTRATA.

I WILL NOT LIFT MY SLIPPERS TOWARD THE
CEILING 190

KALONIKE.

I will not lift my slippers toward the ceiling

LYSISTRATA.

OR CROUCH ON ALL FOURS LIKE THE LIONESS
IN THE CARVING

KALONIKE.

Or crouch on all fours like the lioness in the carving

LYSISTRATA.

AND IF I KEEP THIS OATH LET ME DRINK FROM
THIS BOWL

KALONIKE.

And if I keep this oath let me drink from this bowl 195

LYSISTRATA.

IF NOT, LET MY OWN BOWL BE FILLED WITH
WATER.

KALONIKE.

If not, let my own bowl be filled with water.

LYSISTRATA.

You have all sworn?

MYRRHINE. We have.

LYSISTRATA. Then thus

I sacrifice the victim.

(*Drinks largely.*)

KALONIKE. Save some for us!

Here's to you, darling, and to you, and to you! 200

(*Loud cries off-stage.*)

LAMPITO.

What's all *that* whoozy-goozy?

LYSISTRATA. Just what I told you.

The older women have taken the Akropolis.

Now you, Lampito,
rush back to Sparta. We'll take care of things here. Leave
these girls here for hostages.
205 The rest of you,
up to the Citadel: and mind you push in the bolts.

KALONIKE.
But the men? Won't they be after us?

LYSISTRATA. Just you leave
the men to me. There's not fire enough in the world,
or threats either, to make me open these doors
except on my own terms.

210 KALONIKE. I hope not, by Aphrodite!
After all, we've got a reputation for bitchiness to live up to.
(*Exeunt.*)

PARADOS

CHORAL EPISODE

(*The hillside just under the Akropolis. Enter Chorus of Old Men with burning torches and braziers; much puffing and coughing.*)

KORYPHAIOS(man).
Forward march, Drakes, old friend: never you mind
that damn big log banging hell down on your back.

STROPHE 1

CHORUS(men).
There's this to be said for longevity:
You see things you thought that you'd never see.
5 Look, Strymodoros, who would have thought it?
We've caught it—
the New Femininity!
The wives of our bosom, our board, our bed—
Now, by the gods, they've gone ahead
And taken the Citadel (Heaven knows why!),
10 Profanéd the sacred statuar-y,
And barred the doors,
The subversive whores!

KORYPHAIOS(m).
Shake a leg there, Philurgos, man: the Akropolis or bust!
Put the kindling around here. We'll build one almighty big
15 bonfire for the whole bunch of bitches, every last one;
and the first we fry will be old Lykon's woman.

ANTISTROPHE 1

CHORUS(m).
They're not going to give me the old horselaugh!
No, by Demeter, they won't pull this off!
Think of Kleomenes: even he
Didn't go free
till he brought me his stuff. 20
A good man he was, all stinking and shaggy,
Bare as an eel except for the bag he
Covered his rear with. God, what a mess!
Never a bath in six years, I'd guess.
Pure Sparta, man! 25
He also ran.

KORYPHAIOS(m).
That was a siege, friends! Seventeen ranks strong
we slept at the Gate. And shall we not do as much
against these women, whom God and Euripides hate?
If we don't, I'll turn in my medals from Marathon. 30

STROPHE 2

CHORUS(m).
Onward and upward! A little push,
And we're there.
Ouch, my shoulders! I could wish
For a pair
Of good strong oxen. Keep your eye 35
On the fire there, it mustn't die.
Akh! Akh!
The smoke would make a cadaver cough!

ANTISTROPHE 2

Holy Herakles, a hot spark
Bit my eye! 40
Damn this hellfire, damn this work!
So say I.
Onward and upward just the same.
(Laches, remember the Goddess: for shame!)
Akh! Akh! 45
The smoke would make a cadaver cough!

KORYPHAIOS(m).
At last (and let us give suitable thanks to God
for his infinite mercies) I have managed to bring
my personal flame to the common goal. It breathes, it
lives.
Now, gentlemen, let us consider. Shall we insert 50
the torch, say, into the brazier, and thus extract
a kindling brand? And shall we then, do you think
push on to the gate like valiant sheep? On the whole, yes.
But I would have you consider this, too: if they—
I refer to the women—should refuse to open, 55
what then? Do we set the doors afire
and smoke them out? At ease, men. Meditate.
Akh, the smoke! Woof! What we really need
is the loan of a general or two from the Samos Command.
At least we've got this lumber off our backs. 60
That's something. And now let's look to our fire.

O Pot, brave Brazier, touch my torch with flame!
Victory, Goddess, I invoke thy name!
Strike down these paradigms of female pride,
65 And we shall hang our trophies up inside.

(*Enter Chorus of Old Women on the walls of the Akropolis, carrying jars of water.*)

KORYPHAIOS(woman).
Smoke, girls, smoke! There's smoke all over the place!
Probably fire, too. Hurry, girls! Fire! Fire!

STROPHE I

CHORUS(women).
Nikodike, run!
Or Kalyke's done
70 To a turn, and poor Kritylla's
Smoked like a ham.
Damn
These old men! Are we too late?
I nearly died down at the place
Where we fill our jars:
75 Slaves pushing and jostling—
Such a hustling
I never saw in all my days.

ANTISTROPHE I

But here's water at last.
Haste, sisters, haste!
80 Slosh it on them, slosh it down,
The silly old wrecks!
Sex
Almighty! What they want's
A hot bath? Good. Send one down.
Athena of Athens town,
85 Trito-born!° Helm of Gold!
Cripple the old
Firemen! Help us help them drown!

(*The Old Men capture a woman, Stratyllis.*)

STRATYLLIS.
Let me go! Let me go!
KORYPHAIOS(w). You walking corpses,
have you no shame?
KORYPHAIOS(m). I wouldn't have believed it!
90 An army of women in the Akropolis!
KORYPHAIOS(w).
So we scare you, do we? Grandpa, you've seen
only our pickets yet!

85 **Trito-born** Athene, said to be born near Lake Tritonis, in Libya

KORYPHAIOS(m). Hey, Phaidrias!
Help me with the necks of these jabbering hens!
KORYPHAIOS(w).
Down with your pots, girls! We'll need both hands
if these antiques attack us.
KORYPHAIOS(m). Want your face kicked in? 95
KORYPHAIOS(w).
Want your balls chewed off?
KORYPHAIOS(m). Look out! I've got a stick!
KORYPHAIOS(w).
You lay a half-inch of your stick on Stratyllis,
and you'll never stick again!
KORYPHAIOS(m).
Fall apart!
KORYPHAIOS(w). I'll spit up your guts!
KORYPHAIOS(m). Euripedes!° Master!
How well you knew women!
KORYPHAIOS(w). Listen to him, Rhodippe, 100
up with the pots!
KORYPHAIOS(m). Demolition of God,
what good are your pots?
KORYPHAIOS(w). You refugee from the tomb,
what good is your fire?
KORYPHAIOS(m). Good enough to make a pyre
to barbecue you!
KORYPHAIOS(w). We'll squizzle your kindling!
KORYPHAIOS(m).
You think so?
KORYPHAIOS(w). Yah! Just hang around a while! 105
KORYPHAIOS(m).
Want a touch of my torch?
KORYPHAIOS(w). It needs a good soaping.
KORYPHAIOS(m).
How about you?
KORYPHAIOS(w). Soap for a senile bridegroom!
KORYPHAIOS(m).
Senile? Hold your trap!
KORYPHAIOS(w). Just *you* try to hold it!
KORYPHAIOS(m).
The yammer of women!
KORYPHAIOS(w). Oh is that so?
You're not in the jury room now, you know. 110
KORYPHAIOS(m).
Gentlemen, I beg you, burn off that woman's hair!
KORYPHAIOS(w).
Let it come down!

(*They empty their pots on the men.*)

KORYPHAIOS(m).
What a way to drown!

99 **Euripedes** a tragic dramatist

KORYPHAIOS(w). Hot, hey?
KORYPHAIOS(m). Say,
enough!
KORYPHAIOS(w). Dandruff
115 needs watering. I'll make you
nice and fresh.
KORYPHAIOS(m). For God's sake, you,
hold off!

SCENE I

(*Enter a Commissioner accompanied by four constables.*)

COMMISSIONER.
These degenerate women! What a racket of little drums,
what a yapping for Adonis on every house-top!
It's like the time in the Assembly when I was listening
to a speech—out of order, as usual—by that fool
5 Demostratos,° all about troops for Sicily,°
that kind of nonsense—
and there was his wife
trotting around in circles howling
Alas for Adonis!°—
and Demostratos insisting
we must draft every last Zakynthian that can walk—
10 and his wife up there on the roof,
drunk as an owl, yowling
Oh weep for Adonis!—
and that damned ox Demostratos
mooing away through the rumpus. That's what we get
for putting up with this wretched woman-business!
KORYPHAIOS(m).
15 Sir, you haven't heard the half of it. They laughed at us!
Insulted us! They took pitchers of water
and nearly drowned us! We're still wringing out our
clothes,
for all the world like unhousebroken brats.
COMMISSIONER.
Serves you right, by Poseidon!
20 Whose fault is it if these women-folk of ours
get out of hand? We coddle them,
we teach them to be wasteful and loose. You'll see a
husband
go into a jeweler's. "Look," he'll say,
"jeweler," he'll say, "you remember that gold choker
25 you made for my wife? Well, she went to a dance last night
and broke the clasp. Now, I've got to go to Salamis,
and can't be bothered. Run over to my house tonight,
will you, and see if you can put it together for her."
Or another one goes to a cobbler—a good strong
workman, too,
with an awl that was never meant for child's play. "Here," 30
he'll tell him, "one of my wife's shoes is pinching
her little toe. Could you come up about noon
and stretch it out for her?"
Well, what do you expect?
Look at me, for example, I'm a Public Officer,
and it's one of my duties to pay off the sailors. 35
And where's the money? Up there in the Akropolis!
And those blasted women slam the door in my face!
But what are we waiting for?
—Look here, constable,
stop sniffing around for a tavern, and get us
some crowbars. We'll force their gates! As a matter of fact, 40
I'll do a little forcing myself.

(*Enter Lysistrata, above, with Myrrhine, Kalonike, and the Boiotian.*)

LYSISTRATA. No need of forcing.
Here I am, of my own accord. And all this talk
about locked doors—! We don't need locked doors,
but just the least bit of common sense.
COMMISSIONER.
Is that so, ma'am!
—Where's my constable?
—Constable, 45
arrest that woman, and tie her hands behind her.
LYSISTRATA.
If he touches me, I swear by Artemis
there'll be one scamp dropped from the public payroll
tomorrow!
COMMISSIONER.
Well, constable? You're not afraid, I suppose? Grab her,
two of you, around the middle!
KALONIKE. No, by Pandrosos! 50
Lay a hand on her, and I'll jump on you so hard
your guts will come out the back door!
COMMISSIONER. That's what *you* think!
Where's the sergeant?—Here, you: tie up that trollop first,
the one with the pretty talk!
MYRRHINE. By the Moon-Goddess,
just try! They'll have to scoop you up with a spoon! 55
COMMISSIONER.
Another one!
Officer, seize that woman!
I swear
I'll put an end to this riot!
BOIOTIAN. By the Taurian,
one inch closer, you'll be one screaming baldhead!

5 **Demostratos** Athenian orator and jingoist politician; **Sicily** a reference to the Sicilian Expedition (416 B.C.), in which Athens was decisively defeated 8 **Adonis** fertility god

COMMISSIONER.
Lord, what a mess! And my constables seem ineffective.
60 But—women get the best of us? By God, no!
—Skythians!
Close ranks and forward march!
LYSISTRATA. "Forward," indeed!
By the Two Goddesses, what's the sense in *that?*
They're up against four companies of women
armed from top to bottom.
COMMISSIONER. Forward, my Skythians!
LYSISTRATA.
65 Forward, yourselves, dear comrades!
You grainlettucebeanseedmarket girls!
You garlicandonionbreadbakery girls!
Give it to 'em! Knock 'em down! Scratch 'em!
Tell 'em what you think of 'em!

(*General mêlée; the Skythians yield.*)

—Ah, that's enough!
70 Sound a retreat: good soldiers don't rob the dead.
COMMISSIONER.
A nice day *this* has been for the police!
LYSISTRATA.
Well, there you are.—Did you really think we women
would be driven like slaves? Maybe now you'll admit
that a woman knows something about spirit.
COMMISSIONER. Spirit enough,
75 especially spirits in bottles! Dear Lord Apollo!
KORYPHAIOS(m).
Your Honor, there's no use talking to them. Words
mean nothing whatever to wild animals like these.
Think of the sousing they gave us! and the water
was not, I believe, of the purest.
KORYPHAIOS(w).
80 You shouldn't have come after us. And if you try it again,
you'll be one eye short!—Although, as a matter of fact,
what I like best is just to stay at home and read,
like a sweet little bride: never hurting a soul, no,
never going out. But if you *must* shake hornets' nests,
85 look out for the hornets.

STROPHE

CHORUS(m).
Of all the beasts that God hath wrought
What monster's worse than woman?
Who shall encompass with his thought
Their guile unending? No man.

90 They've seized the Heights, the Rock, the Shrine—
But to what end? I wot not.
Sure there's some clue to their design!
Have you the key? I thought not.

KORYPHAIOS(m).
We might question them, I suppose. But I warn you, sir,
don't believe anything you hear! It would be un-Athenian 95
not to get to the bottom of this plot.
COMMISSIONER. Very well.
My first question is this: Why, so help you God,
did you bar the gates of the Akropolis?
LYSISTRATA. Why?
To keep the money, of course. No money, no war.
COMMISSIONER.
You think that money's the cause of war?
LYSISTRATA. I do. 100
Money brought about that Peisandros° business
and all the other attacks on the State. Well and good!
They'll not get another cent here!
COMMISSIONER. And what will you do?
LYSISTRATA.
What a question! From now on, we intend
to control the Treasury.
COMMISSIONER. Control the Treasury! 105
LYSISTRATA.
Why not? Does that seem strange? After all,
we control our household budgets.
COMMISSIONER. But that's different!
LYSISTRATA.
"Different"? What do you mean?
COMMISSIONER. I mean simply this:
it's the Treasury that pays for National Defense.
LYSISTRATA.
Unnecessary. We propose to abolish war. 110
COMMISSIONER.
Good God.—And National Security?
LYSISTRATA. Leave that to us.
COMMISSIONER.
You?
LYSISTRATA.
Us.
COMMISSIONER.
We're done for, then!
LYSISTRATA. Never mind.
We women will save you in spite of yourselves.
COMMISSIONER. What nonsense!
LYSISTRATA.
If you like. But you must accept it, like it or not.
COMMISSIONER.
Why, this is downright subversion!
LYSISTRATA. Maybe it is. 115
But we're going to save you, Judge.
COMMISSIONER. I don't *want* to be saved.

102 **Peisandros** a plotter against the Athenian democracy

LYSISTRATA.
Tut. The death-wish. All the more reason.
COMMISSIONER. But the idea
of women bothering themselves about peace and war!
LYSISTRATA.
Will you listen to me?
COMMISSIONER. Yes. But be brief, or I'll—
LYSISTRATA.
This is no time for stupid threats.
120 COMMISSIONER. By the gods,
I can't stand any more!
AN OLD WOMAN. Can't stand? Well, well.
COMMISSIONER.
That's enough out of you, you old buzzard!
Now, Lysistrata: tell me what you're thinking.
LYSISTRATA.
Glad to.
Ever since this war began
We women have been watching you men, agreeing with
125 you,
keeping our thoughts to ourselves. That doesn't mean
we were happy: we weren't, for we saw how things were
going;
but we'd listen to you at dinner
arguing this way and that.
—Oh you, and your big
Top Secrets!—
130 And then we'd grin like little patriots
(though goodness knows we didn't feel like grinning) and
ask you:
"Dear, did the Armistice come up in Assembly today?"
And you'd say, "None of your business! Pipe down!," you'd
say.
And so we would.
AN OLD WOMAN. *I* wouldn't have, by God!
COMMISSIONER.
You'd have taken a beating, then!
135 —Go on.
LYSISTRATA.
Well, we'd be quiet. But then, you know, all at once
you men would think up something worse than ever.
Even *I* could see it was fatal. And, "Darling," I'd say,
"have you gone completely mad?" And my husband would
look at me
140 and say, "Wife, you've got your weaving to attend to.
Mind your tongue, if you don't want a slap. 'War's a man's
affair!'"°
COMMISSIONER. Good words, and well pronounced.

143 **War's a man's affair** quoted from Homer's *Iliad,* VI, 492, Hector to his wife Andromache

LYSISTRATA.
You're a fool if you think so.
It was hard enough
to put up with all this banquet-hall strategy.
But then we'd hear you out in the public square: 145
"Nobody left for the draft-quota here in Athens?"
you'd say; and, "No," someone else would say, "not a
man!"
And so we women decided to rescue Greece.
You might as well listen, to us now: you'll have to, later.
COMMISSIONER.
You rescue Greece? Absurd.
LYSISTRATA. You're the absurd one. 150
COMMISSIONER.
You expect me to take orders from a woman?
I'd die first!
LYSISTRATA.
Heavens, if that's what's bothering you, take my veil,
here, and wrap it around your poor head.
KALONIKE. Yes,
and you can have my market-basket, too.
Go home, tighten your girdle, do the washing, mind 155
your beans! "War's
a woman's affair!"
KORYPHAIOS(w). Ground pitchers! Close ranks!

ANTISTROPHE

CHORUS(w).
This is a dance that I know well,
My knees shall never yield.
Wobble and creak I may, but still 160
I'll keep the well-fought field.
Valor and grace march on before,
Love prods us from behind.
Our slogan is EXCELSIOR,
Our watchword SAVE MANKIND. 165
KORYPHAIOS(w).
Women, remember your grandmothers! Remember
that little old mother of yours, what a stinger she was!
On, on, never slacken. There's a strong wind astern!
LYSISTRATA.
O Eros of delight! O Aphrodite! Kyprian!
If ever desire has drenched our breasts or dreamed 170
in our thighs, let it work so now on the men of Hellas
that they shall tail us through the land, slaves, slaves
to Woman, Breaker of Armies!
COMMISSIONER. And if we do?
LYSISTRATA.
Well, for one thing, we shan't have to watch you
going to market, a spear in one hand, and heaven knows 175
what in the other.
KALONIKE. Nicely said, by Aphrodite!

LYSISTRATA.
As things stand now, you're neither men nor women.
Armor clanking with kitchen pans and pots—
you sound like a pack of Korybantes!
COMMISSIONER.
A man must do what a man must do.
180 LYSISTRATA. So I'm told.
But to see a General, complete with Gorgon-shield,
jingling along the dock to buy a couple of herrings!
KALONIKE.
I saw a Captain the other day—lovely fellow he was,
nice curly hair—sitting on his horse; and—can you believe it?—
he'd just bought some soup, and was pouring it into his helmet!
185 And there was a soldier from Thrace
swishing his lance like something out of Euripides,
and the poor fruit-store woman got so scared
that she ran away and let him have his figs free!
COMMISSIONER.
All this is beside the point
190 Will you be so kind
as to tell me how you mean to save Greece?
LYSISTRATA. Of course.
Nothing could be simpler.
COMMISSIONER. I assure you, I'm all ears.
LYSISTRATA.
Do you know anything about weaving?
Say the yarn gets tangled: we thread it
195 this way and that through the skein, up and down,
until it's free. And it's like that with war.
We'll send our envoys
up and down, this way and that, all over Greece,
until it's finished.
COMMISSIONER. Yarn? Thread? Skein?
200 Are you out of your mind? I tell you,
war is a serious business.
LYSISTRATA. So serious
that I'd like to go on talking about weaving.
COMMISSIONER.
All right. Go ahead.
LYSISTRATA. The first thing we have to do
is to wash our yarn, get the dirt out of it.
205 You see? Isn't there too much dirt here in Athens?
You must wash those men away.
Then our spoiled wool—
that's like your job-hunters, out for a life
of no work and big pay. Back to the basket,
citizens or not, allies or not,
or friendly immigrants.
210 And your colonies?
Hanks of wool lost in various places. Pull them
together, weave them into one great whole,
and our voters are clothed for ever.
COMMISSIONER. It would take a woman
to reduce state questions to a matter of carding and weaving.
LYSISTRATA.
You fool! Who were the mothers whose sons sailed off 215
to fight for Athens in Sicily?
COMMISSIONER. Enough!
I beg you, do not call back those memories.
LYSISTRATA. And then,
instead of the love that every woman needs,
we have only our single beds, where we can dream
of our husbands off with the Army.
Bad enough for wives! 220
But what about our girls, getting older every day,
and older, and no kisses?
COMMISSIONER. Men get older, too.
LYSISTRATA.
Not in the same sense.
A soldier's discharged,
and he may be bald and toothless, yet he'll find
a pretty young thing to go to bed with.
But a woman! 225
Her beauty is gone with the first gray hair.
She can spend her time
consulting the oracles and the fortune-tellers,
but they'll never send her a husband.
COMMISSIONER.
Still, if a man can rise to the occasion— 230
LYSISTRATA.
Rise? Rise, yourself!

(*Furiously.*)

Go invest in a coffin!
You've money enough.
I'll bake you
a cake for the Underworld.
And here's your funeral
wreath!

(*She pours water upon him.*)

MYRRHINE. And here's another!

(*More water.*)

KALONIKE. And here's
my contribution!

(*More water.*)

235 LYSISTRATA. What are you waiting for?
All aboard Styx Ferry!
Charon's° calling for you!
It's sailing-time: don't disrupt the schedule!
COMMISSIONER.
The insolence of women! And to me!
No, by God, I'll go back to town and show
240 the rest of the Commission what might happen to them.
(*Exit Commissioner.*)
LYSISTRATA.
Really, I suppose we should have laid out his corpse
on the doorstep, in the usual way.
But never mind.
We'll give him the rites of the dead tomorrow morning.
(*Exit Lysistrata with Myrrhine and Kalonike.*)

PARABASIS

CHORAL EPISODE

ODE I

KORYPHAIOS(m)
Sons of Liberty, awake! The day of glory is at hand.
CHORUS(m).
I smell tyranny afoot, I smell it rising from the land.
I scent a trace of Hippias,° I sniff upon the breeze
A dismal Spartan hogo that suggests King Kleisthenes.°
5 Strip, strip for action, brothers!
Our wives, aunts, sisters, mothers
Have sold us out: the streets are full of godless female rages.
Shall we stand by and let our women confiscate our wages?

EPIRRHEMA I

KORYPHAIOS(m).
Gentlemen, it's a disgrace to Athens, a disgrace
10 to all that Athens stands for, if we allow these grandmas
to jabber about spears and shields and making friends
with the Spartans. What's a Spartan? Give me a wild wolf
any day. No. They want the Tyranny back, I suppose.
Are we going to take that? No. Let us look like
15 the innocent serpent, but be the flower under it,
as the poet sings. And just to begin with,
I propose to poke a number of teeth
down the gullet of that harridan over there.

ANTODE I

KORYPHAIOS(w).
Oh, is that so? When you get home, your own mammá
won't know you!
CHORUS(w).
Who do you think we are, you senile bravos? Well, I'll
show you. 20
I bore the sacred vessels in my eighth year, and at ten
I was pounding out the barley for Athena Goddess; then
They made me Little Bear
At the Braunonian Fair;
I'd held the Holy Basket by the time I was of age, 25
The Blessed Dry figs had adorned my plump décolletage.

ANTEPIRRHEMA I

KORYPHAIOS(w).
A "disgrace to Athens," am I, just at the moment
I'm giving Athens the best advice she ever had?
Don't I pay taxes to the State? Yes, I pay them
in baby boys. And what do you contribute, 30
you impotent horrors? Nothing but waste: all
our Treasury,° dating back to the Persian Wars,
gone! rifled! And not a penny out of your pockets!
Well, then? Can you cough up an answer to that?
Look out for your own gullet, or you'll get a crack 35
from this old brogan that'll make your teeth see stars!

ODE 2

CHORUS(m).
Oh insolence!
Am I unmanned?
Incontinence!
Shall my scarred hand 40
Strike never a blow
To curb this flow-
ing female curse?

Leipsydrion!°
Shall I betray 45
The laurels won
On that great day?
Come, shake a leg,

237 **Charon** god who ferried the souls of the newly dead across the Styx to Hades
3 **Hippias** an Athenian tyrant (d. 490 B.C.) 4 **Kleisthenes** an ambisexual Athenian

32 **Treasury** money originally contributed by Athens and her allies, intended to finance an extension of the sea-war against Persia. Since the failure of the Sicilian Expedition, the contributions of the allies had fallen off; and the fund itself was now being raided by Athenian politicians.
44 **leipsydrion** a place where patriots had gallantly fought

Shed old age, beg
50 The years reverse!

EPIRRHEMA 2

KORYPHAIOS(m).
Give them an inch, and we're done for! We'll have them
launching boats next and planning naval strategy,
sailing down on us like so many Artemisias.
Or maybe they have ideas about the cavalry.
55 That's fair enough, women are certainly good
in the saddle. Just look at Mikon's paintings,
All those Amazons wrestling with all those men!
On the whole, a straitjacket's their best uniform.

ANTODE 2

CHORUS(w).
Tangle with me,
60 And you'll get cramps.
Ferocity
's no use now, Gramps!
By the Two,
I'll get through
65 To you wrecks yet!

I'll scramble your eggs,
I'll burn your beans,
With my two legs.
You'll see such scenes
70 As never yet
Your two eyes met.
A curse? You bet!

ANTEPIRRHEMA 2

KORYPHAIOS(w).
If Lampito stands by me, and that delicious Theban girl,
Ismenia—what good are *you?* You and your seven
75 Resolutions! Resolutions? Rationing Boiotian eels
and making our girls go with them at Hekate's Feast!
That was statesmanship! And we'll have to put up with it
and all the rest of your decrepit legislation
until some patriot—God give him strength!—
80 grabs you by the neck and kicks you off the Rock.

SCENE II

(*Re-enter Lysistrata and her lieutenants.*)

KORYPHAIOS(w) (*Tragic tone*).
Great Queen, fair Architect of our emprise,
Why lookst thou on us with foreboding eyes?

LYSISTRATA.
The behavior of these idiotic women!
There's something about the female temperament
that I can't bear!

KORYPHAIOS(w). What in the world do you mean? 5

LYSISTRATA.
Exactly what I say.

KORYPHAIOS(w). What dreadful thing has happened?
Come, tell us: we're all your friends.

LYSISTRATA. It isn't easy
to say it; yet, God knows, we can't hush it up.

KORYPHAIOS(w).
Well, then? Out with it!

LYSISTRATA. To put it bluntly,
we're dying to get laid.

KORYPHAIOS(w). Almighty God! 10

LYSISTRATA.
Why bring God into it?—No, it's just as I say.
I can't manage them any longer: they've gone man-crazy,
they're all trying to get out.
Why, look:
one of them was sneaking out the back door
over there by Pan's cave; another 15
was sliding down the walls with rope and tackle;
another was climbing aboard a sparrow, ready to take off
for the nearest brothel—I dragged *her* back by the hair!
They're all finding some reason to leave.
Look there!
There goes another one.
—Just a minute, you! 20
Where are you off to so fast?

FIRST WOMAN. I've got to get home.
I've a lot of Milesian wool, and the worms are spoiling it.

LYSISTRATA.
Oh bother you and your worms! Get back inside!

FIRST WOMAN.
I'll be back right away, I swear I will.
I just want to get it stretched out on my bed. 25

LYSISTRATA.
You'll do no such thing. You'll stay right here.

FIRST WOMAN. And my wool?
You want it ruined?

LYSISTRATA. Yes, for all I care.

SECOND WOMAN.
Oh dear! My lovely new flax from Amorgos—
I left it at home, all uncarded!

LYSISTRATA. Another one!
And all she wants is someone to card her flax. 30
Get back in there!

SECOND WOMAN.
But I swear by the Moon-Goddess,

the minute I get it done, I'll be back!
LYSISTRATA. I say No.
If you, why not all the other women as well?
THIRD WOMAN.
O Lady Eileithyia!° Radiant goddess! Thou
35 intercessor for women in childbirth! Stay, I pray thee,
oh stay this parturition. Shall I pollute
a sacred spot?
LYSISTRATA. And what's the matter with *you*?
THIRD WOMAN.
I'm having a baby—any minute now.
LYSISTRATA.
But you weren't pregnant yesterday.
THIRD WOMAN. Well, I am today.
40 Let me go home for a midwife, Lysistrata:
there's not much time.
LYSISTRATA. I never heard such nonsense.
What's that bulging under your cloak?
THIRD WOMAN. A little baby boy.
LYSISTRATA.
It certainly isn't. But it's something hollow,
like a basin or—Why, it's the helmet of Athena!
And you said you were having a baby.
45 THIRD WOMAN. Well, I am! So there!
LYSISTRATA.
Then why the helmet?
THIRD WOMAN. I was afraid that my pains
might begin here in the Akropolis; and I wanted
to drop my chick into it, just as the dear doves do.
LYSISTRATA.
Lies! Evasions!—But at least one thing's clear:
50 you can't leave the place before your purification.
THIRD WOMAN.
But I can't stay here in the Akropolis! Last night I dreamed
of the Snake.
FIRST WOMAN.
And those horrible owls, the noise they make!
I can't get a bit of sleep; I'm just about dead.
LYSISTRATA.
You useless girls, that's enough: Let's have no more lying.
55 Of course you want your men. But don't you imagine
that they want you just as much? I'll give you my word,
their nights must be pretty hard.
Just stick it out!
A little patience, that's all, and our battle's won.
I have heard an Oracle. Should you like to hear it?
FIRST WOMAN.
An Oracle? Yes, tell us!
60 LYSISTRATA. Here is what it says:

34 **Eileithyia** goddess of childbirth

WHEN SWALLOWS SHALL THE HOOPOE SHUN
AND SPURN HIS HOT DESIRE,
ZEUS WILL PERFECT WHAT THEY'VE BEGUN
AND SET THE LOWER HIGHER.
FIRST WOMAN.
Does that mean we'll be on top? 65
LYSISTRATA.
BUT IF THE SWALLOWS SHALL FALL OUT
AND TAKE THE HOOPOE'S BAIT,
A CURSE MUST MARK THEIR HOUR OF DOUBT,
INFAMY SEAL THEIR FATE.
THIRD WOMAN.
I swear, *that* Oracle's all too clear.
FIRST WOMAN. Oh the dear gods! 70
LYSISTRATA.
Let's not be downhearted, girls. Back to our places!
The god has spoken. How can we possibly fail him?
(*Exit Lysistrata with the dissident women.*)

CHORAL EPISODE

STROPHE

CHORUS[m].
I know a little story that I learned way back in school.
Goes like this:
Once upon a time there was a young man—and no fool— 75
Named Melanion; and his
One aversion was marriage. He loathed the very thought.
So he ran off to the hills, and in a special grot
Raised a dog, and spent his days
Hunting rabbits. And it says 80
That he never never never did come home.
It might be called a refuge *from* the womb.
All right,
all right,
all right!
We're as bright as young Melanion, and we hate the very
sight
Of you women! 85
A MAN.
How about a kiss, old lady?
A WOMAN.
Here's an onion for your eye!
A MAN.
A kick in the guts, then?
A WOMAN.
Try, old bristle-tail, just try!
A MAN.
Yet they say Myronides 90
On hands and knees
Looked just as shaggy fore and aft as I!

ANTISTROPHE

CHORUS[w].
Well, *I* know a little story, and it's just as good as yours.
Goes like this:
Once there was a man named Timon—a rough diamond,
of course, 95
And that whiskery face of his
Looked like murder in the shrubbery. By God, he was a son
Of the Furies, let me tell you! And what did he do but run
From the world and all its ways,
100 Cursing mankind! And it says
That his choicest execrations as of then
Were leveled almost wholly at *old* men.
All right,
all right,
all right!
But there's one thing about Timon: he could always stand
the sight
105 Of us women.
A WOMAN.
How about a crack in the jaw, Pop?
A MAN.
I can take it, Ma—no fear!
A WOMAN.
How about a kick in the face?
A MAN.
You'd reveal your old caboose?
A WOMAN.
110 What I'd show,
I'll have you know,
Is an instrument you're too far gone to use.

SCENE III

(*Re-enter Lysistrata.*)

LYSISTRATA.
Oh, quick, girls, quick! Come here!
A WOMAN. What is it?
LYSISTRATA. A man.
A man simply bulging with love.
O Kyprian Queen,°
O Paphian, O Kythereian! Hear us and aid us!
A WOMAN.
Where is this enemy?
LYSISTRATA. Over there, by Demeter's shrine.
A WOMAN.
Damned if he isn't. But who *is* he?

MYRRHINE. My husband. 5
Kinesias.
LYSISTRATA.
Oh, then, get busy! Tease him! Undermine him!
Wreck him! Give him everything—kissing, tickling,
nudging,
whatever you generally torture him with—: give him
everything
except what we swore on the wine we would not give.
MYRRHINE.
Trust me.
LYSISTRATA. I do. But I'll help you get him started. 10
The rest of you women, stay back.

(*Enter Kinesias.*)

KINESIAS. Oh God! Oh my God!
I'm stiff from lack of exercise. All I can do to stand up.
LYSISTRATA.
Halt! Who are you, approaching our lines?
KINESIAS. Me? I.
LYSISTRATA.
A man?
KINESIAS. You have eyes, haven't you?
LYSISTRATA. Go away.
KINESIAS.
Who says so?
LYSISTRATA. Officer of the Day.
KINESIAS. Officer, I beg you, 15
by all the gods at once, bring Myrrhine out.
LYSISTRATA.
Myrrhine? And who, my good sir, are you?
KINESIAS.
Kinesias. Last name's Pennison. Her husband.
LYSISTRATA.
Oh, of course. I beg your pardon. We're glad to see you.
We've heard so much about you. Dearest Myrrhine 20
is always talking about Kinesias—never nibbles an egg
or an apple without saying
"Here's to Kinesias!"
KINESIAS. Do you really mean it?
LYSISTRATA. I do.
When we're discussing men, she always says
"Well, after all, there's nobody like Kinesias!" 25
KINESIAS.
Good God.—Well, then, please send her down here.
LYSISTRATA.
And what do *I* get out of it?
KINESIAS. A standing promise.
LYSISTRATA.
I'll take it up with her.

(*Exit Lysistrata.*)

2 **Kyprian Queen** Aphrodite, goddess of love

KINESIAS. But be quick about it!
Lord, what's life without a wife? Can't eat. Can't sleep.
30 Every time I go home, the place is so empty, so
insufferably sad. Love's killing me, Oh,
hurry!

(*Enter Manes, a slave, with Kinesias' baby; the voice of Myrrhine is heard off-stage.*)

MYRRHINE. But of course I love him! Adore him—
But no,
he hates love. No. I won't go down.

(*Enter Myrrhine, above.*)

KINESIAS. Myrrhine!
Darlingest Myrrhinette! Come down quick!
MYRRHINE.
Certainly not.
35 KINESIAS. Not? But why, Myrrhine?
MYRRHINE.
Why? You don't need me.
KINESIAS. Need you? My God, *look* at me!
MYRRHINE.
So long!

(*Turns to go.*)

KINESIAS. Myrrhine, Myrrhine, Myrrhine!
If not for my sake, for our child!

(*Pinches Baby.*)

—All right, you: pipe up!

BABY.
Mummie! Mummie! Mummie!
KINESIAS. You hear that?
40 Pitiful, I call it. Six days now
with never a bath; no food; enough to break your heart!
MYRRHINE.
My darlingest child! What a father *you* acquired!
KINESIAS.
At least come down for his sake.
MYRRHINE. I suppose I must.
Oh, this mother business!

(*Exit.*)

KINESIAS. How pretty she is! And younger!
The harder she treats me, the more bothered I get.

(*Myrrhine enters, below.*)

45 MYRRHINE. Dearest child,
you're as sweet as your father's horrid. Give me a kiss.
KINESIAS.
Now don't you see how wrong it was to get involved
in this scheming League of women? It's bad
for us both.
MYRRHINE. Keep both hands to yourself!

KINESIAS. But our house
going to rack and ruin?
MYRRHINE. *I* don't care.
KINESIAS. And your knitting 50
all torn to pieces by the chickens? Don't you care?
MYRRHINE.
Not at all.
KINESIAS. And our debt to Aphrodite?
Oh, *won't* you come back?
MYRRHINE. No.—At least, not until you men
make a treaty and stop this war.
KINESIAS. Why, I suppose
that might be arranged.
MYRRHINE. Oh? Well, I suppose 55
I might come down then. But meanwhile,
I've sworn not to.
KINESIAS. Don't worry.—Now let's have fun.
MYRRHINE.
No! Stop it! I said no!
—Although, of course,
I *do* love you.
KINESIAS. I know you do. Darling Myrrhine:
come, shall we?
MYRRHINE. Are you out of your mind? In front of the child? 60
KINESIAS.
Take him home, Manes.

(*Exit Manes with Baby.*)

There. He's gone.
Come on!
There's nothing to stop us now.
MYRRHINE. You devil! But where?
KINESIAS.
In Pan's cave. What could be snugger than that?
MYRRHINE.
But my purification before I go back to the Citadel?
KINESIAS.
Wash in the Klepsydra.°
MYRRHINE. And my oath?
KINESIAS. Leave the oath to me. 65
After all, I'm the man.
MYRRHINE. Well . . . if you say so.
I'll go find a bed.
KINESIAS.
Oh, bother a bed! The ground's good enough for me.
MYRRHINE.
No. You're a bad man, but you deserve something better than dirt.

(*Exit Myrrhine.*)

65 **Klepsydra** a sacred spring beneath the walls of the Akropolis. Kinesias' suggestion has overtones of blasphemy.

KINESIAS.
What a love she is! And how thoughtful!

(*Re-enter Myrrhine.*)

MYRRHINE. Here's your bed.
Now let me get my clothes off.
70 But good horrors!
We haven't a mattress.
KINESIAS. Oh, forget the mattress!
MYRRHINE. No.
Just lying on blankets? Too sordid.
KINESIAS. Give me a kiss.
MYRRHINE.
Just a second.

(*Exit Myrrhine.*)

KINESIAS. I swear, I'll explode!

(*Re-enter Myrrhine.*)

MYRRHINE. Here's your mattress.
I'll just take my dress off.
But look—
where's our pillow?
KINESIAS. I don't *need* a pillow!
75 MYRRHINE. Well, *I* do.

(*Exit Myrrhine.*)

KINESIAS.
I don't suppose even Herakles
would stand for this!

(*Re-enter Myrrhine.*)

MYRRHINE. There we are. Ups-a-daisy!
KINESIAS.
So we are. Well, come to bed.
MYRRHINE. But I wonder:
is everything ready now?
KINESIAS. I can swear to that. Come, darling!
MYRRHINE.
Just getting out of my girdle.
80 But remember, now
what you promised about the treaty.
KINESIAS. Yes, yes, yes!
MYRRHINE.
But no coverlet!
KINESIAS. Damn it, I'll be
your coverlet!
MYRRHINE. Be right back.

(*Exit Myrrhine*)

KINESIAS. This girl and her coverlets
will be the death of me.

(*Re-enter Myrrhine.*)

MYRRHINE. Here we are. Up you go!
KINESIAS.
Up? I've been up for ages.
MYRRHINE. Some perfume? 85
KINESIAS.
No, by Apollo!
MYRRHINE. Yes, by Aphrodite!
I don't care whether you want it or not.

(*Exit Myrrhine.*)

KINESIAS.
For love's sake, hurry!

(*Re-enter Myrrhine.*)

MYRRHINE.
Here, in your hand. Rub it right in.
KINESIAS. Never cared for perfume.
And this is particularly strong. Still, here goes. 90
MYRRHINE.
What a nitwit I am! I brought the Rhodian bottle.
KINESIAS.
Forget it.
MYRRHINE. No trouble at all. You just wait here.

(*Exit Myrrhine.*)

KINESIAS.
God damn the man who invented perfume!

(*Re-enter Myrrhine.*)

MYRRHINE.
At last! The right bottle!
KINESIAS. I've got the rightest
bottle of all, and it's right here waiting for you. 95
Darling, forget everything else. Do come to bed.
MYRRHINE.
Just let me get my shoes off.
—And, by the way,
you'll vote for the treaty?
KINESIAS. I'll think about it.

(*Myrrhine runs away.*)

There! That's done it! The damned woman,
she gets me all bothered, she half kills me, 100
and off she runs! What'll I do? Where
can I get laid?
—And you, little prodding pal,
who's going to take care of *you*? No, you and I
had better get down to old Foxdog's Nursing Clinic.
CHORUS(m).
Alas for the woes of man, alas 105
Specifically for you.
She's brought you to a pretty pass:
What are you going to do?
Split, heart! Sag, flesh! Proud spirit, crack!
Myrrhine's got you on your back. 110
KINESIAS.
The agony, the protraction!
KORYPHAIOS(m). Friend,
What woman's worth a damn?

They bitch us all, world without end.

KINESIAS.

Yet they're so damned sweet, man!

KORYPHAIOS(m).

115 Calamitous, that's what I say.
You should have learned that much today.

CHORUS(m).

O blessed Zeus, roll womankind.
Up into one great ball;
Blast them aloft on a high wind,
120 And once there, let them fall.
Down, down they'll come, the pretty dears,
And split themselves on our thick spears.

(*Exit Kinesias.*)

SCENE IV

(*Enter a Spartan Herald.*)

HERALD.

Gentlemen, Ah beg you will be so kind
as to direct me to the Central Committee.
Ah have a communication.

(*Re-enter Commissioner.*)

COMMISSIONER. Are you a man,
or a fertility symbol?

HERALD. Ah refuse to answer that question!
5 Ah'm a certified herald from Spahta, and Ah've come
to talk about an ahmistice.

COMMISSIONER. Then why
that spear under your cloak?

HERALD. Ah have no speah!

COMMISSIONER.

You don't walk naturally, with your tunic
poked out so. You have a tumor, maybe,
or a hernia?

HERALD. You lost yo' mahnd, man?

10 COMMISSIONER. Well,
something's up, I can see that. And I don't like it.

HERALD.

Colonel, Ah resent this.

COMMISSIONER. So I see. But what *is* it?

HERALD. A staff
with a message from Spahta.

COMMISSIONER. Oh. I know about those staffs.
Well, then, man, speak out: How are things in Sparta?

HERALD.

15 Hahd, Colonel, hahd! We're at a standstill.
Cain't seem to think of anything but women.

COMMISSIONER.

How curious! Tell me, do you Spartans think
that maybe Pan's to blame?

HERALD.

Pan? No. Lampito and her little naked friends.
They won't let a man come nigh them. 20

COMMISSIONER.

How are you handling it?

HERALD. Losing our mahnds,
if y' want to know, and walking around hunched over
lahk men carrying candles in a gale.
The women have swohn they'll have nothing to do with us
until we get a treaty.

COMMISSIONER. Yes. I know. 25
It's a general uprising, sir, in all parts of Greece.
But as for the answer—
Sir: go back to Sparta
and have them send us your Armistice Commission.
I'll arrange things in Athens.
And I may say
that my standing is good enough to make them listen. 30

HERALD.

A man after mah own haht! Seh, Ah thank you.

(*Exit Herald.*)

CHORAL EPISODE

STROPHE

CHORUS(m).

Oh these women! Where will you find
A slavering beast that's more unkind? Where a hotter fire?
Give me a panther, any day.
He's not so merciless as they, 35
And panthers don't conspire.

ANTISTROPHE

CHORUS(w).

We may be hard, you silly old ass,
But who brought you to this stupid pass?
You're the ones to blame.
Fighting with us, your oldest friends, 40
Simply to serve your selfish ends—
Really, you have no shame!

KORYPHAIOS(m).

No, I'm through with women forever.

KORYPHAIOS(w). If you say so.
Still, you might put some clothes on. You look too absurd
standing around naked. Come, get into this cloak. 45

KORYPHAIOS(m).

Thank you; you're right. I merely took it off
because I was in such a temper.

KORYPHAIOS(w). That's much better
Now you resemble a man again.
Why have you been so horrid?
And look: there's some sort of insect in your eye.
Shall I take it out?

50 KORYPHAIOS(m). An insect, is it? So that's
what's been bothering me. Lord, yes: take it out!
KORYPHAIOS(w).
You might be more polite.
—But, heavens!
What an enormous mosquito!
KORYPHAIOS(m). You've saved my life.
That mosquito was drilling an artesian well
in my left eye.
55 KORYPHAIOS(w). Let me wipe
those tears away.—And now: one little kiss?
KORYPHAIOS(m).
No, no kisses.
KORYPHAIOS(w). You're so difficult.
KORYPHAIOS(m).
You impossible women! How you do get around us!
The poet was right: Can't live with you, or without you.
60 But let's be friends.
And to celebrate, you might join us in an Ode.

STROPHE I

CHORUS(m and w).
Let it never be said
That my tongue is malicious:
Both by word and by deed
65 I would set an example that's noble and gracious.
We've had sorrow and care
Till we're sick of the tune.
Is there anyone here
Who would like a small loan?
70 My purse is crammed,
As you'll soon find;
And you needn't pay me back if the Peace gets signed.

STROPHE 2

I've invited to lunch
Some Karystian rips—
75 An esurient bunch,
But I've ordered a menu to water their lips.
I can still make soup
And slaughter a pig.
You're all coming, I hope?
80 But a bath first, I beg!
Walk right up
As though you owned the place,
And you'll get the front door slammed to in your face.

SCENE V

(*Enter Spartan Ambassador, with entourage.*)

KORYPHAIOS(m).
The Commission has arrived from Sparta.

How oddly
they're walking!
Gentlemen, welcome to Athens!
How is life in Lakonia?
AMBASSADOR. Need we discuss that?
Simply use your eyes.
CHORUS(m). The poor man's right:
What a sight!
AMBASSADOR. Words fail me. 5
But come, gentlemen, call in your Commissioners,
and let's get down to a Peace.
CHORAGOS(m). The state we're in! Can't bear
a stitch below the waist. It's a kind of pelvic
paralysis.
COMMISSIONER.
Won't somebody call Lysistrata?—Gentlemen,
we're no better off than you.
AMBASSADOR. So I see. 10
A SPARTAN.
Seh, do y'all feel a certain strain
early in the morning?
AN ATHENIAN.
I do, sir. It's worse than a strain.
A few more days, and there's nothing for us but Kleisthenes,
that broken blossom.
CHORAGOS(m). But you'd better get dressed again.
You know these people going around Athens with chisels, 15
looking for statues of Hermes.°
ATHENIAN. Sir, you are right.
SPARTAN.
He certainly is! Ah'll put mah own clothes back on.

(*Enter Athenian Commissioners.*)

COMMISSIONER.
Gentlemen from Sparta, welcome. This is a sorry business.
SPARTAN (*To one of his own group*).
Colonel, we got dressed just in time. Ah sweah,
if they'd seen us the way we were, there'd have been a new
wah 20
between the states.
COMMISSIONER.
Shall we call the meeting to order?
Now, Lakonians,
what's your proposal?
AMBASSADOR. We propose to consider peace.
COMMISSIONER.
Good. That's on our minds, too.

16 **statues of Hermes** The statues were the Hermai, stone posts set up in various parts of Athens. Just before the sailing of the Sicilian Expedition, a group of anonymous vandals mutilated these statues with chisels. This was considered an unhappy augury.

—Summon Lysistrata.
We'll never get anywhere without her.
25 AMBASSADOR. Lysistrata?
Summon Lysis-*any*body! Only, summon!
KORYPHAIOS[m]. No need to summon:
here she is, herself.

(*Enter Lysistrata.*)

COMMISSIONER. Lysistrata! Lion of women!
This is your hour to be
hard and yielding, outspoken and shy, austere and
30 gentle. You see here
the best brains of Hellas (confused, I admit,
by your devious charming) met as one man
to turn the future over to you.
LYSISTRATA. That's fair enough,
unless you men take it into your heads
35 to turn to each other instead of us. But I'd know
soon enough if you did.
—Where is Reconciliation?
Go, some of you: bring her here.
(*Exeunt two women.*)
And now, women,
lead the Spartan delegates to me: not roughly
or insultingly, as our men handle them, but gently,
40 politely, as ladies should. Take them by the hand,
or by anything else if they won't give you their hands.

(*The Spartans are escorted over.*)

There.—The Athenians next, by any convenient handle.

(*The Athenians are escorted.*)

Stand there, please.—Now, all of you, listen to me.

(*During the following speech the two women reenter, carrying an enormous statue of a naked girl; this is Reconciliation.*)

I'm only a woman, I know; but I've a mind,
45 and, I think, not a bad one: I owe it to my father
and to listening to the local politicians.
So much for that.
Now, gentlemen,
since I have you here, I intend to give you a scolding.
We are all Greeks.
50 Must I remind you of Thermopylai,° of Olympia,
of Delphoi? names deep in all our hearts?
Are they not a common heritage?
Yet you men
go raiding through the country from both sides,
Greek killing Greek, storming down Greek cities—
55 and all the time the Barbarian across the sea
is waiting for his chance!
—That's my first point.

AN ATHENIAN.
Lord! I can hardly contain myself.
LYSISTRATA. As for you Spartans:
Was it so long ago that Perikleides°
came here to beg our help? I can see him still,
his gray face, his sombre gown. And what did he want? 60
An army from Athens. All Messene
was hot at your heels, and the sea-god splitting your land.
Well, Kimon and his men,
four thousand strong, marched out and saved all Sparta.
And what thanks do we get? You come back to murder us. 65
AN ATHENIAN.
They're aggressors, Lysistrata!
A SPARTAN. Ah admit it.
When Ah look at those laigs, Ah sweah Ah'll aggress
mahself!
LYSISTRATA.
And you, Athenians: do you think you're blameless?
Remember that bad time when we were helpless,
and an army came from Sparta, 70
and that was the end of the Thessalian menace,
the end of Hippias and his allies.
And that was Sparta,
and only Sparta; but for Sparta, we'd be
cringing slaves today, not free Athenians.

(*From this point, the male responses are less to Lysistrata than to the statue.*)

A SPARTAN.
A well-shaped speech.
AN ATHENIAN. Certainly it has its points. 75
LYSISTRATA.
Why are we fighting each other? With all this history
of favors given and taken, what stands in the way
of making peace?
AMBASSADOR. Spahta is ready, ma'am,
so long as we get that place back.
LYSISTRATA. What place, man?
AMBASSADOR.
Ah refer to Pylos.
COMMISSIONER. Not a chance, by God! 80
LYSISTRATA.
Give it to them, friend.
COMMISSIONER.
But—what shall we have to bargain with?
LYSISTRATA.
Demand something in exchange.

50 **Thermopylai** a narrow pass where, in 480 B.C., an army of 300 Spartans held out for three days against a vastly superior Persian force 58 **Perikleides** a Spartan ambassador to Athens who successfully urged Athenians to aid Sparta in putting down a rebellion

COMMISSIONER. Good idea.—Well, then:
Cockeville first, and the Happy Hills, and the country
between the Legs of Megara.

AMBASSADOR. Mah government objects.

LYSISTRATA.
85 Over-ruled. Why fuss about a pair of legs?

(*General assent. The statue is removed.*)

AN ATHENIAN.
I want to get out of these clothes and start my plowing.

A SPARTAN.
Ah'll fertilize mahn first, by the Heavenly Twins!

LYSISTRATA.
And so you shall,
once you've made peace. If you are serious,
90 go, both of you, and talk with your allies.

COMMISSIONER.
Too much talk already. No, we'll stand together.
We've only one end in view. All that we want
is our women; and I speak for our allies.

AMBASSADOR.
Mah government concurs.

AN ATHENIAN. So does Karystos.

LYSISTRATA.
95 Good.—But before you come inside
to join your wives at supper, you must perform
the usual lustration. Then we'll open
our baskets for you, and all that we have is yours.
But you must promise upright good behavior
100 from this day on. Then each man home with his woman!

AN ATHENIAN.
Let's get it over with.

A SPARTAN. Lead on. Ah follow.

AN ATHENIAN.
Quick as a cat can wink!

(*Exeunt all but the Choruses.*)

ANTISTROPHE 1

CHORUS[w].
Embroideries and
Twinkling ornaments and
105 Pretty dresses—I hand
Them all over to you, and with never a qualm.
They'll be nice for your daughters
On festival days.
When the girls bring the Goddess
110 The ritual prize.
Come in, one and all:
Take what you will.
I've nothing here so tightly corked that you can't make it
spill.

ANTISTROPHE 2

You may search my house
115 But you'll not find
The least thing of use,
Unless your two eyes are keener than mine.
Your numberless brats
Are half starved? and your slaves?
120 Courage, grandpa! I've lots
Of grain left, and big loaves.
I'll fill your guts,
I'll go the whole hog;
But if you come too close to me, remember: 'ware the dog!

(*Exeunt Choruses.*)

EXODOS

(*A Drunken Citizen enters, approaches the gate, and is halted by a sentry.*)

CITIZEN.
Open. The. Door.

SENTRY. Now, friend, just shove along!
—So you want to sit down. If it weren't such an old joke,
I'd tickle your tail with this torch. Just the sort of gag
this audience appreciates.

CITIZEN. I. Stay. Right. Here.

SENTRY.
Get away from there, or I'll scalp you! The gentlemen
5 from Sparta
are just coming back from dinner.

(*Exit Citizen; the general company reenters; the two Choruses now represent Spartans and Athenians.*)

A SPARTAN. Ah must say,
Ah never tasted better grub.

AN ATHENIAN. And those Lakonians!
They're gentlemen, by the Lord! Just goes to show,
a drink to the wise is sufficient.

COMMISSIONER. And why not?
10 A sober man's an ass.
Men of Athens, mark my words: the only efficient
Ambassador's a drunk Ambassador. Is that clear?
Look: we go to Sparta,
and when we get there we're dead sober. The result?
15 Everyone cackling at everyone else. They make speeches;
and even if we understand, we get it all wrong
when we file our reports in Athens. But today—!
Everybody's happy. Couldn't tell the difference
between *Drink to Me Only* and
The Star-Spangled Athens.

20 What's a few lies,
washed down in good strong drink?

(*Re-enter the Drunken Citizen.*)

SENTRY. God almighty,
he's back again!

CITIZEN. I. Resume. My. Place.

A SPARTAN (*To an Athenian*).
Ah beg yo', seh,
take yo' instrument in yo' hand and play for us.
25 Ah'm told
yo' understand the in*tri*cacies of the floot?
Ah'd lahk to execute a song and dance
in honor of Athens,
and, of cohse, of Spahta.

CITIZEN.
Toot. On. Your. Flute.

(*The following song is a solo—an aria—accompanied by the flute. The Chorus of Spartans begins a slow dance.*)

A SPARTAN.
30 O Memory,
Let the Muse speak once more
In my young voice. Sing glory.
Sing Artemision's shore,
Where Athens fluttered the Persians. *Alalai,*
35 Sing glory, that great
Victory! Sing also
Our Leonidas and his men,
Those wild boars, sweat and blood
Down in a red drench. Then, then
40 The barbarians broke, though they had stood
Numberless as the sands before!

O Artemis,°
Virgin Goddess, whose darts
Flash in our forests: approve
45 This pact of peace and join our hearts,
From this day on, in love.
Huntress, descend!

LYSISTRATA.
All that will come in time.
But now, Lakonians,
take home your wives. Athenians, take yours.
50 Each man be kind to his woman; and you, women,
be equally kind. Never again, pray God,
shall we lose our way in such madness.

KORYPHAIOS (Athenian). And now
let's dance our joy.

42 **Artemis** goddess of virginity, of the hunt, and of childbirth

(*From this point the dance becomes general.*)

CHORUS (Athenian).
Dance, you Graces
Artemis, dance
Dance, Phoibos,° Lord of dancing
Dance, 55
In a scurry of Maenads, Lord Dionysos°
Dance, Zeus Thunderer
Dance, Lady Hera°
Queen of the sky.
Dance, dance, all you gods
Dance witness everlasting of our pact
Evohí Evohé 60
Dance for the dearest
the Bringer of Peace
Deathless Aphrodite!

COMMISSIONER.
Now let us have another song from Sparta.

CHORUS (Spartan).
From Taygetos, from Taygetos,
Lakonian Muse, come down. 65
Sing to the Lord Apollo
Who rules Amyklai Town.

Sing Athena of the House of Brass!°
Sing Leda's Twins,° that chivalry
Resplendent on the shore 70
Of our Eurotas; sing the girls
That dance along before:
Sparkling in dust their gleaming feet,
Their hair a Bacchant fire,
And Leda's daughter, thyrsos° raised, 75
Leads their triumphant choir.

CHORUSES (S and A).
Evohé!
Evohaí!
Evohé!
We pass
Dancing
dancing
to greet
Athena of the House of Brass.

55 **Phoibos** god of the sun 56 **Maenads, Lord Dionysus** The maenads were ecstatic women in the train of Dionysos, god of wine. 57 **Hera** wife of Zeus 68 **Athena of the House of Brass** a temple standing on the Akropolis of Sparta 69 **Leda's Twins** Leda, raped by Zeus, bore quadruplets: two daughters, Helen and Klytaimnestra, and two sons, Kastor and Polydeukes. 75 **thyrsos** a staff twined with ivy, carried by Dionysus and his followers

TOPICS FOR DISCUSSION AND WRITING

1. According to *Lysistrata,* what are the causes of war? What do you think are the causes of war?
2. What connection, if any, is there between the sex strike and the seizure of the Akropolis?
3. An antiwar play might be expected to call attention to cruelty, innocent suffering, and death. How much of this do you find in *Lysistrata?*
4. There is much about sex here. How much is there about love?
5. How much horseplay do you find in the *exodos?* Why?
6. Evaluate the view that the real heroine of the play is not Lysistrata but the nude female statue of Reconciliation.

A NOTE ON *The Medieval Theater*

In A.D. 410 Alaric, King of the Visigoths, crossed the Alps and sacked Rome. In the next five centuries no plays were written in Europe and no theaters were built there. But the drama had encountered an enemy even before Alaric entered Rome: the Christian church had long opposed theatrical entertainments, partly because they included spectacles of nudity, fights with wild beasts, and the like; partly because Christians were fed to lions or were tarred and set afire in entertainments offered to the pagan Romans; and partly because the church's hatred of "falsehood" included among the untruths—the fictions—of literature the art of acting, which involves the impersonation of one man by another, and—even worse—of a woman by a man by means of transvestism. In the fifth century, after a monk attempted to interfere in a gladiatorial combat and was stoned to death, the Roman emperors (who in 378 had adopted Christianity as the official state religion) prohibited public spectacles. For all practical purposes, the theater in Europe ceased to exist, except for quasi-dramatic events such as tournaments and ritual practices in pagan festivals and such meager performances as were put on by itinerant minstrels, owners of performing animals, mimes, jugglers, and puppeteers.

And yet, despite the opposition of Christianity, which held that drama is immoral because it presents false appearances, the drama was reborn within the church in what is known as liturgical drama. A liturgy is a prescribed form of worship, and the forms of worship included the singing of the Mass, in which bread and wine are consecrated as the body and blood of Christ. Some liturgical texts were arranged in dialogue form, with choric chants divided antiphonally, that is with one voice (or set of voices) responding to another. For instance, one of the introductory antiphons for the Easter Mass consists of an exchange in song between a voice or set of voices speaking for an angel and another set of voices speaking for the women who visited Christ's tomb in order to anoint the corpse. The angel asks whom they seek, they reply that they seek Jesus, and the angel explains that Jesus has risen from the tomb. Such a service, with chanting priests and a choir—a voice or voices answering a voice or voices—is a sort of dramatic exchange, but it is not quite drama since there is little or no emphasis on impersonation. Still, before the end of the tenth century it was clear that drama was reborn in the church.

Earlier in this book (pages 3–5), in our essay in which we try to set forth the essence of drama, we discuss the liturgical drama called *Quem Quaeritis* ("Whom do you seek?"), described by Bishop Ethelwold. We need not repeat that discussion here. Suffice it to say that adaptations soon followed; for instance, similar dramatic renditions celebrated the birth of Jesus and the journey of the Magi, and although these compositions probably were not initially conceived of as educational, in time they must have been recognized as a means by which an illiterate congregation could better grasp the miraculous realities. In 1264, some three hundred years after Bishop Ethelwold set down his instructions, Pope Urban IV promulgated a new Feast Day, Corpus Christi (medieval Latin, "body of Christ"), which was finally instituted by Pope Clement V in 1311. Celebrated on the Thursday following Trinity Sunday, and commemorating Christ's sacrifice of his life for the salvation of humankind, Corpus Christi Day occurred

The shepherds visit the newborn Jesus, at the end of the *Second Shepherds' Play.* Left to right: Martha Homes, Anderson Matthews, Ian Schneiderman, and Paul Molder in the Delaware Theater Company's production—1986–87 season. (Photograph by Richard C. Carter.)

nine weeks after Easter Sunday. Although in the modern calendar it falls in late May or in June, in the Middle Ages, because the calendar was inaccurate, Corpus Christi Day fell at a time equivalent to our June or early July. Thus it was a joyful midsummer festival, marked by a procession in which the host, escorted by local dignitaries, was carried through the streets.

Plays soon became attached to the Feast of Corpus Christi, and so, for example, in Italy in the early fourteenth century Corpus Christi Day was celebrated by an almost cosmic cycle of plays on sacred history, in Latin, ranging from the Fall of Lucifer, the Crucifixion of Christ, the Harrowing of Hell, Christ's Ascension, and on up to the Day of Judgment. By the end of the fourteenth century the celebration of Corpus Christi included plays performed not in Latin but in the vernacular, on Old Testament and New Testament subjects, sponsored not only by the Church but by civic organizations. Guilds sponsored plays deemed appropriate; thus, the shipwrights were responsible for the play about Noah's Ark, the bakers for The Last Supper, and so on. (The plays as a group were called "the play of Corpus Christi," but scholars usually call the individual plays **mystery plays** because they were sponsored by various trades or "mysteries," a word derived, like the French *métier,* from the Latin *minister,* "attendant," "servant." The plays are sometimes also called **miracle plays.**)

How does one account for this widespread and vast medieval cyclical drama? Did it "develop" from *Quem Quaeritis,* or was it engendered afresh? In the late nineteenth and early twentieth centuries, scholars customarily held a sort of Darwinian view, suggesting that the late medieval cycles "evolved" out of *Quem Quaeritis.* In this view, the drama gradually but naturally grew, adding one story to another, expanding the length of the stories, inevitably shifting from Latin into the vernacular, and equally inevitably moving out of the church and into the marketplace. The current prevailing scholarly view, however, tends to deemphasize a "natural" evolution and to hold that the plays are the result of self-conscious efforts to set forth scriptural history—a history of the wonders of God—in dramatic form. That is, the plays are now seen as an effort to provide visible evidence explaining the significance of the feast of Corpus Christi.

In England four great cycles of miracle plays are extant: forty-eight plays were done at York, thirty-two at Wakefield, twenty-four at Chester, and forty-three at an unidentified town (formerly thought to be Coventry). Moreover, this sort of medieval drama, enormously popular in the late fourteenth century and in the fifteenth, survived until well into the Renaissance, that is, for several decades after Henry VIII split with the Church of Rome and established the Church of England. The cycles were given at Chester until 1574 and at Coventry (only fourteen miles from Shakespeare's Stratford) until 1581, when Shakespeare was seventeen. They apparently were abandoned not because the people lost interest in religious drama but for two other reasons: (1) Protestantism was hostile to a drama that had developed under Roman Catholic auspices, and (2) better dramatic entertainment was becoming available. The late sixteenth century saw the rise of small companies of professional strolling players, who could put on a better show than could the local amateurs. In 1576, the last year that the plays were staged at Wakefield, James Burbage erected England's first permanent theater, in London.

Something (but not a great deal) is known about the staging of medieval plays. There is evidence of performances on temporary stages made of planks resting on trestles or barrels; there is also evidence of performances in the round (i.e., with the audience on all sides), and of performances on wagons or floats called "pageants." In some towns pageants were drawn to several announced localities where separate audiences waited. In this method of staging, each audience stayed in one place, seeing a succession of scenes, and the wagons traveled on to other audiences waiting at other locations. But it may also be the case, for some vast cycles, that although the wagons were first drawn through the town, they were then assembled in a circle in one place, for instance in a public square, where the plays were performed one by one with the audience in the center of the ring of wagons.

A stage, or a pageant, by the way, might simultaneously display several sets (called *sedes,* literally "seats," or *mansions*) to indicate different locales; a structure representing Hell (the head of a monster, from whose gaping mouth smoke poured forth) might be at one side, and a structure representing Heaven might be at the other. In between were structures representing various places, such as the manger where Jesus was born, the hill where he was crucified, and so forth. There is also evidence that the performers sometimes left their stages and entered the open space (the *platea*) where the audience stood. In short, the productions were closer to our "street theater" than to what goes on in our modern playhouses.

Martial Rose, in *The Wakefield Mystery Plays* (a book with a long introduction to a modernized text of the plays), offers some conjectures about how the town of Wakefield in the mid-fifteenth century may have staged its cycle of thirty-two plays, ranging from the creation of the world through the fall of mankind, the redemption, and the judgment. (It must be remembered that the evidence is very fragmentary, and Rose's account therefore is highly conjectural, but it is as reasonable as any other that has been offered.) Perhaps, Rose says, soon after dawn on Corpus Christi day, twenty or thirty pageants set out on the Corpus Christi procession. Sponsored by the trade guilds—each guild was associated with a particular pageant—the procession of wagons, guildsmen, minstrels, and clergy went to the parish church. Here, at the service, the Host of the Lord was raised, carried out of the church, and carried (with the procession following) to various stations in the town. At each station the pageants would produce, in pantomime, the climax of the play that they would perform in full in the following three days. During the next three days, the plays were performed at only one location (perhaps the market place, the common, or the land adjoining the church), where an audience assembled in a circle around an open space to watch as each pageant entered through an aisle and its actors performed. Rose conjectures that perhaps Heaven and Hell were brought in first and remained in view throughout, while the other wagons came and went. Or possibly the audience assembled in the center, and all of the wagons were assembled around the perimeter of the circle.

The wagon for *The Second Shepherds' Play* might have used two mansions, one for Mak's house and one for Mary and Jesus. The space between and in front of the two mansions (the *platea*) could have served for the fields, though some scholars conjecture a third mansion, a fence, to represent the sheepfold.

For a further discussion of *The Second Shepherds' Play,* see the introduction to the play.

THE WAKEFIELD MASTER

The Second Shepherds' Play

Modernized version by the editors

The anonymous author of five plays in the Wakefield Cycle is called The Wakefield Master. He is thought to have been a clergyman active in the first half of the fifteenth century, but nothing is known for certain about him. (The cycle of thirty-two plays is also known as the Towneley Cycle, from the name of a family that owned the manuscript, but Wakefield is a better designation for two reasons: the manuscript specifically mentions Wakefield, a town in Yorkshire, England, and it is known that a cycle of plays was in fact performed there.)

The Wakefield Cycle probably originated in the late fourteenth century, but it was revised and amplified. The five plays attributed to the Wakefield Master are characterized by the liveliness of the roles and by a distinctive nine-line stanza. The first four lines of each stanza use identical end-rhymes and also internal rhymes. In the last five lines, lines 5 and 9 rhyme, and lines 6, 7, and 8 rhyme. The first four lines each have four stresses, line 5 has only one stress, lines 6, 7, and 8 have three stresses each, and line 9 has two stresses. This stanza is used only in the five plays attributed to the Wakefield Master and in a few passages in other plays that he apparently revised.

From the Wakefield Cycle of thirty-two plays, we print the play called *Secunda Pastorum,* Latin for *The Second Play of the Shepherds,* or *The Second Shepherds' Play,* so called because in the cycle it is the second of two plays on the subject of the revelation of the infant Christ to the shepherds. Of the four Gospels, only Luke, in 2.6–16, specifies that shepherds heard the "good tidings" of the birth of Jesus and journeyed "even unto Bethlehem to see this thing which is come to pass." It is not surprising, however, that in England, with its thriving wool industry, the shepherds would be represented in a dramatization of the Nativity.

COMMENTARY

The Second Shepherds' Play is comic in two senses. First, it is amusing, with its grumbling figures and the sheep-stealer who adopts a dialect in order to impersonate a man of rank and who tries to pass off a stolen lamb as his newborn infant. Second, it is comic in its overall action, that is, in its movement from bad fortune to good fortune (the recovery of the stolen sheep), from sorrow to joy (the news of the birth of Jesus), from the cruelty of nature and of humankind to generosity (the giving of gifts), from winter (in the presentation of the bunch of cherries) to an anticipation of spring and renewed life.

The original text does not include any instructions concerning properties or scenery, but perhaps a cradle, a chair, and a table at one end of the wagon indicated Mak's house, and a cradle and chair at the other end represented the manger. The space between them and in front of them—the *platea*—would serve for the fields. When Mak

Ian Schneiderman, Rory Kelly, Kathryn Gay Wilson, Paul Molder, and Anderson Matthews in the Delaware Theater Company's production of the *Second Shepherds' Play*—1986–87 season. (Photograph by Richard C. Carter.)

steals the sheep in order to take it to his house, perhaps he jumps from the wagon, makes a journey through the audience (the space occupied by the spectators is also the *platea*), and then climbs up at the other end of the wagon. We can, further, imagine an additional detail in the staging: the angel who announces the birth of Christ may have appeared on a platform above the wagon. These comments on the staging of the play are admittedly conjectural, but evidence from other texts indicates that efforts were made to assure that the presentations were theatrically effective.

Something should be said about the language of the original play and about our translation. The anonymous author, writing in the middle of the fifteenth century, used an English that often is close to modern English, and often it is not. Thus, the first line of the original,

> Lord, what these weders are cold! And I am ill happyd,

may be translated fairly literally as

> Lord, how this weather is cold! And I am poorly clothed.

We translate it as:

> Lord, but this weather is cold! And I am ill wrapped.

By substituting "wrapped" for the obscure "happyd," we can spare the reader from consulting a gloss and yet we can also preserve the rhyme of *happyd / nappyd / chappyd* of the original. Or consider the very last lines of the play:

> To sing ar we bun—
> Let take on loft!

Literally this means, "To sing are we bound, / Begin [the song] loudly." We render the last line as "Ring it aloft," which avoids the need to gloss "Let take" as "begin," and which yet preserves the rhyme with "Full oft," as in the original.

THE WAKEFIELD MASTER *The Second Shepherds' Play*

List of Characters

FIRST SHEPHERD [*Coll*]
SECOND SHEPHERD [*Gib*]
THIRD SHEPHERD [*Daw*]
MAK [*a sheep-stealer*]
HIS WIFE [*Gill*]
ANGEL
MARY
CHRIST-CHILD

A field.

FIRST SHEPHERD. Lord, but these weathers are cold!
And I am ill wrapped
I am near-hand dold,° so long have I napped;
My legs they fold, my fingers are chapped.
It is not as I would, for I am all lapped
In sorrow. 5
In storms and tempest,
Now in the east, now in the west,
Woe is him has never rest
Midday nor morrow!

But we simple husbands° that walk on the moor, 10
In faith we are near-hands out of the door.
No wonder, as it stands, if we be poor,
For the tilth of our lands lies fallow as the floor,

2 nearly numb 10 husbandmen, i.e., shepherds

As ye ken.°
15 We are so lamed,
O'ertaxed and maimed,
We are made hand-tamed
By these gentlery men.

Thus they rob us our rest, our Lady them harry!
20 These men that are lord-fast, they make the plough tarry.
What men say is for the best, we find it contrary.
Thus are husbands oppressed, about to miscarry
In life.
Thus hold they us under,
25 Thus they bring us in blunder;
It were great wonder
If ever should we thrive.

There shall come a swain as proud as a po;°
He must borrow my wain, my plough also;
30 Then I am full fain° to grant ere he go.
Thus live we in pain, anger, and woe,
By night, and day.
He must have it for sure,
Though I remain poor;
35 I'll be pushed out of door
If I once say nay.

If he has braid on his sleeve or a badge nowadays,
Woe to him that him grieve or ever gainsays!
No complaint he'll receive, whatever his ways.
40 And yet may none believe one word that he says,
No letter.
He can make his demands
With boasts and commands,
And all because he stands
45 For men who are greater.

It does me good, as I walk thus by mine own,
Of this world for to talk in manner of moan.
To my sheep will I stalk, and hearken anon,°
And there will I halt and sit on a stone
50 Full soon.
For I trust, pardie,°
True men if there be,
We get more company
Ere it be noon.

[*Enter the Second Shepherd, who does not see the First Shepherd.*]

14 know 28 peacock 30 pleased 48 soon 51 by God

SECOND SHEPHERD. Blessings upon us, what may this bemean? 55
Why fares this world thus? Such we seldom have seen.
Lord, these weathers are spiteous, and the winds full keen,
And the frosts so hideous they water mine eyne,°
No lie!
Now in dry, now in wet, 60
Now in snow, now in sleet,
When my shoes freeze to my feet
It is not all easy.

But as far as I've been, or yet as I know,
We poor wedded-men suffer great woe; 65
We sorrow now and again; it falls oft so.
Silly Caple, our hen, both to and fro
She cackles;
But begins she to croak,
To groan or to cluck, 70
Woe is him, our cock,
For he is in her shackles.

These men that are wed have not all their will;
When they're full hard bestead,° they sigh full still.
God knows they are led full hard and full ill; 75
In bower nor in bed they say nought theretil.°
This tide°
My part have I found,
I know my ground!
Woe is him that is bound, 80
For he must abide.

But now late in our lives—a marvel to me,
That I think my heart rives such wonders to see;
Whate'er destiny drives, it must so be—
Some men will have two wives, and some men three 85
In store;
Some are grieved that have any.
But so far ken I—
Woe is him that has many,
For he feels sore. 90

[*Addresses the audience.*]

But, young men, of wooing, for God who you bought,°
Be well ware of wedding, and think in your thought,
"Had I known" is a thing that serves us of nought.
Much constant mourning has wedding home brought,
And griefs, 95
With many a sharp shower;
For thou may catch in an hour

58 eyes 74 oppressed 76 thereto 77 time 91 redeemed

What shall savor full sour
As long as thou lives.

100 For, as e'er read I epistle, I have one for my dear
As sharp as thistle, as rough as a brier;
She is browed like a bristle, with a sour-looking cheer;°
Had she once wet her whistle, she could sing full clear
Her Paternoster.
105 She is as great as a whale,
She has a gallon of gall;
By Him that died for us all,
I would I had run till I had lost her!

[*The First Shepherd interrupts him.*]

FIRST SHEPHERD. The like I never saw! Full deafly ye stand.
SECOND SHEPHERD. Be the devil in thy maw, so
110 tariand!°
Saw thou ought of Daw?
FIRST SHEPHERD. Yea, on pasture-land
Heard I him blaw.° He comes here at hand,
Not far.
Standstill.
SECOND SHEPHERD. Why?
115 FIRST SHEPHERD. For he comes here, think I.
SECOND SHEPHERD. He will tell us both a lie
Unless we beware.

[*Enter the Third Shepherd, a boy, who does not see the others.*]

THIRD SHEPHERD. Christ's cross, my creed, and Saint Nicholas!
Thereof had I need; it is worse than it was.
120 Whoso could take heed and let the world pass,
It is ever in dread and brittle as glass
And slides.
This world fared never sure,
With marvels more and more—
125 Now with rich, now with poor,
Nothing abides.

Never since Noah's flood were such floods seen,
Winds and rains so rude, and storms so keen—
Some stammered, some stood in fear, as I ween,°
130 Now God turn all to good! I say as I mean,
For, ponder:
These floods so they drown,
Both in fields and in town,
And bear all down;

102 face 110 for tarrying 112 blow on his shepherd's pipe 129 fear

And that is a wonder. 135

[*He sees the others.*]

We that walk in the nights, our cattle to keep,
We see sudden sights when other men sleep.
Yet methinks my heart lights; I see rogues peep.
Ye are two tall wights°—I will give my sheep
A turn. 140
But much ill have I meant;
As I walk on this bent,°
I may lightly repent,
My toes if I spurn.°

[*The other two advance.*]

Ah, sir, God you save, and master mine! 145
A drink fain would I have, and somewhat to dine.
FIRST SHEPHERD. Christ's curse, my knave, thou art lazy, I find!
SECOND SHEPHERD. How the boy will rave!. Wait for a time;
You have fed.
Bad luck on your brow; 150
The rogue came just now,
Yet would he, I vow,
Sit down to his bread.
THIRD SHEPHERD. Such servants as I, that sweats and swinks,°
Eats our bread full dry, a sorrow methinks. 155
We are oft wet and weary when master-men winks;°
Yet comes full tardy both dinners and drinks.
But truly.
Both our dame and our sire,
When we have run in the mire, 160
They can nip at our hire,°
And pay us full slowly.

But hear my mind, master: for the bread that I break,
I shall toil thereafter—work as I take.
I shall do but little, sir, and always hold back, 165
For yet lay my supper never on my stomach
In fields.
Why should I complain?
With my staff I can run;
And men say, "A bargain 170
Little profit yields."
FIRST SHEPHERD. You'd be a poor lad to go a-walking
With a man that had but little for spending.

139 men 142 heath 144 perhaps: If I trip, I can easily expiate my evil thoughts 154 works 156 sleeps 161 reduce our wages

SECOND SHEPHERD. Peace, boy, I said. No more jangling,
175 Or I shall make thee afraid, by the heaven's king!
Thy joke—
Where are our sheep, boy?—we scorn.
THIRD SHEPHERD. Sir, this same day at morn
I them left in the corn,°
180 When the dawn broke.

They have pasture good, they can not go wrong.
FIRST SHEPHERD. That is right. By the rood,° these nights are long!
Ere we went, how I would, that one gave us a song.
SECOND SHEPHERD. So I thought as I stood, to mirth us among.
THIRD SHEPHERD. I grant.
185 FIRST SHEPHERD. Let me sing the tenory.
SECOND SHEPHERD. And I the treble so high.
THIRD SHEPHERD. Then the mean falls to me.
Let see how ye chant.

[*They sing.*]

Then Mak enters with a cloak drawn over his tunic.

MAK. Now, Lord, for Thy names seven, that made both beast and bird,
Well more than I can mention, Thy will leaves me
190 unstirred.
I am all uneven; that upsets my brains.
Now would God I were in heaven, for there weep no bairns°
So still.°
FIRST SHEPHERD. Who is that pipes so poor?
195 MAK. Would God ye knew how I were!
Lo, a man that walks on the moor,
And has not all his will.
SECOND SHEPHERD. Mak, where hast thou gone? Tell us tiding.
THIRD SHEPHERD. Is he come? Then each one take
200 heed to his thing.

He takes the cloak from Mak.

MAK. What! Ich° be a yeoman, I tell you, of the king,
The self and the same, agent of a lording,
And sich.
Fie on you! Go hence
205 Out of my presence!
I must have reverence.

179 wheat 182 cross 192 children 193 continuously
201 Mak here adopts a Southern dialect, but slips back into the Northern dialect at times.

Why, who be Ich?
FIRST SHEPHERD. Why make ye it so quaint? Mak, ye do wrong.
SECOND SHEPHERD. Mak, play ye the saint? I think not for long.
THIRD SHEPHERD. I think the rogue can feign, may the devil him hang! 210
MAK. I shall make complaint, and make you all to thwang°
At a word,
And tell even how ye doth.
FIRST SHEPHERD. But, Mak, is that truth?
Now take out that Southern tooth, 215
And put in a turd!
SECOND SHEPHERD. Mak, the devil in your eye! A stroke would I beat you.
THIRD SHEPHERD. Mak, know ye not me? By God, I could grieve you.
MAK. God save you all three! Me thought I had seen you.
Ye are a fair company.
FIRST SHEPHERD. What is it that mean you? 220
SECOND SHEPHERD. Shrew,° peep!
Thus late as thou goes,
What will men suppose?
Thou hast a good nose
For stealing a sheep. 225
MAK. And I am true as steel, all men state;
But a sickness I feel that will not abate:
My belly fares not well; it is out of estate.
THIRD SHEPHERD. Seldom lies the devil dead by the gate.
MAK. Therefore, 230
Full sore am I and sick;
May I stand like a stick
If I've had a bit
For a month and more.
FIRST SHEPHERD. How fares thy wife? By thy hood, what say you? 235
MAK. Lies wallowing—by the rood—by the fire, lo!
And a house full of brood. She drinks well, too;
There's no other good that she will do!
But she
Eats as fast as may be, 240
And every year that we see
She brings forth a baby—
And, some years, two.

Were I even more prosperous and richer by some,
I were eaten out of house and even of home. 245

211 be flogged 221 rogue

Yet is she a foul souse, if ye come near;
There is none that goes or anywhere roams
Worse than she.
Now will ye see what I proffer?
250 To give all in my coffer,
Tomorrow early to offer
Her head-masspenny.°

SECOND SHEPHERD. I know so forwaked° is none in this shire;
I would sleep, if I taked less for my hire.°

255 THIRD SHEPHERD. I am cold and naked, and would have a fire.

FIRST SHEPHERD. I am weary, all ached, and run in the mire—
Watch, thou.

[*Lies down.*]

SECOND SHEPHERD. Nay, I will lie near by,
For I must sleep, truly.

[*Lies down beside him.*]

260 THIRD SHEPHERD. As good a man's son was I
As any of you.

[*Lies down.*]

But, Mak, come thou here. Between us you'll stay.

MAK. Then could I stop you if evil you'd say,
No dread.
265 From my top to my toe,
Manus tuas commendo,
Poncio Pilato;°
May Christ's cross me clear.

Then he gets up, the shepherds still sleeping, and says:

Now's the time for a man that lacks what he would
270 To stalk privily then into a fold,
And nimbly to work then, and be not too bold,
For he might pay for the bargain, if it were told
At the end.
Only time now will tell;
275 But he needs good counsel
Who fain would fare well,
And has little to spend.

[*Mak casts a spell over them.*]

Here about you a circle, as round as a moon,
Till I have done what I will, till that it be noon,
280 May ye lie stone-still till that I have done;
And I shall say theretil a few good words soon:
A height,
Over your heads, my hand I lift.
Out go your eyes! Black out your sight!
But yet I must make better shift 285
If it go right.

[*The shepherds begin to snore.*]

Lord, how they sleep hard. That may ye all hear.
I was never a shepherd, but now will I lere.°
Though the flock be scared, yet shall I draw near.
How! Draw hitherward! Now mends our cheer 290
From sorrow;
A fat sheep, I dare say,
A good fleece, dare I lay.
Pay back when I may,
But this will I borrow. 295

[*He takes the sheep home.*]

How, Gill, art thou in? Get us some light.

WIFE. Who makes such din this time of the night?
I am set for to spin; I don't think there might
Be a penny to win; I curse them, all right!
So fares 300
The housewife that has been
Called from her work by a din.
Thus I earn not a pin
For such small chores.

MAK. Good wife, open the hatch! See'st thou not what I bring? 305

WIFE. I will let you draw the latch. Ah, come in, my sweeting.

MAK. Thou care not a scratch of my long standing.

WIFE. By thy naked neck art thou like for to hang.

MAK. Away!
I am worthy my meat, 310
For in a pinch can I get
More than they that swink and sweat
All the long day. [*Shows her the sheep.*]
Thus it fell to my lot, Gill; I had such grace.

WIFE. It were a foul blot to be hanged for the case. 315

MAK. I have 'scaped, Jelott, oft as hard a place.

WIFE. "But so long goes the pot to the water," men says,
"At last
Comes it home broken."

MAK. Well know I the token, 320
But let it never be spoken.
But come and help fast.

I would it were slain; I would well eat.

252 payment for funeral mass 253 worn out with watching 254 even though I accepted less wages 266–7 "Into thy hands I commend, Pontius Pilate."

288 learn

This twelvemonth was I not so fain of one sheep-meat.
WIFE. Come they ere it be slain, and hear the sheep
325 bleat—
MAK. Then might I be ta'en. That were a cold sweat!
Go bar
The gate-door.
WIFE. Yes, Mak,
And if they're close at thy back—
330 MAK. Then might I get, from all the pack,
The devil and more.
WIFE. A good trick have I spied, since thou know
none:
Here shall we him hide, till they be gone—
In my cradle abide. Let me alone,
335 And I shall lie beside in childbed, and groan.
MAK. Good head!
And I shall say thou was light°
Of a boy-child this night.
WIFE. For sure was the day bright
340 On which I was bred!
This is a good guise and a fair cast;
A woman's advice helps at the last.
I fear someone spies; again go thou fast.
MAK. If I'm gone when they rise, they'll blow a cold
blast.
345 I will go sleep. [*Returns to the shepherds.*]
Still they sleep, these three men,
And I shall softly creep in,
As though I had not been
He who stole their sheep.

[*He resumes his place.*]
[*The First and Second Shepherds awake.*]

FIRST SHEPHERD. *Resurrex a mortruus!*° Give me a
350 hand.
Judas carnas dominus!° I can not well stand;
My foot sleeps, by Jesus, and I totter on land.
I thought that we laid us full near England.
SECOND SHEPHERD. Ah, yea?
355 Lord, but I have slept well!
As fresh as an eel,
As light I me feel
As leaf on a tree.

[*The Third Shepherd awakes.*]

THIRD SHEPHERD. Blessing be herein! My heart so
quakes,
360 My heart is out of skin, hear how it shakes.
Who makes all this din? How my brow aches!

337 delivered 350 garbled Latin: "Resurrection from the dead" 351 "Judas, lord of the flesh"

To the door will I spin. Hark, fellows, wake!
Four we were—
See ye ought of Mak now?
FIRST SHEPHERD. We were up ere thou. 365
SECOND SHEPHERD. Man, I give God a vow,
That he did not stir.
THIRD SHEPHERD. Methought he was lapped in a
wolf-skin.
FIRST SHEPHERD. So are many wrapped now,
namely within.
THIRD SHEPHERD. When we had long napped,
methought with a gin° 370
A fat sheep he trapped; but he made no din.
SECOND SHEPHERD. Be still!
Thy dream makes thee wood;°
It is but phantom, by the rood.
FIRST SHEPHERD. Now God turn all to good, 375
If it be his will.

[*They awaken Mak.*]

SECOND SHEPHERD. Rise, Mak, for shame! Thou
liest right long.
MAK. Now Christ's holy name be us among.
What is this? For Saint Jame, I may not go strong.
I trust I be the same. Ah, my neck has lain wrong 380
Enough.

[*The others help him to his feet.*]

Many thanks! Since yester-even,
Now by Saint Steven,
I was scared by a dream—
That makes me full gruff. 385

I thought Gill began to croak and travail full sad,
Well-nigh at the first cock, of a young lad
To add to our flock. Then be I never glad;
I have more of my stock, more than ever I had.
Ah, my head! 390
A house full of young dolts,
The devil cut up their throats!
Woe is him has many colts,
And only little bread.

I must go home, by your leave, to Gill, as I thought. 395
I pray look up my sleeve, that I steal nought:
I am loath you to grieve, or from you take ought.
[*Leaves.*]
THIRD SHEPHERD. Go forth, ill may'st thou 'chieve!
Now would I we sought,
This morn,

370 trap 373 crazy

400 That we had all our store.
FIRST SHEPHERD. But I will go before;
Let us meet.
SECOND SHEPHERD. Where?
THIRD SHEPHERD. At the crooked thorn. [*They go out.*]

[*Mak outside his own door.*]

MAK. Undo this door! Who is here? How long shall I stand?
405 WIFE. Who is it that's near? Go walk in the quicksand!
MAK. Ah, Gill, what cheer? It is I, Mak, your husband.
WIFE. Then may we see here the devil in a band,°
Sir Guile.
Lo, he comes with a roar,
410 As he were chased by a boar!
I may not work at my chore
A little while.
MAK. Will ye hear what fuss she makes to get her a glose?°
And does naught but shirks, and claws her toes.
WIFE. Why, who wanders, who wakes? Who comes,
415 who goes?
Who brews, who bakes? Who makes us our hose?
And then
It is sad to behold—
Now in hot, now in cold,
420 Full woeful is the household
What lacks a woman.

What end has thou made with the shepherds, Mak?
MAK. The last word that they said when I turned my back
They would look that they had their sheep, all the pack.
425 I think they will not be allayed when they their sheep lack,
Pardie!
But howso the ball fly,
To me they will hie,
And make a foul cry
430 And shout out upon me.

But thou must do it aright.
WIFE. I accord me theretil;
I shall swaddle him right in my cradle.

[*Gill puts the sheep in the cradle.*]

If it were a greater sleight, yet could I help still,
I will lie down straight. Come wrap me.
MAK. I will.

[*Covers her.*]

WIFE. Behind! 435
Come Coll and his mate,
They will nip us full straight.
MAK. But I may cry out, "Wait!"
The sheep if they find.
WIFE. Harken well when they call; they will come anon. 440
Come and make ready all, and sing all alone;
Sing "Lullay" thou shall, for I must groan,
And cry out by the wall on Mary and John,
In pain
Sing "Lullay" so fast 445
When thou hearest at last;
And if I play a false cast,
Don't trust me again.

[*The shepherds meet at the thorn tree.*]

THIRD SHEPHERD. Ah, Coll, good morn. Why sleepest thou not?
FIRST SHEPHERD. Alas, that ever was I born. We have a foul blot— 450
Of a sheep we have been shorn.
THIRD SHEPHERD. The devil! Say what!
SECOND SHEPHERD. Who should do us that scorn? That is a foul plot.
FIRST SHEPHERD. Some shrew.
I have sought with my dogs
All Horbury bogs, 455
And of fifteen hogs°
Found all but one ewe.
THIRD SHEPHERD. Now trust me, if ye will—by Saint Thomas of Kent,
Either Mak or Gill was at that assent.
FIRST SHEPHERD. Peace, man, be still. I saw when he went. 460
Thou slanderest him ill; thou ought to repent
With speed.
SECOND SHEPHERD. Now as ever might thrive I,
Though I should even here die,
It were he, I'd reply, 465
That did that same deed.
THIRD SHEPHERD. Go we thither, let's tread, and run on our feet.
I shall never eat bread, till the truth is complete.
FIRST SHEPHERD No drink in my head, till him I can meet.
SECOND SHEPHERD. I will rest in no stead till that I him greet. 470
My brother,
One pledge I will plight:

407 i.e., bound up 413 explanation

456 young sheep

Till I see him in sight,
Shall I never sleep one night
475 Where I do another.

[*As the shepherds approach Mak's cottage, Mak's Wife begins to groan, and Mak sings a tuneless lullaby.*]

THIRD SHEPHERD. Will ye hear how they hack?°
Our sire can croon.
FIRST SHEPHERD. Heard I never none crack so clear out of tune.
Call to him.
SECOND SHEPHERD. Mak, undo your door soon!
MAK. Who is that spake, as it were noon
480 Aloft?
Who is that, I say?
THIRD SHEPHERD. Good fellows, were it day!
MAK. As much as ye can, [*Opens the door.*]
Sirs, speak soft,

485 Over a sick woman's head that is at malaise;
I had rather be dead than she had any disease.
WIFE. Go elsewhere instead. I may not well wheeze;
Each foot that ye tread makes my nose sneeze.
Ah, me!
490 FIRST SHEPHERD. Tell us, Mak, if ye may,
How fare ye, I say?
MAK. But are ye in this town today?
Now how fare ye?

Ye have run in the mire, and are wet yet;
495 I shall make you a fire, if ye will sit.
A nurse would I hire. Think ye on it?
Well paid is my hire—my dream, this is it—
In season. [*Points to the cradle.*]
I have sons, if ye knew,
500 Well more than a few;
But we must drink as we brew,
And that is but reason.

Ere ye go take some food. Me think that ye sweat.
SECOND SHEPHERD. Nay, neither mends our mood, drink nor meat.
505 MAK. Why, sir, is something not good?
THIRD SHEPHERD. Yea, our sheep that we get
Were stolen as they stood. Our loss is great.
MAK. Sirs, drink!
Had I been there,
Some should have felt it full dear.
FIRST SHEPHERD. Marry, some men hold that ye
510 were,

476 split a note

And that's what I think.
SECOND SHEPHERD. Mak, some men propose that it were ye.
THIRD SHEPHERD. Either ye or your spouse, so say We.
MAK. Now, if ye suppose it of Gill or of me—
Come and search our house, and then may ye see 515
Who had it.
If I any sheep got
Either cow or stot°—
And Gill, my wife, rose not
And here she lies yet— 520
As I am true in zeal, to God here I pray
That this be the first meal that I shall eat this day.

[*Points to the cradle.*]

FIRST SHEPHERD. Mak, as have I weal, be careful, I say:
"He learned early to steal who could not say nay."

[*The shepherds begin to search.*]

WIFE. I shake! 525
Out, thieves, from our home.
Ye come to rob us of our own.
MAK. Hear ye not how she groans?
Your hearts should break.

[*The shepherds approach the cradle.*]

WIFE. Off, thieves, from my son. Nigh him not there. 530
MAK. Know ye how she had done, your hearts would have care.
Ye do wrong, I you warn, that thus come before
To a woman that has born—but I say no more.
WIFE. Ah, my middle!
I pray to God so mild, 535
If ever I you beguiled,
May I eat this child
That lies in this cradle.
MAK. Peace, woman, for God's pain, and cry not so.
You injure your brain, and make me great woe. 540
SECOND SHEPHERD. I think our sheep be slain.
What find ye two?
THIRD SHEPHERD. Our work is in vain; we may as well go.
But hatters!°
I can find no meat,
Salt nor sweet, 545
Nothing to eat—
But two bare platters.

518 heifer 543 confound it

Livestock like this, tame or wild, [*Points to cradle.*]
None, as have I bliss, has smelled so vile.
WIFE. No, so God me bliss, and give me joy of my
550 child.
FIRST SHEPHERD. We have gone amiss; I hold us beguiled.
SECOND SHEPHERD. We're done.
Sir—our Lady him save—
Is your child a knave?°
555 MAK. Any lord might him have,
This child, as his son.

When he wakens he grips, such joy it's to see.
THIRD SHEPHERD. May heirs spring from his hips, happy he be.
But who were his gossips° so soon ready?
560 MAK. Blessings on their lips.
FIRST SHEPHERD. [*Aside.*] Hark now, a lie!
MAK. So God them thanks,
Parkin, and Gibbon Waller, I say,
And gentle John Horne, in good play—
He made us all gay—
565 With his great shanks.
SECOND SHEPHERD. Mak, friends will we be, for we are all one.
MAK. We? No, I'm out for me, for help get I none.
Farewell all three. [*Aside.*] I wish they were gone.
THIRD SHEPHERD. Fair words may there be, but love is there none
570 This year.

[*The shepherds leave the cottage.*]

FIRST SHEPHERD. Gave ye the child anything?
SECOND SHEPHERD. I swear not one farthing.
THIRD SHEPHERD. Quickly back will I fling;
Abide ye me here. [*He runs back.*]

575 Mak, take it to no grief if I come to thy son.
MAK. Nay, thou dost me great mischief, and foul hast thou done.
THIRD SHEPHERD. The child will it not grieve, that daystar one?
Mak, with your leave, let me give your son
But sixpence.
580 MAK. Nay, go way! He sleeps.
THIRD SHEPHERD. Methinks he peeps.
MAK. When he wakens he weeps.
I pray you, go hence!

[*The others return.*]

554 boy 559 godparents

THIRD SHEPHERD. Give me leave him to kiss, and lift up the clout.° [*He lifts up the cover.*]
What the devil is this? He has a long snout! 585
FIRST SHEPHERD. He is shapèd amiss. Let's not wait about.
SECOND SHEPHERD. "Ill-spun weft," iwis, "aye comes foul out."°
A son! [*Recognizes the sheep.*]
He is like to our sheep!
THIRD SHEPHERD. How, Gib, may I peep? 590
FIRST SHEPHERD. "How nature will creep
Where it cannot run!"
SECOND SHEPHERD. This was a quaint gaud and a far cast;°
It was a high fraud.
THIRD SHEPHERD. Yea, sirs, was't.
Let's burn this bawd and bind her fast. 595
A false scold hangs at the last;
So shalt thou.
Will ye see how they swaddle
His four feet in the middle?
Saw I never in a cradle 600
A horned lad ere now.
MAK. Peace, bid I. What! Leave off your care!
I am he that begat, and yond woman him bare.
FIRST SHEPHERD. How named is your brat? "Mak?" Lo, God, Mak's heir. 605
SECOND SHEPHERD. Let be all that. Now God curse his fare,
This boy.
WIFE. A pretty child is he
As sits on a woman's knee;
A dillydown, pardie,
To give a man joy. 610
THIRD SHEPHERD. I know him by the ear-mark; that is a good token.
MAK. I tell you, sirs, hark!—his nose was broken.
I was told by a clerk a spell had been spoken.
FIRST SHEPHERD. This is a false work; my vengeance is woken.
Get weapon! 615
WIFE. He was taken by an elf,
I saw it myself;
When the clock struck twelve
Was he misshapen.
SECOND SHEPHERD. Ye two are most deft, but we're not misled. 620

584 cloth 587 "An ill-spun weft," indeed, "comes ever out foul," i.e., the deformity of the parents appears in the offspring. 593 a clever prank and a sly trick

FIRST SHEPHERD. Since they stand by their theft, let's see them both dead.
MAK. If I trespass eft,° strike off my head.
With you will I be left.
THIRD SHEPHERD. Sirs, let them dread:
625 For this trespass
We will neither curse nor fight,
Strike nor smite;
But hold him tight,
And cast him in canvas.

[*They toss Mak in a sheet, and return to the field.*]

FIRST SHEPHERD. Lord, how I am sore, and ready to burst.
630 Faith, I can do no more; therefore will I rest.
SECOND SHEPHERD. As a sheep of seven score Mak weighed in my fist.
For to sleep anywhere me think that I must.
THIRD SHEPHERD. Now I pray you
Lie on grass yonder.
635 FIRST SHEPHERD. On these thieves I still ponder.
THIRD SHEPHERD. Wherefore should ye wonder?
Do as I say.

[*They lie down and fall asleep.*]
An Angel sings "Gloria in excelsis," and then says:

ANGEL. Rise, herdsmen kind, for now is he born
Who shall take from the fiend what from Adam was drawn;
640 That warlock° to rend, this night is he born.
God is made your friend now at this morn.
He requests
To Bethlehem haste
Where lies that Grace
645 In a crib low placed,
Betwixt two beasts.

[*The Angel withdraws.*]

FIRST SHEPHERD. This was the finest voice that ever yet I heard.
It is a marvel to rejoice, thus to be stirred.
SECOND SHEPHERD. Of God's son so bright he spoke the word.
650 All the wood in a light methought that he made
Appear.
THIRD SHEPHERD. He spoke of a bairn
In Bethlehem born.
FIRST SHEPHERD. That betokens yon starn; [*Points to the star.*]
Let us seek him there. 655
SECOND SHEPHERD. Say, what was his song? Heard ye not how he cracked° it,
Three breves to a long?
THIRD SHEPHERD. Yea, marry, he hacked it:
Was no crotchet wrong, nor nothing that lacked it.
FIRST SHEPHERD. For to sing us among, right as he knacked it,
I can. 660
SECOND SHEPHERD. Let see how ye croon!
Can ye bark at the moon?
THIRD SHEPHERD. Hold your tongues! Have done!
FIRST SHEPHERD. Hark after, then.

[*He sings.*]

SECOND SHEPHERD. To Bethl'em he bade that we be gone; 665
I am afraid that we tarry too long.
THIRD SHEPHERD. Be merry and not sad—of mirth is our song.
Now may we be glad and hasten in throng;
Say not nay.
FIRST SHEPHERD. Go we thither quickly, 670
Though we be wet and weary,
To that child and that lady;
We must never delay.

[*He begins to sing again.*]

SECOND SHEPHERD. The olden prophets bid—let be your din—
Isaiah and David and more than I min°— 675
With great learning they said that in a virgin
Should he light and lie, to atone for our sin,
And slake it,
Our kindred, from woe;
Isaiah said so: 680
Ecce virgo
Concipiet° a child that is naked.
THIRD SHEPHERD. Full glad may we be, and abide that day
That Glory to see, whom all things obey.
Lord, well were me, for once and for aye, 685
Might I kneel on my knee, some word for to say
To that child.
But the angel said

622 again 640 devil

655 In the next few lines the shepherds use technical musical terms in describing the Angel's singing: *cracked,* split a note; *Three breves to a long,* three short notes to one long one; *hacked,* split a note; *crotchet,* a quarter note; *knacked,* trilled.
675 remember 681–2 "Behold, a virgin shall conceive." (Isaiah 7:14)

In a crib was he laid;
690 He was poorly arrayed,
So meek and so mild.

FIRST SHEPHERD. Patriarchs that have been, and prophets beforn,
They desired to have seen this child that is born.
They are gone full clean—they were forlorn.
695 We shall see him, I ween,° ere it be morn,
As token.
When I see him and feel,
Then know I full well
It is true as steel
700 That prophets have spoken:
To so poor as we are that he would appear,
Find us, and declare by his messenger.

SECOND SHEPHERD. Go we now, let us fare; the place is us near.

THIRD SHEPHERD. I am ready, I swear; go we with cheer
705 To that joy.
Lord, if thy will be—
We are simple all three—
Now grant us that we
May comfort thy boy.

[*They enter the stable. The First Shepherd kneels.*]

710 FIRST SHEPHERD. Hail, comely and clean! Hail, young child!
Hail maker, as I mean, of a maiden so mild!
Thou hast beaten, I ween, the warlock so wild:
The beguiler of men, now goes he beguiled.
Lo, he merries!
715 Lo, he laughs, my sweeting!
A welcome meeting.
I here give my greeting:
Have a bob° of cherries.

[*The Second Shepherd kneels.*]

SECOND SHEPHERD. Hail, sovereign savior, for thou hast us sought!
720 Hail, noble child, the flower, who all thing has wrought!
Hail, full of favor, that made all of nought!
Hail! I kneel and I cower. A bird have I brought
To my bairn.
Hail, little tiny mop!°
Of our creed thou art crop;° 725
I would drink of thy cup,
Little day-starn.

[*The Third Shepherd kneels.*]

THIRD SHEPHERD. Hail, darling dear, full of Godhead!
I pray thee be near when that I have need!
Hail, sweet is thy cheer! My heart would bleed 730
To see thee sit here in so poor weed,°
With no pennies.
Hail! Put forth thy hand small.
I bring thee but a ball:
Have it and play withal, 735
And go to the tennis.

MARY. The father of heaven, God omnipotent,
That made all in seven, his son has he sent.
My name did he mention; I conceived ere he went.
I fulfilled God's intention through his might, as he meant; 740
And now is he born.
He keep you from woe!
I shall pray him so.
Tell forth as ye go,
And mind you this morn. 745

FIRST SHEPHERD. Farewell, lady, so fair to behold,
With thy child on thy knee.

SECOND SHEPHERD. But he lies full cold.
Lord, well is me. Now we go, thou behold.

THIRD SHEPHERD. Forsooth, already it seems to be told
Full oft. 750

FIRST SHEPHERD. What grace we have found.

SECOND SHEPHERD. Come forth; now are we sound.

THIRD SHEPHERD. To sing are we bound—
Ring it aloft. [*They go out singing.*]

TOPICS FOR DISCUSSION AND WRITING

1. The play presents two scenes of nativity. What details bind the two scenes together? Does the first nativity strike you as blasphemous? Does the second nativity seem to you to be tacked on? The view in the nineteenth century, and until fairly recently in the twentieth, was that in *The Second Shepherds' Play* we have an example of

695 know 718 bunch

724 moppet, babe 725 head 731 clothing

a virtually independent comic secular play (the business of the sheep-stealing), which is made acceptable by attaching it to a brief dramatization of Christ's nativity. The commonest scholarly view today, however, is that the comedy is subservient to the sacred theme. (For instance, some critics insist that the anachronisms—such as calling on Jesus even before the birth of Jesus has been announced—serve, during the comic scenes, to focus the audience's attention on the profound religious meaning.) Do you find either of these views convincing? To what degree? What other view can you offer?

2. Examine the references to music, chiefly song, with an eye toward seeing how music functions in the play.
3. Exactly why do the shepherds return to Mak's house? Taking into account their motive for returning and the outcome of their return visit, at the risk of being a little heavy-handed, what might one say the moral is for this part of the play? How does such a moral fit with the rest of the play?
4. The medieval punishment for stealing sheep was death, but the shepherds punish Mak only by tossing him in a blanket. Why does the play depart from reality in this respect?
5. After Mak is tossed in a blanket, we hear nothing more about him. If you were directing the play, would you have him go off to his house and watch the rest of the play? Or might you have him sleep on the ground, as the other shepherds do, but remain sleeping, unaware of the good tidings that are granted to the other shepherds? Or should he wake with the others and join them on the journey to Bethlehem? Or can you think of some other staging? Explain your preference.

A NOTE ON *The Elizabethan Theater*

The first permanent structure built in England for plays was The Theatre, built outside the city limits of London in 1576 by James Burbage. It soon had several competitors, but little is known about any of these playhouses. The contract for one, The Fortune (built in 1600), survives; it tells us that the three-storied building was square, 80 feet on the outside, 55 feet on the inside. The stage was 43 feet broad and 27½ feet deep. It has been calculated that about 800 people (the *groundlings*) could stand around the three sides of the stage on the ground that was called the *yard*, and another 1500 could be seated in the three galleries. The other chief pieces of evidence concerning the physical nature of the theater are (1) the "De Witt drawing," which is really a copy of a sketch made by a visitor (c. 1596) to The Swan (see illustration, p. 000), and (2) bits of evidence that can be gleaned from the plays themselves, such as "Enter a Fairy at one door, and Robin Goodfellow at another." Conclusions vary and scholarly tempers run high; the following statements are not indisputable.

Most theaters were polygonal or round structures (Shakespeare calls the theater a "wooden O") with three galleries; the yard was open to the sky. From one side a raised stage (or open *platform*) jutted into the middle. A sort of wooden canopy (the *heavens,* or the *shadow*) projected over the stage and in some theaters rested on two pillars; these pillars could conveniently serve as a hiding place for an actor supposed to be unseen by the other characters. At the rear of the stage there sometimes was a curtained alcove or booth, which when uncurtained might represent a room or a cave. The curtain is often called an *arras,* and it was probably behind this curtain that Polonius hid, only to be stabbed. At the rear of the stage (flanking the curtained space?) there were perhaps also two or three doors, through which entrances and exits were made. Probably the *tiring house* ("attiring house," i.e., dressing room) was behind the stage. Above the alcove or booth was an area that could be used for an *upper stage* (for example, in scenes of people standing on a city's walls); flanking the upper stage were windows, one of which may have served Juliet for her misnamed balcony scene. Some scholars argue that in a yet higher place were musicians, and at the very top—called the *top*—was an opening from which an actor could look; in *Henry VI, Part I,* Joan of Arc appears "on the top, thrusting out a torch burning."

Most of the acting was done on the main stage (the platform), but the "inner stage," "upper stage," "windows," and "top" must have been useful occasionally (if they existed). The *cellar* (beneath the stage) was used, for example, for the voice of the ghost in *Hamlet* and for Ophelia's grave. Though some scenery was used, the absence of a front curtain precluded many elaborate scenic effects (much, however, could be done by carrying banners) and encouraged continuous action. The stage that was a battlefield could in an instant, by the introduction of a throne, become a room in a palace. Two readable books are A. M. Nagler, *Shakespeare's Stage,* and C. Walter Hodges, *The Globe Restored.* Nagler (Ch. 12) also gives information about a second kind of Elizabethan theater—basically a platform at one end of a hall—that catered to a courtly group. For a more detailed study, see Andrew Gurr, *The Shakespearean Stage, 1542–1642,* third edition.

Johannes de Witt, a Continental visitor to London, made a drawing of the Swan Theatre in about the year 1596. The original drawing is lost; this is Arend van Buchel's copy of it. (Historical Pictures, Chicago.)

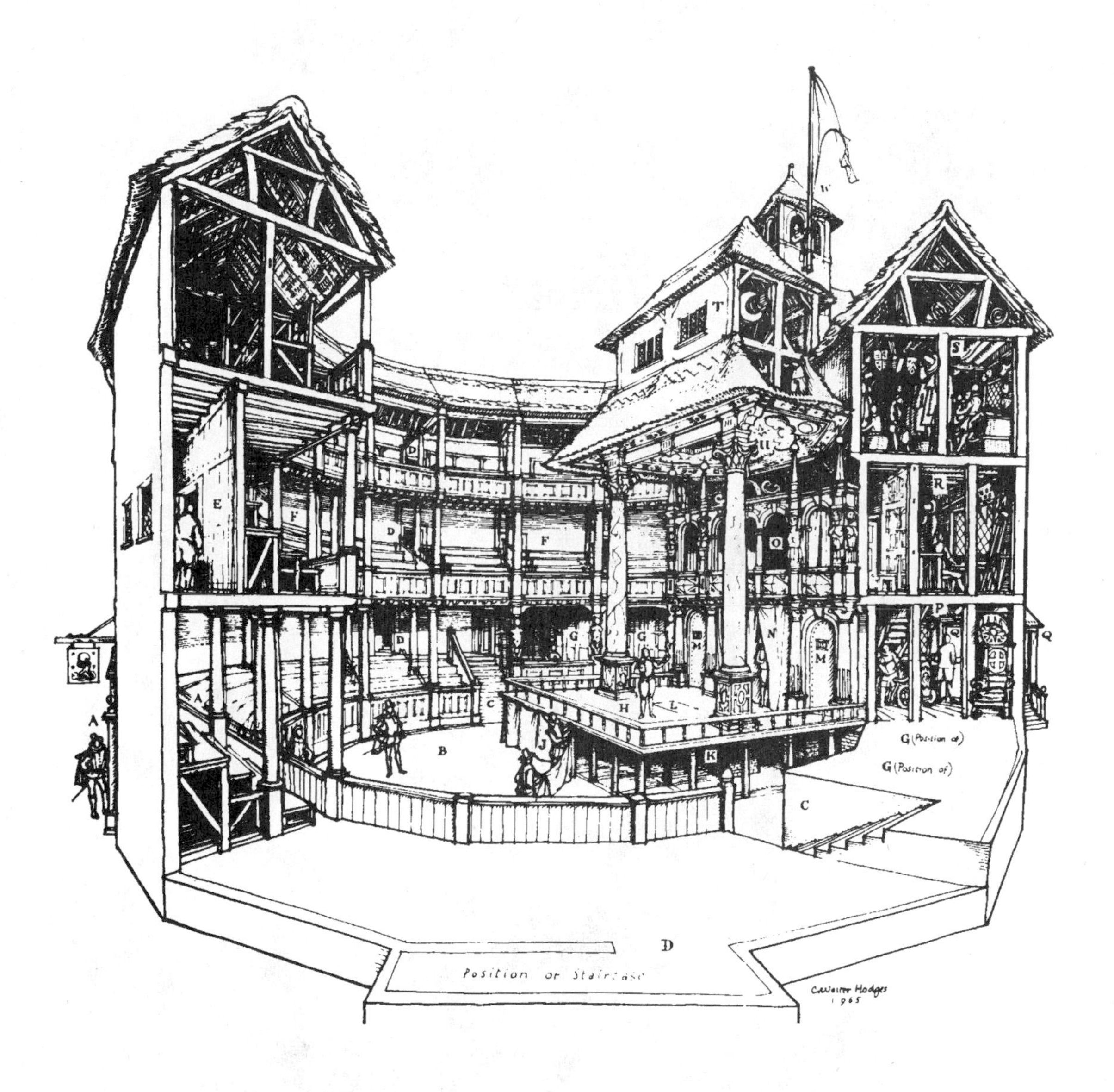

C. Walter Hodges's drawing (1965) of an Elizabethan playhouse.

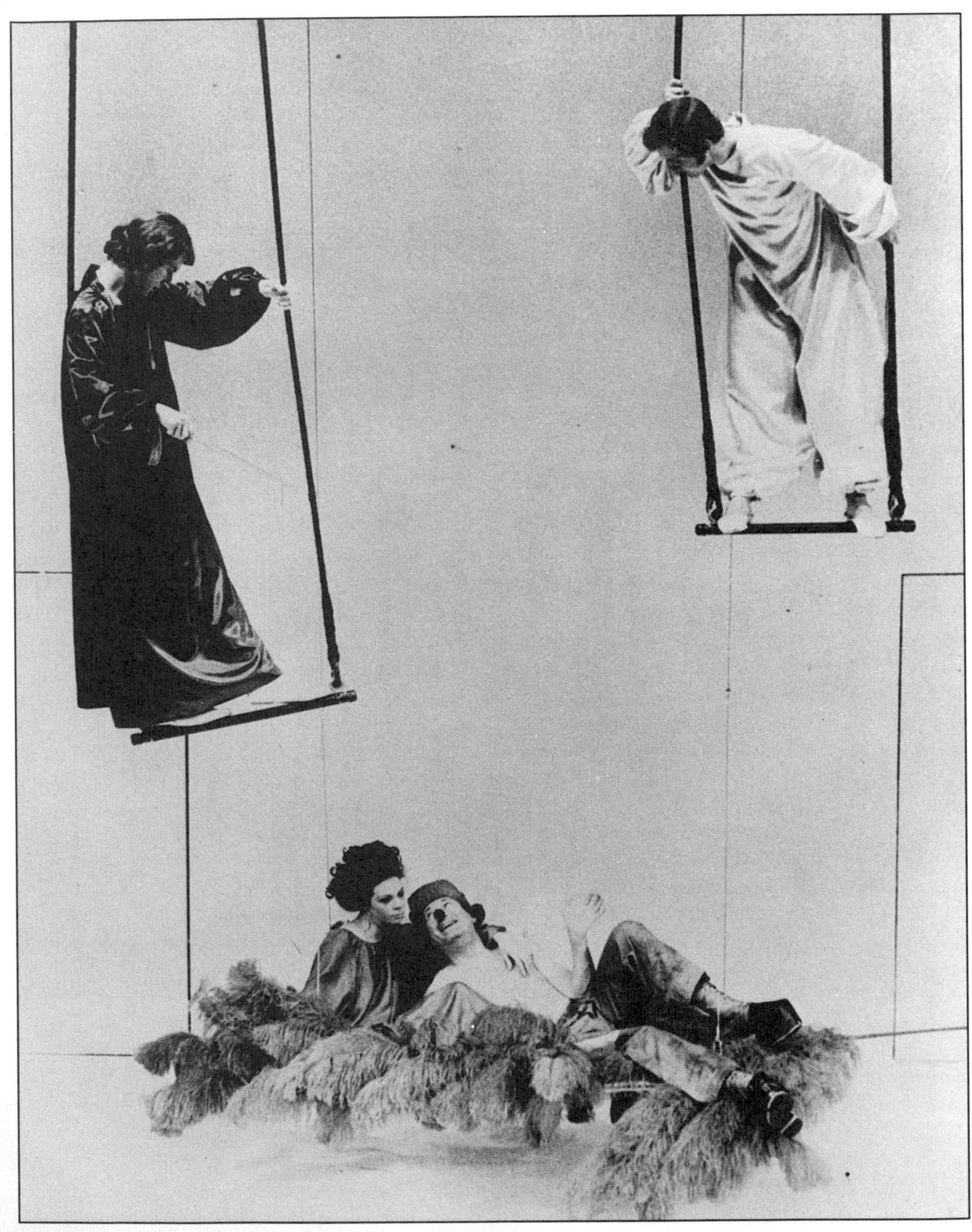

Oberon (Alan Howard), Puck (John Kane), Titania (Sara Kestelman), and Nick Bottom (David Waller) in a 1970 Stratford-upon-Avon production of *A Midsummer Night's Dream* directed by Peter Brook. (Photograph by David Farrell, Shakespeare Centre Library, Stratford-upon-Avon.)

WILLIAM SHAKESPEARE

A Midsummer Night's Dream

Edited by Wolfgang Clemen

William Shakespeare (1564–1616) was born in Stratford, England, of middle-class parents. Nothing of interest is known about his early years, but by 1590 he was acting and writing plays in London. He early worked in all three Elizabethan dramatic genres—tragedy, comedy, and history. *Romeo and Juliet,* for example, was written about 1595, the year of *Richard II,* and in the following year he wrote *A Midsummer Night's Dream.* Other major comedies are *The Merchant of Venice* (1596–97), *As You Like It* (1599–1600), and *Twelfth Night* (1599–1600). His last major works, *The Winter's Tale* (1610–11) and *The Tempest* (1611), are usually called "romances"; these plays have happy endings but they seem more meditative and less joyful than the earlier comedies.

COMMENTARY

Speaking broadly, there are in the Renaissance two comic traditions, which may be called "critical comedy" (or "bitter comedy") and "romantic comedy" (or "sweet comedy"). The former claims, in Hamlet's words, that the "purpose of playing... is to hold, as 'twere, the mirror up to nature; to show virtue her own feature, scorn her own image, and the very age and body of the time his form and pressure." Because it aims to hold a mirror up to the audience, its dramatis personae are usually urban citizens—jealous husbands, foolish merchants, and the like. These are ultimately punished, at times merely by exposure, at times by imprisonment or fines or some such thing. The second kind of comedy, romantic comedy, seeks less to correct than to delight with scenes of pleasant behavior. It does not hold a mirror to the audience: rather, it leads the audience into an elegant dream world where charming gentlefolk live in a timeless world. Thomas Heywood, a playwright contemporary with Shakespeare, briefly set forth the characteristics of both traditions in *An Apology for Actors* (1612). A comedy, he said,

> is pleasantly contrived with merry accidents, and intermixed with apt and witty jests.... and what then is the subject of this harmless mirth? Either in the shape of a clown to show others their slovenly behavior, that they may reform that simplicity in themselves, which others make their sport, ... or to refresh such weary spirits as are tired with labors or study, to moderate the cares and heaviness of the mind, that they may return to their trades and faculties with more zeal and earnestness, after some small soft and pleasant retirement.

When we think of *A Midsummer Night's Dream,* we think not of critical comedy that seeks to reform "slovenly behavior" but of romantic comedy that offers "harmless mirth," "sport," and the refreshing of "such weary spirits as are tired with labors or study." Yet even *A Midsummer Night's Dream* has its touches of critical comedy, its elements that, in Heywood's words, "may reform" by holding up a mirror to unsocial behavior. There is some satire—a little satire of the crabby father, Egeus, and rather more of the young lovers and of the well-meaning rustics who bumblingly stage a play in an effort to please their duke (and to win pensions), but mostly the play is pervaded by genial spirits and a humane vision that make it moral without moralizing. The first book on Shakespeare's morality, Elizabeth Griffith's *The Morality of Shakespeare's Dramas* (1775), rather impatiently dismissed *A Midsummer Night's Dream:* "I shall not trouble my readers with the Fable of this piece, as I can see no general moral that can be deducted from the Argument."

For one thing, all of the people—including the fairies—in *A Midsummer Night's Dream* are basically decent creatures. Egeus is at first irascible, but at the end of the play we hear no more of his insistence that his daughter marry the young man of his choice; Theseus had engaged in youthful indiscretions, but that was long ago and in another country, and now he is the very model of a benevolent ruler; the fairy king and queen bicker, but at the end they are reconciled and they bless the bridal beds of the newlyweds. The rustics, though inept actors and sometimes too impressed by their own theatrical abilities, are men of good intentions. And if in the last act the young aristocratic lovers are a little too confident of their superiority to the rustic actors, we nevertheless feel that they are fundamentally decent; after all, their comments on the performance are more or less in tune with our own.

If *A Midsummer Night's Dream,* then, employs satire only sparingly, what does it do, and what is it about? Perhaps we can get somewhere near to an answer by briefly looking at some of the interrelationships of the stories that make up the intricate plot. There is the story of Theseus and Hippolyta, who will be married in four days; the story of the four young lovers; the story of Bottom and his fellow craftsmen, who are rehearsing a play; and the story of the quarreling fairies. All these stories are related, and eventually come together: the lovers marry on the same day as Theseus and Hippolyta; the craftsmen perform their play at the wedding; the fairies come to witness the wedding and bless it.

One of the play's themes, of course, is love, as shown in the contrasts between the stately love of Theseus and Hippolyta, the changeable romantic love of the four young Athenians, the love of Pyramus and Thisby in the play that the craftsmen are rehearsing, the quarrel between the fairy king and queen, and even Titania's infatuation with Bottom. All these stories play against one another, sometimes very subtly, and sometimes explicitly, as when Lysander, having shifted his affection from Hermia to Helena, says, "Reason says you are the worthier maid" (2.2.116), and Bottom in the next scene accepts Titania's love, saying, "Reason and love keep little company together nowadays" (3.1.146–47). The nature of reason is also implicitly discussed in the play, in the numerous references to "fantasy" and "fancy," or imagination. There is scarcely a scene that does not touch on the matter of the power of the imagination. In the opening scene, for example, Egeus says that Lysander has corrupted Hermia's fantasy (1.1.32), and Duke Theseus tells Hermia that she must perceive her suitors as her father perceives them. The most famous of these references is Theseus's speech on "the lunatic, the lover, and the poet" (5.1.7). In addition to setting the time and place, the images help to define the nature of fantasy: there is an emphasis on night and moonlight during the period of confusion, and then references to the "morning lark," "day," and so on, when Theseus (the spokesman for reason) enters the woods and the lovers are properly paired (4.1.105 ff.). The last scene reintroduces night, and the lovers have moved from the dark wood back to the civilized world of Athens, and the night will bring them to bed. The plot of *A Midsummer Night's Dream*, then, juxtaposes speech against speech, image against image, and scene against scene, telling not simply a story but a story that "grows to something of great constancy, . . . strange and admirable."[1]

WILLIAM SHAKESPEARE *A Midsummer Night's Dream*

[*List of Characters*

THESEUS, *Duke of Athens*
EGEUS, *father to Hermia*
LYSANDER, DEMETRIUS } *in love with Hermia*
PHILOSTRATE, *Master of the Revels to Theseus*
PETER QUINCE, *a carpenter;* PROLOGUE *in the play*
SNUG, *a joiner;* LION *in the play*
NICK BOTTOM, *a weaver;* PYRAMUS *in the play*
FRANCIS FLUTE, *a bellows mender;* THISBY *in the play*
TOM SNOUT, *a tinker;* WALL *in the play*
ROBIN STARVELING, *a tailor;* MOONSHINE *in the play*
HIPPOLYTA, *Queen of the Amazons, betrothed to Theseus*
HERMIA, *daughter to Egeus, in love with Lysander*
HELENA, *in love with Demetrius*
OBERON, *King of the Fairies*
TITANIA, *Queen of the Fairies*
PUCK, *or Robin Goodfellow*
PEASEBLOSSOM, COBWEB, MOTH, MUSTARDSEED } *fairies*
Other FAIRIES *attending their King and Queen*
ATTENDANTS *on Theseus and Hippolyta*

Scene: Athens, and a wood near it.]

[ACT I

SCENE I

The palace of Theseus.]

Enter Theseus, Hippolyta, [*Philostrate,*] *with others.*

THESEUS.
Now, fair Hippolyta, our nuptial hour
Draws on apace. Four happy days bring in
Another moon; but, O, methinks, how slow
This old moon wanes! She lingers°[1] my desires,
Like to a stepdame, or a dowager, 5
Long withering out a young man's revenue.°
HIPPOLYTA.
Four days will quickly steep themselves in night,
Four nights will quickly dream away the time;
And then the moon, like to a silver bow
New-bent in heaven, shall behold the night 10
Of our solemnities.
THESEUS. Go, Philostrate,
Stir up the Athenian youth to merriments,

[1]The degree sign (°) indicates a footnote, which is keyed to the text by line number. Text references are printed in boldface type; the annotation follows in roman type.
I.i.4 **lingers** makes to linger, delays 6 **Long withering out a young man's revenue** diminishing the young man's money (because she must be supported by him)

Awake the pert° and nimble spirit of mirth,
Turn melancholy forth to funerals,
15 The pale companion° is not for our pomp.°
[*Exit Philostrate.*]
Hippolyta, I wooed thee with my sword,°
And won thy love, doing thee injuries;
But I will wed thee in another key,
With pomp, with triumph, and with reveling.

Enter Egeus and his daughter Hermia, and Lysander, and Demetrius.

EGEUS.
20 Happy be Theseus, our renownèd Duke!
THESEUS.
Thanks, good Egeus.° What's the news with thee?
EGEUS.
Full of vexation come I, with complaint
Against my child, my daughter Hermia.
Stand forth, Demetrius. My noble lord,
25 This man hath my consent to marry her.
Stand forth, Lysander. And, my gracious Duke
This man hath bewitched the bosom of my child.
Thou, thou, Lysander, thou hast given her rhymes,
And interchanged love tokens with my child.
30 Thou hast by moonlight at her window sung,
With feigning voice, verses of feigning love,
And stol'n the impression of her fantasy°
With bracelets of thy hair, rings, gauds, conceits,
Knacks,° trifles, nosegays, sweetmeats, messengers
35 Of strong prevailment in unhardened youth.
With cunning hast thou filched my daughter's heart,
Turned her obedience, which is due to me,
To stubborn harshness. And my gracious Duke,
Be it so she will not here before your Grace
40 Consent to marry with Demetrius,
I beg the ancient privilege of Athens:
As she is mine, I may dispose of her,
Which shall be either to this gentleman
Or to her death, according to our law
45 Immediately° provided in that case.
THESEUS.
What say you, Hermia? Be advised, fair maid.
To you your father should be as a god,
One that composed your beauties; yea, and one
To whom you are but as a form in wax
By him imprinted and within his power 50
To leave the figure or disfigure it.
Demetrius is a worthy gentleman.
HERMIA.
So is Lysander.
THESEUS. In himself he is;
But in this kind, wanting your father's voice,°
The other must be held the worthier. 55
HERMIA.
I would my father looked but with my eyes.
THESEUS.
Rather your eyes must with his judgment look.
HERMIA.
I do entreat your Grace to pardon me.
I know not by what power I am made bold,
Nor how it may concern my modesty, 60
In such a presence here to plead my thoughts;
But I beseech your Grace that I may know
The worst that may befall me in this case,
If I refuse to wed Demetrius.
THESEUS.
Either to die the death, or to abjure 65
Forever the society of men.
Therefore, fair Hermia, question your desires;
Know of° your youth, examine well your blood,°
Whether, if you yield not to your father's choice,
You can endure the livery of a nun, 70
For aye to be in shady cloister mewed,°
To live a barren sister all your life,
Chanting faint hymns to the cold fruitless moon.°
Thrice-blessèd they that master so their blood,
To undergo such maiden pilgrimage; 75
But earthlier happy is the rose distilled,°
Than that which, withering on the virgin thorn,
Grows, lives, and dies in single blessedness.
HERMIA.
So will I grow, so live, so die, my lord,
Ere I will yield my virgin patent° up 80
Unto his lordship, whose unwished yoke
My soul consents not to give sovereignty.
THESEUS.
Take time to pause; and, by the next new moon—
The sealing day betwixt my love and me,
For everlasting bond of fellowship— 85

13 **pert** lively 15 **companion** fellow (contemptuous) 15 **pomp** festive procession 16 **I wooed thee with my sword** (Theseus had captured Hippolyta when he conquered the Amazons) 21 **Egeus** (pronounced "E-*gee*-us") 32 **stol'n the impression of her fantasy** fraudulently impressed your image upon her imagination 33–34 **gauds, conceits, Knacks** trinkets, cleverly devised tokens, knick-knacks 45 **Immediately** expressly

54 **But in . . . father's voice** but in this particular respect, lacking your father's approval 68 **Know of** ascertain from 68 **blood** passions 71 **mewed** caged 73 **moon** i.e., Diana, goddess of chastity 76 **distilled** made into perfumes 80 **patent** privilege

Upon that day either prepare to die
For disobedience to your father's will,
Or else to wed Demetrius, as he would,
Or on Diana's altar to protest
90 For aye austerity and single life.

DEMETRIUS.
Relent, sweet Hermia: and Lysander, yield
Thy crazèd title° to my certain right.

LYSANDER.
You have her father's love, Demetrius;
Let me have Hermia's: do you marry him.

EGEUS.
95 Scornful Lysander! True, he hath my love,
And what is mine my love shall render him.
And she is mine, and all my right of her
I do estate unto° Demetrius.

LYSANDER.
I am, my lord, as well derived as he,
100 As well possessed,° my love is more than his;
My fortunes every way as fairly ranked
(If not with vantage°) as Demetrius';
And, which is more than all these boasts can be,
I am beloved of beauteous Hermia.
105 Why should not I then prosecute my right?
Demetrius, I'll avouch it to his head,°
Made love to Nedar's daughter, Helena,
And won her soul; and she, sweet lady, dotes,
Devoutly dotes, dotes in idolatry,
110 Upon this spotted° and inconstant man.

THESEUS.
I must confess that I have heard so much,
And with Demetrius thought to have spoken thereof;
But, being overfull of self-affairs,
My mind did lose it. But, Demetrius, come;
115 And come, Egeus. You shall go with me;
I have some private schooling for you both.
For you, fair Hermia, look you arm yourself
To fit your fancies to your father's will;
Or else the law of Athens yields you up—
120 Which by no means we may extenuate—
To death, or to a vow of single life.
Come, my Hippolyta. What cheer, my love?
Demetrius and Egeus, go along.
I must employ you in some business
125 Against° our nuptial, and confer with you
Of something nearly° that concerns yourselves.

EGEUS.
With duty and desire we follow you

Exeunt [*all but Lysander and Hermia.*]

LYSANDER.
How now, my love! Why is your cheek so pale?
How chance° the roses there do fade so fast?

HERMIA.
Belike° for want of rain, which I could well 130
Beteem° them from the tempest of my eyes.

LYSANDER.
Ay me! For aught that I could ever read,
Could ever hear by tale or history,
The course of true love never did run smooth;
But, either it was different in blood— 135

HERMIA.
O cross! Too high to be enthralled to low!

LYSANDER.
Or else misgraffèd° in respect of years—

HERMIA.
O spite! Too old to be engaged to young!

LYSANDER.
Or else it stood upon the choice of friends—

HERMIA.
O hell! To choose love by another's eyes! 140

LYSANDER.
Or, if there were a sympathy in choice,
War, death, or sickness did lay siege to it,
Making it momentany° as a sound,
Swift as a shadow, short as any dream,
Brief as the lightning in the collied° night, 145
That, in a spleen,° unfolds both heaven and earth,
And ere a man hath power to say "Behold!"
The jaws of darkness do devour it up:
So quick bright things come to confusion.

HERMIA.
If then true lovers have been ever crossed, 150
It stands as an edict in destiny:
Then let us teach our trial patience,°
Because it is a customary cross,
As due to love as thoughts and dreams and sighs,
Wishes and tears, poor Fancy's° followers. 155

LYSANDER.
A good persuasion.° Therefore, hear me, Hermia.
I have a widow aunt, a dowager
Of great revenue, and she hath no child.

92 **crazèd title** flawed claim 98 **estate unto** settle upon 100 **As well possessed** as rich 102 **If not with vantage** if not better 106 **to his head** in his teeth 110 **spotted** i.e., morally stained 125 **Against** in preparation for 126 **nearly** closely

129 **How chance** how does it come that 130 **Belike** perhaps 131 **Beteem** bring forth 137 **misgraffèd** ill matched, misgrafted 143 **momentany** momentary, passing 145 **collied** blackened 146 **spleen** flash 152 **teach our trial patience** teach ourselves to be patient 156 **Fancy's** Love's 156 **persuasion** principle

From Athens is her house remote seven leagues,
160 And she respects me as her only son.
There, gentle Hermia, may I marry thee,
And to that place the sharp Athenian law
Cannot pursue us. If thou lovest me, then,
Steal forth thy father's house tomorrow night;
165 And in the wood, a league without the town,
Where I did meet thee once with Helena,
To do observance to a morn of May,
There will I stay for thee.

HERMIA. My good Lysander!
I swear to thee, by Cupid's strongest bow,
170 By his best arrow with the golden head,°
By the simplicity of Venus' doves,
By that which knitteth souls and prospers loves,
And by that fire which buried the Carthage queen,°
When the false Troyan under sail was seen,
175 By all the vows that ever men have broke,
In number more than ever women spoke,
In that same place thou hast appointed me,
Tomorrow truly will I meet with thee.

LYSANDER.
Keep promise, love. Look, here comes Helena.

Enter Helena.

HERMIA.
180 God speed fair Helena! Whither away?

HELENA.
Call you me fair? That fair again unsay.
Demetrius loves your fair.° O happy fair!
Your eyes are lodestars,° and your tongue's sweet air°
More tunable than lark to shepherd's ear,
185 When wheat is green, when hawthorn buds appear.
Sickness is catching. O, were favor° so,
Yours would I catch, fair Hermia, ere I go;
My ear should catch your voice, my eve your eye,
My tongue should catch your tongue's sweet melody.
190 Were the world mine, Demetrius being bated,°
The rest I'd give to be to you translated.°
O, teach me how you look, and with what art
You sway the motion of Demetrius' heart!

HERMIA.
I frown upon him, yet he loves me still.

HELENA.
195 O that your frowns would teach my smiles such skill!

170 **arrow with the golden head** (Cupid's gold-headed arrows caused love, the leaden ones dislike) 173 **Carthage queen** Dido (who burned herself on a funeral pyre when the Trojan Aeneas left her) 182 **fair** beauty 183 **lodestars** guiding stars 183 **air** music 186 **favor** looks 190 **bated** excepted 191 **translated** transformed

HERMIA.
I give him curses, yet he gives me love.

HELENA.
O that my prayers could such affection move!

HERMIA.
The more I hate, the more he follows me.

HELENA.
The more I love, the more he hateth me.

HERMIA.
200 His folly, Helena, is no fault of mine.

HELENA.
None, but your beauty: would that fault were mine!

HERMIA.
Take comfort. He no more shall see my face;
Lysander and myself will fly this place.
Before the time I did Lysander see,
205 Seemed Athens as a paradise to me.
O, then, what graces in my love do dwell,
That he hath turned a heaven unto a hell!

LYSANDER.
Helen, to you our minds we will unfold.
Tomorrow night, when Phoebe° doth behold
210 Her silver visage in the wat'ry glass,
Decking with liquid pearl the bladed grass,
A time that lovers' flights doth still° conceal,
Through Athens' gates have we devised to steal.

HERMIA.
And in the wood, where often you and I
215 Upon faint primrose beds were wont to lie,
Emptying our bosoms of their counsel sweet,
There my Lysander and myself shall meet,
And thence from Athens turn away our eyes,
To seek new friends and stranger companies.°
220 Farewell, sweet playfellow. Pray thou for us;
And good luck grant thee thy Demetrius!
Keep word, Lysander. We must starve our sight
From lovers' food till tomorrow deep midnight.

LYSANDER.
I will, my Hermia. *Exit Hermia.*
Helena, adieu.
225 As you on him, Demetrius dote on you!
Exit Lysander.

HELENA.
How happy some o'er other some° can be!
Through Athens I am thought as fair as she.
But what of that? Demetrius thinks not so;
He will not know what all but he do know.
230 And as he errs, doting on Hermia's eyes,

209 **Phoebe** the moon 212 **still** always 219 **stranger companies** the company of strangers 226 **some o'er other some** some in comparison with others

So I, admiring of his qualities.
Things base and vile, holding no quantity,°
Love can transpose to form and dignity.
Love looks not with the eyes, but with the mind,
235 And therefore is winged Cupid painted blind.
Nor hath Love's mind of any judgment taste;
Wings, and no eyes, figure° unheedy haste:
And therefore is Love said to be a child,
Because in choice he is so oft beguiled.
240 As waggish boys in game themselves forswear,
So the boy Love is perjured everywhere.
For ere Demetrius looked on Hermia's eyne,°
He hailed down oaths that he was only mine;
And when this hail some heat from Hermia felt,
245 So he dissolved, and show'rs of oaths did melt.
I will go tell him of fair Hermia's flight.
Then to the wood will he tomorrow night
Pursue her; and for this intelligence°
If I have thanks, it is a dear expense:°
250 But herein mean I to enrich my pain,
To have his sight thither and back again.

Exit.

[SCENE II

Quince's house.]

Enter Quince the Carpenter, and Snug the Joiner, and Bottom the Weaver, and Flute the Bellows Mender, and Snout the Tinker, and Starveling the Tailor.°

QUINCE. Is all our company here?

BOTTOM. You were best to call them generally,° man by man, according to the scrip.

QUINCE. Here is the scroll of every man's name, which 5 is thought fit, through all Athens, to play in our interlude° before the Duke and the Duchess, on his wedding day at night.

BOTTOM. First, good Peter Quince, say what the play treats of; then read the names of the actors; and so grow to a 10 point.

232 **holding no quantity** having no proportion (therefore unattractive) 237 **figure** symbolize 242 **eyne** eyes 248 **intelligence** piece of news 249 **dear expense** (1) expense gladly incurred (2) heavy cost (in Demetrius' opinion)
I.ii. s.d. The names of the clowns suggest their trades—**Bottom** skein on which the yarn is wound; **Quince** quines, blocks of wood used for building; **Snug** close-fitting; **Flute** suggesting fluted bellows (for church organs); **Snout** spout of a kettle; **Starveling** an allusion to the proverbial thinness of tailors 2 **generally** (Bottom means "individually") 5 **interlude** dramatic entertainment

QUINCE. Marry,° our play is, "The most lamentable comedy, and most cruel death of Pyramus and Thisby."

BOTTOM. A very good piece of work, I assure you, and a merry. Now, good Peter Quince, call forth your actors by the scroll. Masters, spread yourselves. 15

QUINCE. Answer as I call you. Nick Bottom, the weaver.

BOTTOM. Ready. Name what part I am for, and proceed.

QUINCE. You, Nick Bottom, are set down for Pyramus. 20

BOTTOM. What is Pyramus? A lover, or a tyrant?

QUINCE. A lover that kills himself, most gallant, for love.

BOTTOM. That will ask some tears in the true performing of it: if I do it, let the audience look to their eyes. I will 25 move storms, I will condole° in some measure. To the rest: yet my chief humor° is for a tyrant. I could play Ercles° rarely, or a part to tear a cat in, to make all split.

The raging rocks
And shivering shocks 30
Shall break the locks
Of prison gates;
And Phibbus' car°
Shall shine from afar,
And make and mar 35
The foolish Fates.

This was lofty! Now name the rest of the players. This is Ercles' vein, a tyrant's vein. A lover is more condoling.

QUINCE. Francis Flute, the bellows mender.

FLUTE. Here, Peter Quince. 40

QUINCE. Flute, you must take Thisby on you.

FLUTE. What is Thisby? A wand'ring knight?

QUINCE. It is the lady that Pyramus must love.

FLUTE. Nay, faith, let not me play a woman. I have a beard coming. 45

QUINCE. That's all one.° You shall play it in a mask, and you may speak as small° as you will.

BOTTOM. An° I may hide my face, let me play Thisby too, I'll speak in a monstrous little voice, "Thisne, Thisne!" "Ah Pyramus, my lover dear! Thy Thisby dear, and lady 50 dear!"

QUINCE. No, no; you must play Pyramus: and, Flute, you Thisby.

BOTTOM. Well, proceed.

11 **Marry** (an interjection, originally an oath, "By the Virgin Mary") 26 **condole** lament 27 **humor** disposition 27 **Ercles** Hercules (a part notorious for ranting) 33 **Phibbus' car** (mispronunciation for "Phoebus' car," or chariot, i.e., the sun) 46 **That's all one** it makes no difference 47 **small** softly 48 **An** if

55 QUINCE. Robin Starveling, the tailor.
STARVELING. Here, Peter Quince.
QUINCE. Robin Starveling, you must play Thisby's mother. Tom Snout, the tinker.
SNOUT. Here, Peter Quince.
60 QUINCE. You, Pyramus' father: myself, Thisby's father: Snug, the joiner; you, the lion's part. And I hope here is a play fitted.
SNUG. Have you the lion's part written? Pray you, if it be, give it me, for I am slow of study.
65 QUINCE. You may do it extempore, for it is nothing but roaring.
BOTTOM. Let me play the lion too. I will roar that° I will do any man's heart good to hear me. I will roar, that I will make the Duke say, "Let him roar again, let him roar
70 again."
QUINCE. An you should do it too terribly, you would fright the Duchess and the ladies, that they would shriek; and that were enough to hang us all.
ALL. That would hang us, every mother's son.
75 BOTTOM. I grant you, friends, if you should fright the ladies out of their wits, they would have no more discretion but to hang us: but I will aggravate° my voice so that I will roar you as gently as any sucking dove; I will roar you an 'twere° any nightingale.
80 QUINCE. You can play no part but Pyramus; for Pyramus is a sweet-faced man; a proper° man as one shall see in a summer's day; a most lovely, gentlemanlike man: therefore you must needs play Pyramus.
BOTTOM. Well, I will undertake it. What beard were I
85 best to play it in?
QUINCE. Why, what you will.
BOTTOM. I will discharge it in either your straw-color beard, your orange-tawny beard, your purple-in-grain° beard, or your French-crown-color° beard, your perfit° yel-
90 low.
QUINCE. Some of your French crowns° have no hair at all, and then you will play barefaced.° But, masters, here are your parts; and I am to entreat you, request you, and desire you, to con° them by tomorrow night; and meet me in the
95 palace wood, a mile without the town, by moonlight. There will we rehearse, for if we meet in the city, we shall be dogged with company, and our devices° known. In the meantime I will draw a bill of properties,° such as our play wants. I pray you, fail me not.
BOTTOM. We will meet; and there we may rehearse 100 most obscenely° and courageously. Take pains; be perfit; adieu.
QUINCE. At the Duke's Oak we meet.
BOTTOM. Enough; hold or cut bowstrings.°

Exeunt.

67 **that** so that 77 **aggravate** (Bottom means "moderate") 79 **an 'twere** as if it were 81 **proper** handsome 88 **purple-in-grain** dyed with a fast purple 89 **French-crown-color** color of French gold coin 89 **perfit** perfect 91 **crowns** (1)gold coins (2) heads bald from the French disease (syphilis) 92 **barefaced** (1) bald (2) brazen 94 **con** study 97 **devices** plans

98 **bill of properties** list of stage furnishings 101 **obscenely** (Bottom means "seemly") 104 **hold or cut bowstrings** i.e., keep your word or give it up (?)

[ACT II

SCENE I

A wood near Athens.]

Enter a Fairy at one door, and Robin Goodfellow [*Puck*] *at another.*

PUCK.
How now, spirit! Whither wander you?
FAIRY.
Over Hill, over dale,
Thorough bush, thorough brier,
Over park, over pale.°
Thorough flood, thorough fire, 5
I do wander everywhere,
Swifter than the moon's sphere;°
And I serve the Fairy Queen,
To dew her orbs° upon the green.
The cowslips tall her pensioners° be: 10
In their gold coats spots you see;
Those be rubies, fairy favors,
In this freckles live their savors.°
I must go seek some dewdrops here,
And hang a pearl in every cowslip's ear. 15
Farewell, thou lob° of spirits; I'll be gone.
Our Queen and all her elves come here anon.
PUCK.
The King doth keep his revels here tonight.
Take heed the Queen come not within his sight.
For Oberon is passing fell and wrath,° 20

II.i.4 **pale** enclosed land, park 7 **moon's sphere** (according to the Ptolemaic system the moon was fixed in a hollow sphere that surrounded and revolved about the earth) 9 **orbs** fairy rings, i.e., circles of darker grass 10 **pensioners** bodyguards (referring to Elizabeth I's bodyguard of fifty splendid young noblemen) 12 **favors** gifts 13 **savors** perfumes 16 **lob** lubber, clumsy fellow 20 **passing fell and wrath** very fierce and angry

Because that she as her attendant hath
A lovely boy, stolen from an Indian king;
She never had so sweet a changeling.°
And jealous Oberon would have the child
25 Knight of his train, to trace° the forests wild.
But she perforce withholds the lovèd boy,
Crowns him with flowers, and makes him all her joy.
And now they never meet in grove or green,
By fountain clear, or spangled starlight sheen,°
30 But they do square,° that all their elves for fear
Creep into acorn clips and hide them there.

FAIRY.
Either I mistake your shape and making quite,
Or else you are that shrewd and knavish sprite
Called Robin Goodfellow. Are not you he
35 That frights the maidens of the villagery,°
Skim milk, and sometimes labor in the quern,°
And bootless° make the breathless housewife churn,
And sometime make the drink to bear no barm,°
Mislead night wanderers, laughing at their harm?
40 Those that Hobgoblin call you, and sweet Puck,
You do their work, and they shall have good luck.
Are not you he?

PUCK. Thou speakest aright;
I am that merry wanderer of the night.
I jest to Oberon, and make him smile,
45 When I a fat and bean-fed horse beguile,
Neighing in likeness of a filly foal:
And sometime lurk I in a gossip's° bowl,
In very likeness of a roasted crab;°
And when she drinks, against her lips I bob
50 And on her withered dewlap° pour the ale.
The wisest aunt, telling the saddest° tale,
Sometime for three-foot stool mistaketh me;
Then slip I from her bum, down topples she,
And "tailor"° cries, and falls into a cough;
55 And then the whole quire° hold their hips and laugh,
And waxen° in their mirth, and neeze,° and swear
A merrier hour was never wasted° there.
But, room, fairy! Here comes Oberon.

FAIRY.
And here my mistress. Would that he were gone!

Enter [Oberon,] the King of Fairies, at one door, with his train; and [Titania,] the Queen, at another, with hers.

OBERON.
Ill met by moonlight, proud Titania. 60

TITANIA.
What, jealous Oberon! Fairy, skip hence.
I have forsworn his bed and company.

OBERON.
Tarry, rash wanton;° am not I thy lord?

TITANIA.
Then I must be thy lady: but I know
When thou hast stolen away from fairy land 65
And in the shape of Corin° sat all day,
Playing on pipes of corn,° and versing love
To amorous Phillida. Why art thou here,
Come from the farthest steep of India?
But that, forsooth, the bouncing° Amazon, 70
Your buskined° mistress and your warrior love,
To Theseus must be wedded, and you come
To give their bed joy and prosperity.

OBERON.
How canst thou thus for shame, Titania,
Glance at my credit with Hippolyta, 75
Knowing I know thy love to Theseus?
Didst not thou lead him through the glimmering night
From Perigenia, whom he ravishèd?
And make him with fair Aegles break his faith,
With Ariadne and Antiopa?° 80

TITANIA.
These are the forgeries of jealousy:
And never, since the middle summer's spring,°
Met we on hill, in dale, forest, or mead,
By pavèd° fountain or by rushy brook,
Or in the beachèd margent° of the sea, 85
To dance our ringlets to the whistling wind,
But with thy brawls thou hast disturbed our sport.
Therefore the winds, piping to us in vain,
As in revenge, have sucked up from the sea
Contagious° fogs; which, falling in the land, 90

23 **changeling** usually a child left behind by fairies in exchange for one stolen, but here applied to the stolen child 25 **trace** traverse 29 **starlight sheen** brightly shining starlight 30 **square** clash, quarrel 35 **villagery** villagers 36 **quern** hand mill for grinding grain 37 **bootless** in vain 38 **barm** yeast, froth 47 **gossip's** old woman's 48 **crab** crab apple 50 **dewlap** fold of skin on the throat 51 **saddest** most serious 54 **tailor** (suggesting the posture of a tailor squatting; or a term of abuse: Middle English *taillard,* "thief") 55 **quire** company, choir 56 **waxen** increase 56 **neeze** sneeze 57 **wasted** passed

63 **rash wanton** hasty willful creature 66 **Corin** (like *Phillida,* line 68, a traditional name for a lover in pastoral poetry) 67 **pipes of corn** musical instruments made of grain stalks 70 **bouncing** swaggering 71 **buskined** wearing a hunter's boot (buskin) 78–80 **Perigenia, Aegles, Ariadne, Antiopa** (girls Theseus loved and deserted) 82 **middle summer's spring** beginning of midsummer 84 **pavèd** i.e., with pebbly bottom 85 **margent** margin, shore 90 **contagious** generating pestilence

Hath every pelting° river made so proud,
That they have overborne their continents.°
The ox hath therefore stretched his yoke in vain,
The plowman lost his sweat, and the green corn°
95 Hath rotted ere his youth attained a beard;
The fold stands empty in the drownèd field,
And crows are fatted with the murrion flock;°
The nine men's morris° is filled up with mud;
And the quaint mazes° in the wanton green,°
100 For lack of tread, are undistinguishable.
The human mortals want their winter here;
No night is now with hymn or carol blest.
Therefore the moon, the governess of floods,
Pale in her anger, washes all the air,
105 That rheumatic diseases do abound.
And thorough this distemperature° we see
The seasons alter: hoary-headed frosts
Fall in the fresh lap of the crimson rose,
And on old Hiems' ° thin and icy crown
110 An odorous chaplet° of sweet summer buds
Is, as in mockery, set. The spring, the summer,
The childing° autumn, angry winter, change
Their wonted liveries;° and the mazèd° world,
By their increase, now knows not which is which.
115 And this same progeny of evils comes
From our debate,° from our dissension;
We are their parents and original.

OBERON.
Do you amend it, then; it lies in you:
Why should Titania cross her Oberon?
120 I do but beg a little changeling boy,
To be my henchman.°

TITANIA. Set your heart at rest.
The fairy land buys not° the child of me.
His mother was a vot'ress° of my order,
And, in the spicèd Indian air, by night,
125 Full often hath she gossiped by my side,
And sat with me on Neptune's yellow sands,
Marking th' embarkèd traders on the flood;
When we have laughed to see the sails conceive
And grow big-bellied with the wanton wind;
Which she, with pretty and with swimming gait 130
Following—her womb then rich with my young squire—
Would imitate, and sail upon the land,
To fetch me trifles, and return again,
As from a voyage, rich with merchandise.
But she, being mortal, of that boy did die; 135
And for her sake do I rear up her boy,
And for her sake I will not part with him.

OBERON.
How long within this wood intend you stay?

TITANIA.
Perchance till after Theseus' wedding day.
If you will patiently dance in our round,° 140
And see our moonlight revels, go with us.
If not, shun me, and I will spare° your haunts.

OBERON.
Give me that boy, and I will go with thee.

TITANIA.
Not for thy fairy kingdom. Fairies, away!
We shall chide downright, if I longer stay. 145
Exeunt [*Titania with her train*].

OBERON.
Well, go thy way. Thou shalt not from this grove
Till I torment thee for this injury.
My gentle Puck, come hither. Thou remembʼrest
Since° once I sat upon a promontory,
And heard a mermaid, on a dolphin's back, 150
Uttering such dulcet and harmonious breath,
That the rude sea grew civil° at her song,
And certain stars shot madly from their spheres,
To hear the sea maid's music.

PUCK. I remember.

OBERON.
That very time I saw, but thou couldst not, 155
Flying between the cold moon and the earth,
Cupid all armed. A certain aim he took
At a fair vestal° thronèd by the west,
And loosed his love shaft smartly from his bow,
As it should° pierce a hundred thousand hearts. 160
But I might° see young Cupid's fiery shaft
Quenched in the chaste beams of the wat'ry moon,
And the imperial vot'ress passèd on,
In maiden meditation, fancy-free.°

91 **pelting** petty 92 **continents** containers (i.e.. banks) 94 **corn** grain 97 **murrion flock** flock dead of cattle disease (murrain) 98 **nine men's morris** square cut in the turf (for a game in which each player has nine counters or "men") 99 **quaint mazes** intricate meandering paths on the grass (kept fresh by running along them) 99 **wanton green** grass growing without check 106 **distemperature** disturbance in nature 109 **old Hiems'** the winter's 110 **chaplet** wreath 113 **childing** breeding, fruitful 113 **wonted liveries** accustomed apparel 113 **mazèd** bewildered 116 **debate** quarrel 121 **henchman** page 122 **The fairy land buys not** i.e., even your whole domain could not buy 123 **vot'ress** woman who has taken a vow

140 **round** circular dance 142 **spare** keep away from 149 **Since** when 152 **civil** well behaved 158 **vestal** virgin (possibly an allusion to Elizabeth, the Virgin Queen) 160 **As it should** as if it would 161 **might** could 164 **fancy-free** free from the power of love

165 Yet marked I where the bolt of Cupid fell.
It fell upon a little western flower,
Before milk-white, now purple with love's wound,
And maidens call it love-in-idleness.°
Fetch me that flow'r; the herb I showed thee once:
170 The juice of it on sleeping eyelids laid
Will make or man or woman° madly dote
Upon the next live creature that it sees.
Fetch me this herb, and be thou here again
Ere the leviathan° can swim a league.

PUCK.
175 I'll put a girdle round about the earth
In forty minutes. [*Exit.*]

OBERON. Having once this juice,
I'll watch Titania when she is asleep,
And drop the liquor of it in her eyes.
The next thing then she waking looks upon,
180 Be it on lion, bear, or wolf, or bull,
On meddling monkey, or on busy° ape,
She shall pursue it with the soul of love.
And ere I take this charm from off her sight,
As I can take it with another herb,
185 I'll make her render up her page to me.
But who comes here? I am invisible,
And I will overhear their conference.

Enter Demetrius, Helena following him.

DEMETRIUS.
I love thee not, therefore pursue me not.
Where is Lysander and fair Hermia?
190 The one I'll slay, the other slayeth me.
Thou told'st me they were stol'n unto this wood;
And here am I, and wood° within this wood,
Because I cannot meet my Hermia.
Hence, get thee gone, and follow me no more!

HELENA.
195 You draw me, you hardhearted adamant;°
But yet you draw not iron, for my heart
Is true as steel. Leave you your power to draw,
And I shall have no power to follow you.

DEMETRIUS.
Do I entice you? Do I speak you fair?°
200 Or, rather, do I not in plainest truth
Tell you, I do not nor I cannot love you?

HELENA.
And even for that do I love you the more.
I am your spaniel; and, Demetrius,
The more you beat me, I will fawn on you.
Use me but as your spaniel, spurn me, strike me, 205
Neglect me, lose me; only give me leave,
Unworthy as I am, to follow you.
What worser place can I beg in your love—
And yet a place of high respect with me—
Than to be usèd as you use your dog? 210

DEMETRIUS.
Tempt not too much the hatred of my spirit,
For I am sick when I do look on thee.

HELENA.
And I am sick when I look not on you.

DEMETRIUS.
You do impeach° your modesty too much,
To leave the city, and commit yourself 215
Into the hands of one that loves you not,
To trust the opportunity of night
And the ill counsel of a desert° place
With the rich worth of your virginity.

HELENA.
Your virtue is my privilege.° For that 220
It is not night when I do see your face,
Therefore I think I am not in the night;
Nor doth this wood lack worlds of company,
For you in my respect° are all the world.
Then how can it be said I am alone 225
When all the world is here to look on me?

DEMETRIUS.
I'll run from thee and hide me in the brakes,°
And leave thee to the mercy of wild beasts.

HELENA.
The wildest hath not such a heart as you.
Run when you will, the story shall be changed: 230
Apollo flies, and Daphne° holds the chase;
The dove pursues the griffin;° the mild hind°
Makes speed to catch the tiger; bootless speed,
When cowardice pursues, and valor flies.

DEMETRIUS.
I will not stay° thy questions. Let me go! 235
Or, if thou follow me, do not believe
But I shall do thee mischief in the wood.

168 **love-in-idleness** pansy 171 **or man or woman** either man or woman 174 **leviathan** sea monster, whale 181 **busy** meddlesome 192 **wood** out of my mind (with perhaps an additional pun on "wooed") 195 **adamant** (1) very hard gem (2) loadstone, magnet 199 **speak you fair** speak kindly to you

214 **impeach** expose to reproach 218 **desert** deserted, uninhabited 220 **Your virtue is my privilege** your inherent power is my warrant 224 **in my respect** in my opinion 227 **brakes** thickets 231 **Daphne** a nymph who fled from Apollo (at her prayer she was changed into a laurel tree) 232 **griffin** fabulous monster with an eagle's head and a lion's body 232 **hind** doe 235 **stay** wait for

HELENA.
Ay, in the temple, in the town, the field,
You do me mischief. Fie, Demetrius!
240 Your wrongs do set a scandal on my sex.
We cannot fight for love, as men may do;
We should be wooed, and were not made to woo.
[*Exit Demetrius.*]
I'll follow thee, and make a heaven of hell,
To die upon° the hand I love so well.
[*Exit.*]

OBERON.
245 Fare thee well, nymph: ere he do leave this grove,
Thou shalt fly him, and he shall seek thy love.

Enter Puck.

Hast thou the flower there? Welcome, wanderer.
PUCK.
Ay, there it is.
OBERON. I pray thee, give it me.
I know a bank where the wild thyme blows,
250 Where oxlips and the nodding violet grows,
Quite overcanopied with luscious woodbine,
With sweet musk roses, and with eglantine.
There sleeps Titania sometime of the night,
Lulled in these flowers with dances and delight;
255 And there the snake throws° her enameled skin,
Weed° wide enough to wrap a fairy in.
And with the juice of this I'll streak her eyes,
And make her full of hateful fantasies.
Take thou some of it, and seek through this grove.
260 A sweet Athenian lady is in love
With a disdainful youth. Anoint his eyes;
But do it when the next thing he espies
May be the lady. Thou shalt know the man
By the Athenian garments he hath on.
265 Effect it with some care that he may prove
More fond on her° than she upon her love:
And look thou meet me ere the first cock crow.
PUCK.
Fear not, my lord, your servant shall do so.
Exeunt.

[SCENE II

Another part of the wood.]

Enter Titania, Queen of Fairies, with her train.

TITANIA.
Come, now a roundel° and a fairy song;
Then, for the third part of a minute, hence;
Some to kill cankers in the musk-rose buds,
Some war with reremice° for their leathern wings
To make my small elves coats, and some keep back 5
The clamorous owl, that nightly boots and wonders
At our quaint° spirits. Sing me now asleep.
Then to your offices, and let me rest.

Fairies sing.

1ST FAIRY.
You spotted snakes with double tongue,
Thorny hedgehogs, be not seen; 10
Newts and blindworms,° do no wrong,
Come not near our Fairy Queen.

CHORUS.
Philomele,° with melody
Sing in our sweet lullaby;
Lulla, lulla, lullaby, lulla, lulla, lullaby: 15
Never harm
Nor spell nor charm,
Come our lovely lady nigh;
So, good night, with lullaby.

1ST FAIRY.
Weaving spiders, come not here; 20
Hence, you long-legged spinners, hence!
Beetles black, approach not near;
Worm nor snail, do no offense.

CHORUS.
Philomele, with melody, &c.

2ND FAIRY.
Hence, away! Now all is well. 25
One aloof stand sentinel.
[*Exeunt Fairies. Titania sleeps.*]

Enter Oberon [*and squeezes the flower on Titania's eyelids*].

OBERON.
What thou seest when thou dost wake,
Do it for thy truelove take;
Love and languish for his sake.
Be it ounce,° or cat, or bear, 30
Pard,° or boar with bristled hair,
In thy eye that shall appear
When thou wak'st, it is thy dear.
Wake when some vile thing is near. [*Exit.*]

244 **To die upon** dying by 255 **throws** casts off 256 **Weed** garment 266 **fond on her** foolishly in love with her
II.ii.1 **roundel** dance in a ring

4 **reremice** bats 7 **quaint** dainty 11 **blindworms** small snakes 13 **Philomele** nightingale 30 **ounce** lynx
31 **Pard** leopard

Enter Lysander and Hermia.

LYSANDER.
35 Fair love, you faint with wand'ring in the wood;
And to speak troth,° I have forgot our way.
We'll rest us, Hermia, if you think it good,
And tarry for the comfort of the day.
HERMIA.
Be't so, Lysander. Find you out a bed;
40 For I upon this bank will rest my head.
LYSANDER.
One turf shall serve as pillow for us both,
One heart, one bed, two bosoms, and one troth.
HERMIA.
Nay, good Lysander. For my sake, my dear,
Lie further off yet, do not lie so near.
LYSANDER.
45 O, take the sense,° sweet, of my innocence!
Love takes the meaning° in love's conference.
I mean, that my heart unto yours is knit,
So that but one heart we can make of it:
Two bosoms interchainèd with an oath;
50 So then two bosoms and a single troth.°
Then by your side no bed-room me deny,
For lying so, Hermia, I do not lie.°
HERMIA.
Lysander riddles very prettily.
Now much beshrew° my manners and my pride,
55 If Hermia meant to say Lysander lied.
But, gentle friend, for love and courtesy
Lie further off, in human modesty.
Such separation as may well be said
Becomes a virtuous bachelor and a maid,
60 So far be distant; and, good night, sweet friend.
Thy love ne'er alter till thy sweet life end!
LYSANDER.
Amen, amen, to that fair prayer, say I,
And then end life when I end loyalty!
Here is my bed. Sleep give thee all his rest!
HERMIA.
65 With half that wish the wisher's eyes be pressed!
[*They sleep.*]

Enter Puck.

PUCK.
Through the forest have I gone,
But Athenian found I none,
On whose eyes I might approve°
This flower's force in stirring love.
Night and silence.—Who is here? 70
Weeds° of Athens he doth wear:
This is he, my master said,
Despisèd the Athenian maid;
And here the maiden, sleeping sound,
On the dank and dirty ground. 75
Pretty soul! She durst not lie
Near this lack-love, this kill-courtesy.
Churl,° upon thy eyes I throw
All the power this charm doth owe.°
When thou wak'st, let love forbid 80
Sleep his seat on thy eyelid.
So awake when I am gone.
For I must now to Oberon.
Exit.

Enter Demetrius and Helena, running.

HELENA.
Stay, though thou kill me, sweet Demetrius.
DEMETRIUS.
I charge thee, hence, and do not haunt me thus. 85
HELENA.
O, wilt thou darkling° leave me? Do not so.
DEMETRIUS.
Stay, on thy peril! I alone will go.
[*Exit.*]
HELENA.
O, I am out of breath in this fond° chase!
The more my prayer, the lesser is my grace.
Happy is Hermia, wheresoe'er she lies, 90
For she hath blessèd and attractive eyes.
How came her eyes so bright? Not with salt tears.
If so, my eyes are oft'ner washed than hers.
No, no, I am as ugly as a bear,
For beasts that meet me run away for fear. 95
Therefore no marvel though Demetrius
Do, as a monster, fly my presence thus.
What wicked and dissembling glass of mine
Made me compare with Hermia's sphery eyne?°
But who is here? Lysander! on the ground! 100
Dead? Or asleep? I see no blood, no wound.
Lysander, if you live, good sir, awake.
LYSANDER [*awaking*].
And run through fire I will for thy sweet sake.
Transparent° Helena! Nature shows art,

36 **troth** truth 45 **take the sense** understand the true meaning 46 **Love takes the meaning** lovers understand the true meaning of what they say to each other 50 **troth** faithful love 52 **lie** be untrue 54 **beshrew** curse (but commonly, as here, in a light sense)

68 **approve** try 71 **Weeds** garments 78 **Churl** boorish fellow 79 **owe** possess 86 **darkling** in the dark 88 **fond** (1) doting (2) foolish 99 **sphery eyne** starry eyes 104 **Transparent** bright

105 That through thy bosom makes me see thy heart.
Where is Demetrius? O, how fit a word
Is that vile name to perish on my sword!

HELENA.
Do not say so, Lysander, say not so.
What though he love your Hermia? Lord, what though?
110 Yet Hermia still loves you. Then be content.

LYSANDER.
Content with Hermia! No; I do repent
The tedious minutes I with her have spent.
Not Hermia but Helena I love:
Who will not change a raven for a dove?
115 The will° of man is by his reason swayed
And reason says you are the worthier maid.
Things growing are not ripe until their season:
So I, being young, till now ripe not° to reason.
And touching now the point of human skill,°
120 Reason becomes the marshal to my will,
And leads me to your eyes, where I o'erlook
Love's stories, written in love's richest book.

HELENA.
Wherefore was I to this keen mockery born?
When at your hands did I deserve this scorn?
125 Is't not enough, is't not enough, young man,
That I did never, no, nor ever call,
Deserve a sweet look from Demetrius' eye,
But you must flout° my insufficiency?
Good troth,° you do me wrong, good sooth, you do,
130 In such disdainful manner me to woo.
But fare you well. Perforce I must confess
I thought you lord of more true gentleness.°
O, that a lady, of one man refused,
Should of another therefore be abused!

Exit.

LYSANDER.
135 She sees not Hermia. Hermia, sleep thou there,
And never mayst thou come Lysander near!
For as a surfeit of the sweetest things
The deepest loathing to the stomach brings,
Or as the heresies that men do leave
140 Are hated most of those they did deceive,
So thou, my surfeit and my heresy,
Of all be hated, but the most of me!
And, all my powers, address° your love and might
To honor Helen and to be her knight!

Exit.

HERMIA [*awaking*].
Help me, Lysander, help me! Do thy best 145
To pluck this crawling serpent from my breast!
Ay me, for pity! What a dream was here!
Lysander, look how I do quake with fear.
Methought a serpent eat° my heart away,
And you sat smiling at his cruel prey.° 150
Lysander! What, removed? Lysander! Lord!
What, out of hearing? Gone? No sound, no word?
Alack, where are you? Speak, an if° you hear;
Speak, of° all loves! I swoon almost with fear.
No? Then I well perceive you are not nigh. 155
Either death or you I'll find immediately.

Exit.

[ACT III

SCENE I

The wood. Titania lying asleep.

Enter the clowns: [*Quince, Snug, Bottom, Flute, Snout, and Starveling*].

BOTTOM. Are we all met?

QUINCE. Pat,° pat; and here's a marvail's° convenient place for our rehearsal. This green plot shall be our stage, this hawthorn brake° our tiring house,° and we will do it in action as we will do it before the Duke. 5

BOTTOM. Peter Quince?

QUINCE. What sayest thou, bully° Bottom?

BOTTOM. There are things in this comedy of Pyramus and Thisby that will never please. First, Pyramus must draw a sword to kill himself; which the ladies cannot abide. How 10 answer you that?

SNOUT: By'r lakin,° a parlous° fear.

STARVELING. I believe we must leave the killing out, when all is done.

BOTTOM. Not a whit. I have a device to make all well. 15 Write me a prologue, and let the prologue seem to say, we will do no harm with our swords, and that Pyramus is not killed indeed; and, for the more better assurance, tell them that I Pyramus am not Pyramus, but Bottom the weaver. This will put them out of fear. 20

115 **will** desire 118 **ripe not** have not ripened 119 **touching now . . . human skill** now reaching the fullness of human reason 128 **flout** jeer at 129 **Good troth** indeed (an expletive, like "good sooth") 132 **gentleness** noble character 143 **address** apply

149 **eat** ate (pronounced "et") 150 **prey** act of preying 153 **an if** if 154 **of** for the sake of
III.i.2 **Pat** exactly, on the dot 2 **marvail's** (Quince means "marvelous") 4 **brake** thicket 4 **tiring house** attiring house, dressing room 7 **bully** good fellow 12 **By'r lakin** by our lady (ladykin = little lady) 12 **parlous** perilous, terrible

QUINCE. Well, we will have such a prologue, and it shall be written in eight and six.°

BOTTOM. No, make it two more; let it be written in eight and eight.

25 SNOUT. Will not the ladies be afeared of the lion?

STARVELING. I fear it, I promise you.

BOTTOM. Masters, you ought to consider with yourselves. To bring in—God shield us!—a lion among ladies, is a most dreadful thing. For there is not a more fearful wild 30 fowl than your lion living; and we ought to look to't.

SNOUT. Therefore another prologue must tell he is not a lion.

BOTTOM. Nay, you must name his name, and half his face must be seen through the lion's neck, and he himself 35 must speak through, saying thus, or to the same defect—"Ladies"—or, "Fair ladies—I would wish you"—or, "I would request you"—or, "I would entreat you—not to fear, not to tremble: my life for yours. If you think I come hither as a lion, it were pity of my life.° No, I am no such thing. I 40 am a man as other men are." And there indeed let him name his name, and tell them plainly, he is Snug the joiner.

QUINCE. Well, it shall be so. But there is two hard things; that is, to bring the moonlight into a chamber; for, you know, Pyramus and Thisby meet by moonlight.

45 SNOUT. Doth the moon shine that night we play our play?

BOTTOM. A calendar, a calendar! Look in the almanac; find out moonshine, find out moonshine.

QUINCE. Yes, it doth shine that night.

50 BOTTOM. Why, then may you leave a casement of the great chamber window, where we play, open, and the moon may shine in at the casement.

QUINCE. Ay; or else one must come in with a bush of thorns° and a lantern, and say he comes to disfigure,° or to 55 present, the person of Moonshine. Then, there is another thing: we must have a wall in the great chamber; for Pyramus and Thisby, says the story, did talk through the chink of a wall.

SNOUT. You can never bring in a wall. What say you, 60 Bottom?

BOTTOM. Some man or other must present Wall: and let him have some plaster, or some loam, or some roughcast° about him, to signify Wall; and let him hold his fingers thus, and through that cranny shall Pyramus and Thisby 65 whisper.

22 **in eight and six** in alternate lines of eight and six syllables (ballad stanza) 39 **pity of my life** a bad thing for me 54 **bush of thorns** (legend held that the man in the moon had been placed there for gathering firewood on Sunday) 54 **disfigure** (Quince means "figure," "represent") 63 **roughcast** lime mixed with gravel to plaster outside walls

QUINCE. If that may be, then all is well. Come, sit down, every mother's son, and rehearse your parts. Pyramus, you begin. When you have spoken your speech, enter into that brake; and so everyone according to his cue.

Enter Robin [*Puck*].

PUCK.
What hempen homespuns° have we swagg'ring here, 70
So near the cradle of the Fairy Queen?
What, a play toward!° I'll be an auditor;
An actor too perhaps, if I see cause.

QUINCE. Speak, Pyramus. Thisby, stand forth.

PYRAMUS [*Bottom*].
Thisby, the flowers of odious savors sweet— 75

QUINCE. Odors, odors.

PYRAMUS.
—odors savors sweet:
So hath thy breath, my dearest Thisby dear.
But hark, a voice! Stay thou but here awhile,
And by and by° I will to thee appear. 80

Exit.

PUCK.
A stranger Pyramus than e'er played here!

[*Exit.*]

THISBY [*Flute*]. Must I speak now?

QUINCE. Ay, marry, must you. For you must understand he goes but to see a noise that he heard, and is to come again. 85

THISBY.
Most radiant Pyramus, most lily-white of hue,
Of color like the red rose on triumphant brier,
Most brisky juvenal,° and eke° most lovely Jew,
As true as truest horse, that yet would never tire,
I'll meet thee, Pyramus, at Ninny's° tomb. 90

QUINCE. "Ninus' tomb," man. Why, you must not speak that yet. That you answer to Pyramus. You speak all your part at once, cues and all. Pyramus enter. Your cue is past; it is "never tire."

THISBY.
O—as true as truest horse, that yet would never tire. 95

[*Re-enter Puck, and Bottom with an ass's head.*]

PYRAMUS.
If I were fair, Thisby, I were only thine.

QUINCE. O monstrous! O strange! We are haunted. Pray, masters! Fly, masters! Help!

[*Exeunt all the clowns but Bottom.*]

70 **hempen homespuns** coarse fellows (clad in homespun cloth of hemp) 72 **toward** in preparation 80 **by and by** shortly 88 **juvenal** youth 88 **eke** also 90 **Ninny's** (blunder for "Ninus'"; Ninus was the legendary founder of Nineveh)

PUCK.
I'll follow you, I'll lead you about a round,°
Through bog, through bush, through brake, through
100 brier.
Sometime a horse I'll be, sometime a hound,
A hog, a headless bear, sometime a fire;
And neigh, and bark, and grunt, and roar, and burn,
Like horse, hound, hog, bear, fire, at every turn.
Exit.

105 BOTTOM. Why do they run away? This is a knavery of them to make me afeared.

Enter Snout.

SNOUT. O Bottom, thou art changed! What do I see on thee?

BOTTOM. What do you see? You see an ass head of your
110 own, do you? [*Exit Snout.*]

Enter Quince.

QUINCE. Bless thee, Bottom! Bless thee! Thou art translated.° *Exit.*

BOTTOM. I see their knavery. This is to make an ass of me; to fright me, if they could. But I will not stir from this
115 place, do what they can. I will walk up and down here, and will sing, that they shall hear I am not afraid. [*Sings.*]
The woosel° cock so black of hue,
With orange-tawny bill,
The throstle with his note so true,
120 The wren with little quill°—

TITANIA [*awakening*].
What angel wakes me from my flow'ry bed?

BOTTOM [*sings*].
The finch, the sparrow, and the lark,
The plain-song cuckoo° gray,
Whose note full many a man doth mark,
125 And dares not answer nay—
for, indeed, who would set his wit° to so foolish a bird? Who would give a bird the lie,° though he cry "cuckoo" never so?°

TITANIA.
I pray thee, gentle mortal, sing again:
130 Mine ear is much enamored of thy note;
So is mine eye enthrallèd to thy shape;
And thy fair virtue's force perforce doth move me
On the first view to say, to swear, I love thee.

BOTTOM. Methinks, mistress, you should have little reason for that. And yet, to say the truth, reason and love 135 keep little company together nowadays; the more the pity, that some honest neighbors will not make them friends. Nay, I can gleek° upon occasion.

TITANIA.
Thou art as wise as thou art beautiful.

BOTTOM. Not so, neither; but if I had wit enough to 140 get out of this wood, I have enough to serve mine own turn.

TITANIA.
Out of this wood do not desire to go.
Thou shalt remain here, whether thou wilt or no.
I am a spirit of no common rate.°
The summer still doth tend° upon my state; 145
And I do love thee. Therefore, go with me.
I'll give thee fairies to attend on thee,
And they shall fetch thee jewels from the deep,
And sing, while thou on pressèd flowers dost sleep:
And I will purge thy mortal grossness so, 150
That thou shalt like an airy spirit go.
Peaseblossom! Cobweb! Moth!° And Mustardseed!

Enter four Fairies [*Peaseblossom, Cobweb, Moth, and Mustardseed*].

PEASEBLOSSOM.
Ready.

COBWEB.
And I.

MOTH. And I.

MUSTARDSEED. And I.

ALL. Where shall we go.

TITANIA.
Be kind and courteous to this gentleman;
Hop in his walks, and gambol in his eyes; 155
Feed him with apricocks and dewberries,°
With purple grapes, green figs, and mulberries;
The honey bags steal from the humblebees,°
And for night tapers crop their waxen thighs,
And light them at the fiery glowworm's eyes, 160
To have my love to bed and to arise;
And pluck the wings from painted butterflies,
To fan the moonbeams from his sleeping eyes.
Nod to him, elves, and do him courtesies.

PEASEBLOSSOM.
Hail mortal!

99 **about a round** roundabout 112 **translated** transformed 117 **woosel** ouzel, blackbird 120 **quill** (literally, "reed pipe": here, "piping voice") 123 **the plain-song cuckoo** the cuckoo, who sings a simple song 126 **set his wit** use his intelligence to answer 127 **give a bird the lie** contradict a bird (the cuckoo's song supposedly tells a man he is a cuckold) 128 **never so** ever so often

138 **gleek** make a satirical jest 144 **rate** rank 145 **still doth tend** always waits upon 152 **Moth** (pronounced "mote," and probably a speck rather than an insect is denoted) 156 **apricocks and dewberries** apricots and blackberries 158 **humblebees** bumblebees

COBWEB. Hail!
MOTH. Hail!
165 MUSTARDSEED. Hail!

BOTTOM. I cry your worship's mercy,° heartily: I beseech your worship's name.

COBWEB.
Cobweb.

BOTTOM. I shall desire you of more acquaintance,°
170 good Master Cobweb: if I cut my finger,° I shall make bold with you. Your name, honest gentleman?

PEASEBLOSSOM.
Peaseblossom.

BOTTOM. I pray you, commend me to Mistress Squash,° your mother, and to Master Peascod, your father.
175 Good Master Peaseblossom. I shall desire you of more acquaintance too. Your name, I beseech you, sir?

MUSTARDSEED.
Mustardseed.

BOTTOM. Good Master Mustardseed, I know your patience well. That same cowardly, giantlike ox-beef hath de-
180 voured° many a gentleman of your house. I promise you your kindred hath made my eyes water ere now. I desire you of more acquaintance, good Master Mustardseed.

TITANIA.
Come, wait upon him; lead him to my bower.
The moon methinks looks with a wat'ry eye;
185 And when she weeps. weeps every little flower,
Lamenting some enforcèd° chastity.
Tie up my lover's tongue, bring him silently.
Exit [Titania with Bottom and Fairies].

[SCENE II

Another part of the wood.]

Enter [Oberon,] King of Fairies, and Robin Goodfellow [Puck].

OBERON.
I wonder if Titania be awaked;
Then, what it was that next came in her eye,
Which she must dote on in extremity.°
Here comes my messenger. How now, mad spirit!
5 What night-rule° now about this haunted grove?

PUCK.
My mistress with a monster is in love.
Near to her close° and consecrated bower,
While she was in her dull and sleeping hour,
A crew of patches,° rude mechanicals,°
That work for bread upon Athenian stalls, 10
Were met together to rehearse a play,
Intended for great Theseus' nuptial day.
The shallowest thickskin of that barren sort,°
Who Pyramus presented in their sport,
Forsook his scene, and entered in a brake. 15
When I did him at this advantage take,
An ass's nole° I fixèd on his head.
Anon° his Thisby must be answerèd,
And forth my mimic comes. When they him spy,
As wild geese that the creeping fowler eye, 20
Or russet-pated choughs, many in sort,°
Rising and cawing at the gun's report,
Sever themselves and madly sweep the sky,
So, at his sight, away his fellows fly;
And, at our stamp, here o'er and o'er one falls; 25
He murder cries, and help from Athens calls.
Their sense thus weak, lost with their fears thus strong,
Made senseless things begin to do them wrong;
For briers and thorns at their apparel snatch;
Some sleeves, some hats, from yielders all things catch. 30
I led them on in this distracted fear,
And left sweet Pyramus translated there:
When in that moment, so it came to pass,
Titania waked, and straightway loved an ass.

OBERON.
This falls out better than I could devise. 35
But hast thou yet latched° the Athenian's eyes
With the love juice, as I did bid thee do?

PUCK.
I took him sleeping—that is finished too—
And the Athenian woman by his side;
That, when he waked, of force° she must be eyed. 40

Enter Demetrius and Hermia.

OBERON.
Stand close:° this is the same Athenian.

PUCK.
This is the woman, but not this the man.

166 **I cry your worship's mercy** I beg pardon of your honors 169 **I shall desire you of more acquaintance** I shall want to be better acquainted with you 170 **if I cut my finger** (cobweb was used for stanching blood) 174 **Squash** unripe pea pod 180 **devoured** (because beef is often eaten with mustard) 186 **enforcèd** violated
III.ii.3 **in extremity** to the extreme 5 **night-rule** happenings during the night

7 **close** private, secret 9 **patches** fools, clowns 9 **rude mechanicals** uneducated workingmen 13 **barren sort** stupid group 17 **nole** "noodle," head 18 **Anon** presently 21 **russet-pated . . . in sort** gray-headed jackdaws, many in a flock 36 **latched** fastened (or possibly "moistened") 40 **of force** by necessity 41 **close** concealed

DEMETRIUS.
O, why rebuke you him that loves you so?
Lay breath so bitter on your bitter foe.

HERMIA.
45 Now I but chide; but I should use thee worse,
For thou, I fear, hast given me cause to curse.
If thou hast slain Lysander in his sleep,
Being o'er shoes in blood, plunge in the deep,
And kill me too.
50 The sun was not so true unto the day
As he to me. Would he have stolen away
From sleeping Hermia? I'll believe as soon
This whole° earth may be bored, and that the moon
May through the center creep, and so displease
55 Her brother's° noontide with th' Antipodes.
It cannot be but thou hast murd'red him.
So should a murderer look, so dead,° so grim.

DEMETRIUS.
So should the murdered look; and so should I,
Pierced through the heart with your stern cruelty.
60 Yet you, the murderer, look as bright, as clear,
As yonder Venus in her glimmering sphere.

HERMIA.
What's this to my Lysander? Where is he?
All, good Demetrius, wilt thou give him me?

DEMETRIUS.
I had rather give his carcass to my hounds.

HERMIA.
65 Out, dog! Out, cur! Thou driv'st me past the bounds
Of maiden's patience. Hast thou slain him, then?
Henceforth be never numb'red among men!
O, once tell true! Tell true, even for my sake!
Durst thou have looked upon him being awake?
70 And hast thou killed him sleeping? O brave touch!°
Could not a worm, an adder, do so much?
An adder did it; for with doubler tongue
Than thine, thou serpent, never adder stung.

DEMETRIUS.
You spend your passion on a misprised mood:°
75 I am not guilty of Lysander's blood;
Nor is he dead, for aught that I can tell.

HERMIA.
I pray thee, tell me then that he is well.

DEMETRIUS.
An if I could, what should I get therefore?°

HERMIA.
A privilege, never to see me more.
And from thy hated presence part I so. 80
See me no more, whether he be dead or no.

Exit.

DEMETRIUS.
There is no following her in this fierce vein.
Here therefore for a while I will remain.
So sorrow's heaviness doth heavier grow
For debt that bankrout sleep doth sorrow owe;° 85
Which now in some slight measure it will pay,
If for his tender° here I make some stay.

Lies down [and sleeps].

OBERON.
What hast thou done? Thou has mistaken quite,
And laid the love juice on some truelove's sight.
Of thy misprision° must perforce ensue 90
Some true love turned, and not a false turned true.

PUCK.
Then fate o'errules, that, one man holding troth,
A million fail, confounding oath on oath.°

OBERON.
About the wood go swifter than the wind,
And Helena of Athens look thou find. 95
All fancy-sick° she is and pale of cheer,°
With sighs of love, that costs the fresh blood dear:
By some illusion see thou bring her here.
I'll charm his eyes against she do appear.°

PUCK.
I go, I go; look how I go, 100
Swifter than arrow from the Tartar's bow.

[Exit.]

OBERON.
Flower of this purple dye,
Hit with Cupid's archery,
Sink in apple of his eye.
When his love he doth espy, 105
Let her shine as gloriously
As the Venus of the sky.
When thou wak'st, if she be by,
Beg of her for remedy.

Enter Puck.

PUCK.
Captain of our fairy band, 110
Helena is here at hand;
And the youth, mistook by me,

53 **whole** solid 55 **Her brother's** i.e., the sun's 57 **dead** deadly pale 70 **brave touch** splendid exploit (ironic) 74 **misprised mood** mistaken anger 78 **therefore** in return

85 **For debt . . . sorrow owe** because of the debt that bankrupt sleep owes to sorrow 87 **tender** offer 90 **misprision** mistake 93 **confounding oath on oath** breaking oath after oath 96 **fancy-sick** love-sick 96 **cheer** face 99 **against she do appear** in preparation for her appearance

Pleading for a lover's fee.
Shall we their fond pageant° see?
115 Lord, what fools these mortals be!

OBERON.
Stand aside. The noise they make
Will cause Demetrius to awake.

PUCK.
Then will two at once woo one;
That must needs be sport alone;°
120 And those things do best please me
That befall prepost'rously.

Enter Lysander and Helena.

LYSANDER.
Why should you think that I should woo in scorn?
Scorn and derision never come in tears:
Look, when I vow, I weep; and vows so born,
125 In their nativity all truth appears.
How can these things in me seem scorn to you,
Bearing the badge of faith,° to prove them true?

HELENA.
You do advance° your cunning more and more.
When truth kills truth, O devilish-holy fray!
130 These vows are Hermia's: will you give her o'er?
Weigh oath with oath, and you will nothing weigh.
Your vows to her and me, put in two scales,
Will even weigh; and both as light as tales.

LYSANDER.
I had no judgment when to her I swore.

HELENA.
135 Nor none, in my mind, now you give her o'er.

LYSANDER.
Demetrius loves her, and he loves not you.

DEMETRIUS (*awakening*).
O Helen, goddess, nymph, perfect, divine!
To what, my love, shall I compare thine eyne?
Crystal is muddy. O, how ripe in show°
140 Thy lips, those kissing cherries, tempting grow!
That pure congealèd white, high Taurus'° snow,
Fanned with the eastern wind, turns to a crow
When thou hold'st up thy hand: O, let me kiss
This princess of pure white, this seal of bliss!

HELENA.
145 O spite! O hell! I see you all are bent
To set against me for your merriment:
If you were civil° and knew courtesy,
You would not do me thus much injury.
Can you not hate me, as I know you do,
But you must join in souls to mock me too? 150
If you were men, as men you are in show,
You would not use a gentle° lady so;
To vow, and swear, and superpraise my parts,°
When I am sure you hate me with your hearts.
You both are rivals, and love Hermia; 155
And now both rivals to mock Helena:
A trim° exploit, a many enterprise,
To conjure tears up in a poor maid's eyes
With your derision! None of noble sort
Would so offend a virgin, and extort° 160
A poor soul's patience, all to make you sport.

LYSANDER.
You are unkind, Demetrius. Be not so;
For you love Hermia; this you know I know.
And here, with all good will, with all my heart,
In Hermia's love I yield you up my part; 165
And yours of Helena to me bequeath,
Whom I do love, and will do till my death.

HELENA.
Never did mockers waste more idle° breath.

DEMETRIUS.
Lysander, keep thy Hermia; I will none.
If e'er I loved her, all that love is gone. 170
My heart to her but as guestwise sojourned,
And now to Helen it is home returned,
There to remain.

LYSANDER. Helen, it is not so.

DEMETRIUS.
Disparage not the faith thou dost not know,
Lest, to thy peril, thou aby it dear.° 175
Look, where thy love comes; yonder is thy dear.

Enter Hermia.

HERMIA.
Dark night, that from the eye his° function takes,
The ear more quick of apprehension makes;
Wherein it doth impair the seeing sense,
It pays the hearing double recompense. 180
Thou art not by mine eye, Lysander, found;
Mine ear, I thank it, brought me to thy sound.
But why unkindly didst thou leave me so?

LYSANDER.
Why should he stay, whom love doth press to go?

114 **fond pageant** foolish exhibition 119 **alone** unique, supreme 127 **badge of faith** (Lysander means his tears) 128 **advance** exhibit, display 139 **show** appearance 141 **Taurus'** of the Taurus Mountains (in Turkey) 147 **civil** civilized

152 **gentle** well-born 153 **parts** qualities 157 **trim** splendid (ironical) 160 **extort** wear out by torturing 168 **idle** vain, futile 175 **aby it dear** pay dearly for it 177 **his** its (the eye's)

HERMIA.
185 What love could press Lysander from my side?
LYSANDER.
Lysander's love, that would not let him bide,
Fair Helena, who more engilds the night
Than all yon fiery oes° and eyes of light.
Why seek'st thou me? Could not this make thee know,
190 The hate I bare thee made me leave thee so?
HERMIA.
You speak not as you think: it cannot be.
HELENA.
Lo, she is one of this confederacy!
Now I perceive they have conjoined all three
To fashion this false sport, in spite of me.
195 Injurious° Hermia! Most ungrateful maid!
Have you conspired, have you with these contrived
To bait° me with this foul derision?
Is all the counsel that we two have shared,
The sister's vows, the hours that we have spent,
200 When we have chid the hasty-footed time
For parting us—O, is all forgot?
All school days friendship, childhood innocence?
We, Hermia, like two artificial° gods,
Have with our needles created both one flower,
205 Both on one sampler,° sitting on one cushion,
Both warbling of one song, both in one key;
As if our hands, our sides, voices, and minds,
Had been incorporate.° So we grew together,
Like to a double cherry, seeming parted,
210 But yet an union in partition;
Two lovely berries molded on one stem;
So, with two seeming bodies, but one heart;
Two of the first, like coats in heraldry,
Due but to one, and crownèd with one crest.°
215 And will you rent° our ancient love asunder,
To join with men in scorning your poor friend?
It is not friendly, 'tis not maidenly.
Our sex, as well as I, may chide you for it,
Though I alone do feel the injury.
HERMIA.
220 I am amazèd at your passionate words.
I scorn you not. It seems that you scorn me.
HELENA.
Have you not set Lysander, as in scorn,
To follow me and praise my eyes and face?
And made your other love, Demetrius
(Who even but now did spurn me with his foot), 225
To call me goddess, nymph, divine and rare,
Precious, celestial? Wherefore speaks he this
To her he hates? And wherefore doth Lysander
Deny your love,° so rich within his soul,
And tender me (forsooth) affection, 230
But by your setting on, by your consent?
What though I be not so in grace° as you,
So hung upon with love, so fortunate,
But miserable most, to love unloved?
This you should pity rather than despise. 235
HERMIA.
I understand not what you mean by this.
HELENA.
Ay, do! Persever,° counterfeit sad° looks,
Make mouths° upon me when I turn my back;
Wink each at other; hold the sweet jest up.
This sport, well carried, shall be chronicled. 240
If you have any pity, grace, or manners,
You would not make me such an argument.°
But fare ye well. 'Tis partly my own fault,
Which death or absence soon shall remedy.
LYSANDER.
Stay, gentle Helena; hear my excuse: 245
My love, my life, my soul, fair Helena!
HELENA.
O excellent!
HERMIA.
Sweet, do not scorn her so.
DEMETRIUS.
If she cannot entreat,° I can compel.
LYSANDER.
Thou canst compel no more than she entreat.
Thy threats have no more strength than her weak prayers. 250
Helen, I love thee; by my life, I do!
I swear by that which I will lose for thee,
To prove him false that says I love thee not.
DEMETRIUS.
I say I love thee more than he can do.
LYSANDER.
If thou say so, withdraw and prove it too. 255
DEMETRIUS.
Quick, come!
HERMIA. Lysander, whereto tends all this?

188 **oes** orbs 195 **Injurious** insulting 196–97 **contrived To bait** plotted to assail 203 **artificial** skilled in art 205 **sampler** work of embroidery 208 **incorporate** one body 213–14 **Two of . . . one crest** (Helena apparently envisages a shield on which the coat of arms appears twice but which has a single crest; Helena and Hermia have two bodies but a single heart) 215 **rent** rend, tear

229 **your love** his love for you 232 **in grace** in favor 237 **persever** persevere (but accented on second syllable) 237 **sad** grave 238 **Make mouths** make mocking faces 242 **argument** subject (of scorn) 248 **entreat** prevail by entreating

LYSANDER.
Away, you Ethiope!°
DEMETRIUS. No, no; he'll
Seem to break loose; take on as° you would follow,
But yet come not: you are a tame man, go!
LYSANDER.
260 Hang off, thou cat, thou burr! Vile thing, let loose,
Or I will shake thee from me like a serpent!
HERMIA.
Why are you grown so rude! What change is this,
Sweet love?
LYSANDER.
Thy love! Out, tawny Tartar, out!
Out, loathèd med'cine! O hated potion, hence!
HERMIA.
Do you not jest?
265 HELENA. Yes, sooth;° and so do you.
LYSANDER.
Demetrius, I will keep my word° with thee.
DEMETRIUS.
I would I had your bond, for I perceive
A weak bond holds you. I'll not trust your word.
LYSANDER.
What, should I hurt her, strike her, kill her dead?
270 Although I hate her, I'll not harm her so.
HERMIA.
What, can you do me greater harm than hate?
Hate me! Wherefore? O me! What news, my love!
Am not I Hermia? Are not you Lysander?
I am as fair now as I was erewhile.°
275 Since night° you loved me; yet since night you left me.
Why, then you left me—O, the gods forbid!—
In earnest, shall I say?
LYSANDER. Ay, by my life!
And never did desire to see thee more.
Therefore be out of hope, of question, of doubt;
280 Be certain, nothing truer. 'Tis no jest
That I do hate thee, and love Helena.
HERMIA.
O me! You juggler! You canker blossom!°
You thief of love! What, have you come by night
And stol'n my love's heart from him?
HELENA. Fine, i' faith!
285 Have you no modesty, no maiden shame,
No touch of bashfulness? What, will you tear
Impatient answers from my gentle tongue?
Fie, fie! You counterfeit, you puppet, you!
HERMIA.
Puppet? Why so? Ay, that way goes the game.
Now I perceive that she hath made compare° 290
Between our statures; she hath urged her height,
And with her personage, her tall personage,
Her height, forsooth, she hath prevailed with him.
And are you grown so high in his esteem,
Because I am so dwarfish and so low? 295
How low am I, thou painted maypole? Speak!
How low am I? I am not yet so low
But that my nails can reach unto thine eyes.
HELENA.
I pray you, though you mock me, gentlemen,
Let her not hurt me, I was never curst;° 300
I have no gift at all in shrewishness;
I am a right maid° for my cowardice.
Let her not strike me. You perhaps may think,
Because she is something lower than myself,
That I can match her.
HERMIA. Lower! Hark, again! 305
HELENA.
Good Hermia, do not be so bitter with me.
I evermore did love you, Hermia,
Did ever keep your counsels, never wronged you;
Save that, in love unto Demetrius,
I told him of your stealth unto this wood. 310
He followed you; for love I followed him.
But he hath chid me hence, and threatened me
To strike me, spurn me, nay, to kill me too.
And now, so you will let me quiet go,
To Athens will I bear my folly back. 315
And follow you no further. Let me go.
You see how simple and how fond° I am.
HERMIA.
Why, get you gone. Who is't that hinders you?
HELENA.
A foolish heart, that I leave here behind.
HERMIA.
What, with Lysander?
HELENA. With Demetrius. 320
LYSANDER.
Be not afraid. She shall not harm thee, Helena
DEMETRIUS.
No, sir, she shall not, though you take her part.
HELENA.
O, when she's angry, she is keen and shrewd!°

257 **Ethiope** blackamoor (brunette) 258 **take on as** make a fuss as if 265 **sooth** truly 266 **my word** my promise to fight with you 274 **erewhile** a little while ago 275 **Since night** since the beginning of this night 282 **canker blossom** dog rose (or possibly worm that cankers the blossom)

290 **compare** comparison 300 **curst** quarrelsome 302 **right maid** true young woman 317 **fond** foolish 323 **keen and shrewd** sharp-tongued and shrewish

She was a vixen when she went to school;
325 And though she be but little, she is fierce.

HERMIA.
"Little" again! Nothing but "low" and "little"!
Why will you suffer her to flout me thus?
Let me come to her.

LYSANDER. Get you gone, you dwarf;
You minimus,° of hind'ring knotgrass° made;
You bead, you acorn!

330 DEMETRIUS. You are too officious
In her behalf that scorns your services.
Let her alone. Speak not of Helena;
Take not her part; for, if thou dost intend°
Never so little show of love to her,
Thou shalt aby° it.

335 LYSANDER. Now she holds me not.
Now follow, if thou dar'st, to try whose right,
Of thine or mine, is most in Helena.

DEMETRIUS.
Follow! Nay, I'll go with thee, cheek by jowl.
[*Exeunt Lysander and Demetrius.*]

HERMIA.
You, mistress, all this coil is 'long of you:°
Nay, go not back.

340 HELENA. I will not trust you, I,
Nor longer stay in your curst company.
Your hands than mine are quicker for a fray,
My legs are longer though, to run away.

HERMIA.
I amazed,° and know not what to say.
Exeunt [*Helena and Hermia*].

OBERON.
345 This is thy negligence. Still thou mistak'st,
Or else committ'st thy knaveries willfully.

PUCK.
Believe me, king of shadows, I mistook.
Did you not tell me I should know the man
By the Athenian garments he had on?
350 And so far blameless proves my enterprise,
That I have 'nointed an Athenian's eyes;
And so far am I glad it so did sort,°
As this their jangling I esteem a sport.

OBERON.
Thou see'st these lovers seek a place to fight.
355 Hie therefore, Robin, overcast the night.
The starry welkin° cover thou anon
With drooping fog, as black as Acheron;°
And lead these testy° rivals so astray,
As° one come not within another's way.
Like to Lysander sometime frame thy tongue, 360
Then stir Demetrius up with bitter wrong;°
And sometime rail thou like Demetrius.
And from each other look thou lead them thus,
Till o'er their brows death-counterfeiting sleep
With leaden legs and batty° wings doth creep. 365
Then crush this herb into Lysander's eye,
Whose liquor hath this virtuous° property,
To take from thence all error with his might,
And make his eyeballs roll with wonted sight.
When they next wake, all this derision° 370
Shall seem a dream and fruitless vision.
And back to Athens shall the lovers wend,
With league whose date° till death shall never end.
Whiles I in this affair do thee employ,
I'll to my queen and beg her Indian boy; 375
And then I will her charmèd eye release
From monster's view, and all things shall be peace.

PUCK.
My fairy lord, this must be done with haste,
For night's swift dragons cut the clouds full fast
And yonder shines Aurora's harbinger;° 380
At whose approach, ghosts, wand'ring here and there,
Troop home to churchyards: damnèd spirits all,
That in crossways and floods have burial,
Already to their wormy beds are gone.
For fear lest day should look their shames upon, 385
They willfully themselves exile from light,
And must for aye consort with black-browed night.

OBERON.
But we are spirits of another sort.
I with the Morning's love° have oft made sport;
And, like a forester, the groves may tread, 390
Even till the eastern gate, all fiery-red,
Opening on Neptune with fair blessèd beams,
Turns into yellow gold his salt green streams.
But, notwithstanding, haste; make no delay.
We may effect this business yet ere day. 395
[*Exit.*]

PUCK.
Up and down, up and down,

329 **minimus** smallest thing 329 **knotgrass** (a weed that allegedly stunted one's growth) 333 **intend** give sign, direct (or possibly "pretend") 335 **aby** pay for 339 **all this coil is 'long of you** all this turmoil is brought about by you 344 **amazed** in confusion 352 **sort** turn out 356 **welkin** sky

357 **Acheron** one of the rivers of the underworld 358 **testy** excited, angry 359 **As** that 361 **wrong** insult 365 **batty** batlike 367 **virtuous** potent 370 **derision** i.e., ludicrous delusion 373 **With league whose date** in union whose term 380 **Aurora's harbinger** dawn's herald (i.e., the morning star) 389 **the Morning's love** Aurora (or possibly her lover Cephalus)

I will lead them up and down:
I am feared in field and town:
Goblin,° lead them up and down.
400 Here comes one.

Enter Lysander.

LYSANDER.
Where art thou, proud Demetrius? Speak thou now.
PUCK.
Here, villain; drawn° and ready. Where art thou?
LYSANDER.
I will be with thee straight.
PUCK. Follow me, then,
To plainer° ground.

[*Exit Lysander.*]

Enter Demetrius.

DEMETRIUS. Lysander! Speak again!
405 Thou runaway, thou coward, art thou fled?
Speak! In some bush? Where dost thou hide thy head?
PUCK.
Thou coward, art thou bragging to the stars,
Telling the bushes that thou look'st for wars,
And wilt not come? Come, recreant! Come, thou child!
410 I'll whip thee with a rod. He is defiled
That draws a sword on thee.
DEMETRIUS. Yea, art thou there?
PUCK.
Follow my voice. We'll try no manhood° here.

Exeunt.

[*Enter Lysander.*]

LYSANDER.
He goes before me and still dares me on:
When I come where he calls, then he is gone.
415 The villain is much lighter-heeled than I.
I followed fast, but faster he did fly,
That fallen am I in dark uneven way,
And here will rest me. [*Lies down.*] Come, thou gentle day!
For if but once thou show me thy gray light,
420 I'll find Demetrius, and revenge this spite.

[*Sleeps.*]

[*Enter*] *Robin* [*Puck*] *and Demetrius.*

PUCK.
Ho, ho, ho! Coward, why com'st thou not?
DEMETRIUS.
Abide me,° if thou dar'st; for well I wot°
Thou runn'st before me, shifting every place,
And dar'st not stand, nor look me in the face.
Where art thou now?
PUCK. Come hither. I am here. 425
DEMETRIUS.
Nay, then, thou mock'st me. Thou shalt buy this dear,°
If ever I thy face by daylight see.
Now, go thy way. Faintness constraineth me
To measure out my length on this cold bed.
By day's approach look to be visited.° 430

[*Lies down and sleeps.*]

Enter Helena.

HELENA.
O weary night, O long and tedious night,
Abate° thy hours! Shine comforts from the east,
That I may back to Athens by daylight,
From these that my poor company detest:
And sleep, that sometimes shuts up sorrow's eye, 435
Steal me awhile from mine own company.

Sleep.

PUCK.
Yet but three? Come one more.
Two of both kinds makes up four.
Here she comes, curst° and sad:
Cupid is a knavish lad, 440
Thus to make poor females mad.

[*Enter Hermia.*]

HERMIA.
Never so weary, never so in woe;
Bedabbled with the dew and torn with briers,
I can no further crawl, no further go;
My legs can keep no pace with my desires. 445
Here will I rest me till the break of day.
Heavens shield Lysander, if they mean a fray!

[*Lies down and sleeps.*]

PUCK.
On the ground
Sleep sound:
I'll apply 450
To your eye,
Gentle lover, remedy.

[*Squeezing the juice on Lysander's eye.*]

When thou wak'st,
Thou tak'st
True delight 455

399 **Goblin** Hobgoblin (one of Puck's names) 402 **drawn** with drawn sword 404 **plainer** more level 412 **try no manhood** have no test of valor 422 **Abide me** wait for me 422 **wot** know

426 **buy this dear** pay dearly for this 430 **look to be visited** be sure to be sought out 432 **Abate** make shorter 439 **curst** cross

In the sight
Of thy former lady's eye:
And the country proverb known,
That every man should take his own,
460 In your waking shall be shown.
Jack shall have Jill;
Nought shall go ill;
The man shall have his mare again, and all shall be well.
[*Exit.*]

[ACT IV

SCENE I

The wood. Lysander, Demetrius, Helena, and Hermia, lying asleep.]

Enter [*Titania,*] *Queen of Fairies, and* [*Bottom the*] *Clown, and Fairies; and* [*Oberon,*] *the King, behind them.*

TITANIA.
Come, sit thee down, upon this flow'ry bed,
While I thy amiable cheeks do coy,°
And stick musk roses in thy sleek smooth head,
And kiss thy fair large ears, my gentle joy.
5 BOTTOM. Where's Peaseblossom?
PEASEBLOSSOM.
Ready.
BOTTOM. Scratch my head, Peaseblossom. Where's Mounsieur Cobweb?
COBWEB.
Ready.
10 BOTTOM. Mounsieur Cobweb, good mounsieur, get you your weapons in your hand, and kill me a red-hipped humblebee on the top of a thistle; and, good mounsieur, bring me the honey bag. Do not fret yourself too much in the action, mounsieur; and, good mounsieur, have a care
15 the honey bag break not; I would be loath to have you overflown with a honey bag, signior. Where's Mounsieur Mustardseed?
MUSTARDSEED.
Ready.
BOTTOM. Give me your neaf,° Mounsieur Mustard-
20 seed. Pray you, leave your curtsy,° good mounsieur.
MUSTARDSEED.
What's your will?

IV.i.2 **While I . . . do coy** while I caress your lovely cheeks
19 **neaf** fist, hand 20 **leave your curtsy** i.e., stop bowing, leave your hat on (a curtsy was any gesture of respect)

BOTTOM. Nothing, good mounsieur, but to help Cavalery° Cobweb to scratch. I must to the barber's, mounsieur; for methinks I am marvail's° hairy about the face; and I am such a tender ass, if my hair do but tickle me, I must 25
scratch.
TITANIA.
What, wilt thou hear some music, my sweet love?
BOTTOM. I have a reasonable good ear in music. Let's have the tongs and the bones.°
TITANIA.
Or say, sweet love, what thou desirest to eat. 30
BOTTOM. Truly, a peck of provender. I could munch your good dry oats. Methinks I have a great desire to a bottle° of hay. Good hay, sweet hay, hath no fellow.°
TITANIA.
I have a venturous fairy that shall seek
The squirrel's hoard, and fetch thee new nuts. 35
BOTTOM. I had rather a handful or two of dried peas. But, I pray you, let none of your people stir me: I have an exposition of° sleep come upon me.
TITANIA.
Sleep thou, and I will wind thee in my arms.
Fairies, be gone, and be all ways° away. 40
[*Exeunt Fairies.*]
So doth the woodbine the sweet honeysuckle
Gently entwist; the female ivy° so
Enrings the barky fingers of the elm.
O, how I love thee! How I dote on thee!
[*They sleep.*]

Enter Robin Goodfellow [*Puck*].

OBERON (*advancing*).
Welcome, Good Robin. See'st thou this sweet sight? 45
Her dotage now I do begin to pity:
For, meeting her of late behind the wood,
Seeking sweet favors° for this hateful fool,
I did upbraid her, and fall out with her.
For she his hairy temples then had rounded 50
With coronet of fresh and fragrant flowers;
And that same dew, which sometime° on the buds
Was wont° to swell, like round and orient° pearls,
Stood now within the pretty flouriets'° eyes,

23 **Cavalery** i.e., Cavalier 24 **marvail's** (Bottom means "marvelous") 29 **the tongs and the bones** rustic music, made by tongs struck with metal and by bone clappers held between the fingers 33 **bottle** bundle 33 **fellow** equal
38 **exposition of** (Bottom means "disposition for")
40 **all ways** in every direction 42 **female ivy** (called female because it clings to the elm and is supported by it)
48 **favors** love tokens (probably flowers) 52 **sometime** formerly 53 **Was wont** used to 53 **orient** lustrous
54 **flouriets'** flowerets'

55 Like tears, that did their own disgrace bewail.
When I had at my pleasure taunted her,
And she in mild terms begged my patience,
I then did ask of her her changeling child;
Which straight she gave me, and her fairy sent
60 To bear him to my bower in fairy land.
And now I have the boy, I will undo
This hateful imperfection of her eyes:
And, gentle Puck, take this transformèd scalp
From off the head of this Athenian swain,
65 That, he awaking when the other° do,
May all to Athens back again repair,
And think no more of this night's accidents,°
But as the fierce vexation of a dream.
But first I will release the Fairy Queen.
70 Be as thou wast wont to be;
See as thou wast wont to see.
Dian's bud o'er Cupid's flower
Hath such force and blessèd power.
Now, my Titania, wake you, my sweet Queen.

TITANIA.
75 My Oberon, what visions have I seen!
Methought I was enamored of an ass.

OBERON.
There lies your love.

TITANIA. How came these things to pass?
O, how mine eyes do loathe his visage now!

OBERON.
Silence awhile. Robin, take off this head.
80 Titania, music call; and strike more dead
Than common sleep of all these five the sense.

TITANIA.
Music, ho, music! Such as charmeth sleep!

PUCK.
Now, when thou wak'st, with thine own fool's eyes peep.

OBERON.
Sound, music! [*Music.*] Come, my Queen, take hands with me,
85 And rock the ground whereon these sleepers be.

[*Dance.*]

Now thou and I are new in amity,
And will tomorrow midnight solemnly°
Dance in Duke Theseus' house triumphantly,°
And bless it to all fair prosperity.
90 There shall the pairs of faithful lovers be
Wedded, with Theseus, all in jollity.

PUCK.
Fairy King, attend, and mark:
I do hear the morning lark.

OBERON.
Then, my Queen, in silence sad,°
95 Trip we after night's shade.
We the globe can compass soon,
Swifter than the wand'ring moon.

TITANIA.
Come, my lord; and in our flight,
Tell me how it came this night,
100 That I sleeping here was found
With these mortals on the ground.

Exeunt.

Wind horn. Enter Theseus, and all his train; [*Hippolyta, Egeus*].

THESEUS.
Go, one of you, find out the forester,
For now our observation° is performed;
And since we have the vaward° of the day,
105 My love shall hear the music of my hounds.
Uncouple in the western valley; let them go.
Dispatch, I say, and find the forester.

[*Exit an Attendant.*]

We will, fair Queen, up to the mountain's top,
And mark the musical confusion
110 Of hounds and echo in conjunction.

HIPPOLYTA.
I was with Hercules and Cadmus once,
When in a wood of Crete they bayed° the bear
With hounds of Sparta. Never did I hear
Such gallant chiding; for, besides the groves,
115 The skies, the fountains, every region near
Seemed all one mutual cry. I never heard
So musical a discord, such sweet thunder.

THESEUS.
My hounds are bred out of the Spartan kind,
So flewed, so sanded;° and their heads are hung
120 With ears that sweep away the morning dew;
Crook-kneed, and dew-lapped like Thessalian bulls;
Slow in pursuit, but matched in mouth like bells,
Each under each.° A cry° more tunable
Was never holloed to, nor cheered with horn,
125 In Crete, in Sparta, nor in Thessaly.
Judge when you hear. But, soft!° What nymphs are these?

65 **other** others 67 **accidents** happenings 87 **solemnly** ceremoniously 88 **triumphantly** in festive procession

94 **sad** serious, solemn 103 **observation** observance, i.e., of the rite of May (cf. I.i.167) 104 **vaward** vanguard, i.e., morning 112 **bayed** brought to bay 119 **So flewed, so sanded** i.e., like Spartan hounds, with hanging cheeks and of sandy color 123 **Each under each** of different tone (like the chime of bells) 123 **cry** pack of hounds 126 **soft** stop

EGEUS.
My lord, this is my daughter here asleep;
And this, Lysander; this Demetrius is;
This Helena, old Nedar's Helena:
130 I wonder of their being here together.

THESEUS.
No doubt they rose up early to observe
The rite of May; and, hearing our intent,
Came here in grace of our solemnity.°
But speak, Egeus. Is not this the day
135 That Hermia should give answer of her choice?

EGEUS.
It is, my lord.

THESEUS.
Go, bid the huntsmen wake them with their horns.

Shout within. They all start up. Wind horns.

Good morrow, friends. Saint Valentine is past:
Begin these wood birds but to couple now?°

LYSANDER.
Pardon, my lord.

140 THESEUS. I pray you all, stand up.
I know you two are rival enemies.
How comes this gentle concord in the world,
That hatred is so far from jealousy,°
To sleep by hate, and fear no enmity?

LYSANDER.
145 My lord, I shall reply amazedly,°
Half sleep, half waking: but as yet, I swear,
I cannot truly say how I came here.
But, as I think—for truly would I speak,
And now I do bethink me, so it is—.
150 I came with Hermia hither. Our intent
Was to be gone from Athens, where we might,
Without° the peril of the Athenian law—

EGEUS.
Enough, enough, my lord; you have enough.
I beg the law, the law, upon his head.
155 They would have stol'n away; they would, Demetrius,
Thereby to have defeated° you and me,
You of your wife and me of my consent,
Of my consent that she should be your wife.

DEMETRIUS.
My lord, fair Helen told me of their stealth,°
160 Of this their purpose hither to this wood,
And I in fury hither followed them,
Fair Helena in fancy° following me.
But, my good lord, I wot not by what power—
But by some power it is—my love to Hermia,
Melted as the snow, seems to me now 165
As the remembrance of an idle gaud,°
Which in my childhood I did dote upon;
And all the faith, the virtue° of my heart,
The object and the pleasure of mine eye,
Is only Helena. To her, my lord, 170
Was I betrothed ere I saw Hermia:
But, like a sickness,° did I loathe this food;
But, as in health, come to my natural taste,
Now I do wish it, love it, long for it,
And will for evermore be true to it. 175

THESEUS.
Fair lovers, you are fortunately met.
Of this discourse we more will hear anon.
Egeus, I will overbear your will,
For in the temple, by and by,° with us
These couples shall eternally be knit; 180
And, for the morning now is something worn,°
Our purposed hunting shall be set aside.
Away with us to Athens! Three and three,
We'll hold a feast in great solemnity.
Come, Hippolyta. 185
[*Exeunt Theseus, Hippolyta, Egeus, and train.*]

DEMETRIUS.
These things seem small and undistinguishable
Like far-off mountains turnèd into clouds.

HERMIA.
Methinks I see these things with parted eye,°
When everything seems double.

HELENA. So methinks:
And I have found Demetrius like a jewel, 190
Mine own, and not mine own.

DEMETRIUS. Are you sure
That we are awake? It seems to me
That yet we sleep, we dream. Do not you think
The Duke was here, and bid us follow him?

HERMIA.
Yea, and my father.

HELENA. And Hippolyta. 195

LYSANDER.
And he did bid us follow to the temple.

133 **in grace of our solemnity** in honor of our festival
139 **Begin these . . . couple now** (it was supposed that birds began to mate on February 14, St. Valentine's Day)
143 **jealousy** suspicion 145 **amazedly** confusedly
152 **Without** outside of 156 **defeated** deprived by fraud
159 **stealth** stealthy flight

162 **in fancy** in love, doting 166 **idle gaud** worthless trinket 168 **virtue** power 172 **like a sickness** like one who is sick 179 **by and by** shortly 181 **something worn** somewhat spent 188 **with parted eye** i.e., with the eyes out of focus

DEMETRIUS.
Why, then, we are awake. Let's follow him,
And by the way let us recount our dreams.

[*Exeunt.*]

BOTTOM [*awaking*]. When my cue comes, call me, and
200 I will answer. My next is, "Most fair Pyramus." Heigh-ho! Peter Quince? Flute, the bellows mender? Snout, the tinker? Starveling? God's my life,° stol'n hence, and left me asleep? I have had a most rare vision. I have had a dream, past the wit of man to say what dream it was. Man is but an ass, if he
205 go about° to expound this dream. Methought I was—there is no man can tell what. Methought I was—and methought I had—but man is but a patched° fool if he will offer to say what methought I had. The eye of man hath not heard, the ear of man hath not seen, man's hand is not able to taste, his
210 tongue to conceive, nor his heart to report, what my dream was. I will get Peter Quince to write a ballet° of this dream. It shall be called "Bottom's Dream," because it hath no bottom; and I will sing it in the latter end of a play, before the Duke. Peradventure to make it the more gracious, I shall
215 sing it at her death.°

[*Exit.*]

[SCENE II

Athens. Quince's house.]

Enter Quince, Flute,° Thisby and the rabble [*Snout, Starveling*].

QUINCE. Have you sent to Bottom's house? Is he come home yet?

STARVELING. He cannot be heard of. Out of doubt he is transported.°

5 FLUTE. If he come not, then the play is marred. It goes not forward, doth it?

QUINCE. It is not possible. You have not a man in all Athens able to discharge° Pyramus but he.

FLUTE. No, he hath simply the best wit of any handi-
10 craft man in Athens.

QUINCE. Yea, and the best person too; and he is a very paramour for a sweet voice.

FLUTE. You must say "paragon." A paramour is, God bless us, a thing of nought.°

Enter Snug the Joiner.

15 SNUG. Masters, the Duke is coming from the temple, and there is two or three lords and ladies more married. If our sports had gone forward, we had all been made men.°

FLUTE. O sweet bully Bottom! Thus hath he lost sixpence a day° during his life. He could not have scaped six-
20 pence a day. And the Duke had not given him sixpence a day for playing Pyramus, I'll be hanged. He would have deserved it. Sixpence a day in Pyramus, or nothing.

Enter Bottom.

BOTTOM. Where are these lads? Where are these hearts?

QUINCE. Bottom! O most courageous° day! O most
25 happy hour!

BOTTOM. Masters, I am to discourse wonders: but ask me not what; for if I tell you, I am not true Athenian. I will tell you everything, right as it fell out.

QUINCE. Let us hear, sweet Bottom.

30 BOTTOM. Not a word of me.° All that I will tell you is, that the Duke hath dined. Get your apparel together, good strings to your beards, new ribbons to your pumps; meet presently° at the palace; every man look o'er his part; for the short and the long is, our play is preferred.° In any case, let
35 Thisby have clean linen; and let not him that plays the lion pare his nails. for they shall hang out for the lion's claws. And, most dear actors, eat no onions nor garlic, for we are to utter sweet breath,° and I do not doubt but to hear them say it is a sweet comedy. No more words. Away! Go, away!

[*Exeunt.*]

[ACT V

SCENE I

Athens. The palace of Theseus.]

Enter Theseus, Hippolyta, and Philostrate, [*Lords, and Attendants*].

HIPPOLYTA.
'Tis strange, my Theseus, that these lovers speak of.

THESEUS.
More strange than true. I never may believe
These antique° fables, nor these fairy toys.°

202 **God's my life** an oath (possibly from "God bless my life") 205 **go about** endeavor 207 **patched** (referring to the patchwork dress of jesters) 211 **ballet** ballad 215 **her death** i.e., Thisby's death in the play

IV.ii. s.d. **Flute** (Shakespeare seems to have forgotten that Flute and Thisby are the same person) 4 **transported** carried off (by the fairies) 8 **discharge** play 14 **a thing of nought** a wicked thing

17 **made men** men whose fortunes are made 19–20 **sixpence a day** (a pension) 24 **courageous** brave, splendid 30 **of me** from me 33 **presently** immediately 34 **preferred** put forward, recommended 38 **breath** (1) exhalation (2) words

V.i.3 **antique** (1) ancient (2) grotesque (antic) 3 **fairy toys** trifles about fairies

Lovers and madmen have such seething brains,
5 Such shaping fantasies,° that apprehend
More than cool reason ever comprehends.
The lunatic, the lover and the poet
Are of imagination all compact.°
One sees more devils than vast hell can hold,
10 That is the madman. The lover, all as frantic,
Sees Helen's beauty in a brow of Egypt.°
The poet's eye, in a fine frenzy rolling,
Doth glance from heaven to earth, from earth to heaven;
And as imagination bodies forth
15 The forms of things unknown, the poet's pen
Turns them to shapes, and gives to airy nothing
A local habitation and a name.
Such tricks hath strong imagination,
That, if it would but apprehend some joy,
20 It comprehends some bringer of that joy;°
Or in the night, imagining some fear,°
How easy is a bush supposed a bear!

HIPPOLYTA.
But all the story of the night told over,
And all their minds transfigured so together,
25 More witnesseth than fancy's images,
And grows to something of great constancy;°
But, howsoever, strange and admirable.°

Enter Lovers: Lysander, Demetrius, Hermia and Helena.

THESEUS.
Here come the lovers, full of joy and mirth.
Joy, gentle friends! Joy and fresh days of love
Accompany your hearts!

30 LYSANDER. More than to us
Wait in your royal walks, your board, your bed!

THESEUS.
Come now, what masques,° what dances shall we have,
To wear away this long age of three hours
Between our aftersupper° and bedtime?
35 Where is our usual manager of mirth?
What revels are in hand? Is there no play,
To ease the anguish of a torturing hour?
Call Philostrate.

PHILOSTRATE. Here, mighty Theseus.

THESEUS.
Say, what abridgment° have you for this evening?
40 What masque? What music? How shall we beguile
The lazy time, if not with some delight?

PHILOSTRATE.
There is a brief° how many sports are ripe:°
Make choice of which your Highness will see first.
[*Giving a paper.*]

THESEUS.
"The battle with the Centaurs, to be sung
45 By an Athenian eunuch to the harp."
We'll none of that. That have I told my love,
In glory of my kinsman Hercules.
"The riot of the tipsy Bacchanals,
Tearing the Thracian singer° in their rage."
50 That is an old device;° and it was played
When I from Thebes came last a conqueror.
"The thrice three Muses mourning for the death
Of Learning, late deceased in beggary."
That is some satire, keen and critical,
55 Not sorting with° a nuptial ceremony.
"A tedious brief scene of young Pyramus
And his love Thisby; very tragical mirth."
Merry and tragical? Tedious and brief?
That is, hot ice and wondrous strange snow.
60 How shall we find the concord of this discord?

PHILOSTRATE.
A play there is, my lord, some ten words long,
Which is as brief as I have known a play;
But by ten words, my lord, it is too long,
Which makes it tedious. For in all the play
65 There is not one word apt, one player fitted.
And tragical, my noble lord, it is,
For Pyramus therein doth kill himself.
Which, when I saw rehearsed, I must confess,
Made mine eyes water; but more merry tears
70 The passion° of loud laughter never shed.

THESEUS.
What are they that do play it?

PHILOSTRATE.
Hard-handed men, that work in Athens here,
Which never labored in their minds till now;
And now have toiled their unbreathed° memories
75 With this same play, against° your nuptial.

THESEUS.
And we will hear it.

PHILOSTRATE. No, my noble lord;
It is not for you. I have heard it over,
And it is nothing, nothing in the world;

5 **fantasies** imagination 8 **compact** composed 11 **brow of Egypt** face of a gypsy 20 **It comprehends . . . that joy** it includes an imagined bringer of the joy 21 **fear** object of fear 26 **constancy** consistency (and reality) 27 **admirable** wonderful 32 **masques** courtly entertainments with masked dancers 34 **aftersupper** refreshment served after early supper 39 **abridgment** entertainment (to abridge or shorten the time)

42 **brief** written list 42 **ripe** ready to be presented 49 **Thracian singer** Orpheus 50 **device** show 55 **sorting with** suited to 70 **passion** strong emotion 74 **unbreathed** unexercised 75 **against** in preparation for

Unless you can find sport in their intents,
80 Extremely stretched and conned with cruel pain,
To do you service.

THESEUS. I will hear that play;
For never anything can be amiss,
When simpleness and duty tender it.
Go, bring them in: and take your places, ladies.
[*Exit Philostrate.*]

HIPPOLYTA.
85 I love not to see wretchedness o'ercharged,°
And duty in his service perishing.

THESEUS.
Why, gentle sweet, you shall see no such thing.

HIPPOLYTA.
He says they can do nothing in this kind.°

THESEUS.
The kinder we, to give them thanks for nothing.
90 Our sport shall be to take what they mistake:
And what poor duty cannot do, noble respect
Takes it in might,° not merit.
Where I have come, great clerks° have purposèd
To greet me with premeditated welcomes;
95 Where I have seen them shiver and look pale,
Make periods in the midst of sentences,
Throttle their practiced accent in their fears,
And, in conclusion, dumbly have broke off,
Not paying me a welcome. Trust me, sweet,
100 Out of this silence yet I picked a welcome;
And in the modesty of fearful duty
I read as much as from the rattling tongue
Of saucy and audacious eloquence.
Love, therefore, and tongue-tied simplicity
105 In least speak most, to my capacity.°

[*Enter Philostrate.*]

PHILOSTRATE.
So please your Grace, the Prologue is addressed.°

THESEUS.
Let him approach. [*Flourish trumpets.*]

Enter the Prologue [*Quince*].

PROLOGUE.
If we offend, it is with our good will.
That you should think, we come not to offend,
110 But with good will. To show our simple skill,
That is the true beginning of our end.°
Consider, then, we come but in despite.
We do not come, as minding to content you,
Our true intent is. All for your delight,
We are not here. That you should here repent you, 115
The actors are at hand; and, by their show,°
You shall know all, that you are like to know.

THESEUS. This fellow doth not stand upon points°

LYSANDER. He hath rid his prologue like a rough colt; he knows not the stop.° A good moral, my lord: it is not 120 enough to speak, but to speak true.

HIPPOLYTA. Indeed he hath played on this prologue like a child on a recorder;° a sound. but not in government.°

THESEUS. His speech was like a tangled chain; nothing impaired, but all disordered. Who is next? 125

Enter Pyramus and Thisby and Wall and Moonshine and Lion [*as in dumbshow*].

PROLOGUE.
Gentles, perchance you wonder at this show;
But wonder on, till truth make all things plain.
This man is Pyramus, if you would know;
This beauteous lady Thisby is certain.
This man, with lime and roughcast, doth present 130
Wall, that vile Wall which did these lovers sunder;
And through Wall's chink, poor souls, they are content
To whisper. At the which let no man wonder.
This man, with lantern, dog, and bush of thorn,
Presenteth Moonshine; for, if you will know, 135
By moonshine did these lovers think no scorn
To meet at Ninus' tomb, there, there to woo.
This grisly beast, which Lion hight° by name,
The trusty Thisby, coming first by night,
Did scare away, or rather did affright; 140
And, as she fled, her mantle she did fall,°
Which Lion vile with bloody mouth did stain.
Anon comes Pyramus, sweet youth and tall.°
And finds his trusty Thisby's mantle slain:
Whereat, with blade, with bloody blameful blade, 145
He bravely broached° his boiling bloody breast;
And Thisby, tarrying in mulberry shade,
His dagger drew, and died. For all the rest,
Let Lion, Moonshine, Wall, and lovers twain

85 **wretchedness o'ercharged** lowly people overburdened 88 **in this kind** in this kind of thing (i.e., acting) 92 **Takes it in might** considers the ability, and the effort made 93 **clerks** scholars 105 **to my capacity** according to my understanding 106 **addressed** ready 111 **end** aim

116 **show** (probably referring to a kind of pantomime—"dumb show"—that was to follow, in which the action of the play was acted without words while the Prologue gave his account) 118 **stand upon points** (1) care about punctuation (2) worry about niceties 120 **stop** (1) technical term for the checking of a horse (2) mark of punctuation 123 **recorder** flutelike instrument 123 **government** control 138 **hight** is called 141 **fall** let fall 143 **tall** brave 146 **bravely broached** gallantly stabbed

150 At large° discourse, while here they do remain.
THESEUS. I wonder if the lion be to speak.
DEMETRIUS. No wonder, my lord. One lion may, when many asses do.
Exit Lion, Thisby and Moonshine.

WALL.
In this same interlude it doth befall
155 That I, one Snout by name, present a wall;
And such a wall, as I would have you think,
That had in it a crannied hole or chink,
Through which the lovers, Pyramus and Thisby,
Did whisper often very secretly.
160 This loam, this roughcast, and this stone, doth show
That I am that same wall; the truth is so;
And this the cranny is, right and sinister,°
Through which the fearful lovers are to whisper.

THESEUS. Would you desire lime and hair to speak bet-
165 ter?
DEMETRIUS. It is the wittiest partition° that ever I heard discourse, my lord.
THESEUS. Pyramus draws near the wall. Silence!

PYRAMUS.
O grim-looked night! O night with hue so black!
170 O night, which ever art when day is not!
O night, O night! Alack, alack, alack,
I fear my Thisby's promise is forgot!
And thou, O wall, O sweet, O lovely wall,
That stand'st between her father's ground and mine!
175 Thou wall, O wall, O sweet and lovely wall,
Show me thy chink, to blink through with mine eyne!

[*Wall holds up his fingers.*]

Thanks, courteous wall. Jove shield thee well for this!
But what see I? No Thisby do I see.
O wicked wall, through whom I see no bliss!
180 Cursed be thy stones for thus deceiving me!

THESEUS. The wall, methinks, being sensible,° should curse again.°
PYRAMUS. No, in truth, sir, he should not. "Deceiving me" is Thisby's cue. She is to enter now, and I am to spy her
185 through the wall. You shall see it will fall pat° as I told you. Yonder she comes.

Enter Thisby.

THISBY.
O wall, full often hast thou heard my moans,
For parting my fair Pyramus and me!
My cherry lips have often kissed thy stones,
Thy stones with lime and hair knit up in thee. 190

PYRAMUS.
I see a voice: now will I to the chink,
To spy an I can hear my Thisby's face.
Thisby!

THISBY.
My love thou art, my love I think.

PYRAMUS.
Think what thou wilt, I am thy lover's grace:° 195
And, like Limander,° am I trusty still.

THISBY.
And I like Helen,° till the Fates me kill.

PYRAMUS.
Not Shafalus to Procrus° was so true.

THISBY.
As Shafalus to Procrus, I to you.

PYRAMUS.
O kiss me through the hole of this vile wall! 200

THISBY.
I kiss the wall's hole, not your lips at all.

PYRAMUS.
Wilt thou at Ninny's tomb meet me straightway?

THISBY.
'Tide life, 'tide death,° I come without delay.
[*Exeunt Pyramus and Thisby.*]

WALL.
Thus have I, Wall, my part dischargèd so;
And, being done, this wall away doth go. 205
[*Exit.*]

THESEUS. Now is the moon used° between the two neighbors.
DEMETRIUS. No remedy, my lord, when walls are so willful to hear without warning.°
HIPPOLYTA. This is the silliest stuff that ever I heard. 210
THESEUS. The best in this kind° are but shadows; and the worst are no worse, if imagination amend them.
HIPPOLYTA. It must be your imagination then, and not theirs.
THESEUS. If we imagine no worse of them than they of 215 themselves, they may pass for excellent men. Here come two noble beasts in, a man and a lion.

150 **At large** at length 162 **right and sinister** i.e., running right and left, horizontal 166 **wittiest partition** most intelligent wall (with a pun on "partition," a section of a book or of an oration) 181 **sensible** conscious 182 **again** in return 185 **pat** exactly

195 **thy lover's grace** thy gracious lover 196 **Limander** (Bottom means Leander, but blends him with Alexander) 197 **Helen** (Hero, beloved of Leander, is probably meant) 198 **Shafalus to Procrus** (Cephalus and Procris are meant, legendary lovers) 203 **'Tide life, 'tide death** come (betide) life or death 206 **moon used** (the quartos read thus, the Folio reads *morall downe.* Among suggested emendations are "mural down," and "moon to see") 208–09 **when walls . . . without warning** i.e., when walls are so eager to listen without warning the parents (?) 211 **in this kind** of this sort, i.e., plays (or players?)

Enter Lion and Moonshine.

LION.
You, ladies, you, whose gentle hearts do fear
The smallest monstrous mouse that creeps on floor,
220 May now perchance both quake and tremble here,
When lion rough in wildest rage doth roar.
Then know that I, as Snug the joiner, am
A lion fell,° nor else no lion's dam;
For, if I should as lion come in strife
225 Into this place, 'twere pity on my life.°

THESEUS. A very gentle° beast, and of a good conscience.

DEMETRIUS. The very best at a beast, my lord, that e'er I saw.

230 LYSANDER. The lion is a very fox for his valor.

THESEUS. True; and a goose for his discretion.

DEMETRIUS. Not so, my lord; for his valor cannot carry° his discretion, and the fox carries the goose.

THESEUS. His discretion, I am sure, cannot carry his 235 valor; for the goose carries not the fox. It is well. Leave it to his discretion, and let us listen to the moon.

MOONSHINE.
This lanthorn° doth the hornèd moon present—

DEMETRIUS. He should have worn the horns on his head.°

240 THESEUS. He is no crescent, and his horns are invisible within the circumference.

MOONSHINE.
This lanthorn doth the hornèd moon present;
Myself the man i' th' moon do seem to be.

THESEUS. This is the greatest error of all the rest. The 245 man should be put into the lanthorn. How is it else the man i' th' moon?

DEMETRIUS. He dares not come there for the candle; for, you see, it is already in snuff.°

HIPPOLYTA. I am aweary of this moon. Would he 250 would change!

THESEUS. It appears, by his small light of discretion, that he is in the wane; but yet, in courtesy, in all reason, we must stay the time.

LYSANDER. Proceed, Moon.

255 MOONSHINE. All that I have to say is to tell you that the lanthorn is the moon; I, the man i' th' moon; this thorn bush, my thorn bush; and this dog, my dog.

DEMETRIUS. Why, all these should be in the lanthorn; for all these are in the moon. But, silence! Here comes Thisby. 260

Enter Thisby.

THISBY.
This is old Ninny's tomb. Where is my love?

LION. Oh—[*The Lion roars. Thisby runs off.*]

DEMETRIUS. Well roared, Lion.

THESEUS. Well run, Thisby.

HIPPOLYTA. Well shone, Moon. Truly, the moon shines 265 with a good grace.

[*The Lion shakes Thisby's mantle, and exit.*]

THESEUS. Well moused,° Lion.

DEMETRIUS. And then came Pyramus.

LYSANDER. And so the lion vanished.

Enter Pyramus.

PYRAMUS.
Sweet Moon, I thank thee for thy sunny beams; 270
I thank thee, Moon, for shining now so bright;
For, by thy gracious, golden, glittering gleams,
I trust to take of truest Thisby sight.
But stay, O spite!°
But mark, poor knight, 275
What dreadful dole° is here!
Eyes, do you see?
How can it be?
O dainty duck! O dear!
Thy mantle good, 280
What, stained with blood!
Approach, ye Furies fell!°
O Fates, come, come,
Cut thread and thrum;°
Quail,° crush, conclude, and quell!° 285

THESEUS. This passion, and the death of a dear friend, would go near to make a man look sad.

HIPPOLYTA. Beshrew° my heart, but I pity the man.

PYRAMUS.
O wherefore, Nature, didst thou lions frame?
Since lion vile hath here deflow'red my dear: 290
Which is—no, no—which was the fairest dame
That lived, that loved, that liked, that looked with cheer.°
Come, tears, confound;
Out, sword, and wound
The pap of Pyramus; 295

223 **lion fell** fierce lion (perhaps with a pun on *fell* = "skin") 225 **pity on my life** a dangerous thing for me 226 **gentle** gentlemanly, courteous 233 **carry** carry away 237 **lanthorn** (so spelled, and perhaps pronounced "lant-horn," because lanterns were commonly made of horn) 238–39 **horns on his head** (cuckolds were said to have horns) 248 **in snuff** (1) in need of snuffing (2) resentful

267 **moused** shaken (like a mouse) 274 **spite** vexation 276 **dole** sorrowful thing 282 **fell** fierce 284 **thread and thrum** i.e., everything (*thrum* = the end of the warp thread) 285 **Quail** destroy 285 **quell** kill 288 **Beshrew** curse (but a mild word) 292 **cheer** countenance

Ay, that left pap,
Where heart doth hop.
[*Stabs himself.*]
Thus die I, thus, thus, thus.
Now am I dead,
300 Now am I fled;
My soul is in the sky.
Tongue, lose thy light;
Moon, take thy flight.
[*Exit Moonshine.*]
Now die, die, die, die, die. [*Dies.*]

305 DEMETRIUS. No die, but an ace,° for him; for he is but one.

LYSANDER. Less than an ace, man; for he is dead, he is nothing.

THESEUS. With the help of a surgeon he might yet re-
310 cover, and yet prove an ass.

HIPPOLYTA. How chance° Moonshine is gone before Thisby comes back and finds her lover?

THESEUS. She will find him by starlight. Here she comes; and her passion° ends the play.

[*Enter Thisby.*]

315 HIPPOLYTA. Methinks she should not use a long one for such a Pyramus. I hope she will be brief.

DEMETRIUS. A mote will turn the balance, which Pyramus, which Thisby, is the better; he for a man, God warr'nt us; she for a woman, God bless us!

320 LYSANDER. She hath spied him already with those sweet eyes.

DEMETRIUS. and thus she means,° videlicet:

THISBY.
Asleep, my love?
What, dead, my dove?
325 O Pyramus, arise!
Speak, speak. Quite dumb?
Dead, dead? A tomb
Must cover thy sweet eyes.
These lily lips,
330 This cherry nose,
These yellow cowslip cheeks,
Are gone, are gone.
Lovers, make moan.
His eyes were green as leeks.
335 O Sisters Three,°
Come, come to me,
With hands as pale as milk;
Lay them in gore,
Since you have shore°
340 With shears his thread of silk.
Tongue, not a word.
Come, trusty sword,
Come, blade, my breast imbrue!°
[*Stabs herself.*]
And, farewell, friends.
345 Thus Thisby ends.
Adieu, adieu, adieu. [*Dies.*]

THESEUS. Moonshine and Lion are left to bury the dead.

DEMETRIUS. Ay, and Wall too.

350 BOTTOM [*starting up*]. No, I assure you; the wall is down that parted their fathers. Will it please you to see the epilogue, or to hear a Bergomask dance° between two of our company?

THESEUS. No epilogue, I pray you; for your play needs
355 no excuse. Never excuse, for when the players are all dead, there need none to be blamed. Marry, if he that writ it had played Pyramus and hanged himself in Thisby's garter, it would have been a fine tragedy: and so it is, truly; and very notably discharged. But, come, your Bergomask. Let your
360 epilogue alone.

[*A dance.*]

The iron tongue of midnight hath told° twelve.
Lovers, to bed; 'tis almost fairy time.
I fear we shall outsleep the coming morn,
As much as we this night have overwatched.
365 This palpable-gross° play hath well beguiled
The heavy gait of night. Sweet friends, to bed.
A fortnight hold we this solemnity,
In nightly revels and new jollity. *Exeunt.*

Enter Puck [*with a broom*].

PUCK.
Now the hungry lion roars,
370 And the wolf behowls the moon;
Whilst the heavy plowman snores,
All with weary task fordone.°
Now the wasted° brands do glow,
Whilst the screech owl, screeching loud,
375 Puts the wretch that lies in woe
In remembrance of a shroud.
Now it is the time of night,
That the graves, all gaping wide,
Every one lets forth his sprite,
380 In the churchway paths to glide:

305 **No die, but an ace** not a die (singular of "dice"), but a one-spot on a die 311 **How chance** how does it come that 314 **passion** passionate speech 322 **means** laments 335 **Sisters Three** the three Fates

339 **shore** shorn 343 **imbrue** stain with blood 352 **Bergomask dance** rustic dance 361 **told** counted, tolled 365 **palpable-gross** obviously grotesque 372 **fordone** worn out 373 **wasted** used up

And we fairies, that do run
By the triple Hecate's team,°
From the presence of the sun,
Following darkness like a dream,
385 Now are frolic.° Not a mouse
Shall disturb this hallowed house:
I am sent, with broom, before,
To sweep the dust behind the door.°

Enter King and Queen of Fairies with all their train.

OBERON.
Through the house give glimmering light,
390 By the dead and drowsy fire:
Every elf and fairy sprite
Hop as light as bird from brier;
And this ditty, after me,
Sing, and dance it trippingly.

TITANIA.
395 First, rehearse your song by rote,
To each word a warbling note:
Hand in hand, with fairy grace,
Will we sing, and bless this place.

[*Song and dance.*]

OBERON.
Now, until the break of day,
400 Through this house each fairy stray.
To the best bride-bed will we,
Which by us shall blessèd be;
And the issue there create°
Ever shall be fortunate.
405 So shall all the couples three
Ever true in loving be;
And the blots of Nature's hand
Shall not in their issue stand.
Never mole, harelip, nor scar.
Nor mark prodigious,° such as are 410
Despisèd in nativity.
Shall upon their children be.
With this field-dew consecrate,
Every fairy take his gait,°
And each several° chamber bless, 415
Through this palace, with sweet peace,
And the owner of it blest
Ever shall in safety rest.
Trip away; make no stay;
Meet me all by break of day. 420

Exeunt [*all but Puck*].

PUCK.
If we shadows have offended,
Think but this, and all is mended:
That you have but slumb'red here,
While these visions did appear.
And this weak and idle° theme, 425
No more yielding but° a dream,
Gentles, do not reprehend:
If you pardon, we will mend.
And, as I am an honest Puck,
If we have unearnèd luck 430
Now to scape the serpent's tongue,°
We will make amends ere long;
Else the Puck a liar call:
So, good night unto you all.
Give me your hands,° if we be friends, 435
And Robin shall restore amends.° [*Exit.*]

FINIS

TOPICS FOR DISCUSSION AND WRITING

1. What impression do you get of Theseus in the first scene?
2. Characterize Bottom in the second scene.
3. Take one scene from *A Midsummer Night's Dream* and compose detailed stage directions for it, indicating exactly how you would stage the scene.
4. The love story is really complete by the end of the fourth act. What does the fifth act contribute to the play?
5. What ironies (see the Glossary) do you find in the play?
6. What do you find funny about *A Midsummer Night's Dream*?

382 **triple Hecate's team** i.e., because she had three names: Phoebe in Heaven, Diana on Earth, Hecate in Hades. (Like her chariot—drawn by black horses or dragons—the elves were abroad only at night; but III.ii.388–91 says differently) 385 **frolic** frolicsome 388 **behind the door** i.e., from behind the door (Puck traditionally helped with household chores) 403 **create** created 410 **mark prodigious** ominous birthmark 414 **take his gait** proceed 415 **several** individual 425 **idle** foolish 426 **No more yielding but** yielding no more than 431 **to scape the serpent's tongue** i.e., to escape hisses from the audience 435 **Give me your hands** applaud 436 **restore amends** make amends

The faithful Earl of Kent (James Blendick), unfairly put in the stocks for defending his master King Lear, warns Lear (Len Cariou) that his daughter is turning against him as the Fool (Nicholas Kepros) observes in the Guthrie Theater Company's 1974 production of Shakespeare's *King Lear.* Directed by Michael Langham (Courtesy the Guthrie Theater, Minneapolis.)

WILLIAM SHAKESPEARE

The Tragedy of King Lear

Edited by Russell Fraser

William Shakespeare (1564–1616) was born in Stratford, England, of middle-class parents. Nothing of interest is known about his early years, but by 1590 he was acting and writing plays in London. He early worked in all three Elizabethan dramatic genres—tragedy, comedy, and history. *Romeo and Juliet,* for example, was written about 1595, the year of *Richard II,* and in the following year he wrote *A Midsummer Night's Dream. Julius Caesar* (1599) probably preceded *As You Like It* by one year, and *Hamlet* probably followed *As You Like It* by less than a year. Among the plays that followed *King Lear* (1605–06) were *Macbeth* (1605–06) and several "romances"—plays that have happy endings but that seem more meditative and closer to tragedy than such comedies as *A Midsummer Night's Dream, As You Like It,* and *Twelfth Night.*

COMMENTARY

The best way to understand Shakespeare's tragic vision is, of course, to see and read the tragedies very intelligently, but some help may be gained from a brief consideration of two speeches in *Hamlet.* In the final scene, when Fortinbras and others enter the stage looking for Claudius, they find to their amazement the corpses of Claudius, Gertrude, Laertes, and Hamlet. Horatio, Hamlet's friend, endeavors to bring the visitors up to date:

> What is it you would see?
> If aught of woe or wonder, cease your search.

Fortinbras and his associates are indeed struck with woe and wonder:

> FORTINBRAS. O proud Death,
> What feast is toward in thine eternal cell
> That thou so many princes at a shot
> So bloodily hast struck?
> AMBASSADOR. The sight is dismal.

Horatio seeks to explain: the visitors will hear

> Of carnal, bloody, and unnatural acts,
> Of accidental judgments, casual slaughters,
> Of deaths put on by cunning and forced cause,
> And, in this upshot, purposes mistook
> Fall'n on th'inventors' heads.

The spectators of the play itself have indeed seen "unnatural acts," "deaths put on by cunning," etc., and presumably these spectators have experienced the "woe" and "wonder" that the new arrivals will experience as Horatio sets forth the details.

Let us now look at a second passage from *Hamlet.* The speaker is the despicable Rosencrantz, and there is some flattery of King Claudius in his speech, but the gist of his argument about the death of a king rings true, makes sense:

> The cess of majesty
> Dies not alone, but like a gulf doth draw
> What's near it with it; or it is a massy wheel
> Fixed on the summit of the highest mount.
> To whose huge spokes ten thousand lesser things
> Are mortised and adjoined, which when it falls,
> Each small annexment, petty consequence,
> Attends the boist'rous ruin. Never alone
> Did the King sigh, but with a general groan.

Surely it is understandable that the deaths of, say, Lincoln and Kennedy had a vastly greater effect upon America than the deaths of any number of private citizens. Put crudely, they mattered more.

The speeches together afford some justification of the Elizabethan view that tragedy is concerned with violence done to and by people of high rank. The fall of a person in high position evokes deeper woe and wonder than the snuffing out of a nonentity. The latter may evoke pity, but scarcely awe at the terrifying power of destructiveness or at the weakness that is at the heart of power.

Shakespeare does not merely slap the label of king or prince or general on a character and then assume that greatness has been established. His characters speak great language and perform great deeds. (And, no less important, they have the capacity to suffer greatly.) Lear, in the first scene, gives away—almost seems to create—fertile kingdoms:

> Of all these bounds, even from this line to this.
> With shadowy forests, and with champains riched,
> With plenteous rivers, and wide-skirted meads,
> We make thee lady.

Even in injustice, when he banishes his daughter, Cordelia, for speaking the truth as she sees it, he has a kind of terrible grandeur:

> Let it be so, thy truth then be thy dower!
> For, by the sacred radiance of the sun,
> The mysteries of Hecate and the night,
> By all the operation of the orbs
> From whom we do exist and cease to be,
> Here I disclaim all my paternal care,
> Propinquity and property of blood,
> And as a stranger to my heart and me
> Hold thee from this for ever.

Finally, even in his madness—"a sight most pitiful in the meanest wretch, / Past speaking of in a king"—he has grandeur. To Gloucester's "Is't not the king?" he replies:

> Ay, every inch a king.
> When I do stare, see how the subject quakes.

> I pardon that man's life. What was thy cause?
> Adultery?
> Thou shalt not die: die for adultery! No:
> The wren goes to 't, and the small gilded fly
> Does lecher in my sight.
> Let copulation thrive. . . .

We might contrast Lear's noble voice with Edmund's materialistic comment on the way of the world:

> This is the excellent foppery of the world, that when we are sick in fortune, often the surfeits of our own behavior, we make guilty of our disasters the sun, the moon, and stars; as if we were villains on necessity; fools by heavenly compulsion; knaves, thieves, and treachers by spherical predominance; drunkards, liars, and adulterers by an enforced obedience of planetary influence; and all that we are evil in, by a divine thrusting on. An admirable evasion of whoremaster man, to lay his goatish disposition on the charge of a star. . . . Fut! I should have been that I am, had the maidenliest star in the firmament twinkled on my bastardizing.

Lear seems to be displacing *Hamlet* as the play that speaks to our time. *Hamlet* was especially popular with nineteenth-century audiences, who often found in the uncertain prince an image of their own doubts in a world in which belief in a benevolent divine order was collapsing under the influence of scientific materialism and bourgeois aggressiveness. Many audiences in our age find in *Lear*—where "for many miles about / There's scarce a bush"—a play thoroughly in the spirit of Beckett's *Waiting for Godot,* where the scenery consists of a single tree. Moreover, Lear denounces the hypocrisy of the power structure and exposes the powerlessness of the disenfranchised: "Robes and furred gowns hide all. Plate sin with gold, / And the strong lance of justice hurtless breaks; / Arm it in rags, a pygmy's straw does pierce it." And what of the gods? There are several comments about their nature, but perhaps the most memorable reference to the gods is not a mere comment but one followed by an action: learning that Cordelia is in danger, Albany cries out, "The gods defend her!" and immediately his words are mocked by Lear's entrance on the stage, with the dead Cordelia in his arms.

But the interpretation of *King Lear* as a revelation of the emptiness of life fails to consider at least two things. First, there is an affirmation in those passages in which Lear comes, through heart-rending anguish, to see that he was not what he thought he was. Second, this anagnorisis or recognition is several times associated with love or charity, as when (3.4) Lear invites the Fool to enter the hovel first and then confesses his guilt in having cared too little for humanity. And this care for humanity is seen in Cordelia, who comes—though ineffectually in the long run—to the aid of her father. It is seen, too, in the nameless servant who at the end of 3.7 promises to apply medicine to Gloucester's eyeless sockets; it is seen even in the villainous Edmund, who in dying repents and says, "Some good I mean to do, / Despite mine own nature" (5.3), and who thereupon tries, unsuccessfully, to save Cordelia. No one would say that these actions turn *King Lear* into a happy vision, but it is perverse to ignore them and to refuse to see that in this play love humanizes as surely as egoism dehumanizes. If the play dramatizes human desolation, it also dramatizes the love that, while providing no protection against pain or death, makes a human being's life different from the life of "a dog, a horse, a rat."

WILLIAM SHAKESPEARE *The Tragedy of King Lear*

[*List of Characters*

LEAR, *King of Britain*
KING OF FRANCE
DUKE OF BURGUNDY
DUKE OF CORNWALL, *husband to Regan*
DUKE OF ALBANY, *husband to Goneril*
EARL OF KENT
EARL OF GLOUCESTER
EDGAR, *son to Gloucester*
EDMUND, *bastard son to Gloucester*
CURAN, *a courtier*
OSWALD, *steward to Goneril*
OLD MAN, *tenant to Gloucester*
DOCTOR
LEAR'S FOOL
A CAPTAIN *subordinate to Edmund*
GENTLEMEN *attending on Cordelia*
A HERALD
SERVANTS *to Cornwall*
GONERIL, REGAN, CORDELIA } *daughters to Lear*
KNIGHTS *attending on Lear,* OFFICERS, MESSENGERS, SOLDIERS, ATTENDANTS

Scene: Britain]

ACT I

SCENE I

[*King Lear's palace.*]

Enter Kent, Gloucester, and Edmund.

KENT. I thought the king had more affected°[1] the Duke of Albany° than Cornwall.

GLOUCESTER. It did always seem so to us; but now, in the division of the kingdom, it appears not which of the dukes he values most, for equalities are so weighed that curiosity in neither can make choice of either's moiety.° 5

KENT. Is not this your son, my lord?

GLOUCESTER. His breeding,° sir, hath been at my charge. I have so often blushed to acknowledge him that now I am brazed° to't. 10

KENT. I cannot conceive° you.

GLOUCESTER. Sir, this young fellow's mother could; whereupon she grew round-wombed, and had indeed, sir, a son for her cradle ere she had a husband for her bed. Do you smell a fault? 15

KENT. I cannot wish the fault undone, the issue° of it being so proper.°

GLOUCESTER. But I have a son, sir, by order of law, some year elder than this, who yet is no dearer in my account:° though this knave° came something saucily° to the 20 world before he was sent for, yet was his mother fair, there was good sport at his making, and the whoreson° must be acknowledged. Do you know this noble gentleman, Edmund?

EDMUND. No, my lord. 25

GLOUCESTER. My Lord of Kent. Remember him hereafter as my honorable friend.

EDMUND. My services to your lordship.

KENT. I must love you, and sue° to know you better.

EDMUND. Sir, I shall study deserving. 30

GLOUCESTER. He hath been out° nine years, and away he shall again. The king is coming.

Sound a sennet.° Enter one bearing a coronet,° then King Lear, then the Dukes of Cornwall and Albany, next Goneril, Regan, Cordelia, and Attendants.

LEAR.
Attend the lords of France and Burgundy, Gloucester.

[1] The degree sign (°) indicates a footnote, which is keyed to the text by the line number. Text references are printed in **boldface** type; the annotation follows in lightface type. The notes are Russell Fraser's.
I.i.1 **affected** loved 2 **Albany** Albanacte, whose domain extended "from the river Humber to the point of Caithness" (Holinshed)

5–6 **equalities . . . moiety** shares are so balanced against one another that careful examination by neither can make him wish the other's portion 8 **breeding** upbringing 10 **brazed** made brazen, hardened 11 **conceive** understand (pun follows) 16 **issue** result (child) 17 **proper** handsome 19–20 **account** estimation 20 **knave** fellow (without disapproval) 20 **saucily** (1) insolently (2) lasciviously 22 **whoreson** fellow (literally, son of a whore) 29 **sue** entreat 31 **out** away, abroad 32 s.d. **sennet** set of notes played on a trumpet, signaling the entrance or departure of a procession; **coronet** small crown, intended for Cordelia

GLOUCESTER.
I shall, my lord. *Exit, [with Edmund].*
LEAR.
35 Meantime we shall express our darker purpose.°
Give me the map there. Know that we have divided
In three our kingdom; and 'tis our fast° intent
To shake all cares and business from our age,
Conferring them on younger strengths, while we
40 Unburthened crawl toward death. Our son of Cornwall,
And you our no less loving son of Albany,
We have this hour a constant will to publish°
Our daughters' several° dowers, that future strife
May be prevented° now. The princes, France and Burgundy,
45 Great rivals in our youngest daughter's love,
Long in our court have made their amorous sojourn,
And here are to be answered. Tell me, my daughters
(Since now we will divest us both of rule,
Interest° of territory, cares of state),
50 Which of you shall we say doth love us most,
That we our largest bounty may extend
Where nature doth with merit challenge.° Goneril,
Our eldest-born, speak first.
GONERIL.
Sir, I love you more than word can wield° the matter;
55 Dearer than eyesight, space,° and liberty;
Beyond what can be valued, rich or rare;
No less than life, with grace, health, beauty, honor;
As much as child e'er loved, or father found;
A love that makes breath° poor, and speech unable:°
60 Beyond all manner of so much° I love you.
CORDELIA [*aside*].
What shall Cordelia speak? Love, and be silent.
LEAR.
Of all these bounds, even from this line to this,
With shadowy forests, and with champains riched,°
With plenteous rivers, and wide-skirted meads,°
65 We make thee lady. To thine and Albany's issues°,
Be this perpetual.° What says our second daughter,
Our dearest Regan, wife of Cornwall? Speak.
REGAN.
I am made of that self mettle° as my sister,

35 **darker purpose** hidden intention 37 **fast** fixed
42 **constant . . . publish** fixed intention to proclaim
43 **several** separate 44 **prevented** forestalled
49 **Interest** legal right 52 **nature . . . challenge** natural affection contends with desert for (or lays claim to) bounty
54 **wield** handle 55 **space** scope 59 **breath** language
59 **unable** impotent 60 **Beyond . . . much** beyond all these comparisons 63 **champains riched** enriched plains
64 **wide-skirted meads** extensive grasslands 65 **issues** descendants 66 **perpetual** in perpetuity 68 **self mettle** same material or temperament

And prize me at her worth.° In my true heart
70 I find she names my very deed of love;°
Only she comes too short, that° I profess
Myself an enemy to all other joys
Which the most precious square of sense professes,°
And find I am alone felicitate°
In your dear highness' love.
75 CORDELIA [*aside*]. Then poor Cordelia!
And yet not so, since I am sure my love's
More ponderous° than my tongue.
LEAR.
To thee and thine hereditary ever
Remain this ample third of our fair kingdom,
80 No less in space, validity,° and pleasure
Than that conferred on Goneril. Now, our joy,
Although our last and least;° to whose young love
The vines of France and milk° of Burgundy
Strive to be interest;° what can you say to draw
85 A third more opulent than your sisters? Speak.
CORDELIA.
Nothing, my lord.
LEAR. Nothing?
CORDELIA. Nothing.
LEAR.
Nothing will come of nothing. Speak again.
CORDELIA.
Unhappy that I am, I cannot heave
My heart into my mouth. I love your majesty
90 According to my bond,° no more nor less.
LEAR.
How, how, Cordelia? Mend your speech a little,
Lest you may mar your fortunes.
CORDELIA. Good my lord,
You have begot me, bred me, loved me. I
Return those duties back as are right fit,°
95 Obey you, love you, and most honor you.
Why have my sisters husbands, if they say
They love you all? Haply,° when I shall wed,
That lord whose hand must take my plight° shall carry
Half my love with him, half my care and duty.
100 Sure I shall never marry like my sisters,
To love my father all.

69 **prize . . . worth** value me the same (imperative)
70 **my . . . love** what my love really is (a legalism) 71 **that** in that 73 **Which . . . professes** which the choicest estimate of sense avows 74 **felicitate** made happy 77 **ponderous** weighty 80 **validity** value 82 **least** youngest, smallest
83 **milk** i.e., pastures 84 **interest** closely connected, as interested parties 90 **bond** filial obligation 94 **Return . . . fit** i.e., am correspondingly dutiful 97 **Haply** perhaps
98 **plight** troth plight

LEAR.
But goes thy heart with this?
CORDELIA. Ay, my good lord.
LEAR.
So young, and so untender?
CORDELIA.
So young, my lord, and true.
LEAR.
105 Let it be so, thy truth then be thy dower!
For, by the sacred radiance of the sun,
The mysteries of Hecate° and the night,
By all the operation of the orbs°
From whom we do exist and cease to be,
110 Here I disclaim all my paternal care,
Propinquity and property of blood,°
And as a stranger to my heart and me
Hold thee from this for ever. The barbarous Scythian,°
Or he that makes his generation messes°
115 To gorge his appetite, shall to my bosom
Be as well neighbored, pitied, and relieved,
As thou my sometime° daughter.
KENT. Good my liege—
LEAR.
Peace, Kent!
Come not between the dragon° and his wrath.
120 I loved her most, and thought to set my rest°
On her kind nursery.° Hence and avoid my sight!
So be my grave my peace, as here I give
Her father's heart from her! Call France. Who stirs?
Call Burgundy. Cornwall and Albany,
125 With my two daughters' dowers digest° the third;
Let pride, which she calls plainness, marry her.°
I do invest you jointly with my power,
Preeminence, and all the large effects
That troop with majesty.° Ourself,° by monthly course,
130 With reservation° of an hundred knights,
By you to be sustained, shall our abode
Make with you by due turn. Only we shall retain
The name, and all th' addition° to a king. The sway,
Revènue, execution of the rest,
Belovèd sons, be yours; which to confirm, 135
This coronet° part between you.
KENT. Royal Lear,
Whom I have ever honored as my king,
Loved as my father, as my master followed,
As my great patron thought on in my prayers—
LEAR.
The bow is bent and drawn; make from the shaft.° 140
KENT.
Let it fall° rather, though the fork° invade
The region of my heart. Be Kent unmannerly
When Lear is mad. What wouldst thou do, old man?
Thinkst thou that duty shall have dread to speak
When power to flattery bows? To plainness honor's bound 145
When majesty falls to folly. Reserve thy state,°
And in thy best consideration° check
This hideous rashness. Answer my life my judgment,°
Thy youngest daughter does not love thee least,
Nor are those empty-hearted whose low sounds 150
Reverb° no hollowness.°
LEAR. Kent, on thy life, no more!
KENT.
My life I never held but as a pawn°
To wage° against thine enemies; nor fear to lose it,
Thy safety being motive.°
LEAR. Out of my sight!
KENT.
See better, Lear, and let me still° remain 155
The true blank° of thine eye.
LEAR.
Now by Apollo—
KENT. Now by Apollo, king,
Thou swear'st thy gods in vain.
LEAR. O vassal! Miscreant!°

[*Laying his hand on his sword.*]

ALBANY, CORNWALL. Dear sir, forbear!

107 **mysteries of Hecate** secret rites of Hecate (goddess of the infernal world, and of witchcraft) 108 **operation . . . orbs** astrological influence 111 **Propinquity . . . blood** relationship and common blood 113 **Scythian** type of the savage 114 **makes . . . messes** eats his own offspring 117 **sometime** former 119 **dragon** (1) heraldic device of Britain (2) emblem of ferocity 120 **set my rest** (1) stake my all (a term from the card game of primero) (2) find my rest 121 **nursery** care, nursing 125 **digest** absorb 126 **Let . . . her** Let her pride be her dowry and gain her a husband 128–29 **effects . . . majesty** accompaniments that go with kingship 129 **Ourself** the royal "we" 130 **reservation** the action of reserving a privilege (a legalism)

133 **addition** titles and honors 136 **coronet** the crown that was to have been Cordelia's 140 **make . . . shaft** avoid the arrow 141 **fall** strike 141 **fork** forked head of the arrow 146 **Reserve thy state** retain your kingly authority 147 **best consideration** most careful reflection 148 **Answer . . . judgment** I will stake my life on my opinion 151 **Reverb** reverberate 151 **hollowness** (1) emptiness (2) insincerity 152 **pawn** stake in a wager 153 **wage** (1) wager (2) carry on war 154 **motive** moving cause 155 **still** always 156 **blank** the white spot in the center of the target (at which Lear should aim) 158 **vassal! Miscreant!** base wretch! Misbeliever!

KENT.
160 Kill thy physician, and the fee bestow
Upon the foul disease. Revoke thy gift,
Or, whilst I can vent clamor° from my throat,
I'll tell thee thou dost evil.
LEAR. Hear me, recreant!°
On thine allegiance,° hear me!
165 That thou hast sought to make us break our vows,
Which we durst never yet, and with strained° pride
To come betwixt our sentence° and our power,
Which nor our nature nor our place can bear,
Our potency made good,° take thy reward.
170 Five days we do allot thee for provision°
To shield thee from diseases° of the world,
And on the sixth to turn thy hated back
Upon the kingdom. If, on the tenth day following,
Thy banished trunk° be found in our dominions,
175 The moment is thy death. Away! By Jupiter,
This shall not be revoked.
KENT.
Fare thee well, king. Sith° thus thou wilt appear,
Freedom lives hence, and banishment is here.

[*To Cordelia.*]

The gods to their dear shelter take thee, maid,
180 That justly think'st, and hast most rightly said.

[*To Regan and Goneril.*]

And your large speeches may your deeds approve,°
That good effects° may spring from words of love.
Thus, Kent, O princes, bids you all adieu;
He'll shape his old course° in a country new.
Exit.

Flourish.° Enter Gloucester, with France and Burgundy; Attendants.

GLOUCESTER.
185 Here's France and Burgundy, my noble lord.
LEAR.
My Lord of Burgundy,
We first address toward you, who with this king
Hath rivaled for our daughter. What in the least
Will you require in present° dower with her,
Or cease your quest of love?
BURGUNDY. Most royal majesty, 190
I crave no more than hath your highness offered,
Nor will you tender° less.
LEAR. Right noble Burgundy,
When she was dear° to us, we did hold her so;
But now her price is fallen. Sir, there she stands.
If aught within that little seeming substance,° 195
Or all of it, with our displeasure pieced,°
And nothing more, may fitly like° your grace,
She's there, and she is yours.
BURGUNDY. I know no answer.
LEAR.
Will you, with those infirmities she owes°
Unfriended, new adopted to our hate, 200
Dow'red with our curse, and strangered° with our oath,
Take her, or leave her?
BURGUNDY. Pardon me, royal sir.
Election makes not up° on such conditions.
LEAR.
Then leave her, sir; for, by the pow'r that made me,
I tell you all her wealth. [*To France.*] For you, great king, 205
I would not from your love make such a stray
To° match you where I hate; therefore beseech° you
T' avert your liking a more worthier way°
Than on a wretch whom nature is ashamed
Almost t' acknowledge hers.
FRANCE. This is most strange, 210
That she whom even but now was your best object,°
The argument° of your praise, balm of your age,
The best, the dearest, should in this trice of time
Commit a thing so monstrous to dismantle°
So many folds of favor. Sure her offense 215
Must be of such unnatural degree
That monsters it,° or your fore-vouched° affection
Fall into taint;° which to believe of her

162 **vent clamor** utter a cry 163 **recreant** traitor 164 **On thine allegiance** to forswear, which is to commit high treason 166 **strained** forced (and so excessive) 167 **sentence** judgment, decree 169 **Our . . . good** my royal authority being now asserted 170 **for provision** for making preparation 171 **diseases** troubles 174 **trunk** body 177 **Sith** since 181 **approve** prove true 182 **effects** results 184 **shape . . . course** pursue his customary way 184 s.d. **Flourish** trumpet fanfare

189 **present** immediate 192 **tender** offer 193 **dear** (1) beloved (2) valued at a high price 195 **little seeming substance** person who is (1) inconsiderable (2) outspoken 196 **pieced** added to it 197 **fitly like** please by its fitness 199 **owes** possesses 201 **strangered** made a stranger 203 **Election . . . up** no one can choose 206–07 **make . . . To** stray so far as to 207 **beseech** I beseech 208 **avert . . . way** turn your affections from her and bestow them on a better person 211 **your best object** the one you loved most 212 **argument** subject 214 **dismantle** strip off 217 **That monsters it** as makes it monstrous, unnatural 217 **fore-vouched** previously sworn 218 **Fall into taint** must be taken as having been unjustified all along; i.e., Cordelia was unworthy of your love from the first

Must be a faith that reason without miracle
Should never plant in me.°
220 CORDELIA. I yet beseech your majesty,
If for° I want that glib and oily art
To speak and purpose not,° since what I well intend
I'll do't before I speak, that you make known
It is no vicious blot, murder, or foulness,
225 No unchaste action or dishonored step,
That hath deprived me of your grace and favor;
But even for want of that for which I am richer,
A still-soliciting° eye, and such a tongue
That I am glad I have not, though not to have it
Hath lost° me in your liking.
230 LEAR. Better thou
Hadst not been born than not t' have pleased me better.
FRANCE.
Is it but this? A tardiness in nature°
Which often leaves the history unspoke°
That it intends to do. My Lord of Burgundy,
235 What say you° to the lady? Love's not love
When it is mingled with regards° that stands
Aloof from th' entire point.° Will you have her?
She is herself a dowry.
BURGUNDY. Royal king,
Give but that portion which yourself proposed,
240 And here I take Cordelia by the hand,
Duchess of Burgundy.
LEAR.
Nothing. I have sworn. I am firm.
BURGUNDY.
I am sorry then you have so lost a father
That you must lose a husband.
CORDELIA. Peace be with Burgundy.
245 Since that respects of fortune° are his love,
I shall not be his wife.
FRANCE.
Fairest Cordelia, that art most rich being poor,
Most choice forsaken, and most loved despised,
Thee and thy virtues here I seize upon.
250 Be it lawful I take up what's cast away.
Gods, gods! 'Tis strange that from their cold'st neglect
My love should kindle to inflamed respect.°
Thy dow'rless daughter, king, thrown to my chance,°
Is queen of us, of ours, and our fair France.
Not all the dukes of wat'rish° Burgundy 255
Can buy this unprized precious° maid of me.
Bid them farewell, Cordelia, though unkind.
Thou losest here,° a better where° to find.
LEAR.
Thou hast her, France; let her be thine, for we
Have no such daughter, nor shall ever see 260
That face of hers again. Therefore be gone,
Without our grace, our love, our benison.°
Come, noble Burgundy.
Flourish. Exeunt [Lear, Burgundy, Cornwall, Albany, Gloucester, and Attendants].
FRANCE.
Bid farewell to your sisters.
CORDELIA.
The jewels of our father,° with washed° eyes 265
Cordelia leaves you. I know you what you are,
And, like a sister,° am most loath to call
Your faults as they are named.° Love well our father.
To your professèd° bosoms I commit him.
But yet, alas, stood I within his grace, 270
I would prefer° him to a better place.
So farewell to you both.
REGAN.
Prescribe not us our duty.
GONERIL. Let your study
Be to content your lord, who hath received you
At Fortune's alms.° You have obedience scanted,° 275
And well are worth the want that you have wanted.°
CORDELIA.
Time shall unfold what plighted° cunning hides.
Who covers faults, at last shame them derides.°

219–20 **reason . . . me** my reason would have to be supported by a miracle to make me believe 221 **for** because 222 **purpose not** not mean to do what I promise 228 **still-soliciting** always begging 230 **lost** ruined 232 **tardiness in nature** natural reticence 233 **leaves . . . unspoke** does not announce the action 235 **What say you** i.e., will you have 236 **regards** considerations (the dowry) 236–37 **stands . . . point** have nothing to do with the essential question (love) 245 **respects of fortune** mercenary considerations

252 **inflamed respect** more ardent affection 253 **chance** lot 255 **wat'rish** (1) with many rivers (2) weak, diluted 256 **unprized precious** unappreciated by others, and yet precious 258 **here** in this place 258 **where** other place 262 **benison** blessing 265 **The jewels . . . father** you creatures prized by our father 265 **washed** (1) weeping (2) clearsighted 267 **like a sister** because I am a sister, i.e., loyal, affectionate 268 **as . . . named** by their right and ugly names 269 **professèd** pretending to love 271 **prefer** recommend 275 **At Fortune's alms** as a charitable bequest from Fortune (and so, by extension, as one beggared or cast down by Fortune) 275 **scanted** stinted 276 **worth . . . wanted** deserve to be denied, even as you have denied 277 **plighted** pleated, enfolded 278 **Who . . . derides** Those who hide their evil are finally exposed and shamed ("He that hideth his sons, shall not prosper")

Well may you prosper.

FRANCE. Come, my fair Cordelia.

Exit France and Cordelia.

280 GONERIL. Sister, it is not little I have to say of what most nearly appertains to us both. I think our father will hence tonight.

REGAN. That's most certain, and with you; next month with us.

285 GONERIL. You see how full of changes his age is. The observation we have made of it hath not been little. He always loved our sister most, and with what poor judgment he hath now cast her off appears too grossly.°

REGAN. 'Tis the infirmity of his age; yet he hath ever but
290 slenderly known himself.

GONERIL. The best and soundest of his time° hath been but rash; then must we look from his age to receive not alone the imperfections of long-ingrafted° condition,° but therewithal° the unruly waywardness that infirm and
295 choleric years bring with them.

REGAN. Such unconstant starts° are we like to have from him as this of Kent's banishment.

GONERIL. There is further compliment° of leave-taking between France and him. Pray you, let's hit° together; if our
300 father carry authority with such disposition as he bears,° this last surrender° of his will but offend° us.

REGAN. We shall further think of it.

GONERIL. We must do something, and i' th' heat.°

Exeunt.

SCENE II

[*The Earl of Gloucester's castle.*]

Enter Edmund [*with a letter*].

EDMUND.
Thou, Nature,° art my goddess; to thy law
My services are bound. Wherefore should I
Stand in the plague of custom,° and permit
The curiosity° of nations to deprive me,
5 For that° I am some twelve or fourteen moonshines°

288 **grossly** obviously 291 **of his time** period of his life up to now 293 **long-ingrafted** implanted for a long time 293 **condition** disposition; 294 **therewithal** with them 296 **unconstant starts** impulsive whims 298 **compliment** formal courtesy 299 **hit** agree 300 **carry . . . bears** continues, and in such frame of mind, to wield the sovereign power 301 **last surrender** recent abdication 301 **offend** vex 303 **i' th' heat** while the iron is hot
I.ii.1 **Nature** Edmund's conception of Nature accords with our description of a bastard as a natural child 3 **Stand . . . custom** respect hateful convention 4 **curiosity** nice distinctions 5 **For that** because 5 **moonshines** months

Lag of° a brother? Why bastard? Wherefore base?
When my dimensions are as well compact,°
My mind as generous,° and my shape as true,
As honest° madam's issue? Why brand they us
With base? With baseness? Bastardy? Base? Base? 10
Who, in the lusty stealth of nature, take
More composition° and fierce° quality
Than doth, within a dull, stale, tired bed,
Go to th' creating a whole tribe of fops°
Got° 'tween asleep and wake? Well then, 15
Legitimate Edgar, I must have your land.
Our father's love is to the bastard Edmund
As to th' legitimate. Fine word, "legitimate."
Well, my legitimate, if this letter speed,°
And my invention° thrive, Edmund the base 20
Shall top th' legitimate. I grow, I prosper.
Now, gods, stand up for bastards.

Enter Gloucester.

GLOUCESTER.
Kent banished thus? and France in choler parted?
And the king gone tonight? prescribed° his pow'r?
Confined to exhibition?° All this done 25
Upon the gad?° Edmund, how now? What news?

EDMUND.
So please your lordship, none.

GLOUCESTER.
Why so earnestly seek you to put up° that letter?

EDMUND.
I know no news, my lord.

GLOUCESTER.
What paper were you reading? 30

EDMUND. Nothing, my lord.

GLOUCESTER. No? What needed then that terrible dispatch° of it into your pocket? The quality of nothing hath not such need to hide itself. Let's see. Come, if it be nothing, I shall not need spectacles. 35

EDMUND. I beseech you, sir, pardon me. It is a letter from my brother that I have not all o'er-read; and for so much as I have perused, I find it not fit for your o'erlooking.°

GLOUCESTER. Give me the letter, sir.

EDMUND. I shall offend, either to detain or give it. The 40 contents, as in part I understand them, are to blame.°

6 **Lag of** short of being (in age) 7 **compact** framed 8 **generous** gallant 9 **honest** chaste 12 **composition** completeness 12 **fierce** energetic 14 **fops** fools 15 **Got** begot 19 **speed** prosper 20 **invention** plan 24 **prescribed** limited 25 **exhibition** an allowance or pension 26 **Upon the gad** on the spur of the moment (as if pricked by a gad or goad) 28 **put up** put away, conceal 32–33 **terrible dispatch** hasty putting away 38 **o'erlooking** inspection 41 **to blame** blameworthy

GLOUCESTER. Let's see, let's see.

EDMUND. I hope, for my brother's justification, he wrote this but as an essay or taste° of my virtue.

45 GLOUCESTER (*reads*). "This policy and reverence° of age makes the world bitter to the best of our times;° keeps our fortunes from us till our oldness cannot relish° them. I begin to find an idle and fond° bondage in the oppression of aged tyranny, who sways, not as it hath power, but as it is 50 suffered.° Come to me, that of this I may speak more. If our father would sleep till I waked him, you should enjoy half his revenue° for ever, and live the beloved of your brother, Edgar."

Hum! Conspiracy? "Sleep till I waked him, you should 55 enjoy half his revenue." My son Edgar! Had he a hand to write this? A heart and brain to breed it in? When came you to this? Who brought it?

EDMUND. It was not brought me, my lord; there's the cunning of it. I found it thrown in at the casement of my 60 closet.°

GLOUCESTER. You know the character° to be your brother's?

EDMUND. If the matter were good, my lord, I durst swear it were his; but in respect of that,° I would fain° think 65 it were not.

GLOUCESTER. It is his.

EDMUND. It is his hand, my lord; but I hope his heart is not in the contents.

GLOUCESTER. Has he never before sounded° you in 70 this business?

EDMUND. Never, my lord. But I have heard him oft maintain it to be fit that, sons at perfect° age, and fathers declined, the father should be as ward to the son, and the son manage his revenue.

75 GLOUCESTER. O villain, villain! His very opinion in the letter. Abhorred villain, unnatural, detested,° brutish villain; worse than brutish! Go, sirrah,° seek him. I'll apprehend him. Abominable villain! Where is he?

EDMUND. I do not well know, my lord. If it shall please 80 you to suspend your indignation against my brother till you can derive from him better testimony of his intent, you should run a certain course;° where, if you violently proceed against him, mistaking his purpose, it would make a great gap° in your own honor and shake in pieces the heart of his obedience. I dare pawn down° my life for him that he hath 85 writ this to feel° my affection to your honor, and to no other pretense of danger.°

GLOUCESTER. Think you so?

EDMUND. If your honor judge it meet,° I will place you where you shall hear us confer of this, and by an auricular 90 assurance° have your satisfaction, and that without any further delay than this very evening.

GLOUCESTER. He cannot be such a monster.

EDMUND. Nor is not, sure.

GLOUCESTER. To his father, that so tenderly and en- 95 tirely loves him. Heaven and earth! Edmund, seek him out; wind me into him,° I pray you; frame° the business after your own wisdom. I would unstate myself to be in a due resolution.°

EDMUND. I will seek him, sir, presently;° convey° the 100 business as I shall find means, and acquaint you withal.°

GLOUCESTER. These late° eclipses in the sun and moon portend no good to us. Though the wisdom of nature° can reason° it thus and thus, yet nature finds itself scourged by the sequent effects.° Love cools, friendship falls 105 off,° brothers divide. In cities, mutinies;° in countries, discord; in palaces, treason; and the bond cracked 'twixt son and father. This villain of mine comes under the prediction,° there's son against father; the king falls from bias of nature,° there's father against child. We have seen the best of 110 our time.° Machinations, hollowness,° treachery, and all ruinous disorders follow us disquietly° to our graves. Find out this villain, Edmund; it shall lose thee nothing.° Do it carefully. And the noble and true-hearted Kent banished; his offense, honesty. 'Tis strange. 115

Exit.

44 **essay or taste** test 45 **policy and reverence** policy of reverencing (hendiadys) 46 **best . . . times** best years of our lives (i.e., our youth) 47 **relish** enjoy 48 **idle and fond** foolish 49–50 **who . . . suffered** which rules, not from its own strength, but from our allowance 52 **revenue** income 59–60 **casement . . . closet** window of my room 61 **character** handwriting 64 **in . . . that** in view of what it is 64 **fain** prefer to 69 **sounded** sounded you out 72 **perfect** mature 76 **detested** detestable 77 **sirrah** sir (familiar form of address)

82 **run . . . course** proceed safely, know where you are going 84 **gap** breach 85 **pawn down** stake 86 **feel** test 87 **pretense of danger** dangerous purpose 89 **meet** fit 90–91 **auricular assurance** proof heard with your own ears 97 **wind . . . him** insinuate yourself into his confidence for me 97 **frame** manage 98–99 **unstate . . . resolution** forfeit my earldom to know the truth 100 **presently** at once 100 **convey** manage 101 **withal** with it 102 **late** recent 103–04 **wisdom of nature** scientific learning 104 **reason** explain 104–05 **yet . . . effects** nonetheless our world is punished with subsequent disasters 105–06 **falls off** revolts 106 **mutinies** riots 108–09 **This . . . prediction** my son's villainous behavior is included in these portents, and bears them out 109–10 **bias of nature** natural inclination (the metaphor is from the game of bowls) 110–11 **best . . . time** our best days 111 **hollowness** insincerity 112 **disquietly** unquietly 113 **it . . . nothing** you will not lose by it

EDMUND. This is the excellent foppery° of the world, that when we are sick in fortune, often the surfeits of our own behavior,° we make guilty of our disasters the sun, the moon, and stars; as if we were villains on° necessity; fools by
120 heavenly compulsion; knaves, thieves, and treachers by spherical predominance;° drunkards, liars, and adulterers by an enforced obedience of planetary influence;° and all that we are evil in, by a divine thrusting on.° An admirable evasion of whoremaster° man, to lay his goatish° disposition on
125 the charge of a star. My father compounded° with my mother under the Dragon's Tail,° and my nativity° was under Ursa Major,° so that it follows I am rough and lecherous. Fut!° I should have been that° I am, had the maidenliest star in the firmament twinkled on my bastardizing.
130 Edgar—

Enter Edgar.

and pat he comes, like the catastrophe° of the old comedy. My cue is villainous melancholy, with a sigh like Tom o' Bedlam.°—O, these eclipses do portend these divisions. Fa, sol, la, mi.°

135 EDGAR. How now, brother Edmund; what serious contemplation are you in?

EDMUND. I am thinking, brother, of a prediction I read this other day, what should follow these eclipses.

EDGAR. Do you busy yourself with that?

140 EDMUND. I promise you, the effects he writes of succeed° unhappily: as of unnaturalness° between the child and the parent, death, dearth, dissolutions of ancient amities,° divisions in state, menaces and maledictions against king and nobles, needless diffidences,° banishment of friends, dissi-
145 pation of cohorts,° nuptial breaches, and I know not what.

EDGAR. How long have you been a sectary astronomical?°

EDMUND. Come, come, when saw you my father last?

EDGAR. Why, the night gone by.

EDMUND. Spake you with him? 150

EDGAR. Ay, two hours together.

EDMUND. Parted you in good terms? Found you no displeasure in him by word nor countenance?°

EDGAR. None at all.

EDMUND. Bethink yourself wherein you may have 155 offended him; at my entreaty forbear his presence° until some little time hath qualified° the heat of his displeasure, which at this instant so rageth in him that with the mischief of your person it would scarcely allay.°

EDGAR. Some villain hath done me wrong. 160

EDMUND. That's my fear, brother. I pray you have a continent forbearance° till the speed of his rage goes slower; and, as I say, retire with me to my lodging, from whence I will fitly° bring you to hear my lord speak. Pray ye, go; there's my key. If you do stir abroad, go armed. 165

EDGAR. Armed, brother?

EDMUND. Brother, I advise you to the best. Go armed. I am no honest man if there be any good meaning toward you. I have told you what I have seen and heard; but faintly, nothing like the image and horror° of it. Pray you, away. 170

EDGAR. Shall I hear from you anon?°

EDMUND. I do serve you in this business.

Exit Edgar.

A credulous father, and a brother noble,
Whose nature is so far from doing harms
That he suspects none; on whose foolish honesty 175
My practices° ride easy. I see the business.
Let me, if not by birth, have lands by wit.
All with me's meet° that I can fashion fit.°

Exit.

SCENE III

[The Duke of Albany's palace.]

Enter Goneril, and [Oswald, her] steward.

GONERIL. Did my father strike my gentleman for chiding of his Fool?°

116 **foppery** folly 117–18 **often ... behavior** often caused by our own excesses 119 **on** of 120–21 **treachers ... predominance** traitors because of the ascendancy of a particular star at our birth 121–22 **by ... influence** because we had to submit to the influence of our star 123 **divine thrusting on** supernatural compulsion 124 **whoremaster** lecherous 124 **goatish** lascivious 125 **compounded** (1) made terms (2) formed (a child) 126 **Dragon's Tail** the constellation Draco 126 **nativity** birthday 127 **Ursa Major** the Great Bear 128 **Fut** 'S foot (an impatient oath) 128 **that** what 131 **catastrophe** conclusion 132–33 **My ... Bedlam** I must be doleful, like a lunatic beggar out of Bethlehem (Bedlam) Hospital, the London madhouse 133–34 **Fa, sol, la, mi** Edmund's humming of the musical notes is perhaps prompted by his use of the word *division,* which describes a musical variation 140–41 **succeed** follow 141 **unnaturalness** unkindness 142 **amities** friendships 144 **diffidences** distrusts 144–45 **dissipation of cohorts** falling away of supporters

146–47 **sectary astronomical** believer in astrology 153 **countenance** expression 156 **forbear his presence** keep away from him 157 **qualified** lessened 158–59 **with ... allay** even an injury to you would not appease his anger 161–62 **have ... forbearance** be restrained and keep yourself withdrawn 164 **fitly** at a fit time 170 **image and horror** true horrible picture 171 **anon** in a little while 176 **practices** plots 178 **meet** proper 178 **fashion fit** shape to my purpose I.iii.2 **Fool** court jester

OSWALD. Ay, madam.
GONERIL.
By day and night he wrongs me. Every hour
5 He flashes into one gross crime° or other
That sets us all at odds. I'll not endure it.
His knights grow riotous,° and himself upbraids us
On every trifle. When he returns from hunting,
I will not speak with him. Say I am sick.
10 If you come slack of former services,°
You shall do well; the fault of it I'll answer.°

[*Horns within.*]

OSWALD. He's coming, madam; I hear him.
GONERIL.
Put on what weary negligence you please,
You and your fellows. I'd have it come to question.°
15 If he distaste° it, let him to my sister,
Whose mind and mine I know in that are one,
Not to be overruled. Idle° old man,
That still would manage those authorities
That he hath given away. Now, by my life,
20 Old fools are babes again, and must be used
With checks as flatteries, when they are seen abused.°
Remember what I have said.
OSWALD. Well, madam.
GONERIL.
And let his knights have colder looks among you.
What grows of it, no matter; advise your fellows so.
25 I would breed from hence occasions, and I shall,
That I may speak.° I'll write straight° to my sister
To hold my course. Go, prepare for dinner.

Exeunt.

SCENE IV

[*A hall in the same.*]

Enter Kent [*disguised*].

KENT.
If but as well I other accents borrow
That can my speech defuse,° my good intent
May carry through itself to that full issue°
For which I razed my likeness.° Now, banished Kent,

5 **crime** offense 7 **riotous** dissolute 10 **come . . . services** are less serviceable to him than formerly 11 **answer** answer for 14 **come to question** be discussed openly 15 **distaste** dislike 17 **Idle** foolish 21 **With . . . abused** with restraints as well as soothing words when they are misguided 25–26 **breed . . . speak** find in this opportunities for speaking out 26 **straight** at once
I.iv.2 **defuse** disguise 3 **full issue** perfect result 4 **razed my likeness** shaved off, disguised my natural appearance

If thou canst serve where thou dost stand condemned, 5
So may it come,° thy master whom thou lov'st
Shall find thee full of labors.

Horns within.° *Enter Lear,* [*Knights,*] *and Attendants.*

LEAR. Let me not stay° a jot for dinner; go, get it ready. [*Exit an Attendant.*] How now, what art thou?
KENT. A man, sir. 10
LEAR. What dost thou profess?° What wouldst thou with us?
KENT. I do profess° to be no less than I seem, to serve him truly that will put me in trust, to love him that is honest, to converse with him that is wise and says little, to fear 15 judgment,° to fight when I cannot choose, and to eat no fish.°
LEAR. What art thou?
KENT. A very honest-hearted fellow and as poor as the king. 20
LEAR. If you be'st as poor for a subject as he's for a king, thou art poor enough. What wouldst thou?
KENT. Service.
LEAR. Who wouldst thou serve?
KENT. You. 25
LEAR. Dost thou know me, fellow?
KENT. No, sir, but you have that in your countenance° which I would fain° call master.
LEAR. What's that?
KENT. Authority. 30
LEAR. What services canst thou do?
KENT. I can keep honest counsel,° ride, run, mar a curious tale in telling it,° and deliver a plain message bluntly. That which ordinary men are fit for, I am qualified in, and the best of me is diligence. 35
LEAR. How old art thou?
KENT. Not so young, sir, to love a woman for singing, nor so old to dote on her for anything. I have years on my back forty-eight.
LEAR. Follow me; thou shalt serve me. If I like thee no 40 worse after dinner, I will not part from thee yet. Dinner, ho, dinner! Where's my knave?° My Fool? Go you and call my Fool hither.

[*Exit an Attendant.*]

6 **So . . . come** so may it fall out 7 s.d. **within** offstage 8 **stay** wait 11 **What . . . profess** What do you do? 13 **profess** claim 16 **judgment** by a heavenly or earthly judge 16–17 **eat no fish** (1) I am no Catholic, but a loyal Protestant (2) I am no weakling (3) I use no prostitutes 27 **countenance** bearing 28 **fain** like to 32 **honest counsel** honorable secrets 32–33 **mar . . . it** i.e., I cannot speak like an affected courtier ("curious" = elaborate, as against plain) 42 **knave** boy

Enter Oswald.

You, you, sirrah, where's my daughter?

45 OSWALD. So please you— *Exit.*

LEAR. What says the fellow there? Call the clotpoll° back. [*Exit a Knight.*] Where's my Fool? Ho, I think the world's asleep.

[*Reenter Knight.*]

How now? Where's that mongrel?

50 KNIGHT. He says, my lord, your daughter is not well.

LEAR. Why came not the slave back to me when I called him?

KNIGHT. Sir, he answered me in the roundest° manner, he would not.

55 LEAR. He would not?

KNIGHT. My lord, I know not what the matter is; but to my judgment your highness is not entertained° with that ceremonious affection as you were wont. There's a great abatement of kindness appears as well in the general depen-60 dants° as in the duke himself also and your daughter.

LEAR. Ha? Say'st thou so?

KNIGHT. I beseech you pardon me, my lord, if I be mistaken; for my duty cannot be silent when I think your highness wronged.

65 LEAR. Thou but remem'brest° me of mine own conception.° I have perceived a most faint neglect° of late, which I have rather blamed as mine own jealous curiosity° than as a very pretense° and purpose of unkindness. I will look further into't. But where's my Fool? I have not seen him this 70 two days.

KNIGHT. Since my young lady's going into France, sir, the Fool hath much pined away.

LEAR. No more of that; I have noted it well. Go you and tell my daughter I would speak with her. Go you, call hith-75 er my Fool.

[*Exit an Attendant.*]

Enter Oswald.

O, you, sir, you! Come you hither, sir. Who am I, sir?

OSWALD. My lady's father.

LEAR. "My lady's father"? My lord's knave, you whoreson dog, you slave, you cur!

80 OSWALD. I am none of these, my lord; I beseech your pardon.

LEAR. Do you bandy° looks with me, you rascal?

[*Striking him.*]

OSWALD. I'll not be strucken,° my lord.

KENT. Nor tripped neither, you base football° player.

[*Tripping up his heels.*]

LEAR. I thank thee, fellow. Thou serv'st me, and I'll love 85 thee.

KENT. Come, sir, arise, away. I'll teach you differences.° Away, away. If you will measure your lubber's° length again, tarry; but away. Go to!° Have you wisdom?° So.°

[*Pushes Oswald out.*]

LEAR. Now, my friendly knave, I thank thee. There's 90 earnest° of thy service. [*Giving Kent money.*]

Enter Fool.

FOOL. Let me hire him too. Here's my coxcomb.°

[*Offering Kent his cap.*]

LEAR. How now, my pretty knave? How dost thou?

FOOL. Sirrah, you were best° take my coxcomb.

KENT. Why, Fool? 95

FOOL. Why? For taking one's part that's out of favor. Nay, an° thou canst not smile as the wind sits,° thou'lt catch cold shortly. There, take my coxcomb. Why, this fellow has banished° two on's daughters, and did the third a blessing against his will. If thou follow him, thou must needs wear 100 my coxcomb.—How now, nuncle?° Would I had two coxcombs and two daughters.

LEAR. Why, my boy?

FOOL. If I gave them all my living,° I'd keep my coxcombs myself. There's mine; beg another of thy daughters. 105

LEAR. Take heed, sirrah—the whip.

FOOL. Truth's a dog must to kennel; he must be whipped out, when Lady the Brach° may stand by th' fire and stink.

LEAR. A pestilent gall° to me. 110

FOOL. Sirrah, I'll teach thee a speech.

46 **clotpoll** clodpoll, blockhead 53 **roundest** rudest 57 **entertained** treated 59–60 **dependants** servants 65 **rememb'rest** remindest 65–66 **conception** idea 66 **faint neglect** i.e., "weary negligence" (I.iii.13) 67 **mine . . . curiosity** suspicious concern for my own dignity 68 **very pretense** actual intention

82 **bandy** exchange insolently (metaphor from tennis) 83 **strucken** struck 84 **football** a low game played by idle boys, to the scandal of sensible men 87 **differences** of rank 88 **lubber's** lout's 89 **Go to!** expression of derisive incredulity 89 **Have you wisdom** i.e., Do you know what's good for you? 89 **So** good 91 **earnest** money for services rendered 92 **coxcomb** professional fool's cap, shaped like a coxcomb 94 **you were best** you had better 97 **an** if 97 **smile . . . sits** ingratiate yourself with those in power 99 **banished** alienated (by making them independent) 101 **nuncle** contraction of "mine uncle" 104 **living** property 108 **Brach** bitch 110 **gall** sore

LEAR. Do.
FOOL. Mark it, nuncle.

Have more than thou showest,
115 Speak less than thou knowest,
Lend less than thou owest,°
Ride more than thou goest,°
Learn more than thou trowest,°
Set less than thou throwest;°
120 Leave thy drink and thy whore,
And keep in-a-door,
And thou shalt have more
Than two tens to a score.°

KENT. This is nothing, Fool.
125 FOOL. Then 'tis like the breath of an unfee'd° lawyer—you gave me nothing for't. Can you make no use of nothing, nuncle?
LEAR. Why, no, boy. Nothing can he made out of nothing.
130 FOOL [*to Kent*]. Prithee tell him, so much the rent of his land comes to; he will not believe a fool.
LEAR. A bitter° fool.
FOOL. Dost thou know the difference, my boy, between a bitter fool and a sweet one?
135 LEAR. No, lad; teach me.
FOOL.

That lord that counseled thee
To give away thy land,
Come place him here by me,
Do thou for him stand.
140 The sweet and bitter fool
Will presently appear;
The one in motley° here,
The other found out° there.°

LEAR. Dost thou call me fool, boy?
145 FOOL. All thy other titles thou hast given away; that thou wast born with.
KENT. This is not altogether fool, my lord.
FOOL. No, faith; lords and great men will not let me.° If I had a monopoly° out, they would have part on't. And ladies too, they will not let me have all the fool to myself; 150 they'll be snatching. Nuncle, give me an egg, and I'll give thee two crowns.
LEAR. What two crowns shall they be?
FOOL. Why, after I have cut the egg i' th' middle and eat up the meat, the two crowns of the egg. When thou clovest 155 thy crown i' th' middle and gav'st away both parts, thou bor'st thine ass on thy back o'er the dirt.° Thou hadst little wit in thy bald crown when thou gav'st thy golden one away. If I speak like myself° in this, let him be whipped° that first finds it so. [*Singing.*] 160

Fools had ne'er less grace in a year,
For wise men are grown foppish,
And know not how their wits to wear,
Their manners are so apish.°

LEAR. When were you wont to be so full of songs, sirrah? 165
FOOL. I have used° it, nuncle, e'er since thou mad'st thy daughters thy mothers; for when thou gav'st them the rod, and put'st down thine own breeches, [*Singing.*]

Then they for sudden joy did weep, 170
And I for sorrow sung,
That such a king should play bo-peep°
And go the fools among.

Prithee, nuncle, keep a schoolmaster that can teach thy Fool to lie. I would fain learn to lie. 175
LEAR. And° you lie, sirrah, we'll have you whipped.
FOOL. I marvel what kin thou and thy daughters are. They'll have me whipped for speaking true; thou'lt have me whipped for lying; and sometimes I am whipped for holding my peace. I had rather be any kind o' thing than a fool, 180 and yet I would not be thee, nuncle: thou hast pared thy wit o' both sides and left nothing i' th' middle. Here comes one o' the parings.

Enter Goneril.

LEAR. How now, daughter? What makes that frontlet° on? Methinks you are too much of late i' th' frown. 185
FOOL. Thou wast a pretty fellow when thou hadst no

116 **owest** ownest 117 **goest** walkest 118 **trowest** knowest 119 **Set . . . throwest** bet less than you play for (get odds from your opponent) 122–23 **have . . . score** i.e., come away with more than you had (two tens, or twenty shillings, make a score, or one pound) 125 **unfee'd** unpaid for 132 **bitter** satirical 142 **motley** the drab costume of the professional jester 143 **found out** revealed 143 **there** the Fool points at Lear, as a fool in the grain 148 **let me** i.e., let me have all the folly to myself 149 **monopoly** James I gave great scandal by granting to his "snatching" courtiers royal patents to deal exclusively in some commodity

157 **bor'st . . . dirt** like the foolish and unnatural countryman in Aesop's fable 159 **like myself** like a fool 159 **let . . . whipped** i.e., let the man be whipped for a fool who thinks my true saying to be foolish 161–64 **Fools . . . apish** i.e., fools were never in less favor than now, and the reason is that wise men, turning foolish, and not knowing how to use their intelligence, imitate the professional fools and so make them unnecessary 167 **used** practiced 172 **play bo-peep** (1) act like a child (2) blind himself 176 **And** if 184 **frontlet** frown (literally, ornamental band)

need to care for her frowning. Now thou art an O without a figure.° I am better than thou art now: I am a fool, thou art nothing. [*To Goneril.*] Yes, forsooth, I will hold my tongue.
190 So your face bids me, though you say nothing. Mum, mum,

He that keeps nor crust nor crum,°
Weary of all, shall want° some.

[*Pointing to Lear.*]

That's a shealed peascod.°

GONERIL.
195 Not only, sir, this your all-licensed° Fool,
But other° of your insolent retinue
Do hourly carp and quarrel, breaking forth
In rank° and not-to-be-endurèd riots. Sir,
I had thought by making this well known unto you
200 To have found a safe° redress, but now grow fearful,
By what yourself too late° have spoke and done,
That you protect this course, and put it on
By your allowance;° which if you should, the fault
Would not 'scape censure, nor the redresses sleep,°
205 Which, in the tender of° a wholesome weal,°
Might in their working do you that offense,
Which else were shame, that then necessity
Will call discreet proceeding.°

FOOL. For you know, nuncle,

210 The hedge-sparrow fed the cuckoo° so long
That it had it head bit off by it° young.

So out went the candle, and we were left darkling.°

LEAR. Are you our daughter?

GONERIL.
Come, sir,
215 I would you would make use of your good wisdom
Whereof I know you are fraught° and put away
These dispositions° which of late transport you
From what you rightly are.

FOOL. May not an ass know when the cart draws the horse? Whoop, Jug,° I love thee! 220

LEAR.
Does any here know me? This is not Lear.
Does Lear walk thus? Speak thus? Where are his eyes?
Either his notion° weakens, or his discernings°
Are lethargied°—Ha! Waking? 'Tis not so.
Who is it that can tell me who I am? 225

FOOL. Lear's shadow.

LEAR. I would learn that; for, by the marks of sovereignty,° knowledge, and reason, I should be false° persuaded I had daughters.

FOOL. Which° they will make an obedient father. 230

LEAR. Your name, fair gentlewoman?

GONERIL.
This admiration,° sir, is much o' th' savor°
Of other your° new pranks. I do beseech you
To understand my purposes aright.
As you are old and reverend, should be wise. 235
Here do you keep a hundred knights and squires,
Men so disordered, so deboshed,° and bold,
That this our court, infected with their manners,
Shows° like a riotous inn. Epicurism° and lust
Makes it more like a tavern or a brothel 240
Than a graced° palace. The shame itself doth speak
For instant remedy. Be then desired°
By her, that else will take the thing she begs,
A little to disquantity your train,°
And the remainders° that shall still depend,° 245
To be such men as may besort° your age,
Which know themselves, and you.

LEAR. Darkness and devils!
Saddle my horses; call my train together.
Degenerate° bastard, I'll not trouble thee:
Yet have I left a daughter. 250

GONERIL.
You strike my people, and your disordered rabble
Make servants of their betters.

188 **figure** digit, to give value to the cipher (Lear is a nought) 192 **crum** soft bread inside the loaf 193 **want** lack 194 **shealed peascod** empty pea pod 195 **all-licensed** privileged to take any liberties 196 **other** others 198 **rank** gross 200 **safe** sure 201 **too late** lately 202–03 **put . . . allowance** promote it by your approval 204 **redresses sleep** correction fail to follow 205 **tender of** desire for 205 **weal** state 206–08 **Might . . . proceeding** as I apply it, the correction might humiliate you; but the need to take action cancels what would otherwise be unfilial conduct in me 210 **cuckoo** which lays its eggs in the nests of other birds 211 **it** its 212 **darkling** in the dark 216 **fraught** endowed 217 **dispositions** moods

220 **Jug** Joan (a quotation from a popular song?) 223 **notion** understanding 223 **discernings** faculties 224 **lethargied** paralyzed 227–28 **marks of sovereignty** i.e., tokens that Lear is king, and hence father to his daughters 228 **false** falsely 230 **Which** whom (Lear) 232 **admiration** (affected) wonderment 232 **is . . . savor** smacks much 233 **other your** others of your 237 **deboshed** debauched 239 **Shows** appears 239 **Epicurism** riotous living 241 **graced** dignified 242 **desired** requested 244 **disquantity your train** reduce the number of your dependents 245 **remainders** those who remain 245 **depend** attend on you 246 **besort** befit 249 **Degenerate** unnatural

Enter Albany.

LEAR.
Woe, that too late repents. O, sir, are you come?
Is it your will? Speak, sir. Prepare my horses.
255 Ingratitude! thou marble-hearted fiend,
More hideous when thou show'st thee in a child
Than the sea-monster.

ALBANY. Pray, sir, be patient.

LEAR.
Detested kite,° thou liest.
My train are men of choice and rarest parts,°
260 That all particulars of duty know,
And, in the most exact regard,° support
The worships° of their name. O most small fault,
How ugly didst thou in Cordelia show!
Which, like an engine,° wrenched my frame of nature
265 From the fixed place;° drew from my heart all love,
And added to the gall.° O Lear, Lear, Lear!
Beat at this gate that let thy folly in

[*Striking his head.*]

And thy dear judgment out. Go, go, my people.

ALBANY.
My lord, I am guiltless, as I am ignorant
Of what hath moved you.

270 LEAR. It may be so, my lord.
Hear, Nature, hear; dear goddess, hear:
Suspend thy purpose if thou didst intend
To make this creature fruitful.
Into her womb convey sterility,
275 Dry up in her the organs of increase,°
And from her derogate° body never spring
A babe to honor her. If she must teem,°
Create her child of spleen,° that it may live
And be a thwart disnatured° torment to her.
280 Let it stamp wrinkles in her brow of youth,
With cadent° tears fret° channels in her cheeks,
Turn all her mother's pains and benefits°
To laughter and contempt, that she may feel
How sharper than a serpent's tooth it is
285 To have a thankless child. Away, away!

Exit.

ALBANY.
Now, gods that we adore, whereof comes this?

GONERIL.
Never afflict yourself to know the cause,
But let his disposition° have that scope
As° dotage gives it.

Enter Lear.

LEAR.
What, fifty of my followers at a clap?° 290
Within a fortnight?

ALBANY. What's the matter, sir?

LEAR.
I'll tell thee. [*To Goneril.*] Life and death, I am ashamed
That thou hast power to shake my manhood° thus!
That these hot tears, which break from me perforce,°
Should make thee worth them. Blasts and fogs upon thee! 295
Th' untented woundings° of a father's curse
Pierce every sense about thee! Old fond° eyes,
Beweep° this cause again, I'll pluck ye out
And cast you, with the waters that you loose,°
To temper° clay. Yea, is it come to this? 300
Ha! Let it be so. I have another daughter,
Who I am sure is kind and comfortable.°
When she shall hear this of thee, with her nails
She'll flay thy wolvish visage. Thou shalt find
That I'll resume the shape° which thou dost think 305
I have cast off for ever.

Exit [*Lear, with Kent and Attendants*].

GONERIL. Do you mark that?

ALBANY.
I cannot be so partial, Goneril,
To the great love I bear you°—

GONERIL.
Pray you, content. What, Oswald, ho!

[*To the Fool*].

You, sir, more knave than fool, after your master! 310

FOOL. Nuncle Lear, nuncle Lear, tarry. Take the Fool° with thee.

258 **kite** scavenging bird of prey 259 **parts** accomplishments 261 **exact regard** strict attention to detail 262 **worships** honor 264 **engine** destructive contrivance 264–65 **wrenched . . . place** i.e., disorders my natural self 266 **gall** bitterness 275 **increase** childbearing 276 **derogate** degraded 277 **teem** conceive 278 **spleen** ill humor 279 **thwart disnatured** perverse unnatural 281 **cadent** falling 281 **fret** wear 282 **benefits** the mother's beneficent care of her child

288 **disposition** mood 289 **As** that 290 **at a clap** at one stroke 293 **shake my manhood** i.e., with tears 294 **perforce** involuntarily, against my will 296 **untented woundings** wounds too deep to be probed with a tent (a roll of lint) 297 **fond** foolish 298 **Beweep** if you weep over 299 **loose** (1) let loose (2) lose, as of no avail 300 **temper** mix with and soften 302 **comfortable** ready to comfort 305 **shape** i.e., kingly role 307–08 **I cannot . . . you** i.e., even though my love inclines me to you, I must protest 311 **Fool** (1) the Fool himself (2) the epithet or character of "fool"

A fox, when one has caught her,
And such a daughter,
315 Should sure to the slaughter,
If my cap would buy a halter.°
So the Fool follows after.° *Exit.*

GONERIL.
This man hath had good counsel. A hundred knights!
'Tis politic° and safe to let him keep
320 At point° a hundred knights: yes, that on every dream,
Each buzz,° each fancy, each complaint, dislike,
He may enguard° his dotage with their pow'rs
And hold our lives in mercy.° Oswald, I say!

ALBANY.
Well, you may fear too far.

GONERIL. Safer than trust too far.
325 Let me still take away the harms I fear,
Not fear still to be taken.° I know his heart.
What he hath uttered I have writ my sister.
If she sustain him and his hundred knights,
When I showed th' unfitness—

Enter Oswald.

How now, Oswald?
330 What, have you writ that letter to my sister?

OSWALD. Ay, madam.

GONERIL.
Take you some company,° and away to horse.
Inform her full of my particular° fear,
And thereto add such reasons of your own
335 As may compact° it more. Get you gone,
And hasten your return. [*Exit Oswald.*] No, no, my lord,
This milky gentleness and course° of yours,
Though I condemn not,° yet under pardon,
You are much more attasked° for want of wisdom
340 Than praised for harmful mildness.°

ALBANY.
How far your eyes may pierce I cannot tell;
Striving to better, oft we mar what's well.

GONERIL. Nay then—

ALBANY. Well, well, th' event.° *Exeunt.*

316–17 **halter, after** pronounced "hauter," "auter"
319 **politic** good policy 320 **At point** armed 321 **buzz** rumor 322 **enguard** protect 323 **in mercy** at his mercy 326 **Not . . . taken** rather than remain fearful of being overtaken by them 332 **company** escort 333 **particular** own 335 **compact** strengthen 337 **milky . . . course** mild and gentle way (hendiadys) 338 **condemn not** condemn it not 339 **attasked** taken to task, blamed 340 **harmful mildness** dangerous indulgence 344 **th' event** i.e., we'll see what happens

SCENE V

[*Court before the same.*]

Enter Lear, Kent, and Fool.

LEAR. Go you before to Gloucester with these letters. Acquaint my daughter no further with anything you know than comes from her demand out of the letter.° If your diligence be not speedy, I shall be there afore you.

KENT. I will not sleep, my lord, till I have delivered your letter. *Exit.* 5

FOOL. If a man's brains were in's heels, were't° not in danger of kibes?°

LEAR. Ay, boy.

FOOL. Then I prithee be merry. Thy wit shall not go slipshod.° 10

LEAR. Ha, ha, ha.

FOOL. Shalt° see thy other daughter will use thee kindly;° for though she's as like this as a crab's° like an apple, yet I can tell what I can tell. 15

LEAR. Why, what canst thou tell, my boy?

FOOL. She will taste as like this as a crab does to a crab. Thou canst tell why one's nose stands i' th' middle on's° face?

LEAR. No. 20

FOOL. Why, to keep one's eyes of° either side's nose, that what a man cannot smell out, he may spy into.

LEAR. I did her wrong.

FOOL. Canst tell how an oyster makes his shell?

LEAR. No. 25

FOOL. Nor I neither; but I can tell why a snail has a house.

LEAR. Why?

FOOL. Why, to put's head in; not to give it away to his daughters, and leave his horns° without a case. 30

LEAR. I will forget my nature.° So kind a father! Be my horses ready?

FOOL. Thy asses are gone about 'em. The reason why the seven stars° are no moe° than seven is a pretty° reason.

LEAR. Because they are not eight. 35

FOOL. Yes indeed. Thou wouldst make a good fool.

I.v.3 **than . . . letter** than her reading of the letter brings her to ask 7 **were't** i.e., the brains 8 **kibes** chilblains 10–11 **Thy . . . slipshod** Your brains shall not go in slippers (because you have no brains to be protected from chilblains) 13 **Shalt** thou shalt 13–14 **kindly** (1) affectionately (2) after her kind or nature 14 **crab** crab apple 18 **on's** of his 21 **of** on 30 **horns** (1) snail's horns (2) cuckold's horns 31 **nature** paternal instincts 34 **seven stars** the Pleiades 34 **moe** more 34 **pretty** apt

LEAR. To take't again perforce!° Monster ingratitude!
FOOL. If thou wert my fool, nuncle, I'd have thee beaten for being old before thy time.
40 LEAR. Hows that?
FOOL. Thou shouldst not have been old till thou hadst been wise.
LEAR.
O, let me not be mad, not mad, sweet heaven!
Keep me in temper;° I would not be mad!

[*Enter Gentleman.*]

45 How now, are the horses ready?
GENTLEMAN. Ready, my lord.
LEAR. Come, boy.
FOOL.
She that's a maid now, and laughs at my departure,
Shall not be a maid long, unless things be cut shorter.°

Exeunt.

ACT II

SCENE I

[*The Earl of Gloucester's castle.*]

Enter Edmund and Curan, severally.°

EDMUND. Save° thee, Curan.
CURAN. And you, sir. I have been with your father, and given him notice that the Duke of Cornwall and Regan his duchess will be here with him this night.
5 EDMUND. How comes that?
CURAN. Nay, I know not. You have heard of the news abroad? I mean the whispered ones, for they are yet but ear-kissing arguments.°
EDMUND. Not I. Pray you, what are they?
10 CURAN. Have you heard of no likely° wars toward,° 'twixt the Dukes of Cornwall and Albany?
EDMUND. Not a word.
CURAN. You may do, then, in time. Fare you well, sir.

Exit.

EDMUND.
The duke be here tonight? The better!° best!
15 This weaves itself perforce° into my business.
My father hath set guard to take my brother,
And I have one thing of a queasy question°
Which I must act. Briefness° and Fortune, work!
Brother, a word; descend. Brother, I say!

Enter Edgar.

20 My father watches. O sir, fly this place.
Intelligence° is given where you are hid.
You have now the good advantage of the night.
Have you not spoken 'gainst the Duke of Cornwall?
He's coming hither, now i' th' night, i' th' haste,°
25 And Regan with him. Have you nothing said
Upon his party° 'gainst the Duke of Albany?
Advise yourself°
EDGAR. I am sure on't,° not a word.
EDMUND.
I hear my father coming. Pardon me:
In cunning° I must draw my sword upon you.
30 Draw, seem to defend yourself; now quit you° well.
Yield! Come before my father! Light ho, here!
Fly, brother. Torches, torches!—So farewell.

Exit Edgar.

Some blood drawn on me would beget opinion°

[*Wounds his arm.*]

Of my more fierce endeavor. I have seen drunkards
35 Do more than this in sport. Father, father!
Stop, stop! No help?

Enter Gloucester, and Servants with torches.

GLOUCESTER.
Now, Edmund, where's the villain?
EDMUND.
Here stood he in the dark, his sharp sword out,
Mumbling of wicked charms, conjuring the moon
To stand auspicious mistress.
40 GLOUCESTER. But where is he?
EDMUND.
Look, sir, I bleed.
GLOUCESTER. Where is the villain, Edmund?

37 **To . . . perforce** (1) of Goneril, who has forcibly taken away Lear's privileges; or (2) of Lear, who meditates a forcible resumption of authority 44 **in temper** sane 48–49 **She . . . shorter** The maid who laughs, missing the tragic implications of this quarrel, will not have sense enough to preserve her virginity ("things" = penises)
II.i. s.d. **severally** separately (from different entrances onstage) 1 **Save** God save 7–8 **ear-kissing arguments** subjects whispered in the ear 10 **likely** probable 10 **toward** impending

14 **The better** So much the better 15 **perforce** necessarily 17 **of . . . question** that requires delicate handling (to be "queasy" is to be on the point of vomiting) 18 **Briefness** speed 21 **Intelligence** information 24 **i' th' haste** in great haste 26 **Upon his party** censuring his enmity 27 **Advise yourself** Reflect 27 **on't** of it 29 **In cunning** as a pretense 30 **quit you** acquaint yourself 33 **beget opinion** create the impression

EDMUND.
Fled this way, sir, when by no means he could—
GLOUCESTER.
Pursue him, ho! Go after. [*Exeunt some Servants.*] By no means what?
EDMUND.
45 Persuade me to the murder of your lordship;
But that I told him the revenging gods
'Gainst parricides did all the thunder bend;°
Spoke with how manifold and strong a bond
The child was bound to th' father. Sir, in fine,°
50 Seeing how loathly opposite° I stood
To his unnatural purpose, in fell° motion°
With his preparèd sword he charges home
My unprovided° body, latched° mine arm;
But when he saw my best alarumed° spirits
55 Bold in the quarrel's right,° roused to th' encounter,
Or whether gasted° by the noise I made,
Full suddenly he fled.
GLOUCESTER. Let him fly far.
Not in this land shall he remain uncaught;
And found—dispatch.° The noble duke my master,
60 My worthy arch° and patron, comes tonight.
By his authority I will proclaim it,
That he which finds him shall deserve our thanks,
Bringing the murderous coward to the stake.
He that conceals him, death.°
EDMUND.
65 When I dissuaded him from his intent,
And found him pight° to do it, with curst° speech
I threatened to discover° him. He replied,
"Thou unpossessing° bastard, dost thou think,
If I would stand against thee, would the reposal°
70 Of any trust, virtue, or worth in thee
Make thy words faithed?° No. What I should deny—
As this I would, ay, though thou didst produce
My very character°—I'd turn it all
To thy suggestion,° plot, and damnèd practice.°
75 And thou must make a dullard of the world,°
If they not thought° the profits of my death
Were very pregnant° and potential spirits°
To make thee seek it."
GLOUCESTER.
O strange and fastened° villain!
80 Would he deny his letter, said he? I never got° him.

Tucket° within.

Hark, the duke's trumpets. I know not why he comes.
All ports° I'll bar; the villain shall not 'scape;
The duke must grant me that. Besides, his picture
I will send far and near, that all the kingdom
85 May have due note of him; and of my land,
Loyal and natural° boy, I'll work the means
To make thee capable.°

Enter Cornwall, Regan, and Attendants.

CORNWALL.
How now, my noble friend! Since I came hither,
Which I can call but now, I have heard strange news.
REGAN.
90 If it be true, all vengeance comes too short
Which can pursue th' offender. How dost, my lord?
GLOUCESTER.
O madam, my old heart is cracked, it's cracked.
REGAN.
What, did my father's godson seek your life?
He whom my father named, your Edgar?
GLOUCESTER.
95 O lady, lady, shame would have it hid.
REGAN.
Was he not companion with the riotous knights
That tended upon my father?
GLOUCESTER.
I know not, madam. 'Tis too bad, too bad.
EDMUND.
Yes, madam, he was of that consort.°
REGAN.
100 No marvel then, though he were ill affected.°
'Tis they have put° him on the old man's death
To have th' expense and waste° of his revenues.
I have this present evening from my sister

47 **bend** aim 49 **in fine** finally 50 **loathly opposite** bitterly opposed 51 **fell** deadly 51 **motion** thrust (a term from fencing) 53 **unprovided** unprotected 53 **latched** wounded (lanced) 54 **best alarumed** wholly aroused 55 **Bold . . . right** confident in the rightness of my cause 56 **gasted** struck aghast 59 **dispatch** i.e., he will be killed 60 **arch** chief 64 **death** the same elliptical form that characterizes "dispatch," line 59 66 **pight** determined 66 **curst** angry 67 **discover** expose 68 **unpossessing** beggarly (landless) 69 **reposal** placing 71 **faithed** believed 73 **character** handwriting 74 **suggestion** instigation 74 **practice** device

75 **make . . . world** think everyone stupid 76 **not thought** did not think 77 **pregnant** teeming with incitement 77 **potential spirits** powerful evil spirits 79 **fastened** hardened 80 **got** begot 80 s.d. **Tucket** Cornwall's special trumpet call 82 **ports** exits, of whatever sort 86 **natural** (1) kind (filial) (2) illegitimate 87 **capable** able to inherit 99 **consort** company 100 **ill affected** disposed to evil 101 **put** set 102 **expense and waste** squandering

Been well informed of them, and with such cautions
105 That, if they come to sojourn at my house,
I'll not be there.
CORNWALL. Nor I, assure thee, Regan.
Edmund, I hear that you have shown your father
A childlike° office.
EDMUND. It was my duty, sir.
GLOUCESTER.
He did bewray his practice,° and received
110 This hurt you see, striving to apprehend him.
CORNWALL.
Is he pursued?
GLOUCESTER.
Ay, my good lord.
CORNWALL.
If he be taken, he shall never more
Be feared of doing° harm. Make your own purpose,
How in my strength you please.° For you, Edmund,
115 Whose virtue and obedience° doth this instant
So much commend itself, you shall be ours.
Natures of such deep trust we shall much need;
You we first seize on.
EDMUND. I shall serve you, sir,
Truly, however else.
GLOUCESTER. For him I thank your grace.
CORNWALL.
120 You know not why we came to visit you?
REGAN.
Thus out of season, threading dark-eyed night.
Occasions, noble Gloucester, of some prize,°
Wherein we must have use of your advice.
Our father he hath writ, so hath our sister,
125 Of differences,° which° I best thought it fit
To answer from° our home. The several messengers
From hence attend dispatch.° Our good old friend,
Lay comforts to your bosom,° and bestow
Your needful° counsel to our businesses,
Which craves the instant use.°
130 GLOUCESTER. I serve you, madam.
Your graces are right welcome.
Exeunt. Flourish.

108 **childlike** filial 109 **bewray his practice** disclose his plot 113 **of doing** because he might do 113–14 **Make . . . please** Use my power freely, in carrying out your plans for his capture 115 **virtue and obedience** virtuous obedience 122 **prize** importance 125 **differences** quarrels 125 **which** referring not to "differences," but to the letter Lear has written 126 **from** away from 127 **attend dispatch** are waiting to be sent off 128 **lay . . . bosom** console yourself (about Edgar's supposed treason) 129 **needful** needed 130 **craves . . . use** demands immediate transaction

SCENE II

[*Before Gloucester's castle.*]

Enter Kent and Oswald, severally.

OSWALD. Good dawning° to thee, friend. Art of this house?°
KENT. Ay.
OSWALD. Where may we set our horses?
KENT. I' th' mire. 5
OSWALD. Prithee, if thou lov'st me, tell me.
KENT. I love thee not.
OSWALD. Why then, I care not for thee.
KENT. If I had thee in Lipsbury Pinfold,° I would make thee care for me. 10
OSWALD. Why dost thou use me thus? I know thee not.
KENT. Fellow, I know thee.
OSWALD. What dost thou know me for?
KENT. A knave, a rascal, an eater of broken meats;° a base, proud, shallow, beggarly, three-suited,° hundred- 15 pound,° filthy worsted-stocking° knave; a lily-livered, action-taking,° whoreson, glass-gazing,° superserviceable,° finical° rogue; one-trunk-inheriting° slave; one that wouldst be a bawd in way of good service,° and art nothing but the composition° of a knave, beggar, coward, pander, and the 20 son and heir of a mongrel bitch; one whom I will beat into clamorous whining if thou deniest the least syllable of thy addition.°
OSWALD. Why, what a monstrous fellow art thou, thus to rail on one that is neither known of thee nor knows thee! 25
KENT. What a brazen-faced varlet art thou to deny thou knowest me! Is it two days since I tripped up thy heels and beat thee before the king? [*Drawing his sword.*] Draw, you rogue, for though it be night, yet the moon shines. I'll make

II.ii.1 **dawning** dawn is impending, but not yet arrived 1–2 **Art . . . house** Do you live here? 9 **Lipsbury Pinfold** a pound or pen in which strayed animals are enclosed ("Lipsbury" may denote a particular place, or may be slang for "between my teeth") 14 **broken meats** scraps of food 15 **three-suited** the wardrobe permitted to a servant or "knave" 15–16 **hundred-pound** the extent of Oswald's wealth, and thus a sneer at his aspiring to gentility 16 **worsted-stocking** worn by servants 16–17 **action-taking** one who refuses a fight and goes to law instead 17 **glass-gazing** conceited 17 **superserviceable** sycophantic, serving without principle 18 **finical** overfastidious 18 **one-trunk-inheriting** possessing only a trunkful of goods 19 **bawd . . . service** pimp, to please his master 20 **composition** compound 23 **addition** titles

30 a sop o' th' moonshine° of you. You whoreson cullionly barbermonger,° draw!

OSWALD. Away, I have nothing to do with thee.

KENT. Draw, you rascal. You come with letters against the king, and take Vanity the puppet's° part against the royalty of her father. Draw, you rogue or I'll so carbonado° 35 your shanks. Draw, you rascal. Come your ways!°

OSWALD. Help, ho! Murder! Help!

KENT. Strike, you slave! Stand, rogue! Stand, you neat° slave! Strike!

[*Beating him.*]

40 OSWALD. Help, ho! Murder, murder!

Enter Edmund, with his rapier drawn, Cornwall, Regan, Gloucester, Servants.

EDMUND. How now? What's the matter? Part!

KENT. With you,° goodman boy,° if you please! Come, I'll flesh° ye, come on, young master.

GLOUCESTER. Weapons? Arms? What's the matter 45 here?

CORNWALL. Keep peace, upon your lives. He dies that strikes again. What is the matter?

REGAN. The messengers from our sister and the king.

CORNWALL. What is your difference?° Speak.

50 OSWALD. I am scarce in breath, my lord.

KENT. No marvel, you have so bestirred° your valor. You cowardly rascal, nature disclaims in thee.° A tailor made thee.°

CORNWALL. Thou art a strange fellow. A tailor make a 55 man?

KENT. A tailor, sir. A stonecutter or a painter could not have made him so ill, though they had been but two years o' th' trade.

CORNWALL. Speak yet, how grew your quarrel?

OSWALD. This ancient ruffian, sir, whose life I have 60 spared at suit of° his gray beard—

KENT. Thou whoreson zed,° thou unnecessary letter! My lord, if you will give me leave, I will tread this unbolted° villain into mortar and daub the wall of a jakes° with him. Spare my gray beard, you wagtail!° 65

CORNWALL. Peace, sirrah!
You beastly° knave, know you no reverence?

KENT.
Yes, sir, but anger hath a privilege.

CORNWALL.
Why art thou angry?

KENT.
That such a slave as this should wear a sword, 70
Who wears no honesty. Such smiling rogues as these,
Like rats, oft bite the holy cords° atwain
Which are too intrince° t' unloose; smooth° every passion
That in the natures of their lords rebel,
Being oil to fire, snow to the colder moods; 75
Renege,° affirm, and turn their halcyon beaks°
With every gale and vary° of their masters,
Knowing naught, like dogs, but following.
A plague upon your epileptic° visage!
Smile you° my speeches, as I were a fool? 80
Goose, if I had you upon Sarum Plain,°
I'd drive ye cackling home to Camelot.°

CORNWALL.
What, art thou mad, old fellow?

GLOUCESTER.
How fell you out? Say that.

KENT.
No contraries° hold more antipathy 85
Than I and such a knave.

CORNWALL.
Why dost thou call him knave? What is his fault?

30 **sop . . . moonshine** i.e., Oswald will admit the moonlight, and so sop it up, through the open wounds Kent is preparing to give him 30–31 **cullionly barbermonger** base patron of hairdressers (effeminate man) 34 **Vanity the puppet's** Goneril, here identified with one of the personified characters in the morality plays, which were sometimes put on as puppet shows 35 **carbonado** cut across, like a piece of meat before cooking 36 **Come your ways** Get along! 38 **neat** (1) foppish (2) unmixed, as in "neat wine" 42 **With you** i.e., the quarrel is with you 42 **goodman boy** young man (peasants are "goodmen"; "boy" is a term of contempt) 43 **flesh** introduce to blood (term from hunting) 49 **difference** quarrel 51 **bestirred** exercised 52 **nature . . . thee** nature renounces any part in you 52–53 **A tailor made thee** from the proverb "The tailor makes the man"

61 **at suit of** out of pity for 62 **zed** the letter Z, generally omitted in contemporary dictionaries 63 **unbolted** unsifted, i.e., altogether a villain 64 **jakes** privy 65 **wagtail** a bird that bobs its tail up and down, and thus suggests obsequiousness 67 **beastly** irrational 72 **holy cords** sacred bonds of affection (as between husbands and wives, parents and children) 73 **intrince** entangled, intricate 73 **smooth** appease 76 **Renege** deny 76 **halcyon beaks** the halcyon or kingfisher serves here as a type of the opportunist because, when hung up by the tail or neck, it was supposed to turn with the wind, like a weathervane 77 **gale and vary** varying gale (hendiadys) 79 **epileptic** distorted by grinning 80 **Smile you** do you smile at 81 **Sarum Plain** Salisbury Plain 82 **Camelot** the residence of King Arthur (presumably a particular point, now lost, is intended here) 85 **contraries** opposites

KENT.
His countenance likes° me not.

CORNWALL.
No more perchance does mine, nor his, nor hers.

KENT.
90 Sir, 'tis my occupation to be plain:
I have seen better faces in my time
Than stands on any shoulder that I see
Before me at this instant.

CORNWALL. This is some fellow
Who, having been praised for bluntness, doth affect
95 A saucy roughness, and constrains the garb
Quite from his nature.° He cannot flatter, he;
An honest mind and plain, he must speak truth.
And° they will take it, so; if not, he's plain.
These kind of knaves I know, which in this plainness
100 Harbor more craft and more corrupter ends
Than twenty silly-ducking observants°
That stretch their duties nicely.°

KENT.
Sir, in good faith, in sincere verity,
Under th' allowance° of your great aspect,°
105 Whose influence,° like the wreath of radiant fire
On flick'ring Phoebus' front°—

CORNWALL. What mean'st by this?

KENT. To go out of my dialect,° which you discommend so much. I know, sir, I am no flatterer. He° that beguiled you in a plain accent was a plain knave, which, for
110 my part, I will not be, though I should win your displeasure to entreat me to't.°

CORNWALL.
What was th' offense you gave him?

OSWALD.
I never gave him any.
It pleased the king his master very late°
115 To strike at me, upon his misconstruction;°
When he, compact,° and flattering his displeasure,
Tripped me behind; being down, insulted, railed,
And put upon him such a deal of man°
That worthied him,° got praises of the king
For him attempting who was self-subdued;° 120
And, in the fleshment° of this dread exploit,
Drew on me here again.

KENT. None of these rogues and cowards
But Ajax is their fool.°

CORNWALL. Fetch forth the stocks!
You stubborn° ancient knave, you reverent° braggart, 125
We'll teach you.

KENT. Sir, I am too old to learn.
Call not your stocks for me, I serve the king,
On whose employment I was sent to you.
You shall do small respect, show too bold malice
Against the grace and person° of my master, 130
Stocking his messenger.

CORNWALL.
Fetch forth the stocks. As I have life and honor,
There shall he sit till noon.

REGAN.
Till noon? Till night, my lord, and all night too.

KENT.
Why, madam, if I were your father's dog, 135
You should not use me so.

REGAN. Sir, being his knave, I will.

CORNWALL.
This is a fellow of the selfsame color°
Our sister speaks of. Come, bring away° the stocks.

Stocks brought out.

GLOUCESTER.
Let me beseech your grace not to do so.
His fault is much, and the good king his master 140
Will check° him for't. Your purposed° low correction
Is such as basest and contemnèd'st° wretches

88 **likes** pleases 95–96 **constrains . . . nature** forces the manner of candid speech to be a cloak, not for candor but for craft 98 **And** if 101 **silly-ducking observants** ridiculously obsequious attendants 102 **nicely** punctiliously 104 **allowance** approval 104 **aspect** (1) appearance (2) position of the heavenly bodies 105 **influence** astrological power 106 **Phoebus' front** forehead of the sun 107 **dialect** customary manner of speaking 108 **He** i.e., the sort of candid-crafty man Cornwall has been describing 110–11 **though . . . to't** even if I were to succeed in bringing your graceless person ("displeasure" personified, and in lieu of the expected form, "your grace") to beg me to be a plain knave 114 **very late** recently 115 **misconstruction** misunderstanding

116 **compact** in league with the king 118 **put . . . man** pretended such manly behavior 119 **worthied him** made him seem heroic 120 **For . . . self-subdued** for attacking a man (Oswald) who offered no resistance 121 **fleshment** the bloodthirstiness excited by his first success or "fleshing" 123–24 **None . . . fool** i.e., cowardly rogues like Oswald always impose on fools like Cornwall (who is likened to Ajax: [1] the braggart Greek warrior [2] a jakes or privy 125 **stubborn** rude 125 **reverent** old 130 **grace and person** i.e., Lear as sovereign and in his personal character 137 **color** kind 138 **away** out 141 **check** correct 141 **purposed** intended 142 **contemnèd'st** most despised

For pilf'rings and most common trespasses
Are punished with.
145 The king his master needs must take it ill
That he, so slightly valued in° his messenger,
Should have him thus restrained.

CORNWALL. I'll answer° that.

REGAN.
My sister may receive it much more worse,
To have her gentleman abused, assaulted,
150 For following her affairs. Put in his legs.

[*Kent is put in the stocks.*]

Come, my good lord, away!

[*Exeunt all but Gloucester and Kent.*]

GLOUCESTER.
I am sorry for thee, friend. 'Tis the duke's pleasure,
Whose disposition° all the world well knows
Will not be rubbed° nor stopped. I'll entreat for thee.

KENT.
155 Pray do not, sir. I have watched° and traveled hard.
Some time I shall sleep out, the rest I'll whistle.
A good man's fortune may grow out at heels.°
Give° you good morrow.

GLOUCESTER.
The duke's to blame in this. 'Twill be ill taken.°

Exit.

KENT.
160 Good king, that must approve° the common saw,°
Thou out of heaven's benediction com'st
To the warm sun.°
Approach, thou beacon to this under globe,°
That by thy comfortable° beams I may
165 Peruse this letter. Nothing almost sees miracles
But misery.° I know 'tis from Cordelia,
Who hath most fortunately been informed
Of my obscurèd° course. And shall find time
From this enormous state, seeking to give
Losses their remedies.° All weary and o'er-watched, 170
Take vantage,° heavy eyes, not to behold
This shameful lodging. Fortune, good night;
Smile once more, turn thy wheel.°

Sleeps.

[SCENE III

A wood.]

Enter Edgar.

EDGAR.
I heard myself proclaimed,
And by the happy° hollow of a tree
Escaped the hunt. No port is free, no place
That guard and most unusual vigilance
Does not attend my taking.° Whiles I may 'scape, 5
I will preserve myself; and am bethought°
To take the basest and most poorest shape
That ever penury, in contempt of man,
Brought near to beast;° my face I'll grime with filth,
Blanket° my loins, elf° all my hairs in knots, 10
And with presented° nakedness outface°
The winds and persecutions of the sky.
The country gives me proof° and precedent
Of Bedlam° beggars, who, with roaring voices,
Strike° in their numbed and mortified° bare arms 15
Pins, wooden pricks,° nails, sprigs of rosemary;
And with this horrible object° from low° farms,
Poor pelting° villages, sheepcotes, and mills,
Sometimes with lunatic bans,° sometime with prayers,
Enforce their charity. Poor Turlygod, Poor Tom,° 20
That's something yet: Edgar I nothing am.°

Exit.

146 **slightly valued in** little honored in the person of 147 **answer** answer for 153 **disposition** inclination 154 **rubbed** diverted (metaphor from the game of bowls) 155 **watched** gone without sleep 157 **A . . . heels** Even a good man may have bad fortune 158 **Give** God give 159 **taken** received 160 **approve** confirm 160 **saw** proverb 161–62 **Thou . . . sun** i.e., Lear goes from better to worse, from heaven's blessing or shelter to lack of shelter 163 **beacon . . . globe** i.e., the sun, whose rising Kent anticipates 164 **comfortable** comforting 165–66 **Nothing . . . misery** i.e., True perception belongs only to the wretched 168 **obscurèd** disguised

168–70 **shall . . . remedies** a possible reading: Cordelia, away from this monstrous state of things, will find occasion to right the wrongs we suffer 171 **vantage** advantage (of sleep) 173 **turn thy wheel** i.e., so that Kent, who is at the bottom, may climb upward

II.iii.2 **happy** lucky 5 **attend my taking** watch to capture me 6 **am bethought** have decided 8–9 **penury . . . beast** poverty, to show how contemptible man is, reduced to the level of a beast 10 **Blanket** cover only with a blanket 10 **elf** tangle (into "elflocks," supposed to be caused by elves) 11 **presented** the show of 11 **outface** brave 13 **proof** example 14 **Bedlam** see I.ii.144–45 15 **Strike** stick 15 **mortified** not alive to pain 16 **pricks** skewers 17 **object** spectacle 17 **low** humble 18 **pelting** paltry 19 **bans** curses 20 **Poor . . . Tom** Edgar recites the names a Bedlam beggar gives himself 21 **That's . . . am** There's a chance for me in that I am no longer known for myself

[SCENE IV

Before Gloucester's castle. Kent in the stocks.]

Enter Lear, Fool, and Gentleman.

LEAR.
'Tis strange that they should so depart from home,
And not send back my messenger.
GENTLEMAN. As I learned,
The night before there was no purpose° in them
Of this remove.°
KENT. Hail to thee, noble master.
5 LEAR. Ha!
Mak'st thou this shame thy pastime?°
KENT. No, my lord.
FOOL. Ha, ha, he wears cruel° garters. Horses are tied by the heads, dogs and bears by th' neck, monkeys by th' loins, and men by th' legs. When a man's overlusty at legs,° then
10 he wears wooden netherstocks.°
LEAR.
What's he that hath so much thy place mistook
To set thee here?
KENT. It is both he and she,
Your son and daughter.
LEAR. No.
15 KENT. Yes.
LEAR. No, I say.
KENT. I say yea.
LEAR. No, no, they would not.
KENT. Yes, they have.
20 LEAR. By Jupiter, I swear no!
KENT.
By Juno, I swear ay!
LEAR. They durst not do't;
They could not, would not do't. 'Tis worse than murder
To do upon respect° such violent outrage.
Resolve° me with all modest° haste which way
25 Thou mightst deserve or they impose this usage,
Coming from us.
KENT. My lord, when at their home
I did commend° your highness' letters to them,
Ere I was risen from the place that showed
My duty kneeling, came there a reeking post,°
Stewed° in his haste, half breathless, panting forth 30
From Goneril his mistress salutations,
Delivered letters, spite of intermission,°
Which presently° they read; on° whose contents
They summoned up their meiny,° straight took horse,
Commanded me to follow and attend 35
The leisure of their answer, gave me cold looks,
And meeting here the other messenger,
Whose welcome I perceived had poisoned mine,
Being the very fellow which of late
Displayed° so saucily against your highness, 40
Having more man than wit° about me, drew;
He raised° the house, with loud and coward cries.
Your son and daughter found this trespass worth°
The shame which here it suffers.
FOOL. Winter's not gone yet, if the wild geese fly that 45
way.°

Fathers that wear rags
Do make their children blind,°
But fathers that bear bags°
Shall see their children kind. 50
Fortune, that arrant whore,
Ne'er turns the key° to th' poor.

But for all this, thou shalt have as many dolors° for thy daughters as thou canst tell° in a year.
LEAR.
O, how this mother swells up toward my heart! 55
Hysterica passio,° down, thou climbing sorrow,
Thy element's° below. Where is this daughter?
KENT.
With the earl, sir, here within.
LEAR. Follow me not;
Stay here. *Exit.*
GENTLEMAN.
Made you no more offense but what you speak of? 60
KENT. None.
How chance° the king comes with so small a number?

II.iv.3 **purpose** intention 4 **remove** removal 6 **Mak'st . . . pastime** Are you doing this to amuse yourself? 7 **cruel** (1) painful (2) "crewel," a worsted yarn used in garters 9 **overlusty at legs** (1) a vagabond (2) sexually promiscuous (?) 10 **netherstocks** stockings (as opposed to knee breeches, or upperstocks) 23 **upon respect** (1) on the respect due to the king (2) deliberately 24 **Resolve** inform 24 **modest** becoming 27 **commend** deliver 29 **reeking post** sweating messenger

30 **stewed** steaming 32 **spite of intermission** in spite of the interrupting of my business 33 **presently** at once 33 **on** on the strength of 34 **meiny** retinue 40 **Displayed** showed off 41 **more . . . wit** more manhood than sense 42 **raised** aroused 43 **worth** deserving 45–46 **Winter's . . . way** More trouble is to come, since Cornwall and Regan act so ("geese" is used contemptuously, as in Kent's quarrel with Oswald, II.ii.81) 48 **blind** i.e., indifferent 49 **bags** moneybags 52 **turns the key** i.e., opens the door 53 **dolors** (1) sorrows (2) dollars (English name for Spanish and German coins) 54 **tell** (1) about (2) count 55–56 **mother . . . Hysterica passio** hysteria, causing suffocation or choking 57 **element** proper place 62 **How chance** how does it happen that

FOOL. And° thou hadst been set i' th' stocks for that question, thou'dst well deserved it.

65 KENT. Why, Fool?

FOOL. We'll set thee to school to an ant, to teach thee there's no laboring i' th' winter.° All that follow their noses are led by their eyes but blind men, and there's not a nose among twenty but can smell him that's stinking.° Let go thy

70 hold when a great wheel runs down a hill, lest it break thy neck with following. But the great one that goes upward, let him draw thee after. When a wise man gives thee better counsel, give me mine again. I would have none but knaves follow it since a fool gives it.

75 That sir, which serves and seeks for gain,
And follows but for form,°
Will pack,° when it begins to rain,
And leave thee in the storm.
But I will tarry; the Fool will stay,
80 And let the wise man fly.
The knave turns Fool that runs away,
The Fool no knave,° perdy.°

KENT. Where learned you this, Fool?

FOOL. Not i' th' stocks, fool.

Enter Lear and Gloucester.

LEAR.
85 Deny° to speak with me? They are sick, they are weary,
They have traveled all the night? Mere fetches,°
The images° of revolt and flying off!°
Fetch me a better answer.

GLOUCESTER. My dear lord,
You know the fiery quality° of the duke,
90 How unremovable and fixed he is
In his own course.

LEAR. Vengeance, plague, death, confusion!
Fiery? What quality? Why, Gloucester, Gloucester,
I'd speak with the Duke of Cornwall and his wife.

GLOUCESTER.
Well, my good lord, I have informed them so.

LEAR.
Informed them? Dost thou understand me, man? 95

GLOUCESTER.
Ay, my good lord.

LEAR.
The king would speak with Cornwall. The dear father
Would with his daughter speak, commands—tends°—
service.
Are they informed of this? My breath and blood!
Fiery? The fiery duke, tell the hot duke that— 100
No, but not yet. May be he is not well.
Infirmity doth still neglect all office
Whereto our health is bound.° We are not ourselves
When nature, being oppressed, commands the mind
To suffer with the body. I'll forbear; 105
And am fallen out° with my more headier will°
To take the indisposed and sickly fit
For the sound man. [*Looking on Kent.*] Death on my
state!° Wherefore
Should he sit here? This act persuades me
That this remotion° of the duke and her 110
Is practice° only. Give me my servant forth.°
Go tell the duke and's wife I'd speak with them!
Now, presently!° Bid them come forth and hear me,
Or at their chamber door I'll beat the drum
Till it cry sleep to death.° 115

GLOUCESTER.
I would have all well betwixt you. *Exit.*

LEAR.
O me, my heart, my rising heart! But down!

FOOL. Cry to it, nuncle, as the cockney° did to the eels when she put 'em i' th' paste° alive. She knapped° 'em o' th' coxcombs° with a stick and cried, "Down, wantons,° 120 down!" 'Twas her brother that, in pure kindness to his horse, buttered his hay.°

63 **And** if 66–67 **We'll . . . winter** in the popular fable the ant, unlike the improvident grasshopper, anticipates the winter when none can labor by laying up provisions in the summer; Lear, trusting foolishly to summer days, finds himself unprovided for, and unable to provide, now that "winter" has come 67–69 **All . . . stinking** i.e., all can smell out the decay of Lear's fortunes 76 **form** show 77 **pack** be off 81–82 **The . . . knave** i.e., the faithless man is the true fool, for wisdom requires fidelity; Lear's Fool, who remains faithful, is at least no knave 82 **perdy** by God (French *par Dieu*) 85 **Deny** refuse 86 **fetches** subterfuges, acts of tacking (nautical metaphor) 87 **images** exact likenesses 87 **flying off** desertion 89 **quality** temperament

98 **tends** attends (i.e., awaits); with, possibly, an ironic second meaning, "tenders," or "offers" 103 **Whereto . . . bound** duties which we are required to perform, when in health 106 **fallen out** angry 106 **headier will** headlong inclination 108 **state** royal condition 110 **remotion** (1) removal (2) remaining aloof 111 **practice** pretense 111 **forth** i.e., out of the stocks 113 **presently** at once 115 **cry . . . death** follow sleep, like a cry or pack of hounds, until it kills it 118 **cockney** Londoner (ignorant city dweller) 119 **paste** pastry pie 119 **knapped** rapped 120 **coxcombs** heads 120 **wantons** i.e., playful things (with a sexual implication) 122 **buttered his hay** i.e., the city dweller does from ignorance what the dishonest ostler does from craft: greases the hay the traveler has paid for, so that the horse will not eat

Enter Cornwall, Regan, Gloucester, Servants.

LEAR.
Good morrow to you both.
CORNWALL. Hail to your grace.

Kent here set at liberty.

REGAN.
I am glad to see your highness.
LEAR.
125 Regan, I think you are. I know what reason
I have to think so. If thou shouldst not be glad,
I would divorce me from thy mother's tomb,
Sepulchring an adultress.° [*To Kent.*] O, are you free?
Some other time for that. Beloved Regan,
130 Thy sister's naught.° O Regan, she hath tied
Sharp-toothed unkindness, like a vulture, here.

[*Points to his heart.*]

I can scarce speak to thee. Thou'lt not believe
With how depraved a quality°—O Regan!
REGAN.
I pray you, sir, take patience, I have hope
135 You less know how to value her desert
Than she to scant her duty.°
LEAR. Say? how is that?
REGAN.
I cannot think my sister in the least
Would fail her obligation. If, sir, perchance
She have restrained the riots of your followers,
140 'Tis on such ground, and to such wholesome end,
As clears her from all blame.
LEAR.
My curses on her!
REGAN. O, sir, you are old,
Nature in you stands on the very verge
Of his confine.° You should be ruled, and led
145 By some discretion that discerns your state
Better than you yourself.° Therefore I pray you
That to our sister you do make return,
Say you have wronged her.
LEAR. Ask her forgiveness?
Do you but mark how this becomes the house:°
"Dear daughter, I confess that I am old. 150

[*Kneeling.*]

Age is unnecessary. On my knees I beg
That you'll vouchsafe me raiment, bed, and food."
REGAN.
Good sir, no more. These are unsightly tricks.
Return you to my sister.
LEAR [*rising*]. Never, Regan.
She hath abated° me of half my train, 155
Looked black upon me, struck me with her tongue,
Most serpentlike, upon the very heart.
All the stored vengeances of heaven fall
On her ingrateful top!° Strike her young bones,°
You taking° airs, with lameness.
CORNWALL. Fie, sir, fie! 160
LEAR.
You nimble lightnings, dart your blinding flames
Into her scornful eyes! Infect her beauty,
You fen-sucked° fogs, drawn by the pow'rful sun,
To fall and blister° her pride.
REGAN. O the blest gods!
So will you wish on me when the rash mood is on. 165
LEAR.
No, Regan, thou shalt never have my curse.
Thy tender-hefted° nature shall not give
Thee o'er to harshness. Her eyes are fierce, but thine
Do comfort, and not burn. 'Tis not in thee
To grudge my pleasures, to cut off my train, 170
To bandy° hasty words, to scant my sizes,°
And, in conclusion, to oppose the bolt°
Against my coming in. Thou better knowst
The offices of nature, bond of childhood,°
Effects° of courtesy, dues of gratitude. 175
Thy half o' th' kingdom hast thou not forgot,
Wherein I thee endowed.
REGAN. Good sir, to th' purpose°

Tucket within.

127–28 **divorce . . . adultress** i.e., repudiate your dead mother as having conceived you by another man 130 **naught** wicked 133 **quality** nature 134–36 **I have . . . duty** despite the double negative, the passage means, "I believe that you fail to give Goneril her due, rather than that she fails to fulfill her duty" 143–44 **Nature . . . confine** i.e., you are nearing the end of your life 145–46 **some . . . yourself** some discreet person who understands your condition more than you do

149 **becomes the house** suits my royal and paternal position 155 **abated** curtailed 159 **top** head 159 **young bones** the reference may be to unborn children, rather than to Goneril herself 160 **taking** infecting 163 **fen-sucked** drawn up from swamps by the sun 164 **fall and blister** fall upon and raise blisters 167 **tender-hefted** gently framed 171 **bandy** volley (metaphor from tennis) 171 **scant my sizes** reduce my allowances 172 **oppose the bolt** bar the door 174 **offices . . . childhood** natural duties, a child's duty to its parent 175 **Effects** manifestations 177 **to th' purpose** come to the point

LEAR.
Who put my man i' th' stocks?
CORNWALL. What trumpet's that?
REGAN.
I know't—my sister's. This approves° her letter,
That she would soon be here.

Enter Oswald.

180 Is your lady come?
LEAR.
This is a slave, whose easy borrowed° pride
Dwells in the fickle grace° of her he follows.
Out, varlet,° from my sight.
CORNWALL. What means your grace?
LEAR.
Who stocked my servant? Regan, I have good hope
Thou didst not know on't.

Enter Goneril.

185 Who comes here? O heavens!
If you do love old men, if your sweet sway
Allow° obedience, if you yourselves are old,
Make it° your cause. Send down, and take my part.

[*To Goneril.*]

Art not ashamed to look upon this beard?
190 O Regan, will you take her by the hand?
GONERIL.
Why not by th' hand, sir? How have I offended?
All's not offense that indiscretion finds°
And dotage terms so.
LEAR. O sides,° you are too tough!
Will you yet hold? How came my man i' th' stocks?
CORNWALL.
195 I set him there, sir; but his own disorders°
Deserved much less advancement.°
LEAR. You? Did you?
REGAN.
I pray you, father, being weak, seem so.°
If till the expiration of your month
You will return and sojourn with my sister,
200 Dismissing half your train, come then to me.
I am now from home, and out of that provision
Which shall be needful for your entertainment.°

LEAR.
Return to her, and fifty men dismissed?
No, rather I abjure all roofs, and choose
To wage° against the enmity o' th' air, 205
To be a comrade with the wolf and owl,
Necessity's sharp pinch.° Return with her?
Why, the hot-blooded° France, that dowerless took
Our youngest born, I could as well be brought
To knee° his throne, and, squirelike,° pension beg 210
To keep base life afoot. Return with her?
Persuade me rather to be slave and sumpter°
To this detested groom. [*Pointing at Oswald.*]
GONERIL. At your choice, sir.
LEAR.
I prithee, daughter, do not make me mad.
I will not trouble thee, my child; farewell. 215
We'll no more meet, no more see one another.
But yet thou art my flesh, my blood, my daughter,
Or rather a disease that's in my flesh,
Which I must needs call mine. Thou art a boil,
A plague-sore, or embossèd carbuncle° 220
In my corrupted blood. But I'll not chide thee.
Let shame come when it will, I do not call it.
I do not bid the Thunder-bearer° shoot,
Nor tell tales of thee to high-judging° Jove.
Mend when thou canst, be better at thy leisure, 225
I can be patient, I can stay with Regan,
I and my hundred knights.
REGAN. Not altogether so.
I looked not for you yet, nor am provided
For your fit welcome. Give ear, sir, to my sister,
For those that mingle reason with your passion° 230
Must be content to think you old, and so—
But she knows what she does.
LEAR. Is this well spoken?
REGAN.
I dare avouch° it, sir. What, fifty followers?
Is it not well? What should you need of more?
Yea, or so many, sith that° both charge° and danger 235
Speak 'gainst so great a number? How in one house
Should many people, under two commands,
Hold° amity? 'Tis hard, almost impossible.

179 **approves** confirms 181 **easy borrowed** (1) facile and taken from another (2) acquired without anything to back it up (like money borrowed without security) 182 **grace** favor 183 **varlet** base fellow 187 **Allow** approve of 188 **it** my cause 192 **finds** judges 193 **sides** breast 195 **disorders** misconduct 196 **advancement** promotion 197 **seem so** act weak 202 **entertainment** maintenance

205 **wage** fight 207 **Necessity's sharp pinch** a summing up of the hard choice he has just announced 208 **hot-blooded** passionate 210 **knee** kneel before 210 **squire-like** like a retainer 212 **sumpter** pack horse 220 **embossèd carbuncle** swollen boil 223 **Thunder-bearer** Jupiter 224 **high-judging** (1) supreme (2) judging from heaven 230 **mingle . . . passion** i.e, consider your turbulent behavior coolly and reasonably 233 **avouch** swear by 235 **sith that** since 235 **charge** expense 238 **Hold** preserve

GONERIL.
Why might not you, my lord, receive attendance
240 From those that she calls servants, or from mine?
REGAN.
Why not, my lord? If then they chanced to slack° ye,
We could control them. If you will come to me
(For now I spy a danger), I entreat you
To bring but five-and-twenty. To no more
245 Will I give place or notice.°
LEAR.
I gave you all.
REGAN. And in good time you gave it.
LEAR.
Made you my guardians, my depositaries,°
But kept a reservation° to be followed
With such a number. What, must I come to you
250 With five-and-twenty? Regan, said you so?
REGAN.
And speak't again, my lord. No more with me.
LEAR.
Those wicked creatures yet do look well-favored°
When others are more wicked; not being the worst
Stands in some rank of praise.° [*To Goneril.*] I'll go with thee.
255 Thy fifty yet doth double five-and-twenty,
And thou art twice her love.°
GONERIL. Hear me, my lord.
What need you five-and-twenty? ten? or five?
To follow° in a house where twice so many
Have a command to tend you?
REGAN. What need one?
LEAR.
260 O reason° not the need! Our basest beggars
Are in the poorest thing superfluous.°
Allow not nature more than nature needs,°
Man's life is cheap as beast's. Thou art a lady:
If only to go warm were gorgeous,
265 Why, nature needs not what thou gorgeous wear'st,
Which scarcely keeps thee warm.° But, for true need—
You heavens, give me that patience, patience I need.
You see me here, you gods, a poor old man,
As full of grief as age, wretched in both.
270 If it be you that stirs these daughters' hearts
Against their father, fool° me not so much
To bear° it tamely; touch me with noble anger,
And let not women's weapons, water drops,
Stain my man's cheeks. No, you unnatural hags!
275 I will have such revenges on you both
That all the world shall—I will do such things—
What they are, yet I know not; but they shall be
The terrors of the earth. You think I'll weep.
No, I'll not weep.

Storm and tempest.

280 I have full cause of weeping, but this heart
Shall break into a hundred thousand flaws°
Or ere° I'll weep. O Fool, I shall go mad!
Exeunt Lear, Gloucester, Kent, and Fool.
CORNWALL.
Let us withdraw, 'twill be a storm.
REGAN.
This house is little; the old man and's people
285 Cannot be well bestowed.°
GONERIL.
'Tis his own blame; hath° put himself from rest°
And must needs taste his folly.
REGAN.
For his particular,° I'll receive him gladly,
But not one follower.
GONERIL. So am I purposed.°
290 Where is my Lord of Gloucester?
CORNWALL.
Followed the old man forth.

Enter Gloucester.

He is returned.
GLOUCESTER.
The king is in high rage.
CORNWALL. Whither is he going?
GLOUCESTER.
He calls to horse, but will I know not whither.
CORNWALL.
'Tis best to give him way, he leads himself.°
GONERIL.
295 My lord, entreat him by no means to stay.

241 **slack** neglect 245 **notice** recognition 247 **depositaries** trustees 248 **reservation** condition 252 **well-favored** handsome 253–54 **not . . . praise** i.e., that Goneril is not so bad as Regan is one thing in her favor 256 **her love** i.e., as loving as she 258 **follow** attend on you 260 **reason** scrutinize 261 **Are . . . superfluous** have some trifle not absolutely necessary 262 **needs** i.e., to sustain life 264–66 **If . . . warm** If to satisfy the need for warmth were to be gorgeous, you would not need the clothing you wear, which is worn more for beauty than warmth

271 **fool** humiliate 272 **To bear as** to make me bear 281 **flaws** (1) pieces (2) cracks (3) gusts of passion 282 **Or ere** before 285 **bestowed** lodged 286 **hath** he hath 286 **rest** (1) place of residence (2) repose of mind 288 **his particular** himself personally 289 **purposed** determined 294 **give . . . himself** let him go; he insists on his own way

GLOUCESTER.
Alack, the night comes on, and the high winds
Do sorely ruffle.° For many miles about
There's scarce a bush.
REGAN. O, sir, to willful men
The injuries that they themselves procure
300 Must be their school masters. Shut up your doors.
He is attended with a desperate train,
And what they may incense° him to, being apt
To have his ear abused,° wisdom' bids fear.
CORNWALL.
Shut up your doors, my lord; 'tis a wild night.
305 My Regan counsels well. Come out o' th' storm.
Exeunt.

ACT III

SCENE I

[*A heath.*]

Storm still.° Enter Kent and a Gentleman severally.

KENT.
Who's there besides foul weather?
GENTLEMAN.
One minded like the weather most unquietly.°
KENT.
I know you. Where's the king?
GENTLEMAN.
Contending with the fretful elements;
5 Bids the wind blow the earth into the sea,
Or swell the curlèd waters 'bove the main,°
That things might change° or cease; tears his white hair,
Which the impetuous blasts, with eyeless° rage,
Catch in their fury, and make nothing of;
10 Strives in his little world of man° to outscorn
The to-and-fro conflicting wind and rain.
This night, wherein the cub-drawn° bear would couch,°
The lion, and the belly-pinchèd° wolf
Keep their fur dry, unbonneted° he runs,
And bids what will take all.°
KENT. But who is with him? 15
GENTLEMAN.
None but the Fool, who labors to outjest
His heart-struck injuries.
KENT. Sir, I do know you,
And dare upon the warrant of my note°
Commend a dear thing° to you. There is division,
Although as yet the face of it is covered 20
With mutual cunning, 'twixt Albany and Cornwall;
Who have—as who have not, that° their great stars
Throned° and set high?—servants, who seem no less,°
Which are to France the spies and speculations
Intelligent° of our state. What hath been seen, 25
Either in snuffs and packings° of the dukes,
Or the hard rein which both of them hath borne°
Against the old king, or something deeper,
Whereof perchance, these are but furnishings°—
But, true it is, from France there comes a power° 30
Into this scattered° kingdom, who already,
Wise in our negligence, have secret feet
In some of our best ports, and are at point°
To show their open banner. Now to you:
If on my credit you dare build° so far 35
To° make your speed to Dover, you shall find
Some that will thank you, making° just° report
Of how unnatural and bemadding° sorrow
The king hath cause to plain.°
I am a gentleman of blood and breeding,° 40
And from some knowledge and assurance° offer
This office° to you.
GENTLEMAN.
I will talk further with you.
KENT. No, do not.
For confirmation that I am much more

297 **ruffle** rage 302 **incense** incite 302–03 **being . . . abused** he being inclined to harken to bad counsel III.i. s.d. **still** continually 2 **minded . . . unquietly** disturbed in mind, like the weather 6 **main** land 7 **change** (1) be destroyed (2) be exchanged (i.e., turned upside down) (3) change for the better 8 **eyeless** (1) blind (2) invisible 10 **little . . . man** the microcosm, as opposed to the universe or macrocosm, which it copies in little 12 **cub-drawn** sucked dry by her cubs, and so ravenously hungry 12 **couch** take shelter in its lair 13 **belly-pinchèd** starved

14 **unbonneted** hatless 15 **take all** like the reckless gambler, staking all he has left 18 **warrant . . . note** strength of what I have taken note (of you) 19 **Commend . . . thing** entrust important business 22 **that** whom 22–23 **stars Throned** destinies have throned 23 **seem no less** seem to be so 24–25 **speculations Intelligent** giving intelligence 26 **snuffs and packings** quarrels and plots 27 **hard . . . borne** close and cruel control they have exercised 29 **furnishings** excuses 30 **power** army 31 **scattered** disunited 33 **at point** ready 35 **If . . . build** if you can trust me, proceed 36 **To** as to 37 **making for** making 37 **just** accurate 38 **bemadding** maddening 39 **plain** complain of 40 **blood and breeding** noble family 41 **knowledge and assurance** sure and trustworthy information 42 **office** service (i.e., the trip to Dover)

45 Than my out-wall,° open this purse and take
What it contains. If you shall see Cordelia,
As fear not but you shall, show her this ring,
And she will tell you who that fellow° is
That yet you do not know. Fie on this storm!
50 I will go seek the king.

GENTLEMAN.
Give me your hand. Have you no more to say?

KENT.
Few words, but, to effect,° more than all yet:
That when we have found the king—in which your pain°
That way, I'll this—he that first lights on him,
55 Holla the other. *Exeunt* [*severally*].

SCENE II

[*Another part of the heath.*]

Storm still. Enter Lear and Fool.

LEAR.
Blow, winds, and crack your cheeks. Rage, blow!
You cataracts and hurricanes,° spout
Till you have drenched our steeples, drowned the cocks.°
You sulph'rous and thought-executing° fires,
5 Vaunt-couriers° of oak-cleaving thunderbolts
Singe my white head. And thou, all-shaking thunder,
Strike flat the thick rotundity° o' th' world,
Crack Nature's molds,° all germains spill° at once,
That makes ungrateful° man.

10 FOOL. O nuncle, court holy-water° in a dry house is better than this rain water out o' door. Good nuncle, in; ask thy daughters' blessing. Here's a night pities neither wise men nor fools.

LEAR.
Rumble thy bellyful. Spit, fire. Spout, rain!
15 Nor rain, wind, thunder, fire are my daughters.
I tax° not you, you elements, with unkindness.
I never gave you kingdom, called you children,
You owe me no subscription.° Then let fall
Your horrible pleasure.° Here I stand your slave,
20 A poor, infirm, weak, and despised old man.
But yet I call you servile ministers,°
That will with two pernicious daughters join
Your high-engendered battles° 'gainst a head
So old and white as this. O, ho! 'tis foul.

25 FOOL. He that has a house to put's head in has a good headpiece.°

The codpiece° that will house
Before the head has any,
The head and he° shall louse:
30 So beggars marry many.°
The man that makes his toe
What he his heart should make
Shall of a corn cry woe,
And turn his sleep to wake.°

35 For there was never yet fair woman but she made mouths in a glass.°

Enter Kent.

LEAR.
No, I will be the pattern of all patience,
I will say nothing.

KENT. Who's there?

40 FOOL. Marry,° here's grace and a codpiece; that's a wise man and a fool.°

KENT.
Alas, sir, are you here? Things that love night
Love not such nights as these. The wrathful skies
Gallow° the very wanderers of the dark
45 And make them keep° their caves. Since I was man,
Such sheets of fire, such bursts of horrid° thunder,

45 **out-wall** superficial appearance 48 **fellow** companion 52 **to effect** in their importance 53 **pain** labor
III.ii.2 **hurricanoes** waterspouts 3 **cocks** weathercocks 4 **thought-executing** (1) doing execution as quick as thought (2) executing or carrying out the thought of him who hurls the lightning 5 **Vaunt-couriers** heralds, scouts who range before the main body of the army 7 **rotundity** i.e., not only the sphere of the globe, but the roundness of gestation (Delius) 8 **Nature's molds** the molds or forms in which men are made 8 **all germains spill** destroy the basic seeds of life 9 **ingrateful** ungrateful 10 **court holy-water** flattery 16 **tax** accuse 18 **subscription** allegiance, submission

19 **pleasure** will 21 **ministers** agents 23 **high engendered battles** armies formed in the heavens 26 **headpiece** (1) helmet (2) brain 27 **codpiece** penis (literally, padding worn at the crotch of a man's hose) 29 **he** it 30 **many** i.e., lice 29–30 **The ... many** The man who gratifies his sexual appetites before he has a roof over his head will end up a lousy beggar 31–34 **The ... wake** The man who, ignoring the fit order of things, elevates what is base above what is noble, will suffer for it as Lear has, in banishing Cordelia and enriching her sisters 35–36 **made ... glass** posed before a mirror (irrelevant nonsense, except that it calls to mind the general theme of vanity and folly) 40 **Marry** a mild oath, from "By the Virgin Mary" 40–41 **here's ... fool** Kent's question is unanswered: the king ("grace") is here, and the Fool—who customarily wears an exaggerated codpiece; but which is which is left ambiguous, since Lear has previously been called a codpiece 44 **Gallow** frighten 45 **keep** remain inside 46 **horrid** horrible

Such groans of roaring wind and rain, I never
Remember to have heard. Man's nature cannot carry°
Th' affliction nor the fear.

LEAR. Let the great gods
50 That keep this dreadful pudder° o'er our heads
Find out their enemies now.° Tremble, thou wretch,
That hast within thee undivulgèd crimes
Unwhipped of justice. Hide thee, thou bloody hand,
Thou perjured,° and thou simular° of virtue
55 That art incestuous. Caitiff,° to pieces shake,
That under covert and' convenient seeming°
Has practiced on° man's life. Close° pent-up guilts,
Rive° your concealing continents° and cry
These dreadful summoners grace.° I am a man
More sinned against than sinning.

60 KENT. Alack, bareheaded?
Gracious my lord,° hard by here is a hovel;
Some friendship will it lend you 'gainst the tempest.
Repose you there, while I to this hard house
(More harder than the stones whereof 'tis raised,
65 Which even but now, demanding after° you,
Denied me to come in) return, and force
Their scanted° courtesy.

LEAR. My wits begin to turn.
Come on, my boy. How dost, my boy? Art cold?
I am cold myself. Where is this straw, my fellow?
70 The art° of our necessities is strange,
That can make vile things precious. Come, your hovel.
Poor Fool and knave, I have one part in my heart
That's sorry yet for thee.

FOOL [*Singing.*]
He that has and a little tiny wit,
75 With heigh-ho, the wind and the rain,
Must make content with his fortunes fit,°
Though the rain it raineth every day.

LEAR. True, my good boy. Come, bring us to this hovel.
Exit, [*with Kent*].

FOOL. This is a brave° night to cool a courtesan. I'll
speak a prophecy ere I go: 80

When priests are more in word than matter;
When brewers mar their malt with water;
When nobles are their tailors' tutors,
No heretics burned, but wenches' suitors;°
When every case in law is right, 85
No squire in debt nor no poor knight;
When slanders do not live in tongues;
Nor cutpurses come not to throngs;
When usurers tell their gold i' th' field,°
And bawds and whores do churches build,° 90
Then shall the realm of Albion°
Come to great confusion.
Then comes the time, who lives to see't,
That going shall be used with feet.°

This prophecy Merlin° shall make, for I live before his time. 95
Exit.

SCENE III

[*Gloucester's castle.*]

Enter Gloucester and Edmund.

GLOUCESTER. Alack, alack, Edmund, I like not this
unnatural dealing. When I desired their leave that I might
pity° him, they took from me the use of mine own house,
charged me on pain of perpetual displeasure neither to
speak of him, entreat for him, or any way sustain° him. 5

EDMUND. Most savage and unnatural.

GLOUCESTER. Go to; say you nothing. There is division° between the dukes, and a worse° matter than that. I
have received a letter this night—'tis dangerous to be spoken°—I have locked the letter in my closet.° These injuries 10

48 **carry** endure 50 **pudder** turmoil 51 **Find . . . now** i.e., discover sinners by the terror they reveal 54 **perjured** perjurer 54 **simular** counterfeiter 55 **Caitiff** wretch 56 **seeming** hypocrisy 57 **practiced on** plotted against 57 **Close** hidden 58 **Rive** split open 58 **continents** containers 58–59 **cry . . . grace** beg mercy from the vengeful gods (here figured as officers who summoned a man charged with immorality before the ecclesiastical court) 61 **Gracious my lord** my gracious lord 65 **demanding after** asking for 67 **scanted** stinted 70 **art** magic powers of the alchemists, who sought to transmute base metals into precious 76 **Must . . . fit** must be satisfied with a fortune as tiny as his wit

79 **brave** fine 83–84 **When . . . suitors** the first four prophecies are fulfilled already, and hence "confusion" has come to England: the priest does not suit his action to his words; the brewer adulterates his beer; the nobleman is subservient to his tailor (i.e., cares only for fashion); religious heretics escape, and only those burn (i.e., suffer) who are afflicted with venereal disease 89 **tell . . . field** count their money in the open 85–90 **When . . . build** the last six prophecies, as they are Utopian, are meant ironically; they will never be fulfilled 91 **Albion** England 94 **going . . . feet** people will walk on their feet 95 **Merlin** King Arthur's great magician who, according to Holinshed's Chronicles, lived later than Lear

III.iii.3 **pity** show pity to 5 **sustain** care for 8 **division** falling out 8 **worse** more serious (i.e., the French invasion) 10 **spoken** spoken of 10 **closet** room the king now bears will be revenged home;° there is part of a power° already footed;° we must incline to° the king. I will look° him and privily° relieve him. Go you and maintain talk with the duke, that my charity be not of° him perceived. If he ask for me, I am ill and gone to bed. If I die for it, as no less is threatened me, the king my old master must be relieved. There is strange things toward,° Edmund; pray you be careful. *Exit.*

EDMUND.
This courtesy forbid° thee shall the duke
Instantly know, and of that letter too.
This seems a fair deserving,° and must draw me
That which my father loses no less than all.
The younger rises when the old doth fall.

Exit.

SCENE IV

[*The heath, before a hovel.*]

Enter Lear, Kent, and Fool.

KENT.
Here is the place, my lord. Good my lord, enter.
The tyranny of the open night's too rough
For nature to endure.

Storm still.

LEAR. Let me alone.

KENT.
Good my lord, enter here.

LEAR. Wilt break my heart?°

KENT.
I had rather break mine own. Good my lord, enter.

LEAR.
Thou think'st 'tis much that this contentious storm
Invades us to the skin: so 'tis to thee;
But where the greater malady is fixed,°
The lesser is scarce felt. Thou'dst shun a bear;
But if thy flight lay toward the roaring sea,
Thou'dst meet the bear i' th' mouth.° When the mind's free,°
The body's delicate. The tempest in my mind
Doth from my senses take all feeling else,
Save what beats there. Filial ingratitude,
Is it not as° this mouth should tear this hand
For lifting food to't? But I will punish home.°
No, I will weep no more. In such a night
To shut me out! Pour on, I will endure.
In such a night as this! O Regan, Goneril,
Your old kind father, whose frank° heart gave all—
O, that way madness lies; let me shun that.
No more of that.

KENT. Good my lord, enter here.

LEAR.
Prithee go in thyself; seek thine own ease.
This tempest will not give me leave to ponder
On things would hurt me more, but I'll go in.

[*To the Fool.*]

In, boy; go first. Houseless poverty°—
Nay, get thee in. I'll pray, and then I'll sleep.

Exit [*Fool*].

Poor naked wretches, wheresoe'er you are,
That bide° the pelting of this pitiless storm,
How shall your houseless heads and unfed sides,
Your looped and windowed° raggedness, defend you
From seasons such as these? O, I have ta'en
Too little care of this! Take physic, pomp;°
Expose thyself to feel what wretches feel,
That thou mayst shake the superflux° to them,
And show the heavens more just.

EDGAR [*within*]. Fathom and half, fathom and half!° Poor Tom!

Enter Fool.

FOOL. Come not in here, nuncle, here's a spirit. Help me, help me!

KENT. Give me thy hand. Who's there?

FOOL. A spirit, a spirit. He says his name's Poor Tom.

KENT. What art thou that dost grumble there i' th' straw? Come forth.

Enter Edgar [*disguised as a madman*].

EDGAR. Away! the foul fiend follows me. Through the sharp hawthorn blows the cold wind.° Humh! Go to thy cold bed, and warm thee.

11 **home** to the utmost 12 **power** army 12 **footed** landed 12 **incline to** take the side of 13 **look** search for 13 **privily** secretly 14 **of** by 17 **toward** impending 19 **courtesy forbid** kindness forbidden (i.e., to Lear) 21 **fair deserving** an action deserving reward III.iv.4 **break my heart** i.e., by shutting out the storm which distracts me from thinking 8 **fixed** lodged (in the mind) 11 **i' th' mouth** in the teeth 11 **free** i.e., from care

15 **as** as if 16 **home** to the utmost 20 **frank** liberal (magnanimous) 26 **houseless poverty** the unsheltered poor, abstracted 29 **bide** endure 31 **looped and windowed** full of holes 33 **Take physic, pomp** Take medicine to cure yourselves, you great men 35 **superflux** superfluity 37 **Fathom and half** Edgar, because of the downpour, pretends to take soundings 45–46 **Through . . . wind** a line from the ballad of "The Friar of Orders Gray"

LEAR. Didst thou give all to thy daughters? And art thou come to this?

50 EDGAR. Who gives anything to Poor Tom? Whom the foul fiend hath led through fire and through flame, through ford and whirlpool, o'er bog and quagmire; that hath laid knives under his pillow and halters in his pew,° set ratsbane° by his porridge,° made him proud of heart, to ride on a bay 55 trotting horse over four-inched bridges,° to course° his own shadow for° a traitor. Bless thy five wits,° Tom's a-cold. O, do, de, do, de, do, de. Bless thee from whirlwinds, star-blasting,° and taking.° Do Poor Tom some charity, whom the foul fiend vexes. There could I have him now—and 60 there—and there again—and there.

Storm still.

LEAR.
What, have his daughters brought him to this pass?°
Couldst thou save nothing? Wouldst thou give 'em all?

FOOL. Nay, he reserved a blanket,° else we had been all shamed.

LEAR.
65 Now all the plagues that in the pendulous° air
Hang fated o'er° men's faults light on thy daughters!

KENT. He hath no daughters, sir.

LEAR.
Death, traitor; nothing could have subdued° nature
To such a lowness but his unkind daughters.
70 Is it the fashion that discarded fathers
Should have thus little mercy on° their flesh?
Judicious punishment—'twas this flesh begot
Those pelican° daughters.

EDGAR. Pillicock sat on Pillicock Hill.° Alow, alow, loo, 75 loo!°

FOOL. This cold night will turn us all to fools and madmen.

EDGAR. Take heed o' th' foul fiend; obey thy parents; keep thy word's justice;° swear not; commit not° with man's sworn spouse; set not thy sweet heart on proud array. Tom's 80 a-cold.

LEAR. What hast thou been?

EDGAR. A servingman, proud in heart and mind; that curled my hair, wore gloves in my cap;° served the lust of my mistress' heart, and did the act of darkness with her; 85 swore as many oaths as I spake words, and broke them in the sweet face of heaven. One that slept in the contriving of lust, and waked to do it. Wine loved I deeply, dice dearly; and in woman out-paramoured the Turk.° False of heart, light of ear,° bloody of hand; hog in sloth, fox in stealth, 90 wolf in greediness, dog in madness, lion in prey.° Let not the creaking° of shoes nor the rustling of silks betray thy poor heart to woman. Keep thy foot out of brothels, thy hand out of plackets,° thy pen from lenders' books,° and defy the foul fiend. Still through the hawthorn blows the 95 cold wind; says suum, mun, nonny.° Dolphin° my boy, boy, sessa!° let him trot by.

Storm still.

LEAR. Thou wert better in a grave than to answer° with thy uncovered body this extremity° of the skies. Is man no more than this? Consider him well. Thou owst° the worm 100 no silk, the beast no hide, the sheep no wool, the cat° no perfume. Ha! here's three on's° are sophisticated.° Thou art the thing itself; unaccommodated° man is no more but such a poor, bare, forked° animal as thou art. Off, off, you lendings!° Come, unbutton here. 105

[*Tearing off his clothes.*]

FOOL. Prithee, nuncle, be contented, 'tis a naughty° night to swim in. Now a little fire in a wild° field were like

53 **knives . . . halters . . . ratsbane** the fiend tempts Poor Tom to suicide 53 **pew** gallery or balcony outside a window 54 **porridge** broth 54–55 **ride . . . bridges** i.e., risk his life 55 **course** chase 56 **for** as 56 **five wits** common wit, imagination, fantasy, estimation, memory 57–58 **star-blasting** the evil caused by malignant stars 58 **taking** pernicious influences 61 **pass** wretched condition 63 **blanket** i.e., to cover his nakedness 65 **pendulous** overhanging 66 **fated o'er** destined to punish 68 **subdued** reduced 71 **on** i.e., shown to 73 **pelican** supposed to feed on its parent's blood 74 **Pillicock . . . Hill** probably quoted from a nursery rhyme, and suggested by "pelican"; "pillicock" is a term of endearment and the phallus 74–75 **Alow . . . loo** a hunting call, or the refrain of the song (?)

79 **keep . . . justice** i.e., do not break thy word 79 **commit not** i.e., adultery 84 **gloves . . . cap** i.e., as a pledge from his mistress 89 **out-paramoured the Turk** had more concubines than the sultan 90 **light of ear** ready to hear flattery and slander 91 **prey** preying 92 **creaking** deliberately cultivated, as fashionable 94 **plackets** opening in skirts 94 **pen . . . books** i.e., do not enter your name in the money-lender's account book 96 **suum, mun, nonny** the noise of the wind 96 **Dolphin** the French dauphin (identified by the English with the devil; Poor Tom is pre-sumably quoting from a ballad) 97 **sessa** an interjection: "Go on!" 98 **answer** confront, bear the brunt of 99 **extremity** extreme severity 100 **owst** have taken from 101 **cat** civet cat, whose glands yield perfume 102 **on's** of us 102 **sophisticated** adulterated, made artificial 103 **unaccommodated** uncivilized 104 **forked** two-legged 105 **lendings** borrowed garments 106 **naughty** wicked 107 **wild** barren

an old lecher's heart—a small spark, all the rest on's° body, cold. Look, here comes a walking fire.

Enter Gloucester with a torch.

110 EDGAR. This is the foul fiend Flibbertigibbet.° He begins at curfew,° and walks till the first cock.° He gives the web and the pin,° squints° the eye, and makes the harelip; mildews the white° wheat, and hurts the poor creature of earth.

115 Swithold footed thrice the old;°
He met the nightmare,° and her nine fold;°
Bid her alight°
And her troth plight,°
And aroint° thee, witch, aroint thee!

120 KENT. How fares your grace?
LEAR. What's he?
KENT. Who's there? What is't you seek?
GLOUCESTER. What are you there? Your names?
EDGAR. Poor Tom, that eats the swimming frog, the
125 toad, the todpole, the wall-newt and the water;° that in the fury of his heart, when the foul fiend rages, eats cow-dung for sallets,° swallows the old rat and the ditch-dog,° drinks the green mantle° of the standing° pool; who is whipped from tithing° to tithing, and stocked, punished, and impris-
130 oned; who hath had three suits to his back, six shirts to his body,

Horse to ride, and weapon to wear,
But mice and rats, and such small deer,°
Have been Tom's food for seven long year.°

135 Beware my follower!° Peace, Smulkin,° peace, thou fiend!
GLOUCESTER.
What, hath your grace no better company?
EDGAR.
The Prince of Darkness is a gentleman.
Modo° he's called, and Mahu.°
GLOUCESTER.
Our flesh and blood, my lord, is grown so vile
That it doth hate what gets° it. 140
EDGAR. Poor Tom's a-cold.
GLOUCESTER.
Go in with me. My duty cannot suffer°
T' obey in all your daughters' hard commands.
Though their injunction be to bar my doors
And let this tyrannous night take hold upon you, 145
Yet have I ventured to come seek you out
And bring you where both fire and food is ready.
LEAR.
First let me talk with this philosopher.
What is the cause of thunder?
KENT.
Good my lord, take his offer; go into th' house. 150
LEAR.
I'll talk a word with this same learnèd Theban.°
What is your study?°
EDGAR.
How to prevent° the fiend, and to kill vermin.
LEAR.
Let me ask you one word in private.
KENT.
Importune him once more to go, my lord. 155
His wits begin t' unsettle.
GLOUCESTER. Canst thou blame him?

Storm still.

His daughters seek his death. Ah, that good Kent,
He said it would be thus, poor banished man!
Thou say'st the king grows mad—I'll tell thee, friend,
I am almost mad myself. I had a son, 160
Now outlawed from my blood;° he sought my life
But lately, very late.° I loved him, friend,
No father his son dearer. True to tell thee,
The grief hath crazed my wits. What a night's this!
I do beseech your grace—
LEAR. O, cry you mercy,° sir. 165
Noble philosopher, your company.
EDGAR. Tom's a-cold.
GLOUCESTER.
In, fellow, there, into th' hovel; keep thee warm.

108 **on's** of his 110 **Flibbertigibbet** a figure from Elizabethan demonology 111 **curfew** 9 P.M. 111 **first cock** midnight 112 **web . . . pin** cataract 112 **squints** crosses 113 **white** ripening 115 **Swithold . . . old** Withold (an Anglo-Saxon saint who subdued demons) walked three times across the open country 116 **nightmare** demon 116 **fold** offspring 117 **alight** i.e., from the horse she had possessed 118 **her troth plight** pledge her word 119 **aroint** be gone 125 **todpole . . . water** tadpole, wall lizard, water newt 127 **sallets** salads 127 **ditch-dog** dead dog in a ditch 128 **mantle** scum; **standing** stagnant 129 **tithing** a district comprising ten families 133 **deer** game 133–34 **But . . . year** adapted from a popular romance, "Bevis of Hampton" 135 **follower** familiar

135–38 **Smulkin . . . Modo . . . Mahu** Elizabethan devils, from Samuel Harsnett's *Declaration* of 1603 140 **gets** begets 142 **suffer** permit me 151 **Theban** i.e., Greek philosopher 152 **study** particular scientific study 153 **prevent** balk 161 **outlawed . . . blood** disowned and tainted, like a carbuncle in the corrupted blood 162 **late** recently 165 **cry you mercy** I beg your pardon

LEAR.
Come, let's in all.
KENT. This way, my lord.
LEAR. With him!
170 I will keep still with my philosopher.
KENT.
Good my lord, soothe° him; let him take the fellow.
GLOUCESTER.
Take him you on.°
KENT.
Sirrah, come on; go along with us.
LEAR.
Come, good Athenian.°
GLOUCESTER.
175 No words, no words! Hush.
EDGAR.
Child Rowland to the dark tower came;°
His word was still,° "Fie, foh, and fum,
I smell the blood of a British man."°

Exeunt.

SCENE V

[*Gloucester's castle.*]

Enter Cornwall and Edmund.

CORNWALL. I will have my revenge ere I depart his house.

EDMUND. How, my lord, I may be censured,° that nature thus gives way to loyalty, something fears° me to think
5 of.

CORNWALL. I now perceive it was not altogether your brother's evil disposition made him seek his death; but a provoking merit, set a-work by a reprovable badness in himself.°

10 EDMUND. How malicious is my fortune that I must repent to be just! This is the letter which he spoke of, which approves° him an intelligent party° to the advantages° of France. O heavens, that his treason were not! or not I the detector!

CORNWALL. Go with me to the duchess. 15

EDMUND. If the matter of this paper be certain, you have mighty business in hand.

CORNWALL. True or false, it hath made thee Earl of Gloucester. Seek out where thy father is, that he may be ready for our apprehension.° 20

EDMUND [*aside*]. If I find him comforting° the king, it will stuff his suspicion more fully. I will persever° in my course of loyalty, though the conflict be sore between that and my blood.°

CORNWALL. I will lay trust upon° thee, and thou shalt 25 find a dearer father in my love.

Exeunt.

SCENE VI

[*A chamber in a farmhouse adjoining the castle.*]

Enter Kent and Gloucester.

GLOUCESTER. Here is better than the open air; take it thankfully. I will piece out the comfort with what addition I can. I will not be long from you.

KENT. All the power of his wits have given way to his impatience.° The gods reward your kindness. 5

Exit [*Gloucester*].

Enter Lear, Edgar, and Fool.

EDGAR. Frateretto° calls me, and tells me Nero° is an angler in the lake of darkness. Pray, innocent,° and beware the foul fiend.

FOOL. Prithee, nuncle, tell me whether a madman be a gentleman or a yeoman.° 10

LEAR. A king, a king.

FOOL. No, he's a yeoman that has a gentleman to his son; for he's a mad yeoman that sees his son a gentleman before him.

LEAR.
To have a thousand with red burning spits 15
Come hizzing° in upon 'em—

171 **soothe** humor 172 **you on** with you 174 **Athenian** i.e., philosopher (like "Theban") 176 **Child . . . came** from a lost ballad (?); "child" = a candidate for knighthood; "Rowland" was Charlemagne's nephew, the hero of *The Song of Roland* 177 **His . . . still** his motto was always 177–78 **Fie . . . man** a deliberately absurd linking of the chivalric hero with the nursery tale of Jack the Giant-Killer III.v.3 **censured** judged 4 **something fears** somewhat frightens 8–9 **a provoking . . . himself** a stimulating goodness in Edgar, brought into play by a blamable badness in Gloucester 12 **approves** proves 12 **intelligent party** (1) spy (2) well-informed person 12 **to the advantages** on behalf of

20 **apprehension** arrest 21 **comforting** supporting (a legalism) 22 **persever** persevere 24 **blood** natural feelings 25 **lay trust upon** (1) trust (2) advance III.vi.5 **impatience** raging 6 **Frateretto** Elizabethan devil, from Harsnett's *Declaration* 6 **Nero** who is mentioned by Harsnett, and whose angling is reported by Chaucer in "The Monk's Tale" 7 **innocent** fool 10 **yeoman** farmer (just below a gentleman in rank; the Fool asks what class of man has most indulged his children, and thus been driven mad) 16 **hizzing** hissing

EDGAR. The foul fiend bites my back.

FOOL. He's mad that trusts in the tameness of a wolf, a horse's health, a boy's love, or a whore's oath.

LEAR.
20 It shall be done; I will arraign° them straight.°

[*To Edgar.*]

Come, sit thou here, most learned justice.°

[*To the Fool.*]

Thou, sapient° sir, sit here. Now, you she-foxes—

EDGAR. Look, where he° stands and glares.
Want'st thou eyes at trial, madam?°
25 Come o'er the bourn,° Bessy, to me.

FOOL.
Her boat hath a leak,
And she must not speak
Why she dares not come over to thee.°

EDGAR. The foul fiend haunts Poor Tom in the voice of
30 a nightingale.° Hoppedance° cries in Tom's belly for two white herring.° Croak° not, black angel; I have no food for thee.

KENT.
How do you, sir? Stand you not so amazed.°
Will you lie down and rest upon the cushions?

LEAR.
35 I'll see their trial first. Bring in their evidence.°

[*To Edgar.*]

Thou, robèd man of justice, take thy place.

[*To the Fool.*]

And thou, his yokefellow of equity,°
Bench° by his side. [*To Kent.*] You are o' th' commission;°
Sit you too.

40 EDGAR. Let us deal justly.

Sleepest or wakest thou, jolly shepherd?
Thy sheep be in the corn;°
And for one blast of thy minikin° mouth
Thy sheep shall take no harm.°
Purr, the cat is gray.° 45

LEAR. Arraign her first. 'Tis Goneril, I here take my oath before this honorable assembly, she kicked the poor king her father.

FOOL. Come hither, mistress. Is your name Goneril?

LEAR. She cannot deny it. 50

FOOL. Cry you mercy, I took you for a joint stool.°

LEAR.
And here's another, whose warped looks proclaim
What store° her heart is made on. Stop her there!
Arms, arms, sword, fire! Corruption in the place!°
False justicer, why hast thou let her 'scape? 55

EDGAR. Bless thy five wits!

KENT.
O pity! Sir, where is the patience now
That you so oft have boasted to retain?

EDGAR [*aside*].
My tears begin to take his part so much
They mar my counterfeiting.° 60

LEAR.
The little dogs and all,
Tray, Blanch, and Sweetheart—see, they bark at me.

EDGAR. Tom will throw his head at them. Avaunt, you curs.

Be thy mouth or black or° white, 65
Tooth that poisons if it bite;
Mastiff, greyhound, mongrel grim,
Hound or spaniel, brach° or lym,°
Or bobtail tike, or trundle-tail°—
Tom will make him weep and wail; 70
For, with throwing° thus my head,
Dogs leaped the hatch,° and all are fled.

20 **arraign** bring to trial 20 **straight** straight away 21 **justice** justicer, judge 22 **sapient** wise 23 **he** i.e., a fiend 24 **Want'st ... madam** (to Goneril) i.e., Do you want eyes to look at you during your trial? The fiend serves that purpose 25 **bourn** brook (Edgar quotes from a popular ballad) 26–28 **Her ... thee** the Fool parodies the ballad 30 **nightingale** i.e., the Fool's singing 30 **Hoppedance** Hoberdidance (another devil from Harsnett's *Declaration*) 31 **white herring** unsmoked (as against the black and sulfurous devil?) 31 **Croak** rumble (because his belly is empty) 33 **amazed** astonished 35 **evidence** the evidence of witnesses against them 37 **yokefellow of equity** partner in justice 38 **Bench** sit on the bench 38 **commission** those commissioned as king's justices 42 **corn** wheat 43 **minikin** shrill 41–44 **Sleepest ... harm** probably quoted or adapted from an Elizabethan song 45 **gray** devils were thought to assume the shape of a gray cat 51 **Cry ... stool** proverbial and deliberately impudent apology for overlooking a person; a joint stool was a low stool made by a joiner, perhaps here a stage property to represent Goneril and, in line 52, Regan; "joint stool" can also suggest the judicial bench; hence Goneril may be identified by the Fool, ironically, with those in power, who judge 53 **store** stuff 54 **Corruption ... place** bribery in the court 60 **counterfeiting** i.e., feigned madness 65 **or ... or** either ... or 68 **brach** bitch 68 **lym** bloodhound (from the liam or leash with which he was led) 69 **bobtail ... trundle-tail** short-tailed or long-tailed cur 71 **throwing** jerking (as a hound lifts its head from the ground, the scent having been lost) 72 **leaped the hatch** leaped over the lower half of a divided door (i.e., left in a hurry)

Do, de, de, de. Sessa!° Come, march to wakes° and fairs and
75 market towns. Poor Tom, thy horn° is dry.

LEAR. Then let them anatomize Regan. See what breeds about her heart.° Is there any cause in nature that make° these hard hearts? [*To Edgar.*] You, sir, I entertain° for one of my hundred;° only do not like the fashion of your gar-
80 ments. You will say they are Persian;° but let them be changed.

KENT.
Now, good my lord, lie here and rest awhile.

LEAR.
Make no noise, make no noise; draw the curtains.°
So, so. We'll go to supper i' th' morning.

FOOL. And I'll go to bed at noon.°

Enter Gloucester.

85 GLOUCESTER.
Come hither, friend. Where is the king my master?

KENT.
Here, sir, but trouble him not; his wits are gone.

GLOUCESTER.
Good friend, I prithee take him in thy arms.
I have o'erheard a plot of death upon him.
90 There is a litter ready; lay him in't
And drive toward Dover, friend, where thou shalt meet
Both welcome and protection. Take up thy master.
If thou shouldst dally half an hour, his life,
With thine and all that offer to defend him,
95 Stand in assurèd loss. Take up, take up,
And follow me, that will to some provision°
Give thee quick conduct.°

KENT. Oppressèd nature sleeps.
This rest might yet have balmed thy broken sinews,°
Which, if convenience° will not allow,
Stand in hard cure.° [*To the Fool.*] Come, help to bear thy master.
100 Thou must not stay behind.

GLOUCESTER. Come, come, away!
Exeunt [*all but Edgar*].

EDGAR.
When we our betters see bearing our woes,
We scarcely think our miseries our foes.°
Who alone suffers suffers most i' th' mind,
Leaving free° things and happy shows° behind; 105
But then the mind much sufferance° doth o'erskip
When grief hath mates, and bearing fellowship.°
How light and portable° my pain seems now,
When that which makes me bend makes the king bow.
He childed as I fathered. Tom, away. 110
Mark the high noises,° and thyself bewray°
When false opinion, whose wrong thoughts° defile thee,
In thy just proof repeals and reconciles thee.°
What will hap more° tonight, safe 'scape the king!
Lurk,° lurk. [*Exit.*]

SCENE VII

[*Gloucester's castle.*]

Enter Cornwall, Regan, Goneril, Edmund, and Servants.

CORNWALL [*to Goneril*]. Post speedily to my lord your husband; show him this letter. The army of France is landed. [*To Servants.*] Seek out the traitor Gloucester.
[*Exeunt some of the Servants.*]

REGAN. Hang him instantly.

GONERIL. Pluck out his eyes. 5

CORNWALL. Leave him to my displeasure. Edmund, keep you our sister company. The revenges we are bound° to take upon your traitorous father are not fit for your beholding. Advise the duke where you are going, to a most festinate° preparation. We are bound to the like. Our posts° 10 shall be swift and intelligent° betwixt us. Farewell, dear sister; farewell, my Lord of Gloucester.°

Enter Oswald.

How now? Where's the king?

73 **Sessa** Be off! 73 **wakes** feasts attending the dedication of a church 74 **horn** horn bottle which the Bedlam used in begging a drink (Edgar is suggesting that he is unable to play his role any longer) 75–76 **Then . . . heart** i.e., If the Bedlam's horn is dry, let Regan, whose heart has become as hard as horn, be dissected 76 **make** subjunctive 77 **entertain** engage 78 **hundred** i.e., Lear's hundred knights 79 **Persian** gorgeous (ironically of Edgar's rags) 82 **curtains** Lear imagines himself in bed 84 **And . . . noon** the Fool's last words 95 **provision** maintenance 96 **conduct** direction 97 **balmed . . . sinews** soothed thy racked nerves 98 **convenience** fortunate occasion 99 **Stand . . . cure** will be hard to cure

102 **our foes** enemies peculiar to ourselves 104 **free** carefree 104 **shows** scenes 105 **sufferance** suffering 106 **bearing fellowship** suffering has company 107 **portable** able to be supported or endured 110 **Mark . . . noises** observe the rumors of strife among those in power 110 **bewray** reveal 111 **wrong thoughts** misconceptions 112 **In . . . thee** on the manifesting of your innocence recalls you from outlawry and restores amity between you and your father 113 **What . . . more** whatever else happens 114 **Lurk** hide III.vii.7 **bound** (1) forced (2) purposing to 10 **festinate** speedy 10 **posts** messengers 11 **intelligent** full of information 12 **Lord of Gloucester** Edmund, now elevated to the title

OSWALD.
My Lord of Gloucester hath conveyed him hence.
15 Some five or six and thirty of his knights,
Hot questrists° after him, met him at gate;
Who, with some other of the lords dependants,°
Are gone with him toward Dover, where they boast
To have well-armèd friends.
CORNWALL. Get horses for your mistress.
[*Exit Oswald.*]
20 GONERIL. Farewell, sweet lord, and sister.
CORNWALL.
Edmund, farewell.
[*Exeunt Goneril and Edmund.*]
Go seek the traitor Gloucester,
Pinion him like a thief, bring him before us.
[*Exeunt other Servants.*]
Though well we may not pass upon° his life
Without the form of justice, yet our power
25 Shall do a court'sy to° our wrath, which men
May blame, but not control.

Enter Gloucester, brought in by two or three.

Who's there, the traitor?
REGAN.
Ingrateful fox, 'tis he.
CORNWALL.
Bind fast his corky° arms.
GLOUCESTER.
What means your graces? Good my friends, consider
30 You are my guests. Do me no foul play, friends.
CORNWALL.
Bind him, I say. [*Servants bind him.*]
REGAN. Hard, hard! O filthy traitor.
GLOUCESTER.
Unmerciful lady as you are, I'm none.
CORNWALL.
To this chair bind him. Villain, thou shalt find—
[*Regan plucks his beard.*°]
GLOUCESTER.
By the kind gods, 'tis most ignobly done
35 To pluck me by the beard.
REGAN.
So white, and such a traitor?
GLOUCESTER. Naughty° lady,
These hairs which thou dost ravish from my chin
Will quicken° and accuse thee. I am your host.
With robber's hands my hospitable favors°
You should not ruffle° thus. What will you do? 40
CORNWALL.
Come, sir, what letters had you late° from France?
REGAN.
Be simple-answered,° for we know the truth.
CORNWALL.
And what confederacy have you with the traitors
Late footed in the kingdom?
REGAN.
To whose hands you have sent the lunatic king: 45
Speak.
GLOUCESTER.
I have a letter guessingly° set down,
Which came from one that's of a neutral heart,
And not from one opposed.
CORNWALL. Cunning.
REGAN. And false.
CORNWALL.
Where hast thou sent the king? 50
GLOUCESTER.
To Dover.
REGAN.
Wherefore to Dover? Wast thou not charged at peril°—
CORNWALL.
Wherefore to Dover? Let him answer that.
GLOUCESTER.
I am tied to th' stake, and I must stand the course.°
REGAN.
Wherefore to Dover? 55
GLOUCESTER.
Because I would not see thy cruel nails
Pluck out his poor old eyes; nor thy fierce sister
In his anointed° flesh rash° boarish fangs.
The sea, with such a storm as his bare head
In hell-black night endured, would have buoyed° up 60
And quenched the stellèd° fires.
Yet, poor old heart, he holp° the heavens to rain.
If wolves had at thy gate howled that dearn° time,

16 **questrists** searchers 17 **lords dependants** attendant lords (members of Lear's retinue) 23 **pass upon** pass judgment on 25 **do . . . to** indulge 28 **corky** sapless (because old) 33 s.d. **plucks his beard** a deadly insult 36 **Naughty** wicked

38 **quicken** come to life 39 **hospitable favors** face of your host 40 **ruffle** tear at violently 41 **late** recently 42 **simple-answered** straightforward in answering 47 **guessingly** without certain knowledge 52 **charged at peril** ordered under penalty 54 **course** coursing (in which a relay of dogs baits a bull or bear tied in the pit) 58 **anointed** holy (because king) 58 **rash** strike with the tusk, like a boar 60 **buoyed** risen 61 **stellèd** (1) fixed (as opposed to the planets or wandering stars) (2) starry 62 **holp** helped 63 **dearn** dread

Thou shouldst have said, "Good porter, turn the key."°
65 All cruels else subscribe.° But I shall see
The wingèd° vengeance overtake such children.

CORNWALL.
See't shalt thou never. Fellows, hold the chair.
Upon these eyes of thine I'll set my foot.

GLOUCESTER.
He that will think° to live till he be old,
70 Give me some help.—O cruel! O you gods!

REGAN.
One side will mock° another. Th' other too.

CORNWALL.
If you see vengeance—

FIRST SERVANT. Hold your hand, my lord!
I have served you ever since I was a child;
But better service have I never done you
Than now to bid you hold.

75 REGAN. How now, you dog?

FIRST SERVANT.
If you did wear a beard upon your chin,
I'd shake it° on this quarrel. What do you mean!°

CORNWALL. My villain!°

Draw and fight.

FIRST SERVANT.
Nay, then, come on, and take the chance of anger.

REGAN.
80 Give me thy sword. A peasant stand up thus?

She takes a sword and runs at him behind, kills him.

FIRST SERVANT.
O, I am slain! my lord, you have one eye left
To see some mischief° on him. O!

CORNWALL.
Lest it see more, prevent it. Out, vile jelly.
Where is thy luster now?

GLOUCESTER.
85 All dark and comfortless. Where's my son Edmund?
Edmund, enkindle all the sparks of nature°
To quit° this horrid act.

REGAN. Out, treacherous villain,
Thou call'st on him that hates thee. It was he
That made the overture° of thy treasons to us;
Who is too good to pity thee. 90

GLOUCESTER.
O my follies! Then Edgar was abused.°
Kind gods, forgive me that, and prosper him.

REGAN.
Go thrust him out at gates, and let him smell
His way to Dover.

Exit [one], with Gloucester.

How is't, my lord? How look you?°

CORNWALL.
I have received a hurt. Follow me, lady. 95
Turn out that eyeless villain. Throw this slave
Upon the dunghill. Regan, I bleed apace.
Untimely comes this hurt. Give me your arm.

Exeunt.

SECOND SERVANT.
I'll never care what wickedness I do,
If this man come to good.

THIRD SERVANT. If she live long, 100
And in the end meet the old course of death,°
Women will all turn monsters.

SECOND SERVANT.
Let's follow the old earl, and get the Bedlam
To lead him where he would. His roguish madness
Allows itself to anything.° 105

THIRD SERVANT.
Go thou. I'll fetch some flax and whites of eggs
To apply to his bleeding face. Now heaven help him.

[Exeunt severally.]

ACT IV

SCENE I

[*The heath.*]

Enter Edgar.

EDGAR.
Yet better thus, and known to be contemned,°
Than still contemned and flattered. To be worst,
The lowest and most dejected° thing of fortune,
Stands still in esperance,° lives not in fear:
The lamentable change is from the best, 5

64 **turn the key** i.e., unlock the gate 65 **All . . . subscribe** All cruel creatures but man are compassionate 66 **wingèd** (1) heavenly (2) swift 69 **will think** expects 71 **mock** make ridiculous (because of the contrasts) 77 **shake it** an insult comparable to Regan's plucking of Gloucester's beard 77 **What . . . mean** i.e., What terrible thing are you doing? 78 **villain** serf (with a suggestion of the modern meaning) 82 **mischief** injury 86 **enkindle . . . nature** fan your natural feeling into flame 87 **quit** requite

89 **overture** disclosure 91 **abused** wronged 94 **How look you** How are you? 101 **meet . . . death** die the customary death of old age 104–05 **His . . . anything** his lack of all self-control leaves him open to any suggestion IV.i.1 **known . . . contemned** conscious of being despised 3 **dejected** abased 4 **esperance** hope

The worst returns to laughter.° Welcome then,
Thou unsubstantial air that I embrace!
The wretch that thou hast blown unto the worst
Owes° nothing to thy blasts.

Enter Gloucester, led by an Old Man.

But who comes here?
10 My father, poorly led?° World, world, O world!
But that thy strange mutations make us hate thee,
Life would not yield to age.°

OLD MAN. O, my good lord,
I have been your tenant, and your father's tenant,
These fourscore years.

GLOUCESTER.
15 Away, get thee away; good friend, be gone:
Thy comforts° can do me no good at all;
Thee they may hurt.°

OLD MAN. You cannot see your way.

GLOUCESTER.
I have no way and therefore want° no eyes;
I stumbled when I saw. Full oft 'tis seen,
20 Our means secure us, and our mere defects
Prove our commodities.° Oh, dear son Edgar,
The food° of thy abusèd° father's wrath!
Might I but live to see thee in° my touch,
I'd say I had eyes again!

OLD MAN. How now! Who's there?

EDGAR [*aside*].
25 O gods! Who is't can say, "I am at the worst"?
I am worse than e'er I was.

OLD MAN. 'Tis poor mad Tom.

EDGAR [*aside*].
And worse I may be yet: the worst is not
So long as we can say, "This is the worst."°

OLD MAN.
Fellow, where goest?

GLOUCESTER. Is it a beggar-man?

OLD MAN.
30 Madman and beggar too.

GLOUCESTER.
He has some reason,° else he could not beg.
I' th' last night's storm I such a fellow saw,
Which made me think a man a worm. My son
Came then into my mind, and yet my mind
Was then scarce friends with him. I have heard more since. 35
As flies to wanton° boys, are we to th' gods,
They kill us for their sport.

EDGAR [*aside*]. How should this be?°
Bad is the trade that must play fool to sorrow,
Ang'ring° itself and others. Bless thee, master!

GLOUCESTER.
Is that the naked fellow?

OLD MAN. Ay, my lord. 40

GLOUCESTER.
Then, prithee, get thee gone: if for my sake
Thou wilt o'ertake us hence a mile or twain
I' th' way toward Dover, do it for ancient° love,
And bring some covering for this naked soul,
Which I'll entreat to lead me.

OLD MAN. Alack, sir, he is mad. 45

GLOUCESTER.
'Tis the time's plague,° when madmen lead the blind.
Do as I bid thee, or rather do thy pleasure;°
Above the rest,° be gone.

OLD MAN.
I'll bring him the best 'parel° that I have,
Come on't what will. *Exit.* 50

GLOUCESTER.
Sirrah, naked fellow—

EDGAR.
Poor Tom's a-cold. [*Aside.*] I cannot daub it° further.

GLOUCESTER.
Come hither, fellow.

EDGAR [*aside*].
And yet I must.—Bless thy sweet eyes, they bleed.

GLOUCESTER.
Knowst thou the way to Dover? 55

EDGAR.
Both stile and gate, horse-way and footpath.
Poor Tom hath been scared out of his good wits. Bless thee, good man's son, from the foul fiend! Five fiends have

6 **returns to laughter** changes for the better 9 **Owes** is in debt for 10 **poorly led** (1) led like a poor man, with only one attendant (2) led by a poor man 11–12 **But . . . age** We should not agree to grow old and hence die, except for the hateful mutability of life 16 **comforts** ministrations 17 **hurt** injure 18 **want** require 20–21 **Our . . . commodities** Our resources make us overconfident, while our afflictions make for our advantage 22 **food** i.e., the object on which Gloucester's anger fed 22 **abusèd** deceived 23 **in** i.e., with, by means of 27–28 **the . . . worst** so long as a man continues to suffer (i.e., is still alive), even greater suffering may await him

31 **reason** faculty of reasoning 36 **wanton** (1) playful (2) reckless 37 **How . . . be?** i.e., How can this horror be? 39 **Ang'ring** offending 43 **ancient** (1) the love the Old Man feels, by virtue of his long tenancy (2) the love that formerly obtained between master and man 46 **time's plague** characteristic disorder of this time 47 **thy pleasure** as you like it 48 **the rest** all 49 **'parel** apparel 52 **daub it** lay it on (figure from plastering mortar)

been in Poor Tom at once; of lust, as Obidicut;° Hobbidi-
60 dence, prince of dumbness;° Mahu, of stealing; Modo, of murder; Flibbertigibett, of mopping and mowing;° who since possesses chambermaids and waiting-women. So, bless thee, master!

GLOUCESTER.
Here, take this purse, thou whom the heavens' plagues
65 Have humbled to all strokes:° that I am wretched
Makes thee the happier. Heavens, deal so still!
Let the superfluous° and lust-dieted° man,
That slaves° your ordinance,° that will not see
Because he does not feel, feel your pow'r quickly;
70 So distribution should undo excess,°
And each man have enough. Dost thou know Dover?

EDGAR. Ay, master

GLOUCESTER.
There is a cliff whose high and bending° head
Looks fearfully° in the confinèd deep:°
75 Bring me but to the very brim of it,
And I'll repair the misery thou dost bear
With something rich about me: from that place
I shall no leading need.

EDGAR. Give me thy arm:
Poor Tom shall lead thee. *Exeunt.*

SCENE II

[*Before the Duke of Albany's palace.*]

Enter Goneril and Edmund.

GONERIL.
Welcome, my lord: I marvel our mild husband
Not met° us on the way.

Enter Oswald.

Now, where's your master?

OSWALD.
Madam, within; but never man so changed.
I told him of the army that was landed:
He smiled at it. I told him you were coming; 5
His answer was, "The worse." Of Gloucester's treachery,
And of the loyal service of his son
When I informed him, then he called me sot,°
And told me I had turned the wrong side out:
What most he should dislike seems pleasant to him; 10
What like,° offensive.

GONERIL [*to Edmund*].
Then shall you go no further.
It is the cowish° terror of his spirit,
That dares not undertake:° he'll not feel wrongs,
Which tie him to an answer.° Our wishes on the way 15
May prove effects.° Back, Edmund, to my brother;
Hasten his musters° and conduct his pow'rs.°
I must change names° at home and give the distaff°
Into my husband's hands. This trusty servant
Shall pass between us: ere long you are like to hear, 20
If you dare venture in your own behalf,
A mistress's° command. Wear this; spare speech;
[*Giving a favor.*]
Decline your head.° This kiss, if it durst speak,
Would stretch thy spirits up into the air:
Conceive,° and fare thee well. 25

EDMUND.
Yours in the ranks of death.

GONERIL. My most dear Gloucester!
Exit [*Edmund*].
O, the difference of man and man!
To thee a woman's services are due:
My fool usurps my body.°

OSWALD. Madam, here comes my lord.
Exit.

Enter Albany.

GONERIL.
I have been worth the whistle.°

59 **Obidicut** Hoberdicut, a devil (like the four that follow, from Harsnett's *Declaration*) 60 **dumbness** muteness (like the crimes and afflictions in the next lines, the result of diabolic possession) 61 **mopping and mowing** grimacing and making faces 65 **humbled . . . strokes** brought so low as to bear anything humbly 67 **superfluous** possessed of superfluities 67 **lust-dieted** whose lust is gratified (like Gloucester's) 68 **slaves** (1) tramples, spurns like a slave (2) tears, rends (Old English *slaefan*) (?) 68 **ordinance** law 70 **So . . . excess** Then the man with too much wealth would distribute it among those with too little 73 **bending** overhanging 74 **fearfully** occasioning fear 74 **confinèd deep** the sea, hemmed in below
IV.ii.2 **Not met** did not meet

8 **sot** fool 11 **What like** what he should like 13 **cowish** cowardly 14 **undertake** venture 15 **tie . . . answer** oblige him to retaliate 15–16 **Our . . . effects** Our desires (that you might be my husband), as we journeyed here, may be fulfilled 17 **musters** collecting of troops 17 **conduct his pow'rs** lead his army 18 **change names** i.e., exchange the name of "mistress" for that of "master" 18 **distaff** spinning stick (wifely symbol) 22 **mistress's** lover's (and also, Albany having been disposed of, lady's or wife's) 23 **Decline your head** i.e., that Goneril may kiss him 25 **Conceive** understand (with a sexual implication, that includes "stretch thy spirits," line 24; and "death," line 26: "to die," meaning "to experience sexual intercourse") 29 **My . . . body** My husband wrongfully enjoys me 30 **I whistle** i.e., Once you valued me (the proverb is implied, "It is a poor dog that is not worth the whistling")

30 ALBANY. O Goneril!
You are not worth the dust which the rude wind
Blows in your face. I fear your disposition:°
That nature which contemns° its origin
Cannot be bordered certain in itself;°
35 She that herself will sliver and disbranch°
From her material sap,° perforce must wither
And come to deadly use.°
GONERIL.
No more; the text° is foolish.
ALBANY.
Wisdom and goodness to the vile seem vile:
40 Filths savor but themselves.° What have you done?
Tigers, not daughters, what have you performed?
A father, and a gracious agèd man,
Whose reverence even the head-lugged bear° would lick,
Most barbarous, most degenerate, have you madded.°
45 Could my good brother suffer you to do it?
A man, a prince, by him so benefited!
If that the heavens do not their visible spirits°
Send quickly down to tame these vile offenses,
It will come,
50 Humanity must perforce prey on itself,
Like monsters of the deep.
GONERIL. Milk-livered° man!
That bear'st a cheek for blows, a head for wrongs;
Who hast not in thy brows an eye discerning
Thine honor from thy suffering;° that not know'st
55 Fools do those villains pity who are punished
Ere they have done their mischief.° Where's thy drum?
France spreads his banners in our noiseless° land,
With plumèd helm° thy state begins to threat,°
Whilst thou, a moral° fool, sits still and cries,
"Alack, why does he so?"
ALBANY. See thyself, devil! 60
Proper° deformity seems not in the fiend
So horrid as in woman.
GONERIL. O vain fool!
ALBANY.
Thou changèd and self-covered° thing, for shame,
Be-monster not thy feature.° Were't my fitness°
To let these hands obey my blood,° 65
They are apt enough to dislocate and tear
Thy flesh and bones: howe'er° thou art a fiend,
A woman's shape doth shield thee.
GONERIL.
Marry, your manhood mew°—

Enter a Messenger.

ALBANY. What news? 70
MESSENGER.
O, my good lord, the Duke of Cornwall's dead,
Slain by his servant, going to° put out
The other eye of Gloucester.
ALBANY. Gloucester's eyes!
MESSENGER.
A servant that he bred,° thrilled with remorse,°
Opposed against the act, bending his sword 75
To his great master, who thereat enraged
Flew on him, and amongst them felled° him dead,
But not without that harmful stroke which since
Hath plucked him after.°
ALBANY. This shows you are above,
You justicers,° that these our nether° crimes 80
So speedily can venge.° But, O poor Gloucester!
Lost he his other eye?

32 **disposition** nature 33 **contemns** despises 34 **bordered . . . itself** kept within its normal bounds 35 **sliver and disbranch** cut off 36 **material sap** essential and life-giving sustenance 37 **come . . . use** i.e., be as a dead branch for the burning 38 **text** i.e., on which your sermon is based 40 **Filths . . . themselves** the filthy relish only the taste of filth 43 **head-lugged bear** bear-baited by the dogs, and hence enraged 44 **madded** made mad 47 **visible spirits** avenging spirits in material form 51 **Milk-livered** lily-livered (hence cowardly, the liver being regarded as the seat of courage) 53–54 **discerning . . . suffering** able to distinguish between insults that ought to be resented and ordinary pain that is to be borne 55–56 **Fools . . . mischief** Only fools are sorry for criminals whose intended criminality is prevented by punishment 57 **noiseless** i.e., the drum, signifying preparation for war, is silent 58 **helm** helmet 58 **thy . . . threat** France begins to threaten Albany's realm

59 **moral** moralizing; but also with the implication that morality and folly are one 61 **Proper** (1) natural (to a fiend) (2) fair-appearing 63 **changèd and self-covered** i.e., transformed, by the contorting of her woman's face, on which appears the fiendish behavior she has allowed herself (Goneril has disguised nature by wickedness) 64 **Be-monster . . . feature** do not change your appearance into a fiend's 64 **my fitness** appropriate for me 65 **blood** passion 67 **howe'er** but even if 69 **your manhood mew** (1) coop up or confine (pretended) manhood (2) molt or shed it, if that is what is supposed to "shield" me from you 72 **going to** as he was about to 74 **bred** reared 74 **thrilled with remorse** pierced by compassion 77 **amongst them felled** others assisting, they felled 79 **plucked him after** i.e., brought Cornwall to death with his servant 80 **justicers** judges 80 **nether** committed below (on earth) 81 **venge** avenge

MESSENGER. Both, both, my lord.
This letter, madam, craves° a speedy answer;
'Tis from your sister.
GONERIL [*aside*]. One way I like this well;
85 But being widow, and my Gloucester with her,
May all the building in my fancy pluck
Upon my hateful life.° Another way,°
The news is not so tart.°—I'll read, and answer.
Exit.
ALBANY.
Where was his son when they did take his eyes?
MESSENGER.
Come with my lady hither.
90 ALBANY. He is not here.
MESSENGER.
No, my good lord; I met him back° again.
ALBANY.
Knows he the wickedness?
MESSENGER.
Ay, my good lord; 'twas he informed against him,
And quit the house on purpose, that their punishment
Might have the freer course.
95 ALBANY. Gloucester, I live
To thank thee for the love thou showed'st the king,
And to revenge thine eyes. Come hither, friend:
Tell me what more thou knowst. *Exeunt.*

[SCENE III

The French camp near Dover.]

Enter Kent and a Gentleman.

KENT. Why the King of France is so suddenly gone back, know you no reason?

GENTLEMAN. Something he left imperfect in the state,° which since his coming forth is thought of, which imports° 5 to the kingdom so much fear and danger that his personal return was most required and necessary.

KENT. Who hath he left behind him general?

GENTLEMAN. The Marshal of France, Monsier La Far.

KENT. Did your letters pierce° the queen to any demon- 10 stration of grief?

GENTLEMAN.
Ay, sir; she took them, read them in my presence,
And now and then an ample tear trilled° down
Her delicate cheek: it seemed she was a queen
Over her passion, who most rebel-like
Sought to be king o'er her.
KENT. O, then it moved her. 15
GENTLEMAN.
Not to a rage: patience and sorrow strove
Who should express her goodliest.° You have seen
Sunshine and rain at once: her smiles and tears
Were like a better way:° those happy smilets°
That played on her ripe lip seemed not to know 20
What guests were in her eyes, which parted thence
As pearls from diamonds dropped. In brief,
Sorrow would be a rarity most beloved,
If all could so become it.°
KENT. Made she no verbal question?
GENTLEMAN.
Faith, once or twice she heaved° the name of "father" 25
Pantingly forth, as if it pressed her heart;
Cried, "Sisters! Sisters! Shame of ladies! Sisters!
Kent! Father! Sisters! What, i' th' storm? i' th' night?
Let pity not be believed!"° There she shook
The holy water from her heavenly eyes, 30
And clamor moistened:° then away she started
To deal with grief alone.
KENT. It is the stars,
The stars above us, govern our conditions;°
Else one self mate and make could not beget
Such different issues.° You spoke not with her since? 35
GENTLEMAN. No.
KENT.
Was this before the king returned?
GENTLEMAN. No, since.
KENT.
Well, sir, the poor distressed Lear's i' th' town;
Who sometime in his better tune° remembers
What we are come about, and by no means 40
Will yield to see his daughter.

83 **craves** demands 86–87 **May . . . life** These things (line 85) may send my future hopes, my castles in air, crashing down upon the hateful (married) life I lead now 87 **Another way** looked at another way 88 **tart** sour 91 **back** going back
IV.iii.3 **imperfect . . . state** unsettled in his own kingdom 4 **imports** portends 9 **pierce** impel

12 **trilled** trickled 17 **Who . . . goodliest** which should give her the most becoming expression 19 **Were . . . way** i.e., improved on that spectacle 19 **smilets** little smiles 23–24 **Sorrow . . . it** would be a coveted jewel if it became others as it does her 25 **heaved** expressed with difficulty 29 **Let . . . believed** let it not be believed for pity 31 **clamor moistened** moistened clamor, i.e., mixed (and perhaps assuaged) her outcries with tears 33 **govern our conditions** determine what we are 34–35 **Else . . . issues** otherwise the same husband and wife could not produce such different children 39 **better tune** composed, less jangled intervals

GENTLEMAN. Why, good sir?

KENT.

A sovereign° shame so elbows° him: his own unkindness
That stripped her from his benediction, turned her
To foreign casualties,° gave her dear rights
45 To his dog-hearted daughters: these things sting
His mind so venomously that burning shame
Detains him from Cordelia.

GENTLEMAN. Alack, poor gentleman!

KENT.

Of Albany's and Cornwall's powers you heard not?

GENTLEMAN.

'Tis so;° they are afoot.

KENT.

50 Well, sir, I'll bring you to our master Lear,
And leave you to attend him: some dear cause°
Will in concealment wrap me up awhile;
When I am known aright, you shall not grieve
Lending me this acquaintance. I pray you, go
55 Along with me. [*Exeunt.*]

[SCENE IV

The same. A tent.]

Enter, with drum and colors, Cordelia, Doctor and Soldiers.

CORDELIA.

Alack, 'tis he: why, he was met even now
As mad as the vexed sea; singing aloud;
Crowned with rank femiter and furrow-weeds,
With hardocks, hemlock, nettles, cuckoo-flow'rs,
5 Darnel,° and all the idle weeds that grow
In our sustaining corn.° A century° send forth;
Search every acre in the high-grown field
And bring him to our eye. [*Exit an Officer.*] What can man's wisdom°
In the restoring his bereavèd° sense?
10 He that helps him take all my outward° worth.

42 **sovereign** overpowering 42 **elbows** jog his elbow (i.e., reminds him) 44 **casualties** chances 49 **'tis so** i.e., I have heard of them 51 **dear cause** important reason IV.iv.3–5 **femiter . . . Darnel:** *femiter* fumitory, whose leaves and juice are bitter; *furrow-weeds* weeds that grow in the furrow, or plowed land; *hardocks* hoar or white docks (?), burdocks, harlocks; *hemlock* a poison; *nettles* plants that sting and burn; *cockoo-flow'rs* identified with a plant employed to remedy diseases of the brain; *Darnel* tares, noisome weeds 6 **sustaining corn** life-maintaining wheat 6 **century** sentry (?); troop of a hundred soldiers 8 **What . . . wisdom** what can science accomplish 9 **bereavèd** impaired 10 **outward** material

DOCTOR.

There is means, madam:
Our foster-nurse° of nature is repose,
The which he lacks: that to provoke° in him,
Are many simples operative,° whose power
Will close the eye of anguish.

CORDELIA. All blest secrets, 15
All you unpublished virtues° of the earth,
Spring with my tears! be aidant and remediate°
In the good man's distress! Seek, seek for him,
Lest his ungoverned rage dissolve the life
That wants the means to lead it.°

Enter Messenger.

MESSENGER. News, madam; 20
The British pow'rs are marching hitherward.

CORDELIA.

'Tis known before. Our preparation stands
In expectation of them. O dear father,
It is thy business that I go about;
Therefore° great France 25
My mourning and importuned° tears hath pitied.
No blown° ambition doth our arms incite,
But love, dear love, and our aged father's right:
Soon may I hear and see him! *Exeunt.*

[SCENE V

Gloucester's castle.]

Enter Regan and Oswald.

REGAN.

But are my brother's pow'rs set forth?

OSWALD. Ay, madam.

Himself in person there?

OSWALD. Madam, with much ado:°

Your sister is the better soldier.

REGAN.

Lord Edmund spake not with your lord at home?

OSWALD.

No, madam. 5

REGAN.

What might import° my sister's letter to him?

12 **foster-nurse** fostering nurse 13 **provoke** induce 14 **simples operative** efficacious medicinal herbs 16 **unpublished virtues** i.e., secret remedial herbs 17 **remediate** remedial 20 **wants . . . it** i.e., lacks the reason to control the rage 25 **Therefore** because of that 26 **importuned** importunate 27 **blown** puffed up
IV.v.2 **ado** bother and persuasion 6 **import** purport, carry as its message

OSWALD.
I know not, lady.
REGAN.
Faith, he is posted° hence on serious matter.
It was great ignorance,° Gloucester's eyes being out,
10 To let him live. Where he arrives he moves
All hearts against us: Edmund, I think, is gone,
In pity of his misery, to dispatch
His nighted° life; moreover, to descry
The strength o' th' enemy.
OSWALD.
15 I must needs after him, madam, with my letter.
REGAN.
Our troops set forth tomorrow: stay with us;
The ways are dangerous.
OSWALD. I may not, madam:
My lady charged my duty° in this business.
REGAN.
Why should she write to Edmund? Might not you
20 Transport her purposes° by word? Belike,°
Some things I know not what. I'll love thee much,
Let me unseal the letter.
OSWALD. Madam, I had rather—
REGAN.
I know your lady does not love her husband;
I am sure of that: and at her late° being here
25 She gave strange eliads° and most speaking looks
To noble Edmund. I know you are of her bosom.°
OSWALD. I, madam?
REGAN.
I speak in understanding: y' are; I know't:
Therefore I do advise you, take this note:°
30 My lord is dead; Edmund and I have talked;
And more convenient° is he for my hand
Than for your lady's: you may gather more.°
If you do find him, pray you, give him this;°
And when your mistress hears thus much from you,
35 I pray, desire her call° her wisdom to her.
So, fare you well.
If you do chance to hear of that blind traitor,
Preferment° falls on him that cuts him off.

OSWALD.
Would I could meet him, madam! I should show
What party I do follow.
REGAN. Fare thee well. *Exeunt.* 40

[SCENE VI
Fields near Dover.]

Enter Gloucester and Edgar.

GLOUCESTER.
When shall I come to th' top of that same hill?
EDGAR.
You do climb up it now. Look, how we labor.
GLOUCESTER.
Methinks the ground is even.
EDGAR. Horrible steep.
Hark, do you hear the sea?
GLOUCESTER. No, truly.
EDGAR.
Why then your other senses grow imperfect 5
By your eyes' anguish.°
GLOUCESTER. So may it be indeed.
Methinks thy voice is altered, and thou speak'st
In better phrase and matter than thou didst.
EDGAR.
Y' are much deceived: in nothing am I changed
But in my garments.
GLOUCESTER. Methinks y' are better spoken. 10
EDGAR.
Come on, sir; here's the place: stand still. How fearful
And dizzy 'tis to cast one's eyes so low!
The crows and choughs° that wing the midway air°
Show scarce so gross° as beetles. Half way down
Hangs one that gathers sampire,° dreadful trade! 15
Methinks he seems no bigger than his head.
The fishermen that walk upon the beach
Appear like mice; and yond tall anchoring° bark
Diminished to her cock;° her cock, a buoy
Almost too small for sight. The murmuring surge 20
That on th' unnumb'red idle pebble° chafes
Cannot be heard so high. I'll look no more,
Lest my brain turn and the deficient sight
Topple° down headlong.

8 **is posted** has ridden speedily 9 **ignorance** folly 13 **nighted** (1) darkened, because blinded (2) benighted 18 **charged my duty** ordered me as a solemn duty 20 **Transport her purposes** convey her intentions 20 **Belike** probably 24 **late** recently 25 **eliads** amorous looks 26 **of her bosom** in her confidence 29 **take this note** take note of this 31 **convenient** fitting 32 **gather more** surmise more yourself 33 **this** this advice 35 **call** recall 38 **Preferment** promotion

IV.vi.6 **anguish** pain 13 **choughs** a kind of crow 13 **midway air** i.e., halfway down the cliff 14 **gross** large 15 **sampire** samphire, an aromatic herb associated with Dover Cliffs 18 **anchoring** anchored 19 **cock** cockboat, a small boat usually towed behind the ship 21 **unnumb'red idle pebble** innumerable pebbles, moved to and fro by the waves to no purpose 23–24 **the . . . Topple** my failing sight topple me

GLOUCESTER. Set me where you stand.

EDGAR.

25 Give me your hand: you are now within a foot
Of th' extreme verge: for all beneath the moon
Would I not leap upright.°

GLOUCESTER. Let go my hand.

Here, friend, 's another purse; in it a jewel
Well worth a poor man's taking. Fairies° and gods
30 Prosper it with thee! Go thou further off;
Bid me farewell, and let me hear thee going.

EDGAR.

Now fare ye well, good sir.

GLOUCESTER. With all my heart.

EDGAR [*aside*].

Why I do trifle thus with his despair
Is done to cure it.°

GLOUCESTER. O you mighty gods!

He kneels.

35 This world I do renounce, and in your sights
Shake patiently my great affliction off:
If I could hear it longer and not fall
To quarrel with° your great opposeless° wills,
My snuff° and loathèd part of nature should
40 Burn itself out. If Edgar live, O bless him!
Now, fellow, fare thee well.

He falls.

EDGAR. Gone, sir, farewell.

And yet I know not how° conceit° may rob
The treasury of life, when life itself
Yields to° the theft. Had he been where he thought,
45 By this had thought been past. Alive or dead?
Ho, you sir! friend! Hear you, sir! speak!
Thus might he pass° indeed: yet he revives.
What are you, sir?

GLOUCESTER. Away, and let me die.

EDGAR.

Hadst thou been aught but gossamer, feathers, air,
50 So many fathom down precipitating,°
Thou'dst shivered like an egg: but thou dost breathe;
Hast heavy substance; bleed'st not; speak'st; art sound.
Ten masts at each° make not the altitude
Which thou hast perpendicularly fell:
Thy life's °a miracle. Speak yet again. 55

GLOUCESTER.

But have I fall'n, or no?

EDGAR.

From the dread summit of this chalky bourn.°
Look up a-height;° the shrill-gorged° lark so far
Cannot be seen or heard: do but look up.

GLOUCESTER.

Alack, I have no eyes. 60
Is wretchedness deprived that benefit,
To end itself by death? 'Twas yet some comfort,
When misery could beguile° the tyrant's rage
And frustrate his proud will.

EDGAR. Give me your arm

Up, so. How is't? Feel you° your legs? You stand. 65

GLOUCESTER.

Too well, too well.

EDGAR. This is above all strangeness.

Upon the crown o' th' cliff, what thing was that
Which parted from you?

GLOUCESTER. A poor unfortunate beggar.

EDGAR.

As I stood here below, methought his eyes
Were two full moons; he had a thousand noses, 70
Horns whelked° and waved like the enridgèd° sea:
It was some fiend; therefore; thou happy father,°
Think that the clearest° gods, who make them honors
Of men's impossibilities,° have preserved thee.

GLOUCESTER.

I do remember now: henceforth I'll bear 75
Affliction till it do cry out itself
"Enough, enough," and die. That thing you speak of,
I took it for a man; often 'twould say,
"The fiend, the fiend"—he led me to that place.

EDGAR.

Bear free° and patient thoughts.

Enter Lear [fantastically dressed with wild flowers].

But who comes here? 80

27 **upright** i.e., even up in the air, to say nothing of forward, over the cliff 29 **Fairies** who are supposed to guard and multiply hidden treasure 33–34 **Why . . . it** I play on his despair in order to cure it 37–38 **fall . . . with** rebel against 38 **opposeless** not to be, and not capable of being, opposed 39 **snuff** the guttering (and stinking) wick of a burnt-out candle 42 **how** but what; **conceit** imagination 44 **Yields to** allows 47 **pass** die 50 **precipitating** falling

53 **at each** one on top of the other 55 **life's** survival is 57 **bourn** boundary 58 **a-height** on high 58 **gorged** throated, voiced 63 **beguile** cheat (i.e., by suicide) 65 **Feel you** have you any feeling in 71 **whelked** twisted 71 **enridgèd** i.e., furrowed into waves 72 **happy father** fortunate old man 73 **clearest** purest 73–74 **who . . . impossibilities** who cause themselves to be honored and revered by performing miracles of which men are incapable 80 **free** i.e., emancipated from grief and despair, which fetter the soul

The safer° sense will ne'er accommodate°
His master thus.

LEAR. No, they cannot touch me for coining;° I am the king himself.

EDGAR.
85 O thou side-piercing sight!

LEAR. Nature's above art in that respect.° There's your press-money.° That fellow handles his bow like a crow-keeper;° draw me a clothier's yard.° Look, look a mouse! Peace, peace; this piece of toasted cheese will do't. There's 90 my gauntlet;° I'll prove it on° a giant. Bring up the brown bills.° O, well flown,° bird! i' th' clout, i' th' clout:° hewgh!° Give the word.°

EDGAR. Sweet marjoram.°

LEAR. Pass.

95 GLOUCESTER. I know that voice.

LEAR. Ha! Goneril, with a white heard! They flattered me like a dog,° and told me I had white hairs in my beard ere the black ones were there.° To say "ay" and "no" to everything that I said! "Ay" and "no" too was no good divini-100 ty.° When the rain came to wet me once and the wind to make me chatter; when the thunder would not peace at my bidding; there I found 'em, there I smelt 'em out. Go to, they are not men o' their words: they told me I was everything; 'tis a lie, I am not ague-proof.°

81 **safer** sounder, saner 81 **accommodate** dress, adorn 83 **touch . . . coining** arrest me for minting coins (the king's prerogative) 86 **Nature's . . . respect** i.e., a born king is superior to legal (and hence artificial) inhibition; there is also a glance here at the popular Renaissance debate concerning the relative importance of nature (inspiration) and art (training) 87 **press-money** paid to conscripted soldiers 88 **crow-keeper** a farmer scaring away crows 88 **clothier's yard** the standard English arrow was a cloth-yard long; here the injunction is to draw the arrow back, like a powerful archer, a full yard to the ear 90 **gauntlet** armored glove, thrown down as a challenge 90 **prove it on** maintain my challenge even against 90–91 **brown bills** halberds varnished to prevent rust (here the reference is to the soldiers who carry them) 91 **well flown** falconer's cry; and perhaps a reference to the flight of the arrow 91 **clout** the target shot at 91 **hewgh** imitating the whizzing of the arrow (?) 92 **word** password 93 **Sweet marjoram** herb, used as a remedy for brain disease 97 **like a dog** as a dog flatters 97–98 **I . . . there** I was wise before I had even grown a beard 99–100 **no good divinity** bad theology, because contrary to the biblical saying (II Corinthians 1:18), "Our word toward you was not yea and nay"; see also James 5:12, "But let your yea be yea, and your nay, nay; lest ye fall into condemnation"; and Matthew 5:36–37 104 **ague-proof** secure against fever

GLOUCESTER.
The trick° of that voice I do well remember: 105
Is't not the king?

LEAR. Ay, every inch a king.
When I do stare, see how the subject quakes.
I pardon that man's life. What was thy cause?°
Adultery?
Thou shalt not die: die for adultery! No: 110
The wren goes to't, and the small gilded fly
Does lecher° in my sight.
Let copulation thrive; for Gloucester's bastard son
Was kinder to his father than my daughters
Got° 'tween the lawful sheets. 115
To't, luxury,° pell-mell! for I lack soldiers.°
Behold yond simp'ring dame,
Whose face between her forks presages snow,°
That minces° virtue and does shake the head
To hear of pleasure's name.° 120
The fitchew,° nor the soilèd° horse, goes to't
With a more riotous appetite.
Down from the waist they are Centaurs,°
Though women all above:
But to the girdle° do the gods inherit,° 125
Beneath is all the fiend's.

There's hell, there's darkness, there is the sulphurous pit, burning, scalding, stench, consumption; fie, fie, fie! pah, pah! Give me an ounce of civet;° good apothecary, sweeten my imagination: there's money for thee. 130

GLOUCESTER.
O, let me kiss that hand!

LEAR.
Let me wipe it first; it smells of mortality.°

GLOUCESTER.
O ruined piece of nature! This great world
Shall so wear out to naught.° Dost thou know me?

LEAR. I remember thine eyes well enough. Dost thou 135

105 **trick** intonation 108 **cause** offense 112 **lecher** copulate 115 **Got** begat 116 **luxury** lechery 116 **for . . . soldiers** i.e., (1) whom copulation will supply (?) (2) and am therefore powerless 118 **Whose . . . snow** whose cold demeanor seems to promise chaste behavior ("forks" = legs) 119 **minces** squeamishly pretends to 120 **pleasure's name** the very name of sexual pleasure 121 **fitchew** polecat (and slang for prostitute) 121 **soilèd** put to pasture, and hence wanton with feeding 123 **Centaurs** lustful creatures, half man and half horse 125 **girdle** waist 125 **inherit** possess 129 **civet** perfume 132 **mortality** (1) death (2) existence 133–34 **This . . . nought** i.e., The universe (macrocosm) will decay to nothing in the same way as the little world of man (microcosm)

squiny° at me? No, do thy worst, blind Cupid;° I'll not love.
Read thou this challenge;° mark but the penning of it.

GLOUCESTER.
Were all thy letters suns, I could not see.

EDGAR.
I would not take° this from report: it is,
140 And my heart breaks at it.

LEAR. Read.

GLOUCESTER. What, with the case° of eyes?

LEAR. O, ho, are you there with me?° No eyes in your head, nor no money in your purse? Your eyes are in a heavy
145 case,° your purse in a light,° yet you see how this world goes.

GLOUCESTER.
I see it feelingly.°

LEAR. What, art mad? A man may see how this world goes with no eyes. Look with thine ears: see how yond jus-
150 tice rails upon yond simple° thief. Hark, in thine ear: change places, and, handy-dandy,° which is the justice, which is the thief? Thou hast seen a farmer's dog bark at a beggar?

GLOUCESTER. Ay, sir.

155 LEAR. And the creature run from the cur? There thou mightst behold the great image of authority:° a dog's obeyed in office.°
Thou rascal beadle,° hold thy bloody hand!
Why dost thou lash that whore? Strip thy own back;
160 Thou hotly lusts to use her in that kind°
For which thou whip'st her. The usurer hangs the cozener.°
Through tattered clothes small vices do appear;
Robes and furred gowns° hide all. Plate sin with gold,
And the strong lance of justice hurtless° breaks;
165 Arm it in rags, a pygmy's straw does pierce it.
None does offend, none, I say, none; I'll able° 'em:
Take that° of me, my friend, who have the power
To seal th' accuser's lips. Get thee glass eyes,°
And, like a scurvy politician,° seem
To see the things thou dost not. Now, now, now, now. 170
Pull off my boots: harder, harder: so.

EDGAR.
O, matter and impertinency° mixed!
Reason in madness!

LEAR.
If thou wilt weep my fortunes, take my eyes.
I know thee well enough; thy name is Gloucester: 175
Thou must be patient; we came crying hither:
Thou knowst, the first time that we smell the air
We wawl and cry. I will preach to thee: mark.

GLOUCESTER. Alack, alack the day!

LEAR.
When we are born, we cry that we are come 180
To this great stage of fools. This'° a good block.°
It were a delicate° stratagem, to shoe
A troop of horse with felt: I'll put't in proof;°
And when I have stol'n upon these son-in-laws,
Then, kill, kill, kill, kill, kill, kill! 185

Enter a Gentleman, [with Attendants].

GENTLEMAN.
O, here he is: lay hand upon him. Sir,
Your most dear daughter—

LEAR.
No rescue? What, a prisoner? I am even
The natural fool° of fortune. Use me well;
You shall have ransom. Let me have surgeons; 190
I am cut° to th' brains.

GENTLEMAN. You shall have anything.

LEAR.
No seconds?° all myself?
Why, this would make a man a man of salt,°
To use his eyes for garden water-pots,

136 **squiny** squint, look sideways, like a prostitute 136 **blind Cupid** the sign hung before a brothel 137 **challenge** a reminiscence of lines 89–90 139 **take** believe 142 **case** empty sockets 143 **are . . . me** is that what you tell me 144–45 **heavy case** sad plight (pun on line 142) 145 **light** i.e., empty 147 **feelingly** (1) by touch (2) by feeling pain (3) with emotion 150 **simple** common, of low estate 151 **handy-dandy** i.e., choose, guess (after the children's game—"Handy-dandy, prickly prandy"—of choosing the correct hand) 156 **image of authority** symbol revealing the true meaning of authority 156–57 **a dog's . . . office** i.e., whoever has power is obeyed 158 **beadle** parish constable 160 **kind** i.e., sexual act 161 **The usurer . . . cozener** i.e., The powerful money-lender, in his role as judge, puts to death the petty cheat 163 **Robes . . . gowns** worn by a judge 164 **hurtless** i.e., without hurting the sinner 166 **able** vouch for

167 **that** the immunity just conferred (line 166) 168 **glass eyes** spectacles 169 **scurvy politician** vile politic man 172 **matter and impertinency** sense and nonsense 181 **This** this is 181 **block** various meanings have been suggested, for example, the stump of a tree, on which Lear is supposed to climb; a mounting-block, which suggests "horse" (line 183); a hat (which Lear or another must be made to wear), from the block on which a felt hat is molded, and which would suggest a "felt" (line 183); the proposal here is that "block" be taken to denote the quintain, whose function is to bear blows, "a mere lifeless block" 182 **delicate** subtle 183 **put't in proof** test it 189 **natural fool** born sport (with pun on "natural" = imbecile) 191 **cut** wounded 192 **seconds** supporters 193 **man of salt** i.e., all (salt) tears

195 Ay, and laying autumn's dust.

GENTLEMAN.
Good sir—

LEAR.
I will die bravely,° like a smug° bridegroom.° What!
I will be jovial: come, come; I am a king;
Masters, know you that?

GENTLEMAN.
200 You are a royal one, and we obey you.

LEAR. Then there's life in't.° Come, and you get it, you shall get it by running. Sa, sa, sa, sa.°

Exit [*running; Attendants follow*].

GENTLEMAN.
A sight most pitiful in the meanest wretch,
Past speaking of in a king! Thou hast one daughter
205 Who redeems Nature from the general curse
Which twain have brought her to.°

EDGAR.
Hail, gentle° sir.

GENTLEMAN. Sir, speed° you: what's your will?

EDGAR.
Do you hear aught, sir, of a battle toward?°

GENTLEMAN.
Most sure and vulgar:° every one hears that,
Which can distinguish sound.

210 EDGAR. But, by your favor,
How near's the other army?

GENTLEMAN.
Near and on speedy foot; the main descry
Stands on the hourly thought.°

EDGAR. I thank you, sir: that's all.

GENTLEMAN.
Though that the queen on special cause is here,
Her army is moved on.

215 EDGAR. I thank you, sir.

Exit [*Gentleman*].

GLOUCESTER.
You ever-gentle gods, take my breath from me;
Let not my worser spirit° tempt me again
To die before you please.

EDGAR. Well pray you, father.

GLOUCESTER.
Now, good sir, what are you?

EDGAR.
A most poor man, made tame° to fortune's blows; 220
Who, by the art of known and feeling sorrows,°
Am pregnant° to good pity. Give me your hand,
I'll lead you to some biding.°

GLOUCESTER. Hearty thanks;
The bounty and the benison° of heaven
To boot, and boot.°

Enter Oswald.

OSWALD. A proclaimed prize!° Most happy!° 225
That eyeless head of thine was first framed° flesh
To raise my fortunes. Thou old unhappy traitor,
Briefly thyself remember:° the sword is out
That must destroy thee.

GLOUCESTER. Now let thy friendly° hand
Put strength enough to't. [*Edgar interposes.*]

OSWALD. Wherefore, bold peasant, 230
Dar'st thou support a published° traitor? Hence!
Lest that th' infection of his fortune take
Like hold on thee. Let go his arm.

EDGAR.
Chill° not let go, zir, without vurther 'casion.°

OSWALD.
Let go, slave, or thou diest! 235

EDGAR. Good gentleman, go your gait,° and let poor volk° pass. And chud ha' bin zwaggered° out of my life, 'twould not ha' bin zo long as 'tis by a vortnight. Nay, come not near th' old man; keep out, che vor' ye,° or I'se° try whether your costard° or my ballow° be the harder: chill be 240 plain with you.

OSWALD. Out, dunghill!

They fight.

197 **bravely** (1) smartly attired (2) courageously 197 **smug** spick and span 197 **bridegroom** whose "brave" sexual feats are picked up in the pun on "die" 201 **there's life in't** there's still hope 202 **Sa . . . sa** hunting and rallying cry; also an interjection of defiance 205–06 **general . . . to** (1) universal condemnation which Goneril and Regan have made for (2) damnation incurred by the original sin of Adam and Eve 207 **gentle** noble 207 **speed** God speed 208 **toward** impending 209 **vulgar** common knowledge 212–13 **the main . . . thought** we expect to see the main body of the army any hour 217 **worser spirit** bad angel, evil side of my nature

220 **tame** submissive 221 **art . . . sorrows** instruction of sorrows painfully experienced 222 **pregnant** disposed 223 **biding** place of refuge 224 **benison** blessing 225 **To . . . boot** also, and in the highest degree 225 **proclaimed prize** i.e., one with a price on his head 225 **happy** fortunate (for Oswald) 226 **framed** created 228 **thyself remember** i.e., pray, think of your sins 229 **friendly** i.e., because it offers the death Gloucester covets 231 **published** proclaimed 234 **Chill** I will (Edgar speaks in rustic dialect) 234 **vurther 'casion** further occasion 236 **gait** way 237 **volk** folk 237 **And . . . zwaggered** if I could have been swaggered 239 **che vor' ye** I warrant you 239 **I'se** I shall 240 **costard** head (literally, "apple") 240 **ballow** cudgel

EDGAR. Chill pick your teeth,° zir: come; no matter vor your foins.°

[*Oswald falls.*]

OSWALD.
245 Slave, thou hast slain me. Villain, take my purse:
If ever thou wilt thrive, bury my body,
And give the letters which thou find'st about° me
To Edmund Earl of Gloucester; seek him out
Upon the English party.° O, untimely death!
250 Death! (*He dies.*)

EDGAR.
I know thee well. A serviceable° villain,
As duteous° to the vices of thy mistress
As badness would desire.

GLOUCESTER. What, is he dead?

EDGAR.
Sit you down, father; rest you.
255 Let's see these pockets: the letters that he speaks of
May be my friends. He's dead; I am only sorry
He had no other deathsman.° Let us see:
Leave,° gentle wax;° and, manners, blame us not:
To know our enemies' minds, we rip their hearts;
260 Their papers° is more lawful.

Reads the letter.

"Let our reciprocal vows be remembered. You have many opportunities to cut him off: if your will want not,° time and place will be fruitfully offered. There is nothing done, if he return the conqueror: then am I the prisoner, and his bed 265 my jail; from the loathed warmth whereof deliver me, and supply the place for your labor.

"Your—wife, so I would° say—affectionate servant, and for you her own for venture,°

Goneril."

270 O indistinguished space of woman's will!°
A plot upon her virtuous husband's life;
And the exchange° my brother! Here in the sands
Thee I'll rake up,° the post unsanctified°
Of murderous lechers; and in the mature° time,
With this ungracious paper° strike° the sight 275
Of the death-practiced° duke: for him 'tis well
That of thy death and business I can tell.

GLOUCESTER.
The king is mad: how stiff° is my vile sense,°
That I stand up, and have ingenious° feeling
Of my huge sorrows! Better I were distract:° 280
So should my thoughts be severed from my griefs,
And woes by wrong imaginations° lose
The knowledge of themselves.

Drum afar off

EDGAR. Give me your hand:
Far off, methinks, I hear the beaten drum.
Come, father, I'll bestow° you with a friend. 285

Exeunt.

SCENE VII

[*A tent in the French camp.*]

Enter Cordelia, Kent, Doctor, and Gentleman.

CORDELIA.
O thou good Kent, how shall I live and work,
To match thy goodness? My life will be too short,
And every measure fail me.

KENT.
To be acknowledged, madam, is o'erpaid.
All my reports go° with the modest truth, 5
Nor more nor clipped,° but so.

CORDELIA. Be better suited:°
These weeds° are memories° of those worser hours:
I prithee, put them off.

KENT. Pardon, dear madam:
Yet to be known shortens my made intent:°
My boon I make it,° that you know me not 10
Till time and I think meet.°

243 **Chill . . . teeth** I will knock your teeth out 244 **foins** thrusts 247 **about** upon 249 **party** side 251 **serviceable** ready to be used 252 **duteous** obedient 257 **deathsman** executioner 258 **leave** by your leave 258 **wax** with which the letter is sealed 260 **Their papers** i.e., to rip their papers 262 **if . . . not** if your desire (and lust) be not lacking 267 **would** would like to 267–68 **and . . . venture** i.e., and one who holds you her own for venturing (Edmund had earlier been promised union by Goneril, "If you dare venture in your own behalf," IV.ii.21) 270 **indistinguished . . . will** unlimited range of woman's lust 272 **exchange** substitute 273 **rake up** cover up, bury 273 **post unsanctified** unholy messenger 274 **mature** ripe 275 **ungracious paper** wicked letter 275 **strike** blast 276 **death-practiced** whose death is plotted 278 **stiff** unbending 278 **vile sense** hateful capacity for feeling 279 **ingenious** conscious 280 **distract** distracted, mad 282 **wrong imaginations** delusions 285 **bestow** lodge IV.vii.5 **go** conform 6 **clipped** curtailed 6 **suited** attired 7 **weeds** clothes 7 **memories** reminders 9 **Yet . . . intent** to reveal myself just yet interferes with the plan I have made 10 **My . . . it** I ask this reward 11 **meet** fitting

CORDELIA.
Then be't so, my good lord. [*To the Doctor.*] How does the
king?
DOCTOR.
Madam, sleeps still.
CORDELIA.
O you kind gods!
15 Cure this great breach in his abusèd° nature.
Th' untuned and jarring senses, O, wind up°
Of this child-changèd° father.
DOCTOR. So please your majesty
That we may wake the king: he hath slept long.
CORDELIA.
Be governed by your knowledge, and proceed
20 I' th' sway of° your own will. Is he arrayed?

Enter Lear in a chair carried by Servants.

GENTLEMAN.
Ay, madam; in the heaviness of sleep
We put fresh garments on him.
DOCTOR.
Be by, good madam, when we do awake him;
I doubt not of his temperance.°
CORDELIA. Very well.
DOCTOR.
25 Please you, draw near. Louder the music there!
CORDELIA.
O my dear father, restoration hang
Thy medicine on my lips, and let this kiss
Repair those violent harms that my two sisters
Have in thy reverence° made.
KENT. Kind and dear princess
CORDELIA.
30 Had you not been their father, these white flakes°
Did challenge° pity of them. Was this a face
To be opposed against the warring winds?
To stand against the deep dread-bolted° thunder?
In the most terrible and nimble stroke
35 Of quick, cross° lightning to watch—poor perdu!°—
With this thin helm?° Mine enemy's dog,
Though he had bit me, should have stood that night
Against my fire; and wast thou fain,° poor father,
To hovel thee with swine and rogues° forlorn,
In short and musty straw?° Alack, alack! 40
'Tis wonder that thy life and wits at once
Had not concluded all.° He wakes; speak to him.
DOCTOR.
Madam, do you, 'tis fittest.
CORDELIA.
How does my royal lord? How fares your majesty?
LEAR.
You do me wrong to take me out o' th' grave: 45
Thou art a soul in bliss; but I am bound
Upon a wheel of fire,° that mine own tears
Do scald like molten lead.
CORDELIA. Sir, do you know me?
LEAR.
You are a spirit, I know. Where did you die?
CORDELIA.
Still, still, far wide.° 50
DOCTOR.
He's scarce awake: let him alone awhile.
LEAR.
Where have I been? Where am I? Fair daylight?
I am mightily abused.° I should ev'n die with pity,
To see another thus. I know not what to say.
I will not swear these are my hands: let's see; 55
I feel this pin prick. Would I were assured
Of my condition.
CORDELIA. O, look upon me, sir,
And hold your hand in benediction o'er me.
You must not kneel.
LEAR. Pray, do not mock me:
I am a very foolish fond° old man, 60
Fourscore and upward, not an hour more nor less;
And, to deal plainly,
I fear I am not in my perfect mind.
Methinks I should know you and know this man,
Yet I am doubtful; for I am mainly° ignorant 65
What place this is, and all the skill I have

15 **abusèd** disturbed 16 **wind up** tune 17 **child-changèd** changed, deranged (and also, reduced to a child) by the cruelty of his children 20 **I' . . . of** according to 24 **temperance** sanity 29 **reverence** revered person 30 **flakes** hairs (in long strands) 31 **challenge** claim 33 **deep dread-bolted** deep-voiced and furnished with the dreadful thunderbolt 35 **cross** zigzag 35 **perdu** (1) sentry in a forlorn position (2) lost one 36 **helm** helmet (his scanty hair)

38 **fain** pleased 39 **rogues** vagabonds 40 **short and musty straw** when straw is freshly cut, it is long, and suitable for bedding, given its flexibility and crispness; as it is used, it becomes musty, shreds into pieces, is "short"; in contemporary Maine usage, "short manure" refers to dung mixed with straw that has been broken up, "long manure" to dung mixed with coarse new straw 42 **concluded all** come to a complete end 47 **wheel of fire** torment associated by the Middle Ages with hell, where Lear thinks he is 50 **wide** i.e., of the mark (of sanity) 53 **abused** deluded 60 **fond** in dotage 65 **mainly** entirely

Remembers not these garments, nor I know not
Where I did lodge last night. Do not laugh at me,
For, as I am a man, I think this lady
To be my child Cordelia.

70 CORDELIA. And so I am, I am.

LEAR.
Be your tears wet? Yes, faith. I pray, weep not.
If you have poison for me, I will drink it.
I know you do not love me; for your sisters
Have, as I do remember, done me wrong.
You have some cause, they have not.

75 CORDELIA. No cause, no cause.

LEAR.
Am I in France?

KENT. In your own kingdom, sir.

LEAR. Do not abuse° me.

DOCTOR.
Be comforted, good madam: the great rage,°
You see, is killed in him: and yet it is danger
80 To make him even o'er° the time he has lost.
Desire him to go in; trouble him no more
Till further settling.°

CORDELIA.
Will't please your highness walk?°

LEAR. You must bear with me.
Pray you now, forget and forgive. I am old and foolish.

Exeunt. Mane[n]t° Kent and Gentleman.

85 GENTLEMAN. Holds it true, sir, that the Duke of Cornwall was so slain?

KENT. Most certain, sir.

GENTLEMAN. Who is conductor of his people?

KENT. As 'tis said, the bastard son of Gloucester.

90 GENTLEMAN. They say Edgar, his banished son, is with the Earl of Kent in Germany.

KENT. Report is changeable.° 'Tis time to look about; the powers° of the kingdom approach apace.

GENTLEMAN. The arbitrement° is like to be bloody.
95 Fare you well, sir.

[*Exit.*]

KENT.
My point and period will be throughly wrought,°
Or well or ill, as this day's battle's fought.

Exit.

77 **abuse** deceive 78 **rage** frenzy 80 **even o'er** smooth over by filling in; and hence, "recollect" 82 **settling** calming 83 **walk** perhaps in the sense of "withdraw" 84 **s.d. *Mane[n]t*** remain 92 **Report is changeable** rumors are unreliable 93 **powers** armies 94 **arbitrement** deciding encounter 96 **My . . . wrought** the aim and end, the close of my life, will be completely worked out

ACT V

SCENE I

[*The British camp near Dover.*]

Enter, with drum and colors, Edmund, Regan, Gentlemen, and Soldiers.

EDMUND.
Know° of the duke if his last purpose hold,°
Or whether since he is advised° by aught
To change the course: he's full of alteration
And self-reproving: bring his constant pleasure.°

[*To a Gentleman, who goes out.*]

REGAN.
Our sister's man is certainly miscarried.° 5

EDMUND.
'Tis to be doubted,° madam.

REGAN. Now, sweet lord,
You know the goodness I intend upon you:
Tell me, but truly, but then speak the truth,
Do you not love my sister?

EDMUND. In honored° love.

REGAN.
But have you never found my brother's way 10
To the forfended° place?

EDMUND. That thought abuses° you.

REGAN.
I am doubtful that you have been conjunct
And bosomed with her, as far as we call hers.°

EDMUND.
No, by mine honor, madam.

REGAN.
I shall never endure her: dear my lord, 15
Be not familiar with her.

EDMUND. Fear° me not.—
She and the duke her husband!

Enter, with drum and colors, Albany, Goneril, [and] Soldiers.

GONERIL [*aside*].
I had rather lose the battle than that sister

V.i.1 **Know** learn 1 **last purpose hold** most recent intention (to fight) be maintained 2 **advised** induced 4 **constant pleasure** fixed (final) decision 5 **miscarried** come to grief 6 **doubted** feared 9 **honored** honorable 11 **forfended** forbidden 11 **abuses** (1) deceives (2) demeans, is unworthy of 12–13 **I . . . hers** I fear that you have united with her intimately, in the fullest possible way 16 **Fear** distrust

Should loosen° him and me.

ALBANY.

20 Our very loving sister, well be-met.°
Sir, this I heard, the king is come to his daughter,
With others whom the rigor of our state°
Forced to cry out. Where I could not be honest,°
I never yet was valiant: for this business,
25 It touches us, as° France invades our land,
Not bolds the king, with others, whom, I fear,
Most just and heavy causes make oppose.°

EDMUND.

Sir, you speak nobly.

REGAN. Why is this reasoned?°

GONERIL.

Combine together 'gainst the enemy;
30 For these domestic and particular broils°
Are not the question° here.

ALBANY. Let's then determine
With th' ancient of war° on our proceeding.

EDMUND.

I shall attend you presently at your tent.

REGAN. Sister, you'll go with us?°

35 GONERIL. No.

REGAN.

'Tis most convenient;° pray you, go with us.

GONERIL [*aside*].

O, ho, I know the riddle.°—I will go.

Exeunt both the Armies.

Enter Edgar [disguised].

EDGAR.

If e'er your grace had speech with man so poor,
Hear me one word.

ALBANY [*To those going out*].

I'll overtake you. [*To Edgar.*] Speak.

Exeunt [all but Albany and Edgar].

EDGAR.

40 Before you fight the battle, ope this letter.
If you have victory, let the trumpet sound
For° him that brought it: wretched though I seem,
I can produce a champion that will prove°
What is avouchèd° there. If you miscarry,
Your business of° the world hath so an end, 45
And machination° ceases. Fortune love you.

ALBANY.

Stay till I have read the letter.

EDGAR. I was forbid it.
When time shall serve, let but the herald cry,
And I'll appear again.

ALBANY.

Why, fare thee well: I will o'erlook° thy paper. 50

Exit [Edgar].

Enter Edmund.

EDMUND.

The enemy's in view: draw up your powers.
Here is the guess° of their true strength and forces
By diligent discovery;° but your haste
Is now urged on you.

ALBANY. We will greet° the time.

Exit.

EDMUND.

To both these sisters have I sworn my love; 55
Each jealous° of the other, as the stung
Are of the adder. Which of them shall I take?
Both? One? Or neither? Neither can be enjoyed,
If both remain alive: to take the widow
Exasperates, makes mad her sister Goneril; 60
And hardly° shall I carry out my side,°
Her husband being alive. Now then, we'll use
His countenance° for the battle; which being done,
Let her who would be rid of him devise
His speedy taking off. As for the mercy 65
Which he intends to Lear and to Cordelia,
The battle done, and they within our power,
Shall never see his pardon; for my state
Stands on me to defend, not to debate.°

Exit.

19 **loosen** separate 20 **be-met** met 22 **rigor** state tyranny of our government 23 **honest** honorable 25 **touches us, as** concerns me, only in that 26–27 **Not . . . oppose** and not in that France emboldens the king and others, who have been led, by real and serious grievances, to take up arms against us 28 **reasoned** argued 30 **particular broils** private quarrels 31 **question** issue 32 **th' ancient of war** experienced commanders 34 **us** me (rather than Edmund) 36 **convenient** fitting, desirable 37 **riddle** real reason (for Regan's curious request)

41–42 **sound For** summon 43 **prove** i.e., by trial of combat 44 **avouchèd** maintained 45 **of** in 46 **machination** plotting 50 **o'erlook** read over 52 **guess** estimate 53 **By diligent discovery** obtained by careful reconnoitering 54 **greet** i.e., meet the demands of 56 **jealous** suspicious 61 **hardly** with difficulty 61 **carry . . . side** (1) satisfy my ambition (2) fulfill my bargain (with Goneril) 63 **countenance** authority 68–69 **for . . . debate** my position requires me to act, not to reason about right and wrong

SCENE II

[A field between the two camps.]

Alarum° within. Enter, with drum and colors, Lear, Cordelia, and Soldiers, over the stage; and exeunt.
Enter Edgar and Gloucester.

EDGAR.
Here, father,° take the shadow of this tree
For your good host; pray that the right may thrive.
If ever I return to you again,
I'll bring you comfort.
GLOUCESTER. Grace go with you, sir.
Exit [Edgar].

Alarum and retreat° within. [Re]enter Edgar.

EDGAR.
5 Away, old man; give me thy hand; away!
King Lear hath lost, he and his daughter ta'en:°
Give me thy hand; come on.
GLOUCESTER.
No further, sir; a man may rot even here.
EDGAR.
What, in ill thoughts again? Men must endure
10 Their going hence, even as their coming hither:
Ripeness° is all. Come on.
GLOUCESTER. And that's true too.
Exeunt.

SCENE III

[The British camp near Dover.]

Enter, in conquest, with drum and colors, Edmund; Lear and Cordelia, as prisoners; Soldiers, Captain.

EDMUND.
Some officers take them away: good guard,°
Until their greater pleasures° first be known
That are to censure° them.
CORDELIA. We are not the first
Who with best meaning° have incurred the worst.
5 For thee, oppressèd king, I am cast down;
Myself could else out-frown false Fortune's frown.
Shall we not see these daughters and these sisters?
LEAR.
No, no, no, no! Come, let's away to prison:
We two alone will sing like birds i' th' cage:
When thou dost ask me blessing, I'll kneel down 10
And ask of thee forgiveness: so we'll live,
And pray, and sing, and tell old tales, and laugh
At gilded butterflies,° and hear poor rogues
Talk of court news; and we'll talk with them too,
Who loses and who wins, who's in, who's out; 15
And take upon's the mystery of things,
As if we were God's spies:° and we'll wear out,°
In a walled prison, packs and sects of great ones
That ebb and flow by th' moon.°
EDMUND. Take them away.
LEAR.
Upon such sacrifices, my Cordelia, 20
The gods themselves throw incense.° Have I caught thee?
He that parts us shall bring a brand from heaven,
And fire us hence like foxes.° Wipe thine eyes;
The good years° shall devour them,° flesh and fell,°
Ere they shall make us weep. We'll see 'em starved first. 25
Come. *[Exeunt Lear and Cordelia, guarded.]*
EDMUND.
Come hither, captain; hark.
Take thou this note: go follow them to prison:
One step I have advanced thee; if thou dost
As this instructs thee, thou dost make thy way 30
To noble fortunes: know thou this, that men
Are as the time is:° to be tender-minded
Does not become a sword:° thy great employment
Will not bear question;° either say thou'lt do't,
Or thrive by other means.
CAPTAIN. I'll do't, my lord. 35
EDMUND.
About it; and write happy° when th' hast done.

V.ii. s.d. **Alarum** a trumpet call to battle 1 **father** i.e., venerable old man (Edgar has not yet revealed his identity) 4 s.d. **retreat** signaled by a trumpet 6 **ta'en** captured 11 **Ripeness** maturity, as of fruit that is ready to fall V.iii.1 **good guard** let them be well guarded 2 **their greater pleasures** the will of those in command, the great ones 3 **censure** pass judgment on 4 **meaning** intentions

13 **gilded butterflies** i.e., gorgeously attired courtiers, fluttering after nothing 16–17 **take . . . spies** profess to read the riddle of existence, as if endowed with divine omniscience 17 **wear out** outlast 18–19 **packs . . . moon** intriguing and partisan cliques of those in high station, whose fortunes change every month 20–21 **Upon . . . incense** i.e., the gods approve our renunciation of the world 22–23 **He . . . foxes** No human agency can separate us, but only divine interposition, as of a heavenly torch parting us like foxes that are driven from their place of refuge by fire and smoke 24 **good years** plague and pestilence ("undefined malefic power or agency," *Oxford English Dictionary*) 24 **them** the enemies of Lear and Cordelia 24 **fell** skin 32 **as . . . is** i.e., absolutely determined by the exigencies of the moment 33 **become a sword** befit a soldier 34 **bear question** admit of discussion 36 **write happy** style yourself fortunate

Mark; I say, instantly, and carry it so°
As I have set it down.
CAPTAIN.
I cannot draw a cart, nor eat dried oats;
40 If it be man's work, I'll do't.
Exit Captain.

Flourish. Enter Albany, Goneril, Regan [another Captain, and] Soldiers.

ALBANY.
Sir, you have showed today your valiant strain,°
And fortune led you well: you have the captives
Who were the opposites of° this day's strife:
I do require them of you, so to use them
45 As we shall find their merits° and our safety
May equally determine.
EDMUND. Sir, I thought it fit
To send the old and miserable king
To some retention and appointed guard;°
Whose° age had charms in it, whose title more,
50 To pluck the common bosom on his side,°
And turn our impressed lances in our eyes°
Which do command them. With him I sent the queen:
My reason all the same; and they are ready
Tomorrow, or at further space,° t'appear
55 Where you shall hold your session.° At this time
We sweat and bleed: the friend hath lost his friend;
And the best quarrels, in the heat, are cursed
By those that feel their sharpness.°
The question of Cordelia and her father
Requires a fitter place.
60 ALBANY. Sir, by your patience,
I hold you but a subject° of this war,
Not as a brother.
REGAN. That's as we list to grace° him.
Methinks our pleasure might have been demanded,
Ere you had spoke so far. He led our powers,
65 Bore the commission of my place and person;
The which immediacy may well stand up
And call itself your brother.°
GONERIL. Not so hot:
In his own grace he doth exalt himself
More than in your addition.°
REGAN. In my rights,
By me invested, he compeers° the best. 70
GONERIL.
That were the most,° if he should husband you.°
REGAN.
Jesters do oft prove prophets.
GONERIL. Holla, holla!
That eye that told you so looked but a-squint.°
REGAN.
Lady, I am not well; else I should answer
From a full-flowing stomach.° General, 75
Take thou my soldiers, prisoners, patrimony;°
Dispose of them, of me; the walls is thine:°
Witness the world, that I create thee here
My lord, and master.
GONERIL. Mean you to enjoy him?
ALBANY.
The let-alone° lies not in your good will. 80
EDMUND.
Nor in thine, lord.
ALBANY. Half-blooded° fellow, yes.
REGAN [*to Edmund*].
Let the drum strike, and prove my title thine.°
ALBANY.
Stay yet; hear reason. Edmund, I arrest thee
On capital treason; and in thy attaint°
This gilded serpent [*pointing to Goneril*]. For your claim, fair sister, 85
I bar it in the interest of my wife.
'Tis she is subcontracted° to this lord,
And I, her husband, contradict your banes.°

37 **carry it so** manage the affair in exactly that manner (as if Cordelia had taken her own life) 41 **strain** (1) stock (2) character 43 **opposites of** opponents in 45 **merits** deserts 48 **retention . . . guard** confinement under duly appointed guard 49 **Whose** i.e., Lear's 50 **pluck . . . side** win the sympathy of the people to himself 51 **turn . . . eyes** turn our conscripted lancers against us 54 **further space** a later time 55 **session** trial 57–58 **best . . . sharpness** worthiest causes may be judged badly by those who have been affected painfully by them, and whose passion has not yet cooled 61 **subject of** subordinate in 62 **list to grace** wish to honor

65–67 **Bore . . . brother** was authorized, as my deputy, to take command; his present status, as my immediate representative, entitles him to be considered your equal 69 **your addition** honors you have bestowed on him 70 **compeers** equals 71 **most** most complete investing in your rights 71 **husband you** become your husband 73 **a-squint** cross-eyed 75 **From . . . stomach** angrily 76 **patrimony** inheritance 77 **walls is thine** i.e., Regan's person, which Edmund has stormed and won 80 **let-alone** power to prevent 81 **Half-blooded** bastard, and so only half noble 82 **prove . . . thine** prove by combat your entitlement to my rights 84 **in thy attaint** as a sharer in the treason for which you are impeached 87 **subcontracted** pledged by a contract which is called into question by the existence of a previous contract (Goneril's marriage) 88 **contradict your banes** forbid your announced intention to marry (by citing the precontract)

If you will marry, make your loves° to me;
My lady is bespoke.°

90 GONERIL. An interlude!°

ALBANY.
Thou art armed, Gloucester: let the trumpet sound:
If none appear to prove upon thy person
Thy heinous, manifest, and many treasons,
There is my pledge° [*throwing down a glove*]: I'll make° it on thy heart,
95 Ere I taste bread, thou art in nothing less
Than I have here proclaimed thee.

REGAN. Sick, O, sick!

GONERIL [*aside*].
If not, I'll ne'er trust medicine.

EDMUND [*throwing down a glove*].
There's my exchange:° what in the world he is
That names me traitor, villainlike he lies:°
100 Call by the trumpet:° he that dares approach,
On him, on you—who not?—I will maintain
My truth and honor firmly.

ALBANY.
A herald, ho!

EDMUND. A herald, ho, a herald!

ALBANY.
Trust to thy single virtue;° for thy soldiers,
105 All levied in my name, have in my name
Took their discharge.

REGAN. My sickness grows upon me.

ALBANY.
She is not well; convey her to my tent.

[*Exit Regan, led.*]

Enter a Herald.

Come hither, herald. Let the trumpet sound—
And read out this.

110 CAPTAIN. Sound, trumpet!

A trumpet sounds.

HERALD (*reads*). "If any man of quality or degree° within the lists° of the army will maintain upon Edmund, supposed Earl of Gloucester, that he is a manifold traitor, let him appear by the third sound of the trumpet: he is bold in
115 his defense."

EDMUND. Sound!

First trumpet.

HERALD. Again!

Second trumpet.

HERALD. Again!

Third trumpet.

Trumpet answers within. Enter Edgar, at the third sound, armed, a trumpet before him.°

ALBANY.
Ask him his purpose, why he appears
Upon this call o' th' trumpet.

HERALD. What are you? 120
Your name, your quality,° and why you answer
This present summons?

EDGAR. Know, my name is lost;
By treason's tooth bare-gnawn and canker-bit:°
Yet am I noble as the adversary
I come to cope.°

ALBANY. Which is that adversary? 125

EDGAR.
What's he that speaks for Edmund, Earl of Gloucester?

EDMUND.
Himself: what say'st thou to him?

EDGAR. Draw thy sword,
That if my speech offend a noble heart,
Thy arm do thee justice: here is mine.
Behold it is my privilege, 130
The privilege of mine honors,
My oath, and my profession.° I protest,
Maugre° thy strength, place, youth, and eminence,
Despite thy victor sword and fire-new° fortune,
Thy valor and thy heart,° thou art a traitor, 135
False to thy gods, thy brother, and thy father,
Conspirant° 'gainst this high illustrious prince,
And from th' extremest upward° of thy head
To the descent and dust below thy foot,°
A most toad-spotted traitor.° Say thou "No," 140

89 **loves** love-suits 90 **bespoke** already pledged 90 **interlude** play 94 **pledge** gage 94 **make** prove 97 **medicine** poison 98 **exchange** technical term, denoting the glove Edmund throws down 99 **villainlike he lies** the lie direct, a challenge to mortal combat 100 **trumpet** trumpeter 104 **single virtue** unaided valor 111–12 **quality or degree** rank or position 112 **lists** rolls

118 s.d. **trumpet before him** trumpeter preceding him 121 **quality** rank 123 **canker-bit** eaten by the caterpillar 125 **cope** encounter 130–32 **it . . . profession** my knighthood entitles me to challenge you, and to have my challenge accepted 133 **Maugre** despite 134 **fire-new** fresh from the forge or mint 135 **heart** courage 137 **Conspirant** conspiring, a conspirator 138 **extremest upward** the very top 139 **the . . . foot** your lowest part (sole) and the dust beneath it 140 **toad-spotted traitor** spotted with treason (and hence venomous, as the toad is allegedly marked with spots that exude venom)

This sword, this arm and my best spirits are bent°
To prove upon thy heart, whereto I speak,°
Thou liest.

EDMUND.
In wisdom° I should ask thy name,
But since thy outside looks so fair and warlike,
145 And that thy tongue some say° of breeding breathes,
What safe and nicely° I might well delay°
By rule of knighthood, I disdain and spurn:
Back do I toss these treasons° to thy head;
With the hell-hated° lie o'erwhelm thy heart;
150 Which for they yet glance by and scarcely bruise,
This sword of mine shall give them instant way,
Where they shall rest for ever.° Trumpets, speak!

Alarums. [*They*] *fight.* [*Edmund falls.*]

ALBANY.
Save° him, save him!

GONERIL. This is practice,° Gloucester:
By th' law of war thou wast not bound to answer
155 An unknown opposite;° thou art not vanquished.
But cozened and beguiled.

ALBANY. Shut your mouth, dame,
Or with this paper shall I stop it. Hold, sir;°
Thou° worse than any name, read thine own evil.
No tearing, lady; I perceive you know it.

GONERIL.
160 Say, if I do, the laws are mine, not thine:
Who can arraign me for't?

ALBANY. Most monstrous! O!
Knowst thou this paper?

GONERIL. Ask me not what I know.

Exit.

ALBANY.
Go after her; she's desperate; govern° her.

EDMUND.
What you have charged me with, that have I done;
And more, much more; the time will bring it out. 165
'Tis past, and so am I. But what art thou
That hast this fortune on° me? If thou'rt noble,
I do forgive thee.

EDGAR. Let's exchange charity.°
I am no less in blood° than thou art, Edmund;
If more,° the more th' hast wronged me. 170
My name is Edgar, and thy father's son.
The gods are just, and of our pleasant° vices
Make instruments to plague us:
The dark and vicious place° where thee he got°
Cost him his eyes.

EDMUND. Th' hast spoken right, 'tis true; 175
The wheel is come full circle; I am here.°

ALBANY.
Methought thy very gait did prophesy°
A royal nobleness: I must embrace thee:
Let sorrow split my heart, if ever I
Did hate thee or thy father!

EDGAR. Worthy° prince, I know't. 180

ALBANY.
Where have you hid yourself?
How have you known the miseries of your father?

EDGAR.
By nursing them, my lord. List a brief tale;
And when 'tis told, O, that my heart would burst!
The bloody proclamation to escape° 185
That followed me so near—O, our lives' sweetness,
That we the pain of death would hourly die
Rather than die at once!°—taught me to shift
Into a madman's rags, t' assume a semblance
That very dogs disdained: and in this habit° 190
Met I my father with his bleeding rings,°
Their precious stones new lost; became his guide,
Led him, begged for him, saved him from despair;
Never—O fault!—revealed myself unto him,
Until some half-hour past, when I was armed, 195
Not sure, though hoping, of this good success,
I asked his blessing, and from first to last

141 **bent** directed 142 **whereto I speak** Edgar speaks from the heart, and speaks to the heart of Edmund 143 **wisdom** prudence (since he is not obliged to fight with one of lesser rank) 145 **say** assay (i.e., touch, sign) 146 **safe and nicely** cautiously and punctiliously 146 **delay** i.e., avoid 148 **treasons** accusations of treason 149 **hell-hated** hated like hell 150–52 **Which . . . ever** which accusations of treason, since as yet they do no harm, even though I have hurled them back, I now thrust upon you still more forcibly, with my sword, so that they may remain with you permanently 153 **Save** spare 153 **practice** trickery 155 **opposite** opponent 157 **Hold, sir** to Edmund: "Just a moment!" 158 **Thou** probably Goneril 163 **govern** control

167 **fortune on** victory over 168 **charity** forgiveness and love 169 **blood** lineage 170 **If more** if I am more noble (since legitimate) 172 **of our pleasant** out of our pleasurable 174 **place** i.e., the adulterous bed 174 **got** begot 176 **wheel . . . here** i.e., Fortune's wheel, on which Edmund ascended, has now, in its downward turning, deposited him at the bottom, whence he began 177 **gait did prophesy** carriage did promise 180 **Worthy** honorable 185 **to escape** (my wish) to escape the sentence of death 186–88 **O . . . once** How sweet is life, that we choose to suffer death every hour rather than make an end at once 190 **habit** attire 191 **rings** sockets

Told him our pilgrimage.° But his flawed° heart—
Alack too weak the conflict to support—
200 'Twixt two extremes of passion, joy and grief,
Burst smilingly.

EDMUND. This speech of yours hath moved me,
And shall perchance do good: but speak you on;
You look as you had something more to say.

ALBANY.
If there be more, more woeful, hold it in;
205 For I am almost ready to dissolve,°
Hearing of this.

EDGAR. This would have seemed a period°
To such as love not sorrow; but another,
To amplify too much, would make much more,
And top extremity.°
210 Whilst I was big in clamor,° came there in a man,
Who, having seen me in my worst estate,°
Shunned my abhorred° society; but then, finding
Who 'twas that so endured, with his strong arms
He fastened on my neck, and bellowed out
215 As he'd burst heaven; threw him on my father;
Told the most piteous tale of Lear and him
That ever ear received: which in recounting
His grief grew puissant,° and the strings of life
Began to crack: twice then the trumpets sounded
And there I left him tranced.°

220 ALBANY. But who was this?

EDGAR.
Kent, sir, the banished Kent; who in disguise
Followed his enemy° king, and did him service
Improper for a slave.

Enter a Gentleman, with a bloody knife.

GENTLEMAN.
Help, help, O, help!

EDGAR. What kind of help?

ALBANY. Speak, man.

EDGAR.
What means this bloody knife?

225 GENTLEMAN. 'Tis hot, it smokes;°
It came even from the heart of—O, she's dead!

ALBANY.
Who dead? Speak, man.

GENTLEMAN.
Your lady, sir, your lady: and her sister
By her is poisoned; she confesses it.

EDMUND.
I was contracted° to them both: all three 230
Now marry° in an instant.

EDGAR. Here comes Kent.

ALBANY.
Produce the bodies, be they alive or dead.
[*Exit Gentleman.*]
This judgment of the heavens, that makes us tremble,
Touches us not with pity.

Enter Kent.

O, is this he?
The time will not allow the compliment° 235
Which very manners° urges.

KENT. I am come
To bid my king and master aye° good night:
Is he not here?

ALBANY. Great thing of° us forgot!
Speak, Edmund, where's the king? and where's Cordelia?
See'st thou this object, Kent? 240

The bodies of Goneril and Regan are brought in.

KENT.
Alack, why thus?

EDMUND. Yet° Edmund was beloved:
The one the other poisoned for my sake,
And after slew herself.

ALBANY.
Even so. Cover their faces.

EDMUND.
I pant for life:° some good I mean to do, 245
Despite of mine own nature. Quickly send,
Be brief in it, to th' castle; for my writ°
Is on the life of Lear and on Cordelia:
Nay, send in time.

ALBANY. Run, run, O, run!

EDGAR.
To who, my lord? Who has the office?° Send 250
Thy token of reprieve.°

198 **our pilgrimage** of our (purgatorial) journey
198 **flawed** cracked 205 **dissolve** i.e., into tears
206 **period** limit 207–09 **but . . . extremity** just one woe more, described too fully, would go beyond the extreme limit 210 **big in clamor** loud in lamentation
211 **estate** condition 212 **abhorred** abhorrent
218 **puissant** overmastering 220 **tranced** insensible
222 **enemy** hostile 225 **smokes** steams

230 **contracted** betrothed 231 **marry** i.e., unite in death
235 **compliment** ceremony 236 **very manners** ordinary civility 237 **aye** forever 238 **thing of** matter by
240 **object** sight (the bodies of Goneril and Regan) 241 **Yet** in spite of all 245 **pant for life** gasp for breath 247 **writ** command (ordering the execution) 250 **office** commission
251 **token of reprieve** sign that they are reprieved

EDMUND.
Well thought on: take my sword,
Give it the captain.

EDGAR. Haste thee, for thy life.

[*Exit Messenger.*]

EDMUND.
He hath commission from thy wife and me
255 To hang Cordelia in the prison, and
To lay the blame upon her own despair,
That she fordid° herself.

ALBANY.
The gods defend her! Bear him hence awhile.

[*Edmund is borne off.*]

Enter Lear, with Cordelia in his arms.
[*Gentleman, and others following.*]

LEAR.
Howl, howl, howl, howl! O, you are men of stones:
260 Had I your tongues and eyes, I'd use them so
That heaven's vault should crack. She's gone for ever.
I know when one is dead and when one lives;
She's dead as earth. Lend me a looking-glass;
If that her breath will moist or stain the stone,°
Why, then she lives.

265 KENT. Is this the promised end?°

EDGAR.
Or image° of that horror?

ALBANY. Fall and cease.°

LEAR.
This feather stirs; she lives. If it be so,
It is a chance which does redeem all sorrows
That ever I have felt.

KENT. O my good master.

LEAR.
Prithee, away.

270 EDGAR. 'Tis noble Kent, your friend.

LEAR.
A plague upon you, murderers, traitors all!
I might have saved her; now she's gone for ever.
Cordelia, Cordelia, stay a little. Ha,
What is't thou say'st? Her voice was ever soft,
275 Gentle and low, an excellent thing in woman.
I killed the slave that was a-hanging thee.

GENTLEMAN.
'Tis true, my lords, he did.

LEAR. Did I not, fellow?
I have seen the day, with my good biting falchion°
I would have made them skip: I am old now,
And these same crosses° spoil me.° Who are you? 280
Mine eyes are not o' th' best: I'll tell you straight.°

KENT.
If Fortune brag of two° she loved and hated,
One of them we behold.

LEAR.
This is a dull sight.° Are you not Kent?

KENT. The same,
Your servant Kent. Where is your servant Caius?° 285

LEAR.
He's a good fellow, I can tell you that;
He'll strike, and quickly too: he's dead and rotten.

KENT.
No, my good lord; I am the very man.

LEAR.
I'll see that straight.°

KENT.
That from your first of difference and decay° 290
Have followed your sad steps.

LEAR. You are welcome hither.

KENT.
Nor no man else:° all's cheerless, dark and deadly.
Your eldest daughters have fordone° themselves,
And desperately° are dead.

LEAR. Ay, so I think.

ALBANY.
He knows not what he says, and vain is it 295
That we present us to him.

EDGAR. Very bootless.°

Enter a Messenger.

MESSENGER.
Edmund is dead, my lord.

ALBANY. That's but a trifle here.
You lords and noble friends, know our intent.
What comfort to this great decay may come°
Shall be applied. For us, we° will resign, 300

257 **fordid** destroyed 264 **stone** i.e., the surface of the crystal looking-glass 265 **promised end** doomsday 266 **image** exact likeness 266 **Fall and cease** i.e., Let the heavens fall, and all things finish 268 **redeem** make good 278 **falchion** small curved sword

280 **crosses** troubles 280 **spoil me** i.e., my prowess as a swordsman 281 **tell you straight** recognize you straightaway 282 **two** i.e., Lear, and some hypothetical second, who is also a prime example of Fortune's inconstancy ("loved and hated") 284 **dull sight** (1) melancholy spectacle (2) faulty eyesight (Lear's own, clouded by weeping) 285 **Caius** Kent's name, in disguise 289 **see that straight** attend to that in a moment 290 **your . . . decay** beginning of your decline in fortune 292 **Nor . . . else** no, I am not welcome, nor is anyone else 293 **fordone** destroyed 294 **desperately** in despair 296 **bootless** fruitless 299 **What . . . come** whatever aid may present itself to this great ruined man 300 **us, we** the royal "we"

During the life of this old majesty,
To him our absolute power: [*to Edgar and Kent*] you, to
your rights;
With boot,° and such addition° as your honors
Have more than merited. All friends shall taste
305 The wages of their virtue, and all foes
The cup of their deservings. O, see, see!

LEAR.
And my poor fool° is hanged: no, no, no life?
Why should a dog, a horse, a rat, have life,
And thou no breath at all? Thou'lt come no more,
310 Never, never, never, never, never.
Pray you, undo this button.° Thank you, sir.
Do you see this? Look on her. Look, her lips.
Look there, look there.

He dies.

EDGAR. He faints. My lord, my lord!

KENT.
Break, heart; I prithee, break.

EDGAR. Look up, my lord!

KENT.
315 Vex not his ghost:° O, let him pass! He hates him
That would upon the rack° of this tough world
Stretch him out longer.°

EDGAR. He is gone indeed.

KENT.
The wonder is he hath endured so long:
He but usurped° his life.

ALBANY.
Bear them from hence. Our present business 320
Is general woe. [*To Kent and Edgar.*] Friends of my soul,
you twain,
Rule in this realm and the gored state sustain.

KENT.
I have a journey, sir, shortly to go;
My master calls me, I must not say no.

EDGAR.
The weight of this sad time we must obey,° 325
Speak what we feel, not what we ought to say.
The oldest hath borne most: we that are young
Shall never see so much, nor live so long.

Exeunt, with a dead march.

TOPICS FOR DISCUSSION AND WRITING

1. On the basis of his remarks in the first 36 lines of the play, how would you characterize Gloucester?
2. Coleridge found in Cordelia's "Nothing" (1.1.86) "some little, faulty admixture of pride or sullenness." Do you think that Cordelia is blameworthy here, or can she be exonerated?
3. Characterize the Lear of the first act. Regan and Goneril offer a characterization in 1.1.290–96. Do you find their description acceptable?
4. Explain in a sentence or two what Edmund means by "Nature" in 1.2.1–22. On the basis of 1.2, characterize Edmund.
5. In 1.4, what evidence is there that Lear is perceiving a "recognition" or *anagnorisis* (see Glossary)? On the other hand, which of his speeches in this scene especially indicate that he still has much to learn?
6. At the end of 2.2, Kent is put in the stocks. In a sentence, characterize him on the basis of the last speech in the scene.
7. If you were directing a production of *King Lear,* how would you suggest Kent perform 2.4.1–21? Exactly what tone would you like him to use?
8. The last two lines of 2.4 (Cornwall's speech) are often deleted in performances. Why? What do you think is gained or lost?
9. Characterize Lear in 3.2 and 3.4.
10. In 4.1.19, what does Gloucester mean when he says, "I stumbled when I saw"?

303 **boot** good measure 303 **addition** additional titles and rights 307 **fool** Cordelia ("fool" being a term of endearment; but it is perfectly possible to take the word as referring also to the Fool) 311 **undo this button** i.e., to ease the suffocation Lear feels 315 **Vex . . . ghost** do not trouble his departing spirit 316 **rack** instrument of torture, stretching the victim's joints to dislocation 317 **longer** (1) in time (2) in bodily length 319 **usurped** possessed beyond the allotted term 325 **obey** submit to

11. In 5.3 why does Edmund confess and tell of the plan to murder Lear and Cordelia?
12. What motives do Goneril and Regan have for their behavior? What motive does Edmund have for his?
13. How much self-knowledge do you think Lear achieves?
14. What function does the Fool perform?
15. Some critics insist that Lear dies joyfully, but others insist that he dies angrily and blindly. What can be said on behalf of each of these views? Which view strikes you as truer?
16. In what ways is the subplot (Gloucester and his sons) related to the main plot of Lear and his daughters?
17. Gloucester says: "As flies to wanton boys, are we to th' gods, / They kill us for their sport" (4.1.36). Do you think that this is an adequate summary of the theme of *King Lear*?

The 1983 production of *Le Misanthrope* at the Circle in the Square, New York City.
(Photograph by Martha Swope.)

MOLIÈRE

The Misanthrope

English Version by Richard Wilbur

Jean Baptiste Poquelin (1622–73), who took the name Molière, was born into a prosperous middle-class family. For a while he studied law and philosophy, but by 1643 he was acting. He became the head of a theatrical company that had initial difficulties but later, thanks largely to Molière's comedies, had great successes. In 1662 he married Armande Béjart. The marriage apparently was unhappy, but the capricious and flirtatious Armande proved to be an accomplished actress. Molière continued to act, with great success in comedy, until his death. In one of those improbable things that happen in real life but that are too strange for art, Molière died of a hemorrhage that he suffered while playing the title role in his comedy *The Hypochondriac.* The early plays are highly farcical; among the later and greater plays are *The Highbrow Ladies* (1659), *Tartuffe* (1664), *Don Juan* (1665), *The Misanthrope* (1666), and *The Miser* (1668).

COMMENTARY

The introduction to this book makes the rather obvious point that in both tragedy and comedy we have characters who are motivated by some ideal and that (for example) the tragic hero who hunts out the polluted man in Thebes or who kills his wife because he thinks she is unfaithful is neither more nor less impassioned than the comic lover who writes sonnets to his mistress's eyebrow. Whether the passion is noble or comic depends not on its depth, or its persistence, but on its context, and especially on its object.

The passion for honesty that drives Molière's misanthrope, Alceste, is said by the equable Éliante to have "its noble, heroic side," and her view has found wide acceptance among audiences and readers. Alceste is sometimes seen as a tragic figure caught in a comic world, and the play is sometimes said to be a sort of tragic comedy. Alceste demands honesty, and he fulminates against flattery and other forms of insincerity that apparently compose the entire life of the other figures. Surrounded by trimmers and gossips and worse, he alone (if we except the gentle Éliante) seems to hold to a noble ideal. The only other ideal given much prominence is Philinte's, a code of such easy tolerance that it is at times almost indistinguishable from mere passive acceptance of everything.

What case can be made that Alceste is comic, not tragic? A few points suggest themselves. First, this champion of honesty is in love (or thinks he is) with a coquette. What can be more comic than the apostle of plain-dealing being himself in the power of the irrational, especially when this power deposits him at the feet of Célimène, a woman who employs all the devices that in others infuriate him? Second, his demand for honesty is indiscriminate; he is as offended at trivial courtesies as at the law's injustice.

Philinte "ought to die of self-disgust" for his "crime" of effusively greeting a casual acquaintance whose name he cannot even recall. So disproportionate is Alceste's passion that when he pops onstage in 4.2, saying to Éliante, "Avenge me, Madam," he is funny, though the words in themselves are scarcely amusing.

Alceste's remark about joking provides a thread that may be followed usefully. He cannot take a joke. Whenever he is laughed at, he becomes indignant, but indignation (when motivated by a desire to protect the self from criticism) itself evokes further laughter because of the gap between the indignant man's presentation of himself and his real worth. Comedy does not allow people to strike attitudes. The man who protests that his argument *is* valid, dammit, or that he has a sense of humor, or that his opponent is a fool, is likely to evoke laughter by his monolithic insistence on his merit. When Philinte laughs at the old poem Alceste quotes, Alceste resorts to bitter irony, and when told that his frankness has made him ridiculous, he irritably replies:

> So much the better; just what I wish to hear.
> No news could be more grateful to my ear.
> All men are so detestable in my eyes.
> I should be sorry if they thought me otherwise.

When his persistent refusal to praise a trivial poem moves two auditors to laughter, he again employs frigid irony, and concludes the scene ominously:

> By heavens, Sirs, I really didn't know
> That I was being humorous.
> CÉLIMÈNE. Go, Sir; go;
> Settle your business.
> ALCESTE. I shall, and when I'm through,
> I shall return to settle things with you.

Alceste, unable to laugh at the folly of others, cannot, of course, tolerate laughter at himself. When Philinte puts into practice the frankness Alceste stormily advocates, Alceste's response is the indignation we have been commenting on. A sense of humor (as distinct from derisive laughter) involves the ability to laugh at what one values, and among the things one values is the self. Children can laugh at surprises and at the distress of other children, but they cannot laugh at themselves because they cannot see themselves in perspective, at a distance, as it were. Mature people can laugh at (for example) mimicry of themselves, but the child or the immature adult will, like Alceste, sulk or fly into a rage.

In *The Misanthrope* it is entirely possible that Molière is in some degree mimicking himself. In 1662 Molière at forty married Armande Béjart, a woman less than half his age. The marriage seems to have been unhappy, apparently because his wife enjoyed attracting the attentions of other men. Some critics, pressing this point, assume that if the play is autobiographical, Alceste must be expressing Molière's point of view, and therefore he cannot be a comic figure. If anything, the autobiographic origin shows only that Molière had (which no one has doubted) a sense of humor. He could laugh at himself. Alceste's courtship of Célimène may in some degree represent Molière's unhappy marriage to a flirtatious and unappreciative woman, but the point is that Molière apparently could stand back and laugh at his own exasperation, which Alceste cannot do. (Molière subtitled the play "The Atrabilious Man in Love"; one cannot hear

Alceste speaking thus of himself.) Alceste can only, rather childishly, try to maintain his way, and demand that his special merit be noted and rewarded:

> However high the praise, there's nothing worse
> Than sharing honors with the universe.
> Esteem is founded on comparison:
> To honor all men is to honor none.
> Since you embrace this indiscriminate vice,
> Your friendship comes at far too cheap a price;
> I spurn the easy tribute of a heart
> Which will not set the worthy man apart:
> I choose, Sir, to be chosen; and in fine,
> The friend of mankind is no friend of mine.

Once or twice, when he confesses that his love for Célimène is irrational, he seems to have some perspective, but mostly the scenes of Alceste as lover serve to reveal again and again his consuming egotism. His love is so great, he tells Célimène, that he wishes she were in some peril so that he could prove his love by saving her. Célimène aptly replies that Alceste's is "a strange benevolence indeed."

The argument thus far has tried to make the point that Alceste is funny—funny because (among other things) his anger is indiscriminate and disproportionate, because he is a sort of philosopher and yet is in love, and because his *idée fixe,* frankness, when turned against him, exasperates him. But when we return to Éliante's reference to his "noble, heroic side," and we recall his passion for honesty and his passionate desire to be himself, and when we see the hollowness all about him, the comic figure begins to take on a tragic aspect; and when at the end he departs from the stage unrepentant and bitter, banishing himself from society, we feel that the usual comic plot too has taken on a tragic aspect. But this is hardly to say that Alceste is tragic and *The Misanthrope* a tragedy. One cannot, for example, imagine Alceste committing suicide. He is not a Romeo or an Othello.

MOLIÈRE *The Misanthrope*

List of Characters

ALCESTE, *in love with Célimène*
PHILINTE, *Alceste's friend*
ORONTE, *in love with Célimène*
CÉLIMÈNE, *Alceste's beloved*
ÉLIANTE, *Célimène's cousin*
ARSINOÉ, *a friend of Célimène's*
ACASTE, CLITANDRE } *Marquesses*
BASQUE, *Célimène's servant*
A GUARD *of the Marshalsea*
DUBOIS, *Alceste's valet*

The Scene throughout is in Célimène's house at Paris

ACT 1

SCENE 1

[*Philinte, Alceste*]

PHILINTE. Now, what's got into you?
ALCESTE (*seated*). Kindly leave me alone.
PHILINTE. Come, come, what is it? This lugubrious tone . . .
ALCESTE. Leave me, I said; you spoil my solitude.

PHILINTE. Oh, listen to me, now, and don't be rude.
5 ALCESTE. I choose to be rude, Sir, and to be hard of hearing.
PHILINTE. These ugly moods of yours are not endearing;
Friends though we are, I really must insist . . .
ALCESTE (*abruptly rising*). Friends? Friends, you say? Well, cross me off your list.
I've been your friend till now, as you well know;
10 But after what I saw a moment ago
I tell you flatly that our ways must part.
I wish no place in a dishonest heart.
PHILINTE. Why, what have I done, Alceste? Is this quite just?
ALCESTE. My God, you ought to die of self-disgust.
15 I call your conduct inexcusable, Sir,
And every man of honor will concur.
I see you almost hug a man to death,
Exclaim for joy until you're out of breath,
And supplement these loving demonstrations
20 With endless offers, vows, and protestations;
Then when I ask you "Who was that?" I find
That you can barely bring his name to mind!
Once the man's back is turned, you cease to love him,
And speak with absolute indifference of him!
25 By God, I say it's base and scandalous
To falsify the heart's affections thus;
If I caught myself behaving in such a way,
I'd hang myself for shame, without delay.
PHILINTE. It hardly seems a hanging matter to me;
30 I hope that you will take it graciously
If I extend myself a slight reprieve,
And live a little longer, by your leave.
ALCESTE. How dare you joke about a crime so grave?
PHILINTE. What crime? How else are people to behave?
35 ALCESTE. I'd have them be sincere, and never part
With any word that isn't from the heart.
PHILINTE. When someone greets us with a show of pleasure,
It's but polite to give him equal measure,
Return his love the best that we know how,
40 And trade him offer for offer, vow for vow.
ALCESTE. No, no, this formula you'd have me follow,
However fashionable, is false and hollow,
And I despise the frenzied operations
Of all these barterers of protestations,
45 These lavishers of meaningless embraces,
These utterers of obliging commonplaces,
Who court and flatter everyone on earth
And praise the fool no less than the man of worth.
Should you rejoice that someone fondles you,
Offers his love and service, swears to be true, 50
And fills your ears with praises of your name,
When to the first damned fop he'll say the same?
No, no: no self-respecting heart would dream
Of prizing so promiscuous an esteem;
However high the praise, there's nothing worse 55
Than sharing honors with the universe.
Esteem is founded on comparison:
To honor all men is to honor none.
Since you embrace this indiscriminate vice,
Your friendship comes at far too cheap a price; 60
I spurn the easy tribute of a heart
Which will not set the worthy man apart:
I choose, Sir, to be chosen; and in fine,
The friend of mankind is no friend of mine.
PHILINTE. But in polite society, custom decrees 65
That we show certain outward courtesies. . . .
ALCESTE. Ah, no! we should condemn with all our force
Such false and artificial intercourse.
Let men behave like men; let them display
Their inmost hearts in everything they say; 70
Let the heart speak, and let our sentiments
Not mask themselves in silly compliments.
PHILINTE. In certain cases it would be uncouth
And most absurd to speak the naked truth;
With all respect for your exalted notions, 75
It's often best to veil one's true emotions.
Wouldn't the social fabric come undone
If we were wholly frank with everyone?
Suppose you met with someone you couldn't bear;
Would you inform him of it then and there? 80
ALCESTE. Yes.
PHILINTE. Then you'd tell old Emilie it's pathetic
The way she daubs her features with cosmetic
And plays the gay coquette at sixty-four?
ALCESTE. I would.
PHILINTE. And you'd call Dorilas a bore,
And tell him every ear at court is lame 85
From hearing him brag about his noble name?
ALCESTE. Precisely.
PHILINTE. Ah, you're joking.
ALCESTE. *Au contraire:*
In this regard there's none I'd choose to spare.
All are corrupt; there's nothing to be seen
In court or town but aggravates my spleen. 90
I fall into deep gloom and melancholy
When I survey the scene of human folly,
Finding on every hand base flattery,
Injustice, fraud, self-interest, treachery. . . .
Ah, it's too much; mankind has grown so base, 95
I mean to break with the whole human race.

PHILINTE. This philosophic rage is a bit extreme;
You've no idea how comical you seem;
Indeed, we're like those brothers in the play
100 Called *School for Husbands,* one of whom was prey . . .
ALCESTE. Enough, now! None of your stupid similes.
PHILINTE. Then let's have no more tirades, if you please.
The world won't change, whatever you say or do;
And since plain speaking means so much to you,
105 I'll tell you plainly that by being frank
You've earned the reputation of a crank,
And that you're thought ridiculous when you rage
And rant against the manners of the age.
ALCESTE. So much the better; just what I wish to hear.
110 No news could be more grateful to my ear.
All men are so detestable in my eyes,
I should be sorry if they thought me wise.
PHILINTE. Your hatred's very sweeping, is it not?
ALCESTE. Quite right: I hate the whole degraded lot.
PHILINTE. Must all poor human creatures be
115 embraced,
Without distinction, by your vast distaste?
Even in these bad times, there are surely a few . . .
ALCESTE. No, I include all men in one dim view:
Some men I hate for being rogues: the others
120 I hate because they treat the rogues like brothers,
And, lacking a virtuous scorn for what is vile,
Receive the villain with a complaisant smile.
Notice how tolerant people choose to be
Toward that bold rascal who's at law with me.
125 His social polish can't conceal his nature;
One sees at once that he's a treacherous creature;
No one could possibly be taken in
By those soft speeches and that sugary grin.
The whole world knows the shady means by which
130 The low-brow's grown so powerful and rich,
And risen to a rank so bright and high
That virtue can but blush, and merit sigh.
Whenever his name comes up in conversation,
None will defend his wretched reputation;
135 Call him knave, liar, scoundrel, and all the rest,
Each head will nod, and no one will protest.
And yet his smirk is seen in every house,
He's greeted everywhere with smiles and bows,
And when there's any honor that can be got
140 By pulling strings, he'll get it, like as not.
My God! It chills my heart to see the ways
Men come to terms with evil nowadays;
Sometimes, I swear, I'm moved to flee and find
Some desert land unfouled by humankind.
145 PHILINTE. Come, let's forget the follies of the times
And pardon mankind for its petty crimes;
Let's have an end of rantings and of railings,
And show some leniency toward human failings.
This world requires a pliant rectitude;
Too stern a virtue makes one stiff and rude; 150
Good sense views all extremes with detestation,
And bids us to be noble in moderation.
The rigid virtues of the ancient days
Are not for us; they jar with all our ways
And ask of us too lofty a perfection. 155
Wise men accept their times without objection,
And there's no greater folly, if you ask me,
Than trying to reform society.
Like you, I see each day a hundred and one
Unhandsome deeds that might be better done, 160
But still, for all the faults that meet my view,
I'm never known to storm and rave like you.
I take men as they are, or let them be,
And teach my soul to bear their frailty;
And whether in court or town, whatever the scene, 165
My phlegm's as philosophic as your spleen.
ALCESTE. This phlegm which you so eloquently commend,
Does nothing ever rile it up, my friend?
Suppose some man you trust should treacherously
Conspire to rob you of your property, 170
And do his best to wreck your reputation?
Wouldn't you feel a certain indignation?
PHILINTE. Why, no. These faults of which you so complain
Are part of human nature, I maintain,
And it's no more a matter for disgust 175
That men are knavish, selfish and unjust,
Than that the vulture dines upon the dead,
And wolves are furious, and apes ill-bred.
ALCESTE. Shall I see myself betrayed, robbed, torn to bits,
And not . . . Oh, let's be still and rest our wits. 180
Enough of reasoning, now. I've had my fill.
PHILINTE. Indeed, you would do well, Sir, to be still.
Rage less at your opponent, and give some thought
To how you'll win this lawsuit that he's brought.
ALCESTE. I assure you I'll do nothing of the sort. 185
PHILINTE. Then who will plead your case before the court?
ALCESTE. Reason and right and justice will plead for me.
PHILINTE. Oh, Lord. What judges do you plan to see?
ALCESTE. Why, none. The justice of my cause is clear.
PHILINTE. Of course, man; but there's politics to fear. . . . 190
ALCESTE. No, I refuse to lift a hand. That's flat.
I'm either right, or wrong.

PHILINTE. Don't count on that.
ALCESTE. No, I'll do nothing.
PHILINTE. Your enemy's influence
Is great, you know . . .
ALCESTE. That makes no difference.
PHILINTE. It will; you'll see.
195 ALCESTE. Must honor bow to guile?
If so, I shall be proud to lose the trial.
PHILINTE. O, really . . .
ALCESTE. I'll discover by this case
Whether or not men are sufficiently base
And impudent and villainous and perverse
200 To do me wrong before the universe.
PHILINTE. What a man!
ALCESTE. Oh, I could wish, whatever the cost,
Just for the beauty of it, that my trial were lost.
PHILINTE. If people heard you talking so, Alceste,
They'd split their sides. Your name would be a jest.
ALCESTE. So much the worse for jesters.
205 PHILINTE. May I enquire
Whether this rectitude you so admire,
And these hard virtues you're enamored of
Are qualities of the lady whom you love?
It much surprises me that you, who seem
210 To view mankind with furious disesteem,
Have yet found something to enchant your eyes
Amidst a species which you so despise.
And what is more amazing, I'm afraid,
Is the most curious choice your heart has made.
215 The honest Éliante is fond of you,
Arsinoé, the prude, admires you too;
And yet your spirit's been perversely led
To choose the flighty Célimène instead,
Whose brittle malice and coquettish ways
220 So typify the manners of our days.
How is it that the traits you most abhor
Are bearable in this lady you adore?
Are you so blind with love that you can't find them?
Or do you contrive, in her case, not to mind them?
225 ALCESTE. My love for that young widow's not the kind
That can't perceive defects; no, I'm not blind.
I see her faults, despite my ardent love,
And all I see I fervently reprove.
And yet I'm weak; for all her falsity,
230 That woman knows the art of pleasing me,
And though I never cease complaining of her,
I swear I cannot manage not to love her.
Her charm outweighs her faults; I can but aim
To cleanse her spirit in my love's pure flame.
235 PHILINTE. That's no small task; I wish you all success.
You think then that she loves you?
ALCESTE. Heavens, yes!

I wouldn't love her did she not love me.
PHILINTE. Well, if her taste for you is plain to see,
Why do these rivals cause you such despair?
ALCESTE. True love, Sir, is possessive, and cannot bear 240
To share with all the world. I'm here today
To tell her she must send that mob away.
PHILINTE. If I were you, and had your choice to make,
Éliante, her cousin, would be the one I'd take;
That honest heart, which cares for you alone, 245
Would harmonize far better with your own.
ALCESTE. True, true: each day my reason tells me so;
But reason doesn't rule in love, you know.
PHILINTE. I fear some bitter sorrow is in store;
This love . . .

SCENE 2

[*Oronte, Alceste, Philinte*]

ORONTE (*to Alceste*). The servants told me at the door
That Éliante and Célimène were out,
But when I heard, dear Sir, that you were about,
I came to say, without exaggeration,
That I hold you in the vastest admiration, 5
And that it's always been my dearest desire
To be the friend of one I so admire.
I hope to see my love of merit requited,
And you and I in friendship's bond united.
I'm sure you won't refuse—if I may be frank— 10
A friend of my devotedness—and rank.

During this speech of Oronte's, Alceste is abstracted, and seems unaware that he is being spoken to. He only breaks off his reverie when Oronte says:

It was for you, if you please, that my words were intended.
ALCESTE. For me, Sir?
ORONTE. Yes, for you. You're not offended?
ALCESTE. By no means. But this much surprises me. . . .
The honor comes most unexpectedly. . . . 15
ORONTE. My high regard should not astonish you;
The whole world feels the same. It is your due.
ALCESTE. Sir . . .
ORONTE. Why, in all the State there isn't one
Can match your merits; they shine, Sir, like the sun.
ALCESTE. Sir . . .
ORONTE. You are higher in my estimation 20
Than all that's most illustrious in the nation.
ALCESTE. Sir . . .
ORONTE. If I lie, may heaven strike me dead!
To show you that I mean what I have said,

Permit me, Sir, to embrace you most sincerely,
25 And swear that I will prize our friendship dearly.
Give me your hand. And now, Sir, if you choose,
We'll make our vows.

ALCESTE. Sir . . .

ORONTE. What! You refuse?

ALCESTE. Sir, it's a very great honor you extend:
But friendship is a sacred thing, my friend;
30 It would be profanation to bestow
The name of friend on one you hardly know.
All parts are better played when well-rehearsed;
Let's put off friendship, and get acquainted first.
We may discover it would be unwise
35 To try to make our natures harmonize.

ORONTE. By heaven! You're sagacious to the core;
This speech has made me admire you even more.
Let time, then, bring us closer day by day;
Meanwhile, I shall be yours in every way.
40 If, for example, there should be anything
You wish at court, I'll mention it to the King.
I have his ear, of course; it's quite well known
That I am much in favor with the throne.
In short, I am your servant. And now, dear friend,
45 Since you have such fine judgment, I intend
To please you, if I can, with a small sonnet
I wrote not long ago. Please comment on it,
And tell me whether I ought to publish it.

ALCESTE. You must excuse me, Sir; I'm hardly fit
To judge such matters.

ORONTE. Why not?

50 ALCESTE. I am, I fear,
Inclined to be unfashionably sincere.

ORONTE. Just what I ask; I'd take no satisfaction
In anything but your sincere reaction.
I beg you not to dream of being kind.

55 ALCESTE. Since you desire it, Sir, I'll speak my mind.

ORONTE. *Sonnet.* It's a sonnet. . . . *Hope* . . . The poem's addressed
To a lady who wakened hopes within my breast.
Hope . . . this is not the pompous sort of thing,
Just modest little verses, with a tender ring.

ALCESTE. Well, we shall see.

60 ORONTE. *Hope* . . . I'm anxious to hear
Whether the style seems properly smooth and clear,
And whether the choice of words is good or bad.

ALCESTE. We'll see, we'll see.

ORONTE. Perhaps I ought to add
That it took me only a quarter-hour to write it.

65 ALCESTE. The time's irrelevant, Sir: kindly recite it.

ORONTE (*reading*).
Hope comforts us awhile, 'tis true,
Lulling our cares with careless laughter,
And yet such joy is full of rue,
My Phyllis, if nothing follows after.

PHILINTE. I'm charmed by this already; the style's delightful. 70

ALCESTE (*sotto voce, to Philinte*). How can you say that? Why, the thing is frightful.

ORONTE. *Your fair face smiled on me awhile,*
But was it kindness so to enchant me?
'Twould have been fairer not to smile,
If hope was all you meant to grant me. 75

PHILINTE. What a clever thought! How handsomely you phrase it!

ALCESTE (*sotto voce, to Philinte*). You know the thing is trash. How dare you praise it?

ORONTE. *If it's to be my passion's fate.*
Thus everlastingly to wait,
Then death will come to set me free: 80
For death is fairer than the fair;
Phyllis, to hope is to despair
When one must hope eternally.

PHILINTE. The close is exquisite—full of feeling and grace.

ALCESTE (*sotto voce, aside*). Oh, blast the close; you'd better close your face 85
Before you send your lying soul to hell.

PHILINTE. I can't remember a poem I've liked so well.

ALCESTE (*sotto voce, aside*). Good Lord!

ORONTE (*to Philinte*). I fear you're flattering me a bit.

PHILINTE. Oh, no!

ALCESTE (*sotto voce, aside*). What else d'you call it, you hypocrite?

ORONTE (*to Alceste*). But you, Sir, keep your promise now: don't shrink 90
From telling me sincerely what you think.

ALCESTE. Sir, these are delicate matters; we all desire
To be told that we've the true poetic fire.
But once, to one whose name I shall not mention,
I said, regarding some verse of his invention, 95
That gentlemen should rigorously control
That itch to write which often afflicts the soul;
That one should curb the heady inclination
To publicize one's little avocation;
And that in showing off one's works of art 100
One often plays a very clownish part.

ORONTE. Are you suggesting in a devious way
That I ought not . . .

ALCESTE. Oh, that I do not say.
Further, I told him that no fault is worse
Than that of writing frigid, lifeless verse, 105
And that the merest whisper of such a shame
Suffices to destroy a man's good name.

ORONTE. D'you mean to say my sonnet's dull and trite?
ALCESTE. I don't say that. But I went on to cite
110 Numerous cases of once-respected men
Who came to grief by taking up the pen.
ORONTE. And am I like them? Do I write so poorly?
ALCESTE. I don't say that. But I told this person, "Surely
You're under no necessity to compose;
115 Why you should wish to publish, heaven knows.
There's no excuse for printing tedious rot
Unless one writes for bread, as you do not.
Resist temptation, then, I beg of you;
Conceal your pastimes from the public view;
120 And don't give up, on any provocation,
Your present high and courtly reputation,
To purchase at a greedy printer's shop
The name of silly author and scribbling fop."
These were the points I tried to make him see.
125 ORONTE. I sense that they are also aimed at me;
But now—about my sonnet—I'd like to be told . . .
ALCESTE. Frankly, that sonnet should be pigeonholed.
You've chosen the worst models to imitate.
The style's unnatural. Let me illustrate:
130 For example, *Your fair face smiled on me awhile,*
Followed by, *'Twould have been fairer not to smile!*
Or this: *such joy is full of rue;*
Or this: *For death is fairer than the fair;*
Or, *Phyllis, to hope is to despair*
135 *When one must hope eternally!*
This artificial style, that's all the fashion,
Has neither taste, nor honesty, nor passion;
It's nothing but a sort of wordy play,
And nature never spoke in such a way.
140 What, in this shallow age, is not debased?
Our fathers, though less refined, had better taste;
I'd barter all that men admire today
For one old love song I shall try to say:
If the King had given me for my own
145 *Paris, his citadel,*
And I for that must leave alone
Her whom I love so well,
I'd say then to the Crown,
Take back your glittering town;
150 *My darling is more fair, I swear,*
My darling is more fair.
The rhyme's not rich, the style is rough and old,
But don't you see that it's the purest gold
Beside the tinsel nonsense now preferred,
155 And that there's passion in its every word?
If the King had given me for my own
Paris, his citadel,
And I for that must leave alone
Her whom I love so well,
160 *I'd say then to the Crown,*
Take back your glittering town;
My darling is more fair, I swear,
My darling is more fair.
There speaks a loving heart. (*To Philinte.*) You're laughing, eh?
165 Laugh on, my precious wit. Whatever you say,
I hold that song's worth all the bibelots
That people hail today with ah's and oh's.
ORONTE. And I maintain my sonnet's very good.
ALCESTE. It's not at all surprising that you should.
170 You have your reasons; permit me to have mine
For thinking that you cannot write a line.
ORONTE. Others have praised my sonnet to the skies.
ALCESTE. I lack their art of telling pleasant lies.
ORONTE. You seem to think you've got no end of wit.
175 ALCESTE. To praise your verse, I'd need still more of it.
ORONTE. I'm not in need of your approval, Sir.
ALCESTE. That's good; you couldn't have it if you were.
ORONTE. Come now, I'll lend you the subject of my sonnet;
I'd like to see you try to improve upon it.
180 ALCESTE. I might, by chance, write something just as shoddy;
But then I wouldn't show it to everybody.
ORONTE. You're most opinionated and conceited.
ALCESTE. Go find your flatterers, and be better treated.
ORONTE. Look here, my little fellow, pray watch your tone.
185 ALCESTE. My great big fellow, you'd better watch your own.
PHILINTE (*stepping between them*). Oh, please, please, gentlemen! This will never do.
ORONTE. The fault is mine, and I leave the field to you.
I am your servant, Sir, in every way.
ALCESTE. And I, Sir, am your most abject valet.

SCENE 3

[*Philinte, Alceste*]

PHILINTE. Well, as you see, sincerity in excess
Can get you into a very pretty mess;
Oronte was hungry for appreciation. . . .
ALCESTE. Don't speak to me.
PHILINTE. What?
ALCESTE. No more conversation.
PHILINTE. Really, now . . .

ALCESTE. Leave me alone.
PHILINTE. If I . . .
5 ALCESTE. Out of my sight!
PHILINTE. But what . . .
ALCESTE. I won't listen.
PHILINTE. But . . .
ALCESTE. Silence!
PHILINTE. Now, is it polite . . .
ALCESTE. By heaven, I've had enough. Don't follow me.
PHILINTE. Ah, you're just joking. I'll keep you company.

ACT 2

SCENE 1

[*Alceste, Célimène*]

ALCESTE. Shall I speak plainly, Madam? I confess
Your conduct gives me infinite distress,
And my resentment's grown too hot to smother.
Soon, I foresee, we'll break with one another.
5 If I said otherwise, I should deceive you;
Sooner or later, I shall be forced to leave you,
And if I swore that we shall never part,
I should misread the omens of my heart.
CÉLIMÈNE. You kindly saw me home, it would appear,
10 So as to pour invectives in my ear.
ALCESTE. I've no desire to quarrel. But I deplore
Your inability to shut the door
On all these suitors who beset you so.
There's what annoys me, if you care to know.
CÉLIMÈNE. Is it my fault that all these men pursue
15 me?
Am I to blame if they're attracted to me?
And when they gently beg an audience,
Ought I to take a stick and drive them hence?
ALCESTE. Madam, there's no necessity for a stick;
20 A less responsive heart would do the trick.
Of your attractiveness I don't complain;
But those your charms attract, you then detain
By a most melting and receptive manner,
And so enlist their hearts beneath your banner.
25 It's the agreeable hopes which you excite
That keep these lovers round you day and night;
Were they less liberally smiled upon,
That sighing troop would very soon be gone.
But tell me, Madam, why is it that lately
30 This man Clitandre interests you so greatly?
Because of what high merits do you deem
Him worthy of the honor of your esteem?
Is it that your admiring glances linger
On the splendidly long nail of his little finger?
Or do you share the general deep respect 35
For the blond wig he chooses to affect?
Are you in love with his embroidered hose?
Do you adore his ribbons and his bows?
Or is it that this paragon bewitches
Your tasteful eye with his vast German breeches? 40
Perhaps his giggle, or his falsetto voice,
Makes him the latest gallant of your choice?
CÉLIMÈNE. You're much mistaken to resent him so.
Why I put up with him you surely know:
My lawsuit's very shortly to be tried, 45
And I must have his influence on my side.
ALCESTE. Then lose your lawsuit, Madam, or let it drop;
Don't torture me by humoring such a fop.
CÉLIMÈNE. You're jealous of the whole world, Sir.
ALCESTE. That's true,
Since the whole world is well-received by you. 50
CÉLIMÈNE. That my good nature is so unconfined
Should serve to pacify your jealous mind;
Were I to smile on one, and scorn the rest,
Then you might have some cause to be distressed.
ALCESTE. Well, if I mustn't be jealous, tell me, then, 55
Just how I'm better treated than other men.
CÉLIMÈNE. You know you have my love. Will that not do?
ALCESTE. What proof have I that what you say is true?
CÉLIMÈNE. I would expect, Sir, that my having said it
Might give the statement a sufficient credit. 60
ALCESTE. But how can I be sure that you don't tell
The selfsame thing to other men as well?
CÉLIMÈNE. What a gallant speech! How flattering to me!
What a sweet creature you make me out to be!
Well then, to save you from the pangs of doubt, 65
All that I've said I hereby cancel out;
Now, none but yourself shall make a monkey of you:
Are you content?
ALCESTE. Why, why am I doomed to love you?
I swear that I shall bless the blissful hour
When this poor heart's no longer in your power! 70
I make no secret of it: I've done my best
To exorcise this passion from my breast;
But thus far all in vain; it will not go;
It's for my sins that I must love you so.
CÉLIMÈNE. Your love for me is matchless, Sir; that's clear. 75
ALCESTE. Indeed, in all the world it has no peer;
Words can't describe the nature of my passion,

And no man ever loved in such a fashion.
CÉLIMÈNE. Yes, it's a brand-new fashion, I agree:
80 You show your love by castigating me,
And all your speeches are enraged and rude.
I've never been so furiously wooed.
ALCESTE. Yet you could calm that fury, if you chose.
Come, shall we bring our quarrels to a close?
85 Let's speak with open hearts, then, and begin . . .

SCENE 2

[*Célimène, Alceste, Basque*]

CÉLIMÈNE. What is it?
BASQUE. Acaste is here.
CÉLIMÈNE. Well, send him in.

SCENE 3

[*Célimène, Alceste*]

ALCESTE. What! Shall we never be alone at all?
You're always ready to receive a call,
And you can't bear, for ten ticks of the clock,
Not to keep open house for all who knock.
5 CÉLIMÈNE. I couldn't refuse him: he'd be most put out.
ALCESTE. Surely that's not worth worrying about.
CÉLIMÈNE. Acaste would never forgive me if he guessed
That I consider him a dreadful pest.
ALCESTE. If he's a pest, why bother with him then?
10 CÉLIMÈNE. Heavens! One can't antagonize such men;
Why, they're the chartered gossips of the court,
And have a say in things of every sort.
One must receive them, and be full of charm;
They're no great help, but they can do you harm,
15 And though your influence be ever so great,
They're hardly the best people to alienate.
ALCESTE. I see, dear lady, that you could make a case
For putting up with the whole human race;
These friendships that you calculate so nicely . . .

SCENE 4

[*Alceste, Célimène, Basque*]

BASQUE. Madam, Clitandre is here as well.
ALCESTE. Precisely.
CÉLIMÈNE. Where are you going?
ALCESTE. Elsewhere.
CÉLIMÈNE. Stay.
ALCESTE. No, no.
CÉLIMÈNE. Stay, Sir.
ALCESTE. I can't.
CÉLIMÈNE. I wish it.
ALCESTE. No, I must go.
I beg you, Madam, not to press the matter;
5 You know I have no taste for idle chatter.
CÉLIMÈNE.
Stay. I command you.
ALCESTE. No, I cannot stay.
CÉLIMÈNE.
Very well; you have my leave to go away.

SCENE 5

[*Éliante, Philinte, Acaste, Clitandre, Alceste, Célimène, Basque*]

ÉLIANTE (*to Célimène*). The Marquesses have kindly come to call.
Were they announced?
CÉLIMÈNE. Yes. Basque, bring chairs for all.

Basque provides the chairs, and exits.

(*To Alceste.*) You haven't gone?
ALCESTE. No; and I shan't depart
Till you decide who's foremost in your heart.
CÉLIMÈNE. Oh, hush.
5 ALCESTE. It's time to choose; take them, or me.
CÉLIMÈNE. You're mad.
ALCESTE. I'm not, as you shall shortly see.
CÉLIMÈNE. Oh?
ALCESTE. You'll decide.
CÉLIMÈNE. You're joking now, dear friend.
ALCESTE. No, no; you'll choose; my patience is at an end.
CLITANDRE. Madam, I come from court, where poor Cléonte
10 Behaved like a perfect fool, as is his wont.
Has he no friend to counsel him, I wonder,
And teach him less unerringly to blunder?
CÉLIMÈNE. It's true, the man's a most accomplished dunce;
His gauche behavior charms the eye at once;
15 And every time one sees him, on my word,
His manner's grown a trifle more absurd.
ACASTE. Speaking of dunces, I've just now conversed
With old Damon, who's one of the very worst;
I stood a lifetime in the broiling sun
20 Before his dreary monologue was done.
CÉLIMÈNE. Oh, he's a wondrous talker, and has the power
To tell you nothing hour after hour:
If, by mistake, he ever came to the point,
The shock would put his jawbone out of joint.
25 ÉLIANTE (*to Philinte*). The conversation takes its usual turn,

And all our dear friends' ears will shortly burn.
CLITANDRE. Timante's a character, Madam.
CÉLIMÈNE. Isn't he, though?
A man of mystery from top to toe,
Who moves about in a romantic mist
30 On secret missions which do not exist.
His talk is full of eyebrows and grimaces;
How tired one gets of his momentous faces;
He's always whispering something confidential
Which turns out to be quite inconsequential;
35 Nothing's too slight for him to mystify;
He even whispers when he says "good-bye."
ACASTE. Tell us about Géralde.
CÉLIMÈNE. That tiresome ass.
He mixes only with the titled class,
And fawns on dukes and princes, and is bored
40 With anyone who's not as least a lord.
The man's obsessed with rank, and his discourses
Are all of hounds and carriages and horses;
He uses Christian names with all the great,
And the word Milord, with him, is out of date.
45 CLITANDRE. He's very taken with Bélise, I hear.
CÉLIMÈNE. She is the dreariest company, poor dear.
Whenever she comes to call, I grope about
To find some topic which will draw her out,
But, owing to her dry and faint replies,
50 The conversation wilts, and droops, and dies.
In vain one hopes to animate her face
By mentioning the ultimate commonplace;
But sun or shower, even hail or frost
Are matters she can instantly exhaust.
55 Meanwhile her visit, painful though it is,
Drags on and on through mute eternities,
And though you ask the time, and yawn, and yawn,
She sits there like a stone and won't be gone.
ACASTE. Now for Adraste.
CÉLIMÈNE. Oh, that conceited elf
60 Has a gigantic passion for himself;
He rails against the court, and cannot bear it
That none will recognize his hidden merit;
All honors given to others give offense
To his imaginary excellence.
CLITANDRE. What about young Cléon? His house,
65 they say,
Is full of the best society, night and day.
CÉLIMÈNE. His cook has made him popular, not he:
It's Cléon's table that people come to see.
ÉLIANTE. He gives a splendid dinner, you must admit.
70 CÉLIMÈNE. But must he serve himself along with it?
For my taste, he's a most insipid dish
Whose presence sours the wine and spoils the fish.
PHILINTE. Damis, his uncle, is admired no end.
What's your opinion, Madam?
CÉLIMÈNE. Why, he's my friend.
PHILINTE. He seems a decent fellow, and rather clever. 75
CÉLIMÈNE. He works too hard at cleverness, however.
I hate to see him sweat and struggle so
To fill his conversation with bons mots.
Since he's decided to become a wit
His taste's so pure that nothing pleases it; 80
He scolds at all the latest books and plays,
Thinking that wit must never stoop to praise,
That finding fault's a sign of intellect,
That all appreciation is abject,
And that by damning everything in sight 85
One shows oneself in a distinguished light.
He's scornful even of our conversations:
Their trivial nature sorely tries his patience;
He folds his arms, and stands above the battle,
And listens sadly to our childish prattle. 90
ACASTE. Wonderful, Madam! You've hit him off
precisely.
CLITANDRE. No one can sketch a character so nicely.
ALCESTE. How bravely, Sirs, you cut and thrust at all
These absent fools, till one by one they fall:
But let one come in sight, and you'll at once 95
Embrace the man you lately called a dunce,
Telling him in a tone sincere and fervent
How proud you are to be his humble servant.
CLITANDRE. Why pick on us? *Madame's* been
speaking, Sir.
And you should quarrel, if you must, with her. 100
ALCESTE. No, no, by God, the fault is yours, because
You lead her on with laughter and applause,
And make her think that she's the more delightful
The more her talk is scandalous and spiteful.
Oh, she would stoop to malice far, far less 105
If no such claque approved her cleverness.
It's flatterers like you whose foolish praise
Nourishes all the vices of these days.
PHILINTE. But why protest when someone ridicules
Those you'd condemn, yourself, as knaves or fools? 110
CÉLIMÈNE. Why, Sir? Because he loves to make a fuss.
You don't expect him to agree with us,
When there's an opportunity to express
His heaven-sent spirit of contrariness?
What other people think, he can't abide; 115
Whatever they say, he's on the other side;
He lives in deadly terror of agreeing;
'Twould make him seem an ordinary being.
Indeed, he's so in love with contradiction,
He'll turn against his most profound conviction 120
And with a furious eloquence deplore it,
If only someone else is speaking for it.

ALCESTE. Go on, dear lady, mock me as you please;
You have your audience in ecstasies.
125 PHILINTE. But what she says is true: you have a way
Of bridling at whatever people say;
Whether they praise or blame, your angry spirit
Is equally unsatisfied to hear it.
ALCESTE. Men, Sir, are always wrong, and that's the reason
130 That righteous anger's never out of season;
All that I hear in all their conversation
Is flattering praise or reckless condemnation.
CÉLIMÈNE. But...
ALCESTE. No, no, Madam, I am forced to state
That you have pleasures which I deprecate,
135 And that these others, here, are much to blame
For nourishing the faults which are your shame.
CLITANDRE. I shan't defend myself, Sir; but I vow
I'd thought this lady faultless until now.
ACASTE. I see her charms and graces, which are many;
140 But as for faults, I've never noticed any.
ALCESTE. I see them, Sir; and rather than ignore them,
I strenuously criticize her for them.
The more one loves, the more one should object
To every blemish, every least defect.
145 Were I this lady, I would soon get rid
Of lovers who approved of all I did,
And by their slack indulgence and applause
Endorsed my follies and excused my flaws.
CÉLIMÈNE. If all hearts beat according to your measure,
150 The dawn of love would be the end of pleasure;
And love would find its perfect consummation
In ecstasies of rage and reprobation.
ÉLIANTE. Love, as a rule, affects men otherwise,
And lovers rarely love to criticize.
155 They see their lady as a charming blur,
And find all things commendable in her.
If she has any blemish, fault, or shame,
They will redeem it by a pleasing name.
The pale-faced lady's lily-white, perforce;
160 The swarthy one's a sweet brunette, of course;
The spindly lady has a slender grace;
The fat one has a most majestic pace;
The plain one, with her dress in disarray,
They classify as *beauté negligée;*
165 The hulking one's a goddess in their eyes,
The dwarf, a concentrate of Paradise;
The haughty lady has a noble mind;
The mean one's witty, and the dull one's kind;
The chatterbox has liveliness and verve,
170 The mute one has a virtuous reserve.
So lovers manage, in their passion's cause,
To love their ladies even for their flaws.
ALCESTE. But I still say ...
CÉLIMÈNE. I think it would be nice
To stroll around the gallery once or twice.
What! You're not going, Sirs?
CLITANDRE AND ACASTE. No, Madam, no. 175
ALCESTE. You seem to be in terror lest they go.
Do what you will, Sirs; leave, or linger on,
But I shan't go till after you are gone.
ACASTE. I'm free to linger, unless I should perceive
Madame is tired, and wishes me to leave. 180
CLITANDRE. And as for me, I needn't go today
Until the hour of the King's *coucher.*
CÉLIMÈNE (*to Alceste*). You're joking, surely?
ALCESTE. Not in the least; we'll see
Whether you'd rather part with them, or me.

SCENE 6

[*Alceste, Célimène, Éliante, Acaste, Philinte, Clitandre, Basque*]

BASQUE (*to Alceste*). Sir, there's a fellow here who bids me state
That he must see you, and that it can't wait.
ALCESTE. Tell him that I have no such pressing affairs.
BASQUE. It's a long tailcoat that this fellow wears,
With gold all over.
CÉLIMÈNE (*to Alceste*). You'd best go down and see. 5
Or—have him enter.

SCENE 7

[*Alceste, Célimène, Éliante, Acaste, Philinte, Clitandre, Guard*]

ALCESTE (*confronting the Guard*). Well, what do you want with me?
Come in, Sir.
GUARD. I've a word, Sir, for your ear.
ALCESTE. Speak it aloud, Sir; I shall strive to hear.
GUARD. The Marshals have instructed me to say
You must report to them without delay. 5
ALCESTE. Who? Me, Sir?
GUARD. Yes, Sir; you.
ALCESTE. But what do they want?
PHILINTE (*to Alceste*). To scotch your silly quarrel with Oronte.
CÉLIMÈNE (*to Philinte*). What quarrel?
PHILINTE. Oronte and he have fallen out
Over some verse he spoke his mind about;
The Marshals wish to arbitrate the matter. 10
ALCESTE. Never shall I equivocate or flatter!
PHILINTE. You'd best obey their summons; come, let's go.

ALCESTE. How can they mend our quarrel, I'd like to know?
Am I to make a cowardly retraction,
15 And praise those jingles to his satisfaction?
I'll not recant; I've judged that sonnet rightly.
It's bad.
PHILINTE. But you might say so more politely....
ALCESTE. I'll not back down; his verses make me sick.
PHILINTE. If only you could be more politic!
But come, let's go.
20 ALCESTE. I'll go, but I won't unsay
A single word.
PHILINTE. Well, let's be on our way.
ALCESTE. Till I am ordered by my lord the King
To praise that poem, I shall say the thing
Is scandalous, by God, and that the poet
25 Ought to be hanged for having the nerve to show it.
(*To Clitandre and Acaste, who are laughing.*) By heaven, Sirs, I really didn't know
That I was being humorous.
CÉLIMÈNE. Go, Sir, go;
Settle your business.
ALCESTE. I shall, and when I'm through,
I shall return to settle things with you.

ACT 3

SCENE 1

[*Clitandre, Acaste*]

CLITANDRE. Dear Marquess, how contented you appear;
All things delight you, nothing mars your cheer.
Can you, in perfect honesty, declare
That you've a right to be so debonair?
5 ACASTE. By Jove, when I survey myself, I find
No cause whatever for distress of mind.
I'm young and rich; I can in modesty
Lay claim to an exalted pedigree;
And owing to my name and my condition
10 I shall not want for honors and position.
Then as to courage, that most precious trait,
I seem to have it, as was proved of late
Upon the field of honor, where my bearing,
They say, was very cool and rather daring.
15 I've wit, of course; and taste in such perfection
That I can judge without the least reflection,
And at the theater, which is my delight,
Can make or break a play on opening night,
And lead the crowd in hisses or bravos,
20 And generally be known as one who knows.
I'm clever, handsome, gracefully polite;
My waist is small, my teeth are strong and white.
As for my dress, the world's astonished eyes
Assure me that I bear away the prize.
I find myself in favor everywhere, 25
Honored by men, and worshiped by the fair;
And since these things are so, it seems to me
I'm justified in my complacency.
CLITANDRE. Well, if so many ladies hold you dear,
Why do you press a hopeless courtship here? 30
ACASTE. Hopeless, you say? I'm not the sort of fool
That likes his ladies difficult and cool.
Men who are awkward, shy, and peasantish
May pine for heartless beauties, if they wish,
Grovel before them, bear their cruelties, 35
Woo them with tears and sighs and bended knees,
And hope by dogged faithfulness to gain
What their poor merits never could obtain.
For men like me, however, it makes no sense
To love on trust, and foot the whole expense. 40
Whatever any lady's merits be,
I think, thank God, that I'm as choice as she;
That if my heart is kind enough to burn
For her, she owes me something in return;
And that in any proper love affair 45
The partners must invest an equal share.
CLITANDRE. You think, then, that our hostess favors you?
ACASTE. I've reason to believe that that is true.
CLITANDRE. How did you come to such a mad conclusion?
You're blind, dear fellow. This is sheer delusion. 50
ACASTE. All right, then: I'm deluded and I'm blind.
CLITANDRE. Whatever put the notion in your mind?
ACASTE. Delusion.
CLITANDRE. What persuades you that you're right?
ACASTE. I'm blind.
CLITANDRE. But have you any proofs to cite?
ACASTE. I tell you I'm deluded.
CLITANDRE. Have you, then, 55
Received some secret pledge from Célimène?
ACASTE. Oh, no: she scorns me.
CLITANDRE. Tell me the truth, I beg.
ACASTE. She just can't bear me.
CLITANDRE. Ah, don't pull my leg.
Tell me what hope she's given you, I pray.
ACASTE. I'm hopeless, and it's you who win the day. 60
She hates me thoroughly, and I'm so vexed
I mean to hang myself on Tuesday next.
CLITANDRE. Dear Marquess, let us have an armistice
And make a treaty. What do you say to this?
If ever one of us can plainly prove 65

That Célimène encourages his love,
The other must abandon hope, and yield,
And leave him in possession of the field.
ACASTE. Now there's a bargain that appeals to me;
70 With all my heart, dear Marquess, I agree.
But hush.

SCENE 2

[*Célimène, Acaste, Clitandre*]

CÉLIMÈNE. Still here?
CLITANDRE. 'Twas love that stayed our feet.
CÉLIMÈNE. I think I heard a carriage in the street.
Whose is it? D'you know?

SCENE 3

[*Célimène, Acaste, Clitandre, Basque*]

BASQUE. Arsinoé is here,
Madame.
CÉLIMÈNE. Arsinoé, you say? Oh, dear.
BASQUE. Éliante is entertaining her below.
CÉLIMÈNE. What brings the creature here, I'd like to know?
5 ACASTE. They say she's dreadfully prudish, but in fact
I think her piety . . .
CÉLIMÈNE. It's all an act.
At heart she's worldly, and her poor success
In snaring men explains her prudishness.
It breaks her heart to see the beaux and gallants
10 Engrossed by other women's charms and talents,
And so she's always in a jealous rage
Against the faulty standards of the age.
She lets the world believe that she's a prude
To justify her loveless solitude,
15 And strives to put a brand of moral shame
On all the graces that she cannot claim.
But still she'd love a lover; and Alceste
Appears to be the one she'd love the best.
His visits here are poison to her pride;
20 She seems to think I've lured him from her side;
And everywhere, at court or in the town,
The spiteful, envious woman runs me down.
In short, she's just as stupid as can be,
Vicious and arrogant in the last degree,
25 And . . .

SCENE 4

[*Arsinoé, Célimène, Clitandre, Acaste*]

CÉLIMÈNE. Ah! What happy chance has brought you here?
I've thought about you ever so much, my dear.
ARSINOÉ.
I've come to tell you something you should know.
CÉLIMÈNE. How good of you to think of doing so!

Clitandre and Acaste go out, laughing.

SCENE 5

[*Arsinoé, Célimène*]

ARSINOÉ. It's just as well those gentlemen didn't tarry.
CÉLIMÈNE. Shall we sit down?
ARSINOÉ. That won't be necessary.
Madam, the flame of friendship ought to burn
Brightest in matters of the most concern,
And as there's nothing which concerns us more 5
Than honor, I have hastened to your door
To bring you, as your friend, some information
About the status of your reputation.
I visited, last night, some virtuous folk,
And, quite by chance, it was of you they spoke; 10
There was, I fear, no tendency to praise
Your light behavior and your dashing ways.
The quantity of gentlemen you see
And your by now notorious coquetry
Were both so vehemently criticized 15
By everyone, that I was much surprised.
Of course, I needn't tell you where I stood;
I came to your defense as best I could,
Assured them you were harmless, and declared
Your soul was absolutely unimpaired. 20
But there are some things, you must realize,
One can't excuse, however hard one tries,
And I was forced at last into conceding
That your behavior, Madam, is misleading,
That it makes a bad impression, giving rise 25
To ugly gossip and obscene surmise,
And that if you were more *overtly* good,
You wouldn't be so much misunderstood.
Not that I think you've been unchaste—no! no!
The saints preserve me from a thought so low! 30
But mere good conscience never did suffice:
One must avoid the outward show of vice.
Madam, you're too intelligent, I'm sure,
To think my motives anything but pure
In offering you this counsel—which I do 35
Out of a zealous interest in you.
CÉLIMÈNE. Madam, I haven't taken you amiss;
I'm very much obliged to you for this;
And I'll at once discharge the obligation
By telling you about *your* reputation. 40
You've been so friendly as to let me know
What certain people say of me, and so

I mean to follow your benign example
By offering you a somewhat similar sample.
45 The other day, I went to an affair
And found some most distinguished people there
Discussing piety, both false and true.
The conversation soon came round to you.
Alas! Your prudery and bustling zeal
50 Appeared to have a very slight appeal.
Your affectation of a grave demeanor,
Your endless talk of virtue and of honor,
The aptitude of your suspicious mind
For finding sin where there is none to find,
55 Your towering self-esteem, that pitying face
With which you contemplate the human race,
Your sermonizings and your sharp aspersions
On people's pure and innocent diversions—
All these were mentioned, Madam, and, in fact,
60 Were roundly and concertedly attacked.
"What good," they said, "are all these outward shows,
When everything belies her pious pose?
She prays incessantly; but then, they say,
She beats her maids and cheats them of their pay;
65 She shows her zeal in every holy place,
But still she's vain enough to paint her face;
She holds that naked statues are immoral,
But with a naked *man* she'd have no quarrel."
Of course, I said to everybody there
70 That they were being viciously unfair;
But still they were disposed to criticize you,
And all agreed that someone should advise you
To leave the morals of the world alone,
And worry rather more about your own.
75 They felt that one's self-knowledge should be great
Before one thinks of setting others straight;
That one should learn the art of living well
Before one threatens other men with hell,
And that the Church is best equipped, no doubt,
80 To guide our souls and root our vices out.
Madam, you're too intelligent, I'm sure,
To think my motives anything but pure
In offering you this counsel—which I do
Out of a zealous interest in you.
85 ARSINOÉ. I dared not hope for gratitude, but I
Did not expect so acid a reply;
I judge, since you've been so extremely tart,
That my good counsel pierced you to the heart.
CÉLIMÈNE. Far from it, Madam. Indeed, it seems to me
90 We ought to trade advice more frequently.
One's vision of oneself is so defective
That it would be an excellent corrective.
If you are willing, Madam, let's arrange
Shortly to have another frank exchange
In which we'll tell each other, *entre nous,* 95
What you've heard tell of me, and I of you.
ARSINOÉ. Oh, people never censure you, my dear;
It's me they criticize. Or so I hear.
CÉLIMÈNE. Madam, I think we either blame or praise
According to our taste and length of days. 100
There is a time of life for coquetry,
And there's a season, too, for prudery.
When all one's charms are gone, it is, I'm sure,
Good strategy to be devout and pure:
It makes one seem a little less forsaken. 105
Some day, perhaps, I'll take the road you've taken:
Time brings all things. But I have time aplenty,
And see no cause to be a prude at twenty.
ARSINOÉ. You give your age in such a gloating tune
That one would think I was an ancient crone; 110
We're not so far apart, in sober truth,
That you can mock me with a boast of youth!
Madam, you baffle me. I wish I knew
What moves you to provoke me as you do.
CÉLIMÈNE. For my part, Madam, I should like to
know 115
Why you abuse me everywhere you go.
Is it my fault, dear lady, that your hand
Is not, alas, in very great demand?
If men admire me, if they pay me court
And daily make me offers of the sort 120
You'd dearly love to have them make to you,
How can I help it? What would you have me do?
If what you want is lovers, please feel free
To take as many as you can from me.
ARSINOÉ. Oh, come. D'you think the world is losing
sleep 125
Over the flock of lovers which you keep,
Or that we find it difficult to guess
What price you pay for their devotedness?
Surely you don't expect us to suppose
Mere merit could attract so many beaux? 130
It's not your virtue that they're dazzled by;
Nor is it virtuous love for which they sigh.
You're fooling no one, Madam; the world's not blind;
There's many a lady heaven has designed
To call men's noblest, tenderest feelings out, 135
Who has no lovers dogging her about;
From which it's plain that lovers nowadays
Must be acquired in bold and shameless ways,
And only pay one court for such reward
As modesty and virtue can't afford. 140
Then don't be quite so puffed up, if you please,
About your tawdry little victories;
Try, if you can, to be a shade less vain,
And treat the world with somewhat less disdain.

145 If one were envious of your amours,
One soon could have a following like yours;
Lovers are no great trouble to collect
If one prefers them to one's self-respect.
CÉLIMÈNE. Collect them then, my dear; I'd love to see
150 You demonstrate that charming theory;
Who knows, you might . . .
ARSINOÉ. Now, Madam, that will do;
It's time to end this trying interview.
My coach is late in coming to your door,
Or I'd have taken leave of you before.
CÉLIMÈNE. Oh, please don't feel that you must rush
155 away;
I'd be delighted, Madam, if you'd stay.
However, lest my conversation bore you,
Let me provide some better company for you;
This gentleman, who comes most apropos,
160 Will please you more than I could do, I know.

SCENE 6

[*Alceste, Célimène, Arsinoé*]

CÉLIMÈNE. Alceste, I have a little note to write
Which simply must go out before tonight;
Please entertain *Madame;* I'm sure that she
Will overlook my incivility.

SCENE 7

[*Alceste, Arsinoé*]

ARSINOÉ. Well, Sir, our hostess graciously contrives
For us to chat until my coach arrives;
And I shall be forever in her debt
For granting me this little tête-à-tête.
5 We women very rightly give our hearts
To men of noble character and parts,
And your especial merits, dear Alceste,
Have roused the deepest sympathy in my breast.
Oh, how I wish they had sufficient sense
10 At court, to recognize your excellence!
They wrong you greatly, Sir. How it must hurt you
Never to be rewarded for your virtue!
ALCESTE. Why, Madam, what cause have I to feel
aggrieved?
What great and brilliant thing have I achieved?
15 What service have I rendered to the King
That I should look to him for anything?
ARSINOÉ. Not everyone who's honored by the State
Has done great services. A man must wait
Till time and fortune offer him the chance.
20 Your merit, Sir, is obvious at a glance,
And . . .
ALCESTE. Ah, forget my merit; I am not neglected.
The court, I think, can hardly be expected
To mine men's souls for merit, and unearth
Our hidden virtues and our secret worth.
ARSINOÉ. *Some* virtues, though are far too bright to
hide; 25
Yours are acknowledged, Sir, on every side.
Indeed, I've heard you warmly praised of late
By persons of considerable weight.
ALCESTE. This fawning age has praise for everyone,
And all distinctions, Madam, are undone. 30
All things have equal honor nowadays,
And no one should be gratified by praise.
To be admired, one only need exist,
And every lackey's on the honors list.
ARSINOÉ. I only wish, Sir, that you had your eye 35
On some position at court, however high;
You'd only have to hint at such a notion
For me to set the proper wheels in motion;
I've certain friendships I'd be glad to use
To get you any office you might choose. 40
ALCESTE. Madam, I fear that any such ambition
Is wholly foreign to my disposition.
The soul God gave me isn't of the sort
That prospers in the weather of a court.
It's all too obvious that I don't possess 45
The virtues necessary for success.
My one great talent is for speaking plain;
I've never learned to flatter or to feign;
And anyone so stupidly sincere
Had best not seek a courtier's career. 50
Outside the court, I know, one must dispense
With honors, privilege, and influence;
But still one gains the right, forgoing these,
Not to be tortured by the wish to please.
One needn't live in dread of snubs and slights, 55
Nor praise the verse that every idiot writes,
Nor humor silly Marquesses, nor bestow
Politic sighs on Madam So-and-So.
ARSINOÉ. Forget the court, then; let the matter rest.
But I've another cause to be distressed 60
About your present situation, Sir.
It's to your love affair that I refer.
She whom you love, and who pretends to love you,
Is, I regret to say, unworthy of you.
ALCESTE. Why, Madam? Can you seriously intend 65
To make so grave a charge against your friend?
ARSINOÉ. Alas, I must. I've stood aside too long
And let that lady do you grievous wrong;
But now my debt to conscience shall be paid:
I tell you that your love has been betrayed. 70
ALCESTE. I thank you, Madam; you're extremely kind.

Such words are soothing to a lover's mind.
ARSINOÉ. Yes, though she *is* my friend, I say again
You're very much too good for Célimène.
75 She's wantonly misled you from the start.
ALCESTE. You may be right; who knows another's heart?
But ask yourself if it's the part of charity
To shake my soul with doubts of her sincerity.
ARSINOÉ. Well, if you'd rather be a dupe than doubt her,
80 That's your affair. I'll say no more about her.
ALCESTE. Madam, you know that doubt and vague suspicion
Are painful to a man in my position;
It's most unkind to worry me this way
Unless you've some real proof of what you say.
ARSINOÉ. Sir, say no more: all doubts shall be
85 removed,
And all that I've been saying shall be proved.
You've only to escort me home, and there
We'll look into the heart of this affair.
I've ocular evidence which will persuade you
90 Beyond a doubt, that Célimène's betrayed you.
Then, if you're saddened by that revelation,
Perhaps I can provide some consolation.

ACT 4

SCENE 1

[*Éliante, Philinte*]

PHILINTE. Madam, he acted like a stubborn child;
I thought they never would be reconciled;
In vain we reasoned, threatened, and appealed;
He stood his ground and simply would not yield.
5 The Marshals, I feel sure, have never heard
An argument so splendidly absurd.
"No, gentlemen," said he, "I'll not retract.
His verse is bad: extremely bad, in fact.
Surely it does the man no harm to know it.
10 Does it disgrace him, not to be a poet?
A gentleman may be respected still,
Whether he writes a sonnet well or ill.
That I dislike his verse should not offend him;
In all that touches honor, I commend him;
15 He's noble, brave, and virtuous—but I fear
He can't in truth be called a sonneteer.
I'll gladly praise his wardrobe; I'll endorse
His dancing, or the way he sits a horse;
But, gentlemen, I cannot praise his rhyme.
20 In fact, it ought to be a capital crime
For anyone so sadly unendowed
To write a sonnet, and read the thing aloud."
At length he fell into a gentler mood
And, striking a concessive attitude,
He paid Oronte the following courtesies. 25
"Sir, I regret that I'm so hard to please,
And I'm profoundly sorry that your lyric
Failed to provoke me to a panegyric."
After these curious words, the two embraced,
And then the hearing was adjourned—in haste. 30
ÉLIANTE. His conduct has been very singular lately;
Still, I confess that I respect him greatly.
The honesty in which he takes such pride
Has—to my mind—its noble, heroic side.
In this false age, such candor seems outrageous; 35
But I could wish that it were more contagious.
PHILINTE. What most intrigues me in our friend Alceste
Is the grand passion that rages in his breast.
The sullen humors he's compounded of
Should not, I think, dispose his heart to love; 40
But since they do, it puzzles me still more
That he should choose your cousin to adore.
ÉLIANTE. It does, indeed, belie the theory
That love is born of gentle sympathy,
And that the tender passion must be based 45
On sweet accords of temper and of taste.
PHILINTE. Does she return his love, do you suppose?
ÉLIANTE. Ah, that's a difficult question, Sir. Who knows?
How can we judge the truth of her devotion?
Her heart's a stranger to its own emotion. 50
Sometimes it thinks it loves, when no love's there;
At other times it loves quite unaware.
PHILINTE. I rather think Alceste is in for more
Distress and sorrow than he's bargained for;
Were he of my mind, Madam, his affection 55
Would turn in quite a different direction,
And we would see him more responsive to
The kind regard which he receives from you.
ÉLIANTE. Sir, I believe in frankness, and I'm inclined,
In matters of the heart, to speak my mind. 60
I don't oppose his love for her; indeed,
I hope with all my heart that he'll succeed,
And were it in my power, I'd rejoice
In giving him the lady of his choice.
But if, as happens frequently enough 65
In love affairs, he meets with a rebuff—
If Célimène should grant some rival's suit—
I'd gladly play the role of substitute;
Nor would his tender speeches please me less
Because they'd once been made without success. 70

PHILINTE. Well, Madam, as for me, I don't oppose
Your hopes in this affair; and heaven knows
That in my conversations with the man
I plead your cause as often as I can.
75 But if those two should marry, and so remove
All chance that he will offer you his love,
Then I'll declare my own, and hope to see
Your gracious favor pass from him to me.
In short, should you be cheated of Alceste,
80 I'd be most happy to be second best.
ÉLIANTE. Philinte, you're teasing.
PHILINTE. Ah, Madam, never fear;
No words of mine were ever so sincere,
And I shall live in fretful expectation
Till I can make a fuller declaration.

SCENE 2

[*Alceste, Éliante, Philinte*]

ALCESTE. Avenge me, Madam! I must have satisfaction,
Or this great wrong will drive me to distraction!
ÉLIANTE. Why, what's the matter? What's upset you so?
ALCESTE. Madam, I've had a mortal, mortal blow.
5 If Chaos repossessed the universe,
I swear I'd not be shaken any worse.
I'm ruined. . . . I can say no more. . . . My soul . . .
ÉLIANTE. Do try, Sir, to regain your self-control.
ALCESTE. Just heaven! Why were so much beauty and grace
10 Bestowed on one so vicious and so base?
ÉLIANTE. Once more, Sir, tell us. . . .
ALCESTE. My world has gone to wrack;
I'm—I'm betrayed; she's stabbed me in the back.
Yes, Célimène (who would have thought it of her?)
Is false to me, and has another lover.
ÉLIANTE. Are you quite certain? Can you prove these
15 things?
PHILINTE. Lovers are prey to wild imaginings
And jealous fancies. No doubt there's some mistake. . . .
ALCESTE. Mind your own business, Sir, for heaven's sake.
(*To Éliante.*) Madam, I have the proof that you demand
20 Here in my pocket, penned by her own hand.
Yes, all the shameful evidence one could want
Lies in this letter written to Oronte—
Oronte! whom I felt sure she couldn't love,
And hardly bothered to be jealous of.
25 PHILINTE. Still, in a letter, appearances may deceive;
This may not be so bad as you believe.
ALCESTE. Once more I beg you, Sir, to let me be;
Tend to your own affairs; leave mine to me.
ÉLIANTE. Compose yourself, this anguish that you feel . . .
ALCESTE. Is something, Madam, you alone can heal. 30
My outraged heart, beside itself with grief,
Appeals to you for comfort and relief.
Avenge me on your cousin, whose unjust
And faithless nature has deceived my trust;
Avenge a crime your pure soul must detest. 35
ÉLIANTE. But how, Sir?
ALCESTE. Madam, this heart within my breast
Is yours; pray take it; redeem my heart from her,
And so avenge me on my torturer.
Let her be punished by the fond emotion,
The ardent love, the bottomless devotion, 40
The faithful worship which this heart of mine
Will offer up to yours as to a shrine.
ÉLIANTE. You have my sympathy, Sir, in all you suffer;
Nor do I scorn the noble heart you offer;
But I suspect you'll soon be mollified, 45
And this desire for vengeance will subside.
When some beloved hand has done us wrong
We thirst for retribution—but not for long;
However dark the deed that she's committed,
A lovely culprit's very soon acquitted. 50
Nothing's so stormy as an injured lover,
And yet no storm so quickly passes over.
ALCESTE. No, Madam, no—this is no lovers' spat;
I'll not forgive her; it's gone too far for that;
My mind's made up; I'll kill myself before 55
I waste my hopes upon her any more.
Ah, here she is. My wrath intensifies.
I shall confront her with her tricks and lies,
And crush her utterly, and bring you then
A heart no longer slave to Célimène. 60

SCENE 3

[*Célimène, Alceste*]

ALCESTE (*aside*). Sweet heaven, help me to control my passion.
CÉLIMÈNE (*aside*). Oh, Lord.
(*To Alceste.*) Why stand there staring in that fashion?
And what d'you mean by those dramatic sighs,
And that malignant glitter in your eyes?
ALCESTE. I mean that sins which cause the blood to freeze 5
Look innocent beside your treacheries;
That nothing Hell's or Heaven's wrath could do
Ever produced so bad a thing as you.
CÉLIMÈNE. Your compliments were always sweet and pretty.

10 ALCESTE. Madam, it's not the moment to be witty.
No, blush and hang your head; you've ample reason,
Since I've the fullest evidence of your treason.
Ah, this is what my sad heart prophesied;
Now all my anxious fears are verified;
15 My dark suspicion and my gloomy doubt
Divined the truth, and now the truth is out.
For all your trickery, I was not deceived;
It was my bitter stars that I believed.
But don't imagine that you'll go scot-free;
20 You shan't misuse me with impunity.
I know that love's irrational and blind;
I know the heart's not subject to the mind,
And can't be reasoned into beating faster;
I know each soul is free to choose its master;
25 Therefore had you but spoken from the heart,
Rejecting my attention from the start,
I'd have no grievance, or at any rate
I could complain of nothing but my fate.
Ah, but so falsely to encourage me—
30 That was a treason and a treachery
For which you cannot suffer too severely,
And you shall pay for that behavior dearly.
Yes, now I have no pity, not a shred;
My temper's out of hand; I've lost my head.
35 Shocked by the knowledge of your double-dealings,
My reason can't restrain my savage feelings;
A righteous wrath deprives me of my senses,
And I won't answer for the consequences.
CÉLIMÈNE. What does this outburst mean? Will you please explain?
40 Have you, by any chance, gone quite insane?
ALCESTE. Yes, yes, I went insane the day I fell
A victim to your black and fatal spell,
Thinking to meet with some sincerity
Among the treacherous charms that beckoned me.
CÉLIMÈNE. Pooh. Of what treachery can you
45 complain?
ALCESTE. How sly you are, how cleverly you feign!
But you'll not victimize me any more.
Look: here's a document you've seen before.
This evidence, which I acquired today,
50 Leaves you, I think, without a thing to say.
CÉLIMÈNE. Is this what sent you into such a fit?
ALCESTE. You should be blushing at the sight of it.
CÉLIMÈNE. Ought I to blush? I truly don't see why.
ALCESTE. Ah, now you're being bold as well as sly;
55 Since there's no signature, perhaps you'll claim . . .
CÉLIMÈNE. I wrote it, whether or not it bears my name.
ALCESTE. And you can view with equanimity
This proof of your disloyalty to me!
CÉLIMÈNE. Oh, don't be so outrageous and extreme.
ALCESTE. You take this matter lightly, it would seem. 60
Was it no wrong to me, no shame to you,
That you should send Oronte this billet-doux?
CÉLIMÈNE
Oronte! Who said it was for him?
ALCESTE. Why, those
Who brought me this example of your prose.
But what's the difference? If you wrote the letter 65
To someone else, it pleases me no better.
My grievance and your guilt remain the same.
CÉLIMÈNE. But need you rage, and need I blush for shame,
If this was written to a *woman* friend?
ALCESTE. Ah! Most ingenious. I'm impressed no end; 70
And after that incredible evasion
Your guilt is clear. I need no more persuasion.
How dare you try so clumsy a deception?
D'you think I'm wholly wanting in perception?
Come, come, let's see how brazenly you'll try 75
To bolster up so palpable a lie:
Kindly construe this ardent closing section
As nothing more than sisterly affection!
Here, let me read it. Tell me, if you dare to,
That this is for a woman . . .
CÉLIMÈNE. I don't care to. 80
What right have you to badger and berate me,
And so highhandedly interrogate me?
ALCESTE. Now, don't be angry; all I ask of you
Is that you justify a phrase or two . . .
CÉLIMÈNE. No, I shall not. I utterly refuse, 85
And you may take those phrases as you choose.
ALCESTE. Just show me how this letter could be meant
For a woman's eyes, and I shall be content.
CÉLIMÈNE. No, no, it's for Oronte; you're perfectly right.
I welcome his attentions with delight, 90
I prize his character and his intellect,
And everything is just as you suspect.
Come, do your worst now; give your rage free rein;
But kindly cease to bicker and complain.
ALCESTE (*aside*). Good God! Could anything be more inhuman? 95
Was ever a heart so mangled by a woman?
When I complain of how she has betrayed me,
She bridles, and commences to upbraid me!
She tries my tortured patience to the limit;
She won't deny her guilt; she glories in it! 100
And yet my heart's too faint and cowardly
To break these chains of passion, and be free,
To scorn her as it should, and rise above
This unrewarded, mad, and bitter love.

105 (*To Célimène.*) Ah, traitress, in how confident a fashion
You take advantage of my helpless passion,
And use my weakness for your faithless charms
To make me once again throw down my arms!
But do at least deny this black transgression;
110 Take back that mocking and perverse confession;
Defend this letter and your innocence,
And I, poor fool, will aid in your defense.
Pretend, pretend, that you are just and true,
And I shall make myself believe in you.

115 CÉLIMÈNE. Oh, stop it. Don't be such a jealous dunce,
Or I shall leave off loving you at once.
Just why should I *pretend?* What could impel me
To stoop so low as that? And kindly tell me
Why, if I loved another, I shouldn't merely
120 Inform you of it, simply and sincerely!
I've told you where you stand, and that admission
Should altogether clear me of suspicion;
After so generous a guarantee,
What right have you to harbor doubts of me?
125 Since women are (from natural reticence)
Reluctant to declare their sentiments,
And since the honor of our sex requires
That we conceal our amorous desires,
Ought any man for whom such laws are broken
130 To question what the oracle has spoken?
Should he not rather feel an obligation
To trust that most obliging declaration?
Enough, now. Your suspicions quite disgust me;
Why should I love a man who doesn't trust me?
135 I cannot understand why I continue,
Fool that I am, to take an interest in you.
I ought to choose a man less prone to doubt,
And give you something to be vexed about.

ALCESTE. Ah, what a poor enchanted fool I am;
140 These gentle words, no doubt, were all a sham,
But destiny requires me to entrust
My happiness to you, and so I must.
I'll love you to the bitter end, and see
How false and treacherous you dare to be.

145 CÉLIMÈNE. No, you don't really love me as you ought.

ALCESTE. I love you more than can be said or thought;
Indeed, I wish you were in such distress
That I might show my deep devotedness.
Yes, I could wish that you were wretchedly poor,
150 Unloved, uncherished, utterly obscure;
That fate had set you down upon the earth
Without possessions, rank, or gentle birth;
Then, by the offer of my heart, I might
Repair the great injustice of your plight;
155 I'd raise you from the dust, and proudly prove
The purity and vastness of my love.

CÉLIMÈNE. This is a strange benevolence indeed!
God grant that I may never be in need....
Ah, here's Monsier Dubois, in quaint disguise.

SCENE 4

[*Célimène, Alceste, Dubois*]

ALCESTE. Well, why this costume? Why those frightened eyes?
What ails you?

DUBOIS. Well, Sir, things are most mysterious.

ALCESTE. What do you mean?

DUBOIS. I fear they're very serious.

ALCESTE. What?

DUBOIS. Shall I speak more loudly?

ALCESTE. Yes; speak out.

DUBOIS. Isn't there someone here, Sir?

ALCESTE. Speak, you lout! 5
Stop wasting time.

DUBOIS. Sir, we must slip away.

ALCESTE. How's that?

DUBOIS. We must decamp without delay.

ALCESTE. Explain yourself.

DUBOIS. I tell you we must fly.

ALCESTE. What for?

DUBOIS. We mustn't pause to say good-by.

ALCESTE. Now what d'you mean by all of this, you clown? 10

DUBOIS. I mean, Sir, that we've got to leave this town.

ALCESTE. I'll tear you limb from limb and joint from joint
If you don't come more quickly to the point.

DUBOIS. Well, Sir, today a man in a black suit,
Who wore a black and ugly scowl to boot, 15
Left us a document scrawled in such a hand
As even Satan couldn't understand.
It bears upon your lawsuit, I don't doubt;
But all hell's devils couldn't make it out.

ALCESTE. Well, well, go on. What then? I fail to see 20
How this event obliges us to flee.

DUBOIS. Well, Sir, an hour later, hardly more,
A gentleman who's often called before
Came looking for you in an anxious way.
Not finding you, he asked me to convey 25
(Knowing I could be trusted with the same)
The following message.... Now, what *was* his name?

ALCESTE. Forget his name, you idiot. What did he say?

DUBOIS. Well, it was one of your friends, Sir, anyway.
He warned you to begone, and he suggested 30
That if you stay, you may well he arrested.

ALCESTE. What? Nothing more specific? Think, man, think!

DUBOIS. No, Sir. He had me bring him pen and ink,
And dashed you off a letter which, I'm sure,
35 Will render things distinctly less obscure.
ALCESTE. Well—let me have it!
CÉLIMÈNE. What *is* this all about?
ALCESTE. God knows; but I have hopes of finding out.
How long am I to wait, you blitherer?
DUBOIS (*after a protracted search for the letter*). I must have left it on your table, Sir.
ALCESTE. I ought to . . .
40 CÉLIMÈNE. No, no, keep your self-control;
Go find out what's behind this rigmarole.
ALCESTE. It seems that fate, no matter what I do,
Has sworn that I may not converse with you;
But, Madam, pray permit your faithful lover
45 To try once more before the day is over.

ACT 5

SCENE 1

[*Alceste, Philinte*]

ALCESTE. No, it's too much. My mind's made up, I tell you.
PHILINTE. Why should this blow, however hard, compel you . . .
ALCESTE. No, no, don't waste your breath in argument;
Nothing you say will alter my intent;
5 This age is vile, and I've made up my mind
To have no further commerce with mankind.
Did not truth, honor, decency, and the laws
Oppose my enemy and approve my cause?
My claims were justified in all men's sight;
10 I put my trust in equity and right;
Yet, to my horror and the world's disgrace,
Justice is mocked, and I have lost my case!
A scoundrel whose dishonesty is notorious
Emerges from another lie victorious!
15 Honor and right condone his brazen fraud,
While rectitude and decency applaud!
Before his smirking face, the truth stands charmed,
And virtue conquered, and the law disarmed!
His crime is sanctioned by a court decree!
20 And not content with what he's done to me,
The dog now seeks to ruin me by stating
That I composed a book now circulating,
A book so wholly criminal and vicious
That even to speak its title is seditious!
25 Meanwhile Oronte, my rival, lends his credit
To the same libelous tale, and helps to spread it!
Oronte! a man of honor and of rank,
With whom I've been entirely fair and frank;
Who sought me out and forced me, willy-nilly,
To judge some verse I found extremely silly; 30
And who, because I properly refused
To flatter him, or see the truth abused,
Abets my enemy in a rotten slander!
There's the reward of honesty and candor!
The man will hate me to the end of time 35
For failing to commend his wretched rhyme!
And not this man alone, but all humanity
Do what they do from interest and vanity;
They prate of honor, truth, and righteousness,
But lie, betray, and swindle nonetheless. 40
Come then: man's villainy is too much to bear;
Let's leave this jungle and this jackal's lair.
Yes! treacherous and savage race of men,
You shall not look upon my face again.
PHILINTE. Oh, don't rush into exile prematurely; 45
Things aren't as dreadful as you make them, surely.
It's rather obvious, since you're still at large,
That people don't believe your enemy's charge.
Indeed, his tale's so patently untrue
That it may do more harm to him than you. 50
ALCESTE. Nothing could do that scoundrel any harm:
His frank corruption is his greatest charm,
And, far from hurting him, a further shame
Would only serve to magnify his name.
PHILINTE. In any case, his bald prevarication 55
Has done no injury to your reputation,
And you may feel secure in that regard.
As for your lawsuit, it should not be hard
To have the case reopened, and contest
This judgment . . .
ALCESTE. No, no, let the verdict rest. 60
Whatever cruel penalty it may bring,
I wouldn't have it changed for anything.
It shows the times' injustice with such clarity
That I shall pass it down to our posterity
As a great proof and signal demonstration 65
Of the black wickedness of this generation.
It may cost twenty thousand francs; but I
Shall pay their twenty thousand, and gain thereby
The right to storm and rage at human evil,
And send the race of mankind to the devil. 70
PHILINTE. Listen to me . . .
ALCESTE. Why? What can you possibly say?
Don't argue, Sir; your labor's thrown away.
Do you propose to offer lame excuses
For men's behavior and the times' abuses?
PHILINTE. No, all you say I'll readily concede. 75
This is a low, conniving age indeed;

Nothing but trickery prospers nowadays,
And people ought to mend their shabby ways.
Yes, man's a beastly creature; but must we then
80 Abandon the society of men?
Here in the world, each human frailty
Provides occasion for philosophy,
And that is virtue's noblest exercise;
If honesty shone forth from all men's eyes,
85 If every heart were frank and kind and just,
What could our virtues do but gather dust
(Since their employment is to help us bear
The villainies of men without despair)?
A heart well-armed with virtue can endure....

90 ALCESTE. Sir, you're a matchless reasoner, to be sure;
Your words are fine and full of cogency;
But don't waste time and eloquence on me.
My reason bids me go, for my own good.
My tongue won't lie and flatter as it should;
95 God knows what frankness it might next commit,
And what I'd suffer on account of it.
Pray let me wait for Célimène's return
In peace and quiet. I shall shortly learn,
By her response to what I have in view,
100 Whether her love for me is feigned or true.

PHILINTE. Till then, let's visit Éliante upstairs.

ALCESTE. No, I am too weighed down with somber cares.
Go to her, do; and leave me with my gloom
Here in the darkened corner of this room.

105 PHILINTE. Why, that's no sort of company, my friend;
I'll see if Éliante will not descend.

SCENE 2

[*Célimène, Oronte, Alceste*]

ORONTE. Yes, Madam, if you wish me to remain
Your true and ardent lover, you must deign
To give me some more positive assurance.
All this suspense is quite beyond endurance.
5 If your heart shares the sweet desires of mine,
Show me as much by some convincing sign;
And here's the sign I urgently suggest:
That you no longer tolerate Alceste,
But sacrifice him to my love, and sever
10 All your relations with the man forever.

CÉLIMÈNE. Why do you suddenly dislike him so?
You praised him to the skies not long ago.

ORONTE. Madam, that's not the point. I'm here to find
Which way your tender feelings are inclined.
15 Choose, if you please, between Alceste and me,
And I shall stay or go accordingly.

ALCESTE (*emerging from the corner*). Yes, Madam, choose; this gentleman's demand
Is wholly just, and I support his stand.
I too am true and ardent; I too am here
To ask you that you make your feelings clear. 20
No more delays, now; no equivocation;
The time has come to make your declaration.

ORONTE. Sir, I've no wish in any way to be
An obstacle to your felicity.

ALCESTE. Sir, I've no wish to share her heart with you; 25
That may sound jealous, but at least it's true.

ORONTE. If, weighing us, she leans in your direction . . .

ALCESTE. If she regards you with the least affection . . .

ORONTE. I swear I'll yield her to you there and then.

ALCESTE. I swear I'll never see her face again. 30

ORONTE. Now, Madam, tell us what we've come to hear.

ALCESTE. Madam, speak openly and have no fear.

ORONTE. Just say which one is to remain your lover.

ALCESTE. Just name one name, and it will all be over.

ORONTE. What! Is it possible that you're undecided? 35

ALCESTE. What! Can your feelings possibly be divided?

CÉLIMÈNE. Enough: this inquisition's gone too far:
How utterly unreasonable you are!
Not that I couldn't make the choice with ease;
My heart has no conflicting sympathies; 40
I know full well which one of you I favor,
And you'd not see me hesitate or waver.
But how can you expect me to reveal
So cruelly and bluntly what I feel?
I think it altogether too unpleasant 45
To choose between two men when both are present;
One's heart has means more subtle and more kind
Of letting its affections be divined,
Nor need one be uncharitably plain
To let a lover know he loves in vain. 50

ORONTE. No, no, speak plainly; I for one can stand it.
I beg you to be frank.

ALCESTE. And I demand it.
The simple truth is what I wish to know,
And there's no need for softening the blow.
You've made an art of pleasing everyone, 55
But now your days of coquetry are done.
You have no choice now, Madam, but to choose,
For I'll know what to think if you refuse;
I'll take your silence for a clear admission
That I'm entitled to my worst suspicion. 60

ORONTE. I thank you for this ultimatum, Sir,
And I may say I heartily concur.

CÉLIMÈNE. Really, this foolishness is very wearing.

Must you be so unjust and overbearing?
65 Haven't I told you why I must demur?
Ah, here's Éliante; I'll put the case to her.

SCENE 3

[*Éliante, Philinte, Célimène, Oronte, Alceste*]

CÉLIMÈNE. Cousin, I'm being persecuted here
By these two persons, who, it would appear,
Will not be satisfied till I confess
Which one I love the more, and which the less,
5 And tell the latter to his face that he
Is henceforth banished from my company.
Tell me, has ever such a thing been done?
ÉLIANTE. You'd best not turn to me; I'm not the one
To back you in a matter of this kind.
10 I'm all for those who frankly speak their mind.
ORONTE. Madam, you'll search in vain for a defender.
ALCESTE. You're beaten, Madam, and may as well surrender.
ORONTE. Speak, speak, you must; and end this awful strain.
ALCESTE. Or don't, and your position will be plain.
15 ORONTE. A single word will close this painful scene.
ALCESTE. But if you're silent, I'll know what you mean.

SCENE 4

[*Arsinoé, Célimène, Éliante, Alceste, Philinte, Acaste, Clitandre, Oronte*]

ACASTE (*to Célimène*). Madam, with all due deference, we two
Have come to pick a little bone with you.
CLITANDRE (*to Oronte and Alceste*). I'm glad you're present, Sirs, as you'll soon learn,
Our business here is also your concern.
ARSINOÉ (*to Célimène*). Madam, I visit you so soon
5 again
Only because of these two gentlemen,
Who came to me indignant and aggrieved
About a crime too base to be believed.
Knowing your virtue, having such confidence in it,
10 I couldn't think you guilty for a minute,
In spite of all their telling evidence;
And, rising above our little difference,
I've hastened here in friendship's name to see
You clear yourself of this great calumny.
15 ACASTE. Yes, Madam, let us see with what composure
You'll manage to respond to this disclosure.
You lately sent Clitandre this tender note.
CLITANDRE. And this one, for Acaste, you also wrote.
ACASTE (*to Oronte and Alceste*). You'll recognize this writing, Sirs, I think;
20 The lady is so free with pen and ink
That you must know it all too well, I fear.
But listen: this is something you should hear.

"How absurd you are to condemn my light-heartedness in society, and to accuse me of being happiest in the company of others. Nothing could be more unjust; and 25 if you do not come to me instantly and beg pardon for saying such a thing, I shall never forgive you as long as I live. Our big bumbling friend the Viscount . . ."

What a shame that he's not here.

"Our big bumbling friend the Viscount, whose name 30 stands first in your complaint, is hardly a man to my taste; and ever since the day I watched him spend three-quarters of an hour spitting into a well, so as to make circles in the water, I have been unable to think highly of him. As for the little Marquess . . ." 35

In all modesty, gentlemen, that is I.

"As for the little Marquess, who sat squeezing my hand for such a long while yesterday, I find him in all respects the most trifling creature alive; and the only things of value about him are his cape and his sword. As for the 40 man with the green ribbons . . ."

(*To Alceste.*) It's your turn now, Sir.

"As for the man with the green ribbons, he amuses me now and then with his bluntness and his bearish ill-humor; but there are many times indeed when I think 45 him the greatest bore in the world. And as for the sonneteer . . ."

(*To Oronte.*) Here's your helping.

"And as for the sonneteer, who has taken it into his head to be witty, and insists on being an author in the teeth of 50 opinion, I simply cannot be bothered to listen to him, and his prose wearies me quite as much as his poetry. Be assured that I am not always so well-entertained as you suppose; that I long for your company more than I dare to say, at all these entertainments to which people drag 55 me; and that the presence of those one loves is the true and perfect seasoning to all one's pleasures."

CLITANDRE. And now for me.

"Clitandre, whom you mention, and who so pesters me with his saccharine speeches, is the last man on earth for 60 whom I could feel any affection. He is quite mad to suppose that I love him, and so are you, to doubt that you are loved. Do come to your senses; exchange your sup-

The Court Theatre production of *The Misanthrope.* Left to right: Ann Dowd, John Mahoney, Joe Lauck, Sam Tsoutsouvas, Wanda Bimson, Richard Gilbert-Hill, George Tynan, and Maureen Gallagher. (Photograph by Dawn Murray.)

positions for his; and visit me as often as possible, to help
65 me bear the annoyance of his unwelcome attentions."

It's sweet character that these letters show,
And what to call it, Madam, you well know.
Enough. We're off to make the world acquainted
With this sublime self-portrait that you've painted.
70 ACASTE. Madam I'll make no farewell oration;
No, you're not worthy of my indignation.
Far choicer hearts than yours, as you'll discover,
Would like this little Marquess for a lover.

SCENE 5

[*Célimène, Éliante, Arsinoé, Alceste, Oronte, Philinte*]

ORONTE. So! After all those loving letters you wrote,
You turn on me like this and cut my throat!
And your dissembling faithless heart, I find,
Has pledged itself by turns to all mankind!
5 How blind I've been! But now I clearly see;
I thank you, Madam, for enlightening me.
My heart is mine once more, and I'm content;
The loss of it shall be your punishment.
(*To Alceste.*) Sir, she is yours; I'll seek no more to stand
10 Between your wishes and this lady's hand.

SCENE 6

[*Célimène, Éliante, Arsinoé, Alceste, Philinte*]

ARSINOÉ (*to Célimène*). Madam I'm forced to speak. I'm far too stirred
To keep my counsel after what I've heard.
I'm shocked and staggered by your want of morals.
It's not my way to mix in others' quarrels;
5 But really, when this fine and noble spirit,
This man of honor and surpassing merit,
Laid down the offering of his heart before you,
How *could* you . . .
ALCESTE. Madam, permit me, I implore you,
To represent myself in this debate.
10 Don't bother, please, to be my advocate.
My heart, in any case, could not afford
To give your services their due reward;
And if I chose, for consolation's sake,
Some other lady, 'twould not be you I'd take.
ARSINOÉ. What makes you think you could, Sir? And
15 how dare you
Imply that I've been trying to ensnare you?
If you can for a moment entertain
Such flattering fancies, you're extremely vain.
I'm not so interested as you suppose
20 In Célimène's discarded gigolos.
Get rid of that absurd illusion, do.
Women like me are not for such as you.
Stay with this creature, to whom you're so attached;
I've never seen two people better matched.

SCENE 7

[*Célimène, Éliante, Alceste, Philinte*]

ALCESTE (*to Célimène*). Well, I've been still throughout this exposé,
Till everyone but me has said his say.
Come, have I shown sufficient self-restraint?
And may I now...
CÉLIMÈNE. Yes, make your just complaint.
Reproach me freely, call me what you will; 5
You've every right to say I've used you ill.
I've wronged you, I confess it; and in my shame
I'll make no effort to escape the blame.
The anger of those others I could despise;
My guilt toward you I sadly recognize. 10
Your wrath is wholly justified, I fear;
I know how culpable I must appear,
I know all things bespeak my treachery,
And that, in short, you've grounds for hating me.
Do so; I give you leave.
ALCESTE. Ah, traitress—how, 15
How should I cease to love you, even now?
Though mind and will were passionately bent
On hating you, my heart would not consent.
(*To Éliante and Philinte.*) Be witness to my madness, both of you;
See what infatuation drives one to; 20
But wait; my folly's only just begun,
And I shall prove to you before I'm done
How strange the human heart is, and how far
From rational we sorry creatures are.
(*To Célimène.*) Woman, I'm willing to forget your shame, 25
And clothe your treacheries in a sweeter name;
I'll call them youthful errors, instead of crimes,
And lay the blame on these corrupting times.
My one condition is that you agree
To share my chosen fate, and fly with me 30
To that wild, trackless, solitary place
In which I shall forget the human race.
Only by such a course can you atone
For those atrocious letters; by that alone
Can you remove my present horror of you, 35
And make it possible for me to love you.
CÉLIMÈNE. What! *I* renounce the world at my young age,
And die of boredom in some hermitage?
ALCESTE. Ah, if you really loved me as you ought,
You wouldn't give the world a moment's thought; 40
Must you have me, and all the world beside?

CÉLIMÈNE. Alas, at twenty one is terrified
Of solitude. I fear I lack the force
And depth of soul to take so stern a course.
45 But if my hand in marriage will content you,
Why, there's a plan which I might well consent to,
And . . .
ALCESTE. No, I detest you now. I could excuse
Everything else, but since you thus refuse
To love me wholly as a wife should do,
50 And see the world in me, as I in you,
Go! I reject your hand and disenthrall
My heart from your enchantments, once for all.

SCENE 8

[*Éliante, Alceste, Philinte*]

ALCESTE (*to Éliante*). Madam, your virtuous beauty has no peer;
Of all this world you only are sincere;
I've long esteemed you highly, as you know;
Permit me ever to esteem you so,
5 And if I do not now request your hand,
Forgive me, Madam, and try to understand.
I feel unworthy of it; I sense that fate
Does not intend me for the married state,
That I should do you wrong by offering you
My shattered heart's unhappy residue, 10
And that in short . . .
ÉLIANTE. Your argument's well taken:
Nor need you fear that I shall feel forsaken.
Were I to offer him this hand of mine,
Your friend Philinte, I think, would not decline.
PHILINTE. Ah, Madam, that's my heart's most cherished goal, 15
For which I'd gladly give my life and soul.
ALCESTE (*to Éliante and Philinte*). May you be true to all you now profess,
And so deserve unending happiness.
Meanwhile betrayed and wronged in everything,
I'll flee this bitter world where vice is king, 20
And seek some spot unpeopled and apart
Where I'll be free to have an honest heart.
PHILINTE. Come, Madam, let's do everything we can
To change the mind of this unhappy man.

TOPICS FOR DISCUSSION AND WRITING

1. Does Alceste want to win or lose his lawsuit? Why?
2. Alceste bases his claims on reason. Do you think his own tone is always reasonable? Is his love of Célimène reasonable?
3. Jean-Jacques Rousseau said (in 1758) that Alceste is a man "who detests the morals of his age . . . who precisely because he loves mankind, despises in them the wrong they inflict upon one another." In somewhat the same vein, Jean-Louis Barrault, who often performed the role of Alceste, said that Alceste "loved people too well. That was why he couldn't stand them as they were." How much evidence do you find of this love?
4. Evaluate François Mauriac's comment:

   In a world where a decent man . . . has so many reasons if not for protest, at least for examining his own conscience, Alceste only attacks the most harmless practices, those "lies" which do not take anyone in but which are necessary if social life is to go on at all. . . . In a world where injustice is rife, where crime is everywhere, he is up in arms against trivialities. He feels no horror for what is really horrible—beginning with himself. All his attacks are directed to things outside himself; he only compares himself with other people in order to demonstrate his own superiority.

5. Like King Lear, Alceste is greatly distressed at the discrepancy between reality and appearance, between what is said and what is believed or felt. But why—at least to some degree—does Alceste's distress strike you as funny?
6. Alceste scarcely appears in the third act. Is there any decline of interest? If not, why not? Is it reasonable to argue that Molière has not lost sight of the issues, that (for example) Acaste in 3.1 gives us something of Alceste and that Arsinoé in 3.5 gives us a sample of the outspokenness Alceste desires? Do you find Arsinoé's sincerity engaging?
7. What is the difference between Éliante's view of Alceste and Philinte's view? What do you think are the strengths and weaknesses of Philinte's speech on "philosophy" and "virtue" in 5.1.80–89?
8. Philinte's marriage to Éliante is in accord with the usual ending of comedy, but what is the dramatic relevance of Molière's emphasis on the unromantic aspects of the marriage?
9. If we grant that Alceste's sincerity is at least in part rooted in self-love, does it follow that an audience sees no validity in his indictment of society?

HENRIK IBSEN

A Doll's House

Translated by Michael Meyer

Henrik Ibsen (1828–1906) was born in Skien, Norway, of wealthy parents who soon after his birth lost their money. Ibsen worked as a pharmacist's apprentice, but at the age of 22 he had written his first play, a promising melodrama entitled *Cataline.* He engaged in theater work first in Norway and then in Denmark and Germany. By 1865 his plays had won him a state pension that enabled him to settle in Rome. After writing romantic, historic, and poetic plays, he turned to realistic drama with *The League of Youth* (1869). Among the major realistic "problem plays" are *A Doll's House* (1879), *Ghosts* (1881), and *An Enemy of the People* (1882). In *The Wild Duck* (1884) he moved toward a more symbolic tragic comedy, and his last plays, written in the nineties, are highly symbolic.

COMMENTARY

Before he was forty Ibsen had written two masterpieces of poetic drama, *Brand* (1866) and *Peer Gynt* (1867). But a few years later he came to feel, along with many others, that the future of dramatic literature was not in poetic language, but in language that closely resembled ordinary speech. He devoted his subsequent efforts to prose drama, and we find him, in his letters, occasionally prophesying that poetic drama has no future and warning his translators to avoid all expressions that depart from "everyday speech." In the 1870s and 1880s he wrote the so-called "problem plays" (including *A Doll's House, Ghosts,* and *An Enemy of the People*) that for the next 75 years made his name familiar to the English-speaking world. A problem play, or "play of ideas," or *pièce à thèse,* is concerned with some troublesome social institution, its author hoping to arouse the audience to do something about the problem (for example, to modify the divorce laws, to extend the ballot, to alter the tax structure). The more successful the play, the more it ensures its own demise, for when the social institutions have been altered and the problem has been solved, the play has no relevance to experience; it is merely a thing of historical importance, a museum curio. The violent reviews that *A Doll's House, Ghosts* and some of Ibsen's other plays engendered are evidence that more was at stake than aesthetic matters; discussions of the plays inevitably became discussions of divorce, venereal disease, incest, etc. Almost a century has passed, and readers have found that Ibsen has something more to offer than thoughts on how to improve society.

First of all, we have come to see that Ibsen's prose dramas, which he said were written in "the straightforward plain language spoken in daily life," are more than realistic copies of aspects of behavior. With Ibsen, realism often becomes a form of symbolism. Let's begin with the stage and its setting. When the curtain goes up on a performance

Sam Waterston as Helmer and Liv Ullmann as Nora in the 1975 production directed by Tormod Skagestad. (Photograph: The Joseph Abeles Collection.)

of *A Doll's House,* the audience sees "a comfortably and tastefully but not expensively furnished room." Additional details, such as "engravings on the walls," and "a small bookcase with leather-bound books," tell us much about the kind of people who live here. We shall learn more about these people when we see the clothes that they wear and hear the words that they speak, but even now—from seeing their living room—we know that they are people who hold the conventional middle-class values. The leather-bound books in the bookcase, for example, are more for show than for reading.

In some plays there are several sets—sometimes in sharp contrast—but in *A Doll's House* there is only one set, and perhaps we come to feel that this omnipresent room is a sort of prison that stifles its inhabitants or, as the title of the play implies, that this room keeps its inhabitants at a distance from the realities of life. At the end of the play, Nora escapes from this box and enters the real world. We might look, too, at the ways in which some of the furniture and the properties work in the play. Very early, when Torvald begins to lecture Nora about incurring debts, she "goes over towards the stove." It is scarcely too subtle to conclude that she is seeking a place of warmth or security when confronted by Torvald's chilling words. We may not *consciously* come to this conclusion, but that doesn't matter. Indeed, later in this act, Torvald, sitting near the stove, says quite naturally, "Ah, how cozy and peaceful it is here."

Or consider the use Ibsen makes of the Christmas tree. In Act 1, when Nora's world is still relatively undisturbed, the tree, adorned with candles and flowers, is in the center of the stage. By the end of this act Nora is terrified, and when the curtain goes up for the second act, we see the tree thrust into a corner, "stripped and disheveled," with burnt-down candles. Again, we may not consciously concede that Ibsen, through the tree, is telling us something about Nora, but surely the tree—at first gay, then forlorn—somehow has an impact on us.

Speaking of candles, or of lighting, in the second act a stage direction tells us, as Nora's terror grows, "During the following scene, it begins to grow dark." Later in the scene, when Dr. Rank confesses he loves Nora and thereby adds to her confusion, Nora seeks to regain her composure by ordering the maid to bring in a lamp—a natural desire, given her sense that she is threatened sexually, but also a symbol of illumination, for now the secret is out in the open. Finally, in the last act, when Nora forcefully explains to Torvald that she now sees things clearly, they are sitting on opposite sides of a table with a lighted lamp on it.

The costumes, too, tell us a good deal, In the first act Nora wears ordinary clothing, but in the middle of the second act she puts on a long, "multi-colored shawl" when she frantically rehearses her tarantella. The shawl, of course, is supposed to be appropriate to the Italian dance, but surely its multitude of colors also helps to express Nora's conflicting emotions, her near hysteria, expressed too in the fact that "her hair works loose and falls over her shoulders," but "she ignores it." The shawl and her disheveled hair, then, *speak* to us as clearly as the dialogue does.

In the middle of the third act, after the party and just before the showdown, Nora appears in her "Italian costume," and Helmer wears "evening dress" under an open black cloak. She is dressed for a masquerade (her whole life has been a masquerade, it turns out), and Torvald's formal suit and black cloak help to express the stiffness and the blight that have forced her to present a false front throughout their years of marriage. A little later, after Nora sees that she has never really known her husband for the selfish creature he is, she leaves the stage, and when she returns she is in street clothes. The pretense is over. She is no longer Torvald's "doll." When she finally leaves the stage—leaving the house—she puts on her shawl. This is not the many-colored shawl she used in rehearsing the dance, but the "large, black shawl" she wears when she returns from the dance. The blackness of this shawl helps to express the death of her old way of life; Nora is now aware that life is not a play.

Gestures, like costumes, are part of Ibsen's dramatic language. Helmer playfully pulls Nora's ear, showing his affection—and his power; Nora claps her hands; Mrs Linde (an old friend of Nora's) tries to read but is unable to concentrate, and so forth. All such gestures clearly and naturally convey states of mind. One of the most delightful and revealing gestures in the play occurs when, in the third act, Helmer demonstrates to Mrs. Linde the ugliness of knitting ("Look—arms all huddled up") and the elegance of embroidering ("you take the needle in your right hand and go in and out in a slow, easy movement—like this"). None of his absurd remarks throughout the play is quite so revealing of his absurdity as is this silly demonstration.

Like the setting, the costumes, and the gestures, the sound effects in a play are important. Footsteps on stairs, or the swish and slight thud of a letter dropping into a mailbox on the door, can have an electrifying effect. In *A Doll's House* the music of the tarantella communicates Nora's frenzy, but the most famous sound effect is reserved for the very end of the play, when Nora walks out on Helmer: "The street door is slammed shut downstairs."

What does the play add up to? Before we try to answer such a question, it may be useful to mention that Ibsen actually knew a woman who had forged a check to pay for a trip that her husband's health required. When the husband learned the truth, he turned on her and had her committed to an asylum, though later, for the sake of their children, he allowed her to return to their home. This episode apparently set Ibsen thinking, and when he set to work on *A Doll's House* he jotted down some "Notes for a Modern Tragedy":

> There are two kinds of moral law, two kinds of conscience, one in man and a completely different one in woman. They do not understand each other; but in matters of practical living the woman is judged by man's law, as if she were not a woman but a man.
>
> The wife in the play ends up quite bewildered and not knowing right from wrong; her natural instincts on the one side and her faith in authority on the other leave her completely confused.

Of course, Ibsen probably began by thinking about the real woman who forged a check to pay for the trip to save her sick husband, but the passage just quoted is the earliest writing relevant to the play. As Ibsen worked on the play, he (not surprisingly) produced characters and a plot that have a life of their own; but even if they depart from his preliminary note, these characters and this plot add up to something. (A *plot* is what happens; a *theme* is what the happenings add up to.) Some readers see in *A Doll's House* a play about a woman's place in a man's world, or a play about women's rights, but Ibsen himself (years after writing the play) said he had a larger theme: "I am not even sure what women's rights really are. To me it has been a question of human rights." Certainly the play deals, as Ibsen implies, with the enslavement of one person by another. At last Torvald dimly seems to recognize that Nora is a human being, not a doll; and Nora perceives that such a recognition could lead to "a true marriage."

HENRIK IBSEN *A Doll's House*

List of Characters

TORVALD HELMER, *a lawyer*
NORA, *his wife*
DR. RANK
MRS. LINDE
NILS KROGSTAD, *also a lawyer*
THE HELMERS' THREE SMALL CHILDREN
ANNE-MARIE, *their nurse*
HELEN, *the maid*
A PORTER

Scene: The action takes place in the Helmers' apartment.

ACT 1

A comfortably and tastefully, but not expensively furnished room. Backstage right a door leads out to the hall; backstage left, another door to Helmer's study. Between these two doors stands a piano. In the middle of the left-hand wall is a door, with a window downstage of it. Near the window, a round table with armchairs and a small sofa. In the right-hand wall, slightly upstage, is a door; downstage of this, against the same wall, a stove lined with porcelain tiles, with a couple of armchairs and a rocking-chair in front of it. Between the stove and the side door is a small table. Engravings on the wall. A what-not with china and other bric-a-brac; a small bookcase with leather-bound books. A carpet on the floor; a fire in the stove. A winter day.

A bell rings in the hall outside. After a moment we hear the front door being opened. Nora enters the room, humming contentedly to herself. She is wearing outdoor clothes and carrying a lot of parcels, which she puts down on the table right. She leaves the door to the hall open; through it, we can see a Porter carrying a Christmas tree and a basket. He gives these to the Maid, who has opened the door for them.

NORA. Hide that Christmas tree away, Helen. The children mustn't see it before I've decorated it this evening. (*To the Porter, taking out her purse.*) How much—?

PORTER. A shilling.

NORA. Here's half a crown. No, keep it.

The Porter touches his cap and goes. Nora closes the door. She continues to laugh happily to herself as she removes her coat, etc. She takes from her pocket a bag containing macaroons and eats a couple. Then she tiptoes across and listens at her husband's door.

NORA. Yes, he's here. (*Starts humming again as she goes over to the table, right.*)

HELMER (*from his room*). Is that my skylark twittering out there?

NORA (*opening some of the parcels*). It is!

HELMER. Is that my squirrel rustling?

NORA. Yes!

HELMER. When did my squirrel come home?

NORA. Just now. (*Pops the bag of macaroons in her pocket and wipes her mouth.*) Come out here, Torvald, and see what I've bought.

HELMER. You mustn't disturb me! (*Short pause; then he opens the door and looks in, his pen in his hand.*) Bought, did you say? All that? Has my little squanderbird been overspending again?

NORA. Oh, Torvald, surely we can let ourselves go a little this year! It's the first Christmas we don't have to scrape.

HELMER. Well, you know, we can't afford to be extravagant.

NORA. Oh yes, Torvald, we can be a little extravagant now. Can't we? Just a tiny bit? You've got a big salary now, and you're going to make lots and lots of money.

HELMER. Next year, yes. But my new salary doesn't start till April.

NORA. Pooh; we can borrow till then.

HELMER. Nora! (*Goes over to her and takes her playfully by the ear.*) What a little spendthrift you are! Suppose I were to borrow fifty pounds today, and you spent it all over Christmas, and then on New Year's Eve a tile fell off a roof on to my head—

NORA (*puts her hand over his mouth*). Oh, Torvald! Don't say such dreadful things!

HELMER. Yes, but suppose something like that did happen? What then?

NORA. If anything as frightful as that happened, it wouldn't make much difference whether I was in debt or not.

HELMER. But what about the people I'd borrowed from?

NORA. Them? Who cares about them? They're strangers.

HELMER. Oh, Nora, Nora, how like a woman! No, but seriously, Nora, you know how I feel about this. No debts! Never borrow! A home that is founded on debts can never be a place of freedom and beauty. We two have stuck it out bravely up to now; and we shall continue to do so for the short time we still have to.

NORA (*goes over towards the stove*). Very well, Torvald. As you say.

HELMER (*follows her*). Now, now! My little songbird mustn't droop her wings. What's this? Is little squirrel sulking? (*Takes out his purse.*) Nora; guess what I've got here!

NORA (*turns quickly*). Money!

HELMER. Look. (*Hands her some banknotes.*) I know how these small expenses crop up at Christmas.

NORA (*counts them*). One—two—three—four. Oh, thank you, Torvald, thank you! I should be able to manage with this.

HELMER. You'll have to.

NORA. Yes, yes, of course I will. But come over here, I want to show you everything I've bought. And so cheaply! Look, here are new clothes for Ivar—and a sword. And a horse and a trumpet for Bob. And a doll and a cradle for Emmy—they're nothing much, but she'll pull them apart in a few days. And some bits of material and handkerchiefs for the maids. Old Anne-Marie ought to have had something better, really.

HELMER. And what's in that parcel?

NORA (*cries*). No, Torvald, you mustn't see that before this evening!

HELMER. Very well. But now, tell me, you little spendthrift, what do you want for Christmas?

NORA. Me? Oh, pooh, I don't want anything.

HELMER. Oh, yes, you do. Now tell me, what, within reason, would you most like?

NORA. No, I really don't know. Oh, yes—Torvald —!

HELMER. Well?

NORA (*plays with his coat-buttons; not looking at him*). If you really want to give me something, you could—you could—

HELMER. Come on, out with it.

NORA (*quickly*). You could give me money, Torvald. Only as much as you feel you can afford; then later I'll buy something with it.

HELMER. But, Nora —

NORA. Oh yes, Torvald dear, please! Please! Then I'll wrap up the notes in pretty gold paper and hang them on the Christmas tree. Wouldn't that be fun?

HELMER. What's the name of that little bird that can never keep any money?

NORA. Yes, yes, squanderbird; I know. But let's do as I say, Torvald; then I'll have time to think about what I need most. Isn't that the best way? Mm?

HELMER (*smiles*). To be sure it would be, if you could keep what I give you and really buy yourself something with it. But you'll spend it on all sorts of useless things for the house, and then I'll have to put my hand in my pocket again.

NORA. Oh, but Torvald —

HELMER. You can't deny it, Nora dear. (*Puts his arm round her waist.*) The squanderbird's a pretty little creature, but she gets through an awful lot of money. It's incredible what an expensive pet she is for a man to keep.

NORA. For shame! How can you say such a thing? I save every penny I can.

HELMER (*laughs*). That's quite true. Every penny you can. But you can't.

NORA (*hums and smiles, quietly gleeful*). Hm. If you only knew how many expenses we larks and squirrels have, Torvald.

HELMER. You're a funny little creature. Just like your father used to be. Always on the look-out for some way to get money, but as soon as you have any it just runs through your fingers, and you never know where it's gone. Well, I suppose I must take you as you are. It's in your blood. Yes, yes, yes, these things are hereditary, Nora.

NORA. Oh, I wish I'd inherited more of Papa's qualities.

HELMER. And I wouldn't wish my darling little songbird to be any different from what she is. By the way, that reminds me. You look awfully—how shall put it?—awfully guilty today.

NORA. Do I?

HELMER. Yes, you do. Look me in the eyes.

NORA (*looks at him*). Well?

HELMER (*wags his finger*). Has my little sweet-tooth been indulging herself in town today, by any chance?

NORA. No, how can you think such a thing?

HELMER. Not a tiny little digression into a pastry shop?

NORA. No, Torvald, I promise —

HELMER. Not just a wee jam tart?

NORA. Certainly not.

HELMER. Not a little nibble at a macaroon?

NORA. No, Torvald—I promise you, honestly—

HELMER. There, there. I was only joking.

NORA (*goes over to the table, right*). You know I could never act against your wishes.

HELMER. Of course not. And you've given me your word— (*Goes over to her.*) Well, my beloved Nora, you keep your little Christmas secrets to yourself. They'll be revealed this evening, I've no doubt, once the Christmas tree has been lit.

NORA. Have you remembered to invite Dr. Rank?

HELMER. No. But there's no need; he knows he'll be dining with us. Anyway, I'll ask him when he comes this morning. I've ordered some good wine. Oh, Nora, you can't imagine how I'm looking forward to this evening.

NORA. So am I. And, Torvald, how the children will love it!

HELMER. Yes, it's a wonderful thing to know that one's position is assured and that one has an ample income. Don't you agree? It's good to know that, isn't it?

NORA. Yes, it's almost like a miracle.

HELMER. Do you remember last Christmas? For three whole weeks you shut yourself away every evening to make flowers for the Christmas tree, and all those other things you were going to surprise us with. Ugh, it was the most boring time I've ever had in my life.

NORA. I didn't find it boring.

HELMER (*smiles*). But it all came to nothing in the end, didn't it?

NORA. Oh, are you going to bring that up again? How could I help the cat getting in and tearing everything to bits?

HELMER. No, my poor little Nora, of course you couldn't. You simply wanted to make us happy, and that's all that matters. But it's good that those hard times are past.

NORA. Yes, it's wonderful.

HELMER. I don't have to sit by myself and be bored. And you don't have to tire your pretty eyes and your delicate little hands—

NORA (*claps her hands*). No, Torvald, that's true, isn't it—I don't have to any longer? Oh, it's really all just like a miracle. (*Takes his arm.*) Now, I'm going to tell you what I thought we might do, Torvald. As soon as Christmas is over— (*A bell rings in the hall.*) Oh, there's the doorbell. (*Tidies up one or two things in the room.*) Someone's coming. What a bore.

HELMER. I'm not at home to any visitors. Remember!

MAID (*in the doorway*). A lady's called, madam. A stranger.

NORA. Well, ask her to come in.

MAID. And the doctor's here too, sir.

HELMER. Has he gone to my room?

MAID. Yes, sir.

Helmer goes into his room. The Maid shows in Mrs. Linde, who is dressed in traveling clothes, and closes the door.

MRS. LINDE (*shyly and a little hesitantly*). Good evening, Nora.

NORA (*uncertainly*). Good evening—

MRS. LINDE. I don't suppose you recognize me.

NORA. No, I'm afraid I—Yes, wait a minute—surely— (*Exclaims.*) Why, Christine! Is it really you?

MRS. LINDE. Yes, it's me.

NORA. Christine! And I didn't recognize you! But how could I—? (*More quietly.*) How you've changed, Christine!

MRS. LINDE. Yes, I know. It's been nine years—nearly ten—

NORA. Is it so long? Yes, it must be. Oh, these last eight years have been such a happy time for me! So you've come to town? All that way in winter! How brave of you!

MRS. LINDE. I arrived by the steamer this morning.

NORA. Yes, of course—to enjoy yourself over Christmas. Oh, how splendid! We'll have to celebrate! But take off your coat. You're not cold, are you? (*Helps her off with it.*) There! Now let's sit down here by the stove and be comfortable. No, you take the armchair. I'll sit here in the rocking-chair. (*Clasps Mrs. Linde's hands.*) Yes, now you look like your old self. It was just at first that—you've got a little paler, though, Christine. And perhaps a bit thinner.

MRS. LINDE. And older, Nora. Much, much older.

NORA. Yes, perhaps a little older. Just a tiny bit. Not much. (*Checks herself suddenly and says earnestly.*) Oh, but how thoughtless of me to sit here and chatter away like this! Dear, sweet Christine, can you forgive me?

MRS. LINDE. What do you mean, Nora?

NORA (*quietly*). Poor Christine, you've become a widow.

MRS. LINDE. Yes. Three years ago.

NORA. I know, I know—I read it in the papers. Oh, Christine, I meant to write to you so often, honestly. But I always put it off, and something else always cropped up.

MRS. LINDE. I understand, Nora dear.

NORA. No, Christine, it was beastly of me. Oh, my poor darling, what you've gone through! And he didn't leave you anything?

MRS. LINDE. No.

NORA. No children, either?

MRS. LINDE. No.

NORA. Nothing at all, then?

MRS. LINDE. Not even a feeling of loss or sorrow.

NORA (*looks incredulously at her*). But, Christine, how is that possible?

MRS. LINDE (*smiles sadly and strokes Nora's hair*). Oh, these things happen, Nora.

NORA. All alone. How dreadful that must be for you. I've three lovely children. I'm afraid you can't see them now, because they're out with nanny. But you must tell me everything—

MRS. LINDE. No, no, no. I want to hear about you.

NORA. No, you start. I'm not going to be selfish today, I'm just going to think about you. Oh, but there's one thing I *must* tell you. Have you heard of the wonderful luck we've just had?

MRS. LINDE. No. What?

NORA. Would you believe it—my husband's just been made manager of the bank!

MRS. LINDE. Your husband? Oh, how lucky—!

NORA. Yes, isn't it? Being a lawyer is so uncertain, you know, especially if one isn't prepared to touch any case that isn't—well—quite nice. And of course Torvald's been very firm about that—and I'm absolutely with him. Oh, you can imagine how happy we are! He's joining the bank in the New Year, and he'll be getting a big salary, and lots of percentages too. From now on we'll be able to live quite differently—we'll be able to do whatever we want. Oh, Christine, it's such a relief! I feel so happy! Well, I mean, it's lovely to have heaps of money and not to have to worry about anything. Don't you think?

MRS. LINDE. It must be lovely to have enough to cover one's needs, anyway.

NORA. Not just our needs! We're going to have heaps and heaps of money!

MRS. LINDE (*smiles*). Nora, Nora, haven't you grown up yet? When we were at school you were a terrible little spendthrift.

NORA (*laughs quietly*). Yes, Torvald still says that. (*Wags her finger.*) But "Nora, Nora" isn't as silly as you think. Oh, we've been in no position for me to waste money. We've both had to work.

MRS. LINDE. You too?

NORA. Yes, little things—fancy work, crocheting, embroidery and so forth. (*Casually.*) And other things too. I suppose you know Torvald left the Ministry when we got married? There were no prospects of promotion in his department, and of course he needed more money. But the first year he overworked himself quite dreadfully. He had to take on all sorts of extra jobs, and worked day and night. But it was too much for him, and he became frightfully ill. The doctors said he'd have to go to a warmer climate.

MRS. LINDE. Yes, you spent a whole year in Italy, didn't you?

NORA. Yes. It wasn't easy for me to get away, you know. I'd just had Ivar. But of course we had to do it. Oh, it was a marvelous trip! And it saved Torvald's life. But it cost an awful lot of money, Christine.

MRS. LINDE. I can imagine.

NORA. Two hundred and fifty pounds. That's a lot of money, you know.

MRS. LINDE. How lucky you had it.

NORA. Well, actually, we got it from my father.

MRS. LINDE. Oh, I see. Didn't he die just about that time?

NORA. Yes, Christine, just about then. Wasn't it dreadful, I couldn't go and look after him. I was expecting little Ivar any day. And then I had my poor Torvald to care for—we really didn't think he'd live. Dear, kind Papa! I never saw him again, Christine. Oh, it's the saddest thing that's happened to me since I got married.

MRS. LINDE. I know you were very fond of him. But you went to Italy—?

NORA. Yes. Well, we had the money, you see, and the doctors said we mustn't delay. So we went the month after Papa died.

MRS. LINDE. And your husband came back completely cured?

NORA. Fit as a fiddle!

MRS. LINDE. But—the doctor?

NORA. How do you mean?

MRS. LINDE. I thought the maid said that the gentleman who arrived with me was the doctor.

NORA. Oh yes, that's Doctor Rank, but he doesn't come because anyone's ill. He's our best friend, and he looks us up at least once every day. No, Torvald hasn't had a moment's illness since we went away. And the children are fit and healthy and so am I. (*Jumps up and claps her hands.*) Oh God, oh God, Christine, isn't it a wonderful thing to be alive and happy! Oh, but how beastly of me! I'm only talking about myself. (*Sits on a footstool and rests her arms on Mrs. Linde's knee.*) Oh, please don't be angry with me! Tell me, is it really true you didn't love your husband? Why did you marry him, then?

MRS. LINDE. Well, my mother was still alive; and she was helpless and bedridden. And I had my two little brothers to take care of. I didn't feel I could say no.

NORA. Yes, well, perhaps you're right. He was rich then, was he?

MRS. LINDE. Quite comfortably off, I believe. But his business was unsound, you see, Nora. When he died it went bankrupt, and there was nothing left.

NORA. What did you do?

MRS. LINDE. Well, I had to try to make ends meet somehow, so I started a little shop, and a little school, and anything else I could turn my hand to. These last three years have been just one endless slog for me, without a moment's rest. But now it's over, Nora. My poor dear mother doesn't need me any more; she's passed away. And the boys don't need me either; they've got jobs now and can look after themselves.

NORA. How relieved you must feel—

MRS. LINDE. No, Nora. Just unspeakably empty. No one to live for any more. (*Gets up restlessly.*) That's why I couldn't bear to stay out there any longer, cut off from the world. I thought it'd be easier to find some work here that will exercise and occupy my mind. If only I could get a regular job—office work of some kind—

NORA. Oh but, Christine, that's dreadfully exhausting; and you look practically finished already. It'd be much better for you if you could go away somewhere.

MRS. LINDE (*goes over to the window*). I have no Papa to pay for my holidays, Nora.

NORA (*gets up*). Oh, please don't be angry with me.

MRS. LINDE. My dear Nora, it's I who should ask you not to be angry. That's the worst thing about this kind of situation—it makes one so bitter. One has no one to work for; and yet one has to be continually sponging for jobs. One has to live; and so one becomes completely egocentric. When you told me about this luck you've just had with Torvald's new job—can you imagine?—I was happy not so much on your account, as on my own.

NORA. How do you mean? Oh, I understand. You mean Torvald might be able to do something for you?

MRS. LINDE. Yes, I was thinking that.

NORA. He will too, Christine. Just you leave it to me. I'll lead up to it so delicately, so delicately; I'll get him in the right mood. Oh, Christine, I do so want to help you.

MRS. LINDE. It's sweet of you to bother so much about me, Nora. Especially since you know so little of the worries and hardships of life.

NORA. I? You say *I* know little of—?

MRS. LINDE (*smiles*). Well, good heavens—those bits of fancy work of yours—well, really—! You're a child, Nora.

NORA (*tosses her head and walks across the room*). You shouldn't say that so patronizingly.

MRS. LINDE. Oh?

NORA. You're like the rest. You all think I'm incapable of getting down to anything serious—

MRS. LINDE. My dear—

NORA. You think I've never had any worries like the rest of you.

MRS. LINDE. Nora dear, you've just told me about all your difficulties—

NORA. Pooh—that! (*Quietly.*) I haven't told you about the big thing.

MRS. LINDE. What big thing? What do you mean?

NORA. You patronize me, Christine; but you shouldn't. You're proud that you've worked so long and so hard for your mother.

MRS. LINDE. I don't patronize anyone, Nora. But you're right—I am both proud and happy that I was able to make my mother's last months on earth comparatively easy.

NORA. And you're also proud of what you've done for your brothers.

MRS. LINDE. I think I have a right to be.

NORA. I think so too. But let me tell you something, Christine. I too have done something to be proud and happy about.

MRS. LINDE. I don't doubt it. But—how do you mean?

NORA. Speak quietly! Suppose Torvald should hear! He mustn't, at any price—no one must know, Christine—no one but you.

MRS. LINDE. But what is this?

NORA. Come over here. (*Pulls her down on to the sofa beside her.*) Yes, Christine—I too have done something to be happy and proud about. It was I who saved Torvald's life.

MRS. LINDE. Saved his—? How did you save it?

NORA. I told you about our trip to Italy. Torvald couldn't have lived if he hadn't managed to get down there—

MRS. LINDE. Yes, well—your father provided the money—

NORA (*smiles*). So Torvald and everyone else thinks. But—

MRS. LINDE. Yes?

NORA. Papa didn't give us a penny. It was I who found the money.

MRS. LINDE. You? All of it?

NORA. Two hundred and fifty pounds. What do you say to that?

MRS. LINDE. But Nora, how could you? Did you win a lottery or something?

NORA (*scornfully*). Lottery? (*Sniffs.*) What would there be to be proud of in that?

MRS. LINDE. But where did you get it from, then?

NORA (*hums and smiles secretively*). Hm; tra-la-la-la!

MRS. LINDE. You couldn't have borrowed it.

NORA. Oh? Why not?

MRS. LINDE. Well, a wife can't borrow money without her husband's consent.

NORA (*tosses her head*). Ah, but when a wife has a little business sense, and knows how to be clever—

MRS. LINDE. But Nora, I simply don't understand—

NORA. You don't have to. No one has said I borrowed the money. I could have got it in some other way. (*Throws herself back on the sofa.*) I could have got it from an admirer. When a girl's as pretty as I am—

MRS. LINDE. Nora, you're crazy!

NORA. You're dying of curiosity now, aren't you, Christine?

MRS. LINDE. Nora dear, you haven't done anything foolish?

NORA (*sits up again*). Is it foolish to save one's husband's life?

MRS. LINDE. I think it's foolish if without his knowledge you—

NORA. But the whole point was that he mustn't know! Great heavens, don't you see? He hadn't to know how dangerously ill he was. I was the one they told that his life was in danger and that only going to a warm climate could save him. Do you suppose I didn't try to think of other ways of getting him down there? I told him how wonderful it would be for me to go abroad like other young wives; I cried and prayed; I asked him to remember my condition, and said he ought to be nice and tender to me; and then I suggested he might quite easily borrow the money. But then he got almost angry with me, Christine. He said I was frivolous, and that it was his duty as a husband not to pander to my moods and caprices—I think that's what he called them. Well, well, I thought, you've got to be saved somehow. And then I thought of a way—

MRS. LINDE. But didn't your husband find out from your father that the money hadn't come from him?

NORA. No, never. Papa died just then. I'd thought of letting him into the plot and asking him not to tell. But since he was so ill—! And as things turned out, it didn't become necessary.

MRS. LINDE. And you've never told your husband about this?

NORA. For heaven's sake, no! What an idea! He's frightfully strict about such matters. And besides—he's so proud of being a *man*—it'd be so painful and humiliating for him to know that he owed anything to me. It'd completely wreck our relationship. This life we have built together would no longer exist.

MRS. LINDE. Will you never tell him?

NORA (*thoughtfully, half-smiling*). Yes—some time, perhaps. Years from now, when I'm no longer pretty. You mustn't laugh! I mean of course, when Torvald no longer loves me as he does now; when it no longer amuses him to see me dance and dress up and play the fool for him. Then it might be useful to have something up my sleeve. (*Breaks off.*) Stupid, stupid, stupid! That time will never come. Well, what do you think of my big secret, Christine? I'm not completely useless, am I? Mind you, all this has caused me a frightful lot of worry. It hasn't been easy for me to meet my obligations punctually. In case you don't know, in the world of business there are things called quarterly installments and interest, and they're a terrible problem to cope with. So I've had to scrape a little here and save a little there as best I can. I haven't been able to save much on the housekeeping money, because Torvald likes to live well; and I couldn't let the children go short of clothes—I couldn't take anything out of what he gives me for them. The poor little angels!

MRS. LINDE. So you've had to stint yourself, my poor Nora?

NORA. Of course. Well, after all, it was my problem. Whenever Torvald gave me money to buy myself new clothes, I never used more than half of it; and I always bought what was cheapest and plainest. Thank heaven anything suits me, so that Torvald's never noticed. But it made me a bit sad sometimes, because it's lovely to wear pretty clothes. Don't you think?

MRS. LINDE. Indeed it is.

NORA. And then I've found one or two other sources of income. Last winter I managed to get a lot of copying to do. So I shut myself away and wrote every evening, late into the night. Oh, I often got so tired, so tired. But it was great fun, though, sitting there working and earning money. It was almost like being a man.

MRS. LINDE. But how much have you managed to pay off like this?

NORA. Well, I can't say exactly. It's awfully difficult to keep an exact check on these kind of transactions. I only know I've paid everything I've managed to scrape together. Sometimes I really didn't know where to turn. (*Smiles.*) Then I'd sit here and imagine some rich old gentleman had fallen in love with me—

MRS. LINDE. What! What gentleman?

NORA. Silly! And that now he'd died and when they opened his will it said in big letters: "Everything I possess is to be paid forthwith to my beloved Mrs. Nora Helmer in cash."

MRS. LINDE. But, Nora dear, who was this gentleman?

NORA. Great heavens, don't you understand? There wasn't any old gentleman; he was just something I used to dream up as I sat here evening after evening wondering how on earth I could raise some money. But what does it matter? The old bore can stay imaginary as far as I'm concerned, because now I don't have to worry any longer! (*Jumps up.*) Oh, Christine, isn't it wonderful? I don't have to worry any more! No more troubles! I can play all day with the children, I can fill the house with pretty things, just the way Torvald likes. And, Christine, it'll soon be spring, and the air'll be fresh and the skies blue, —and then perhaps we'll be able to take a little trip somewhere. I shall be able to see the sea again. Oh, yes, yes, it's a wonderful thing to be alive and happy!

The bell rings in the hall.

MRS. LINDE (*gets up*). You've a visitor. Perhaps I'd better go.

NORA. No, stay. It won't be for me. It's someone for Torvald—

MAID (*in the door*). Excuse me, madam, a gentleman's called who says he wants to speak to the master. But I didn't know—seeing as the doctor's with him—

NORA. Who is this gentleman?

KROGSTAD (*in the doorway*). It's me, Mrs. Helmer.

Mrs. Linde starts, composes herself, and turns away to the window.

NORA (*takes a step toward him and whispers tensely*). You? What is it? What do you want to talk to my husband about?

KROGSTAD. Business—you might call it. I hold a

minor post in the bank, and I hear your husband is to become our new chief—

NORA. Oh—then it isn't—?

KROGSTAD. Pure business, Mrs. Helmer. Nothing more.

NORA. Well, you'll find him in his study.

Nods indifferently as she closes the hall door behind him. Then she walks across the room and sees to the stove.

MRS. LINDE. Nora, who was that man?

NORA. A lawyer called Krogstad.

MRS. LINDE. It was him, then.

NORA. Do you know that man?

MRS. LINDE. I used to know him—some years ago. He was a solicitor's clerk in our town, for a while.

NORA. Yes, of course, so he was.

MRS. LINDE. How he's changed!

NORA. He was very unhappily married, I believe.

MRS. LINDE. Is he a widower now?

NORA. Yes, with a lot of children. Ah, now it's alight.

She closes the door of the stove and moves the rocking-chair a little to one side.

MRS. LINDE. He does—various things now, I hear?

NORA. Does he? It's quite possible—I really don't know. But don't let's talk about business. It's so boring.

Dr. Rank enters from Helmer's study.

RANK (*still in the doorway*). No, no, my dear chap, don't see me out. I'll go and have a word with your wife. (*Closes the door and notices Mrs. Linde.*) Oh, I beg your pardon. I seem to be *de trop* here too.

NORA. Not in the least. (*Introduces them.*) Dr. Rank. Mrs. Linde.

RANK. Ah! A name I have often heard in this house. I believe I passed you on the stairs as I came up.

MRS. LINDE. Yes. Stairs tire me; I have to take them slowly.

RANK. Oh, have you hurt yourself?

MRS. LINDE. No, I'm just a little run down.

RANK. Ah, is that all? Then I take it you've come to town to cure yourself by a round of parties?

MRS. LINDE. I have come here to find work.

RANK. Is that an approved remedy for being run down?

MRS. LINDE. One has to live, Doctor.

RANK. Yes, people do seem to regard it as a necessity.

NORA. Oh, really, Dr. Rank. I bet you want to stay alive.

RANK. You bet I do. However miserable I sometimes feel, I still want to go on being tortured for as long as possible. It's the same with all my patients; and with people who are morally sick, too. There's a moral cripple in with Helmer at this very moment—

MRS. LINDE (*softly*). Oh!

NORA. Whom do you mean?

RANK. Oh, a lawyer fellow called Krogstad—you wouldn't know him. He's crippled all right; morally twisted. But even he started off by announcing, as though it were a matter of enormous importance, that he had to live.

NORA. Oh? What did he want to talk to Torvald about?

RANK. I haven't the faintest idea. All I heard was something about the bank.

NORA. I didn't know that Krog—that this man Krogstad had any connection with the bank

RANK. Yes, he's got some kind of job down there. (*To Mrs. Linde.*) I wonder if in your part of the world you too have a species of human being that spends its time fussing around trying to smell out moral corruption? And when they find a case they give him some nice, comfortable position so that they can keep a good watch on him. The healthy ones just have to lump it.

MRS. LINDE. But surely it's the sick who need care most?

RANK (*shrugs his shoulders*). Well, there we have it. It's that attitude that's turning human society into a hospital.

Nora, lost in her own thoughts, laughs half to herself and claps her hands.

RANK. Why are you laughing? Do you really know what society is?

NORA. What do I care about society? I think it's a bore. I was laughing at something else—something frightfully funny. Tell me, Dr. Rank—will everyone who works at the bank come under Torvald now?

RANK. Do you find that particularly funny?

NORA (*smiles and hums*). Never you mind! Never you mind! (*Walks around the room.*) Yes, I find it very amusing to think that we—I mean, Torvald—has obtained so much influence over so many people. (*Takes the paper bag from her pocket.*) Dr. Rank, would you like a small macaroon?

RANK. Macaroons! I say! I thought they were forbidden here.

NORA. Yes, well, these are some Christine gave me.

MRS. LINDE. What? I—?

NORA. All right, all right, don't get frightened. You weren't to know Torvald had forbidden them. He's afraid they'll ruin my teeth. But, dash it—for once—! Don't you agree, Dr. Rank? Here! (*Pops a macaroon into his mouth.*) You too, Christine. And I'll have one too. Just a little one. Two at the most. (*Begins to walk around again.*) Yes, now I feel really, really happy. Now there's just one thing in the world I'd really love to do.

RANK. Oh? And what is that?

NORA. Just something I'd love to say to Torvald.

RANK. Well, why don't you say it?

NORA. No, I daren't. It's too dreadful.

MRS. LINDE. Dreadful?

RANK. Well, then, you'd better not. But you can say it to us. What is it you'd so love to say to Torvald?

NORA. I've the most extraordinary longing to say: "Bloody hell!"

RANK. Are you mad?

MRS. LINDE. My dear Nora—!

RANK. Say it. Here he is.

NORA (*hiding the bag of macaroons*). Ssh! Ssh!

Helmer, with his overcoat on his arm and his hat in his hand, enters from his study.

NORA (*goes to meet him*). Well, Torvald dear, did you get rid of him?

HELMER. Yes, he's just gone.

NORA. May I introduce you—? This is Christine. She's just arrived in town.

HELMER. Christine—? Forgive me, but I don't think—

NORA. Mrs. Linde, Torvald dear. Christine Linde.

HELMER. Ah. A childhood friend of my wife's, I presume?

MRS. LINDE. Yes, we knew each other in earlier days.

NORA. And imagine, now she's traveled all this way to talk to you.

HELMER. Oh?

MRS. LINDE. Well, I didn't really—

NORA. You see, Christine's frightfully good at office work, and she's mad to come under some really clever man who can teach her even more than she knows already—

HELMER. Very sensible, madam.

NORA. So when she heard you'd become head of the bank—it was in her local paper—she came here as quickly as she could and—Torvald, you will, won't you? Do a little something to help Christine? For my sake?

HELMER. Well, that shouldn't be impossible. You are a widow, I take it, Mrs. Linde?

MRS. LINDE. Yes.

HELMER. And you have experience of office work?

MRS. LINDE. Yes, quite a bit.

HELMER. Well then, it's quite likely I may be able to find some job for you—

NORA (*claps her hands*). You see, you see!

HELMER. You've come at a lucky moment, Mrs. Linde.

MRS. LINDE. Oh, how can I ever thank you—?

HELMER. There's absolutely no need. (*Puts on his overcoat.*) But now I'm afraid I must ask you to excuse me—

RANK. Wait. I'll come with you.

He gets his fur coat from the hall and warms it at the stove.

NORA. Don't be long, Torvald dear.

HELMER. I'll only be an hour.

NORA. Are you going too, Christine?

MRS. LINDE (*puts on her outdoor clothes*). Yes, I must start to look round for a room.

HELMER. Then perhaps we can walk part of the way together.

NORA (*helps her*). It's such a nuisance we're so cramped here—I'm afraid we can't offer to—

MRS. LINDE. Oh, I wouldn't dream of it. Goodbye, Nora dear, and thanks for everything.

NORA. *Au revoir.* You'll be coming back this evening, of course. And you too, Dr. Rank. What? If you're well enough? Of course you'll be well enough. Wrap up warmly, though.

They go out, talking, into the hall. Children's voices are heard from the stairs.

NORA. Here they are! Here they are!

She runs out and opens the door. Anne-Marie, the nurse, enters with the children.

NORA. Come in, come in! (*Stoops down and kisses them.*) Oh, my sweet darlings—! Look at them, Christine! Aren't they beautiful?

RANK. Don't stand here chattering in this draught!

HELMER. Come, Mrs. Linde. This is for mothers only.

Dr. Rank, Helmer, and Mrs. Linde go down the stairs. The nurse brings the children into the room. Nora follows, and closes the door to the hall.

NORA. How well you look! What red cheeks you've got! Like apples and roses! (*The children answer her inaudibly as she talks to them.*) Have you had fun? That's splendid. You gave Emmy and Bob a ride on the sledge? What, both together? I say! What a clever boy you are, Ivar! Oh, let me hold her for a moment, Anne-Marie! My sweet little baby doll! (*Takes the smallest child from the nurse and dances with her.*) Yes, yes, Mummy will dance with Bob too. What? Have you been throwing snowballs? Oh, I wish I'd been there! No, don't—I'll undress them myself, Anne-Marie. No, please let me; it's such fun. Go inside and warm yourself; you look frozen. There's some hot coffee on the stove. (*The nurse goes into the room on the left. Nora takes off the children's outdoor clothes and throws them anywhere while they all chatter simultaneously.*) What? A big dog ran after you? But he didn't bite you? No, dogs don't bite lovely little baby dolls. Leave those parcels alone, Ivar. What's in them? Ah, wouldn't you like to know! No, no; it's nothing nice. Come on, let's play a game. What shall we play? Hide and seek. Yes, let's play hide and seek. Bob shall hide first. You want me to? All right, let me hide first.

Nora and the children play around the room, and in the adjacent room to the left, laughing and shouting. At length Nora hides under the table. The children rush in, look, but cannot find her. Then they hear her half-stifled laughter, run to the table, lift up the cloth, and see her. Great excitement. She crawls out as though to frighten them. Further excitement. Meanwhile, there has been a knock on the door leading from the hall, but no one has noticed it. Now the door is half-opened and Krogstad enters. He waits for a moment; the game continues.

KROGSTAD. Excuse me, Mrs. Helmer—

NORA (*turns with a stifled cry and half jumps up*). Oh! What do you want?

KROGSTAD. I beg your pardon; the front door was ajar. Someone must have forgotten to close it.

NORA (*gets up*). My husband is not at home, Mr. Krogstad.

KROGSTAD. I know.

NORA. Well, what do want here, then?

KROGSTAD. A word with you.

NORA. With—? (*To the children, quietly.*) Go inside to Anne-Marie. What? No, the strange gentleman won't do anything to hurt Mummy. When he's gone we'll start playing again.

She takes the children into the room on the left and closes the door behind them.

NORA (*uneasy, tense*). You want to speak to me?

KROGSTAD. Yes.

NORA. Today? But it's not the first of the month yet.

KROGSTAD. No, it is Christmas Eve. Whether or not you have a merry Christmas depends on you.

NORA. What do you want? I can't give you anything today—

KROGSTAD. We won't talk about that for the present. There's something else. You have a moment to spare?

NORA. Oh, yes. Yes, I suppose so; though—

KROGSTAD. Good. I was sitting in the café down below and I saw your husband cross the street—

NORA. Yes.

KROGSTAD. With a lady.

NORA. Well?

KROGSTAD. Might I be so bold as to ask: was not that lady a Mrs. Linde?

NORA. Yes.

KROGSTAD. Recently arrived in town?

NORA. Yes, today.

KROGSTAD. She is a good friend of yours, is she not?

NORA. Yes, she is. But I don't see—

KROGSTAD. I used to know her too once.

NORA. I know.

KROGSTAD. Oh? You've discovered that. Yes, I thought you would. Well then, may I ask you a straight question: is Mrs. Linde to be employed at the bank?

NORA. How dare you presume to cross-examine me, Mr. Krogstad? You, one of my husband's employees? But since you ask, you shall have an answer. Yes, Mrs. Linde is to be employed by the bank. And I arranged it, Mr. Krogstad. Now you know.

KROGSTAD. I guessed right, then.

NORA (*walks up and down the room*). Oh, one has a little influence, you know. Just because one's a woman it doesn't necessarily mean that— When one is in a humble position, Mr. Krogstad, one should think twice before offending someone who—hm—

KROGSTAD. —who has influence?

NORA. Precisely.

KROGSTAD (*changes his tone*). Mrs. Helmer, will you have the kindness to use your influence on my behalf?

NORA. What? What do you mean?

KROGSTAD. Will you be so good as to see that I keep my humble position at the bank?

NORA. What do you mean? Who is thinking of removing you from your position?

KROGSTAD. Oh, you don't need to play innocent with me. I realize it can't be very pleasant for your friend to risk bumping into me; and now I also realize whom I have to thank for being hounded out like this.

NORA. But I assure you—

KROGSTAD. Look, let's not beat about the bush. There's still time, and I'd advise you to use your influence to stop it.

NORA. But, Mr. Krogstad, I have no influence!

KROGSTAD. Oh? I thought you just said—

NORA. But I didn't mean it like that! I? How on earth could you imagine that I would have any influence over my husband?

KROGSTAD. Oh, I've known your husband since we were students together. I imagine he has his weaknesses like other married men.

NORA. If you speak impertinently of my husband, I shall show you the door.

KROGSTAD. You're a bold woman, Mrs. Helmer.

NORA. I'm not afraid of you any longer. Once the New Year is in, I'll soon be rid of you.

KROGSTAD (*more controlled*). Now listen to me, Mrs. Helmer. If I'm forced to, I shall fight for my little job at the bank as I would fight for my life.

NORA. So it sounds.

KROGSTAD. It isn't just the money; that's the last thing I care about. There's something else—well, you might as well know. It's like this, you see. You know of course, as everyone else does, that some years ago I committed an indiscretion.

NORA. I think I did hear something—

KROGSTAD. It never came into court; but from that day, every opening was barred to me. So I turned my hand to the kind of business you know about. I had to do something; and I don't think I was one of the worst. But now I want to give up all that. My sons are growing up; for their sake, I must try to regain what respectability I can. This job in the bank was the first step on the ladder. And now your husband wants to kick me off that ladder back into the dirt.

NORA. But my dear Mr. Krogstad, it simply isn't in my power to help you.

KROGSTAD. You say that because you don't want to help me. But I have the means to make you.

NORA. You don't mean you'd tell my husband that I owe you money?

KROGSTAD. And if I did?

NORA. That'd be a filthy trick! (*Almost in tears.*) This secret that is my pride and my joy—that he should hear about it in such a filthy, beastly way—hear about it from you! It'd involve me in the most dreadful unpleasantness—

KROGSTAD. Only—unpleasantness?

NORA (*vehemently*). All right, do it! You'll be the one who'll suffer. It'll show my husband the kind of man you are, and then you'll never keep your job.

KROGSTAD. I asked you whether it was merely domestic unpleasantness you were afraid of.

NORA. If my husband hears about it, he will of course immediately pay you whatever is owing. And then we shall have nothing more to do with you.

KROGSTAD (*takes a step closer*). Listen, Mrs. Helmer. Either you've a bad memory or else you know very little about financial transactions. I had better enlighten you.

NORA. What do you mean?

KROGSTAD. When your husband was ill, you came to me to borrow two hundred and fifty pounds.

NORA. I didn't know anyone else.

KROGSTAD. I promised to find that sum for you—

NORA. And you did find it.

KROGSTAD. I promised to find that sum for you on certain conditions. You were so worried about your husband's illness and so keen to get the money to take him abroad that I don't think you bothered much about the details. So it won't be out of place if I refresh your memory. Well—I promised to get you the money in exchange for an I.O.U., which I drew up.

NORA. Yes, and which I signed.

KROGSTAD. Exactly. But then I added a few lines naming your father as security for the debt. This paragraph was to be signed by your father.

NORA. Was to be? He did sign it.

KROGSTAD. I left the date blank for your father to fill in when he signed this paper. You remember, Mrs. Helmer?

NORA. Yes, I think so—

KROGSTAD. Then I gave you back this I.O.U. for you to post to your father. Is that not correct?

NORA. Yes.

KROGSTAD. And of course you posted it at once; for within five or six days you brought it along to me with your father's signature on it. Whereupon I handed you the money.

NORA. Yes, well. Haven't I repaid the installments as agreed?

KROGSTAD. Mm—yes, more or less. But to return to what we were speaking about—that was a difficult time for you just then, wasn't it, Mrs. Helmer?

NORA. Yes, it was.

KROGSTAD. And your father was very ill, if I am not mistaken.

NORA. He was dying.

KROGSTAD. He did in fact die shortly afterwards?

NORA. Yes.

KROGSTAD. Tell me, Mrs. Helmer, do you by any chance remember the date of your father's death? The day of the month, I mean.

NORA. Papa died on the twenty-ninth of September.

KROGSTAD. Quite correct; I took the trouble to confirm it. And that leaves me with a curious little problem—(*Takes out a paper.*)—which I simply cannot solve.

NORA. Problem? I don't see—

KROGSTAD. The problem, Mrs. Helmer, is that your father signed this paper three days after his death.

NORA. What? I don't understand—

KROGSTAD. Your father died on the twenty-ninth of September. But look at this. Here your father has dated his signature the second of October. Isn't that a curious little problem, Mrs. Helmer? (*Nora is silent.*) Can you suggest any explanation? (*She remains silent.*) And there's another curious thing. The words "second of October" and the year are written in a hand which is not your father's, but which I seem to know. Well, there's a simple explanation to that. Your father could have forgotten to write in the date when he signed, and someone else could have added it before the news came of his death. There's nothing criminal about that. It's the signature itself I'm wondering about. It *is* genuine, I suppose, Mrs. Helmer? It was your father who wrote his name here?

NORA (*after a short silence, throws back her head and looks defiantly at him*). No, it was not. It was I who wrote Papa's name there.

KROGSTAD. Look, Mrs. Helmer, do you realize this is a dangerous admission?

NORA. Why? You'll get your money.

KROGSTAD. May I ask you a question? Why didn't you send this paper to your father?

NORA. I couldn't. Papa was very ill. If I'd asked him to sign this, I'd have had to tell him what the money was for.

But I couldn't have told him in his condition that my husband's life was in danger. I couldn't have done that!

KROGSTAD. Then you would have been wiser to have given up your idea of a holiday.

NORA. But I couldn't! It was to save my husband's life. I couldn't put it off.

KROGSTAD. But didn't it occur to you that you were being dishonest towards me?

NORA. I couldn't bother about that. I didn't care about you. I hated you because of all the beastly difficulties you'd put in my way when you knew how dangerously ill my husband was.

KROGSTAD. Mrs. Helmer, you evidently don't appreciate exactly what you have done. But I can assure you that it is no bigger nor worse a crime than the one I once committed, and thereby ruined my whole social position.

NORA. You? Do you expect me to believe that you would have taken a risk like that to save your wife's life?

KROGSTAD. The law does not concern itself with motives.

NORA. Then the law must be very stupid.

KROGSTAD. Stupid or not, if I show this paper to the police, you will be judged according to it.

NORA. I don't believe that. Hasn't a daughter the right to shield her father from worry and anxiety when he's old and dying? Hasn't a wife the right to save her husband's life? I don't know much about the law, but there must be something somewhere that says that such things are allowed. You ought to know about that, you're meant to be a lawyer, aren't you? You can't be a very good lawyer, Mr. Krogstad.

KROGSTAD. Possibly not. But business, the kind of business we two have been transacting—I think you'll admit I understand something about that? Good. Do as you please. But I tell you this. If I get thrown into the gutter for a second time, I shall take you with me.

He bows and goes out through the hall.

NORA (*stands for a moment in thought, then tosses her head*). What nonsense! He's trying to frighten me! I'm not that stupid. (*Busies herself gathering together the children's clothes; then she suddenly stops.*) But—? No, it's impossible. I did it for love, didn't I?

CHILDREN (*in the doorway, left*). Mummy, the strange gentleman's gone out into the street.

NORA. Yes, yes, I know. But don't talk to anyone about the strange gentleman. You hear? Not even to Daddy.

CHILDREN. No, Mummy. Will you play with us again now?

NORA. No, no. Not now.

CHILDREN. Oh but, Mummy, you promised!

NORA. I know, but I can't just now. Go back to the nursery. I've a lot to do. Go away, my darlings, go away. (*She pushes them gently into the other room, and closes the door behind them. She sits on the sofa, takes up her embroidery, stitches for a few moments, but soon stops.*) No! (*Throws the embroidery aside, gets up, goes to the door leading to the hall, and calls.*) Helen! Bring in the Christmas tree! (*She goes to the table on the left and opens the drawer in it; then pauses again.*) No, but it's utterly impossible!

MAID (*enters with the tree*). Where shall I put it, madam?

NORA. There, in the middle of the room.

MAID. Will you be wanting anything else?

NORA. No, thank you, I have everything I need.

The maid puts down the tree and goes out.

NORA (*busy decorating the tree*). Now—candles here—and flowers here. That loathsome man! Nonsense, nonsense, there's nothing to be frightened about. The Christmas tree must be beautiful. I'll do everything that you like, Torvald. I'll sing for you, dance for you—

Helmer, with a bundle of papers under his arm, enters.

NORA. Oh—are you back already?

HELMER. Yes. Has anyone been here?

NORA. Here? No.

HELMER. That's strange. I saw Krogstad come out of the front door.

NORA. Did you? Oh yes, that's quite right—Krogstad was here for a few minutes.

HELMER. Nora, I can tell from your face, he's been here and asked you to put in a good word for him.

NORA. Yes.

HELMER. And you were to pretend you were doing it of your own accord? You weren't going to tell me he'd been here? He asked you to do that too, didn't he?

NORA. Yes, Torvald. But—

HELMER. Nora, Nora! And you were ready to enter into such a conspiracy? Talking to a man like that, and making him promises—and then, on top of it all, to tell me an untruth!

NORA. An untruth?

HELMER. Didn't you say no one had been here? (*Wags his finger.*) My little songbird must never do that again. A songbird must have a clean beak to sing with; otherwise she'll start twittering out of tune. (*Puts his arm round her waist.*) Isn't that the way we want things? Yes, of course it is. (*Lets go of her.*) So let's hear no more about that. (*Sits down in front of the stove.*) Ah, how cozy and peaceful it is here. (*Glances for a few moments at his papers.*)

NORA (*busy with the tree; after a short silence*). Torvald.

HELMER. Yes.

NORA. I'm terribly looking forward to that fancy dress ball at the Stenborgs on Boxing Day.

HELMER. And I'm terribly curious to see what you're going to surprise me with.

NORA. Oh, it's so maddening.

HELMER. What is?

NORA. I can't think of anything to wear. It all seems so stupid and meaningless.

HELMER. So my little Nora's come to that conclusion, has she?

NORA (*behind his chair, resting her arms on its back*). Are you very busy, Torvald?

HELMER. Oh—

NORA. What are those papers?

HELMER. Just something to do with the bank.

NORA. Already?

HELMER. I persuaded the trustees to give me authority to make certain immediate changes in the staff and organization. I want to have everything straight by the New Year.

NORA. Then that's why this poor man Krogstad—

HELMER. Hm.

NORA (*still leaning over his chair, slowly strokes the back of his head*). If you hadn't been so busy, I was going to ask you an enormous favour, Torvald.

HELMER. Well, tell me. What was it to be?

NORA. You know I trust your taste more than anyone's. I'm so anxious to look really beautiful at the fancy dress ball. Torvald, couldn't you help me to decide what I shall go as, and what kind of costume I ought to wear?

HELMER. Aha! So little Miss Independent's in trouble and needs a man to rescue her, does she?

NORA. Yes, Torvald. I can't get anywhere without your help.

HELMER. Well, well, I'll give the matter thought. We'll find something.

NORA. Oh, how kind of you! (*Goes back to the tree. Pause.*) How pretty these red flowers look! But, tell me, is it so dreadful, this thing that Krogstad's done?

HELMER. He forged someone else's name. Have you any idea what that means?

NORA. Mightn't he have been forced to do it by some emergency?

HELMER. He probably just didn't think—that's what usually happens. I'm not so heartless as to condemn a man for an isolated action.

NORA. No, Torvald, of course not!

HELMER. Men often succeed in reestablishing themselves if they admit their crime and take their punishment.

NORA. Punishment?

HELMER. But Krogstad didn't do that. He chose to try and trick his way out of it; and that's what has morally destroyed him.

NORA. You think that would—?

HELMER. Just think how a man with that load on his conscience must always be lying and cheating and dissembling; how he must wear a mask even in the presence of those who are dearest to him, even his own wife and children! Yes, the children. That's the worst danger, Nora.

NORA. Why?

HELMER. Because an atmosphere of lies contaminates and poisons every corner of the home. Every breath that the children draw in such a house contains the germs of evil.

NORA (*comes closer behind him*). Do you really believe that?

HELMER. Oh, my dear, I've come across it so often in my work at the bar. Nearly all young criminals are the children of mothers who are constitutional liars.

NORA. Why do you say mothers?

HELMER. It's usually the mother; though of course the father can have the same influence. Every lawyer knows that only too well. And yet this fellow Krogstad has been sitting at home all these years poisoning his children with his lies and pretenses. That's why I say that, morally speaking, he is dead. (*Stretches out his hands toward her.*) So my pretty little Nora must promise me not to plead his case. Your hand on it. Come, come, what's this? Give me your hand. There. That's settled, now. I assure you it'd be quite impossible for me to work in the same building as him. I literally feel physically ill in the presence of a man like that.

NORA (*draws her hand from his and goes over to the other side of the Christmas tree*). How hot it is in here! And I've so much to do.

HELMER (*gets up and gathers his papers*). Yes, and I must try to get some of this read before dinner. I'll think about your costume too. And I may even have something up my sleeve to hang in gold paper on the Christmas tree. (*Lays his hand on her head.*) My precious little songbird!

He goes into his study and closes the door.

NORA (*softly, after a pause*). It's nonsense. It must be. It's impossible. It *must* be impossible!

NURSE (*in the doorway, left*). The children are asking if they can come in to Mummy.

NORA. No, no, no; don't let them in! You stay with them, Anne-Marie.

NURSE. Very good, madam. (*Closes the door.*)

NORA (*pale with fear*). Corrupt my little children—! Poison my home! (*Short pause. She throws back her head.*) It isn't true! It *couldn't* be true!

ACT 2

The same room. In the corner by the piano the Christmas tree stands, stripped and disheveled, its candles burned to their sockets. Nora's outdoor clothes lie on the sofa. She is alone in the room, walking restlessly to and fro. At length she stops by the sofa and picks up her coat.

NORA (*drops the coat again*). There's someone coming! (*Goes to the door and listens.*) No, it's no one. Of course—no one'll come today, it's Christmas Day. Nor tomorrow. But perhaps—! (*Opens the door and looks out.*) No. Nothing in the letter-box. Quite empty. (*Walks across the room.*) Silly, silly. Of course he won't do anything. It couldn't happen. It isn't possible. Why, I've three small children.

The Nurse, carrying a large cardboard box, enters from the room on the left.

NURSE. I found those fancy dress clothes at last, madam.

NORA. Thank you. Put them on the table.

NURSE (*does so*). They're all rumpled up.

NORA. Oh, I wish I could tear them into a million pieces!

NURSE. Why, madam! They'll be all right. Just a little patience.

NORA. Yes, of course. I'll go and get Mrs. Linde to help me.

NURSE. What, out again? In this dreadful weather? You'll catch a chill, madam.

NORA. Well, that wouldn't be the worst. How are the children?

NURSE. Playing with their Christmas presents, poor little dears. But—

NORA. Are they still asking to see me?

NURSE. They're so used to having their Mummy with them.

NORA. Yes, but, Anne-Marie, from now on I shan't be able to spend so much time with them.

NURSE. Well, children get used to anything in time.

NORA. Do you think so? Do you think they'd forget their mother if she went away from them—for ever?

NURSE. Mercy's sake, madam! For ever!

NORA. Tell me, Anne-Marie—I've so often wondered. How could you bear to give your child away—to strangers?

NURSE. But I had to when I came to nurse my little Miss Nora.

NORA. Do you mean you wanted to?

NURSE. When I had the chance of such a good job? A poor girl what's got into trouble can't afford to pick and choose. That good-for-nothing didn't lift a finger.

NORA. But your daughter must have completely forgotten you.

NURSE. Oh no, indeed she hasn't. She's written to me twice, once when she got confirmed and then again when she got married.

NORA (*hugs her*). Dear old Anne-Marie, you were a good mother to me.

NURSE. Poor little Miss Nora, you never had any mother but me.

NORA. And if my little ones had no one else, I know you would—no, silly, silly, silly! (*Opens the cardboard box.*) Go back to them, Anne-Marie. Now I must—Tomorrow you'll see how pretty I shall look.

NURSE. Why, there'll be no one at the ball as beautiful as my Miss Nora.

She goes into the room, left.

NORA (*begins to unpack the clothes from the box, but soon throws them down again*). Oh, if only I dared to go out! If I could be sure no one would come, and nothing would happen while I was away! Stupid, stupid! No one will come. I just mustn't think about it. Brush this muff. Pretty gloves, pretty gloves! Don't think about it, don't think about it! One, two, three, four, five, six— (*Cries.*) Ah—they're coming—!

She begins to run toward the door, but stops uncertainly. Mrs. Linde enters from the hall where she has been taking off her outdoor clothes.

NORA. Oh, it's you, Christine. There's no one else out there, is there? Oh, I'm so glad you've come.

MRS. LINDE. I hear you were at my room asking for me.

NORA. Yes, I just happened to be passing. I want to ask you to help me with something. Let's sit down here on the sofa. Look at this. There's going to be a fancy dress ball tomorrow night upstairs at Consul Stenborg's, and Torvald wants me to go as a Neapolitan fisher-girl and dance the tarantella. I learned it on Capri.

MRS. LINDE. I say, are you going to give a performance?

NORA. Yes, Torvald says I should. Look, here's the dress. Torvald had it made for me in Italy; but now it's all so torn, I don't know—

MRS. LINDE. Oh, we'll soon put that right; the stitching's just come away. Needle and thread? Ah, here we are.

NORA. You're being awfully sweet.

MRS. LINDE (*sews*). So you're going to dress up tomorrow, Nora? I must pop over for a moment to see how you look. Oh, but I've completely forgotten to thank you for that nice evening yesterday.

NORA (*gets up and walks across the room*). Oh, I didn't think it was as nice as usual. You ought to have come to town a little earlier, Christine. . . . Yes, Torvald understands how to make a home look attractive.

MRS. LINDE. I'm sure you do, too. You're not your

father's daughter for nothing. But, tell me. Is Dr. Rank always in such low spirits as he was yesterday?

NORA. No, last night it was very noticeable. But he's got a terrible disease; he's got spinal tuberculosis, poor man. His father was a frightful creature who kept mistresses and so on. As a result Dr. Rank has been sickly ever since he was a child—you understand—

MRS. LINDE (*puts down her sewing*). But, my dear Nora, how on earth did you get to know about such things?

NORA (*walks about the room*). Oh, don't be silly, Christine—when one has three children, one comes into contact with women who—well, who know about medical matters, and they tell one a thing or two.

MRS. LINDE (*sews again; a short silence*). Does Dr. Rank visit you every day?

NORA. Yes, every day. He's Torvald's oldest friend, and a good friend to me too. Dr. Rank's almost one of the family.

MRS. LINDE. But, tell me—is he quite sincere? I mean, doesn't he rather say the sort of thing he thinks people want to hear?

NORA. No, quite the contrary. What gave you that idea?

MRS. LINDE. When you introduced me to him yesterday, he said he'd often heard my name mentioned here. But later I noticed your husband had no idea who I was. So how could Dr. Rank—?

NORA. Yes, that's quite right, Christine. You see, Torvald's so hopelessly in love with me that he wants to have me all to himself—those were his very words. When we were first married, he got quite jealous if I as much as mentioned any of my old friends back home. So naturally, I stopped talking about them. But I often chat with Dr. Rank about that kind of thing. He enjoys it, you see.

MRS. LINDE. Now listen, Nora. In many ways you're still a child; I'm a bit older than you and have a little more experience of the world. There's something I want to say to you. You ought to give up this business with Dr. Rank.

NORA. What business?

MRS. LINDE. Well, everything. Last night you were speaking about this rich admirer of yours who was going to give you money—

NORA. Yes, and who doesn't exist—unfortunately. But what's that got to do with—?

MRS. LINDE. Is Dr. Rank rich?

NORA. Yes.

MRS. LINDE. And he has no dependents?

NORA. No, no one. But—

MRS. LINDE. And he comes here to see you every day?

NORA. Yes, I've told you.

MRS. LINDE. But how dare a man of his education be so forward?

NORA. What on earth are you talking about?

MRS. LINDE. Oh, stop pretending, Nora. Do you think I haven't guessed who it was who lent you that two hundred pounds?

NORA. Are you out of your mind? How could you imagine such a thing? A friend, someone who comes here every day! Why, that'd be an impossible situation!

MRS. LINDE. Then it really wasn't him?

NORA. No, of course not. I've never for a moment dreamed of—anyway, he hadn't any money to lend then. He didn't come into that till later.

MRS. LINDE. Well, I think that was a lucky thing for you, Nora dear.

NORA. No, I could never have dreamed of asking Dr. Rank— Though I'm sure that if I ever did ask him—

MRS. LINDE. But of course you won't.

NORA. Of course not. I can't imagine that it should ever become necessary. But I'm perfectly sure that if I did speak to Dr. Rank—

MRS. LINDE. Behind your husband's back?

NORA. I've got to get out of this other business; and *that's* been going on behind his back. I've *got* to get out of it.

MRS. LINDE. Yes, well, that's what I told you yesterday. But—

NORA (*walking up and down*). It's much easier for a man to arrange these things than a woman—

MRS. LINDE. One's own husband, yes.

NORA. Oh, bosh. (*Stops walking.*) When you've completely repaid a debt, you get your I.O.U. back, don't you?

MRS. LINDE. Yes, of course.

NORA. And you can tear it into a thousand pieces and burn the filthy, beastly thing!

MRS. LINDE (*looks hard at her, puts down her sewing, and gets up slowly*). Nora, you're hiding something from me.

NORA. Can you see that?

MRS. LINDE. Something has happened since yesterday morning. Nora, what is it?

NORA (*goes toward her*). Christine! (*Listens.*) Ssh! There's Torvald. Would you mind going into the nursery for a few minutes? Torvald can't bear to see sewing around. Anne-Marie'll help you.

MRS. LINDE (*gathers some of her things together*). Very well. But I shan't leave this house until we've talked this matter out.

She goes into the nursery, left. As she does so, Helmer enters from the hall.

NORA (*runs to meet him*). Oh, Torvald dear, I've been so longing for you to come back!

HELMER. Was that the dressmaker?

NORA. No, it was Christine. She's helping me mend my costume. I'm going to look rather splendid in that.

HELMER. Yes, that was quite a bright idea of mine, wasn't it?

NORA. Wonderful! But wasn't it nice of me to give in to you?

HELMER (*takes her chin in his hand*). Nice—to give in to your husband? All right, little silly, I know you didn't mean it like that. But I won't disturb you. I expect you'll be wanting to try it on.

NORA. Are you going to work now?

HELMER. Yes. (*Shows her a bundle of papers.*) Look at these. I've been down to the bank— (*Turns to go into his study.*)

NORA. Torvald.

HELMER (*stops*). Yes.

NORA. If little squirrel asked you really prettily to grant her a wish—

HELMER. Well?

NORA. Would you grant it to her?

HELMER. First I should naturally have to know what it was.

NORA. Squirrel would do lots of pretty tricks for you if you granted her wish.

HELMER. Out with it, then.

NORA. Your little skylark would sing in every room—

HELMER. My little skylark does that already.

NORA. I'd turn myself into a little fairy and dance for you in the moonlight, Torvald.

HELMER. Nora, it isn't that business you were talking about this morning?

NORA (*comes closer*). Yes, Torvald—oh, please! I beg of you!

HELMER. Have you really the nerve to bring that up again?

NORA. Yes, Torvald, yes, you must do as I ask! You must let Krogstad keep his place at the bank!

HELMER. My dear Nora, his is the job I'm giving to Mrs. Linde.

NORA. Yes, that's terribly sweet of you. But you can get rid of one of the other clerks instead of Krogstad.

HELMER. Really, you're being incredibly obstinate. Just because you thoughtlessly promised to put in a word for him, you expect me to—

NORA. No, it isn't that, Helmer. It's for your own sake. That man writes for the most beastly newspapers—you said so yourself. He could do you tremendous harm. I'm so dreadfully frightened of him—

HELMER. Oh, I understand. Memories of the past. That's what's frightening you.

NORA. What do you mean?

HELMER. You're thinking of your father, aren't you?

NORA. Yes, yes. Of course. Just think what those dreadful men wrote in the papers about Papa! The most frightful slanders. I really believe it would have lost him his job if the Ministry hadn't sent you down to investigate, and you hadn't been so kind and helpful to him.

HELMER. But my dear little Nora, there's a considerable difference between your father and me. Your father was not a man of unassailable reputation. But I am; and I hope to remain so all my life.

NORA. But no one knows what spiteful people may not dig up. We could be so peaceful and happy now, Torvald—we could be free from every worry—you and I and the children. Oh, please, Torvald, please—!

HELMER. The very fact of your pleading his cause makes it impossible for me to keep him. Everyone at the bank already knows that I intend to dismiss Krogstad. If the rumor got about that the new manager had allowed his wife to persuade him to change his mind—

NORA. Well, what then?

HELMER. Oh, nothing, nothing. As long as my little Miss Obstinate gets her way— Do you expect me to make a laughing-stock of myself before my entire staff—give people the idea that I am open to outside influence? Believe me, I'd soon feel the consequences! Besides—there's something else that makes it impossible for Krogstad to remain in the bank while I am its manager.

NORA. What is that?

HELMER. I might conceivably have allowed myself to ignore his moral obloquies—

NORA. Yes, Torvald, surely?

HELMER. And I hear he's quite efficient at his job. But we—well, we were schoolfriends. It was one of those friendships that one enters into over-hastily and so often comes to regret later in life. I might as well confess the truth. We—well, we're on Christian name terms. And the tactless idiot makes no attempt to conceal it when other people are present. On the contrary, he thinks it gives him the right to be familiar with me. He shows off the whole time, with "Torvald this," and "Torvald that." I can tell you, I find it damned annoying. If he stayed, he'd make my position intolerable.

NORA. Torvald, you can't mean this seriously.

HELMER. Oh? And why not?

NORA. But it's so petty.

HELMER. What did you say? Petty? You think *I* am petty?

NORA. No, Torvald dear, of course you're not. That's just why—

HELMER. Don't quibble! You call my motives petty. Then I must be petty too. Petty! I see. Well, I've had enough of this. (*Goes to the door and calls into the hall.*) Helen!

NORA. What are you going to do?

HELMER (*searching among his papers*). I'm going to settle this matter once and for all. (*The Maid enters.*) Take this letter downstairs at once. Find a messenger and see that he delivers it. Immediately! The address is on the envelope. Here's the money.

MAID. Very good, sir. (*Goes out with the letter.*)

HELMER (*putting his papers in order*). There now, little Miss Obstinate.

NORA (*tensely*). Torvald—what was in that letter?

HELMER. Krogstad's dismissal.

NORA. Call her back, Torvald! There's still time. Oh, Torvald, call her back! Do it for my sake—for your own sake—for the children! Do you hear me, Torvald? Please do it! You don't realize what this may do to us all!

HELMER. Too late.

NORA. Yes. Too late.

HELMER. My dear Nora, I forgive you this anxiety. Though it is a bit of an insult to me. Oh, but it is! Isn't it an insult to imply that I should be frightened by the vindictiveness of a depraved hack journalist? But I forgive you, because it so charmingly testifies to the love you bear me. (*Takes her in his arms.*) Which is as it should be, my own dearest Nora. Let what will happen, happen. When the real crisis comes, you will not find me lacking in strength or courage. I am man enough to bear the burden for us both.

NORA (*fearfully*). What do you mean?

HELMER. The whole burden, I say—

NORA (*calmly*). I shall never let you do that.

HELMER. Very well. We shall share it, Nora—as man and wife. And that is as it should be. (*Caresses her.*) Are you happy now? There, there, there; don't look at me with those frightened little eyes. You're simply imagining things. You go ahead now and do your tarantella, and get some practice on that tambourine. I'll sit in my study and close the door. Then I won't hear anything, and you can make all the noise you want. (*Turns in the doorway.*) When Dr. Rank comes, tell him where to find me. (*He nods to her, goes into his room with his papers, and closes the door.*)

NORA (*desperate with anxiety, stands as though transfixed, and whispers*). He said he'd do it. He will do it. He will do it, and nothing'll stop him. No, never that. I'd rather anything. There must be some escape—Some way out—! (*The bell rings in the hall.*) Dr. Rank—! Anything but that! Anything, I don't care—!

She passes her hand across her face, composes herself, walks across, and opens the door to the hall. Dr. Rank is standing there, hanging up his fur coat. During the following scene, it begins to grow dark.

NORA. Good evening, Dr. Rank. I recognized your ring. But you mustn't go to Torvald yet. I think he's busy.

RANK. And—you?

NORA (*as he enters the room and she closes the door behind him*). Oh, you know very well I've always time to talk to you.

RANK. Thank you. I shall avail myself of that privilege as long as I can.

NORA. What do you mean by that? As long as you *can?*

RANK. Yes. Does that frighten you?

NORA. Well, it's rather a curious expression. Is something going to happen?

RANK. Something I've been expecting to happen for a long time. But I didn't think it would happen quite so soon.

NORA (*seizes his arm*). What is it? Dr. Rank, you must tell me!

RANK (*sits down by the stove*). I'm on the way out. And there's nothing to be done about it.

NORA (*sighs with relief*). Oh, it's you—?

RANK. Who else? No, it's no good lying to oneself. I am the most wretched of all my patients, Mrs. Helmer. These last few days I've been going through the books of this poor body of mine, and I find I am bankrupt. Within a month I may be rotting up there in the churchyard.

NORA. Ugh, what a nasty way to talk!

RANK. The facts aren't exactly nice. But the worst is that there's so much else that's nasty to come first. I've only one more test to make. When that's done I'll have a pretty accurate idea of when the final disintegration is likely to begin. I want to ask you a favour. Helmer's a sensitive chap, and I know how he hates anything ugly. I don't want him to visit me when I'm in hospital—

NORA. Oh but, Dr. Rank—

RANK. I don't want him there. On any pretext. I shan't have him allowed in. As soon as I know the worst, I'll send you my visiting card with a black cross on it, and then you'll know that the final filthy process has begun.

NORA. Really, you're being quite impossible this evening. And I did hope you'd be in a good mood.

RANK. With death on my hands? And all this to atone for someone else's sin? Is there justice in that? And in every single family, in one way or another, the same merciless law of retribution is at work—

NORA (*holds her hands to her ears*). Nonsense! Cheer up! Laugh!

RANK. Yes, you're right. Laughter's all the damned thing's fit for. My poor innocent spine must pay for the fun my father had as a gay young lieutenant.

NORA (*at the table, left*). You mean he was too fond of asparagus and *foie gras?*

RANK. Yes, and truffles too.

NORA. Yes, of course, truffles, yes. And oysters too, I suppose?

RANK. Yes, oysters, oysters. Of course.

NORA. And all that port and champagne to wash them down. It's too sad that all those lovely things should affect one's spine.

RANK. Especially a poor spine that never got any pleasure out of them.

NORA. Oh yes, that's the saddest thing of all.

RANK (*looks searchingly at her*). Hm—

NORA (*after a moment*). Why did you smile?

RANK. No, it was you who laughed.

NORA. No, it was you who smiled, Dr. Rank!

RANK (*gets up*). You're a worse little rogue than I thought.

NORA. Oh, I'm full of stupid tricks today.

RANK. So it seems.

NORA (*puts both her hands on his shoulders*). Dear, dear Dr. Rank, you mustn't die and leave Torvald and me.

RANK. Oh, you'll soon get over it. Once one is gone, one is soon forgotten.

NORA (*looks at him anxiously*). Do you believe that?

RANK. One finds replacements, and then—

NORA. Who will find a replacement?

RANK. You and Helmer both will, when I am gone. You seem to have made a start already, haven't you? What was this Mrs. Linde doing here yesterday evening?

NORA. Aha! But surely you can't be jealous of poor Christine?

RANK. Indeed I am. She will be my successor in this house. When I have moved on, this lady will—

NORA. Ssh—don't speak so loud! She's in there!

RANK. Today again? You see!

NORA. She's only come to mend my dress. Good heavens, how unreasonable you are! (*Sits on the sofa.*) Be nice now, Dr. Rank. Tomorrow you'll see how beautifully I shall dance; and you must imagine that I'm doing it just for you. And for Torvald of course; obviously. (*Takes some things out of the box.*) Dr. Rank, sit down here and I'll show you something.

RANK (*sits*). What's this?

NORA. Look here! Look!

RANK. Silk stockings!

NORA. Flesh-colored. Aren't they beautiful? It's very dark in here now, of course, but tomorrow— No, no, no; only the soles. Oh well, I suppose you can look a bit higher if you want to.

RANK. Hm—

NORA. Why are you looking so critical? Don't you think they'll fit me?

RANK. I can't really give you a qualified opinion on that.

NORA (*looks at him for a moment*). Shame on you! (*Flicks him on the ear with the stockings.*) Take that. (*Puts them back in the box.*)

RANK. What other wonders are to be revealed to me?

NORA. I shan't show you anything else. You're being naughty.

She hums a little and looks among the things in the box.

RANK (*after a short silence*). When I sit here like this being so intimate with you, I can't think—I cannot imagine what would have become of me if I had never entered this house.

NORA (*smiles*). Yes, I think you enjoy being with us, don't you?

RANK (*more quietly, looking into the middle distance*). And now to have to leave it all—

NORA. Nonsense. You're not leaving us.

RANK (*as before*). And not to be able to leave even the most wretched token of gratitude behind; hardly even a passing sense of loss; only an empty place, to be filled by the next comer.

NORA. Suppose I were to ask you to—? No—

RANK. To do what?

NORA. To give me proof of your friendship—

RANK. Yes, yes?

NORA. No, I mean—to do me a very great service—

RANK. Would you really for once grant me that happiness?

NORA. But you've no idea what it is.

RANK. Very well, tell me, then.

NORA. No, but, Dr. Rank, I can't. It's far too much—I want your help and advice, and I want you to do something for me.

RANK. The more the better. I've no idea what it can be. But tell me. You do trust me, don't you?

NORA. Oh, yes, more than anyone. You're my best and truest friend. Otherwise I couldn't tell you. Well then, Dr. Rank—there's something you must help me to prevent. You know how much Torvald loves me—he'd never hesitate for an instant to lay down his life for me—

RANK (*leans over toward her*). Nora—do you think he is the only one—?

NORA (*with a slight start*). What do you mean?

RANK. Who would gladly lay down his life for you?

NORA (*sadly*). Oh, I see.

RANK. I swore to myself I would let you know that before I go. I shall never have a better opportunity. . . . Well, Nora, now you know that. And now you also know that you can trust me as you can trust nobody else.

NORA (*rises; calmly and quietly*). Let me pass, please.

RANK (*makes room for her but remains seated*). Nora—

NORA (*in the doorway to the hall*). Helen, bring the lamp. (*Goes over to the stove.*) Oh, dear Dr. Rank, this was really horrid of you.

RANK (*gets up*). That I have loved you as deeply as anyone else has? Was that horrid of me?

NORA. No—but that you should go and tell me. That was quite unnecessary—

RANK. What do you mean? Did you know, then—?

The Maid enters with the lamp, puts it on the table, and goes out.

RANK. Nora—Mrs. Helmer—I am asking you, did you know this?

NORA. Oh, what do I know, what did I know, what didn't I know—I really can't say. How could you be so stupid, Dr. Rank? Everything was so nice.

RANK. Well, at any rate now you know that I am ready to serve you, body and soul. So—please continue.

NORA (*looks at him*). After this?

RANK. Please tell me what it is.

NORA. I can't possibly tell you now.

RANK. Yes, yes! You mustn't punish me like this. Let me be allowed to do what I can for you.

NORA. You can't do anything for me now. Anyway, I don't need any help. It was only my imagination—you'll see. Yes, really. Honestly. (*Sits in the rocking chair, looks at him, and smiles.*) Well, upon my word you *are* a fine gentleman, Dr. Rank. Aren't you ashamed of yourself, now that the lamp's been lit?

RANK. Frankly, no. But perhaps I ought to say—*adieu?*

NORA. Of course not. You will naturally continue to visit us as before. You know quite well how Torvald depends on your company.

RANK. Yes, but you?

NORA. Oh, I always think it's enormous fun having you here.

RANK. That was what misled me. You're a riddle to me, you know. I'd often felt you'd just as soon be with me as with Helmer.

NORA. Well, you see, there are some people whom one loves, and others whom it's almost more fun to be with.

RANK. Oh yes, there's some truth in that.

NORA. When I was at home, of course I loved Papa best. But I always used to think it was terribly amusing to go down and talk to the servants; because they never told me what I ought to do; and they were such fun to listen to.

RANK. I see. So I've taken their place?

NORA (*jumps up and runs over to him*). Oh, dear, sweet Dr. Rank, I didn't mean that at all. But I'm sure you understand—I feel the same about Torvald as I did about Papa.

MAID (*enters from the hall*). Excuse me, madam. (*Whispers to her and hands her a visiting card.*)

NORA (*glances at the card*). Oh! (*Puts it quickly in her pocket.*)

RANK. Anything wrong?

NORA. No, no, nothing at all. It's just something that—it's my new dress.

RANK. What? But your costume is lying over there.

NORA. Oh—that, yes—but there's another—I ordered it specially—Torvald mustn't know—

RANK. Ah, so that's your big secret?

NORA. Yes, yes. Go in and talk to him—he's in his study—keep him talking for a bit—

RANK. Don't worry. He won't get away from me. (*Goes into Helmer's study.*)

NORA (*to the Maid*). Is he waiting in the kitchen?

MAID. Yes, madam, he came up the back way—

NORA. But didn't you tell him I had a visitor?

MAID. Yes, but he wouldn't go.

NORA. Wouldn't go?

MAID. No, madam, not until he'd spoken with you.

NORA. Very well, show him in; but quietly. Helen, you mustn't tell anyone about this. It's a surprise for my husband.

NORA. Very good, madam. I understand. (*Goes.*)

NORA. It's happening. It's happening after all. No, no, no, it can't happen, it mustn't happen.

She walks across and bolts the door of Helmer's study. The Maid opens the door in the hall to admit Krogstad, and closes it behind him. He is wearing an overcoat, heavy boots, and a fur cap.

NORA (*goes towards him*). Speak quietly. My husband's at home.

KROGSTAD. Let him hear.

NORA. What do you want from me?

KROGSTAD. Information.

NORA. Hurry up, then. What is it?

KROGSTAD. I suppose you know I've been given the sack.

NORA. I couldn't stop it, Mr. Krogstad. I did my best for you, but it didn't help.

KROGSTAD. Does your husband love you so little? He knows what I can do to you, and yet he dares to—

NORA. Surely you don't imagine I told him?

KROGSTAD. No. I didn't really think you had. It wouldn't have been like my old friend Torvald Helmer to show that much courage—

NORA. Mr. Krogstad, I'll trouble you to speak respectfully of my husband.

KROGSTAD. Don't worry, I'll show him all the respect he deserves. But since you're so anxious to keep this matter hushed up, I presume you're better informed than you were yesterday of the gravity of what you've done?

NORA. I've learned more than you could ever teach me.

KROGSTAD. Yes, a bad lawyer like me—

NORA. What do you want from me?

KROGSTAD. I just wanted to see how things were with

you, Mrs. Helmer. I've been thinking about you all day. Even duns and hack journalists have hearts, you know.

NORA. Show some heart, then. Think of my little children.

KROGSTAD. Have you and your husband thought of mine? Well, let's forget that. I just wanted to tell you, you don't need to take this business too seriously. I'm not going to take any action, for the present.

NORA. Oh, no—you won't, will you? I knew it.

KROGSTAD. It can all be settled quite amicably. There's no need for it to become public. We'll keep it among the three of us.

NORA. My husband must never know about this.

KROGSTAD. How can you stop him? Can you pay the balance of what you owe me?

NORA. Not immediately.

KROGSTAD. Have you any means of raising the money during the next few days?

NORA. None that I would care to use.

KROGSTAD. Well, it wouldn't have helped anyway. However much money you offered me now I wouldn't give you back that paper.

NORA. What are you going to do with it?

KROGSTAD. Just keep it. No one else need ever hear about it. So in case you were thinking of doing anything desperate—

NORA. I am.

KROGSTAD. Such as running away—

NORA. I am.

KROGSTAD. Or anything more desperate—

NORA. How did you know?

KROGSTAD. —just give up the idea.

NORA. How did you know?

KROGSTAD. Most of us think of that at first. I did. But I hadn't the courage—

NORA (*dully*). Neither have I.

KROGSTAD (*relieved*). It's true, isn't it? You haven't the courage either?

NORA. No. I haven't. I haven't.

KROGSTAD. It'd be a stupid thing to do anyway. Once the first little domestic explosion is over. . . . I've got a letter in my pocket here addressed to your husband—

NORA. Telling him everything?

KROGSTAD. As delicately as possible.

NORA (*quickly*). He must never see that letter. Tear it up. I'll find the money somehow—

KROGSTAD. I'm sorry, Mrs. Helmer, I thought I'd explained—

NORA. Oh, I don't mean the money I owe you. Let me know how much you want from my husband, and I'll find it for you.

KROGSTAD. I'm not asking your husband for money.

NORA. What do you want, then?

KROGSTAD. I'll tell you. I want to get on my feet again, Mrs. Helmer. I want to get to the top. And your husband's going to help me. For eighteen months now my record's been clean. I've been in hard straits all that time; I was content to fight my way back inch by inch. Now I've been chucked back into the mud, and I'm not going to be satisfied with just getting back my job. I'm going to get to the top, I tell you. I'm going to get back into the bank, and it's going to be higher up. Your husband's going to create a new job for me—

NORA. He'll never do that!

KROGSTAD. Oh, yes he will. I know him. He won't dare to risk a scandal. And once I'm in there with him, you'll see! Within a year I'll be his right-hand man. It'll be Nils Krogstad who'll be running that bank, not Torvald Helmer!

NORA. That will never happen.

KROGSTAD. Are you thinking of—?

NORA. Now I *have* the courage.

KROGSTAD. Oh, you can't frighten me. A pampered little pretty like you—

NORA. You'll see! You'll see!

KROGSTAD. Under the ice? Down in the cold, black water? And then, in the spring, to float up again, ugly, unrecognizable, hairless—?

NORA. You can't frighten me.

KROGSTAD. And you can't frighten me. People don't do such things, Mrs. Helmer. And anyway, what'd be the use? I've got him in my pocket.

NORA. But afterwards? When I'm no longer—?

KROGSTAD. Have you forgotten that then your reputation will be in my hands? (*She looks at him speechlessly.*) Well, I've warned you. Don't do anything silly. When Helmer's read my letter, he'll get in touch with me. And remember, its your husband who's forced me to act like this. And for that I'll never forgive him. Goodbye, Mrs. Helmer. (*He goes out through the hall.*)

NORA (*runs to the hall door, opens it a few inches, and listens*). He's going. He's not going to give him the letter. Oh, no, no, it couldn't possibly happen. (*Opens the door a little wider.*) What's he doing? Standing outside the front door. He's not going downstairs. Is he changing his mind? Yes, he—!

A letter falls into the letter-box. Krogstad's footsteps die away down the stairs.

NORA (*with a stifled cry, runs across the room towards the table by the sofa. A pause*). In the letter-box. (*Steals timidly over towards the hall door.*) There it is! Oh, Torvald, Torvald! Now we're lost!

MRS. LINDE (*enters from the nursery with Nora's cos-*

tume). Well, I've done the best I can. Shall we see how it looks—?

NORA (*whispers hoarsely*). Christine, come here.

MRS. LINDE (*throws the dress on the sofa*). What's wrong with you? You look as though you'd seen a ghost!

NORA. Come here. Do you see that letter? There—look—through the glass of the letter-box.

MRS. LINDE. Yes, yes, I see it.

NORA. That letter's from Krogstad—

MRS. LINDE. Nora! It was Krogstad who lent you the money!

NORA. Yes. And now Torvald's going to discover everything.

MRS. LINDE. Oh, believe me, Nora, it'll be best for you both.

NORA. You don't know what's happened. I've committed a forgery—

MRS. LINDE. But, for heaven's sake—!

NORA. Christine, all I want is for you to be my witness.

MRS. LINDE. What do you mean? Witness what?

NORA. If I should go out of my mind—and it might easily happen—

MRS. LINDE. Nora!

NORA. Or if anything else should happen to me—so that I wasn't here any longer—

MRS. LINDE. Nora, Nora, you don't know what you're saying!

NORA. If anyone should try to take the blame, and say it was all his fault—you understand—?

MRS. LINDE. Yes, yes—but how can you think—?

NORA. Then you must testify that it isn't true, Christine. I'm not mad—I know exactly what I'm saying—and I'm telling you, no one else knows anything about this. I did it entirely on my own. Remember that.

MRS. LINDE. All right. But I simply don't understand—

NORA. Oh, how could you understand? A—miracle—is about to happen.

MRS. LINDE. Miracle?

NORA. Yes. A miracle. But it's so frightening, Christine. It *mustn't* happen, not for anything in the world.

MRS. LINDE. I'll go over and talk to Krogstad.

NORA. Don't go near him. He'll only do something to hurt you.

MRS. LINDE. Once upon a time he'd have done anything for my sake.

NORA. He?

MRS. LINDE. Where does he live?

NORA. Oh, how should I know—? Oh, yes, wait a moment—! (*Feels in her pocket.*) Here's his card. But the letter, the letter—!

HELMER (*in his study, knocks on the door*). Nora!

NORA (*cries in alarm*). What is it?

HELMER. Now, now, don't get alarmed. We're not coming in; you've closed the door. Are you trying on your costume?

NORA. Yes, yes—I'm trying on my costume. I'm going to look so pretty for you, Torvald.

MRS. LINDE (*who has been reading the card*). Why, he lives just around the corner.

NORA. Yes; but it's no use. There's nothing to be done now. The letter's lying there in the box.

MRS. LINDE. And your husband has the key?

NORA. Yes, he always keeps it.

MRS. LINDE. Krogstad must ask him to send the letter back unread. He must find some excuse—

NORA. But Torvald always opens the box at just about this time—

MRS. LINDE. You must stop him. Go in and keep him talking. I'll be back as quickly as I can.

She hurries out through the hall.

NORA (*goes over to Helmer's door, opens it and peeps in*). Torvald!

HELMER (*offstage*). Well, may a man enter his own drawing room again? Come on, Rank, now we'll see what— (*In the doorway.*) But what's this?

NORA. What, Torvald dear?

HELMER. Rank's been preparing me for some great transformation scene.

RANK (*in the doorway*). So I understood. But I seem to have been mistaken.

NORA. Yes, no one's to be allowed to see me before tomorrow night.

HELMER. But, my dear Nora, you look quite worn out. Have you been practicing too hard?

NORA. No, I haven't practiced at all yet.

HELMER. Well, you must.

NORA. Yes, Torvald, I must, I know. But I can't get anywhere without your help. I've completely forgotten everything.

HELMER. Oh, we'll soon put that to rights.

NORA. Yes, help me, Torvald. Promise me you will? Oh, I'm so nervous. All those people—! You must forget everything except me this evening. You mustn't think of business—I won't even let you touch a pen. Promise me, Torvald?

HELMER. I promise. This evening I shall think of nothing but you—my poor, helpless little darling. Oh, there's just one thing I must see to— (*Goes towards the hall door.*)

NORA. What do you want out there?

HELMER. I'm only going to see if any letters have come.

NORA. No, Torvald, no!
HELMER. Why, what's the matter?
NORA. Torvald, I beg you. There's nothing there.
HELMER. Well, I'll just make sure.

He moves towards the door. Nora runs to the piano and plays the first bar of the tarantella.

HELMER (*at the door, turns*). Aha!
NORA. I can't dance tomorrow if I don't practice with you now.
HELMER (*goes over to her*). Are you really so frightened, Nora dear?
NORA. Yes, terribly frightened. Let me start practicing now, at once—we've still time before dinner. Oh, do sit down and play for me, Torvald dear. Correct me, lead me, the way you always do.
HELMER. Very well, my dear, if you wish it.

He sits down at the piano. Nora seizes the tambourine and a long multi-colored shawl from the cardboard box, wraps the latter hastily around her, then takes a quick leap into the center of the room.

NORA. Play for me! I want to dance!

Helmer plays and Nora dances. Dr. Rank stands behind Helmer at the piano and watches her.

HELMER (*as he plays*). Slower, slower!
NORA. I can't!
HELMER. Not so violently, Nora.
NORA. I must!
HELMER (*stops playing*). No, no, this won't do at all.
NORA (*laughs and swings her tambourine*). Isn't that what I told you?
RANK. Let me play for her.
HELMER (*gets up*). Yes, would you? Then it'll be easier for me to show her.

Rank sits down at the piano and plays. Nora dances more and more wildly. Helmer has stationed himself by the stove and tries repeatedly to correct her but she seems not to hear him. Her hair works loose and falls over her shoulders; she ignores it and continues to dance. Mrs. Linde enters.

MRS. LINDE (*stands in the doorway as though tongue-tied*). Ah—!
NORA (*as she dances*). Oh, Christine, we're having such fun!
HELMER. But, Nora darling, you're dancing as if your life depended on it.
NORA. It does.
HELMER. Rank, stop it! This is sheer lunacy. Stop it, I say!

Rank ceases playing. Nora suddenly stops dancing.

HELMER (*goes over to her*). I'd never have believed it. You've forgotten everything I taught you.
NORA (*throws away the tambourine*). You see!
HELMER. I'll have to show you every step.
NORA. You see how much I need you! You must show me every step of the way. Right to the end of the dance. Promise me you will, Torvald?
HELMER. Never fear. I will.
NORA. You mustn't think about anything but me—today or tomorrow. Don't open any letters—don't even open the letter-box—
HELMER. Aha, you're still worried about that fellow—
NORA. Oh, yes, yes, him too.
HELMER. Nora, I can tell from the way you're behaving, there's a letter from him already lying there.
NORA. I don't know. I think so. But you mustn't read it now. I don't want anything ugly to come between us till it's all over.
RANK (*quietly, to Helmer*). Better give her her way.
HELMER (*puts his arm round her*). My child shall have her way. But tomorrow night, when your dance is over—
NORA. Then you will be free.
MAID (*appears in the doorway, right*). Dinner is served, madam.
NORA. Put out some champagne, Helen.
MAID. Very good, madam. (*Goes.*)
HELMER. I say! What's this, a banquet?
NORA. We'll drink champagne until dawn! (*Calls.*) And, Helen! Put out some macaroons! Lots of macaroons—for once!
HELMER (*takes her hands in his*). Now, now, now. Don't get so excited. Where's my little songbird, the one I know?
NORA. All right. Go and sit down—and you too, Dr. Rank. I'll be with you in a minute. Christine, you must help me put my hair up.
RANK (*quietly, as they go*). There's nothing wrong, is there? I mean, she isn't—er—expecting—?
HELMER. Good heavens no, my dear chap. She just gets scared like a child sometimes—I told you before—

They go out right.

NORA. Well?
MRS. LINDE. He's left town.
NORA. I saw it from your face.
MRS. LINDE. He'll be back tomorrow evening. I left a note for him.
NORA. You needn't have bothered. You can't stop anything now. Anyway, it's wonderful really, in a way—sitting here and waiting for the miracle to happen.

MRS. LINDE. Waiting for what?

NORA. Oh, you wouldn't understand. Go in and join them. I'll be with you in a moment.

Mrs. Linde goes into the dining-room.

NORA (*stands for a moment as though collecting herself. Then she looks at her watch.*). Five o'clock. Seven hours till midnight. Then another twenty-four hours till midnight tomorrow. And then the tarantella will be finished. Twenty-four and seven? Thirty-one hours to live.

HELMER (*appears in the doorway, right*). What's happened to my little songbird?

NORA (*runs to him with her arms wide*). Your songbird is here!

ACT 3

The same room. The table which was formerly by the sofa has been moved into the center of the room; the chairs surround it as before. The door to the hall stands open. Dance music can be heard from the floor above. Mrs. Linde is seated at the table, absent-mindedly glancing through a book. She is trying to read, but seems unable to keep her mind on it. More than once she turns and listens anxiously towards the front door.

MRS. LINDE (*looks at her watch*). Not here yet. There's not much time left. Please God he hasn't—! (*Listens again.*) Ah, here he is. (*Goes out into the hall and cautiously opens the front door. Footsteps can be heard softly ascending the stairs. She whispers.*) Come in. There's no one here.

KROGSTAD (*in the doorway*). I found a note from you at my lodgings. What does this mean?

MRS. LINDE. I must speak with you.

KROGSTAD. Oh? And must our conversation take place in this house?

MRS. LINDE. We couldn't meet at my place; my room has no separate entrance. Come in. We're quite alone. The maid's asleep, and the Helmers are at the dance upstairs.

KROGSTAD (*comes into the room*). Well, well! So the Helmers are dancing this evening? Are they indeed?

MRS. LINDE. Yes. why not?

KROGSTAD. True enough. Why not?

MRS. LINDE. Well, Krogstad. You and I must have a talk together.

KROGSTAD. Have we two anything further to discuss?

MRS. LINDE. We have a great deal to discuss.

KROGSTAD. I wasn't aware of it.

MRS. LINDE. That's because you've never really understood me.

KROGSTAD. Was there anything to understand? It's the old story, isn't it—a woman chucking a man because something better turns up?

MRS. LINDE. Do you really think I'm so utterly heartless? You think it was easy for me to give you up?

KROGSTAD. Wasn't it?

MRS. LINDE. Oh, Nils, did you really believe that?

KROGSTAD. Then why did you write to me the way you did?

MRS. LINDE. I had to. Since I had to break with you, I thought it my duty to destroy all the feelings you had for me.

KROGSTAD (*clenches his fists*). So that was it. And you did this for money!

MRS. LINDE. You mustn't forget I had a helpless mother to take care of, and two little brothers. We couldn't wait for you, Nils. It would have been so long before you'd had enough to support us.

KROGSTAD. Maybe. But you had no right to cast me off for someone else.

MRS. LINDE. Perhaps not. I've often asked myself that.

KROGSTAD (*more quietly*). When I lost you, it was just as though all solid ground had been swept from under my feet. Look at me. Now I am a shipwrecked man, clinging to a spar.

MRS. LINDE. Help may be near at hand.

KROGSTAD. It was near. But then you came, and stood between it and me.

MRS. LINDE. I didn't know, Nils. No one told me till today that this job I'd found was yours.

KROGSTAD. I believe you, since you say so. But now you know, won't you give it up?

MRS. LINDE. No—because it wouldn't help you even if I did.

KROGSTAD. Wouldn't it? I'd do it all the same.

MRS. LINDE. I've learned to look at things practically. Life and poverty have taught me that.

KROGSTAD. And life has taught me to distrust fine words.

MRS. LINDE. Then it's taught you a useful lesson. But surely you still believe in actions?

KROGSTAD. What do you mean?

MRS. LINDE. You said you were like a shipwrecked man clinging to a spar.

KROGSTAD. I have good reason to say it.

MRS. LINDE. I'm in the same position as you. No one to care about, no one to care for.

KROGSTAD. You made your own choice.

MRS. LINDE. I had no choice—then.

KROGSTAD. Well?

MRS. LINDE. Nils, suppose we two shipwrecked souls could join hands?

KROGSTAD. What are you saying?

MRS. LINDE. Castaways have a better chance of survival together than on their own.

KROGSTAD. Christine!

MRS. LINDE. Why do you suppose I came to this town?

KROGSTAD. You mean—you came because of me?

MRS. LINDE. I must work if I'm to find life worth living. I've always worked, for as long as I can remember; it's been the greatest joy of my life—my only joy. But now I'm alone in the world, and I feel so dreadfully lost and empty. There's no joy in working just for oneself. Oh, Nils, give me something—someone—to work for.

KROGSTAD. I don't believe all that. You're just being hysterical and romantic. You want to find an excuse for self-sacrifice.

MRS. LINDE. Have you ever known me to be hysterical?

KROGSTAD. You mean you really—? Is it possible? Tell me—you know all about my past?

MRS. LINDE. Yes.

KROGSTAD. And you know what people think of me here?

MRS. LINDE. You said just now that with me you might have become a different person.

KROGSTAD. I know I could have.

MRS. LINDE. Couldn't it still happen?

KROGSTAD. Christine—do you really mean this? Yes—you do—I see it in your face. Have you really the courage—?

MRS. LINDE. I need someone to be a mother to; and your children need a mother. And you and I need each other. I believe in you, Nils. I am afraid of nothing—with you.

KROGSTAD (*clasps her hands*). Thank you, Christine—thank you! Now I shall make the world believe in me as you do! Oh—but I'd forgotten—

MRS. LINDE (*listens*). Ssh! The tarantella! Go quickly, go!

KROGSTAD. Why? What is it?

MRS. LINDE. You hear that dance? As soon as it's finished, they'll be coming down.

KROGSTAD. All right, I'll go. It's no good, Christine. I'd forgotten—you don't know what I've just done to the Helmers.

MRS. LINDE. Yes, Nils. I know.

KROGSTAD. And yet you'd still have the courage to—?

MRS. LINDE. I know what despair can drive a man like you to.

KROGSTAD. Oh, if only I could undo this!

MRS. LINDE. You can. Your letter is still lying in the box.

KROGSTAD. Are you sure?

MRS. LINDE. Quite sure. But—

KROGSTAD (*looks searchingly at her*). Is that why you're doing this? You want to save your friend at any price? Tell me the truth. Is that the reason?

MRS. LINDE. Nils, a woman who has sold herself once for the sake of others doesn't make the same mistake again.

KROGSTAD. I shall demand my letter back.

MRS. LINDE. No, no.

KROGSTAD. Of course I shall. I shall stay here till Helmer comes down. I'll tell him he must give me back my letter—I'll say it was only to do with my dismissal, and that I don't want him to read it—

MRS. LINDE. No, Nils, you mustn't ask for that letter back.

KROGSTAD. But—tell me—wasn't that the real reason you asked me to come here?

MRS. LINDE. Yes—at first, when I was frightened. But a day has passed since then, and in that time I've seen incredible things happen in this house. Helmer must know the truth. This unhappy secret of Nora's must be revealed. They must come to a full understanding; there must be an end of all these shiftings and evasions.

KROGSTAD. Very well. If you're prepared to risk it. But one thing I can do—and at once—

MRS. LINDE (*listens*). Hurry! Go, go! The dance is over. We aren't safe here another moment.

KROGSTAD. I'll wait for you downstairs.

MRS. LINDE. Yes, do. You can see me home.

KROGSTAD. I've never been so happy in my life before!

He goes out through the front door. The door leading from the room into the hall remains open.

MRS. LINDE (*tidies the room a little and gets her hat and coat*). What a change! Oh, what a change! Someone to work for—to live for! A home to bring joy into! I won't let this chance of happiness slip through my fingers. Oh, why don't they come? (*Listens.*) Ah, here they are. I must get my coat on.

She takes her hat and coat. Helmer's and Nora's voices become audible outside. A key is turned in the lock and Helmer leads Nora almost forcibly into the hall. She is dressed in an Italian costume with a large black shawl. He is in evening dress, with a black cloak.

NORA (*still in the doorway, resisting him*). No, no, no—not in here! I want to go back upstairs. I don't want to leave so early.

HELMER. But my dearest Nora—

NORA. Oh, please, Torvald, please! Just another hour!

HELMER. Not another minute, Nora, my sweet. You know what we agreed. Come along, now. Into the drawing-room. You'll catch cold if you stay out here.

He leads her, despite her efforts to resist him, gently into the room.

MRS. LINDE. Good evening.

NORA. Christine!

HELMER. Oh, hullo, Mrs. Linde. You still here?

MRS. LINDE. Please forgive me. I did so want to see Nora in her costume.

NORA. Have you been sitting here waiting for me?

MRS. LINDE. Yes. I got here too late, I'm afraid. You'd already gone up. And I felt I really couldn't go back home without seeing you.

HELMER (*takes off Nora's shawl*). Well, take a good look at her. She's worth looking at, don't you think? Isn't she beautiful, Mrs. Linde?

MRS. LINDE. Oh, yes, indeed—

HELMER. Isn't she unbelievably beautiful? Everyone at the party said so. But dreadfully stubborn she is, bless her pretty little heart. What's to be done about that? Would you believe it, I practically had to use force to get her away!

NORA. Oh, Torvald, you're going to regret not letting me stay—just half an hour longer.

HELMER. Hear that, Mrs. Linde? She dances her tarantella—makes a roaring success—and very well deserved—though possibly a trifle too realistic—more so than was aesthetically necessary, strictly speaking. But never mind that. Main thing is—she had a success—roaring success. Was I going to let her stay on after that and spoil the impression? No, thank you. I took my beautiful little Capri signorina—my capricious little Capricienne, what?—under my arm—a swift round of the ballroom, a curtsey to the company, and, as they say in novels, the beautiful apparition disappeared! An exit should always be dramatic, Mrs. Linde. But unfortunately that's just what I can't get Nora to realize. I say, it's hot in here. (*Throws his cloak on a chair and opens the door to his study.*) What's this? It's dark in here. Ah, yes, of course—excuse me. (*Goes in and lights a couple of candles.*)

NORA (*whispers swiftly, breathlessly*). Well?

MRS. LINDE (*quietly*). I've spoken to him.

NORA. Yes?

MRS. LINDE. Nora—you must tell your husband everything.

NORA (*dully*). I knew it.

MRS. LINDE. You've nothing to fear from Krogstad. But you must tell him.

NORA. I shan't tell him anything.

MRS. LINDE. Then the letter will.

NORA. Thank you, Christine. Now I know what I must do. Ssh!

HELMER (*returns*). Well, Mrs. Linde, finished admiring her?

MRS. LINDE. Yes. Now I must say good night.

HELMER. Oh, already? Does this knitting belong to you?

MRS. LINDE (*takes it*). Thank you, yes. I nearly forgot it.

HELMER. You knit, then?

MRS. LINDE. Why, yes.

HELMER. Know what? You ought to take up embroidery.

MRS. LINDE. Oh? Why?

HELMER. It's much prettier. Watch me, now. You hold the embroidery in your left hand, like this, and then you take the needle in your right hand and go in and out in a slow, easy movement—like this. I am right, aren't I?

MRS. LINDE. Yes, I'm sure—

HELMER. But knitting, now—that's an ugly business—can't help it. Look—arms all huddled up—great clumsy needles going up and down—makes you look like a damned Chinaman. I say, that really was a magnificent champagne they served us.

MRS. LINDE. Well, good night, Nora. And stop being stubborn. Remember!

HELMER. Quite right, Mrs. Linde!

MRS. LINDE. Good night, Mr. Helmer.

HELMER (*accompanies her to the door*). Good night, good night! I hope you'll manage to get home all right? I'd gladly—but you haven't far to go, have you? Good night, good night. (*She goes. He closes the door behind her and returns.*) Well, we've got rid of her at last. Dreadful bore that woman is!

NORA. Aren't you very tired, Torvald?

HELMER. No, not in the least.

NORA. Aren't you sleepy?

HELMER. Not a bit. On the contrary, I feel extraordinarily exhilarated. But what about you? Yes, you look very sleepy and tired.

NORA. Yes, I am very tired. Soon I shall sleep.

HELMER. You see, you see! How right I was not to let you stay longer!

NORA. Oh, you're always right, whatever you do.

HELMER (*kisses her on the forehead*). Now my little songbird's talking just like a real big human being. I say, did you notice how cheerful Rank was this evening?

NORA. Oh? Was he? I didn't have a chance to speak with him.

HELMER. I hardly did. But I haven't seen him in such a jolly mood for ages. (*Looks at her for a moment, then comes closer.*) I say, it's nice to get back to one's home again, and be all alone with you. Upon my word, you're a distractingly beautiful young woman.

NORA. Don't look at me like that, Torvald!

HELMER. What, not look at my most treasured possession? At all this wonderful beauty that's mine, mine alone, all mine.

NORA (*goes round to the other side of the table*). You mustn't talk to me like that tonight.

HELMER (*follows her*). You've still the tarantella in your blood, I see. And that makes you even more desirable. Listen! Now the other guests are beginning to go. (*More quietly.*) Nora—soon the whole house will be absolutely quiet.

NORA. Yes, I hope so.

HELMER. Yes, my beloved Nora, of course you do! Do you know—when I'm out with you among other people like we were tonight, do you know why I say so little to you, why I keep so aloof from you, and just throw you an occasional glance? Do you know why I do that? It's because I pretend to myself that you're my secret mistress, my clandestine little sweetheart, and that nobody knows there's anything at all between us.

NORA. Oh, yes, yes, yes—I know you never think of anything but me.

HELMER. And then when we're about to go, and I wrap the shawl round your lovely young shoulders, over this wonderful curve of your neck—then I pretend to myself that you are my young bride, that we've just come from the wedding, that I'm taking you to my house for the first time—that, for the first time, I am alone with you—quite alone with you, as you stand there young and trembling and beautiful. All evening I've had no eyes for anyone but you. When I saw you dance the tarantella, like a huntress, a temptress, my blood grew hot, I couldn't stand it any longer! That was why I seized you and dragged you down here with me—

NORA. Leave me, Torvald! Get away from me! I don't want all this.

HELMER. What? Now, Nora, you're joking with me. Don't want, don't want—? Aren't I your husband—?

There is a knock on the front door.

NORA (*starts*). What was that?

HELMER (*goes toward the hall*). Who is it?

RANK (*outside*). It's me. May I come in for a moment?

HELMER (*quietly, annoyed*). Oh, what does he want now? (*Calls.*) Wait a moment. (*Walks over and opens the door.*) Well! Nice of you not to go by without looking in.

RANK. I thought I heard your voice, so I felt I had to say goodbye. (*His eyes travel swiftly around the room.*) Ah, yes—these dear rooms, how well I know them. What a happy, peaceful home you two have.

HELMER. You seemed to be having a pretty happy time yourself upstairs.

RANK. Indeed I did. Why not? Why shouldn't one make the most of this world? As much as one can, and for as long as one can. The wine was excellent—

HELMER. Especially the champagne.

RANK. You noticed that too? It's almost incredible how much I managed to get down.

NORA. Torvald drank a lot of champagne too, this evening.

RANK. Oh?

NORA. Yes. It always makes him merry afterwards.

RANK. Well, why shouldn't a man have a merry evening after a well-spent day?

HELMER. Well-spent? Oh, I don't know that I can claim that.

RANK (*slaps him across the back*). I can, though, my dear fellow!

NORA. Yes, of course, Dr. Rank—you've been carrying out a scientific experiment today, haven't you?

RANK. Exactly.

HELMER. Scientific experiment! Those are big words for my little Nora to use!

NORA. And may I congratulate you on the finding?

RANK. You may indeed.

NORA. It was good, then?

RANK. The best possible finding—both for the doctor and the patient. Certainty.

NORA (*quickly*). Certainty?

RANK. Absolute certainty. So aren't I entitled to have a merry evening after that?

NORA. Yes, Dr. Rank. You were quite right to.

HELMER. I agree. Provided you don't have to regret it tomorrow.

RANK. Well, you never get anything in this life without paying for it.

NORA. Dr. Rank—you like masquerades, don't you?

RANK. Yes, if the disguises are sufficiently amusing.

NORA. Tell me. What shall we two wear at the next masquerade?

HELMER. You little gadabout! Are you thinking about the next one already?

RANK. We two? Yes, I'll tell you. You must go as the Spirit of Happiness—

HELMER. You try to think of a costume that'll convey that.

RANK. Your wife need only appear as her normal, everyday self—

HELMER. Quite right! Well said! But what are you going to be? Have you decided that?

RANK. Yes, my dear friend. I have decided that.

HELMER. Well?

RANK. At the next masquerade, I shall be invisible.

HELMER. Well, that's a funny idea.

RANK. There's a big, black hat—haven't you heard of the invisible hat? Once it's over your head, no one can see you any more.

HELMER (*represses a smile*). Ah yes, of course.

RANK. But I'm forgetting what I came for. Helmer, give me a cigar. One of your black Havanas.

HELMER. With the greatest pleasure. (*Offers him the box.*)

RANK (*takes one and cuts off the tip*). Thank you.

NORA (*strikes a match*). Let me give you a light.

RANK. Thank you. (*She holds out the match for him. He lights his cigar.*) And now—goodbye.

HELMER. Goodbye, my dear chap, goodbye.

NORA. Sleep well, Dr. Rank.

RANK. Thank you for that kind wish.

NORA. Wish me the same.

RANK. You? Very well—since you ask. Sleep well. And thank you for the light. (*He nods to them both and goes.*)

HELMER (*quietly*). He's been drinking too much.

NORA (*abstractedly*). Perhaps.

Helmer takes his bunch of keys from his pocket and goes out into the hall.

NORA. Torvald, what do you want out there?

HELMER. I must empty the letter-box. It's absolutely full. There'll be no room for the newspapers in the morning.

NORA. Are you going to work tonight?

HELMER. You know very well I'm not. Hullo, what's this? Someone's been at the lock.

NORA. At the lock—?

HELMER. Yes, I'm sure of it. Who on earth—? Surely not one of the maids? Here's a broken hairpin. Nora, it's yours—

NORA (*quickly*). Then it must have been the children.

HELMER. Well, you'll have to break them of that habit. Hm, hm. Ah, that's done it. (*Takes out the contents of the box and calls into the kitchen.*) Helen! Put out the light on the staircase. (*Comes back into the drawing-room with the letters in his hand and closes the door to the hall.*) Look at this! You see how they've piled up? (*Glances through them.*) What on earth's this?

NORA (*at the window*). The letter! Oh, no, Torvald, no!

HELMER. Two visiting cards—from Rank.

NORA. From Dr. Rank?

HELMER (*looks at them*). Peter Rank, M.D. They were on top. He must have dropped them in as he left.

NORA. Has he written anything on them?

HELMER. There's a black cross above his name. Look. Rather gruesome, isn't it? It looks just as though he was announcing his death.

NORA. He is.

HELMER. What? Do you know something? Has he told you anything?

NORA. Yes. When these cards come, it means he's said goodbye to us. He wants to shut himself up in his house and die.

HELMER. Ah, poor fellow. I knew I wouldn't be seeing him for much longer. But so soon—! And now he's going to slink away and hide like a wounded beast.

NORA. When the time comes, it's best to go silently. Don't you think so, Torvald?

HELMER (*walks up and down*). He was so much a part of our life. I can't realize that he's gone. His suffering and loneliness seemed to provide a kind of dark background to the happy sunlight of our marriage. Well, perhaps it's best this way. For him, anyway. (*Stops walking.*) And perhaps for us too, Nora. Now we have only each other. (*Embraces her.*) Oh, my beloved wife—I feel as though I could never hold you close enough. Do you know, Nora, often I wish some terrible danger might threaten you, so that I could offer my life and my blood, everything, for your sake.

NORA (*tears herself loose and says in a clear, firm voice*). Read your letters now, Torvald.

HELMER. No, no. Not tonight. Tonight I want to be with you, my darling wife—

NORA. When your friend is about to die—?

HELMER. You're right. This news has upset us both. An ugliness has come between us; thoughts of death and dissolution. We must try to forget them. Until then—you go to your room; I shall go to mine.

NORA (*throws her arms round his neck*). Good night, Torvald! Good night!

HELMER (*kisses her on the forehead*). Good night, my darling little songbird. Sleep well, Nora. I'll go and read my letters.

He goes into the study with the letters in his hand, and closes the door.

NORA (*wild-eyed, fumbles around, seizes Helmer's cloak, throws it round herself and whispers quickly, hoarsely*). Never see him again. Never. Never. Never. (*Throws the shawl over her head.*) Never see the children again. Them too. Never. Never. Oh—the icy black water! Oh—that bottomless—that—! Oh, if only it were all over! Now he's got it—he's reading it. Oh, no, no! Not yet! Goodbye, Torvald! Goodbye, my darlings!

She turns to run into the hall. As she does so, Helmer throws open his door and stands there with an open letter in his hand.

HELMER. Nora!

NORA (*shrieks*). Ah—!

HELMER. What is this? Do you know what is in this letter?

NORA. Yes, I know. Let me go! Let me go!

HELMER (*holds her back*). Go? Where?

NORA (*tries to tear herself loose*). You mustn't try to save me, Torvald!

HELMER (*staggers back*). Is it true? Is it true, what he writes? Oh, my God! No, no—it's impossible, it can't be true!

NORA. It *is* true. I've loved you more than anything else in the world.

HELMER. Oh, don't try to make silly excuses.

NORA (*takes a step toward him*). Torvald—

HELMER. Wretched woman! What have you done?

NORA. Let me go! You're not going to suffer for my sake. I won't let you!

HELMER. Stop being theatrical. (*Locks the front door.*) You're going to stay here and explain yourself. Do you understand what you've done? Answer me! Do you understand?

NORA (*looks unflinchingly at him and, her expression growing colder, says*). Yes. Now I am beginning to understand.

HELMER (*walking around the room*). Oh, what a dreadful awakening! For eight whole years—she who was my joy and my pride—a hypocrite, a liar—worse, worse—a criminal! Oh, the hideousness of it! Shame on you, shame!

Nora is silent and stares unblinkingly at him.

HELMER (*stops in front of her*). I ought to have guessed that something of this sort would happen. I should have foreseen it. All your father's recklessness and instability—be quiet!—I repeat, all your father's recklessness and instability he has handed on to you. No religion, no morals, no sense of duty! Oh, how I have been punished for closing my eyes to his faults! I did it for your sake. And now you reward me like this.

NORA. Yes. Like this.

HELMER. Now you have destroyed all my happiness. You have ruined my whole future. Oh, it's too dreadful to contemplate! I am in the power of a man who is completely without scruples. He can do what he likes with me, demand what he pleases, order me to do anything—I dare not disobey him. I am condemned to humiliation and ruin simply for the weakness of a woman.

NORA. When I am gone from this world, you will be free.

HELMER. Oh, don't be melodramatic. Your father was always ready with that kind of remark How would it help me if you were "gone from this world," as you put it? It wouldn't assist me in the slightest. He can still make all the facts public; and if he does, I may quite easily be suspected of having been an accomplice in your crime. People may think that I was behind it—that it was I who encouraged you! And for all this I have to thank you, you whom I have carried on my hands through all the years of our marriage! Now do you realize what you've done to me?

NORA (*coldly calm*). Yes.

HELMER. It's so unbelievable I can hardly credit it. But we must try to find some way out. Take off that shawl. Take it off, I say! I must try to buy him off somehow. This thing must be hushed up at any price. As regards our relationship—we must appear to be living together just as before. Only *appear*, of course. You will therefore continue to reside here. That is understood. But the children shall be taken out of your hands. I dare no longer entrust them to you. Oh, to have to say this to the woman I once loved so dearly—and whom I still—! Well, all that must be finished. Henceforth there can be no question of happiness; we must merely strive to save what shreds and tatters— (*The front door bell rings. Helmer starts.*) What can that be? At this hour? Surely not—? He wouldn't—? Hide yourself, Nora. Say you're ill.

Nora does not move. Helmer goes to the door of the room and opens it. The maid is standing half-dressed in the hall.

MAID. A letter for madam.

HELMER. Give it to me. (*Seizes the letter and shuts the door.*) Yes, it's from him. You're not having it. I'll read this myself.

NORA. Read it.

HELMER (*by the lamp*). I hardly dare to. This may mean the end for us both. No, I must know. (*Tears open the letter hastily; reads a few lines; looks at a piece of paper which is enclosed with it; utters a cry of joy.*) Nora! (*She looks at him questioningly.*) Nora! No—I must read it once more. Yes, yes, it's true! I am saved! Nora, I am saved!

NORA. What about me?

HELMER. You too, of course. We're both saved, you and I. Look! He's returning your I.O.U. He writes that he is sorry for what has happened—a happy accident has changed his life—oh, what does it matter what he writes? We are saved, Nora! No one can harm you now. Oh, Nora, Nora—no, first let me destroy this filthy thing. Let me see—! (*Glances at the I.O.U.*) No, I don't want to look at it. I shall merely regard the whole business as a dream. (*He tears the I.O.U. and both letters into pieces, throws them into the stove, and watches them burn.*) There. Now they're destroyed. He wrote that ever since Christmas Eve you've been—oh, these must have been three dreadful days for you, Nora.

NORA. Yes. It's been a hard fight.

HELMER. It must have been terrible—seeing no way out except—no, we'll forget the whole sordid business. We'll just be happy and go on telling ourselves over and over again: "It's over! It's over!" Listen to me, Nora. You don't seem to realize. It's over! Why are you looking so pale? Ah, my poor little Nora, I understand. You can't believe that I have forgiven you. But I have, Nora. I swear it to you. I have forgiven you everything. I know that what you did you did for your love of me.

NORA. That is true.

HELMER. You have loved me as a wife should love her husband. It was simply that in your inexperience you chose the wrong means. But do you think I love you any the less because you don't know how to act on your own initiative? No, no. Just lean on me. I shall counsel you. I shall guide you. I would not be a true man if your feminine helplessness did not make you doubly attractive in my eyes. You mustn't mind the hard words I said to you in those first dreadful moments when my whole world seemed to be tumbling about my ears. I have forgiven you, Nora. I swear it to you; I have forgiven you.

NORA. Thank you for your forgiveness.

She goes out through the door, right.

HELMER. No, don't go— (*Looks in.*) What are you doing there?

NORA (*offstage*). Taking off my fancy dress.

HELMER (*by the open door*). Yes, do that. Try to calm yourself and get your balance again, my frightened little songbird. Don't be afraid. I have broad wings to shield you. (*Begins to walk around near the door.*) How lovely and peaceful this little home of ours is, Nora. You are safe here; I shall watch over you like a hunted dove which I have snatched unharmed from the claws of the falcon. Your wildly beating little heart shall find peace with me. It will happen, Nora; it will take time, but it will happen, believe me. Tomorrow all this will seem quite different. Soon everything will be as it was before. I shall no longer need to remind you that I have forgiven you; your own heart will tell you that it is true. Do you really think I could ever bring myself to disown you, or even to reproach you? Ah, Nora, you don't understand what goes on in a husband's heart. There is something indescribably wonderful and satisfying for a husband in knowing that he has forgiven his wife—forgiven her unreservedly, from the bottom of his heart. It means that she has become his property in a double sense; he has, as it were, brought her into the world anew; she is now not only his wife but also his child. From now on that is what you shall be to me, my poor, helpless, bewildered little creature. Never be frightened of anything again, Nora. Just open your heart to me. I shall be both your will and your conscience. What's this? Not in bed? Have you changed?

NORA (*in her everyday dress*). Yes, Torvald. I've changed.

HELMER. But why now—so late—?

NORA. I shall not sleep tonight.

HELMER. But, my dear Nora—

NORA (*looks at her watch*). It isn't that late. Sit down here, Torvald. You and I have a lot to talk about.

She sits down on one side of the table.

HELMER. Nora, what does this mean? You look quite drawn—

NORA. Sit down. It's going to take a long time. I've a lot to say to you.

HELMER (*sits down on the other side of the table*). You alarm me, Nora. I don't understand you.

NORA. No, that's just it. You don't understand me. And I've never understood you—until this evening. No, don't interrupt me. Just listen to what I have to say. You and I have got to face facts, Torvald.

HELMER. What do you mean by that?

NORA (*after a short silence*). Doesn't anything strike you about the way we're sitting here?

HELMER. What?

NORA. We've been married for eight years. Does it occur to you that this is the first time that we two, you and I, man and wife, have ever had a serious talk together?

HELMER. Serious? What do you mean, serious?

NORA. In eight whole years—no, longer—ever since we first met—we have never exchanged a serious word on a serious subject.

HELMER. Did you expect me to drag you into all my worries—worries you couldn't possibly have helped me with?

NORA. I'm not talking about worries. I'm simply saying that we have never sat down seriously to try to get to the bottom of anything.

HELMER. But, my dear Nora, what on earth has that got to do with you?

NORA. That's just the point. You have never understood me. A great wrong has been done to me, Torvald. First by Papa, and then by you.

HELMER. What? But we two have loved you more than anyone in the world!

NORA (*shakes her head*). You have never loved me. You just thought it was fun to be in love with me.

HELMER. Nora, what kind of a way is this to talk?

NORA. It's the truth, Torvald. When I lived with Papa, he used to tell me what he thought about everything, so that I never had any opinions but his. And if I did have any of my own, I kept them quiet, because he wouldn't have liked them. He called me his little doll, and he played with me just the way I played with my dolls. Then I came here to live in your house

HELMER. What kind of a way is that to describe our marriage?

NORA (*undisturbed*). I mean, then I passed from Papa's hands into yours. You arranged everything the way you wanted it, so that I simply took over your taste in everything—or pretended I did—I don't really know—I think it was a little of both—first one and then the other. Now I look back on it, it's as if I've been living here like a pauper, from hand to mouth. I performed tricks for you, and you gave me food and drink. But that was how you wanted it. You and Papa have done me a great wrong. It's your fault that I have done nothing with my life.

HELMER. Nora, how can you be so unreasonable and ungrateful? Haven't you been happy here?

NORA. No; never. I used to think I was; but I haven't ever been happy.

HELMER. Not—not happy?

NORA. No. I've just had fun. You've always been very kind to me. But our home has never been anything but a playroom. I've been your doll-wife, just as I used to be Papa's doll-child. And the children have been my dolls. I used to think it was fun when you came in and played with me, just as they think it's fun when I go in and play games with them. That's all our marriage has been, Torvald.

HELMER. There may be a little truth in what you say, though you exaggerate and romanticize. But from now on it'll be different. Playtime is over. Now the time has come for education.

NORA. Whose education? Mine or the children's?

HELMER. Both yours and the children's, my dearest Nora.

NORA. Oh, Torvald, you're not the man to educate me into being the right wife for you.

HELMER. How can you say that?

NORA. And what about me? Am I fit to educate the children?

HELMER. Nora!

NORA. Didn't you say yourself a few minutes ago that you dare not leave them in my charge?

HELMER. In a moment of excitement. Surely you don't think I meant it seriously?

NORA. Yes. You were perfectly right. I'm not fitted to educate them. There's something else I must do first. I must educate myself. And you can't help me with that. It's something I must do by myself. That's why I'm leaving you.

HELMER (*jumps up*). What did you say?

NORA. I must stand on my own feet if I am to find out the truth about myself and about life. So I can't go on living here with you any longer.

HELMER. Nora, Nora!

NORA. I'm leaving you now, at once. Christine will put me up for tonight—

HELMER. You're out of your mind! You can't do this! I forbid you!

NORA. It's no use your trying to forbid me any more. I shall take with me nothing but what is mine. I don't want anything from you, now or ever.

HELMER. What kind of madness is this?

NORA. Tomorrow I shall go home—I mean, to where I was born. It'll be easiest for me to find some kind of a job there.

HELMER. But you're blind! You've no experience of the world—

NORA. I must try to get some, Torvald.

HELMER. But to leave your home, your husband, your children! Have you thought what people will say?

NORA. I can't help that. I only know that I must do this.

HELMER. But this is monstrous! Can you neglect your most sacred duties?

NORA. What do you call my most sacred duties?

HELMER. Do I have to tell you? Your duties towards your husband, and your children.

NORA. I have another duty which is equally sacred.

HELMER. You have not. What on earth could that be?

NORA. My duty towards myself.

HELMER. First and foremost you are a wife and a mother.

NORA. I don't believe that any longer. I believe that I am first and foremost a human being, like you—or anyway, that I must try to become one. I know most people think as you do, Torvald, and I know there's something of the sort to be found in books. But I'm no longer prepared to accept what people say and what's written in books. I must think things out for myself, and try to find my own answer.

HELMER. Do you need to ask where your duty lies in your own home? Haven't you an infallible guide in such matters—your religion?

NORA. Oh, Torvald, I don't really know what religion means.

HELMER. What are you saying?

NORA. I only know what Pastor Hansen told me when I went to confirmation. He explained that religion meant this and that. When I get away from all this and can think things out on my own, that's one of the questions I want to look into. I want to find out whether what Pastor Hansen said was right—or anyway, whether it is right for me.

HELMER. But it's unheard of for so young a woman to behave like this! If religion cannot guide you, let me at least appeal to your conscience. I presume you have some moral feelings left? Or—perhaps you haven't? Well, answer me.

NORA. Oh, Torvald, that isn't an easy question to answer.

I simply don't know. I don't know where I am in these matters. I only know that these things mean something quite different to me from what they do to you. I've learned now that certain laws are different from what I'd imagined them to be; but I can't accept that such laws can be right. Has a woman really not the right to spare her dying father pain, or save her husband's life? I can't believe that.

HELMER. You're talking like a child. You don't understand how society works.

NORA. No, I don't. But now I intend to learn. I must try to satisfy myself which is right, society or I.

HELMER. Nora, you're ill; you're feverish. I almost believe you're out of your mind.

NORA. I've never felt so sane and sure in my life.

HELMER. You feel sure that it is right to leave your husband and your children?

NORA. Yes. I do.

HELMER. Then there is only one possible explanation.

NORA. What?

HELMER. That you don't love me any longer.

NORA. No, that's exactly it.

HELMER. Nora! How can you say this to me?

NORA. Oh, Torvald, it hurts me terribly to have to say it, because you've always been so kind to me. But I can't help it. I don't love you any longer.

HELMER (*controlling his emotions with difficulty*). And you feel quite sure about this too?

NORA. Yes, absolutely sure. That's why I can't go on living here any longer.

HELMER. Can you also explain why I have lost your love?

NORA. Yes, I can. It happened this evening, when the miracle failed to happen. It was then that I realized you weren't the man I'd thought you to be.

HELMER. Explain more clearly. I don't understand you.

NORA. I've waited so patiently, for eight whole years—well, good heavens, I'm not such a fool as to suppose that miracles occur every day. Then this dreadful thing happened to me, and then I *knew:* "Now the miracle will take place!" When Krogstad's letter was lying out there, it never occurred to me for a moment that you would let that man trample over you. I *knew* that you would say to him: "Publish the facts to the world." And when he had done this—

HELMER. Yes, what then? When I'd exposed my wife's name to shame and scandal—

NORA. Then I was certain that you would step forward and take all the blame on yourself, and say: "I am the one who is guilty!"

HELMER. Nora!

NORA. You're thinking I wouldn't have accepted such a sacrifice from you? No, of course I wouldn't! But what would my word have counted for against yours? That was the miracle I was hoping for, and dreading. And it was to prevent it happening that I wanted to end my life.

HELMER. Nora, I would gladly work for you night and day, and endure sorrow and hardship for your sake. But no man can be expected to sacrifice his honor, even for the person he loves.

NORA. Millions of women have done it.

HELMER. Oh, you think and talk like a stupid child

NORA. That may be. But you neither think nor talk like the man I could share my life with. Once you'd got over your fright—and you weren't frightened of what might threaten me, but only of what threatened you—once the danger was past, then as far as you were concerned it was exactly as though nothing had happened. I was your little songbird just as before—your doll whom henceforth you would take particular care to protect from the world because she was so weak and fragile. (*Gets up.*) Torvald, in that moment I realized that for eight years I had been living here with a complete stranger, and had borne him three children—! Oh, I can't bear to think of it! I could tear myself to pieces!

HELMER (*sadly*). I see it, I see it. A gulf has indeed opened between us. Oh, but Nora—couldn't it be bridged?

NORA. As I am now, I am no wife for you.

HELMER. I have the strength to change.

NORA. Perhaps—if your doll is taken from you.

HELMER. But to be parted—to be parted from you! No, no, Nora, I can't conceive of it happening!

NORA (*goes into the room, right*). All the more necessary that it should happen.

She comes back with her outdoor things and a small traveling bag, which she puts down on a chair by the table.

HELMER. Nora, Nora, not now! Wait till tomorrow!

NORA (*puts on her coat*). I can't spend the night in a strange man's house.

HELMER. But can't we live here as brother and sister, then—?

NORA (*fastens her hat*). You know quite well it wouldn't last. (*Puts on her shawl.*) Goodbye, Torvald. I don't want to see the children. I know they're in better hands than mine. As I am now, I can be nothing to them.

HELMER. But some time, Nora—some time—?

NORA. How can I tell? I've no idea what will happen to me.

HELMER. But you are my wife, both as you are and as you will be.

NORA. Listen, Torvald. When a wife leaves her husband's house, as I'm doing now, I'm told that according to the law he is freed of any obligations towards her. In any case, I release you from any such obligations. You mustn't feel bound to me in any way, however small, just as I shall not feel bound to you. We must both be quite free. Here is your ring back. Give me mine.

HELMER. That too?

NORA. That too.

HELMER. Here it is.

NORA. Good. Well, now it's over. I'll leave the keys here. The servants know about everything to do with the house—much better than I do. Tomorrow, when I have left town, Christine will come to pack the things I brought here from home. I'll have them sent on after me.

HELMER. This is the end then! Nora, will you never think of me any more?

NORA. Yes, of course. I shall often think of you and the children and this house.

HELMER. May I write to you, Nora?

NORA. No. Never. You mustn't do that.

HELMER. But at least you must let me send you—

NORA. Nothing. Nothing.

HELMER. But if you should need help?—

NORA. I tell you, no. I don't accept things from strangers.

HELMER. Nora—can I never be anything but a stranger to you?

NORA (*picks up her bag*). Oh, Torvald! Then the miracle of miracles would have to happen.

HELMER. The miracle of miracles?

NORA. You and I would both have to change so much that—oh, Torvald, I don't believe in miracles any longer.

HELMER. But I want to believe in them. Tell me. We should have to change so much that—?

NORA. That life together between us two could become a marriage. Goodbye.

She goes out through the hall.

HELMER (*sinks down on a chair by the door and buries his face in his hands*). Nora! Nora! (*Looks round and gets up.*) Empty! She's gone! (*A hope strikes him.*) The miracle of miracles—?

The street door is slammed shut downstairs.

TOPICS FOR DISCUSSION AND WRITING

1. Near the beginning of the play, how does Mrs. Linde's presence help to define Nora's character? How does Nora's response to Krogstad's entrance tell us something about Nora?
2. What does Dr. Rank contribute to the play? If he were eliminated, what would be lost?
3. In view of the fact that the last act several times seems to be moving toward a "happy ending" (e.g., Krogstad promises to recall his letter), what is wrong with the alternate ending (see page 304) that Ibsen reluctantly provided for a German production?
4. Can it be argued that although at the end Nora goes out to achieve self-realization, her abandonment of her children—especially to Torvald's loathsome conventional morality—is a crime? (By the way, exactly why does Nora leave the children? She seems to imply, in some passages, that because she forged a signature she is unfit to bring them up. But do you agree with her?)
5. Michael Meyer, in his splendid biography, *Henrik Ibsen,* says that the play is not so much about women's rights as about "the need of every individual to find out the kind of person he or she really is, and to strive to become that person." What evidence can you offer to support this interpretation?
6. In *The Quintessence of Ibsenism* Bernard Shaw says that Ibsen, reacting against a common theatrical preference for strange situations, "saw that . . . the more familiar the situation, the more interesting the play. Shakespear had put ourselves on the stage but not our situations. Our uncles seldom murder our fathers and . . . marry our mothers. . . . Ibsen . . . gives us not only ourselves, but ourselves in our own situations. The things that happen to his stage figures are things that happen to us. One consequence is that his plays are much more important to us than Shakespear's. Another is that they are capable both of hurting us cruelly and of filling us with excited hopes of escape from idealistic tyrannies, and with visions of intenser life in the future." How much of this do you believe?

CONTEXTS FOR *A DOLL'S HOUSE*

Remarks by Ibsen

1. [The University Library, Oslo, has the following preliminary notes for *A Doll's House:*]

Notes for the tragedy of modern times

Rome 19.10.78

There are two kinds of moral law, two kinds of conscience, one in man and a completely different one in woman. They do not understand each other; but in matters of practical living the woman is judged by man's law, as if she were not a woman but a man.

The wife in the play ends up quite bewildered and not knowing right from wrong; her natural instincts on the one side and her faith in authority on the other leave her completely confused.

A woman cannot be herself in contemporary society, it is an exclusively male society with laws drafted by men, and with counsel and judges who judge feminine conduct from the male point of view.

She has committed a crime, and she is proud of it; because she did it for love of her husband and to save his life. But the husband, with his conventional views of honor, stands on the side of the law and looks at the affair with male eyes.

Mental conflict. Depressed and confused by her faith in authority, she loses faith in her moral right and ability to bring up her children. Bitterness. A mother in contemporary society, just as certain insects go away and die when she has done her duty in the propagation of the race [*sic*]. Love of life, of home and husband and children and family. Now and then, woman-like, she shrugs off her thoughts. Sudden return of dread and terror. Everything must be borne alone. The catastrophe approaches, ineluctably, inevitably. Despair, resistance, defeat.

[*The following note was later added in the margin:*]

Krogstad has done some dishonest business, and thus made a bit of money; but his prosperity does not help him, he cannot recover his honour.

2. [Because Norwegian works were not copyrighted in Germany, German theaters could stage and freely adapt Ibsen's works without his consent. When he heard that a German director was going to change the ending to a happy one, Ibsen decided that he had better do the adaptation himself, though he characterized it as "a barbaric outrage" against the play.]

NORA. . . . Where we could make a real marriage out of our lives together. Goodbye. (*Begins to go.*)

HELMER. Go then! (*Seizes her arm.*) But first you shall see your children for the last time!

NORA. Let me go! I will not see them! I cannot!

HELMER (*draws her over to the door, left*). You shall see them. (*Opens the door and says softly.*) Look, there they are asleep, peaceful and carefree. Tomorrow, when they wake up and call for their mother, they will be—motherless.

NORA (*trembling*). Motherless . . . !

HELMER. As you once were.

NORA. Motherless! (*Struggles with herself, lets her travelling bag fall, and says.*) Oh, this is a sin against myself, but I cannot leave them. (*Half sinks down by the door.*)

HELMER (*joyfully, but softly*). Nora!

(*The curtain falls.*)

3. *Speech at the Banquet of the Norwegian League for Women's Rights*

Christiania, May 26, 1898

[A month after the official birthday celebrations were over, Ibsen and his wife were invited to a banquet in his honor given by the leading Norwegian feminist society.]

I am not a member of the Women's Rights League. Whatever I have written has been without any conscious thought of making propaganda. I have been more the poet and less the social philosopher than people generally seem inclined to believe. I thank you for the toast, but must disclaim the honor of having consciously worked for the women's rights movement. I am not even quite clear as to just what this women's rights movement really is. To me it has seemed a problem of mankind in general. And if you read my books carefully you will understand this. True enough, it is desirable to solve the woman problem, along with all the others; but that has not been the whole purpose. My task has been the *description of humanity.* To be sure, whenever such a description is felt to be reasonably true, the reader will read his own feelings and sentiments into the work of the poet. These are then attributed to the poet; but incorrectly so. Every reader remolds the work beautifully and neatly, each according to his own personality. Not only those who write but also those who read are poets. They are collaborators. They are often more poetical than the poet himself.

OSCAR WILDE

The Importance of Being Earnest

A Trivial Comedy for Serious People

Oscar Wilde (1854–1900) was born in Dublin. He distinguished himself as a student at Trinity College, Dublin, and at Oxford and then turned to a career of writing, lecturing, and in other ways making himself a public figure in England: his posture as an aesthete (he was alleged to have walked down Piccadilly with a flower in his hand) was caricatured by Gilbert and Sullivan in *Patience.* But it became no laughing matter when in 1895 he was arrested and convicted of homosexuality. After serving two years at hard labor, he was released from jail. He then went to France, where he lived under an assumed name until he died. His Irish birth did not ally him to the Irish Renaissance at the end of the nineteenth century; when W. B. Yeats was writing plays on Irish legends, Wilde was writing drawing-room comedies.

COMMENTARY

The gist of the plot of *The Importance of Being Earnest* is the gist of the plot of many comedies: a young man and a young woman wish to marry, but an apparently insurmountable obstacle interposes. The obstacle, however, is surmounted, and so at the end we get a happy, united society. Wilde doubles the lovers, giving us two young men and two young women, but this is scarcely an innovation, for we get two pairs of lovers in several of Shakespeare's comedies, including *A Midsummer Night's Dream,* which, after what has been called an obstacle race to the altar, similarly concludes with all of the lovers happily paired.

Our entry on *farce* in the Glossary suggests that farce is "a sort of comedy based not on clever language or subtleties of character, but on broadly humorous situations," such as a man mistakenly entering the ladies' locker room. Generally the emphasis in farce is on surprise and on swift physical action, with much frantic hiding under beds, desperate putting on of absurd disguises, and so forth. But it is widely (though not universally) agreed that *The Importance of Being Earnest* is a farce, an utterly improbable play with virtually no connection with life as we know or feel it. Those who hold this view, however, see this play as unique, the one farce that depends on language rather than physical action. Writing in 1902, at a revival staged seven years after the original production of *The Importance of Being Earnest,* Max Beerbohm said:

> In scheme, of course, it is a hackneyed farce—the story of a young man coming up to London "on the spree," and of another young man going down conversely to the country, and of the complications that ensue. . . . [But] the fun depends mainly on what the characters say, rather than on what they do. They speak a kind of beautiful nonsense—the language of high comedy, twisted into fantasy. Throughout the dialogue is the horse-play of a distinguished intellect and a distinguished imagination—a horse-play among words and ideas, conducted with poetic dignity.

A scene from the 1947 Theatre Guild production, directed by John Gielgud, with Gielgud as John Worthing, J. P., Pamela Browne as Gwendolen, Margaret Rutherford as Lady Bracknell, and Robert Fleming as Algernon. (Photograph courtesy of the New York Public Library Vandamm Collection.)

A few critics, however, have insisted that under the glittering but apparently trivial surface (Wilde said this play was "written by a butterfly for butterflies") there are serious topics, and that Wilde is indeed saying serious things—disguised as nonsense—about society. He is, in this view, joking in earnest; that is, he is writing satirically and only pretending to be playful. (On *satire,* see the Glossary entry.) Among the topics that critics have singled out are marriage, money, education, sincerity (the importance—or unimportance—of being earnest), class relationships, and death. In effect, the question comes down to this: When we hear, for instance, Lady Bracknell commenting on the absurd circumstances of Jack's infancy, do our minds turn to a criticism of the snobbish speaker, or do they (delighting in the absurd speech) relish the lines themselves and take pleasure in the speaker? Here is the passage in question:

> To be born, or at any rate, bred in a handbag, whether it had handles or not, seems to me to display a contempt for the ordinary decencies of family life that reminds one of the worst excesses of the French Revolution. And I presume you know what that unfortunate movement led to?

Readers are invited to try thinking about the play both ways—as a work of art divorced from reality, and as a work of art that repeatedly if indirectly comments on life—and to come to their own conclusions about the truth of the two views we have set forth. Possibly they will conclude, with Algernon, that "The truth is rarely pure, and never simple."

OSCAR WILDE *The Importance of Being Earnest*

List of Characters

JOHN WORTHING, J. P.
ALGERNON MONCRIEFF
REV. CANON CHASUBLE, D.D
MERRIMAN, *butler*
LANE, *manservant*
LADY BRACKNELL
HON.[1] GWENDOLEN FAIRFAX
CECILY CARDEW
MISS PRISM, *governess*

ACT 1

Morning room in Algernon's flat in Half-Moon Street. The room is luxuriously and artistically furnished. The sound of a piano is heard in the adjoining room. Lane is arranging afternoon tea on the table, and after the music has ceased, Algernon enters.

[1]**Hon.** The prefix *Hon.* (Honorable) indicates that she is the daughter of a viscount or a baron.

ALGERNON. Did you hear what I was playing, Lane?

LANE. I didn't think it polite to listen, sir.

ALGERNON. I'm sorry for that, for your sake. I don't play accurately—anyone can play accurately—but I play with wonderful expression. As far as the piano is concerned, sentiment is my forte. I keep science for Life.

LANE. Yes, sir.

ALGERNON. And, speaking of the science of Life, have you got the cucumber sandwiches cut for Lady Bracknell?

LANE. Yes, sir. (*Hands them on a salver.*)

ALGERNON (*inspects them, takes two, and sits down on the sofa*). Oh! . . . by the way, Lane, I see from your book that on Thursday night, when Lord Shoreman and Mr. Worthing were dining with me, eight bottles of champagne are entered as having been consumed.

LANE. Yes, sir; eight bottles and a pint.

ALGERNON. Why is it that at a bachelor's establishment the servants invariably drink the champagne? I ask merely for information.

LANE. I attribute it to the superior quality of the wine, sir. I have often observed that in married households the champagne is rarely of a first-rate brand.

ALGERNON. Good heavens! Is marriage so demoralizing as that?

LANE. I believe it *is* a very pleasant state, sir. I have had very little experience of it myself up to the present. I have only been married once. That was in consequence of a misunderstanding between myself and a young person.

ALGERNON (*languidly*). I don't know that I am much interested in your family life, Lane.

LANE. No, sir; it is not a very interesting subject. I never think of it myself.

ALGERNON. Very natural, I am sure. That will do, Lane, thank you.

LANE. Thank you, sir.

Lane goes out.

ALGERNON. Lane's views on marriage seem somewhat lax. Really, if the lower orders don't set us a good example, what on earth is the use of them? They seem, as a class, to have absolutely no sense of moral responsibility.

Enter Lane.

LANE. Mr. Ernest Worthing.

Enter Jack. Lane goes out.

ALGERNON. How are you, my dear Ernest? What brings you up to town?

JACK. Oh, pleasure, pleasure! What else should bring one anywhere? Eating as usual, I see, Algy!

ALGERNON (*stiffly*). I believe it is customary in good society to take some slight refreshment at five o'clock. Where have you been since last Thursday?

JACK (*sitting down on the sofa*). In the country.

ALGERNON. What on earth do you do there?

JACK (*pulling off his gloves*). When one is in town one amuses oneself. When one is in the country one amuses other people. It is excessively boring.

ALGERNON. And who are the people you amuse?

JACK (*airily*). Oh, neighbors, neighbors.

ALGERNON. Got nice neighbors in your part of Shropshire?

JACK. Perfectly horrid! Never speak to one of them.

ALGERNON. How immensely you must amuse them! (*Goes over and takes sandwich.*) By the way, Shropshire is your country, is it not?

JACK. Eh? Shropshire? Yes, of course. Hallo! Why all these cups? Why cucumber sandwiches? Why such reckless extravagance in one so young? Who is coming to tea?

ALGERNON. Oh! merely Aunt Augusta and Gwendolen.

JACK. How perfectly delightful!

ALGERNON. Yes, that is all very well; but I am afraid Aunt Augusta won't quite approve of your being here.

JACK. May I ask why?

ALGERNON. My dear fellow, the way you flirt with Gwendolen is perfectly disgraceful. It is almost as bad as the way Gwendolen flirts with you.

JACK. I am in love with Gwendolen. I have come up to town expressly to propose to her.

ALGERNON. I thought you had come up for pleasure? . . . I call that business.

JACK. How utterly unromantic you are!

ALGERNON. I really don't see anything romantic in proposing. It is very romantic to be in love. But there is nothing romantic about a definite proposal. Why, one may be accepted. One usually is, I believe. Then the excitement is all over. The very essence of romance is uncertainty. If ever I get married, I'll certainly try to forget the fact.

JACK. I have no doubt about that, dear Algy. The Divorce Court was specially invented for people whose memories are so curiously constituted.

ALGERNON. Oh! there is no use speculating on that subject. Divorces are made in Heaven— (*Jack puts out his hand to take a sandwich. Algernon at once interferes.*) Please don't touch the cucumber sandwiches. They are ordered especially for Aunt Augusta. (*Takes one and eats it.*)

JACK. Well, you have been eating them all the time.

ALGERNON. That is quite a different matter. She is my aunt. (*Takes plate from below.*) Have some bread and butter. The bread and butter is for Gwendolen. Gwendolen is devoted to bread and butter.

JACK (*advancing to table and helping himself*). And very good bread and butter it is too.

ALGERNON. Well, my dear fellow, you need not eat as if you were going to eat it all. You behave as if you were married to her already. You are not married to her already, and I don't think you ever will be.

JACK. Why on earth do you say that?

ALGERNON. Well, in the first place, girls never marry the men they flirt with. Girls don't think it right.

JACK. Oh, that is nonsense!

ALGERNON. It isn't. It is a great truth. It accounts for the extraordinary number of bachelors that one sees all over the place. In the second place, I don't give my consent.

JACK. Your consent!

ALGERNON. My dear fellow, Gwendolen is my first cousin. And before I allow you to marry her, you will have to clear up the whole question of Cecily. (*Rings bell.*)

JACK. Cecily! What on earth do you mean? What do you mean, Algy, by Cecily! I don't know anyone of the name of Cecily.

Enter Lane.

ALGERNON. Bring me that cigarette case Mr. Worthing left in the smoking room the last time he dined here.

LANE. Yes, sir.

Lane goes out.

JACK. Do you mean to say you have had my cigarette case all this time? I wish to goodness you had let me know. I have been writing frantic letters to Scotland Yard[2] about it. I was very nearly offering a large reward.

ALGERNON. Well, I wish you would offer one. I happen to be more than usually hard up.

JACK. There is no good offering a large reward now that the thing is found.

Enter Lane with the cigarette case on a salver. Algernon takes it at once. Lane goes out.

ALGERNON. I think that is rather mean of you, Ernest, I must say. (*Opens case and examines it.*) However, it makes no matter, for, now that I look at the inscription inside, I find that the thing isn't yours after all.

JACK. Of course it's mine. (*Moving to him.*) You have seen me with it a hundred times, and you have no right whatsoever to read what is written inside. It is a very ungentlemanly thing to read a private cigarette case.

ALGERNON. Oh! It is absurd to have a hard and fast rule about what one should read and what one shouldn't. More than half of modern culture depends on what one shouldn't read.

JACK. I am quite aware of the fact, and I don't propose to discuss modern culture. It isn't the sort of thing one should talk of in private. I simply want my cigarette case back.

ALGERNON. Yes; but this isn't your cigarette case. This cigarette case is a present from someone of the name of Cecily, and you said you didn't know anyone of that name.

JACK. Well, if you want to know, Cecily happens to be my aunt.

ALGERNON. Your aunt!

JACK. Yes. Charming old lady she is, too. Lives at Tunbridge Wells.[3] Just give it back to me, Algy.

ALGERNON (*retreating to back of sofa*). But why does she call herself little Cecily if she is your aunt and lives at Tunbridge Wells? (*Reading.*) "From little Cecily with her fondest love."

JACK (*moving to sofa and kneeling upon it*). My dear fellow, what on earth is there in that? Some aunts are tall, some aunts are not tall. That is a matter that surely an aunt may be allowed to decide for herself. You seem to think that every aunt should be exactly like your aunt! That is absurd. For Heaven's sake give me back my cigarette case. (*Follows Algernon round the room.*)

ALGERNON. Yes. But why does your aunt call you her uncle? "From little Cecily, with her fondest love to her dear Uncle Jack." There is no objection, I admit, to an aunt being a small aunt, but why an aunt, no matter what her size may be, should call her own nephew her uncle, I can't quite make out. Besides, your name isn't Jack at all, it is Ernest.

JACK. It isn't Ernest; it's Jack.

ALGERNON. You have always told me it was Ernest. I have introduced you to everyone as Ernest. You answer to the name of Ernest. You look as if your name was Ernest. You are the most earnest-looking person I ever saw in my life. It is perfectly absurd your saying that your name isn't Ernest. It's on your cards. Here is one of them (*taking it from case*). "Mr. Ernest Worthing, B.4, The Albany."[4] I'll keep this as a proof that your name is Ernest if ever you attempt to deny it to me, or to Gwendolen, or to any one else. (*Puts the card in his pocket.*)

JACK. Well, my name is Ernest in town and Jack in the country, and the cigarette case was given to me in the country.

ALGERNON. Yes, but that does not account for the fact that your small Aunt Cecily, who lives at Tunbridge Wells, calls you her dear uncle. Come, old boy, you had much better have the thing out at once.

JACK. My dear Algy, you talk exactly as if you were a dentist. It is very vulgar to talk like a dentist when one isn't a dentist. It produces a false impression.

ALGERNON. Well, that is exactly what dentists always do. Now, go on! Tell me the whole thing. I may mention that I have always suspected you of being a confirmed and secret Bunburyist; and I am quite sure of it now.

JACK. Bunburyist? What on earth do you mean by a Bunburyist?

ALGERNON. I'll reveal to you the meaning of that incomparable expression as soon as you are kind enough to inform me why you are Ernest in town and Jack in the country.

JACK. Well, produce my cigarette case first.

ALGERNON. Here it is. (*Hands cigarette case.*) Now produce your explanation, and pray make it improbable. (*Sits on sofa.*)

JACK. My dear fellow, there is nothing improbable about my explanation at all. In fact it's perfectly ordinary. Old Mr. Thomas Cardew, who adopted me when I was a little boy, made me in his will guardian to his granddaughter, Miss Cecily Cardew. Cecily, who addresses me as her uncle from motives of respect that you could not possibly

[2]**Scotland Yard** headquarters of the London Police

[3]**Tunbridge Wells** a fashionable town south of London in Kent

[4]**The Albany** fashionable apartments in Piccadilly near the center of London

appreciate, lives at my place in the country under the charge of her admirable governess, Miss Prism.

ALGERNON. Where is that place in the country, by the way?

JACK. That is nothing to you, dear boy. You are not going to be invited.... I may tell you candidly that the place is not in Shropshire.

ALGERNON. I suspected that, my dear fellow! I have Bunburyed all over Shropshire on two separate occasions. Now, go on. Why are you Ernest in town and Jack in the country?

JACK. My dear Algy, I don't know whether you will be able to understand my real motives. You are hardly serious enough. When one is placed in the position of guardian, one has to adopt a very high moral tone on all subjects. It's one's duty to do so. And as a high moral tone can hardly be said to conduce very much to either one's health or one's happiness, in order to get up to town I have always pretended to have a younger brother of the name of Ernest, who lives in the Albany, and gets into the most dreadful scrapes. That, my dear Algy, is the whole truth pure and simple.

ALGERNON. The truth is rarely pure and never simple. Modern life would be very tedious if it were either, and modern literature a complete impossibility!

JACK. That wouldn't be at all a bad thing.

ALGERNON. Literary criticism is not your forte, my dear fellow. Don't try it. You should leave that to people who haven't been at a University. They do it so well in the daily papers. What you really are is a Bunburyist. I was quite right in saying you were a Bunburyist. You are one of the most advanced Bunburyists I know.

JACK. What on earth do you mean?

ALGERNON. You have invented a very useful younger brother called Ernest, in order that you may be able to come up to town as often as you like. I have invented an invaluable permanent invalid called Bunbury, in order that I may be able to go down into the country whenever I choose. Bunbury is perfectly invaluable. If it wasn't for Bunbury's extraordinary bad health, for instance, I wouldn't be able to dine with you at Willis's[5] tonight, for I have been really engaged to[6] Aunt Augusta for more than a week.

JACK. I haven't asked you to dine with me anywhere tonight.

ALGERNON. I know. You are absurdly careless about sending out invitations. It is very foolish of you. Nothing annoys people so much as not receiving invitations.

JACK. You had much better dine with your Aunt Augusta.

ALGERNON. I haven't the smallest intention of doing anything of the kind. To begin with, I dined there on Monday, and once a week is quite enough to dine with one's own relations. In the second place, whenever I do dine there I am always treated as a member of the family, and sent down with[7] either no woman at all, or two. In the third place, I know perfectly well whom she will place me next to, tonight. She will place me next Mary Farquhar, who always flirts with her own husband across the dinner table. That is not very pleasant. Indeed, it is not even decent ... and that sort of thing is enormously on the increase. The amount of women in London who flirt with their own husbands is perfectly scandalous. It looks so bad. It is simply washing one's clean linen in public. Besides, now that I know you to be a confirmed Bunburyist I naturally want to talk to you about Bunburying. I want to tell you the rules.

JACK. I'm not a Bunburyist at all. If Gwendolen accepts me, I am going to kill my brother, indeed I think I'll kill him in any case. Cecily is a little too much interested in him. It is rather a bore. So I am going to get rid of Ernest. And I strongly advise you to do the same with Mr. ... with your invalid friend who has the absurd name.

ALGERNON. Nothing will induce me to part with Bunbury, and if you ever get married, which seems to be extremely problematic, you will be very glad to know Bunbury. A man who marries without knowing Bunbury has a very tedious time of it.

JACK. That is nonsense. If I marry a charming girl like Gwendolen, and she is the only girl I ever saw in my life that I would marry, I certainly won't want to know Bunbury.

ALGERNON. Then your wife will. You don't seem to realize, that in married life three is company and two is none.

JACK (*sententiously*). That, my dear young friend, is the theory that the corrupt French Drama has been propounding for the last fifty years.

ALGERNON. Yes; and that the happy English home has proved in half the time.

JACK. For heaven's sake, don't try to be cynical. It's perfectly easy to be cynical.

ALGERNON. My dear fellow, it isn't easy to be anything nowadays. There's such a lot of beastly competition about. (*The sound of an electric bell is heard.*) Ah! that must be Aunt Augusta. Only relatives, or creditors, ever ring in that Wagnerian manner.[8] Now, if I get her out of the way for ten minutes, so that you can have an opportunity for proposing to Gwendolen, may I dine with you tonight at Willis's?

JACK. I suppose so, if you want to.

ALGERNON. Yes, but you must be serious about it. I

[5]**Willis's** popular restaurant
[6]**engaged to** i.e., promised to attend her dinner party
[7]**sent down with** i.e., ordered to escort
[8]**Wagnerian manner** loudly

hate people who are not serious about meals. It is so shallow of them.

Enter Lane.

LANE. Lady Bracknell and Miss Fairfax.

Algernon goes forward to meet them. Enter Lady Bracknell and Gwendolen.

LADY BRACKNELL. Good afternoon, dear Algernon, I hope you are behaving very well.

ALGERNON. I'm feeling very well, Aunt Augusta.

LADY BRACKNELL. That's not quite the same thing. In fact the two things rarely go together. (*Sees Jack and bows to him with icy coldness.*)

ALGERNON (*to Gwendolen*). Dear me, you are smart![9]

GWENDOLEN. I am always smart! Am I not, Mr. Worthing?

JACK. You're quite perfect, Miss Fairfax.

GWENDOLEN. Oh! I hope I am not that. It would leave no room for developments, and I intend to develop in many directions. (*Gwendolen and Jack sit down together in the corner.*)

LADY BRACKNELL. I'm sorry if we are a little late, Algernon, but I was obliged to call on dear Lady Harbury. I hadn't been there since her poor husband's death. I never saw a woman so altered; she looks quite twenty years younger. And now I'll have a cup of tea and one of those nice cucumber sandwiches you promised me.

ALGERNON. Certainly, Aunt Augusta. (*Goes over to tea table.*)

LADY BRACKNELL. Won't you come and sit here, Gwendolen?

GWENDOLEN. Thanks, mamma, I'm quite comfortable where I am.

ALGERNON (*picking up empty plate in horror*). Good heavens! Lane! Why are there no cucumber sandwiches? I ordered them specially.

LANE (*gravely*). There were no cucumbers in the market this morning, sir. I went down twice.

ALGERNON. No cucumbers!

LANE. No, sir. Not even for ready money.

ALGERNON. That will do, Lane, thank you.

LANE. Thank you, sir. (*Goes out.*)

ALGERNON. I am greatly distressed, Aunt Augusta, about there being no cucumbers, not even for ready money.

LADY BRACKNELL. It really makes no matter, Algernon. I had some crumpets[10] with Lady Harbury, who seems to me to be living entirely for pleasure now.

ALGERNON. I hear her hair has turned quite gold from grief.

LADY BRACKNELL. It certainly has changed its color. From what cause I, of course, cannot say. (*Algernon crosses and hands tea.*) Thank you. I've quite a treat for you tonight, Algernon. I am going to send you down with Mary Farquhar. She is such a nice woman, and so attentive to her husband. It's delightful to watch them.

ALGERNON. I am afraid, Aunt Augusta, I shall have to give up the pleasure of dining with you tonight after all.

LADY BRACKNELL (*frowning*). I hope not, Algernon. It would put my table completely out. Your uncle would have to dine upstairs. Fortunately he is accustomed to that.

ALGERNON. It is a great bore, and, I need hardly say, a terrible disappointment to me, but the fact is I have just had a telegram to say that my poor friend Bunbury is very ill again. (*Exchanges glances with Jack*). They seem to think I should be with him.

LADY BRACKNELL. It is very strange. This Mr. Bunbury seems to suffer from curiously bad health.

ALGERNON. Yes; poor Bunbury is a dreadful invalid.

LADY BRACKNELL. Well, I must say, Algernon, that I think it is high time that Mr. Bunbury made up his mind whether he was going to live or to die. This shilly-shallying with the question is absurd. Nor do I in any way approve of the modern sympathy with invalids. I consider it morbid. Illness of any kind is hardly a thing to be encouraged in others. Health is the primary duty of life. I am always telling that to your poor uncle, but he never seems to take much notice . . . as far as any improvement in his ailments goes. I should be much obliged if you would ask Mr. Bunbury, from me, to be kind enough not to have a relapse on Saturday, for I rely on you to arrange my music for me. It is my last reception, and one wants something that will encourage conversation, particularly at the end of the season[11] when everyone has practically said whatever they had to say, which, in most cases, was probably not much.

ALGERNON. I'll speak to Bunbury, Aunt Augusta, if he is still conscious, and I think I can promise you he'll be all right by Saturday. Of course the music is a great difficulty. You see, if one plays good music, people don't listen, and if one plays bad music, people don't talk. But I'll run over the program I've drawn out, if you will kindly come into the next room for a moment.

LADY BRACKNELL. Thank you, Algernon. It is very thoughtful of you. (*Rising, and following Algernon.*) I'm sure the program will be delightful, after a few expurgations. French songs I cannot possibly allow. People always seem to think that they are improper, and either look shocked,

[9]**smart** elegantly dressed
[10]**crumpets** lightly toasted bread (similar to English muffins)
[11]**season** the social season

which is vulgar, or laugh, which is worse. But German sounds a thoroughly respectable language, and, indeed I believe is so. Gwendolen, you will accompany me.

GWENDOLEN. Certainly, mamma.

Lady Bracknell and Algernon go into the music room; Gwendolen remains behind.

JACK. Charming day it has been, Miss Fairfax.

GWENDOLEN. Pray don't talk to me about the weather, Mr. Worthing. Whenever people talk to me about the weather, I always feel quite certain that they mean something else. And that makes me so nervous.

JACK. I do mean something else.

GWENDOLEN. I thought so. In fact, I am never wrong.

JACK. And I would like to be allowed to take advantage of Lady Bracknell's temporary absence . . .

GWENDOLEN. I would certainly advise you to do so. Mamma has a way of coming back suddenly into a room that I have often had to speak to her about.

JACK (*nervously*). Miss Fairfax, ever since I met you I have admired you more than any girl . . . I have ever met since . . . I met you.

GWENDOLEN. Yes, I am quite aware of the fact. And I often wish that in public, at any rate, you had been more demonstrative. For me you have always had an irresistible fascination. Even before I met you I was far from indifferent to you. (*Jack looks at her in amazement.*) We live, as I hope you know, Mr. Worthing, in an age of ideals. The fact is constantly mentioned in the more expensive monthly magazines, and has reached the provincial pulpits, I am told; and my ideal has always been to love someone of the name of Ernest. There is something in that name that inspires absolute confidence. The moment Algernon first mentioned to me that he had a friend called Ernest, I knew I was destined to love you.

JACK. You really love me, Gwendolen?

GWENDOLEN. Passionately!

JACK. Darling! You don't know how happy you've made me.

GWENDOLEN. My own Ernest!

JACK. But you don't really mean to say that you couldn't love me if my name wasn't Ernest?

GWENDOLEN. But your name is Ernest.

JACK. Yes, I know it is. But supposing it was something else? Do you mean to say you couldn't love me then?

GWENDOLEN (*glibly*). Ah! that is clearly a metaphysical speculation, and like most metaphysical speculations has very little reference at all to the actual facts of real life, as we know them.

JACK. Personally, darling, to speak quite candidly, I don't much care about the name of Ernest . . . I don't think the name suits me at all.

GWENDOLEN. It suits you perfectly. It is a divine name. It has a music of its own. It produces vibrations.

JACK. Well, really, Gwendolen, I must say that I think there are lots of other much nicer names. I think Jack, for instance, a charming name.

GWENDOLEN. Jack? . . . No, there is very little music in the name Jack, if any at all, indeed. It does not thrill. It produces absolutely no vibrations. . . . I have known several Jacks, and they all, without exception, were more than usually plain. Besides, Jack is a notorious domesticity for John! And I pity any woman who is married to a man called John. She would probably never be allowed to know the entrancing pleasure of a single moment's solitude. The only really safe name is Ernest.

JACK. Gwendolen, I must get christened at once—I mean we must get married at once. There is no time to be lost.

GWENDOLEN. Married, Mr. Worthing?

JACK (*astounded*). Well . . . surely. You know that I love you, and you led me to believe, Miss Fairfax, that you were not absolutely indifferent to me.

GWENDOLEN. I adore you. But you haven't proposed to me yet. Nothing has been said at all about marriage. The subject has not even been touched on.

JACK. Well . . . may I propose to you now?

GWENDOLEN. I think it would be an admirable opportunity. And to spare you any possible disappointment, Mr. Worthing, I think it only fair to tell you quite frankly beforehand that I am fully determined to accept you.

JACK. Gwendolen!

GWENDOLEN. Yes, Mr. Worthing, what have you got to say to me?

JACK. You know what I have got to say to you.

GWENDOLEN. Yes, but you don't say it.

JACK. Gwendolen, will you marry me? (*Goes on his knees.*)

GWENDOLEN. Of course I will, darling. How long you have been about it! I am afraid you have had very little experience in how to propose.

JACK. My own one, I have never loved anyone in the world but you.

GWENDOLEN. Yes, but men often propose for practice. I know my brother Gerald does. All my girl friends tell me so. What wonderfully blue eyes you have, Ernest! They are quite, quite blue. I hope you will always look at me just like that, especially when there are other people present.

Enter Lady Bracknell.

LADY BRACKNELL. Mr. Worthing! Rise sir, from this semi-recumbent posture. It is most indecorous.

GWENDOLEN. Mamma! (*He tries to rise; she restrains*

him.) I must beg you to retire. This is no place for you. Besides, Mr. Worthing has not quite finished yet.

LADY BRACKNELL. Finished what, may I ask?

GWENDOLEN. I am engaged to Mr. Worthing, Mamma. (*They rise together.*)

LADY BRACKNELL. Pardon me, you are not engaged to anyone. When you do become engaged to someone, I, or your father, should his health permit him, will inform you of the fact. An engagement should come on a young girl as a surprise, pleasant or unpleasant, as the case may be. It is hardly a matter that she could be allowed to arrange for herself. . . . And now I have a few questions to put to you, Mr. Worthing. While I am making these inquiries, you, Gwendolen, will wait for me below in the carriage.

GWENDOLEN (*reproachfully*). Mamma!

LADY BRACKNELL. In the carriage, Gwendolen! (*Gwendolen goes to the door. She and Jack blow kisses to each other behind Lady Bracknell's back. Lady Bracknell looks vaguely about as if she could not understand what the noise was. Finally turns round.*) Gwendolen, the carriage!

GWENDOLEN. Yes, Mamma. (*Goes out, looking back at Jack.*)

LADY BRACKNELL (*sitting down*). You can take a seat, Mr. Worthing. (*Looks in her pocket for notebook and pencil.*)

JACK. Thank you, Lady Bracknell, I prefer standing.

LADY BRACKNELL (*pencil and notebook in hand*). I feel bound to tell you that you are not down on my list of eligible young men, although I have the same list as the dear Duchess of Bolton has. We work together, in fact. However, I am quite ready to enter your name, should your answers be what a really affectionate mother requires. Do you smoke?

JACK. Well, yes, I must admit I smoke.

LADY BRACKNELL. I am glad to hear it. A man should always have an occupation of some kind. There are far too many idle men in London as it is. How old are you?

JACK. Twenty-nine.

LADY BRACKNELL. A very good age to be married at. I have always been of opinion that a man who desires to get married should know either everything or nothing. Which do you know?

JACK (*after some hesitation*). I know nothing, Lady Bracknell.

LADY BRACKNELL. I am pleased to hear it. I do not approve of anything that tampers with natural ignorance. Ignorance is like a delicate exotic fruit; touch it and the bloom is gone. The whole theory of modern education is radically unsound. Fortunately in England, at any rate, education produces no effect whatsoever. If it did, it would prove a serious danger to the upper classes, and probably lead to acts of violence in Grosvenor Square. What is your income?

JACK. Between seven and eight thousand a year.

LADY BRACKNELL (*makes a note in her book*). In land, or in investments?

JACK. In investments, chiefly.

LADY BRACKNELL. That is satisfactory. What between the duties expected of one during one's lifetime, and the duties[12] exacted from one after one's death, land has ceased to be either a profit or a pleasure. It gives one position, and prevents one from keeping it up. That's all that can he said about land.

JACK. I have a country house with some land, of course, attached to it, about fifteen hundred acres, I believe; but I don't depend on that for my real income. In fact, as far as I can make out, the poachers are the only people who make anything out of it.

LADY BRACKNELL. A country house! How many bedrooms? Well, that point can be cleared up afterwards. You have a town house, I hope? A girl with a simple, unspoiled nature, like Gwendolen, could hardly be expected to reside in the country.

JACK. Well, I own a house in Belgrave Square, but it is let by the year to Lady Bloxham. Of course, I can get it back whenever I like, at six months' notice.

LADY BRACKNELL. Lady Bloxham? I don't know her.

JACK. Oh, she goes about very little. She is a lady considerably advanced in years.

LADY BRACKNELL. Ah, nowadays that is no guarantee of respectability of character. What number in Belgrave Square?

JACK. 149.

LADY BRACKNELL (*shaking her head*). The unfashionable side. I thought there was something. However, that could easily be altered.

JACK. Do you mean the fashion, or the side?

LADY BRACKNELL (*sternly*). Both, if necessary, I presume. What are your politics?

JACK. Well, I am afraid I really have none. I am a Liberal Unionist.

LADY BRACKNELL. Oh, they count as Tories. They dine with us. Or come in the evening, at any rate. Now to minor matters. Are your parents living?

JACK. I have lost both my parents.

LADY BRACKNELL. To lose one parent, Mr. Worthing, may be regarded as a misfortune; to lose both looks like carelessness. Who was your father? He was evidently a man of some wealth. Was he born in what the Radical papers call the purple of commerce, or did he rise from the ranks of the aristocracy?

JACK. I am afraid I really don't know. The fact is, Lady Bracknell, I said I had lost my parents. It would be nearer the truth to say that my parents seem to have lost me . . . I

[12] **duties** inheritance taxes

don't actually know who I am by birth. I was . . . well, I was found.

LADY BRACKNELL. Found!

JACK. The late Mr. Thomas Cardew, an old gentleman of a very charitable and kindly disposition, found me, and gave me the name of Worthing, because he happened to have a first-class ticket for Worthing in his pocket at the time. Worthing is a place in Sussex. It is a seaside resort.

LADY BRACKNELL. Where did the charitable gentleman who had a first-class ticket for this seaside resort find you?

JACK (*gravely*). In a handbag.

LADY BRACKNELL. A handbag?

JACK (*very seriously*). Yes, Lady Bracknell. I was in a handbag—a somewhat large, black leather handbag, with handles to it—an ordinary handbag in fact.

LADY BRACKNELL. In what locality did this Mr. James, or Thomas, Cardew come across this ordinary handbag?

JACK. In the cloakroom at Victoria Station. It was given to him in mistake for his own.

LADY BRACKNELL. The cloakroom at Victoria Station?

JACK. Yes. The Brighton line.

LADY BRACKNELL. The line is immaterial. Mr. Worthing, I confess I feel somewhat bewildered by what you have just told me. To be born, or at any rate bred, in a handbag, whether it had handles or not, seems to me to display a contempt for the ordinary decencies of family life that reminds one of the worst excesses of the French Revolution. And I presume you know what that unfortunate movement led to? As for the particular locality in which the handbag was found, a cloakroom at a railway station might serve to conceal a social indiscretion—had probably, indeed, been used for that purpose before now—but it could hardly be regarded as an assured basis for a recognized position in good society.

JACK. May I ask you then what you would advise me to do? I need hardly say I would do anything in the world to ensure Gwendolen's happiness.

LADY BRACKNELL. I would strongly advise you, Mr. Worthing, to try and acquire some relations as soon as possible, and to make a definite effort to produce at any rate one parent, of either sex, before the season is quite over.

JACK. Well, I don't see how I could possibly manage to do that. I can produce the handbag at any moment. It is in my dressing room at home. I really think that should satisfy you, Lady Bracknell.

LADY BRACKNELL. Me, sir! What has it to do with me? You can hardly imagine that I and Lord Bracknell would dream of allowing our only daughter—a girl brought up with the utmost care—to marry into a cloakroom, and form an alliance with a parcel. Good morning, Mr. Worthing!

(*Lady Bracknell sweeps out in majestic indignation.*)

JACK. Good morning! (*Agernon, from the other room, strikes up the Wedding March. Jack looks perfectly furious, and goes to the door.*) For goodness' sake don't play that ghastly tune, Algy! How idiotic you are!

The music stops and Algernon enters cheerily.

ALGERNON. Didn't it go off all right, old boy? You don't mean to say Gwendolen refused you? I know it is a way she has. She is always refusing people. I think it is most ill-natured of her.

JACK. Oh, Gwendolen is as right as a trivet.[13] As far as she is concerned, we are engaged. Her mother is perfectly unbearable. Never met such a Gorgon[14]. . . I don't really know what a Gorgon is like, but I am quite sure that Lady Bracknell is one. In any case, she is a monster, without being a myth, which is rather unfair. . . . I beg your pardon, Algy, I suppose I shouldn't talk about your own aunt in that way before you.

ALGERNON. My dear boy, I love hearing my relations abused. It is the only thing that makes me put up with them at all. Relations are simply a tedious pack of people, who haven't got the remotest knowledge of how to live, nor the smallest instinct about when to die.

JACK. Oh, that is nonsense!

ALGERNON. It isn't!

JACK. Well, I won't argue about the matter. You always want to argue about things.

ALGERNON. That is exactly what things were originally made for.

JACK. Upon my word, if I thought that, I'd shoot myself. . . . (*A pause.*) You don't think there is any chance of Gwendolen becoming like her mother in about a hundred and fifty years, do you, Algy?

ALGERNON. All women become like their mothers. That is their tragedy. No man does. That's his.

JACK. Is that clever?

ALGERNON. It is perfectly phrased! and quite as true as any observation in civilized life should be.

JACK. I am sick to death of cleverness. Everybody is clever nowadays. You can't go anywhere without meeting clever people. The thing has become an absolute public nuisance. I wish to goodness we had a few fools left.

ALGERNON. We have.

JACK. I should extremely like to meet them. What do they talk about?

[13]**trivet** proverbial expression meaning reliable (like a trivet used to support a kettle over a fire)
[14]**Gorgon** mythical female figure with writhing snakes for hair; her face turned anyone who looked at her into stone

ALGERNON. The fools? Oh! about the clever people, of course.

JACK. What fools.

ALGERNON. By the way, did you tell Gwendolen the truth about your being Ernest in town, and Jack in the country?

JACK (*in a very patronizing manner*). My dear fellow, the truth isn't quite the sort of thing one tells to a nice, sweet, refined girl. What extraordinary ideas you have about the way to behave to a woman!

ALGERNON. The only way to behave to a woman is to make love[15] to her, if she is pretty, and to someone else, if she is plain.

JACK. Oh, that is nonsense.

ALGERNON. What about your brother? What about the profligate Ernest?

JACK. Oh, before the end of the week I shall have got rid of him. I'll say he died in Paris of apoplexy. Lots of people die of apoplexy, quite suddenly, don't they?

ALGERNON. Yes, but it's hereditary, my dear fellow. It's a sort of thing that runs in families. You had much better say a severe chill.

JACK. You are sure a severe chill isn't hereditary, or anything of that kind?

ALGERNON. Of course it isn't!

JACK. Very well, then. My poor brother Ernest is carried off suddenly, in Paris, by a severe chill. That gets rid of him.

ALGERNON. But I thought you said that . . . Miss Cardew was a little too much interested in your poor brother Ernest? Won't she feel his loss a good deal?

JACK. Oh, that is all right. Cecily is not a silly romantic girl, I am glad to say. She has got a capital appetite, goes long walks, and pays no attention at all to her lessons.

ALGERNON. I would rather like to see Cecily.

JACK. I will take very good care you never do. She is excessively pretty, and she is only eighteen.

ALGERNON. Have you told Gwendolen yet that you have an excessively pretty ward who is only just eighteen?

JACK. Oh! one doesn't blurt these things out to people. Cecily and Gwendolen are perfectly certain to be extremely great friends. I'll bet you anything you like that half an hour after they have met, they will be calling each other sister.

ALGERNON. Women only do that when they have called each other a lot of other things first. Now, my dear boy, if we want to get a good table at Willis's, we really must go and dress. Do you know it is nearly seven?

JACK (*irritably*). Oh! it always is nearly seven.

ALGERNON. Well, I'm hungry.

JACK. I never knew you when you weren't. . . .

[15]**make love** to pay court to her, to woo

ALGERNON. What shall we do after dinner? Go to a theater?

JACK. Oh no! I loathe listening.

ALGERNON. Well, let us go to the Club?

JACK. Oh, no! I hate talking.

ALGERNON. Well, we might trot round to the Empire[16] at ten?

JACK. Oh no! I can't bear looking at things. It is so silly.

ALGERNON. Well, what shall we do?

JACK. Nothing!

ALGERNON. It is awfully hard work doing nothing. However, I don't mind hard work where there is no definite object of any kind.

Enter Lane.

LANE. Miss Fairfax.

Enter Gwendolen, Lane goes out.

ALGERNON. Gwendolen, upon my word!

GWENDOLEN. Algy, kindly turn your back. I have something very particular to say to Mr. Worthing.

ALGERNON. Really, Gwendolen, I don't think I can allow this at all.

GWENDOLEN. Algy, you always adopt a strictly immoral attitude towards life. You are not quite old enough to do that. (*Algernon retires to the fireplace.*)

JACK. My own darling!

GWENDOLEN. Ernest, we may never be married. From the expression on mamma's face I fear we never shall. Few parents nowadays pay any regard to what their children say to them. The old-fashioned respect for the young is fast dying out. Whatever influence I ever had over mamma, I lost at the age of three. But although she may prevent us from becoming man and wife, and I may marry someone else, and marry often, nothing that she can possibly do can alter my eternal devotion to you.

JACK. Dear Gwendolen!

GWENDOLEN. The story of your romantic origin, as related to me by mamma, with unpleasing comments, has naturally stirred the deeper fibers of my nature. Your Christian name has an irresistible fascination. The simplicity of your character makes you exquisitely incomprehensible to me. Your town address at the Albany I have. What is your address in the country?

JACK. The Manor House, Woolton, Hertfordshire.

Algernon, who has been carefully listening, smiles to himself and writes the address on his shirt-cuff. Then picks up the Railway Guide.

GWENDOLEN. There is a good postal service, I sup-

[16]**Empire** a music hall or variety theater

pose? It may be necessary to do something desperate. That of course will require serious consideration. I will communicate with you daily.

JACK. My own one!

GWENDOLEN. How long do you remain in town?

JACK. Till Monday.

GWENDOLEN. Good! Algy, you may turn round now.

ALGERNON. Thanks, I've turned round already.

GWENDOLEN. You may also ring the bell.

JACK. You will let me see you to your carriage, my own darling?

GWENDOLEN. Certainly.

JACK (*to Lane, who now enters*). I will see Miss Fairfax out.

LANE. Yes, sir. (*Jack and Gwendolen go off.*)

Lane presents several letters on a salver to Algernon. It is to be surmised that they are bills, as Algernon, after looking at the envelopes, tears them up.

ALGERNON. A glass of sherry, Lane.

LANE. Yes, sir.

ALGERNON. Tomorrow, Lane, I'm going Bunburying.

LANE. Yes, sir.

ALGERNON. I shall probably not be back till Monday. You can put up my dress clothes, my smoking jacket, and all the Bunbury suits .

LANE. Yes, sir. (*Handing sherry.*)

ALGERNON. I hope tomorrow will be a fine day, Lane.

LANE. It never is, sir.

ALGERNON. Lane, you're a perfect pessimist.

LANE. I do my best to give satisfaction, sir.

Enter Jack. Lane goes off.

JACK. There's a sensible, intellectual girl! the only girl I ever cared for in my life. (*Algernon is laughing immoderately.*) What on earth are you so amused at?

ALGERNON. Oh, I'm a little anxious about poor Bunbury, that is all.

JACK. If you don't take care, your friend Bunbury will get you into a serious scrape some day.

ALGERNON. I love scrapes. They are the only things that are never serious.

JACK. Oh, that's nonsense, Algy. You never talk anything but nonsense.

ALGERNON. Nobody ever does.

Jack looks indignantly at him, and leaves the room. Algernon lights a cigarette, reads his shirt-cuV, and smiles.

ACT DROP[17]

[17]**act drop** a curtain lowered in a theater during intermission

ACT 2

Garden at the Manor House. A flight of gray stone steps leads up to the house. The garden, an old-fashioned one, full of roses. Time of year, July. Basket chairs, and a table covered with books, are set under a large yew tree.

Miss Prism discovered seated at the table. Cecily is at the back, watering flowers.

MISS PRISM (*calling*). Cecily, Cecily! Surely such a utilitarian occupation as the watering of flowers is rather Moulton's duty than yours? Especially at a moment when intellectual pleasures await you. Your German grammar is on the table. Pray open it at page fifteen. We will repeat yesterday's lesson.

CECILY (*coming over very slowly*). But I don't like German. It isn't at all a becoming language. I know perfectly well that I look quite plain after my German lesson.

MISS PRISM. Child, you know how anxious your guardian is that you should improve yourself in every way. He laid particular stress on your German, as he was leaving for town yesterday. Indeed, he always lays stress on your German when he is leaving for town.

CECILY. Dear Uncle Jack is so very serious! Sometimes he is so serious that I think he cannot be quite well.

MISS PRISM (*drawing herself up*). Your guardian enjoys the best of health, and his gravity of demeanor is especially to be commended in one so comparatively young as he is. I know no one who has a higher sense of duty and responsibility.

CECILY. I suppose that is why he often looks a little bored when we three are together.

MISS PRISM. Cecily! I am surprised at you. Mr. Worthing has many troubles in his life. Idle merriment and triviality would be out of place in his conversation. You must remember his constant anxiety about that unfortunate young man his brother.

CECILY. I wish Uncle Jack would allow that unfortunate young man, his brother, to come down here sometimes. We might have a good influence over him, Miss Prism. I am sure you certainly would. You know German, and geology, and things of that kind influence a man very much. (*Cecily begins to write in her diary.*)

MISS PRISM (*shaking her head*). I do not think that even I could produce any effect on a character that according to his own brother's admission is irretrievably weak and vacillating. Indeed I am not sure that I would desire to reclaim him. I am not in favor of this modern mania for turning bad people into good people at a moment's notice. As a man sows so let him reap.[1] You must put away your diary, Cecily. I really don't see why you should keep a diary at all.

CECILY. I keep a diary in order to enter the wonderful secrets of my life. If I didn't write them down, I should probably forget all about them.

MISS PRISM. Memory, my dear Cecily, is the diary that we all carry about with us.

CECILY. Yes, but it usually chronicles the things that have never happened, and couldn't possibly have happened. I believe that Memory is responsible for nearly all the three-volume novels that Mudie[2] sends us.

MISS PRISM. Do not speak slightingly of the three-volume novel, Cecily. I wrote one myself in earlier days.

CECILY. Did you really, Miss Prism? How wonderfully clever you are! I hope it did not end happily? I don't like novels that end happily. They depress me so much.

MISS PRISM. The good ended happily, and the bad unhappily. That is what Fiction means.

CECILY. I suppose so. But it seems very unfair. And was your novel ever published?

MISS PRISM. Alas! no. The manuscript unfortunately was abandoned. (*Cecily starts.*) I used the word in the sense of lost or mislaid. To your work, child, these speculations are profitless.

CECILY (*smiling*). But I see dear Dr. Chasuble coming up through the garden.

MISS PRISM (*rising and advancing*). Dr. Chasuble! This is indeed a pleasure.

Enter Canon Chasuble.

CHASUBLE. And how are we this morning? Miss Prism, you are, I trust, well?

CECILY. Miss Prism has just been complaining of a slight headache. I think it would do her so much good to have a short stroll with you in the Park, Dr. Chasuble.

MISS PRISM. Cecily, I have not mentioned anything about a headache.

CECILY. No, dear Miss Prism, I know that, but I felt instinctively that you had a headache. Indeed I was thinking about that, and not about my German lesson, when the Rector came in.

CHASUBLE. I hope, Cecily, you are not inattentive.

CECILY. Oh, I am afraid I am.

CHASUBLE. That is strange. Were I fortunate enough to be Miss Prism's pupil, I would hang upon her lips. (*Miss Prism glares.*) I spoke metaphorically.—My metaphor was drawn from bees. Ahem! Mr. Worthing, I suppose, has not returned from town yet?

MISS PRISM. We do not expect him till Monday afternoon.

CHASUBLE. Ah yes, he usually likes to spend his Sunday in London. He is not one of those whose sole aim is enjoyment, as, by all accounts, that unfortunate young man his brother seems to be. But I must not disturb Egeria[3] and her pupil any longer.

MISS PRISM. Egeria? My name is Laetitia, Doctor.

CHASUBLE (*bowing*). A classical allusion merely, drawn from the Pagan authors. I shall see you both no doubt at Evensong?[4]

MISS PRISM. I think, dear Doctor, I will have a stroll with you. I find I have a headache after all, and a walk might do it good.

CHASUBLE. With pleasure, Miss Prism, with pleasure. We might go as far as the schools and back.

MISS PRISM. That would he delightful. Cecily, you will read your Political Economy in my absence. The chapter on the Fall of the Rupee you may omit. It is somewhat too sensational. Even these metallic problems have their melodramatic side. (*Goes down the garden with Dr. Chasuble.*)

CECILY (*picks up books and throws them back on table*). Horrid Political Economy! Horrid Geography! Horrid, horrid German!

Enter Merriman with a card on a salver.

MERRIMAN. Mr. Ernest Worthing has just driven over from the station. He has brought his luggage with him.

CECILY (*takes the card and reads it*). "Mr. Ernest Worthing, B.4, The Albany, W." Uncle Jack's brother! Did you tell him Mr. Worthing was in town?

MERRIMAN. Yes, Miss. He seemed very much disappointed. I mentioned that you and Miss Prism were in the garden. He said he was anxious to speak to you privately for a moment.

CECILY. Ask Mr. Ernest Worthing to come here. I suppose you had better talk to the housekeeper about a room for him.

MERRIMAN. Yes, Miss. (*Merriman goes off.*)

CECILY. I have never met any really wicked person before. I feel rather frightened. I am so afraid he will look just like everyone else.

Enter Algernon, very gay and debonair.

He does!

ALGERNON (*raising his hat*). You are my little cousin Cecily, I'm sure.

[1]**As . . . reap** Galatians 6.7
[2]**Mudie** a lending library
[3]**Egeria** mythical Roman female advisor of statesmen
[4]**Evensong** evening church service

CECILY. You are under some strange mistake. I am not little. In fact, I believe I am more than usually tall for my age. (*Algernon is rather taken aback.*) But I am your cousin Cecily. You, I see from your card, are Uncle Jack's brother, my cousin Ernest, my wicked cousin Ernest.

ALGERNON. Oh! I am not really wicked at all, Cousin Cecily. You mustn't think that I am wicked.

CECILY. If you are not, then you have certainly been deceiving us all in a very inexcusable manner. I hope you have not been leading a double life, pretending to be wicked and being really good all the time. That would he hypocrisy.

ALGERNON (*looks at her in amazement*). Oh! Of course I have been rather reckless.

CECILY. I am glad to hear it.

ALGERNON. In fact, now you mention the subject, I have been very bad in my own small way.

CECILY. I don't think you should he so proud of that, though I am sure it must have been very pleasant.

ALGERNON. It is much pleasanter being here with you.

CECILY. I can't understand how you are here at all. Uncle Jack won't be back till Monday afternoon.

ALGERNON. That is a great disappointment. I am obliged to go up by the first train on Monday morning. I have a business appointment that I am anxious . . . to miss!

CECILY. Couldn't you miss it anywhere but in London?

ALGERNON. No: the appointment is in London.

CECILY. Well, I know, of course, how important it is not to keep a business engagement, if one wants to retain any sense of the beauty of life, but still I think you had better wait till Uncle Jack arrives. I know he wants to speak to you about your emigrating.

ALGERNON. About my what?

CECILY. Your emigrating. He has gone up to buy your outfit.

ALGERNON. I certainly wouldn't let Jack buy my outfit. He has no taste in neckties at all.

CECILY. I don't think you will require neckties. Uncle Jack is sending you to Australia.

ALGERNON. Australia! I'd sooner die.

CECILY. Well, he said at dinner on Wednesday night, that you would have to choose between this world, the next world, and Australia.

ALGERNON. Oh, well! The accounts I have received of Australia and the next world are not particularly encouraging. This world is good enough for me, Cousin Cecily.

CECILY. Yes, but are you good enough for it?

ALGERNON. I'm afraid I'm not that. That is why I want you to reform me. You might make that your mission, if you don't mind, Cousin Cecily.

CECILY. I'm afraid I've no time, this afternoon.

ALGERNON. Well would you mind my reforming myself this afternoon?

CECILY. It is rather Quixotic of you. But I think you should try.

ALGERNON. I will. I feel better already.

CECILY. You are looking a little worse.

ALGERNON. That is because I am hungry.

CECILY. How thoughtless of me. I should have remembered that when one is going to lead an entirely new life, one requires regular and wholesome meals. Won't you come in?

ALGERNON. Thank you. Might I have a buttonhole first?[5] I never have any appetite unless I have a buttonhole first.

CECILY. A Maréchal Niel?[6] (*Picks up scissors.*)

ALGERNON. No, I'd sooner have a pink rose.

CECILY. Why? (*Cuts a flower.*)

ALGERNON. Because you are like a pink rose, Cousin Cecily.

CECILY. I don't think it can be right for you to talk to me like that. Miss Prism never says such things to me.

ALGERNON. Then Miss Prism is a shortsighted old lady. (*Cecily puts the rose in his buttonhole.*) You are the prettiest girl I ever saw.

CECILY. Miss Prism says that all good looks are a snare.

ALGERNON. They are a snare that every sensible man would like to be caught in.

CECILY. Oh, I don't think I would care to catch a sensible man. I shouldn't know what to talk to him about.

They pass into the house. Miss Prism and Dr. Chasuble return.

MISS PRISM. You are too much alone, dear Dr. Chasuble. You should get married. A misanthrope I can understand—a womanthrope, never!

CHASUBLE (*with a scholar's shudder*). Believe me, I do not deserve so neologistic a phrase. The precept as well as the practice of the Primitive Church was distinctly against matrimony.

MISS PRISM (*sententiously*). That is obviously the reason why the Primitive Church has not lasted up to the present day. And you do not seem to realize, dear Doctor, that by persistently remaining single, a man converts himself into a permanent public temptation. Men should be more careful; this very celibacy leads weaker vessels astray.

CHASUBLE. But is a man not equally attractive when married?

MISS PRISM. No married man is ever attractive except to his wife.

CHASUBLE. And often, I've been told, not even to her.

MISS PRISM. That depends on the intellectual sympa-

[5]**buttonhole** a flower for the buttonhole of a man's jacket
[6]**Maréchal Niel** a variety of rose

thies of the woman. Maturity can always be depended on. Ripeness can be trusted. Young women are green. (*Dr. Chasuble starts.*) I spoke horticulturally. My metaphor was drawn from fruits. But where is Cecily?

CHASUBLE. Perhaps she followed us to the schools.

Enter Jack slowly from the back of the garden. He is dressed in the deepest mourning, with crepe hatband and black gloves.

MISS PRISM. Mr. Worthing!

CHASUBLE. Mr. Worthing?

MISS PRISM. This is indeed a surprise. We did not look for you till Monday afternoon.

JACK (*shakes Miss Prism's hand in a tragic manner*). I have returned sooner than I expected. Dr. Chasuble, I hope you are well?

CHASUBLE. Dear Mr. Worthing, I trust this garb of woe does not betoken some terrible calamity?

JACK. My brother.

MISS PRISM. More shameful debts and extravagance?

CHASUBLE. Still leading his life of pleasure?

JACK (*shaking his head*). Dead!

CHASUBLE. Your brother Ernest dead?

JACK. Quite dead.

MISS PRISM. What a lesson for him! I trust he will profit by it.

CHASUBLE. Mr. Worthing, I offer you my sincere condolence. You have at least the consolation of knowing that you were always the most generous and forgiving of brothers.

JACK. Poor Ernest! He had many faults, but it is a sad, sad blow.

CHASUBLE. Very sad indeed. Were you with him at the end?

JACK. No. He died abroad; in Paris, in fact. I had a telegram last night from the manager of the Grand Hotel.

CHASUBLE. Was the cause of death mentioned?

JACK. A severe chill, it seems.

MISS PRISM. As a man sows, so shall he reap.

CHASUBLE (*raising his hand*). Charity, dear Miss Prism, charity! None of us are perfect. I myself am peculiarly susceptible to draughts. Will the interment take place here?

JACK. No. He seems to have expressed a desire to be buried in Paris.

CHASUBLE. In Paris! (*Shakes his head.*) I fear that hardly points to any very serious state of mind at the last. You would no doubt wish me to make some slight allusion to this tragic domestic affliction next Sunday. (*Jack presses his hand convulsively.*) My sermon on the meaning of the manna in the wilderness can be adapted to almost any occasion, joyful, or, as in the present case, distressing. (*All sigh.*) I have preached it at harvest celebrations, christening, confirmations, on days of humiliation and festal days. The last time I delivered it was in the Cathedral, as a charity sermon on behalf of the Society for the Prevention of Discontent among the Upper Orders. The Bishop, who was present, was much struck by some of the analogies I drew.

JACK. Ah! that reminds me, you mentioned christenings I think, Dr. Chasuble? I suppose you know how to christen all right? (*Dr. Chasuble looks astounded.*) I mean, of course, you are continually christening, aren't you?

MISS PRISM. It is, I regret to say, one of the Rector's most constant duties in this parish. I have often spoken to the poorer classes on the subject. But they don't seem to know what thrift is.

CHASUBLE. But is there any particular infant in whom you are interested, Mr. Worthing? Your brother was, I believe, unmarried, was he not?

JACK. Oh yes.

MISS PRISM (*bitterly*). People who live entirely for pleasure usually are.

JACK. But it is not for any child, dear Doctor. I am very fond of children. No! the fact is, I would like to be christened myself this afternoon, if you have nothing better to do.

CHASUBLE. But surely, Mr. Worthing, you have been christened already?

JACK. I don't remember anything about it.

CHASUBLE. But have you any grave doubts on the subject?

JACK. I certainly intend to have. Of course I don't know if the thing would bother you in any way, or if you think I am a little too old now.

CHASUBLE. Not at all. The sprinkling, and, indeed, the immersion of adults is a perfectly canonical practice.

JACK. Immersion!

CHASUBLE. You need have no apprehensions. Sprinkling is all that is necessary, or indeed I think advisable. Our weather is so changeable. At what hour would you wish the ceremony performed?

JACK. Oh, I might trot round about five if that would suit you.

CHASUBLE. Perfectly, perfectly! In fact I have two similar ceremonies to perform at that time. A case of twins that occurred recently in one of the outlying cottages on your own estate. Poor Jenkins the carter, a most hard-working man.

JACK. Oh! I don't see much fun in being christened along with other babies. It would be childish. Would half-past five do?

CHASUBLE. Admirably! Admirably! (*Takes out watch.*) And now, dear Mr. Worthing, I will not intrude any longer into a house of sorrow. I would merely beg you not to be too much bowed down by grief. What seems to us bitter trials are often blessings in disguise.

MISS PRISM. This seems to me a blessing of an extremely obvious kind.

Enter Cecily from the house.

CECILY. Uncle Jack! Oh, I am pleased to see you back. But what horrid clothes you have got on. Do go and change them.

MISS PRISM. Cecily!

CHASUBLE. My child! My child! (*Cecily goes towards Jack; he kisses her brow in a melancholy manner.*)

CECILY. What is the matter, Uncle Jack? Do look happy! You look as if you had toothache, and I have got such a surprise for you. Who do you think is in the dining room? Your brother!

JACK. Who?

CECILY. Your brother Ernest. He arrived about half an hour ago.

JACK. What nonsense! I haven't got a brother.

CECILY. Oh, don't say that. However badly he may have behaved to you in the past he is still your brother. You couldn't be so heartless as to disown him. I'll tell him to come out. And you will shake hands with him, won't you, Uncle Jack? (*Runs back into the house.*)

CHASUBLE. These are very joyful tidings.

MISS PRISM. After we had all been resigned to his loss, his sudden return seems to me peculiarly distressing.

JACK. My brother is in the dining room? I don't know what it all means. I think it is perfectly absurd.

Enter Algernon and Cecily hand in hand. They come slowly up to Jack.

JACK. Good heavens! (*Motions Algernon away.*)

ALGERNON. Brother John, I have come down from town to tell you that I am very sorry for all the trouble I have given you, and that I intend to lead a better life in the future. (*Jack glares at him and does not take his hand.*)

CECILY. Uncle Jack, you are not going to refuse your own brother's hand?

JACK. Nothing will induce me to take his hand. I think his coming down here disgraceful. He knows perfectly well why.

CECILY. Uncle Jack, do be nice. There is some good in everyone. Ernest has just been telling me about his poor invalid friend Mr. Bunbury whom he goes to visit so often. And surely there must be much good in one who is kind to an invalid, and leaves the pleasures of London to sit by a bed of pain.

JACK. Oh! he has been talking about Bunbury, has he?

CECILY. Yes, he has told me all about poor Mr. Bunbury, and his terrible state of health.

JACK. Bunbury! Well, I won't have him talk to you about Bunbury or about anything else. It is enough to drive one perfectly frantic.

ALGERNON. Of course I admit that the faults were all on my side. But I must say that I think that Brother John's coldness to me is peculiarly painful. I expected a more enthusiastic welcome, especially considering it is the first time I have come here.

CECILY. Uncle Jack, if you don't shake hands with Ernest I will never forgive you.

JACK. Never forgive me?

CECILY. Never, never, never!

JACK. Well, this is the last time I shall ever do it. (*Shakes hands with Algernon and glares.*)

CHASUBLE. It's pleasant, is it not, to see so perfect a reconciliation? I think we might leave the two brothers together.

MISS PRISM. Cecily, you will come with us.

CECILY. Certainly, Miss Prism. My little task of reconciliation is over.

CHASUBLE. You have done a beautiful action today, dear child.

MISS PRISM. We must not be premature in our judgments.

CECILY. I feel very happy. (*They all go off except Jack and Algernon.*)

JACK. You young scoundrel, Algy, you must get out of this place as soon as possible. I don't allow any Bunburying here.

Enter Merriman.

MERRIMAN. I have put Mr. Ernest's things in the room next to yours, sir. I suppose that is all right?

JACK. What?

MERRIMAN. Mr. Ernest's luggage, sir. I have unpacked it and put it in the room next to your own.

JACK. His luggage?

MERRIMAN. Yes, sir. Three portmanteaus,[7] a dressing case, two hatboxes, and a large luncheon basket.

ALGERNON. I am afraid I can't stay more than a week this time.

JACK. Merriman, order the dogcart[8] at once. Mr. Ernest has been suddenly called back to town.

MERRIMAN. Yes, sir. (*Goes back into the house.*)

ALGERNON. What a fearful liar you are, Jack. I have not been called back to town at all.

JACK. Yes, you have.

ALGERNON. I haven't heard anyone call me.

[7]**portmanteaus** large suitcases
[8]**dogcart** a vehicle drawn by a horse and accommodating two persons

JACK. Your duty as a gentleman calls you back.

ALGERNON. My duty as a gentleman has never interfered with my pleasures in the smallest degree.

JACK. I can quite understand that.

ALGERNON. Well, Cecily is a darling.

JACK. You are not to talk of Miss Cardew like that. I don't like it.

ALGERNON. Well, I don't like your clothes. You look perfectly ridiculous in them. Why on earth don't you go up and change? It is perfectly childish to be in deep mourning for a man who is actually staying for a whole week with you in your house as a guest. I call it grotesque.

JACK. You are certainly not staying with me for a whole week as a guest or anything else. You have got to leave . . . by the four-five train.

ALGERNON. I certainly won't leave you so long as you are in mourning. It would be most unfriendly. If I were in mourning you would stay with me, I suppose. I should think it very unkind if you didn't.

JACK. Well, will you go if I change my clothes?

ALGERNON. Yes, if you are not too long. I never saw anybody take so long to dress, and with such little result.

JACK. Well, at any rate, that is better than being always overdressed as you are.

ALGERNON. If I am occasionally a little overdressed, I make up for it by being always immensely overeducated.

JACK. Your vanity is ridiculous, your conduct an outrage, and your presence in my garden utterly absurd. However, you have got to catch the four-five, and I hope you will have a pleasant journey back to town. This Bunburying, as you call it, has not been a great success for you. (*Goes into the house.*)

ALGERNON. I think it has been a great success. I'm in love with Cecily, and that is everything.

Enter Cecily at the back of the garden. She picks up the can and begins to water the flowers.

But I must see her before I go, and make arrangements for another Bunbury. Ah, there she is.

CECILY. Oh, I merely came back to water the roses. I thought you were with Uncle Jack.

ALGERNON. He's gone to order the dogcart for me.

CECILY. Oh, is he going to take you for a nice drive?

ALGERNON. He's going to send me away.

CECILY. Then have we got to part?

ALGERNON. I am afraid so. It's a very painful parting.

CECILY. It is always painful to part from people whom one has known for a very brief space of time. The absence of old friends one can endure with equanimity. But even a momentary separation from anyone to whom one has just been introduced is almost unbearable.

ALGERNON. Thank you.

Enter Merriman.

MERRIMAN. The dogcart is at the door, sir.

(*Algernon looks appealing at Cecily.*)

CECILY. It can wait, Merriman . . . for . . . five minutes.

MERRIMAN. Yes, miss.

Exit Merriman.

ALGERNON. I hope, Cecily, I shall not offend you if I state quite frankly and openly that you seem to me to be in every way the visible personification of absolute perfection.

CECILY. I think your frankness does you great credit, Ernest. If you will allow me, I will copy your remarks into my diary. (*Goes over to table and begins writing in diary.*)

ALGERNON. Do you really keep a diary? I'd give anything to look at it. May I?

CECILY. Oh no. (*Puts her hand over it.*) You see, it is simply a very young girl's record of her own thoughts and impressions, and consequently meant for publication. When it appears in volume form I hope you will order a copy. But pray, Ernest, don't stop. I delight in taking down from dictation. I have reached "absolute perfection." You can go on. I am quite ready for more.

ALGERNON (*somewhat taken aback*). Ahem! Ahem!

CECILY. Oh, don't cough, Ernest. When one is dictating one should speak fluently and not cough. Besides, I don't know how to spell a cough. (*Writes as Algernon speaks.*)

ALGERNON (*speaking very rapidly*). Cecily, ever since I first looked upon your wonderful and incomparable beauty, I have dared to love you wildly, passionately, devotedly, hopelessly.

CECILY. I don't think that you should tell me that you love me wildly, passionately, devotedly, hopelessly. Hopelessly doesn't seem to make much sense, does it?

ALGERNON. Cecily.

Enter Merriman.

MERRIMAN. The dogcart is waiting, sir.

ALGERNON. Tell it to come round next week, at the same hour.

MERRIMAN (*looks at Cecily, who makes no sign*). Yes, sir.

Merriman retires.

CECILY. Uncle Jack would be very much annoyed if he knew you were staying on till next week, at the same hour.

ALGERNON. Oh, I don't care about Jack. I don't care for anybody in the whole world but you. I love you, Cecily. You will marry me, won't you?

CECILY. You silly boy! Of course. Why, we have been engaged for the last three months.

ALGERNON. For the last three months?

CECILY. Yes, it will be exactly three months on Thursday.

ALGERNON. But how did we become engaged?

CECILY. Well, ever since dear Uncle Jack first confessed to us that he had a younger brother who was very wicked and bad, you of course have formed the chief topic of conversation between myself and Miss Prism. And of course a man who is much talked about is always very attractive. One feels there must be something in him, after all. I daresay it was foolish of me, but I fell in love with you, Ernest.

ALGERNON. Darling. And when was the engagement actually settled?

CECILY. On the 14th of February last. Worn out by your entire ignorance of my existence, I determined to end the matter one way or the other, and after a long struggle with myself I accepted you under this dear old tree here. The next day I bought this little ring in your name, and this is the little bangle with the true lovers' knot I promised you always to wear.

ALGERNON. Did I give you this? It's very pretty, isn't it?

CECILY. Yes, you've wonderfully good taste, Ernest. It's the excuse I've always given for your leading such a bad life. And this is the box in which I keep all your dear letters. (*Kneels at table, opens box, and produces letters tied up with blue ribbon.*)

ALGERNON. My letters! But, my own sweet Cecily, I have never written you any letters.

CECILY. You need hardly remind me of that, Ernest. I remember only too well that I was forced to write your letters for you. I wrote always three times a week, and sometimes oftener.

ALGERNON. Oh, do let me read them, Cecily?

CECILY. Oh, I couldn't possibly. They would make you far too conceited. (*Replaces box.*) The three you wrote me after I had broken off the engagement are so beautiful, and so badly spelled, that even now I can hardly read them without crying a little.

ALGERNON. But was our engagement ever broken off?

CECILY. Of course it was. On the 22nd of last March. You can see the entry if you like. (*Shows diary.*) "Today I broke off my engagement with Ernest. I feel it is better to do so. The weather still continues charming."

ALGERNON. But why on earth did you break it off? What had I done? I had done nothing at all. Cecily, I am very much hurt indeed to hear you broke it off. Particularly when the weather was so charming.

CECILY. It would hardly have been a really serious engagement if it hadn't been broken off at least once. But I forgave you before the week was out.

ALGERNON (*crossing to her, and kneeling*). What a perfect angel you are, Cecily.

CECILY. You dear romantic boy. (*He kisses her, she puts her fingers through his hair.*) I hope your hair curls naturally, does it?

ALGERNON. Yes, darling, with a little help from others.

CECILY. I am so glad.

ALGERNON. You'll never break off our engagement again. Cecily?

CECILY. I don't think I could break it off now that I have actually met you. Besides, of course, there is the question of your name.

ALGERNON. Yes, of course. (*Nervously.*)

CECILY. You must not laugh at me, darling, but it had always been a girlish dream of mine to love someone whose name was Ernest. (*Algernon rises, Cecily also.*) There is something in that name that seems to inspire absolute confidence. I pity any poor married woman whose husband is not called Ernest.

ALGERNON. But, my dear child, do you mean to say you could not love me if I had some other name?

CECILY. But what name?

ALGERNON. Oh, any name you like—Algernon—for instance. . . .

CECILY. But I don't like the name of Algernon.

ALGERNON. Well, my own dear, sweet, loving little darling, I really can't see why you should object to the name of Algernon. It is not at all a bad name. In fact, it is rather an aristocratic name. Half of the chaps who get into the Bankruptcy Court are called Algernon. But seriously, Cecily . . . (*moving to her*) if my name was Algy, couldn't you love me?

CECILY (*rising*). I might respect you, Ernest, I might admire your character, but I fear that I should not be able to give you my undivided attention.

ALGERNON. Ahem! Cecily! (*Picking up hat.*) Your Rector here is, I suppose, thoroughly experienced in the practice of all the rites and ceremonials of the Church?

CECILY. Oh, yes. Dr. Chasuble is a most learned man. He has never written a single book, so you can imagine how much he knows.

ALGERNON. I must see him at once on a most important christening—I mean on most important business.

CECILY. Oh!

ALGERNON. I shan't be away more than half an hour.

CECILY. Considering that we have been engaged since February the 14th, and that I only met you today for the first time, I think it is rather hard that you should leave me for so long a period as half an hour. Couldn't you make it twenty minutes?

ALGERNON. I'll be back in no time. (*Kisses her and rushes down the garden.*)

CECILY. What an impetuous boy he is! I like his hair so much. I must enter his proposal in my diary.

Enter Merriman.

MERRIMAN. A Miss Fairfax just called to see Mr. Worthing. On very important business, Miss Fairfax states.

CECILY. Isn't Mr. Worthing in his library?

MERRIMAN. Mr. Worthing went over in the direction of the Rectory some time ago.

CECILY. Pray ask the lady to come out here; Mr. Worthing is sure to be back soon. And you can bring tea.

MERRIMAN. Yes, Miss. (*Goes out.*)

CECILY. Miss Fairfax! I suppose one of the many good elderly women who are associated with Uncle Jack in some of his philanthropic work in London. I don't quite like women who are interested in philanthropic work. I think it is so forward of them.

Enter Merriman.

MERRIMAN. Miss Fairfax.

Enter Gwendolen. Exit Merriman.

CECILY (*advancing to meet her*). Pray let me introduce myself to you. My name is Cecily Cardew.

GWENDOLEN. Cecily Cardew? (*Moving to her and shaking hands.*) What a very sweet name! Something tells me that we are going to be great friends. I like you already more than I can say. My first impressions of people are never wrong.

CECILY. How nice of you to like me so much after we have known each other such a comparatively short time. Pray sit down.

GWENDOLEN (*still standing up*). I may call you Cecily, may I not?

CECILY. With pleasure!

GWENDOLEN. And you will always call me Gwendolen, won't you?

CECILY. If you wish.

GWENDOLEN. Then that is all quite settled, is it not?

CECILY. I hope so. (*A pause. They both sit down together.*)

GWENDOLEN. Perhaps this might be a favorable opportunity for my mentioning who I am. My father is Lord Bracknell. You have never heard of papa, I suppose?

CECILY. I don't think so.

GWENDOLEN. Outside the family circle, papa, I am glad to say, is entirely unknown. I think that is quite as it should be. The home seems to me to be the proper sphere for the man. And certainly once a man begins to neglect his domestic duties he becomes painfully effeminate, does he not? And I don't like that. It makes men so very attractive. Cecily, mamma, whose views on education are remarkably strict, has brought me up to be extremely shortsighted; it is part of her system; so do you mind my looking at you through my glasses?

CECILY. Oh! not at all, Gwendolen. I am very fond of being looked at.

GWENDOLEN (*after examining Cecily carefully through a lorgnette*). You are here on a short visit, I suppose.

CECILY. Oh no! I live here.

GWENDOLEN (*severely*). Really? Your mother, no doubt, or some female relative of advanced years, resides here also?

CECILY. Oh no! I have no mother, nor, in fact, any relations.

GWENDOLEN. Indeed?

CECILY. My dear guardian, with the assistance of Miss Prism, has the arduous task of looking after me.

GWENDOLEN. Your guardian?

CECILY. Yes, I am Mr. Worthing's ward.

GWENDOLEN. Oh! It is strange he never mentioned to me that he had a ward. How secretive of him! He grows more interesting hourly. I am not sure, however, that the news inspires me with feelings of unmixed delight. (*Rising and going to her.*) I am very fond of you, Cecily; I have liked you ever since I met you! But I am bound to state that now that I know that you are Mr. Worthing's ward, I cannot help expressing a wish you were—well, just a little older than you seem to be—and not quite so very alluring in appearance. In fact, if I may speak candidly—

CECILY. Pray do! I think that whenever one has anything unpleasant to say, one should always be quite candid.

GWENDOLEN. Well, to speak with perfect candor, Cecily, I wish that you were fully forty-two, and more than usually plain for your age. Ernest has a strong upright nature. He is the very soul of truth and honor. Disloyalty would be as impossible to him as deception. But even men of the noblest possible moral character are extremely susceptible to the influence of the physical charms of others. Modern, no less than Ancient History, supplies us with many most painful examples of what I refer to. If it were not so, indeed, History would be quite unreadable.

CECILY. I beg your pardon, Gwendolen, did you say Ernest?

GWENDOLEN. Yes.

CECILY. Oh, but it is not Ernest Worthing who is my guardian. It is his brother—his elder brother.

GWENDOLEN (*sitting down again*). Ernest never mentioned to me that he had a brother.

CECILY. I am sorry to say they have not been on good terms for a long time.

GWENDOLEN. Ah! that accounts for it. And now that I think of it I have never heard any man mention his brother. The subject seems distasteful to most men. Cecily, you have lifted a load from my mind. I was growing almost anxious. It would have been terrible if any cloud had come across a friendship like ours, would it not? Of course you are quite, quite sure that it is not Mr. Ernest Worthing who is your guardian?

CECILY. Quite sure. (*A pause.*) In fact, I am going to be his.

GWENDOLEN (*inquiringly*). I beg your pardon?

CECILY (*rather shy and confidingly*). Dearest Gwendolen, there is no reason why I should make a secret of it to you. Our little country newspaper is sure to chronicle the fact next week. Mr. Ernest Worthing and I are engaged to be married.

GWENDOLEN (*quite politely, rising*). My darling Cecily, I think there must be some slight error. Mr. Ernest Worthing is engaged to me. The announcement will appear in the *Morning Post* on Saturday at the latest.

CECILY. (*very politely, rising*). I am afraid you must be under some misconception. Ernest proposed to me exactly ten minutes ago. (*Shows diary.*)

GWENDOLEN (*examines diary through her lorgnette carefully*). It is very curious, for he asked me to be his wife yesterday afternoon at 5:30. If you would care to verify the incident, pray do so. (*Produces diary of her own.*) I never travel without my diary. One should always have something sensational to read in the train. I am so sorry, dear Cecily, if it is any disappointment to you, but I am afraid I have the prior claim.

CECILY. It would distress me more than I can tell you, dear Gwendolen, if it caused you any mental or physical anguish, but I feel bound to point out that since Ernest proposed to you he clearly has changed his mind.

GWENDOLEN (*meditatively*). If the poor fellow has been entrapped into any foolish promise I shall consider it my duty to rescue him at once, and with a firm hand.

CECILY (*thoughtfully and sadly*). Whatever unfortunate entanglement my dear boy may have got into, I will never reproach him with it after we are married.

GWENDOLEN. Do you allude to me, Miss Cardew, as an entanglement? You are presumptuous. On an occasion of this kind it becomes more than a moral duty to speak one's mind. It becomes a pleasure.

CECILY. Do you suggest, Miss Fairfax, that I entrapped Ernest into an engagement? How dare you? This is no time for wearing the shallow mask of manners. When I see a spade I call it a spade.

GWENDOLEN (*satirically*). I am glad to say that I have never seen a spade. It is obvious that our social spheres have been widely different.

Enter Merriman, followed by the footman. He carries a salver, tablecloth, and plate stand. Cecily is about to retort. The presence of the servants exercises a restraining influence, under which both girls chafe.

MERRIMAN. Shall I lay tea here as usual, Miss?

CECILY (*sternly, in a calm voice*). Yes, as usual. (*Merriman begins to clear table and lay cloth. A long pause. Cecily and Gwendolen glare at each other.*)

GWENDOLEN. Are there many interesting walks in the vicinity, Miss Cardew?

CECILY. Oh! yes! a great many. From the top of one of the hills quite close one can see five counties.

GWENDOLEN. Five counties! I don't think I should like that; I hate crowds.

CECILY (*sweetly*). I suppose that is why you live in town? (*Gwendolen bites her lip, and beats her foot nervously with her parasol.*)

GWENDOLEN (*looking round*). Quite a well-kept garden this is, Miss Cardew.

CECILY. So glad you like it, Miss Fairfax.

GWENDOLEN. I had no idea there were any flowers in the country.

CECILY. Oh, flowers are as common here, Miss Fairfax, as people are in London.

GWENDOLEN. Personally I cannot understand how anybody manages to exist in the country, if anybody who is anybody does. The country always bores me to death.

CECILY. Ah! This is what the newspapers call agricultural depression, is it not? I believe the aristocracy are suffering very much from it just at present. It is almost an epidemic amongst them, I have been told. May I offer you some tea, Miss Fairfax?

GWENDOLEN (*with elaborate politeness*). Thank you. (*Aside.*) Detestable girl! But I require tea!

CECILY (*sweetly*). Sugar?

GWENDOLEN (*superciliously*). No, thank you. Sugar is not fashionable any more. (*Cecily looks angrily at her, takes up the tongs and puts four lumps of sugar into the cup.*)

CECILY (*severely*). Cake or bread and butter?

GWENDOLEN (*in a bored manner*). Bread and butter, please. Cake is rarely seen at the best houses nowadays.

CECILY (*cuts a very large slice of cake and puts it on the tray*). Hand that to Miss Fairfax.

Merriman does so, and goes out with footman. Gwendolen drinks the tea and makes a grimace. Puts down cup at once, reaches out her hand to the bread and butter, looks at it, and finds it is cake. Rises in indignation.

GWENDOLEN. You have filled my tea with lumps of sugar, and though I asked most distinctly for bread and butter, you have given me cake. I am known for the gentleness of my disposition, and the extraordinary sweetness of my nature, but I warn you, Miss Cardew, you may go too far.

CECILY (*rising*). To save my poor, innocent, trusting boy from the machinations of any other girl there are no lengths to which I would not go.

GWENDOLEN. From the moment I saw you I distrusted you. I felt that you were false and deceitful. I am never deceived in such matters. My first impressions of people are invariably right

CECILY. It seems to me. Miss Fairfax, that I am trespassing on your valuable time. No doubt you have many other calls of a similar character to make in the neighborhood.

Enter Jack.

GWENDOLEN (*catches sight of him*). Ernest! My own Ernest!

JACK. Gwendolen! Darling! (*Offers to kiss her.*)

GWENDOLEN (*drawing back*). A moment! May I ask if you are engaged to be married to this young lady? (*Points to Cecily*).

JACK (*laughing*). To dear little Cecily! Of course not! What could have put such an idea into your pretty little head?

GWENDOLEN. Thank you. You may! (*Offers her cheek.*)

CECILY (*very sweetly*). I knew there must be some misunderstanding, Miss Fairfax. The gentleman whose arm is at present round your waist is my dear guardian, Mr. John Worthing.

GWENDOLEN. I beg your pardon?

CECILY. This is Uncle Jack.

GWENDOLEN (*receding*). Jack! Oh!

Enter Algernon.

CECILY. Here is Ernest.

ALGERNON (*goes straight over to Cecily without noticing anyone else*). My own love! (*Offers to kiss her.*)

CECILY (*drawing back*). A moment, Ernest! May I ask you—are you engaged to be married to this young lady?

ALGERNON (*looking round*). To what young lady? Good heavens! Gwendolen!

CECILY. Yes, to good heavens, Gwendolen, I mean to Gwendolen.

ALGERNON (*laughing*). Of course not. What could have put such an idea into your pretty little head?

CECILY. Thank you. (*Presenting her cheek to be kissed.*) You may. (*Algernon kisses her.*)

GWENDOLEN. I felt there was some slight error, Miss Cardew. The gentleman who is now embracing you is my cousin, Mr. Algernon Moncrieff.

CECILY (*breaking away from Algernon*). Algernon Moncrieff! Oh! (*The two girls move towards each other and put their arms around each other's waists as if for protection.*)

CECILY. Are you called Algernon?

ALGERNON. I cannot deny it.

CECILY. Oh!

GWENDOLEN. Is your name really John?

JACK (*standing rather proudly*). I could deny it if I liked. I could deny anything if I liked. But my name certainly is John. It has been John for years.

CECILY (*to Gwendolen*). A gross deception has been practiced on both of us.

GWENDOLEN. My poor wounded Cecily!

CECILY. My sweet wronged Gwendolen!

GWENDOLEN (*slowly and seriously*). You will call me sister, will you not? (*They embrace. Jack and Algernon groan and walk up and down.*)

CECILY (*rather brightly*). There is just one question I would like to be allowed to ask my guardian.

GWENDOLEN. An admirable idea! Mr. Worthing, there is just one question I would like to be permitted to put to you. Where is your brother Ernest? We are both engaged to be married to your brother Ernest, so it is a matter of some importance to us to know where your brother Ernest is at present.

JACK (*slowly and hesitatingly*). Gwendolen—Cecily—it is very painful for me to be forced to speak the truth. It is the first time in my life that I have ever been reduced to such a painful position, and I am really quite inexperienced in doing anything of the kind. However, I will tell you quite frankly that I have no brother Ernest. I have no brother at all. I never had a brother in my life, and I certainly have not the smallest intention of ever having one in the future.

CECILY (*surprised*). No brother at all?

JACK (*cheerily*). None!

GWENDOLEN (*severely*). Had you never a brother of any kind?

JACK (*pleasantly*). Never. Not even of any kind.

GWENDOLEN. I am afraid it is quite clear, Cecily, that neither of us is engaged to be married to anyone.

CECILY. It is not a very pleasant position for a young girl suddenly to find herself in. Is it?

GWENDOLEN. Let us go into the house. They will hardly venture to come after us there.

CECILY. No, men are so cowardly, aren't they?

They retire into the house with scornful looks.

JACK. This ghastly state of things is what you call Bunburying, I suppose?

ALGERNON. Yes, and a perfectly wonderful Bunbury it is. The most wonderful Bunbury I have ever had in my life.

JACK. Well, you've no right whatsoever to Bunbury here.

ALGERNON. That is absurd. One has a right to Bunbury anywhere one chooses. Every serious Bunburyist knows that.

JACK. Serious Bunburyist? Good heavens!

ALGERNON. Well, one must be serious about something, if one wants to have any amusement in life. I happen to be serious about Bunburying. What on earth you are serious about I haven't got the remotest idea. About everything, I should fancy. You have such an absolutely trivial nature.

JACK. Well, the only small satisfaction I have in the whole of this wretched business is that your friend Bunbury is quite exploded. You won't be able to run down to the country quite so often as you used to do, dear Algy. And a very good thing too.

ALGERNON. Your brother is a little off color, isn't he, dear Jack? You won't be able to disappear to London quite so frequently as your wicked custom was. And not a bad thing either.

JACK. As for your conduct towards Miss Cardew, I must say that your taking in a sweet, simple, innocent girl like that is quite inexcusable. To say nothing of the fact that she is my ward.

ALGERNON. I can see no possible defense at all for your deceiving a brilliant, clever, thoroughly experienced young lady like Miss Fairfax. To say nothing of the fact that she is my cousin.

JACK. I wanted to be engaged to Gwendolen, that is all. I love her.

ALGERNON. Well, I simply wanted to be engaged to Cecily. I adore her.

JACK. There is certainly no chance of your marrying Miss Cardew.

ALGERNON. I don't think there is much likelihood, Jack, of you and Miss Fairfax being united.

JACK. Well, that is no business of yours.

ALGERNON. If it was my business, I wouldn't talk about it. (*Begins to eat muffins.*) It is very vulgar to talk about one's business. Only people like stockbrokers do that, and then merely at dinner parties.

JACK. How you can sit there, calmly eating muffins when we are in this horrible trouble, I can't make out. You seem to me to be perfectly heartless.

ALGERNON. Well, I can't eat muffins in an agitated manner. The butter would probably get on my cuffs. One should always eat muffins quite calmly. It is the only way to eat them.

JACK. I say it's perfectly heartless your eating muffins at all, under the circumstances.

ALGERNON. When I am in trouble, eating is the only thing that consoles me. Indeed, when I am in really great trouble, as anyone who knows me intimately will tell you, I refuse everything except food and drink. At the present moment I am eating muffins because I am unhappy. Besides, I am particularly fond of muffins. (*Rising.*)

JACK (*rising*). Well, there is no reason why you should eat them all in that greedy way. (*Takes muffins from Algernon.*)

ALGERNON (*offering teacake*). I wish you would have teacake instead. I don't like teacake.

JACK. Good heavens! I suppose a man may eat his own muffins in his own garden.

ALGERNON. But you have just said it was perfectly heartless to eat muffins.

JACK. I said it was perfectly heartless of you, under the circumstances. That is a very different thing.

ALGERNON. That may be. But the muffins are the same. (*He seizes the muffin dish from Jack.*)

JACK. Algy, I wish to goodness you would go.

ALGERNON. You can't possibly ask me to go without having some dinner. It's absurd. I never go without my dinner. No one ever does, except vegetarians and people like that. Besides I have just made arrangements with Dr. Chasuble to be christened at a quarter to six under the name of Ernest.

JACK. My dear fellow, the sooner you give up that nonsense the better. I made arrangements this morning with Dr. Chasuble to be christened myself at 5:30, and I naturally will take the name of Ernest. Gwendolen would wish it. We can't both be christened Ernest. It's absurd. Besides, I have a perfect right to be christened if I like. There is no evidence at all that I have ever been christened by anybody. I should think it extremely probable I never was, and so does Dr. Chasuble. It is entirely different in your case. You have been christened already.

ALGERNON. Yes, but I have not been christened for years.

JACK. Yes, but you have been christened. That is the important thing.

ALGERNON. Quite so. So I know my constitution can stand it. If you are not quite sure about your ever having been christened, I must say I think it rather dangerous your venturing on it now. It might make you very unwell. You can hardly have forgotten that someone very closely connected with you was very nearly carried off this week in Paris by a severe chill.

JACK. Yes, but you said yourself that a severe chill was not hereditary.

ALGERNON. It usen't to be, I know—but I daresay it is now. Science is always making wonderful improvements in things.

JACK (*picking up the muffin dish*). Oh, that is nonsense; you are always talking nonsense.

ALGERNON. Jack, you are at the muffins again! I wish you wouldn't. There are only two left. (*Takes them.*) I told you I was particularly fond of muffins.

JACK. But I hate teacake.

ALGERNON. Why on earth then do you allow teacake to be served up for your guests? What ideas you have of hospitality!

JACK. Algernon! I have already told you to go. I don't want you here. Why don't you go!

ALGERNON. I haven't quite finished my tea yet! and there is one muffin left. (*Jack groans, and sinks into a chair. Algernon still continues eating.*)

ACT 3

Morning room at the Manor House. Gwendolen and Cecily are at the window, looking out into the garden.

GWENDOLEN. The fact that they did not follow us at once into the house, as anyone else would have done, seems to me to show that they have some sense of shame left.

CECILY. They have been eating muffins. That looks like repentance.

GWENDOLEN (*after a pause*). They don't seem to notice us at all. Couldn't you cough?

CECILY. But I haven't got a cough.

GWENDOLEN. They're looking at us. What effrontery!

CECILY. They're approaching. That's very forward of them.

GWENDOLEN. Let us preserve a dignified silence.

CECILY. Certainly. It's the only thing to do now.

Enter Jack followed by Algernon. They whistle some dreadful popular air from a British opera.

GWENDOLEN. This dignified silence seems to produce an unpleasant effect.

CECILY. A most distasteful one.

GWENDOLEN. But we will not be the first to speak.

CECILY. Certainly not.

GWENDOLEN. Mr. Worthing, I have something very particular to ask you. Much depends on your reply.

CECILY. Gwendolen, your common sense is invaluable. Mr. Moncrieff, kindly answer me the following question. Why did you pretend to be my guardian's brother?

ALGERNON. In order that I might have an opportunity of meeting you.

CECILY (*to Gwendolen*). That certainly seems a satisfactory explanation, does it not?

GWENDOLEN. Yes, dear, if you can believe him.

CECILY. I don't. But that does not affect the wonderful beauty of his answer.

GWENDOLEN. True. In matters of grave importance, style, not sincerity, is the vital thing. Mr. Worthing, what explanation can you offer to me for pretending to have a brother? Was it in order that you might have an opportunity of coming up to town to see me as often as possible?

JACK. Can you doubt it, Miss Fairfax?

GWENDOLEN. I have the gravest doubts upon the subject. But I intend to crush them. This is not the moment for German skepticism. (*Moving to Cecily.*) Their explanations appear to be quite satisfactory, especially Mr. Worthing's. That seems to me to have the stamp of truth upon it.

CECILY. I am more than content with what Mr. Moncrieff said. His voice alone inspires one with absolute credulity.

GWENDOLEN. Then you think we should forgive them?

CECILY. Yes. I mean no.

GWENDOLEN. True! I had forgotten. There are principles at stake that one cannot surrender. Which of us should tell them? The task is not a pleasant one.

CECILY. Could we not both speak at the same time?

GWENDOLEN. An excellent idea! I nearly always speak at the same time as other people. Will you take the time from me?

CECILY. Certainly. (*Gwendolen beats time with uplifted finger.*)

GWENDOLEN AND CECILY (*speaking together*). Your Christian names are still an insuperable barrier. That is all!

JACK AND ALGERNON (*speaking together*). Our Christian names! Is that all? But we are going to be christened this afternoon.

GWENDOLEN (*to Jack*). For my sake you are prepared to do this terrible thing?

JACK. I am.

CECILY (*to Algernon*). To please me you are ready to face this fearful ordeal?

ALGERNON. I am!

GWENDOLEN. How absurd to talk of the equality of the sexes! Where questions of self-sacrifice are concerned, men are infinitely beyond us.

JACK. We are. (*Clasps hands with Algernon.*)

CECILY. They have moments of physical courage of which we women know absolutely nothing.

GWENDOLEN (*to Jack*). Darling!

ALGERNON (*to Cecily*). Darling! (*They fall into each other's arms.*)

Enter Merriman. When he enters he coughs loudly, seeing the situation.

MERRIMAN. Ahem! Ahem! Lady Bracknell.

JACK. Good heavens!

Enter Lady Bracknell. The couples separate in alarm. Exit Merriman.

LADY BRACKNELL. Gwendolen! What does this mean?

GWENDOLEN. Merely that I am engaged to be married to Mr. Worthing, Mamma.

LADY BRACKNELL. Come here. Sit down. Sit down immediately. Hesitation of any kind is a sign of mental decay in the young, of physical weakness in the old. (*Turns to Jack.*) Apprised, sir, of my daughter's sudden flight by her trusty maid, whose confidence I purchased by means of a small coin, I followed her at once by a luggage train. Her unhappy father is, I am glad to say, under the impression that she is attending a more than usually lengthy lecture by the University Extension Scheme on the Influence of a permanent income on Thought. I do not propose to undeceive him. Indeed I have never undeceived him on any question. I would consider it wrong. But of course, you will clearly understand that all communication between yourself and my daughter must cease immediately from this moment. On this point, as indeed on all points, I am firm.

JACK. I am engaged to be married to Gwendolen, Lady Bracknell!

LADY BRACKNELL. You are nothing of the kind, sir. And now as regards Algernon! . . . Algernon!

ALGERNON. Yes, Aunt Augusta.

LADY BRACKNELL. May I ask if it is in this house that your invalid friend Mr. Bunbury resides?

ALGERNON (*stammering*). Oh! No! Bunbury doesn't live here. Bunbury is somewhere else at present. In fact, Bunbury is dead.

LADY BRACKNELL. Dead! When did Mr. Bunbury die? His death must have been extremely sudden.

ALGERNON (*airily*). Oh! I killed Bunbury this afternoon. I mean poor Bunbury died this afternoon.

LADY BRACKNELL. What did he die of?

ALGERNON. Bunbury? Oh, he was quite exploded.

LADY BRACKNELL. Exploded! Was he the victim of a revolutionary outrage? I was not aware that Mr. Bunbury was interested in social legislation. If so, he is well punished for his morbidity.

ALGERNON. My dear Aunt Augusta, I mean he was found out! The doctors found out that Bunbury could not live, that is what I mean—so Bunbury died.

LADY BRACKNELL. He seems to have had great confidence in the opinion of his physicians. I am glad, however, that he made up his mind at the last to some definite course of action, and acted upon proper medical advice. And now that we have finally got rid of this Mr. Bunbury, may I ask, Mr. Worthing, who is that young person whose hand my nephew Algernon is now holding in what seems to me a peculiarly unnecessary manner?

JACK. That lady is Miss Cecily Cardew, my ward. (*Lady Bracknell bows coldly to Cecily.*)

ALGERNON. I am engaged to be married to Cecily, Aunt Augusta.

LADY BRACKNELL. I beg your pardon?

CECILY. Mr. Moncrieff and I are engaged to be married, Lady Bracknell.

LADY BRACKNELL (*with a shiver, crossing to the sofa and sitting down*). I do not know whether there is anything peculiarly exciting in the air of this particular part of Hertfordshire, but the number of engagements that go on seems to be considerably above the proper average that statistics have laid down for our guidance. I think some preliminary inquiry on my part would not be out of place. Mr. Worthing, is Miss Cardew at all connected with any of the larger railway stations in London? I merely desire information. Until yesterday I had no idea that there were any families or persons whose origin was a Terminus.[1] (*Jack looks perfectly furious, but restrains himself*)

JACK (*in a cold, clear voice*). Miss Cardew is the granddaughter of the late Mr. Thomas Cardew of 149 Belgrave Square, S.W.; Gervase Park, Dorking, Surrey; and the Sporran, Fifeshire, N. B.[2]

LADY BRACKNELL. That sounds not unsatisfactory. Three addresses always inspire confidence, even in tradesmen. But what proof have I of their authenticity?

JACK. I have carefully preserved the Court Guides of the period. They are open to your inspection, Lady Bracknell.

LADY BRACKNELL (*grimly*). I have known strange errors in that publication.

JACK. Miss Cardew's family solicitors are Messrs. Markby, Markby, and Markby.

LADY BRACKNELL. Markby, Markby, and Markby? A firm of the very highest position in their profession. Indeed I am told that one of the Mr. Markbys is occasionally to be seen at dinner parties. So far I am satisfied.

JACK (*very irritably*). How extremely kind of you, Lady Bracknell! I have also in my possession, you will be pleased to hear, certificates of Miss Cardew's birth, baptism, whooping cough, registration, vaccination, confirmation, and the measles; both the German and the English variety.

LADY BRACKNELL. Ah! A life crowded with incident, I see; though perhaps somewhat too exciting for a young girl. I am not myself in favour of premature experiences. (*Rises, looks at her watch.*) Gwendolen! the time approaches for our departure. We have not a moment to lose. As a matter of form, Mr. Worthing, I had better ask you if Miss Cardew has any little fortune?

JACK. Oh! about a hundred and thirty thousand pounds in the Funds.[3] That is all. Good-bye, Lady Bracknell. So pleased to have seen you.

LADY BRACKNELL (*sitting down again*). A moment, Mr. Worthing. A hundred and thirty thousand pounds! And in the Funds! Miss Cardew seems to me a most attractive young lady, now that I look at her. Few girls of the present day have any really solid qualities, any of the qualities that last, and improve with time. We live, I regret to say, in an age of surfaces. (*To Cecily.*) Come over here, dear. (*Cecily goes across.*) Pretty child! your dress is sadly simple, and your hair seems almost as Nature might have left it. But we

[1] **Terminus** railway station
[2] **N.B.** North Britain, i.e., Scotland
[3] **Funds** interest-bearing government bonds

can soon alter all that. A thoroughly experienced French maid produces a really marvelous result in a very brief space of time. I remember recommending one to young Lady Lancing, and after three months her own husband did not know her.

JACK. And after six months nobody knew her.

LADY BRACKNELL (*glares at Jack for a few moments. Then bends, with a practiced smile, to Cecily*). Kindly turn round, sweet child. (*Cecily turns completely round.*) No, the side view is what I want. (*Cecily presents her profile.*) Yes, quite as I expected. There are distinct social possibilities in your profile. The two weak points in our age are its want of principle and its want of profile. The chin a little higher, dear. Style largely depends on the way the chin is worn. They are worn very high, just at present. Algernon!

ALGERNON. Yes, Aunt Augusta!

LADY BRACKNELL. There are distinct social possibilities in Miss Cardew's profile.

ALGERNON. Cecily is the sweetest, dearest, prettiest girl in the whole world. And I don't care twopence about social possibilities.

LADY BRACKNELL. Never speak disrespectfully of Society, Algernon. Only people who can't get into it do that. (*To Cecily.*) Dear child, of course you know that Algernon has nothing but his debts to depend upon. But I do not approve of mercenary marriages. When I married Lord Bracknell I had no fortune of any kind. But I never dreamed for a moment of allowing that to stand in my way. Well, I suppose I must give my consent.

ALGERNON. Thank you, Aunt Augusta.

LADY BRACKNELL. Cecily, you may kiss me!

CECILY (*kisses her*). Thank you, Lady Bracknell.

LADY BRACKNELL. You may also address me as Aunt Augusta for the future.

CECILY. Thank you, Aunt Augusta.

LADY BRACKNELL. The marriage, I think, had better take place quite soon.

ALGERNON. Thank you, Aunt Augusta.

CECILY. Thank you, Aunt Augusta.

LADY BRACKNELL. To speak frankly, I am not in favor of long engagements. They give people the opportunity of finding out each other's character before marriage, which I think is never advisable.

JACK. I beg your pardon for interrupting you, Lady Bracknell, but this engagement is quite out of the question. I am Miss Cardew's guardian, and she cannot marry without my consent until she comes of age. That consent I absolutely decline to give.

LADY BRACKNELL. Upon what grounds, may I ask? Algernon is an extremely, I may almost say an ostentatiously, eligible young man. He has nothing, but he looks everything. What more can one desire?

JACK. It pains me very much to have to speak frankly to you, Lady Bracknell, about your nephew, but the fact is that I do not approve at all of his moral character. I suspect him of being untruthful. (*Algernon and Cecily look at him in indignant amazement.*)

LADY BRACKNELL. Untruthful! My nephew Algernon? Impossible! He is an Oxonian.[4]

JACK. I fear there can be no possible doubt about the matter. This afternoon during my temporary absence in London on an important question of romance, he obtained admission to my house by means of the false pretense of being my brother. Under an assumed name he drank, I've just been informed by my butler, an entire pint bottle of my Perrier-Jouet, Brut, '89; wine I was specially reserving for myself. Continuing his disgraceful deception, he succeeded in the course of the afternoon in alienating the affections of my only ward. He subsequently stayed to tea, and devoured every single muffin. And what makes his conduct all the more heartless is, that he was perfectly well aware from the first that I have no brother, that I never had a brother, and that I don't intend to have a brother, not even of any kind. I distinctly told him so myself yesterday afternoon.

LADY BRACKNELL. Ahem! Mr. Worthing, after careful consideration I have decided entirely to overlook my nephew's conduct to you.

JACK. That is very generous of you, Lady Bracknell. My own decision, however, is unalterable. I decline to give my consent.

LADY BRACKNELL (*to Cecily*). Come here, sweet child. (*Cecily goes over.*) How old are you, dear?

CECILY. Well, I am really only eighteen, but I always admit to twenty when I go to evening parties.

LADY BRACKNELL. You are perfectly right in making some slight alteration. Indeed, no woman should ever be quite accurate about her age. It looks so calculating. . . . (*In a meditative manner.*) Eighteen, but admitting to twenty at evening parties. Well, it will not be very long before you are of age and free from the restraints of tutelage. So I don't think your guardian's consent is, after all, a matter of any importance.

JACK. Pray excuse me, Lady Bracknell, for interrupting you again, but it is only fair to tell you that according to the terms of her grandfather's will Miss Cardew does not come legally of age till she is thirty-five.

LADY BRACKNELL. That does not seem to me to be a grave objection. Thirty-five is a very attractive age. London society is full of women of the very highest birth who have, of their own free choice, remained thirty-five for years. Lady Dumbleton is an instance in point. To my own knowledge she has been thirty-five ever since she arrived at the age of

[4]**Oxonian** a graduate of Oxford

forty, which was many years ago now. I see no reason why our dear Cecily should not be even still more attractive at the age you mention than she is at present. There will be a large accumulation of property.

CECILY. Algy, could you wait for me till I was thirty-five?

ALGERNON. Of course I could, Cecily. You know I could.

CECILY. Yes, I felt it instinctively, but I couldn't wait all that time. I hate waiting even five minutes for anybody. It always makes me rather cross. I am not punctual myself, I know, but I do like punctuality in others, and waiting, even to be married, is quite out of the question.

ALGERNON. Then what is to be done, Cecily?

CECILY. I don't know, Mr. Moncrieff.

LADY BRACKNELL. My dear Mr. Worthing, as Miss Cardew states positively that she cannot wait till she is thirty-five—a remark which I am bound to say seems to me to show a somewhat impatient nature—I would beg of you to reconsider your decision.

JACK. But my dear Lady Bracknell, the matter is entirely in your own hands. The moment you consent to my marriage with Gwendolen, I will most gladly allow your nephew to form an alliance with my ward.

LADY BRACKNELL (*rising and drawing herself up*). You must be quite aware that what you propose is out of the question.

JACK. Then a passionate celibacy is all that any of us can look forward to.

LADY BRACKNELL. That is not the destiny I propose for Gwendolen. Algernon, of course, can choose for himself. (*Pulls out her watch.*) Come, dear (*Gwendolen rises*), we have already missed five, if not six, trains. To miss any more might expose us to comment on the platform.

Enter Dr. Chasuble.

CHASUBLE. Everything is quite ready for the christenings.

LADY BRACKNELL. The christenings, sir! Is not that somewhat premature?

CHASUBLE (*looking rather puzzled, and pointing to Jack and Algernon*). Both these gentlemen have expressed a desire for immediate baptism.

LADY BRACKNELL. At their age? The idea is grotesque and irreligious! Algernon, I forbid you to be baptized. I will not hear of such excesses. Lord Bracknell would be highly displeased if he learned that that was the way in which you wasted your time and money.

CHASUBLE. Am I to understand then that there are to be no christenings at all this afternoon?

JACK. I don't think that, as things are now, it would be of much practical value to either of us, Dr. Chasuble.

CHASUBLE. I am grieved to hear such sentiments from you, Mr. Worthing. They savor of the heretical views of the Anabaptists, views that I have completely refuted in four of my unpublished sermons. However, as your present mood seems to be one peculiarly secular, I will return to the church at once. Indeed, I have just been informed by the pew-opener that for the last hour and a half Miss Prism has been waiting for me in the vestry.

LADY BRACKNELL (*starting*). Miss Prism! Did I hear you mention a Miss Prism?

CHASUBLE. Yes, Lady Bracknell. I am on my way to join her.

LADY BRACKNELL. Pray allow me to detain you for a moment. This matter may prove to be one of vital importance to Lord Bracknell and myself. Is this Miss Prism a female of repellent aspect, remotely connected with education?

CHASUBLE (*somewhat indignantly*). She is the most cultivated of ladies, and the very picture of respectability.

LADY BRACKNELL. It is obviously the same person. May I ask what position she holds in your household?

CHASUBLE (*severely*). I am a celibate, madam.

JACK (*interposing*). Miss Prism, Lady Bracknell, has been for the last three years Miss Cardew's esteemed governess and valued companion.

LADY BRACKNELL. In spite of what I hear of her, I must see her at once. Let her be sent for.

CHASUBLE (*looking off*). She approaches; she is nigh.

Enter Miss Prism hurriedly.

MISS PRISM. I was told you expected me in the vestry, dear Canon. I have been waiting for you there for an hour and three-quarters. (*Catches sight of Lady Bracknell, who has fixed her with a stony glare. Miss Prism grows pale and quails. She looks anxiously round as if desirous to escape.*)

LADY BRACKNELL (*in a severe, judicial voice*). Prism! (*Miss Prism bows her head in shame.*) Come here, Prism! (*Miss Prism approaches in a humble manner.*) Prism! where is that baby? (*General consternation. The Canon starts back in horror. Algernon and Jack pretend to be anxious to shield Cecily and Gwendolen from hearing the details of a terrible public scandal.*) Twenty-eight years ago, Prism, you left Lord Bracknell's house, Number 104, Upper Grosvenor Square, in charge of a perambulator that contained a baby of the male sex. You never returned. A few weeks later, through the elaborate investigations of the Metropolitan police, the perambulator was discovered at midnight standing by itself in a remote corner of Bayswater. It contained the manuscript of a three-volume novel of more than usually revolting sentimentality. (*Miss Prism starts in involuntary indignation.*) But the baby was not there. (*Everyone looks at Miss Prism.*) Prism! Where is that baby? (*A pause.*)

MISS PRISM. Lady Bracknell, I admit with shame that I do not know. I only wish I did. The plain facts of the case are these. On the morning of the day you mention, a day that is forever branded on my memory, I prepared as usual to take the baby out in its perambulator. I had also with me a somewhat old, but capacious handbag in which I had intended to place the manuscript of a work of fiction that I had written during my few unoccupied hours. In a moment of mental abstraction, for which I can never forgive myself, I deposited the manuscript in the bassinette and placed the baby in the handbag.

JACK (*who has been listening attentively*). But where did you deposit the handbag?

MISS PRISM. Do not ask me, Mr. Worthing.

JACK. Miss Prism, this is a matter of no small importance to me. I insist on knowing where you deposited the handbag that contained that infant.

MISS PRISM. I left it in the cloakroom of one of the larger railway stations in London.

JACK. What railway station?

MISS PRISM (*quite crushed*). Victoria. The Brighton line. (*Sinks into a chair.*)

JACK. I must retire to my room for a moment. Gwendolen, wait here for me.

GWENDOLEN. If you are not too long, I will wait here for you all my life. (*Exit Jack in great excitement.*)

CHASUBLE. What do you think this means, Lady Bracknell?

LADY BRACKNELL. I dare not even suspect, Dr. Chasuble. I need hardly tell you that in families of high position strange coincidences are not supposed to occur. They are hardly considered the thing.

Noises heard overhead as if someone was throwing trunks about. Every one looks up.

CECILY. Uncle Jack seems strangely agitated

CHASUBLE. Your guardian has a very emotional nature.

LADY BRACKNELL. This noise is extremely unpleasant. It sounds as if he was having an argument. I dislike arguments of any kind. They are always vulgar, and often convincing.

CHASUBLE (*looking up*). It has stopped now. (*The noise is redoubled.*)

LADY BRACKNELL. I wish he would arrive at some conclusion.

GWENDOLEN. This suspense is terrible. I hope it will last.

Enter Jack with a handbag of black leather in his hand.

JACK (*rushing over to Miss Prism*). Is this the handbag, Miss Prism? Examine it carefully before you speak. The happiness of more than one life depends on your answer.

MISS PRISM (*calmly*). It seems to be mine. Yes, here is the injury it received through the upsetting of a Gower Street omnibus in younger and happier days. Here is the stain on the lining caused by the explosion of a temperance beverage, an incident that occurred at Leamington. And here, on the lock, are my initials. I had forgotten that in an extravagant mood I had had them placed there. The bag is undoubtedly mine. I am delighted to have it so unexpectedly restored to me. It has been a great inconvenience being without it all these years.

JACK (*in a pathetic voice*). Miss Prism, more is restored to you than this handbag. I was the baby you placed in it.

MISS PRISM (*amazed*). You?

JACK (*embracing her*). Yes . . . mother!

MISS PRISM (*recoiling in indignant astonishment*). Mr. Worthing. I am unmarried!

JACK. Unmarried! I do not deny that is a serious blow. But after all, who has the right to cast a stone against one who has suffered? Cannot repentance wipe out an act of folly? Why should there be one law for men, and another for women? Mother, I forgive you. (*Tries to embrace her again.*)

MISS PRISM (*still more indignant*). Mr. Worthing, there is some error. (*Pointing to Lady Bracknell.*) There is the lady who can tell you who you really are.

JACK (*after a pause*). Lady Bracknell, I hate to seem inquisitive, but would you kindly inform me who I am?

LADY BRACKNELL. I am afraid that the news I have to give you will not altogether please you. You are the son of my poor sister, Mrs. Moncrieff, and consequently Algernon's elder brother.

JACK. Algy's elder brother! Then I have a brother after all. I knew I had a brother! I always said I had a brother! Cecily—how could you have ever doubted that I had a brother? (*Seizes hold of Algernon.*) Dr. Chasuble, my unfortunate brother. Miss Prism, my unfortunate brother. Gwendolen, my unfortunate brother. Algy, you young scoundrel, you will have to treat me with more respect in the future. You have never behaved to me like a brother in all your life.

ALGERNON. Well, not till today, old boy, I admit. I did my best, however, though I was out of practice.

(*Shakes hands.*)

GWENDOLEN (*to Jack*). My own! But what own are you? What is your Christian name, now that you have become someone else?

JACK. Good heavens! . . . I had quite forgotten that point. Your decision on the subject of my name is irrevocable, I suppose?

GWENDOLEN. I never change, except in my affections.

CECILY. What a noble nature you have, Gwendolen!

JACK. Then the question had better be cleared up at

once. Aunt Augusta, a moment. At the time when Miss Prism left me in the handbag, had I been christened already?

LADY BRACKNELL. Every luxury that money could buy, including christening, had been lavished on you by your fond and doting parents.

JACK. Then I was christened! That is settled. Now, what name was I given? Let me know the worst.

LADY BRACKNELL. Being the eldest son you were naturally christened after your father.

JACK (*irritably*). Yes, but what was my father's Christian name?

LADY BRACKNELL (*meditatively*). I cannot at the present moment recall what the General's Christian name was. But I have no doubt he had one. He was eccentric, I admit. But only in later years. And that was the result of the Indian climate, and marriage, and indigestion, and other things of that kind.

JACK. Algy! Can't you recollect what our father's Christian name was?

ALGERNON. My dear boy, we were never even on speaking terms. He died before I was a year old.

JACK. His name would appear in the Army Lists of the period, I suppose, Aunt Augusta?

LADY BRACKNELL. The General was essentially a man of peace, except in his domestic life. But I have no doubt his name would appear in any military directory.

JACK. The Army Lists of the last forty years are here. These delightful records should have been my constant study. (*Rushes to bookcase and tears the books out.*) M. Generals . . . Mallam, Maxbohm, Magley—what ghastly names they have—Markby, Migsby, Mobbs, Moncrieff! Lieutenant 1840, Captain, Lieutenant-Colonel, Colonel, General 1869, Christian names, Ernest John. (*Puts book very quietly down and speaks quite calmly.*) I always told you, Gwendolen, my name was Ernest, didn't I? Well, it is Ernest after all. I mean it naturally is Ernest.

LADY BRACKNELL. Yes, I remember now that the General was called Ernest. I knew I had some particular reason for disliking the name.

GWENDOLEN. Ernest! My own Ernest! I felt from the first that you could have no other name!

JACK. Gwendolen, it is a terrible thing for a man to find out suddenly that all his life he has been speaking nothing but the truth. Can you forgive me?

GWENDOLEN. I can. For I feel that you are sure to change.

JACK. My own one!

CHASUBLE (*to Miss Prism*). Laetitia! (*Embraces her.*)

MISS PRISM (*enthusiastically*). Frederick! At last!

ALGERNON. Cecily! (*Embraces her.*) At last!

JACK. Gwendolen! (*Embraces her.*) At last!

LADY BRACKNELL. My nephew, you seem to be displaying signs of triviality.

JACK. On the contrary, Aunt Augusta, I've now realized for the first time in my life the vital Importance of Being Earnest.

TABLEAU

TOPICS FOR DISCUSSION AND WRITING

1. Speaking of this play, Wilde said in an interview: "It has as its philosophy . . . that we should treat all the trivial things of life seriously, and all the serious things of life with sincere and studied triviality." Was he kidding? To what extent does the play dramatize such a view?
2. Can it be argued that the play presents a fanciful world utterly remote from the real world, and that attempts to see it as in any way related to our world do it an injustice? If this is the case, what value does the play have?
3. Describe some of Wilde's chief devices of verbal humor. Once such device, for instance, is to turn a proverb inside out, as with the proverbial "Marriages are made in heaven." What other examples of this device do you find? And what other kinds of humor?
4. What are Lady Bracknell's values? What is your response to her—not to her values, but to her? Why?
5. Take one part of one act—Lady Bracknell's examination of Jack in Act 1 would be a good choice—and indicate what stage business you would use if you were directing the play. A simple example: When Lady Bracknell finishes questioning Jack about his finances and his social standing, she might close her notebook and invitingly pat the seat beside her as she says, "Now to minor matters. Are your parents living?" A little later, when Jack confesses that he cannot identify his parents, she might tear the page out of her notebook.

BERNARD SHAW

Arms and the Man

A Pleasant Play

Bernard Shaw (1856–1950) was born in Dublin of Anglo-Irish stock. His father drank too much, and his mother—something of an Ibsenite "new woman"—went to London to make her way as singer and voice teacher. Shaw worked in a Dublin real estate office for a while (he did not attend a college or university), and then followed his mother to London, where he wrote critical reviews and five novels (1879–83) before turning playwright. His first play, begun with William Archer (playwright and translator of Ibsen), was abandoned in 1885 and then entirely revised by Shaw into *Widowers' Houses* (1892). He had already shown, in a critical study entitled *The Quintessence of Ibsenism* (1891), that he regarded the stage as a pulpit and soap box; before the nineteenth century was over, he wrote nine more plays, in order (he said) to espouse socialism effectively. *Arms and the Man* (1894) is among his early comic masterpieces, but at least a dozen of his plays have established themselves in the repertoire, including one tragedy, *Saint Joan.*

COMMENTARY

Though *Arms and the Man* (1894), Shaw's fourth attempt at playwriting, was at first a financial failure, it is unquestionably a theatrical success. It was a great hit on the first night, but the actors, encouraged by the laughter, later played broadly for laughs and thus succeeded in killing much of the humor. The first night, however, was marked not only by a restrained (and therefore successful) performance, but by a more personal triumph of Shaw's. At the end of the play he appeared onstage in response to the applause; as the cheers died down a solitary "boo" came from the gallery. "My dear fellow," Shaw (1856–1950) replied pleasantly, "I quite agree with you; but what are we two against so many?" The night was Shaw's, and the line was so successful that 17 years later when someone booed at another of his plays, Shaw is reported to have used it again with equal success.

The play's subsequent failure, however, was probably due not merely to the actors but to the audience. The British public had not yet learned to laugh at military heroics, and its ears still rang with Tennyson's glorification of the Light Brigade which bravely did its duty and annihilated itself. Gilbert and Sullivan had, in *The Pirates of Penzance,* however, begun to chip away the gilt which covers the unpleasant idea of dying in battle:

> Go, ye heroes, go to glory.
> Though you die in combat gory
> Ye shall live in song and story.
> Go to immortality.
> Go to death, and go to slaughter;

Raina retrieves the photograph she left for Captain Bluntschli in the pocket of her father's coat in a scene from the 1980 production in the Guthrie Theater, Minneapolis, directed by Michael Langham. (Photograph by Bruce Goldstein.)

Die, and every Cornish daughter
With her tears your grave shall water.
Go, ye heroes, go and die!

But Gilbert and Sullivan were considered jesters, not social critics. Nine weeks after the opening of *Arms and the Man,* Shaw himself pointed out in an essay in *The New Review* that no one confused H.M.S. Pinafore with a real ship, but he insisted that *Arms and the Man* realistically portrays a real war. How unreceptive the public was to a play that pooh-poohed heroics and showed a soldier who preferred chocolates to cartridges can be seen in the comment by the Prince of Wales (later Edward VII) that the author was mad, and a statement was circulated that "His Royal Highness regretted that the play should have shown so disrespectful an attitude as was betrayed by the character of the chocolate-cream soldier."

Many in the first audiences that saw *Arms and the Man* concluded that the play was a libel on heroism; Captain Bluntschli's insistence that it is a soldier's duty "to live as long as we can, and kill as many of the enemy as we can," was regarded as the central point of the drama. Bluntschli's line was shocking, for in imperial England one did not proclaim, in effect, that a soldier's duty is not to die for his country but to make the enemy soldier die for his. But the play is less about war than about the pseudo-romance of war, and perhaps we can generalize and say it is an attack not on war but on dangerous (and silly) romantic ideas. Battles are not usually won by patriotic brainless heroes; they are won by clever men. Similarly, successful marriages cannot be based on a woman's infatuation with a clean uniform and a handsome profile, or on a man's vision of a woman on a pedestal. The romance of war is one of Shaw's targets; the romance of romance is another.

Like most comedy, *Arms and the Man* criticizes foibles, and, like most comic authors, Shaw assumes that our behavior ought to be rational. But we should here note an important way in which Shavian comedy differs from most other comedy. Most comic dramatists poke fun at the individual who deviates from society's norm. The assumption is, this is to say, that society is rational and that the occasional deviant (the miser, the jealous husband, the braggart) is irrational and ought to behave like the majority. Shaw's plays, however, generally make fun of society as a whole and insist that only the deviant is rational. In *Arms and the Man,* for instance, Captain Bluntschli is at odds with the conventional view, but Shaw goes on to demonstrate that Bluntschli is sensible and that the conventional view is foolish. Although Shaw's plays thus differ from most comedies, they are nevertheless allied to traditional comedy in their insistence that deviations from reason are absurd.

Society's irrationality is caricatured in the aristocrats who in the beginning are opposed to Bluntschli. Raina and Sergius hold the conventional romantic view of war, and Bluntschli at first appears absurd. But as the play progresses we see that Bluntschli's view is sound and that the heroic view of war is, though prevalent, unsound. Shaw is thus not merely standing ideas on their head for the sake of a momentary laugh, as, say, Wilde does when he solemnly proclaims that divorces are made in heaven. Rather, Shaw dramatizes the absurdity of some commonly accepted concepts and seriously suggests that a whole army except for one man *can* be out of step. Beneath the tomfoolery, Shaw is often in earnest; he wants us to see life as it really is and not as our preconceptions tell us it should or must be. An oculist once told him, Shaw wrote, that he had normal vision, but when he assumed his sight was like most people's, the oculist explained that Shaw was highly fortunate because only a small minority has normal vision. His mind, Shaw went on to say, was in this sense normal: though untypical, it was undamaged and saw clearly the fuzzy minds of his contemporaries.

But life as Shaw says it is may not be life as it really is; Shaw's view may be as one-sided as that of the romanticists he depicts. His countryman, William Butler Yeats (who could not quite be called Shaw's friend, for he quoted approvingly Wilde's observation that "Mr. Bernard Shaw has no enemies but is intensely disliked by all his friends") found Shaw's realistic view not only offensive but unlifelike: "I listened to *Arms and the Man* with admiration and hatred. It seemed to me inorganic, logical straightness and not the crooked road of life, yet I stood aghast before its energy." Perhaps Shaw's rational view, then, is as false and one-sided as the one-sided view of a comic figure. His anti-romantic vision, his "logical straightness," is, one might say with Yeats, cold, mechanistic, unlifelike—and amusing. "I had a nightmare," Yeats wrote, after seeing Shaw's *Arms and the Man,* "that I was haunted by a sewing-machine, that clicked and shone, but the incredible thing was that the machine smiled, smiled perpetually."

BERNARD SHAW *Arms and the Man*

List of Characters

CATHERINE PETKOFF, *a Bulgarian lady*
RAINA, *her daughter*
LOUKA, *the Petkoffs' maid*
BLUNTSCHLI, *a Swiss officer*
NICOLA, *the Petkoffs' butler*
PETKOFF, *a major in the Bulgarian Army*
SERGIUS, *Raina's fiancé, a captain in the Bulgarian Army*

ACT 1

Night. A lady's bedchamber in Bulgaria, in a small town near the Dragoman Pass, late in November in the year 1885. Through an open window with a little balcony a peak of the Balkans, wonderfully white and beautiful in the starlit snow, seems quite close at hand, though it is really miles away. The interior of the room is not like anything to be seen in the west of Europe. It is half rich Bulgarian, half cheap Viennese. Above the head of the bed, which stands against a little wall cutting off the left hand corner of the room, is a painted wooden shrine, blue and gold, with an ivory image of Christ, and a light hanging before it in a pierced metal ball suspended by three chains. The principal seat, placed towards the other side of the room and opposite the window, is a Turkish ottoman. The counterpane and hangings of the bed, the window curtains, the little carpet, and all the ornamental textile fabrics in the room are oriental and gorgeous; the paper on the walls is occidental and paltry. The washstand, against the wall on the side nearest the ottoman and window, consists of an enamelled iron basin with a pail beneath it in a painted metal frame, and a single towel on the rail at the side. The dressing table, between the bed and the window, is a common pine table, covered with a cloth of many colours, with an expensive toilet mirror on it. The door is on the side nearest the bed; and there is a chest of drawers between. This chest of drawers is also covered by a variegated native cloth; and on it there is a pile of paper-backed novels, a box of chocolate creams, and a miniature easel with a large photograph of an extremely handsome officer, whose lofty bearing and magnetic glance can be felt even from the portrait. The room is lighted by a candle on the chest of drawers, and another on the dressing table with a box of matches beside it.

The window is hinged doorwise and stands wide open. Outside, a pair of wooden shutters, opening outwards, also stand open. On the balcony a young lady, intensely conscious of the romantic beauty of the night, and of the fact that her own youth and beauty are part of it, is gazing at the snowy Balkans. She is in her nightgown, well covered by a long mantle of furs, worth, on a moderate estimate, about three times the furniture of the room.

Her reverie is interrupted by her mother, Catherine Petkoff, a woman over forty, imperiously energetic, with magnificent black hair and eyes, who might be a very splendid specimen of the wife of a mountain farmer, but is determined to be a Viennese lady, and to that end wears a fashionable tea gown on all occasions.

CATHERINE (*entering hastily, full of good news*). Raina! (*She pronounces it RahEEna, with the stress on the ee.*) Raina! (*She goes to the bed, expecting to find Raina there.*) Why, where—? (*Raina looks into the room.*) Heavens, child! are you out in the night air instead of in your bed? Youll catch your death. Louka told me you were asleep.

RAINA (*dreamily*). I sent her away. I wanted to be alone. The stars are so beautiful! What is the matter?

CATHERINE. Such news! There has been a battle.

RAINA (*her eyes dilating*). Ah! (*She comes eagerly to Catherine.*)

CATHERINE. A great battle at Slivnitza! A victory! And it was won by Sergius.

RAINA (*with a cry of delight*). Ah! (*They embrace rapturously.*) Oh, mother! (*Then, with sudden anxiety*) Is father safe?

CATHERINE. Of course! he sends me the news. Sergius is the hero of the hour, the idol of the regiment.

RAINA. Tell me, tell me. How was it? (*Ecstatically*) Oh, mother! mother! mother! (*She pulls her mother down on the ottoman; and they kiss one another frantically.*)

CATHERINE (*with surging enthusiasm*). You cant guess how splendid it is. A cavalry charge! think of that! He defied our Russian commanders—acted without orders—led a charge on his own responsibility—headed it himself—was the first man to sweep through their guns. Cant you see it, Raina: our gallant splendid Bulgarians with their swords and eyes flashing, thundering down like an avalanche and scattering the wretched Serbs and their dandified Austrian officers like chaff. And you! you kept Sergius waiting a year before you would be betrothed to him. Oh, if you have a drop of Bulgarian blood in your veins, you will worship him when he comes back.

RAINA. What will he care for my poor little worship after the acclamations of a whole army of heroes? But no matter: I am so happy! so proud! (*She rises and walks about excitedly.*) It proves that all our ideas were real after all.

CATHERINE (*indignantly*). Our ideas real! What do you mean?

RAINA. Our ideas of what Sergius would do. Our patriotism. Our heroic ideals. I sometimes used to doubt whether they were anything but dreams. Oh, what faithless little creatures girls are! When I buckled on Sergius's sword he looked so noble: it was treason to think of disillusion or humiliation or failure. And yet—and yet— (*She sits down again suddenly.*) Promise me youll never tell him.

CATHERINE. Dont ask me for promises until I know what I'm promising.

RAINA. Well, it came into my head just as he was holding me in his arms and looking into my eyes, that perhaps we only had our heroic ideas because we are so fond of reading Byron and Pushkin, and because we were so delighted with the opera that season at Bucharest. Real life is so seldom like that! indeed never, as far as I knew it then. (*Remorsefully*) Only think, mother: I doubted him: I wondered whether all his heroic qualities and his soldiership might not prove mere imagination when he went into a real battle. I had an uneasy fear that he might cut a poor figure there beside all those clever officers from the Tsar's court.

CATHERINE. A poor figure! Shame on you! The Serbs have Austrian officers who are just as clever as the Russians; but we have beaten them in every battle for all that.

RAINA (*laughing and snuggling against her mother*). Yes: I was only a prosaic little coward. Oh, to think that it was all true! that Sergius is just as splendid and noble as he looks! that the world is really a glorious world for women who can see its glory and men who can act its romance! What happiness! what unspeakable fulfilment!

(*They are interrupted by the entry of Louka, a handsome proud girl in a pretty Bulgarian peasant's dress with double apron, so defiant that her servility to Raina is almost insolent. She is afraid of Catherine, but even with her goes as far as she dares.*)

LOUKA. If you please, madam, all the windows are to be closed and the shutters made fast. They say there may be shooting in the streets. (*Raina and Catherine rise together, alarmed.*) The Serbs are being chased right back through the pass; and they say they may run into the town. Our cavalry will be after them; and our people will be ready for them, you may be sure, now theyre running away. (*She goes out on the balcony, and pulls the outside shutters to; then steps back into the room.*)

CATHERINE (*businesslike, housekeeping instincts aroused*). I must see that everything is made safe downstairs.

RAINA. I wish our people were not so cruel. What glory is there in killing wretched fugitives?

CATHERINE. Cruel! Do you suppose they would hesitate to kill you—or worse?

RAINA (*to Louka*). Leave the shutters so that I can just close them if I hear any noise.

CATHERINE (*authoritatively, turning on her way to the door*). Oh no, dear: you must keep them fastened. You would be sure to drop off to sleep and leave them open. Make them fast, Louka.

LOUKA. Yes, madam. (*She fastens them.*)

RAINA. Dont be anxious about me. The moment I hear a shot, I shall blow out the candles and roll myself up in bed with my ears well covered.

CATHERINE. Quite the wisest thing you can do, my love. Goodnight.

RAINA. Goodnight. (*Her emotion comes back for a moment.*) Wish me joy. (*They kiss.*) This is the happiest night of my life—if only there are no fugitives.

CATHERINE. Go to bed, dear; and dont think of them. (*She goes out.*)

LOUKA (*secretly to Raina*). If you would like the shutters open, just give them a push like this. (*She pushes them: they open: she pulls then to again.*) One of them ought to be bolted at the bottom; but the bolt's gone.

RAINA (*with dignity, reproving her*). Thanks, Louka; but we must do what we are told. (*Louka makes a grimace.*) Goodnight.

LOUKA (*carelessly*). Goodnight. (*She goes out, swaggering.*)

(*Raina, left alone, takes off her fur cloak and throws it on the ottoman. Then she goes to the chest of drawers, and adores the portrait there with feelings that are beyond all expression. She does not kiss it or press it to her breast, or show it any mark of bodily affection; but she takes it in her hands and elevates it, like a priestess.*)

RAINA (*looking up at the picture*). Oh, I shall never be unworthy of you any more, my soul's hero: never, never, never. (*She replaces it reverently. Then she selects a novel from the little pile of books. She turns over the leaves dreamily; finds her page; turns the book inside out at it; and, with a happy sigh, gets into bed and prepares to read herself to sleep. But before abandoning herself to fiction, she raises her eyes once more, thinking of the blessed reality, and murmurs*) My hero! my hero!

(*A distant shot breaks the quiet of the night. She starts, listening; and two more shots, much nearer, follow, startling her so that she scrambles out of bed, and hastily blows out the candle on the chest of drawers. Then, putting her fingers in her ears, she runs to the dressing table, blows out the light there, and hurries back to bed in the dark, nothing being visible but the glimmer of the light in the pierced ball before the image, and the starlight seen through the slits at the top of the shutters. The firing breaks out again: there is a startling fusillade quite close at hand. Whilst it is still echoing, the shutters disappear, pulled open from without; and for an instant the rectangle of snowy starlight flashes out with the figure of a man silhouetted in black upon it. The shutters close immediately; and the room is dark again. But the silence is now broken by the sound of panting. Then there is a scratch; and the flame of a match is seen in the middle of the room.*)

RAINA (*crouching on the bed*). Who's there? (*The match is out instantly.*) Who's there? Who is that?

A MAN'S VOICE (*in the darkness, subduedly, but threateningly*). Sh—sh! Dont call out; or youll be shot. Be good; and no harm will happen to you. (*She is heard leaving her bed, and making for the door.*) Take care: it's no use trying to run away.

RAINA. But who—

THE VOICE (*warning*). Remember: if you raise your voice my revolver will go off. (*Commandingly*) Strike a light and let me see you. Do you hear? (*Another moment of silence and darkness as she retreats to the chest of drawers. Then she lights a candle; and the mystery is at an end. He is a man of about 35, in a deplorable plight, bespattered with mud and blood and snow, his belt and the strap of his revolver case keeping together the torn ruins of the blue tunic of a Serbian artillery officer. All that the candlelight and his unwashed unkempt condition make it possible to discern is that he is of middling stature and undistinguished appearance, with strong neck and shoulders, roundish obstinate-looking head covered with short crisp bronze curls, clear quick eyes and good brows and mouth, hopelessly prosaic nose like that of a strong-minded baby, trim soldierlike carriage and energetic manner, and with all his wits about him in spite of his desperate predicament: even with a sense of the humor of it, without, however, the least intention of trifling with it or throwing away a chance. Reckoning up what he can guess about Raina: her age, her social position, her character, and the extent to which she is frightened, he continues, more politely but still most determinedly*) Excuse my disturbing you; but you recognize my uniform? Serb! If I'm caught I shall be killed. (*Menacingly*) Do you understand that?

RAINA. Yes.

THE MAN. Well, I dont intend to get killed if I can help it. (*Still more formidably*) Do you understand that? (*He locks the door quickly but quietly.*)

RAINA (*disdainfully*). I suppose not. (*She draws herself up superbly, and looks him straight in the face, adding, with cutting emphasis*) Some soldiers, I know, are afraid to die.

THE MAN (*with grim good humor*). All of them, dear lady, all of them, believe me. It is our duty to live as long as we can. Now, if you raise an alarm—

RAINA (*cutting him short*). You will shoot me. How do you know that *I* am afraid to die?

THE MAN (*cunningly*). Ah; but suppose I dont shoot you, what will happen then? A lot of your cavalry will burst into this pretty room of yours and slaughter me here like a pig; for I'll fight like a demon: they shant get me into the street to amuse themselves with: I know what they are. Are you prepared to receive that sort of company in your present undress? (*Raina, suddenly conscious of her nightgown, instinctively shrinks and gathers it more closely about her neck. He watches her and adds pitilessly*) Hardly presentable, eh? (*She turns to the ottoman. He raises his pistol instantly, and cries*) Stop! (*She stops.*) Where are you going?

RAINA (*with dignified patience*). Only to get my cloak.

THE MAN (*passing swiftly to the ottoman and snatching the cloak*). A good idea! I'll keep the cloak; and you'll take care that nobody comes in and sees you without it. This is a better weapon than the revolver: eh? (*He throws the pistol down on the ottoman.*)

RAINA (*revolted*). It is not the weapon of a gentleman!

THE MAN. It's good enough for a man with only you to stand between him and death. (*As they look at one another for a moment, Raina hardly able to believe that even a Serbian officer can be so cynically and selfishly unchivalrous, they are startled by a sharp fusillade in the street. The chill of imminent death hushes the man's voice as he adds*) Do you hear? If you are going to bring those blackguards in on me you shall receive them as you are.

(*Clamor and disturbance. The pursuers in the street batter at the house door, shouting* Open the door! Open the door! Wake up, will you! *A man servant's voice calls to them angrily from within* This is Major Petkoff's house: you cant come in here; *but a renewal of the clamor, and a torrent of blows on the door, end with his letting a chain down with a clank, followed by a rush of heavy footsteps and a din of triumphant yells, dominated at last by the voice of Catherine, indignantly addressing an officer with* What does this mean, sir? Do you know where you are? *The noise subsides suddenly.*)

LOUKA (*outside, knocking at the bedroom door*). My lady! my lady! get up quick and open the door. If you dont they will break it down.

(*The fugitive throws up his head with the gesture of a man who sees that it is all over with him, and drops the manner he has been assuming to intimidate Raina.*)

THE MAN (*sincerely and kindly*). No use, dear: I'm done for. (*Flinging the cloak to her*) Quick! wrap yourself up: theyre coming.

RAINA. Oh, thank you. (*She wraps herself up with intense relief.*)

THE MAN (*between his teeth*). Dont mention it.

RAINA (*anxiously*). What will you do?

THE MAN (*grimly*). The first man in will find out. Keep out of the way; and dont look. It wont last long; but it will not be nice. (*He draws his sabre and faces the door, waiting.*)

RAINA (*impulsively*). I'll help you. I'll save you.

THE MAN. You cant.

RAINA. I can. I'll hide you. (*She drags him towards the window.*) Here! behind the curtains.

THE MAN (*yielding to her*). Theres just half a chance, if you keep your head.

RAINA (*drawing the curtain before him*). S-sh! (*She makes for the ottoman.*)

THE MAN (*putting out his head*). Remember—

RAINA (*running back to him*). Yes?

THE MAN. —nine soldiers out of ten are born fools.

RAINA. Oh! (*She draws the curtain angrily before him.*)

THE MAN (*looking out at the other side*). If they find me, I promise you a fight: a devil of a fight.

(*She stamps at him. He disappears hastily. She takes off her cloak, and throws it across the foot of the bed. Then, with a sleepy, disturbed air, she opens the door. Louka enters excitedly.*)

LOUKA. One of those beasts of Serbs has been seen climbing up the waterpipe to your balcony. Our men want to search for him; and they are so wild and drunk and furious. (*She makes for the other side of the room to get as far from the door as possible.*) My lady says you are to dress at once and to— (*She sees the revolver lying on the ottoman, and stops, petrified.*)

RAINA (*as if annoyed at being disturbed*). They shall not search here. Why have they been let in?

CATHERINE (*coming in hastily*). Raina, darling, are you safe? Have you seen anyone or heard anything?

RAINA. I heard the shooting. Surely the soldiers will not dare come in here?

CATHERINE. I have found a Russian officer, thank Heaven: he knows Sergius. (*Speaking through the door to someone outside*) Sir: will you come in now. My daughter will receive you.

(*A young Russian officer, in Bulgarian uniform, enters, sword in hand.*)

OFFICER (*with soft feline politeness and stiff military carriage*). Good evening, gracious lady. I am sorry to intrude; but there is a Serb hiding on the balcony. Will you and the gracious lady your mother please to withdraw whilst we search?

RAINA (*petulantly*). Nonsense, sir: you can see that there is no one on the balcony.

(*She throws the shutters wide open and stands with her back to the curtain where the man is hidden, pointing to *the moonlit balcony. A couple of shots are fired right under the window; and a bullet shatters the glass opposite Raina, who winks and gasps, but stands her ground; whilst Catherine screams, and the officer, with a cry of* Take care! *rushes to the balcony.*)

THE OFFICER (*on the balcony, shouting savagely down to the street*). Cease firing, you fools: do you hear? Cease firing, damn you! (*He glares down for a moment; then turns to Raina, trying to resume his polite manner.*) Could anyone have got in without your knowledge? Were you asleep?

RAINA. No: I have not been to bed.

THE OFFICER (*impatiently, coming back into the room*). Your neighbors have their heads so full of runaway Serbs that they see them everywhere. (*Politely*) Gracious lady: a thousand pardons. Good night.

(*Military bow, which Raina returns coldly. Another to Catherine, who follows him out. Raina closes the shutters. She turns and sees Louka, who has been watching the scene curiously.*)

RAINA. Dont leave my mother, Louka, until the soldiers go away.

(*Louka glances at Raina, at the ottoman, at the curtain; then purses her lips secretively, laughs insolently, and goes out. Raina, highly offended by this demonstration, follows her to the door, and shuts it behind her with a slam, locking it violently. The man immediately steps out from behind the curtain, sheathing his sabre. Then, dismissing the danger from his mind in a businesslike way, he comes affably to Raina.*)

THE MAN. A narrow shave; but a miss is as good as a mile. Dear young lady: your servant to the death. I wish for your sake I had joined the Bulgarian army instead of the other one. I am not a native Serb.

RAINA (*haughtily*). No: you are one of the Austrians who set the Serbs on to rob us of our national liberty, and who officer their army for them. We hate them!

THE MAN. Austrian! not I. Dont hate me, dear young lady. I am a Swiss, fighting merely as a professional soldier. I joined the Serbs because they came first on the road from Switzerland. Be generous: youve beaten us hollow.

RAINA. Have I not been generous?

THE MAN. Noble! Heroic! But I'm not saved yet. This particular rush will soon pass through; but the pursuit will go on all night by fits and starts. I must take my chance to get off in a quiet interval. (*Pleasantly*) You dont mind my waiting just a minute or two, do you?

RAINA (*putting on her most genteel society manner*). Oh, not at all. Wont you sit down?

THE MAN. Thanks. (*He sits on the foot of the bed.*)

(*Raina walks with studied elegance to the ottoman and sits down. Unfortunately she sits on the pistol, and jumps up with a shriek. The man, all nerves, shies like a frightened horse to the other side of the room.*)

THE MAN (*irritably*). Dont frighten me like that. What is it?

RAINA. Your revolver! It was staring that officer in the face all the time. What an escape!

THE MAN (*vexed at being unnecessarily terrified*). Oh, is that all?

RAINA (*staring at him rather superciliously as she conceives a poorer and poorer opinion of him, and feels proportionately more and more at her ease*). I am sorry I frightened you. (*She takes up the pistol and hands it to him.*) Pray take it to protect yourself against me.

THE MAN (*grinning wearily at the sarcasm as he takes the pistol*). No use, dear young lady: there's nothing in it. It's not loaded. (*He makes a grimace at it, and drops it disparagingly into his revolver case.*)

RAINA. Load it by all means.

THE MAN. Ive no ammunition. What use are cartridges in battle? I always carry chocolate instead; and I finished the last cake of that hours ago.

RAINA (*outraged in her most cherished ideals of manhood*). Chocolate! Do you stuff your pockets with sweets—like a schoolboy—even in the field?

THE MAN (*grinning*). Yes: isnt it contemptible? (*Hungrily*). I wish I had some now.

RAINA. Allow me. (*She sails away scornfully to the chest of drawers, and returns with the box of confectionery in her hand.*) I am sorry I have eaten them all except these. (*She offers him the box.*)

THE MAN (*ravenously*). Youre an angel! (*He gobbles the contents.*) Creams! Delicious! (*He looks anxiously to see whether there are any more. There are none: he can only scrape the box with his fingers and suck them. When that nourishment is exhausted he accepts the inevitable with pathetic good humor, and says, with grateful emotion*) Bless you, dear lady! You can always tell an old soldier by the inside of his holsters and cartridge boxes. The young ones carry pistols and cartridges: the old ones, grub. Thank you. (*He hands back the box. She snatches it contemptuously from him and throws it away. He shies again, as if she had meant to strike him.*) Ugh! Dont do things so suddenly, gracious lady. It's mean to revenge yourself because I frightened you just now.

RAINA (*loftily*). Frighten me! Do you know, sir, that though I am only a woman, I think I am at heart as brave as you.

THE MAN. I should think so. You havent been under fire for three days as I have. I can stand two days without showing it much; but no man can stand three days: I'm as nervous as a mouse. (*He sits down on the ottoman, and takes his head in his hands.*) Would you like to see me cry?

RAINA (*alarmed*). No.

THE MAN. If you would, all you have to do is to scold me just as if I were a little boy and you my nurse. If I were in camp now, theyd play all sorts of tricks on me.

RAINA (*a little moved*). I'm sorry. I wont scold you. (*Touched by the sympathy in her tone, he raises his head and looks gratefully at her: she immediately draws back and says stiffly*) You must excuse me: our soldiers are not like that. (*She moves away from the ottoman.*)

THE MAN. Oh yes they are. There are only two sorts of soldiers: old ones and young ones. Ive served fourteen years: half of your fellows never smelt powder before. Why, how is it that youve just beaten us? Sheer ignorance of the art of war, nothing else. (*indignantly*) I never saw anything so unprofessional.

RAINA (*ironically*). Oh! was it unprofessional to beat you?

THE MAN. Well, come! is it professional to throw a regiment of cavalry on a battery of machine guns, with the dead certainty that if the guns go off not a horse or man will ever get within fifty yards of the fire? I couldn't believe my eyes when I saw it.

RAINA (*eagerly turning to him, as all her enthusiasm and her dreams of glory rush back on her*). Did you see the great cavalry charge? Oh, tell me about it. Describe it to me.

THE MAN. You never saw a cavalry charge, did you?

RAINA. How could I?

THE MAN. Ah, perhaps not. No: of course not! Well, it's a funny sight. It's like slinging a handful of peas against a window pane: first one comes; then two or three close behind him; and then all the rest in a lump.

RAINA (*her eyes dilating as she raises her clasped hands ecstatically*). Yes, first One! the bravest of the brave!

THE MAN (*prosaically*). Hm! you should see the poor devil pulling at his horse.

RAINA. Why should he pull at his horse?

THE MAN (*impatient of so stupid a question*). It's running away with him, of course; do you suppose the fellow wants to get there before the others and be killed? Then they all come. You can tell the young ones by their wildness and their slashing. The old ones come bunched up under the number one guard: they know that theyre mere projectiles, and that it's no use trying to fight. The wounds are mostly broken knees, from the horses cannoning together.

RAINA. Ugh! But I dont believe the first man is a coward. I know he is a hero!

THE MAN (*goodhumoredly*). Thats what youd have said if youd seen the first man in the charge today.

RAINA (*breathless, forgiving him everything*). Ah, I knew it! Tell me. Tell me about him.

THE MAN. He did it like an operatic tenor. A regular handsome fellow, with flashing eyes and lovely moustache, shouting his war-cry and charging like Don Quixote at the windmills. We did laugh.

RAINA. You dared to laugh!

THE MAN. Yes; but when the sergeant ran up as white as a sheet, and told us theyd sent us the wrong ammunition, and that we couldnt fire a round for the next ten minutes, we laughed at the other side of our mouths. I never felt so sick in my life; though Ive been in one or two very tight places. And I hadnt even a revolver cartridge: only chocolate. We'd no bayonets: nothing. Of course, they just cut us to bits. And there was Don Quixote flourishing like a drum major, thinking he'd done the cleverest thing ever known, whereas he ought to be courtmartialled for it. Of all the fools ever let loose on a field of battle, that man must be the very maddest. He and his regiment simply committed suicide; only the pistol missed fire: thats all.

RAINA (*deeply wounded, but steadfastly loyal to her ideals*). Indeed! Would you know him again if you saw him?

THE MAN. Shall I ever forget him!

(*She again goes to the chest of drawers. He watches her with a vague hope that she may have something more for him to eat. She takes the portrait from its stand and brings it to him.*)

RAINA. That is a photograph of the gentleman—the patriot and hero—to whom I am betrothed.

THE MAN (*recognizing it with a shock*). I'm really very sorry. (*Looking at her*) Was it fair to lead me on? (*He looks at the portrait again.*) Yes: thats Don Quixote: not a doubt of it. (*He stifles a laugh.*)

RAINA (*quickly*). Why do you laugh?

THE MAN (*apologetic, but still greatly tickled*). I didnt laugh, I assure you. At least I didnt mean to. But when I think of him charging the windmills and imagining he was doing the finest thing— (*He chokes with suppressed laughter.*)

RAINA (*sternly*). Give me back the portrait, sir.

THE MAN (*with sincere remorse*). Of course. Certainly. I'm really very sorry. (*He hands her the picture. She deliberately kisses it and looks him straight in the face before returning to the chest of drawers to replace it. He follows her, apologizing.*) Perhaps I'm quite wrong, you know: no doubt I am. Most likely he had got wind of the cartridge business somehow, and knew it was a safe job.

RAINA. That is to say, he was a pretender and a coward! You did not dare say that before.

THE MAN (*with a comic gesture of despair*). It's no use, dear lady: I cant make you see it from the professional point of view.

(*As he turns away to get back to the ottoman, a couple of distant shots threaten renewed trouble.*)

RAINA (*sternly, as she sees him listening to the shots*). So much the better for you!

THE MAN (*turning*). How?

RAINA. You are my enemy; and you are at my mercy. What would I do if I were a professional soldier?

THE MAN. Ah, true, dear young lady: youre always right. I know how good youve been to me: to my last hour I shall remember those three chocolate creams. It was unsoldierly; but it was angelic.

RAINA (*coldly*). Thank you. And now I will do a soldierly thing. You cannot stay here after what you have just said about my future husband; but I will go out on the balcony and see whether it is safe for you to climb down into the street. (*She turns to the window.*)

THE MAN (*changing countenance*). Down that waterpipe! Stop! Wait! I cant! I darent! The very thought of it makes me giddy. I came up it fast enough with death behind me. But to face it now in cold blood—! (*He sinks on the ottoman.*) It's no use: I give up: I'm beaten. Give the alarm. (*He drops his head on his hands in the deepest dejection.*)

RAINA (*disarmed by pity*). Come: dont be disheartened. (*She stoops over him almost maternally: he shakes his head.*) Oh, you are a very poor soldier: a chocolate cream soldier! Come, cheer up! it takes less courage to climb down than to face capture: remember that.

THE MAN (*dreamily, lulled by her voice*). No: capture only means death; and death is sleep: oh, sleep, sleep, sleep, undisturbed sleep! Climbing down the pipe means doing something—exerting myself —thinking! Death ten times over first.

RAINA (*softly and wonderingly, catching the rhythm of his weariness*). Are you as sleepy as that?

THE MAN. Ive not had two hours undisturbed sleep since I joined. I havent closed my eyes for forty-eight hours.

RAINA (*at her wit's end*). But what am I to do with you?

THE MAN (*staggering up, roused by her desperation*). Of course. I must do something. (*He shakes himself; pulls himself together; and speaks with rallied vigor and courage.*) You see, sleep or no sleep, hunger or no hunger, tired or not tired, you can always do a thing when you know it must be done. Well, that pipe must be got down: (*he hits himself on the chest*) do you hear that, you chocolate cream soldier? (*He turns to the window.*)

RAINA (*anxiously*). But if you fall?

THE MAN. I shall sleep as if the stones were a feather bed. Goodbye. (*He makes boldly for the window; and his hand is on the shutter when there is a terrible burst of firing in the street beneath.*)

RAINA (*rushing to him*). Stop! (*She seizes him recklessly, and pulls him quite round.*) Theyll kill you.

THE MAN (*coolly, but attentively*). Never mind: this sort of thing is all in my day's work. I'm bound to take my chance. (*Decisively*) Now do what I tell you. Put out the candle; so that they shant see the light when I open the shutters. And keep away from the window, whatever you do. If they see me theyre sure to have a shot at me.

RAINA (*clinging to him*). Theyre sure to see you: it's bright moonlight. I'll save you. Oh, how can you be so indifferent! You want me to save you, dont you?

THE MAN. I really dont want to be troublesome. (*She shakes him in her impatience.*) I am not indifferent, dear young lady, I assure you. But how is it to be done?

RAINA. Come away from the window. (*She takes him firmly back to the middle of the room. The moment she releases him he turns mechanically towards the window again. She seizes him and turns him back, exclaiming*) Please! (*He becomes motionless, like a hypnotized rabbit, his fatigue gaining fast on him. She releases him, and addresses him patronizingly.*) Now listen. You must trust to our hospitality. You do not yet know in whose house you are. I am a Petkoff.

THE MAN. A pet what?

RAINA (*rather indignantly*). I mean that I belong to the family of the Petkoffs, the richest and best known in our country.

THE MAN. Oh yes, of course. I beg your pardon. The Petkoffs, to be sure. How stupid of me!

RAINA. You know you never heard of them until this moment. How can you stoop to pretend!

THE MAN. Forgive me: I'm too tired to think; and the change of subject was too much for me. Dont scold me.

RAINA. I forgot. It might make you cry. (*He nods, quite seriously. She pouts and then resumes her patronizing tone.*) I must tell you that my father holds the highest command of any Bulgarian in our army. He is (*proudly*) a Major.

THE MAN (*pretending to be deeply impressed*). A Major. Bless me! Think of that!

RAINA. You showed great ignorance in thinking that it was necessary to climb up to the balcony because ours is the only private house that has two rows of windows. There is a flight of stairs inside to get up and down by.

THE MAN. Stairs! How grand! You live in great luxury indeed, dear young lady.

RAINA. Do you know what a library is?

THE MAN. A library? A roomful of books?

RAINA. Yes. We have one, the only one in Bulgaria.

THE MAN. Actually a real library! I should like to see that.

RAINA (*affectedly*). I tell you these things to show you that you are not in the house of ignorant country folk who would kill you the moment they saw your Serbian uniform, but among civilized people. We go to Bucharest every year for the opera season; and I have spent a whole month in Vienna.

THE MAN. I saw that, dear young lady. I saw at once that you knew the world.

RAINA. Have you ever seen the opera of Ernani?

THE MAN. Is that the one with the devil in it in red velvet, and a soldiers' chorus?

RAINA (*contemptuously*). No!

THE MAN (*stifling a heavy sigh of weariness*). Then I dont know it.

RAINA. I thought you might have remembered the great scene where Ernani, flying from his foes just as you are tonight, takes refuge in the castle of his bitterest enemy, an old Castilian noble. The noble refuses to give him up. His guest is sacred to him.

THE MAN (*quickly, waking up a little*). Have your people got that notion?

RAINA (*with dignity*). My mother and I can understand that notion, as you call it. And if instead of threatening me with your pistol as you did you had simply thrown yourself as a fugitive on our hospitality, you would have been as safe as in your father's house.

THE MAN. Quite sure?

RAINA (*turning her back on him in disgust*). Oh, it is useless to try to make you understand.

THE MAN. Dont be angry: you see how awkward it would be for me if there was any mistake. My father is a very hospitable man: he keeps six hotels; but I couldnt trust him as far as that. What about your father?

RAINA. He is away at Slivnitza fighting for his country. I answer for your safety. There is my hand in pledge of it. Will that reassure you? (*She offers him her hand.*)

THE MAN (*looking dubiously at his own hand*). Better not touch my hand, dear young lady. I must have a wash first.

RAINA (*touched*). That is very nice of you. I see that you are a gentleman.

THE MAN (*puzzled*). Eh?

RAINA. You must not think I am surprised. Bulgarians of really good standing—people in our position—wash their hands nearly every day. So you see I can appreciate your delicacy. You may take my hand. (*She offers it again.*)

THE MAN (*kissing it with his hands behind his back*). Thanks, gracious young lady: I feel safe at last. And now would you mind breaking the news to your mother? I had better not stay here secretly longer than is necessary.

RAINA. If you will be so good as to keep perfectly still whilst I am away.

THE MAN. Certainly.

(*He sits down on the ottoman. Raina goes to the bed and wraps herself in the fur cloak. His eyes close. She goes to the door. Turning for a last look at him, she sees that he is dropping off to sleep.*)

RAINA (*at the door*). You are not going asleep, are you? (*He murmurs inarticulately: she runs to him and shakes him.*) Do you hear? Wake up: you are falling asleep.

THE MAN. Eh? Falling aslee—? Oh no: not the least in the world: I was only thinking. It's all right: I'm wide awake.

RAINA (*severely*). Will you please stand up while I am away. (*He rises reluctantly.*) All the time, mind.

THE MAN (*standing unsteadily*). Certainly. Certainly: you may depend on me.

(*Raina looks doubtfully at him. He smiles weakly. She goes reluctantly, turning again at the door, and almost catching him in the act of yawning. She goes out.*)

THE MAN (*drowsily*). Sleep, sleep, sleep, sleep, slee— (*The words trail off into a murmur. He wakes again with a shock on the point of falling.*) Where am I? Thats what I want to know: where am I? Must keep awake. Nothing keeps me awake except danger: remember that: (*intently*) danger, danger, danger, dan— (*trailing off again: another shock*) Wheres danger? Mus' find it. (*He starts off vaguely round the room in search of it.*) What am I looking for? Sleep—danger—dont know. (*He stumbles against the bed.*) Ah yes: now I know. All right now. I'm to go to bed, but not to sleep. Be sure not to sleep, because of danger. Not to lie down either, only sit down. (*He sits on the bed. A blissful expression comes into his face.*) Ah!

(*With a happy sigh he sinks back at full length; lifts his boots into the bed with a final effort; and falls fast asleep instantly. Catherine comes in, followed by Raina.*)

RAINA (*looking at the ottoman*). He's gone! I left him here.

CATHERINE. Here! Then he must have climbed down from the—

RAINA (*seeing him*). Oh! (*She points.*)

CATHERINE (*scandalized*). Well! (*She strides to the bed, Raina following until she is opposite her on the other side.*) He's fast asleep. The brute!

RAINA (*anxiously*). Sh!

CATHERINE (*shaking him*). Sir! (*Shaking him again, harder*) Sir!! (*Vehemently, shaking very hard*) Sir!!!

RAINA (*catching her arm*). Dont, mamma; the poor darling is worn out. Let him sleep.

CATHERINE (*letting him go, and turning amazed to Raina*). The poor darling! Raina!!!

(*She looks sternly at her daughter. The man sleeps profoundly.*)

ACT 2

The sixth of March, 1886. In the garden of Major Petkoff's house. It is a fine spring morning: the garden looks fresh and pretty. Beyond the paling the tops of a couple of minarets can be seen, shewing that there is a valley there, with the little town in it. A few miles further the Balkan mountains rise and shut in the landscape. Looking towards them from within the garden, the side of the house is seen on the left, with a garden door reached by a little flight of steps. On the right the stable yard, with its gateway, encroaches on the garden. There are fruit bushes along the paling and house, covered with washing spread out to dry. A path runs by the house, and rises by two steps at the corner, where it turns out of sight. In the middle, a small table, with two bent wood chairs at it, is laid for breakfast with Turkish coffee pot, cups, rolls, etc.; but the cups have been used and the bread broken. There is a wooden garden seat against the wall on the right.

Louka, smoking a cigaret, is standing between the table and the house, turning her back with angry disdain on a man servant who is lecturing her. He is a middle-aged man of cool temperament and low but clear and keen intelligence, with the complacency of the servant who values himself on his rank in servitude, and the imperturbability of the accurate calculator who has no illusions. He wears a white Bulgarian costume: jacket with embroidered border, sash, wide knickerbockers, and decorated gaiters. His head is shaved up to the crown, giving him a high Japanese forehead. His name is Nicola.

NICOLA. Be warned in time, Louka: mend your manners. I know the mistress. She is so grand that she never dreams that any servant could dare be disrespectful to her; but if she once suspects that you are defying her, out you go.

LOUKA. I do defy her. I will defy her. What do I care for her?

NICOLA. If you quarrel with the family, I never can marry you. It's the same as if you quarrelled with me!

LOUKA. You take her part against me, do you?

NICOLA (*sedately*). I shall always be dependent on the good will of the family. When I leave their service and start a shop in Sofia, their custom will be half my capital: their bad word would ruin me.

LOUKA. You have no spirit. I should like to catch them saying a word against me!

NICOLA (*pityingly*). I should have expected more sense from you, Louka. But youre young: youre young!

LOUKA. Yes; and you like me the better for it, dont you? But I know some family secrets they wouldnt care to have told, young as I am. Let them quarrel with me if they dare!

NICOLA (*with compassionate superiority*). Do you know what they would do if they heard you talk like that?

LOUKA. What could they do?

NICOLA. Discharge you for untruthfulness. Who would believe any stories you told after that? Who would give you another situation? Who in this house would dare be seen speaking to you ever again? How long would your father be left on his little farm? (*She impatiently throws away the end of her cigaret, and stamps on it.*) Child: you dont know the power such high people have over the like of you and me when we try to rise out of our poverty against them. (*He goes close to her and lowers his voice.*) Look at me, ten years in their service. Do you think I know no secrets? I know things about the mistress that she wouldnt have the master know for a thousand levas. I know things about him that she wouldnt let him hear the last of for six months if I blabbed them to her. I know things about Raina that would break off her match with Sergius if—

LOUKA (*turning on him quickly*). How do you know? I never told you!

NICOLA (*opening his eyes cunningly*). So thats your little secret, is it? I thought it might be something like that. Well, you take my advice and be respectful; and make the mistress feel that no matter what you know or dont know, she can depend on you to hold your tongue and serve the family faithfully. Thats what they like; and thats how youll make most out of them.

LOUKA (*with searching scorn*). You have the soul of a servant, Nicola.

NICOLA (*complacently*). Yes: thats the secret of success in service.

(*A loud knocking with a whip handle on a wooden door is heard from the stable yard.*)

MALE VOICE OUTSIDE. Hollo! Hollo there! Nicola!

LOUKA. Master! back from the war!

NICOLA (*quickly*). My word for it, Louka, the war's over. Off with you and get some fresh coffee. (*He runs out into the stable yard.*)

LOUKA (*as she collects the coffee pot and cups on the tray, and carries it into the house*). Youll never put the soul of a servant into me.

(*Major Petkoff comes from the stable yard, followed by Nicola. He is a cheerful, excitable, insignificant, unpolished man of about 50, naturally unambitious except as to his income and his importance in local society, but just now greatly pleased with the military rank which the war has thrust on him as a man of consequence in his town. The fever of plucky patriotism which the Serbian attack roused in all the Bulgarians has pulled him through the war; but he is obviously glad to be home again.*)

PETKOFF (*pointing to the table with his whip*). Breakfast out here, eh?

NICOLA. Yes, sir. The mistress and Miss Raina have just gone in.

PETKOFF (*sitting down and taking a roll*). Go in and say Ive come; and get me some fresh coffee.

NICOLA. It's coming, sir. (*He goes to the house door. Louka, with fresh coffee, a clean cup, and a brandy bottle on her tray, meets him.*) Have you told the mistress?

LOUKA. Yes: she's coming.

(*Nicola goes into the house. Louka brings the coffee to the table.*)

PETKOFF. Well: the Serbs havnt run away with you, have they?

LOUKA. No, sir.

PETKOFF. Thats right. Have you brought me some cognac?

LOUKA (*putting the bottle on the table*). Here, sir.

PETKOFF. Thats right.

(*He pours some into his coffee. Catherine, who, having at this early hour made only a very perfunctory toilet, wears a Bulgarian apron over a once brilliant but now half worn-out dressing gown, and a colored handkerchief tied over her thick black hair, comes from the house with Turkish slippers on her bare feet, looking astonishingly handsome and stately under all the circumstances. Louka goes into the house.*)

CATHERINE. My dear Paul: what a surprise for us! (*She stoops over the back of his chair to kiss him.*) Have they brought you fresh coffee?

PETKOFF. Yes: Louka's been looking after me. The war's over. The treaty was signed three days ago at Bucharest; and the decree for our army to demobilize was issued yesterday.

CATHERINE (*springing erect, with flashing eyes*). Paul: have you let the Austrians force you to make peace?

PETKOFF (*submissively*). My dear: they didnt consult me. What could *I* do? (*She sits down and turns away from him.*) But of course we saw to it that the treaty was an honorable one. It declares peace—

CATHERINE (*outraged*). Peace!

PETKOFF (*appeasing her*). —but not friendly relations: remember that. They wanted to put that in; but I insisted on its being struck out. What more could I do?

CATHERINE. You could have annexed Serbia and made Prince Alexander Emperor of the Balkans. Thats what I would have done.

PETKOFF. I dont doubt it in the least, my dear. But I should have had to subdue the whole Austrian Empire first; and that would have kept me too long away from you. I missed you greatly.

CATHERINE (*relenting*). Ah! (*She stretches her hand affectionately across the table to squeeze his.*)

PETKOFF. And how have you been, my dear?

CATHERINE. Oh, my usual sore throats: thats all.

PETKOFF (*with conviction*). That comes from washing your neck every day. Ive often told you so.

CATHERINE. Nonsense, Paul!

PETKOFF (*over his coffee and cigaret*). I dont believe in going too far with these modern customs. All this washing cant be good for the health: it's not natural. There was an Englishman at Philippopolis who used to wet himself all over with cold water every morning when he got up. Disgusting! It all comes from the English: their climate makes them so dirty that they have to be perpetually washing themselves. Look at my father! he never had a bath in his life; and he lived to be ninety-eight, the healthiest man in Bulgaria. I dont mind a good wash once a week to keep up my position; but once a day is carrying the thing to a ridiculous extreme.

CATHERINE. You are a barbarian at heart still, Paul. I hope you behaved yourself before all those Russian officers.

PETKOFF. I did my best. I took care to let them know that we have a library.

CATHERINE. Ah; but you didnt tell them that we have an electric bell in it? I have had one put up.

PETKOFF. Whats an electric bell?

CATHERINE. You touch a button; something tinkles in the kitchen; and then Nicola comes up.

PETKOFF. Why not shout for him?

CATHERINE. Civilized people never shout for their servants. Ive learnt that while you were away.

PETKOFF. Well, I'll tell you something Ive learnt too. Civilized people dont hang out their washing to dry where visitors can see it; so youd better have all that (*indicating the clothes on the bushes*) put somewhere else.

CATHERINE. Oh, thats absurd, Paul: I dont believe really refined people notice such things.

SERGIUS (*knocking at the stable gates*). Gate, Nicola!

PETKOFF. Theres Sergius. (*Shouting*) Hollo, Nicola!

CATHERINE. Oh, dont shout, Paul: it really isnt nice.

PETKOFF. Bosh! (*He shouts louder than before.*) Nicola!

NICOLA (*appearing at the house door*). Yes, sir.

PETKOFF. Are you deaf? Dont you hear Major Saranoff knocking? Bring him round this way. (*He pronounces the name with the stress on the second syllable: SaRAHnoff.*)

NICOLA. Yes, Major. (*He goes into the stable yard.*)

PETKOFF. You must talk to him, my dear, until Raina takes him off our hands. He bores my life out about our not promoting him. Over my head, if you please.

CATHERINE. He certainly ought to be promoted when he marries Raina. Besides, the country should insist on having at least one native general.

PETKOFF. Yes; so that he could throw away whole brigades instead of regiments. It's no use, my dear: he hasnt the slightest chance of promotion until we're quite sure that the peace will be a lasting one.

NICOLA (*at the gate, announcing*). Major Sergius Saranoff!

(*He goes into the house and returns presently with a third chair, which he places at the table. He then withdraws. Major Sergius Saranoff, the original of the portrait in Raina's room, is a tall romantically handsome man, with the physical hardihood, the high spirit, and the susceptible imagination of an untamed mountaineer chieftain. But his remarkable personal distinction is of a characteristically civilized type. The ridges of his eyebrows, curving with an interrogative twist round the projections at the outer corners; his jealously observant eye; his nose, thin, keen, and apprehensive in spite of the pugnacious high bridge and large nostril; his assertive chin would not be out of place in a Parisian salon, showing that the clever imaginative barbarian has an acute critical faculty which has been thrown into intense activity by the arrival of western civilization in the Balkans. The result is precisely what the advent of nineteenth-century thought first produced in England: to wit, Byronism. By his brooding on the perpetual failure, not only of others, but of himself, to live up to his ideals; by his consequent cynical scorn for humanity; by his jejune credulity as to the absolute validity of his concepts and the unworthiness of the world in disregarding them; by his wincings and mockeries under the sting of the petty disillusions which every hour spent among men brings to his sensitive observation, he has acquired the half tragic, half ironic air, the mysterious moodiness, the suggestion of a strange and terrible history that has left nothing but undying remorse, by which Childe Harold fascinated the grandmothers of his English contemporaries. It is clear that here or nowhere is Raina's ideal hero. Catherine is hardly less enthusiastic about him than her daughter, and much less reserved in showing her enthusiasm. As he enters from the stable gate, she rises effusively to greet him. Petkoff is distinctly less disposed to make a fuss about him.*)

PETKOFF. Here already, Sergius! Glad to see you.

CATHERINE. My dear Sergius! (*She holds out both her hands.*)

SERGIUS (*kissing them with scrupulous gallantry*). My dear mother, if I may call you so.

PETKOFF (*drily*). Mother-in-law, Sergius: mother-in-law! Sit down; and have some coffee.

SERGIUS. Thank you: none for me. (*He gets away from the table with a certain distaste for Petkoff's enjoyment of it, and posts himself with conscious dignity against the rail of the steps leading to the house.*)

CATHERINE. You look superb. The campaign has improved you, Sergius. Everybody here is mad about you. We were all wild with enthusiasm about that magnificent cavalry charge.

SERGIUS (*with grave irony*). Madam: it was the cradle and the grave of my military reputation.

CATHERINE. How so?

SERGIUS. I won the battle the wrong way when our worthy Russian generals were losing it the right way. In short, I upset their plans, and wounded their self-esteem. Two Cossack colonels had their regiments routed on the most correct principles of scientific warfare. Two major-generals got killed strictly according to military etiquette. The two colonels are now major-generals; and I am still a simple major.

CATHERINE. You shall not remain so, Sergius. The women are on your side; and they will see that justice is done you.

SERGIUS. It is too late. I have only waited for the peace to send in my resignation.

PETKOFF (*dropping his cup in his amazement*). Your resignation!

CATHERINE. Oh, you must withdraw it!

SERGIUS (*with resolute measured emphasis, folding his arms*). I never withdraw.

PETKOFF (*vexed*). Now who could have supposed you were going to do such a thing?

SERGIUS (*with fire*). Everyone that knew me. But enough of myself and my affairs. How is Raina; and where is Raina?

RAINA (*suddenly coming round the corner of the house and standing at the top of the steps in the path*). Raina is here.

(*She makes a charming picture as they turn to look at her. She wears an underdress of pale green silk, draped with an overdress of thin ecru canvas embroidered with gold. She is crowned with a dainty eastern cap of gold tinsel. Sergius goes impulsively to meet her. Posing regally, she presents her hand: he drops chivalrously on one knee and kisses it.*)

PETKOFF (*aside to Catherine, beaming with parental pride*). Pretty, isnt it? She always appears at the right moment.

CATHERINE (*impatiently*). Yes; she listens for it. It is an abominable habit.

(*Sergius leads Raina forward with splendid gallantry. When they arrive at the table, she turns to him with a bend of the head: he bows; and thus they separate, he coming to his place and she going behind her father's chair.*)

RAINA (*stooping and kissing her father*). Dear father! Welcome home!

PETKOFF (*patting her cheek*). My little pet girl.

(*He kisses her. She goes to the chair left by Nicola for Sergius, and sits down.*)

CATHERINE. And so youre no longer a soldier, Sergius.

SERGIUS. I am no longer a soldier. Soldiering, my dear madam, is the coward's art of attacking mercilessly when you are strong, and keeping out of harm's way when you are weak. That is the whole secret of successful fighting. Get your enemy at a disadvantage; and never, on any account, fight him on equal terms.

PETKOFF. They wouldnt let us make a fair standup fight of it. However, I suppose soldiering has to be a trade like any other trade.

SERGIUS. Precisely. But I have no ambition to shine as a tradesman; so I have taken the advice of that bagman of a captain that settled the exchange of prisoners with us at Pirot, and given it up.

PETKOFF. What! that Swiss fellow? Sergius: Ive often thought of that exchange since. He over-reached us about those horses.

SERGIUS. Of course he over-reached us. His father was a hotel and livery stable keeper; and he owed his first step to his knowledge of horse-dealing. (*With mock enthusiasm*) Ah, he was a soldier: every inch a soldier! If only I had bought the horses for my regiment instead of foolishly leading it into danger, I should have been a field-marshal now!

CATHERINE. A Swiss? What was he doing in the Serbian army?

PETKOFF. A volunteer, of course: keen on picking up his profession. (*Chuckling*) We shouldnt have been able to begin fighting if these foreigners hadnt shown us how to do it: we knew nothing about it; and neither did the Serbs. Egad, there'd have been no war without them!

RAINA. Are there many Swiss officers in the Serbian army?

PETKOFF. No. All Austrians, just as our officers were all Russians. This was the only Swiss I came across. I'll never trust a Swiss again. He humbugged us into giving him fifty ablebodied men for two hundred worn-out chargers. They werent even eatable!

SERGIUS. We were two children in the hands of that consummate soldier, Major: simply two innocent little children.

RAINA. What was he like?

CATHERINE. Oh, Raina, what a silly question!

SERGIUS. He was like a commercial traveller in uniform. Bourgeois to his boots!

PETKOFF (*grinning*). Sergius: tell Catherine that queer story his friend told us about how he escaped after Slivnitza. You remember. About his being hid by two women.

SERGIUS (*with bitter irony*). Oh yes: quite a romance! He was serving in the very battery I so unprofessionally charged. Being a thorough soldier, he ran away like the rest of them, with our cavalry at his heels. To escape their sabres he climbed a waterpipe and made his way into the bedroom of a young Bulgarian lady. The young lady was enchanted by his persuasive commercial traveller's manners. She very modestly entertained him for an hour or so, and then called in her mother lest her conduct should appear unmaidenly. The old lady was equally fascinated; and the fugitive was sent on his way in the morning, disguised in an old coat belonging to the master of the house, who was away at the war.

RAINA (*rising with marked stateliness*). Your life in the camp has made you coarse, Sergius. I did not think you would have repeated such a story before me. (*She turns away coldly.*)

CATHERINE (*also rising*). She is right, Sergius. If such women exist, we should be spared the knowledge of them.

PETKOFF. Pooh! nonsense! what does it matter?

SERGIUS (*ashamed*). No, Petkoff: I was wrong. (*To Raina, with earnest humility*) I beg your pardon. I have behaved abominably. Forgive me, Raina. (*She bows reservedly.*) And you too, madam. (*Catherine bows graciously and sits down. He proceeds solemnly, again addressing Raina.*) The glimpses I have had of the seamy side of life during the last few months have made me cynical; but I should not have brought my cynicism here: least of all into your presence, Raina. I— (*Here, turning to the others, he is evidently going to begin a long speech when the Major interrupts him.*)

PETKOFF. Stuff and nonsense, Sergius! Thats quite enough fuss about nothing: a soldier's daughter should be able to stand up without flinching to a little strong conversation. (*He rises.*) Come: it's time for us to get to business. We have to make up our minds how those three regiments are to get back to Philippopolis: theres no forage for them on the Sofia route. (*He goes towards the house.*) Come along. (*Sergius is about to follow him when Catherine rises and intervenes.*)

CATHERINE. Oh, Paul, cant you spare Sergius for a few moments? Raina has hardly seen him yet. Perhaps I can help you to settle about the regiments.

SERGIUS (*protesting*). My dear madam, impossible: you—

CATHERINE (*stopping him playfully*). You stay here, my dear Sergius: theres no hurry. I have a word or two to say to Paul. (*Sergius instantly bows and steps back.*) Now, dear (*taking Petkoff's arm*): come and see the electric bell.

PETKOFF. Oh, very well, very well.

(They go into the house together affectionately. Sergius, left alone with Raina, looks anxiously at her, fearing that she is still offended. She smiles, and stretches out her arms to him.)

SERGIUS (*hastening to her*). Am I forgiven?

RAINA (*placing her arms on his shoulders as she looks up at him with admiration and worship*). My hero! My king!

SERGIUS. My queen! (*He kisses her on the forehead.*)

RAINA. How I have envied you, Sergius! You have been out in the world, on the field of battle, able to prove yourself there worthy of any woman in the world; whilst I have had to sit at home inactive—dreaming—useless—doing nothing that could give me the right to call myself worthy of any man.

SERGIUS. Dearest: all my deeds have been yours. You inspired me. I have gone through the war like a knight in a tournament with his lady looking down at him!

RAINA. And you have never been absent from my thoughts for a moment. (*Very solemnly*) Sergius: I think we two have found the higher love. When I think of you, I feel that I could never do a base deed, or think an ignoble thought.

SERGIUS. My lady and my saint! (*He clasps her reverently.*)

RAINA (*returning his embrace*). My lord and my—

SERGIUS. Sh-sh! Let me be the worshipper, dear. You little know how unworthy even the best man is of a girl's pure passion!

RAINA. I trust you. I love you. You will never disappoint me, Sergius. (*Louka is heard singing within the house. They quickly release each other.*) I cant pretend to talk indifferently before her: my heart is too full. (*Louka comes from the house with her tray. She goes to the table, and begins to clear it, with her back turned to them.*) I will get my hat; and then we can go out until lunch time. Wouldnt you like that?

SERGIUS. Be quick. If you are away five minutes, it will seem five hours. (*Raina runs to the top of the steps, and turns there to exchange looks with him and wave him a kiss with both hands. He looks after her with emotion for a moment; then turns slowly away, his face radiant with the loftiest exaltation. The movement shifts his field of vision, into the corner of which there now comes the tail of Louka's double apron. His attention is arrested at once. He takes a stealthy look at her, and begins to twirl his moustache mischievously, with his left hand akimbo on his hip. Finally, striking the ground with his heels in something of a cavalry swagger, he strolls over to the other side of the table, opposite her, and says*) Louka: do you know what the higher love is?

LOUKA (*astonished*). No, sir.

SERGIUS. Very fatiguing thing to keep up for any length of time, Louka. One feels the need of some relief after it.

LOUKA (*innocently*). Perhaps you would like some coffee, sir? (*She stretches her hand across the table for the coffee pot.*)

SERGIUS (*taking her hand*). Thank you, Louka.

LOUKA (*pretending to pull*). Oh, sir, you know I didnt mean that. I'm surprised at you!

SERGIUS (*coming clear of the table and drawing her with him*). I am surprised at myself, Louka. What would Sergius, the hero of Slivnitza, say if he saw me now? What would Sergius, the apostle of the higher love, say if he saw me now? What would the half dozen Sergiuses who keep popping in and out of this handsome figure of mine say if they caught us here? (*Letting go her hand and slipping his arm dexterously round her waist*) Do you consider my figure handsome, Louka?

LOUKA. Let me go, sir. I shall be disgraced. (*She struggles: he holds her inexorably.*) Oh, will you let go?

SERGIUS (*looking straight into her eyes*). No.

LOUKA. Then stand back where we cant be seen. Have you no common sense?

SERGIUS. Ah! thats reasonable. (*He takes her into the stable yard gateway, where they are hidden from the house.*)

LOUKA (*plaintively*). I may be seen from the windows: Miss Raina is sure to be spying about after you.

SERGIUS (*stung: letting her go*). Take care, Louka. I may be worthless enough to betray the higher love; but do not you insult it.

LOUKA (*demurely*). Not for the world, sir, I'm sure. May I go on with my work, please, now?

SERGIUS (*again putting his arm round her*). You are a provoking little witch, Louka. If you were in love with me, would you spy out of windows on me?

LOUKA. Well, you see, sir, since you say you are half a dozen different gentlemen all at once, I should have a great deal to look after.

SERGIUS (*charmed*). Witty as well as pretty. (*He tries to kiss her.*)

LOUKA (*avoiding him*). No: I dont want your kisses. Gentlefolk are all alike: you making love to me behind Miss Raina's back; and she doing the same behind yours.

SERGIUS (*recoiling a step*). Louka!

LOUKA. It shows how little you really care.

SERGIUS (*dropping his familiarity, and speaking with freezing politeness*). If our conversation is to continue, Louka, you will please remember that a gentleman does not discuss the conduct of the lady he is engaged to with her maid.

LOUKA. It's so hard to know what a gentleman considers right. I thought from your trying to kiss me that you had given up being so particular.

SERGIUS (*turning away from her and striking his forehead as he comes back into the garden from the gateway*). Devil! devil!

LOUKA. Ha! ha! I expect one of the six of you is very like me, sir; though I am only Miss Raina's maid. (*She goes back to her work at the table, taking no further notice of him.*)

SERGIUS (*speaking to himself*). Which of the six is the real man? thats the question that torments me. One of them is a hero, another a buffoon, another a humbug, another perhaps a bit of a blackguard. (*He pauses, and looks furtively at Louka as he adds, with deep bitterness*) And one, at least, is a coward: jealous, like all cowards. (*He goes to the table.*) Louka.

LOUKA. Yes?

SERGIUS. Who is my rival?

LOUKA. You shall never get that out of me, for love or money.

SERGIUS. Why?

LOUKA. Never mind why. Besides, you would tell that I told you; and I should lose my place.

SERGIUS (*holding out his right hand in affirmation*). No! on the honor of a—(*he checks himself; and his hand drops, nerveless, as he concludes sardonically*)—of a man capable of behaving as I have been behaving for the last five minutes. Who is he?

LOUKA. I dont know. I never saw him. I only heard his voice through the door of her room.

SERGIUS. Damnation! How dare you?

LOUKA (*retreating*). Oh, I mean no harm: youve no right to take up my words like that. The mistress knows all about it. And I tell you that if that gentleman ever comes here again, Miss Raina will marry him, whether he likes it or not. I know the difference between the sort of manner you and she put on before one another and the real manner.

(*Sergius shivers as if she had stabbed him. Then, setting his face like iron, he strides grimly to her, and grips her above the elbows with both hands.*)

SERGIUS. Now listen you to me.

LOUKA (*wincing*). Not so tight; youre hurting me,

SERGIUS. That doesnt matter. You have stained my honor by making me a party to your eavesdropping. And you have betrayed your mistress.

LOUKA (*writhing*). Please—

SERGIUS. That shows that you are an abominable little clod of common clay, with the soul of a servant. (*He lets her go as if she were an unclean thing, and turns away, dusting his hands of her, to the bench by the wall, where he sits down with averted head, meditating gloomily.*)

LOUKA (*whimpering angrily with her hands up her sleeves, feeling her bruised arms*). You know how to hurt with your tongue as well as with your hands. But I dont care, now Ive found out that whatever clay I'm made of, youre made of the same. As for her, she's a liar; and her fine airs are a cheat; and I'm worth six of her.

(*She shakes the pain off hardily; tosses her head; and sets to work to put the things on the tray. He looks doubtfully at her. She finishes packing the tray, and laps the cloth over the edges, so as to carry all out together. As she stoops to lift it, he rises.*)

SERGIUS. Louka! (*She stops and looks defiantly at him.*) A gentleman has no right to hurt a woman under any circumstances. (*With profound humility, uncovering his head*) I beg your pardon.

LOUKA. That sort of apology may satisfy a lady. Of what use is it to a servant?

SERGIUS (*rudely crossed in his chivalry, throws it off with a bitter laugh, and says slightingly*). Oh! you wish to be paid for the hurt! (*He puts on his shako, and takes some money from his pocket.*)

LOUKA (*her eyes filling with tears in spite of herself*). No: I want my hurt made well.

SERGIUS (*sobered by her tone*). How?

(*She rolls up her left sleeve; clasps her arm with the thumb and fingers of her right hand; and looks down at the bruise. Then she raises her head and looks straight at him. Finally, with a superb gesture, she presents her arm to be kissed. Amazed, he looks at her; at the arm; at her again; hesitates; and then, with shuddering intensity, exclaims* Never! *and gets away as far as possible from her. Her arm drops. Without a word, and with unaffected dignity, she takes her tray, and is approaching the house when Raina returns, wearing a hat and jacket in the height of the Vienna fashion of the previous year, 1885. Louka makes way proudly for her, and then goes into the house.*)

RAINA. I'm ready. Whats the matter? (*Gaily*) Have you been flirting with Louka?

SERGIUS (*hastily*). No, no. How can you think such a thing?

RAINA (*ashamed of herself*). Forgive me, dear: it was only a jest. I am so happy today.

(*He goes quickly to her, and kisses her hand remorsefully. Catherine comes out and calls to them from the top of the steps.*)

CATHERINE (*coming down to them*). I am sorry to disturb you, children; but Paul is distracted over those three regiments. He doesnt know how to send them to Philippopolis; and he objects to every suggestion of mine. You must go and help him, Sergius. He is in the library.

RAINA (*disappointed*). But we are just going out for a walk.

SERGIUS. I shall not be long. Wait for me just five minutes. (*He runs up the steps to the door.*)

RAINA (*following him to the foot of the steps and looking*

up at him with timid coquetry). I shall go round and wait in full view of the library windows. Be sure you draw father's attention to me. If you are a moment longer than five minutes, I shall go in and fetch you, regiments or no regiments.

SERGIUS (*laughing*). Very well. (*He goes in.*)

(*Raina watches him until he is out of her sight. Then, with a perceptible relaxation of manner, she begins to pace up and down the garden in a brown study.*)

CATHERINE. Imagine their meeting that Swiss and hearing the whole story! The very first thing your father asked for was the old coat we sent him off in. A nice mess you have got us into!

RAINA (*gazing thoughtfully at the gravel as she walks*). The little beast!

CATHERINE. Little beast! What little beast?

RAINA. To go and tell! Oh, if I had him here, I'd cram him with chocolate creams til he couldnt ever speak again!

CATHERINE. Dont talk such stuff. Tell me the truth, Raina. How long was he in your room before you came to me?

RAINA (*whisking round and recommencing her march in the opposite direction*). Oh, I forget.

CATHERINE. You cannot forget! Did he really climb up after the soldiers were gone; or was he there when that officer searched the room?

RAINA. No. Yes: I think he must have been there then.

CATHERINE. You think! Oh, Raina! Raina! Will anything ever make you straightforward? If Sergius finds out, it will be all over between you.

RAINA (*with cool impertinence*). Oh, I know Sergius is your pet. I sometimes wish you could marry him instead of me. You would just suit him. You would pet him, and spoil him, and mother him to perfection.

CATHERINE (*opening her eyes very widely indeed*). Well, upon my word!

RAINA (*capriciously: half to herself*). I always feel a longing to do or say something dreadful to him—to shock his propriety—to scandalize the five senses out of him. (*To Catherine, perversely*) I dont care whether he finds out about the chocolate cream soldier or not. I half hope he may. (*She again turns and strolls flippantly away up the path to the corner of the house.*)

CATHERINE. And what should I be able to say to your father, pray?

RAINA (*over her shoulder, from the top of the two steps*). Oh, poor father! As if he could help himself! (*She turns the corner and passes out of sight.*)

CATHERINE (*looking after her, her fingers itching*). Oh, if you were only ten years younger! (*Louka comes from the house with a salver, which she carries hanging down by her side.*) Well?

LOUKA. Theres a gentleman just called, madam. A Serbian officer.

CATHERINE (*flaming*). A Serb! And how dare he—(*Checking herself bitterly*) Oh, I forgot. We are at peace now. I suppose we shall have them calling every day to pay their compliments. Well: if he is an officer why dont you tell your master? He is in the library with Major Saranoff. Why do you come to me?

LOUKA. But he asks for you, madam. And I dont think he knows who you are: he said the lady of the house. He gave me this little ticket for you. (*She takes a card out of her bosom; puts it on the salver; and offers it to Catherine.*)

CATHERINE (*reading*). "Captain Bluntschli"? Thats a German name.

LOUKA. Swiss, madam, I think.

CATHERINE (*with a bound that makes Louka jump back*). Swiss! What is he like?

LOUKA (*timidly*). He has a big carpet bag, madam.

CATHERINE. Oh Heavens! he's come to return the coat. Send him away: say we're not at home: ask him to leave his address and I'll write to him. Oh stop: that will never do. Wait! (*She throws herself into a chair to think it out. Louka waits.*) The master and Major Saranoff are busy in the library, arnt they?

LOUKA. Yes, madam.

CATHERINE (*decisively*). Bring the gentleman out here at once. (*Peremptorily*) And be very polite to him. Dont delay. Here (*impatiently snatching the salver from her*): leave that here; and go straight back to him.

LOUKA. Yes, madam (*going*).

CATHERINE. Louka!

LOUKA (*stopping*). Yes, madam.

CATHERINE. Is the library door shut?

LOUKA. I think so, madam.

CATHERINE. If not, shut it as you pass through.

LOUKA. Yes, madam (*going*).

CATHERINE. Stop! (*Louka stops.*) He will have to go that way (*indicating the gate of the stable yard.*) Tell Nicola to bring his bag here after him. Dont forget.

LOUKA (*surprised*). His bag?

CATHERINE. Yes: here: as soon as possible. (*Vehemently*) Be quick! (*Louka runs into the house. Catherine snatches her apron off and throws it behind a bush. She then takes up the salver and uses it as a mirror, with the result that the handkerchief tied round her head follows the apron. A touch to her hair and a shake to her dressing gown make her presentable.*) Oh, how? how? how can a man be such a fool! Such a moment to select! (*Louka appears at the door of the house, announcing Captain Bluntschli. She stands aside at the top of the steps to let him pass before she goes in again. He is the man of the midnight adventure in Raina's room, clean, well brushed, smartly uniformed, and out of trouble, but still unmistakably the same man. The moment Louka's back is turned, Catherine swoops on him with impetuous, urgent, coaxing appeal.*) Captain Bluntschli: I am very glad to see you; but you must leave this house at once. (*He raises his eyebrows.*) My husband has just returned with my future son-in-law; and they know nothing. If they did, the consequences would be terrible. You are a foreigner: you do not feel our national animosities as we do. We still hate the Serbs: the effect of the peace on my husband has been to make him feel like a lion baulked of his prey. If he discovers our secret, he will never forgive me; and my daughter's life will hardly be safe. Will you, like the chivalrous gentleman and soldier you are, leave at once before he finds you here?

BLUNTSCHLI (*disappointed, but philosophical*). At once, gracious lady. I only came to thank you and return the coat you lent me. If you will allow me to take it out of my bag and leave it with your servant as I pass out, I need detain you no further. (*He turns to go into the house.*)

CATHERINE (*catching him by the sleeve*). Oh, you must not think of going back that way. (*Coaxing him across to the stable gates*) This is the shortest way out. Many thanks. So glad to have been of service to you. Good-bye.

BLUNTSCHLI. But my bag?

CATHERINE. It shall be sent on. You will leave me your address.

BLUNTSCHLI. True. Allow me.

(*He takes out his cardcase, and stops to write his address, keeping Catherine in an agony of impatience. As he hands her the card, Petkoff, hatless, rushes from the house in a fluster of hospitality, followed by Sergius.*)

PETKOFF (*as he hurries down the steps*). My dear Captain Bluntschli—

CATHERINE. Oh Heavens! (*She sinks on the seat against the wall.*)

PETKOFF (*too preoccupied to notice her as he shakes Bluntschli's hand heartily*). Those stupid people of mine thought I was out here, instead of in the—haw!—library (*he cannot mention the library without betraying how proud he is of it*). I saw you through the window. I was wondering why you didnt come in. Saranoff is with me: you remember him, dont you?

SERGIUS (*saluting humorously, and then offering his hand with great charm of manner*). Welcome, our friend the enemy!

PETKOFF. No longer the enemy, happily. (*Rather anxiously*) I hope youve called as a friend, and not about horses or prisoners.

CATHERINE. Oh, quite as a friend, Paul. I was just asking Captain Bluntschli to stay to lunch; but he declares he must go at once.

SERGIUS (*sardonically*). Impossible, Bluntschli. We want you here badly. We have to send on three cavalry regiments to Philippopolis; and we dont in the least know how to do it.

BLUNTSCHLI (*suddenly attentive and businesslike*). Philippopolis? The forage is the trouble, I suppose.

PETKOFF (*eagerly*). Yes: thats it. (*To Sergius*) He sees the whole thing at once.

BLUNTSCHLI. I think I can show you how to manage that.

SERGIUS. Invaluable man! Come along!

(*Towering over Bluntschli, he puts his hand on his shoulder and takes him to the steps, Petkoff following. Raina comes from the house as Bluntschli puts his foot on the first step.*)

RAINA. Oh! The chocolate cream soldier!

(*Bluntschli stands rigid. Sergius, amazed, looks at Raina, then at Petkoff, who looks back at him and then at his wife.*)

CATHERINE (*with commanding presence of mind*). My dear Raina, dont you see that we have a guest here? Captain Bluntschli: one of our new Serbian friends.

(*Raina bows: Bluntschli bows.*)

RAINA. How silly of me! (*She comes down into the centre of the group, between Bluntschli and Petkoff.*) I made a beautiful ornament this morning for the ice pudding; and that stupid Nicola has just put down a pile of plates on it and spoilt it. (*To Bluntschli, winningly*) I hope you didnt think that you were the chocolate cream soldier, Captain Bluntschli.

BLUNTSCHLI (*laughing*). I assure you I did. (*Stealing a whimsical glance at her*) Your explanation was a relief.

PETKOFF (*suspiciously, to Raina*). And since when, pray, have you taken to cooking?

CATHERINE. Oh, whilst you were away. It is her latest fancy.

PETKOFF (*testily*). And has Nicola taken to drinking? He used to be careful enough. First he shows Captain Bluntschli out here when he knew quite well I was in the library; and then he goes downstairs and breaks Raina's chocolate soldier. He must— (*Nicola appears at the top of the steps with the bag. He descends; places it respectfully before Bluntschli; and waits for further orders. General amazement. Nicola, unconscious of the effect he is producing, looks perfectly satisfied with himself. When Petkoff recovers his power of speech, he breaks out at him with*) Are you mad, Nicola?

NICOLA (*taken aback*). Sir?

PETKOFF. What have you brought that for?

NICOLA. My lady's orders, Major. Louka told me that—

CATHERINE (*interrupting him*). My orders! Why should I order you to bring Captain Bluntschli's luggage out here? What are you thinking of, Nicola?

NICOLA (*after a moment's bewilderment, picking up the bag as he addresses Bluntschli with the very perfection of servile discretion*). I beg your pardon, Captain, I am sure. (*To Catherine*) My fault, madame: I hope youll overlook it.

(*He bows, and is going to the steps with the bag, when Petkoff addresses him angrily.*)

PETKOFF. Youd better go and slam that bag, too, down on Miss Raina's ice pudding! (*This is too much for Nicola. The bag drops from his hand almost on his master's toes, eliciting a roar of*) Begone, you butter-fingered donkey.

NICOLA (*snatching up the bag, and escaping into the house*). Yes, Major.

CATHERINE. Oh, never mind. Paul: dont be angry.

PETKOFF (*blustering*). Scoundrel! He's got out of hand while I was away. I'll teach him. Infernal blackguard! The sack next Saturday! I'll clear out the whole establishment—

(*He is stifled by the caresses of his wife and daughter, who hang round his neck, petting him.*)

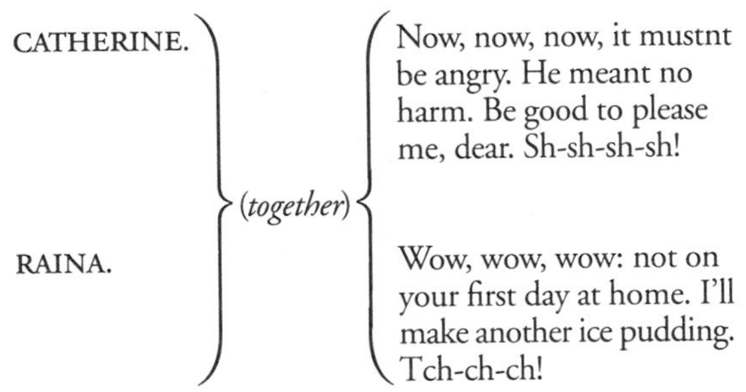

CATHERINE. } (*together*) { Now, now, now, it mustnt be angry. He meant no harm. Be good to please me, dear. Sh-sh-sh-sh!

RAINA. } (*together*) { Wow, wow, wow: not on your first day at home. I'll make another ice pudding. Tch-ch-ch!

PETKOFF (*yielding*). Oh well, never mind. Come, Bluntschli: lets have no more nonsense about going away. You know very well youre not going back to Switzerland yet. Until you do go back youll stay with us.

RAINA. Oh, do, Captain Bluntschli.

PETKOFF (*to Catherine*). Now, Catherine: it's of you he's afraid. Press him: and he'll stay.

CATHERINE. Of course I shall be only too delighted if (*appealingly*) Captain Bluntschli really wishes to stay. He knows my wishes.

BLUNTSCHLI (*in his driest military manner*). I am at madam's orders.

SERGIUS (*cordially*). That settles it!

PETKOFF (*heartily*). Of course!

RAINA. You see you must stay.

BLUNTSCHLI (*smiling*). Well, if I must, I must.

(*Gesture of despair from Catherine.*)

ACT 3

In the library after lunch. It is not much of a library. Its literary equipment consists of a single fixed shelf stocked with old paper-covered novels, broken-backed, coffee-stained, torn and thumbed; and a couple of little hanging shelves with a few gift books on them: the rest of the wall space being occupied by trophies of war and the chase. But it is a most comfortable sitting room. A row of three large windows shows a mountain panorama, just now seen in one of its friendliest aspects in the mellowing afternoon light. In the corner next the right hand window a square earthenware stove, a perfect tower of glistening pottery, rises nearly to the ceiling and guarantees plenty of warmth. The ottoman is like that in Raina's room, and similarly placed; and the window seats are luxurious with decorated cushions. There is one object, however, hopelessly out of keeping with its surroundings. This is a small kitchen table, much the worse for wear, fitted as a writing table with an old canister full of pens, an eggcup filled with ink, and a deplorable scrap of heavily used pink blotting paper.

At the side of this table, which stands to the left of anyone facing the window, Bluntschli is hard at work with a couple of maps before him, writing orders. At the head of it sits Sergius, who is supposed to be also at work, but is actually gnawing the feather of a pen, and contemplating Bluntschli's quick, sure, businesslike progress with a mixture of envious irritation at his own incapacity and awestruck wonder at an ability which seems to him almost miraculous, though its prosaic character forbids him to esteem it. The Major is comfortably established on the ottoman, with a newspaper in his hand and the tube of his hookah within easy reach. Catherine sits at the stove, with her back to them, embroidering. Raina, reclining on the divan, is gazing in a daydream out at the Balkan landscape, with a neglected novel in her lap.

The door is on the same side as the stove, farther from the window. The button of the electric bell is at the opposite side, behind Bluntschli.

PETKOFF (*looking up from his paper to watch how they are getting on at the table*). Are you sure I cant help in any way, Bluntschli?

BLUNTSCHLI (*without interrupting his writing or looking up*). Quite sure, thank you. Saranoff and I will manage it.

SERGIUS (*grimly*). Yes: we'll manage it. He finds out what to do; draws up the orders; and I sign em. Division of labor! (*Bluntschli passes him a paper.*) Another one? Thank you. (*He plants the paper squarely before him; sets his chair carefully parallel to it; and signs with his cheek on his elbow and his protruded tongue following the movements of his pen*).

This hand is more accustomed to the sword than to the pen.

PETKOFF. It's very good of you, Bluntschli: it is indeed, to let yourself be put upon in this way. Now are you quite sure I can do nothing?

CATHERINE (*in a low warning tone*). You can stop interrupting, Paul.

PETKOFF (*starting and looking round at her*). Eh? Oh! Quite right. (*He takes his newspaper up again, but presently lets it drop.*) Ah, you havnt been campaigning, Catherine: you dont know how pleasant it is for us to sit here, after a good lunch, with nothing to do but enjoy ourselves. Theres only one thing I want to make me thoroughly comfortable.

CATHERINE. What is that?

PETKOFF. My old coat. I'm not at home in this one: I feel as if I were on parade.

CATHERINE. My dear Paul, how absurd you are about that old coat! It must be hanging in the blue closet where you left it.

PETKOFF. My dear Catherine, I tell you Ive looked there. Am I to believe my own eyes or not? (*Catherine rises and crosses the room to press the button of the electric bell.*) What are you showing off that bell for? (*She looks at him majestically, and silently resumes her chair and her needlework.*) My dear: if you think the obstinacy of your sex can make a coat out of two old dressing gowns of Raina's, your waterproof, and my mackintosh, youre mistaken. Thats exactly what the blue closet contains at present.

(*Nicola presents himself.*)

CATHERINE. Nicola: go to the blue closet and bring your master's old coat here: the braided one he wears in the house.

NICOLA. Yes, madame. (*He goes out.*)

PETKOFF. Catherine.

CATHERINE. Yes, Paul.

PETKOFF. I bet you any piece of jewelry you like to order from Sofia against a week's housekeeping money that the coat isnt there.

CATHERINE. Done, Paul!

PETKOFF (*excited by the prospect of a gamble*). Come: heres an opportunity for some sport. Wholl bet on it? Bluntschli: I'll give you six to one.

BLUNTSCHLI (*imperturbably*). It would be robbing you, Major. Madame is sure to be right. (*Without looking up, he passes another batch of papers to Sergius.*)

SERGIUS (*also excited*). Bravo, Switzerland! Major: I bet my best charger against an Arab mare for Raina that Nicola finds the coat in the blue closet.

PETKOFF (*eagerly*). Your best char—

CATHERINE (*hastily interrupting him*). Dont be foolish, Paul. An Arabian mare will cost you 50,000 levas.

RAINA (*suddenly coming out of her picturesque revery*). Really, mother, if you are going to take the jewelry, I dont see why you should grudge me my Arab.

(*Nicola comes back with the coat, and brings it to Petkoff, who can hardly believe his eyes.*)

CATHERINE. Where was it, Nicola?

NICOLA. Hanging in the blue closet, madame.

PETKOFF. Well, I am d—

CATHERINE (*stopping him*). Paul!

PETKOFF. I could have sworn it wasnt there. Age is beginning to tell on me. I'm getting hallucinations. (*To Nicola*) Here: help me to change. Excuse me, Bluntschli. (*He begins changing coats, Nicola acting as valet.*) Remember: I didnt take that bet of yours, Sergius. Youd better give Raina that Arab steed yourself, since youve roused her expectations. Eh, Raina? (*He looks round at her; but she is again rapt in the landscape. With a little gush of parental affection and pride, he points her out to them, and says*) She's dreaming, as usual.

SERGIUS. Assuredly she shall not be the loser.

PETKOFF. So much the better for her. *I* shant come off so cheaply, I expect. (*The change is now complete. Nicola goes out with the discarded coat.*) Ah, now I feel at home at last. (*He sits down and takes his newspaper with a grunt of relief.*)

BLUNTSCHLI (*to Sergius, handing a paper*). Thats the last order.

PETKOFF (*jumping up*). What! Finished?

BLUNTSCHLI. Finished.

PETKOFF (*with childlike envy*). Havnt you anything for me to sign?

BLUNTSCHLI. Not necessary. His signature will do.

PETKOFF (*inflating his chest and thumping it*). Ah well, I think weve done a thundering good day's work. Can I do anything more?

BLUNTSCHLI. You had better both see the fellows that are to take these. (*Sergius rises.*) Pack them off at once; and show them that Ive marked on the orders the time they should hand them in by. Tell them that if they stop to drink or tell stories—if theyre five minutes late, theyll have the skin taken off their backs.

SERGIUS (*stiffening indignantly*). I'll say so. (*He strides to the door.*) And if one of them is man enough to spit in my face for insulting him, I'll buy his discharge and give him a pension. (*He goes out.*)

BLUNTSCHLI (*confidentially*). Just see that he talks to them properly, Major, will you?

PETKOFF (*officiously*). Quite right, Bluntschli, quite right. I'll see to it. (*He goes to the door importantly, but hesitates on the threshold.*) By the bye, Catherine, you may as well come too. Theyll be far more frightened of you than of me.

CATHERINE (*putting down her embroidery*). I daresay I

had better. You would only splutter at them. (*She goes out, Petkoff holding the door for her and following her.*)

BLUNTSCHLI. What an army! They make cannons out of cherry trees; and the officers send for their wives to keep discipline!

(*He begins to fold and docket the papers. Raina, who has risen from the divan, marches slowly down the room with her hands clasped behind her, and looks mischievously at him.*)

RAINA. You look ever so much nicer than when we last met. (*He looks up, surprised.*) What have you done to yourself?

BLUNTSCHLI. Washed; brushed; good night's sleep and breakfast. Thats all.

RAINA. Did you get back safely that morning?

BLUNTSCHLI. Quite, thanks.

RAINA. Were they angry with you for running away from Sergius's charge?

BLUNTSCHLI (*grinning*). No: they were glad; because theyd all just run away themselves.

RAINA (*going to the table, and leaning over it towards him*). It must have made a lovely story for them: all that about me and my room.

BLUNTSCHLI. Capital story. But I only told it to one of them: a particular friend.

RAINA. On whose discretion you could absolutely rely?

BLUNTSCHLI. Absolutely.

RAINA. Hm! He told it all to my father and Sergius the day you exchanged the prisoners. (*She turns away and strolls carelessly across to the other side of the room.*)

BLUNTSCHLI (*deeply concerned, and half incredulous*). No! You dont mean that, do you?

RAINA (*turning, with sudden earnestness*). I do indeed. But they dont know that it was in this house you took refuge. If Sergius knew, he would challenge you and kill you in a duel.

BLUNTSCHLI. Bless me! then dont tell him.

RAINA. Please be serious, Captain Bluntschli. Can you not realize what it is to me to deceive him? I want to be quite perfect with Sergius: no meanness, no smallness, no deceit. My relation to him is the one really beautiful and noble part of my life. I hope you can understand that.

BLUNTSCHLI (*sceptically*). You mean that you wouldnt like him to find out that the story about the ice pudding was a—a—a—You know.

RAINA (*wincing*). Ah, dont talk of it in that flippant way. I lied: I know it. But I did it to save your life. He would have killed you. That was the second time I ever uttered a falsehood. (*Bluntschli rises quickly and looks doubtfully and somewhat severely at her.*) Do you remember the first time?

BLUNTSCHLI. I! No. Was I present?

RAINA. Yes; and I told the officer who was searching for you that you were not present.

BLUNTSCHLI. True. I should have remembered it.

RAINA (*greatly encouraged*). Ah, it is natural that you should forget it first. It cost you nothing: it cost me a lie! A lie!

(*She sits down on the ottoman, looking straight before her with her hands clasped around her knee. Bluntschli, quite touched, goes to the ottoman with a particularly reassuring and considerate air, and sits down beside her.*)

BLUNTSCHLI. My dear young lady, dont let this worry you. Remember: I'm a soldier. Now what are the two things that happen to a soldier so often that he comes to think nothing of them? One is hearing people tell lies (*Raina recoils.*) the other is getting his life saved in all sorts of ways by all sorts of people.

RAINA (*rising in indignant protest*). And so he becomes a creature incapable of faith and gratitude.

BLUNTSCHLI (*making a wry face*). Do you like gratitude? I dont. If pity is akin to love, gratitude is akin to the other thing.

RAINA. Gratitude! (*Turning on him*) If you are incapable of gratitude you are incapable of any noble sentiment. Even animals are grateful. Oh, I see now exactly what you think of me! You were not surprised to hear me lie. To you it was something I probably did every day! every hour! That is how men think of women. (*She paces the room tragically.*)

BLUNTSCHLI (*dubiously*). Theres reason in everything. You said youd told only two lies in your whole life. Dear young lady: isnt that rather a short allowance? I'm quite a straightforward man myself; but it wouldnt last me a whole morning.

RAINA (*staring haughtily at him*). Do you know, sir, that you are insulting me?

BLUNTSCHLI. I cant help it. When you strike that noble attitude and speak in that thrilling voice, I admire you; but I find it impossible to believe a single word you say.

RAINA (*superbly*). Captain Bluntschli!

BLUNTSCHLI (*unmoved*). Yes?

RAINA (*standing over him, as if she could not believe her senses*). Do you mean what you said just now? Do you know what you said just now?

BLUNTSCHLI. I do.

RAINA (*gasping*). I! I!!! (*She points to herself incredulously, meaning "I, Raina Petkoff tell lies!" He meets her gaze unflinchingly. She suddenly sits down beside him, and adds, with a complete change of manner from the heroic to a babyish familiarity*) How did you find me out?

BLUNTSCHLI (*promptly*). Instinct, dear young lady. Instinct, and experience of the world.

RAINA (*wonderingly*). Do you know, you are the first man I ever met who did not take me seriously?

BLUNTSCHLI. You mean, dont you, that I am the first man that has ever taken you quite seriously?

RAINA. Yes: I suppose I do mean that. (*Cosily, quite at her ease with him*) How strange it is to be talked to in such a way! You know, Ive always gone on like that.

BLUNTSCHLI. You mean the—?

RAINA. I mean the noble attitude and the thrilling voice. (*They laugh together.*) I did it when I was a tiny child to my nurse. She believed in it. I do it before my parents. They believe in it. I do it before Sergius. He believes in it.

BLUNTSCHLI. Yes; he's a little in that line himself, isnt he?

RAINA (*startled*). Oh! Do you think so?

BLUNTSCHLI. You know him better than I do.

RAINA. I wonder—I wonder is he? If I thought that—! (*Discouraged*) Ah, well; what does it matter? I suppose, now youve found me out, you despise me.

BLUNTSCHLI (*warmly, rising*). No, my dear young lady, no, no, no a thousand times. It's part of your youth: part of your charm. I'm like all the rest of them: the nurse, your parents, Sergius: I'm your infatuated admirer.

RAINA (*pleased*). Really?

BLUNTSCHLI (*slapping his breast smartly with his hand, German fashion*). Hand aufs Herz! Really and truly.

RAINA (*very happy*). But what did you think of me for giving you my portrait?

BLUNTSCHLI (*astonished*). Your portrait! You never gave me your portrait.

RAINA (*quickly*). Do you mean to say you never got it?

BLUNTSCHLI. No. (*He sits down beside her, with renewed interest, and says, with some complacency*) When did you send it to me?

RAINA (*indignantly*). I did not send it to you. (*She turns her head away, and adds, reluctantly*) It was in the pocket of that coat.

BLUNTSCHLI (*pursing his lips and rounding his eyes*). Oh-o-oh! I never found it. It must be there still.

RAINA (*springing up*). There still! for my father to find the first time he puts his hand in his pocket! Oh, how could you be so stupid?

BLUNTSCHLI (*rising also*). It doesnt matter: I suppose it's only a photograph: how can he tell who it was intended for? Tell him he put it there himself.

RAINA (*bitterly*). Yes: that is so clever! isnt it? (*Distractedly*) Oh! what shall I do?

BLUNTSCHLI. Ah, I see. You wrote something on it. That was rash.

RAINA (*vexed almost to tears*). Oh, to have done such a thing for you, who care no more—except to laugh at me—oh! Are you sure nobody has touched it?

BLUNTSCHLI. Well, I cant be quite sure. You see, I couldnt carry it about with me all the time: one cant take much luggage on active service.

RAINA. What did you do with it?

BLUNTSCHLI. When I got through to Pirot I had to put it in safe keeping somehow. I thought of the railway cloak room; but thats the surest place to get looted in modern warfare. So I pawned it.

RAINA. Pawned it!!!

BLUNTSCHLI. I know it doesnt sound nice: but it was much the safest plan. I redeemed it the day before yesterday. Heaven only knows whether the pawnbroker cleared out the pockets or not.

RAINA (*furious: throwing the words right into his face*). You have a low shopkeeping mind. You think of things that would never come into a gentleman's head.

BLUNTSCHLI (*phlegmatically*). Thats the Swiss national character, dear lady. (*He returns to the table.*)

RAINA. Oh, I wish I had never met you. (*She flounces away, and sits at the window fuming. Louka comes in with. a heap of letters and telegrams on her salver, and crosses, with her bold free gait, to the table. Her left sleeve is looped up to the shoulder with a brooch, shewing her naked arm, with a broad gilt bracelet covering the bruise.*)

LOUKA (*to Bluntschli*). For you. (*She empties the salver with a fling on to the table.*) The messenger is waiting. (*She is determined not to be civil to an enemy, even if she must bring him his letters.*)

BLUNTSCHLI (*to Raina*). Will you excuse me: the last postal delivery that reached me was three weeks ago. These are the subsequent accumulations. Four telegrams: a week old. (*He opens one.*) Oho! Bad news!

RAINA (*rising and advancing a little remorsefully*). Bad news?

BLUNTSCHLI. My father's dead. (*He looks at the telegram with his lips pursed, musing on the unexpected change in his arrangements. Louka crosses herself hastily.*)

RAINA. Oh, how very sad!

BLUNTSCHLI. Yes: I shall have to start for home in an hour. He has left a lot of big hotels behind him to be looked after. (*He takes up a fat letter in a long blue envelope.*) Here's a whacking letter from the family solicitor. (*He puts out the enclosures and glances over them.*) Great Heavens! Seventy! Two hundred! (*In a crescendo of dismay*) Four hundred! Four thousand!! Nine thousand six hundred!!! What on earth am I to do with them all?

RAINA (*timidly*). Nine thousand hotels?

BLUNTSCHLI. Hotels! nonsense. If you only knew! Oh, it's too ridiculous! Excuse me: I must give my fellow orders about starting. (*He leaves the room hastily, with the documents in his hand.*)

LOUKA (*knowing instinctively that she can annoy Raina*

by disparaging Bluntschli). He has not much heart, that Swiss. He has not a word of grief for his poor father.

RAINA (*bitterly*). Grief! A man who has been doing nothing but killing people for years! What does he care? What does any soldier care?

(*She goes to the door, restraining her tears with difficultly.*)

LOUKA. Major Saranoff has been fighting too; and he has plenty of heart left. (*Raina, at the door, draws herself up haughtily and goes out.*) Aha! I thought you wouldnt get much feeling out of your soldier.

(*She is following Raina when Nicola enters with an armful of logs for the stove.*)

NICOLA (*grinning amorously at her*). Ive been trying all the afternoon to get a minute alone with you, my girl. (*His countenance changes as he notices her arm.*) Why, what fashion is that of wearing your sleeve, child?

LOUKA (*proudly*). My own fashion.

NICOLA. Indeed! If the mistress catches you, she'll talk to you. (*He puts the logs down, and seats himself comfortably on the ottoman.*)

LOUKA. Is that any reason why you should take it on yourself to talk to me?

NICOLA. Come! Dont be so contrary with me. Ive some good news for you. (*She sits down beside him. He takes out some paper money. Louka, with an eager gleam in her eyes, tries to snatch it; but he shifts it quickly to his left hand, out of her reach.*) See! a twenty leva bill! Sergius gave me that, out of pure swagger. A fool and his money are soon parted. Theres ten levas more. The Swiss gave me that for backing up the mistress' and Raina's lies about him. He's no fool, he isnt. You should have heard old Catherine downstairs as polite as you please to me, telling me not to mind the Major being a little impatient; for they knew what a good servant I was—after making a fool and a liar of me before them all! The twenty will go to our savings; and you shall have the ten to spend if youll only talk to me so as to remind me I'm a human being. I get tired of being a servant occasionally.

LOUKA. Yes: sell your manhood for 30 levas and buy me for 10! (*Rising scornfully*) Keep your money. You were born to be a servant. I was not. When you set up your shop you will only be everybody's servant instead of somebody's servant. (*She goes moodily to the table and seats herself regally in Sergius's chair.*)

NICOLA (*picking up his logs, and going to the stove*). Ah, wait til you see. We shall have our evenings to ourselves; and I shall be master in my own house, I promise you. (*He throws the logs down and kneels at the stove.*)

LOUKA. You shall never be master in mine.

NICOLA (*turning, still on his knees, and squatting down rather forlornly on his calves, daunted by her implacable disdain*). You have a great ambition in you, Louka. Remember if any luck comes to you, it was I that made a woman of you.

LOUKA. You!

NICOLA (*scrambling up and going to her*). Yes, me. Who was it made you give up wearing a couple of pounds of false black hair on your head and reddening your lips and cheeks like any other Bulgarian girl! I did. Who taught you to trim your nails, and keep your hands clean, and be dainty about yourself, like a fine Russian lady! Me: do you hear that? me! (*She tosses her head defiantly; and he turns away, adding more coolly*) Ive often thought that if Raina were out of the way, and you just a little less of a fool and Sergius just a little more of one, you might come to be one of my grandest customers, instead of only being my wife and costing me money.

LOUKA. I believe you would rather be my servant than my husband. You would make more out of me. Oh, I know that soul of yours.

NICOLA (*going closer to her for greater emphasis*). Never you mind my soul; but just listen to my advice. If you want to be a lady, your present behavior to me wont do at all, unless when we're alone. It's too sharp and impudent; and impudence is a sort of familiarity: it shows affection for me. And dont you try being high and mighty with me, either. Youre like all country girls: you think it's genteel to treat a servant the way I treat a stableboy. Thats only your ignorance; and dont you forget it. And dont be so ready to defy everybody. Act as if you expected to have your own way, not as if you expected to be ordered about. The way to get on as a lady is the same as the way to get on as a servant: youve got to know your place: thats the secret of it. And you may depend on me to know my place if you get promoted. Think over it, my girl. I'll stand by you: one servant should always stand by another.

LOUKA (*rising impatiently*). Oh, I must behave in my own way. You take all the courage out of me with your cold-blooded wisdom. Go and put those logs in the fire: thats the sort of thing you understand.

(*Before Nicola can retort, Sergius comes in. He checks himself a moment on seeing Louka; then goes to the stove.*)

SERGIUS (*to Nicola*). I am not in the way of your work, I hope.

NICOLA (*in a smooth, elderly manner*). Oh no, sir: thank you kindly. I was only speaking to this foolish girl about her habit of running up here to the library whenever she gets a chance, to look at the books. Thats the worst of her education, sir: it gives her habits above her station. (*To Louka*) Make that table tidy, Louka, for the Major. (*He goes out sedately. Louka, without looking at Sergius, pretends to arrange the papers on the table. He crosses slowly to her, and studies the arrangement of her sleeve reflectively.)*

SERGIUS. Let me see: is there a mark there? (*He turns up the bracelet and sees the bruise made by his grasp. She stands motionless, not looking at him: fascinated, but on her guard.*) Ffff! Does it hurt?

LOUKA. Yes.

SERGIUS. Shall I cure it?

LOUKA (*instantly withdrawing herself proudly, but still not looking at him*). No. You cannot cure it now.

SERGIUS (*masterfully*). Quite sure? (*He makes a movement as if to take her in his arms.*)

LOUKA. Dont trifle with me, please. An officer should not trifle with a servant.

SERGIUS (*indicating the bruise with a merciless stroke of his forefinger*). That was no trifle, Louka.

LOUKA (*flinching; then looking at him for the first time*). Are you sorry?

SERGIUS (*with measured emphasis, folding his arms*). I am never sorry.

LOUKA (*wistfully*). I wish I could believe a man could be as unlike a woman as that. I wonder are you really a brave man?

SERGIUS (*unaffectedly, relaxing his attitude*). Yes: I am a brave man. My heart jumped like a woman's at the first shot; but in the charge I found that I was brave. Yes: that at least is real about me.

LOUKA. Did you find in the charge that the men whose fathers are poor like mine were any less brave than the men who are rich like you?

SERGIUS (*with bitter levity*). Not a bit. They all slashed and cursed and yelled like heroes. Psha! the courage to rage and kill is cheap. I have an English bull terrier who has as much of that sort of courage as the whole Bulgarian nation, and the whole Russian nation at its back. But he lets my groom thrash him, all the same. Thats your soldier all over! No, Louka: your poor men can cut throats; but they are afraid of their officers; they put up with insults and blows; they stand by and see one another punished like children: aye, and help to do it when they are ordered. And the officers!!! Well (*with a short harsh laugh*), *I* am an officer. Oh (*fervently*), give me the man who will defy to the death any power on earth or in heaven that sets itself up against his own will and conscience: he alone is the brave man.

LOUKA. How easy it is to talk! Men never seem to me to grow up: they all have schoolboy's ideas. You dont know what true courage is.

SERGIUS (*ironically*). Indeed! I am willing to be instructed. (*He sits on the ottoman, sprawling magnificently.*)

LOUKA. Look at me! How much am I allowed to have my own will? I have to get your room ready for you: to sweep and dust, to fetch and carry. How could that degrade me if it did not degrade you to have it done for you? But (*with subdued passion*) if I were Empress of Russia, above everyone in the world, then!! Ah then, though according to you I could show no courage at all, you should see, you should see.

SERGIUS. What would you do, most noble Empress?

LOUKA. I would marry the man I loved, which no other queen in Europe has the courage to do. If I loved you, though you would be as far beneath me as I am beneath you, I would dare to be the equal of my inferior. Would you dare as much if you loved me? No: if you felt the beginnings of love for me you would not let it grow. You would not dare: you would marry a rich man's daughter because you would be afraid of what other people would say of you.

SERGIUS (*bounding up*). You lie: it is not so, by all the stars! If I loved you, and I were the Czar himself, I would set you on the throne by my side. You know that I love another woman, a woman as high above you as heaven is above earth. And you are jealous of her.

LOUKA. I have no reason to be. She will never marry you now. The man I told you of has come back. She will marry the Swiss.

SERGIUS (*recoiling*). The Swiss!

LOUKA. A man worth ten of you. Then you can come to me; and I will refuse you. You are not good enough for me. (*She turns to the door.*)

SERGIUS (*springing after her and catching her fiercely in his arms*). I will kill the Swiss; and afterwards I will do as I please with you.

LOUKA (*in his arms, passive and steadfast*). The Swiss will kill you, perhaps. He has beaten you in love. He may beat you in war.

SERGIUS (*tormentedly*). Do you think I believe that she—she! whose worst thoughts are higher than your best ones, is capable of trifling with another man behind my back?

LOUKA. Do you think she would believe the Swiss if he told her now that I am in your arms?

SERGIUS (*releasing her in despair*). Damnation! Oh, damnation! Mockery! mockery everywhere! everything I think is mocked by everything I do. (*He strikes himself frantically on the breast.*) Coward! liar! fool! Shall I kill myself like a man, or live and pretend to laugh at myself? (*She again turns to go.*) Louka! (*She stops near the door.*) Remember: you belong to me.

LOUKA (*turning*). What does that mean? An insult?

SERGIUS (*commandingly*). It means that you love me, and that I have had you here in my arms, and will perhaps have you there again. Whether that is an insult I neither know nor care: take it as you please. But (*vehemently*) I will not be a coward and a trifler. If I choose to love you, I dare marry you, in spite of all Bulgaria. If these hands ever touch you again, they shall touch my affianced bride.

LOUKA. We shall see whether you dare keep your word. And take care. I will not wait long.

SERGIUS (*again folding his arms and standing motionless in the middle of the room*). Yes: we shall see. And you shall wait my pleasure. (*Bluntschli, much preoccupied, with his papers still in his hand, enters, leaving the door open for Louka to go out. He goes across to the table, glancing at her as he passes. Sergius, without altering his resolute attitude, watches him steadily. Louka goes out, leaving the door open.*)

BLUNTSCHLI (*absently, sitting at the table as before, and putting down his papers*). Thats a remarkable looking young woman.

SERGIUS (*gravely, without moving*). Captain Bluntschli.

BLUNTSCHLI. Eh?

SERGIUS. You have deceived me. You are my rival. I brook no rivals. At six o'clock I shall be in the drilling-ground on the Klissoura road, alone, on horseback, with my sabre. Do you understand?

BLUNTSCHLI (*staring, but sitting quite at his ease*). Oh, thank you: thats a cavalry man's proposal. I'm in the artillery; and I have the choice of weapons. If I go, I shall take a machine gun. And there shall be no mistake about the cartridges this time.

SERGIUS (*flushing, but with deadly coldness*). Take care, sir. It is not our custom in Bulgaria to allow invitations of that kind to be trifled with.

BLUNTSCHLI (*warmly*). Pooh! Dont talk to me about Bulgaria. You dont know what fighting is. But have it your own way. Bring your sabre along. I'll meet you.

SERGIUS (*fiercely delighted to find his opponent a man of spirit*). Well said, Switzer. Shall I lend you my best horse?

BLUNTSCHLI. No; damn your horse! thank you all the same, my dear fellow. (*Raina comes in, and hears the next sentence.*) I shall fight you on foot. Horseback's too dangerous; I dont want to kill you if I can help it.

RAINA (*hurrying forward anxiously*). I have heard what Captain Bluntschli said, Sergius. You are going to fight. Why? (*Sergius turns away in silence; and goes to the stove, where he stands watching her as she continues, to Bluntschli.*) What about?

BLUNTSCHLI. I dont know: he hasnt told me. Better not interfere, dear young lady. No harm will be done: Ive often acted as sword instructor. He wont be able to touch me; and I'll not hurt him. It will save explanations. In the morning I shall be off home; and youll never see me or hear of me again. You and he will then make it up and live happily ever after.

RAINA (*turning away deeply hurt, almost with a sob in her voice*). I never said I wanted to see you again.

SERGIUS (*striding forward*). Ha! That is a confession.

RAINA (*haughtily*). What do you mean?

SERGIUS. You love that man!

RAINA (*scandalized*). Sergius!

SERGIUS. You allow him to make love to you behind my back, just as you treat me as your affianced husband behind his. Bluntschli: you knew our relations; and you deceived me. It is for that that I call you to account, not for having received favors *I* never enjoyed.

BLUNTSCHLI (*jumping up indignantly*). Stuff! Rubbish! I have received no favors. Why, the young lady doesnt even know whether I'm married or not.

RAINA (*forgetting herself*). Oh! (*Collapsing on the. ottoman*) Are you?

SERGIUS. You see the young lady's concern, Captain Bluntschli. Denial is useless. You have enjoyed the privilege of being received in her own room, late at night—

BLUNTSCHLI (*interrupting him pepperily*). Yes, you blockhead! she received me with a pistol at her head. Your cavalry were at my heels. I'd have blown out her brains if she'd uttered a cry.

SERGIUS (*taken aback*). Bluntschli! Raina: is this true?

RAINA (*rising in wrathful majesty*). Oh, how dare you, how dare you?

BLUNTSCHLI. Apologize, man: apologize. (*He resumes his seat at the table.*)

SERGIUS (*with the old measured emphasis, folding his arms*). I never apologize!

RAINA (*passionately*). This is the doing of that friend of yours, Captain Bluntschli. It is he who is spreading this horrible story about me. (*She walks about excitedly.*)

BLUNTSCHLI. No: he's dead. Burnt alive.

RAINA (*stopping. shocked*). Burnt alive!

BLUNTSCHLI. Shot in the hip in a woodyard. Couldnt drag himself out. Your fellows' shells set the timber on fire and burnt him, with half a dozen other poor devils in the same predicament.

RAINA. How horrible!

SERGIUS. And how ridiculous! Oh, war! war! the dream of patriots and heroes! A fraud, Bluntschli. A hollow sham, like love.

RAINA (*outraged*). Like love! You say that before me!

BLUNTSCHLI. Come, Saranoff: that matter is explained.

SERGIUS. A hollow sham, I say. Would you have come back here if nothing had passed between you except at the muzzle of your pistol? Raina is mistaken about your friend who was burnt. He was not my informant.

RAINA. Who then? (*Suddenly guessing the truth*) Ah, Louka! my maid! my servant! You were with her this morning all that time after—after—Oh, what sort of god is this I have been worshipping! (*He meets her gaze with sardonic enjoyment of her disenchantment. Angered all the more, she goes closer to him, and says, in a lower, intenser tone*) Do you know that I looked out of the window as I went upstairs, to have another sight of my hero; and I saw something I did not understand then. I know now that you were making love to her.

SERGIUS (*with grim humor*). You saw that?

RAINA. Only too well. (*She turns away, and throws herself on the divan under the centre window, quite overcome.*)

SERGIUS (*cynically*). Raina: our romance is shattered. Life's a farce.

BLUNTSCHLI (*to Raina, whimsically*). You see: he's found himself out now.

SERGIUS (*going to him*). Bluntschli: I have allowed you to call me a blockhead. You may now call me a coward as well. I refuse to fight you. Do you know why?

BLUNTSCHLI. No; but it doesn't matter. I didnt ask the reason when you cried on; and I dont ask the reason now that you cry off. I'm a professional soldier! I fight when I have to, and am very glad to get out of it when I havnt to. Youre only an amateur: you think fighting's an amusement.

SERGIUS (*sitting down at the table, nose to nose with him*). You shall hear the reason all the same, my professional. The reason is that it takes two men—real men—men of heart, blood and honor—to make a genuine combat. I could no more fight with you than I could make love to an ugly woman. Youve no magnetism: youre not a man: youre a machine.

BLUNTSCHLI (*apologetically*). Quite true, quite true. I always was that sort of chap. I'm very sorry.

SERGIUS. Psha!

BLUNTSCHLI. But now that youve found that life isnt a farce, but something quite sensible and serious, what further obstacle is there to your happiness?

RAINA (*rising*). You are very solicitous about my happiness and his. Do you forget his new love—Louka? It is not you that he must fight now, but his rival, Nicola.

SERGIUS. Rival!! (*Bounding half across the room.*)

RAINA. Dont you know that theyre engaged?

SERGIUS. Nicola! Are fresh abysses opening? Nicola!

RAINA (*sarcastically*). A shocking sacrifice, isnt it? Such beauty! such intellect! such modesty! wasted on a middle-aged servant man. Really, Sergius, you cannot stand by and allow such a thing. It would be unworthy of your chivalry.

SERGIUS (*losing all self-control*). Viper! Viper! (*He rushes to and fro, raging.*)

BLUNTSCHLI. Look here, Saranoff: youre getting the worst of this.

RAINA (*getting angrier*). Do you realize what he has done, Captain Bluntschli? He has set this girl as a spy on us; and her reward is that he makes love to her.

SERGIUS. False! Monstrous!

RAINA. Monstrous! (*Confronting him*) Do you deny that she told you about Captain Bluntschli being in my room?

SERGIUS. No; but—

RAINA (*interrupting*). Do you deny that you were making love to her when she told you?

SERGIUS. No; but I tell you—

RAINA (*cutting him short contemptuously*). It is unnecessary to tell us anything more. That is quite enough for us. (*She turns away from him and sweeps majestically back to the window.*)

BLUNTSCHLI (*quietly, as Sergius, in an agony of mortification, sinks on the ottoman, clutching his averted head between his fists*). I told you you were getting the worst of it, Saranoff.

SERGIUS. Tiger cat!

RAINA (*running excitedly to Bluntschli*). You hear this man calling me names, Captain Bluntschli?

BLUNTSCHLI. What else can he do, dear lady? He must defend himself somehow. Come (*very persuasively*): dont quarrel. What good does it do?

(*Raina, with a gasp, sits down on the ottoman, and after a vain effort to look vexedly at Bluntschli, falls a victim to her sense of humor, and actually leans back babyishly against the writhing shoulder of Sergius.*)

SERGIUS. Engaged to Nicola! Ha! ha! Ah well, Bluntschli, you are right to take this huge imposture of a world coolly.

RAINA (*quaintly to Bluntschli, with an intuitive guess at his state of mind*). I daresay you think us a couple of grown-up babies, dont you?

SERGIUS (*grinning savagely*). He does: he does. Swiss civilization nurse-tending Bulgarian barbarism, eh?

BLUNTSCHLI (*blushing*). Not at all, I assure you. I'm only very glad to get you two quieted. There! there! let's be pleasant and talk it over in a friendly way. Where is this other young lady?

RAINA. Listening at the door, probably.

SERGIUS (*shivering as if a bullet had struck him, and speaking with quiet but deep indignation*). I will prove that that, at least, is a calumny. (*He goes with dignity to the door and opens it. A yell of fury bursts from him as he looks out. He darts into the passage, and returns dragging in Louka, whom he flings violently against the table, exclaiming*) Judge her, Bluntschli. You, the cool impartial man: judge the eavesdropper.

(*Louka stands her ground, proud and silent.*)

BLUNTSCHLI (*shaking his head*). I mustnt judge her. I once listened myself outside a tent when there was a mutiny brewing. It's all a question of the degree of provocation. My life was at stake.

LOUKA. My love was at stake. I am not ashamed.

RAINA (*contemptuously*). Your love! Your curiosity, you mean.

LOUKA (*facing her and returning her contempt with interest*). My love, stronger than anything you can feel, even for your chocolate cream soldier.

SERGIUS (*with quick suspicion, to Louka*). What does that mean?

LOUKA (*fiercely*). I mean—

SERGIUS (*interrupting her slightingly*). Oh, I remember: the ice pudding. A paltry taunt, girl!

(*Major Petkoff enters, in his shirtsleeves.*)

PETKOFF. Excuse my shirtsleeves, gentlemen. Raina: somebody has been wearing that coat of mine: I'll swear it. Somebody with a differently shaped back. It's all burst open at the sleeve. Your mother is mending it. I wish she'd make haste: I shall catch cold. (*He looks more attentively at them.*) Is anything the matter?

RAINA. No. (*She sits down at the stove, with a tranquil air.*)

SERGIUS. Oh no. (*He sits down at the end of the table, as at first.*)

BLUNTSCHLI (*who is already seated*). Nothing. Nothing.

PETKOFF (*sitting down on the ottoman in his old place*). Thats all right. (*He notices Louka.*) Anything the matter, Louka?

LOUKA. No, sir.

PETKOFF (*genially*). Thats all right. (*He sneezes*) Go and ask your mistress for my coat, like a good girl, will you?

(*Nicola enters with the coat. Louka makes a pretense of having business in the room by taking the little table with the hookah away to the wall near the windows.*)

RAINA (*rising quickly as she sees the coat on Nicola's arm*). Here it is, papa. Give it to me, Nicola; and do you put some more wood on the fire.

(*She takes the coat, and brings it to the Major, who stands up to put it on. Nicola attends to the fire.*)

PETKOFF (*to Raina, teasing her affectionately*). Aha! Going to be very good to poor old papa just for one day after his return from the wars, eh?

RAINA (*with solemn reproach*). Ah, how can you say that to me, father?

PETKOFF. Well, well, only a joke, little one. Come: give me a kiss. (*She kisses him.*) Now give me the coat.

RAINA. No: I am going to put it on for you. Turn your back. (*He turns his back and feels behind him with his arms for the sleeves. She dexterously takes the photograph from the pocket and throws it on the table before Bluntschli, who covers it with a sheet of paper under the very nose of Sergius, who looks on amazed, with his suspicions roused in the highest degree. She then helps Petkoff on with his coat.*) There, dear! Now are you comfortable?

PETKOFF. Quite, little love. Thanks. (*He sits down; and Raina returns to her seat near the stove.*) Oh, by the bye, Ive found something funny. Whats the meaning of this? (*He puts his hand into the picked pocket.*) Eh? Hallo! (*He tries the other pocket.*) Well, I could have sworn—! (*Much puzzled, he tries the breast pocket.*) I wonder— (*trying the original pocket*). Where can it—? (*He rises, exclaiming*) Your mother's taken it!

RAINA (*very red*). Taken what?

PETKOFF. Your photograph, with the inscription "Raina, to her Chocolate Cream Soldier: a Souvenir." Now you know theres something more in this than meets the eye; and I'm going to find it out. (*Shouting*) Nicola!

NICOLA (*coming to him*). Sir!

PETKOFF. Did you spoil any pastry of Miss Raina's this morning?

NICOLA. You heard Miss Raina say that I did, sir.

PETKOFF. I know that, you idiot. Was it true?

NICOLA. I am sure Miss Raina is incapable of saying anything that is not true, sir.

PETKOFF. Are you? Then I'm not. (*Turning to the others*) Come: do you think I dont see it all? (*He goes to Sergius, and slaps him on the shoulder.*) Sergius: youre the chocolate cream soldier, arnt you?

SERGIUS (*starting up*). I! A chocolate cream soldier! Certainly not.

PETKOFF. Not! (*He looks at them. They are all very serious and very conscious.*) Do you mean to tell me that Raina sends things like that to other men?

SERGIUS (*enigmatically*). The world is not such an innocent place as we used to think, Petkoff.

BLUNTSCHLI (*rising*). It's all right, Major. I'm the chocolate cream soldier. (*Petkoff and Sergius are equally astonished.*) The gracious young lady saved my life by giving me chocolate creams when I was starving: shall I ever forget their flavor! My late friend Stolz told you the story of Pirot. I was the fugitive.

PETKOFF. You! (*He gasps.*) Sergius: do you remember how those two women went on this morning when we mentioned it? (*Sergius smiles cynically. Petkoff confronts Raina severely.*) Youre a nice young woman, arnt you?

RAINA (*bitterly*). Major Saranoff has changed his mind. And when I wrote that on the photograph, I did not know that Captain Bluntschli was married.

BLUNTSCHLI (*startled into vehement protest*). I'm not married.

RAINA (*with deep reproach*). You said you were.

BLUNTSCHLI. I did not. I positively did not. I never was married in my life.

PETKOFF (*exasperated*). Raina: will you kindly inform me, if I am not asking too much, which of these gentlemen you are engaged to?

RAINA. To neither of them. This young lady (*introducing Louka, who faces them all proudly*) is the object of Major Saranoff's affections at present.

PETKOFF. Louka! Are you mad, Sergius? Why, this girl's engaged to Nicola.

NICOLA. I beg your pardon, sir. There is a mistake. Louka is not engaged to me.

PETKOFF. Not engaged to you, you scoundrel! Why, you had twenty-five levas from me on the day of your betrothal; and she had that gilt bracelet from Miss Raina.

NICOLA (*with cool unction*). We gave it out so, sir. But it was only to give Louka protection. She had a soul above her station; and I have been no more than her confidential servant. I intend, as you know, sir, to set up a shop later on in Sofia; and I look forward to her custom and recommendation should she marry into the nobility. (*He goes out with impressive discretion, leaving them all staring after him.*)

PETKOFF (*breaking the silence*). Well, I am—hm!

SERGIUS. This is either the finest heroism or the most crawling baseness. Which is it, Bluntschli?

BLUNTSCHLI. Never mind whether it's heroism or baseness. Nicola's the ablest man Ive met in Bulgaria. I'll make him manager of a hotel if he can speak French and German.

LOUKA (*suddenly breaking out at Sergius*). I have been insulted by everyone here. You set them the example. You owe me an apology.

(*Sergius, like a repeating clock of which the spring has been touched, immediately begins to fold his arms.*)

BLUNTSCHLI (*before he can speak*). It's no use. He never apologizes.

LOUKA. Not to you, his equal and his enemy. To me his poor servant, he will not refuse to apologize.

SERGIUS (*approvingly*). You are right. (*He bends his knee in his grandest manner.*) Forgive me.

LOUKA. I forgive you. (*She timidly gives him her hand, which he kisses.*) That touch makes me your affianced wife.

SERGIUS (*springing up*). Ah! I forgot that.

LOUKA (*coldly*). You can withdraw if you like.

SERGIUS. Withdraw! Never! You belong to me.

(*He puts his arm about her. Catherine comes in and finds Louka in Sergius's arms, with all the rest gazing at them in bewildered astonishment.*)

CATHERINE. What does this mean?

(*Sergius releases Louka.*)

PETKOFF. Well, my dear, it appears that Sergius is going to marry Louka instead of Raina. (*She is about to break out indignantly at him: he stops her by exclaiming testily*) Dont blame me: Ive nothing to do with it. (*He retreats to the stove.*)

CATHERINE. Marry Louka! Sergius: you are bound by your word to us!

SERGIUS (*folding his arms*). Nothing binds me.

BLUNTSCHLI (*much pleased by this piece of common sense*). Saranoff: your hand. My congratulations. These heroics of yours have their practical side after all. (*To Louka*) Gracious young lady: the best wishes of a good Republican! (*He kisses her hand, to Raina's great disgust, and returns to his seat.*)

CATHERINE. Louka: you have been telling stories.

LOUKA. I have done Raina no harm.

CATHERINE (*haughtily*) Raina!

(*Raina, equally indignant, almost snorts at the liberty.*)

LOUKA. I have a right to call her Raina: she calls me Louka. I told Major Saranoff she would never marry him if the Swiss gentleman came back.

BLUNTSCHLI (*rising, much surprised*). Hallo!

LOUKA (*turning to Raina*). I thought you were fonder of him than of Sergius. You know best whether I was right.

BLUNTSCHLI. What nonsense! I assure you, my dear Major, my dear Madame, the gracious young lady simply saved my life, nothing else. She never cared two straws for me. Why, bless my heart and soul, look at the young lady and look at me. She, rich, young, beautiful, with her imagination full of fairy princes and noble natures and cavalry charges and goodness knows what! And I, a commonplace Swiss soldier who hardly knows what a decent life is after fifteen years of barracks and battles: a vagabond, a man who has spoiled all his chances in life through an incurably romantic disposition, a man—

SERGIUS (*starting as if a needle had pricked him and interrupting Bluntschli in incredulous amazement*). Excuse me, Bluntschli: what did you say had spoiled your chances in life?

BLUNTSCHLI (*promptly*). An incurably romantic disposition. I ran away from home twice when I was a boy. I went into the army instead of into my father's business. I climbed the balcony of this house when a man of sense would have dived into the nearest cellar. I came sneaking back here to have another look at the young lady when any other man of my age would have sent the coat back—

PETKOFF. My coat!

BLUNTSCHLI. —yes: thats the coat I mean—would have sent it back and gone quietly home. Do you suppose I am the sort of fellow a young girl falls in love with? Why, look at our ages! I'm thirty-four: I dont suppose the young lady is much over seventeen. (*This estimate produces a marked sensation, all the rest turning and staring at one another. He proceeds innocently.)* All that adventure which was life or death to me, was only a schoolgirl's game to her—chocolate creams and hide and seek. Heres the proof! (*He takes the photograph from the table.*) Now, I ask you, would a woman who took the affair seriously have sent me this and written on it "Raina, to her Chocolate Cream Soldier: a Souvenir"? (*He exhibits the photograph triumphantly, as if it settled the matter beyond all possibility of refutation.*)

PETKOFF. Thats what I was looking for. How the deuce did it get there? (*He comes from the stove to look at it, and sits down on the ottoman.*)

BLUNTSCHLI (*to Raina, complacently*). I have put everything right, I hope, gracious young lady.

RAINA (*going to the table to face him*). I quite agree with your account of yourself. You are a romantic idiot. (*Bluntschli is unspeakably taken aback.*) Next time, I hope you will know the difference between a schoolgirl of seventeen and a woman of twenty-three.

BLUNTSCHLI (*stupefied*). Twenty-three!

(*Raina snaps the photograph contemptuously from his hand; tears it up; throws the pieces in his face; and sweeps back to her former place.*)

SERGIUS (*with grim enjoyment of his rival's discomfiture*). Bluntschli: my one last belief is gone. Your sagacity is a fraud, like everything else. You have less sense than even I!

BLUNTSCHLI (*overwhelmed*). Twenty-three! Twenty-three!! (*He considers.*) Hm. (*Swiftly making up his mind and coming to his host*) In that case, Major Petkoff, I beg to propose formally to become a suitor for your daughter's hand, in place of Major Saranoff retired.

RAINA. You dare!

BLUNTSCHLI. If you were twenty-three when you said those things to me this afternoon, I shall take them seriously.

CATHERINE (*loftily polite*). I doubt, sir, whether you quite realize either my daughter's position or that of Major Sergius Saranoff, whose place you propose to take. The Petkoffs and the Saranoffs are known as the richest and most important families in the country. Our position is almost historical: we can go back for twenty years.

PETKOFF. Oh, never mind that, Catherine. (*To Bluntschli*) We should be most happy, Bluntschli, if it were only a question of your position; but hang it, you know, Raina is accustomed to a very comfortable establishment. Sergius keeps twenty horses.

BLUNTSCHLI. But who wants twenty horses? We're not going to keep a circus.

CATHERINE (*severely*). My daughter, sir, is accustomed to a first-rate stable.

RAINA. Hush, mother: youre making me ridiculous.

BLUNTSCHLI. Oh well, if it comes to a question of an establishment, here goes! (*He darts impetuously to the table; seizes the papers in the blue envelope; and turns to Sergius.*) How many horses did you say?

SERGIUS. Twenty, noble Switzer.

BLUNTSCHLI. I have two hundred horses. (*They are amazed.*) How many carriages?

SERGIUS. Three.

BLUNTSCHLI. I have seventy. Twenty-four of them will hold twelve inside, besides two on the box, without counting the driver and conductor. How many tablecloths have you?

SERGIUS. How the deuce do I know?

BLUNTSCHLI. Have you four thousand?

SERGIUS. No.

BLUNTSCHLI. I have. I have nine thousand six hundred pairs of sheets and blankets, with two thousand four hundred eider-down quilts. I have ten thousand knives and forks, and the same quantity of dessert spoons. I have three hundred servants. I have six palatial establishments, besides two livery stables, a tea garden, and a private house. I have four medals for distinguished services; I have the rank of an officer and the standing of a gentleman; and I have three native languages. Show me any man in Bulgaria that can offer as much!

PETKOFF (*with childish awe*). Are you Emperor of Switzerland?

BLUNTSCHLI. My rank is the highest known in Switzerland: I am a free citizen.

CATHERINE. Then, Captain Bluntschli, since you are my daughter's choice—

RAINA (*mutinously*). He's not.

CATHERINE (*ignoring her*). —I shall not stand in the way of her happiness. (*Petkoff is about to speak.*) That is Major Petkoff's feeling also.

PETKOFF. Oh, I shall be only too glad. Two hundred horses! Whew!

SERGIUS. What says the lady?

RAINA (*pretending to sulk*). The lady says that he can keep his tablecloths and his omnibuses. I am not here to be sold to the highest bidder. (*She turns her back on him.*)

BLUNTSCHLI. I wont take that answer. I appealed to you as a fugitive, a beggar, and a starving man. You accepted me. You gave me your hand to kiss, your bed to sleep in, and your roof to shelter me.

RAINA. I did not give them to the Emperor of Switzerland.

BLUNTSCHLI. Thats just what I say. (*He catches her by the shoulders and turns her face-to-face with him.*) Now tell us whom you did give them to.

RAINA (*succumbing with a shy smile*). To my chocolate cream soldier.

BLUNTSCHLI (*with a boyish laugh of delight*). Thatll do. Thank you. (*He looks at his watch and suddenly becomes businesslike.*) Time's up, Major. Youve managed those regiments so well that youre sure to be asked to get rid of some of the infantry of the Timok division. Send them home by way of Lom Palanka. Saranoff: Dont get married until I come back: I shall be here punctually at five in the evening on Tuesday fortnight. Gracious ladies (*his heels click*) good evening. (*He makes them a military bow, and goes.*)

SERGIUS. What a man! Is he a man!

TOPICS FOR DISCUSSION AND WRITING

1. What is Shaw getting at in his description (page 336) of the furniture in Petkoff's house?
2. Raina ends as a realist, but at the outset she is not merely the opposite, a self-deceived romanticist. Do you think the characterization—and the play—would be better if her transformation were from wholehearted romanticist to realist? Aristotle's terms *peripeteia* (reversal) and *anagnorisis* (recognition) are commonly used in discussions of tragedy (see page 30), but they can also be useful in discussions of comedy. What reversals and recognitions do you find in *Arms and the Man*? When Sergius is disenchanted, he claims (page 358) that war is "a hollow sham, like love." Is this recognition the point toward which the play has been moving? Explain.
3. Nicola is not essential to the plot. What, then, does he contribute to the play?
4. Sir Max Beerbohm says in a critique of *Arms and the Man* that we first cudgel our brains over the meaning of Sergius's marriage to Louka and finally must conclude that it has no meaning. Sergius marries her, Sir Max says, merely because Bluntschli will marry Raina, and the symmetry of the plot demands that Sergius marry someone and Louka is the only available unmarried woman. Do you think this marriage is a dramatic weakness? Explain.
5. Shaw once said: "It is the business of a writer of comedy to wound the susceptibilities of his audience. The classic definition of his function is 'the chastening of morals by ridicule.'" Does *Arms and the Man* wound your susceptibilities? If so, to any purpose? Is the play a serious examination of the nature of soldiers and of war? Or does the clowning, especially in the third act, pretty much obliterate any intellectual content? Explain.
6. Sergius says to Bluntschli: "Youre not a man: youre a machine." On page 33 we quoted Bergson's view that figures who respond mechanically are often the objects of laughter because they are absurdly inadequate in their responses to the complexities of life. Does Bluntschli provide an example of Bergson's "mechanical encrusted on the living"? Or, on the contrary, does he embody a mental flexibility that lets him cut through the encrustations of society? And can it be argued that the romantic Sergius is Bergson's mechanical man?
7. One of the chief theories of laughter is neatly stated in Thomas Hobbes's *Leviathan* (1651):

   Sudden Glory, is the passion which maketh those Grimaces called laughter; and is caused either by some sudden act of their own, that pleaseth them; or by the apprehension of some deformed thing in another, in comparison whereof they suddenly applaud themselves.

   If *Arms and the Man* evokes laughter, is the laughter of Hobbes's sort? Does Hobbes's theory cover any or all laughable occurrences you can think of?

Leigh Lawson (left), Judy Parfitt (center), and Caroline Langrisile (right) in a recent production of *The Cherry Orchard.* (Photograph by Donald Cooper © PHOTOSTAGE.)

ANTON CHEKHOV

The Cherry Orchard

Translated by Laurence Senelick

Anton Chekhov (1860–1904) received his medical degree from the University of Moscow in 1884, but he had already published some stories. His belief that his medical training assisted him in writing about people caused some people to find him cold, but on the whole the evidence suggests that he was a genial, energetic young man with considerable faith in reason and (as befitted a doctor) in science, and with very little faith in religion and in heroics. His major plays are *The Seagull* (1896), *Uncle Vanya* (1899), *Three Sisters* (1901), and, finally, *The Cherry Orchard* (1903), written during his last illness.

COMMENTARY

At the end of *The Cherry Orchard,* the old servant Firs, forgotten by the family he has long served, wanders onto the stage, locked within the house that is no longer theirs. Is he comic, in his mutterings, in his old-maidish frettings about Leonid Andreevich's inadequate coat, and in his implicit realization that although he is concerned about the aristocrats the aristocrats are unconcerned about him? Or is he tragic, dying in isolation? Or neither? The comedy is scarcely uproarious; if there is humor in his realization that his life has been trivial, this humor is surely tinged with melancholy. And the "tragic" reading is also ambiguous: first, the text does not say that he dies; second, if it can be assumed that he dies, the death of an ill eighty-seven-year-old man can scarcely seem untimely; and third, Firs does not seem particularly concerned about dying.

If this play ends with a death, then, it is not the sort of death that Byron had in mind when he said, "All tragedies are finished by a death, / All comedies are ended by a marriage." We are in the dramatic world that Shaw spoke of when he said that "the curtain no longer comes down on a hero slain or married: it comes down when the audience has seen enough of the life presented to it, . . . and must either leave the theatre or miss its last train."

Chekhov insisted that *The Cherry Orchard* was a comedy, but what sort of comedy? In the latter part of the last act there is almost a proposal of marriage, but, typically, it never gets made. For two years everyone has joked about the anticipated marriage between Lopakhin and Varya, but when these two are thrust together they are overcome by embarrassment, and the interview is dissipated in small talk. Not that (of course) a comedy must end with a marriage; marriage is only the conventional way of indicating a happy union, or reunion, that symbolizes the triumph of life. But in this play we *begin* with a reunion—the family is reunited in the ancestral home—and we end with a separation, the inhabitants scattering when the home is sold.

Another way of getting at *The Cherry Orchard* is to notice that in this play, although there are innumerable references to Time between the first speech, when Lopakhin says "Train's in, thank God! What's the time?" and the last act, where there is much talk about catching the outbound train, Time does not function as it usually functions either in tragedy or in comedy. In tragedy we usually feel: if there had only been more time.... For example, in *Romeo and Juliet* Friar Laurence writes a letter to Romeo, explaining that Juliet will take a potion that will put her in a temporary, deathlike trance, but the letter is delayed, Romeo mistakenly hears that Juliet is dead, and he kills himself. A few moments after his suicide Juliet revives. Had Friar Laurence's message arrived on schedule, or had Romeo not been so quick to commit suicide, no great harm would have been done. In *King Lear,* Edmund repents that he has ordered a soldier to kill Cordelia, and a messenger hurries out to change the order, but he is too late.

If in tragedy we usually feel the pressure of time, in comedy there is usually a sense of leisure. Things are difficult now, but in the course of time they will work themselves out. Sooner or later people will realize that the strange goings-on are due to the existence of identical twins; sooner or later the stubborn parents will realize that they cannot forever stand in the way of young lovers; sooner or later the money will turn up and all will be well. In the world of comedy, one is always safe in relying on time. In *The Cherry Orchard,* Lopakhin insists, correctly enough, that the family must act *now* if it is to save the orchard: "You've got to decide once and for all—time won't stand still." There is ample time to act on Lopakhin's suggestion that the orchard be leased for summer houses, and the play covers a period from May to October; but the plan is not acted on because to the aristocrats any sort of selling is unthinkable, and although one Pishchik is in the course of time miraculously redeemed from financial ruin by some Englishmen who discover and buy "some kind of white clay" on *his* land, time brings Mme. Ranevskaya and her brother Gaev no such good fortune. So far as the main happenings in the play are concerned, time neither presses nor preserves; it only passes.

During the passage of time in this play, the orchard is lost (tragic?) and the characters reveal themselves to be funny (comic?). The loss of the orchard is itself a happening of an uncertain kind. It stands, partly, for the end of an old way of life. But if that way once included intelligent and gracious aristocrats, it also included slavery, and in any case it now is embodied in the irresponsible heirs we see on the stage—Mme. Ranevskaya and her brother Gaev, along with their deaf and near-senile servant Firs. For Gaev the orchard is important chiefly because it lends prestige, since it is mentioned in the encyclopedia. Mme. Ranevskaya sees more to it. For her it is "all white" and it is "young again, full of happiness"; we are momentarily touched by her vision, but there is yet another way of seeing the orchard: for Trofimov, a student who envisions a new society as an orchard for all people, the ancestral cherry orchard is haunted by the serfs of the bad old days. Moreover, although the orchard is much talked about, it seems to have decayed to a trivial ornament. Long ago its crop was regularly harvested, pickled, and sold, thus providing food and income, but now "nobody remembers" the pickling formula and nobody buys the crop. There seems to be some truth to Lopakhin's assertion that "the only remarkable thing about this cherry orchard is that it's very big," and although one must point out that this remark is made by a despised merchant, Lopakhin is neither a fool nor the "money grubber" that Gaev thinks he is. Lopakhin delights in nature put to use. He "cleared forty thousand net" from poppies, "And when my poppies bloomed, it was like a picture!" His enthusiasm for the flowers is undercut for us only a little, if at all, by the fact that they were of use to him and to others.

Lopakhin's serious concern, whether for his poppies or for the future of the cherry orchard, contrasts interestingly with Mme. Ranevskaya's and with Gaev's sporadic passion for the orchard. Mme. Ranevskaya says, "Without the cherry orchard, I couldn't make sense of my life," and she doubtless means what she says; but that her words have not much relation to reality is indicated by her meaningless addition, "If it really has to be sold, then sell me along with the orchard." After the orchard has been sold, Gaev confesses, "everything's fine now. Until the sale of the cherry orchard, we were all upset, distressed, but then, when the dilemma was settled, finally, irrevocably, everyone calmed down, even became cheerful . . . I'm a bank employee. . . . Lyuba, anyway, you're looking better, that's for sure." His sister agrees: "Yes. My nerves are better, that's true. . . . I'm sleeping well. Carry my things out, Yasha. It's time." She returns to her lover in Paris, Gaev goes off to a job in the bank, and though we can imagine that the orchard will continue to be an occasional topic of conversation, we cannot imagine that the loss has in any way changed them. The play ends, but things will go on in the same way; neither a tragic nor a comic action has been completed.

The characters no less than the action are tragicomic. Their longings would touch the heart if only these people did not so quickly digress or engage in little actions that call their depth into doubt. Charlotta laments that she had no proper passport and that her deceased parents may not have been married: "Where I came from and who I am I don't know." And then, having touched on the mighty subject of one's identity, the subject that is the stuff of tragedy in which heroes endure the worst in order to know who they are, she begins to eat a cucumber, and somehow that simple and entirely necessary act diminishes her dignity—though it does not totally dissipate our glimpse of her alienation. In the same scene, when Yepikhodov confesses that although he reads "all kinds of remarkable books" he "cannot discover [his] own inclinations," we hear another echo of the tragic hero's quest for self-knowledge, but we also hear an echo from the world of comedy, say of the pedant who guides his life by a textbook. Yepikhodov, perhaps like a tragic hero, is particularly concerned with whether to live or to shoot himself; but this racking doubt is diminished by his prompt explanation that since he may someday decide on suicide, he always carries a revolver, which he proceeds to show to his listeners. Almost all of the characters bare their souls, but their slightly addled minds and their hungry bodies expose them to a gentle satirical treatment so that they evoke a curious amused pathos. One can, for example, sympathize with Mme. Ranevskaya's despair—but one cannot forget that she is scatterbrained and that domestic duties and local pieties occupy her mind only occasionally and that her disreputable lover in Paris means as much as the orchard she thinks she cannot live without. And when Gaev says, "Word of honor I'll swear, by whatever you like, that the estate won't be sold," we know that he has very little honor and even less ability to focus on the problem (mostly he takes refuge in thoughts about billiards, and somehow his habit of eating candy does not enhance his status in our eyes) and that the estate will be sold.

Finally, something must be said about the ambiguous treatment of the future. We know, from his correspondence, that Chekhov looked forward to a new and happier society. Russia, like much of the rest of Europe, was ceasing to be an agrarian society, but if the death throes were evident, one could not be so confident about the birth pangs. Something of the presence of two worlds is hinted at in the stage direction at the beginning of the second act, where we see the estate with its orchard, and also "Further off are telegraph poles, and way in the distance, dimly sketched on the horizon, is a large town." The telegraph poles and the town silently represent the new industrial society, but Trofimov the student speaks at length of the glorious possibilities of the future, and his speeches were sufficiently close to the bone for the censor to delete two passages sharply critical of the present. But we cannot take Trofimov's speeches quite at face value. He is a student, but he is almost thirty and still has not received his degree. His speeches in Act 2 are moving, especially those on the need to work rather than to talk if the future is to be better than the past, but we cannot quite rid ourselves of the suspicion that Trofimov talks rather than works. Certainly he is contemptuous of the merchant Lopakhin, who delights in work. And, worse, Trofimov frets too much about his overshoes, thinks he is "above love," and is so confounded by Mme. Ranevskaya's remark, "At your age, not to have a mistress!" that he falls down a flight of stairs. None of these personal failings invalidates his noble view of the future; certainly none of them turns this view into a comic pipedream, and yet all of these things, along with a certain nostalgia that we feel for the past, do suffuse even his noblest statements about the future with a delicate irony that puts them, along with the much praised but totally neglected cherry orchard, firmly in the tragicomic world. One understands why Chekhov called the play a comedy, and one understands why Stanislavsky (who directed the first production and played the part of Gaev) told Chekhov, "It is definitely not a comedy . . . but a tragedy." Perhaps neither of the men fully wanted to see the resonant ambiguities in the play.

ANTON CHEKHOV *The Cherry Orchard*

List of Characters[1]

RANEVSKAYA, LYUBOV ANDREEVNA, *a landowner* (Lyoo-BAWFF Ahn-DRAY-eff-nah Rahn-YEHFF-skei-ah)

ANYA, *her daughter, age 17* (AHN-yah)

VARYA, *her adopted daughter, age 24* (VAHR-yah)

GAEV, LEONID ANDREEVICH, *Ranevskaya's brother* (Lyaw-NEED Ahn-DRAY-eech GEI-ehff)

LOPAKHIN, YERMOLAI ALEKSEICH, *a businessman* (Yehr-mah-LEI Ah-lihk-SAY-eech Lah-PAH-kheen)

TROFIMOV, PYOTR SERGEEVICH, *a student* (PYAW-tr Ser-GAY-veech Trah-FEE-mawff)

SIMEONOV-PISHCHIK, BORIS BORISOVICH, *a landowner* (Seem-YAWN-awff PEESH-cheek)

CHARLOTTA IVANOVNA, *a governess* (Sharh-LAW-tah Ee-VAHN-awff-nah)

YEPIKHODOV, SEMYON PANTELEEVICH, *a bookkeeper* (Sim-YAHN Pahn-til-YAY-eech Ippy-KHAW-dawff)

DUNYASHA, *a parlor-maid* (Doon-YAH-shah)

[1] Unlike earlier dramatists like Gogol or Ostrovsky, Chekhov seldom resorts to word play in naming the characters in his full-length pieces, but to a Russian ear, certain associations can be made. *Lyubov* means "love" (perhaps Amy is the English equivalent), and a kind of indiscriminate love is indeed the soul of Ranevskaya's character. *Gaev* suggests *gaer,* buffoon, while *Lopakhin* may be derived from either *lopata,* a shovel, or *lopat',* to shovel food down one's gullet—both words of the earth, earthy. *Simeonov-Pishchik* is a Dickensian combination of a noble boyar name and a silly one reminiscent of *pishchat',* to chirp. A similar English appellation might be Montmorency-Tweet. [All notes are by the translator.]

FIRS NIKOLAEVICH, *a footman, an old fellow of 87* (FEERRSS Nee-kaw-LEI-yeh-veech)
YASHA, *a young manservant* (YAH-shah)
A TRAMP
THE STATIONMASTER
A POSTAL CLERK
GUESTS, SERVANTS

The action takes place on Madam Ranevskaya's estate.

ACT 1

A room, which is still known as the Nursery. One of the doors opens into Anya's bedroom. Dawn, soon the sun will be up. It is already May, the cherry trees are in blossom, but it is chilly in the orchard, there is a frost. The windows in the room are shut.

(*Enter Dunyasha carrying a candle, and Lopakhin holding a book.*)

LOPAKHIN. Train's in, thank God. What's the time?

DUNYASHA. Almost two. (*Blows out the candle.*) Daylight already.

LOPAKHIN. But just how late was the train? Must have been two hours at least. (*Yawns and stretches.*) I'm a fine one, made quite a fool of myself! Drove over here on purpose, so as to meet them at the station, and fell asleep just like that . . . dozed off in a chair. Annoying . . . but you should have woken me up.

DUNYASHA. I thought you'd gone. (*Listening.*) Listen, it sounds like they're coming.

LOPAKHIN (*listening*). No . . . the luggage has to be brought in, and what-have-you. . . . (*Pause.*) Lyubov Andreevna's been living abroad five years now. I wonder what she's like these days. . . . She's a good sort of person. An easygoing, unpretentious person. I remember, when I was a lad of about fifteen, my late father—at that time he kept a shop here in the village—punched me in the face with his fist, blood was pouring from my nose. . . . We'd come into the yard for some reason or other, and he was tipsy. Lyubov Andreevna, I remember as if it were yesterday, she was still a young lady, so slender, led me to the washbasin, right here in this very room, the nursery. "Don't cry," says she "peasant boy, it'll heal in time for your wedding . . ." (*Pause.*) Peasant boy. . . . My father, it's true, was a peasant, and here am I in a white waistcoat and tan shoes. Like a pig rooting in a pastry shop. . . . Now here am I, rich, plenty of money, but if you think it over and consider, once a peasant, always a peasant. . . . (*Leafs through the book.*) I was reading this book and couldn't make head or tail of it. Reading and dozed off.

(*Pause.*)

DUNYASHA. The dogs didn't sleep all night, they sense the mistress coming home.

LOPAKHIN. What's got into you, Dunyasha, you're such a . . .

DUNYASHA. My hands are trembling. I'm going to swoon.

LOPAKHIN. You're much too delicate, Dunyasha. Dressing up like a lady, fixing your hair like one too. Mustn't do that. Mustn't forget who you are.

(*Yepikhodov enters with a bouquet; he is wearing a jacket and brightly polished boots, which squeak noisily. On entering, he drops the bouquet.*)

YEPIKHODOV (*picks up the bouquet*). Here, the gardener sent them, he says to stick 'em in the dining room. (*He hands Dunyasha the bouquet.*)

LOPAKHIN. And bring me some beer.

DUNYASHA. Very good. (*She exits.*)

YEPIKHODOV. Three degrees of frost this morning, but the cherries are all in bloom. I can't condone our climate. (*He sighs.*) I can't. I mean, it doesn't seem to make an effort. Look, Yermolai Alekseich, allow me to append, I bought myself some boots the day before yesterday, and they, I make bold to assert, squeak so much, it's quite out of the question. What should I grease them with?

LOPAKHIN. Leave me alone. You're a pest.

YEPIKHODOV. Every day something unlucky happens to me. But I don't complain, I'm used to it. I even smile.

(*Dunyasha enters and gives Lopakhin some beer.*)

YEPIKHODOV. I'm on my way. (*Bumps into a chair which falls over.*) There. . . . (*As if triumphant*) You see, pardon the expression, what a circumstance, incidentally. . . . It's simply, you might say conspicuous! (*He exits.*)

DUNYASHA. Just let me tell you, Yermolai Alekseich, Yepikhodov proposed to me.

LOPAKHIN. Ah!

DUNYASHA. I don't know what to do. . . . He's a quiet sort, but sometimes he starts talking away, and you can't understand a thing. It's nice and it's sensitive, only you can't understand it. I kind of like him. He's madly in love with me. He's an unlucky sort of fellow, something happens every day. So we've nicknamed him: twenty-two troubles. . . .

LOPAKHIN (*hearkening*). Listen, I think they're coming. . . .

DUNYASHA. Coming! What's the matter with me . . . I'm all over chills.

LOPAKHIN. They are coming. Let's go meet them. Will she recognize me? We haven't set eyes on one another for five years.

DUNYASHA (*in a flurry*). I'll faint this minute.... Ach, I'll faint!

(*We hear the sounds of two carriages drawing up to the house. Lopakhin and Dunyasha exeunt quickly. The stage is empty. Noises begin in the adjoining rooms. Firs, leaning on a stick, hurries across the stage; he has just been to meet Lyubov Andreevna: he is wearing an old suit of livery and a top hat; he mutters something to himself but no words can be made out. The offstage noises keep growing louder. A voice: "Let's go through here." Lyubov Andreevna, Anya, and Charlotta Ivanovna with a lapdog on a leash, the three dressed in travelling clothes, Varya in an overcoat and kerchief, Gaev, Simeonov-Pishchik, Lopakhin, Dunyasha with a bundle and a parasol, servants carrying suitcases—all pass through the room.*)

ANYA. Let's go through here. Mama, do you remember what room this was?

LYUBOV ANDREEVNA (*joyously, through tears*). The nursery!

VARYA. It's cold, my hands are numb. (*To Lyubov Andreevna*) Your rooms, the white and the violet, are still the same as ever, Mama dear.

LYUBOV ANDREEVNA. The nursery, my darling, beautiful room.... I slept here when I was a little girl.... (*She weeps.*) And now I'm like a little girl.... (*She kisses her brother and Varya and then her brother again.*) And Varya is just the same as before, looks like a nun. And I recognized Dunyasha.... (*Kisses Dunyasha.*)

GAEV. The train was two hours late. What's going on? What kind of organization is that?

CHARLOTTA (*to Pishchik*). My dog, he even eats nuts.

PISHCHIK (*astounded*). Can you imagine!

(*They all go out, except for Anya and Dunyasha.*)

DUNYASHA. We've been waiting and waiting. (*Helps to remove Anya's overcoat and hat.*)

ANYA. I couldn't sleep the four nights on the train ... now I'm so frozen.

DUNYASHA. You left during Lent, then there was snow, frost, and now? My darling! (*She laughs and kisses her.*) We kept waiting for you, my sweet, my precious ... I'll tell you now, I can't keep it back another minute....

ANYA (*weary*). Now what ...

DUNYASHA. Yepikhodov the bookkeeper proposed to me right after Easter.

ANYA. You've got a one-track mind.... (*Setting her hair to rights.*) I've lost all my hair-pins.... (*She is very tired, practically staggering.*)

DUNYASHA. I just don't know what to think. He loves me, loves me so much!

ANYA (*peering through the door to her room, tenderly*). My room, my windows, as if I'd never gone away. I'm home! Tomorrow morning I'll get up, I'll run through the orchard.... Oh, if only I could get some sleep! I couldn't sleep the whole way. I was worried to death.

DUNYASHA. Day before yesterday, Pyotr Sergeich arrived.

ANYA (*joyfully*). Petya!

DUNYASHA. Sleeping in the bathhouse, practically lives there. "I'm afraid," says he, "of being a bother." (*Looking at her pocket watch*) Somebody ought to wake him up, but Varvara Mikhailovna gave the order not to. "You mustn't wake him up," she says.

(*Enter Varya, with a key-ring on her belt.*)

VARYA. Dunyasha, coffee immediately.... Mama dear is asking for coffee.

DUNYASHA. Right this minute. (*She exits.*)

VARYA. Well, thank God, you've come back. You're home again. (*Caressing her.*) My darling's come back! My beauty's come back!

ANYA. I've had so much to put up with.

VARYA. I can imagine!

ANYA. I left during Holy Week, it was so cold then. Charlotta kept on talking the whole way, performing card tricks. Why you stuck me with Charlotta....

VARYA. You couldn't have travelled by yourself, precious. Seventeen years old!

ANYA. We got to Paris, it was cold there too, snowing. I speak awful French. Mama was living on a fifth floor walkup, she had all sorts of French visitors, ladies, some old Catholic priest with a little book, so smoky and tawdry. And all of a sudden I started pitying Mama, pitying her so, I took her head between my hands and couldn't let go. Then Mama kept hugging me, crying....

VARYA (*through tears*). Don't talk about it, don't talk about it ...

ANYA. The villa near Menton she'd already sold, she had nothing left, nothing. And I hadn't a kopek left either, we barely got this far. And Mama doesn't understand! We sit down to dine at a station, and she orders the most expensive meal and gives each waiter a ruble tip. Charlotta's the same way. And Yasha insists on his share too, it's simply horrible. Of course Mama has her own valet Yasha, we brought him back....

VARYA. I saw the loafer....

ANYA. Well, how is everything? Have we paid off the interest?

VARYA. What with?

ANYA. Oh dear, oh dear....

VARYA. In August the estate's to be auctioned off....

ANYA. Oh dear....

LOPAKHIN (*sticking his head in the door and bleating*). Me-e-eh.... (*Exits.*)

VARYA (*through tears*). I'd like to smack him one.... (*Shakes her fist.*)

ANYA (*embraces Varya, quietly*). Varya, has he proposed? (*Varya shakes her head.*) He *does* love you.... Why don't you talk it over, what are you waiting for?

VARYA. I don't think anything will come of it for us. He's got so much work, no time for me ... and pays me no attention. May he go with God, it's hard for me even to get to see him ... Everybody talks about our wedding, everybody's congratulating us, but as a matter of fact, there's nothing to it, it's all like a dream.... (*In a different tone*) You've got a new brooch like a bumble-bee.

ANYA (*sadly*). Mama bought it. (*Goes to her room, speaks merrily, like a child.*) And in Paris I went up in a balloon!

VARYA. My darling's come back! My beauty's come back!

(*Dunyasha has returned with a coffee-pot and is making coffee.*)

VARYA (*stands near the door*). I go about the whole day, darling, with my household chores and dream and dream. If only there were a rich man for you to marry, I'd be at peace too, I'd go to a hermitage, then to Kiev ... to Moscow, and so I'd keep on going to holy places ... I'd go on and on. Glorious!...

ANYA. Birds are singing in the orchard. What's the time now?

VARYA. Must be three. Time for you to be asleep, dearest. (*Going into Anya's room.*) Glorious!

(*Yasha enters with a lap rug, and a travelling bag.*)

YASHA (*crosses the stage; affectedly*). May I pass through here?

DUNYASHA. A body'd hardly recognize you, Yasha. How you've changed abroad.

YASHA. Mm.... Who are you?

DUNYASHA. When you left here, I was so high.... (*Measures from the floor.*) Dunyasha, Fyodor Kozoedov's daughter. You don't remember!

YASHA. Mm ... some tomato! (*Glances around, embraces her; she shrieks and drops a saucer. Yasha hurriedly exits.*)

VARYA (*in the doorway, crossly*). Now what was that?

DUNYASHA (*through tears*). I broke a saucer....

VARYA. That's good luck.

ANYA (*entering from her room*). We ought to warn Mama that Petya's here....

VARYA. I gave orders not to wake him.

ANYA (*pensively*). Six years ago, a month after father died, brother Grisha drowned in the river, a sweet little boy, seven years old. Mama couldn't stand it, she went away, went away without looking back.... (*Shivers.*) How I understand her, if she only knew! (*Pause.*) And Petya Trofimov was Grisha's tutor, he might remind ...

(*Enter Firs in a jacket and white vest.*)

FIRS (*goes to the coffee pot; preoccupied*). The mistress will take her coffee in here.... (*Putting on white gloves*) Coffee ready? (*Sternly to Dunyasha*) You! where's the cream?

DUNYASHA. Ach, my God.... (*Exits hurriedly.*)

FIRS (*fussing with the coffee-pot*). Ech, you're half-baked.... (*Mumbles to himself*) Come home from Paris.... And the master went to Paris once upon a time ... by coach.... (*Laughs.*)

VARYA. Firs, what are you on about?

FIRS. What's wanted? (*Joyfully*) My mistress has come home! I've been waiting! Now I can die.... (*Weeps with joy.*)

(*Enter Lyubov Andreevna, Gaev, and Simeonov-Pishchik, the last in a peasant coat of excellent cloth and wide trousers. Gaev, on entering, moves his arms and torso as if he were playing billiards.*)

LYUBOV ANDREEVNA. How does it go? Let me remember.... Yellow to the corner! Doublet to the center!

GAEV. Red to the corner! Once upon a time, sister we used to sleep together in this very room, and now I'm already fifty-one years old, strange as it seems....

LOPAKHIN. Yes, time flies.

GAEV. How's that?

LOPAKHIN. Time, I say, flies.

GAEV. It smells of cheap perfume in here.

ANYA. I'm going to bed. Good night, Mama. (*Kisses her mother.*)

LYUBOV ANDREEVNA. My precious little princess. (*Kisses her hands.*) Are you glad you're home? I can't pull myself together.

ANYA. Good night, Uncle.

GAEV (*kisses her face, hands*). God bless you. How like your mother you are! (*To his sister*) Lyuba, you were just the same at her age.

(*Anya gives her hand to Lopakhin and Pishchik, exits, and shuts the door behind her.*)

LYUBOV ANDREEVNA. She's very tired.

PISHCHIK. Must be a long trip.

VARYA (*to Lopakhin and Pishchik*). Well, gentlemen? Three o'clock, by this time you've worn out your welcome.

LYUBOV ANDREEVNA (*laughing*). You never change, Varya. (*Draws Varya to her and kisses her.*) First I'll have some coffee, then everybody will go. (*Firs puts a cushion under her feet.*) Thank you, dear. I've grown accustomed to coffee. I drink it night and day. Thank you, old dear. (*Kisses Firs.*)

VARYA. I'll see if all the luggage was brought in. . . . (*Exits.*)

LYUBOV ANDREEVNA. Can I really be sitting here? (*Laughs.*) I feel like jumping up and down and swinging my arms. (*Hides her face in her hands.*) But suppose I'm dreaming! God knows, I love my country, love it tenderly. I couldn't look at it from the carriage, couldn't stop crying. (*Through tears*) However, must drink some coffee. Thank you, Firs, thank you, my old dear. I'm so glad you're still alive.

FIRS. Day before yesterday.

GAEV. He doesn't hear well.

LOPAKHIN. I've got to leave for Kharkov around five. What a nuisance! I wanted to have a look at you, to talk. . . . You're still as lovely as ever.

PISHCHIK (*breathing hard*). Even gotten prettier. . . . Dressed in Parisian fashions. . . . "Lost my cart with all four wheels. Lost my heart head over heels."

LOPAKHIN. Your brother, Leonid Andreich here, says that I'm a boor, a money-grubbing peasant, but it doesn't make the least bit of difference to me. Let him talk. The only thing I want is for you to believe in me as you once did, for your wonderful, heart-breaking eyes to look at me as they once did. Merciful God! My father was your grandfather's serf and your father's, but you, you personally, did so much for me once that I forgot it all and love you like my own kin—more than my own kin.

LYUBOV ANDREEVNA. I can't sit still. I just can't. . . . (*Leaps up and walks about in great excitement.*) I won't survive the joy. . . . Laugh at me, I'm silly. . . . My dear bookcase! (*Kisses the bookcase.*) My little table.

GAEV. While you were away, Nanny died.

LYUBOV ANDREEVNA (*sits and drinks coffee*). Yes, may she rest in peace. They wrote me.

GAEV. And Anastasy died. Cross-eyed Petrusha left me and now he's working in town for the police. (*Takes a box from his pocket and eats caramels out of it.*)

PISHCHIK. My dear daughter Dashenka . . . says to say hello. . . .

LOPAKHIN. I'd like to tell you something very enjoyable, cheery. (*Looking at his watch.*) I have to go now, never time for a chat . . . well, here it is in two or three words. As you already know, the cherry orchard will be sold to pay your debts, the auction is set for August 22nd but don't you fret, dear lady, don't lose any sleep, there's a way out. . . . Here's my plan. Please pay attention! Your estate lies only thirteen miles from town, the railroad runs alongside it, and if the cherry orchard were divided into building lots and then leased out for summer cottages, you'd be making at the very least twenty-five thousand a year.

GAEV. Excuse me, what poppycock!

LYUBOV ANDREEVNA. I don't quite understand you, Yermolai Alekseich.

LOPAKHIN. You'll get out of the tenants about twenty-five rubles a year per two-and-a-half acres at the very least, and if you advertise now, I'll willingly bet anything that by fall there won't be a single unoccupied plot, it'll all be grabbed up. In a word, congratulations, you're saved. Wonderful location, deep river. Only, of course, we'll have to put it to rights, fix it up . . . for example, say, pull down all the old sheds, and this house, which is absolutely worthless, chop down the old cherry orchard.

LYUBOV ANDREEVNA. Chop it down? My dear, forgive me, but you don't understand anything. If there's one thing of interest in the entire district, even outstanding, it's none other than our cherry orchard.

LOPAKHIN. The only outstanding thing about this orchard is that it's enormous. The cherries grow once in two years, and there's no way of getting rid of them, nobody buys them.

GAEV. This orchard is cited in the Encyclopedia.

LOPAKHIN (*glancing at his watch*). If we don't think up something and come to some decision, then on the twenty-second of August the cherry orchard and the whole estate will be sold at auction. Make up your mind! There's no other way out, I promise you. Absolutely none!

FIRS. In the old days, some forty–fifty years back—cherries were dried, preserved, pickled, made into jam, and sometimes . . .

GAEV. Be quiet, Firs.

FIRS. And sometimes whole cartloads of dried cherries were sent to Moscow and Kharkov. Then there was money! And in those days the dried cherries were soft, juicy, sweet, tasty. . . . They knew a recipe then. . . .

LYUBOV ANDREEVNA. And where's that recipe today?

FIRS. Forgotten. Nobody remembers.

PISHCHIK (*to Lyubov*). What's going on in Paris? How was it? You ate frogs?

LYUBOV ANDREEVNA. I ate crocodiles.

PISHCHIK. Can you imagine . . .

LOPAKHIN. Up till now there were only gentry and peasants in the country, but now the summer tourists have sprung up. Every town, even the smallest, is surrounded these days by summer cottages. And I'll bet that during the next twenty-odd years the summer tourist will multiply fantastically. Now he only drinks tea on his veranda, but it might just happen that on his puny two-and-a-half acres, he goes in for farming and then your cherry orchard will become happy, rich, lush. . . .

GAEV (*getting indignant*). What poppycock!

(*Enter Varya and Yasha.*)

VARYA. Mama dear, here are two telegrams for you. (*Selects a key; with a jangle opens the old bookcase.*) Here they are.

LYUBOV ANDREEVNA. This is from Paris. (*Tears up the telegrams, without reading them.*) I'm through with Paris.

GAEV. Lyuba, do you know how old that bookcase is? A week ago I pulled out the bottom drawer, and I looked, and there were numbers burnt into it. This bookcase was built exactly one hundred years ago. How do you like that? Maybe we ought to celebrate its anniversary. An inanimate object, but all the same, any way you look at it, a case to hold books.

PISHCHIK (*astounded*). A hundred years . . . Can you imagine! . . .

GAEV. Yes. . . . This thing. . . . (*Clasping the bookcase*) Dear, venerable bookcase! I salute your existence, which for over a century has been dedicated to the enlightened idealism of virtue and justice. Your mute appeal to constructive endeavor has not faltered in the course of a century, upholding (*through tears*) in generations of our line, courage, faith in a better future and nurturing within us ideals of decency and social consciousness.

(*Pause.*)

LOPAKHIN. Yes. . . .

LYUBOV ANDREEVNA. You're still the same, Lyonya.

GAEV (*somewhat embarrassed*). Carom to the right corner! Red to the center!

LOPAKHIN (*glancing at his watch*). Well, my time's up.

YASHA (*handing medicine to Lyubov*). Maybe you'll take your pills now. . . .

PISHCHIK. Shouldn't take medicine, dearest lady. . . . It does no good, or harm. . . . Give that here . . . most respected lady. (*He takes the pills, shakes them into his palm, blows on them, pops them into his mouth and drinks some beer.*) There!

LYUBOV ANDREEVNA (*alarmed*). You've gone crazy!

PISHCHIK. I took all the pills.

LOPAKHIN. What a glutton!

(*They all laugh.*)

FIRS. The gentleman stayed with us during Holy Week, ate half-a-bucket of cucumbers. . . . (*Mumbles.*)

LYUBOV ANDREEVNA. What is he on about?

VARYA. For three years now he's been mumbling like that. We're used to it.

YASHA. Senility.

(*Charlotta Ivanovna crosses the stage in a white dress. She is very slender, tightly laced, with a pair of pincenez on a cord at her belt.*)

LOPAKHIN. Excuse me, Charlotta Ivanovna, I haven't yet had time to say hello to you. (*Tries to kiss her hand.*)

CHARLOTTA (*pulling her hand away*). If I let you kiss a hand, then next you'd be after a elbow, then a shoulder. . . .

LOPAKHIN. My unlucky day. (*Everybody laughs.*) Charlotta Ivanovna, show us a trick!

LYUBOV ANDREEVNA. Charlotta, show us a trick!

CHARLOTTA. No reason. I want to go to bed. (*Exits.*)

LOPAKHIN. We'll see each other again in three weeks. (*Kisses Lyubov Andreevna's hand.*) Meanwhile good-bye. It's time. (*To Gaev*) Be seeing you. (*Exchanges kisses with Pishchik*) Be seeing you. (*Gives his hand to Varya, then to Firs and Yasha*) I don't want to go. (*To Lyubov Andreevna*) If you think over this business of the cottages and decide, then let me know, I'll arrange a loan of fifty thousand or so. Give it some serious thought.

VARYA (*angrily*). Well, go once and for all!

LOPAKHIN. I'm going, I'm going. . . . (*He leaves.*)

GAEV. Boor. However, I apologize. . . . Varya's going to marry him, that's Varya's little fiancé!

VARYA. Don't say anything uncalled for, Uncle dear.

LYUBOV ANDREEVNA. Anyway, Varya, I shall be delighted. He's a good man.

PISHCHIK. A man, you've got to tell the truth . . . most worthy. . . . And my Dashenka . . . also says that . . . says all sorts of things. (*Snores but immediately wakes up.*) But by the way, most respected lady, will you lend me . . . two hundred forty rubles . . . tomorrow I've got to pay the interest on the mortgage.

VARYA (*alarmed*). We haven't got any, we haven't got any!

LYUBOV ANDREEVNA. As a matter of fact, I haven't a thing.

PISHCHIK. It'll turn up. (*Laughs.*) I never lose hope. There, I think, all is lost, I'm ruined, lo and behold!—the railroad runs across my land and . . . pays me for it. And then, watch, something else will happen, if not today, tomorrow . . . Dashenka will win two hundred thousand . . . she's got a lottery ticket.

LYUBOV ANDREEVNA. The coffee's finished, now we can go to bed.

FIRS (*brushes Gaev's clothes, scolding*). You didn't put on them trousers again. What am I going to do with you!

VARYA (*quietly*). Anya's asleep. (*Quietly opens a window.*) The sun's up already, it's not so cold. Look, Mama dear: what wonderful trees! My God, the air! The starlings are singing.

GAEV (*opens another window*). The orchard's all white. You haven't forgotten, Lyuba? There's that long pathway leading straight on, straight on, like a stretched ribbon, it glistens on moonlit nights. You remember? You haven't forgotten?

LYUBOV ANDREEVNA (*looks through the window at the orchard*). O my childhood, my innocence! I slept in this nursery, gazed out at the orchard, happiness awoke with me every morning, and it was just the same then, nothing has changed. (*Laughs with joy.*) All, all white! O my orchard! After the dark, drizzly autumn and the cold winter, you're young again, full of happiness, the heavenly angels haven't forsaken you.... If only I could lift this heavy stone from off my chest and shoulders, if only I could forget my past!

GAEV. Yes, and the orchard will be sold for debts, strange as it seems.

LYUBOV ANDREEVNA. Look, our poor Mama is walking through the orchard ... in a white dress! (*Laughs with joy.*) There she is.

GAEV. Where?

VARYA. God be with you, Mama dear.

LYUBOV ANDREEVNA. There's nobody there, it just seemed so to me. At the right, by the turning to the summerhouse, a white sapling is bent over, looking like a woman.... (*Enter Trofimov in a shabby student's uniform and eyeglasses.*) What a marvelous orchard! White bunches of blossoms, blue sky ...

TROFIMOV. Lyubov Andreevna! (*She stares round at him.*) I'll only pay my respects and then leave at once. (*Kisses her hand fervently.*) They told me to wait till morning, but I didn't have the patience....

(*Lyubov Andreevna stares in bewilderment.*)

VARYA (*through tears*). This is Petya Trofimov.

TROFIMOV. Petya Trofimov, one-time tutor to your Grisha.... Can I have changed so much?

(*Lyubov Andreevna embraces him and weeps quietly.*)

GAEV (*embarrassed*). Come, come, Lyuba.

VARYA (*weeps*). Didn't I tell you, Petya, to wait till tomorrow.

LYUBOV ANDREEVNA. My Grisha ... my little boy ... Grisha ... son....

VARYA. There's no help for it, Mama dear. God's will be done.

TROFIMOV (*gently, through tears*). All right, all right....

LYUBOV ANDREEVNA (*quietly weeping*). A little boy lost, drowned.... What for? What for, my friend? (*More quietly*) Anya's asleep in there, and I'm shouting ... making noise.... Well now, Petya? Why have you become so homely? Why have you aged so?

TROFIMOV. On the train an old peasant woman called me "the mangy gent."

LYUBOV ANDREEVNA. You were just a boy in those days, a dear little student, but now your hair is thinning, eyeglasses. Are you really still a student? (*Goes to the door.*)

TROFIMOV. I suppose I'll be a perpetual student.

LYUBOV ANDREEVNA (*kisses her brother, then Varya*). Well, let's go to bed.... You've aged too, Leonid.

PISHCHIK (*follows her*). That means it's time for bed.... Och, my gout. I'll stay over with you.... And if you would, Lyubov Andreevna, my soul, tomorrow morning early ... two hundred forty rubles....

GAEV. He never gives up.

PISHCHIK. Two hundred forty rubles ... to pay the interest on the mortgage.

LYUBOV ANDREEVNA. I haven't any money, dovie.

PISHCHIK. We'll pay it back, dear lady.... A trifling sum....

LYUBOV ANDREEVNA. Well, all right, Leonid will let you have it.... You give it to him, Leonid.

GAEV. I'll give it to him all right, hold out your pockets.

LYUBOV ANDREEVNA. What can we do, give it to him.... He needs it.... He'll pay it back.

(*Lyubov Andreevna, Trofimov, Pishchik, and Firs exeunt. Gaev, Varya and Yasha remain.*)

GAEV. My sister still hasn't outgrown the habit of squandering money. (*To Yasha.*) Out of the way, my good man, you smell like a chicken-coop.

YASHA (*with a sneer*). But you're just the same as you always were, Leonid Andreich.

GAEV. Hows that? (*To Varya*) What did he say?

VARYA (*to Yasha*). Your mother's come from the village, ever since yesterday she's been sitting in the servant's hall, wanting to see you....

YASHA. To hell with her!

VARYA. Ach, disgraceful!

YASHA. That's all I need. She might have come tomorrow. (*Exits.*)

VARYA. Mama dear is just as she was before, she hasn't changed a bit. If it were in her power, she'd give away everything.

GAEV. Yes.... (*Pause.*) If a large number of cures is suggested for a particular disease, that means the disease is incurable. I think, wrack my brains, I've come up with all sorts of solutions, all sorts, and that means, actually, none. It would be nice to inherit a fortune from somebody, nice if we married off our Anya to a very rich man, nice to go off to Yaroslavl and try our luck with our auntie the Countess. Auntie's really very, very wealthy.

VARYA (*weeps*). If only God would help us.

GAEV. Stop snivelling. Auntie's very wealthy, but she isn't fond of us. In the first place, Sister married a courtroom lawyer, not a nobleman.... (*Anya appears in the doorway.*) Married a commoner and behaved herself, well, you can't say very virtuously. She's a good, kind, splendid person, I love her very much, but, no matter how much you consider the extenuating circumstances, even so, it must be admitted she's depraved. You can feel it in her slightest movement.

VARYA (*whispering*). Anya's standing in the doorway.

GAEV. Hows that? (*Pause.*) Extraordinary, something's got in my right eye. . . . My sight's beginning to fail. And Thursday, when I was at the County Court . . .

(*Anya enters.*)

VARYA. Why aren't you asleep, Anya?

ANYA. I can't fall asleep. I can't.

GAEV. My little tadpole. (*Kisses Anya's face, hands.*) My little girl. . . . (*Through tears*) You're not my niece, you're my angel, you're everything to me. Believe me, believe . . .

ANYA. I believe you, Uncle. Everybody loves you, respects you . . . but, dear Uncle, you must keep still, simply keep still. What were you saying just now about my Mama, your own sister? Why did you say that?

GAEV. Yes, yes. . . . (*Hides his face in his hands.*) In fact, it was terrible! My God! God, save me! And today I made a speech to the bookcase . . . like a fool! And as soon as I'd finished, I realized what a fool I'd been.

VARYA. True, Uncle dear, you ought to keep still. Just keep still. That's all.

ANYA. If you keep still, you'll be more at peace with yourself.

GAEV. I'll keep still. (*Kisses Anya's and Varya's hands.*) I'll keep still. Only this is business. Thursday I was at the County Court, well, some friends gathered around, started a conversation about this and that, six of one, half a dozen of the other, and it turns out it's possible to borrow money on an I.O.U. to pay the interest to the bank.

VARYA. If only God would help us!

GAEV. I'll go there on Tuesday and have another talk. (*To Varya*) Stop snivelling. (*To Anya*) Your Mama will talk to Lopakhin, he won't refuse her, of course. . . . And you, when you're rested up, will go to Yaroslavl to your grandmother the Countess. That way we'll have action in three directions—and our business is in the bag! We'll pay off the interest. I'm positive. . . . (*Pops a caramel into his mouth.*) Word of honor. I'll swear by whatever you like, the estate won't be sold! (*Excited*) I swear by my happiness! Here's my hand on it, call me a trashy, dishonorable man if I permit that auction! I swear with all my heart!

ANYA (*a more peaceful mood comes over her, she is happy*). You're so good, Uncle, so clever! (*Embraces her uncle.*) Now I feel calm! I'm calm! I'm happy!

(*Enter Firs.*)

FIRS (*scolding*). Leonid Andreich, have you no fear of God? When are you going to bed?

GAEV. Right now, right now. Go along, Firs. I'll even undress myself, how about that. Well, children, beddy-bye. . . . Details tomorrow, but for now go to bed. (*Kisses Anya and Varya.*) I'm a man of the 'eighties.[1]. . . . People don't put much stock in that period, but all the same I can say I've suffered considerably for my convictions in my time. It's not for nothing I'm loved by the peasant. You've got to know the peasant! You've got to know with what . . .

ANYA. You're at it again, Uncle!

VARYA. You must keep still, Uncle dear.

FIRS (*angrily*). Leonid Andreich!

GAEV. Coming, coming. . . . Go to bed. Two cushion carom to the center! I pocket the white . . . (*Exits followed by Firs, hobbling.*)

ANYA. Now I'm calm. I don't want to go to Yaroslavl. I don't like Grandmama, but just the same, I'm calm. Thanks to Uncle. (*Sits down.*)

VARYA. I must get some sleep. I'm off. Oh, there was some unpleasantness while you were away. As you probably know, only the old servants live in the old quarters; Yefimushka, Polya, Yevstignei, oh, and Karp. They started letting certain tramps spend the night with them—I held my peace. Only then, I hear they're spreading the rumor that I gave orders to feed them nothing but peas. Out of stinginess, you see. . . . And this was all Yevstignei's doing. . . . Fine, thinks I. If that's how things are, thinks I, then just you wait. I send for Yevstignei. . . . (*Yawns.*) Up he trots. . . . What's wrong with you, I say, Yevstignei . . . you're such a nincompoop. . . . (*Glancing at Anya.*) Anechka! (*Pause.*) Fallen asleep! . . . (*Takes Anya by the arm.*) Let's go to bed. . . . Let's go! . . . (*Leads her.*) My darling has fallen asleep! Let's go. . . .

(*They exeunt. Far beyond the orchard a shepherd is playing his pipes. Trofimov crosses the stage and, seeing Anya and Varya, stops short.*)

VARYA. Ssh. . . . She's asleep . . . asleep. . . . Let's go, dearest.

ANYA (*softly, half-asleep*). I'm so tired. . . . all the bells. . . . Uncle . . . dear . . . and mama and uncle . . .

VARYA. Let's go, dearest, let's go. . . . (*Exits into Anya's room.*)

TROFIMOV (*moved*). My sunshine! My springtime!

[1]**A man of the 'eighties** The 1880s, when Russia was ruled by the reactionary Alexander III, was a period of intensive political repression. Revolutionary movements were forcibly suppressed, as were the more liberal journals, and social activism virtually ceased. The intelligentsia took refuge in the passive resistance of Tolstoyanism and a tame dabbling in "art for art's sake" (which explains Gaev's chatter about the decadents, mentioned in Act 2). The feeling of social and political impotence led to the torpid aimlessness that is a common theme in Chekhov's works.

ACT 2

A field. An old, long-abandoned shrine leaning to one side. Beside it a well, large stones which were once, obviously, tombstones, and an old bench. At one side, towering poplars cast their shadows; here the cherry orchard begins. Further off are telegraph poles, and way in the distance, dimly sketched on the horizon, is a large town, which can be seen only in the best and clearest weather. A road to Gaev's estate can be seen. Soon the sun will set. Charlotta, Yasha, and Dunyasha are sitting on the bench. Yepikhodov stands nearby and strums a guitar; everyone sits rapt in thought. Charlotta is wearing an old peaked cap; she has taken a rifle off her shoulder and is adjusting a buckle on the strap.

CHARLOTTA (*pensively*). I haven't got a proper passport. I don't know how old I am, and I always have the impression I'm still a young thing. When I was a little girl, my father and Mama used to go from fairground to fairground, giving performances, rather good ones. And I would jump the *salto mortale*[1] and do all sorts of different stunts. And when Papa and Mama died, a German lady took me to her house and started teaching me. Fine. I grew up, then turned into a governess. But where I'm from and who I am—I don't know. . . . Who my parents were, maybe they weren't married. . . . I don't know. (*Pulls a cucumber from her pocket and eats it.*) I don't know anything. (*Pause.*) I would so like to talk, but there's no one to talk with. . . . No one.

YEPIKHODOV (*strums his guitar and sings*). "What care I for the noisy world, what are friends and foes to me. . . ." How pleasant to play the mandolin!

DUNYASHA. That's a guitar, not a mandolin. (*Looks in a hand-mirror and powders her nose.*)

YEPIKHODOV. To a lovesick lunatic, this is a mandolin. . . . (*Sings quietly*) "Were but my heart aflame with the spark of requited love. . . ."

(*Yasha joins in.*)

CHARLOTTA. These people are rotten singers. . . . Fooey! A pack of hyenas.

DUNYASHA (*to Yasha*). Anyway, how lucky you were to live abroad.

YASHA. Yes, of course. I can't disagree with you there. (*Yawns, then lights a cigar.*)

YEPIKHODOV. Stands to reason. Abroad everything has long since attained its complete maturation point.

YASHA. Goes without saying.

YEPIKHODOV. I'm a cultured fellow, I read all kinds of remarkable books, but somehow I can't figure out my own inclinations, what I personally want, to live or to shoot myself, strictly speaking, but nevertheless I always carry a revolver on my person. Here it is. . . . (*Displays a revolver.*)

CHARLOTTA. I'm done. Now I'll go. (*Slips the gun over her shoulder.*) Yepikhodov, you're a very clever fellow and a very frightening one; the women ought to love you madly. Brr! (*Exiting*) These clever people are all so stupid there's no one for me to talk to. . . . No one. . . . All alone, alone, I've got no one and . . . who I am, why I am, I don't know. (*Exits.*)

YEPIKHODOV. Strictly speaking, not flying off on tangents, I must declare concerning myself, by the way, that Fate treats me ruthlessly, as a storm does a rowboat. If, suppose, I'm wrong about this, then why when I woke up this morning, to give but a single example, I look and there on my chest is a terrifically huge spider. . . . This big. (*Uses both hands to show.*) Or then again, I'll take some beer, so as to drink it, and there, lo and behold, is something in the highest degree improper, such as a cockroach. . . . (*Pause.*) Have you read Buckle?[2] (*Pause.*) I should like to trouble you with a couple of words, Avdotya Fyodorovna.

DUNYASHA. Go ahead.

YEPIKHODOV. I'm desirous of seeing you in private. . . . (*Sighs.*)

DUNYASHA. (*embarrassed*). All right . . . only first bring me my shawl . . . It's next to the cupboard . . . it's getting damp.

YEPIKHODOV. All right, ma'am . . . I'll fetch it, ma'am. . . . Now I know what I must do with my revolver. . . . (*Takes the guitar and exits playing it.*)

YASHA. Twenty-two troubles! Pretty stupid, take it from me. (*Yawns.*)

DUNYASHA. God forbid he should shoot himself. (*Pause.*) I've gotten jittery, always worrying. When I was still a little girl, they took me to the master's house, now I'm out of touch with the simple life, and my hands are white, as white as can be, like a young lady's. I've gotten sensitive, so delicate, ladylike, afraid of everything. . . . Awfully so. And,

[1] ***Salto mortale*** death-defying leap

[2] **Buckle** Henry Thomas Buckle—pronounced Bucklee—(1821–62), whose *History of Civilization in England* (1857, 1861) posited that skepticism was the handmaiden of progress and that credulity (for which, read religion) retarded civilization's advance. He enjoyed immense popularity among progressive Russians in the 1860s, but by the end of the century seemed outmoded. Chekhov himself had read Buckle when a youth and quoted him approvingly in his early correspondence; as the years wore on, however, he began to take issue with many of Buckle's contentions. In *The Cherry Orchard,* he uses the reference to indicate that Yepikhodov's attempts at self-education are jejune and far behind the times.

Yasha, if you deceive me, then I don't know what'll happen to my nerves.

YASHA (*kisses her*). Some tomato! Of course, every girl ought to know just how far to go, and if there's one thing I hate, it's a girl who misbehaves herself.

DUNYASHA. I love you ever so much, you're educated, you can discuss anything.

(*Pause.*)

YASHA (*yawns*). Yes'm. . . . The way I look at it, it's like this: if a girl loves somebody, that means she's immoral. (*Pause.*) Nice smoking a cigar in the fresh air. . . . (*Listening*) Someone's coming this way. . . . The gentry. . . . (*Dunyasha impulsively embraces him.*) Go home, as if you'd been to the river for a swim, take this road or you'll run into them and they'll think I've been going out with you. I couldn't stand that.

DUNYASHA (*coughs quietly*). I've got a headache from your cigar. . . . (*Exits.*)

(*Yasha remains sitting beside the shrine. Enter Lyubov Andreevna, Gaev, and Lopakhin.*)

LOPAKHIN. You've got to decide once and for all—time won't stand still. It's really quite a dead issue. Do you agree to rent land for cottages or not? Answer in one word: yes or no? Just one word!

LYUBOV ANDREEVNA. Who's been smoking those revolting cigars here? . . . (*Sits.*)

GAEV. Now that the railroad's in operation it's become convenient. (*Sits.*) You ride to town and have lunch . . . yellow to the center! I ought to stop off at home, play one game. . . .

LYUBOV ANDREEVNA. You'll have time.

LOPAKHIN. Just one word! (*Pleading.*) Give me an answer!

GAEV (*yawning*). Hows that?

LYUBOV ANDREEVNA (*looking into her purse*). Yesterday I had lots of money, but today there's very little. My poor Varya for economy's sake feeds everybody milk soup, in the kitchen the old people get nothing but peas, and somehow I'm spending recklessly. . . . (*Drops the purse, scattering gold coins.*) Oh dear, spilled all over the place. . . . (*Annoyed.*)

YASHA. Allow me, I'll pick them up at once. (*Gathers the money.*)

LYUBOV ANDREEVNA. That's sweet of you, Yasha. And why did I go into town for lunch. . . . That shabby restaurant of yours with its music, the tablecloths smelt of soap. . . . Why drink so much, Lyonya? Why eat so much? Why talk so much? Today in the restaurant you started in talking a lot again and all off the subject. About the 'seventies, about the decadents. And who to? Talking to waiters about the decadents!

LOPAKHIN. Yes.

GAEV (*waves his hands*). I'm incorrigible, it's obvious. . . . (*Irritably, to Yasha*) What's the matter, forever whirling around in front of us. . . .

YASHA (*laughing*). I can't hear your voice without laughing.

GAEV (*to his sister*). Either he goes, or I do. . . .

LYUBOV ANDREEVNA. Go away, Yasha, run along.

YASHA (*handing the purse to Lyubov Andreevna*). I'll go right now. (*Barely restraining his laughter.*) This very minute. . . . (*Exits.*)

LOPAKHIN. Rich old Deriganov intends to purchase your estate. They say he's coming to the auction.

LYUBOV ANDREEVNA. Where did you hear that?

LOPAKHIN. They were discussing it in town.

GAEV. Our aunt in Yaroslavl promised to send something, but when and how much she'll send I don't know.

LOPAKHIN. How much is she sending? A hundred thousand? Two hundred?

LYUBOV ANDREEVNA. Well . . . ten or fifteen thousand—and we're grateful for that much.

LOPAKHIN. Excuse me, but such frivolous people as you, my friends, such unbusinesslike, peculiar people I never encountered before. Somebody tells you in plain Russian your estate is going to he sold, but you simply refuse to understand.

LYUBOV ANDREEVNA. But what are we going to do? Inform us, what?

LOPAKHIN. I inform you every day. Every day I tell you one and the same thing. Both the cherry orchard and the land have got to be leased as lots for cottages, do it right now, immediately—the auction is staring you in the face! Will you understand! Decide once and for all that there'll be cottages, they'll lend you as much money as you want, and then you'll be saved.

LYUBOV ANDREEVNA. Summer cottages and summer tourists—it's so vulgar, excuse me.

GAEV. I agree with you wholeheartedly.

LOPAKHIN. I'll either burst into tears or scream or fall down in a faint. It's too much for me! You're wearing me out! (*To Gaev*) You old woman!

GAEV. How's that?

LOPAKHIN. Old woman! (*Starts to exit.*)

LYUBOV ANDREEVNA (*frightened*). No, don't go, stay, dovie. Please! Maybe we'll think of something.

LOPAKHIN. What's there to think about?

LYUBOV ANDREEVNA. Don't go, please. With you here somehow it's jollier. . . . (*Pause.*) I keep anticipating something, as if the house were about to collapse on top of us.

GAEV (*in deep meditation*). Off the cushion to the corner . . . double to the center. . . .

LYUBOV ANDREEVNA. We've sinned so very much. . . .

LOPAKHIN. What kind of sins have you got. . . .

GAEV (*pops a caramel into his mouth*). They say I've eaten up my whole estate in caramels. . . . (*Laughs*)

LYUBOV ANDREEVNA. Oh, my sins. . . . I've always thrown money around recklessly, like a maniac, and married a man who produced nothing but debts. My husband died of champagne—he drank frightfully—and then, to my misfortune, I fell in love with another man, had an affair, and just at that time—this was my first punishment, dropped right on my head—the river over there . . . my little boy drowned, and I went abroad, went for good, so as never to return, never see that river again . . . I shut my eyes, ran away, beside myself, and *he* came after me . . . cruelly, brutally. I bought a villa near Menton, because *he* fell ill there, and for three years I didn't know what it was to rest day or night: the invalid exhausted me, my heart shrivelled up. But the next year, when the villa was sold for debts, I went to Paris, and there he robbed me, ran off and had an affair with another woman, I tried to poison myself . . . so silly, so shameful . . . and suddenly I had a longing for Russia, for my country, my little girl. . . . (*Wipes away her tears.*) Lord, Lord, be merciful, forgive me my sins! Don't punish me anymore! (*Takes a telegram out of her pocket.*) I received this today from Paris. . . . He begs my forgiveness, implores me to come back. . . . (*Tears up telegram.*) Sounds like music somewhere. (*Listens.*)

GAEV. That's our famous Jewish orchestra. You remember, four fiddles, a flute and a double bass.

LYUBOV ANDREEVNA. Does it still exist? We ought to hire them sometime and throw a party.

LOPAKHIN (*listening*). I don't hear it. . . . (*Sings softly*) "And for cash the Prussians will Frenchify the Russians." (*Laughs.*) What a play I saw at the theatre yesterday, very funny.

LYUBOV ANDREEVNA. And most likely there was nothing funny about it. It's not for you to look at plays, you should look at yourselves more. You all lead such gray lives, you talk such utter nonsense.

LOPAKHIN. That's true. I've got to admit, our life is idiotic. . . . (*Pause.*) My daddy was a peasant, an ignoramus, he didn't understand anything, didn't teach me but kept getting drunk and beating me with a stick. When you come down to it, I'm the same kind of idiot and ignoramus. I never studied anything, my handwriting is terrible, I write, I'm ashamed to show it to people, like a pig.

LYUBOV ANDREEVNA. You ought to get married, my friend.

LOPAKHIN. Yes . . . that's true.

LYUBOV ANDREEVNA. You should marry our Varya; she's a good girl.

LOPAKHIN. Yes.

LYUBOV ANDREEVNA. I adopted her from the common folk, she works the livelong day, but the main thing is she loves you. Yes and you've cared for her for a long time.

LOPAKHIN. Why not? I'm not against it. . . . She's a good girl.

(*Pause.*)

GAEV. They've offered me a position at the bank. Six thousand a year. . . . Did you hear?

LYUBOV ANDREEVNA. You indeed! Stay where you are. . . .

(*Firs enters; he is carrying an overcoat.*)

FIRS (*to Gaev*). Please, sir, put it on, it's damp here.

GAEV (*putting on the overcoat*). You're a pest, my man.

FIRS. Never you mind. . . . You went out this morning, didn't tell me. (*Inspects him.*)

LYUBOV ANDREEVNA. How old you're getting, Firs!

FIRS. What's wanted?

LOPAKHIN. The mistress says, you're getting very old!

FIRS. I've lived a long time. They were planning my wedding, long before your daddy was even born. . . . (*Laughs.*) And when the serfs was freed,[3] I was already head valet. Those days I didn't hanker to be freed, I stayed by the masters. . . . (*Pause.*) And I remember, everybody was glad, but what they was glad about, they didn't know themselves.

LOPAKHIN. It used to be nice all right. For instance, you got flogged.

FIRS (*not having heard*). I'll say. The peasants stood by the masters, the masters stood by the peasants, but now everything is topsy-turvy, can't figure out nothing.

GAEV. Keep quiet, Firs. Tomorrow I have to go to town. They promised to introduce me to some general, who might make us a loan on an I.O.U.

LOPAKHIN. Nothing'll come of it. And you won't pay the interest, you can be sure.

LYUBOV ANDREEVNA. He's raving. There are no such generals.

(*Enter Trofimov, Anya, and Varya.*)

GAEV. And here comes our crowd.

ANYA. Mama's sitting down.

[3]**When the serfs was freed** The serfs were emancipated by Alexander II in 1861, two years before Lincoln followed suit. Under the terms of the Emancipation Act, peasants were allotted land but had to pay back the government in annual installments, the sum used to indemnify former landowners. House serfs, on the other hand, were allotted no land. Both these conditions caused tremendous hardship and were responsible for great unrest among the newly manumitted. So there is more than a grain of truth in Firs's jeremiad.

LYUBOV ANDREEVNA (*tenderly*). Come, come.... My darlings.... (*kissing Anya and Varya.*) If only you both knew how much I love you. Sit beside me, that's right.

(*Everyone sits down.*)

LOPAKHIN. Our perpetual student is always stepping out with the ladies.

TROFIMOV. None of your business.

LOPAKHIN. Soon he'll be fifty and he'll still be a student.

TROFIMOV. Stop your idiotic jokes.

LOPAKHIN. What are you getting angry about, you crank?

TROFIMOV. Stop pestering me.

LOPAKHIN (*laughs*). May I ask, what's your opinion of me?

TROFIMOV. Here's my opinion, Yermolai Alekseich. You're a rich man, soon you'll be a millionaire. And in the same way a wild beast that devours everything that crosses its path is necessary to the conversion of matter, *you're* necessary.

(*Everyone laughs.*)

VARYA. Petya, tell us about the planets instead.

LYUBOV ANDREEVNA. No, let's go with yesterday's conversation.

TROFIMOV. What was that about?

GAEV. About human pride.

TROFIMOV. Yesterday we talked for quite a while, but we didn't get anywhere. In a proud man, according to you, there's something mystical. It may be your viewpoint's the right one, but if we reason it out simply, without frills, what pride can there be, is there any sense to it, if Man is poorly constructed physiologically, if the vast majority is crude, unthinking, profoundly wretched? We ought to stop admiring ourselves. We should just work.

GAEV. You'll die nonetheless.

TROFIMOV. Who knows? What does that mean—you'll die? Maybe Man has a hundred senses and with death only five, the ones known to us, perish, but the remaining ninety-five live on.

LYUBOV ANDREEVNA. Aren't you clever, Petya....

LOPAKHIN (*ironically*). Awfully!

TROFIMOV. Mankind moves forward, perfecting its powers. Everything that's unattainable for us now will some day come within our grasp and our understanding, only we've got to work to help the Truth seekers with all our might. Here in Russia very few people do any work at the moment. The vast majority of educated people, as I know them, are searching for nothing, do nothing, and so far aren't capable of work. They call themselves intellectuals, but they refer to their servants by pet names, treat the peasants like animals, are poorly informed, read nothing serious, do absolutely nothing, just talk about science, barely understand art. They're all intense, they all have glum faces, and all they talk about is major concerns, they philosophize, but meanwhile anybody can see that the working class is abominably fed, sleeps without pillows, thirty or forty to a single room, everywhere bedbugs, foul odors, dampness, moral filth.... And obviously all our nice chitchat serves only to shut our own eyes and other people's. Show me, where are the day-care centers we do so much talking about so often, where are the reading rooms? People only write about them in novels, in fact there aren't any. There's only dirt, vulgarity, Asiatic bestiality.... I distrust and don't care for very intense faces, I distrust intense conversations. It's better to keep still!

LOPAKHIN. Take me, I get up before five every morning, I work from dawn to dusk, well, I always have money on hand, my own and other people's, and I notice what the people around me are like. You only have to start in business to find out how few honest, decent people there are. Sometimes, when I can't sleep, I think: "Lord, you gave us vast forests, boundless fields, the widest horizons, and living here, we ourselves ought to be regular giants."

LYUBOV ANDREEVNA. What do you need giants for? . . . They're only useful in fairy tales, anywhere else they're scary.

(*Far upstage Yepikhodov crosses and plays his guitar.*)

LYUBOV ANDREEVNA (*dreamily*). There goes Yepikhodov....

ANYA (*dreamily*). There goes Yepikhodov....

GAEV. The sun is setting ladies and gentlemen.

TROFIMOV. Yes.

GAEV (*quietly, as if declaiming*). Oh, Nature, wondrous creature, aglow with eternal radiance, beautiful yet impassive, you, whom we call Mother, merging within yourself Life and Death, you vitalize and you destroy....

VARYA (*pleading*). Uncle dear!

ANYA. Uncle, you're at it again!

TROFIMOV. You'd better bank the yellow to the center doublet.

GAEV. I'll keep still, keep still.

(*Everyone sits down, absorbed in thought. The only sound is Firs softly muttering. Suddenly a distant sound is heard, as if from the sky, the sound of a snapped string, dying away, mournfully.*)

LYUBOV ANDREEVNA. What's that?

LOPAKHIN. I don't know. Somewhere far off in a mineshaft a bucket dropped. But somewhere very far off.

GAEV. Or perhaps it was some kind of bird . . . such as a heron.

TROFIMOV. Or an owl . . .

LYUBOV ANDREEVNA (*shivers*). Unpleasant anyway.

(*Pause.*)

FIRS. Before the disaster it was the same: the screech-owl hooted and the samovar hummed non-stop.

GAEV. Before what disaster?

FIRS. Before the serfs were freed.

(*Pause.*)

LYUBOV ANDREEVNA. Come everyone, let's go home. Evening's coming on. (*To Anya*) You've got tears in your eyes.... What is it, my little girl? (*Kisses her.*)

ANYA. Nothing special, Mama. Never mind.

TROFIMOV. Someone's coming.

(*A Tramp appears, in a shabby white peaked cap, and an overcoat; he's tipsy.*)

TRAMP. Allow me to inquire, can I reach the station straight on from here?

GAEV. You can. Follow that road.

TRAMP. I'm extremely obliged to you. (*Coughs.*) Splendid weather.... (*Declaiming*) "Brother mine, suffering brother.... come to Volga, whose laments ..." (*To Varya*) Mademoiselle, bestow some thirty kopeks on a famished fellow Russian....

(*Varya is alarmed, screams.*)

LOPAKHIN (*angrily*). That'll be enough of that!

LYUBOV ANDREEVNA (*flustered*). Take this ... here you are.... (*Looks in her purse.*) No silver.... Never mind, here's a gold-piece for you....

TRAMP. Extremely obliged to you! (*Exits.*)

(*Laughter.*)

VARYA (*frightened*). I'm going.... I'm going.... Ach, Mama dear, there's nothing in the house for people to eat, and you gave him a gold-piece.

LYUBOV ANDREEVNA. What can you do with a silly like me! I'll let you have everything I've got when we get home. Yermolai Alekseich, lend me some more!

LOPAKHIN. Gladly.

LYUBOV ANDREEVNA. Come along, ladies and gentlemen, it's time. And look, Varya, we've made quite a match for you, congratulations.

VARYA (*through tears*). You mustn't joke about this, Mama.

LOPAKHIN. Oldphelia, get thee to a nunnery.[4]...

[4]**Oldphelia** Lopakhin is apparently an avid theatre-goer and misquotes from one of the many bad Russian translations of Shakespeare. The reference is to Hamlet's admonition to Ophelia.

GAEV. My hands are trembling: it's been a long time since I played billiards.

LOPAKHIN. Oldphelia, oh nymph, in thy horizons be all my sins remembered!

LYUBOV ANDREEVNA. Come along, ladies and gentlemen. Almost time for supper.

VARYA. He scared me. My heart's pounding so.

LOPAKHIN. I remind you, ladies and gentlemen, on the twenty-second of August the estate will be auctioned off. Think about that!... Think!...

(*Exeunt everyone except Trofimov and Anya.*)

ANYA (*laughing*). Thank the tramp, he scared off Varya, now we're alone.

TROFIMOV. Varya's afraid we'll suddenly fall in love with one another, so she hangs around us all day long. Her narrow mind can't comprehend that we're above love. Avoiding the petty and specious that keeps us from being free and happy, that's the goal and meaning of our life. Forward! We march irresistibly toward the shining star, glowing there in the distance! Forward! No dropping behind, friends!

ANYA (*stretching up her arms*). You speak so well! (*Pause.*) It's wonderful here today.

TROFIMOV. Yes, superb weather.

ANYA. What you have done to me, Petya, why have I stopped loving the cherry orchard as I did? I loved it so tenderly, there seemed to me no finer place on earth than our orchard.

TROFIMOV. All Russia is our orchard. The world is wide and beautiful and there are many wonderful places in it. (*Pause.*) Just think, Anya: your grandfather, great-grandfather and all your ancestors were slave-owners, owners of living souls, and from every cherry in the orchard, every leaf, every tree trunk there must be human beings watching you, you must hear voices.... To own living souls—it's really corrupted all of you, those who lived before and those living now, so that your mother, you, your uncle, no longer notice that you're living in debt, at other peoples' expense, at the expense of those people whom you wouldn't even let beyond your front hall.... We're at least two hundred years behind the times, we've still got absolutely nothing, no definite attitude to the past, we just philosophize, complain we're depressed or drink vodka. Yet it's so clear that before we start living in the present, we must first atone for our past, finish with it, and we can atone for it only through suffering, only through extraordinary, incessant labor. Understand that, Anya.

ANYA. The house we live in hasn't been our house for a long time, and I'll go away, I give you my word.

TROFIMOV. If you have the housekeeper's keys, throw them down the well and go away. Be free as the wind.

ANYA (*enraptured*). You speak so well!

TROFIMOV. Believe me, Anya, believe! I'm not yet thirty, I'm young. I'm still a student, but I've already undergone so much! When winter comes, I'm starved, sick, worried, poor as a beggar, and—where haven't I been chased by Fate, where haven't I been! And yet, always, every moment of the day and night, my soul has been full of inexplicable presentiments. I foresee happiness, Anya, I can see it already. . . .

ANYA (*dreamily*). The moon's on the rise.

(*We can hear Yepikhodov playing the same gloomy tune as before on his guitar. The moon comes up. Somewhere near the poplars Varya is looking for Anya and calling: "Anya! Where are you?"*)

TROFIMOV. Yes, the moon's on the rise. (*Pause.*) Here's happiness, here it comes, drawing closer and closer, I can already hear its footsteps. And if we don't see it, can't recognize it, what's wrong with that? Others will see it!

VARYA'S VOICE. Anya! Where are you?

TROFIMOV. That Varya again! (*Angrily*) Appalling!

ANYA. So what? Let's go down to the river. It's nice there.

TROFIMOV. Let's go. (*They exit.*)

VARYA'S VOICE. Anya! Anya!

ACT 3

The drawing room, separated from the ballroom by an arch. A chandelier is alight. We can hear, as if in the hallway, a Jewish orchestra, the same mentioned in Act 2. Evening. Grand-rond is being played in the ballroom. Simeonov-Pishchik's voice: "Promenade à une paire!" Enter the drawing room: in the first couple Pishchik and Charlotta Ivanovna, in the second Trofimov and Lyubov Andreevna, in the third Anya and the Postal Clerk, in the fourth Varya and the Stationmaster, etc. Varya is weeping quietly and while dancing, wipes away the tears. In the last couple Dunyasha. They go through the drawing-room. Pishchik calls out: "Grand-rond balancez!" and "Les cavaliers à genoux et remerciez vos dames!" Firs in a tail-coat crosses the room with seltzer bottle on a tray. Pishchik and Trofimov enter the room.

PISHCHIK. I've got high blood pressure, I've already had two strokes, it's tough dancing, but as the saying goes, when you run with the pack, bark or don't bark, but keep on wagging your tail. Actually I've got the constitution of a horse. My late father, what a cut-up, rest in peace, used to talk of our ancestry as if our venerable line, the Simeonov-Pishchiks, were descended from the very horse Caligula made a Senator. . . . (*Sits down.*) But here's my problem: no money! A hungry dog believes only in meat. . . . (*Snores and immediately wakes up.*) Just like me. . . . I can't think of anything but money. . . .

TROFIMOV. As a matter of fact, there is something horsey about your build.

PISHCHIK. So what . . . a horse is a fine beast . . . you could sell a horse. . . .

(*We hear billiards played in the next room. Varya appears under the arch in the ballroom.*)

TROFIMOV (*teasing*). Madam Lopakhin! Madam Lopakhin!

VARYA (*angrily*). Mangy gent!

TROFIMOV. Yes, I'm a mangy gent and proud of it!

VARYA (*brooding bitterly*). Here we've hired musicians and what are we going to pay them with? (*Exits.*)

TROFIMOV (*to Pishchik*). If the energy you've wasted in the course of a lifetime tracking down money to pay off interest had gone into something else, then you probably could have turned the world upside-down.

PISHCHIK. Nietzche[1] . . . a philosopher . . . the greatest, most famous . . . a man of immense intellect, says in his works it's justifiable to counterfeit money.

TROFIMOV. So you've read Nietzsche?

PISHCHIK. Well . . . Dashenka told me. But now I'm in such straits that if it came to counterfeiting money . . . Day after tomorrow three hundred rubles to pay . . . I've already borrowed a hundred and thirty. . . . (*Feeling his pockets, alarmed.*) The money's gone! I've lost the money! (*Through tears*) Where's the money? (*Gleefully*) Here it is, in the lining. . . . I was really sweating for a minute.

(*Enter Lyubov Andreevna and Charlotta Ivanovna.*)

LYUBOV ANDREEVNA (*humming a lively dance*). Why is Lyonya taking so long? What's he doing in town? (*To Dunyasha*) Dunyasha, offer the musicians some tea. . . .

TROFIMOV. The auction didn't come off, in all likelihood.

LYUBOV ANDREEVNA. And the musicians arrived at the wrong time and we started the ball at the wrong time. . . . Well, never mind. . . . (*Sits down and hums softly.*)

CHARLOTTA (*hands Pishchik a deck of cards*). Here's a deck of cards for you, think of one particular card.

[1]**Nietzsche** Friedrich Wilhelm Nietzsche (1844–1900), whose philosophy encourages a new "master" morality for Supermen and instigates revolt against the conventional constraints of Western civilization

PISHCHIK. I've got one.

CHARLOTTA. Now shuffle the deck. Very good. Hand it over. O my dear Mister Pishchik. Ein, zwei, drei! Now look at it, it's in your breast pocket. . . .

PISHCHIK (*pulling a card from his breast pocket*). Eight of spades, absolutely right! (*Astounded*) Can you imagine!

CHARLOTTA (*holds deck of cards on her palm, to Trofimov*). Tell me quick, which card's on top.

TROFIMOV. What? Well, the queen of spades.

CHARLOTTA. Right! (*To Pishchik*) Well? Which card's on top?

PISHCHIK. The ace of hearts.

CHARLOTTA. Right! (*Claps her hand over her palm, the deck of cards disappears.*) Isn't it lovely weather today! (*She is answered by a mysterious feminine voice, as if from beneath the floor: "Oh yes, marvellous weather, Madam."*) You're so nice, my ideal. . . .

VOICE. Madam, I been liking you ferry much.

STATIONMASTER (*applauding*). Lady ventriloquist, bravo!

PISHCHIK (*astounded*). Can you imagine! Bewitching Charlotta Ivanovna. . . . I'm simply in love with you. . . .

CHARLOTTA. In love? (*Shrugging*) What do you know about love? *Guter Mensch, aber schlechter Musikant.*[2]

TROFIMOV (*claps Pishchik on the shoulder*). Good old horse. . . .

CHARLOTTA. Please pay attention, one more trick. (*Takes a rug from a chair.*) Here is a very nice rug. I'd like to sell it . . . (*Shakes it out.*) What am I offered?

PISHCHIK (*astounded*). Can you imagine!

CHARLOTTA. Ein, zwei, drei! (*Quickly lifts the lowered rug.*)

(*Behind the rug stands Anya, who curtsies, runs to her mother, embraces her, and runs back to the ballroom amid the general delight.*)

LYUBOV ANDREEVNA (*applauding*). Bravo, bravo!

CHARLOTTA. One more! Ein, zwei, drei! (*Raises the rug.*)

(*Behind the rug stands Varya, who bows.*)

PISHCHIK (*astounded*). Can you imagine!

CHARLOTTA. The end! (*Throws the rug at Pishchik, curtsies, and runs into the ballroom.*)

PISHCHIK (*scurrying after her*). You little rascal! . . . How do you like that! How do you like that! (*Exits.*)

LYUBOV ANDREEVNA. And Leonid still isn't back. I don't understand what he can be doing in town all this time! Everything must be over there, either the estate is sold or the auction didn't take place, but why keep us in suspense so long?

VARYA (*trying to solace her*). Uncle dear bought it, I'm sure of it.

TROFIMOV (*sarcastically*). Sure.

VARYA. Granny sent him power of attorney, so he could buy it in her name and transfer the debt. She did it for Anya. And I'm sure, God willing, that Uncle dear bought it.

LYUBOV ANDREEVNA. Granny in Yaroslavl sent fifty thousand to buy the estate in her name—she doesn't trust us—but that money won't even manage to pay off the interest. (*Hides her face in her hands.*) Today my fate will be decided, my fate. . . .

TROFIMOV (*teases Varya*). Madam Lopakhin!

VARYA (*angrily*). Perpetual student! Twice already you've been expelled from the university.

LYUBOV ANDREEVNA. Why are you getting angry, Varya? He teases you about Lopakhin, what of it? You want to—then marry Lopakhin, he's a good man, an interesting person. You don't want to—don't get married; nobody's forcing you, sweetheart. . . .

VARYA. I regard this as a serious matter, Mama dear, I've got to speak frankly. He's a good man, I like him.

LYUBOV ANDREEVNA. Then marry him. I don't understand what you're waiting for!

VARYA. Mama dear, I can't propose to him myself. It's been two years now they've talked about him, everyone's talking, but he either keeps still or makes jokes. I understand. He's getting rich, involved in business, no time for me. If only I'd had some money, even a little, just a hundred rubles, I'd have dropped everything and gone far away. I'd have gone to a convent.

TROFIMOV. Glorious!

VARYA (*to Trofimov*). A student ought to act intelligent! (*In a soft voice, tearfully*) How homely you've become, Petya. How old you've grown! (*To Lyubov Andreevna, no longer weeping*) Only I can't do without work, Mama dear. I have to do something every minute.

(*Enter Yasha.*)

YASHA (*barely restraining his laughter*). Yepikhodov broke a billiard cue!

(*He exits.*)

VARYA. What's Yepikhodov doing here? Who allowed him to play billiards? I don't understand these people. (*She exits.*)

LYUBOV ANDREEVNA. Don't tease her, Petya, can't you see she's sad enough without that?

TROFIMOV. She's just too officious, poking her nose in other people's business. All summer long she couldn't leave us alone, me or Anya. She was afraid a romance might

[2] ***Guter Mensch, aber schlechter Musikant*** a good man, but a poor musician

spring up between us. What concern is it of hers? And anyway, I didn't show any signs of it, I'm so removed from banality. We're above love!

LYUBOV ANDREEVNA. Well then, I must be beneath love. (*Extremely upset*) Why isn't Leonid back? If only I knew whether the estate were sold or not. Calamity seems so incredible to me that I don't even know what to think, I'm at a loss.... I could scream right this minute.... I could do something absurd. Save me, Petya. Say something, tell me....

TROFIMOV. Whether the estate's sold today or not—what's the difference? Its been over and done with for a long time now, no turning back, the bridges are burnt. Calm down, dear lady. You mustn't deceive yourself, for once in your life you've got to look the truth straight in the eye.

LYUBOV ANDREEVNA. What truth? You can see where truth is and where falsehood is, but I seem to have lost my sight. I can't see anything. You boldly settle all the important questions, but tell me, dovie, isn't that because you're young, because you haven't had time to suffer through any of your problems? You boldly look forward, but isn't that because you don't see and don't expect anything awful, because life is still concealed from your young eyes? You're more courageous and more sincere and more profound than we are, but stop and think, be indulgent if only in your fingertips, spare me. Why, I was born here, here lived my father and my mother, my grandfather, I love this house, without the cherry orchard, I couldn't make sense of my life, and if it really has to be sold, then sell me along with the orchard.... (*Embraces Trofimov, kisses him on the forehead.*) Why, my son was drowned here.... (*Weeps.*) Show me some pity, dear, kind man.

TROFIMOV. You know I sympathize wholeheartedly.

LYUBOV ANDREEVNA. But you should say so differently, differently.... (*Takes out a handkerchief, a telegram falls to the floor.*) My heart is so heavy today, you can't imagine. Here it's too noisy for me, my soul shudders at every sound, I shudder all over, but I can't go off by myself, it would terrify me to be alone in silence. Don't blame me, Petya ... I love you like my own flesh-and-blood. I'd gladly have given you Anya's hand, believe me, only, dovie, you've got to study, got to finish your course. You don't do anything, Fate simply hustles you from place to place, it's so odd.... Isn't that right? Isn't it? And something's got to be done about your beard, to make it grow somehow.... (*Laughs.*) You look funny!

TROFIMOV (*picks up telegram*). I've no desire to be a fashion-plate.

LYUBOV ANDREEVNA. This telegram's from Paris. Every day I get one. Yesterday too and today. That wild man has fallen ill again, something's wrong with him again.... He begs my forgiveness, implores me to come back, and actually I feel I ought to go to Paris, stay with him for a while. You look so stern, Petya, but what's to be done, dove, what am I to do, he's ill, he's lonely, unhappy, and who's there to look after him, who'll keep him out of mischief, who'll give him his medicine at the right time? And what's there to hide or keep mum about, I love him, it's obvious. I love him, I love him.... It's a millstone around my neck, it's dragging me to the depths, but I love that stone and I can't live without it. (*Presses Trofimov's hand.*) Don't think harshly of me, Petya, don't say anything, don't talk....

TROFIMOV (*through tears*). Forgive my frankness, for God's sake: but he robbed you blind!

LYUBOV ANDREEVNA. No, no, no, don't talk that way.... (*Puts her hands over her ears.*)

TROFIMOV. Why, he's a scoundrel, you're the only one who doesn't realize it! He's an insignificant scoundrel, a nonentity....

LYUBOV ANDREEVNA (*getting angry, but restraining herself*). You're twenty-six or twenty-seven, but you're still a sophomoric schoolboy!

TROFIMOV. So what!

LYUBOV ANDREEVNA. You should act like a man, at your age you should understand people in love. And you should be in love yourself ... you should fall in love! (*Angrily*) Yes, yes! And there's no purity in you, you're simply "puritanical," a ridiculous crank, a freak....

TROFIMOV (*horrified*). What is she saying!

LYUBOV ANDREEVNA. "I am above love!" You're not above love, but simply, as our Firs here says, you're half-baked. At your age not to have a mistress!...

TROFIMOV (*horrified*). This is horrible! What is she saying! (*Rushes to the ballroom clutching his head.*) This is horrible ... I can't stand it, I'm going.... (*Exits, but immediately returns.*) All is over between us! (*Exits into the hall.*)

LYUBOV ANDREEVNA (*shouting after him*). Petya, wait! You funny man, I was joking! Petya!

(*We hear in the hallway, someone running up the stairs and suddenly falling back down with a crash. Anya and Varya shriek, but immediately laughter is heard.*)

LYUBOV ANDREEVNA. What's going on in there?

(*Anya runs in.*)

ANYA (*laughing*). Petya fell down the stairs! (*Runs out.*)

LYUBOV ANDREEVNA. What a character that Petya is!...

(*The Stationmaster stops in the center of the ballroom and recites Aleksei Tolstoi's "The Fallen Woman." The guests listen, but barely has he recited a few lines, when the strains of a waltz reach them from the hallway, and the recitation breaks off. Everyone dances. Enter from the hall, Trofimov, Anya, Varya, and Lyubov Andreevna.*)

LYUBOV ANDREEVNA. Well, Petya. . . . well, my pure-in-heart. I apologize . . . let's go dance. . . . (*Dances with Trofimov.*)

(*Anya and Varya dance.*)

(*Firs enters, leaves his stick by the side-door. Yasha also enters the drawing room, watching the dancers.*)

YASHA. How're you doing, Gramps?

FIRS. I'm none too well. In the old days we had generals, barons, admirals dancing at our parties, but now we send for the postal clerk and the stationmaster, yes and they don't come a-running. Somehow I've gotten weak. The late master, the grandfather, doctored everybody with sealing wax for every ailment. I've took sealing wax every day now for twenty-odd years, and maybe more; maybe that's why I'm still alive.

YASHA. You bore me stiff, Gramps. (*Yawns.*) How about dropping dead.

FIRS. Ech, you're . . . half-baked! (*Mutters.*)

(*Trofimov and Lyubov Andreevna dance in the ballroom, then in the drawing-room.*)

LYUBOV ANDREEVNA. Merci, I'm going to sit down a bit. . . . (*Sits down.*) I'm tired.

(*Enter Anya.*)

ANYA (*agitated*). Just now in the kitchen some man was saying that the cherry orchard has already been sold.

LYUBOV ANDREEVNA. Sold to whom?

ANYA. He didn't say. He left. (*Dances with Trofimov.*)

(*They both exeunt into the ballroom.*)

YASHA. It was some old coot babbling away there. A stranger.

FIRS. And Leonid Andreich still isn't back, still not returned. He's got on a light topcoat, for between seasons, see if he don't catch cold. Ech, these striplings!

LYUBOV ANDREEVNA. I'll die this instant. Yasha, go and find out whom it's been sold to.

YASHA. He went away a long time ago, that old man. (*Laughs.*)

LYUBOV ANDREEVNA (*somewhat annoyed*). Well, what are you laughing about? What's made you so happy?

YASHA. Yepikhodov's awfully funny. Empty-headed fellow. Twenty-two troubles.

LYUBOV ANDREEVNA. Firs, if the estate is sold, then where will you go?

FIRS. Wherever you order, there I'll go.

LYUBOV ANDREEVNA. Why do you look like that? Aren't you well? You know you ought to go to bed. . . .

FIRS. Yes— (*With a grin*) I go to bed, and with me gone, who'll serve, who'll take care of things? I'm the only one in the whole house.

YASHA (*to Lyubov Andreevna*). Lyubov Andreevna! Let me ask you a favor, be so kind! If you go off to Paris again, take me with you, please. For me to stay around here is absolutely out of the question. (*Glances around, lowers his voice*) Why bring it up, you see for yourself, an uncivilized country, immoral people, besides it's boring, in the kitchen they feed us disgusting stuff and there's that Firs going around, muttering all sorts of uncalled-for remarks. Take me with you, be so kind!

(*Enter Pishchik.*)

PISHCHIK. Allow me to request . . . a little waltz, loveliest of ladies. . . . (*Lyubov Andreevna goes with him.*) Enchanting lady, I'll borrow that hundred and eighty rubles off you just the same . . . I'll borrow . . . (*Dances*) a hundred and eighty rubles. . . .

(*They pass into the ballroom.*)

YASHA (*singing softly*). "Wilt thou learn my soul's unrest . . ."

(*In the ballroom a figure in a gray top-hat and checked trousers waves its arms and jumps up and dawn; shouts of "Bravo, Charlotta Ivanovna!"*)

DUNYASHA (*stops to powder her nose*). The young mistress orders me to dance—lots of gentlemen and few ladies—but dancing makes my head swim, my heart pound. Firs Nikolaevich, just now the clerk from the post-office told me something that took my breath away.

(*The music subsides.*)

FIRS. Well, what did he tell you?

DUNYASHA. You, he says, are like a flower.

YASHA (*yawns*). Ignorance. . . . (*Exits.*)

DUNYASHA. Like a flower. . . . I'm such a sensitive girl, I'm frightfully fond of compliments.

FIRS. You'll get your head turned.

(*Enter Yepikhodov.*)

YEPIKHODOV. Avdotya Fyodorovna, you refuse to see me . . . as if I were some sort of bug. (*Sighs.*) Ech, life!

DUNYASHA. What can I do for you?

YEPIKHODOV. No doubt you may be right. (*Sighs.*) But, of course, if it's considered from a standpoint, then you, I venture to express myself thus, pardon my outspokenness, positively drove me into a state of mind. I know my fate, every day something unlucky happens to me, and I've grown accustomed to that long ago, so that I look upon my destiny with a smile. You gave me your word, and although I . . .

DUNYASHA. Please, we'll talk later on, but now leave me alone. I'm dreaming now. (*Plays with her fan.*)

YEPIKHODOV. I suffer misfortune every day, and I, I venture to express myself thus, merely smile, even laugh.

(*Enter Varya from the ballroom.*)

VARYA. Haven't you gone yet, Semyon? What a really disrespectful person you are. (*To Dunyasha.*) Clear out of here, Dunyasha. (*To Yepikhodov.*) First you play billiards and break the cue, and now you're strolling around the drawing room like a guest.

YEPIKHODOV. To make demands on me, allow me to inform you, you can't.

VARYA. I'm not making demands on you, I'm just telling you. The only thing you know is walking from place to place, instead of attending to business. We keep a bookkeeper but nobody knows what for.

YEPIKHODOV (*offended*). Whether I work or whether I walk or whether I eat or whether I play billiards may only be discussed by people of understanding, my elders.

VARYA. You dare to talk to me that way? (*Flying into a rage*) You dare? You mean I don't understand anything? Get out of here! This minute!

YEPIKHODOV (*alarmed*). I request you to express yourself in a tactful fashion.

VARYA (*beside herself*). This very minute, out of here! Out! (*He goes to the door, she follows him.*) Twenty-two troubles! Don't draw another breath here! Don't let me set eyes on you! (*Yepikhodov exits, behind the door his voice:*)

YEPIKHODOV'S VOICE. I'm going to complain about you.

VARYA. So, you're coming back? (*Seizes the stick, left near the door by Firs.*) Come on . . . come on . . . come on, I'll show you. . . . Well, are you coming? Are you coming? So take this. . . . (*Swings the stick.*)

(*At the same moment, Lopakhin enters.*)

LOPAKHIN. My humble thanks.

VARYA (*angrily and sarcastically*). My fault!

LOPAKHIN. Don't mention it. Thank you kindly for the pleasant surprise.

VARYA. It's not worth thanks. (*Starts out, then looks back and asks gently.*) I didn't hurt you?

LOPAKHIN. No, it's nothing. Raised an enormous bump though.

(*Voices in the ballroom: "Lopakhin's arrived! Yermolai Alekseich!"*)

PISHCHIK. Sights to be seen, sounds to be heard. . . . (*He and Lopakhin kiss.*) You smell a little of cognac, my dear boy, my bucko. But we were making merry here too.

(*Enter Lyubov Andreevna.*)

LYUBOV ANDREEVNA. Is that you, Yermolai Alekseich? Why so long? Where's Leonid?

LOPAKHIN. Leonid Andreich returned with me, he's on his way. . . .

LYUBOV ANDREEVNA (*agitated*). Well, what? Was there an auction? Tell me!

LOPAKHIN (*embarrassed, afraid to display his joy*). The auction was over by four o'clock. . . . We missed the train, had to wait till half-past nine. (*Sighs heavily.*) Oof! My head's in a bit of a whirl. . . .

(*Enter Gaev; his right hand is holding packages, his left is wiping away tears.*)

LYUBOV ANDREEVNA. Lyonya, what? Well, Lyonya? (*Impatiently, tearfully*) Hurry up, for God's sake. . . .

GAEV (*not answering her, only waves his hand, to Firs, weeping*). Here, take this. . . . There's anchovies, Kerch herring. . . . I didn't eat a thing all day. . . . What I've been through!

(*The door to the billiard room opens. We hear the sounds of the balls and Yasha's voice: "Seven and Eighteen!" Gaev's expression shifts, he stops crying.*)

GAEV. I'm awfully tired. Firs, help me change. (*Exits through the ballroom, followed by Firs.*)

PISHCHIK. What happened at the auction? Tell us!

LYUBOV ANDREEVNA. Is the cherry orchard sold?

LOPAKHIN. Sold.

LYUBOV ANDREEVNA. Who bought it?

LOPAKHIN. I bought it.

(*Pause. Lyubov Andreevna is overcome; she would fall, were she not standing beside an armchair and a table. Varya takes the keys from her belt, throws them on the floor in the middle of the drawing room and exits.*)

LOPAKHIN. I bought it! Wait, ladies and gentlemen, please for a minute, my head's in a muddle, I can't talk. . . . (*Laughs.*) We showed up at the auction, Deriganov was there already. Leonid Andreich only had fifty thousand, and Deriganov right off bid thirty over and above the mortgage. I get the picture, I pitched into him, bid forty. He forty-five. I fifty-five. I mean, he kept adding by fives, I by tens. . . . Well, it ended. Over and above the mortgage I bid ninety thousand, it was knocked down to me. Now the cherry orchard's mine. Mine! (*Chuckling.*) My God, Lord, the cherry orchard's mine! Tell me I'm drunk, out of my mind, that I'm imagining it all. . . . (*Stamps his feet.*) Don't laugh at me!

Early twentieth-century production of *The Cherry Orchard,* presented at the Moscow Art Theater.
(Photograph: Culver Pictures.)

If only my father and grandfather could rise up from their graves and see all that's happened, how their Yermolai, beaten, half-literate Yermolai, who used to run around barefoot in the wintertime; how this same Yermolai bought the estate, the most beautiful thing in the world. I bought the estate where grandfather and father were slaves, where they weren't even allowed in the kitchen. I'm asleep, this is only one of my dreams, it only looks this way. . . . This is a figment of your imagination, hidden by the shadows of ignorance. . . . (*Picks up the keys, smiles gently.*) She threw down the keys, she wants to show that she's no longer mistress here. . . . (*Jingles the keys.*) Well, it's all the same. (*We hear the orchestra tuning up.*) Hey, musicians, play, I want to hear you! Come on, everybody, see how Yermolai Lopakhin will swing an axe in the cherry orchard, how the trees'll come tumbling to the ground!! We'll build cottages, and our grandchildren and great-grandchildren will see a new life here. . . . Music, play! (*The music plays, Lyubov Andreevna has sunk into a chair, crying bitterly.*) (*Reproachfully*) Why, oh, why didn't you listen to me? My poor, dear lady, you can't undo it now. (*Tearfully*) Oh, if only this were all over quickly, if somehow our clumsy, unhappy life could be changed quickly.

PISHCHIK (*takes him by the arm; in an undertone*). She's crying. Let's go into the ballroom, leave her alone. . . . Let's go. . . . (*Drags him by the arm and leads him into the ballroom.*)

LOPAKHIN. So what? Music, play louder! Let everything be the way I want it! (*Ironically*) Here comes the new landlord, the owner of the cherry orchard! (*He accidentally bumps into a small table and almost knocks over the candelabrum.*) I can pay for everything! (*Exits with Pishchik.*)

(*No one is left in the ballroom or drawing room except Lyubov Andreevna, who is sitting, all bunched up, weeping bitterly. The music is playing, softly. Anya and Trofimov hurry in. Anya goes up to her mother and kneels before her. Trofimov remains at the entrance to the ballroom.*)

ANYA. Mama! . . . Mama, you're crying? Dear, kind, good Mama, my own, my beautiful, I love you . . . I bless you. The cherry orchard's sold, there isn't any more, that's true, true, true, but don't cry, Mama, you've got your life ahead of you, you've got your good, pure heart . . . Come with me, come, dearest, away from here, come! . . . We'll plant a new orchard, more splendid than this one, you'll see it, you'll understand, and joy, peaceful, profound joy will sink into your heart, like the sun at nightfall, and you'll smile, Mama! Come, dearest! Come! . . .

ACT 4

First Act set. Neither curtains on the windows, nor pictures on the walls, a few sticks of furniture remain, piled up in a corner, as if for sale. A feeling of emptiness. Near the door to the outside and at the back of the stage are piled suitcases, travelling bags, etc. At the left the door is open, and through it we can hear the voices of Varya and Anya. Lopakhin stands waiting. Yasha is holding a tray of champagne glasses. In the hallway, Yepikhodov is tying up a carton. Offstage, at the back, a hum. It's the peasants come to say good-bye. Gaev's voice: "Thank you, friends, thank you."

YASHA. The common folk have come to say good-bye. I'm of the opinion, Yermolai Alekseich, they're decent enough people, but they aren't too bright.

(*The hum subsides. Enter through the hall Lyubov Andreevna and Gaev. She isn't crying, but is pale, her face twitches, she can't talk.*)

GAEV. You gave them your purse, Lyuba. You mustn't! You mustn't!

LYUBOV ANDREEVNA. I couldn't help it! I couldn't help it!

(*Both exit.*)

LOPAKHIN (*through the door, after them*). Please, I humbly beseech you! A little drink at parting. It didn't occur to me to bring any from town, and at the station I only found one bottle. Please! (*Pause.*) How about it, ladies and gentlemen? Don't you want any? (*Walks away from the door.*) Had I known, I wouldn't have bought it. Well, I won't drink any either. (*Yasha carefully sets the tray on a chair.*) You drink up, Yasha, anyway.

YASHA. To those departing! And happy days to the stay-at-homes! (*Drinks.*) This champagne isn't the genuine article, you can take it from me.

LOPAKHIN. Eight rubles a bottle. (*Pause.*) It's cold as hell in here.

YASHA. They didn't stoke up today, it doesn't matter, we're leaving. (*Laughs.*)

LOPAKHIN. What's that for?

YASHA. Sheer satisfaction.

LOPAKHIN. Outside it's October, but sunny and mild, like summer. Good building weather. (*Glances at his watch, at the door.*) Ladies and gentlemen, remember, until the train leaves, there's forty-seven minutes in all! Which means, in twenty minutes we start for the station. Get a move on.

(*Enter from outdoors Trofimov in an overcoat.*)

TROFIMOV. Seems to me it's time to go now. The horses are at the door. Where the hell are my galoshes? Disappeared. (*Through the door*) Anya, my galoshes aren't here! I can't find them!

LOPAKHIN. And I have to be in Kharkov. I'll accompany you on the same train. I'm staying all winter in Kharkov. I've been hanging around here with you, I'm worn out doing nothing. I can't be without work, I don't even know what to do with my hands. They dangle something strange, like somebody else's.

TROFIMOV. We'll be going soon, and you can return to your productive labor.

LOPAKHIN. Do have a little drink.

TROFIMOV. None for me.

LOPAKHIN. Looks like off to Moscow now?

TROFIMOV. Yes, I'll see them as far as town, but tomorrow off to Moscow.

LOPAKHIN. Yes.... Hey, the professors are holding off on lectures, I'll bet they're waiting for your arrival!

TROFIMOV. None of your business.

LOPAKHIN. How many years have you been studying at the University?

TROFIMOV. Think up something fresher. That's old and stale. (*Looks for his galoshes.*) By the way, we probably won't see each other again, so let me give you a piece of advice as a farewell: don't wave your arms! Break yourself of that habit—arm-waving. And also cottage-building, figuring that eventually tourists will turn into private householders, figuring in that way is just the same as arm-waving.... When you come down to it, I'm fond of you anyhow. You've got delicate, gentle fingers, like an artist, you've got a delicate, gentle soul....

LOPAKHIN (*embraces him*). Good-bye, dear boy. Thanks for everything. If you need it, borrow some money from me for the road.

TROFIMOV. What for? No need.

LOPAKHIN. But you've got none!

TROFIMOV. I do. Thank you. I received some for a translation. Here it is, in my pocket. (*Anxiously*) But my galoshes are gone!

VARYA (*from the next room*). Take your nasty things! (*She flings a pair of rubber galoshes on stage.*)

TROFIMOV. What are you upset about, Varya? Hm.... But these aren't *my* galoshes!

LOPAKHIN. Last spring I planted twenty-seven hundred acres of poppies, and now I've cleared forty thousand net. And when my poppies bloomed, it was like a picture! Here's what I'm driving at, I cleared forty thousand, which means I offer you a loan because I'm able to. Why turn up your nose? I'm a peasant... plain and simple.

TROFIMOV. Your father was a peasant, mine, a druggist, but from that absolutely nothing follows. (*Lopakhin pulls out his wallet.*) Don't bother, don't bother.... Even if you gave me two hundred thousand, I wouldn't take it. I'm a free man. And everything that's valued so highly and fondly by all of you, rich men and beggars, hasn't the slightest sway over me, it's like fluff floating in the air. I can manage without you, I can pass you by. I'm strong and proud. Humanity is moving toward the most exalted truth, the most exalted happiness possible on earth, and I'm in the front ranks!

LOPAKHIN. Will you get there?

TROFIMOV. I'll get there. (*Pause.*) I'll get there, or I'll show others the way to get there.

(*We hear in the distance an axe striking a tree.*)

LOPAKHIN. Well, good-bye, my boy. Time to go. We turn up our noses at each other, but life keeps slipping by. When I work a long time nonstop, then my thoughts are sharper, and even I seem to know why I exist. But, brother, how many people there are in Russia who have no reason to exist. Well, what's the difference, that's not what makes the world go round. Leonid Andreich, they say, took a position, he'll be in the bank, six thousand a year.... Only he won't keep at it, too lazy....

ANYA (*in the doorway*). Mama begs you: until she's gone, not to chop down the orchard.

TROFIMOV. I mean really, haven't you got any tact.... (*Exits through the hall.*)

LOPAKHIN. Right away, right away.... These people, honestly! (*Exits after him.*)

ANYA. Did they take Firs to the hospital?

YASHA. I told them to this morning. They took him, I should think.

ANYA (*to Yepikhodov, who is crossing through the ballroom*). Semyon Panteleich, please find out whether Firs was taken to the hospital.

YASHA (*offended*). I told Yegor this morning. Why ask ten times?

YEPIKHODOV. Superannuated Firs, in my conclusive opinion, is past all repairing, he should be gathered to his fathers. And I can only envy him. (*Sets a suitcase on top of a cardboard hatbox and crushes it.*) Well, look at that, naturally. I should have known. (*Exits.*)

YASHA (*mocking*). Twenty-two troubles....

YEPIKHODOV. Well, it could have happened to anybody.

VARYA (*from behind door*). Have they sent Firs to the hospital?

ANYA. They have.

VARYA. Then why didn't they take the letter to the doctor?

ANYA. We'll have to send someone after them.... (*Exits.*)

VARYA (*from the adjoining room*). Where's Yasha? Tell him his mother's arrived, wants to say good-bye to him.

YASHA (*waves his hand*). They simply try my patience.

(*Dunyasha in the meantime has been fussing with the luggage; now that Yasha is alone, she comes up to him.*)

DUNYASHA. If only you'd take one little look at me, Yasha. You're going away . . . you're leaving me behind. . . . (*Weeps and throws herself around his neck.*)

YASHA. What's to cry about? (*Drinks champagne.*) In six days I'll be in Paris again. Tomorrow we'll board an express train and dash away, just try and spot us. Somehow I can't believe it. Vive la France! . . . It doesn't suit me, here, I can't live . . . nothing going on. I've seen enough ignorance—fed up. (*Drinks champagne.*) What's there to cry about? Behave respectably, then you won't have to cry.

DUNYASHA (*powdering her nose, looks in a hand-mirror*). Drop me a line from Paris. I really loved you, Yasha, loved you so! I'm a soft-hearted creature, Yasha!

YASHA. Someone's coming in here. (*Fusses around with the luggage, humming softly.*)

(*Enter Lyubov Andreevna, Gaev, Anya, and Charlotta Ivanovna.*)

GAEV. We should be off. Not much time left. (*Looking at Yasha*) Who's that smelling of herring?

LYUBOV ANDREEVNA. In about ten minutes we ought to be getting into the carriages . . . (*Casting a glance around the room.*) Good-bye, dear old house, old grandfather. Winter will pass, spring will come again, but you won't be here anymore, they'll tear you down. How much these walls have seen! (*Kissing her daughter ardently.*) My precious, you're radiant, your eyes are sparkling like two diamonds. Are you glad? Very?

ANYA. Very! A new life is beginning, Mama!

GAEV. As a matter of fact, everything's fine now. Until the sale of the cherry orchard, we were all upset, distressed, but then, when the dilemma was settled, finally, irrevocably, everyone calmed down, even became cheerful. . . . I'm a bank employee, now; I'm a financier . . . yellow to the center, and you, Lyuba, anyway, you're looking better, that's for sure.

LYUBOV ANDREEVNA. Yes. My nerves are better, that's true. (*They help her on with her hat and coat.*) I'm sleeping well. Carry my things out, Yasha. It's time. (*To Anya*) My little girl, we'll see each other soon. . . . I'm off to Paris, I'll live there on that money your granny in Yaroslavl sent us to buy the estate—hurray for Granny!—but that money won't last long.

ANYA. Mama, you'll come back soon . . . won't you? I'll study, pass the examination at the high school, and then I'll work to help you. Mama, we'll be together and read all sorts of books . . . won't we? (*Kisses her mother's hand.*) We'll read in the autumn evenings, we'll read lots of books, and before us a new, wonderful world will open up. . . . (*Dreaming*) Mama, come back. . . .

LYUBOV ANDREEVNA. I'll come back, my treasure. (*Embraces her daughter.*)

(*Enter Lopakhin. Charlotta is quietly singing a song.*)

GAEV. Charlotta's happy! She's singing.

CHARLOTTA (*picks up a bundle that looks like a swaddled baby*). Rock-a-bye, baby, on-the-tree-top. (*We hear a baby crying: "Waa! Waa!"*) Hush, my sweet, my dear little boy. (*"Waa! Waa!"*) I'm so sorry for you! (*Tossing back the bundle.*) Will you please find me a position! I can't keep on this way.

LOPAKHIN. We'll find one, Charlotta Ivanovna, don't worry.

GAEV. Everyone's dropping us, Varya's leaving . . . we've suddenly become superfluous.

CHARLOTTA. There's no place to live in town. Have to go away. . . . (*Hums.*) It doesn't matter.

(*Enter Pishchik.*)

LOPAKHIN. The freak of nature! . . .

PISHCHIK (*out of breath*). Oy, let me catch my breath. . . . I'm winded . . . my most honored. . . . Give me some water. . . .

GAEV. After money, I suppose? Your humble servant, I'll keep out of temptation's way. . . . (*Exits.*)

PISHCHIK (*out of breath*). I haven't been to see you for a long time . . . loveliest of ladies. . . . (*To Lopakhin*) You here . . . glad to see you . . . a man of the widest intellect . . . take . . . go on. . . . (*Hands money to Lopakhin.*) Four hundred rubles. . . . I still owe you eight hundred and forty. . . .

LOPAKHIN (*bewildered, shrugs*). It's like a dream. . . . Where did you get this?

PISHCHIK. Wait. . . . Hot. . . . Most amazing thing happened. Some Englishmen stopped by my place and found some kind of white clay on the land. . . . (*To Lyubov Andreevna*) And four hundred for you . . . beautiful lady, divine. . . . (*Hands her money.*) The rest later. (*Drinks water.*) Just now some young man on the train was relating that a certain . . . great philosopher recommends jumping off roofs . . . "Jump!"—he says, and in that lies the whole problem. (*Astounded.*) Can you imagine! Water! . . .

LOPAKHIN. Who were these Englishmen?

PISHCHIK. I leased them the lot with the clay for twenty-four years. . . . But now, excuse me, no time. . . . Have to run along . . . I'm going to Znoikov's . . . Kardamonov's . . . I owe everybody. . . . (*Drinks.*) I wish you health. . . . On Thursday I'll drop by. . . .

LYUBOV ANDREEVNA. We're just about to move to town, and tomorrow I'll be abroad.

PISHCHIK. What? (*Agitated*) Why to town? Goodness, look at the furniture . . . the suitcases . . . well, never mind. . . . (*Through tears*) Never mind. Persons of the highest intelligence . . . those Englishmen. . . . Never mind. . . . Be happy. . . . God will aid you. . . . Never mind. . . . Everything in this world comes to an end. . . . (*Kisses Lyubov Andreevna's hand.*) And should rumor reach you that my end has come, just remember this very thing—a horse, and say: "There was on earth thus-and-such . . . Simeonov-Pishchik . . . rest in peace." . . . Incredible weather . . . yes. . . . (*Exits, overcome with emotion, but immediately reappears in the doorway and says*) Dashenka says to say hello! (*Exits.*)

LYUBOV ANDREEVNA. Now we can go. I'm leaving with two things on my mind. First—that Firs is ill. (*Glancing at her watch.*) There's still five minutes. . . .

ANYA. Mama, they've already sent Firs to the hospital. Yasha sent him this morning.

LYUBOV ANDREEVNA. My second anxiety is Varya. She's used to early rising and working, and now without work, she's like a fish out of water. She's got thin, she's got pale, she cries, poor thing. . . . (*Pause.*) You know this perfectly well, Yermolai Alekseich: I had dreamt . . . of marrying her to you, yes and it certainly looked as if you were ready to get married. (*Whispers to Anya, who nods to Charlotta, and both leave.*) She loves you, you're fond of her, I don't know, I just don't know why you seem to avoid each other. I don't understand.

LOPAKHIN. Personally I don't understand either, I admit. It's all sort of strange. . . . If there's still time, then I'm ready right now. . . . Let's settle it right away—and there's an end to it, but if it weren't for you I feel I wouldn't propose.

LYUBOV ANDREEVNA. That's excellent. All it takes is one little minute. I'll call her right now. . . .

LOPAKHIN. And there's champagne for the occasion. (*Looks in the glasses.*) Empty, somebody drank it already. (*Yasha coughs.*) I should say, lapped it up. . . .

LYUBOV ANDREEVNA (*lively*). Fine! We'll leave . . . Yasha, allez! I'll call her. . . . (*In the doorway*) Varya, drop everything, come here. Come on! (*Exits with Yasha.*)

LOPAKHIN (*glancing at his watch*). Yes. . . . (*Pause. Behind the door a stifled laugh, whispering, finally Varya enters.*)

VARYA (*scrutinizes the luggage for a long time*). That's odd, I just can't find it. . . .

LOPAKHIN. What are you looking for?

VARYA. I packed it myself and can't remember. (*Pause.*)

LOPAKHIN. Where are you off to now, Varvara Mikhailovna?

VARYA. Me? To the Ragulins'. . . . I've agreed to take charge of their household . . . as a housekeeper, or something.

LOPAKHIN. That's in Yashnevo? On to seventy miles from here. (*Pause.*) So ends life in this house. . . .

VARYA (*examining the luggage*). Where in the world is it. . . . Or maybe I packed it in the trunk. . . . Yes, life in this house is ended . . . there won't be any more.

LOPAKHIN. And I'll be riding to Kharkov soon . . . by the same train. Lots of business. But I'm leaving Yepikhodov on the grounds . . . I hired him.

VARYA. That so!

LOPAKHIN. Last year by this time it was snowing already, if you remember, but now it's mild, sunny. Except that it's cold. . . . About three degrees of frost.

VARYA. I haven't noticed. (*Pause.*) And besides our thermometer is broken. . . .

(*Pause. Voice from the yard through the door: "Yermolai Alekseich!"*)

LOPAKHIN (*as if expecting this call for a long time*). Right away! (*Rushes out.*)

(*Varya, sitting on the floor, laying her head on a pile of dresses, quietly sobs. The door opens, Lyubov Andreevna enters cautiously.*)

LYUBOV ANDREEVNA. Well? (*Pause.*) We've got to go.

VARYA (*has stopped crying, wipes her eyes*). Yes, it's time, Mama dear. I'll get to the Ragulins today, if only I don't miss the train. . . .

LYUBOV ANDREEVNA (*in the doorway*). Anya, put your things on!

(*Enter Anya, then Gaev, Charlotta Ivanovna. Gaev has on a heavy overcoat with a hood. The servants and coach man foregather. Yepikhodov fusses around with the luggage.*)

LYUBOV ANDREEVNA. Now we can be on our way.

ANYA (*joyously*). On our way!

GAEV. My friends, beloved friends! Leaving this house forever, can I be silent, can I restrain myself from expressing at parting those feelings which now fill my whole being . . .

ANYA (*entreating*). Uncle!

VARYA. Uncle dear, you mustn't!

GAEV (*depressed*). Bank the yellow to the center . . . I'll keep still. . . .

(*Enter Trofimov, then Lopakhin.*)

TROFIMOV. Well, ladies and gentlemen, time to go!

LOPAKHIN. Yepikhodov, my overcoat!

LYUBOV ANDREEVNA. I'll sit just one more minute. It's as if I'd never before seen what the walls are like in this house, what the ceilings are like, and now I gaze at them greedily, with such tender love. . . .

GAEV. I remember when I was six, on Trinity Sunday I

sat in this window and watched my father driving to church....

LYUBOV ANDREEVNA. Is all the luggage loaded?

LOPAKHIN. Everything, I think. (*Putting on his overcoat, to Yepikhodov*) You there, Yepikhodov, see that everything's in order.

YEPIKHODOV (*talks in a hoarse voice*). Don't worry, Yermolai Alekseich!

LOPAKHIN. What's the matter with your voice?

YEPIKHODOV. I just drank some water, swallowed something.

YASHA (*contemptuously*). Ignorance....

LYUBOV ANDREEVNA. We're leaving—and not a soul will be left here....

LOPAKHIN. Until next spring.

VARYA (*pulls a parasol out of a bundle, looking as if she were about to hit somebody. Lopakhin pretends to be scared*). What are you ... what are you doing ... it never crossed my mind....

TROFIMOV. Ladies and gentlemen, let's get into the carriages.... It's high time! The train'll be here any minute!

VARYA. Petya, here they are, your galoshes, next to the suitcase. (*Tearfully*) And yours are so muddy, so old....

TROFIMOV (*putting on his galoshes*). Let's go, ladies and gentlemen!...

GAEV (*overcome with emotion, afraid he'll cry*). The train ... the station.... Followshot to the center, white doublet to the corner....

LYUBOV ANDREEVNA. Let's go!

LOPAKHIN. Everybody here? Nobody there? (*Locking the side door on the left.*) Things stored here, have to lock up. Let's go!...

ANYA. Good-bye, house! Good-bye, old life!

TROFIMOV. Hello, new life! (*Exits with Anya.*)

(*Varya casts a glance around the room and exits unhurriedly. Exeunt Yasha and Charlotta with a lapdog.*)

LOPAKHIN. Which means, till spring. Come along, ladies and gentlemen.... Till we meet again!... (*Exits.*)

(*Lyubov Andreevna and Gaev are left alone. As if they had been waiting for this, they throw themselves around one another's neck and sob with restraint, quietly, afraid of someone hearing them.*)

GAEV (*in despair*). Sister dear, sister dear....

LYUBOV ANDREEVNA. Oh, my darling, my sweet, beautiful orchard!... My life, my youth, my happiness, good-bye!... Good-bye!...

(*Anya's voice, gaily, appealing: "Mama!" Trofimov's voice, gaily, excited: "Yoo-hoo!"*)

LYUBOV ANDREEVNA. One last look at the walls, the windows.... Our poor mother loved to walk about in this room....

GAEV. Sister dear, sister dear!...

ANYA'S VOICE. Mama!...

TROFIMOV'S VOICE. Yoo-hoo!...

LYUBOV ANDREEVNA. We're coming!

(*They exeunt. The stage is empty. We hear the doors being locked with a key, then the carriages driving off. It grows quiet. In the silence there is the dull thud of the axe against a tree, sounding forlorn and doleful. We hear footsteps. From the door at right Firs appears. He's dressed as always, in a jacket and white vest, slippers on his feet. He is ill.*)

FIRS (*crosses to the door, tries the knob*). Locked. They've gone.... (*Sits on the sofa.*) Forgot about me.... Never mind.... I'll sit here a bit.... And I guess Leonid Andreich didn't put on his fur-coat, went out in his topcoat.... (*Sighs, anxiously.*) I didn't see to it.... Young striplings! (*Mutters something that cannot be understood.*) This life's gone by like I hadn't lived. (*Lies down.*) I'll lie down a bit.... Ain't no strength in you, nothing left, nothing.... Ech, you're ... half-baked!... (*Lies immobile.*)

(*We hear the distant sound, as if from the sky, the sound of a snapped string, dying away mournfully. Silence ensues, and all we hear far away in the orchard is the thud of an axe on a tree.*)

TOPICS FOR DISCUSSION AND WRITING

1. What do you make of the fact that the opening stage directions specify that the setting for the first act is a room that "is still known as the Nursery"?
2. What do the costumes communicate? (Consider, for example, the brief description of Lopakhin's costume on p. 369.)
3. Characterize Lyubov Andreevna.
4. Can some of the characters clearly be called comic? Do some of these characters help to make Lyubov Andreevna less comic?
5. How might the theme of the play be stated?
6. How seriously do you take Gaev's thoughts?

7. In your opinion, why is Firs in the play?
8. What do you make of the sound of the breaking string at the end of the play?
9. Chekhov said that he wrote "a comedy, in places even a farce." But the director, Stanislavsky, replied, "This is not a comedy or a farce; . . . it is a tragedy." What can be said for each of these views? Try to specify speeches or scenes that can be used to support these judgments. For instance, when Trofimov falls downstairs, is the episode farcical?

JOHN MILLINGTON SYNGE

Riders to the Sea

John Millington Synge (1871–1909) was born in Dublin of Protestant English stock. After his graduation from Trinity College, Dublin, where he specialized in languages—Gaelic, Latin, Greek, Hebrew—he went to Paris and tried to eke out a living by writing criticism of French literature. William Butler Yeats, in Paris in 1896, urged him to return to Ireland so that he might steep himself in the speech of the common people and record a life never described in literature. Synge took the advice and then in his few remaining years wrote six plays, three of which are masterpieces: *Riders to the Sea* (1904), *The Playboy of the Western World* (1907) and *Deidre of the Sorrows* (1909). He died of cancer in his thirty-eighth year.

COMMENTARY

Synge first visited the Aran Islands (three rocky places off the west coast of Ireland, inhabited by Gaelic-speaking fishermen) in the summer of 1898. From this visit and subsequent ones he derived the material for *The Aran Islands,* an account of life there, full of observations and bits of folklore he had picked up. In it one can find something of the origins of *Riders to the Sea:* descriptions of bringing horses across the sound, including an account of an old woman who had a vision of her drowned son riding on a horse; a reference to a coffin untimely made out of boards prepared for another person; and a reference to a body that floated ashore some weeks after the man drowned.

In writing the play Synge chose among the innumerable things he saw and heard, selecting (as any artist does) from the welter or chaos of experience to put together a unified story. One need not compare *Riders to the Sea* (in which everything is related to everything else) with *The Aran Islands* (in which we have a wonderful grab bag of scarcely related details) to see that the careful arrangement of physical happenings and dialogue gives us more than a slice of life, more than a picture of a certain kind of Irish life. Synge's art extends beyond his plot to his language. The islanders spoke Gaelic, and Synge claimed that his English was close to a translation of their language; but the speeches—as distinct from the words—are Synge's, just as Macbeth's "I am in blood / Stepped in so far, that, should I wade no more, / Returning were as tedious as go o'er" is Shakespeare's creation although the individual words are pretty much the property of any literate American or Englishman. The speeches Synge creates, no less than his plot, belong to the world of art, though the speeches and the events are made up of the materials of Aran life.

Synge chose the peasant idiom because it seemed to him to have beauty and even

A scene from the Abbey Theatre production of *Riders to the Sea,* Dublin, 1980.
(Photograph: Rod Tuach.)

grandeur, while at the same time it was rooted in people who lived an elemental existence. He saw no need to choose between beauty and truth: beauty without truth led writers of the late nineteenth century (he believed) to highly wrought yet trivial or even meaningless verse, and truth without beauty to dull pictures of humankind's insignificance. It is partly by making "every speech . . . as fully flavored as a nut or apple" that Synge produced a work that (although it deals with multiple deaths) is not depressing but is, like every work of art, stimulating: "Let you go down each day, and see the sheep aren't jumping in on the rye, and if the jobber comes you can sell the pig with the black feet if there is a good price going." Even the speeches on the inevitable end of humankind have, while they call attention to a person's ignominious remains, richness and dignity: "And isn't it a pitiful thing when there is nothing left of a man who was a great rower and fisher, but a bit of an old shirt and a plain stocking?" Throughout the play this artful use of language communicates a picture of heroism and humbleness that is reassuring as well as grievous, nowhere more so than in Maurya's final speech, which calls attention to the hardness of life and the inevitability of death in such a way as almost to offer a kind of reassurance.

Early in the play Maurya speaks "querulously" and rakes the fire "aimlessly." Finally, after the death of Bartley, Maurya derives some comfort from the thought that "Bartley will have a fine coffin out of the white boards," and Michael "a clean burial in the far north." She has been "hard set," known despair, seen the worst that can happen ("They're all gone now, and there isn't anything more the sea can do to me"), and now from the vantage point of one stripped of all that one has cherished, she can utter with dignity the most terrible facts of life. This is the heart of Synge's drama. The word *drama* is from the Greek verb *dran,* "to do," "to accomplish"; in *Riders to the Sea* the thing accomplished is not only the identification of Michael's clothing and the death of Bartley, but the shift in Maurya's mind.

We have been talking at some length about *Riders to the Sea* as a drama, but we have said nothing about it as a tragedy. Two of Synge's fellow Irishmen have left brief interesting comments on the play, especially on the play's relation to classical tragedy. William Butler Yeats, Synge's older contemporary, called it "quite Greek"; but James Joyce, Synge's younger contemporary, who regarded himself as one who adhered to Aristotle's *Poetics,* after reading *Riders to the Sea* sniffily remarked that "Synge isn't an Aristotelian." Joyce was especially bothered by the brevity of the play; in a program note to a production of the play, he wondered "whether a brief tragedy be possible or not (a point on which Aristotle had some doubts)," though he did go on to say that *Riders to the Sea* is "the work of a tragic poet." One might learn something by considering the play in the light of some of Aristotle's remarks. This is not to say that if the play doesn't hew to Aristotle's prescriptions it is defective—and indeed Aristotle is sometimes confusing and sometimes contradictory. Still, here are a few of his comments, extracted from the fuller text of *The Poetics* that we print on pages 70–75. You may want to evaluate their relevance to *Riders to the Sea,* partly in an effort to see the strengths or weaknesses of the play, partly in an effort to see the strengths or weaknesses of *The Poetics.*

1. "Tragedy [imitates] persons [who are] above [the level of our world]" (page 71).

2. "Tragedy . . . is an imitation of an action of high importance, complete and of some amplitude; in language enhanced by . . . beauties. . . . By the beauties enhancing the language I mean rhythm and melody" (page 71).
3. "[One of] the chief means by which tragedy moves us [is] Irony of events. . . . Irony is a reversal in the course of events, . . . and, as I say, in accordance with probability or necessity" (pages 72–73).
4. ". . . tragedy is an imitation of a whole and complete action of some amplitude. . . . as to amplitude, the invariable rule dictated by the nature of the action is the fuller the more beautiful so long as the outline remains clear" (page 72).
5. ". . . it is not the poet's business to tell what has happened, but the kind of things that would happen—what is possible according to probability or necessity" (page 72).
6. "The action imitated must contain incidents that evoke fear and pity, besides being a complete action; but this effect is accentuated when these incidents occur logically as well as unexpectedly, which will be more sensational if they happen arbitrarily, by chance" (page 73).
7. ". . . tragedy, to be at its finest, . . . should . . . imitate fearful and pitiful events. . . . pity is induced by undeserved misfortune, and fear by the misfortunes of normal people" (pages 73–74).
8. "[Tragedy shows] the kind of man who neither is distinguished for excellence and virtue, nor comes to grief on account of baseness and vice, but on account of some error" (page 74).

JOHN MILLINGTON SYNGE *Riders to the Sea*

List of Characters

MAURYA, *an old woman*
BARTLEY, *her son*
CATHLEEN, *her daughter*
NORA, *a younger daughter*
MEN *and* WOMEN

Scene. An island off the West of Ireland.

Cottage kitchen, with nets, oil-skins, spinning-wheel, some new boards standing by the wall, etc. Cathleen, a girl of about twenty, finishes kneading cake, and puts it down in the pot-oven by the fire; then wipes her hands, and begins to spin at the wheel. Nora, a young girl, puts her head in at the door.

NORA (*in a low voice*). Where is she?

CATHLEEN. She's lying down, God help her, and may be sleeping, if she's able.

Nora comes in softly, and takes a bundle from under her shawl.

CATHLEEN (*spinning the wheel rapidly*). What is it you have?

NORA. The young priest is after bringing them. It's a shirt and a plain stocking were got off a drowned man in Donegal.

Cathleen stops her wheel with a sudden movement, and leans out to listen.

NORA. We're to find out if it's Michael's they are, some time herself will be down looking by the sea.

CATHLEEN. How would they be Michael's, Nora? How would he go the length of that way to the far north?

NORA. The young priest says he's known the like of it. "If it's Michael's they are," says he, "you can tell herself he's got a clean burial by the grace of God, and if they're not his, let no one say a word about them, for she'll be getting her death," says he, "with crying and lamenting."

The door which Nora half-closed is blown open by a gust of wind.

CATHLEEN (*looking out anxiously*). Did you ask him would he stop Bartley going this day with the horses to the Galway fair?

NORA. "I won't stop him," says he, "but let you not be afraid. Herself does be saying prayers half through the night, and the Almighty God won't leave her destitute," says he, "with no son living."

CATHLEEN. Is the sea bad by the white rocks, Nora?

NORA. Middling bad, God help us. There's a great roaring in the west, and it's worse it'll be getting when the tide's turned to the wind.

She goes over to the table with the bundle.

Shall I open it now?

CATHLEEN. Maybe she'd wake up on us, and come in before we'd done. (*Coming to the table.*) It's a long time we'll be, and the two of us crying.

NORA (*goes to the inner door and listens*). She's moving about on the bed. She'll be coming in a minute.

CATHLEEN. Give me the ladder, and I'll put them up in the turf-loft, the way she won't know of them at all, and maybe when the tide turns she'll be going down to see would he be floating from the east.

They put the ladder against the gable of the chimney; Cathleen goes up a few steps and hides the bundle in the turf-loft. Maurya comes from the inner room.

MAURYA (*looking up at Cathleen and speaking querulously*). Isn't it turf enough you have for this day and evening?

CATHLEEN. There's a cake baking at the fire for a short space (*throwing down the turf*) and Bartley will want it when the tide turns if he goes to Connemara.

Nora picks up the turf and puts it round the pot-oven.

MAURYA (*sitting down on a stool at the fire*). He won't go this day with the wind rising from the south and west. He won't go this day, for the young priest will stop him surely.

NORA. He'll not stop him, mother, and I heard Eamon Simon and Stephen Pheety and Colum Shawn saying he would go.

MAURYA. Where is he itself?

NORA. He went down to see would there be another boat sailing in the week, and I'm thinking it won't be long till he's here now, for the tide's turning at the green head, and the hooker's[1] tacking from the east.

CATHLEEN. I hear some one passing the big stones.

NORA (*looking out*). He's coming now, and he in a hurry.

BARTLEY (*comes in and looks round the room. Speaking sadly and quietly*). Where is the bit of new rope, Cathleen, was bought in Connemara?

CATHLEEN (*coming down*). Give it to him, Nora; it's on a nail by the white boards. I hung it up this morning, for the pig with the black feet was eating it.

NORA (*giving him a rope*). Is that it, Bartley?

MAURYA. You'd do right to leave that rope, Bartley, hanging by the boards. (*Bartley takes the rope.*) It will be wanting in this place, I'm telling you, if Michael is washed up to-morrow morning, or the next morning, or any morning in the week, for it's a deep grave we'll make him by the grace of God.

BARTLEY (*beginning to work with the rope*). I've no halter the way I can ride down on the mare, and I must go now quickly. This is the one boat going for two weeks or beyond it, and the fair will be a good fair for horses I heard them saying below.

MAURYA. It's a hard thing they'll be saying below if the body is washed up and there's no man in it to make the coffin, and I after giving a big price for the finest white boards you'd find in Connemara.

She looks round at the boards.

BARTLEY. How would it be washed up, and we after looking each day for nine days, and a strong wind blowing a while back from the west and south?

MAURYA. If it wasn't found itself, that wind is raising the sea, and there was a star up against the moon, and it rising in the night. If it was a hundred horses, or a thousand horses you had itself, what is the price of a thousand horses against a son where there is one son only?

BARTLEY (*working at the halter, to Cathleen*). Let you go down each day, and see the sheep aren't jumping in on the rye, and if the jobber comes you can sell the pig with the black feet if there is a good price going.

MAURYA. How would the like of her get a good price for a pig?

BARTLEY (*to Cathleen*). If the west wind holds with the last bit of the moon let you and Nora get up weed enough for another cock for the kelp.[2] It's hard set we'll be from this day with no one in it but one man to work.

MAURYA. It's hard set we'll be surely the day you're drownd'd with the rest. What way will I live and the girls with me, and I an old woman looking for the grave?

Bartley lays down the halter, takes off his old coat, and puts on a newer one of the same flannel.

[1] **hooker** sailing boat

[2] **kelp** seaweed (used for fertilizer)

BARTLEY (*to Nora*). Is she coming to the pier?

NORA (*looking out*). She's passing the green head and letting fall her sails.

BARTLEY (*getting his purse and tobacco*). I'll have half an hour to go down, and you'll see me coming again in two days, or in three days, or maybe in four days if the wind is bad.

MAURYA (*turning round to the fire, and putting her shawl over her head*). Isn't it a hard and cruel man won't hear a word from an old woman, and she holding him from the sea?

CATHLEEN. It's the life of a young man to be going on the sea, and who would listen to an old woman with one thing and she saying it over?

BARTLEY (*taking the halter*). I must go now quickly. I'll ride down on the red mare, and the gray pony'll run behind me. . . . The blessing of God on you.

He goes out.

MAURYA (*crying out as he is in the door*). He's gone now, God spare us, and we'll not see him again. He's gone now, and when the black night is falling I'll have no son left me in the world.

CATHLEEN. Why wouldn't you give him your blessing and he looking round in the door? Isn't it sorrow enough is on every one in this house without your sending him out with an unlucky word behind him, and a hard word in his ear?

Maurya takes up the tongs and begins raking the fire aimlessly without looking round.

NORA (*turning towards her*). You're taking away the turf from the cake.

CATHLEEN (*crying out*). The Son of God forgive us, Nora, we're after forgetting his bit of bread.

She comes over to the fire.

NORA. And it's destroyed he'll be going till dark night, and he after eating nothing since the sun went up.

CATHLEEN (*turning the cake out of the oven*). It's destroyed he'll be, surely. There's no sense left on any person in a house where an old woman will be talking for ever.

Maurya sways herself on her stool.

CATHLEEN (*cutting off some of the bread and rolling it in a cloth; to Maurya*). Let you go down now to the spring well and give him this and he passing. You'll see him then and the dark word will be broken, and you can say "God speed you," the way he'll be easy in his mind.

MAURYA (*taking the bread*). Will I be in it as soon as himself?

CATHLEEN. If you go now quickly.

MAURYA (*standing up unsteadily*). It's hard set I am to walk.

CATHLEEN (*looking at her anxiously*). Give her the stick, Nora, or maybe she'll slip on the big stones.

NORA. What stick?

CATHLEEN. The stick Michael brought from Connemara.

MAURYA (*taking a stick Nora gives her*). In the big world the old people do be leaving things after them for their sons and children, but in this place it is the young men do be leaving things behind for them that do be old.

She goes out slowly. Nora goes over to the ladder.

CATHLEEN. Wait, Nora, maybe she'd turn back quickly. She's that sorry, God help her, you wouldn't know the thing she'd do.

NORA. Is she gone around by the bush?

CATHLEEN (*looking out*). She's gone now. Throw it down quickly, for the Lord knows when she'll be out of it again.

NORA (*getting the bundle from the loft*). The young priest said he'd be passing to-morrow, and we might go down and speak to him below if it's Michael's they are surely.

CATHLEEN (*taking the bundle*). Did he say what way they were found?

NORA (*coming down*). "There were two men," says he, "and they rowing round with poteen[3] before the cocks crowed, and the oar of one of them caught the body, and they passing the black cliffs of the north."

CATHLEEN (*trying to open the bundle*). Give me a knife, Nora, the strings perished with the salt water, and there's a black knot on it you wouldn't loosen in a week.

NORA (*giving her a knife*). I've heard tell it was a long way to Donegal.

CATHLEEN (*cutting the string*). It is surely. There was a man in here a while ago—the man sold us that knife—and he said if you set off walking from the rock beyond, it would be seven days you'd be in Donegal.

NORA. And what time would a man take, and he floating?

Cathleen opens the bundle and takes out a bit of a stocking. They look at them eagerly.

CATHLEEN (*in a low voice*). The Lord spare us, Nora! isn't it a queer hard thing to say if it's his they are surely?

NORA. I'll get his shirt off the hook the way we can put the one flannel on the other. (*She looks through some clothes hanging in the corner.*) It's not with them, Cathleen, and where will it be?

CATHLEEN. I'm thinking Bartley put it on him in the

[3]**poteen** illegal whiskey

morning, for his own shirt was heavy with the salt in it. (*Pointing to the corner.*) There's a bit of a sleeve was of the same stuff. Give me that and it will do.

Nora brings it to her and they compare the flannel.

CATHLEEN. It's the same stuff, Nora; but if it is itself aren't there great rolls of it in the shops of Galway, and isn't it many another man may have a shirt of it as well as Michael himself?

NORA (*who has taken up the stocking and counted the stitches, crying out*). It's Michael, Cathleen, it's Michael; God spare his soul, and what will herself say when she hears this story, and Bartley on the sea?

CATHLEEN (*taking the stocking*). It's a plain stocking.

NORA. It's the second one of the third pair I knitted, and I put up three score stitches, and I dropped four of them.

CATHLEEN (*counts the stitches*). It's that number is in it. (*Crying out.*) Ah, Nora, isn't it a bitter thing to think of him floating that way to the far north, and no one to keen[4] him but the black hags that do be flying on the sea?

NORA (*swinging herself round, and throwing out her arms on the clothes*). And isn't it a pitiful thing when there is nothing left of a man who was a great rower and fisher, but a bit of an old shirt and a plain stocking?

CATHLEEN (*after an instant*). Tell me is herself coming, Nora? I hear a little sound on the path.

NORA (*looking out*). She is, Cathleen. She's coming up to the door.

CATHLEEN. Put these things away before she'll come in. Maybe it's easier she'll be after giving her blessing to Bartley, and we won't let on we've heard anything the time he's on the sea.

NORA (*helping Cathleen to close the bundle*). We'll put them here in the corner.

They put them into a hole in the chimney corner. Cathleen goes back to the spinning-wheel.

NORA. Will she see it was crying I was?

CATHLEEN. Keep your back to the door the way the light'll not be on you.

Nora sits down at the chimney corner, with her back to the door. Maurya comes in very slowly, without looking at the girls, and goes over to her stool at the other side of the fire. The cloth with the bread is still in her hand. The girls look at each other, and Nora points to the bundle of bread.

CATHLEEN (*after spinning for a moment*). You didn't give him his bit of bread?

[4]**keen** lament

Maurya begins to keen softly, without turning round.

CATHLEEN. Did you see him riding down?

Maurya goes on keening.

CATHLEEN (*a little impatiently*). God forgive you; isn't it a better thing to raise your voice and tell what you seen, than to be making lamentation for a thing that's done? Did you see Bartley, I'm saying to you.

MAURYA (*with a weak voice*). My heart's broken from this day.

CATHLEEN (*as before*). Did you see Bartley?

MAURYA. I seen the fearfulest thing.

CATHLEEN (*leaves her wheel and looks out*). God forgive you; he's riding the mare now over the green head, and the gray pony behind him.

MAURYA (*starts, so that her shawl falls back from her head and shows her white tossed hair. With a frightened voice*). The gray pony behind him.

CATHLEEN (*coming to the fire*). What is it ails you, at all?

MAURYA (*speaking very slowly*). I've seen the fearfulest thing any person has seen, since the day Bride Dara seen the dead man with the child in his arms.

CATHLEEN AND NORA. Uah.

They crouch down in front of the old woman at the fire.

NORA. Tell us what it is you seen.

MAURYA. I went down to the spring well, and I stood there saying a prayer to myself. Then Bartley came along, and he riding on the red mare with the gray pony behind him. (*She puts up her hands, as if to hide something from her eyes.*) The Son of God spare us, Nora!

CATHLEEN. What is it you seen?

MAURYA. I seen Michael himself.

CATHLEEN (*speaking softly*). You did not, mother; it wasn't Michael you seen, for his body is after being found in the far north, and he's got a clean burial by the grace of God.

MAURYA (*a little defiantly*). I'm after seeing him this day, and he riding and galloping. Bartley came first on the red mare; and I tried to say "God speed you," but something choked the words in my throat. He went by quickly; and "the blessing of God on you," says he, and I could say nothing. I looked up then, and I crying, at the gray pony, and there was Michael upon it—with fine clothes on him, and new shoes on his feet.

CATHLEEN (*begins to keen*). It's destroyed we are from this day. It's destroyed, surely.

NORA. Didn't the young priest say the Almighty God wouldn't leave her destitute with no son living?

MAURYA (*in a low voice, but clearly*). It's little the like of him knows of the sea. . . . Bartley will be lost now, and let you call in Eamon and make me a good coffin out of the white boards, for I won't live after them. I've had a husband, and a husband's father, and six sons in this house—six fine men, though it was a hard birth I had with every one of them and they coming to the world—and some of them were found and some of them were not found, but they're gone now the lot of them. . . . There were Stephen, and Shawn, were lost in the great wind, and found after in the Bay of Gregory of the Golden Mouth, and carried up the two of them on the one plank, and in by that door.

She pauses for a moment, the girls start as if they heard something through the door that is half open behind them.

NORA (*in a whisper*). Did you hear that, Cathleen? Did you hear a noise in the north-east?

CATHLEEN (*in a whisper*). There's some one after crying out by the seashore.

MAURYA (*continues without hearing anything*). There was Sheamus and his father, and his own father again, were lost in a dark night, and not a stick or sign was seen of them when the sun went up. There was Patch after was drowned out of a curagh[5] that turned over. I was sitting here with Bartley, and he a baby, lying on my two knees, and I seen two women, and three women, and four women coming in, and they crossing themselves, and not saying a word. I looked out then, and there were men coming after them, and they holding a thing in the half of a red sail, and water dripping out of it—it was a dry day, Nora—and leaving a track to the door.

She pauses again with her hand stretched out towards the door. It opens softly and old women begin to come in, crossing themselves on the threshold, and kneeling down in front of the stage with red petticoats over their heads.

MAURYA (*half in a dream, to Cathleen*). Is it Patch, or Michael, or what is it at all?

CATHLEEN. Michael is after being found in the far north, and when he is found there how could he be here in this place?

MAURYA. There does be a power of young men floating round in the sea, and what way would they know if it was Michael they had, or another man like him, for when a man is nine days in the sea, and the wind blowing, it's hard set his own mother would be to say what man was it.

CATHLEEN. It's Michael, God spare him, for they're after sending us a bit of his clothes from the far north.

She reaches out and hands Maurya the clothes that belonged to Michael. Maurya stands up slowly and takes them in her hand. Nora looks out.

NORA. They're carrying a thing among them and there's water dripping out of it and leaving a track by the big stones.

CATHLEEN (*in a whisper to the women who have come in*). Is it Bartley it is?

ONE OF THE WOMEN. It is surely, God rest his soul.

Two younger women come in and pull out the table. Then men carry in the body of Bartley, laid on a plank, with a bit of sail over it, and lay it on the table.

CATHLEEN (*to the women, as they are doing so*). What way was he drowned?

ONE OF THE WOMEN. The gray pony knocked him into the sea, and he was washed out where there is a great surf on the white rocks.

Maurya has gone over and knelt down at the head of the table. The women are keening softly and swaying themselves with a slow movement. Cathleen and Nora kneel at the other end of the table. The men kneel near the door.

MAURYA (*raising her head and speaking as if she did not see the people around her*). They're all gone now, and there isn't anything more the sea can do to me. . . . I'll have no call now to be up crying and praying when the wind breaks from the south, and you can hear the surf is in the east, and the surf is in the west, making a great stir with the two noises, and they hitting one on the other. I'll have no call now to be going down and getting Holy Water in the dark nights after Samhain,[6] and I won't care what way the sea is when the other women will be keening. (*To Nora.*) Give me the Holy Water, Nora, there's a small sup still on the dresser.

Nora gives it to her.

MAURYA (*drops Michael's clothes across Bartley's feet, and sprinkles the Holy Water over him*). It isn't that I haven't prayed for you, Bartley, to the Almighty God. It isn't that I haven't said prayers in the dark night till you wouldn't know what I'ld be saying; but it's a great rest I'll have now, and it's time surely. It's a great rest I'll have now, and great sleeping in the long nights after Samhain, if it's only a bit of wet flour we do have to eat, and maybe a fish that would be stinking.

She kneels down again, crossing herself, and saying prayers under her breath.

CATHLEEN (*to an old man*). Maybe yourself and Eamon would make a coffin when the sun rises. We have

[5]**curagh** unstable vessel of tarred canvas on a wood frame; canoe

[6]**Samhain** November 1, All Saints' Day

fine white boards herself bought, God help her, thinking Michael would be found, and I have a new cake you can eat while you'll be working.

THE OLD MAN (*looking at the boards*). Are there nails with them?

CATHLEEN. There are not, Colum; we didn't think of the nails.

ANOTHER MAN. It's a great wonder she wouldn't think of the nails, and all the coffins she's seen made already.

CATHLEEN. It's getting old she is, and broken.

Maurya stands up again very slowly and spreads out the pieces of Michael's clothes beside the body, sprinkling them with the last of the Holy Water.

NORA (*in a whisper to Cathleen*). She's quiet now and easy; but the day Michael was drowned you could hear her crying out from this to the spring well. It's fonder she was of Michael, and would any one have thought that?

CATHLEEN (*slowly and clearly*). An old woman will be soon tired with anything she will do, and isn't it nine days herself is after crying and keening, and making great sorrow in the house?

MAURYA (*puts the empty cup mouth downwards on the table, and lays her hands together on Bartley's feet*). They're all together this time, and the end is come. May the Almighty God have mercy on Bartley's soul, and on Michael's soul, and on the souls of Sheamus and Patch, and Stephen and Shawn (*bending her head*); and may He have mercy on my soul, Nora, and on the soul of every one is left living in the world.

She pauses, and the keen rises a little more loudly from the women, then sinks away.

MAURYA (*continuing*). Michael has a clean burial in the far north, by the grace of the Almighty God. Bartley will have a fine coffin out of the white boards, and a deep grave surely. What more can we want than that? No man at all can be living for ever, and we must be satisfied.

She kneels down again and the curtain falls slowly.

TOPICS FOR DISCUSSION AND WRITING

1. What is revealed about Maurya's state of mind by her speech (page 397): "He won't go this day with the wind rising from the south and west. He won't go this day, for the young priest will stop him surely." Why is her reference to the need for the rope (page 397) one of the strongest arguments she can propose for Bartley's staying?
2. Characterize the priest. What is his function in the play?
3. What is implied by Maurya's vision of Michael "with fine clothes on him, and new shoes on his feet" (page 399)?
4. Trace the foreshadowing of Bartley's death.
5. Nora and Cathleen hear someone calling out by the seashore (page 400). Why doesn't Maurya hear the noise? Why does Synge not have a stage direction calling for a cry?
6. Does the fact that Maurya has forgotten the coffin-nails indicate (as Cathleen says, page 401) that she is "broken"?
7. Evaluate James Joyce's complaint that the catastrophe is brought about by a pony rather than by the sea. It has been suggested that a reply can be made to Joyce: Bartley is knocked into the sea by the gray pony, but this is not an accident, for the ghost of his brother Michael is riding the pony, and Irish ghosts commonly seek to bring the living into the realm of the dead. Do you think this reply is satisfactory, or does it introduce a red herring?
8. In addition to the conflict between human beings and nature, what conflicts do you find in the play?

Robin Bailey, Lesley Sharp, Barbara Jefford, and Richard Pasco in a 1987 National Theatre production of *Six Characters in Search of an Author.* (Photograph: Donald Cooper © PHOTOSTAGE.)

LUIGI PIRANDELLO

Six Characters in Search of an Author

A Comedy in the Making

English Version by Edward Storer

Luigi Pirandello (1867–1936) was born in Sicily, the son of the owner of a profitable sulfur mine. Pirandello studied at Rome and then at Bonn, where in 1891 he received a doctorate for a thesis on Sicilian dialect. Back in Rome he wrote poetry, fiction, and literary criticism, and taught Italian at a teachers college. Troubles came thick: his family, and his wife's, suffered financial setbacks, and his wife became intermittently insane. But from 1917 onward he had great success in the theater with many of his forty or so plays. Among the best-known plays are *Right You Are (If You Think You Are)* (1917), *Six Characters in Search of an Author* (1921), and *Henry IV* (1922). In 1934 Pirandello was awarded the Nobel Prize. Curiously, this philosophic skeptic was a supporter of Italian fascism, and he gave his Nobel medal to be melted down for Mussolini's Abyssinian campaign.

COMMENTARY

In an essay on *Six Characters in Search of an Author,* published several years after the play, Pirandello wryly noted that he had the "misfortune" to be a philosophical writer. Such a writer, he explained, is not content to present characters and stories for the pleasure of presenting them, but is moved by a "profound spiritual need." Something should be said, then, of Pirandello's philosophy, which can be found not only in the plays and in his essay on *Six Characters,* but also in an essay of 1908 entitled "Umorismo" ("Humor"). Reality is fluid, and beyond the grasp of reason. But man *has* reason, and he cannot tolerate a fluid, irrational world, so he sets up reasonable—but false—categories. He creates laws, codes of ethics, religions, and other "communal lies," but in certain dreadful moments he may become aware that these creations are distortions of reality.

In *Six Characters,* take as an example this speech by the Father:

> Each of us when he appears before his fellows is clothed in a certain dignity. But every man knows what unconfessable things pass within the secrecy of his own heart. One gives way to the temptation, only to rise from it again, afterwards, with a great eagerness to re-establish one's dignity, as if it were a tombstone to place on the grave of one's shame, and a monument to hide and sign the memory of our weaknesses. Everybody's in the same case. Some folks haven't the courage to say certain things, that's all!

Now, such an attack on the apparent dignity of human beings is not unprecedented.

King Lear, for example, offers an even more terrifying indictment of man's hypocrisy, penetrating the fair outside to the "mischief" that breeds about the heart. But Lear's remarks are the remarks of an overwrought speaker, and though we cannot dismiss his insights, we do not take them as the whole truth. Lear forces on us the awareness of the vast discrepancy between appearance and reality, but (1) we do not doubt that there *is* a reality, and (2) the play itself offers evidence that reality is not exactly what the tragic hero, at the height of his agony, perceives it to be. We remember, for example, Cordelia in *King Lear,* and we know that goodness and love are not mere illusions.

Pirandello went beyond suggesting that dignity is an illusion; he suggested that the idea of any sort of coherent personality is an illusion, and that all experience is illusory. Men have, of course, for centuries touched on the idea that what we call reality may be only illusion. One thinks, for example, of Plato, and of Shakespeare's numerous references to the world as a stage. Near the end of *Macbeth,* for example, the protagonist says:

> Life's but a walking shadow, a poor player
> That struts and frets his hour upon the stage
> And then is heard no more. It is a tale
> Told by an idiot, full of sound and fury
> Signifying nothing.

But such a passage is the remark of a particular character, not of Shakespeare. It is not Shakespeare but Macbeth who—finding that he cannot enjoy the crown for which he has given up his humanity and his soul—says that life signifies nothing. To the viewer of *Macbeth,* the significance is fairly clear: the violence that Macbeth does to others he unknowingly does also to himself, and this man who acts as though the lives of others have no significance comes to find his own life lacking any. In short, though Macbeth finds no significance in life, the play clearly implies one. Or take the end of *A Midsummer Night's Dream,* when Puck, in the epilogue, says:

> If we shadows have offended,
> Think but this, and all is mended:
> That you have but slumb'red here,
> While these visions did appear.
> And this weak and idle theme,
> No more yielding but a dream.

Shakespeare is graciously suggesting that his "weak and idle" play yields no more than a dream—but, first, we recognize these words for the modest untruth that they are, and, second, we know that the play itself refutes them, since in this play the several dreams in fact are not "weak and idle" (that is, foolish) but accurate indications of what happens. Macbeth and Puck, then, are not Shakespeare's spokesmen—but Pirandello's Father in *Six Characters* is indeed Pirandello's spokesman when he explains to the superficial Manager that the Manager's "reality is a mere transitory and fleeting illusion, taking this form today and that tomorrow, according to the conditions, according to your will, your sentiments, which in turn are controlled by an intellect that shows them to you today in one manner and tomorrow . . . who knows how?" After all, the Father explains, each day we see things differently; we dismiss as illusions what we earlier took for reality, and we will later dismiss as illusions what we at this moment take for reality:

> Well, sir, if you think of all those illusions that mean nothing to you now, of all those things which don't even *seem* to you to exist any more, while once they *were* for you, don't you feel that—I won't say these boards—but the very earth under your feet is sinking away from you when you reflect that in the same way this *you* as you feel it today—all this present reality of yours—is fated to seem a mere illusion to you tomorrow?

In effect Pirandello is saying that both external reality and personality are fluid, incoherent, elusive, and, for all practical purposes, unreal.

This extreme relativism had been introduced earlier in the play, especially in the Father's speech on conscience, which rejects the concept of personality, of a dominant ego:

> We believe this conscience to be a single thing, but it is many-sided. There is one for this person, and another for that. Diverse consciences. So we have this illusion of being one person for all, of having a personality that is unique in all our acts. But it isn't true. We perceive this when, tragically perhaps, in something we do, we are as it were, suspended, caught up in the air on a kind of hook. Then we perceive that all of us was not in that act, and that it would be an atrocious injustice to judge us by that action alone, as if all our existence were summed up in that one deed.

And the Father is not Pirandello's only spokesman. For example, the churlish Son scoffs at the Father but makes a similar point: "He [the Father] thinks he has got at the meaning of it all. Just as if each one of us in every circumstance of life couldn't find his own explanation of it!"

We have said that Pirandello suggested it was his "misfortune" to be a philosophical writer, and we have tried to sketch the philosophy underlying the play. But *Six Characters* is a play rather than a philosophic treatise, and we should not neglect Pirandello's vivid characterizations and his energetic conflicts. He memorably embodies in his play his vision of characters struggling to express themselves and to achieve reality even though they have no faith in reality. When the Manager impatiently explains to the Father, "Drama is action, sir, action and not confounded philosophy," Pirandello is making a little joke at the expense of those who are impatient with ideas in drama, but he has throughout taken care to embody his philosophy in the theatrical action of a tragicomedy. The serious concerns of the characters seem absurd to the Actors, and the Actors' efforts to impersonate the Characters seem ludicrous to the Characters. The tragic aspects of the play are obvious—for example, the drowning of the little Child, the suicide of the Boy, the emotional paralysis of the Son. Some of the comic aspects are equally obvious—especially the satire on the theater, and the occasional deflation of the Father (he has "aspirations towards a certain moral sanity," but he visits a brothel). But the struggle of the deeply feeling Characters against the shallow Actors can only be characterized as tragicomic. That the chief spokesman for the Characters, the Father, argues against the concept of personality yet desperately seeks to achieve a full reality in a play to be performed by Actors whom he regards as less real than himself, is perhaps the tragicomic paradox at the heart of the play.

LUIGI PIRANDELLO *Six Characters in Search of an Author*

Characters of the Comedy in the Making

THE FATHER	THE BOY
THE MOTHER	THE CHILD
THE STEPDAUGHTER	(*The last two do not speak.*)
THE SON	MADAME PACE

Actors of the Company

THE MANAGER	PROPERTY MAN
LEADING LADY	PROMPTER
LEADING MAN	MACHINIST
SECOND LADY LEAD	MANAGER'S SECRETARY
L'INGÉNUE	DOOR-KEEPER
JUVENILE LEAD	SCENE-SHIFTERS

OTHER ACTORS AND ACTRESSES

Scene: Daytime. The stage of a theater.

N.B. The Comedy is without acts or scenes. The performance is interrupted once, without the curtain being lowered, when the Manager and the chief characters withdraw to arrange a scenario. A second interruption of the action takes place when, by mistake, the stage hands let the curtain down.

ACT 1

The spectators will find the curtain raised and the stage as it usually is during the daytime. It will be half dark, and empty, so that from the beginning the public may have the impression of an impromptu performance.

Prompter's box and a small table and chair for the Manager.

Two other small tables and several chairs scattered about as during rehearsals.

The Actors and Actresses of the company enter from the back of the stage: first one, then another, then two together; nine or ten in all. They are about to rehearse a Pirandello play: Mixing It Up. *Some of the company move off towards their dressing rooms. The Prompter, who has the "book" under his arm, is waiting for the Manager in order to begin the rehearsal.*

The Actors and Actresses, some standing, some sitting, chat and smoke. One perhaps reads a paper; another cons his part.

Finally, the Manager enters and goes to the table prepared for him. His Secretary brings him his mail, through which he glances. The Prompter takes his seat, turns on a light, and opens the "book."

THE MANAGER (*throwing a letter down on the table*). I can't see. (*To Property Man.*) Let's have a little light, please!

PROPERTY MAN. Yes, sir, yes, at once. (*A light comes down on to the stage.*)

THE MANAGER (*clapping his hands*). Come along! Come along! Second act of "Mixing It Up." (*Sits down.*)

(*The Actors and Actresses go from the front of the stage to the wings, all except the three who are to begin the rehearsal.*)

THE PROMPTER (*reading the "book"*). "Leo Gala's house. A curious room serving as dining-room and study."

THE MANAGER (*to Property Man*). Fix up the old red room.

PROPERTY MAN (*noting it down*). Red set. All right!

THE PROMPTER (*continuing to read from the "book"*). "Table already laid and writing desk with books and papers. Book-shelves. Exit rear to Leo's bedroom. Exit left to kitchen. Principal exit to right."

THE MANAGER (*energetically*). Well, you understand: The principal exit over there; here, the kitchen. (*Turning to actor who is to play the part of Socrates.*) You make your entrances and exits here. (*To Property Man.*) The baize doors at the rear, and curtains.

PROPERTY MAN (*noting it down*). Right!

PROMPTER (*reading as before*). "When the curtain rises, Leo Gala, dressed in cook's cap and apron, is busy beating an egg in a cup. Philip, also dressed as a cook, is beating another egg. Guidi Venanzi is seated and listening."

LEADING MAN (*to Manager*). Excuse me, but must I absolutely wear a cook's cap?

THE MANAGER (*annoyed*). I imagine so. It says so there anyway. (*Pointing to the "book."*)

LEADING MAN. But it's ridiculous!

THE MANAGER (*jumping up in a rage*). Ridiculous? Ridiculous? Is it my fault if France won't send us any more good comedies, and we are reduced to putting on Pirandello's works; where nobody understands anything, and where the author plays the fool with us all? (*The Actors grin. The Manager goes to Leading Man and shouts.*) Yes sir, you put on the cook's cap and beat eggs. Do you suppose that with all this egg-beating business you are on an ordinary stage? Get that out of your head. You represent the shell of the eggs you are beating! (*Laughter and comments among the Actors.*) Silence! and listen to my explanations, please! (*To Leading Man.*) "The empty form of reason without the fullness of instinct, which is blind."—You stand for reason, your wife is instinct. It's a mixing up of the parts, according to which you who act your own part become the puppet of yourself. Do you understand?

LEADING MAN. I'm hanged if I do.

THE MANAGER. Neither do I. But let's get on with it. It's sure to be a glorious failure anyway. (*Confidentially.*) But I say, please face three-quarters. Otherwise, what with the abstruseness of the dialogue, and the public that won't be able to hear you, the whole thing will go to hell. Come on! come on!

PROMPTER. Pardon sir, may I get into my box? There's a bit of a draught.

THE MANAGER. Yes, yes, of course!

(*At this point, the Door-Keeper has entered from the stage door and advances towards the Manager's table, taking off his braided cap. During this maneuver, the Six Characters enter, and stop by the door at back of stage, so that when the Door-Keeper is about to announce their coming to the Manager, they are already on the stage. A tenuous light surrounds them, almost as if irradiated by them—the faint breath of their fantastic reality.*

This light will disappear when they come forward towards the actors. They preserve, however, something of the dream lightness in which they seem almost suspended; but this does not detract from the essential reality of their forms and expressions.

He who is known as The Father is a man of about 50: hair, reddish in color, thin at the temples; he is not bald, however; thick moustaches, falling over his still fresh mouth, which often opens in an empty and uncertain smile. He is fattish, pale; with an especially wide forehead. He has blue, oval-shaped eyes, very clear and piercing. Wears light trousers and a dark jacket. He is alternatively mellifluous and violent in his manner.

The Mother seems crushed and terrified as if by an intolerable weight of shame and abasement. She is dressed in modest black and wears a thick widow's veil of crêpe. When she lifts this, she reveals a wax-like face. She always keeps her eyes downcast.

The Stepdaughter is dashing, almost impudent, beautiful. She wears mourning too, but with great elegance. She shows contempt for the timid half-frightened manner of the wretched Boy (14 years old, and also dressed in black): on the other hand, she displays a lively tenderness for her little sister, The Child (about four), who is dressed in white, with a black silk sash at the waist.

The Son (22) is tall, severe in his attitude of contempt for The Father, supercilious and indifferent to The Mother. He looks as if he had come on the stage against his will.)

DOOR-KEEPER (*cap in hand*). Excuse me, sir . . .

THE MANAGER (*rudely*). Eh? What is it?

DOOR-KEEPER (*timidly*). These people are asking for you, sir.

THE MANAGER (*furious*). I am rehearsing, and you know perfectly well no one's allowed to come in during rehearsals! (*Turning to the Characters.*) Who are you, please? What do you want?

THE FATHER (*coming forward a little, followed by the others who seem embarrassed*). As a matter of fact . . . we have come here in search of an author . . .

THE MANAGER (*half angry, half amazed*). An author? What author?

THE FATHER. Any author, sir.

THE MANAGER. But there's no author here. We are not rehearsing a new piece.

THE STEPDAUGHTER (*vivaciously*). So much the better, so much the better! We can be your new piece.

AN ACTOR (*coming forward from the others*). Oh, do you hear that?

THE FATHER (*to Stepdaughter*). Yes, but if the author isn't here . . . (*to Manager*) unless you would be willing . . .

THE MANAGER. You are trying to be funny.

THE FATHER. No, for Heaven's sake, what are you saying? We bring you a drama, sir.

THE STEPDAUGHTER. We may be your fortune.

THE MANAGER. Will you oblige me by going away? We haven't time to waste with mad people.

THE FATHER (*mellifluously*). Oh sir, you know well that life is full of infinite absurdities, which, strangely enough, do not even need to appear plausible, since they are true.

THE MANAGER. What the devil is he talking about?

THE FATHER. I say that to reverse the ordinary process may well be considered a madness: that is, to create credible situations, in order that they may appear true. But permit me to observe that if this be madness, it is the sole *raison d'être*[1] of your profession, gentlemen. (*The Actors look hurt and perplexed.*)

THE MANAGER (*getting up and looking at him*). So our profession seems to you one worthy of madmen then?

THE FATHER. Well, to make seem true that which isn't true . . . without any need . . . for a joke as it were . . . Isn't that your mission, gentlemen: to give life to fantastic characters on the stage?

THE MANAGER (*interpreting the rising anger of the Company*). But I would beg you believe, my dear sir, that the profession of the comedian is a noble one. If today, as

[1] ***raison d'être*** French, "reason for being"

things go, the playwrights give us stupid comedies to play and puppets to represent instead of men, remember we are proud to have given life to immortal works here on these very boards! (*The Actors, satisfied, applaud their Manager.*)

THE FATHER (*interrupting furiously*). Exactly, perfectly, to living beings more alive than those who breathe and wear clothes: beings less real perhaps, but truer! I agree with you entirely. (*The Actors look at one another in amazement.*)

THE MANAGER. But what do you mean? Before, you said . . .

THE FATHER. No, excuse me, I meant it for you, sir, who were crying out that you had no time to lose with madmen, while no one better than yourself knows that nature uses the instrument of human fantasy in order to pursue her high creative purpose.

THE MANAGER. Very well,—but where does all this take us?

THE FATHER. Nowhere! It is merely to show you that one is born to life in many forms, in many shapes, as tree, or as stone, as water, as butterfly, or as woman. So one may also be born a character in a play.

THE MANAGER (*with feigned comic dismay*). So you and these other friends of yours have been born characters?

THE FATHER. Exactly, and alive as you see! (*Manager and Actors burst out laughing.*)

THE FATHER (*hurt*). I am sorry you laugh, because we carry in us a drama, as you can guess from this woman here veiled in black.

THE MANAGER (*losing patience at last and almost indignant*). Oh, chuck it! Get away please! Clear out of here! (*To Property Man.*) For Heaven's sake, turn them out!

THE FATHER (*resisting*). No, no, look here, we . . .

THE MANAGER (*roaring*). We come here to work, you know.

LEADING ACTOR. One cannot let oneself be made such a fool of.

THE FATHER (*determined, coming forward*). I marvel at your incredulity, gentlemen. Are you not accustomed to see the characters created by an author spring to life in yourselves and face each other? Just because there is no "book" (*pointing to the Prompter's box*) which contains us, you refuse to believe . . .

THE STEPDAUGHTER (*advances towards Manager, smiling and coquettish*). Believe me, we are really six most interesting characters, sir; side-tracked however.

THE FATHER. Yes, that is the word! (*To Manager all at once.*) In the sense, that is, that the author who created us alive no longer wished, or was no longer able, materially to put us into a work of art. And this was a real crime, sir; because he who has had the luck to be born a character can laugh even at death. He cannot die. The man, the writer, the instrument of the creation will die, but his creation does not die. And to live for ever, it does not need to have extraordinary gifts or to be able to work wonders. Who was Sancho Panza? Who was Don Abbondio?[2] Yet they live eternally because—live germs as they were—they had the fortune to find a fecundating matrix, a fantasy which could raise and nourish them: make them live for ever!

THE MANAGER. That is quite all right. But what do you want here, all of you?

THE FATHER. We want to live.

THE MANAGER (*ironically*). For Eternity?

THE FATHER. No, sir, only for a moment . . . in you.

AN ACTOR. Just listen to him!

LEADING LADY. They want to live, in us . . . !

JUVENILE LEAD (*pointing to the Stepdaughter*). I've no objection, as far as that one is concerned!

THE FATHER. Look here! look here! The comedy has to be made. (*To the Manager.*) But if you and your actors are willing, we can soon concert it among ourselves.

THE MANAGER (*annoyed*). But what do you want to concert? We don't go in for concerts here. Here we play dramas and comedies!

THE FATHER. Exactly! That is just why we have come to you.

THE MANAGER. And where is the "book"?

THE FATHER. It is in us! (*The Actors laugh.*) The drama is in us, and we are the drama. We are impatient to play it. Our inner passion drives us on to this.

THE STEPDAUGHTER (*disdainful, alluring, treacherous, full of impudence*). My passion, sir! Ah, if you only knew! My passion for him! (*Points to the Father and makes a pretense of embracing him. Then she breaks out into a loud laugh.*)

THE FATHER (*angrily*). Behave yourself! And please don't laugh in that fashion.

THE STEPDAUGHTER. With your permission, gentlemen, I, who am a two months' orphan, will show you how I can dance and sing. (*Sings and then dances* Prenez garde à Tchou-Tchin-Tchou.[3])

Les chinois sont un peuple malin,
De Shangaî à Pékin,

[2]**Sancho Panza . . . Don Abbondio** characters in novels: squire in Cervantes' *Don Quixote* and priest in Manzoni's *I Promessi Sposi* (*The Betrothed*)

[3]***Prenez garde . . . Tchou*** This French popular song is an adaptation of "Chu-Chin Chow," an old Broadway show tune. Translation: "The Chinese are a sly people; / From Shanghai to Peking, / They've stuck up warning signs: / Beware of Tchou-Tchin-Tchou." (This is more amusing in French: *chou* means "cabbage.")

Ils ont mis des écriteaux partout:
Prenez garde à Tchou-Tchin-Tchou.

ACTORS AND ACTRESSES. Bravo! Well done! Tip-top!

THE MANAGER. Silence! This isn't a café concert, you know! (*Turning to the Father in consternation.*) Is she mad?

THE FATHER. Mad? No, she's worse than mad.

THE STEPDAUGHTER (*to Manager*). Worse? Worse? Listen! Stage this drama for us at once! Then you will see that at a certain moment I . . . when this little darling here. . . . (*Takes the Child by the hand and leads her to the Manager.*) Isn't she a dear? (*Takes her up and kisses her.*) Darling! Darling! (*Puts her down again and adds feelingly.*) Well, when God suddenly takes this dear little child away from that poor mother there; and this imbecile here (*seizing hold of the Boy roughly and pushing him forward*) does the stupidest things, like the fool he is, you will see me run away. Yes, gentlemen, I shall be off. But the moment hasn't arrived yet. After what has taken place between him and me (*indicates the Father with a horrible wink*) I can't remain any longer in this society, to have to witness the anguish of this mother here for that fool. . . . (*Indicates the Son.*) Look at him! Look at him! See how indifferent, how frigid he is, because he is the legitimate son. He despises me, despises him (*pointing to the Boy*), despises this baby here; because . . . we are bastards. (*Goes to the Mother and embraces her.*) And he doesn't want to recognize her as his mother—she who is the common mother of us all. He looks down upon her as if she were only the mother of us three bastards. Wretch! (*She says all this very rapidly, excitedly. At the word "bastards" she raises her voice, and almost spits out the final "Wretch!"*)

THE MOTHER (*to the Manager, in anguish*). In the name of these two little children, I beg you. . . . (*She grows faint and is about to fall.*) Oh God!

THE FATHER (*coming forward to support her as do some of the Actors*). Quick, a chair, a chair for this poor widow!

THE ACTORS. Is it true? Has she really fainted?

THE MANAGER. Quick, a chair! Here!

(*One of the Actors brings a chair, the others proffer assistance. The Mother tries to prevent the Father from lifting the veil which covers her face.*)

THE FATHER. Look at her! Look at her!

THE MOTHER. No, no; stop it please!

THE FATHER (*raising her veil*). Let them see you!

THE MOTHER (*rising and covering her face with her hands, in desperation*). I beg you, sir, to prevent this man from carrying out his plan which is loathsome to me.

THE MANAGER (*dumbfounded*). I don't understand at all. What is the situation? (*To the Father.*) Is this lady your wife?

THE FATHER. Yes, gentlemen: my wife!

THE MANAGER. But how can she be a widow if you are alive? (*The Actors find relief for their astonishment in a loud laugh.*)

THE FATHER. Don't laugh! Don't laugh like that, for Heaven's sake. Her drama lies just here in this: she has had a lover, a man who ought to be here.

THE MOTHER (*with a cry*). No! No!

THE STEPDAUGHTER. Fortunately for her, he is dead. Two months ago as I said. We are in mourning, as you see.

THE FATHER. He isn't here, you see, not because he is dead. He isn't here—look at her a moment and you will understand—because her drama isn't a drama of the love of two men for whom she was incapable of feeling anything except possibly a little gratitude—not for me but for the other. She isn't a woman, she is a mother, and her drama—powerful, sir, I assure you—lies, as a matter of fact, all in these four children she has had by two men.

THE MOTHER. I had them? Have you got the courage to say that I wanted them? (*To the Company.*) It was his doing. It was he who gave me that other man, who forced me to go away with him.

THE STEPDAUGHTER. It isn't true.

THE MOTHER (*startled*). Not true, isn't it?

THE STEPDAUGHTER. No, it isn't true, it just isn't true.

THE MOTHER. And what can you know about it?

THE STEPDAUGHTER. It isn't true. Don't believe it. (*To Manager.*) Do you know why she says so? For that fellow there. (*Indicates the Son.*) She tortures herself, destroys herself on account of the neglect of that son there; and she wants him to believe that if she abandoned him when he was only two years old, it was because he (*indicates the Father*) made her do so.

THE MOTHER (*vigorously*). He forced me to it, and I call God to witness it. (*To the Manager.*) Ask him (*indicates Husband*) if it isn't true. Let him speak. You (*to Daughter*) are not in a position to know anything about it.

THE STEPDAUGHTER. I know you lived in peace and happiness with my father while he lived. Can you deny it?

THE MOTHER. No, I don't deny it. . . .

THE STEPDAUGHTER. He was always full of affection and kindness for you. (*To the Boy, angrily.*) It's true, isn't it? Tell them! Why don't you speak, you little fool?

THE MOTHER. Leave the poor boy alone. Why do you want to make me appear ungrateful, daughter? I don't want to offend your father. I have answered him that I didn't abandon my house and my son through any fault of mine, nor from any wilful passion.

THE FATHER. It is true. It was my doing.

LEADING MAN (*to the Company*). What a spectacle!

LEADING LADY. We are the audience this time.

JUVENILE LEAD. For once, in a way.

THE MANAGER (*beginning to get really interested*). Let's hear them out. Listen!

THE SON. Oh yes, you're going to hear a fine bit now. He will talk to you of the Demon of Experiment.

THE FATHER. You are a cynical imbecile. I've told you so already a hundred times. (*To the Manager.*) He tries to make fun of me on account of this expression which I have found to excuse myself with.

THE SON (*with disgust*). Yes, phrases! phrases!

THE FATHER. Phrases! Isn't everyone consoled when faced with a trouble or fact he doesn't understand, by a word, some simple word, which tells us nothing and yet calms us?

THE STEPDAUGHTER. Even in the case of remorse. In fact, especially then.

THE FATHER. Remorse? No, that isn't true. I've done more than use words to quiet the remorse in me.

THE STEPDAUGHTER. Yes, there was a bit of money too. Yes, yes, a bit of money. There were the hundred lire he was about to offer me in payment, gentlemen. . . . (*Sensation of horror among the Actors.*)

THE SON (*to the Stepdaughter*). This is vile.

THE STEPDAUGHTER. Vile? There they were in a pale blue envelope on a little mahogany table in the back of Madame Pace's shop. You know Madame Pace—one of those ladies who attract poor girls of good family into their ateliers, under the pretext of their selling *robes et manteaux.*[4]

THE SON. And he thinks he has bought the right to tyrannize over us all with those hundred lire he was going to pay; but which, fortunately—note this, gentlemen—he had no chance of paying.

THE STEPDAUGHTER. It was a near thing, though, you know! (*Laughs ironically.*)

THE MOTHER (*protesting*). Shame, my daughter, shame!

THE STEPDAUGHTER. Shame indeed! This is my revenge! I am dying to live that scene . . . The room . . . I see it . . . Here is the window with the mantles exposed, there the divan, the looking-glass, a screen, there in front of the window the little mahogany table with the blue envelope containing one hundred lire. I see it. I see it. I could take hold of it. . . . But you, gentlemen, you ought to turn your backs now: I am almost nude, you know. But I don't blush: I leave that to him. (*Indicating Father.*)

THE MANAGER. I don't understand this at all.

THE FATHER. Naturally enough. I would ask you, sir, to exercise your authority a little here, and let me speak before you believe all she is trying to blame me with. Let me explain.

[4] ***robes et manteaux*** French, "dresses and coats"

THE STEPDAUGHTER. Ah yes, explain it in your own way.

THE FATHER. But don't you see that the whole trouble lies here? In words, words. Each one of us has within him a whole world of things, each man of us his own special world. And how can we ever come to an understanding if I put in the words I utter the sense and value of things as I see them; while you who listen to me must inevitably translate them according to the conception of things each one of you has within himself. We think we understand each other, but we never really do. Look here! This woman (*indicating the Mother*) takes all my pity for her as a specially ferocious form of cruelty.

THE MOTHER. But you drove me away.

THE FATHER. Do you hear her? I drove her away! She believes I really sent her away.

THE MOTHER. You know how to talk, and I don't; but, believe me, sir (*to Manager*), after he had married me . . . who knows why? . . . I was a poor insignificant woman. . . .

THE FATHER. But, good Heavens! it was just for your humility that I married you. I loved this simplicity in you. (*He stops when he sees she makes signs to contradict him, opens his arms wide in sign of desperation, seeing how hopeless it is to make himself understood.*) You see she denies it. Her mental deafness, believe me, is phenomenal, the limit: (*touches his forehead*) deaf, deaf, mentally deaf! She has plenty of feeling. Oh yes, a good heart for the children; but the brain—deaf, to the point of desperation—!

THE STEPDAUGHTER. Yes, but ask him how his intelligence has helped us.

THE FATHER. If we could see all the evil that may spring from good, what should we do? (*At this point the Leading Lady, who is biting her lips, with rage at seeing the Leading Man flirting with the Stepdaughter, comes forward and speaks to the Manager.*)

LEADING LADY. Excuse me, but are we going to rehearse today?

MANAGER. Of course, of course; but let's hear them out.

JUVENILE LEAD. This is something quite new.

L'INGÉNUE. Most interesting!

LEADING LADY. Yes, for the people who like that kind of thing. (*Casts a glance at Leading Man.*)

THE MANAGER (*to Father*). You must please explain yourself quite clearly. (*Sits down.*)

THE FATHER. Very well then: listen! I had in my service a poor man, a clerk, a secretary of mine, full of devotion, who became friends with her. (*Indicating the Mother.*) They understood one another, were kindred souls in fact, without, however, the least suspicion of any evil existing. They were incapable even of thinking of it.

THE STEPDAUGHTER. So he thought of it—for them!

THE FATHER. That's not true. I meant to do good to them—and to myself, I confess, at the same time. Things had come to the point that I could not say a word to either of them without their making a mute appeal, one to the other, with their eyes. I could see them silently asking each other how I was to be kept in countenance, how I was to be kept quiet. And this, believe me, was just about enough of itself to keep me in a constant rage, to exasperate me beyond measure.

THE MANAGER. And why didn't you send him away then—this secretary of yours?

THE FATHER. Precisely what I did, sir. And then I had to watch this poor woman drifting forlornly about the house like an animal without a master, like an animal one has taken in out of pity.

THE MOTHER. Ah yes . . . !

THE FATHER (*suddenly turning to the Mother*). It's true about the son anyway, isn't it?

THE MOTHER. He took my son away from me first of all.

THE FATHER. But not from cruelty. I did it so that he should grow up healthy and strong by living in the country.

THE STEPDAUGHTER (*pointing to him ironically*). As one can see.

THE FATHER (*quickly*). Is it my fault if he has grown up like this? I sent him to a wet nurse in the country, a peasant, as *she* did not seem to me strong enough, though she is of humble origin. That was, anyway, the reason I married her. Unpleasant all this may be, but how can it be helped? My mistake possibly, but there we are! All my life I have had these confounded aspirations towards a certain moral sanity. (*At this point the Stepdaughter bursts into a noisy laugh.*) Oh, stop it! Stop it! I can't stand it.

THE MANAGER. Yes, please stop it, for Heaven's sake.

THE STEPDAUGHTER. But imagine moral sanity from him, if you please—the client of certain ateliers like that of Madame Pace!

THE FATHER. Fool! That is the proof that I am a man! This seeming contradiction, gentlemen, is the strongest proof that I stand here a live man before you. Why, it is just for this very incongruity in my nature that I have had to suffer what I have. I could not live by the side of that woman (*indicating the Mother*) any longer; but not so much for the boredom she inspired me with as for the pity I felt for her.

THE MOTHER. And so he turned me out—.

THE FATHER. —well provided for! Yes, I sent her to that man, gentlemen . . . to let her go free of me.

THE MOTHER. And to free himself.

THE FATHER. Yes, I admit it. It was also a liberation for me. But great evil has come of it. I meant well when I did it; and I did it more for her sake than mine. I swear it. (*Crosses his arms on his chest; then turns suddenly to the Mother.*) Did I ever lose sight of you until that other man carried you off to another town, like the angry fool he was? And on account of my pure interest in you . . . my pure interest, I repeat, that had no base motive in it . . . I watched with the tenderest concern the new family that grew up around her. She can bear witness to this. (*Points to the Stepdaughter.*)

THE STEPDAUGHTER. Oh yes, that's true enough. When I was a kiddie, so so high, you know, with plaits over my shoulders and knickers longer than my skirts, I used to see him waiting outside the school for me to come out. He came to see how I was growing up.

THE FATHER. This is infamous, shameful!

THE STEPDAUGHTER. No. Why?

THE FATHER. Infamous! infamous! (*Then excitedly to Manager, explaining.*) After she (*indicating the Mother*) went away, my house seemed suddenly empty. She was my incubus, but she filled my house. I was like a dazed fly alone in the empty rooms. This boy here (*indicating the Son*) was educated away from home, and when he came back, he seemed to me to be no more mine. With no mother to stand between him and me, he grew up entirely for himself, on his own, apart, with no tie of intellect or affection binding him to me. And then—strange but true—I was driven, by curiosity at first and then by some tender sentiment, towards her family, which had come into being through my will. The thought of her began gradually to fill up the emptiness I felt all around me. I wanted to know if she were happy in living out the simple daily duties of life. I wanted to think of her as fortunate and happy because far away from the complicated torments of my spirit. And so, to have proof of this, I used to watch that child coming out of school.

THE STEPDAUGHTER. Yes, yes. True. He used to follow me in the street and smiled at me, waved his hand, like this. I would look at him with interest, wondering who he might be. I told my mother, who guessed at once. (*The Mother agrees with a nod.*) Then she didn't want to send me to school for some days; and when I finally went back, there he was again—looking so ridiculous—with a paper parcel in his hands. He came close to me, caressed me, and drew out a fine straw hat from the parcel, with a bouquet of flowers—all for me!

THE MANAGER. A bit discursive this, you know!

THE SON (*contemptuously*). Literature! Literature!

THE FATHER. Literature indeed! This is life, this is passion!

THE MANAGER. It may be, but it won't act.

THE FATHER. I agree. This is only the part leading up. I don't suggest this should be staged. She (*pointing to the Stepdaughter*), as you see, is no longer the flapper with plaits down her back—

THE STEPDAUGHTER. —and knickers showing below the skirt!

THE FATHER. The drama is coming now, sir; something new, complex, most interesting.

THE STEPDAUGHTER. As soon as my father died . . .

THE FATHER. —there was absolute misery for them. They came back here, unknown to me. Through her stupidity! (*Pointing to the Mother.*) It is true she can barely write her own name; but she could anyhow have got her daughter to write to me that they were in need . . .

THE MOTHER. And how was I to divine all this sentiment in him?

THE FATHER. That is exactly your mistake, never to have guessed any of my sentiments.

THE MOTHER. After so many years apart, and all that had happened . . .

THE FATHER. Was it my fault if that fellow carried you away? It happened quite suddenly; for after he had obtained some job or other, I could find no trace of them; and so, not unnaturally, my interest in them dwindled. But the drama culminated unforeseen and violent on their return, when I was impelled by my miserable flesh that still lives. . . . Ah! what misery, what wretchedness is that of the man who is alone and disdains debasing *liaisons*! Not old enough to do without women, and not young enough to go and look for one without shame. Misery? It's worse than misery; it's a horror; for no woman can any longer give him love; and when a man feels this. . . . One ought to do without, you say? Yes, yes, I know. Each of us when he appears before his fellows is clothed in a certain dignity. But every man knows what unconfessable things pass within the secrecy of his own heart. One gives way to the temptation, only to rise from it again, afterwards, with a great eagerness to re-establish one's dignity, as if it were a tombstone to place on the grave of one's shame, and a monument to hide and sign the memory of our weaknesses. Everybody's in the same case. Some folks haven't the courage to say certain things, that's all!

THE STEPDAUGHTER. All appear to have the courage to do them though.

THE FATHER. Yes, but in secret. Therefore, you want more courage to say these things. Let a man but speak these things out, and folks at once label him a cynic. But it isn't true. He is like all the others, better indeed, because he isn't afraid to reveal with the light of the intelligence the red shame of human bestiality on which most men close their eyes so as not to see it. Woman—for example, look at her case! She turns tantalizing inviting glances on you. You seize her. No sooner does she feel herself in your grasp than she closes her eyes. It is the sign of her mission, the sign by which she says to man: "Blind yourself, for I am blind."

THE STEPDAUGHTER. Sometimes she can close them no more: when she no longer feels the need of hiding her shame to herself, but dry-eyed and dispassionately, sees only that of the man who has blinded himself without love. Oh, all these intellectual complications make me sick, disgust me—all this philosophy that uncovers the beast in man, and then seeks to save him, excuse him . . . I can't stand it, sir. When a man seeks to "simplify" life bestially, throwing aside every relic of humanity, every chaste aspiration, every pure feeling, all sense of ideality, duty, modesty, shame . . . then nothing is more revolting and nauseous than a certain kind of remorse—crocodiles' tears, that's what it is.

THE MANAGER. Let's come to the point. This is only discussion.

THE FATHER. Very good, sir! But a fact is like a sack which won't stand up when it's empty. In order that it may stand up, one has to put into it the reason and sentiment which have caused it to exist. I couldn't possibly know that after the death of that man, they had decided to return here, that they were in misery, and that she (*pointing to the Mother*) had gone to work as a modiste, and at a shop of the type of that of Madame Pace.

THE STEPDAUGHTER. A real high-class modiste, you must know, gentlemen. In appearance, she works for the leaders of the best society; but she arranges matters so that these elegant ladies serve her purpose . . . without prejudice to other ladies who are . . . well . . . only so so.

THE MOTHER. You will believe me, gentlemen, that it never entered my mind that the old hag offered me work because she had her eye on my daughter.

THE STEPDAUGHTER. Poor mamma! Do you know, sir, what that woman did when I brought her back the work my mother had finished? She would point out to me that I had torn one of my frocks, and she would give it back to my mother to mend. It was I who paid for it, always I; while this poor creature here believed she was sacrificing herself for me and these two children here, sitting up at night sewing Madame Pace's robes.

THE MANAGER. And one day you met there . . .

THE STEPDAUGHTER. Him, him. Yes sir, an old client. There's a scene for you to play! Superb!

THE FATHER. She, the Mother arrived just then . . .

THE STEPDAUGHTER (*treacherously*). Almost in time!

THE FATHER (*crying out*). No, in time! in time! Fortunately I recognized her . . . in time. And I took them back home with me to my house. You can imagine now her position and mine; she, as you see her; and I who cannot look her in the face.

THE STEPDAUGHTER. Absurd! How can I possibly be expected—after that—to be a modest young miss, a fit person to go with his confounded aspirations for "a solid moral sanity"?

THE FATHER. For the drama lies all in this—in the conscience that I have, that each one of us has. We believe this conscience to be a single thing, but it is many-sided. There is one for this person, and another for that. Diverse consciences. So we have this illusion of being one person for all, of having a personality that is unique in all our acts. But it isn't true. We perceive this when, tragically perhaps, in something we do, we are as it were, suspended, caught up in the air on a kind of hook. Then we perceive that all of us was not in that act, and that it would be an atrocious injustice to judge us by that action alone, as if all our existence were summed up in that one deed. Now do you understand the perfidy of this girl? She surprised me in a place, where she ought not to have known me, just as I could not exist for her; and she now seeks to attach to me a reality such as I could never suppose I should have to assume for her in a shameful and fleeting moment of my life. I feel this above all else. And the drama, you will see, acquires a tremendous value from this point. Then there is the position of the others . . . his. . . . (*Indicating the Son.*)

THE SON (*shrugging his shoulders scornfully*). Leave me alone! I don't come into this.

THE FATHER. What? You don't come into this?

THE SON. I've got nothing to do with it, and don't want to have; because you know well enough I wasn't made to be mixed up in all this with the rest of you.

THE STEPDAUGHTER. We are only vulgar folk! He is the fine gentleman. You may have noticed, Mr. Manager, that I fix him now and again with a look of scorn while he lowers his eyes—for he knows the evil he has done me.

THE SON (*scarcely looking at her*). I?

THE STEPDAUGHTER. You! you! I owe my life on the streets to you. Did you or did you not deny us, with your behavior, I won't say the intimacy of home, but even that mere hospitality which makes guests feel at their ease? We were intruders who had come to disturb the kingdom of your legitimacy. I should like to have you witness, Mr. Manager, certain scenes between him and me. He says I have tyrannized over everyone. But it was just his behavior which made me insist on the reason for which I had come into the house,—this reason he calls "vile"—into his house, with my mother who is his mother too. And I came as mistress of the house.

THE SON. It's easy for them to put me always in the wrong. But imagine, gentlemen, the position of a son, whose fate it is to see arrive one day at his home a young woman of impudent bearing, a young woman who inquires for his father, with whom who knows what business she has. This young man has then to witness her return bolder than ever, accompanied by that child there. He is obliged to watch her treat his father in an equivocal and confidential manner. She asks for money of him in a way that lets one suppose he must give it to her, *must,* do you understand, because he has every obligation to do so.

THE FATHER. But I have, as a matter of fact, this obligation. I owe it to your mother.

THE SON. How should I know? When had I ever seen or heard of her? One day there arrive with her (*indicating Stepdaughter*) that lady and this baby here. I am told: "This is *your* mother too, you know." I divine from her manner (*indicating Stepdaughter again*) why it is they have come home. I had rather not say what I feel and think about it. I shouldn't even care to confess to myself. No action can therefore be hoped for from me in this affair. Believe me, Mr. Manager, I am an "unrealized" character, dramatically speaking; and I find myself not at all at ease in their company. Leave me out of it, I beg you.

THE FATHER. What? It is just because you are so that . . .

THE SON. How do you know what I am like? When did you ever bother your head about me?

THE FATHER. I admit it. I admit it. But isn't that a situation in itself? This aloofness of yours which is so cruel to me and to your mother, who returns home and sees you almost for the first time grown up, who doesn't recognize you but knows you are her son. . . . (*Pointing out the Mother to the Manager.*) See, she's crying!

THE STEPDAUGHTER (*angrily, stamping her foot*). Like a fool!

THE FATHER (*indicating Stepdaughter*). She can't stand him, you know. (*Then referring again to the Son.*) He says he doesn't come into the affair, whereas he is really the hinge of the whole action. Look at that lad who is always clinging to his mother, frightened and humiliated. It is on account of this fellow here. Possibly his situation is the most painful of all. He feels himself a stranger more than the others. The poor little chap feels mortified, humiliated at being brought into a home out of charity as it were. (*In confidence.*) He is the image of his father. Hardly talks at all. Humble and quiet.

THE MANAGER. Oh, we'll cut him out. You've no notion what a nuisance boys are on the stage. . . .

THE FATHER. He disappears soon, you know. And the baby too. She is the first to vanish from the scene. The drama consists finally in this: when that mother reenters my house, her family born outside of it, and shall we say superimposed on the original, ends with the death of the little girl, the tragedy of the boy and the flight of the elder daughter. It cannot go on, because it is foreign to its surroundings. So after much torment, we three remain: I, the mother, that son. Then, owing to the disappearance of that extraneous family, we too find ourselves strange to one another. We find we are living in an atmosphere of mortal desolation which is the revenge, as he (*indicating Son*) scornfully said of the Demon of Experiment, that unfortunately hides in me. Thus, sir, you see when faith is lacking, it becomes impossible to create certain states of happiness, for we lack the necessary humility. Vaingloriously, we try to substitute ourselves for this faith, creating thus for the rest of the world a reality which we believe after their fashion, while, actually, it doesn't exist. For each one of us has his own reality to be respected before God, even when it is harmful to one's very self.

THE MANAGER. There is something in what you say. I assure you all this interests me very much. I begin to think there's the stuff for a drama in all this, and not a bad drama either.

THE STEPDAUGHTER (*coming forward*). When you've got a character like me . . .

THE FATHER (*shutting her up, all excited to learn the decision of the Manager*). You be quiet!

THE MANAGER (*reflecting, heedless of interruption*). It's new . . . hem . . . yes. . . .

THE FATHER. Absolutely new!

THE MANAGER. You've got a nerve though, I must say, to come here and fling it at me like this . . .

THE FATHER. You will understand, sir, born as we are for the stage . . .

THE MANAGER. Are you amateur actors then?

THE FATHER. No, I say born for the stage, because . . .

THE MANAGER. Oh, nonsense. You're an old hand, you know.

THE FATHER. No sir, no. We act that rôle for which we have been cast, that rôle which we are given in life. And in my own case, passion itself, as usually happens, becomes a trifle theatrical when it is exalted.

THE MANAGER. Well, well, that will do. But you see, without an author. . . . I could give you the address of an author if you like . . .

THE FATHER. No, no. Look here! You must be the author.

THE MANAGER. I? What are you talking about?

THE FATHER. Yes, you, you! Why not?

THE MANAGER. Because I have never been an author: that's why.

THE FATHER. Then why not turn author now? Everybody does it. You don't want any special qualities. Your task is made much easier by the fact that we are all here alive before you. . . .

THE MANAGER. It won't do.

THE FATHER. What? When you see us live our drama. . . .

THE MANAGER. Yes, that's all right. But you want someone to write it.

THE FATHER. No, no. Someone to take it down, possibly, while we play it, scene by scene! It will be enough to sketch it out at first, and then try it over.

THE MANAGER. Well . . . I am almost tempted. It's a bit of an idea. One might have a shot at it.

THE FATHER. Of course. You'll see what scenes will come out of it. I can give you one, at once . . .

THE MANAGER. By Jove, it tempts me. I'd like to have a go at it. Let's try it out. Come with me to my office. (*Turning to the Actors.*) You are at liberty for a bit, but don't step out of the theatre for long. In a quarter of an hour, twenty minutes, all back here again! (*To the Father.*) We'll see what can be done. Who knows if we don't get something really extraordinary out of it?

THE FATHER. There's no doubt about it. They (*indicating the Characters*) had better come with us too, hadn't they?

THE MANAGER. Yes, yes. Come on! come on! (*Moves away and then turning to the Actors.*) Be punctual, please! (*Manager and the Six Characters cross the stage and go off. The other Actors remain, looking at one another in astonishment.*)

LEADING MAN. Is he serious? What the devil does he want to do?

JUVENILE LEAD. This is rank madness.

THIRD ACTOR. Does he expect to knock up a drama in five minutes?

JUVENILE LEAD. Like the improvisers!

LEADING LADY. If he thinks I'm going to take part in a joke like this. . . .

JUVENILE LEAD. I'm out of it anyway.

FOURTH ACTOR. I should like to know who they are. (*Alludes to Characters.*)

THIRD ACTOR. What do you suppose? Madmen or rascals!

JUVENILE LEAD. And he takes them seriously!

L'INGÉNUE. Vanity! He fancies himself as an author now.

LEADING MAN. It's absolutely unheard of. If the stage has come to this . . . well I'm . . .

FIFTH ACTOR. It's rather a joke.

THIRD ACTOR. Well, we'll see what's going to happen next.

(*Thus talking, the Actors leave the stage; some going out by the little door at the back; others retiring to their dressing-rooms.*

The curtain remains up.

The action of the play is suspended for twenty minutes.)

ACT 2

The stage call-bells ring to warn the company that the play is about to begin again.

The Stepdaughter comes out of the Manager's office along with the Child and the Boy. As she comes out of the office, she cries:—

Nonsense! nonsense! Do it yourselves! I'm not going to mix myself up in this mess. (*Turning to the Child and coming quickly with her on to the stage.*) Come on, Rosetta, let's run!

(*The Boy follows them slowly, remaining a little behind and seeming perplexed.*)

THE STEPDAUGHTER (*stops, bends over the Child and takes the latter's face between her hands*). My little darling! You're frightened, aren't you? You don't know where we are, do you? (*Pretending to reply to a question of the Child.*) What is the stage? It's a place, baby, you know, where people play at being serious, a place where they act comedies. We've got to act a comedy now, dead serious, you know; and you're in it also, little one. (*Embraces her, pressing the little head to her breast, and rocking the Child for a moment.*) Oh darling, darling, what a horrid comedy you've got to play! What a wretched part they've found for you! A garden . . . a fountain . . . look . . . just suppose, kiddie, it's here. Where, you say? Why, right here in the middle. It's all pretense you know. That's the trouble, my pet: it's all make-believe here. It's better to imagine it, though, because if they fix it up for you, it'll only be painted cardboard, painted cardboard for the rockery, the water, the plants. . . . Ah, but I think a baby like this one would sooner have a make-believe fountain than a real one, so she could play with it. What a joke it'll be for the others! But for you, alas! not quite such a joke: you who are real, baby dear, and really play by a real fountain that is big and green and beautiful, with ever so many bamboos around it that are reflected in the water, and a whole lot of little ducks swimming about. . . . No, Rosetta, no, your mother doesn't bother about you on account of that wretch of a son there. I'm in the devil of a temper, and as for that lad. . . . (*Seizes Boy by the arm to force him to take one of his hands out of his pockets.*) What have you got there? What are you hiding? (*Pulls his hand out of his pocket, looks into it and catches the glint of a revolver.*) Ah! where did you get this? (*The Boy, very pale in the face, looks at her, but does not answer.*) Idiot! If I'd been in your place, instead of killing myself, I'd have shot one of those two, or both of them: father and son.

(*The Father enters from the office, all excited from his work. The Manager follows him.*)

THE FATHER. Come on, come on dear! Come here for a minute! We've arranged everything. It's all fixed up.

THE MANAGER (*also excited*). If you please, young lady, there are one or two points to settle still. Will you come along?

THE STEPDAUGHTER (*following him towards the office*). Ouff! what's the good, if you've arranged everything.

(*The Father, Manager and Stepdaughter go back into the office again* [*off*] *for a moment. At the same time, the Son, followed by the Mother, comes out.*)

THE SON (*looking at the three entering office*). Oh this is fine, fine! And to think I can't even get away!

(*The Mother attempts to look at him, but lowers her eyes immediately when he turns away from her. She then sits down. The Boy and the Child approach her. She casts a glance again at the Son, and speaks with humble tones, trying to draw him into conversation.*)

THE MOTHER. And isn't my punishment the worst of all? (*Then seeing from the Son's manner that he will not bother himself about her.*) My God! Why are you so cruel? Isn't it enough for one person to support all this torment? Must you then insist on others seeing it also?

THE SON (*half to himself, meaning the Mother to hear, however*). And they want to put it on the stage! If there was at least a reason for it! He thinks he has got at the meaning of it all. Just as if each one of us in every circumstance of life couldn't find his own explanation of it! (*Pauses.*) He complains he was discovered in a place where he ought not to have been seen, in a moment of his life which ought to have remained hidden and kept out of the reach of that convention which he has to maintain for other people. And what about my case? Haven't I had to reveal what no son ought ever to reveal: how father and mother live and are man and wife for themselves quite apart from that idea of father and mother which we give them? When this idea is revealed, our life is then linked at one point only to that man and that woman; and as such it should shame them, shouldn't it?

(*The Mother hides her face in her hands. From the dressing-rooms and the little door at the back of the stage the Actors and Stage Manager return, followed by the Property Man, and the Prompter. At the same moment, the Manager comes out of his office, accompanied by the Father and the Stepdaughter.*)

THE MANAGER. Come on, come on, ladies and gentlemen! Heh! you there, machinist!

MACHINIST. Yes sir?

THE MANAGER. Fix up the parlor with the floral decorations. Two wings and a drop with a door will do. Hurry up!

(*The Machinist runs off at once to prepare the scene, and arranges it while the Manager talks with the Stage Manager, the Property Man, and the Prompter on matters of detail.*)

THE MANAGER (*to Property Man*). Just have a look, and see if there isn't a sofa or a divan in the wardrobe . . .

PROPERTY MAN. There's the green one.

THE STEPDAUGHTER. No no! Green won't do. It was yellow, ornamented with flowers—very large! and most comfortable!

PROPERTY MAN. There isn't one like that.

THE MANAGER. It doesn't matter. Use the one we've got.

THE STEPDAUGHTER. Doesn't matter? It's most important!

THE MANAGER. We're only trying it now. Please don't interfere. (*To Property Man.*) See if we've got a shop window—long and narrowish.

THE STEPDAUGHTER. And the little table! The little mahogany table for the pale blue envelope!

PROPERTY MAN (*to Manager*). There's that little gilt one.

THE MANAGER. That'll do fine.

THE FATHER. A mirror.

THE STEPDAUGHTER. And the screen! We must have a screen. Otherwise how can I manage?

PROPERTY MAN. That's all right, Miss. We've got any amount of them.

THE MANAGER (*to the Stepdaughter*). We want some clothes pegs too, don't we?

THE STEPDAUGHTER. Yes, several, several!

THE MANAGER. See how many we've got and bring them all.

PROPERTY MAN. All right!

(*The Property Man hurries off to obey his orders. While he is putting the things in their places, the Manager talks to the Prompter and then with the Characters and the Actors.*)

THE MANAGER (*to Prompter*). Take your seat. Look here: this is the outline of the scenes, act by act. (*Hands him some sheets of paper.*) And now I'm going to ask you to do something out of the ordinary.

PROMPTER. Take it down in shorthand?

THE MANAGER (*pleasantly surprised*). Exactly! Can you do shorthand?

PROMPTER. Yes, a little.

THE MANAGER. Good! (*Turning to a Stage Hand.*) Go and get some paper from my office, plenty, as much as you can find.

(*The Stage Hand goes off, and soon returns with a handful of paper which he gives to the Prompter.*)

THE MANAGER (*to Prompter*). You follow the scenes as we play them, and try and get the points down, at any rate the most important ones. (*Then addressing the Actors.*) Clear the stage, ladies and gentlemen! Come over here (*pointing to the left*) and listen attentively.

LEADING LADY. But, excuse me, we . . .

THE MANAGER (*guessing her thought*). Don't worry! You won't have to improvise.

LEADING MAN. What have we to do then?

THE MANAGER. Nothing. For the moment you just watch and listen. Everybody will get his part written out afterwards. At present we're going to try the thing as best we can. They're going to act now.

THE FATHER (*as if fallen from the clouds into the confusion of the stage*). We? What do you mean, if you please, by a rehearsal?

THE MANAGER. A rehearsal for them. (*Points to the Actors.*)

THE FATHER. But since we are the characters . . .

THE MANAGER. All right: "characters" then, if you insist on calling yourselves such. But here, my dear sir, the characters don't act. Here the actors do the acting. The characters are there, in the "book" (*pointing towards Prompter's box*)—when there is a "book"!

THE FATHER. I won't contradict you; but excuse me, the actors aren't the characters. They want to be, they pretend to be, don't they? Now if these gentlemen here are fortunate enough to have us alive before them . . .

THE MANAGER. Oh, this is grand! You want to come before the public yourselves then?

THE FATHER. As we are. . . .

THE MANAGER. I can assure you it would be a magnificent spectacle!

LEADING MAN. What's the use of us here anyway then?

THE MANAGER. You're not going to pretend that you can act? It makes me laugh! (*The Actors laugh.*) There, you see, they are laughing at the notion. But, by the way, I must cast the parts. That won't be difficult. They cast themselves. (*To the Second Lady Lead.*) You play the Mother. (*To the Father.*) We must find her a name.

THE FATHER. Amalia, sir.

THE MANAGER. But that is the real name of your wife. We don't want to call her by her real name.

THE FATHER. Why ever not, if it is her name? . . . Still, perhaps, if that lady must . . . (*Makes a slight motion of the hand to indicate the Second Lady Lead.*) I see this woman here (*means the Mother*) as Amalia. But do as you like. (*Gets more and more confused.*) I don't know what to say to you. Already, I begin to hear my own words ring false, as if they had another sound . . .

THE MANAGER. Don't you worry about it. It'll be our job to find the right tones. And as for her name, if you want her Amalia, Amalia it shall be; and if you don't like it, we'll find another! For the moment though, we'll call the characters in this way: (*To Juvenile Lead.*) You are the Son. (*To the Leading Lady.*) You naturally are the Stepdaughter. . . .

THE STEPDAUGHTER (*excitedly*). What? what? I, that woman there? (*Bursts out laughing.*)

THE MANAGER (*angry*). What is there to laugh at?

LEADING LADY (*indignant*). Nobody has ever dared to laugh at me. I insist on being treated with respect; otherwise I go away.

THE STEPDAUGHTER. No, no, excuse me . . . I am not laughing at you. . . .

THE MANAGER (*to Stepdaughter*). You ought to feel honored to be played by . . .

LEADING LADY (*at once, contemptuously*). "That woman there" . . .

THE STEPDAUGHTER. But I wasn't speaking of you, you know. I was speaking of myself—whom I can't see at all in you! That is all. I don't know . . . but . . . you . . . aren't in the least like me. . . .

THE FATHER. True: Here's the point. Look here, sir, our temperaments, our souls. . . .

THE MANAGER. Temperament, soul, be hanged! Do you suppose the spirit of the piece is in you? Nothing of the kind!

THE FATHER. What, haven't we our own temperaments, our own souls?

THE MANAGER. Not at all. Your soul or whatever you like to call it takes shape here. The actors give body and form to it, voice and gesture. And my actors—I may tell you—have given expression to much more lofty material than this little drama of yours, which may or may not hold up on the stage. But if it does, the merit of it, believe me, will be due to my actors.

THE FATHER. I don't dare contradict you, sir; but, believe me, it is a terrible suffering for us who are as we are, with these bodies of ours, these features to see. . . .

THE MANAGER (*cutting him short and out of patience*). Good heavens! The make-up will remedy all that, man, the make-up. . . .

THE FATHER. Maybe. But the voice, the gestures . . .

THE MANAGER. Now, look here! On the stage, you as yourself, cannot exist. The actor here acts you, and that's an end to it!

THE FATHER. I understand. And now I think I see why our author who conceived us as we are, all alive, didn't want to put us on the stage after all. I haven't the least desire to offend your actors. Far from it! But when I think that I am to be acted by . . . I don't know by whom. . . .

LEADING MAN (*on his dignity*). By me, if you've no objection!

THE FATHER (*humbly, mellifluously*). Honored, I assure you, sir. (*Bows.*) Still, I must say that try as this gentleman may, with all his good will and wonderful art, to absorb me into himself. . . .

LEADING MAN. Oh chuck it! "Wonderful art!" Withdraw that, please!

THE FATHER. The performance he will give, even doing his best with make-up to look like me. . . .

LEADING MAN. It will certainly be a bit difficult! (*The Actors laugh.*)

THE FATHER. Exactly! It will be difficult to act me as I really am. The effect will be rather—apart from the make-up—according as to how he supposes I am, as he senses me—if he does sense me—and not as I inside of myself feel myself to be. It seems to me then that account should be taken of this by everyone whose duty it may become to criticize us. . . .

THE MANAGER. Heavens! The man's starting to think about the critics now! Let them say what they like. It's up to us to put on the play if we can. (*Looking around.*) Come on! come on! Is the stage set? (*To the Actors and Characters.*) Stand back—stand back! Let me see, and don't let's lose any more time! (*To the Stepdaughter.*) Is it all right as it is now?

THE STEPDAUGHTER. Well, to tell the truth, I don't recognize the scene.

THE MANAGER. My dear lady, you can't possibly suppose that we can construct that shop of Madame Pace piece by piece here? (*To the Father.*) You said a white room with flowered wall paper, didn't you?

THE FATHER. Yes.

THE MANAGER. Well then. We've got the furniture right more or less. Bring that little table a bit further forward. (*The Stage Hands obey the order. To Property Man.*) You go and find an envelope, if possible, a pale blue one; and give it to that gentleman. (*Indicates Father.*)

PROPERTY MAN. An ordinary envelope?

MANAGER AND FATHER. Yes, yes, an ordinary envelope.

PROPERTY MAN. At once, sir. (*Exit.*)

THE MANAGER. Ready, everyone! First scene—the Young Lady. (*The Leading Lady comes forward.*) No, no, you must wait. I meant her. (*Indicating the Stepdaughter.*) You just watch—

THE STEPDAUGHTER (*adding at once*). How I shall play it, how I shall live it! . . .

LEADING LADY (*offended*). I shall live it also, you may be sure, as soon as I begin!

THE MANAGER (*with his hands to his head*). Ladies and gentlemen, if you please! No more useless discussions! Scene I: the Young Lady with Madame Pace: Oh! (*Looks around as if lost.*) And this Madame Pace, where is she?

THE FATHER. She isn't with us, sir.

THE MANAGER. Then what the devil's to be done?

THE FATHER. But she is alive too.

THE MANAGER.Yes, but where is she?

THE FATHER. One minute. Let me speak! (*Turning to the Actresses.*) If these ladies would be so good as to give me their hats for a moment. . . .

THE ACTRESSES (*half surprised, half laughing, in chorus*). What? Why? Our hats? What does he say?

THE MANAGER. What are you going to do with the ladies' hats? (*The Actors laugh.*)

THE FATHER. Oh nothing. I just want to put them on these pegs for a moment. And one of the ladies will be so kind as to take off her mantle. . . .

THE ACTORS. Oh, what d'you think of that? Only the mantle? He must be mad.

SOME ACTRESSES. But why? Mantles as well?

THE FATHER. To hang them up here for a moment. Please be so kind, will you?

THE ACTRESSES (*taking off their hats, one or two also their cloaks, and going to hang them on the racks*). After all, why not? There you are! This is really funny. We've got to put them on show.

THE FATHER. Exactly; just like that, on show.

THE MANAGER. May we know why?

THE FATHER. I'll tell you. Who knows if, by arranging the stage for her, she does not come here herself, attracted by the very articles of her trade? (*Inviting the Actors to look towards the exit at back of stage.*) Look! Look!

(*The door at the back of stage opens and Madame Pace enters and takes a few steps forward. She is a fat, oldish woman with puffy oxygenated hair. She is rouged and powdered, dressed with a comical elegance in black silk. Round her waist is a long silver chain from which hangs a pair of scissors. The Stepdaughter runs over to her at once amid the stupor of the Actors.*)

THE STEPDAUGHTER (*turning towards her*). There she is! There she is!

THE FATHER (*radiant*). It's she! I said so, didn't I! There she is!

THE MANAGER (*conquering his surprise, and then becoming indignant*). What sort of a trick is this?

LEADING MAN (*almost at the same time*). What's going to happen next?

JUVENILE LEAD. Where does *she* come from?

L'INGÉNUE. They've been holding her in reserve, I guess.

THE LEADING LADY. A vulgar trick!

THE FATHER (*dominating the protests*). Excuse me, all of you! Why are you so anxious to destroy in the name of a vulgar, commonplace sense of truth, this reality which comes to birth attracted and formed by the magic of the stage itself, which has indeed more right to live here than you, since it is much truer than you—if you don't mind my saying so? Which is the actress among you who is to play Madame Pace? Well, here is Madame Pace herself. And you will allow, I fancy, that the actress who acts her will be less true than this woman here, who is herself in person. You see my daughter recognized her and went over to her at once. Now you're going to witness the scene!

(*But the scene between the Stepdaughter and Madame Pace has already begun despite the protest of the Actors and the reply of the Father. It has begun quietly, naturally, in a manner impossible for the stage. So when the Actors, called to attention by the Father, turn round and see Madame Pace, who has placed one hand under the Stepdaughter's chin to raise her head, they observe her at first with great attention, but hearing her speak in an unintelligible manner their interest begins to wane.*)

THE MANAGER. Well? well?

LEADING MAN. What does she say?

LEADING LADY. One can't hear a word.

JUVENILE LEAD. Louder! Louder please!

THE STEPDAUGHTER (*leaving Madame Pace, who smiles a Sphinx-like smile, and advancing towards the Actors*). Louder? Louder? What are you talking about? These aren't matters which can be shouted at the top of one's voice. If I have spoken them out loud, it was to shame him and have my revenge. (*Indicates Father.*) But for Madame it's quite a different matter.

THE MANAGER. Indeed? indeed? But here, you know, people have got to make themselves heard, my dear. Even we who are on the stage can't hear you. What will it be when the public's in the theatre? And anyway, you can very well speak up now among yourselves, since we shan't be present to listen to you as we are now. You've got to pretend to be alone in a room at the back of a shop where no one can hear you.

(*The Stepdaughter coquettishly and with a touch of malice makes a sign of disagreement two or three times with her finger.*)

THE MANAGER. What do you mean by no?

THE STEPDAUGHTER (*sotto voce, mysteriously*). There's someone who will hear us if she (*indicating Madame Pace*) speaks out loud.

THE MANAGER (*in consternation*). What? Have you got someone else to spring on us now? (*The Actors burst out laughing.*)

THE FATHER. No, no sir. She is alluding to me. I've got to be here—there behind that door, in waiting; and Madame Pace knows it. In fact, if you will allow me, I'll go there at once, so I can be ready. (*Moves away.*)

THE MANAGER (*stopping him*). No! Wait! wait! We

must observe the conventions of the theatre. Before you are ready. . . .

THE STEPDAUGHTER (*interrupting him*). No, get on with it at once! I'm just dying, I tell you, to act this scene. If he's ready, I'm more than ready.

THE MANAGER (*shouting*). But, my dear young lady, first of all, we must have the scene between you and this lady. . . . (*Indicates Madame Pace.*) Do you understand? . . .

THE STEPDAUGHTER. Good Heavens! She's been telling me what you know already: that mama's work is badly done again, that the material's ruined; and that if I want her to continue to help us in our misery I must be patient. . . .

MADAME PACE (*coming forward with an air of great importance*). Yes indeed, sir, I no wanta take advantage of her, no wanta be hard. . . .

(*Note: Madame Pace is supposed to talk in a jargon half Italian, half English.*)

THE MANAGER (*alarmed*). What? What? She talks like that? (*The Actors burst out laughing again.*)

THE STEPDAUGHTER (*also laughing*). Yes yes, that's the way she talks, half English, half Italian! Most comical it is!

MADAME PACE. Itta seem not verra polite gentlemen laugha atta me eeff I trya best speaka English.

THE MANAGER. *Diamine!*[5] Of course! Of course! Let her talk like that! Just what we want. Talk just like that, Madame, if you please! The effect will be certain. Exactly what was wanted to put a little comic relief into the crudity of the situation. Of course she talks like that! Magnificent!

THE STEPDAUGHTER. Magnificent? Certainly! When certain suggestions are made to one in language of that kind, the effect is certain, since it seems almost a joke. One feels inclined to laugh when one hears her talk about an "old signore" "who wanta talka nicely with you." Nice old signore, eh, Madame?

MADAME PACE. Not so old my dear, not so old! And even if you no lika him, he won't make any scandal!

THE MOTHER (*jumping up amid the amazement and consternation of the Actors, who had not been noticing her. They move to restrain her.*). You old devil! You murderess!

THE STEPDAUGHTER (*running over to calm her Mother*). Calm yourself, Mother, calm yourself! Please don't. . . .

THE FATHER (*going to her also at the same time*). Calm yourself! Don't get excited! Sit down now!

THE MOTHER. Well then, take that woman away out of my sight!

THE STEPDAUGHTER (*to Manager*). It is impossible for my mother to remain here.

THE FATHER (*to Manager*). They can't be here together. And for this reason, you see: that woman there was not with us when we came. . . . If they are on together, the whole thing is given away inevitably, as you see.

THE MANAGER. It doesn't matter. This is only a first rough sketch—just to get an idea of the various points of the scene, even confusedly. . . . (*Turning to the Mother and leading her to her chair.*) Come along, my dear lady, sit down now, and let's get on with the scene. . . .

Meanwhile, the Stepdaughter, coming forward again, turns to Madame Pace.

THE STEPDAUGHTER. Come on, Madame, come on!

MADAME PACE (*offended*). No, no, *grazie*. I do not do anything witha your mother present.

THE STEPDAUGHTER. Nonsense! Introduce this "old signore" who wants to talk nicely to me. (*Addressing the Company imperiously.*) We've got to do this scene one way or another, haven't we? Come on! (*To Madame Pace.*) You can go!

MADAME PACE. Ah yes! I go 'way! I go 'way! Certainly! (*Exits furious.*)

THE STEPDAUGHTER (*to the Father*). Now you make your entry. No, you needn't go over there. Come here. Let's suppose you've already come in. Like that, yes! I'm here with bowed head, modest like. Come on! Out with your voice! Say "Good morning, Miss" in that peculiar tone, that special tone. . . .

THE MANAGER. Excuse me, but are you the Manager, or am I? (*To the Father who looks undecided and perplexed.*) Get on with it, man! Go down there to the back of the stage. You needn't go off. Then come right forward here.

(*The Father does as he is told, looking troubled and perplexed at first. But as soon as he begins to move, the reality of the action affects him, and he begins to smile and to be more natural. The Actors watch intently.*)

THE MANAGER (*sotto voce, quickly to the Prompter in his box*). Ready! ready! Get ready to write now.

THE FATHER (*coming forward and speaking in a different tone*). Good afternoon, Miss!

THE STEPDAUGHTER (*head bowed down slightly, with restrained disgust*). Good afternoon!

THE FATHER (*looks under her hat which partly covers her face. Perceiving she is very young, he makes an exclamation, partly of surprise, partly of fear lest he compromise himself in a risky adventure*). Ah . . . but . . . ah . . . I say . . . this is not the first time that you have come here, is it?

THE STEPDAUGHTER (*modestly*). No sir.

THE FATHER. You've been here before, eh? (*Then seeing her nod agreement.*) More than once? (*Waits for her to answer, looks under her hat, smiles, and then says:*) Well then, there's no need to be so shy, is there? May I take off your hat?

[5] ***Diamine*** Italian, "I'll be damned!"

THE STEPDAUGHTER (*anticipating him and with veiled disgust*). No sir . . . I'll do it myself. (*Takes it off quickly.*)

(*The Mother, who watches the progress of the scene with the Son and the other two children who cling to her, is on thorns; and follows with varying expressions of sorrow, indignation, anxiety, and horror the words and actions of the other two. From time to time she hides her face in her hands and sobs.*)

THE MOTHER. Oh, my God, my God!

THE FATHER (*playing his part with a touch of gallantry*). Give it to me! I'll put it down. (*Takes hat from her hands.*) But a dear little head like yours ought to have a smarter hat. Come and help me choose one from the stock, won't you?

L'INGÉNUE (*interrupting*). I say . . . those are our hats you know.

THE MANAGER (*furious*). Silence! silence! Don't try and be funny, if you please.... We're playing the scene now, I'd have you notice. (*To the Stepdaughter.*) Begin again, please!

THE STEPDAUGHTER (*continuing*). No thank you, sir.

THE FATHER. Oh, come now. Don't talk like that. You must take it. I shall be upset if you don't. There are some lovely little hats here; and then—Madame will be pleased. She expects it, anyway, you know.

THE STEPDAUGHTER. No, no! I couldn't wear it!

THE FATHER. Oh, you're thinking about what they'd say at home if they saw you come in with a new hat? My dear girl, there's always a way round these little matters, you know.

THE STEPDAUGHTER (*all keyed up*). No, it's not that. I couldn't wear it because I am . . . as you see . . . you might have noticed . . .

(*Showing her black dress.*)

THE FATHER. . . . in mourning! Of course: I beg your pardon: I'm frightfully sorry....

THE STEPDAUGHTER (*forcing herself to conquer her indignation and nausea*). Stop! Stop! It's I who must thank you. There's no need for you to feel mortified or specially sorry. Don't think any more of what I've said. (*Tries to smile.*) I must forget that I am dressed so....

THE MANAGER (*interrupting and turning to the Prompter.*) Stop a minute! Stop! Don't write that down. Cut out that last bit. (*Then to the Father and Stepdaughter.*) Fine! it's going fine! (*To the Father only.*) And now you can go on as we arranged. (*To the Actors.*) Pretty good that scene, where he offers her the hat, eh?

THE STEPDAUGHTER. The best's coming now. Why can't we go on?

THE MANAGER. Have a little patience! (*To the Actors.*) Of course, it must be treated rather lightly.

LEADING MAN. Still, with a bit of go in it!

LEADING LADY. Of course! It's easy enough! (*To Leading Man.*) Shall you and I try it now?

LEADING MAN. Why, yes! I'll prepare my entrance. (*Exit in order to make his entrance.*)

THE MANAGER (*to Leading Lady*). See here! The scene between you and Madame Pace is finished. I'll have it written out properly after. You remain here . . . oh, where are you going?

LEADING LADY. One minute. I want to put my hat on again. (*Goes over to hat-rack and puts her hat on her head.*)

THE MANAGER. Good! You stay here with your head bowed down a bit.

THE STEPDAUGHTER. But she isn't dressed in black.

LEADING LADY. But I shall be, and much more effectively than you.

THE MANAGER (*to Stepdaughter*). Be quiet please, and watch! You'll be able to learn something. (*Clapping his hands.*) Come on! come on! Entrance, please!

(*The door at rear of stage opens, and the Leading Man enters with the lively manner of an old gallant. The rendering of the scene by the Actors from the very first words is seen to be quite a different thing, though it has not in any way the air of a parody. Naturally, the Stepdaughter and the Father, not being able to recognize themselves in the Leading Lady and the Leading Man, who deliver their words in different tones and with a different psychology, express, sometimes with smiles, sometimes with gestures, the impression they receive.*)

LEADING MAN. Good afternoon, Miss....

THE FATHER (*at once unable to contain himself*). No!

(*The Stepdaughter, noticing the way the Leading Man enters, bursts out laughing.*)

THE MANAGER (*furious*). Silence! and you please just stop that laughing. If we go on like this, we shall never finish.

THE STEPDAUGHTER. Forgive me, sir, but it's natural enough. This lady (*indicating Leading Lady*) stands there still; but if she is supposed to be me, I can assure you that if I heard anyone say "Good afternoon" in that manner and in that tone, I should burst out laughing as I did.

THE FATHER. Yes, yes; the manner, the tone....

THE MANAGER. Nonsense! Rubbish! Stand aside and let me see the action.

LEADING MAN. If I've got to represent an old fellow who's coming into a house of an equivocal character....

THE MANAGER. Don't listen to them, for Heaven's sake! Do it again! It goes fine. (*Waiting for the Actors to begin again.*) Well?

LEADING MAN. Good afternoon, Miss.

LEADING LADY. Good afternoon.

LEADING MAN (*imitating the gesture of the Father when he looked under the hat, and then expressing quite clearly first satisfaction and then fear*). Ah, but . . . I say . . . this is not the first time that you have come here, is it?

THE MANAGER. Good, but not quite so heavily. Like this. (*Acts himself.*) "This isn't the first time you have come here" . . . (*To Leading Lady.*) And you say: "No sir.

LEADING LADY. No, sir.

LEADING MAN. You've been here before, more than once.

THE MANAGER. No, no, stop! Let her nod "yes" first. "You've been here before, eh?"

(*The Leading Lady lifts up her head slightly and closes her eyes as though in disgust. Then she inclines her head twice.*)

THE STEPDAUGHTER (*unable to contain herself*). Oh my God! (*Puts a hand to her mouth to prevent herself from laughing.*)

THE MANAGER (*turning round*). What's the matter?

THE STEPDAUGHTER. Nothing, nothing!

THE MANAGER (*to Leading Man*). Go on!

LEADING MAN. You've been here before, eh? Well then, there's no need to be shy, is there? May I take off your hat?

(*The Leading Man says this last speech in such a tone and with such gestures that the Stepdaughter, though she has her hand to her mouth, cannot keep from laughing.*)

LEADING LADY (*indignant*). I'm not going to stop here to be made a fool of by that woman there.

LEADING MAN. Neither am I! I'm through with it!

THE MANAGER (*shouting to Stepdaughter*). Silence! for once and all, I tell you!

THE STEPDAUGHTER. Forgive me! forgive me!

THE MANAGER. You haven't any manners: that's what it is! You go too far.

THE FATHER (*endeavoring to intervene*). Yes, it's true, but excuse her. . . .

THE MANAGER. Excuse what? It's absolutely disgusting.

THE FATHER. Yes, sir, but believe me, it has such a strange effect when . . .

THE MANAGER. Strange? Why strange? Where is it strange?

THE FATHER. No, Sir; I admire your actors—this gentleman here, this lady; but they are certainly not us!

THE MANAGER. I should hope not. Evidently they cannot be you, if they are actors.

THE FATHER. Just so: actors! Both of them act our parts exceedingly well. But, believe me, it produces quite a different effect on us. They want to be us, but they aren't, all the same.

THE MANAGER. What is it then anyway?

THE FATHER. Something that is . . . that is theirs—and no longer ours . . .

THE MANAGER. But naturally, inevitably. I've told you so already.

THE FATHER. Yes, I understand . . . I understand . . .

THE MANAGER. Well then, let's have no more of it! (*Turning to the Actors.*) We'll have the rehearsals by ourselves, afterwards, in the ordinary way. I never could stand rehearsing with the author present. He's never satisfied! (*Turning to Father and Stepdaughter.*) Come on! Let's get on with it again; and try and see if you can't keep from laughing.

THE STEPDAUGHTER. Oh, I shan't laugh any more. There's a nice little bit coming from me now: you'll see.

THE MANAGER. Well then: when she says "Don't think any more of what I've said, I must forget, etc.," you (*addressing the Father*) come in sharp with "I understand"; and then you ask her . . .

THE STEPDAUGHTER (*interrupting*). What?

THE MANAGER. Why she is in mourning.

THE STEPDAUGHTER. Not at all! See here: when I told him that it was useless for me to be thinking about my wearing mourning, do you know how he answered me? "Ah well," he said, "then let's take off this little frock."

THE MANAGER. Great! Just what we want, to make a riot in the theater!

THE STEPDAUGHTER. But it's the truth!

THE MANAGER. What does that matter? Acting is our business here. Truth up to a certain point, but no further.

THE STEPDAUGHTER. What do you want to do then?

THE MANAGER. You'll see, you'll see! Leave it to me.

THE STEPDAUGHTER. No sir! What you want to do is to piece together a little romantic sentimental scene out of my disgust, out of all the reasons, each more cruel and viler than the other, why I am what I am. He is to ask me why I'm in mourning; and I'm to answer with tears in my eyes, that it is just two months since papa died. No sir, no! He's got to say to me, as he did say, "Well, let's take off this little dress at once." And I, with my two months' mourning in my heart, went there behind that screen, and with these fingers tingling with shame . . .

THE MANAGER (*running his hands through his hair*). For Heaven's sake! What are you saying?

THE STEPDAUGHTER (*crying out excitedly*). The truth! The truth!

THE MANAGER. It may be. I don't deny it, and I can understand all your horror; but you must surely see that you can't have this kind of thing on the stage. It won't go.

THE STEPDAUGHTER. Not possible, eh? Very well! I'm much obliged to you—but I'm off.

THE MANAGER. Now be reasonable! Don't lose your temper!

THE STEPDAUGHTER. I won't stop here! I won't! I can see you fixed it all up with him in your office. All this talk about what is possible for the stage . . . I understand! He wants to get at his complicated "cerebral drama," to have his famous remorses and torments acted; but I want to act my part, *my part!*

THE MANAGER (*annoyed, shaking his shoulders*). Ah! Just *your* part! But, if you will pardon me, there are other parts than yours: His (*indicating the Father*) and hers (*indicating the Mother*)! On the stage you can't have a character becoming too prominent and overshadowing all the others. The thing is to pack them all into a neat little framework and then act what is actable. I am aware of the fact that everyone has his own interior life which he wants very much to put forward. But the difficulty lies in this fact: to set out just so much as is necessary for the stage, taking the other characters into consideration, and at the same time hint at the unrevealed interior life of each. I am willing to admit, my dear young lady, that from your point of view it would be a fine idea if each character could tell the public all his troubles in a nice monologue or a regular one-hour lecture. (*Good humoredly.*) You must restrain yourself, my dear, and in your own interest, too; because this fury of yours, this exaggerated disgust you show, may make a bad impression, you know. After you have confessed to me that there were others before him at Madame Pace's and more than once . . .

THE STEPDAUGHTER (*bowing her head, impressed*). It's true. But remember those others mean him for me all the same.

THE MANAGER (*not understanding*). What? The others? What do you mean?

THE STEPDAUGHTER. For one who has gone wrong, sir, he who was responsible for the first fault is responsible for all that follow. He is responsible for my faults, was, even before I was born. Look at him, and see if it isn't true!

THE MANAGER. Well, well! And does the weight of so much responsibility seem nothing to you? Give him a chance to act it, to get it over!

THE STEPDAUGHTER. How? How can he act all his "noble remorses," all his "moral torments," if you want to spare him the horror of being discovered one day—after he had asked her what he did ask her—in the arms of her, that already fallen woman, that child, sir, that child he used to watch come out of school? (*She is moved.*)

(*The Mother at this point is overcome with emotion, and breaks out into a fit of crying. All are touched. A long pause.*)

THE STEPDAUGHTER (*as soon as the Mother becomes a little quieter, adds resolutely and gravely*). At present, we are unknown to the public. Tomorrow, you will act us as you wish, treating us in your own manner. But do you really want to see drama, do you want to see it flash out as it really did?

THE MANAGER. Of course! That's just what I do want, so I can use as much of it as is possible.

THE STEPDAUGHTER. Well then, ask that Mother there to leave us.

THE MOTHER (*changing her low plaint into a sharp cry*). No! No! Don't permit it, sir, don't permit it!

THE MANAGER. But it's only to try it.

THE MOTHER. I can't bear it. I can't.

THE MANAGER. But since it has happened already . . . I don't understand!

THE MOTHER. It's taking place now. It happens all the time. My torment isn't a pretended one. I live and feel every minute of my torture. Those two children there—have you heard them speak? They can't speak any more. They cling to me to keep my torment actual and vivid for me. But for themselves, they do not exist, they aren't any more. And she (*indicating the Stepdaughter*) has run away, she has left me, and is lost. If I now see her here before me, it is only to renew for me the tortures I have suffered for her too.

THE FATHER. The eternal moment! She (*indicating the Stepdaughter*) is here to catch me, fix me, and hold me eternally in the stocks for that one fleeting and shameful moment of my life. She can't give it up! And you, sir, cannot either fairly spare me it.

THE MANAGER. I never said I didn't want to act it. It will form, as a matter of fact, the nucleus of the whole first act right up to her surprise. (*Indicates the Mother.*)

THE FATHER. Just so! This is my punishment: the passion in all of us that must culminate in her final cry.

THE STEPDAUGHTER. I can hear it still in my ears. It's driven me mad, that cry!—You can put me on as you like; it doesn't matter. Fully dressed, if you like—provided I have at least the arm bare; because, standing like this (*she goes close to the Father and leans her head on his breast*) with my head so, and my arms round his neck, I saw a vein pulsing in my arm here; and then, as if that live vein had awakened disgust in me, I closed my eyes like this, and let my head sink on his breast. (*Turning to the Mother.*) Cry out, mother! Cry out! (*Buries head in Father's breast, and with her shoulders raised as if to prevent her hearing the cry, adds in tones of intense emotion:*) Cry out as you did then!

THE MOTHER (*coming forward to separate them*). No! My daughter, my daughter! (*And after having pulled her away from him.*) You brute! you brute! She is my daughter! Don't you see she's my daughter?

THE MANAGER (*walking backwards towards footlights*). Fine! fine! Damned good! And then, of course—curtain!

THE FATHER (*going towards him excitedly*). Yes, of course, because that's the way it really happened.

THE MANAGER (*convinced and pleased*). Oh, yes, no doubt about it. Curtain here, curtain!

(*At the reiterated cry of the Manager, the Machinist lets the curtain down, leaving the Manager and the Father in front of it before the footlights.*)

THE MANAGER. The darned idiot! I said "curtain" to show the act should end there, and he goes and lets it down in earnest. (*To the Father, while he pulls the curtain back to go on to the stage again.*) Yes, yes, it's all right. Effect certain! That's the right ending. I'll guarantee the first act at any rate.

ACT 3

When the curtain goes up again, it is seen that the Stage Hands have shifted the bit of scenery used in the last part, and have rigged up instead at the back of the stage a drop, with some trees, and one or two wings. A portion of a fountain basin is visible. The Mother is sitting on the right with the two children by her side. The Son is on the same side, but away from the others. He seems bored, angry, and full of shame. The Father and the Stepdaughter are also seated towards the right front. On the other side (left) are the Actors, much in the positions they occupied before the curtain was lowered. Only the Manager is standing up in the middle of the stage, with his hand closed over his mouth in the act of meditating.

THE MANAGER (*shaking his shoulders after a brief pause*). Ah yes: the second act! Leave it to me, leave it all to me as we arranged, and you'll see! It'll go fine!

THE STEPDAUGHTER. Our entry into his house (*indicates Father*) in spite of him.... (*Indicates the Son.*)

THE MANAGER (*out of patience*). Leave it to me, I tell you!

THE STEPDAUGHTER. Do let it be clear, at any rate, that it is in spite of my wishes.

THE MOTHER (*from her corner, shaking her head*). For all the good that's come of it....

THE STEPDAUGHTER (*turning towards her quickly*). It doesn't matter. The more harm done us, the more remorse for him.

THE MANAGER (*impatiently*). I understand! Good Heavens! I understand! I'm taking it into account.

THE MOTHER (*supplicatingly*). I beg you, sir, to let it appear quite plain that for conscience' sake I did try in every way....

THE STEPDAUGHTER (*interrupting indignantly and continuing for the Mother*).... to pacify me, to dissuade me from spiting him. (*To Manager.*) Do as she wants: satisfy her, because it is true! I enjoy it immensely. Anyhow, as you can see, the meeker she is, the more she tries to get at his heart, the more distant and aloof does he become.

THE MANAGER. Are we going to begin this second act or not?

THE STEPDAUGHTER. I'm not going to talk any more now. But I must tell you this: you can't have the whole action take place in the garden, as you suggest. It isn't possible!

THE MANAGER. Why not?

THE STEPDAUGHTER. Because he (*indicates the Son again*) is always shut up alone in his room. And then there's all the part of that poor dazed-looking boy there which takes place indoors.

THE MANAGER. Maybe! On the other hand, you will understand—we can't change scenes three or four times in one act.

THE LEADING MAN. They used to once.

THE MANAGER. Yes, when the public was up to the level of that child there.

THE LEADING LADY. It makes the illusion easier.

THE FATHER (*irritated*). The illusion! For Heaven's sake, don't say illusion. Please don't use that word, which is particularly painful for us.

THE MANAGER (*astounded*). And why, if you please?

THE FATHER. It's painful, cruel, really cruel; and you ought to understand that.

THE MANAGER. But why? What ought we to say then? The illusion, I tell you, sir, which we've got to create for the audience....

THE LEADING MAN. With our acting.

THE MANAGER. The illusion of a reality.

THE FATHER. I understand; but you, perhaps, do not understand us. Forgive me! You see ... here for you and your actors, the thing is only—and rightly so ... a kind of game....

THE LEADING LADY (*interrupting indignantly*). A game! We're not children here, if you please! We are serious actors.

THE FATHER. I don't deny it. What I mean is the game,

or play, of your art, which has to give, as the gentleman says, a perfect illusion of reality.

THE MANAGER. Precisely—!

THE FATHER. Now, if you consider the fact that we (*indicates himself and the other five Characters*), as we are, have no other reality outside of this illusion....

THE MANAGER (*astonished, looking at his Actors, who are also amazed*). And what does that mean?

THE FATHER (*after watching them for a moment with a wan smile*). As I say, sir, that which is a game of art for you is our sole reality. (*Brief pause. He goes a step or two nearer the Manager and adds:*) But not only for us, you know, by the way. Just you think it over well. (*Looks him in the eyes.*) Can you tell me who you are?

THE MANAGER (*perplexed, half smiling*). What? Who am I? I am myself.

THE FATHER. And if I were to tell you that that isn't true, because you and I . . . ?

THE MANAGER. I should say you were mad—! (*The Actors laugh.*)

THE FATHER. You're quite right to laugh: because we are all making believe here. (*To Manager.*) And you can therefore object that it's only for a joke that that gentleman there (*indicates the Leading Man*), who naturally is himself, has to be me, who am on the contrary myself—this thing you see here. You see I've caught you in a trap! (*The Actors laugh.*)

THE MANAGER (*annoyed*). But we've had all this over once before. Do you want to begin again?

THE FATHER. No, no! That wasn't my meaning! In fact, I should like to request you to abandon this game of art (*looking at the Leading Lady as if anticipating her*) which you are accustomed to play here with your actors, and to ask you seriously once again: who are you?

THE MANAGER (*astonished and irritated, turning to his Actors*). If this fellow here hasn't got a nerve! A man who calls himself a character comes and asks me who I am!

THE FATHER (*with dignity, but not offended*). A character, sir, may always ask a man who he is. Because a character has really a life of his own, marked with his especial characteristics; for which reason he is always "somebody." But a man—I'm not speaking of you now—may very well be "nobody."

THE MANAGER. Yes, but you are asking these questions of me, the boss, the manager! Do you understand?

THE FATHER. But only in order to know if you, as you really are now, see yourself as you once were with all the illusions that were yours then, with all the things both inside and outside of you as they seemed to you—as they were then indeed for you. Well, sir, if you think of all those illusions that mean nothing to you now, of all those things which don't even *seem* to you to exist any more, while once they *were* for you, don't you feel that—I won't say these boards—but the very earth under your feet is sinking away from you when you reflect that in the same way this *you* as you feel it today—all this present reality of yours—is fated to seem a mere illusion to you tomorrow?

THE MANAGER (*without having understood much, but astonished by the specious argument*). Well, well! And where does all this take us anyway?

THE FATHER. Oh, nowhere! It's only to show you that if we (*indicating the Characters*) have no other reality beyond the illusion, you too must not count overmuch on your reality as you feel it today, since, like that of yesterday, it may prove an illusion for you tomorrow.

THE MANAGER (*determining to make fun of him*). Ah, excellent! Then you'll be saying next that you, with this comedy of yours that you brought here to act, are truer and more real than I am.

THE FATHER (*with the greatest seriousness*). But of course; without doubt!

THE MANAGER. Ah, really?

THE FATHER. Why, I thought you'd understand that from the beginning.

THE MANAGER. More real than I?

THE FATHER. If your reality can change from one day to another....

THE MANAGER. But everyone knows it can change. It is always changing, the same as anyone else's.

THE FATHER (*with a cry*). No, sir, not ours! Look here! That is the very difference! Our reality doesn't change: it can't change! It can't be other than what it is, because it is already fixed for ever. It's terrible. Ours is an immutable reality which should make you shudder when you approach us if you are really conscious of the fact that your reality is a mere transitory and fleeting illusion, taking this form today and that tomorrow, according to the conditions, according to your will, your sentiments, which in turn are controlled by an intellect that shows them to you today in one manner and tomorrow . . . who knows how? . . . Illusions of reality represented in this fatuous comedy of life that never ends, nor can ever end! Because if tomorrow it were to end . . . then, why, all would be finished.

THE MANAGER. Oh for God's sake, will you *at least* finish with this philosophizing and let us try and shape this comedy which you yourself have brought me here? You argue and philosophize a bit too much, my dear sir. You know you seem to me almost, almost . . . (*Stops and looks him over from head to foot.*) Ah, by the way, I think you introduced yourself to me as a—what shall . . . we say—a "character," created by an author who did not afterward care to make a drama of his own creations.

THE FATHER. It is the simple truth, sir.

THE MANAGER. Nonsense! Cut that out, please! None

of us believes it, because it isn't a thing, as you must recognize yourself, which one can believe seriously. If you want to know, it seems to me you are trying to imitate the manner of a certain author whom I heartily detest—I warn you—although I have unfortunately bound myself to put on one of his works. As a matter of fact, I was just starting to rehearse it, when you arrived. (*Turning to the Actors.*) And this is what we've gained—out of the frying-pan into the fire!

THE FATHER. I don't know to what author you may be alluding, but believe me I feel what I think; and I seem to be philosophizing only for those who do not think what they feel, because they blind themselves with their own sentiment. I know that for many people this self-blinding seems much more "human"; but the contrary is really true. For man never reasons so much and becomes so introspective as when he suffers; since he is anxious to get at the cause of his sufferings, to learn who has produced them, and whether it is just or unjust that he should have to bear them. On the other hand, when he is happy, he takes his happiness as it comes and doesn't analyze it, just as if happiness were his right. The animals suffer without reasoning about their sufferings. But take the case of a man who suffers and begins to reason about it. Oh no! it can't be allowed! Let him suffer like an animal, and then—ah yes, he is "human"!

THE MANAGER. Look here! Look here! You're off again, philosophizing worse than ever.

THE FATHER. Because I suffer, sir! I'm not philosophizing: I'm crying aloud the reason of my sufferings.

THE MANAGER (*makes brusque movement as he is taken with a new idea*). I should like to know if anyone has ever heard of a character who gets right out of his part and perorates and speechifies as you do. Have you ever heard of a case? I haven't.

THE FATHER. You have never met such a case, sir, because authors, as a rule, hide the labor of their creations. When the characters are really alive before their author, the latter does nothing but follow them in their action, in other words, in the situations which they suggest to him; and he has to will them the way they will themselves—for there's trouble if he doesn't. When a character is born, he acquires at once such an independence, even of his own author, that he can be imagined by everybody even in many other situations where the author never dreamed of placing him; and so he acquires for himself a meaning which the author never thought of giving him.

THE MANAGER. Yes, yes, I know this.

THE FATHER. What is there then to marvel at in us? Imagine such a misfortune for characters as I have described to you: to be born of an author's fantasy, and be denied life by him; and then answer me if these characters left alive, and yet without life, weren't right in doing what they did do and are doing now, after they have attempted everything in their power to persuade him to give them their stage life. We've all tried him in turn, I, she (*indicating the Stepdaughter*) and she (*indicating the Mother*).

THE STEPDAUGHTER. It's true. I too have sought to tempt him, many, many times, when he has been sitting at his writing table, feeling a bit melancholy, at the twilight hour. He would sit in his armchair too lazy to switch on the light, and all the shadows that crept into his room were full of our presence coming to tempt him. (*As if she saw herself still there by the writing table, and was annoyed by the presence of the Actors.*) Oh, if you would only go away, go away and leave us alone—mother here with that son of hers—I with that child—that boy there always alone—and then I with him (*just hints at the Father*)—and then I alone, alone ... in those shadows! (*Makes a sudden movement as if in the vision she has of herself illuminating those shadows she wanted to seize hold of herself.*) Ah! my life! my life! Oh, what scenes we proposed to him—and I tempted him more than any of the others!

THE FATHER. Maybe. But perhaps it was your fault that he refused to give us life: because you were too insistent, too troublesome.

THE STEPDAUGHTER. Nonsense! Didn't he make me so himself? (*Goes close to the Manager to tell him as if in confidence.*) In my opinion he abandoned us in a fit of depression, of disgust for the ordinary theater as the public knows it and likes it.

THE SON. Exactly what it was, sir; exactly that!

THE FATHER. Not at all! Don't believe it for a minute. Listen to me! You'll be doing quite right to modify, as you suggest, the excesses both of this girl here, who wants to do too much, and of this young man, who won't do anything at all.

THE SON. No, nothing!

THE MANAGER. You too get over the mark occasionally, my dear sir, if I may say so.

THE FATHER. I? When? Where?

THE MANAGER. Always! Continuously! Then there's this insistence of yours in trying to make us believe you are a character. And then too, you must really argue and philosophize less, you know, much less.

THE FATHER. Well, if you want to take away from me the possibility of representing the torment of my spirit which never gives me peace, you will be suppressing me: that's all. Every true man, sir, who is a little above the level of the beasts and plants does not live for the sake of living, without knowing how to live; but he lives so as to give a meaning and a value of his own to life. For me this is *everything.* I cannot give up this, just to represent a mere fact as she (*indicating the Stepdaughter*) wants. It's all very well for her, since her "vendetta" lies in the "fact." I'm not going to do it. It destroys my *raison d'être.*

THE MANAGER. Your *raison d'être*! Oh, we're going ahead fine! First she starts off, and then you jump in. At this rate, we'll never finish.

THE FATHER. Now, don't be offended! Have it your own way—provided, however, that within the limits of the parts you assign us each one's sacrifice isn't too great.

THE MANAGER. You've got to understand that you can't go on arguing at your own pleasure. Drama is action, sir, action and not confounded philosophy.

THE FATHER. All right. I'll do just as much arguing and philosophizing as everybody does when he is considering his own torments.

THE MANAGER. If the drama permits! But for Heaven's sake, man, let's get along and come to the scene.

THE STEPDAUGHTER. It seems to me we've got too much action with our coming into his house. (*Indicating Father.*) You said, before, you couldn't change the scene every five minutes.

THE MANAGER. Of course not. What we've got to do is to combine and group up all the facts in one simultaneous, close-knit action. We can't have it as you want, with your little brother wandering like a ghost from room to room, hiding behind doors and meditating a project which—what did you say it did to him?

THE STEPDAUGHTER. Consumes him, sir, wastes him away!

THE MANAGER. Well, it may be. And then at the same time, you want the little girl there to be playing in the garden . . . one in the house, and the other in the garden: isn't that it?

THE STEPDAUGHTER. Yes, in the sun, in the sun! That is my only pleasure: to see her happy and careless in the garden after the misery and squalor of the horrible room where we all four slept together. And I had to sleep with her—I, do you understand?—with my vile contaminated body next to hers; with her folding me fast in her loving little arms. In the garden, whenever she spied me, she would run to take me by the hand. She didn't care for the big flowers, only the little ones; and she loved to show me them and pet me.

THE MANAGER. Well then, we'll have it in the garden. Everything shall happen in the garden; and we'll group the other scenes there. (*Calls a Stage Hand.*) Here, a backcloth with trees and something to do as a fountain basin. (*Turning round to look at the back of the stage.*) Ah, you've fixed it up. Good! (*To Stepdaughter.*) This is just to give an idea, of course. The Boy, instead of hiding behind the doors, will wander about here in the garden, hiding behind the trees. But it's going to be rather difficult to find a child to do that scene with you where she shows you the flowers. (*Turning to the Boy.*) Come forward a little, will you please? Let's try it now! Come along! come along! (*Then seeing him come shyly forward, full of fear and looking lost.*) It's a nice business, this lad here. What's the matter with him? We'll have to give him a word or two to say. (*Goes close to him, puts a hand on his shoulders, and leads him behind one of the trees.*) Come on! come on! Let me see you a little! Hide here . . . yes, like that. Try and show your head just a little as if you were looking for someone. . . . (*Goes back to observe the effect, when the Boy at once goes through the action.*) Excellent! fine! (*Turning to Stepdaughter.*) Suppose the little girl there were to surprise him as he looks round, and run over to him, so we could give him a word or two to say?

THE STEPDAUGHTER. It's useless to hope he will speak, as long as that fellow there is here. . . . (*Indicates the Son.*) You must send him away first.

THE SON (*jumping up*). Delighted! Delighted! I don't ask for anything better. (*Begins to move away.*)

THE MANAGER (*at once stopping him*). No! No! Where are you going? Wait a bit!

(*The Mother gets up alarmed and terrified at the thought that he is really about to go away. Instinctively she lifts her arms to prevent him, without, however, leaving her seat.*)

THE SON (*to Manager, who stops him*). I've got nothing to do with this affair. Let me go, please! Let me go!

THE MANAGER. What do you mean by saying you've got nothing to do with this?

THE STEPDAUGHTER (*calmly, with irony*). Don't bother to stop him: he won't go away.

THE FATHER. He has to act the terrible scene in the garden with his mother.

THE SON (*suddenly resolute and with dignity*). I shall act nothing at all. I've said so from the very beginning. (*To the Manager.*) Let me go!

THE STEPDAUGHTER (*going over to the Manager*). Allow me? (*Puts down the Manager's arm which is restraining the Son.*) Well, go away then, if you want to! (*The Son looks at her with contempt and hatred. She laughs and says:*) You see, he can't, he can't go away! He is obliged to stay here, indissolubly bound to the chain. If I, who fly off when that happens which has to happen, because I can't bear him—if I am still here and support that face and expression of his, you can well imagine that he is unable to move. He has to remain here, has to stop with that nice father of his, and that mother whose only son he is. (*Turning to the Mother.*) Come on, mother, come along! (*Turning to Manager to indicate her.*) You see, she was getting up to keep him back. (*To the Mother, beckoning her with her hand.*) Come on! come on! (*Then to Manager.*) You can imagine how little she wants to show these actors of yours what she really feels; but so eager is she to get near him that. . . . There, you see? She is willing to act her part. (*And in fact, the Mother approaches him; and as soon as the Stepdaughter has finished speaking, opens her arms to signify that she consents.*)

THE SON (*suddenly*). No! no! If I can't go away, then I'll stop here; but I repeat: I act nothing!

THE FATHER (*to Manager excitedly*). You can force him, sir.

THE SON. Nobody can force me.

THE FATHER. I can.

THE STEPDAUGHTER. Wait a minute, wait ... First of all, the baby has to go to the fountain.... (*Runs to take the Child and leads her to the fountain.*)

THE MANAGER. Yes, yes of course; that's it. Both at the same time.

(*The Second Lady Lead and the Juvenile Lead at this point separate themselves from the group of Actors. One watches the Mother attentively; the other moves about studying the movements and manner of the Son whom he will have to act.*)

THE SON (*to Manager*). What do you mean by both at the same time? It isn't right. There was no scene between me and her. (*Indicates the Mother.*) Ask her how it was!

THE MOTHER. Yes, it's true. I had come into his room....

THE SON. Into my room, do you understand? Nothing to do with the garden.

THE MANAGER. It doesn't matter. Haven't I told you we've got to group the action?

THE SON (*observing the Juvenile Lead studying him*). What do you want?

THE JUVENILE LEAD. Nothing! I was just looking at you.

THE SON (*turning towards the Second Lady Lead*). Ah! she's at it too: to re-act her part! (*Indicating the Mother.*)

THE MANAGER. Exactly! And it seems to me that you ought to be grateful to them for their interest.

THE SON. Yes, but haven't you yet perceived that it isn't possible to live in front of a mirror which not only freezes us with the image of ourselves, but throws our likeness back at us with a horrible grimace?

THE FATHER. That is true, absolutely true. You must see that.

THE MANAGER (*to Second Lady Lead and Juvenile Lead*). He's right! Move away from them!

THE SON. Do as you like. I'm out of this!

THE MANAGER. Be quiet, you, will you? And let me hear your mother! (*To Mother.*) You were saying you had entered....

THE MOTHER. Yes, into his room, because I couldn't stand it any longer. I went to empty my heart to him of all the anguish that tortures me.... But as soon as he saw me come in....

THE SON. Nothing happened! There was no scene. I went away, that's all! I don't care for scenes!

THE MOTHER. It's true, true. That's how it was.

THE MANAGER. Well now, we've got to do this bit between you and him. It's indispensable.

THE MOTHER. I'm ready ... when you are ready. If you could only find a chance for me to tell him what I feel here in my heart.

THE FATHER (*going to Son in a great rage*). You'll do this for your mother, for your mother, do you understand?

THE SON (*quite determined*). I do nothing!

THE FATHER (*taking hold of him and shaking him*). For God's sake, do as I tell you! Don't you hear your mother asking you for a favor? Haven't you even got the guts to be a son?

THE SON (*taking hold of the Father*). No! No! And for God's sake stop it, or else.... (*General agitation. The Mother frightened, tries to separate them*).

THE MOTHER (*pleading*). Please! please!

THE FATHER (*not leaving hold of the Son*). You've got to obey, do you hear?

THE SON (*almost crying from rage*). What does it mean, this madness you've got? (*They separate.*) Have you no decency, that you insist on showing everyone our shame? I won't do it! I won't! And I stand for the will of our author in this. He didn't want to put us on the stage, after all!

THE MANAGER. Man alive! You came here....

THE SON (*indicating Father*). *He* did! I didn't!

THE MANAGER. Aren't you here now?

THE SON. It was his wish, and he dragged us along with him. He's told you not only the things that did happen, but also things that have never happened at all.

THE MANAGER. Well, tell me then what did happen. You went out of your room without saying a word?

THE SON. Without a word, so as to avoid a scene!

THE MANAGER. And then what did you do?

THE SON. Nothing ... walking in the garden.... (*Hesitates for a moment with expression of gloom.*)

THE MANAGER (*coming closer to him, interested by his extraordinary reserve*). Well, well ... walking in the garden....

THE SON (*exasperated*). Why on earth do you insist? It's horrible!

(*The Mother trembles, sobs, and looks towards the fountain.*)

THE MANAGER (*slowly observing the glance and turning towards the Son with increasing apprehension*). The baby?

THE SON. There in the fountain....

THE FATHER (*pointing with tender pity to the Mother*). She was following him at the moment....

THE MANAGER (*to the Son anxiously*). And then you....

THE SON. I ran over to her; I was jumping in to drag

her out when I saw something that froze my blood . . . the boy standing stock still, with eyes like a madman's, watching his little drowned sister, in the fountain! (*The Stepdaughter bends over the fountain to hide the Child. She sobs.*) Then. . . . (*A revolver shot rings out behind the trees where the Boy is hidden.*)

THE MOTHER (*with a cry of terror runs over in that direction together with several of the Actors amid general confusion*). My son! My son! (*Then amid the cries and exclamations one hears her voice.*) Help! Help!

THE MANAGER (*pushing the Actors aside while they lift up the Boy and carry him off*). Is he really wounded?

SOME ACTORS. He's dead! dead!

OTHER ACTORS. No, no, it's only make-believe, it's only pretense!

THE FATHER (*with a terrible cry*). Pretense? Reality, sir, reality!

THE MANAGER. Pretense? Reality? To hell with it all! Never in my life has such a thing happened to me. I've lost a whole day over these people, a whole day!

TOPICS FOR DISCUSSION AND WRITING

1. Consult the Glossary (page 791) for a definition of *chorus character*. How many chorus characters do you find in *Six Characters*?
2. The Father says that the characters are more real than the actors themselves. Put his argument into your own words.
3. Explain the Father's assertion (page 412) that "a fact is like a sack which won't stand up when it is empty."
4. Argue for or against the view that *Six Characters* is really only a lurid melodrama.
5. The Father and the Stepdaughter are eager to achieve existence by having their play acted out, but the Son wants to remain an "unrealized character." Judging him as a character in a play, do you think that he is less fully "realized" than the Father and the Stepdaughter? Judging him as a human being, do you think that he is less fully realized?
6. Are the members of the acting troupe richly or thinly characterized? Which group do we know better, the actors or the six characters?

EUGENE O'NEILL

Desire under the Elms

Eugene O'Neill (1888–1953), the son of an actor, was born in a hotel room near Broadway and spent his early years traveling with his parents throughout the United States. He entered Princeton University in 1906 but left before the end of his first year. In 1909 he traveled to Honduras looking for gold, contracted malaria, and returned to the United States in 1910. After touring briefly with his father's company, he shipped to Buenos Aires, jumped ship there, did odd jobs, shipped to South Africa, and returned to the United States in 1911. The following year he learned that he had tuberculosis. In a sanatorium he began seriously reading plays, and in 1916 he joined the Provincetown Players, who put on some of his one-act plays. His first major play, *The Emperor Jones* (1920), produced by the Provincetown Players in New York, was followed in rapid succession by such plays as *Anna Christie* (1921), *Desire under the Elms* (1924), *Strange Interlude* (1928), and *Ah, Wilderness!* (1933). In time he was awarded four Pulitzer Prizes (one, posthumous, was for *Long Day's Journey into Night,* written in 1940, but not produced until 1955), and a Nobel Prize.

COMMENTARY

Although tragic drama traditionally depicted the fall of kings and princes, as early as the sixteenth century there were tragedies with middle-class protagonists. Playwrights sought to justify their new tragedies against conservative critical theory. The standard argument in favor of the older heroic tragedy is that only the fall of a great man can excite pity and fear, whereas the fall of an ordinary man—someone like ourselves—is not awe-inspiring but merely pathetic. Great passions, the argument runs, are found only in great people; a king, for example, can avenge his honor, but a shopkeeper has no honor to avenge. More specifically, the fall of a great hero is more tragic than the fall of an ordinary citizen because it is a bigger fall, and because it necessarily has greater reverberations. When a king falls, a kingdom trembles.

On the other hand, advocates of bourgeois tragedy generally insist that tragic drama derives much of its impact from our sympathy for (or identification with) the tragic hero, and this identification is, presumably, more likely to be achieved when the hero resembles us. Furthermore, democratic supporters of middle-class tragedy say, all people are potentially great, and rank is irrelevant to largeness of spirit.

Paradoxically, O'Neill's characters achieve their greatness through passions that might be thought of as base. When *Desire under the Elms* was first produced, it was denounced for its depiction of greed, lechery, adultery, and murder, and the entire cast of the Los Angeles production was arrested for publicly performing "filth." But whatever grandeur the characters have is rooted in their primal feelings. Thus Eben's stepmother,

Desire under the Elms at the Greenwich Village Theatre, 1924.
(Museum of the City of New York; The Theater Collection.)

Abbie, drawn irresistibly to her stepson and sensing his passionate interest in her, says, "Hain't the sun strong an' hot? Ye kin feel it burnin' into the earth—Nature—makin' thin's grow—bigger 'n' bigger—burnin' inside ye—makin' ye want t' grow—into somethin' else—till ye're jined with it—an' its your'n—but it owns ye, too—an' makes ye grow bigger—like a tree—like them elums—(*She laughs again softly, holding his eyes. He takes a step toward her, compelled against his will.*) Nature'll beat ye, Eben. Ye might's well own up t' it fust 's last." Or consider these words of Ephraim's, Abbie's husband and Eben's father. He is talking about his passionate devotion to his rocky New England farm: "When ye kin make corn sprout out o' stones, God's livin' in yew!... God's hard, not easy! God's in the stones! Build my church on a rock—out o' stones an' I'll be in them! That's what He meant t' Peter!"

One critic, assuming that O'Neill accepted the view that Aristotle's word *hamartia* refers to a tragic flaw, argues that Ephraim "has dedicated his entire life to God, who is, of course, only an image of his own ego." Really "only an image of his own ego"? We shall let the reader decide whether or not Ephraim's devotion to God is, in the context of the play, a tragic fault, but we want to take advantage of this space to give the reader one of O'Neill's comments about the play. (For additional comments, see "Contexts for *Desire under the Elms*," pages 455–56.) The passage, from a letter of March 26, 1925, is addressed to a theater critic, George Jean Nathan:

> What I think everyone missed in *Desire* is the quality in it I set most store by—the attempt to give an epic tinge to New England's inhibited life-lust, to make its inexpressiveness poetically expressive, to release it. It's just that—the poetical (in the broadest and deepest sense) vision illuminating even the most sordid and mean blind alleys of life—which I'm convinced is, and is to be, *my* concern and justification as a dramatist.

EUGENE O'NEILL *Desire under the Elms*

List of Characters

EPHRAIM CABOT

SIMEON, PETER, EBEN — *his sons*

ABBIE PUTNAM

YOUNG GIRL, TWO FARMERS, THE FIDDLER, THE SHERIFF, OTHER FOLK *from the neighboring farms*

The action of the entire play takes place in, and immediately outside of, the Cabot farmhouse in New England, in the year 1850. The south end of the house faces front to a stone wall with a wooden gate at center opening on a country road. The house is in good condition but in need of paint. Its walls are a sickly grayish, the green of the shutters faded. Two enormous elms are on each side of the house. They bend their trailing branches down over the roof. They appear to protect and at the same time subdue. There is a sinister maternity in their aspect, a crushing, jealous absorption. They have developed from their intimate contact with the life of man in the house an appalling humaneness. They brood oppressively over the house. They are like exhausted women resting their sagging breasts and hands and hair on its roof, and when it rains their tears trickle down monotonously and rot on the shingles.

There is a path running from the gate around the right corner of the house to the front door. A narrow porch is on this side. The end wall facing us has two windows in its upper story, two larger ones on the floor below. The two upper are those of the father's bedroom and that of the brothers. On the left, ground floor, is the kitchen—on the right, the parlor, the shades of which are always drawn down.

PART 1

SCENE 1

Exterior of the farmhouse. It is sunset of a day at the beginning of summer in the year 1850. There is no wind and everything is still. The sky above the roof is suffused with deep colors, the green of the elms glows, but the house is in shadow, seeming pale and washed out by contrast.

A door opens and Eben Cabot comes to the end of the porch and stands looking down the road to the right. He has a large bell in his hand and this he swings mechanically, awakening a deafening clangor. Then he puts his hands on his hips and stares up at the sky. He sighs with a puzzled awe and blurts out with halting appreciation.

EBEN. God! Purty! (*His eyes fall and he stares about him frowningly. He is twenty-five, tall and sinewy. His face is well-formed, good-looking, but its expression is resentful and defensive. His defiant, dark eyes remind one of a wild animal's in captivity. Each day is a cage in which he finds himself trapped but inwardly unsubdued. There is a fierce repressed vitality about him. He has black hair, mustache, a thin curly trace of beard. He is dressed in rough farm clothes.*

He spits on the ground with intense disgust, turns and goes back into the house.

Simeon and Peter come in from their work in the fields. They are tall men, much older than their half-brother [*Simeon is thirty-nine and Peter thirty-seven*], *built on a squarer, simpler model, fleshier in body, more bovine and homelier in face, shrewder and more practical. Their shoulders stoop a bit from years of farm work. They clump heavily along in their clumsy thick-soled boots caked with earth. Their clothes, their faces, hands, bare arms and throats are earth-stained. They smell of earth. They stand together for a moment in front of the house and, as if with the one impulse, stare dumbly up at the sky, leaning on their hoes. Their faces have a compressed, unresigned expression. As they look upward, this softens.*)

SIMEON (*grudgingly*). Purty.

PETER. Ay-eh.

SIMEON (*suddenly*). Eighteen year ago.

PETER. What?

SIMEON. Jenn. My woman. She died.

PETER. I'd fergot.

SIMEON. I rec'lect—now an' agin. Makes it lonesome. She'd hair long's a hoss' tail—an' yaller like gold!

PETER. Waal—she's gone. (*This with indifferent finality—then after a pause*) They's gold in the West, Sim.

SIMEON (*still under the influence of sunset—vaguely*). In the sky?

PETER. Waal—in a manner o' speakin'—thar's the promise. (*growing excited*) Gold in the sky—in the West—Golden Gate—Californi-a!—Goldest West—fields o' gold!

SIMEON (*excited in his turn*). Fortunes layin' just atop o' the ground waitin' t' be picked! Solomon's mines, they says! (*For a moment they continue looking up at the sky—then their eyes drop.*)

PETER (*with sardonic bitterness*). Here—it's stones atop o' the ground—stones atop o' stones—makin' stone walls—year atop o' year—him 'n' yew 'n' me 'n' then Eben—makin' stone walls fur him to fence us in!

SIMEON. We've wuked. Give our strength. Give our years. Plowed 'em under in the ground—(*he stamps rebelliously*)—rottin'—makin' soil for his crops! (*a pause*) Waal—the farm pays good for hereabouts.

PETER. If we plowed in Californi-a, they'd be lumps o' gold in the furrow!

SIMEON. Californi-a's t'other side o' earth, a'most. We got t' calc'late—

PETER (*after a pause*). 'Twould be hard fur me, too, to give up what we've 'arned here by our sweat. (*A pause, Eben sticks his head out of the dining-room window, listening.*)

SIMEON. Ay-eh. (*a pause*) Mebbe—he'll die soon.

PETER (*doubtfully*). Mebbe.

SIMEON. Mebbe—fur all we knows—he's dead now.

PETER. Ye'd need proof.

SIMEON. He's been gone two months—with no word.

PETER. Left us in the fields an evenin' like this. Hitched up an' druv off into the West. That's plum onnateral. He hain't never been off this farm 'ceptin' t' the village in thirty year or more, not since he married Eben's maw. (*A pause. Shrewdly*) I calc'late we might git him declared crazy by the court.

SIMEON. He skinned 'em too slick. He got the best o' all on 'em. They'd never b'lieve him crazy. (*a pause*) We got t' wait—till he's under ground.

EBEN (*with a sardonic chuckle*). Honor thy father! (*They turn, startled, and stare at him. He grins, then scowls.*) I pray he's died. (*They stare at him. He continues matter-of-factly*) Supper's ready.

SIMEON *and* PETER (*together*). Ay-eh.

EBEN (*gazing up at the sky*). Sun's downin' purty.

SIMEON *and* PETER (*together*). Ay-eh. They's gold in the West.

EBEN. Ay-eh. (*pointing*) Yonder atop o' the hill pasture, ye mean?

SIMEON *and* PETER (*together*). In Californi-a!

EBEN. Hunh? (*Stares at them indifferently for a second, then drawls*) Waal—supper's gittin' cold. (*He turns back into kitchen.*)

SIMEON (*startled—smacks his lips*). I air hungry!

PETER (*sniffing*). I smells bacon!

SIMEON (*with hungry appreciation*). Bacon's good!

PETER (*in same tone*). Bacon's bacon! (*They turn, shouldering each other, their bodies bumping and rubbing together as they hurry clumsily to their food, like two friendly oxen toward their evening meal. They disappear around the right corner of house and can be heard entering the door.*)

SCENE 2

The color fades from the sky. Twilight begins. The interior of the kitchen is now visible. A pine table is at center, a cookstove in the right rear corner, four rough wooden chairs, a tallow candle on the table. In the middle of the rear wall is fastened a big advertising poster with a ship in full sail and the word "California" in big letters. Kitchen utensils hang from nails. Everything is neat and in order but the atmosphere is of a men's camp kitchen rather than that of a home.

Places for three are laid. Eben takes boiled potatoes and bacon from the stove and puts them on the table, also a loaf of bread and a crock of water. Simeon and Peter shoulder in, slump down in their chairs without a word. Eben joins them. The three eat in silence for a moment, the two elder as naturally unrestrained as beasts of the field, Eben picking at his food without appetite, glancing at them with a tolerant dislike.

SIMEON (*suddenly turns to Eben*). Looky here! Ye'd oughtn't t' said that, Eben.

PETER. 'Twa'n't righteous.

EBEN. What?

SIMEON. Ye prayed he'd died.

EBEN. Waal—don't yew pray it? (*a pause*)

PETER. He's our Paw.

EBEN (*violently*). Not mine!

SIMEON (*dryly*). Ye'd not let no one else say that about yer Maw! Ha! (*He gives one abrupt sardonic guffaw. Peter grins.*)

EBEN (*very pale*). I meant—I hain't his'n—I hain't like him—he hain't me!

PETER (*dryly*). Wait till ye've growed his age!

EBEN (*intensely*). I'm Maw—every drop o' blood! (*A pause. They stare at him with indifferent curiosity.*)

PETER (*reminiscently*). She was good t' Sim 'n' me. A good step maw's scurse.

SIMEON. She was good t' everyone.

EBEN (*greatly moved, gets to his feet and makes an awkward bow to each of them—stammering*). I be thankful t' ye. I'm her—her heir. (*He sits down in confusion.*)

PETER (*after a pause—judicially*). She was good even t' him.

EBEN (*fiercely*). An' fur thanks he killed her!

SIMEON (*after a pause*). No one never kills nobody. It's allus somethin'. That's the murderer.

EBEN. Didn't he slave Maw t' death?

PETER. He's slaved himself t' death. He's slaved Sim 'n' me 'n' yew t' death—on'y none o' us hain't died—yit.

SIMEON. It's somethin'—drivin' him—t' drive us!

EBEN (*vengefully*). Waal—I hold him t' jedgment! (*then scornfully*) Somethin'! What's somethin'?

SIMEON. Dunno.

EBEN (*sardonically*). What's drivin' yew to Californi-a, mebbe? (*They look at him in surprise.*) Oh, I've heerd ye! (*then, after a pause*) But ye'll never go t' the gold fields!

PETER (*assertively*). Mebbe!

EBEN. Whar'll ye git the money?

PETER. We kin walk. It's an a'mighty ways—Californi-a—but if yew was t' put all the steps we've walked on this farm end t' end we'd be in the moon!

EBEN. The Injuns'll skulp ye on the plains.

SIMEON (*with grim humor*). We'll mebbe make 'em pay a hair fur a hair!

EBEN (*decisively*). But t'ain't that. Ye won't never go because ye'll wait here fur yer share o' the farm, thinkin' allus he'll die soon.

SIMEON (*after a pause*). We've a right.

PETER. Two-thirds belongs t'us.

EBEN (*jumping to his feet*). Ye've no right! She wa'n't yewr Maw! It was her farm! Didn't he steal it from her? She's dead. It's my farm.

SIMEON (*sardonically*). Tell that t' Paw—when he comes! I'll bet ye a dollar he'll laugh—fur once in his life. Ha! (*He laughs himself in one single mirthless bark.*)

PETER (*amused in turn, echoes his brother*). Ha!

SIMEON (*after a pause*). What've ye got held agin us, Eben? Year arter year it's skulked in yer eye—somethin'.

PETER. Ay-eh.

EBEN. Ay-eh. They's somethin'. (*suddenly exploding*) Why didn't ye never stand between him 'n' my Maw when he was slavin' her to her grave—t' pay her back fur the kindness she done t' yew? (*There is a long pause. They stare at him in surprise.*)

SIMEON. Waal—the stock'd got t' be watered.

PETER. 'R they was woodin' t' do.

SIMEON. 'R plowin'.

PETER. 'R hayin'.

SIMEON. 'R spreadin' manure.

PETER. 'R weedin'.

SIMEON. 'R prunin'.

PETER. 'R milkin'.

EBEN (*breaking in harshly*). An' makin' walls—stone atop o' stone—makin' walls till yer heart's a stone ye heft up out o' the way o' growth onto a stone wall t' wall in yer heart!

SIMEON (*matter-of-factly*). We never had no time t' meddle.

PETER (*to Eben*). Yew was fifteen afore yer Maw died—an' big fur yer age. Why didn't ye never do nothin'?

EBEN (*harshly*). They was chores t' do, wa'n't they? (*a pause—then slowly*) It was on'y arter she died I come to think o' it. Me cookin'—doin' her work—that made me know her, suffer her sufferin'—she'd come back t' help—come back t' bile potatoes—come back t' fry bacon—come back t' bake biscuits—come back all cramped up t' shake the fire, an' carry ashes, her eyes weepin' an' bloody with smoke an' cinders same's they used t' be. She still comes back—stands by the stove thar in the evenin'—she can't find it nateral sleepin' an' restin' in peace. She can't git used t' bein' free—even in her grave.

SIMEON. She never complained none.

EBEN. She'd got too tired. She'd got too used t' bein' too tired. That was what he done. (*with vengeful passion*) An' sooner'r later, I'll meddle. I'll say the thin's I didn't say then t' him! I'll yell 'em at the top o' my lungs. I'll see t' it my Maw gits some rest an' sleep in her grave! (*He sits down again, relapsing into a brooding silence. They look at him with a queer indifferent curiosity.*)

PETER (*after a pause*). Whar in tarnation d'ye s'pose he went, Sim?

SIMEON. Dunno. He druv off in the buggy, all spick an' span, with the mare all breshed an' shiny, druv off clackin' his tongue an' wavin' his whip. I remember it right well. I was finishin' plowin', it was spring an' May an' sunset, an' gold in the West, an' he druv off into it. I yells "Whar ye goin', Paw?" an' he hauls up by the stone wall a jiffy. His old snake's eyes was glitterin' in the sun like he'd been drinkin' a jugful an' he says with a mule's grin: "Don't ye run away till I come back!"

PETER. Wonder if he knowed we was wantin' fur Californi-a?

SIMEON. Mebbe. I didn't say nothin' and he says, lookin' kinder queer an' sick: "I been hearin' the hens cluckin' an' the roosters crowin' all the durn day. I been listenin' t' the cows lowin' an' everythin' else kickin' up till I can't stand it no more. It's spring an' I'm feelin' damned," he says. "Damned like an old bare hickory tree fit on'y fur burnin'," he says. An' then I calc'late I must've looked a mite hopeful, fur he adds real spry and vicious: "But don't git no fool idee I'm dead. I've sworn t' live a hundred an' I'll do it, if on'y t' spite yer sinful greed! An' now I'm ridin' out t' learn God's message t' me in the spring, like the prophets done. An' yew git back t' yer plowin'," he says. An' he druv off singin' a hymn. I thought he was drunk—'r I'd stopped him goin'.

EBEN (*scornfully*). No, ye wouldn't! Ye're scared o' him. He's stronger—inside—than both o' ye put together!

PETER (*sardonically*). An' yew—be yew Samson?

EBEN. I'm gittin' stronger. I kin feel it growin' in me—growin' an' growin'—till it'll bust out—! (*He gets up and puts on his coat and a hat. They watch him, gradually breaking into grins. Eben avoids their eyes sheepishly.*) I'm goin' out fur a spell—up the road.

PETER. T' the village?

SIMEON. T' see Minnie?

EBEN (*defiantly*). Ay-eh!

PETER (*jeeringly*). The Scarlet Woman!

SIMEON. Lust—that's what's growin' in ye!

EBEN. Waal—she's purty!

PETER. She's been purty fur twenty year!

SIMEON. A new coat o' paint'll make a heifer out of forty.

EBEN. She hain't forty!

PETER. If she hain't, she's teeterin' on the edge.

EBEN (*desperately*). What d'yew know—

PETER. All they is . . . Sim knew her—an' then me arter—

SIMEON. An' Paw kin tell yew somethin' too! He was fust!

EBEN. D'ye mean t' say he . . . ?

SIMEON (*with a grin*). Ay-eh! We air his heirs in everythin'!

EBEN (*intensely*). That's more to it! That grows on it! It'll bust soon! (*then violently*) I'll go smash my fist in her face! (*He pulls open the door in rear violently.*)

SIMEON (*with a wink at Peter—drawlingly*). Mebbe—but the night's wa'm—purty—by the time ye git thar mebbe ye'll kiss her instead!

PETER. Sart'n he will! (*They both roar with coarse laughter. Eben rushes out and slams the door—then the outside front door—comes around the corner of the house and stands still by the gate, staring up at the sky.*)

SIMEON (*looking after him*). Like his Paw.

PETER. Dead spit an' image!

SIMEON. Dog'll eat dog!

PETER. Ay-eh. (*Pause. With yearning*) Mebbe a year from now we'll be in Californi-a.

SIMEON. Ay-eh. (*A pause. Both yawn.*) Let's git t'bed. (*He blows out the candle. They go out door in rear. Eben stretches his arms up to the sky—rebelliously.*)

EBEN. Waal—thar's a star, an' somewhar's they's him, an' here's me, an' thar's Min up the road—in the same night. What if I does kiss her? She's like t'night, she's soft 'n' wa'm, her eyes kin wink like a star, her mouth's wa'm, her arms're wa'm, she smells like a wa'm plowed field, she's purty . . . Ay-eh! By God A'mighty she's purty, an' I don't give a damn how many sins she's sinned afore mine or who she's sinned 'em with, my sin's as purty as any one on 'em! (*He strides off down the road to the left.*)

SCENE 3

It is the pitch darkness just before dawn. Eben comes in from the left and goes around to the porch, feeling his way, chuckling bitterly and cursing half-aloud to himself.

EBEN. The cussed old miser! (*He can be heard going in the front door. There is a pause as he goes upstairs, then a loud knock on the bedroom door of the brothers.*) Wake up!

SIMEON (*startedly*). Who's thar?

EBEN (*pushing open the door and coming in, a lighted candle in his hand. The bedroom of the brothers is revealed. Its ceiling is the sloping roof. They can stand upright only close to the center dividing wall of the upstairs. Simeon and Peter are in a double bed, front. Eben's cot is to the rear. Eben has a mixture of silly grin and vicious scowl on his face*). I be!

PETER (*angrily*). What in hell's-fire . . . ?

EBEN. I got news fur ye! Ha! (*He gives one abrupt sardonic guffaw.*)

SIMEON (*angrily*). Couldn't ye hold it 'til we'd got our sleep?

EBEN. It's nigh sunup. (*then explosively*) He's gone an' married agen!

SIMEON *and* PETER (*explosively*). Paw?

EBEN. Got himself hitched to a female 'bout thirty-five—an' purty, they says . . .

SIMEON (*aghast*). It's a durn lie!

PETER. Who says?

SIMEON. They been stringin' ye!

EBEN. Think I'm a dunce, do ye? The hull village says. The preacher from New Dover, he brung the news—told it t'our preacher—New Dover, that's whar the old loon got himself hitched—that's whar the woman lived—

PETER (*no longer doubting—stunned*). Waal . . . !

SIMEON (*the same*). Waal . . . !

EBEN (*sitting down on a bed—with vicious hatred*). Ain't he a devil out o' hell? It's jest t' spite us—the damned old mule!

PETER (*after a pause*). Everythin'll go t' her now.

SIMEON. Ay-eh. (*A pause—dully*) Waal—if it's done—

PETER. It's done us. (*pause—then persuasively*) They's gold in the fields o' Californi-a, Sim. No good a-stayin' here now.

SIMEON. Jest what I was a-thinkin'. (*then with decision*) S'well fust's last! Let's light out and git this mornin'.

PETER. Suits me.

EBEN. Ye must like walkin'.

SIMEON (*sardonically*). If ye'd grow wings on us we'd fly thar!

EBEN. Ye'd like ridin' better—on a boat, wouldn't ye? (*Fumbles in his pocket and takes out a crumpled sheet of foolscap.*) Waal, if ye sign this ye kin ride on a boat. I've had it writ out an' ready in case ye'd ever go. It says fur three hundred dollars t' each ye agree yewr shares o' the farm is sold t' me. (*They look suspiciously at the paper. A pause.*)

SIMEON (*wonderingly*). But if he's hitched agen—

PETER. An' whar'd yew git that sum o' money, anyways?

EBEN (*cunningly*). I know whar it's hid. I been waitin'—Maw told me. She knew whar it lay fur years, but she was waitin' . . . It's her'n—the money he hoarded from her farm an' hid from Maw. It's my money by rights now.

PETER. Whar's it hid?

EBEN (*cunningly*). Whar yew won't never find it without me. Maw spied on him—'r she'd never knowed. (*A pause. They look at him suspiciously, and he at them.*) Waal, is it fa'r trade?

SIMEON. Dunno.

PETER. Dunno.

SIMEON (*looking at window*). Sky's grayin'.

PETER. Ye better start the fire, Eben.

SIMEON. An' fix some vittles.

EBEN. Ay-eh. (*Then with a forced jocular heartiness*) I'll git ye a good one. If ye're startin' t' hoof it t' Californi-a ye'll need somethin' that'll stick t' yer ribs. (*He turns to the door, adding meaningly*) But ye kin ride on a boat if ye'll swap. (*He stops at the door and pauses. They stare at him.*)

SIMEON (*suspiciously*). Whar was ye all night?

EBEN (*defiantly*). Up t' Min's. (*then slowly*) Walkin' thar, fust I felt 's if I'd kiss her; then I got a-thinkin' on' what ye'd said o' him an' her an' I says, I'll bust her nose fur that! Then I got t' the village an' heerd the news an' I got madder'n hell an' run all the way t' Min's not knowin' what I'd do—(*He pauses—then sheepishly but more defiantly*) Waal—when I seen her, I didn't hit her—nor I didn't kiss her nuther—I begun t' beller like a calf an' cuss at the same time, I was so durn mad—an' she got scared—an' I jest grabbed holt an' tuk her! (*Proudly*) Yes, sirree! I tuk her. She may've been his'n—an' your'n, too—but she's mine now!

SIMEON (*dryly*). In love, air yew?

EBEN (*with lofty scorn*). Love! I don't take no stock in sech slop!

PETER (*winking at Simeon*). Mebbe Eben's aimin' t' marry, too.

SIMEON. Min'd make a true faithful he'pmeet! (*They snicker.*)

EBEN. What do I care fur her—'ceptin' she's round an' wa'm? The p'int is she was his'n—an' now she belongs t' me! (*He goes to the door—then turns—rebelliously.*) An' Min hain't sech a bad un. They's worse'n Min in the world, I'll bet ye! Wait'll we see this cow the Old Man's hitched t'! She'll beat Min, I got a notion! (*He starts to go out.*)

SIMEON (*suddenly*). Mebbe ye'll try t' make her your'n, too?

PETER. Ha! (*He gives a sardonic laugh of relish at this idea.*)

EBEN (*spitting with disgust*). Her—here—sleepin' with him—stealin' my Maw's farm! I'd as soon pet a skunk 'r kiss a snake! (*He goes out. The two stare after him suspiciously. A pause. They listen to his steps receding.*)

PETER. He's startin' the fire.

SIMEON. I'd like t' ride t' Californi-a—but—

PETER. Min might o' put some scheme in his head.

SIMEON. Mebbe it's all a lie 'bout Paw marryin'. We'd best wait an' see the bride.

PETER. An' don't sign nothin' till we does!

SIMEON. Nor till we've tested it's good money! (*then with a grin*) But if Paw's hitched we'd be sellin' Eben somethin' we'd never git nohow!

PETER. We'll wait an' see. (*then with sudden vindictive anger*) An' till he comes, let's yew 'n' me not wuk a lick, let Eben tend to thin's if he's a mind t', let's us jest sleep an' eat an' drink likker, an' let the hull damned farm go t' blazes!

SIMEON (*excitedly*). By God, we've 'arned a rest! We'll play rich fur a change. I hain't a-going to stir outa bed till breakfast's ready.

PETER. An' on the table!

SIMEON (*after a pause—thoughtfully*). What d'ye calc'late she'll be like—our new Maw? Like Eben thinks?

PETER. More'n likely.

SIMEON (*vindictively*). Waal—I hope she's a she-devil that'll make him wish he was dead an' livin' in the pit o' hell fur comfort!

PETER (*fervently*). Amen!

SIMEON (*imitating his father's voice*). "I'm ridin' out t' learn God's message t' me in the spring like the prophets done," he says. I'll bet right then an' thar he knew plumb well he was goin' whorin', the stinkin' old hypocrite!

SCENE 4

Same as Scene 2—shows the interior of the kitchen with a lighted candle on table. It is gray dawn outside. Simeon and Peter are just finishing their breakfast. Eben sits before his plate of untouched food, brooding frowningly.

PETER (*glancing at him rather irritably*). Lookin' glum don't help none.

SIMEON (*sarcastically*). Sorrowin' over his lust o' the flesh!

PETER (*with a grin*). Was she yer fust?

EBEN (*angrily*). None o' yer business. (*a pause*) I was thinkin' o' him. I got a notion he's gittin' near—I kin feel him comin' on like yew kin feel malaria chill afore it takes ye.

PETER. It's too early yet.

SIMEON. Dunno. He'd like t' catch us nappin'—jest t' have somethin' t' hoss us 'round over.

PETER (*mechanically gets to his feet. Simeon does the same*). Waal—let's git t' wuk. (*They both plod mechanically toward the door before they realize. Then they stop short.*)

SIMEON (*grinning*). Ye're a cussed fool, Pete—and I be wuss! Let him see we hain't wukin'! We don't give a durn!

PETER (*as they go back to the table*). Not a damned durn! It'll serve t' show him we're done with him. (*They sit down again. Eben stares from one to the other with surprise.*)

SIMEON (*grins at him*). We're aimin' t' start bein' lilies o' the field.

PETER. Nary a toil 'r spin 'r lick o' wuk do we put in!

SIMEON. Ye're sole owner—till he comes—that's what ye wanted. Waal, ye got t' be sole hand, too.

PETER. The cows air bellerin'. Ye better hustle at the milkin'.

EBEN (*with excited joy*). Ye mean ye'll sign the paper?

SIMEON (*dryly*). Mebbe.

PETER. Mebbe.

SIMEON. We're considerin'. (*peremptorily*) Ye better git t' wuk.

EBEN (*with queer excitement*). It's Maw's farm agen! It's my farm! Them's my cows! I'll milk my durn fingers off fur cows o' mine! (*He goes out door in rear, they stare after him indifferently.*)

SIMEON. Like his Paw.

PETER. Dead spit 'n' image!

SIMEON. Waal—let dog eat dog! (*Eben comes out of front door and around the corner of the house. The sky is beginning to grow flushed with sunrise. Eben stops by the gate and stares around him with glowing, possessive eyes. He takes in the whole farm with his embracing glance of desire.*)

EBEN. It's purty! It's damned purty! It's mine! (*He suddenly throws his head back boldly and glares with hard, defiant eyes at the sky.*) Mine, d'ye hear? Mine! (*He turns and walks quickly off left, rear, toward the barn. The two brothers light their pipes.*)

SIMEON (*putting his muddy boots up on the table, tilting back his chair, and puffing defiantly*). Waal—this air solid comfort—fur once.

PETER. Ay-eh. (*He follows suit. A pause. Unconsciously they both sigh.*)

SIMEON (*suddenly*). He never was much o' a hand at milkin', Eben wa'n't.

PETER (*with a snort*). His hands air like hoofs! (*a pause*)

SIMEON. Reach down the jug thar! Let's take a swaller. I'm feelin' kind o' low.

PETER. Good idee! (*He does so—gets two glasses—they pour out drinks of whisky.*) Here's t' the gold in Californi-a!

SIMEON. An' luck t' find it! (*They drink—puff resolutely—sigh—take their feet down from the table.*)

PETER. Likker don't pear t' sot right.

SIMEON. We hain't used t' it this early. (*A pause. They become very restless.*)

PETER. Gittin' close in this kitchen.

SIMEON (*with immense relief*). Let's git a breath o' air. (*They arise briskly and go out rear—appear around house and stop by the gate. They stare up at the sky with a numbed appreciation.*)

PETER. Purty!

SIMEON. Ay-eh. Gold's t' the East now.

PETER. Sun's startin' with us fur the Golden West.

SIMEON (*staring around the farm, his compressed face tightened, unable to conceal his emotion*). Waal—it's our last mornin'—mebbe.

PETER (*the same*). Ay-eh.

SIMEON (*stamps his foot on the earth and addresses it desperately*). Waal—ye've thirty year o' me buried in ye—spread out over ye—blood an' bone an' sweat—rotted away—fertilizin' ye—richin' yer soul—prime manure, by God, that's what I been t' ye!

PETER. Ay-eh! An' me!

SIMEON. An' yew, Peter. (*He sighs—then spits.*) Waal—no use'n cryin' over spilt milk.

PETER. They's gold in the West—an' freedom, mebbe. We been slaves t' stone walls here.

SIMEON (*defiantly*). We hain't nobody's slaves from this out—nor nothin's slaves nuther. (*a pause—restlessly*) Speakin' o' milk, wonder how Eben's managin'?

PETER. I s'pose he's managin'.

SIMEON. Mebbe we'd ought t' help—this once.

PETER. Mebbe. The cows knows us.

SIMEON. An' likes us. They don't know him much.

PETER. An' the hosses, an' pigs, an' chickens. They don't know him much.

SIMEON. They knows us like brothers—an' likes us! (*proudly*) Hain't we raised 'em t' be fust-rate, number one prize stock?

PETER. We hain't—not no more.

SIMEON (*dully*). I was fergittin'. (*then resignedly*) Waal, let's go help Eben a spell an' git waked up.

PETER. Suits me. (*They are starting off down left, rear, for the barn when Eben appears from there hurrying toward them, his face excited.*)

EBEN (*breathlessly*). Waal—har they be! The old mule an' the bride! I seen 'em from the barn down below at the turnin'.

PETER. How could ye tell that far?

EBEN. Hain't I as far-sight as he's near-sight? Don't I know the mare 'n' buggy, an' two people settin' in it? Who else . . . ? An' I tell ye I kin feel 'em a-comin', too! (*He squirms as if he had the itch.*)

PETER (*beginning to be angry*). Waal—let him do his own unhitchin'!

SIMEON (*angry in his turn*). Let's hustle in an' git our bundles an' be a-goin' as he's a-comin'. I don't want never t' step inside the door agen arter he's back. (*They both start back around the corner of the house. Eben follows them.*)

EBEN (*anxiously*). Will ye sign it afore ye go?

PETER. Let's see the color o' the old skinflint's money an' we'll sign. (*They disappear left. The two brothers clump upstairs to get their bundles. Eben appears in the kitchen, runs to the window, peers out, comes back and pulls up a strip of flooring in under stove, takes out a canvas bag and puts it on table, then sets the floorboard back in place. The two brothers appear a moment after. They carry old carpet bags.*)

EBEN (*puts his hand on bag guardingly*). Have ye signed?

SIMEON (*shows paper in his hand*). Ay-eh. (*greedily*) Be that the money?

EBEN (*opens bag and pours out pile of twenty-dollar gold pieces*). Twenty-dollar pieces—thirty on 'em. Count 'em. (*Peter does so, arranging them in stacks of five, biting one or two to test them.*)

PETER. Six hundred. (*He puts them in bag and puts it inside his shirt carefully.*)

SIMEON (*handing paper to Eben*). Har ye be.

EBEN (*after a glance, folds it carefully and hides it under his shirt—gratefully*). Thank yew.

PETER. Thank yew fur the ride.

SIMEON. We'll send ye a lump o' gold fur Christmas. (*A pause. Eben stares at them and they at him.*)

PETER (*awkwardly*). Waal—we're a-goin'.

SIMEON. Comin' out t' the yard?

EBEN. No. I'm waitin' in here a spell. (*Another silence. The brothers edge awkwardly to door in rear—then turn and stand.*)

SIMEON. Waal—good-by.

PETER. Good-by.

EBEN. Good-by. (*They go out. He sits down at the table, faces the stove and pulls out the paper. He looks from it to the stove. His face, lighted up by the shaft of sunlight from the window, has an expression of trance. His lips move. The two brothers come out to the gate.*)

PETER (*looking off toward barn*). Thar he be—unhitchin'.

SIMEON (*with a chuckle*). I'll bet ye he's riled!

PETER. An' thar she be.

SIMEON. Let's wait 'n' see what our new Maw looks like.

PETER (*with a grin*). An' give him our partin' cuss!

SIMEON (*grinning*). I feel like raisin' fun. I feel light in my head an' feet.

PETER. Me, too. I feel like laffin' till I'd split up the middle.

SIMEON. Reckon it's the likker?

PETER. No. My feet feel itchin' t' walk an' walk—an' jump high over thin's—an'. . . .

SIMEON. Dance? (*a pause*)

PETER (*puzzled*). It's plumb onnateral.

SIMEON (*a light coming over his face*). I calc'late it's 'cause school's out. It's holiday. Fur once we're free!

PETER (*dazedly*). Free?

SIMEON. The halter's broke—the harness is busted—the fence bars is down—the stone walls air crumblin' an' tumblin'! We'll be kickin' up an' tearin' away down the road!

PETER (*drawing a deep breath—oratorically*). Anybody that wants this stinkin' old rock-pile of a farm kin hev it. 'Tain't our'n, no sirree!

SIMEON (*takes the gate off its hinges and puts it under his arm*). We harby 'bolishes shet gates an' open gates, an' all gates, by thunder!

PETER. We'll take it with us fur luck an' let 'er sail free down some river.

SIMEON (*as a sound of voices comes from left, rear*). Har they comes! (*The two brothers congeal into two stiff, grim-visaged statues. Ephraim Cabot and Abbie Putnam come in. Cabot is seventy-five, tall and gaunt, with great, wiry, concentrated power, but stoop-shouldered from toil. His face is as hard as if it were hewn out of a boulder, yet there is a weakness in it, a pretty pride in its own narrow strength. His eyes are small, close together, and extremely near-sighted, blinking continually in the effort to focus on objects, their stare having a straining, ingrowing quality. He is dressed in his dismal black Sunday suit. Abbie is thirty-five, buxom, full of vitality. Her round face is pretty but marred by its rather gross sensuality. There is strength and obstinacy in her jaw, a hard determination in her eyes, and about her whole personality the same unsettled, untamed, desperate quality which is so apparent in Eben.*)

CABOT (*as they enter—a queer strangled emotion in his dry cracking voice*). Har we be t' hum, Abbie.

ABBIE (*with lust for the word*). Hum! (*Her eyes gloating on the house without seeming to see the two stiff figures at the gate.*) It's purty—purty! I can't b'lieve it's r'ally mine.

CABOT (*sharply*). Yewr'n? Mine! (*He stares at her penetratingly. She stares back. He adds relentingly.*) Our'n—mebbe! It was lonesome too long. I was growin' old in the spring. A hum's got t' hev a woman.

ABBIE (*her voice taking possession*). A woman's got t' hev a hum!

CABOT (*nodding uncertainly*). Ay-eh. (*then irritably*) Whar be they? Ain't thar nobody about—'r wukin'—'r nothin'?

ABBIE (*sees the brothers. She returns their stare of cold appraising contempt with interest—slowly*). Thar's two men loafin' at the gate an' starin' at me like a couple o' strayed hogs.

CABOT (*straining his eyes*). I kin see 'em—but I can't make out. . . .

SIMEON. It's Simeon.

PETER. It's Peter.

CABOT (*exploding*). Why hain't ye wukin'?

SIMEON (*dryly*). We're waitin' t' welcome ye hum—yew an' the bride!

CABOT (*confusedly*). Huh? Waal—this be yer new Maw, boys. (*She stares at them and they at her.*)

SIMEON (*turns away and spits contemptuously*). I see her!

PETER (*spits also*). An' I see her!

ABBIE (*with the conqueror's conscious superiority*). I'll go in an' look at *my* house. (*She goes slowly around to porch.*)

SIMEON (*with a snort*). *Her* house!

PETER (*calls after her*). Ye'll find Eben inside. Ye better not tell him it's *yewr* house.

ABBIE (*mouthing the name*). Eben. (*then quietly*) I'll tell Eben.

CABOT (*with a contemptuous sneer*). Ye needn't heed Eben. Eben's a dumb fool—like his Maw—soft an' simple!

SIMEON (*with his sardonic burst of laughter*). Ha! Eben's a chip o' yew—spit 'n' image—hard 'n' bitter's a hickory tree! Dog'll eat dog. He'll eat ye yet, old man!

CABOT (*commandingly*). Ye git t' wuk!

SIMEON (*as Abbie disappears in house—winks at Peter and says tauntingly*). So that thar's our new Maw, be it? Whar in hell did ye dig her up? (*He and Peter laugh.*)

PETER. Ha! Ye'd better turn her in the pen with the other sows. (*They laugh uproariously, slapping their thighs.*)

CABOT (*so amazed at their effrontery that he stutters in confusion*). Simeon! Peter! What's come over ye? Air ye drunk?

SIMEON. We're free, old man—free o' yew an' the hull damned farm! (*They grow more and more hilarious and excited.*)

PETER. An' we're startin' out fur the gold fields o' Californi-a!

SIMEON. Ye kin take this place an' burn it!

PETER. An' bury it—fur all we cares!

SIMEON. We're free, old man! (*He cuts a caper.*)

PETER. Free! (*He gives a kick in the air.*)

SIMEON (*in a frenzy*). Whoop!

PETER. Whoop! (*They do an absurd Indian war dance about the old man who is petrified between rage and the fear that they are insane.*)

SIMEON. We're free as Injuns! Lucky we don't sculp ye!

PETER. An' burn yer barn an' kill the stock!

SIMEON. An' rape yer new woman! Whoop! (*He and*

Peter stop their dance, holding their sides, rocking with wild laughter.)

CABOT (*edging away*). Lust fur gold—fur the sinful, easy gold o' Californi-a! It's made ye mad!

SIMEON (*tauntingly*). Wouldn't ye like us to send ye back some sinful gold, ye old sinner?

PETER. They's gold besides what's in Californi-a! (*He retreats back beyond the vision of the old man and takes the bag of money and flaunts it in the air above his head, laughing.*)

SIMEON. And sinfuller, too!

PETER. We'll be voyagin' on the sea! Whoop! (*He leaps up and down.*)

SIMEON. Livin' free! Whoop! (*He leaps in turn.*)

CABOT (*suddenly roaring with rage*). My cuss on ye!

SIMEON. Take our'n in trade fur it! Whoop!

CABOT. I'll hev ye both chained up in the asylum!

PETER. Ye old skinflint! Good-by!

SIMEON. Ye old blood sucker! Good-by!

CABOT. Go afore I . . . !

PETER. Whoop! (*He picks a stone from the road. Simeon does the same.*)

SIMEON. Maw'll be in the parlor.

PETER. Ay-eh! One! Two!

CABOT (*frightened*). What air ye . . . ?

PETER. Three! (*They both throw, the stones hitting the parlor window with a crash of glass, tearing the shade.*)

SIMEON. Whoop!

PETER. Whoop!

CABOT (*in a fury now, rushing toward them*). If I kin lay hands on ye—I'll break yer bones fur ye! (*But they beat a capering retreat before him, Simeon with the gate still under his arm. Cabot comes back, panting with impotent rage. Their voices as they go off take up the song of the gold-seekers to the old tune of "Oh, Susannah!"*)

"I jumped aboard the Liza ship,
And traveled on the sea,
And every time I thought of home
I wished it wasn't me!
Oh! Californi-a,
That's the land fur me!
I'm off to Californi-a!
With my wash bowl on my knee."

(*In the meantime, the window of the upper bedroom on right is raised and Abbie sticks her head out. She looks down at Cabot—with a sigh of relief.*)

ABBIE. Waal—that's the last o' them two, hain't it? (*He doesn't answer. Then in possessive tones*) This here's a nice bedroom, Ephraim. It's a r'al nice bed. Is it my room, Ephraim?

CABOT (*grimly—without looking up*). Our'n! (*She cannot control a grimace of aversion and pulls back her head slowly and shuts the window. A sudden horrible thought seems to enter Cabot's head.*) They been up to somethin'! Mebbe—mebbe they've pizened the stock—'r somethin'! (*He almost runs off down toward the barn. A moment later the kitchen door is slowly pushed open and Abbie enters. For a moment she stands looking at Eben. He does not notice her at first. Her eyes take him in penetratingly with a calculating appraisal of his strength as against hers. But under this her desire is dimly awakened by his youth and good looks. Suddenly he becomes conscious of her presence and looks up. Their eyes meet. He leaps to his feet, glowering at her speechlessly.*)

ABBIE (*in her most seductive tones which she uses all through this scene*). Be you—Eben? I'm Abbie—(*She laughs.*) I mean, I'm yer new Maw.

EBEN (*viciously*). No, damn ye!

ABBIE (*as if she hadn't heard—with a queer smile*). Yer Paw's spoke a lot o' yew. . . .

EBEN. Ha!

ABBIE. Ye mustn't mind him. He's an old man. (*A long pause. They stare at each other.*) I don't want t' pretend playin' Maw t' ye, Eben. (*admiringly*) Ye're too big an' too strong fur that. I want t' be frens with ye. Mebbe with me fur a fren ye'd find ye'd like livin' here better. I kin make it easy fur ye with him, mebbe. (*with a scornful sense of power*) I calc'late I kin git him t' do most anythin' fur me.

EBEN (*with bitter scorn*). Ha! (*They stare again, Eben obscurely moved, physically attracted to her—in forced stilted tones*) Yew kin go t' the devil!

ABBIE (*calmly*). If cussin' me does ye good, cuss all ye've a mind t'. I'm all prepared t' have ye agin me—at fust. I don't blame ye nuther. I'd feel the same at any stranger comin' t' take my Maw's place. (*He shudders. She is watching him carefully.*) Yew must've cared a lot fur yewr Maw, didn't ye? My Maw died afore I'd growed. I don't remember her none. (*A pause.*) But yew won't hate me long, Eben. I'm not the wust in the world—an' yew an' me've got a lot in common. I kin tell that by lookin' at ye. Waal—I've had a hard life, too—oceans o' trouble an' nuthin' but wuk fur reward. I was a orphan early an' had t' wuk fur others in other folks' hums. Then I married an' he turned out a drunken spreer an' so he had to wuk fur others an' me too agen in other folks' hums, an' the baby died, an' my husband got sick an' died too, an' I was glad sayin' now I'm free fur once, on'y I diskivered right away all I was free fur was t' wuk agen in other folks' hums, doin' other folks' wuk till I'd most give up hope o' ever doin' my own wuk in my own hum, an' then your Paw come. . . . (*Cabot appears returning from the barn. He comes to the gate and looks down the road the brothers have gone. A faint strain of their retreating voices is heard: "Oh, Californi-a! That's the place for me." He stands glowering, his fist clenched, his face grim with rage.*)

EBEN (*fighting against his growing attraction and sympathy harshly*). An' bought yew—like a harlot! (*She is stung and flushes angrily. She has been sincerely moved by the recital of her troubles. He adds furiously*) An' the price he's payin' ye—this farm—was my Maw's, damn ye!—an' mine now!

ABBIE (*with a cool laugh of confidence*). Yewr'n? We'll see 'bout that! (*then strongly*) Waal—what if I did need a hum? What else'd I marry an old man like him fur?

EBEN (*maliciously*). I'll tell him ye said that!

ABBIE (*smiling*). I'll say ye're lyin' a-purpose—an' he'll drive ye off the place!

EBEN. Ye devil!

ABBIE (*defying him*). This be my farm—this be my hum—this be my kitchen—!

EBEN (*furiously, as if he were going to attack her*). Shut up, damn ye!

ABBIE (*walks up to him—a queer coarse expression of desire in her face and body—slowly*). An' upstairs—that be my bedroom—an' my bed! (*He stares into her eyes, terribly confused and torn. She adds softly*) I hain't bad nor mean—'ceptin' fur an enemy—but I got t' fight fur what's due me out o' life, if I ever 'spect t' git it. (*Then putting her hand on his arm—seductively*) Let's yew 'n' me be frens, Eben.

EBEN (*stupidly—as if hypnotized*). Ay-eh. (*Then furiously flinging off her arm*) No, ye durned old witch! I hate ye! (*He rushes out the door.*)

ABBIE (*looks after him smiling satisfiedly—then half to herself, mouthing the word*). Eben's nice. (*She looks at the table, proudly.*) I'll wash up *my* dishes now. (*Eben appears outside, slamming the door behind him. He comes around corner, stops on seeing his father, and stands staring at him with hate.*)

CABOT (*raising his arms to heaven in the fury he can no longer control*). Lord God o' Hosts, smite the undutiful sons with Thy wust cuss!

EBEN (*breaking in violently*). Yew 'n' yewr God! Allus cussin' folks—allus naggin' 'em!

CABOT (*oblivious to him—summoningly*). God o' the old! God o' the lonesome!

EBEN (*mockingly*). Naggin' His sheep t' sin! T' hell with yewr God! (*Cabot turns. He and Eben glower at each other.*)

CABOT (*harshly*). So it's yew. I might've knowed it. (*shaking his finger threateningly at him*) Blasphemin' fool! (*then quickly*) Why hain't ye t' wuk?

EBEN. Why hain't yew? They've went. I can't wuk it all alone.

CABOT (*contemptuously*). Nor noways! I'm wuth ten o' ye yit, old's I be! Ye'll never be more'n half a man! (*then, matter-of-factly*) Waal—let's git t' the barn. (*They go. A last faint note of the "Californi-a" song is heard from the distance. Abbie is washing her dishes.*)

PART 2

SCENE 1

The exterior of the farmhouse, as in Part 1—a hot Sunday afternoon two months later. Abbie, dressed in her best, is discovered sitting in a rocker at the end of the porch. She rocks listlessly, enervated by the heat, staring in front of her with bored, half-closed eyes.

Eben sticks his head out of his bedroom window. He looks around furtively and tries to see—or hear—if anyone is on the porch, but although he has been careful to make no noise, Abbie has sensed his movement. She stops rocking, her face grows animated and eager, she waits attentively. Eben seems to feel her presence, he scowls back his thoughts of her and spits with exaggerated disdain—then withdraws back into the room. Abbie waits, holding her breath as she listens with passionate eagerness for every sound within the house.

Eben comes out. Their eyes meet. His falter, he is confused, he turns away and slams the door resentfully. At this gesture, Abbie laughs tantalizingly, amused but at the same time piqued and irritated. He scowls, strides off the porch to the path and starts to walk past her to the road with a grand swagger of ignoring her existence. He is dressed in his store suit, spruced up, his face shines from soap and water. Abbie leans forward on her chair, her eyes hard and angry now, and, as he passes her, gives a sneering, taunting chuckle.

EBEN (*stung—turns on her furiously*). What air yew cacklin' 'bout?

ABBIE (*triumphant*). Yew!

EBEN. What about me?

ABBIE. Ye look all slicked up like a prize bull.

EBEN (*with a sneer*). Waal—ye hain't so durned purty yerself, be ye? (*They stare into each other's eyes, his held by hers in spite of himself, hers glowingly possessive. Their physical attraction becomes a palpable force quivering in the hot air.*)

ABBIE (*softly*). Ye don't mean that, Eben. Ye may think ye mean it, mebbe, but ye don't. Ye can't. It's agin nature, Eben. Ye been fightin' yer nature ever since the day I come—tryin' t' tell yerself I hain't purty t'ye. (*She laughs a low humid laugh without taking her eyes from his. A pause—her body squirms desirously—she murmurs languorously.*) Hain't the sun strong an' hot? Ye kin feel it burnin' into the earth—Nature—makin' thin's grow—bigger 'n' bigger—burnin' inside ye—makin' ye want t' grow—into somethin' else—till ye're jined with it—an' it's your'n—but it owns ye, too—an' makes ye grow bigger—like a tree—like them elums— (*She laughs again softly, holding his eyes. He takes a step toward her, compelled against his will.*) Nature'll beat ye, Eben. Ye might's well own up t' it fust 's last.

EBEN (*trying to break from her spell—confusedly*). If Paw'd hear ye goin' on.... (*resentfully*) But ye've made such a damned idjit out o' the old devil ...! (*Abbie laughs.*)

ABBIE. Waal—hain't it easier fur yew with him changed softer?

EBEN (*defiantly*). No. I'm fightin' him—fightin' yew—fightin' fur Maw's right t' her hum! (*This breaks her spell for him. He glowers at her.*) An' I'm onto ye. Ye hain't foolin' me a mite. Ye're aimin' t' swaller up everythin' an' make it your'n. Waal, you'll find I'm a heap sight bigger hunk nor yew kin chew! (*He turns from her with a sneer.*)

ABBIE (*trying to regain her ascendancy—seductively*). Eben!

EBEN. Leave me be! (*He starts to walk away.*)

ABBIE (*more commandingly*). Eben!

EBEN (*stops—resentfully*). What d'ye want?

ABBIE (*trying to conceal a growing excitement*). Whar air ye goin'?

EBEN (*with malicious nonchalance*). Oh—up the road a spell.

ABBIE. T' the village?

EBEN (*airily*). Mebbe.

ABBIE (*excitedly*). T' see that Min, I s'pose?

EBEN. Mebbe.

ABBIE (*weakly*). What d'ye want t' waste time on her fur?

EBEN (*revenging himself now—grinning at her*). Ye can't beat Nature, didn't ye say? (*He laughs and again starts to walk away.*)

ABBIE (*bursting out*). An ugly old hake!

EBEN (*with a tantalizing sneer*). She's purtier'n yew be!

ABBIE. That every wuthless drunk in the country has....

EBEN (*tauntingly*). Mebbe—but she's better'n yew. She owns up fa'r 'n' squar' t' her doin's.

ABBIE (*furiously*). Don't ye dare compare....

EBEN. She don't go sneakin' an' stealin'—what's mine.

ABBIE (*savagely seizing on his weak point*). Your'n? Yew mean—my farm?

EBEN. I mean the farm yew sold yerself fur like any other old whore—my farm!

ABBIE (*stung—fiercely*). Ye'll never live t' see the day when even a stinkin' weed on it'll belong t' ye! (*then in a scream*) Git out o' my sight! Go on t' yer slut—disgracin' yer Paw 'n' me! I'll git yer Paw t' horsewhip ye off the place if I want t'! Ye're only livin' here 'cause I tolerate ye! Git along! I hate the sight o' ye! (*She stops, panting and glaring at him.*)

EBEN (*returning her glance in kind*). An' I hate the sight o' yew! (*He turns and strides off up the road. She follows his retreating figure with concentrated hate. Old Cabot appears coming up from the barn. The hard, grim expression of his face has changed. He seems in some queer way softened, mellowed. His eyes have taken on a strange, incongruous dreamy quality. Yet there is no hint of physical weakness about him—rather he looks more robust and younger. Abbie sees him and turns away quickly with unconcealed aversion. He comes slowly up to her.*)

CABOT (*mildly*). War yew an' Eben quarrelin' agen?

ABBIE (*shortly*). No.

CABOT. Ye was talkin' a'mighty loud. (*He sits down on the edge of porch.*)

ABBIE (*snappishly*). If ye heerd us they hain't no need askin' questions.

CABOT. I didn't hear what ye said.

ABBIE (*relieved*). Waal—it wa'n't nothin' t' speak on.

CABOT (*after a pause*). Eben's queer.

ABBIE (*bitterly*). He's the dead spit 'n' image o' yew!

CABOT (*queerly interested*). D'ye think so, Abbie? (*After a pause, ruminatingly*) Me 'n' Eben's allus fit 'n' fit. I never could b'ar him noways. He's so thunderin' soft—like his Maw.

ABBIE (*scornfully*). Ay-eh! 'Bout as soft as yew be!

CABOT (*as if he hadn't heard*). Mebbe I been too hard on him.

ABBIE (*jeeringly*). Waal—ye're gittin' soft now—soft as slop! That's what Eben was sayin'.

CABOT (*his face instantly grim and ominous*). Eben was sayin'? Waal, he'd best not do nothin' t' try me 'r he'll soon diskiver.... (*A pause. She keeps her face turned away. His gradually softens. He stares up at the sky.*) Purty, hain't it?

ABBIE (*crossly*). I don't see nothin' purty.

CABOT. The sky. Feels like a wa'm field up thar.

ABBIE (*sarcastically*). Air yew aimin' t' buy up over the farm too? (*She snickers contemptuously.*)

CABOT (*strangely*). I'd like t' own my place up thar. (*a pause*) I'm gittin' old, Abbie. I'm gittin' ripe on the bough. (*A pause. She stares at him mystified. He goes on.*) It's allus lonesome cold in the house—even when it's bilin' hot outside. Hain't yew noticed?

ABBIE. No.

CABOT. It's wa'm down t' the barn—nice smellin' an' warm—with the cows. (*a pause*) Cows is queer.

ABBIE. Like yew?

CABOT. Like Eben. (*a pause*) I'm gittin' t' feel resigned t' Eben—jest as I got t' feel 'bout his Maw. I'm gittin' t' learn to b'ar his softness—jest like her'n. I calc'late I c'd a'most take t' him—if he wa'n't sech a dumb fool! (*a pause*) I s'pose it's old age a-creepin' in my bones.

ABBIE (*indifferently*). Waal—ye hain't dead yet.

CABOT (*roused*). No, I hain't, yew bet—not by a hell of a sight—I'm sound 'n' tough as hickory! (*then moodily*) But arter three score and ten the Lord warns ye t' prepare. (*a pause*) That's why Eben's come in my head. Now that his cussed sinful brothers is gone their path t' hell, they's no one left but Eben.

ABBIE (*resentfully*). They's me, hain't they? (*Agitatedly*) What's all this sudden likin' ye tuk to Eben? Why don't ye say nothin' 'bout me? Hain't I yer lawful wife?

CABOT (*simply*). Ay-eh. Ye be. (*A pause—he stares at her desirously—his eyes grow avid—then with a sudden movement he seizes her hands and squeezes them, declaiming in a queer camp meeting preacher's tempo*) Yew air my Rose o' Sharon! Behold, yew air fair; yer eyes air doves; yer lips air like scarlet; yer two breasts air like two fawns; yer navel be like a round goblet; yer belly be like a heap o' wheat.... (*He covers her hand with kisses. She does not seem to notice. She stares before her with hard angry eyes.*)

ABBIE (*jerking her hands away—harshly*). So ye're plannin' t' leave the farm t' Eben, air ye?

CABOT (*dazedly*). Leave ...? (*then with resentful obstinacy*) I hain't a-givin' it t' no one!

ABBIE (*remorselessly*). Ye can't take it with ye.

CABOT (*thinks a moment—then reluctantly*). No, I calc'late not. (*after a pause—with a strange passion*) But if I could, I would, by the Etarnal! 'R if I could, in my dyin' hour, I'd set it afire an' watch it burn—this house an' every ear o' corn an' every tree down t' the last blade o' hay! I'd sit an' know it was all a-dying with me an' no one else'd ever own what was mine, what I'd made out o' nothin' with my own sweat 'n' blood! (*a pause—then he adds with a queer affection*) 'Ceptin' the cows. Them I'd turn free.

ABBIE (*harshly*). An' me?

CABOT (*with a queer smile*). Ye'd be turned free, too.

ABBIE (*furiously*). So that's the thanks I git fur marryin' ye—t' have ye change kind to Eben who hates ye, an' talk o' turnin' me out in the road.

CABOT (*hastily*). Abbie! Ye know I wa'n't....

ABBIE (*vengefully*). Just let me tell ye a thing or two 'bout Eben! Whar's he gone? T' see that harlot, Min! I tried fur t' stop him. Disgracin' yew an' me—on the Sabbath, too!

CABOT (*rather guiltily*). He's a sinner—nateral-born. It's lust eatin' his heart.

ABBIE (*enraged beyond endurance—wildly vindictive*). An' his lust fur me! Kin ye find excuses fur that?

CABOT (*stares at her—after a dead pause*). Lust—fur yew?

ABBIE (*defiantly*). He was tryin' t' make love t' me—when ye heerd us quarrelin'.

CABOT (*stares at her—then a terrible expression of rage comes over his face—he springs to his feet shaking all over*). By the A'mighty God—I'll end him!

ABBIE (*frightened now for Eben*). No! Don't ye!

CABOT (*violently*). I'll git the shotgun an' blow his soft brains t' the top o' them elums!

ABBIE (*throwing her arms around him*). No, Ephraim!

CABOT (*pushing her away violently*). I will, by God!

ABBIE (*in a quieting tone*). Listen, Ephraim. 'Twa'n't nothin' bad—on'y a boy's foolin'—'twa'n't meant serious—jest jokin' an' teasin'....

CABOT. Then why did ye say—lust?

ABBIE. It must hev sounded wusser'n I meant. An' I was mad at thinkin'—ye'd leave him the farm.

CABOT (*quieter but still grim and cruel*). Waal then, I'll horsewhip him off the place if that much'll content ye.

ABBIE (*reaching out and taking his hand*). No. Don't think o' me! Ye mustn't drive him off. 'Tain't sensible. Who'll ye get to help ye on the farm? They's no one hereabouts.

CABOT (*considers this—then nodding his appreciation*). Ye got a head on ye. (*then irritably*) Waal, let them stay. (*He sits down on the edge of the porch. She sits beside him. He murmurs contemptuously*) I oughtn't t' git riled so—at that 'ere fool calf. (*a pause*) But har's the p'int. What son o' mine'll keep on here t' the farm—when the Lord does call me? Simeon an' Peter air gone t' hell—an' Eben's follerin' 'em.

ABBIE. They's me.

CABOT. Ye're on'y a woman.

ABBIE. I'm yewr wife.

CABOT. That hain't me. A son is me—my blood—mine. Mine ought t' git mine. An' then it's still mine—even though I be six foot under. D'ye see?

ABBIE (*giving him a look of hatred*). Ay-eh. I see. (*She becomes very thoughtful, her face growing shrewd, her eyes studying Cabot craftily.*)

CABOT. I'm gittin' old—ripe on the bough. (*then with a sudden forced reassurance*) Not but what I hain't a hard nut t' crack even yet—an' fur many a year t' come! By the Etarnal, I kin break most o' the young fellers' backs at any kind o' work any day o' the year!

ABBIE (*suddenly*). Mebbe the Lord'll give *us* a son.

CABOT (*turns and stares at her eagerly*). Ye mean—a son—t' me 'n' yew?

ABBIE (*with a cajoling smile*). Ye're a strong man yet, hain't ye? 'Tain't noways impossible, be it? We know that. Why d'ye stare so? Hain't ye never thought o' that afore? I been thinkin' o' it all along. Ay-eh—an' I been prayin' it'd happen, too.

CABOT (*his face growing full of joyous pride and a sort of religious ecstasy*). Ye been prayin', Abbie?—fur a son?—t' us?

ABBIE. Ay-eh. (*with a grim resolution*) I want a son now.

CABOT (*excitedly clutching both of her hands in his*). It'd be the blessin' o' God, Abbie—the blessin' o' God A'mighty on me—in my old age—in my lonesomeness! They hain't nothin' I wouldn't do fur ye then, Abbie. Ye'd hev on'y ask it—anythin' ye'd a mind t'!

ABBIE (*interrupting*). Would ye will the farm t' me then—t' me an' it ...?

CABOT (*vehemently*). I'd do anythin' ye axed, I tell ye! I

swar it! May I be everlastin' damned t' hell if I wouldn't! (*He sinks to his knees pulling her down with him. He trembles all over with the fervor of his hopes.*) Pray t' the Lord agen, Abbie. It's the Sabbath! I'll jine ye! Two prayers air better nor one. "An' God hearkened unto Rachel"! An' God hearkened unto Abbie! Pray, Abbie! Pray fur him to hearken! (*He bows his head, mumbling. She pretends to do likewise but gives him a side glance of scorn and triumph.*)

SCENE 2

About eight in the evening. The interior of the two bedrooms on the top floor is shown—Eben is sitting on the side of his bed in the room on the left. On account of the heat he has taken off everything but his undershirt and pants. His feet are bare. He faces front, brooding moodily, his chin propped on his hands, a desperate expression on his face.

In the other room Cabot and Abbie are sitting side by side on the edge of their bed, an old four-poster with feather mattress. He is in his night shirt, she in her nightdress. He is still in the queer, excited mood into which the notion of a son has thrown him. Both rooms are lighted dimly and flickeringly by tallow candles.

CABOT. The farm needs a son.

ABBIE. I need a son.

CABOT. Ay-eh. Sometimes ye air the farm an' sometimes the farm be yew. That's why I clove t' ye in my lonesomeness. (*A pause. He pounds his knee with his fist.*) Me an' the farm has got t' beget a son!

ABBIE. Ye'd best go t' sleep. Ye're gittin' thin's all mixed.

CABOT (*with an impatient gesture*). No, I hain't. My mind's clear's a bell. Ye don't know me, that's it. (*He stares hopelessly at the floor.*)

ABBIE (*indifferently*). Mebbe. (*In the next room Eben gets up and paces up and down distractedly. Abbie hears him. Her eyes fasten on the intervening wall with concentrated attention. Eben stops and stares. Their hot glances seem to meet through the wall. Unconsciously he stretches out his arms for her and she half rises. Then aware, he mutters a curse at himself and flings himself face downward on the bed, his clenched fists above his head, his face buried in the pillow. Abbie relaxes with a faint sigh but her eyes remain fixed on the wall; she listens with all her attention for some movement from Eben.*)

CABOT (*suddenly raises his head and looks at her—scornfully*). Will ye ever know me—'r will any man 'r woman? (*Shaking his head*) No. I calc'late 't wa'n't t' be. (*He turns away. Abbie looks at the wall. Then, evidently unable to keep silent about his thoughts, without looking at his wife, he puts out his hand and clutches her knee. She starts violently, looks at him, sees he is not watching her, concentrates again on the wall and pays no attention to what he says.*) Listen, Abbie. When I come here fifty odd year ago—I was jest twenty an the strongest an' hardest ye ever seen—ten times as strong an' fifty times as hard as Eben. Waal—this place was nothin' but fields o' stones. Folks laughed when I tuk it. They couldn't know what I knowed. When he kin make corn sprout out o' stones, God's livin' in yew! They wa'n't strong enuf fur that! They reckoned God was easy. They laughed. They don't laugh no more. Some died hereabouts. Some went West an' died. They're all under ground—fur follerin' arter an easy God. God hain't easy. (*He shakes his head slowly.*) An' I growed hard. Folks kept allus sayin' he's a hard man like 'twas sinful t' be hard, so's at last I said back at 'em: Waal then, by thunder, ye'll git me hard an' see how ye like it! (*Then suddenly*) But I give in t' weakness once. 'Twas arter I'd been here two year. I got weak—despairful—they was so many stones. They was a party leavin', givin' up, goin' West. I jined 'em. We tracked on 'n' on. We come t' broad medders, plains, whar the soil was black an' rich as gold. Nary a stone. Easy. Ye'd on'y to plow an' sow an' then set an' smoke yer pipe an' watch thin's grow. I could o' been a rich man—but somethin' in me fit me an' fit me—the voice o' God sayin': "This hain't wuth nothin' t' Me. Get ye back t' hum!" I got afeerd o' that voice an' I lit out back t' hum here, leavin' my claim an' crops t' whoever'd a mind t' take 'em. Ay-eh. I actoolly give up what was rightful mine! God's hard, not easy! God's in the stones! Build my church on a rock—out o' stones an' I'll be in them! That's what He meant t' Peter! (*He sighs heavily—a pause*) Stones. I picked 'em up an' piled 'em into walls. Ye kin read the years o' my life in them walls, every day a hefted stone, climbin' over the hills up and down, fencin' in the fields that was mine, whar I'd made thin's grow out o' nothin'—like the will o' God, like the servant o' His hand. It wa'n't easy. It was hard an' He made me hard fur it. (*He pauses.*) All the time I kept gittin' lonesomer. I tuk a wife. She bore Simeon an' Peter. She was a good woman. She wuked hard. We was married twenty year. She never knowed me. She helped but she never knowed what she was helpin'. I was allus lonesome. She died. After that it wa'n't so lonesome fur a spell. (*a pause*) I lost count o' the years. I had no time t' fool away countin' 'em. Sim an' Peter helped. The farm growed. It was all mine! When I thought o' that I didn't feel lonesome. (*a pause*) But ye can't hitch yer mind t' one thin' day an' night. I tuk another wife—Eben's Maw. Her folks was contestin' me at law over my deeds t' the farm—my farm! That's why Eben keeps a'talkin' his fool talk o' this bein' his Maw's farm. She bore Eben. She was purty—but soft. She tried t' be hard. She couldn't. She never knowed me nor nothin'. It was lonesomer 'n hell with her. After a matter o' sixteen odd years, she died. (*a pause*) I lived with the boys. They hated me 'cause I was hard. I hated them 'cause they was soft. They coveted the farm without knowin' what it meant. It made me bitter 'n wormwood. It aged me—them coveting what I'd made fur mine. Then this spring the call come—the voice o' God cryin' in my wilderness, in my lonesomeness—t' go out an' seek an' find! (*Turning to her with strange passion*) I sought ye an' I found ye! Yew air my Rose o' Sharon! Yer eyes air like. . . . (*She has turned a blank face, resentful eyes to his. He stares at her for a moment—then harshly*) Air ye any the wiser fur all I've told ye?

ABBIE (*confusedly*). Mebbe.

CABOT (*pushing her away from him—angrily*). Ye don't know nothin'—nor never will. If ye don't hev a son t' redeem ye . . . (*this in a tone of cold threat*)

ABBIE (*resentfully*). I've prayed, hain't I?

CABOT (*bitterly*). Pray agen—fur understandin'!

ABBIE (*a veiled threat in her tone*). Ye'll have a son out o' me, I promise ye.

CABOT. How kin ye promise?

ABBIE. I got second-sight mebbe. I kin foretell. (*She gives a queer smile.*)

CABOT. I believe ye have. Ye give me the chills sometimes. (*He shivers.*) It's cold in this house. It's oneasy. They's thin's pokin' about in the dark—in the corners. (*He pulls on his trousers, tucking in his night shirt, and pulls on his boots.*)

ABBIE (*surprised*). Whar air ye goin'?

CABOT (*queerly*). Down whar it's restful—whar it's warm—down t' the barn. (*bitterly*) I kin talk t' the cows. They know. They know the farm an' me. They'll give me peace. (*He turns to go out the door.*)

ABBIE (*a bit frightenedly*). Air ye ailin' tonight, Ephraim?

CABOT. Growin'. Growin' ripe on the bough. (*He turns and goes, his boots clumping down the stairs. Eben sits up with a start, listening. Abbie is conscious of his movement and stares at the wall. Cabot comes out of the house around the corner and stands by the gate, blinking at the sky. He stretches up his hands in a tortured gesture*) God A'mighty, call from the dark! (*He listens as if expecting an answer. Then his arms drop, he shakes his head and plods off toward the barn. Eben and Abbie stare at each other through the wall. Eben sighs heavily and Abbie echoes it. Both become terribly nervous, uneasy. Finally Abbie gets up and listens, her ear to the wall. He acts as if he saw every move she was making, he becomes resolutely still. She seems driven into a decision—goes out the door in rear determinedly. His eyes follow her. Then as the door of his room is opened softly, he turns away, waits in an attitude of strained fixity. Abbie stands for a second staring at him, her eyes burning with desire. Then with a little cry she runs over and throws her arms about his neck, she pulls his head back and covers his mouth with kisses. At first, he submits dumbly; then he puts his arms about her neck and returns her kisses, but finally, suddenly aware of his hatred, he hurls her away from him, springing to his feet. They stand speechless and breathless, panting like two animals.*)

ABBIE (*at last—painfully*). Ye shouldn't, Eben—ye shouldn't—I'd make ye happy!

EBEN (*harshly*). I don't want t' be happy—from yew!

ABBIE (*helplessly*). Ye do, Eben! Ye do! Why d'ye lie?

EBEN (*viciously*). I don't take t'ye, I tell ye! I hate the sight o' ye!

ABBIE (*with an uncertain troubled laugh*). Waal, I kissed ye anyways—an' ye kissed back—yer lips was burnin'—ye can't lie 'bout that! (*intensely*). If ye don't care, why did ye kiss me back—why was yer lips burnin'?

EBEN (*wiping his mouth*). It was like pizen on 'em (*then tauntingly*) When I kissed ye back, mebbe I thought 'twas someone else.

ABBIE (*wildly*). Min?

EBEN. Mebbe.

ABBIE (*torturedly*). Did ye go t' see her? Did ye r'ally go? I thought ye mightn't. Is that why ye throwed me off jest now?

EBEN (*sneeringly*). What if it be?

ABBIE (*raging*). Then ye're a dog, Eben Cabot!

EBEN (*threateningly*). Ye can't talk that way t' me!

ABBIE (*with a shrill laugh*). Can't I? Did ye think I was in love with ye—a weak thin' like yew? Not much! I on'y wanted ye fur a purpose o' my own—an' I'll hev ye fur it yet 'cause I'm stronger'n yew be!

EBEN (*resentfully*). I knowed well it was on'y part o' yer plan t' swaller everythin'!

ABBIE (*taughtingly*). Mebbe!

EBEN (*furious*). Git out o' my room!

ABBIE. This air my room an' ye're on'y hired help!

EBEN (*threateningly*). Git out afore I murder ye!

ABBIE (*quite confident now*). I hain't a mite afeerd. Ye want me, don't ye? Yes, ye do! An' yer Paw's son'll never kill what he wants! Look at yer eyes! They's lust fur me in 'em, burnin' 'em up! Look at yer lips now! They're tremblin' an' longin' t' kiss me, an' yer teeth t'bite! (*He is watching her now with a horrible fascination. She laughs a crazy triumphant laugh.*) I'm a-goin' t' make all o' this hum my hum! They's one room hain't mine yet, but it's a-goin' t' be tonight. I'm a-goin' down now an' light up! (*She makes him a mocking bow.*) Won't ye come courtin' me in the best parlor, Mister Cabot?

EBEN (*staring at her—horribly confused—dully*). Don't ye dare! It hain't been opened since Maw died an' was laid out thar! Don't ye. . . . (*But her eyes are fixed on his so burningly that his will seems to wither before hers. He stands swaying toward her helplessly.*)

ABBIE (*holding his eyes and putting all her will into her words as she backs out the door*). I'll expect ye afore long, Eben.

EBEN (*stares after her for a while, walking toward the*

door. A light appears in the parlor window. He murmurs) In the parlor? (*This seems to arouse connotations for he comes back and puts on his white shirt, collar, half ties the tie mechanically, puts on coat, takes his hat, stands barefooted looking about him in bewilderment, mutters wonderingly*) Maw! Whar air yew? (*Then goes slowly toward the door in rear.*)

SCENE 3

A few minutes later. The interior of the parlor is shown. A grim, repressed room like a tomb in which the family has been interred alive. Abbie sits on the edge of the horsehair sofa. She has lighted all the candles and the room is revealed in all its preserved ugliness. A change has come over the woman. She looks awed and frightened now, ready to run away.

The door is opened and Eben appears. His face wears an expression of obsessed confusion. He stands staring at her, his arms hanging disjointedly from his shoulders, his feet bare, his hat in his hand.

ABBIE (*after a pause—with a nervous, formal politeness*). Won't ye set?

EBEN (*dully*). Ay-eh. (*Mechanically he places his hat carefully on the floor near the door and sits stiffly beside her on the edge of the sofa. A pause. They both remain rigid, looking straight ahead with eyes full of fear.*)

ABBIE. When I fust came in—in the dark—they seemed somethin' here.

EBEN (*simply*). Maw.

ABBIE. I kin still feel—somethin'....

EBEN. It's Maw.

ABBIE. At fust I was feered o' it. I wanted t' yell an' run. Now—since yew come—seems like it's growin' soft an' kind t' me. (*Addressing the air—queerly*) Thank yew.

EBEN. Maw allus loved me.

ABBIE. Mebbe it knows I love yew too. Mebbe that makes it kind t' me.

EBEN (*dully*). I dunno. I should think she'd hate ye.

ABBIE (*with certainty*). No. I kin feel it don't—not no more.

EBEN. Hate yer fur stealin' her place—here in her hum—settin' in her parlor whar she was laid— (*He suddenly stops, staring stupidly before him.*)

ABBIE. What is it, Eben?

EBEN (*in a whisper*). Seems like Maw didn't want me t' remind ye.

ABBIE (*excitedly*). I knowed, Eben! It's kind t' me! It don't b'ar me no grudges fur what I never knowed an' couldn't help!

EBEN. Maw b'ars him a grudge.

ABBIE. Waal, so does all o' us.

EBEN. Ay-eh. (*with passion*) I does, by God!

ABBIE (*taking one of his hands in hers and patting it*) Thar! Don't git riled thinkin' o' him. Think o' yer Maw who's kind t' us. Tell me about yer Maw, Eben.

EBEN. They hain't nothin' much. She was kind. She was good.

ABBIE (*putting one arm over his shoulder. He does not seem to notice—passionately*) I'll be kind an' good t' ye!

EBEN. Sometimes she used t' sing fur me.

ABBIE. I'll sing fur ye!

EBEN. This was her hum. This was her farm.

ABBIE. This is my hum! This is my farm!

EBEN. He married her t' steal 'em. She was soft an' easy. He couldn't 'preciate her.

ABBIE. He can't 'preciate me!

EBEN. He murdered her with his hardness.

ABBIE. He's murderin' me!

EBEN. She died. (*a pause*) Sometimes she used to sing fur me. (*He bursts into a fit of sobbing.*)

ABBIE (*both arms around him—with wild passion*). I'll sing fur ye! I'll die fur ye! (*In spite of her overwhelming desire for him, there is a sincere maternal love in her manner and voice—a horribly frank mixture of lust and mother love.*) Don't cry, Eben! I'll take yer Maw's place! I'll be everythin' she was t' ye! Let me kiss ye, Eben! (*She pulls his head around. He makes a bewildered pretense of resistance. She is tender.*) Don't be afeered! I'll kiss ye pure, Eben—same 's if I was a Maw t' ye—an' ye kin kiss me back 's if yew was my son—my boy—sayin' goodnight t' me! Kiss me, Eben. (*They kiss in restrained fashion. Then suddenly wild passion overcomes her. She kisses him lustfully again and again and he flings his arms about her and returns her kisses. Suddenly, as in the bedroom, he frees himself from her violently and springs to his feet. He is trembling all over, in a strange state of terror. Abbie strains her arms toward him with fierce pleading.*) Don't ye leave me, Eben! Can't ye see it hain't enuf—lovin' ye like a Maw—can't ye see it's got t' be that an' more—much more—a hundred times more—fur me t' be happy—fur yew t' be happy?

EBEN (*to the presence he feels in the room*). Maw! Maw! What d'ye want? What air ye tellin' me?

ABBIE. She's tellin' ye t' love me. She knows I love ye an' I'll be good t' ye. Can't ye feel it? Don't ye know? She's tellin' ye t' love me, Eben!

EBEN. Ah-eh. I feel—mebbe she—but—I can't figger out—why—when ye've stole her place—here in her hum—in the parlor whar she was—

ABBIE (*fiercely*). She knows I love ye!

EBEN (*his face suddenly lighting up with a fierce triumphant grin*). I see it! I sees why. It's her vengeance on him—so's she kin rest quiet in her grave!

ABBIE (*wildly*). Vengeance o' God on the hull o' us!

What d'we give a durn? I love ye, Eben! God knows I love ye! (*She stretches out her arms for him.*)

EBEN (*throws himself on his knees beside the sofa and grabs her in his arms—releasing all his pent-up passion*). An' I love yew, Abbie !—now I kin say it! I been dyin' fur want o' ye—every hour since ye come! I love ye! (*Their lips meet in a fierce, bruising kiss.*)

SCENE 4

Exterior of the farmhouse. It is just dawn. The front door at right is opened.

Eben comes out and walks around to the gate. He is dressed in his working clothes. He seems changed. His face wears a bold and confident expression, he is grinning to himself with evident satisfaction. As he gets near the gate, the window of the parlor is heard opening and the shutters are flung back and Abbie sticks her head out. Her hair tumbles over her shoulders in disarray, her face is flushed, she looks at Eben with tender, languorous eyes and calls softly.

ABBIE. Eben. (*As he turns—playfully*) Jest one more kiss afore ye go. I'm goin' to miss ye fearful all day.

EBEN. An' me yew, ye kin bet! (*He goes to her. They kiss several times. He draws away, laughingly.*) Thar. That's enuf, hain't it? Ye won't hev none left fur next time.

ABBIE. I got a million o' 'em left fur yew! (*then a bit anxiously*) D'ye r'ally love me, Eben?

EBEN (*emphatically*). I like ye better'n any gal I ever knowed! That's gospel!

ABBIE. Likin' hain't lovin'.

EBEN. Waal then—I love ye. Now air yew satisfied?

ABBIE. Ay-eh, I be. (*She smiles at him adoringly.*)

EBEN. I better git t' the barn. The old critter's liable t' suspicion an' come sneakin' up.

ABBIE (*with a confident laugh*). Let him! I kin allus pull the wool over his eyes. I'm goin' t' leave the shutters open and let in the sun 'n' air. This room's been dead long enuf. Now it's goin' t' be my room!

EBEN (*frowning*). Ay-eh.

ABBIE. We made it our'n last night, didn't we? We give it life—our lovin' did. (*a pause*)

EBEN (*with a strange look*). Maw's gone back t' her grave. She kin sleep now.

ABBIE. May she rest in peace! (*then tenderly rebuking*) Ye oughtn't t' talk o' sad thin's—this mornin'.

EBEN. It jest come up in my mind o' itself.

ABBIE. Don't let it. (*He doesn't answer. She yawns.*) Waal, I'm a-goin' t' steal a wink o' sleep. I'll tell the Old Man I hain't feelin' pert. Let him git his own vittles.

EBEN. I see him comin' from the barn Ye better look smart an' git upstairs.

ABBIE. Ay-eh. Good-by. Don't fergit me. (*She throws him a kiss. He grins—then squares his shoulders and awaits his father confidently. Cabot walks slowly up from the left, staring up at the sky with a vague face.*)

EBEN (*jovially*). Mornin', Paw. Star-gazin' in daylight?

CABOT. Purty, hain't it?

EBEN (*looking around him possessively*). It's a durned purty farm.

CABOT. I mean the sky.

EBEN (*grinning*). How d'ye know? Them eyes o' your'n can't see that fur. (*This tickles his humor and he slaps his thigh and laughs.*) Ho-ho! That's a good un!

CABOT (*grimly sarcastic*). Ye're feelin' right chipper, hain't ye? Whar'd ye steal the likker?

BERN (*good-naturedly*). 'Taint likker. Jest life. (*Suddenly holding out his hand—soberly*). Yew 'n' me is quits. Let's shake hands.

CABOT (*suspiciously*). What's come over ye?

EBEN. Then don't. Mebbe it's jest as well. (*a moment's pause*) What's come over me? (*queerly*) Didn't ye feel her passin'—goin' back t' her grave?

CABOT (*dully*). Who?

EBEN. Maw. She kin rest now an' sleep content. She's quit with ye.

CABOT (*confusedly*). I rested. I slept good—down with the cows. They know how t' sleep. They're teachin' me.

EBEN (*suddenly jovial again*). Good fur the cows! Waal—ye better git t' work.

CABOT (*grimly amused*). Air yew bossin' me, ye calf?

EBEN (*beginning to laugh*). Ah-eh! I'm bossin' yew! Ha-ha-ha! see how ye like it! Ha-ha-ha! I'm the prize rooster o' this roost. Ha-ha-ha! (*He goes off toward tho barn laughing.*)

CABOT (*looks after him with scornful pity*). Soft-headed. Like his Maw. Dead spit 'n' image. No hope in him! (*He spits with contemptuous disgust.*) A born fool! (*Then matter-of-factly*) Waal—I'm gittin' peckish. (*He goes toward door.*)

PART 3

SCENE 1

A night in late spring the following year. The kitchen and the two bedrooms upstairs are shown. The two bedrooms are dimly lighted by a tallow candle in each. Eben is sitting on the side of the bed in his room, his chin propped on his fists, his face a study of the struggle he is making to understand his conflicting emotions. The noisy laughter and music from below where a kitchen dance is in progress annoy and distract him. He scowls at the floor. In the next room a cradle stands beside the double bed.

In the kitchen all is festivity. The stove has been taken down to give more room to the dancers. The chairs, with wooden benches added, have been pushed back against the walls. On these are seated, squeezed in tight against one another, farmers and their wives and their young folks of both sexes from the neighboring farms. They are all chattering and laughing loudly. They evidently have some secret joke in common. There is no end of winking, of nudging, of meaning nods of the head toward Cabot who, in a state of extreme hilarious excitement increased by the amount he has drunk, is standing near the rear door where there is a small keg of whisky and serving drinks to all the men. In the left corner, front, dividing the attention with her husband, Abbie is sitting in a rocking chair, a shawl wrapped about her shoulders. She is very pale, her face is thin and drawn, her eyes are fixed anxiously on the open door in rear as if waiting for someone.

The Musician is tuning up his fiddle, seated in the far right corner. He is a lanky young fellow with a long, weak face. His pale eyes blink incessantly and he grins about him slyly with a greedy malice.

ABBIE (*suddenly turning to a young girl on her right*). Whar's Eben?

YOUNG GIRL (*eying her scornfully*). I dunno, Mrs. Cabot. I hain't seen Eben in ages. (*meaningly*) Seems like he's spent most o' his time t' hum since yew come.

ABBIE (*vaguely*). I tuk his Maw's place.

YOUNG GIRL. Ay-eh. So I've heerd. (*She turns away to retail this bit of gossip to her mother sitting next to her. Abbie turns to her left to a big stoutish middle-aged man whose flushed face and staring eyes show the amount of "likker" he has consumed.*)

ABBIE. Ye hain't seen Eben, hev ye?

MAN. No, I hain't. (*then he adds with a wink*) If yew hain't, who would?

ABBIE. He's the best dancer in the county. He'd ought t' come an' dance.

MAN (*with a wink*). Mebbe he's doin' the dutiful an' walkin' the kid t' sleep. It's a boy, hain't it?

ABBIE (*nodding vaguely*). Ay-eh—born two weeks back—purty's a picter.

MAN. They all is—t' their Maws. (*then in a whisper, with a nudge and a leer*) Listen, Abbie—if ye ever git tired o' Eben, remember me! Don't fergit now! (*He looks at her uncomprehending face for a second—then grunts disgustedly.*) Waal—guess I'll likker agin. (*He goes over and joins Cabot who is arguing noisily with an old farmer over cows. They all drink.*)

ABBIE (*this time appealing to nobody in particular*). Wonder what Eben's a-doin'? (*Her remark is repeated down the line with many a guffaw and titter until it reaches the fiddler. He fastens his blinking eyes on Abbie.*)

FIDDLER (*raising his voice*). Bet I kin tell ye, Abbie, what Eben's doin'! He's down t' the church offerin' up prayers o' thanksgivin'. (*They all titter expectantly.*)

MAN. What fur? (*Another titter.*)

FIDDLER. 'Cause unto him a—(*He hesitates just long enough.*)—brother is born! (*A roar of laughter. They all look from Abbie to Cabot. She is oblivious, staring at the door. Cabot, although he hasn't heard the words, is irritated by the laughter and steps forward, glaring about him. There is an immediate silence.*)

CABOT. What're ye all bleatin' about—like a flock o' goats? Why don't ye dance, damn ye? I axed ye here t' dance—t' eat, drink an' be merry—an' thar ye set cacklin' like a lot o' wet hens with the pip! Ye've swilled my likker an' guzzled my vittles like hogs, hain't ye? Then dance fur me, can't ye? That's fa'r an' squar', hain't it? (*A grumble of resentment goes around but they are all evidently in too much awe of him to express it openly.*)

FIDDLER (*slyly*). We're waitin' fur Eben. (*a suppressed laugh*)

CABOT (*with a fierce exultation*). T'hell with Eben! Eben's done fur now! I got a new son! (*his mood switching with drunken suddenness*) But ye needn't t' laugh at Eben, none o' ye! He's my blood, if he be a dumb fool. He's better nor any o' yew! He kin do a day's work a'most up t' what I kin—an' that'd put any o' yew pore critters t' shame!

FIDDLER. An' he kin do a good night's work, too! (*a roar of laughter*)

CABOT. Laugh, ye damn fools! Ye're right jist the same, Fiddler. He kin work day an' night too, like I kin, if need be!

OLD FARMER (*from behind the keg where he is weaving drunkenly back and forth—with great simplicity*). They hain't many t' touch ye, Ephraim—a son at seventy-six. That's a hard man fur ye! I be on'y sixty-eight an' I couldn't do it. (*a roar of laughter in which Cabot joins uproariously*)

CABOT (*slapping him on the back*). I'm sorry fur ye, Hi. I'd never suspicion sech weakness from a boy like yew!

OLD FARMER. An' I never reckoned yew had it in ye nuther, Ephraim. (*There is another laugh.*)

CABOT (*suddenly grim*). I got a lot in me—a hell of a lot—folks don't know on. (*turning to the Fiddler*) Fiddle 'er up, durn ye! Give 'em somethin' t' dance t'! What air ye, an ornament? Hain't this a celebration? Then grease yer elbow an' go it!

FIDDLER (*seizes a drink which the Old Farmer holds out to him and downs it*). Here goes! (*He starts to fiddle "Lady of the Lake." Four young fellows and four girls form in two lines and dance a square dance. The Fiddler shouts directions for the different movements, keeping his words in the rhythm of the music and interspersing them with jocular personal remarks to the dancers themselves. The people seated along the walls stamp their feet and clap their hands in unison. Cabot is especially active in this respect. Only Abbie remains apathetic, staring at the door as if she were alone in a silent room.*)

FIDDLER. Swing your partner t' the right! That's it, Jim! Give her a b'ar hug! Her Maw hain't lookin'. (*laughter*) Change partners! That suits ye, don't it, Essie, now ye got Reub afore ye? Look at her redden up, will ye! Waal, life is short an' so's love, as the feller says. (*laughter*)

CABOT (*excitedly, stamping his foot*). Go it, boys! Go it, gals!

FIDDLER (*with a wink at the others*). Ye're the spryest seventy-six ever I sees, Ephraim! Now if ye'd on'y good eye-sight . . . ! (*Suppressed laughter. He gives Cabot no chance to retort but roars*) Promenade! Ye're walkin' like a bride down the aisle, Sarah! Waal, while they's life they's allus hope, I've heerd tell. Swing your partner to the left! Gosh A'mighty, look at Johnny Cook high-steppin'! They hain't goin' t'be much strength left fur howin' in the corn lot t'morrow. (*laughter*)

CABOT. Go it! Go it! (*Then suddenly, unable to restrain himself any longer, he prances into the midst of the dancers, scattering them, waving his arms about wildly.*) Ye're all hoofs! Git out o' my road! Give me room! I'll show ye dancin'. Ye're all too soft! (*He pushes them roughly away. They crowd back toward the walls, muttering, looking at him resentfully.*)

FIDDLER (*jeeringly*). Go it, Ephraim! Go it! (*He starts "Pop Goes the Weasel," increasing the tempo with every verse until at the end he is fiddling crazily as fast as he can go.*)

CABOT (*starts to dance, which he does very well and with tremendous vigor. Then he begins to improvise, cuts incredibly grotesque capers, leaping up and cracking his heels together, prancing around in a circle with body bent in an Indian war dance, then suddenly straightening up and kicking as high as he can with both legs. He is like a monkey on a string. And all the while he intersperses his antics with shouts and derisive comments*). Whoop! Here's dancin' fur ye! Whoop! See that! Seventy-six, if I'm a day! Hard as iron yet! Beatin' the young 'uns like I allus done! Look at me! I'd invite ye t' dance on my hundredth birthday on'y ye'll all be dead by then. Ye're a sickly generation! Yer hearts air pink, not red! Yer veins is full o' mud an' water! I be the on'y man in the county! Whoop! See that! I'm a Injun! I've killed Injuns in the West afore ye was born—an' skulped 'em too! They's a arrer wound on my backside I c'd show ye! The hull tribe chased me. I outrun 'em all—with the arrer stuck in me! An' I tuk vengeance on 'em. Ten eyes fur an eye, that was my motter! Whoop! Look at me! I kin kick the ceilin' off the room! Whoop!

FIDDLER (*stops playing—exhaustedly*). God A'mighty, I got enuf. Ye got the devil's strength in ye.

CABOT (*delightedly*). Did I beat yew, too? Wa'al, ye played smart. Hev a swig. (*He pours whisky for himself and Fiddler. They drink. The others watch Cabot silently with cold, hostile eyes. There is a dead pause. The Fiddler rests. Cabot leans against the keg, panting, glaring around him confusedly. In the room above, Eben gets to his feet and tiptoes out the door in rear, appearing a moment later in the other bedroom. He moves silently, even frightenedly, toward the cradle and stands there looking down at the baby. His face is as vague as his reactions are confused, but there is a trace of tenderness, of interested discovery. At the same moment that he reaches the cradle, Abbie seems to sense something. She gets up weakly and goes to Cabot.*)

ABBIE. I'm goin' up t' the baby.

CABOT (*with real solicitude*). Air ye able fur the stairs? D'ye want me t' help ye, Abbie?

ABBIE. No. I'm able. I'll be down agen soon.

CABOT. Don't ye git wore out! He needs ye, remember—our son does! (*He grins affectionately, patting her on the back. She shrinks from his touch.*)

ABBIE (*dully*). Don't—tech me. I'm goin'—up. (*She goes. Cabot looks after her. A whisper goes around the room. Cabot turns. It ceases. He wipes his forehead streaming with sweat. He is breathing pantingly.*)

CABOT. I'm a-goin' out t' git fresh air. I'm feelin' a mite dizzy. Fiddle up thar! Dance, all o' ye! Here's likker fur them as wants it. Enjoy yerselves. I'll be back. (*He goes, closing the door behind him.*)

FIDDLER (*sarcastically*). Don't hurry none on our account! (*A suppressed laugh. He imitates Abbie.*) Whar's Eben? (*more laughter*)

A WOMAN (*loudly*). What's happened in this house is plain as the nose on yer face! (*Abbie appears in the doorway upstairs and stands looking in surprise and adoration at Eben who does not see her.*)

A MAN. Ssshh! He's li'ble t' be listenin' at the door. That'd be like him. (*Their voices die to an intensive whispering. Their faces are concentrated on this gossip. A noise as of dead leaves in the wind comes from the room. Cabot has come out from the porch and stands by the gate, leaning on it, staring at the sky blinkingly. Abbie comes across the room silently. Eben does not notice her until quite near.*)

EBEN (*starting*). Abbie!

ABBIE. Ssshh! (*She throws her arms around him. They kiss—then bend over the cradle together.*) Ain't he purty?—dead spit 'n' image o' yew!

EBEN (*pleased*). Air he? I can't tell none.

ABBIE. E-zactly like!

EBEN (*frowningly*). I don't like this. I don't like lettin' on what's mine's his'n. I been doin' that all my life. I'm gittin' t' the end o' b'arin' it!

ABBIE (*putting her finger on his lips*). We're doin' the best we kin. We got t' wait. Somethin's bound t' happen. (*She puts her arms around him.*) I got t' go back.

EBEN. I'm goin' out. I can't b'ar it with the fiddle playin' an' the laughin'.

ABBIE. Don't git feelin' low. I love ye, Eben. Kiss me. (*He kisses her. They remain in each other's arms.*)

CABOT (*at the gate, confusedly*). Even the music can't drive it out—somethin'. Ye kin feel it droppin' off the elums, climbin' up the roof, sneakin' down the chimney, pokin' in the comers! They's no peace in houses, they's no rest livin' with folks. Somethin's always livin' with ye. (*with a deep sigh*) I'll go t' the barn an' rest a spell. (*He goes wearily toward the barn.*)

FIDDLER (*tuning up*). Let's celebrate the old skunk gittin' fooled! We kin have some fun now he's went. (*He starts to fiddle "Turkey in the Straw." There is real merriment now. The young folks get up to dance.*)

SCENE 2

A half hour later—exterior.

Eben is standing by the gate looking up at the sky, an expression of dumb pain bewildered by itself on his face. Cabot appears, returning from the barn, walking wearily, his eyes on the ground. He sees Eben and his whole mood immediately changes. He becomes excited, a cruel, triumphant grin comes to his lips, he strides up and slaps Eben on the back. From within comes the whining of the fiddle and the noise of stamping feet and laughing voices.

CABOT. So har ye be!

EBEN (*startled, stares at him with hatred for a moment—then dully*). Ay-eh.

CABOT (*surveying him jeeringly*). Why hain't ye been in t' dance? They was all axin' fur ye.

EBEN. Let 'em ax!

CABOT. They's a hull pasel o' purty gals.

EBEN. T' hell with 'em!

CABOT. Ye'd ought t' be marryin' one o' 'em soon.

EBEN. I hain't marryin' no one.

CABOT. Ye might 'arn a share o' a farm that way.

EBEN (*with a sneer*). Like yew did, ye mean? I hain't that kind.

CABOT (*stung*). Ye lie! 'Twas yer Maw's folks aimed t' steal my farm from me.

EBEN. Other folks don't say so. (*after a pause—defiantly*) An' I got a farm, anyways!

CABOT (*derisively*). Whar?

EBEN (*stamps a foot on the ground*). Har!

CABOT (*throws his head back and laughs coarsely*). Ho-ho! Ye hev, hev ye? Waal, that's a good un!

EBEN (*controlling himself—grimly*). Ye'll see!

CABOT (*stares at him suspiciously, trying to make him out—a pause—then with scornful confidence*). Ay-eh. I'll see. So'll ye. It's ye that's blind—blind as a mole underground. (*Eben suddenly laughs, one short sardonic bark: "Ha." A pause. Cabot peers at him with renewed suspicion.*) Whar air ye hawin' 'bout? (*Eben turns away without answering. Cabot grows angry.*) God A'mighty, yew air a dumb dunce! They's nothin' in that thick skull o' your'n but noise—like a empty keg it be! (*Eben doesn't seem to hear—Cabot's rage grows.*) Yewr farm! God A'mighty! If ye wa'n't a born donkey ye'd know ye'll never own stick nor stone on it, specially now arter him bein' born. It's his'n, I tell ye—his'n arter I die—but I'll live a hundred jest t' fool ye all—an' he'll be growed then—yewr age a'most! (*Eben laughs again his sardonic "Ha." This drives Cabot into a fury.*) Ha? Ye think ye kin git 'round that someways, do ye? Waal, it'll be her'n, too—Abbie's—ye won't git 'round her—she knows yer tricks—she'll be too much fur ye—she wants the farm her'n—she was afeerd o' ye—she told me ye was sneakin' 'round tryin' t' make love t' her t' git her on yer side . . . ye . . . ye mad fool, ye! (*He raises his clenched fists threateningly.*)

EBEN (*is confronting him choking with rage*). Ye lie, ye old skunk! Abbie never said no sech thing!

CABOT (*suddenly triumphant when he sees how shaken Eben is*). She did. An' I says, I'll blow his brains t' the top o' them elums—an' she says no, that hain't sense, who'll ye git t'help ye on the farm in his place—an' then she says yew'n me ought t' have a son—I know we kin, she says—an' I says, if we do, ye kin have anythin' I've got ye've a mind t'. An' she says, I wants Eben cut off so's this farm'll be mine when ye die! (*with terrible gloating*) An' that's what's happened, hain't it? An' the farm's her'n! An' the dust o' the road—that's you'rn! Ha! Now who's hawin'?

EBEN (*has been listening, petrified with grief and rage—suddenly laughs wildly and brokenly*). Ha-ha-ha! So that's her sneakin' game—all along!—like I suspicioned at fust—t' swaller it all—an' me, too . . . ! (*madly*) I'll murder her! (*He springs toward the porch but Cabot is quicker and gets in between.*)

CABOT. No, ye don't!

EBEN. Git out o' my road! (*He tries to throw Cabot aside. They grapple in what becomes immediately a murderous struggle. The old man's concentrated strength is too much for Eben. Cabot gets one hand on his throat and presses him back across the stone wall. At the same moment, Abbie comes out on the porch. With a stifled cry she runs toward them.*)

ABBIE. Eben! Ephraim! (*She tugs at the hand on Eben's throat.*) Let go, Ephraim! Ye're chokin' him!

CABOT (*removes his hand and flings Eben sideways full length on the grass, gasping and choking. With a cry, Abbie kneels beside him, trying to take his head on her lap, but he pushes her away. Cabot stands looking down with fierce triumph*). Ye needn't t've fret, Abbie, I wa'n't aimin' t' kill him. He hain't wuth hangin' fur—not by a hell of a sight! (*more and more triumphantly*) Seventy-six an' him not thirty yit—an' look whar he be fur thinkin' his Paw was easy! No, by God, I hain't easy! An' him upstairs, I'll raise him t' be like me! (*He turns to leave them.*) I'm goin' in an' dance—sing an' celebrate! (*He walks to the porch—then turns with a great grin.*) I don't calc'late it's left in him, but if he gits pesky, Abbie, ye jest sing out. I'll come a-runnin' an' by the Etarnal, I'll put him across my knee an' birch him! Ha-ha-ha! (*He goes into the house laughing. A moment later his loud "whoop" is heard.*)

ABBIE (*tenderly*). Eben. Air ye hurt? (*She tries to kiss him but he pushes her violently away and struggles to a sitting position.*)

EBEN (*gaspingly*). T'hell—with ye!

ABBIE (*not believing her ears*). It's me, Eben—Abbie—don't ye know me?

EBEN (*glowering at her with hatred*). Ay-eh—I know ye—now! (*He suddenly breaks down, sobbing weakly.*)

ABBIE (*fearfully*). Eben—what's happened t' ye—why did ye look at me 's if ye hated me?

EBEN (*violently, between sobs and gasps*). I do hate ye! Ye're a whore—a damn trickin' whore!

ABBIE (*shrinking back horrified*). Eben! Ye don't know what ye're sayin'!

EBEN (*scrambling to his feet and following her—accusingly*). Ye're nothin' but a stinkin' passel o' lies! Ye've been lyin' t' me every word ye spoke, day an' night, since we fust—done it. Ye've kept' sayin' ye loved me. . . .

ABBIE (*frantically*). I do love ye! (*She takes his hand but he flings hers away.*)

EBEN (*unheeding*). Ye've made a fool o' me—a sick, dumb fool—a-purpose! Ye've been on'y playin' yer sneakin', stealin' game all along—gittin' me t' lie with ye so's ye'd hev a son he'd think was his'n, an' makin' him promise he'd give ye the farm and let me eat dust, if ye did git him a son! (*staring at her with anguished, bewildered eyes*) They must be a devil livin' in ye! 'Tain't human t' be as bad as that be!

ABBIE (*stunned—dully*). He told yew . . . ?

EBEN. Hain't it true? It hain't no good in yew lyin'.

ABBIE (*pleadingly*). Eben, listen—ye must listen—it was long ago—afore we done nothin'—yew was scornin' me—goin' t' see Min—when I was lovin' ye—an' I said it t' him t' git vengeance on ye!

EBEN (*unheedingly. With tortured passion*). I wish ye was dead! I wish I was dead along with ye afore this come! (*ragingly*) But I'll git my vengeance too! I'll pray Maw t' come back t' help me—t' put her cuss on yew an' him!

ABBIE (*brokenly*). Don't ye, Eben! Don't ye! (*She throws herself on her knees before him, weeping.*) I didn't mean t' do bad t'ye! Fergive me, won't ye?

EBEN (*not seeming to hear her—fiercely*). I'll git squar' with the old skunk—an' yew! I'll tell him the truth 'bout the son he's so proud o'! Then I'll leave ye here t' pizen each other— with Maw comin' out o' her grave at nights—an' I'll go t' the gold fields o' Californi-a whar Sim an' Peter be!

ABBIE (*terrified*). Ye won't—leave me? Ye can't!

EBEN (*with fierce determination*). I'm a-goin', I tell ye! I'll git rich thar an' come back an' fight him fur the farm he stole—an' I'll kick ye both out in the road—t' beg an' sleep in the woods—an' yer son along with ye—t' starve an' die! (*He is hysterical at the end.*)

ABBIE (*with a shudder—humbly*). He's yewr son, too, Eben.

EBEN (*torturedly*). I wish he never was born! I wish he'd die this minit! I wish I'd never sot eyes on him! It's him—yew havin' him—a-purpose t' steal—that's changed everythin'!

ABBIE (*gently*). Did ye believe I loved ye—afore he come?

EBEN. Ay-eh—like a dumb ox!

ABBIE. An' ye don't believe no more?

EBEN. B'lieve a lyin' thief! Ha!

ABBIE (*shudders—then humbly*). An did ye r'ally love me afore?

EBEN (*brokenly*). Ay-eh—an' ye was trickin' me!

ABBIE. An' ye don't love me now!

EBEN (*violently*). I hate ye, I tell ye!

ABBIE. An' ye're truly goin' West—goin' t' leave me—all account o' him being born?

EBEN. I'm a-goin' in the mornin'—or may God strike me t' hell!

ABBIE (*after a pause—with a dreadful cold intensity—slowly*). If that's what his comin's done t' me—killin' yewr love—takin' yew away—my on'y joy—the on'y joy I've ever knowed—like heaven t' me—purtier'n heaven—then I hate him, too, even if I be his Maw!

EBEN (*bitterly*). Lies! Ye love him! He'll steal the farm fur ye! (*brokenly*) But 'tain't the farm so much—not no more—it's yew foolin' me—gittin' me t' love ye—lyin' yew loved me—jest t' git a son t' steal!

ABBIE (*distractedly*). He won't steal! I'd kill him fust! I do love ye! I'll prove t' ye . . . !

EBEN (*harshly*). 'Tain't no use lyin' no more. I'm deaf t' ye! (*He turns away.*) I hain't seein' ye agen. Good-by!

ABBIE (*pale with anguish*). Hain't ye even goin' t' kiss me—not once—arter all we loved?

EBEN (*in a hard voice*). I hain't wantin' t' kiss ye never agen! I'm wantin' t' forgit I ever sot eyes on ye!

ABBIE. Eben!—ye mustn't—wait a spell—I want t' tell ye. . . .

EBEN. I'm a-goin' in t' git drunk. I'm agoin' t' dance.

ABBIE (*clinging to his arm—with passionate earnestness*). If I could make it—'s if he'd never come up between us—if I could prove t' ye I wa'n't schemin' t' steal from ye—so's everythin' could be jest the same with us, lovin' each other jest the same, kissin' an' happy the same's we've been happy afore he come—if I could do it—ye'd love me agen, wouldn't ye? Ye'd kiss me agen? Ye wouldn't never leave me, would ye?

EBEN (*moved*). I calc'late not. (*Then shaking her hand off his arm—with a bitter smile*) But ye hain't God, be ye?

ABBIE (*exultantly*). Remember ye've promised! (*Then with strange intensity*) Mebbe I kin take back one thin' God does!

EBEN (*peering at her*). Ye're gittin' cracked, hain't ye? (*Then going towards door*) I'm a-goin' t' dance.

ABBIE (*calls after him intensely*). I'll prove t' ye! I'll prove I love ye better'n. . . . (*He goes in the door, not seeming to hear. She remains standing where she is, looking after him—then she finishes desperately*) Better'n everythin' else in the world!

SCENE 3

Just before dawn in the morning—shows the kitchen and Cabot's bedroom.

In the kitchen, by the light of a tallow candle on the table, Eben is sitting, his chin propped on his hands, his drawn face blank and expressionless. His carpetbag is on the floor beside him. In the bedroom, dimly lighted by a small whale-oil lamp, Cabot lies asleep. Abbie is bending over the cradle, listening, her face full of terror yet with an undercurrent of desperate triumph. Suddenly, she breaks down and sobs, appears about to throw herself on her knees beside the cradle; but the old man turns restlessly, groaning in his sleep, and she controls herself, and shrinking away from the cradle with a gesture of horror, backs swiftly toward the door in rear and goes out. A moment later she comes into the kitchen and, running to Eben, flings her arms about his neck and kisses him wildly. He hardens himself, he remains unmoved and cold, he keeps his eyes straight ahead.

ABBIE (*hysterically*). I done it, Eben! I told ye I'd do it! I've proved I love ye—better'n everythin'—so's ye can't never doubt me no more!

EBEN (*dully*). Whatever ye done, it hain't no good now.

ABBIE (*wildly*). Don't ye say that! Kiss me, Eben, won't ye? I need ye t' kiss me arter what I done! I need ye t' say ye love me!

EBEN (*kisses her without emotion—dully*). That's fur good-by. I'm a-goin' soon.

ABBIE. No! No! Ye won't go—not now!

EBEN (*going on with his own thoughts*). I been a-thinkin'—an' I hain't goin' t' tell Paw nothin'. I'll leave Maw t' take vengeance on ye. If I told him, the old skunk'd jest be stinkin' mean enuf to take it out on that baby. (*His voice showing emotion in spite of him*) An' I don't want nothin' bad t' happen t' him. He hain't t' blame fur yew. (*He adds with a certain queer pride*) An' he looks like me! An' by God, he's mine! An' some day I'll be a-comin' back an' . . . !

ABBIE (*too absorbed in her own thoughts to listen to him—pleadingly*). They's no cause fur ye t' go now—they's no sense—it's all the same's it was—they's nothin' come b'tween us now—arter what I done!

EBEN (*something in her voice arouses him. He stares at her a bit frightenedly*). Ye look mad, Abbie. What did ye do?

ABBIE. I—I killed him, Eben.

EBEN (*amazed*). Ye killed him?

ABBIE (*dully*). Ay-eh.

EBEN (*recovering from his astonishment—savagely*). An' serves him right! But we got t' do somethin' quick t' make it look s'if the old skunk'd killed himself when he was drunk. We kin prove by 'em all how drunk he got.

ABBIE (*wildly*). No! No! Not him! (*Laughing distractedly*). But that's what I ought t' done, hain't it? I oughter killed him instead! Why didn't ye tell me?

EBEN (*appalled*). Instead? What d'ye mean?

ABBIE. Not him.

EBEN (*his face grown ghastly*). Not—not that baby!

ABBIE (*dully*). Ay-eh!

EBEN (*falls to his knees as if he'd been struck—his voice trembling with horror*). Oh, God A'mighty! A'mighty God! Maw, whar was ye, why didn't ye stop her?

ABBIE (*simply*). She went back t' her grave that night we fust done it, remember? I hain't felt her about since. (*A pause. Eben hides his head in his hands, trembling all over as if he had the ague. She goes on dully*). I left the piller over his little face. Then he killed himself. He stopped breathin'. (*She begins to weep softly.*)

EBEN (*rage beginning to mingle with grief*). He looked like me. He was mine, damn ye!

ABBIE (*slowly and brokenly*). I didn't want t' do it. I hated myself, fur doin' it. I loved him. He was so purty—dead spit 'n' image o' yew. But I loved yew more—an' yew was goin' away—far off whar I'd never see ye agen, never kiss ye, never feel ye pressed agin me agen—an' ye said ye hated me fur havin' him—ye said ye hated him an' wished he was dead—ye said if it hadn't been fur him comin' it'd be the same's afore between us.

EBEN (*unable to endure this, springs to his feet in a fury, threatening her, his twitching fingers seeming to reach out for her throat*). Ye lie! I never said—I never dreamed ye'd—I'd cut off my head afore I'd hurt his finger!

ABBIE (*piteously, sinking on her knees*). Eben, don't ye look at me like that—hatin' me—not after what I done fur ye—fur us—so's we could be happy agen—

EBEN (*furiously now*). Shut up, or I'll kill ye! I see yer game now—the same old sneakin' trick—ye're aimin' t' blame me fur the murder ye done!

ABBIE (*moaning—putting her hands over her ears*). Don't ye, Eben! Don't ye! (*She grasps his legs.*)

EBEN (*his mood suddenly changing to horror, shrinks away from her*). Don't ye tech me! Ye're pizen! How could ye—t' murder a pore little critter— Ye must've swapped yer soul t' hell! (*suddenly raging*) Ha! I kin see why ye done it! Not the lies ye jest told—but 'cause ye wanted t' steal agen—steal the last thin' ye'd left me—my part o' him—no, the hull o' him—ye saw he looked like me—ye knowed he was all mine—an' ye couldn't b'ar it—I know ye! Ye killed him fur bein' mine! (*All this has driven him almost insane. He makes a rush past her for the door—then turns—shaking both fists at her, violently.*) But I'll take vengeance now! I'll git the Sheriff! I'll tell him everythin'! Then I'll sing "I'm off to Californi-a!" an' go—gold—Golden Gate—gold sun—fields o' gold in the West! (*This last he half shouts, half croons incoherently, suddenly breaking off passionately.*) I'm a-goin' fur the Sheriff t' come an' git ye! I want ye tuk away, locked up from me! I can't stand t'luk at ye! Murderer an' thief 'r not, ye still tempt me! I'll give ye up t' the Sheriff! (*He turns and runs out, around the corner of house, panting and sobbing, and breaks into a swerving sprint down the road.*)

ABBIE (*struggling to her feet, runs to the door, calling after him*). I love ye, Eben! I love ye! (*She stops at the door weakly, swaying, about to fall.*) I don't care what ye do—if ye'll on'y love me agen—(*She falls limply to the floor in a faint.*)

SCENE 4

About an hour later. Same as Scene 3. Shows the kitchen and Cabot's bedroom. It is after dawn. The sky is brilliant with the sunrise.

In the kitchen, Abbie sits at the table, her body limp and exhausted, her head bowed down over her arms, her face hidden. Upstairs, Cabot is still asleep but awakens with a start. He looks toward the window and gives a snort of surprise and irritation—throws back the covers and begins hurriedly pulling on his clothes. Without looking behind him, he begins talking to Abbie whom he supposes beside him.

CABOT. Thunder 'n' lightnin', Abbie! I hain't slept this late in fifty year! Looks 's if the sun was full riz a'most. Must've been the dancin' an' likker. Must be gittin' old. I hope Eben's t' wuk. Ye might've tuk the trouble t' rouse me, Abbie. (*He turns—sees no one there—surprised.*) Waal—whar air she? Gittin' vittles, I calc'late. (*He tiptoes to the cradle and peers down—proudly*) Mornin', sonny. Purty's a picter! Sleepin' sound. He don't beller all night like most o' 'em. (*He goes quietly out the door in rear—a few moments later enters kitchen—sees Abbie—with satisfaction*) So thar ye be. Ye got any vittles cooked?

ABBIE (*without moving*). No.

CABOT (*coming to her, almost sympathetically*). Ye feelin' sick?

ABBIE. No.

CABOT (*pats her on shoulder. She shudders*). Ye'd best lie down a spell. (*half jocularly*) Yer son'll be needin' ye soon. He'd ought t' wake up with a gnashin' appetite, the sound way he's sleepin'.

ABBIE (*shudders—then in a dead voice*). He ain't never goin' to wake up.

CABOT (*jokingly*). Takes after me this mornin'. I ain't slept so late in . . .

ABBIE. He's dead.

CABOT (*stares at her—bewilderedly*). What . . .

ABBIE. I killed him.

CABOT (*stepping back from her—aghast*). Air ye drunk —'r crazy—'r . . . !

ABBIE (*suddenly lifts her head and turns on him—wildly*). I killed him, I tell ye! I smothered him. Go up an' see if ye don't b'lieve me! (*Cabot stares at her a second, then bolts out the rear door, can be heard bounding up the stairs, and rushes into the bedroom and over to the cradle. Abbie has sunk back lifelessly into her former position. Cabot puts his hand down on the body in the crib. An expression of fear and horror comes over his face.*)

CABOT (*shrinking away—tremblingly*). God A'mighty! God A'mighty. (*He stumbles out the door—in a short while returns to the kitchen—comes to Abbie, the stunned expression still on his face—hoarsely*). Why did ye do it? Why? (*As she doesn't answer, he grabs her violently by the shoulder and shakes her.*) I ax ye why ye done it! Ye'd better tell me 'r . . . !

ABBIE (*gives him a furious push which sends him staggering back and springs to her feet—with wild rage and hatred*). Don't ye dare tech me! What right hev ye t' question me 'bout him? He wa'n't yewr son! Think I'd have a son by yew? I'd die fust! I hate the sight o' ye an' allus did! It's yew I should've murdered, if I'd had good sense! I hate ye! I love Eben. I did from the fust. An' he was Eben's son—mine an' Eben's—not your'n!

CABOT (*stands looking at her dazedly—a pause—finding his words with an effort—dully*). That was it—what I felt—pokin' round the corners—while ye lied—holdin' herself from me—sayin' ye'd a'ready conceived—(*He lapses into crushed silence—then with a strange emotion*) He's dead, sart'n. I felt his heart. Pore little critter! (*He blinks back one tear, wiping his sleeve across his nose.*)

ABBIE (*hysterically*). Don't ye! Don't ye! (*She sobs unrestrainedly.*)

CABOT (*with a concentrated effort that stiffens his body into a rigid line and hardens his face into a stony mask—through his teeth to himself*). I got t' be—like a stone—a rock o' jedgment! (*A pause. He gets complete control over himself—harshly*) If he was Eben's, I be glad he air gone! An' mebbe I suspicioned it all along. I felt they was somethin' onnateral—somewhars—the house got so lonesome—an' cold—drivin' me down t' the barn—t' the beasts o' the field. . . . Ay-eh. I must've suspicioned—somethin'. Ye didn't fool me—not altogether, leastways—I'm too old a bird—

growin' ripe on the bough. . . . (*He becomes aware he is wandering, straightens again, looks at Abbie with a cruel grin.*) So ye'd liked t' hev murdered me 'stead o' him, would ye? Waal, I'll live to a hundred! I'll live t' see ye hung! I'll deliver ye up t' the jedgment o' God an' the law! I'll git the Sheriff now. (*Starts for the door.*)

ABBIE (*dully*). Ye needn't. Eben's gone fur him.

CABOT (*amazed*). Eben—gone fur the Sheriff?

ABBIE. Ay-eh.

CABOT. T'inform agen ye?

ABBIE. Ay-eh.

CABOT (*considers this—a pause—then in a hard voice*). Waal, I'm thankful fur him savin' me the trouble. I'll git t' wuk. (*He goes to the door—then turns—in a voice full of strange emotion*) He'd ought t' been my son, Abbie. Ye'd ought t' loved me. I'm a man. If ye'd loved me, I'd never told no Sheriff on ye no matter what ye did, if they was t' brile me alive!

ABBIE (*defensively*). They's more to it nor yew know, makes him tell.

CABOT (*dryly*). Fur yewr sake, I hope they be. (*He goes out—comes around to the gate—stares up at the sky. His control relaxes. For a moment he is old and weary. He murmurs despairingly*) God A'mighty, I be lonesomer'n ever! (*He hears running footsteps from the left, immediately is himself again. Eben runs in, panting exhaustedly, wild-eyed and mad looking. He lurches through the gate. Cabot grabs him by the shoulder. Eben stares at him dumbly.*) Did ye tell the Sheriff?

EBEN (*nodding stupidly*). Ay-eh.

CABOT (*gives him a push away that sends him sprawling—laughing with withering contempt*). Good fur ye! A prime chip o' yer Maw ye be! (*He goes toward the barn, laughing harshly. Eben scrambles to his feet. Suddenly Cabot turns—grimly threatening*) Git off this farm when the Sheriff takes her—or, by God, he'll have t' come back an' git me fur murder, too! (*He stalks off. Eben does not appear to have heard him. He runs to the door and comes into the kitchen. Abbie looks up with a cry of anguished joy. Eben stumbles over and throws himself on his knees beside her—sobbing brokenly.*)

EBEN. Fergive me!

ABBIE (*happily*). Eben! (*She kisses him and pulls his head over against her breast.*)

EBEN. I love ye! Fergive me!

ABBIE (*ecstatically*). I'd fergive ye all the sins in hell fur sayin' that! (*She kisses his head, pressing it to her with a fierce passion of possession.*)

EBEN (*brokenly*). But I told the Sheriff. He's comin' fur ye!

ABBIE. I kin b'ar what happens t' me—now!

EBEN. I woke him up. I told him. He says, wait 'til I git dressed. I was waiting. I got to thinkin' o' yew. I got to thinkin' how I'd loved ye. It hurt like somethin' was bustin' in my chest an' head. I got t' cryin. I knowed sudden I loved ye yet, an' allus would love ye!

ABBIE (*caressing his hair—tenderly*). My boy, hain't ye?

EBEN. I begun t' run back. I cut across the fields an' through the woods. I thought ye might have time t' run away—with me—an' . . .

ABBIE (*shaking her head*). I got t' take my punishment—t' pay fur my sin.

EBEN. Then I want t' share it with ye.

ABBIE. Ye didn't do nothin'.

EBEN. I put it in yer head. I wisht he was dead! I as much as urged ye t' do it!

ABBIE. No. It was me alone!

EBEN. I'm as guilty as yew be! He was the child o' our sin.

ABBIE (*lifting her head as if defying God*). I don't repent that sin! I hain't askin' God t' fergive that!

EBEN. Nor me—but it led up t' the other—an' the murder ye did, ye did 'count o' me—an' it's my murder, too, I'll tell the Sheriff—an' if ye deny it, I'll say we planned it t'gether—an' they'll all b'lieve me, fur they suspicion everythin' we've done, an' it'll seem likely an' true to 'em. An' it is true—way down. I did help ye—somehow.

ABBIE (*laying her head on his—sobbing*). No! I don't want ye t' suffer!

EBEN. I got t' pay fur my part o' the sin! An' I'd suffer wuss leavin' ye, goin' West, thinkin' o' ye day an' night, bein' out when yew was in—(*lowering his voice*)—'r bein' alive when yew was dead. (*a pause*) I want t' share with ye, Abbie—prison 'r death 'r hell 'r anythin'! (*He looks into her eyes and forces a trembling smile.*) If I'm sharin' with ye, I won't feel lonesome, leastways.

ABBIE (*weakly*). Eben! I won't let ye! I can't let ye!

EBEN (*kissing her—tenderly*). Ye can't he'p yerself. I got ye beat fur once!

ABBIE (*forcing a smile—adoringly*). I hain't beat—s'long's I got ye!

EBEN (*hears the sound of feet outside*). Ssshh! Listen! They've come t' take us!

ABBIE. No, it's him. Don't give him no chance to fight ye, Eben. Don't say nothin'—no matter what he says. An' I won't neither. (*It is Cabot. He comes up from the barn in a great state of excitement and strides into the house and then into the kitchen. Eben is kneeling beside Abbie, his arm around her, hers around him. They stare straight ahead.*)

CABOT (*stares at them, his face hard. A long pause—vindictively*). Ye make a slick pair o' murderin' turtle doves! Ye'd ought t' be both hung on the same limb an' left thar t' swing in the breeze an' rot—a warnin' t' old fools like me t' b'ar their lonesomeness alone—an' fur young fools like ye t' hobble their lust. (*A pause. The excitement returns to his face, his eyes snap, he looks a bit crazy.*) I couldn't work today. I couldn't take no interest. T' hell with the farm! I'm leavin' it! I've turned the cows an' other stock loose! I've druv 'em into the woods whar they kin be free! By freein' em, I'm freein' myself! I'm quittin' here today! I'll set fire t' house an' barn an' watch 'em burn, an' I'll leave yer Maw t' haunt the ashes, an' I'll will the fields back t' God, so that nothin' human kin never touch 'em! I'll be a-goin' to Californi-a—t' jine Simeon an' Peter—true sons o' mine if they be dumb fools—an' the Cabots'll find Solomon's Mines t'gether! (*He suddenly cuts a mad caper.*) Whoop! What was the song they sung? "Oh, Californi-a! That's the land fur me." (*He sings this—then gets on his knees by the floorboard under which the money was hid.*) An' I'll sail thar on one o' the finest clippers I kin find! I've got the money! Pity ye didn't know whar this was hidden so's ye could steal . . . (*He has pulled up the board. He stares—feels—stares again. A pause of dead silence. He slowly turns, slumping into a sitting position on the floor, his eyes like those of a dead fish, his face the sickly green of an attack of nausea. He swallows painfully several times—forces a weak smile at last.*) So—ye did steal it!

EBEN (*emotionlessly*). I swapped it t' Sim an' Peter fur their share o' the farm—t' pay their passage t' Californi-a.

CABOT (*with one sardonic*). Ha! (*He begins to recover. Gets slowly to his feet—strangely*) I calc'late God give it to 'em—not yew! God's hard, not easy! Mebbe they's easy gold in the West but it hain't God's gold. It hain't fur me. I kin hear His voice warnin' me agen t' be hard an' stay on my farm. I kin see his hand usin' Eben t' steal t' keep me from weakness. I kin feel I be in the palm o' His hand, His fingers guidin' me. (*A pause—then he mutters sadly*) It's a-goin' t' be lonesomer now than ever it war afore—an' I'm gittin' old, Lord—ripe on the bough. . . . (*Then stiffening*) Waal—what d'ye want? God's lonesome, hain't He? God's hard an' lonesome! (*A pause. The Sheriff with two men comes up the road from the left. They move cautiously to the door. The Sheriff knocks on it with the butt of his pistol.*)

SHERIFF. Open in the name o' the law! (*They start.*)

CABOT. They've come fur ye. (*He goes to the rear door.*) Come in, Jim! (*The three men enter. Cabot meets them in doorway.*) Jest a minit, Jim. I got 'em safe here. (*The Sheriff nods. He and his companions remain in the doorway.*)

EBEN (*suddenly calls*). I lied this mornin', Jim. I helped her to do it. Ye kin take me, too.

ABBIE (*brokenly*). No!

CABOT. Take 'em both. (*He comes forward—stares at Eben with a trace of grudging admiration*) Purty good—fur yew! Waal, I got t' round up the stock. Good-by.

EBEN. Good-by.

ABBIE. Good-by. (*Cabot turns and strides past the men—comes out and around the corner of the house, his shoulders squared, his face stony, and stalks grimly toward the barn. In the meantime the Sheriff and men have come into the room.*)

SHERIFF (*embarrassedly*). Waal—we'd best start.

ABBIE. Wait. (*Turns to Eben*) I love ye, Eben.

EBEN. I love ye, Abbie. (*They kiss. The three men grin and shuffle embarrassedly. Eben takes Abbie's hand. They go out the door in rear, the men following, and come from the house, walking hand in hand to the gate. Eben stops there and points to the sunrise sky.*) Sun's a-risin'. Purty, hain't it?

ABBIE. Ay-eh. (*They both stand for a moment looking up raptly in attitudes strangely aloof and devout.*)

SHERIFF (*looking around at the farm enviously—to his companion*) It's a jim-dandy farm, no denyin'. Wished I owned it!

TOPICS FOR DISCUSSION AND WRITING

1. Before we see Ephraim Cabot in the fourth scene, we hear a good deal about him in the first three scenes. What sort of person do we expect him to be? To what extent does he fulfill the audience's expectations?
2. What kind of woman was Eben's mother? How do you know?
3. Some critics have suggested that the characters are fairly obvious stereotypes: Abbie is the sex-driven woman, Eben is the rebellious son, Ephraim is the tyrannical father. Do you agree? If not, why?
4. At least one student of O'Neill argued that the play should have begun with the third scene, which might have included necessary bits of exposition from the first two scenes. What do you think, and why?
5. The "telepathic" scene in which Abbie and Eben stare at each other through the wall has been criticized as a flaw in an otherwise chiefly realistic play. (See O'Neill's response in his letter to Sophus K. Winther, on page 456.) What is your opinion?
6. O'Neill is explicit about the symbolism of the elms. What other symbols does he use in the play? How effective do you find them?

CONTEXTS FOR *DESIRE UNDER THE ELMS*

Remarks by Eugene O'Neill

Tragic Beauty

I have been accused of unmitigated gloom. Is this a pessimistic view of life? I do not think so. There is a skin deep optimism and another higher optimism, not skin deep, which is usually confounded with pessimism. To me, the tragic alone has that significant beauty which is truth. It is the meaning of life—and the hope. The noblest is eternally the most tragic. The people who succeed and do not push on to a greater failure are the spiritual middle classers. Their stopping at success is the proof of their compromising insignificance. How pretty their dreams must have been! The man who pursues the mere attainable should be sentenced to get it—and keep it. Let him rest on his laurels and enthrone him in a Morris chair, in which laurels and hero may wither away together. Only through the unattainable does man achieve a hope worth living and dying for—and so attain himself. He with the spiritual guerdon of a hope in hopelessness, is nearest to the stars and the rainbow's foot.

—*New York Tribune,* February 13, 1921

Letter to Grace Dupre Hills, March 21, 1925

Desire, briefly, is a tragedy of the possessive—the pitiful longing of man to build his own heaven here on earth by glutting his sense of power with ownership of land, people, money—but principally the land and other people's lives. It is the creative yearning of the uncreative spirit which never achieves anything but a momentary clutch of failing fingers on the equally temporal tangible. This, in brief, is the background of the drama in *Desire.* Of course, there's more to it than that, and the above is so crude as to misrepresent, but it's the best I can do. I love to write plays but I hate to write about them.

As for my philosophy, that's a hard one. I have so many brands depending so much on the weather and the state of my digestion. Call me a tragic optimist. I believe everything I doubt and I doubt everything I believe. And no motto at this moment strikes me as a better one than the ancient "Hew to the line and let the chips fall where they may!"

Sincerely,
Eugene O'Neill

Letter to Arthur Hobson Quinn, April 3, 1925

It's not in me to pose much as a "misunderstood one," but it does seem discouragingly (that is, if one lacked a sense of ironic humor!) evident to me that most of my critics don't want to see what I'm trying to do or how I'm trying to do it, although I flatter myself that end and means are characteristic, individual and positive enough not to be mistaken for anyone else's, or for those of any "modern" or "premodern" school. To be called a "sordid realist" one day, a "grim, pessimistic Naturalist" the next, a "lying Moral Romanticist" the next, etc. is quite perplexing—not to add the *Times* editorial that settled *Desire* once and for all by calling it a "Neo-Primitive," a Matisse of the drama, as it were! So I'm really longing to explain and try and convince some sympathetic ear that I've tried to make myself a melting pot for all these methods, seeing some virtues for my ends in each of them, and thereby, if there is enough real fire in me, boil down to my own technique. But where I feel myself most neglected is just where I set most store by myself—as a bit of a poet, who has labored with the spoken word to evolve original rhythms of beauty, where beauty apparently isn't—*Jones, Ape, God's Chillun, Desire,* etc.—and to see the transfiguring nobility of tragedy, in as near the Greek sense as one can grasp it, in seemingly the most ignoble, debased lives. And just here is where I am a most confirmed mystic, too, for I'm always, always trying to interpret Life in terms of lives, never just lives in terms of character. I'm always acutely conscious of the Force behind—Fate, God, our biological past creating our present, whatever one calls it—Mystery certainly—and of the one eternal tragedy of Man in his glorious, self-destructive struggle to make the Force express him instead of being, as an animal is, an infinitesimal incident in its expression. And my profound conviction is that this is the only subject worth writing about and that it is possible—or can be—to develop a tragic expression in terms of transfigured modern values and symbols in the theater which may to some degree bring home to members of a modern audience their ennobling identity with the tragic figures on the stage. Of course, this is very much of a dream, but where the theater is concerned, one must have a dream, and the Greek dream in tragedy is the noblest ever!

Letter to Sophus Keith Winther, July 7, 1933

Dear Dr. Winther,

I have read your book[1] and am most enthusiastic about it. Congratulations on a splendid job. It impresses me as a searching critical analysis, finely conceived and soundly carried out. What particularly strikes me is that you have so illuminatingly revealed the relationship of the plays to the mental and spiritual background of their time, and shown

[1]Winther had sent O'Neill a book-length manuscript on O'Neill. It was published in the following year, under the title of *Eugene O'Neill: A Critical Study.*

that background as inseparable from the work—something no one else has so far troubled to do except sketchily, yet which is so essential to any true comprehension of what I have attempted to accomplish. I am also delighted with the way you dispose of the "gloomy," "pessimistic," "one-sided" nonsense which has always greeted every play of mine until it has become a meaningless cliché of criticism which uses catchwords to defend itself from understanding. . . .

Naturally, there are a few points where I don't agree with you—something you say about the danger of mysticism, for example. To me the danger lies more in no mysticism. We tend complacently to regard the unknown as non-existent because it is unknown to us—but drama should keep a place for intuitive vision or it loses an inherent, powerful value.

And what you say about mental telepathy in *Desire* and *Electra.* I hadn't defined it to myself as that, but I certainly believe that under special, stress conditions of extreme passionate tension, where one person is emotionally "tuned in" on another, so to speak, that some sort of super-awareness is possible at a crucial moment. Or call it due to an extraordinary intensification of the functions of the senses—one hears a sound too low for ordinary hearing, etc. That science has not got this in its card index seems to me simply because it is obviously barred from ever sitting in on such rare occasions. But, after all, as I interpret the latest scientific-mystical dogmas, we seem to become more and more merely other electrical plants, and, accepting that, emotional thought transference strikes me as much less incredible than my radio set!

I mention the above, not by way of criticism, but because the points brought up are extremely interesting to me. I am a great believer in all we don't know about ourselves, but inclined to skepticism about what we think we know.

Again, my grateful appreciation—and all good wishes to you.

Cordially,
Eugene O'Neill

BERTOLT BRECHT

The Good Woman of Setzuan

Translated by Eric Bentley

Bertolt Brecht (1898–1956) was born in Germany of middle-class parents, attended public schools and then entered the University of Munich to study medicine, but after one year was drafted for military service in World War I and served as a medical orderly for about a year. At the end of the war he returned to a shattered Germany, and during most of the twenties he seems to have been more or less an anarchist; in any case, his earliest poems and plays (e.g., *The Threepenny Opera,* 1928) cannot be called Communist, though around 1928 he seems to have become a believer in Communism. With the rise of Hitler, Brecht left Germany (1933), spending most of the years 1933 to 1939 in Denmark, 1940 in Finland, and 1941 to 1948 in the United States. Most of his best-known plays (including *The Good Woman of Setzuan,* 1938–1941) were written during his fifteen years of exile. His return in 1948 to Germany—to East Berlin—was somewhat equivocal, for he obtained Austrian citizenship (1950) and arranged for the copyright to his work to be held by a publisher in West Berlin. He died suddenly, of a thrombosis, in 1956.

COMMENTARY

Earlier drama interested Brecht enormously, but he believed that it was obsolete and he devoted a fair amount of his time to trying to adapt it to the twentieth century. (His most popular play, *The Threepenny Opera,* is an adaptation of John Gay's *The Beggar's Opera,* and at the time of his death he was working on an adaptation of Shakespeare's *Coriolanus.* Accused of plagiarism, he replied that in literature as in life he did not recognize the idea of private property.)

Roughly speaking, earlier tragedy, as Brecht saw it, depicted a hero who, inevitably driven to the wall, performed some terrible deed and then became aware of all of its implications, thus achieving full understanding of himself and his fate. Interpreting Aristotle's comments on tragedy, Brecht went on to say that tragedy customarily sought to cause the audience to identify itself with the tragic hero and through the identification to undergo an emotional cleansing or catharsis. Here is one of Brecht's characteristically earthy and acerbic comments:

> The drama of our time still follows Aristotle's recipe for achieving what he calls catharsis (the spiritual cleansing of the spectator). In Aristotelian drama the plot leads the hero into situations where he reveals his innermost being. All the incidents shown have the object of driving the hero into spiritual conflicts. It is a possibly blasphemous but quite useful comparison if one turns one's mind to the burlesque shows on Broadway, where

Shen Te (center) begs the gods not to leave her alone in this cruel world.
(Photograph: Liz Lauren.)

> the public, with yells of "Take it off!" forces the girls to expose their bodies more and more. The individual whose innermost being is thus driven into the open then of course comes to stand for Man with a capital M. Everyone (including every spectator) is then carried away by the momentum of the events portrayed, so that in a performance of *Oedipus* one has for all practical purposes an auditorium full of little Oedipuses, an auditorium full of Emperor Joneses for a performance of *The Emperor Jones.*[1]

Now, in opposition to what he called "Aristotelian drama," drawing partly on German critical theories about the difference between drama and epic, Brecht developed the idea of "non-Aristotelian" or "epic drama." Whereas the usual play is set in the present and implies that what is happening on the stage happens *now,* to all of us, the epic traditionally is a story set in the past and is quite frankly about how things *used to be.* Because the readers of an epic, the argument goes, are detached individuals capable of using their minds critically, but the spectators at an Aristotelian drama are part of a mob, their reason having been subordinated to a communal emotion. "Epic drama," then, in opposition to traditional Aristotelian drama, seeks to create a detachment comparable to that which the epic creates.

Brecht's word for this quality is *Verfremdung,* i.e., detachment, estrangement, alienation. The point of estranging the dramatic action from the audience is to make the audience regard it critically and thus see it more clearly, unobscured by emotional prejudices. To induce this estrangement, to shatter a sense of community between actors and audience, Brecht interrupted the action of his plays with such devices as songs, addresses to the audience, and slogans projected onto the stage, and he insisted on highly stylized acting (Chaplin was one of his heroes) and unrealistic scenery. Brecht's ideal audience at an epic drama is critically aware of—not emotionally overcome by—what it sees on the stage. Brecht thus rejected tragedy of the sort that Yeats characterized as "a drowning and breaking of the dykes that separate man from man," and he insisted, in contrast to Yeats, that detachment is not limited to the spectator at a comedy.

Every play gives some image of the world; according to Brecht the Aristotelian play shows a static world, for in the hero's agony it claims to reveal with increasing clarity how things inevitably are. The epic play, however, shows a dynamic or changing world, or a world that can be—must be—changed. (The direction in which Brecht wanted the change to go is clear enough; he was a Communist.)

> The dramatic [i.e., Aristotelian] theatre's spectator says: Yes, I have felt like that too—Just like me—It's only natural—It'll never change—The sufferings of this man appall me, because they are inescapable—That's great art; it all seems the most obvious thing in the world—I weep when they weep, I laugh when they laugh.
>
> The epic theatre's spectator says: I'd never have thought it—That's not the way—That's extraordinary, hardly believable—It's got to stop—The sufferings of this man appall me, because they are unnecessary—That's great art: nothing obvious in it—I laugh when they weep, I weep when they laugh.[2]

Brecht put the distinctions between the two kinds of drama into the following tabular

[1] *Brecht on Theatre,* translated by John Willett (New York: Hill and Wang; London: Methuen & Co., 1964), p. 87.

[2] *Brecht on Theatre,* p. 71.

form, but one should keep in mind that he was talking about emphases, not utter opposites:[3]

DRAMATIC THEATRE	EPIC THEATRE
plot	narrative
implicates the spectator in a stage situation	turns the spectator into an observer, but
wears down his capacity for action	arouses his capacity for action
provides him with sensations	forces him to take decisions
experience	picture of the world
the spectator is involved in something	he is made to face something
suggestion	argument
instinctive feelings are preserved	brought to the point of recognition
the spectator is in the thick of it, shares the experience	the spectator stands outside, studies
the human being is taken for granted	the human being is the object of the inquiry
he is unalterable	he is alterable and able to alter
eyes on the finish	eyes on the course
one scene makes another	each scene for itself
growth	montage
linear development	in curves
evolutionary determinism	jumps
man as a fixed point	man as a process
thought determines being	social being determines thought
feeling	reason

It was with this scaffolding that Brecht built his plays. His interest was not in passionate tragic heroes who reveal their greatness when they assert themselves and do a deed of horror that affronts a mysterious metaphysical order that demands their life in expiation, but with the no less momentous issues of How do we survive? Must little people be imposed on? Above all, What is to be done?

Such plays do not seek to evoke the woe or wonder that Shakespeare spoke of in connection with tragedy, for these emotions induce a sense of the inevitability of guilt and suffering, and send us out of the theater reconciled to the naturalness of our present condition. For Brecht, what is "natural" is not guilty actions but generous actions. (Brecht would argue that the following speech is counter-balanced by many other speeches because epic drama shows several sides, but it seems evident that the speech represents Brecht's own thinking.) Shen Te, the charitable prostitute, says in another version of *The Good Woman of Setzuan:*

Why are you so bad?

[3]The list is reprinted from *Brecht on Theatre,* translated by John Willett, p. 37.

> You tread on your fellow man.
> Isn't it a strain?
> Your veins swell with your efforts to be greedy.
> Extended naturally, a hand gives and receives with equal ease.

But somehow, according to Brecht, in our present (i.e., capitalistic) society, we find that we are forced into unnatural postures; Shen Te finds that she cannot continue to be charitable without the aid of a cruel "cousin" (she is so torn by the problem that she invents this person in order to protect herself from her own generous impulses). Moreover, in our society love itself must become savage: Shen Te so loves her child, and so fears that he may encounter a life of poverty, that she determines for his sake to be ruthless in her business dealings, and she determines also (further irony) to shield the child from knowledge of her activities so that he will grow up to be good—in a world in which goodness cannot survive.

These life-and-death issues are treated tragicomically. First, and least important, the play mingles gods and mortals, like Plautus' *Amphitryon,* a mixture which caused Plautus to introduce the word tragicomedy. And what gods they are, mouthing amiable pieties, getting a black eye when they intervene in a mortal quarrel, and finally, in a concluding scene that is funny and terrible, ascending to heaven on a cloud, singing, smiling, and waving to Shen Te, who is crying for help. More important, in this immensely earnest play that seeks to face some of the darkest facts of our life as it is, there are a good many comic figures and there is a good deal of wry wit. One example will have to suffice. Yang Sun wants to be sure that his wife will be frugal.

> YANG SUN. Can you sleep on a straw mattress the size of that book?
> SHEN TE. The two of us?
> YANG SUN. The one of you.
> SHEN TE. In that case, no.

More broadly, *The Good Woman of Setzuan,* like all comedies, calls attention to incongruity, but here the incongruity is not from some sort of unlovely behavior needlessly adopted in a smiling world where things will work out all right; rather, the incongruity is generosity in a corrupt world. Shen Te is funny in her persistent innocence and goodness—but she is not only funny, she is compelling (despite Brecht's theories?) and deeply sympathetic, as when she persists in loving the deceitful Yang Sun:

> SHEN TE.
> When I heard his cunning laugh, I was afraid
> But when I saw the holes in his shoes, I loved him dearly.

At the end, the play does not let us rest content, as tragedy and comedy in their different ways traditionally do. An epilogue invites us to work out a sequel:

> We feel deflated too. We too are nettled
> To see the curtain down and nothing settled.
> How could a better ending be arranged?
> Could one change people? Can the world be changed?
> Would new gods do the trick? Will atheism?
> Moral rearmament? Materialism?
> It is for you to find a way, my friends,

To help good men arrive at happy ends.
You write the happy ending to the play!
There must, there must, there's got to be a way!

Probably Brecht assumed that Marx had shown us the way out: Change the economic basis of society and you will find a new human nature. Still, at rehearsals of his plays Brecht sometimes quoted his own Galileo: "I'm not trying to show that I'm in the right, but to find out whether."

BERTOLT BRECHT *The Good Woman of Setzuan*

List of Characters

WONG, *a water seller*
THREE GODS
SHEN TE, *a prostitute, later a shopkeeper*
MRS. SHIN, *former owner of Shen Te's shop*
A FAMILY OF EIGHT *(husband, wife, brother, sister-in-law, grandfather, nephew, niece, boy)*
AN UNEMPLOYED MAN
A CARPENTER
MRS. MI TZU, *Shen Te's landlady*
YANG SUN, *an unemployed pilot, later a factory manager*
AN OLD WHORE
A POLICEMAN
AN OLD MAN
AN OLD WOMAN, *his wife*
MR. SHU FU, *a barber*
MRS. YANG, *mother of Yang Sun*
GENTLEMEN, VOICES, CHILDREN *(three), etc.*

PROLOGUE

(At the gates of the half-westernized city of Setzuan. Evening. Wong the Water Seller introduces himself to the audience.)*

WONG. I sell water here in the city of Setzuan. It isn't easy. When water is scarce, I have long distances to go in search of it, and when it is plentiful, I have no income. But in our part of the world there is nothing unusual about poverty. Many people think only the gods can save the situation. And I hear from a cattle merchant—who travels a lot—that some of the highest gods are on their way here at this very moment. Informed sources have it that heaven is quite disturbed at all the complaining. I've been coming out here to the city gates for three days now to bid these gods welcome. I want to be the first to greet them. What about those fellows over there? No, no, they *work.* And that one there has ink on his fingers, he's no god, he must be a clerk from the cement factory. *Those* two are another story. They look as though they'd like to beat you. But gods don't need to beat you, do they? (*Enter Three Gods.*) What about those three? Old-fashioned clothes—dust on their feet—they *must* be gods! (*He throws himself at their feet.*) Do with me what you will, illustrious ones!

FIRST GOD (*with an ear trumpet*). Ah! (*He is pleased.*) So we were expected?

WONG (*giving them water*). Oh, yes. And I *knew* you'd come.

FIRST GOD. We need somewhere to stay the night. You know of a place?

WONG. The whole town is at your service, illustrious ones! What sort of a place would you like?

(*The Gods eye each other.*)

FIRST GOD. Just try the first house you come to, my son.
WONG. That would be Mr. Fo's place.
FIRST GOD. Mr. Fo.
WONG. One moment! (*He knocks at the first house.*)
VOICE FROM MR. FO'S. No!

(*Wong returns a little nervously.*)

WONG. It's too bad. Mr. Fo isn't in. And his servants don't dare do a thing without his consent. He'll have a fit when he finds out who they turned away, won't he?

FIRST GOD (*smiling*). He will, won't he?

*So Brecht's first MS. Brecht must later have learned that Setzuan (usually spelled Szechwan) is not a city but a province and he adjusted the printed German text. I have kept the earlier reading as such mythology seems to me more Brechtian than Brecht's own second thoughts."—E.B.

WONG. One moment! The next house is Mr. Cheng's. Won't he be thrilled?

FIRST GOD. Mr. Cheng.

(*Wong knocks.*)

VOICE FROM MR. CHENG'S. Keep your gods. We have our own troubles!

WONG (*back with the Gods*). Mr. Cheng is very sorry, but he has a houseful of relations. I think some of them are a bad lot, and naturally, he wouldn't like you to see them.

THIRD GOD. Are we so terrible?

WONG. Well, only with bad people, of course. Everyone knows the province of Kwan is always having floods.

SECOND GOD. Really? How's *that*?

WONG. Why, because they're so irreligious.

SECOND GOD. Rubbish. It's because they neglected the dam.

FIRST GOD (*to Second*). Sh! (*To Wong.*) You're still in hopes, aren't you, my son?

WONG. Certainly. All Setzuan is competing for the honor! What happened up to now is pure coincidence. I'll be back. (*He walks away, but then stands undecided.*)

SECOND GOD. What did I tell you?

THIRD GOD. It *could* be pure coincidence.

SECOND GOD. The same coincidence in Shun, Kwan, and Setzuan? People just aren't religious any more, let's face the fact. Our mission has failed!

FIRST GOD. Oh come, we might run into a good person any minute.

THIRD GOD. How did the resolution read? (*Unrolling a scroll and reading from it.*) "The world can stay as it is if enough people are found living lives worthy of human beings." Good people, that is. Well, what about this Water Seller himself? *He's* good, or I'm very much mistaken.

SECOND GOD. You're very much mistaken. When he gave us a drink, I had the impression there was something odd about the cup. Well, look! (*He shows the cup to the First God.*)

FIRST GOD. A false bottom!

SECOND GOD. The man is a swindler.

FIRST GOD. Very well, count *him* out. That's one man among millions. And as a matter of fact, we only need one on *our* side. These atheists are saying, "The world must be changed because no one can *be* good and *stay* good." No one, eh? I say: let us find one—just one—and we have those fellows where we want them!

THIRD GOD (*to Wong*). Water Seller, is it so hard to find a place to stay?

WONG. Nothing could be easier. It's just me. I don't go about it right.

THIRD GOD. Really? (*He returns to the others. A Gentleman passes by.*)

WONG. Oh dear, they're catching on. (*He accosts the Gentleman.*) Excuse the intrusion, dear sir, but three Gods have just turned up. Three of the very highest. They need a place for the night. Seize this rare opportunity—to have real gods as your guests!

GENTLEMAN (*laughing*). A new way of finding free rooms for a gang of crooks.

(*Exit Gentleman.*)

WONG (*shouting at him*). Godless rascal! Have you no religion, gentlemen of Setzuan? (*Pause.*) Patience, illustrious ones! (*Pause.*) There's only one person left. Shen Te, the prostitute. She *can't* say no. (*Calls up to a window.*) Shen Te!

(*Shen Te opens the shutters and looks out.*)

WONG. *They're* here, and nobody wants them. Will you take them?

SHEN TE. Oh, no, Wong, I'm expecting a gentleman.

WONG. Can't you forget about him for tonight?

SHEN TE. The rent has to be paid by tomorrow or I'll be out on the street.

WONG. This is no time for calculation, Shen Te.

SHEN TE. Stomachs rumble even on the Emperor's birthday, Wong.

WONG. Setzuan is one big dung hill!

SHEN TE. Oh, very well! I'll hide till my gentleman has come and gone. Then I'll take them. (*She disappears.*)

WONG. They mustn't see her gentleman or they'll know what she is.

FIRST GOD (*who hasn't heard any of this*). I think it's hopeless.

(*They approach Wong.*)

WONG (*jumping, as he finds them behind him*). A room has been found, illustrious ones! (*He wipes sweat off his brow.*)

SECOND GOD. Oh, good.

THIRD GOD. Let's see it.

WONG (*nervously*). Just a minute. It has to be tidied up a bit.

THIRD GOD. Then we'll sit down here and wait.

WONG (*still more nervous*). No, no! (*Holding himself back.*) Too much traffic, you know.

THIRD GOD (*with a smile*). Of course, if you *want* us to move.

(*They retire a little. They sit on a doorstep. Wong sits on the ground.*)

WONG (*after a deep breath*). You'll be staying with a single girl—the finest human being in Setzuan!

THIRD GOD. That's nice.

WONG (*to the audience*). They gave me such a look when I picked up my cup just now.

THIRD GOD. You're worn out, Wong.
WONG. A little, maybe.
FIRST GOD. Do people here have a hard time of it?
WONG. The good ones do.
FIRST GOD. What about yourself?
WONG. You mean I'm not good. That's true. And I don't have an easy time either!

(During this dialogue, a Gentleman has turned up in front of Shen Te's house, and has whistled several times. Each time Wong has given a start.)

THIRD GOD (*to Wong, softly*). Psst! I think he's gone now.
WONG (*confused and surprised*). Ye-e-es.

(The Gentleman has left now, and Shen Te has come down to the street.)

SHEN TE (*softly*). Wong!

(Getting no answer, she goes off down the street. Wong arrives just too late, forgetting his carrying pole.)

WONG (*softly*). Shen Te! Shen Te! (*To himself.*) So she's gone off to earn the rent. Oh dear, I can't go to the gods *again* with no room to offer them. Having failed in the service of the gods, I shall run to my den in the sewer pipe down by the river and hide from their sight!

(He rushes off. Shen Te returns, looking for him, but finding the gods. She stops in confusion.)

SHEN TE. You are the illustrious ones? My name is Shen Te. It would please me very much if my simple room could be of use to you.
THIRD GOD. Where is the Water Seller, Miss . . . Shen Te?
SHEN TE. I missed him, somehow.
FIRST GOD. Oh, he probably thought you weren't coming, and was afraid of telling us.
THIRD GOD (*picking up the carrying pole*). We'll leave this with you. He'll be needing it.

(Led by Shen Te, they go into the house. It grows dark, then light. Dawn. Again escorted by Shen Te, who leads them through the half-light with a little lamp, the Gods take their leave.)

FIRST GOD. Thank you, thank you, dear Shen Te, for your elegant hospitality! We shall not forget! And give our thanks to the Water Seller—he showed us a good human being.
SHEN TE. Oh, *I'm* not good. Let me tell you something: when Wong asked me to put you up, I hesitated.
FIRST GOD. It's all right to hesitate if you then go ahead! And in giving us that room you did much more than you knew. You proved that good people still exist, a point that has been disputed of late—even in heaven. Farewell!
SECOND GOD. Farewell!
THIRD GOD. Farewell!
SHEN TE. Stop, illustrious ones! I'm not sure you're right. I'd like to be good, it's true, but there's the rent to pay. And that's not all: I sell myself for a living. Even so I can't make ends meet, there's too much competition. I'd like to honor my father and mother and speak nothing but the truth and not covet my neighbor's house. I should love to stay with one man. But how? How is it done? Even breaking only a *few* of your commandments, I can hardly manage.
FIRST GOD (*clearing his throat*). These thoughts are but, um, the misgivings of an unusually good woman!
THIRD GOD. Goodbye, Shen Te! Give our regards to the Water Seller!
SECOND GOD. And above all: be good! Farewell!
FIRST GOD. Farewell!
THIRD GOD. Farewell!

(They start to wave goodbye.)

SHEN TE. But everything is so expensive, I don't feel sure I can do it!
SECOND GOD. That's not in our sphere. We never meddle with economics.
THIRD GOD. One moment.

(They stop.)

Isn't it true she might do better if she had more money?
SECOND GOD. Come, come! How could we ever account for it Up Above?
FIRST GOD. Oh, there are ways.

(They put their heads together and confer in dumb show.)

(To Shen Te, with embarrassment.) As you say you can't pay your rent, well, um, we're not paupers, so of course we *insist* on paying for our room. (*Awkwardly thrusting money into her hands.*) There! (*Quickly.*) But don't tell anyone! The incident is open to misinterpretation.
SECOND GOD. It certainly is!
FIRST GOD (*defensively*). But there's no law against it! It was never decreed that a god mustn't pay hotel bills!

(The Gods leave.)

SCENE 1

(A small tobacco shop. The shop is not as yet completely furnished and hasn't started doing business.)

SHEN TE (*to the audience*). It's three days now since the gods left. When they said they wanted to pay for the room,

I looked down at my hand, and there was more than a thousand silver dollars! I bought a tobacco shop with the money, and moved in yesterday. I don't own the building, of course, but I can pay the rent, and I hope to do a lot of good here. Beginning with Mrs. Shin, who's just coming across the square with her pot. She had the shop before me, and yesterday she dropped in to ask for rice for her children.

(*Enter Mrs. Shin. Both women bow.*)

How do you do, Mrs. Shin.

MRS. SHIN. How do you do, Miss Shen Te. You like your new home?

SHEN TE. Indeed, yes. Did your children have a good night?

MRS. SHIN. In that hovel? The youngest is coughing already.

SHEN TE. Oh, dear!

MRS. SHIN. You're going to learn a thing or two in these slums.

SHEN TE. Slums? That's not what you said when you sold me the shop!

MRS. SHIN. Now don't start nagging! Robbing me and my innocent children of their home and then calling it a slum! That's the limit! (*She weeps.*)

SHEN TE (*tactfully*). I'll get your rice.

MRS. SHIN. And a little cash while you're at it.

SHEN TE. I'm afraid I haven't sold anything yet.

MRS. SHIN (*screeching*). I've got to have it. Strip the clothes from my back and then cut my throat, will you? I know what I'll do: I'll leave my children on your doorstep! (*She snatches the pot out of Shen Te's hands.*)

SHEN TE. Please don't be angry. You'll spill the rice.

(*Enter an elderly Husband and Wife with their shabbily-dressed Nephew.*)

WIFE. Shen Te, dear! You've come into money, they tell me. And we haven't a roof over our heads! A tobacco shop. We had one too. But it's gone. Could we spend the night here, do you think?

NEPHEW (*appraising the shop*). Not bad!

WIFE. He's our nephew. We're inseparable!

MRS. SHIN. And who are these . . . ladies and gentlemen?

SHEN TE. They put me up when I first came in from the country. (*To the audience.*) Of course, when my small purse was empty, they put me out on the street, and they may be afraid I'll do the same to them. (*To the newcomers, kindly.*) Come in, and welcome, though I've only one little room for you—it's behind the shop.

HUSBAND. That'll do. Don't worry.

WIFE (*bringing Shen Te some tea*). We'll stay over here, so we won't be in your way. Did you make it a tobacco shop in memory of your first real home? We can certainly give you a hint or two! That's one reason we came.

MRS. SHIN (*to Shen Te*). Very nice! As long as you have a few customers too!

HUSBAND. Sh! A customer!

(*Enter an Unemployed Man, in rags.*)

UNEMPLOYED MAN. Excuse me. I'm unemployed.

(*Mrs. Shin laughs.*)

SHEN TE. Can I help you?

UNEMPLOYED MAN. Have you any damaged cigarettes? I thought there might be some damage when you're unpacking.

WIFE. What nerve, begging for tobacco! (*Rhetorically.*) Why don't they ask for bread?

UNEMPLOYED MAN. Bread is expensive. One cigarette butt and I'll be a new man.

SHEN TE (*giving him cigarettes*). That's very important—to be a new man. You'll be my first customer and bring me luck.

(*The Unemployed Man quickly lights a cigarette, inhales, and goes off, coughing.*)

WIFE. Was that right, Shen Te, dear?

MRS. SHIN. If this is the opening of a shop, you can hold the closing at the end of the week.

HUSBAND. I bet he had money on him.

SHEN TE. Oh, no, he said he hadn't!

NEPHEW. How d'you know he wasn't lying?

SHEN TE (*angrily*). How do you know he was?

WIFE (*wagging her head*). You're too good, Shen Te, dear. If you're going to keep this shop, you'll have to learn to say No.

HUSBAND. Tell them the place isn't yours to dispose of. Belongs to . . . some relative who insists on all accounts being strictly in order . . .

MRS. SHIN. That's right! What do you think you are—a philanthropist?

SHEN TE (*laughing*). Very well, suppose I ask you for my rice back, Mrs. Shin?

WIFE (*combatively, at Mrs. Shin*). So that's *her* rice?

(*Enter the Carpenter, a small man.*)

MRS. SHIN (*who, at the sight of him, starts to hurry away*). See you tomorrow, Miss Shen Te! (*Exit Mrs. Shin.*)

CARPENTER. Mrs. Shin, it's you I want!

WIFE (*to Shen Te*). Has she some claim on you?

SHEN TE. She's hungry. That's a claim.

CARPENTER. Are you the new tenant? And filling up the shelves already? Well, they're not yours, till they're paid for, ma'am. I'm the carpenter, so I should know.

SHEN TE. I took the shop "furnishings included."
CARPENTER. You're in league with that Mrs. Shin, of course. All right: I demand my hundred silver dollars.
SHEN TE. I'm afraid I haven't got a hundred silver dollars.
CARPENTER. Then you'll find it. Or I'll have you arrested.
WIFE (*whispering to Shen Te*). That relative: make it a cousin.
SHEN TE. Can't it wait till next month?
CARPENTER. No!
SHEN TE. Be a little patient, Mr. Carpenter, I can't settle all claims at once.
CARPENTER. Who's patient with me? (*He grabs a shelf from the wall.*) Pay up—or I take the shelves back!
WIFE. Shen Te! Dear! Why don't you let your . . . cousin settle this affair? (*To Carpenter.*) Put your claim in writing. Shen Te's cousin will see you get paid.
CARPENTER (*derisively*). Cousin, eh?
HUSBAND. Cousin, yes.
CARPENTER. I know these cousins!
NEPHEW. Don't be silly. He's a personal friend of mine.
HUSBAND. What a man! Sharp as a razor!
CARPENTER. All right. I'll put my claim in writing. (*Puts shelf on floor, sits on it, writes out bill.*)
WIFE (*to Shen Te*). He'd tear the dress off your back to get his shelves. Never recognize a claim! That's my motto.
SHEN TE. He's done a job, and wants something in return. It's shameful that I can't give it to him. What will the gods say?
HUSBAND. You did your bit when you took *us* in.

(*Enter the Brother, limping, and the Sister-in-Law, pregnant.*)

BROTHER (*to Husband and Wife*). So this is where you're hiding out! There's family feeling for you! Leaving us on the corner!
WIFE (*embarrassed, to Shen Te*). It's my brother and his wife. (*To them.*) Now stop grumbling, and sit quietly in that corner. (*To Shen Te.*) It can't be helped. She's in her fifth month.
SHEN TE. Oh yes. Welcome!
WIFE (*to the couple*). Say thank you.

(*They mutter something.*)

The cups are there. (*To Shen Te.*) Lucky you bought this shop when you did!
SHEN TE (*laughing and bringing tea*). Lucky indeed!

(*Enter Mrs. Mi Tzu, the landlady.*)

MRS. MI TZU. Miss Shen Te? I am Mrs. Mi Tzu, your landlady. I hope our relationship will be a happy one? I like to think I give my tenants modern, personalized service. Here is your lease. (*To the others, as Shen Te reads the lease.*) There's nothing like the opening of a little shop, is there? A moment of true beauty! (*She is looking around.*) Not very much on the shelves, of course. But everything in the gods' good time! Where are your references, Miss Shen Te?
SHEN TE. Do I *have* to have references?
MRS. MI TZU. After all, I haven't a notion who you are!
HUSBAND. Oh, *we'd* be glad to vouch for Miss Shen Te! We'd go through fire for her!
MRS. MI TZU. And who may *you* be?
HUSBAND (*stammering*). Ma Fu, tobacco dealer.
MRS. MI TZU. Where is your shop, Mr. . . . Ma Fu?
HUSBAND. Well, um, I haven't a shop—I've just sold it.
MRS. MI TZU. I see. (*To Shen Te.*) Is there no one else that knows you?
WIFE (*whispering to Shen Te*). Your cousin! Your cousin!
MRS. MI TZU. This is a respectable house, Miss Shen Te. I never sign a lease without certain assurances.
SHEN TE (*slowly, her eyes downcast*). I have . . . a cousin.
MRS. MI TZU. On the square? Let's go over and see him. What does he do?
SHEN TE (*as before*). He lives . . . in another city.
WIFE (*prompting*). Didn't you say he was in Shung?
SHEN TE. That's right. Shung.
HUSBAND (*prompting*). I had his name on the tip of my tongue. Mr. . . .
SHEN TE (*with an effort*). Mr. . . . Shui . . . Ta.
HUSBAND. That's it! Tall, skinny fellow!
SHEN TE. Shui Ta!
NEPHEW (*to Carpenter*). You were in touch with him, weren't you? About the shelves?
CARPENTER (*surlily*). Give him this bill. (*He hands it over.*) I'll be back in the morning. (*Exit Carpenter.*)
NEPHEW (*calling after him, but with his eyes on Mrs. Mi Tzu*). Don't worry! Mr. Shui Ta pays on the nail!
MRS. MI TZU (*looking closely at Shen Te*). I'll be happy to make his acquaintance, Miss Shen Te. (*Exit Mrs. Mi Tzu.*)

(*Pause.*)

WIFE. By tomorrow morning she'll know more about you than you do yourself.
SISTER-IN-LAW (*to Nephew*). This thing isn't built to last.

(*Enter Grandfather.*)

WIFE. It's Grandfather! (*To Shen Te.*) Such a good old soul!

(*The Boy enters.*)

BOY (*over his shoulder*). Here they are!

WIFE. And the boy, how he's grown! But he always could eat enough for ten.

(*Enter the Niece.*)

WIFE (*to Shen Te*). Our little niece from the country. There are more of us now than in your time. The less we had, the more there were of us; the more there were of us, the less we had. Give me the key. We must protect ourselves from unwanted guests. (*She takes the key and locks the door.*) Just make yourself at home. I'll light the little lamp.

NEPHEW (*a big joke*). I hope her cousin doesn't drop in tonight! The strict Mr. Shui Ta!

(*Sister-in-Law laughs.*)

BROTHER (*reaching for a cigarette*). One cigarette more or less . . .

HUSBAND. One cigarette more or less.

(*They pile into the cigarettes. The Brother hands a jug of wine round.*)

NEPHEW. Mr. Shui Ta'll pay for it!

GRANDFATHER (*gravely, to Shen Te*). How do you do?

(*Shen Te, a little taken aback by the belatedness of the greeting, bows. She has the Carpenter's bill in one hand, the landlady's lease in the other.*)

WIFE. How about a bit of a song? To keep Shen Te's spirits up?

NEPHEW. Good idea. Grandfather: you start!

Song of the Smoke

GRANDFATHER.
I used to think (before old age beset me)
That brains could fill the pantry of the poor.
But where did all my cerebration get me?
I'm just as hungry as I was before.
So what's the use?
See the smoke float free
Into ever colder coldness!
It's the same with me.

HUSBAND.
The straight and narrow path leads to disaster
And so the crooked path I tried to tread.
That got me to disaster even faster.
(They say we shall be happy when we're dead.)
So what's the use, etc.

NIECE.
You older people, full of expectation,
At any moment now you'll walk the plank!
The future's for the younger generation!
Yes, even if that future is a blank.
So what's the use, etc.

NEPHEW (*to the Brother*). Where'd you get that wine?

SISTER-IN-LAW (*answering for the Brother*). He pawned the sack of tobacco.

HUSBAND (*stepping in*). What? That tobacco was all we had to fall back on! You pig!

BROTHER. *You'd* call a man a pig because your wife was frigid! Did you refuse to drink it?

(*They fight. The shelves fall over.*)

SHEN TE (*imploringly*). Oh, don't! Don't break everything! Take it, take it all, but don't destroy a gift from the gods!

WIFE (*disparagingly*). This shop isn't big enough. I should never have mentioned it to Uncle and the others. When *they* arrive, it's going to be disgustingly overcrowded.

SISTER-IN-LAW. And did you hear our gracious hostess? She cools off quick!

(*Voices outside. Knocking at the door.*)

UNCLE'S VOICE. Open the door!

WIFE. Uncle? Is that you, Uncle?

UNCLE'S VOICE. Certainly, it's me. Auntie says to tell you she'll have the children here in ten minutes.

WIFE (*to Shen Te*). I'll have to let him in.

SHEN TE (*who scarcely hears her*).
The little lifeboat is swiftly sent down
Too many men too greedily
Hold on to it as they drown.

SCENE 1A

(*Wong's den in a sewer pipe.*)

WONG (*crouching there*). All quiet! It's four days now since I left the city. The gods passed this way on the second day. I heard their steps on the bridge over there. They must be a long way off by this time, so I'm safe.

(*Breathing a sigh of relief, he curls up and goes to sleep. In his dream the pipe becomes transparent, and the Gods appear.*)

(*Raising an arm, as if in self-defense.*) I know, I know, illustrious ones! I found no one to give you a room—not in all Setzuan! There, it's out. Please continue on your way!

FIRST GOD (*mildly*). But you did find someone. Someone who took us in for the night, watched over us in our sleep, and in the early morning lighted us down to the street with a lamp.

WONG. It was . . . Shen Te, that took you in?

THIRD GOD. Who else?

WONG. And I ran away! "She isn't coming," I thought, "she just can't afford it."

GODS (*singing*).
O you feeble, well-intentioned, and yet feeble chap!
Where there's need the fellow thinks there is no
goodness!
When there's danger he thinks courage starts to ebb
away!
Some people only see the seamy side!
What hasty judgment! What premature desperation!

WONG. I'm *very* ashamed, illustrious ones.

FIRST GOD. Do us a favor, Water Seller. Go back to Setzuan. Find Shen Te, and give us a report on her. We hear that she's come into a little money. Show interest in her goodness—for no one can be good for long if goodness is not in demand. Meanwhile we shall continue the search, and find other good people. After which, the idle chatter about the impossibility of goodness will stop!

(*The Gods vanish.*)

SCENE 2

(*A knocking.*)

WIFE. Shen Te! Someone at the door. Where is she anyway?

NEPHEW. She must be getting the breakfast. Mr. Shui Ta will pay for it.

(*The Wife laughs and shuffles to the door. Enter Mr. Shui Ta and the Carpenter.*)

WIFE. Who is it?

SHUI TA. I am Miss Shen Te's cousin.

WIFE. What?

SHUI TA. My name is Shui Ta.

WIFE. Her cousin?

NEPHEW. Her cousin?

NIECE. But that was a joke. She hasn't got a cousin.

HUSBAND. So early in the morning?

BROTHER. What's all the noise?

SISTER-IN-LAW. This fellow says he's her cousin.

BROTHER. Tell him to prove it.

NEPHEW. Right. If you're Shen Te's cousin, prove it by getting the breakfast.

SHUI TA (*whose regime begins as he puts out the lamp to save oil. Loudly, to all present, asleep or awake*). Would you all please get dressed! Customers will be coming! I wish to open my shop!

HUSBAND. *Your* shop? Doesn't it belong to our good friend Shen Te?

(*Shui Ta shakes his head.*)

SISTER-IN-LAW. So we've been cheated. Where *is* the little liar?

SHUI TA. Miss Shen Te has been delayed. She wishes me to tell you there will be nothing she can do—now I am here.

WIFE (*bowled over*). I thought she was *good!*

NEPHEW. Do you have to believe *him*?

HUSBAND. *I* don't.

NEPHEW. Then do something.

HUSBAND. Certainly! I'll send out a search party at once. You, you, you, and you, go out and look for Shen Te.

(*As the Grandfather rises and makes for the door.*)

Not you, Grandfather, you and I will hold the fort.

SHUI TA. You won't find Miss Shen Te. She has suspended her hospitable activity for an unlimited period. There are too many of you. She asked me to say: this is a tobacco shop, not a gold mine.

HUSBAND. Shen Te never said a thing like that. Boy, food! There's a bakery on the corner. Stuff your shirt full when they're not looking!

SISTER-IN-LAW. Don't overlook the raspberry tarts.

HUSBAND. And don't let the policeman see you.

(*The Boy leaves.*)

SHUI TA. Don't you depend on this shop now? Then why give it a bad name, by stealing from the bakery?

NEPHEW. Don't listen to him. Let's find Shen Te. She'll give him a piece of her mind.

SISTER-IN-LAW. Don't forget to leave us some breakfast.

(*Brother, Sister-in-Law, and Nephew leave.*)

SHUI TA (*to the Carpenter*). You see, Mr. Carpenter, nothing has changed since the poet, eleven hundred years ago, penned these lines:

> A governor was asked what was needed
> To save the freezing people in the city.
> He replied:
> "A blanket ten thousand feet long
> To cover the city and all its suburbs."

(*He starts to tidy up the shop.*)

CARPENTER. Your cousin owes me money. I've got witnesses. For the shelves.

SHUI TA. Yes, I have your bill. (*He takes it out of his pocket.*) Isn't a hundred silver dollars rather a lot?

CARPENTER. No deductions! I have a wife and children.

SHUI TA. How many children?

CARPENTER. Three.
SHUI TA. I'll make you an offer. Twenty silver dollars.

(*The Husband laughs.*)

CARPENTER. You're crazy. Those shelves are real walnut.
SHUI TA. Very well. Take them away.
CARPENTER. What?
SHUI TA. They cost too much. Please take them away.
WIFE. Not bad! (*And she, too, is laughing.*)
CARPENTER (*a little bewildered*). Call Shen Te, someone! (*To Shui Ta.*) She's good!
SHUI TA. Certainly. She's ruined.
CARPENTER (*provoked into taking some of the shelves*). All right, you can keep your tobacco on the floor.
SHUI TA (*to the Husband*). Help him with the shelves.
HUSBAND (*grins and carries one shelf over to the door where the Carpenter now is*). Goodbye, shelves!
CARPENTER (*to the Husband*). You dog! You want my family to starve?
SHUI TA. I repeat my offer. I have no desire to keep my tobacco on the floor. Twenty silver dollars.
CARPENTER (*with desperate aggressiveness*). One hundred!

(*Shui Ta shows indifference, looks through the window. The Husband picks up several shelves.*)

(*To Husband.*) You needn't smash them against the doorpost, you idiot! (*To Shui Ta.*) These shelves were made to measure. They're no use anywhere else!
SHUI TA. Precisely.

(*The Wife squeals with pleasure.*)

CARPENTER (*giving up, sullenly*). Take the shelves. Pay what you want to pay.
SHUI TA (*smoothly*). Twenty silver dollars.

(*He places two large coins on the table. The Carpenter picks them up.*)

HUSBAND (*brings the shelves back in*). And quite enough too!
CARPENTER (*slinking off*). Quite enough to get drunk on.
HUSBAND (*happily*). Well, we got rid of *him!*
WIFE (*weeping with fun, gives a rendition of the dialogue just spoken*). "Real walnut," says he. "Very well, take them away," says his lordship. "I have children," says he. "Twenty silver dollars," says his lordship. "They're no use anywhere else," says he. "Precisely," said his lordship! (*She dissolves into shrieks of merriment.*)
SHUI TA. And now: go!
HUSBAND. What's that?
SHUI TA. You're thieves, parasites. I'm giving you this chance. Go!
HUSBAND (*summoning all his ancestral dignity*). That sort deserves no answer. Besides, one should never shout on an empty stomach.
WIFE. Where's that boy?
SHUI TA. Exactly. The boy. I want no stolen goods in this shop. (*Very loudly.*) I strongly advise you to leave! (*But they remain seated, noses in the air. Quietly.*) As you wish.

(*Shui Ta goes to the door. A Policeman appears. Shui Ta bows.*)

I am addressing the officer in charge of this precinct?
POLICEMAN. That's right, Mr., um . . . what was the name, sir?
SHUI TA. Mr. Shui Ta.
POLICEMAN. Yes, of course, sir.

(*They exchange a smile.*)

SHUI TA. Nice weather we're having.
POLICEMAN. A little on the warm side, sir.
SHUI TA. Oh, a little on the warm side.
HUSBAND (*whispering to the Wife*). If he keeps it up till the boy's back, we're done for. (*Tries to signal Shui Ta.*)
SHUI TA (*ignoring the signal*). Weather, of course, is one thing indoors, another out on the dusty street!
POLICEMAN. Oh, quite another, sir!
WIFE (*to the Husband*). It's all right as long as he's standing in the doorway—the boy will see him.
SHUI TA. Step inside for a moment! It's quite cool indoors. My cousin and I have just opened the place. And we attach the greatest importance to being on good terms with the, um, authorities.
POLICEMAN (*entering*). Thank you, Mr. Shui Ta. It *is* cool!
HUSBAND (*whispering to the Wife*). And now the boy *won't* see him.
SHUI TA (*showing Husband and Wife to the Policeman*). Visitors, I think my cousin knows them. They were just leaving.
HUSBAND (*defeated*). Ye-e-es, we were . . . just leaving.
SHUI TA. I'll tell my cousin you couldn't wait.

(*Noise from the street. Shouts of "Stop, thief!"*)

POLICEMAN. What's that?

(*The Boy is in the doorway with cakes and buns and rolls spilling out of his shirt. The Wife signals desperately to him to leave. He gets the idea.*)

No, you don't! (*He grabs the Boy by the collar.*) Where's all this from?
BOY (*vaguely pointing*). Down the street.

POLICEMAN (*grimly*). So that's it. (*Prepares to arrest the Boy.*)

WIFE (*stepping in*). And *we* knew nothing about it. (*To the Boy.*) Nasty little thief!

POLICEMAN (*dryly*). Can you clarify the situation, Mr. Shui Ta?

(*Shui Ta is silent.*)

POLICEMAN (*who understands silence*). Aha. You're all coming with me—to the station.

SHUI TA. I can hardly say how sorry I am that *my* establishment . . .

WIFE. Oh, he saw the boy leave not ten minutes ago!

SHUI TA. And to conceal the theft asked a policeman in?

POLICEMAN. Don't listen to her, Mr. Shui Ta, I'll be happy to relieve you of their presence one and all! (*To all three.*) Out! (*He drives them before him.*)

GRANDFATHER (*leaving last. Gravely*). Good morning!

POLICEMAN. Good morning!

(*Shui Ta, left alone, continues to tidy up. Mrs. Mi Tzu breezes in.*)

MRS. MI TZU. *You're* her cousin, are you? Then have the goodness to explain what all this means—police dragging people from a respectable house! By what right does your Miss Shen Te turn my property into a house of assignation?—Well, as you see, I know all!

SHUI TA. Yes. My cousin has the worst possible reputation: that of being poor.

MRS. MI TZU. No sentimental rubbish, Mr. Shui Ta. Your cousin was a common . . .

SHUI TA. Pauper. Let's use the uglier word.

MRS. MI TZU. I'm speaking of her conduct, not her earnings. But there must have *been* earnings, or how did she buy all this? Several elderly gentlemen took care of it, I suppose. I repeat: this is a respectable house! I have tenants who prefer not to live under the same roof with such a person.

SHUI TA (*quietly*). How much do you want?

MRS. MI TZU (*he is ahead of her now*). I beg your pardon.

SHUI TA. To reassure yourself. To reassure your tenants. How much will it cost?

MRS. MI TZU. You're a cool customer.

SHUI TA (*picking up the lease*). The rent is high. (*He reads on.*) I assume it's payable by the month?

MRS. MI TZU. Not in her case.

SHUI TA (*looking up*). What?

MRS. MI TZU. Six months rent payable in advance. Two hundred silver dollars.

SHUI TA. Six . . . ! Sheer usury! And where am I to find it?

MRS. MI TZU. You should have thought of that before.

SHUI TA. Have you no heart, Mrs. Mi Tzu? It's true Shen Te acted foolishly, being kind to all those people, but she'll improve with time. I'll see to it she does. She'll work her fingers to the bone to pay her rent, and all the time be as quiet as a mouse, as humble as a fly.

MRS. MI TZU. Her social background . . .

SHUI TA. Out of the depths! She came out of the depths! And before she'll go back there, she'll work, sacrifice, shrink from nothing. . . . Such a tenant is worth her weight in gold, Mrs. Mi Tzu.

MRS. MI TZU. It's silver we were talking about, Mr. Shui Ta. Two hundred silver dollars or . . .

(*Enter the Policeman.*)

POLICEMAN. Am I intruding, Mr. Shui Ta?

MRS. MI TZU. This tobacco shop is well-known to the police, I see.

POLICEMAN. Mr. Shui Ta has done us a service, Mrs. Mi Tzu. I am here to present our official felicitations!

MRS. MI TZU. That means less than nothing to me, sir. Mr. Shui Ta, all I can say is: I hope your cousin will find my terms acceptable. Good day, gentlemen. (*Exit.*)

SHUI TA. Good day, ma'am.

(*Pause.*)

POLICEMAN. Mrs. Mi Tzu a bit of a stumbling block, sir?

SHUI TA. She wants six months' rent in advance.

POLICEMAN. And you haven't got it, eh?

(*Shui Ta is silent.*)

But surely you can get it, sir? A man like you?

SHUI TA. What about a woman like Shen Te?

POLICEMAN. You're not staying, sir?

SHUI TA. No, and I won't be back. Do you smoke?

POLICEMAN (*taking two cigars, and placing them both in his pocket*). Thank you, sir—I see your point. Miss Shen Te—let's mince no words—Miss Shen Te lived by selling herself. "What else could she have done?" you ask. "How else was she to pay the rent?" True. But the fact remains, Mr. Shui Ta, it is not respectable. Why not? A very deep question. But, in the first place, love—love isn't bought and sold like cigars, Mr. Shui Ta. In the second place, it isn't respectable to go waltzing off with someone that's paying his way, so to speak—it must be for love! Thirdly and lastly, as the proverb has it: not for a handful of rice but for love! (*Pause. He is thinking hard.*) "Well," you may say, "and what good is all this wisdom if the milk's already spilt?" Miss

Shen Te is what she is. Is *where* she is. We have to face the fact that if she doesn't get hold of six months' rent pronto, she'll be back on the streets. The question then as I see it—everything in this world is a matter of opinion—the question as I see it is: *how* is she to get hold of this rent? How? Mr. Shui Ta: I don't know. (*Pause.*) I take that back, sir. It's just come to me. A husband. We must find her a husband!

(*Enter a little Old Woman.*)

OLD WOMAN. A good cheap cigar for my husband, we'll have been married forty years tomorrow and we're having a little celebration.

SHUI TA. Forty years? And you still want to celebrate?

OLD WOMAN. As much as we can afford to. We have the carpet shop across the square. We'll be good neighbors, I hope?

SHUI TA. I hope so too.

POLICEMAN (*who keeps making discoveries*). Mr. Shui Ta, you know what we need? We need capital. And how do we acquire capital? We get married.

SHUI TA (*to Old Woman*). I'm afraid I've been pestering this gentleman with my personal worries.

POLICEMAN (*lyrically*). We can't pay six months' rent, so what do we do? We marry money.

SHUI TA. That might not be easy.

POLICEMAN. Oh, I don't know. She's a good match. Has a nice, growing business. (*To the Old Woman.*) What do you think?

OLD WOMAN (*undecided*). Well—

POLICEMAN. Should she put an ad in the paper?

OLD WOMAN (*not eager to commit herself*). Well, if *she* agrees—

POLICEMAN. I'll write it for her. *You* lend us a hand, and *we* write an ad for you! (*He chuckles away to himself, takes out his notebook, wets the stump of a pencil between his lips, and writes away.*)

SHUI TA (*slowly*). Not a bad idea.

POLICEMAN. "What . . . *respectable* . . . man . . . with small capital . . . widower . . . not excluded . . . desires . . . marriage . . . into flourishing . . . tobacco shop?" And now let's add: "am . . . pretty . . ." No! . . . "Prepossessing appearance."

SHUI TA. If you don't think that's an exaggeration?

OLD WOMAN. Oh, not a bit. I've seen her.

(*The Policeman tears the page out of his notebook, and hands it over to Shui Ta.*)

SHUI TA (*with horror in his voice*). How much luck we need to keep our heads above water! How many ideas! How many friends! (*To the Policeman.*) Thank you, sir. I think I see my way clear.

SCENE 3

(*Evening in the municipal park. Noise of a plane overhead. Yang Sun, a young man in rags, is following the plane with his eyes: one can tell that the machine is describing a curve above the park. Yang Sun then takes a rope out of his pocket, looking anxiously about him as he does so. He moves toward a large willow. Enter Two Prostitutes, one old, the other the Niece whom we have already met.*)

NIECE. Hello. Coming with me?

YANG SUN (*taken aback*). If you'd like to buy me a dinner.

OLD WHORE. Buy you a dinner! (*To the Niece.*) Oh, we know him—it's the unemployed pilot. Waste no time on him!

NIECE. But he's the only man left in the park. And it's going to rain.

OLD WHORE. Oh, how do you know?

(*And they pass by. Yang Sun again looks about him, again takes his rope, and this time throws it round a branch of the willow tree. Again he is interrupted. It is the Two Prostitutes returning—and in such a hurry they don't notice him.*)

NIECE. It's going to pour!

(*Enter Shen Te.*)

OLD WHORE. There's that *gorgon* Shen Te! That *drove* your family out into the cold!

NIECE. It wasn't her. It was that cousin of hers. She offered to *pay* for the cakes. I've nothing against her.

OLD WHORE. I have, though. (*So that Shen Te can hear.*) Now where could the little lady be off to? She may be rich now but that won't stop her snatching our young men, will it?

SHEN TE. I'm going to the tearoom by the pond.

NIECE. Is it true what they say? You're marrying a widower—with three children?

SHEN TE. Yes. I'm just going to see him.

YANG SUN (*his patience at breaking point*). Move on there! This is a park, not a whorehouse!

OLD WHORE. Shut your mouth!

(*But the Two Prostitutes leave.*)

YANG SUN. Even in the farthest corner of the park, even when it's raining, you can't get rid of them! (*He spits.*)

SHEN TE (*overhearing this*). And what right have you to scold them? (*But at this point she sees the rope.*) Oh!

YANG SUN. Well, what are you staring at?
SHEN TE. That rope. What is it for?
YANG SUN. Think! Think! I haven't a penny. Even if I had, I wouldn't spend it on you. I'd buy a drink of water.

(*The rain starts.*)

SHEN TE (*still looking at the rope*). What is the rope for? You mustn't!
YANG SUN. What's it to you? Clear out!
SHEN TE (*irrelevantly*). It's raining.
YANG SUN. Well, don't try to come under this tree.
SHEN TE. Oh, no. (*She stays in the rain.*)
YANG SUN. Now go away. (*Pause.*) For one thing, I don't like your looks, you're bow-legged.
SHEN TE (*indignantly*). That's not true!
YANG SUN. Well, don't show 'em to me. Look, it's raining. You better come under this tree.

(*Slowly, she takes shelter under the tree.*)

SHEN TE. Why did you want to do it?
YANG SUN. You really want to know? (*Pause.*) To get rid of you! (*Pause.*) You know what a flyer is?
SHEN TE. Oh yes, I've met a lot of pilots. At the tearoom.
YANG SUN. You call *them* flyers? Think they know what a machine *is?* Just 'cause they have leather helmets? They gave the airfield director a bribe, that's the way *those* fellows got up in the air! Try one of them out sometime. "Go up to two thousand feet," tell him, "then let it fall, then pick it up again with a flick of the wrist at the last moment." Know what he'll say to that? "It's not in my contract." Then again, there's the landing problem. It's like landing on your own backside. It's no different, planes are human. Those fools don't understand. (*Pause.*) And I'm the biggest fool for reading the book on flying in the Peking school and skipping the page where it says: "we've got enough flyers and we don't need you." I'm a mail pilot and no mail. You understand that?
SHEN TE (*shyly*). Yes. I do.
YANG SUN. No, you don't. You'd never understand that.
SHEN TE. When we were little we had a crane with a broken wing. He made friends with us and was very good-natured about our jokes. He would strut along behind us and call out to stop us going too fast for him. But every spring and autumn when the cranes flew over the villages in great swarms, he got quite restless. (*Pause.*) I understood that. (*She bursts out crying.*)
YANG SUN. Don't!
SHEN TE (*quieting down*). No.
YANG SUN. It's bad for the complexion.
SHEN TE (*sniffing*). I've stopped.

(*She dries her tears on her big sleeve. Leaning against the tree, but not looking at her, he reaches for her face.*)

YANG SUN. You can't even wipe your own face. (*He is wiping it for her with his handkerchief. Pause.*)
SHEN TE (*still sobbing*). I don't know *anything!*
YANG SUN. You interrupted me! What for?
SHEN TE. It's such a rainy day. You only wanted to do ... *that* because it's such a rainy day.

(*To the audience.*)

In our country
The evenings should never be somber
High bridges over rivers
The grey hour between night and morning
And the long, long winter:
Such things are dangerous
For, with all the misery,
A very little is enough
And men throw away an unbearable life.

(*Pause.*)

YANG SUN. Talk about yourself for a change.
SHEN TE. What about me? I have a shop.
YANG SUN (*incredulous*). You have a shop, do you? Never thought of walking the streets?
SHEN TE. I *did* walk the streets. Now I have a shop.
YANG SUN (*ironically*). A gift of the gods, I suppose!
SHEN TE. How did you know?
YANG SUN (*even more ironical*). One fine evening the gods turned up saying: here's some money!
SHEN TE (*quickly*). One fine morning.
YANG SUN (*fed up*). This isn't much of an entertainment.

(*Pause.*)

SHEN TE. I can play the zither a little. (*Pause.*) And I can mimic men. (*Pause.*) I got the shop, so the first thing I did was to give my zither away. I can be as stupid as a fish now, I said to myself, and it won't matter.

I'm rich now, I said
I walk alone, I sleep alone
For a whole year, I said
I'll have nothing to do with a man.

YANG SUN. And now you're marrying one! The one at the tearoom by the pond?

(*Shen Te is silent.*)

YANG SUN. What do you know about love?
SHEN TE. Everything.
YANG SUN. Nothing. (*Pause.*) Or d'you just mean you enjoyed it?
SHEN TE. No.
YANG SUN (*again without turning to look at her, he strokes her cheek with his hand*). You like that?

SHEN TE. Yes.

YANG SUN (*breaking off*). You're easily satisfied, I must say. (*Pause.*) What a town!

SHEN TE. You have no friends?

YANG SUN (*defensively*). Yes, I have! (*Change of tone.*) But they don't want to hear I'm still unemployed. "What?" they ask. "Is there still water in the sea?" You have friends?

SHEN TE (*hesitating*). Just a . . . cousin.

YANG SUN. Watch him carefully.

SHEN TE. He only came once. Then he went away. He won't be back.

(*Yang Sun is looking away.*)

But to be without hope, they say, is to be without goodness!

(*Pause.*)

YANG SUN. Go on talking. A voice is a voice.

SHEN TE. Once, when I was a little girl, I fell, with a load of brushwood. An old man picked me up. He gave me a penny too. Isn't it funny how people who don't have very much like to give some of it away? They must like to show what they can do, and how could they show it better than by being kind? Being wicked is just like being clumsy. When we sing a song, or build a machine, or plant some rice, we're being kind. You're kind.

YANG SUN. You make it sound easy.

SHEN TE. Oh, no. (*Little pause.*) Oh! A drop of rain!

YANG SUN. Where'd you feel it?

SHEN TE. Between the eyes.

YANG SUN. Near the right eye? Or the left?

SHEN TE. Near the left eye.

YANG SUN. Oh, good. (*He is getting sleepy.*) So you're through with men, eh?

SHEN TE (*with a smile*). But I'm not bow-legged.

YANG SUN. Perhaps not.

SHEN TE. Definitely not.

(*Pause.*)

YANG SUN (*leaning wearily against the willow*). I haven't had a drop to drink all day, I haven't eaten anything for *two* days. I couldn't love you if I tried.

(*Pause.*)

SHEN TE. I like it in the rain.

(*Enter Wong the Water Seller, singing.*)

The Song of the Water Seller in the Rain

"Buy my water," I am yelling
And my fury restraining
For no water I'm selling
'Cause it's raining, 'cause it's raining!
I keep yelling: "Buy my water!"
But no one's buying
Athirst and dying
And drinking and paying!
Buy water!
Buy water, you dogs!

Nice to dream of lovely weather!
Think of all the consternation
Were there no precipitation
Half a dozen years together!
Can't you hear them shrieking: "Water!"
Pretending they adore me!
They all would go down on their knees before me!
Down on your knees!
Go down on your knees, you dogs!

What are lawns and hedges thinking?
What are fields and forests saying?
"At the cloud's breast we are drinking!
And we've no idea who's paying!"
I keep yelling: "Buy my water!"
But no one's buying
Athirst and dying
And drinking and paying!
Buy water!
Buy water, you dogs!

(*The rain has stopped now. Shen Te sees Wong and runs toward him.*)

SHEN TE. Wong! You're back! Your carrying pole's at the shop.

WONG. Oh, thank you, Shen Te. And how is life treating *you*?

SHEN TE. I've just met a brave and clever man. And I want to buy him a cup of your water.

WONG (*bitterly*). Throw back your head and open your mouth and you'll have all the water you need—

SHEN TE (*tenderly*).
I want *your* water, Wong
The water that has tired you so
The water that you carried all this way
The water that is hard to sell because it's been raining
I need it for the young man over there—he's a flyer!
A flyer is a bold man:
Braving the storms
In company with the clouds
He crosses the heavens
And brings to friends in far-away lands
The friendly mail!

(*She pays Wong, and runs over to Yang Sun with the cup. But Yang Sun is fast asleep.*)

(*Calling to Wong, with a laugh.*) He's fallen asleep! Despair and rain and I have worn him out!

SCENE 3A

(*Wong's den. The sewer pipe is transparent, and the Gods again appear to Wong in a dream.*)

WONG (*radiant*). I've seen her, illustrious ones! And she hasn't changed!

FIRST GOD. That's good to hear.

WONG. She loves someone.

FIRST GOD. Let's hope the experience gives her the strength to stay good!

WONG. It does. She's doing good deeds all the time.

FIRST GOD. Ah? What sort? What sort of good deeds, Wong?

WONG. Well, she has a kind word for everybody.

FIRST GOD (*eagerly*). And then?

WONG. Hardly anyone leaves her shop without tobacco in his pocket—even if he can't pay for it.

FIRST GOD. Not bad at all. Next?

WONG. She's putting up a family of eight.

FIRST GOD (*gleefully, to the Second God*). Eight! (*To Wong.*) And that's not all, of course!

WONG. She bought a cup of water from me even though it was raining.

FIRST GOD. Yes, yes, yes, all these smaller good deeds!

WONG. Even they run into money. A little tobacco shop doesn't make so much.

FIRST GOD (*sententiously*). A prudent gardener works miracles on the smallest plot.

WONG. She hands out rice every morning. That eats up half her earnings.

FIRST GOD (*a little disappointed*). Well, as a beginning . . .

WONG. They call her the Angel of the Slums—whatever the Carpenter may say!

FIRST GOD. What's this? A carpenter speaks ill of her?

WONG. Oh, he only says her shelves weren't paid for in full.

SECOND GOD (*who has a bad cold and can't pronounce his n's and m's*). What's this? Not paying a carpenter? Why was that?

WONG. I suppose she didn't have the money.

SECOND GOD (*severely*). One pays what one owes, that's in our book of rules! First the letter of the law, then the spirit!

WONG. But it wasn't Shen Te, illustrious ones, it was her cousin. She called *him* in to help.

SECOND GOD. Then her cousin must never darken her threshold again!

WONG. Very well, illustrious ones! But in fairness to Shen Te, let me say that her cousin is a businessman.

FIRST GOD. Perhaps we should inquire what is customary? I find business quite unintelligible. But everybody's doing it. Business! Did the Seven Good Kings do business? Did Kung the Just sell fish?

SECOND GOD. In any case, such a thing must not occur again!

(*The Gods start to leave.*)

THIRD GOD. Forgive us for taking this tone with you, Wong, we haven't been getting enough sleep. The rich recommend us to the poor, and the poor tell us they haven't enough room.

SECOND GOD. Feeble, feeble, the best of them!

FIRST GOD. No great deeds! No heroic daring!

THIRD GOD. On such a *small* scale!

SECOND GOD. Sincere, yes, but what is actually *achieved?*

(*One can no longer hear them.*)

WONG (*calling after them*). I've thought of something, illustrious ones: Perhaps you shouldn't ask—too—much—all—at—once!

SCENE 4

(*The square in front of Shen Te's tobacco shop. Beside Shen Te's place, two other shops are seen: the carpet shop and a barber's. Morning. Outside Shen Te's the Grandfather, the Sister-in-Law, the Unemployed Man, and Mrs. Shin stand waiting.*)

SISTER-IN-LAW. She's been out all night again.

MRS. SHIN. No sooner did we get rid of that crazy cousin of hers than Shen Te herself starts carrying on! Maybe she does give us an ounce of rice now and then, but can you depend on her? Can you depend on her?

(*Loud voices from the Barber's.*)

VOICE OF SHU FU. What are you doing in my shop? Get out—at once!

VOICE OF WONG. But sir. They all let me sell . . .

(*Wong comes staggering out of the barber's shop pursued by Mr. Shu Fu, the barber, a fat man carrying a heavy curling iron.*)

SHU FU. Get out, I said! Pestering my customers with your slimy old water! Get out! Take your cup!

(*He holds out the cup. Wong reaches out for it. Mr. Shu Fu strikes his hand with the curling iron, which is hot. Wong howls.*)

You had it coming, my man!

(*Puffing, he returns to his shop. The Unemployed Man picks up the cup and gives it to Wong.*)

UNEMPLOYED MAN. You can report that to the police.

WONG. My hand! It's smashed up!

UNEMPLOYED MAN. Any bones broken?

WONG. I can't move my fingers.

UNEMPLOYED MAN. Sit down. I'll put some water on it.

(*Wong sits.*)

MRS. SHIN. The water won't cost you anything.

SISTER-IN-LAW. You might have got a bandage from Miss Shen Te till she took to staying out all night. It's a scandal.

MRS. SHIN (*despondently*). If you ask me, she's forgotten we ever existed!

(*Enter Shen Te down the street, with a dish of rice.*)

SHEN TE (*to the audience*). How wonderful to see Setzuan in the early morning! I always used to stay in bed with my dirty blanket over my head afraid to wake up. This morning I saw the newspapers being delivered by little boys, the streets being washed by strong men, and fresh vegetables coming in from the country on ox carts. It's a long walk from where Yang Sun lives, but I feel lighter at every step. They say you walk on air when you're in love, but it's even better walking on the rough earth, on the hard cement. In the early morning, the old city looks like a great rubbish heap. Nice, though—with all its little lights. And the sky, so pink, so transparent, before the dust comes and muddies it! What a lot you miss if you never see your city rising from its slumbers like an honest old craftsman pumping his lungs full of air and reaching for his tools, as the poet says! (*Cheerfully, to her waiting guests.*) Good morning, everyone, here's your rice! (*Distributing the rice, she comes upon Wong.*) Good morning, Wong, I'm quite lightheaded today. On my way over, I looked at myself in all the shop windows. I'd love to be beautiful.

(*She slips into the carpet shop. Mr. Shu Fu has just emerged from his shop.*)

SHU FU (*to the audience*). It surprises me how beautiful Miss Shen Te is looking today! I never gave her a passing thought before. But now I've been gazing upon her comely form for exactly three minutes! I begin to suspect I am in love with her. She is overpoweringly attractive! (*Crossly, to Wong.*) Be off with you, rascal!

(*He returns to his shop. Shen Te comes back out of the carpet shop with the Old Man its proprietor and his wife—whom we have already met—the Old Woman. Shen Te is wearing a shawl. The Old Man is holding up a looking glass for her.*)

OLD WOMAN. Isn't it lovely? We'll give you a reduction because there's a little hole in it.

SHEN TE (*looking at another shawl on the Old Woman's arm*). The other one's nice too.

OLD WOMAN (*smiling*). Too bad there's no hole in that!

SHEN TE. That's right. My shop doesn't make very much.

OLD WOMAN. And your good deeds eat it all up! Be more careful, my dear . . .

SHEN TE (*trying on the shawl with the hole*). Just now, I'm lightheaded! Does the color suit me?

OLD WOMAN. You'd better ask a man.

SHEN TE (*to the Old Man*). Does the color suit me?

OLD MAN. You'd better ask your young friend.

SHEN TE. I'd like to have your opinion.

OLD MAN. It suits you, very well. But wear it this way: the dull side out.

(*Shen Te pays up.*)

OLD WOMAN. If you decide you don't like it, you can exchange it. (*She pulls Shen Te to one side.*) Has he got money?

SHEN TE (*with a laugh*). Yang Sun? Oh, no.

OLD WOMAN. Then how're you going to pay your rent?

SHEN TE. I'd forgotten about that.

OLD WOMAN. And next Monday is the first of the month! Miss Shen Te, I've got something to say to you. After we (*indicating her husband*) got to know you, we had our doubts about that marriage ad. We thought it would be better if you'd let *us* help you. Out of our savings. We reckon we could lend you two hundred silver dollars. We don't need anything in writing—you could pledge us your tobacco stock.

SHEN TE. You're prepared to lend money to a person like me?

OLD WOMAN. It's folks like you that need it. We'd think twice about lending anything to your cousin.

OLD MAN (*coming up*). All settled, my dear?

SHEN TE. I wish the gods could have heard what your wife was just saying, Mr. Ma. They're looking for good people who're happy—and helping me makes you happy because you know it was love that got me into difficulties!

(*The old couple smile knowingly at each other.*)

OLD MAN. And here's the money, Miss Shen Te.

(*He hands her an envelope. Shen Te takes it. She bows. They bow back. They return to their shop.*)

SHEN TE (*holding up her envelope*). Look, Wong, here's six months' rent! Don't you believe in miracles now? And how do you like my new shawl?

WONG. For the young fellow I saw you with in the park?

(*Shen Te nods.*)

MRS. SHIN. Never mind all that. It's time you took a look at his hand!

SHEN TE. Have you hurt your hand?

MRS. SHIN. That barber smashed it with his hot curling iron. Right in front of our eyes.

SHEN TE (*shocked at herself*). And I never noticed! We must get you to a doctor this minute or who knows what will happen?

UNEMPLOYED MAN. It's not a doctor he should see, it's a judge. He can ask for compensation. The barber's filthy rich.

WONG. You think I have a chance?

MRS. SHIN (*with relish*). If it's really good and smashed. But is it?

WONG. I think so. It's very swollen. Could I get a pension?

MRS. SHIN. You'd need a witness.

WONG. Well, you all saw it. You could all testify.

(*He looks round. The Unemployed Man, the Grandfather, and the Sister-in-Law are all sitting against the wall of the shop eating rice. Their concentration on eating is complete.*)

SHEN TE (*to Mrs. Shin*). You saw it yourself.

MRS. SHIN. I want nothin' to do with the police. It's against my principles.

SHEN TE (*to Sister-in-Law*). What about you?

SISTER-IN-LAW. Me? I wasn't looking.

SHEN TE (*to the Grandfather, coaxingly*). Grandfather, *you'll* testify, won't you?

SISTER-IN-LAW. And a lot of good that will do. He's simple-minded.

SHEN TE (*to the Unemployed Man*). You seem to be the only witness left.

UNEMPLOYED MAN. My testimony would only hurt him. I've been picked up twice for begging.

SHEN TE. Your brother is assaulted, and you shut your eyes?
He is hit, cries out in pain, and you are silent?
The beast prowls, chooses and seizes his victim, and you say:
"Because we showed no displeasure, he has spared us."
If no one present will be a witness, I will. I'll say *I* saw it.

MRS. SHIN (*solemnly*). The name for that is perjury.

WONG. I don't know if I can accept that. Though maybe I'll have to. (*Looking at his hand.*) Is it swollen enough, do you think? The swelling's not going down?

UNEMPLOYED MAN. No, no, the swelling's holding up well.

WONG. Yes. It's *more* swollen if anything. Maybe my wrist is broken after all. I'd better see a judge at once.

(*Holding his hand very carefully, and fixing his eyes on it, he runs off. Mrs. Shin goes quickly into the barber's shop.*

UNEMPLOYED MAN (*seeing her*). She is getting on the right side of Mr. Shu Fu.

SISTER-IN-LAW. You and I can't change the world, Shen Te.

SHEN TE. Go away! Go away all of you!

(*The Unemployed Man, the Sister-in-Law, and the Grandfather stalk off, eating and sulking.*)

(*To the audience.*)

They've stopped answering
They stay put
They do as they're told
They don't care
Nothing can make them look up
But the smell of food.

(*Enter Mrs. Yang, Yang Sun's mother, out of breath.*)

MRS. YANG. Miss. Shen Te. My son has told me everything. I am Mrs. Yang, Sun's mother. Just think. He's got an offer. Of a job as a pilot. A letter has just come. From the director of the airfield in Peking!

SHEN TE. So he can fly again? Isn't that wonderful!

MRS. YANG (*less breathlessly all the time*). They won't give him the job for nothing. They want five hundred silver dollars.

SHEN TE. We can't let money stand in his way, Mrs. Yang!

MRS. YANG. If only you could help him out!

SHEN TE. I have the shop. I can try! (*She embraces Mrs. Yang.*) I happen to have two hundred with me now. Take it. (*She gives her the old couple's money.*) It was a loan but they said I could repay it with my tobacco stock.

MRS. YANG. And they were calling Sun the Dead Pilot of Setzuan! A friend in need!

SHEN TE. We must find another three hundred.

MRS. YANG. How?

SHEN TE. Let me think. (*Slowly.*) I know someone who can help. I didn't want to call on his services again, he's hard and cunning. But a flyer must fly. And I'll make this the last time.

(*Distant sound of a plane.*)

MRS. YANG. If the man you mentioned can do it. . . . Oh, look, there's the morning mail plane, heading for Peking!

SHEN TE. The pilot can see us, let's wave!

(*They wave. The noise of the engine is louder.*)

MRS. YANG. You know that pilot up there?

SHEN TE. Wave, Mrs. Yang! I know the pilot who *will* be up there. He gave up hope. But he'll do it now. One man to raise himself above the misery, above us all.

(*To the audience.*)

Yang Sun, my lover:
Braving the storms
In company with the clouds
Crossing the heavens
And bringing to friends in far-away lands
The friendly mail!

SCENE 4A

(*In front of the inner curtain. Enter Shen Te, carrying Shui Ta's mask. She sings.*)

The Song of Defenselessness

In our country
A useful man needs luck
Only if he finds strong backers can he prove himself
  useful
The good can't defend themselves and
Even the gods are defenseless.

Oh, why don't the gods have their own ammunition
And launch against badness their own expedition
Enthroning the good and preventing sedition
And bringing the world to a peaceful condition?

Oh, why don't the gods do the buying and selling
Injustice forbidding, starvation dispelling
Give bread to each city and joy to each dwelling?
Oh, why don't the gods do the buying and selling?

(*She puts on Shui Ta's mask and sings in his voice.*)

You can only help one of your luckless brothers
By trampling down a dozen others

Why is it the gods do not feel indignation
And come down in fury to end exploitation
Defeat all defeat and forbid desperation
Refusing to tolerate such toleration?

Why is it?

SCENE 5

(*Shen Te's tobacco shop. Behind the counter, Mr. Shui Ta, reading the paper. Mrs. Shin is cleaning up. She talks and he takes no notice.*)

MRS. SHIN. And when certain' rumors get about, what *happens* to a little place like this? It goes to pot. *I* know. So, if you want my advice, Mr. Shui Ta, find out just what exactly has been going on between Miss Shen Te and that Yang Sun from Yellow Street. And remember: a certain interest in Miss Shen Te has been expressed by the barber next door, a man with twelve houses and only one wife, who, for that matter, is likely to drop off at any time. A certain interest has been expressed. (*She relishes the phrase.*) He was even inquiring about her means and, if *that* doesn't prove a man is getting serious, what would? (*Still getting no response, she leaves with her bucket.*)

YANG SUN'S VOICE. Is that Miss Shen Te's tobacco shop?

MRS. SHIN'S VOICE. Yes, it is, but it's Mr. Shui Ta who's here today.

(*Shui Ta runs to the looking glass with the short, light steps of Shen Te, and is just about to start primping, when he realizes his mistake, and turns away, with a short laugh. Enter Yang Sun. Mrs. Shin enters behind him and slips into the back room to eavesdrop.*)

YANG SUN. I am Yang Sun.

(*Shui Ta bows.*)

Is Miss Shen Te in?

SHUI TA: No.

YANG SUN. I guess you know our relationship? (*He is inspecting the stock.*) Quite a place! And I thought she was just talking big. I'll be flying again, all right. (*He takes a cigar, solicits and receives a light from Shui Ta.*) You think we can squeeze the other three hundred out of the tobacco stock?

SHUI TA. May I ask if it is your intention to sell at once?

YANG SUN. It was decent of her to come out with the two hundred but they aren't much use with the other three hundred still missing.

SHUI TA. Shen Te was overhasty promising so much. She might have to sell the shop itself to raise it. Haste, they say, is the wind that blows the house down.

YANG SUN. Oh, she isn't a girl to keep a man waiting. For one thing or the other, if you take my meaning.

SHUI TA. I take your meaning.

YANG SUN (*leering*). Uh, huh.

SHUI TA. Would you explain what the five hundred silver dollars are for?

YANG SUN. Trying to sound me out? Very well. The director of the Peking airfield is a friend of mine from flying school. I give him five hundred: he gets me the job.

SHUI TA. The price is high.

YANG SUN. Not as these things go. He'll have to fire one of the present pilots—for negligence. Only the man he has in mind isn't negligent. Not easy, you understand. You needn't mention that part of it to Shen Te.

SHUI TA (*looking intently at Yang Sun*). Mr. Yang Sun, you are asking my cousin to give up her possessions, leave her friends, and place her entire fate in your hands. I presume you intend to marry her?

YANG SUN. I'd be prepared to.

(*Slight pause.*)

SHUI TA. Those two hundred silver dollars would pay the rent here for six months. If you were Shen Te wouldn't you be tempted to continue in business?

YANG SUN. What? Can you imagine Yang Sun the Flyer behind a counter? (*In an oily voice.*) "A strong cigar or a mild one, worthy sir?" Not in this century!

SHUI TA. My cousin wishes to follow the promptings of her heart, and, from her own point of view, she may even have what is called the right to love. Accordingly, she has commissioned me to help you to this post. There is nothing here that I am not empowered to turn immediately into cash. Mrs. Mi Tzu, the landlady, will advise me about the sale.

(*Enter Mrs. Mi Tzu.*)

MRS. MI TZU. Good morning, Mr. Shui Ta, you wish to see me about the rent? As you know it falls due the day after tomorrow.

SHUI TA. Circumstances have changed, Mrs. Mi Tzu: my cousin is getting married. Her future husband here, Mr. Yang Sun, will be taking her to Peking. I am interested in selling the tobacco stock.

MRS. MI TZU. How much are you asking, Mr. Shui Ta?

YANG SUN. Three hundred sil—

SHUI TA. Five hundred silver dollars.

MRS. MI TZU. How much did she pay for it, Mr. Shui Ta?

SHUI TA. A thousand. And very little has been sold.

MRS. MI TZU. She was robbed. But I'll make you a special offer if you'll promise to be out by the day after tomorrow. Three hundred silver dollars.

YANG SUN (*shrugging*). Take it, man, take it.

SHUI TA. It is not enough.

YANG SUN. Why not? Why not? Certainly, it's enough.

SHUI TA. Five hundred silver dollars.

YANG SUN. But why? We only need three!

SHUI TA (*to Mrs. Mi Tzu*). Excuse me. (*Takes Yang Sun on one side.*) The tobacco stock is pledged to the old couple who gave my cousin the two hundred.

YANG SUN. Is it in writing?

SHUI TA. No.

YANG SUN (*to Mrs. Mi Tzu*). Three hundred will do.

MRS. MI TZU. Of course, I need an assurance that Miss Shen Te is not in debt.

YANG SUN. Mr. Shui Ta?

SHUI TA. She is not in debt.

YANG SUN. When can you let us have the money?

MRS. MI TZU. The day after tomorrow. And remember: I'm doing this because I have a soft spot in my heart for young lovers! (*Exit.*)

YANG SUN (*calling after her*). Boxes, jars and sacks—three hundred for the lot and the pain's over! (*To Shui Ta.*) Where else can we raise money by the day after tomorrow?

SHUI TA. Nowhere. Haven't you enough for the trip and the first few weeks?

YANG SUN. Oh, certainly.

SHUI TA. How much, exactly?

YANG SUN. Oh, I'll dig it up, if I have to steal it.

SHUI TA. I see.

YANG SUN. Well, don't fall off the roof. I'll get to Peking somehow.

SHUI TA. Two people can't travel for nothing.

YANG SUN (*not giving Shui Ta a chance to answer*). I'm leaving *her* behind. No millstones round *my* neck!

SHUI TA. Oh.

YANG SUN. Don't look at me like that!

SHUI TA. How precisely is my cousin to live?

YANG SUN. Oh, you'll think of something.

SHUI TA. A small request, Mr. Yang Sun. Leave the two hundred silver dollars here until you can show me two tickets for Peking.

YANG SUN. You learn to mind your own business, Mr. Shui Ta.

SHUI TA. I'm afraid Miss Shen Te may not wish to sell the shop when she discovers that . . .

YANG SUN. You don't know women. She'll want to. Even then.

SHUI TA (*a slight outburst*). She is a human being, sir! And not devoid of common sense!

YANG SUN. Shen Te is a woman: she *is* devoid of common sense. I only have to lay my hand on her shoulder, and church bells ring.

SHUI TA (*with difficulty*). Mr. Yang Sun!

YANG SUN. Mr. Shui Whatever-it-is!

SHUI TA. My cousin is devoted to you . . . because . . .

YANG SUN. Because I have my hands on her breasts. Give me a cigar. (*He takes one for himself, stuffs a few more in his pocket, then changes his mind and takes the whole box.*) Tell her I'll marry her, then bring me the three hundred. Or let her bring it. One or the other. (*Exit.*)

MRS. SHIN (*sticking her head out of the back room*). Well, he has your cousin under his thumb, and doesn't care if all Yellow Street knows it!

SHUI TA (*crying out*). I've lost my shop! And he doesn't love me! (*He runs berserk through the room, repeating these lines incoherently. Then stops suddenly, and addresses Mrs. Shin.*) Mrs. Shin, you grew up in the gutter, like me. Are we lacking in hardness? I doubt it. If you steal a penny from me, I'll take you by the throat till you spit it out! You'd do the same to me. The times are bad, this city is hell, but we're like ants, we keep coming, up and up the walls, however smooth! Till bad luck comes. Being in love, for instance. *One* weakness is enough, and love is the deadliest.

MRS. SHIN (*emerging from the back room*). You should have a little talk with Mr. Shu Fu the Barber. He's a real gentleman and just the thing for your cousin. (*She runs off.*)

SHUI TA.
A caress becomes a stranglehold
A sigh of love turns to a cry of fear
Why are there vultures circling in the air?
A girl is going to meet her lover.

(*Shui Ta sits down and Mr. Shu Fu enters with Mrs. Shin.*)

Mr. Shu Fu?

SHU FU. Mr. Shui Ta.

(*They both bow.*)

SHUI TA. I am told that you have expressed a certain interest in my cousin Shen Te. Let me set aside all propriety and confess: she is at this moment in grave danger.

SHU FU. Oh, dear!

SHUI TA. She has lost her shop, Mr. Shu Fu.

SHU FU. The charm of Miss Shen Te, Mr. Shui Ta, derives from the goodness, not of her shop, but of her heart. Men call her the Angel of the Slums.

SHUI TA. Yet her goodness has cost her two hundred silver dollars in a single day: we must put a stop to it.

SHU FU. Permit me to differ, Mr. Shui Ta. Let us rather, open wide the gates to such goodness! Every morning, with pleasure tinged by affection, I watch her charitable ministrations. For they are hungry, and she giveth them to eat! Four of them, to be precise. Why only four? I ask. Why not four hundred? I hear she has been seeking shelter for the homeless. What about my humble cabins behind the cattle run? They are at her disposal. And so forth. And so on. Mr. Shui Ta, do you think Miss Shen Te could be persuaded to listen to certain ideas of mine? Ideas like these?

SHUI TA. Mr. Shu Fu, she would be honored.

(*Enter Wong and the Policeman. Mr. Shu Fu turns abruptly away and studies the shelves.*)

WONG. Is Miss Shen Te here?

SHUI TA. No.

WONG. I am Wong the Water Seller. You are Mr. Shui Ta?

SHUI TA. I am.

WONG. I am a friend of Shen Te's.

SHUI TA. An intimate friend, I hear.

WONG (*to the Policeman*). You see? (*To Shui Ta.*) It's because of my hand.

POLICEMAN. He hurt his hand, sir, that's a fact.

SHUI TA (*quickly*). You need a sling, I see. (*He takes a shawl from the back room, and throws it to Wong.*)

WONG. But that's her new shawl!

SHUI TA. She has no more use for it.

WONG. But she bought it to please someone!

SHUI TA. It happens to be no longer necessary.

WONG (*making the sling*). She is my only witness.

POLICEMAN. Mr. Shui Ta, your cousin is supposed to have seen the Barber hit the Water Seller with a curling iron.

SHUI TA. I'm afraid my cousin was not present at the time.

WONG. But she was, sir! Just ask her! Isn't she in?

SHUI TA (*gravely*). Mr. Wong, my cousin has her own troubles. You wouldn't wish her to add to them by committing perjury?

WONG. But it was she that told me to go to the judge!

SHUI TA. Was the judge supposed to heal your hand?

(*Mr. Shu Fu turns quickly around. Shui Ta bows to Shu Fu, and vice versa.*)

WONG (*taking the sling off, and putting it back*). I see how it is.

POLICEMAN. Well, I'll be on my way. (*To Wong.*) And you be careful. If Mr. Shu Fu wasn't a man who tempers justice with mercy, as the saying is, you'd be in jail for libel. Be off with you!

(*Exit Wong, followed by Policeman.*)

SHUI TA. Profound apologies, Mr. Shu Fu.

SHU FU. Not at all, Mr. Shui Ta. (*Pointing to the shawl.*) The episode is over?

SHUI TA. It may take her time to recover. There are some fresh wounds.

SHU FU. We shall be discreet. Delicate. A short vacation could be arranged . . .

SHUI TA. First, of course, you and she would have to talk things over.

SHU FU. At a small supper in a small, but high-class, restaurant.

SHUI TA. I'll go and find her. (*Exit into back room.*)

MRS. SHIN (*sticking her head in again*). Time for congratulations, Mr. Shu Fu?

SHU FU. Ah, Mrs. Shin! Please inform Miss Shen Te's guests they may take shelter in the cabins behind the cattle run!

(*Mrs. Shin nods, grinning.*)

(*To the audience.*) Well? What do you think of me, ladies and gentlemen? What could a man do more? Could he be less selfish? More farsighted? A small supper in a small but . . . Does that bring rather vulgar and clumsy thoughts into your mind? Ts, ts, ts. Nothing of the sort will occur. She won't even be touched. Not even accidentally while passing the salt. An exchange of ideas only. Over the flowers on the table—white chrysanthemums, by the way (*He writes down a note of this.*) —yes, over the white chrysanthemums, two young souls will . . . shall I say "find each other"? We shall NOT exploit the misfortune of others. Understanding? Yes. An offer of assistance? Certainly. But quietly. Almost inaudibly. Perhaps with a single glance. A glance that could also—mean more.

MRS. SHIN (*coming forward*). Everything under control, Mr. Shu Fu?

SHU FU. Oh, Mrs. Shin, what do you know about this worthless rascal Yang Sun?

MRS. SHIN. Why, he's the most worthless rascal . . .

SHU FU. Is he really? You're sure? (*As she opens her mouth.*) From now on, he doesn't exist! Can't be found anywhere!

(*Enter Yang Sun.*)

YANG SUN. What's been going on here?

MRS. SHIN. Shall I call Mr. Shui Ta, Mr. Shu Fu? He wouldn't want strangers in here!

SHU FU. Mr. Shui Ta is in conference with Miss Shen Te. Not to be disturbed!

YANG SUN. Shen Te here? I didn't see her come in. What kind of conference?

SHU FU (*not letting him enter the back room*). Patience, dear sir! And if by chance I have an inkling who you are, pray take note that Miss Shen Te and I are about to announce our engagement.

YANG SUN. What?

MRS. SHIN. You didn't expect that, did you?

(*Yang Sun is trying to push past the barber into the back room when Shen Te comes out.*)

SHU FU. My dear Shen Te, ten thousand apologies! Perhaps you . . .

YANG SUN. What is it, Shen Te? Have you gone crazy?

SHEN TE (*breathless*). My cousin and Mr. Shu Fu have come to an understanding. They wish me to hear Mr. Shu Fu's plans for helping the poor.

YANG SUN. Your cousin wants to part us.

SHEN TE. Yes.

YANG SUN. And you've agreed to it?

SHEN TE. Yes.

YANG SUN. They told you I was bad.

(*Shen Te is silent.*)

And suppose I am. Does that make me need you less? I'm low, Shen Te, I have no money, I don't do the right thing but at least I put up a fight! (*He is near her now, and speaks in an undertone.*) Have you no eyes? Look at him. Have you forgotten already?

SHEN TE. No.

YANG SUN. How it was raining?

SHEN TE. No.

YANG SUN. How you cut me down from the willow tree? Bought me water? Promised me money to fly with?

SHEN TE (*shakily*). Yang Sun, what do you want?

YANG SUN. I want you to come with me.

SHEN TE (*in a small voice*). Forgive me, Mr. Shu Fu, I want to go with Mr. Yang Sun.

YANG SUN. We're lovers you know. Give me the key to the shop.

(*Shen Te takes the key from around her neck. Yang Sun puts it on the counter. To Mrs. Shin.*)

Leave it under the mat when you're through. Let's go, Shen Te.

SHU FU. But this is rape! Mr. Shui Ta!!

YANG SUN (*to Shen Te*). Tell him not to shout.

SHEN TE. Please don't shout for my cousin, Mr. Shu Fu. He doesn't agree with me, I know, but he's wrong. (*To the audience.*)

> I want to go with the man I love
> I don't want to count the cost
> I don't want to consider if it's wise
> I don't want to know if he loves me
> I want to go with the man I love.

YANG SUN. That's the spirit.

(*And the couple leave.*)

SCENE 5A

(*In front of the inner curtain. Shen Te in her wedding clothes, on the way to her wedding.*)

SHEN TE. Something terrible has happened. As I left the shop with Yang Sun, I found the old carpet dealer's wife waiting in the street, trembling all over. She told me her husband had taken to his bed—sick with all the worry and excitement over the two hundred silver dollars they lent me. She said it would be best if I gave it back now. Of course, I had to say I would. She said she couldn't quite trust my cousin Shui Ta or even my fiancé Yang Sun. There were tears in her eyes. With my emotions in an uproar, I threw myself into Yang Sun's arms, I couldn't resist him. The things he'd said to Shui Ta had taught Shen Te nothing. Sinking into his arms, I said to myself:

To let no one perish, not even oneself
To fill everyone with happiness, even oneself
Is so good

How could I have forgotten those two old people? Yang Sun swept me away like a small hurricane. But he's not a bad man, and he loves me. He'd rather work in the cement factory than owe his flying to a crime. Though, of course, flying *is* a great passion with Sun. Now, on the way to my wedding, I waver between fear and joy.

SCENE 6

(*The "private dining room" on the upper floor of a cheap restaurant in a poor section of town. With Shen Te: the Grandfather, the Sister-in-Law, the Niece, Mrs. Shin, the Unemployed Man. In a corner, alone, a Priest. A Waiter pouring wine. Downstage, Yang Sun talking to his mother. He wears a dinner jacket.*)

YANG SUN. Bad news, Mamma. She came right out and told me she can't sell the shop for me. Some idiot is bringing a claim because he lent her the two hundred she gave you.

MRS. YANG. What did *you* say? Of course, you can't marry her now.

YANG SUN. It's no use saying anything to *her.* I've sent for her cousin, Mr. Shui Ta. He said there was nothing in writing.

MRS. YANG. Good idea. I'll go out and look for him. Keep an eye on things.

(*Exit Mrs. Yang. Shen Te has been pouring wine.*)

SHEN TE (*to the audience, pitcher in hand*). I wasn't mistaken in him. He's bearing up well. Though it must have been an awful blow—giving up flying. I do love him so. (*Calling across the room to him.*) Sun, you haven't drunk a toast with the bride!

YANG SUN. What do we drink to?

SHEN TE. Why, to the future!

YANG SUN. When the bridegroom's dinner jacket won't be a hired one!

SHEN TE. But when the bride's dress will still get rained on sometimes!

YANG SUN. To everything we ever wished for!

SHEN TE. May all our dreams come true!

(*They drink.*)

YANG SUN (*with loud conviviality*). And now, friends, before the wedding gets under way, I have to ask the bride a few questions. I've no idea what kind of a wife she'll make, and it worries me. (*Wheeling on Shen Te.*) For example. Can you make five cups of tea with three tea leaves?

SHEN TE. No.

YANG SUN. So I won't be getting very much tea. Can you sleep on a straw mattress the size of that book? (*He points to the large volume the Priest is reading.*)

SHEN TE. The two of us?

YANG SUN. The one of you.

SHEN TE. In that case, no.

YANG SUN. What a wife! I'm shocked!

(*While the audience is laughing, his mother returns. With a shrug of her shoulders, she tells Yang Sun the expected guest hasn't arrived. The Priest shuts the book with a bang, and makes for the door.*)

MRS. YANG. Where are *you* off to? It's only a matter of minutes.

PRIEST (*watch in hand*). Time goes on, Mrs. Yang, and I've another wedding to attend to. Also a funeral.

MRS. YANG (*irately*). D'you think we planned it this way? I was hoping to manage with one pitcher of wine, and we've run through two already. (*Points to empty pitcher. Loudly.*) My dear Shen Te, I don't know where your cousin can be keeping himself!

SHEN TE. My cousin?

MRS. YANG. Certainly. I'm old fashioned enough to think such a close relative should attend the wedding.

SHEN TE. Oh, Sun, is it the three hundred silver dollars?

YANG SUN (*not looking her in the eye*). Are you deaf? Mother says she's old fashioned. And I say I'm considerate. We'll wait another fifteen minutes.

HUSBAND. Another fifteen minutes.

MRS. YANG (*addressing the company*). Now you all know, don't you, that my son is getting a job as a mail pilot?

SISTER-IN-LAW. In Peking, too, isn't it?

MRS. YANG. In Peking, too! The two of us are moving to Peking!

SHEN TE. Sun, tell your mother Peking is out of the question now.

YANG SUN. Your cousin'll tell her. If he agrees. I don't agree.

SHEN TE (*amazed, and dismayed*). Sun!

YANG SUN. I hate this godforsaken Setzuan. What people! Know what they look like when I half close my eyes? Horses! Whinnying, fretting, stamping, screwing their necks up! (*Loudly.*) And what is it the thunder says? They are su-per-flu-ous! (*He hammers out the syllables.*) They've run their last race! They can go trample themselves to death! (*Pause.*) I've got to get out of here.

SHEN TE. But I've promised the money to the old couple.

YANG SUN. And since you always do the wrong thing, it's lucky your cousin's coming. Have another drink.

SHEN TE (*quietly*). My cousin can't be coming.

YANG SUN. How d'you mean?

SHEN TE. My cousin can't be where I am.

YANG SUN. Quite a conundrum!

SHEN TE (*desperately*). Sun, I'm the one that loves you. Not my cousin. He was thinking of the job in Peking when he promised you the old couple's money—

YANG SUN. Right. And that's why he's bringing the three hundred silver dollars. Here—to my wedding.

SHEN TE. He is not bringing the three hundred silver dollars.

YANG SUN. Huh? What makes you think that?

SHEN TE (*looking into his eyes*). He says you only bought one ticket to Peking.

(*Short pause.*)

YANG SUN. That was yesterday. (*He pulls two tickets part way out of his inside pocket, making her look under his coat.*) Two tickets. I don't want Mother to know. She'll get left behind. I sold her furniture to buy these tickets, so you see . . .

SHEN TE. But what's to become of the old couple?

YANG SUN. What's to become of me? Have another drink. Or do you believe in moderation? If I drink, I fly again. And if you drink, you may learn to understand me.

SHEN TE: You want to fly. But I can't help you.

YANG SUN. "Here's a plane, my darling—but it's only got one wing!"

(*The Waiter enters.*)

WAITER. Mrs. Yang! Mrs. Yang!

MRS. YANG. Yes?

WAITER. Another pitcher of wine, ma'am?

MRS. YANG. We have enough, thanks. Drinking makes me sweat.

WAITER. Would you mind paying, ma'am?

MRS. YANG (*to everyone*). Just be patient a few moments longer, everyone, Mr. Shui Ta is on his way over! (*To the Waiter.*) Don't be a spoilsport.

WAITER. I can't let you leave till you've paid your bill, ma'am.

MRS. YANG. But they know me here!

WAITER. That's just it.

PRIEST (*ponderously getting up*). I humbly take my leave. (*And he does.*)

MRS. YANG (*to the others, desperately*). Stay where you are, everybody! The priest says he'll be back in two minutes!

YANG SUN. It's no good, Mamma. Ladies and gentlemen, Mr. Shui Ta still hasn't arrived and the priest has gone home. We won't detain you any longer.

(*They are leaving now.*)

GRANDFATHER (*in the doorway, having forgotten to put his glass down*). To the bride! (*He drinks, puts down the glass, and follows the others.*)

(*Pause.*)

SHEN TE. Shall I go too?

YANG SUN. You? Aren't you the bride? Isn't this your wedding? (*He drags her across the room, tearing her wedding dress.*) If we can wait, you can wait. Mother calls me her falcon. She wants to see me in the clouds. But I think it may be St. Nevercome's Day before she'll go to the door and see my plane thunder by. (*Pause. He pretends the guests are still present.*) Why such a lull in the conversation, ladies and gentlemen? Don't you like it here? The ceremony is only slightly postponed—because an important guest is expected at any moment. Also because the bride doesn't know what love is. While we're waiting, the bridegroom will sing a little song. (*He does so.*)

The Song of St. Nevercome's Day

On a certain day, as is generally known,
One and all will be shouting: Hooray, hooray!
For the beggar maid's son has a solid-gold throne
And the day is St. Nevercome's Day
On St. Nevercome's, Nevercome's, Nevercome's Day
He'll sit on his solid-gold throne

Oh, hooray, hooray! That day goodness will pay!
That day badness will cost you your head!
And merit and money will smile and be funny
While exchanging salt and bread
On St. Nevercome's, Nevercome's, Nevercome's Day
While exchanging salt and bread

And the grass, oh, the grass will look down at the sky
And the pebbles will roll up the stream
And all men will be good without batting an eye
They will make of our earth a dream
On St. Nevercome's, Nevercome's, Nevercome's Day
They will make of our earth a dream

And as for me, that's the day I shall be
A flyer and one of the best
Unemployed man, you will have work to do
Washerwoman, you'll get your rest
On St. Nevercome's, Nevercome's, Nevercome's Day
Washerwoman, you'll get your rest.

MRS. YANG. It looks like he's not coming.

(*The three of them sit looking at the door.*)

SCENE 6A

(*Wong's den. The sewer pipe is again transparent and again the Gods appear to Wong in a dream.*)

WONG. I'm so glad you've come, illustrious ones. It's Shen Te. She's in great trouble from following the rule about loving thy neighbor. Perhaps she's *too* good for this world!

FIRST GOD. Nonsense! You are eaten up by lice and doubts!

WONG. Forgive me, illustrious one, I only meant you might deign to intervene.

FIRST GOD. Out of the question! My colleague here intervened in some squabble or other only yesterday. (*He points to the Third God who has a black eye.*) The results are before us!

WONG. She had to call on her cousin again. But not even he could help. I'm afraid the shop is done for.

THIRD GOD (*a little concerned*). Perhaps we should help after all?

FIRST GOD. The gods help those that help themselves.

WONG. What if we *can't* help ourselves, illustrious ones?

(*Slight pause.*)

SECOND GOD. Try, anyway! Suffering ennobles!

FIRST GOD. Our faith in Shen Te is unshaken!

THIRD GOD. We certainly haven't found any *other* good people. You can see where we spend our nights from the straw on our clothes.

WONG. You might help her find her way by—

FIRST GOD. The good man finds his own way here below!

SECOND GOD. The good woman too.

FIRST GOD. The heavier the burden, the greater her strength!

THIRD GOD. We're only onlookers, you know.

FIRST GOD. And everything will be all right in the end, O ye of little faith!

(*They are gradually disappearing through these last lines.*)

SCENE 7

(*The yard behind Shen Te's shop. A few articles of furniture on a cart. Shen Te and Mrs. Shin are taking the washing off the line.*)

MRS. SHIN. If you ask me, you should fight tooth and nail to keep the shop.

SHEN TE. How can I? I have to sell the tobacco to pay back the two hundred silver dollars today.

MRS. SHIN. No husband, no tobacco, no house and home! What are you going to live on?

SHEN TE. I can work. I can sort tobacco.

MRS. SHIN. Hey, look, Mr. Shui Ta's trousers! He must have left here stark naked!

SHEN TE. Oh, he may have another pair, Mrs. Shin.

MRS. SHIN. But if he's gone for good as you say, why has he left his pants behind?

SHEN TE. Maybe he's thrown them away.

MRS. SHIN. Can I take them?

SHEN TE. Oh, no.

(*Enter Mr. Shu Fu, running.*)

SHU FU. Not a word! Total silence! I know all. You have sacrificed your own love and happiness so as not to hurt a dear old couple who had put their trust in you! Not in vain does this district—for all its malevolent tongues!—call you the Angel of the Slums! That young man couldn't rise to your level, so you left him. And now, when I see you closing up the little shop, that veritable haven of rest for the multitude, well, I cannot, I cannot let it pass. Morning after morning I have stood watching in the doorway not unmoved—while you graciously handed out rice to the wretched. Is that never to happen again? Is the good woman of Setzuan to disappear? If only you would allow *me* to assist you! Now don't say anything! No assurances, no exclamations of gratitude! (*He has taken out his check book.*) Here! A blank check. (*He places it on the cart.*) Just my signature. Fill it out as you wish. Any sum in the world. I herewith retire from the scene, quietly, unobtrusively, making no claims, on tiptoe, full of veneration, absolutely selflessly . . . (*He has gone.*)

MRS. SHIN. Well! You're saved. There's always some idiot of a man . . . Now hurry! Put down a thousand silver dollars and let me fly to the bank before he comes to his senses.

SHEN TE. I can pay you for the washing without any check.

MRS. SHIN. What? You're not going to cash it just because you might have to marry him? Are you crazy? Men like him *want* to be led by the nose! Are you still thinking of that flyer? All Yellow Street knows how he treated you!

SHEN TE.

When I heard his cunning laugh, I was afraid
But when I saw the holes in his shoes, I loved him dearly.

MRS. SHIN. Defending that good for nothing after all that's happened!

SHEN TE (*staggering as she holds some of the washing*). Oh!

MRS. SHIN (*taking the washing from her, dryly*). So you feel dizzy when you stretch and bend? There couldn't be a little visitor on the way? If that's it, you can forget Mr. Shu Fu's blank check: it wasn't meant for a christening present!

(*She goes to the back with a basket. Shen Te's eyes follow Mrs. Shin for a moment. Then she looks down at her own body, feels her stomach, and a great joy comes into her eyes.*)

SHEN TE. O joy! A new human being is on the way. The world awaits him. In the cities the people say: he's got to be reckoned with, this new human being! (*She imagines a little boy to be present, and introduces him to the audience.*)

This is my son, the well-known flyer!
Say: Welcome
To the conqueror of unknown mountains and unreachable regions
Who brings us our mail across the impassable deserts!

(*She leads him up and down by the hand.*) Take a look at the world, my son. That's a tree. Tree, yes. Say: "Hello, tree!" And bow. Like this. (*She bows.*) Now you know each other. And, look, here comes the Water Seller. He's a friend, give him your hand. A cup of fresh water for my little son, please. Yes, it *is* a warm day. (*Handing the cup.*) Oh dear, a policeman, we'll have to make a circle round *him.* Perhaps we can pick a few cherries over there in the rich Mr. Pung's garden. But we mustn't be seen. You want cherries? Just like children with fathers. No, no, you can't go straight at them like that. Don't pull. We must learn to be reasonable. Well, have it your own way. (*She has let him make for the cherries.*) Can you reach? Where to put them? Your mouth is the best place. (*She tries one herself.*) Mmm, they're good. But the policeman, we must run! (*They run.*) Yes, back to the street. Calm now, so no one will notice us. (*Walking the street with her child, she sings.*)

Once a plum—'twas in Japan—
Made a conquest of a man
But the man's turn soon did come
For he gobbled up the plum

(*Enter Wong, with a Child by the hand. He coughs.*)

SHEN TE. Wong!

WONG. It's about the Carpenter, Shen Te. He's lost his shop, and he's been drinking. His children are on the streets. This is one. Can you help?

SHEN TE (*to the child*). Come here, little man. (*Takes him down to the footlights. To the audience.*)

You there! A man is asking you for shelter!
A man of tomorrow says: what about today?
His friend the conqueror, whom you know,
Is his advocate!

(*To Wong.*) He can live in Mr. Shu Fu's cabins. I may have to go there myself. I'm going to have a baby. That's a secret—don't tell Yang Sun—we'd only be in his way. Can you find the Carpenter for me?

WONG. I knew you'd think of something. (*To the Child.*) Goodbye, son, I'm going for your father.

SHEN TE. What about your hand, Wong? I wanted to help, but my cousin . . .

WONG. Oh, I can get along with one hand, don't worry. (*He shows how he can handle his pole with his left hand alone.*)

SHEN TE. But your right hand! Look, take this cart, sell everything that's on it, and go to the doctor with the money . . .

WONG. She's still good. But first I'll bring the Carpenter. I'll pick up the cart when I get back. (*Exit Wong.*)

SHEN TE (*to the Child*). Sit down over here, son, till your father comes.

(*The Child sits crosslegged on the ground. Enter the Husband and Wife, each dragging a large, full sack.*)

WIFE (*furtively*). You're alone, Shen Te, dear?

(*Shen Te nods. The Wife beckons to the Nephew offstage. He comes on with another sack.*)

Your cousin's away?

(*Shen Te nods.*)

He's not coming back?

SHEN TE. No. I'm giving up the shop.

WIFE. That's why we're here. We want to know if we can leave these things in your new home. Will you do us this favor?

SHEN TE. Why, yes, I'd be glad to.

HUSBAND (*cryptically*). And if anyone asks about them, say they're yours.

SHEN TE. Would anyone ask?

WIFE (*with a glance back at her Husband*). Oh, someone might. The police, for instance. They don't seem to like us. Where can we put it?

SHEN TE. Well, I'd rather not get in any more trouble . . .

WIFE. Listen to her! The good woman of Setzuan!

(*Shen Te is silent.*)

HUSBAND. There's enough tobacco in those sacks to give us a new start in life. We could have our own tobacco factory!

SHEN TE (*slowly*). You'll have to put them in the back room.

(*The sacks are taken offstage, where the Child is left alone. Shyly glancing about him, he goes to the garbage can, starts playing with the contents, and eating some of the scraps. The others return.*)

WIFE. We're counting on you, Shen Te!

SHEN TE. Yes. (*She sees the Child and is shocked.*)

HUSBAND. We'll see you in Mr. Shu Fu's cabins.

NEPHEW. The day after tomorrow.

SHEN TE. Yes. Now, go. Go! I'm not feeling well.

(*Exeunt all three, virtually pushed off.*)

He is eating the refuse in the garbage can!
Only look at his little grey mouth!

(*Pause. Music.*)

As this is the world *my* son will enter
I will study to defend him.
To be good to you, my son,
I shall be a tigress to all others
If I have to.
And I shall have to.

(*She starts to go.*) One more time, then. I hope really the last.

(*Exit Shen Te, taking Shui Ta's trousers. Mrs. Shin enters and watches her with marked interest. Enter the Sister-in-Law and the Grandfather.*)

SISTER-IN-LAW. So it's true, the shop has closed down. And the furniture's in the back yard. It's the end of the road!

MRS. SHIN (*pompously*). The fruit of high living, selfishness, and sensuality! Down the primrose path to Mr. Shu Fu's cabins—with you!

SISTER-IN-LAW. Cabins? Rat holes! He gave them to us because his soap supplies only went mouldy there!

(*Enter the Unemployed Man.*)

UNEMPLOYED MAN. Shen Te is moving?

SISTER-IN-LAW. Yes. She was sneaking away.

MRS. SHIN. She's ashamed of herself, and no wonder!

UNEMPLOYED MAN. Tell her to call Mr. Shui Ta or she's done for this time!

SISTER-IN-LAW. Tell her to call Mr. Shui Ta or *we're* done for this time!

(*Enter Wong and Carpenter, the latter with a Child on each hand.*)

CARPENTER. So we'll have a roof over our heads for a change!

MRS. SHIN. Roof? Whose roof?

CARPENTER. Mr. Shu Fu's cabins. And we have little Feng to thank for it. (*Feng, we find, is the name of the child already there; his Father now takes him. To the other two.*) Bow to your little brother, you two! (*The Carpenter and the two new arrivals bow to Feng.*)

(*Enter Shui Ta.*)

UNEMPLOYED MAN. Sst! Mr. Shui Ta!

(*Pause.*)

SHUI TA. And what is this crowd here for, may I ask?

WONG. How do you do, Mr. Shui Ta? This is the Carpenter. Miss Shen Te promised him space in Mr. Shu Fu's cabins.

SHUI TA. That will not be possible.

CARPENTER. We can't go there after all?

SHUI TA. All the space is needed for other purposes.

SISTER-IN-LAW. You mean we have to get out? But we've got nowhere to go.

SHUI TA. Miss Shen Te finds it possible to provide employment. If the proposition interests you, you may stay in the cabins.

SISTER-IN-LAW (*with distaste*). You mean *work?* Work for Miss Shen Te?

SHUI TA. Making tobacco, yes. There are three bales here already. Would you like to get them?

SISTER-IN-LAW (*trying to bluster*). We have our own tobacco! We were in the tobacco business before you were born!

SHUI TA (*to the Carpenter and the Unemployed Man*). You *don't* have your own tobacco. What about you?

(*The Carpenter and the Unemployed Man get the point, and go for the sacks. Enter Mrs. Mi Tzu.*)

MRS. MI TZU. Mr. Shui Ta? I've brought you your three hundred silver dollars.

SHUI TA. I'll Sign your lease instead. I've decided not to sell.

MRS. MI TZU. What? You don't need the money for that flyer?

SHUI TA. No.

MRS. MI TZU. And you can pay six months' rent?

SHUI TA (*takes the barber's blank check from the cart and fills it out*). Here is a check for ten thousand silver dollars.

On Mr. Shu Fu's account. Look! (*He shows her the signature on the check.*) Your six months' rent will be in your hands by seven this evening. And now, if you'll excuse me.

MRS. MI TZU. So it's Mr. Shu Fu now. The flyer has been given his walking papers. These modern girls! In my day they'd have said she was flighty. That poor, deserted Mr. Yang Sun!

(*Exit Mrs. Mi Tzu. The Carpenter and the Unemployed Man drag the three sacks back on the stage.*)

CARPENTER (*to Shui Ta*). I don't know why I'm doing this for you.

SHUI TA. Perhaps your children want to eat, Mr. Carpenter.

SISTER-IN-LAW (*catching sight of the sacks*). Was my brother-in-law here?

MRS. SHIN. Yes, he was.

SISTER-IN-LAW. I thought as much. I know those sacks! That's our tobacco!

SHUI TA. Really? I thought it came from my back room? Shall we consult the police on the point?

SISTER-IN-LAW (*defeated*). No.

SHUI TA. Perhaps you will show me the way to Mr. Shu Fu's cabins?

(*Shui Ta goes off, followed by the Carpenter and his two older children, the Sister-in-Law, the Grandfather, and the Unemployed Man. Each of the last three drags a sack. Enter Old Man and Old Woman.*)

MRS. SHIN. A pair of pants—missing from the clothes line one minute—and next minute on the honorable backside of Mr. Shui Ta!

OLD WOMAN. We thought Miss Shen Te was here.

MRS. SHIN (*preoccupied*). Well, she's not.

OLD MAN. There was something she was going to give us.

WONG. She was going to help me too. (*Looking at his hand.*) It'll be too late soon. But she'll be back. This cousin has never stayed long.

MRS. SHIN (*approaching a conclusion*). No, he hasn't, has he?

SCENE 7A

(*The sewer pipe: Wong asleep. In his dream, he tells the Gods his fears. The Gods seem tired from all their travels. They stop for a moment and look over their shoulders at the Water Seller.*)

WONG. Illustrious ones, I've been having a bad dream. Our beloved Shen Te was in great distress in the rushes down by the rivers—the spot where the bodies of suicides are washed up. She kept staggering and holding her head down as if she was carrying something and it was dragging her down into the mud. When I called out to her, she said she had to take your Book of Rules to the other side, and not get it wet, or the ink would all come off. You had talked to her about the virtues, you know, the time she gave you shelter in Setzuan.

THIRD GOD. Well, but what do you suggest, my dear Wong?

WONG. Maybe a little relaxation of the rules, Benevolent One, in view of the bad times.

THIRD GOD. As for instance?

WONG. Well, um, good-will, for instance, might do instead of love?

THIRD GOD. I'm afraid that would create new problems.

WONG. Or, instead of justice, good sportsmanship?

THIRD GOD. That would only mean more work.

WONG. Instead of honor, outward propriety?

THIRD GOD. Still more work! No, no! The rules will have to stand, my dear Wong!

(*Wearily shaking their heads, all three journey on.*)

SCENE 8

(*Shui Ta's tobacco factory in Shu Fu's cabins. Huddled together behind bars, several families, mostly women and children. Among these people the Sister-in-Law, the Grandfather, the Carpenter, and his three children. Enter Mrs. Yang followed by Yang Sun.*)

MRS. YANG (*to the audience*). There's something I just *have* to tell you: strength and wisdom are wonderful things. The strong and wise Mr. Shui Ta has transformed my son from a dissipated good-for-nothing into a model citizen. As you may have heard, Mr. Shui Ta opened a small tobacco factory near the cattle runs. It flourished. Three months ago—I shall never forget it—I asked for an appointment, and Mr. Shui Ta agreed to see us—me and my son. I can see him now as he came through the door to meet us . . .

(*Enter Shui Ta, from a door.*)

SHUI TA. What can I do for you, Mrs. Yang?

MRS. YANG. This morning the police came to the house. We find you've brought an action for breach of promise of marriage. In the name of Shen Te. You also claim that Sun came by two hundred silver dollars by improper means.

SHUI TA. That is correct.

MRS. YANG. Mr. Shui Ta, the money's all gone. When the Peking job didn't materialize, he ran through it all in three days. I know he's a good-for-nothing. He sold my furniture. He was moving to Peking without me. Miss Shen Te thought highly of him at one time.

SHUI TA. What do *you* say, Mr. Yang Sun?

YANG SUN. The money's gone.

SHUI TA (*to Mrs. Yang*). Mrs. Yang, in consideration of my cousin's incomprehensible weakness for your son, I am prepared to give him another chance. He can have a job—here. The two hundred silver dollars will be taken out of his wages.

YANG SUN. So it's the factory or jail?

SHUI TA. Take your choice.

YANG SUN. May I speak with Shen Te?

SHUI TA. You may not.

(*Pause.*)

YANG SUN (*sullenly*). Show me where to go.

MRS. YANG. Mr. Shui Ta, you are kindness itself: the gods will reward you! (*To Yang Sun.*) And honest work will make a man of you, my boy.

(*Yang Sun follows Shui Ta into the factory. Mrs. Yang comes down again to the footlights.*)

Actually, honest work didn't agree with him—at first. And he got no opportunity to distinguish himself till—in the third week—when the wages were being paid....

(*Shui Ta has a bag of money. Standing next to his foreman—the former Unemployed Man—he counts out the wages. It is Yang Sun's turn.*)

UNEMPLOYED MAN (*reading*). Carpenter, six silver dollars. Yang Sun, six silver dollars.

YANG SUN (*quietly*). Excuse me, sir. I don't think it can be more than five. May I see? (*He takes the foreman's list.*) It says six working days. But that's a mistake, sir. I took a day off for court business. And I won't take what I haven't earned, however miserable the pay is!

UNEMPLOYED MAN. Yang Sun. Five silver dollars. (*To Shui Ta.*) A rare case, Mr. Shui Ta!

SHUI TA. How is it the book says six when it should say five?

UNEMPLOYED MAN. I must've made a mistake, Mr. Shui Ta. (*With a look at Yang Sun.*) It won't happen again.

SHUI TA (*taking Yang Sun aside*). You don't hold back, do you? You give your all to the firm. You're even honest. Do the foreman's mistakes always favor the workers?

YANG SUN. He does have ... friends.

SHUI TA. Thank you. May I offer you any little recompense?

YANG SUN. Give me a trial period of one week, and I'll prove my intelligence is worth more to you than my strength.

MRS. YANG (*still down at the footlights*). Fighting words, fighting words! That evening, I said to Sun: "If you're a flyer, then fly, my falcon! Rise in the world!" And he got to be foreman. Yes, in Mr. Shui Ta's tobacco factory, he worked real miracles.

(*We see Yang Sun with his legs apart standing behind the workers who are handing along a basket of raw tobacco above their heads.*)

YANG SUN. Faster! Faster! You, there, d'you think you can just stand around now you're not foreman any more? It'll be your job to lead us in song. Sing!

(*Unemployed Man starts singing. The others join in the refrain.*)

Song of the Eighth Elephant

Chang had seven elephants—all much the same—
But then there was Little Brother
The seven, they were wild, Little Brother, he was tame
And to guard them Chang chose Little Brother
Run faster!
Mr. Chang has a forest park
Which must be cleared before tonight
And already it's growing dark!

When the seven elephants cleared that forest park
Mr. Chang rode high on Little Brother
While the seven toiled and moiled till dark
On his big behind sat Little Brother
Dig faster!
Mr. Chang has a forest park
Which must be cleared before tonight
And already it's growing dark!

And the seven elephants worked many an hour
Till none of them could work another
Old Chang, he looked sour, on the seven, he did glower
But gave a pound of rice to Little Brother
What was that?
Mr. Chang has a forest park
Which must be cleared before tonight
And already it's growing dark!

And the seven elephants hadn't any tusks
The one that had the tusks was Little Brother!
Seven are no match for one, if the one has a gun!
How old Chang did laugh at Little Brother!
Keep on digging!
Mr. Chang has a forest park
Which must be cleared before tonight
And already it's growing dark!

(*Smoking a cigar, Shui Ta strolls by. Yang Sun, laughing, has joined in the refrain of the third stanza and speeded up the tempo of the last stanza by clapping his hands.*)

MRS. YANG. And that's why I say: strength and wisdom are wonderful things. It took the strong and wise Mr. Shui Ta to bring out the best in Yang Sun. A real superior man is like a bell. If you ring it, it rings, and if you don't, it don't, as the saying is.

SCENE 9

(*Shen Te's shop, now an office with club chairs and fine carpets. It is raining. Shui Ta, now fat, is just dismissing the Old Man and Old Woman. Mrs. Shin, in obviously new clothes, looks on, smirking.*)

SHUI TA. No! I can NOT tell you when we expect her back.

OLD WOMAN. The two hundred silver dollars came today. In an envelope. There was no letter, but it must be from Shen Te. We want to write and thank her. May we have her address?

SHUI TA. I'm afraid I haven't got it.

OLD MAN (*pulling Old Woman's sleeve*). Let's be going.

OLD WOMAN. She's got to come back some time! (*They move off, uncertainly, worried. Shui Ta bows.*)

MRS. SHIN. They lost the carpet shop because they couldn't pay their taxes. The money arrived too late.

SHUI TA. They could have come to me.

MRS. SHIN. People don't like coming to you.

SHUI TA (*sits suddenly, one hand to his head*). I'm dizzy.

MRS. SHIN. After all, you *are* in your seventh month. But old Mrs. Shin will be there in your hour of trial! (*She cackles feebly.*)

SHUI TA (*in a stifled voice*). Can I count on that?

MRS. SHIN. We all have our price, and mine won't be too high for the great Mr. Shui Ta! (*She opens Shui Ta's collar.*)

SHUI TA. It's for the child's sake. All of this.

MRS. SHIN. "All for the child," of course.

SHUI TA. I'm so fat. People must notice.

MRS. SHIN. Oh no, they think it's 'cause you're rich.

SHUI TA (*more feelingly*). What will happen to the child?

MRS. SHIN. You ask that nine times a day. Why, it'll have the best that money can buy!

SHUI TA. He must never see Shui Ta.

MRS. SHIN. Oh, no. Always Shen Te.

SHUI TA. What about the neighbors? There are rumors, aren't there?

MRS. SHIN. As long as Mr. Shu Fu doesn't find out, there's nothing to worry about. Drink this.

(*Enter Yang Sun in a smart business suit, and carrying a businessman's brief case. Shui Ta is more or less in Mrs. Shin's arms.*)

YANG SUN (*surprised*). I seem to be in the way.

SHUI TA (*ignoring this, rises with an effort*). Till tomorrow, Mrs. Shin.

(*Mrs. Shin leaves with a smile, putting her new gloves on.*)

YANG SUN. Gloves now! She couldn't be fleecing you? And since when did *you* have a private life? (*Taking a paper from the brief case.*) You haven't been at your best lately, and things are getting out of hand. The police want to close us down. They say that at the most they can only permit twice the lawful number of workers.

SHUI TA (*evasively*). The cabins are quite good enough.

YANG SUN. For the workers maybe, not for the tobacco. They're too damp. We must take over some of Mrs. Mi Tzu's buildings.

SHUI TA. Her price is double what I can pay.

YANG SUN. Not unconditionally. If she has me to stroke her knees she'll come down.

SHUI TA. I'll never agree to that.

YANG SUN. What's wrong? Is it the rain? You get so irritable whenever it rains.

SHUI TA. Never! I will never . . .

YANG SUN. Mrs. Mi Tzu'll be here in five minutes. *You* fix it. And Shu Fu will be with her. . . . What's all that noise?

(*During the above dialogue, Wong is heard off stage calling: "The good Shen Te, where is she? Which of you has seen Shen Te, good people? Where is Shen Te?" A knock. Enter Wong.*)

WONG. Mr. Shui Ta, I've come to ask when Miss Shen Te will be back, it's six months now . . . There are rumors. People say something's happened to her.

SHUI TA. I'm busy. Come back next week.

WONG (*excited*). In the morning there was always rice on her doorstep—for the needy. It's been there again lately!

SHUI TA. And what do people conclude from this?

WONG. That Shen Te is still in Setzuan! She's been . . . (*He breaks off.*)

SHUI TA. She's been what? Mr. Wong, if you're Shen Te's friend, talk a little less about her, that's my advice to you.

WONG. I don't want your advice! Before she disappeared, Miss Shen Te told me something very important—she's pregnant!

YANG SUN. What? What was that?

SHUI TA (*quickly*). The man is lying.

WONG. A good woman isn't so easily forgotten, Mr. Shui Ta.

(*He leaves. Shui Ta goes quickly into the back room.*)

YANG SUN (*to the audience*). Shen Te pregnant? So that's why. Her cousin sent her away, so I wouldn't get wind of it. I have a son, a Yang appears on the scene, and what happens? Mother and child vanish into thin air! That scoundrel, that unspeakable . . . (*The sound of sobbing is heard from the back room.*) What was that? Someone sobbing? Who was it? Mr. Shui Ta the Tobacco King doesn't weep his heart out. And where does the rice come from that's on the doorstep in the morning?

(*Shui Ta returns. He goes to the door and looks out into the rain.*)

Where is she?

SHUI TA. Sh! It's nine o'clock. But the rain's so heavy, you can't hear a thing.

YANG SUN. What do you want to hear?

SHUI TA. The mail plane.

YANG SUN. What?

SHUI TA. I've been told *you* wanted to fly at one time. Is that all forgotten?

YANG SUN. Flying mail is night work. I prefer the daytime. And the firm is very dear to me—after all it belongs to my ex-fiancée, even if she's not around. And she's not, is she?

SHUI TA. What do you mean by that?

YANG SUN. Oh, well, let's say I haven't altogether—lost interest.

SHUI TA. My cousin might like to know that.

YANG SUN. I might not be indifferent—if I found she was being kept under lock and key.

SHUI TA. By whom?

YANG SUN. By you.

SHUI TA. What could you do about it?

YANG SUN. I could submit for discussion—my position in the firm.

SHUI TA. You are now my Manager. In return for a more appropriate position, you might agree to drop the enquiry into your ex-fiancée's whereabouts?

YANG SUN. I might.

SHUI TA. What position *would* be more appropriate?

YANG SUN. The one at the top.

SHUI TA. My own? (*Silence.*) And if I preferred to throw you out on your neck?

YANG SUN. I'd come back on my feet. With suitable escort.

SHUI TA. The police?

YANG SUN. The police.

SHUI TA. And when the police found no one?

YANG SUN. I might ask them not to overlook the back room. (*Ending the pretense.*) In short, Mr. Shui Ta, my interest in this young woman has not been officially terminated. I should like to see more of her. (*Into Shui Ta's face.*) Besides, she's pregnant and needs a friend. (*He moves to the door.*) I shall talk about it with the Water Seller. (*Exit.*)

(*Shui Ta is rigid for a moment, then he quickly goes into the back room. He returns with Shen Te's belongings: underwear, etc. He takes a long look at the shawl of the previous scene. He then wraps the things in a bundle which, upon hearing a noise, he hides under the table. Enter Mrs. Mi Tzu and Mr. Shu Fu. They put away their umbrellas and galoshes.*)

MRS. MI TZU. I thought your manager was here, Mr. Shui Ta. He combines charm with business in a way that can only be to the advantage of all of us.

SHU FU. You sent for us, Mr. Shui Ta?

SHUI TA. The factory is in trouble.

SHU FU. It always is.

SHUI TA. The police are threatening to close us down unless I can show that the extension of our facilities is imminent.

SHU FU. Mr. Shui Ta, I'm sick and tired of your constantly expanding projects. I place cabins at your cousin's disposal; you make a factory of them. I hand your cousin a check; you present it. Your cousin disappears and you find the cabins too small and talk of yet more . . .

SHUI TA. Mr. Shu Fu, I'm authorized to inform you that Miss Shen Te's return is now imminent.

SHU FU. Imminent? It's becoming his favorite word.

MRS. MI TZU. Yes, what does it mean?

SHUI TA. Mrs. Mi Tzu, I can pay you exactly half what you asked for your buildings. Are you ready to inform the police that I am taking them over?

MRS. MI TZU. Certainly, if I can take over your manager.

SHU FU. What?

MRS. MI TZU. He's so efficient.

SHUI TA. I'm afraid I need Mr. Yang Sun.

MRS. MI TZU. So do I.

SHUI TA. He will call on you tomorrow.

SHU FU. So much the better. With Shen Te likely to turn up at any moment, the presence of that young man is hardly in good taste.

SHUI TA. So we have reached a settlement. In what was once the good Shen Te's little shop we are laying the foundations for the great Mr. Shui Ta's twelve magnificent super tobacco markets. You will bear in mind that though they call me the Tobacco King of Setzuan, it is my cousin's interests that have been served . . .

VOICES (*off*). The police, the police! Going to the tobacco shop! Something must have happened! (*etcetera.*)

(*Enter Yang Sun, Wong, and the Policeman.*)

POLICEMAN. Quiet there, quiet, quiet! (*They quiet down.*) I'm sorry, Mr. Shui Ta, but there's a report that you've been depriving Miss Shen Te of her freedom. Not that I believe all I hear, but the whole city's in an uproar.

SHUI TA. That's a lie.

POLICEMAN. Mr. Yang Sun has testified that he heard someone sobbing in the back room.

SHU FU. Mrs. Mi Tzu and myself will testify that no one here has been sobbing.

MRS. MI TZU. We have been quietly smoking our cigars.

POLICEMAN. Mr. Shui Ta, I'm afraid I shall have to take a look at that room. (*He does so. The room is empty.*) No one there, of course, sir.

YANG SUN. But I heard sobbing. What's that? (*He finds the clothes.*)

WONG. Those are Shen Te's things. (*To crowd.*) Shen Te's clothes are here!

VOICES (*Off. In sequence*). Shen Te's clothes! They've been found under the table! Body of murdered girl still missing! Tobacco King suspected!

POLICEMAN. Mr. Shui Ta, unless you can tell us where the girl is, I'll have to ask you to come along.

SHUI TA. I do not know.

POLICEMAN. I can't say how sorry I am, Mr. Shui Ta. (*He shows him the door.*)

SHUI TA. Everything will be cleared up in no time. There are still judges in Setzuan.

YANG SUN. I heard sobbing!

SCENE 9A

(*Wong's den. For the last time, the Gods appear to the Water Seller in his dream. They have changed and show signs of a long journey, extreme fatigue, and plenty of mishaps. The First no longer has a hat; the Third has lost a leg; all Three are barefoot.*)

WONG. Illustrious ones, at last you're here. Shen Te's been gone for months and today her cousin's been arrested. They think he murdered her to get the shop. But I had a dream and in this dream Shen Te said her cousin was keeping her prisoner. You must find her for us, illustrious ones!

FIRST GOD. We've found very few good people anywhere, and even they didn't keep it up. Shen Te is still the only one that stayed good.

SECOND GOD. If she *has* stayed good.

WONG. Certainly she has. But she's vanished.

FIRST GOD. That's the last straw. All is lost!

SECOND GOD. A little moderation, dear colleague!

FIRST GOD (*plaintively*). What's the good of moderation now? If she can't be found, we'll have to resign! The world is a terrible place! Nothing but misery, vulgarity, and waste! Even the countryside isn't what it used to be. The trees are getting their heads chopped off by telephone wires, and there's such a noise from all the gunfire, and I can't stand those heavy clouds of smoke, and—

THIRD GOD. The place is absolutely unlivable! Good intentions bring people to the brink of the abyss, and good deeds push them over the edge. I'm afraid our book of rules is destined for the scrap heap—

SECOND GOD. It's people! They're a worthless lot!

THIRD GOD. The world is too cold!

SECOND GOD. It's people! They are too weak!

FIRST GOD. Dignity, dear colleagues, dignity! Never despair! As for this world, didn't we agree that we only have to find one human being who can stand the place? Well, we found her. True, we lost her again. We must find her again, that's all! And at once!

(*They disappear.*)

SCENE 10

(*Courtroom. Groups: Shu Fu and Mrs. Mi Tzu; Yang Sun and Mrs. Yang; Wong, the Carpenter, the Grandfather, the Niece, the Old Man, the Old Woman; Mrs. Shin, the Policeman; the Unemployed Man, the Sister-in-Law.*)

OLD MAN. So much power isn't good for one man.

UNEMPLOYED MAN. And he's going to open twelve super tobacco markets!

WIFE. One of the judges is a friend of Mr. Shu Fu's.

SISTER-IN-LAW. Another one accepted a present from Mr. Shui Ta only last night. A great fat goose.

OLD WOMAN (*to Wong*). And Shen Te is nowhere to be found.

WONG. Only the gods will ever know the truth.

POLICEMAN. Order in the court! My lords the judges!

(*Enter the Three Gods in judges' robes. We overhear their conversation as they pass along the footlights to their bench.*)

THIRD GOD. We'll never get away with it, our certificates were so badly forged.

SECOND GOD. My predecessor's "sudden indigestion" will certainly cause comment.

FIRST GOD. But he *had* just eaten a whole goose.

UNEMPLOYED MAN. Look at that! *New* judges!

WONG. New judges. And what good ones!

(*The Third God hears this, and turns to smile at Wong. The Gods sit. The First God beats on the bench with his gavel. The Policeman brings in Shui Ta who walks with lordly steps. He is whistled at.)*

POLICEMAN (*to Shui Ta*). Be prepared for a surprise. The judges have been changed.

(*Shui Ta turns quickly round, looks at them, and staggers.*)

NIECE. What's the matter now?
WIFE. The great Tobacco King nearly fainted.
HUSBAND. Yes, as soon as he saw the new judges.
WONG. Does *he* know who they are?

(*Shui Ta picks himself up, and the proceedings open.*)

FIRST GOD. Defendant Shui Ta, you are accused of doing away with your cousin Shen Te in order to take possession of her business. Do you plead guilty or not guilty?
SHUI TA. Not guilty, my lord.
FIRST GOD (*thumbing through the documents of the case*). The first witness is the Policeman. I shall ask him to tell us something of the respective reputations of Miss Shen Te and Mr. Shui Ta.
POLICEMAN. Miss Shen Te was a young lady who aimed to please, my lord. She liked to live and let live, as the saying goes. Mr. Shui Ta, on the other hand, is a man of principle. Though the generosity of Miss Shen Te forced him at times to abandon half measures, unlike the girl, he was always on the side of the law, my lord. One time, he even unmasked a gang of thieves to whom his too trustful cousin had given shelter. The evidence, in short, my lord, proves that Mr. Shui Ta was *incapable* of the crime of which he stands accused!
FIRST GOD. I see. And are there others who could testify along, shall we say, the same lines?

(*Shu Fu rises.*)

POLICEMAN (*whispering to Gods*). Mr. Shu Fu—a very important person.
FIRST GOD (*inviting him to speak*). Mr. Shu Fu!
SHU FU. Mr. Shui Ta is a businessman, my lord. Need I say more?
FIRST GOD. Yes.
SHU FU. Very well, I will. He is Vice President of the Council of Commerce and is about to be elected a Justice of the Peace. (*He returns to his seat.*)
WONG. Elected! *He* gave him the job!

(*With a gesture the First God asks who Mrs. Mi Tzu is.*)

POLICEMAN. Another very important person. Mrs. Mi Tzu.
FIRST GOD (*inviting her to speak*). Mrs. Mi Tzu!
MRS. MI TZU. My lord, as Chairman of the Committee on Social Work, I wish to call attention to just a couple of eloquent facts: Mr. Shui Ta not only has erected a model factory with model housing in our city, he is a regular contributor to our home for the disabled. (*She returns to her seat.*)
POLICEMAN (*whispering*). And she's a great friend of the judge that ate the goose!
FIRST GOD (*to the Policeman*). Oh, thank you. What next? (*To the Court, genially.*) Oh, yes. We should find out if any of the evidence is less favorable to the Defendant.

(*Wong, the Carpenter, the Old Man, the Old Woman, the Unemployed Man, the Sister-in-Law, and the Niece come for ward.*)

POLICEMAN (*whispering*). Just the riff raff, my lord.
FIRST GOD (*addressing the "riff raff"*). Well, um, riff raff—do you know anything of the Defendant, Mr. Shui Ta?
WONG. Too much, my lord.
UNEMPLOYED MAN. What don't we know, my lord?
CARPENTER. He ruined us.
SISTER-IN-LAW. He's a cheat.
NIECE. Liar.
WIFE. Thief.
BOY. Blackmailer.
BROTHER. Murderer.
FIRST GOD. Thank you. We should now let the Defendant state his point of view.
SHUI TA. I only came on the scene when Shen Te was in danger of losing what I had understood was a gift from the gods. Because I did the filthy jobs which someone had to do, they hate me. My activities were held down to the minimum, my lord.
SISTER-IN-LAW. He had us arrested!
SHUI TA. Certainly. You stole from the bakery!
SISTER-IN-LAW. Such concern for the bakery! You didn't want the shop for yourself, I suppose!
SHUI TA. I didn't want the shop overrun with parasites.
SISTER-IN-LAW. We had nowhere else to go.
SHUI TA. There were too many of you.
WONG. What about this old couple: Were *they* parasites?
OLD MAN. We lost our shop because of you!
SISTER-IN-LAW. And we gave your cousin money!
SHUI TA. My cousin's fiancé was a flyer. The money had to go to *him*.
WONG. Did you care whether he flew or not? Did you care whether she married him or not? You wanted her to marry someone else! (*He points at Shu Fu.*)
SHUI TA. The flyer unexpectedly turned out to be a scoundrel.
YANG SUN (*jumping up*). Which was the reason you made him your Manager?

SHUI TA. Later on he improved.

WONG. And when he improved, you sold him to her? (*He points out Mrs. Mi Tzu.*)

SHUI TA. She wouldn't let me have her premises unless she had him to stroke her knees!

MRS. MI TZU. What? The man's a pathological liar. (*To him.*) Don't mention my property to me as long as you live! Murderer! (*She rustles off, in high dudgeon.*)

YANG SUN (*pushing in*). My lord, I wish to speak for the Defendant.

SISTER-IN-LAW. Naturally. He's your employer.

UNEMPLOYED MAN. And the worst slave driver in the country.

MRS. YANG. That's a lie! My lord, Mr. Shui Ta is a great man. He . . .

YANG SUN. He's this and he's that, but he is not a murderer, my lord. Just fifteen minutes before his arrest I heard Shen Te's voice in his own back room.

FIRST GOD. Oh? Tell us more!

YANG SUN. I heard sobbing, my lord!

FIRST GOD. But lots of women sob, we've been finding.

YANG SUN. Could I fail to recognize her voice?

SHU FU. No, you made her sob so often yourself, young man!

YANG SUN. Yes. But I also made her happy. Till he (*pointing at Shui Ta*) decided to sell her to you!

SHUI TA. Because you didn't love her.

WONG. Oh, no: it was for the money, my lord!

SHUI TA. And what was the money for, my lord? For the poor! And for Shen Te so she could go on being good!

WONG. For the poor? That he sent to his sweatshops? And why didn't you let Shen Te be good when you signed the big check?

SHUI TA. For the child's sake, my lord.

CARPENTER. What about *my* children? What did he do about them?

(*Shui Ta is silent.*)

WONG. The shop was to be a fountain of goodness. That was the gods' idea. You came and spoiled it!

SHUI TA. If I hadn't, it would have run dry!

MRS. SHIN. There's a lot in that, my lord.

WONG. What have you done with the good Shen Te, bad man? She *was* good, my lords, she was, I swear it! (*He raises his hand in an oath.*)

THIRD GOD. What's happened to your hand, Water Seller?

WONG (*pointing to Shui Ta*). It's all his fault, my lord, *she* was going to send me to a doctor— (*To Shui Ta.*) You were her worst enemy!

SHUI TA. I was her only friend!

WONG. Where is she then? Tell us where your good friend is!

(*The excitement of this exchange has run through the whole crowd.*)

ALL. Yes, where is she? Where is Shen Te? (*etcetera.*)

SHUI TA. Shen Te had to go.

WONG. Where? Where to?

SHUI TA. I cannot tell you! I cannot tell you!

ALL. Why? Why did she have to go away? (*etcetera.*)

WONG (*into the din with the first words, but talking on beyond the others*). Why not, why not? Why did she have to go away?

SHUI TA (*shouting*). Because you'd all have torn her to shreds, that's why! My lords, I have a request. Clear the court! When only the judges remain, I will make a confession.

ALL (*except Wong, who is silent, struck by the new turn of events*). So he's guilty? He's confessing! (*etcetera.*)

FIRST GOD (*using the gavel*). Clear the court!

POLICEMAN. Clear the court!

WONG. Mr. Shui Ta has met his match this time.

MRS. SHIN (*with a gesture toward the judges*). You're in for a little surprise.

(*The court is cleared. Silence.*)

SHUI TA. Illustrious ones!

(*The Gods look at each other, not quite believing their ears.*)

SHUI TA. Yes, I recognize you!

SECOND GOD (*taking matters in hand, sternly*). What have you done with our good woman of Setzuan?

SHUI TA. I have a terrible confession to make: I am she! (*He takes off his mask, and tears away his clothes. Shen Te stands there.*)

SECOND GOD. Shen Te!

SHEN TE. Shen Te, yes. Shui Ta *and* Shen Te. Both.

Your injunction
To be good and yet to live
Was a thunderbolt:
It has torn me in two
I can't tell how it was
But to be good to others
And myself at the same time
I could not do it
Your world is not an easy one, illustrious ones!
When we extend our hand to a beggar, he tears it
off for us
When we help the lost, we are lost ourselves.

And so
Since not to eat is to die
Who can long refuse to be bad?
As I lay prostrate beneath the weight of good intentions
Ruin stared me in the face
It was when I was unjust that I ate good meat
And hobnobbed with the mighty
Why?
Why are bad deeds rewarded?
Good ones punished?
I enjoyed giving
I truly wished to be the Angel of the Slums
But washed by a foster-mother in the water of the gutter
I developed a sharp eye
The time came when pity was a thorn in my side
And, later, when kind words turned to ashes in my mouth
And anger took over
I became a wolf
Find me guilty, then, illustrious ones,
But know:
All that I have done I did
To help my neighbor
To love my lover
And to keep my little one from want
For your great, godly deeds, I was too poor, too small.

(*Pause.*)

FIRST GOD (*shocked*). Don't go on making yourself miserable, Shen Te! We're overjoyed to have found you!

SHEN TE. I'm telling you I'm the bad man who committed all those crimes!

FIRST GOD (*using—or failing to use—his ear trumpet*). The good woman who did all those good deeds?

SHEN TE. Yes, but the bad man too!

FIRST GOD (*as if something had dawned*). Unfortunate coincidences! Heartless neighbors!

THIRD GOD (*shouting in his ear*). But how is she to continue?

FIRST GOD. Continue? Well, she's a strong, healthy girl . . .

SECOND GOD. You didn't hear what she said!

FIRST GOD. I heard every word! She is confused, that's all! (*He begins to bluster.*) And what about this book of rules—we can't renounce our rules, can we? (*More quietly.*) Should the world be changed? How? By whom? The world should *not* be changed! (*At a sign from him, the lights turn pink, and music plays.*)

And now the hour of parting is at hand.
Dost thou behold, Shen Te, yon fleecy cloud?
It is our chariot. At a sign from me
'Twill come and take us back from whence we came
Above the azure vault and silver stars . . .

SHEN TE. No! Don't go, illustrious ones!

FIRST GOD.

Our cloud has landed now in yonder field
From whence it will transport us back to heaven.
Farewell, Shen Te, let not thy courage fail thee . . .

(*Exeunt Gods.*)

SHEN TE. What about the old couple? They've lost their shop! What about the Water Seller and his hand? And I've got to defend myself against the barber, because I don't love him! And against Sun, because I do love him! How? How?

(*Shen Te's eyes follow the Gods as they are imagined to step into a cloud which rises and moves forward over the orchestra and up beyond the balcony.*)

FIRST GOD (*from on high*). We have faith in you, Shen Te!

SHEN TE. There'll be a child. And he'll have to be fed. I can't stay here. Where shall I go?

FIRST GOD. Continue to be good, good woman of Setzuan!

SHEN TE. I need my bad cousin!

FIRST GOD. But not very often!

SHEN TE. Once a week at least!

FIRST GOD. Once a month will be quite enough!

SHEN TE (*shrieking*). No, no! Help!

(*But the cloud continues to recede as the Gods sing.*)

Valedictory Hymn

What rapture, oh, it is to know
A good thing when you see it
And having seen a good thing, oh,
What rapture 'tis to flee it

Be good, sweet maid of Setzuan
Let Shui Ta be clever
Departing, we forget the man
Remember your endeavor

ÒBecause through all the length of days
Her goodness faileth never
Sing hallelujah! May Shen Te's
Good name live on forever!

SHEN TE. Help!

TOPICS FOR DISCUSSION AND WRITING

1. It has been said that Brecht's "characters are social types without a private psychological side." Do you agree? And if so, do you think this is a shortcoming in his work? Explain.
2. In your opinion why does Shen Te assume the mask of Shui Ta?
3. It has been said that drama is the art of preparation—meaning that speeches and scenes generate suspense that is interestingly fulfilled. How important would you say suspense is in *The Good Woman*?
4. Brecht was a didactic writer, unashamed of preaching. What would you say is his message in this play? How acceptable to you is the message? Why? And would you say that Brecht presents the message interestingly? Explain.
5. Originally Brecht set the play in the Berlin of the 1920s. What do you think is gained or lost by setting it in a rather mythical China?

GERTRUDE STEIN

The Mother of Us All

Gertrude Stein (1874–1946), experimental poet, novelist, essayist, autobiographer, and playwright, was born into a prosperous American family of German-Jewish background living in Allegheny, Pennsylvania (now part of Pittsburgh). From 1875 to 1879 the family lived in Europe, then returned to the United States and settled in Oakland, California. (Of Oakland she later said, "There is no there there.")

Stein graduated from Radcliffe College, and then, on the recommendation of the philosopher and psychologist William James, she studied medicine at Johns Hopkins, intending to become a physiological psychologist, but she dropped out before completing her last semester. Financially independent (her parents had died and left her with adequate financial resources), in 1902 she moved to London, and then in 1903 she joined her brother Leo in Paris, where she spent the rest of her life except for a period in the French countryside when the Germans occupied Paris during World War II. "America is my country," she said, "and Paris is my home town and it is as it has come to be." She and Leo promoted and collected such modern French painters as Cézanne, Renoir, Gauguin, and Manet, and especially two younger painters, Picasso and Matisse, though in time she and Leo went their separate ways. Gertrude Stein is also known for offering hospitality and abundant advice (not all of it welcome) to Americans in Paris, including Hemingway, Paul Robeson, and Richard Wright.

Stein's best-known works are *Three Lives* (1909), three stories about women, and a memoir of her early years in Paris entitled *The Autobiography of Alice B. Toklas* (1933). Toklas moved into Stein's apartment in 1909 and remained her housekeeper, typist, editor, and lover until Stein's death 37 years later. Stein wrote about 70 works that she called plays—some no longer than a few lines—but only one, *Yes Is for a Very Young Man,* comes at all near to being a conventional play. Her best-known dramatic works are *Four Saints in Three Acts* (1927, 1934) and *The Mother of Us All* (1945–46), both of which were set to music by Virgil Thomson.

COMMENTARY

An opera is a dramatic text set to music. One can make distinctions between grand opera (an opera on a serious theme, with the whole text set to music), comic opera (a story that ends happily, set to music but usually with some spoken dialogue), operetta (an amusing dramatic performance with songs and spoken dialogue), and a play with incidental music; but for our purposes we need say only that in 1945–46 Gertrude Stein wrote a play called *The Mother of Us All* with the understanding that the composer Virgil Thomson (who had previously set to music Stein's *Four Saints in Three Acts*) would compose the music. Stein completed the text but died before she could hear any of the music that Thomson wrote for it.

Stein was not interested in what we might think of as drama of the conventional sort, that is, plays in which characters speak realistically and engage in an action that

Susan B. Anthony (Mignon Dunn) on "Ship of State" in *The Mother of Us All,* 1976, at the Santa Fe Opera. (Photograph by Ken Howard.)

ultimately comes to a resolution—an action of the sort that Aristotle had in mind when he said that a dramatic plot has a beginning, a middle, and an end. In an essay called "Plays," originally delivered as a lecture in 1934, she says that when she was a child she liked to read a play by Shakespeare because "there were so many little bits in it that were lively words." She goes on to make two distinctions, first between dramatic poetry and other kinds of poetry, and then between poetic drama and prose drama:

> In the poetry of plays words are more lively words than in any other kind of poetry and if one naturally liked lively words and I naturally did one likes to read plays in poetry. I always as a child read all the plays I could get hold of that were in poetry. Plays in prose do not read so well. The words in prose are livelier when they are not a play. I am not saying anything about why, it is just a fact.

As to the first assertion, that words are more "lively" in a poetic play than in a nondramatic poem such as a sonnet, for instance, perhaps an explanation (assuming that one thinks Stein may have a point) might go as follows: A nondramatic poem is usually the utterance of a single speaker (for instance, a man lamenting the death of his beloved), whereas a drama plays many voices against each other, so that in a drama there is, so to speak, a music of harmonizing (even if conflicting) voices. As to Stein's belief that "Plays in prose do not read so well" and that "The words in prose are livelier when they are not in a play," one can easily grasp her point. In short stories and novels—even those that can be called highly realistic—the prose often has an intensity that much of the language of prose drama does not have. For instance, the narrator of a story can quickly and even movingly describe the setting, whereas the dramatist ploddingly tells us that at the left of the stage are two chairs, etc., etc. Similarly, the writer of fiction can give us a scrap of dialogue and can then enter the mind of the speaker, perhaps describing that character's state of mind with effective metaphors, whereas the playwright will have to give extensive dialogue if we are to know the speaker's thoughts.

Later in her talk on "Plays" Stein tells us how she came to write plays while living in Paris. (Stein's language and thinking here, as always, are unusual, as you doubtless have recognized from the few passages that we have already quoted.)

> I had just come home from a pleasant dinner party and I realized then as anybody can know that something is always happening.
>
> Something is always happening, anybody knows a quantity of stories of people's lives that are always happening, there are always plenty for the newspapers and there are always plenty in private life. Everybody knows so many stories and what is the use of telling another story. What is the use of telling a story since there are so many and everybody knows so many and tells so many. In the country it is perfectly extraordinary how many complicated dramas go on all the time. And everybody knows them, so why tell another one. There is always a story going on.
>
> So naturally what I wanted to do in my play was what everybody did not always know nor always tell. By everybody I do of course include myself by always I do of course include myself.
>
> And so I wrote, What Happened, A Play.

For the nominal subject of her last play—really an opera, because Stein knew that Virgil Thomson would set it to music—Stein chose Susan B. Anthony (1820–1906), the American reformer and advocate of women's rights, notably the right to control property and wages, the right to coeducation, and the right to vote. More than any other single person Anthony was responsible for extending the vote to women, though it was not until 14 years after her death that the Nineteenth Amendment, giving women the right to vote—the "Anthony Amendment"—was passed. (Anthony had energetically worked for The Fourteenth Amendment, which in 1868 extended the vote to black males, but she had been unsuccessful in her effort to have that amendment include women. In 1872 she registered and voted in order to test the legality of the Fourteenth Amendment. She was arrested, tried, found guilty, and fined, but she refused to pay on the grounds that the law was unfair. The case went to the Supreme Court of the United States, where it was decided against Anthony and her followers.)

One might think that the events of Susan B. Anthony's life might afford the material for a play, but Stein was not interested in writing a biographical or conventional historical drama. In fact, she flouts history by including characters who were not contemporaries; for instance, Stein includes a young friend, Donald Gallup, who was not born until seven years after Anthony's death, and another friend, Joseph Barry (called Jo the Loiterer in the play), who was not born until eleven years after Anthony's death. Even some of the characters whose lives did overlap Anthony's, such as Stein and Virgil Thomson, to say nothing of John Adams and Daniel Webster, never met her. In one of her novels, *Lucy Church Amiably,* Stein says, "Supposing everyone lived at the same time what would they say?" *The Mother of Us All* provides an answer to that question; Stein brings together people from different periods, and lets them converse, or, perhaps more accurately, lets them express their thoughts in the presence of others. Although she carefully read *History of Women's Suffrage,* a work by Anthony and others, as well as documents about Daniel Webster, Stein's chief interest apparently is not history; rather, it is the play—the music, we might say—of voices in conversation. Stein's Susan B. Anthony is less an historic figure than an heroic, mythic (and thus properly operatic) figure, the Mother of Us All.

The Susan B. Anthony who is the Mother of Us All is an archetypal figure, but she is also an individual, a real person, not simply the creation of society. Perhaps something of her individuality and her emphasis on the individuality of each person is suggested when she says to Jo the Loiterer, "A crowd is never allowed but each one of you can come in." Anthony is a "one," a distinctive personality. Interestingly, unlike most protagonists, she does not develop, and we might therefore think of her as something of a symbol, a static representation of, say, anti-patriarchal thinking, especially since the last scene shows us a statue of Susan B. Anthony. Does this lifeless monument at the end indicate what she has been all along, an idea rather than a human being? On the contrary, the Anthony of the play is never so abstract or heroic that she ceases to be profoundly human, a distinctive voice that holds our ear.

Gertrude Stein must have felt some sense of identity with Susan B. Anthony. Like Stein, Anthony was unmarried, and like Stein she had a close female companion, Anna Howard Shaw, who for 18 years worked closely with Anthony. *The Mother of Us All* is Stein's last work, and one can easily think that in part she used Anthony as a way of talking about herself, a way of summing up her own career as an anti-establishment figure, a person dedicated to individuality. Further, Stein may also have felt that just as

Anthony died without seeing her ideals fulfilled, so Stein, dying of cancer, would not live to see her goals (and her reputation) solidly established.

Still, for the reader, or for the hearer and viewer of the opera, the work is not about Gertrude Stein but about Susan B. Anthony, or rather about Anthony and her America as imagined by Stein. In particular it is about Anthony's dedication to the idea of female independence and her resistance to patriarchal authority of the sort that is comically embodied in John Adams and Daniel Webster, men who put women on a pedestal so that they will not be troubled by women as real people. Stein is true to Anthony in emphasizing not the matter of the vote for women but marriage as an oppressive social institution that reduced women to property. This point is made, for instance, in a comic bit of dialogue when Jo the Loiterer speaks of buying something and a listener thinks he is speaking of buying a wife.

We hope that what we have said thus far is true, but we know that it is too solemn. *The Mother of Us All*, however serious a comment on nineteenth- and early twentieth-century society, is for the most part highly amusing, most notably of course in the debates between Webster and Susan B. (The debates are imaginary; Webster died in 1852, just as Susan B. began to give herself full-time to her causes.) In contrast to Susan B.'s direct speech ("I am not married and the reason why is that I have had to do what I have had to do") is the grotesque rhetoric of Webster and the VIP's. Here, for instance, is a typical passage of political hot air: "When the mariner has been tossed for many days, in thick weather, and on an unknown sea, he naturally avails himself of the first pause in the storm." A second example: "Mr. President I shall enter on no encomium upon Massachusetts she need none. There she is behold her and judge for yourself." This is the language of nineteenth-century public oratory, but today it strikes us as lifeless—a way of *not* communicating—especially in comparison with the language of Susan. Webster is so bound by parliamentary conventions that he addresses Susan B. in the third person ("the honorable member") and he uses the masculine pronoun "he" when speaking of her. (One can almost say that for Webster, women do not exist.) We are not surprised to hear that Webster has slept through the speeches of others (a comic touch), but perhaps we are surprised to hear Susan B.'s comment: "The right to sleep is given to no woman" (a comic touch, but one that makes a telling point). Or, again, Webster orates, "I resist it today and always. Who ever falters or whoever flies I continue the contest." Constance Fletcher (born after Webster had died) comments approvingly, "Dear man, he can make us glad that we have had so great so dear a man," but Susan B. cuts through the nonsense with, "Hush, this is slush."

Most of the critical commentaries on Gertrude Stein concentrate on her experiments with language, for instance her attempt in *Tender Buttons* (1914) to achieve in words the effects of abstract painting. But we can make a case that the essential, enduring Gertrude Stein is to be found not in these experiments but in her understanding of American society and especially in her efforts to show the role of women in American life.

A Note on the Characters: As the preceding comment indicates, the play includes historical characters from the nineteenth century and also persons of Stein's acquaintance in the twentieth century, as well as imaginary characters.

The chief historical figures are Susan B. Anthony (1820–1906), social reformer; Anna Howard Shaw (1847–1919), woman-suffrage leader; Daniel Webster (1782–1852), American statesman and orator; John Adams (1735–1826), second president of the United States; Andrew Johnson (1808–75), seventeenth president of the United States; Ulysses S. Grant (1822–85), eighteenth president of the United States; Thaddeus Stevens (1792–1868), statesman and abolitionist; Anthony Comstock (1844–1915), self-appointed censor of books and plays; Lillian Russell (1861–1922), American singer and actress.

Among the people whom Stein knew were: Constance Fletcher, (1858–1938), the author of novels and plays; Donald Gallup (b. 1913), an American soldier who met Stein when the war ended in 1945 and who later edited some of her work; Joseph Barry (b. 1917), a journalist who is called "the loiterer" because in his student days he had been arrested while picketing and was charged with loitering.

GERTRUDE STEIN *The Mother of Us All*

ACT 1

(*Prologue sung by Virgil T.*)

Pity the poor persecutor.
Why,
If money is money isn't money money,
Why,
Pity the poor persecutor,
Why,
Is money money or isn't money money.
Why.
Pity the poor persecutor.
Pity the poor persecutor because the poor persecutor always gets to be poor
Why,
Because the persecutor gets persecuted
Because is money money or isn't money money,
That's why,
When the poor persecutor is persecuted he has to cry,
Why,
Because the persecutor always ends by being persecuted,
That is the reason why.

(*Virgil T. after he has sung his prelude begins to sit.*)

VIRGIL T. Begins to sit. Begins to sit. He begins to sit. That's why. Begins to sit. He begins to sit. And that is the reason why.

ACT 1—SCENE 1

DANIEL WEBSTER.
He digged a pit, he digged it deep he digged it for his brother.
Into the pit he did fall in the pit he digged for tother.

ALL THE CHARACTERS.
Daniel was my father's name,
My father's name was Daniel.

JO THE LOITERER.
Not Daniel.

CHRIS THE CITIZEN.
Not Daniel in the lion's den.

ALL THE CHARACTERS.
My father's name was Daniel.

G. S.
My father's name was Daniel, Daniel and a bear, a bearded Daniel,
not Daniel in the lion's den not Daniel, yes Daniel my father had
a beard my father's name was Daniel,

DANIEL WEBSTER.
He digged a pit he digged it deep he digged it for his brother,
Into the pit he did fall in the pit he digged for tother.

INDIANA ELLIOT. Choose a name.

SUSAN B. ANTHONY. Susan B. Anthony is my name to choose a name is feeble, Susan B. Anthony is my name, a name can only be a name my name can only be my name, I have a name, Susan B. Anthony is my name, to choose a name is feeble.

INDIANA ELLIOT. Yes that's easy, Susan B. Anthony is that kind of a name but my name Indiana Elliot. What's in a name.

SUSAN B. ANTHONY. Everything.

G. S. My father's name was Daniel he had a black beard he was not tall not at all tall, he had a black beard his name was Daniel.

ALL THE CHARACTERS. My father had a name his name was Daniel.

JO THE LOITERER. Not Daniel

CHRIS THE CITIZEN. Not Daniel not Daniel in the lion's den not Daniel.

SUSAN B. ANTHONY. I had a father, Daniel was not his name.

INDIANA ELLIOT. I had no father no father.

DANIEL WEBSTER. He digged a pit he digged it deep he digged it for his brother, into the pit he did fall in the pit he digged for tother.

ACT 1—SCENE 2

JO THE LOITERER. I want to tell

CHRIS THE CITIZEN. Very well

JO THE LOITERER. I want to tell oh hell.

CHRIS THE CITIZEN. Oh very well.

JO THE LOITERER. I want to tell oh hell I want to tell about my wife.

CHRIS THE CITIZEN. And have you got one.

JO THE LOITERER. No not one.

CHRIS THE CITIZEN. Two then

JO THE LOITERER. No not two.

CHRIS. How many then

JO THE LOITERER. I haven't got one. I want to tell oh hell about my wife I haven't got one.

CHRIS THE CITIZEN. Well.

JO THE LOITERER. My wife, she had a garden.

CHRIS THE CITIZEN. Yes

JO THE LOITERER. And I bought one.

CHRIS THE CITIZEN. A wife.

No said Jo I was poor and I bought a garden. And then said Chris. She said, said Jo, she said my wife said one tree in my garden was her tree in her garden. And said Chris, Was it. Jo, We quarreled about it. And then said Chris. And then said Jo, we took a train and we went where we went. And then said Chris. She gave me a little package said Jo. And was it a tree said Chris. No it was money said Jo. And was she your wife said Chris, yes said Jo when she was funny, How funny said Chris. Very funny said Jo. Very funny said Jo. To be funny you have to take everything in the kitchen and put it on the floor, you have to take all your money and all your jewels and put them near the door you have to go to bed then and leave the door ajar. That is the way you do when you are funny.

CHRIS THE CITIZEN. Was she funny.

JO THE LOITERER. Yes she was funny.

(*Chris and Jo put their arms around each other.*)

ANGEL MORE. Not any more I am not a martyr any more, not any more.

Be a martyr said Chris.

ANGEL MORE. Not any more. I am not a martyr any more. Surrounded by sweet smelling flowers I fell asleep three times.

Darn and wash and patch, darn and wash and patch, darn and wash and patch darn and wash and patch.

JO THE LOITERER. Anybody can be accused of loitering.

CHRIS BLAKE A CITIZEN. Any loiterer can be accused of loitering.

HENRIETTA M. Daniel Webster needs an artichoke.

ANGEL MORE. Susan B. is cold in wet weather.

HENRY B. She swore an oath she'd quickly come to any one to any one.

ANTHONY COMSTOCK. Caution and curiosity, oil and obligation, wheels and appurtenances, in the way of means.

VIRGIL T. What means.

JOHN ADAMS. I wish to say I also wish to stay, I also wish to go away, I also wish I endeavor to also wish.

ANGEL MORE. I wept on a wish.

JOHN ADAMS. Whenever I hear any one say of course, do I deny it, yes I do deny it whenever I hear any one say of course I deny it, I do deny it.

THADDEUS S. Be mean.

DANIEL WEBSTER. Be there.

HENRIETTA M. Be where

CONSTANCE FLETCHER. I do and I do not declare that roses and wreaths, wreaths and roses around and around, blind as a bat, curled as a hat and a plume, be mine when I die, farewell to a thought, he left all alone, be firm in despair dear dear never share, dear dear, dear dear, I Constance Fletcher dear dear, I am a dear, I am dear dear I am a dear, here there everywhere. I bow myself out.

INDIANA ELLIOT. Anybody else would be sorry.

SUSAN B. ANTHONY. Hush, I hush, you hush, they hush, we hush. Hush.

GLOSTER HEMING AND ISABEL WENTWORTH. We, hush, dear as we are, we are very dear to us and to you we hush, we hush you say hush, dear hush. Hush dear.

ANNA HOPE. I open any door, that is the way that any day is today, any day is today I open any door every door a door.

LILLIAN RUSSELL. Thank you.

ANTHONY COMSTOCK. Quilts are not crazy, they are kind.

JENNY REEFER. My goodness gracious me.

ULYSSES S. GRANT. He knew that his name was not Eisenhower. Yes he knew it. He did know it.

HERMAN ATLAN. He asked me to come he did ask me.

DONALD GALLUP. I chose a long time, a very long time, four hours are a very long time, I chose, I took a very long time, I took a very long time. Yes I took a very long time to choose, yes I did.

T. T. AND A. A. They missed the boat yes they did they missed the boat.

JO A LOITERER. I came again but not when I was expected, but yes when I was expected because they did expect me.

CHRIS THE CITIZEN. I came to dinner.

(*They all sit down.*)

CURTAIN

ACT 1—SCENE 3

(*Susan B. Anthony and Daniel Webster seated in two straight-backed chairs not too near each other. Jo the Loiterer comes in.*)

JO THE LOITERER. I don't know where a mouse is I don't know what a mouse is. What is a mouse.

ANGEL MORE. I am a mouse

JO THE LOITERER. Well

ANGEL MORE. Yes Well

JO THE LOITERER. All right well. Well what is a mouse

ANGEL MORE. I am a mouse

JO THE LOITERER. Well if you are what is a mouse

ANGEL MORE. You know what a mouse is, I am a mouse.

JO THE LOITERER. Yes well, And she.

(*Susan B. dressed like a Quakeress turns around.*)

SUSAN B. I hear a sound.

JO THE LOITERER. Yes well

DANIEL WEBSTER. I do not hear a sound. When I am told.

SUSAN B. ANTHONY. Silence.

(*Everybody is silent.*)

SUSAN B. ANTHONY. Youth is young, I am not old.

DANIEL WEBSTER. When the mariner has been tossed for many days, in thick weather, and on an unknown sea, he naturally avails himself of the first pause in the storm.

SUSAN B. ANTHONY. For instance. They should always fight. They should be martyrs. Some should be martyrs. Will they. They will.

DANIEL WEBSTER. We have thus heard sir what a resolution is.

SUSAN B. ANTHONY. I am resolved.

DANIEL WEBSTER. When this debate sir was to be resumed on Thursday it so happened that it would have been convenient for me to be elsewhere.

SUSAN B. I am here, ready to be here. Ready to be where. Ready to be here. It is my habit.

DANIEL WEBSTER. The honorable member complained that I had slept on his speech.

SUSAN B. The right to sleep is given to no woman.

DANIEL WEBSTER. I did sleep on the gentleman's speech; and slept soundly.

SUSAN B. I too have slept soundly when I have slept, yes when I have slept I too have slept soundly.

DANIEL WEBSTER. Matches and over matches.

SUSAN B. I understand you undertake to overthrow my undertaking.

DANIEL WEBSTER. I can tell the honorable member once for all that he is greatly mistaken, and that he is dealing with one of whose temper and character he has yet much to learn.

SUSAN B. I have declared that patience is never more than patient. I too have declared, that I who am not patient am patient.

DANIEL WEBSTER. What interest asks he has South Carolina in a canal in Ohio.

SUSAN B. What interest have they in me, what interest have I in them, who holds the head of whom, who can bite their lips to avoid a swoon.

DANIEL WEBSTER. The harvest of neutrality had been great, but we had gathered it all.

SUSAN B. Near hours are made not by shade not by heat not by joy, I always know that not now rather not now, yes and I do not stamp but I know that now yes now is now. I have never asked any one to forgive me.

DANIEL WEBSTER. On yet another point I was still more unaccountably misunderstood.

SUSAN B. Do we do what we have to do or do we have to do what we do. I answer.

DANIEL WEBSTER. Mr. President I shall enter on no encomium upon Massachusetts she need none. There she is behold her and judge for yourselves.

SUSAN B. I enter into a tabernacle I was born a believer in peace, I say fight for the right, be a martyr and live, be a coward and die, and why, because they, yes they, sooner or later go away. They leave us here. They come again. Don't forget, they come again.

DANIEL WEBSTER. So sir I understand the gentleman and am happy to find I did not misunderstand him.

SUSAN B. I should believe, what they ask, but they know, they know.

DANIEL WEBSTER. It has been to us all a copious fountain of national, social and personal happiness.

SUSAN B. Shall I protest, not while I live and breathe, I shall protest, shall I protest, shall I protest while I live and breathe.

DANIEL WEBSTER. When my eyes shall be turned to behold for the last time the sun in heaven.

SUSAN B. Yes.

JO THE LOITERER. I like a mouse

ANGEL MORE. I hate mice.

JO THE LOITERER. I am not talking about mice, I am talking about a mouse. I like a mouse.

ANGEL MORE. I hate a mouse.

JO THE LOITERER. Now do you.

CURTAIN

INTERLUDE

(*Susan B. A Short Story.*)

Yes I was said Susan.

You mean you are, said Anne.

No said Susan no.

When this you see remember me said Susan B.

I do said Anne.

After a while there was education. Who is educated said Anne.

Susan began to follow, she began to follow herself. I am not tired said Susan. No not said Anne. No I am not said Susan. This was the beginning. They began to travel not to travel you know but to go from one place to another place. In each place Susan B. said here I am I am here. Well said Anne. Do not let it trouble you said Susan politely. By the time she was there she was polite. She often thought about politeness. She said politeness was so agreeable. Is it said Anne. Yes said Susan yes I think so that is to say politeness is agreeable that is to say it could be agreeable if everybody were polite but when it is only me, ah me, said Susan B.

Anne was reproachful why do you not speak louder she said to Susan B. I speak as loudly as I can said Susan B. I even speak louder I even speak louder than I can. Do you really said Anne. Yes I really do said Susan B. it was dark and as it was dark it was necessary to speak louder or very softly, very softly. Dear me said Susan B., if it was not so early I would be sleepy. I myself said Anne never like to look at a newspaper. You are entirely right said Susan B. only I disagree with you. You do said Anne. You know very well I do said Susan B.

Men said Susan B. are so conservative, so selfish, so boresome and said Susan B. they are so ugly, and said Susan B. they are gullible, anybody can convince them, listen said Susan B. they listen to me. Well said Anne anybody would. I know said Susan B. I know anybody would I know that.

Once upon a time any day was full of occupation. You were never tired said Anne. No I was never tired said Susan B. And now, said Anne. Now I am never tired said Susan B. Let us said Anne let us think about everything. No said Susan B. no, no no, I know, I know said Susan B. no, said Susan B. No. But said Anne. But me no buts said Susan B. I know, now you like every one, every one and you each one and you they all do, they all listen to me, utterly unnecessary to deny, why deny, they themselves will they deny that they listen to me but let them deny it, all the same they do they do, listen to me all the men do, see them said Susan B., do see them, see them, why not, said Susan B., they are men, and men, well of course they know that they cannot either see or hear unless I tell them so, poor things said Susan B. I do not pity them. Poor things. Yes said Anne they are poor things. Yes said Susan B. they are poor things. They are poor things said Susan B. men are poor things. Yes they are said Anne. Yes they are said Susan B. and nobody pities them. No said Anne no, nobody pities them. Very likely said Susan B. More than likely, said Anne. Yes said Susan B. yes.

It was not easy to go away but Susan B. did go away. She kept on going away and every time she went away she went away again. Oh my said Susan B. why do I go away, I go away because if I did not go away I would stay. Yes of course said Anne yes of course, if you did not go away you would stay. Yes of course said Susan B. Now said Susan B., let us not forget that in each place men are the same just the same, they are conservative, they are selfish and they listen to me. Yes they do said Anne. Yes they do said Susan B.

Susan B. was right, she said she was right and she was right. Susan B. was right. She was right because she was right. It is easy to be right, everybody else is wrong so it is easy to be right, and Susan B. was right, of course she was right, it is easy to be right, everybody else is wrong it is easy to be right. And said Susan B., in a way yes in a way yes really in a way, in a way really it is useful to be right. It does what it does, it does do what it does, if you are right, it does do what it does. It is very remarkable said Anne. Not very remarkable said Susan B. not very remarkable, no not very remarkable. It is not very remarkable really not very remarkable said Anne. No said Susan B. no not very remarkable.

And said Susan B. that is what I mean by not very remarkable.

Susan B. said she would not leave home. No said Susan B. I will not leave home. Why not said Anne. Why not said

Susan B. all right I will I always have I always will. Yes you always will said Anne. Yes I always will said Susan B. In a little while anything began again and Susan B. said she did not mind. Really and truly said Susan B. really and truly I do not mind. No said Anne you do not mind, no said Susan B. no really and truly truly and really I do not mind. It was very necessary never to be cautious said Susan B. Yes said Anne it is very necessary.

In a little while they found everything very mixed. It is not really mixed said Susan B. How can anything be really mixed when men are conservative, dull, monotonous, deceived, stupid, unchanging and bullies, how said Susan B. how when men are men can they be mixed. Yes said Anne, yes men are men, how can they when men are men how can they be mixed yes how can they. Well said Susan B. let us go on they always listen to me. Yes said Anne yes they always listen to you. Yes said Susan B. yes they always listen to me.

ACT 2

ANDREW J. It is cold weather.
HENRIETTA M. In winter.
ANDREW J. Wherever I am

(*Thaddeus S. comes in singing a song.*)

THADDEUS S. I believe in public school education, I do not believe in free masons I believe in public school education, I do not believe that every one can do whatever he likes because (a pause) I have not always done what I liked, but, I would, if I could, and so I will, I will do what I will, I will have my will, and they, when the they, where are they, beside a poll, Gallup the poll. It is remarkable that there could be any nice person by the name of Gallup, but there is, yes there is, that is my decision.

ANDREW J. Bother your decision, I tell you it is cold weather.

HENRIETTA M. In winter.

ANDREW J. Wherever I am.

CONSTANCE FLETCHER. Antagonises is a pleasant name, antagonises is a pleasant word, antagonises has occurred, bless you all and one.

JOHN ADAMS. Dear Miss Constance Fletcher, it is a great pleasure that I kneel at your feet, but I am Adams, I kneel at the feet of none, not any one, dear Miss Constance Fletcher dear dear Miss Constance Fletcher I kneel at your feet, you would have ruined my father if I had had one but I have had one and you had ruined him, dear Miss Constance Fletcher if I had not been an Adams I would have kneeled at your feet.

CONSTANCE FLETCHER. And kissed my hand.

J. ADAMS (*shuddering*). And kissed your hand.

CONSTANCE FLETCHER. What a pity, no not what a pity it is better so, but what a pity what a pity it is what a pity.

J. ADAMS. Do not pity me kind beautiful lovely Miss Constance Fletcher do not pity me, no do not pity me, I am an Adams and not pitiable.

CONSTANCE FLETCHER. Dear dear me if he had not been an Adams he would have kneeled at my feet and he would have kissed my hand. Do you mean that you would have kissed my hand or my hands, dear Mr. Adams.

J. ADAMS. I mean that I would have first kneeled at your feet and then I would have kissed one of your hands and then I would still kneeling have kissed both of your hands, if I had not been an Adams.

CONSTANCE FLETCHER. Dear me Mr. Adams dear me.

ALL THE CHARACTERS. If he had not been an Adams he would have kneeled at her feet and he would have kissed one of her hands, and then still kneeling he would have kissed both of her hands still kneeling if he had not been an Adams.

ANDREW J. It is cold weather.

HENRIETTA M. In winter.

ANDREW J. Wherever I am.

THADDEUS S. When I look at him I fly, I mean when he looks at me he can cry.

LILLIAN RUSSELL. It is very naughty for men to quarrel so.

HERMAN ATLAN. They do quarrel so.

LILLIAN RUSSELL. It is very naughty of them very naughty.

(*Jenny Reefer begins to waltz with Herman Atlan.*)

A SLOW CHORUS. Naughty men, they quarrel so
Quarrel about what.
About how late the moon can rise.
About how soon the earth can turn.
About how naked are the stars.
About how black are blacker men.
About how pink are pinks in spring.
About what corn is best to pop.
About how many feet the ocean has dropped.
Naughty men naughty men, they are always always quarreling.

JENNY REEFER. Ulysses S. Grant was not the most earnest nor the most noble of men, but he was not always quarreling.

DONALD GALLUP. No he was not.

JO THE LOITERER. Has everybody forgotten Isabel Wentworth. I just want to say has everybody forgotten Isabel Wentworth.

CHRIS THE CITIZEN. Why shouldn't everybody forget Isabel Wentworth.

JO THE LOITERER. Well that is just what I want to know I just want to know if everybody has forgotten Isabel Wentworth. That is all I want to know I just want to know if everybody has forgotten Isabel Wentworth.

ACT 2—SCENE 2

SUSAN B. Shall I regret having been born, will I regret having been born, shall and will, will and shall, I regret having been born.

ANNE. Is Henrietta M. a sister of Angel More.

SUSAN B. No, I used to feel that sisters should be sisters, and that sisters prefer sisters, and I.

ANNE. Is Angel More the sister of Henrietta M. It is important that I know important.

SUSAN B. Yes important.

ANNE. An Indiana Elliot are there any other Elliots beside Indiana Elliot. It is important that I should know, very important.

SUSAN B. Should one work up excitement, or should one turn it low so that it will explode louder, should one work up excitement should one.

ANNE. Are there any other Elliots beside Indiana Elliot, had she sisters or even cousins, it is very important that I should know, very important.

SUSAN B. A life is never given for a life, when a life is given a life is gone, if no life is gone there is no room for more life, life and strife, I give my life, that is to say, I live my life every day.

ANNE. And Isabel Wentworth, is she older or younger than she was it is very important very important that I should know just how old she is. I must have a list I must of how old every one is, it is very important.

SUSAN B. I am ready.

ANNE. We have forgotten we have forgotten Jenny Reefer, I don't know even who she is, it is very important that I know who Jenny Reefer is very important.

SUSAN B. And perhaps it is important to know who Lillian Russell is, perhaps it is important.

ANNE. It is not important to know who Lillian Russell is.

SUSAN B. Then you do know.

ANNE. It is not important for me to know who Lillian Russell is.

SUSAN B. I must choose I do choose, men and women women and men I do choose. I must choose colored or white white or colored I must choose, I must choose, weak or strong, strong or weak I must choose.

(*All the men coming forward together.*)

SUSAN B. I must choose

JO THE LOITERER. Fight fight fight, between the nigger and the white.

CHRIS THE CITIZEN. And the women.

ANDREW J. I wish to say that little men are bigger than big men, that they know how to drink and to get drunk. They say I was a little man next to that big man, nobody can say what they do say nobody can.

CHORUS OF ALL THE MEN. No nobody can, we feel that way too, no nobody can.

ANDREW JOHNSON. Begin to be drunk when you can so be a bigger man than a big man, you can.

CHORUS OF MEN. You can.

ANDREW J. I often think, I am a bigger man than a bigger man. I often think I am.

(*Andrew J. moves around and as he moves around he sees himself in a mirror.*)

Nobody can say little as I am I am not bigger than anybody bigger bigger bigger (and then in a low whisper) bigger than him bigger than him.

JO THE LOITERER. Fight fight between the big and the big never between the little and the big.

CHRIS THE CITIZEN. They don't fight.

(*Virgil T. makes them all gather around him.*)

VIRGIL T. Hear me he says hear me in every way I have satisfaction, I sit I stand I walk around and I am grand, and you all know it.

CHORUS OF MEN. Yes we all know it. That's that.

And Said VIRGIL T. I will call you up one by one and then you will know which one is which, I know, then you will be known. Very well, Henry B.

HENRY B. (*comes forward*). I almost thought that I was Tommy I almost did I almost thought I was Tommy W. but if I were Tommy W. I would never come again, not if I could do better no not if I could do better.

VIRGIL T. Useless. John Adams. (*John Adams advances.*) Tell me are you the real John Adams you know I sometimes doubt it not really doubt it you know but doubt it.

JOHN ADAMS. If you were silent I would speak.

JO THE LOITERER. Fight fight fight between day and night.

CHRIS THE CITIZEN. Which is day and which is night.

JO THE LOITERER. Hush, which.

JOHN ADAMS. I ask you Virgil T. do you love women, I do. I love women but I am never subdued by them never.

VIRGIL T. He is no good. Andrew J. and Thaddeus S. better come together.

JO THE LOITERER. He wants to fight fight fight between.

CHRIS. Between what.
JO THE LOITERER. Between the dead.
ANDREW J. I tell you I am bigger bigger is not biggest is not bigger. I am bigger and just to the last minute, I stick, it's better to stick than to die, it's better to itch than to cry, I have tried them all.
VIRGIL T. You bet you have.
THADDEUS S. I can be carried in dying but I will never quit trying.
JO THE LOITERER. Oh go to bed when all is said oh go to bed, everybody, let's hear the women.
CHRIS THE CITIZEN. Fight fight between the nigger and the white and the women.

(*Andrew J. and Thaddeus S. begin to quarrel violently.*)

Tell me said Virgil T. tell me I am from Missouri.

(*Everybody suddenly stricken dumb.*)
(*Daniel advances holding Henrietta M. by the hand.*)

DANIEL. Ladies and gentlemen let me present you let me present to you Henrietta M. it is rare in this troubled world to find a woman without a last name rare delicious and troubling, ladies and gentlemen let me present Henrietta M.

CURTAIN

ACT 2—SCENE 3

SUSAN B. I do not know whether I am asleep or awake, awake or asleep, asleep or awake. Do I know.
JO THE LOITERER. I know, you are awake Susan B.

(*A snowy landscape. A negro man and a negro woman.*)

SUSAN B. Negro man would you vote if you only can and not she.
NEGRO MAN. You bet.
SUSAN B. I fought for you that you could vote would you vote if they would not let me.
NEGRO MAN. Holy gee.
SUSAN B. (*moving down in the snow*). If I believe that I am right and I am right if they believe that they are right and they are not in the right, might, might, might there be what might be.
NEGRO MAN AND WOMAN (*following her*). All right Susan B. all right.
SUSAN B. How then can we entertain a hope that they will act differently, we may pretend to go in good faith but there will be no faith in us.
DONALD GALLUP. Let me help you Susan B.
SUSAN B. And if you do and I annoy you what will you do.
DONALD GALLUP. But I will help you Susan B.
SUSAN B. I tell you if you do and I annoy you what will you do.
DONALD GALLUP. I wonder if I can help you Susan B.
SUSAN B. I wonder.

(*Andrew G., Thaddeus and Daniel Webster come in together.*)

We are the chorus of the V.I.P. Very important persons to every one who can hear and see, we are the chorus of the V.I.P.
SUSAN B. Yes, so they are. I am important but not that way, not that way.
THE THREE V.I.P.'s. We you see we V.I.P. very important to any one who can hear or you can see, just we three, of course lots of others but just we three, just we three we are the chorus of V.I.P. Very important persons to any one who can hear or can see.
SUSAN B. My constantly recurring thought and prayer now are that no word or act of mine may lessen the might of this country in the scale of truth and right.
THE CHORUS OF V.I.P.
DANIEL WEBSTER. When they all listen to me.
THADDEUS S. When they all listen to me.
ANDREW J. When they all listen to him, by him I mean me.
DANIEL WEBSTER. By him I mean me.
THADDEUS S. It is not necessary to have any meaning I am he, he is me I am a V.I.P.
THE THREE. We are the V.I.P. the very important persons, we have special rights, they ask us first and they wait for us last and wherever we are well there we are everybody knows we are there, we are the V.I.P. Very important persons for everybody to see.
JO THE LOITERER. I wished that I knew the difference between rich and poor, I used to think I was poor, now I think I am rich and I am rich, quite rich not very rich quite rich, I wish I knew the difference between rich and poor.
CHRIS THE CITIZEN. Ask her, ask Susan B. I always ask, I find they like it and I like it, and if I like it, and if they like it, I am not rich and I am not poor, just like that Jo just like that.
JO THE LOITERER. Susan B. listen to me, what is the difference between rich and poor poor and rich no use to ask the V.I.P., they never answer me but you Susan B. you answer, answer me.
SUSAN B. Rich, to be rich, is to be so rich that when they are rich they have it to be that they do not listen and when they do they do not hear, and to be poor to be poor, is to be so poor they listen and listen and what they hear well what do they hear, they hear that they listen, they listen to hear, that is what it is to be poor, but I, I Susan B., there is

no wealth nor poverty, there is no wealth, what is wealth, there is no poverty, what is poverty, has a pen ink, has it.

JO THE LOITERER. I had a pen that was to have ink for a year and it only lasted six weeks.

SUSAN B. Yes I know Jo. I know.

CURTAIN

ACT 2—SCENE 4

(*A Meeting.*)

SUSAN B. (*on the platform*). Ladies there is no neutral position for us to assume. If we say we love the cause and then sit down at our ease, surely does our action speak the lie.

And now will Daniel Webster take the platform as never before.

DANIEL WEBSTER. Coming and coming alone, no man is alone when he comes, when he comes when he is coming he is not alone and now ladies and gentlemen I have done, remember that remember me remember each one.

SUSAN B. And now Virgil T. Virgil T. will bow and speak and when it is necessary they will know that he is he.

VIRGIL T. I make what I make, I make a noise, there is a poise in making a noise.

(*An interruption at the door.*)

JO THE LOITERER. I have behind me a crowd, are we allowed.

SUSAN B. A crowd is never allowed but each one of you can come in.

CHRIS THE CITIZEN. But if we are allowed then we are a crowd.

SUSAN B. No, this is the cause, and a cause is a pause. Pause before you come in.

JO THE LOITERER. Yes ma'am.

(*All the characters crowd in. Constance Fletcher and Indiana Elliot leading*).

DANIEL WEBSTER. I resist it today and always. Who ever falters or whoever flies I continue the contest.

(*Constance Fletcher and Indiana Elliot bowing low say*). Dear man, he can make us glad that we have had so great so dear a man here with us now and now we bow before him here, this dear this dear great man.

SUSAN B. Hush, this is slush. Hush.

JOHN ADAMS. I cannot be still when still and until I see Constance Fletcher dear Constance Fletcher noble Constance Fletcher and I spill I spill over like a thrill and a trill, dear Constance Fletcher there is no cause in her presence, how can there be a cause. Women what are women. There is Constance Fletcher, men what are men, there is Constance Fletcher, Adams, yes, Adams, I am John Adams, there is Constance Fletcher, when this you see listen to me, Constance, no I cannot call her Constance I can only call her Constance Fletcher.

INDIANA ELLIOT. And how about me.

JO THE LOITERER. Whist shut up I have just had an awful letter from home, shut up.

INDIANA ELLIOT. What did they say.

JO THE LOITERER. They said I must come home and not marry you.

INDIANA. Who ever said we were going to marry.

JO THE LOITERER. Believe me I never did.

INDIANA. Disgrace to the cause of women, out. (*And she shoves him out.*)

JO THE LOITERER. Help Susan B. help me.

SUSAN B. I know that we suffer, and as we suffer we grow strong, I know that we wait and as we wait we are bold, I know that we are beaten and as we are beaten we win, I know that men know that this is not so but it is so, I know, yes I know.

JO THE LOITERER. There didn't I tell you she knew best, you just give me a kiss and let me alone.

DANIEL WEBSTER. I who was once old am now young, I who was once weak am now strong, I who have left every one behind am now overtaken.

SUSAN B. I undertake to overthrow your undertaking.

JO THE LOITERER. You bet.

CHRIS THE CITIZEN. I always repeat everything I hear.

JO THE LOITERER. You sure do.

(*While all this is going on, all the characters are crowding up on the platform.*)

(THEY SAY).
Now we are all here there is nobody down there to hear, now if it is we're always like that there would be no reason why anybody should cry, because very likely if at all it would be so nice to be the head, we are the head we have all the bread.

JO THE LOITERER. And the butter too.

CHRIS THE CITIZEN. And Kalamazoo.

SUSAN B. (*advancing*). I speak to those below who are not there who are not there who are not there. I speak to those below to those below who are not there to those below who are not there.

CURTAIN

ACT 2—SCENE 5

SUSAN B. Will they remember that it is true that neither they that neither you, will they marry will they carry, aloud, the right to know that even if they love them so, they are alone to live and die, they are alone to sink and swim they are alone to have what they own, to have no idea but that they are here, to struggle and thirst to do everything first, because until it is done there is no other one.

(*Jo the Loiterer leads in Indiana Elliot in wedding attire, followed by John Adams and Constance Fletcher and followed by Daniel Webster and Angel More. All the other characters follow after. Anne and Jenny Reefer come and stand by Susan B. Ulysses S. Grant sits down in a chair right behind the procession.*)

ANNE. Marriage.
JENNY REEFER. Marry marriage.
SUSAN B. I know I know and I have told you so, but if no one marries how can there be women to tell men, women to tell men.
ANNE. What
JENNY REEFER. Women should not tell men.
SUSAN B. Men can not count, they do not know that two and two make four if women do not tell them so. There is a devil creeps into men when their hands are strengthened. Men want to be half slave half free. Women want to be all slave or all free, therefore men govern and women know, and yet.
ANNE. Yet.
JENNY REEFER. There is no yet in paradise.
SUSAN B. Let them marry.

(*The marrying commences.*)

JO THE LOITERER. I tell her if she marries me do I marry her.
INDIANA ELLIOT. Listen to what he says so you can answer, have you the ring.
JO THE LOITERER. You did not like the ring and mine is too large.
INDIANA ELLIOT. Hush.
JO THE LOITERER. I wish my name was Adams.
INDIANA ELLIOT. Hush.
JOHN ADAMS. I never marry I have been twice divorced but I have never married, fair Constance Fletcher fair Constance Fletcher do you not admire me that I never can married be. I who have been twice divorced. Dear Constance Fletcher dear dear Constance Fletcher do you not admire me.
CONSTANCE FLETCHER. So beautiful. It is so beautiful to meet you here, so beautiful, so beautiful to meet you here dear, dear John Adams, so beautiful to meet you here.
DANIEL WEBSTER. When I have joined and not having joined have separated and not having separated have led, and not having led have thundered, when I having thundered have provoked and having provoked have dominated, may I dear Angel More not kneel at your feet because I cannot kneel my knees are not kneeling knees but dear Angel More be my Angel More for evermore.
ANGEL MORE. I join the choir that is visible, because the choir that is visible is as visible.
DANIEL WEBSTER. As what Angel More.
ANGEL MORE. As visible as visible, do you not hear me, as visible.
DANIEL WEBSTER. You do not and I do not.
ANGEL MORE. What.
DANIEL WEBSTER. Separate marriage from marriage.
ANGEL MORE. And why not.
DANIEL WEBSTER. And.

(*Just at this moment Ulysses S. Grant makes his chair pound on the floor.*)

ULYSSES S. GRANT. As long as I sit I am sitting, silence again as you were, you were all silent, as long as I sit I am sitting.
ALL TOGETHER. We are silent, as we were.
SUSAN B. We are all here to celebrate the civil and religious marriage of Jo the Loiterer and Indiana Elliot.
JO THE LOITERER. Who is civil and who is religious.
ANNE. Who is, listen to Susan B. She knows.

(*The Brother of Indiana Elliot rushes in.*)

Nobody knows who I am but I forbid the marriage, do we know whether Jo the Loiterer is a bigamist or a grandfather or an uncle or a refugee. Do we know, no we do not know and I forbid the marriage, I forbid it, I am Indiana Elliot's brother and I forbid it, I am known as Herman Atlan and I forbid it, I am known as Anthony Comstock and I forbid it. I am Indiana Elliot's brother and I forbid it.
JO THE LOITERER. Well well well, I knew that ring of mine was too large, It could not fall off on account of my joints but I knew it was too large.
INDIANA ELLIOT. I renounce my brother.
JO THE LOITERER. That's right my dear that's all right.
SUSAN B. What is marriage, is marriage protection or religion, is marriage renunciation or abundance, is marriage a stepping-stone or an end. What is marriage.
ANNE. I will never marry.
JENNY REEFER. If I marry I will divorce but I will not marry because if I did marry, I would be married.

(*Ulysses S. Grant pounds his chair.*)

ULYSSES S. GRANT. Didn't I say I do not like noise, I do not like cannon balls, I do not like storms, I do not like talking, I do not like noise. I like everything and everybody to be silent and what I like I have. Everybody be silent.
JO THE LOITERER. I know I was silent, everybody can tell just by listening to me just how silent I am, dear General, dear General Ulysses, dear General Ulysses Simpson dear

General Ulysses Simpson Grant, dear dear sir, am I not a perfect example of what you like, am I not silent.

(*Ulysses S. Grant's chair pounds and he is silent.*)

SUSAN B. I am not married and the reason why is that I have had to do what I have had to do, I have had to be what I have had to be, I could never be one of two I could never be two in one as married couples do and can, I am but one all one, one and all one, and so I have never been married to any one.

ANNE. But I I have been, I have been married to what you have been to that one.

SUSAN B. No no, no, you may be married to the past one, the one that is not the present one, no one can be married to the present one, the one, the one, the present one.

JENNY REEFER. I understand you undertake to overthrow their undertaking.

SUSAN B. I love the sound of these, one over two, two under one, three under four, four over more.

ANNE. Dear Susan B. Anthony thank you.

JOHN ADAMS. All this time I have been lost in my thoughts in my thoughts of thee beautiful thee, Constance Fletcher, do you see, I have been lost in my thoughts of thee.

CONSTANCE FLETCHER. I am blind and therefore I dream.

DANIEL WEBSTER. Dear Angel More, dear Angel More, there have been men who have stammered and stuttered but not, not I.

ANGEL MORE. Speak louder.

DANIEL WEBSTER. Not I.

THE CHORUS. Why the hell don't you all get married, why don't you, we want to go home, why don't you.

JO THE LOITERER. Why don't you.

INDIANA ELLIOT. Why don't you.

INDIANA ELLIOT'S BROTHER. Why don't you because I am here.

The crowd remove him forcibly

SUSAN B. ANTHONY (*suddenly*). They are married all married and their children women as well as men will have the vote, they will they will, they will have the vote.

CURTAIN

ACT 2—SCENE 6

(*Susan B. doing her house-work in her house.*)

Enter ANNE. Susan B. they want you.

SUSAN B. Do they

ANNE. Yes. You must go.

SUSAN B. No.

JENNY REEFER. (*Comes in*) Oh yes they want to know if you are here.

SUSAN B. Yes still alive. Painters paint and writers write and soldiers drink and fight and I am still alive.

ANNE. They want you.

SUSAN B. And when they have me.

JENNY REEFER. Then they will want you again.

SUSAN B. Yes I know, they love me so, they tell me so and they tell me so, but I, I do not tell them so because I know, they will not do what they could do and I I will be left alone to die but they will not have done what I need to have done to make it right that I live lived my life and fight.

JO THE LOITERER (*at the window*). Indiana Elliot wants to come in, she will not take my name she says it is not all the same, she says that she is Indiana Elliot and that I am Jo, and that she will not take my name and that she will always tell me so. Oh yes she is right of course she is right it is not all the same Indiana Elliot is her name, she is only married to me, but there is no difference that I can see, but all the same there she is and she will not change her name, yes it is all the same.

SUSAN B. Let her in.

INDIANA ELLIOT. Oh Susan B. they want you they have to have you, can I tell them you are coming I have not changed my name can I tell them you are coming and that you will do everything.

SUSAN B. No but there is no use in telling them so, they won't vote my laws, there is always a clause, there is always a pause, they won't vote my laws.

(*Andrew Johnson puts his head in at the door.*)

ANDREW JOHNSON. Will the good lady come right along.

THADDEUS STEVENS (*behind him*). We are waiting, will the good lady not keep us waiting, will the good lady not keep us waiting.

SUSAN B. You you know so well that you will not vote my laws.

STEVENS. Dear lady remember humanity comes first.

SUSAN B. You mean men come first, women, you will not vote my laws, how can you dare when you do not care, how can you dare, there is no humanity in humans, there is only law, and you will not because you know so well that there is no humanity there are only laws, you know it so well that you will not you will not vote my laws.

(*Susan B. goes back to her housework. All the characters crowd in.*)

CHORUS. Do come Susan B. Anthony do come nobody no nobody can make them come the way you make them come, do come do come Susan B. Anthony, it is your duty, Susan B. Anthony, you know you know your duty, you come, do come, come.

SUSAN B. ANTHONY. I suppose I will be coming, is it because you flatter me, is it because if I do not come you will forget me and never vote my laws, you will never vote my laws even if I do come but if I do not come you will never vote my laws, come or not come it always comes to the same thing it comes to their not voting my laws, not voting my laws, tell me all you men tell me you know you will never vote my laws.

ALL THE MEN. Dear kind lady we count on you, and as we count on you so can you count on us.

SUSAN B. ANTHONY. Yes but I work for you I do, I say never again, never again, never never, and yet I know I do say no but I do not mean no, I know I always hope that if I go that if I go and go and go, perhaps then you men will vote my laws but I know how well I know, a little this way a little that way you steal away, you steal a piece away you steal yourselves away, you do not intend to stay and vote my laws, and still when you call I go, I go, I go, I say no, no, no, and I go, but no, this time no, this time you have to do more than promise, you must write it down that you will vote my laws, but no, you will pay no attention to what is written, well then swear by my hearth, as you hope to have a home and hearth, swear after I work for you swear that you will vote my laws, but no, no oaths, no thoughts, no decisions, no intentions, no gratitude, no convictions, no nothing will make you pass my laws. Tell me can any of you be honest now, and say you will not pass my laws.

JO THE LOITERER. I can I can be honest I can say I will not pass your laws, because you see I have no vote, no loiterer has a vote so it is easy Susan B. Anthony easy for one man among all these men to be honest and to say I will not pass your laws. Anyway Susan B. Anthony what are your laws. Would it really be all right to pass them, if you say so it is all right with me. I have no vote myself but I'll make them as long as I don't have to change my name don't have to don't have to change my name.

T. STEVENS. Thanks dear Susan B. Anthony, thanks we all know that whatever happens we all can depend upon you to do your best for any cause which is a cause, and any cause is a cause and because any cause is a cause therefore you will always do your best for any cause, and now you will be doing your best for this cause our cause the cause.

SUSAN B. Because. Very well is it snowing.

CHORUS. Not just now.

SUSAN B. ANTHONY. Is it cold.

CHORUS. A little.

SUSAN B. ANTHONY. I am not well

CHORUS. But you look so well and once started it will be all right.

SUSAN B. ANTHONY. All right

CURTAIN

ACT 2—SCENE 7

(*Susan B. Anthony busy with her housework.*)

ANNE (*comes in*). Oh it was wonderful, wonderful, they listen to nobody the way they listen to you.

SUSAN B. Yes it is wonderful as the result of my work for the first time the word male has been written into the constitution of the United States concerning suffrage. Yes it is wonderful.

ANNE. But

SUSAN B. Yes but, what is man, what are they. I do not say that they haven't kind hearts, if I fall down in a faint, they will rush to pick me up, if my house is on fire, they will rush in to put the fire out and help me, yes they have kind hearts but they are afraid, afraid, they are afraid, they are afraid. They fear women, they fear each other, they fear their neighbor, they fear other countries and then they hearten themselves in their fear by crowding together and following each other, and when they crowd together and follow each other they are brutes, like animals who stampede, and so they have written in the name male into the United States constitution, because they are afraid of black men because they are afraid of women, because they are afraid afraid. Men are afraid.

ANNE (*timidly*). And women.

SUSAN B. Ah women often have not any sense of danger, after all a hen screams pitifully when she sees an eagle but she is only afraid for her children, men are afraid for themselves, that is the real difference between men and women.

ANNE. But Susan B. why do you not say these things out loud.

SUSAN B. Why not, because if I did they would not listen they not alone would not listen they would revenge themselves. Men have kind hearts when they are not afraid but they are afraid afraid afraid. I say they are afraid, but if I were to tell them so their kindness would turn to hate. Yes the Quakers are right, they are not afraid because they do not fight, they do not fight.

ANNE. But Susan B. you fight and you are not afraid.

SUSAN B. I fight and I am not afraid, I fight but I am not afraid.

ANNE. And you will win.

SUSAN B. Win what, win what.

ANNE. Win the vote for women.

SUSAN B. Yes some day some day the women will vote and by that time.

ANNE. By that time oh wonderful time.

SUSAN B. By that time it will do them no good because having the vote they will become like men, they will be afraid, having the vote will make them afraid, oh I know it, but I will fight for the right, for the right to vote for them even though they become like men, become afraid like men, become like men.

(*Anne bursts into tears. Jenny Reefer rushes in.*)

JENNY REEFER. I have just converted Lillian Russell to the cause of woman's suffrage, I have converted her, she will give all herself and all she earns oh wonderful day I know you will say, here she comes isn't she beautiful.

(*Lillian Russell comes in followed by all the women in the chorus. Women crowding around, Constance Fletcher in the background.*)

LILLIAN RUSSELL. Dear friends, it is so beautiful to meet you all, so beautiful, so beautiful to meet you all.

(*John Adams comes in and sees Constance Fletcher.*)

JOHN ADAMS. Dear friend beautiful friend, there is no beauty where you are not.

CONSTANCE FLETCHER. Yes dear friend but look look at real beauty look at Lillian Russell look at real beauty.

JOHN ADAMS. Real beauty real beauty is all there is of beauty and why should my eye wander where no eye can look without having looked before. Dear friend I kneel to you because dear friend each time I see you I have never looked before, dear friend you are an open door.

(*Daniel Webster strides in, the women separate.*)

DANIEL WEBSTER. What what is it, what is it, what is the false and the true and I say to you you Susan B. Anthony, you know the false from the true and yet you will not wait you will not wait, I say you will you will wait. When my eyes, and I have eyes when my eyes, beyond that I seek not to penetrate the veil, why should you want what you have chosen, when mine eyes, why do you want that the curtain may rise, why when mine eyes, why should the vision be opened to what lies behind, why, Susan B. Anthony fight the fight that is the fight, that any fight may be a fight for the right. I hear that you say that the word male should not be written into the constitution of the United States of America, but I say, I say, that so long that the gorgeous ensign of the republic, still full high advanced, its arms and trophies streaming in their original luster not a stripe erased or polluted not a single star obscured.

JO THE LOITERER. She has decided to change her name.

INDIANA ELLIOT. Not because it is his name but it is such a pretty name, Indiana Loiterer is such a pretty name I think all the same he will have to change his name, he must be Jo Elliot, yes he must, it is what he has to do, he has to be Jo Elliot and I am going to be Indiana Loiterer, dear friends, all friends is it not a lovely name, Indiana Loiterer all the same.

JO THE LOITERER. All right I never fight, nobody will know it's men, but what can I do, if I am not she and I am not me, what can I do, if a name is not true, what can I do but do as she tells me.

ALL THE CHORUS. She is quite right, Indiana Loiterer is so harmonious, so harmonious, Indiana Loiterer is so harmonious.

(*All the men come in.*)

What did she say.

JO. I was talking not she but nobody no nobody ever wants to listen to me.

ALL THE CHORUS (*men and women.*) Susan B. Anthony was very successful we are all very grateful to Susan B. Anthony because she was so successful, she worked for the votes for women and she worked for the vote for colored men and she was so successful, they wrote the word male into the constitution of the United States of America, dear Susan B. Anthony. Dear Susan B., whenever she wants to be and she always wants to be she is always so successful so very successful.

SUSAN B. So successful.

CURTAIN

ACT 2—SCENE 8

(*The Congressional Hall, the replica of the statue of Susan B. Anthony and her comrades in the suffrage fight.*)

ANNE (*alone in front of the statuary*). The Vote. Women have the vote. They have it each and every one, it is glorious glorious glorious.

SUSAN B. ANTHONY (*behind the statue*). Yes women have the vote, all my long life of strength and strife, all my long life, women have it, they can vote, every man and every woman have the vote, the word male is not there any more, that is to say, that is to say.

(*Silence. Virgil T. comes in very nicely, he looks around and sees Anne.*)

VIRGIL T. Very well indeed, very well indeed, you are looking very well indeed, have you a chair anywhere, very well indeed, as we sit, we sit, some day very soon some day they will vote sitting and that will be a very successful day any day, every day.

(*Henry B. comes in. He looks all around at the statue and then he sighs.*)

HENRY B. Does it really mean that women are as white and cold as marble does it really mean that.

(*Angel More comes in and bows gracefully to the sculptured group.*)

ANGEL MORE. I can always think of dear Daniel Webster daily.

(John Adams comes in and looks around, and then carefully examines the statue.)

JOHN ADAMS. I think that they might have added dear delicate Constance Fletcher I do think they might have added her wonderful profile, I do think they might have, I do, I really do. *(Andrew Johnson shuffles in.)*

ANDREW JOHNSON. I have no hope in black or white in white or black in black or black or white or white, no hope.

(Thaddeus Stevens comes in, he does not address anybody, he stands before the statue and frowns.)

THADDEUS S. Rob the cradle, rob it, rob the robber, rob him, rob whatever there is to be taken, rob, rob the cradle, rob it.

DANIEL WEBSTER *(he sees nothing else)*. Angel More, more more Angel More, did you hear me, can you hear shall you hear me, when they come and they do come, when they go and they do go, Angel More can you will you shall you may you might you would you hear me, when they have lost and won, when they have won and lost, when words are bitter and snow is white, Angel More come to me and we will leave together.

ANGEL MORE. Dear sir, not leave, stay.

HENRIETTA M. I have never been mentioned again. *(She curtseys.)*

CONSTANCE FLETCHER. Here I am, I am almost blind but here I am, dear dear here I am, I cannot see what is so white, here I am.

JOHN ADAMS *(kissing her hand)*. Here you are, blind as a bat and beautiful as a bird, here you are, white and cold as marble, beautiful as marble, yes that is marble but you you are the living marble dear Constance Fletcher, you are.

CONSTANCE FLETCHER. Thank you yes I am here, blind as a bat, I am here.

INDIANA ELLIOT. I am sorry to interrupt so sorry to interrupt but I have a great deal to say about marriage, either one or the other married must be economical, either one or the other, if either one or the other of a married couple are economical then a marriage is successful, if not not, I have a great deal to say about marriage, and dear Susan B. Anthony was never married, how wonderful it is to be never married how wonderful. I have a great deal to say about marriage.

SUSAN B. ANTHONY *(voice from behind the statue)*. It is a puzzle, I am not puzzled but it is a puzzle, if there are no children there are no men and women, and if there are men and women, it is rather horrible, and if it is rather horrible, then there are children, I am not puzzled but it is very puzzling, women and men vote and children, I am not puzzled but it is very puzzling.

GLOSTER HEMING. I have only been a man who has a very fine name, and it must be said I made it up yes I did, so many do why not I, so many do, so many do, and why not two, when anybody might, and you can vote and you can dote with any name. Thank you.

ISABEL WENTWORTH. They looked for me and they found me, I like to talk about it. It is very nearly necessary not to be noisy not to be noisy and hope, hope and hope, no use in enjoying men and women no use, I wonder why we are all happy, yes.

ANNIE HOPE. There is another Anne and she believes, I am hopey hope and I do not believe I have been in California and Kalamazoo, and I do not believe I burst into tears and I do not believe.

(They all crowd closer together and Lillian Russell who comes in stands quite alone.)

LILLIAN RUSSELL. I can act so drunk that I never drink, I can drink so drunk that I never act, I have a curl I was a girl and I am old and fat but very handsome for all that.

(Anthony Comstock comes in and glares at her.)

ANTHONY COMSTOCK. I have heard that they have thought that they would wish that one like you could vote a vote and help to let the ones who want do what they like, I have heard that even you, and I am through, I cannot hope that there is dope, oh yes a horrid word. I have never heard, short.

JENNY REEFER. I have hope and faith, not charity no not charity, I have hope and faith, no not, not charity, no not charity.

ULYSSES S. GRANT. Women are women, soldiers are soldiers, men are not men, lies are not lies, do, and then a dog barks, listen to him and then a dog barks, a dog barks a dog barks any dog barks, listen to him any dog barks. *(He sits down.)*

HERMAN ATLAN. I am not loved any more, I was loved oh yes I was loved but I am not loved any more. I am not, was I not, I knew I would refuse what a woman would choose and so I am not loved any more, not loved any more.

DONALD GALLUP. Last but not least, first and not best, I am tall as a man, I am firm as a clam, and I never change, from day to day.

(Jo the Loiterer and Chris a Citizen.)

JO THE LOITERER. Let us dance and sing, Chrissy Chris, wet and not in debt, I am a married man and I know how I show I am a married man. She votes, she changes her name and she votes.

(*They all crowd together in front of the statue, there is a moment of silence and then a chorus.*)

CHORUS. To vote the vote, the vote we vote, can vote do vote will vote could vote, the vote the vote.

JO THE LOITERER. I am the only one who cannot vote, no loiterer can vote.

INDIANA ELLIOT. I am a loiterer Indiana Loiterer and I can vote.

JO THE LOITERER. You only have the name, you have not got the game.

CHORUS. The vote the vote we will have the vote.

LILLIAN RUSSELL. It is so beautiful to meet you all here so beautiful.

ULYSSES S. GRANT. Vote the vote, the army does not vote, the general generals, there is no vote, bah vote.

THE CHORUS. The vote we vote we note the vote.

(*They all bow and smile to the statue. Suddenly Susan B.'s voice is heard.*)

SUSAN B.'S VOICE. We cannot retrace our steps, going forward may be the same as going backwards. We cannot retrace our steps, retrace our steps. All my long life, all my life, we do not retrace our steps, all my long life, but.

(*A silence a long silence.*)

But—we do not retrace our steps, all my long life, and here, here we are here, in marble and gold, did I say gold, yes I said gold, in marble and gold and where—

(*A silence.*)

Where is where, in my long life of effort and strife, dear life, life is strife, in my long life, it will not come and go, I tell you so, it will stay it will pay but

(*A long silence.*)

But do I want what we have got, has it not gone, what made it live, has it not gone because now it is had, in my long life in my long life

(*Silence.*)

Life is strife, I was a martyr all my life not to what I won but to what was done.

(*Silence.*)

Do you know because I tell you so, or do you know, do you know.

(*Silence.*)

My long life, my long life.

CURTAIN

TOPICS FOR DISCUSSION AND WRITING

1. Virgil Thomson suggested that the 1948 production at Western Reserve University might use a set and staging that were "visually a sort of evocation of a 19th-century photograph album." (See Thomson's letter to Nadine Miles, p. 515, for further details.) What do you think of the idea? Why?
2. Is the opera anti-male, or on the contrary simply anti-patriarchal?
3. In Stein's libretto, in the last scene of the last act (2.8) Susan B. Anthony sings only from behind a statue of herself. In the first production, however, at Columbia University in 1947, during this scene she twice crossed the stage before taking her place on the pedestal, i.e., before becoming a statue. What, if anything, can be said on behalf of this staging?
4. Richard Bridgman, in *Gertrude Stein in Pieces,* says that the opera ends bleakly in the recognition of SBA's failure. To what extent, if any, do you agree?

CONTEXTS FOR *THE MOTHER OF US ALL*

Virgil Thomson: Letters and Other Writings

Virgil Thomson (1896–1989), music critic and composer, met Gertrude Stein in Paris in 1926 and later collaborated with her on two operas, *Four Saints in Three Acts* and *The Mother of Us All.* In the following selections (letters, an essay, and a passage from his autobiography) he discusses *The Mother of Us All.*

How The Mother of Us All *Was Created*

The Mother of Us All is an opera about American public and private life in the nineteenth century. That was a time, rare in history, when great issues were debated in great language. As in the Greece of Pericles and Demosthenes, in the Rome of Caesar and Cicero, in the England of Pitt and Burke, historical changes of the utmost gravity were argued in noble prose by Webster, Clay and Calhoun in the Senate, by Beecher and Emerson in the pulpit, by Douglas and Lincoln on the partisan political platform.

These changes, which became burning issues after the Missouri Compromise of 1820, dealt with political, economic, racial and sexual equality. And the advocated reforms—excepting woman suffrage—were all embodied in the Constitution by 1870. In fifty glorious and tragic years the United States grew up. We ceased to be an eighteenth-century country and became a twentieth-century one. Surely, it had long seemed to me, surely somewhere in this noble history and in its oratory there must be the theme, and perhaps even the words, of a musico-dramatic spectacle that would be a pleasure to compose.

So it came about that in 1945, when Douglas Moore, for the Alice M. Ditson Fund of Columbia University, asked me to write an opera, I turned with this theme to my old friend and former operatic collaborator, Gertrude Stein. She liked it and began at once to read and reread the words of the period. She exhausted the American Library in Paris and the librarian obtained more books for her from the New York Public Library. She asked me if I minded her making feminism the central theme and Susan B. Anthony the heroine. I did not. And so she began to write.

She showed me the first two scenes in October, 1945. In March, 1946, she sent me the whole libretto. It was her last completed work. In May and June we talked about it, agreed on some transpositions in the order of the scenes and on the possibility of certain cuts, these to be left eventually to my discretion. She obtained also the promise of the painter, Maurice Grosser, who had added to our earlier opera, *Four Saints in Three Acts,* a workable scenario for staging, that he would do the same for *The Mother of Us All.* In July she died. I had not yet composed any of the music.

The composing was begun Oct. 12, 1946, and seven of the eight scenes that make up the opera were finished by Dec. 10. Then I played and sang them to my friends—tried them out, so to speak. And in January, 1947, I composed the epilogue, in which Susan B. Anthony, dead and turned to marble, sings as a statue from her pedestal her own (and Gertrude Stein's own) funeral oration. The opera was orchestrated during February and March; and it was produced, beginning May 9, at the Brander Mathews Theatre at Columbia.

Since then it has been given in Cleveland, Denver, New Orleans and other cities, and just last month at Sanders Theatre in Cambridge, Mass. The Phoenix Theatre performances tomorrow and on April 23 will mark its first revival in New York and its first performance anywhere by a wholly professional cast.

The libretto deals with real persons and invented persons, with historical celebrities and with their friends and neighbors. The celebrities speak in the style of their historic utterances, sometimes even in quotations from them. The others speak straight American.

There is little in the libretto that is not directly comprehensible. All the same, its dialogue is far more an expression of the characters themselves than a vehicle for advancing the plot. As in real life, the people of the play, especially when more than two are present, rarely answer one another or even listen. They tend rather to say what is urgently on their own minds.

In Shakespeare and Shaw the characters talk mostly about what they have done or are going to do, defending their past and future actions with argument, poetry and wit. In Gertrude Stein's plays they rarely defend their actions. They merely give you their own emotional and character background. The language of Stein's later plays is the essence of American English, but their story-line is that of Corneille and Racine and the court ballets of Molière. They are French classical theatre in the American dialect.

The music of *The Mother of Us All* is an evocation of nineteenth-century America, with its gospel hymns and cocky marches, its sentimental ballads, waltzes, darn-fool ditties and intoned sermons. Only in descriptions of weather, which has no period, does it engage the dissonant elements. Like the libretto, which deals with the attitudes and speeches, the playgames and the passions of our Victorian forebears, it is a memory book. It is a souvenir of all those sounds and kinds of tunes that were once the music of rural America and that are still the basic idiom of our country because they are the oldest vernacular still remembered here and used.

Virgil Thomson: Three Letters

To a Correspondent March 21, 1947

I am not too happy at seeing my score called whimsical. Also, I think the idea that Miss Stein and I are primarily wits is, if you will permit me, both antiquated and inaccurate. I should appreciate it if you could refer to *The Mother of Us All*—both the words and the music—as a serious work on a serious theme. That theme is not "the war between the sexes" but woman suffrage. There is comedy in it, of course; but referring to it as witty, whimsical, and charming does not give a resembling picture of it any more than those same adjectives would of *Hamlet.* I am sorry to be so critical, because I know you have spent a great deal of thought on the paragraph which you sent me. But since you have asked for my cooperation, I should be most grateful, and so would Miss Stein if she were living, for some word that would not place us quite so definitely with the amusers.

Always cordially yours,

To Nadine Miles December 22, 1948

Dear Miss Miles:

Mr. Shepherd tells me that you are in charge of the production of my opera *The Mother of Us All,* and I am delighted to hear it. If I can be of any help to you, please do not hesitate to write me about anything that bothers you. You are certain to run into a nasty set change just before the final scene of the opera. The music at this point is not long enough, and a silent wait is not desirable dramatically. I should like to write a rather noisy intermezzo to cover this change. Will two minutes be enough, or do you need three? I shall try to make it adjustable, so that cuts or repetitions can be operated to make it fit your stagehands' timing.

Mr. Shepherd asked me to tell you about a production idea which we were not able to put into execution at Columbia University but which I have always hoped could be realized. That is to make the opera visually a sort of evocation of a 19th-century photograph album. A permanent frame for the stage would be helpful in this regard, and so would a special curtain designed somewhat like the cover of such an album. Since 19th-century photographs were often hand-colored, one would not need to limit the sets and costumes to gray or sepia tints. Grays and warm browns could give the chief tone to the color composition of the stage but a whole range of pinks, red, purples, and other bright colors could be added in the costumes. In this way a variety of color could be achieved while keeping the spectacle at all times in harmony. The stage movement could be regulated, with or without aid of a choreographer, to suggest photographic poses. I do not mean a series of motionless tableaux vivants, though certain moments might be impressive if held a little. I see the whole rather as a series of such motionless tableaux but with the singers moving constantly from one to another. Each character could move in a different and characteristic way, since each speaks and sings in a different way and since the costumes are also intended to accentuate contrasts of character and decade. All these contrasts risk turning the opera into a costume party unless there is some deliberate overall stylization. It has long seemed to me that the photograph album idea could solve this problem effectively and that the addition of regulated movement would help. Any movement or histrionic effort of a naturalistic character would, of course, interfere.

Do not hesitate to add dancers to any of the scenes where these may seem appropriate to you. Real dancing can only heighten the effect of the movements executed by the singers. . . .

The V.I.P. scene can be pointed up perhaps by vaudeville routines of a pseudo-military character. In general, heightening the spectacle by choreographic means seems to me thoroughly desirable. I have even thought of adding a ballet to the opera but I don't know exactly where I could put it.

Most sincerely yours,

To Arthur Shepherd January 12, 1949

Dear Mr. Shepherd:

The idea of using a subject from 19th-century American political history was mine; also that of using direct quotation from the oratory of the period. The selection of the characters and their arrangement into a play I left to Miss Stein. She transformed my proposal about the oratory of the period into a method whereby Susan B. Anthony, Daniel Webster, and others speak as they really spoke.

I suggested my ideas to her in the fall of 1945 in Paris, and she wrote the first two scenes immediately. The libretto was finished during the course of the winter and sent to me in the early spring of '46, I being then in New York. In the late spring we discussed it in Paris. She died in July of that year before I had begun the actual composition, which was done during the early and middle part of the following winter.

The Mother of Us All was Miss Stein's last completed work. It represents an attempt to revivify history, to show historical movements and personalities as these appeared to those personalities themselves and to others living at the time. That time, of course, was not a specific moment but a whole epoch in the life of our country, the last epoch about which any of us can have, through his own memories or through those of persons he has known in his lifetime, a feeling of having been there.

Always faithfully yours,

Virgil Thomson: from
Virgil Thomson by Virgil Thomson

I began *The Mother of Us All* on October 10 of 1946. On December 10 the voice-and-piano score was complete up to the last scene. I waited a month before composing that, feeling that I must back off and view the rest. In order to find out what the rest was like, I invited friends to hear me play and sing it. Through performing it for others, as I had done for seven years with *Four Saints,* I could find out how it moved and learn its ways. In January, I composed the final scene; by this time a partial cast was learning roles, with Jack Beeson as *répétiteur.* Otto Luening, who was to conduct, had as yet no orchestral score; but that was not urgent, since we were not opening till May.

The production was for Columbia University's Brander

Matthews Theatre, where the house was small but the pit commodious. The cast was part professionals and part students; no one was paid for working in the show. The scenery and costumes were by Paul du Pont; staging was by the choreographer John Taras to a scenario, as before, by Maurice Grosser. I cast all the roles myself, holding auditions in my Hotel Chelsea drawing room. For minor parts we used Columbia students and trained them for understudying the leads. Among the finer singers who took part were Dorothy Dow (later of La Scala) and Teresa Stich-Randall (Mozart specialist and *Kammersängerin,* who now sings everywhere). The names of Belva Kibler, Hazel Gravell, Jean Handzlik, and Alice Howland are remembered by many in the music world, those too of William Horne and Everett Anderson. The stage was beautiful for sight and sound, though not to be compared to my Negroes-and-cellophane *Four Saints.*

The student orchestral players were pretty poor; and Luening, an experienced opera man, was patient, to prevent nervousness on stage. The instrumental textures, therefore, which I had laid out with transparency in mind, were likely to come out on any night with holes in them. Nevertheless, after the fourth or fifth performance, when I felt the players knew their parts as well as they ever would, I asked Luening to speed up the pacing. "Can you take twenty minutes off the running time?" I said. "Can do," he answered. And with no cuts made, the next performance came out shorter by that much.

Everybody up-to-date came to hear the new opera, and the press was receptive. The Music Critics' Circle, though reluctant to honor a member, even voted it a special award. Koussevitzky, still angry over criticisms, said to his neighbor (textually), "I do not like it to say it, but I like it." And wrote me to offer a commission for another opera. My colleague Samuel Barber, perhaps also smarting, remarked of my plain-as-Dick's-hatband harmony, "I hope you won't mind my stealing a few of your chords."

From its beginning, *The Mother of Us All* has often been produced by colleges, though it was never designed for amateurs and is difficult for young voices. I have not seen all these productions by any means; but in all that I have seen some charm has come through, for there is in both text and music a nostalgia for nineteenth-century rural America which makes any presentation warm and touching. Western Reserve gave it in Cleveland at elegant Severance Hall; and the orchestra, Cleveland's Philharmonia, was first class. Harvard performances in the Civil War memorial Sanders Theater, with only students singing (and not vocal students either), were so perfectly paced by their conductor, Victor Yellin, then a graduate student, that audiences laughed and applauded, wept at the end. Even at the University of Denver, with everything else precarious, an ingenious stage direction gave the spectacle security, enough at least for Stravinsky to comprehend. But it was not till eighteen years after its birth that it got interesting scenery. Then in 1965, at the University of California; Los Angeles, with Jan Popper conducting, an impressive young soprano, Barbara Gordon (my discovery), singing the role of Susan B., and with myself having coached everybody, including the choreographer, a visual investiture was created by David Hilberman which was as original, evocative, and appropriate as what Florine Stettheimer had created in 1934 for *Four Saints.*

The originality of this scenery lay in its representing neither buildings nor landscapes, but, of all things, people. It consisted of a set of giant cutouts painted to illustrate nineteenth-century ladies and gentlemen, for all the world like colored prints from some Victorian magazine. And all these flats could be moved horizontally to closed-in or to open stage-positions. They were dark blue in color, a tone rarely effective in painted scenery but one which, when lightly rubbed with red, can take light in glowing vibrant ways. And to the profiled figures slight additions of flowering branches, brief cases, flags, gave to outdoor scenes, to a departure, to a political meeting complete evocation. Moreover, the gigantic proportions of these pictured people reduced our singing actors to human size, a desideratum in not overlarge Schoenberg Hall, where any smaller scaling of the scenery tends to make giants of the actors and to trivialize them. The *Mother* sets were, in addition, airy. For all their largeness and somber color, they did not weigh on the spirit or box-in the play, but gave it space and lightness, as if great distances lay all about and the stage were just the segment of a continent.

TENNESSEE WILLIAMS

The Glass Menagerie

Nobody, not even the rain, has such small hands.

—e. e. cummings

Tennessee Williams (1914–83) was born Thomas Lanier Williams in Columbus, Mississippi. During his childhood his family moved to St. Louis, where his father had accepted a job as manager of a shoe company. Williams has written that neither he nor his sister Rose could adjust to the change from the South to the Midwest, but the children had already been deeply troubled. Nevertheless, at the age of sixteen he achieved some distinction as a writer when his prize-winning essay in a nationwide contest was published. After high school he attended the University of Missouri but flunked ROTC and was therefore withdrawn from school by his father. He worked in a shoe factory for a while, then attended Washington University, where he wrote several plays. He finally graduated from the University of Iowa with a major in playwrighting. After graduation he continued to write, supporting himself with odd jobs such as waiting on tables and running elevators. His first commercial success was *The Glass Menagerie* (produced in Chicago in 1944, and in New York in 1945); among his other plays are *A Streetcar Named Desire* (1947), *Cat on a Hot Tin Roof* (1955), and *Suddenly Last Summer* (1958).

COMMENTARY

Broadly speaking, drama has been divided into two sorts, *conventional* (also called presentational, stylized, or symbolic) and, on the other hand, *realistic* (or naturalistic). Conventional drama, such as the ancient Greek plays of Sophocles or the Elizabethan plays of Shakespeare, makes little pretense of offering an accurate transcription of the surface reality. For instance, in real life we all speak prose, but in Sophocles's *Oedipus the King* it is conventional for the characters to speak verse; a man living in a remote region is summoned and appears on stage a few minutes later; moments after blinding himself, Oedipus enters, not writhing in pain but speaking eloquently. Similarly, in Shakespeare's plays, which were staged during the daytime in an unroofed theater, if a character enters carrying a torch the audience understands, by means of this convention, that the scene—acted in full light—is taking place at night. (A *convention* is literally a "coming together"; the audience and the theatrical personnel come together—reach an understanding—and pretend that what is shown onstage is real.)

Most drama before the middle of the nineteenth century was highly conventional, partly because it had to be. The vast size of a Greek theater required the actors to gesticulate broadly and to speak loudly, even if they were supposed to be whispering inconspicuously. Similarly, before the development of advanced techniques of lighting,

This is a scene from the opening production of *The Glass Menagerie* at The Playhouse in New York on March 31, 1945, starring Lorette Taylor, Julie Hayden, Eddie Dowling, and Anthony Ross. (Reproduced by courtesy of the New York Public Library, The Billy Rose Theater Collection.)

night scenes necessarily were played in the daylight, or, if played in roofed theaters that used artificial illumination, they were played with only a suggestion of darkness. If a character looked upward and spoke of the moon, the audience agreed to pretend that the moon was visible. But around the middle of the nineteenth century, new techniques of lighting allowed for relatively realistic effects of, say, the breaking of dawn, or the gradual coming of night. Moreover, the temper of the times (largely dominated by a scientific spirit—which, for instance, invented the art of photography) favored an art that seemed close to the surface of life. The announced aim of art, or at least of some artists, was to give "a slice of life."

In fact, of course, even the most realistic play is in some ways conventional. For two and a half hours the characters do not digress, and they never seem to have to go to the bathroom. The audience looks at "real" furniture displayed in what seems to be a "real" room, but in fact most of the furniture faces the footlights, and the room is missing a wall (see, for instance, the illustration of the set for *A Doll's House* on page 270) so that the audience may see what goes on in it. At the end of the act the curtain drops, and the audience, knowing that there will be an intermission of fifteen minutes, troops out into the lobby. When the audience returns, it understands from the dialogue (and maybe the program note) that the time is now the next day, or the next week. We are scarcely aware of these conventions because, having grown up with them, we have assimilated them, just as we hardly think it is odd that a photograph in a newspaper is black and white, when in real life the images are colored. Similarly, in film and on television—media that are largely realistic—we are not surprised when we get a close-up of a head, even though such a shot is a convention, since in real life we don't suddenly see heads without bodies.

Although the conventions of realism dominated the serious theater in the later nineteenth century, the very end of the century and the first third of the twentieth century saw a vigorous rebellion against them. Just as the realism of the nineteenth century owed much to a new spirit of scientific thinking (especially to studies of the influence of the environment on the individual), so this new movement owed much to a new science, psychology. Some plays now sought to give not the external reality or surface appearance of life but the inner reality, life as *felt* rather than as seen. Thus, instead of the setting closely imitating a room as the scientific eye sees it, the walls might veer crazily, to represent (or symbolize) the way the main character perceives his or her irrational or oppressive world. (For a bit more on this, see the entry on *expressionism* in the Glossary.)

Tennessee Williams's *The Glass Menagerie* is largely in this expressionistic tradition. Its link to psychology—to feeling rather than seeing—is suggested in the first sentence of the Production Notes, where Williams calls it a "memory play." Notice too that in the Production Notes he says that the play "can be presented with unusual freedom of convention." He does not mean that the play is free from conventions; rather, he means that the conventions are not the old established ones but are relatively fresh ones, invented for the moment. Similarly, when he speaks of expressionist plays as being "unconventional," he does not mean that they do not employ conventions. Rather, he means that they are untraditional, relatively novel, employing new conventions. "Expressionism," he says,

> and all other unconventional techniques in drama have only one valid aim, and that is a closer approach to truth. When a play employs unconventional techniques, it is not, or certainly shouldn't be, trying to escape its responsibility of dealing with reality, or interpreting experience, but is actually or should be attempting to find a closer approach, a more penetrating and vivid expression of things as they are.

In fact, when *The Glass Menagerie* was staged in New York, the conspicuously unrealistic convention of projecting words on a screen was not used, but the New York production nevertheless was essentially unrealistic, following, for instance, his comment that "The lighting in the play is not realistic. . . . Shafts of light are focused on selected areas or actors . . . The light upon Laura should be distinct from the others, having a peculiar pristine clarity such as light used in early religious portraits of female saints or madonnas." Jo Mielziner, who did the sets for this play and for many of Williams's other plays, makes a helpful comment in *Designing for the Theatre:*

> If he had written plays in the days before the technical development of translucent and transparent scenery, I believe he would have invented it. . . . My use of translucent and transparent scenic interior walls was not just another trick. It was a true reflection of the contemporary playwright's interest in—and at times obsession with—the exploration of the inner man. Williams was writing not only a memory play but a play of influences that were not confined within the walls of a room.

TENNESSEE WILLIAMS *The Glass Menagerie*

List of Characters

AMANDA WINGFIELD, *the mother. A little woman of great but confused vitality clinging frantically to another time and place. Her characterization must be carefully created, not copied from type. She is not paranoiac, but her life is paranoia. There is much to admire in Amanda, and as much to love and pity as there is to laugh at. Certainly she has endurance and a kind of heroism, and though her foolishness makes her unwittingly cruel at times, there is tenderness in her slight person.*

LAURA WINGFIELD, *her daughter. Amanda, having failed to establish contact with reality, continues to live vitally in her illusions, but Laura's situation is even graver. A childhood illness has left her crippled, one leg slightly shorter than the other, and held in a brace. This defect need not be more than suggested on the stage. Stemming from this, Laura's separation increases till she is like a piece of her own glass collection, too exquisitely fragile to move from the shelf.*

TOM WINGFIELD, *her son. And the narrator of the play. A poet with a job in a warehouse. His nature is not remorseless, but to escape from a trap he has to act without pity.*

JIM O'CONNOR, *the gentleman caller. A nice, ordinary, young man.*

Scene: An alley in St. Louis.

Part 1: Preparation for a Gentleman Caller.
Part 2: The Gentleman Calls.

Time: Now and the Past.

SCENE 1

The Wingfield apartment is in the rear of the building, one of those vast hive-like conglomerations of cellular living-units that flower as warty growths in overcrowded urban centers of lower middle-class population and are symptomatic of the impulse of this largest and fundamentally enslaved section of American society to avoid fluidity and differentiation and to exist and function as one interfused mass of automatism.

The apartment faces an alley and is entered by a fire-escape, a structure whose name is a touch of accidental poetic truth, for all of these huge buildings are always burning with the slow and implacable fires of human desperation. The fire escape is included in the set—that is, the landing of it and steps descending from it.

The scene is memory and is therefore non-realistic. Memory takes a lot of poetic license. It omits some details; others are exaggerated, according to the emotional value of the articles it touches, for memory is seated predominantly in the heart. The interior is therefore rather dim and poetic.

At the rise of the curtain, the audience is faced with the dark, grim rear wall of the Wingfield tenement. This building, which runs parallel to the footlights, is flanked on both sides by dark, narrow alleys which run into murky canyons of tangled clotheslines, garbage cans and the sinister latticework of neighboring fire-escapes. It is up and down these side alleys that exterior entrances and exits are made, during the play. At the end of Tom's opening commentary, the dark tenement wall slowly reveals (by means of a transparency) the interior of the ground floor Wingfield apartment.

Downstage is the living room, which also serves as a sleeping room for Laura, the sofa unfolding to make her bed. Upstage, center, and divided by a wide arch or second proscenium with transparent faded portieres (or second curtain), is the dining room. In an old-fashioned what-not in the living room are seen scores of transparent glass animals. A blown-up photograph of the father hangs on the wall of the living room, facing the audience, to the left of the archway. It is the face of a very handsome young man in a doughboy's First World War cap. He is gallantly smiling, ineluctably smiling, as if to say, "I will be smiling forever."

The audience hears and sees the opening scene in the dining room through both the transparent fourth wall of the building and the transparent gauze portieres of the dining-room arch. It is during this revealing scene that the fourth wall slowly ascends, out of sight.

This transparent exterior wall is not brought down again until the very end of the play, during Tom's final speech.

The narrator is an undisguised convention of the play. He takes whatever license with dramatic convention as is convenient to his purposes.

Tom enters dressed as a merchant sailor from alley, stage left, and strolls across the front of the stage to the fire-escape. There he stops and lights a cigarette. He addresses the audience.

TOM. Yes, I have tricks in my pocket, I have things up my sleeve. But I am the opposite of a stage magician. He gives you illusion that has the appearance of truth. I give you truth in the pleasant disguise of illusion. To begin with, I turn back time. I reverse it to that quaint period, the thirties, when the huge middle class of America was matriculating in a school for the blind. Their eyes had failed them, or they had failed their eyes, and so they were having their fingers pressed forcibly down on the fiery Braille alphabet of a dissolving economy. In Spain there was revolution. Here there was only shouting and confusion. In Spain there was Guernica. Here there were disturbances of labor, sometimes pretty violent, in otherwise peaceful cities such as Chicago, Cleveland, Saint Louis. . . . This is the social background of the play.

(**Music.**)

The play is memory. Being a memory play, it is dimly lighted, it is sentimental, it is not realistic. In memory everything seems to happen to music. That explains the fiddle in the wings. I am the narrator of the play, and also a character in it. The other characters are my mother, Amanda, my sister, Laura, and a gentleman caller who appears in the final scenes. He is the most realistic character in the play, being an emissary from a world of reality that we were somehow set apart from. But since I have a poet's weakness for symbols, I am using this character also as a symbol; he is the long delayed but always expected something that we live for. There is a fifth character in the play who doesn't appear except in this larger-than-life photograph over the mantel. This is our father who left us a long time ago. He was a telephone man who fell in love with long distances; he gave up his job with the telephone company and skipped the light fantastic out of town. . . . The last we heard of him was a picture post-card from Mazatlan, on the Pacific coast of Mexico, containing a message of two words—"Hello—Good-bye!" and no address. I think the rest of the play will explain itself. . . .

Amanda's voice becomes audible through the portieres.

(**Legend on Screen: "Où Sont Les Neiges."**)

He divides the portieres and enters the upstage area. Amanda and Laura are seated at a drop-leaf table. Eating is indicated by gestures without food or utensils. Amanda faces the audience. Tom and Laura are seated in profile. The interior has lit up softly and through the scrim we see Amanda and Laura seated at the table in the upstage area.

AMANDA (*calling*). Tom?

TOM. Yes, Mother.

AMANDA. We can't say grace until you come to the table!

TOM. Coming, Mother. (*He bows slightly and withdraws, reappearing a few moments later in his place at the table.*)

AMANDA (*to her son*). Honey, don't *push* with your *fingers.* If you have to push with something, the thing to push with is a crust of bread. And chew—chew! Animals have sections in their stomachs which enable them to digest food without mastication, but human beings are supposed to chew their food before they swallow it down. Eat food leisurely, son, and really enjoy it. A well-cooked meal has lots of delicate flavors that have to be held in the mouth for appreciation. So chew your food and give your salivary glands a chance to function!

(*Tom deliberately lays his imaginary fork down and pushes his chair back from the table.*)

TOM. I haven't enjoyed one bite of this dinner because of your constant directions on how to eat it. It's you that makes me rush through meals with your hawk-like attention to every bite I take. Sickening—spoils my appetite—all this discussion of animals' secretion—salivary glands—mastication!

AMANDA (*lightly*). Temperament like a Metropolitan star! (*He rises and crosses downstage.*) You're not excused from the table.

TOM. I am getting a cigarette.

AMANDA. You smoke too much.

(*Laura rises.*)

LAURA. I'll bring in the blanc mange.

(*He remains standing with his cigarette by the portieres during the following.*)

AMANDA (*rising*). No, sister, no, sister—you be the lady this time and I'll be the darky.

LAURA. I'm already up.

AMANDA. Resume your seat, little sister—I want you to stay fresh and pretty—for gentlemen callers!

LAURA. I'm not expecting any gentlemen callers.

AMANDA (*crossing out to kitchenette. Airily*). Sometimes they come when they are least expected! Why, I remember one Sunday afternoon in Blue Mountain—(*Enters kitchenette.*)

TOM. I know what's coming!

LAURA. Yes. But let her tell it.

TOM. Again?

LAURA. She loves to tell it.

(*Amanda returns with bowl of dessert.*)

AMANDA. One Sunday afternoon in Blue Mountain—your mother received—*seventeen!*—gentlemen callers! Why, sometimes there weren't chairs enough to accommodate them all. We had to send the nigger over to bring in folding chairs from the parish house.

TOM (*remaining at portieres*). How did you entertain those gentlemen callers?

AMANDA. I understood the art of conversation!

TOM. I bet you could talk.

AMANDA. Girls in those days *knew* how to talk, I can tell you.

TOM. Yes?

(**Image: Amanda as a Girl on a Porch Greeting Callers.**)

AMANDA. They knew how to entertain their gentlemen callers. It wasn't enough for a girl to be possessed of a pretty face and a graceful figure—although I wasn't slighted in either respect. She also needed to have a nimble wit and a tongue to meet all occasions.

TOM. What did you talk about?

AMANDA. Things of importance going on in the world! Never anything coarse or common or vulgar. (*She addresses Tom as though he were seated in the vacant chair at the table though he remains by portieres. He plays this scene as though he held the book.*) My callers were gentlemen—all! Among my callers were some of the most prominent young planters of the Mississippi Delta—planters and sons of planters!

(*Tom motions for music and a spot of light on Amanda. Her eyes lift, her face glows, her voice becomes rich and elegiac.*)

(**Screen Legend: "Où Sont Les Neiges."**)

There was young Champ Laughlin who later became vice-president of the Delta Planters Bank. Hadley Stevenson who was drowned in Moon Lake and left his widow one hundred and fifty thousand in Government bonds. There were the Cutrere brothers, Wesley and Bates. Bates was one of my bright particular beaux! He got in a quarrel with that wild Wainright boy. They shot it out on the floor of Moon Lake Casino. Bates was shot through the stomach. Died in the ambulance on his way to Memphis. His widow was also well provided for, came into eight or ten thousand acres, that's all. She married him on the rebound—never loved her—carried my picture on him the night he died! And there was that boy that every girl in the Delta had set her cap for! That beautiful, brilliant young Fitzhugh boy from Green County!

TOM. What did he leave his widow?

AMANDA. He never married! Gracious, you talk as though all of my old admirers had turned up their toes to the daisies!

TOM. Isn't this the first you mentioned that still survives?

AMANDA. That Fitzhugh boy went North and made a fortune—came to be known as the Wolf of Wall Street! He had the Midas touch, whatever he touched turned to gold! And I could have been Mrs. Duncan J. Fitzhugh, mind you! But—I picked your *father!*

LAURA (*rising*). Mother, let me clear the table.

AMANDA. No dear, you go in front and study your typewriter chart. Or practice your shorthand a little. Stay fresh and pretty!—It's almost time for our gentlemen callers to start arriving. (*She flounces girlishly toward the kitchenette.*) How many do you suppose we're going to entertain this afternoon?

(*Tom throws down the paper and jumps up with a groan.*)

LAURA (*alone in the dining room*). I don't believe we're going to receive any, Mother.

AMANDA (*reappearing, airily*). What? No one—not one? You must be joking! (*Laura nervously echoes her laugh. She slips in a fugitive manner through the half-open portieres and draws them gently behind her. A shaft of very clear light is thrown on her face against the faded tapestry of the curtains.*) (**Music: "The Glass Menagerie" Under Faintly.**) (*Lightly*) Not one gentleman caller? It can't be true! There must be a flood, there must have been a tornado!

LAURA. It isn't a flood, it's not a tornado, Mother. I'm just not popular like you were in Blue Mountain. . . . (*Tom utters another groan. Laura glances at him with a faint, apologetic smile. Her voice catching a little*) Mother's afraid I'm going to be an old maid.

(**The Scene Dims Out with "Glass Menagerie" Music.**)

SCENE 2

"Laura, Haven't You Ever Liked Some Boy"

On the dark stage the screen is lighted with the image of blue roses. Gradually Laura's figure becomes apparent and the screen goes out. The music subsides. Laura is seated in the delicate ivory chair at the small clawfoot table. She wears a dress of soft violet material for a kimono—her hair tied back from her forehead with a ribbon. She is washing and polishing her collection of glass.

Amanda appears on the fire-escape steps. At the sound of her ascent, Laura catches her breath, thrusts the bowl of ornaments away and seats herself stiffly before the diagram of the typewriter keyboard as though it held her spellbound. Something has happened to Amanda. It is written in her face as she climbs to the landing: a look that is grim and hopeless and a little absurd.

She has on one of those cheap or imitation velvety-looking cloth coats with imitation fur collar. Her hat is five or six years old, one of those dreadful cloche hats that were worn in the late twenties, and she is clasping an enormous black patent-leather pocketbook with nickel clasp and initials. This is her full-dress outfit, the one she usually wears to the D.A.R.

Before entering she looks through the door. She purses her lips, opens her eyes wide, rolls them upward and shakes her head. Then she slowly lets herself in the door. Seeing her mother's expression Laura touches her lips with a nervous gesture.

LAURA. Hello, Mother, I was—(*She makes a nervous gesture toward the chart on the wall. Amanda leans against the shut door and stares at Laura with a martyred look.*)

AMANDA. Deception? Deception? (*She slowly removes her hat and gloves, continuing the swift suffering stare. She lets the hat and gloves fall on the floor—a bit of acting.*)

LAURA (*shakily*). How was the D.A.R. meeting? (*Amanda slowly opens her purse and removes a dainty white handkerchief which she shakes out delicately and delicately touches to her lips and nostrils.*) Didn't you go to the D.A.R. meeting, Mother?

AMANDA (*faintly, almost inaudibly*).—No.—No. (*Then more forcibly*) I did not have the strength—to go to the D.A.R. In fact, I did not have the courage! I waited to find a hole in the ground and hide myself in it forever! (*She crosses slowly to the wall and removes the diagram of the typewriter keyboard. She holds it in front of her for a second, staring at it sweetly and sorrowfully—then bites her lips and tears it in two pieces.*)

LAURA (*faintly*). Why did you do that, Mother? (*Amanda repeats the same procedure with the chart of the Gregg Alphabet.*) Why are you—

AMANDA. Why? Why? How old are you, Laura?

LAURA. Mother, you know my age.

AMANDA. I thought that you were an adult; it seems that I was mistaken. (*She crosses slowly to the sofa and sinks down and stares at Laura.*)

LAURA. Please don't stare at me, Mother.

(*Amanda closes her eyes and lowers her head. Count ten.*)

AMANDA. What are we going to do, what is going to become of us, what is the future?

(*Count ten.*)

LAURA. Has something happened, Mother? (*Amanda draws a long breath and takes out the handkerchief again. Dabbing process.*) Mother, has—something happened?

AMANDA. I'll be all right in a minute. I'm just bewildered—(*count five*)—by life. . . .

LAURA. Mother, I wish that you would tell me what's happened.

AMANDA. As you know, I was supposed to be inducted into my office at the D.A.R. this afternoon. (**Image: A Swarm of Typewriters.**) But I stopped off at Rubicam's Business College to speak to your teachers about your having a cold and ask them what progress they thought you were making down there.

LAURA. Oh. . . .

AMANDA. I went to the typing instructor and introduced myself as your mother. She didn't know who you were. Wingfield, she said. We don't have any such student enrolled at the school! I assured her she did, that you had been going to classes since early in January. "I wonder," she said, "if you could be talking about that terribly shy little girl who dropped out of school after only a few days' attendance?" "No," I said, "Laura, my daughter, has been going to school every day for the past six weeks!" "Excuse me," she said. She took the attendance book out and there was your name, unmistakably printed, and all the dates you were absent until they decided that you had dropped out of school. I still said, "No, there must have been some mistake! There must have been some mix-up in the records!" And she said, "No—I remember her perfectly now. Her hand shook so that she couldn't hit the right keys! The first time we gave a speed-test, she broke down completely—was sick at the stomach and almost had to be carried into the wash-room! After that morning she never showed up any more. We phoned the house but never got any answer"—while I was working at Famous and Barr, I suppose, demonstrating those—Oh! I felt so weak I could barely keep on my feet. I had to sit down while they got me a glass of water! Fifty dollars' tuition, all of our plans—my hopes and ambitions for you—just gone up the spout, just gone up the spout like that. (*Laura draws a long breath and gets awkwardly to her feet. She crosses to the victrola and winds it up.*) What are you doing?

LAURA. Oh! (*She releases the handle and returns to her seat.*)

AMANDA. Laura, where have you been going when you've gone out pretending that you were going to business college?

LAURA. I've just been going out walking.

AMANDA. That's not true.

LAURA. It is. I just went walking.

AMANDA. Walking? Walking? In winter? Deliberately courting pneumonia in that light coat? Where did you walk to, Laura?

LAURA. It was the lesser of two evils, Mother. (**Image: Winter Scene in Park.**) I couldn't go back up. I—threw up—on the floor!

AMANDA. From half past seven till after five thirty every day you mean to tell me you walked around in the park, because you wanted to make me think that you were still going to Rubicam's Business College?

LAURA. It wasn't as bad as it sounds. I went inside places to get warmed up.

AMANDA. Inside where?

LAURA. I went in the art museum and the birdhouses at the Zoo. I visited the penguins every day! Sometimes I did without lunch and went to the movies. Lately I've been spending most of my afternoons in the Jewel-box, that big glass house where they raise the tropical flowers.

AMANDA. You did all this to deceive me, just for the deception? (*Laura looks down.*) Why?

LAURA. Mother, when you're disappointed, you get that awful suffering look on your face, like the picture of Jesus' mother in the museum!

AMANDA. Hush!

LAURA. I couldn't face it.

(*Pause. A whisper of strings.*)

(**Legend: "The Crust of Humility."**)

AMANDA (*hopelessly fingering the huge pocketbook*). So what are we going to do the rest of our lives? Stay home and watch the parades go by? Amuse ourselves with the glass menagerie, darling? Eternally play those worn-out phonograph records your father left as a painful reminder of him? We won't have a business career—we've given that up because it gave us nervous indigestion! (*Laughs wearily.*) What is there left but dependency all our lives? I know so well what becomes of unmarried women who aren't prepared to occupy a position. I've seen such pitiful cases in the South—barely tolerated spinsters living upon the grudging patronage of sister's husband or brother's wife!—stuck away in some little mousetrap of a room—encouraged by one in-law to visit another—little birdlike women without any nest—eating the crust of humility all their life! Is that the future that we've mapped out for ourselves? I swear it's the only alternative I can think of! It isn't a very pleasant alternative, is it? Of course—some girls *do marry.* (*Laura twists her hands nervously.*) Haven't you ever liked some boy?

LAURA. Yes. I liked one once. (*Rises.*) I came across his picture a while ago.

AMANDA (*with some interest*). He gave you his picture?

LAURA. No, it's in the year-book.

AMANDA (*disappointed*). Oh—a high-school boy.

(**Screen Image: Jim as a High-School Hero Bearing a Silver Cup.**)

LAURA. Yes. His name was Jim. (*Laura lifts the heavy annual from the clawfoot table.*) Here he is in *The Pirates of Penzance.*

AMANDA (*absently*). The what?

LAURA. The operetta the senior class put on. He had a wonderful voice and we sat across the aisle from each other Mondays, Wednesdays and Fridays in the Aud. Here he is with the silver cup for debating! See his grin?

AMANDA (*absently*). He must have had a jolly disposition.

LAURA. He used to call me—Blue Roses.

(**Image: Blue Roses.**)

AMANDA. Why did he call you such a name as that?

LAURA. When I had that attack of pleurosis—he asked me what was the matter when I came back. I said pleurosis—he thought that I said Blue Roses! So that's what he always called me after that. Whenever he saw me, he'd holler, "Hello, Blue Roses!" I didn't care for the girl that he went out with. Emily Meisenbach. Emily was the best-dressed girl at Soldan. She never struck me, though, as being sincere.... It says in the Personal Section—they're engaged. That's—six years ago! They must be married by now.

AMANDA. Girls that aren't cut out for business careers usually wind up married to some nice man. (*Gets up with a spark of revival.*) Sister, that's what you'll do!

(*Laura utters a startled, doubtful laugh. She reaches quickly for a piece of glass.*)

LAURA. But, Mother—

AMANDA. Yes? (*Crossing to photograph.*)

LAURA (*in a tone of frightened apology*). I'm—crippled!

(**Image: Screen.**)

AMANDA. Nonsense! Laura, I've told you never, never to use that word. Why, you're not crippled, you just have a little defect—hardly noticeable, even! When people have some slight disadvantage like that, they cultivate other things to make up for it—develop charm—and vivacity—and—*charm!* That's all you have to do! (*She turns again to the photograph.*) One thing your father had *plenty of*—was *charm!*

(*Tom motions to the fiddle in the wings.*)

(**The Scene Fades Out with Music.**)

SCENE 3

(**Legend on the Screen: "After the Fiasco—"**)

Tom speaks from the fire-escape landing.

TOM. After the fiasco at Rubicam's Business College, the idea of getting a gentleman caller for Laura began to play a more important part in Mother's calculations. It became an obsession. Like some archetype of the universal unconscious, the image of the gentleman caller haunted our small apartment.... (**Image: Young Man at Door with Flowers.**) An evening at home rarely passed without some allusion to this image, this specter, this hope.... Even when he wasn't mentioned, his presence hung in Mother's preoccupied look and in my sister's frightened, apologetic manner—hung like a sentence passed upon the Wingfields! Mother was a woman of action as well as words. She began to take logical steps in the planned direction. Late that winter and in the early spring—realizing that extra money would be needed to properly feather the nest and plume the bird—she conducted a vigorous campaign on the telephone, roping in subscribers to one of those magazines for matrons called The *Home-maker's Companion,* the type of journal that features the serialized sublimations of ladies of letters who think in terms of delicate cup-like breasts, slim, tapering waists, rich, creamy thighs, eyes like wood-smoke in autumn, fingers that soothe and caress like strains of music, bodies as powerful as Etruscan sculpture.

(**Screen Image: Glamor Magazine Cover.**)

(*Amanda enters with phone on long extension cord. She is spotted in the dim stage.*)

AMANDA. Ida Scott? This is Amanda Wingfield! We *missed* you at the D.A.R. last Monday! I said to myself: She's probably suffering with that sinus condition! How is that sinus condition? Horrors! Heaven have mercy!—You're a Christian martyr, yes, that's what you are, a Christian martyr! Well, I just now happened to notice that your subscription to the *Companion*'s about to expire! Yes, it expires with the next issue, honey!—just when that wonderful new serial by Bessie Mae Hopper is getting off to such an exciting start. Oh, honey, it's something that you can't miss! You remember how *Gone With the Wind* took everybody by storm? You simply couldn't go out if you hadn't read it. All everybody *talked* was Scarlett O'Hara. Well, this is a book that critics already compare to *Gone With the Wind.* It's the *Gone With the Wind* of the post-World War generation!—What?—Burning? Oh, honey, don't let them burn, go take a look in the oven and I'll hold the wire! Heavens—I think she's hung up!

(**Dim Out.**)

(**Legend on Screen: "You Think I'm in Love with Continental Shoemakers?"**)

(*Before the stage is lighted, the violent voices of Tom and Amanda are heard. They are quarreling behind the portieres. In front of them stands Laura with clenched hands and panicky expression. A clear pool of light on her figure throughout this scene.*)

TOM. What in Christ's name am I—

AMANDA (*shrilly*). Don't you use that—

TOM. Supposed to do!

AMANDA. Expression! Not in my—

TOM. Ohhh!

AMANDA. Presence! Have you gone out of your senses?

TOM. I have, that's true, *driven* out!

AMANDA. What is the matter with you, you—big—big—IDIOT!

TOM. Look—I've got *no thing,* no single thing—

AMANDA. Lower your voice!

TOM. In my life here that I can call my OWN! Everything is—

AMANDA. Stop that shouting!

TOM. Yesterday you confiscated my books! You had the nerve to—

AMANDA. I took that horrible novel back to the library —yes! That hideous book by that insane Mr. Lawrence. (*Tom laughs wildly.*) I cannot control the output of diseased minds or people who cater to them—(*Tom laughs still more wildly.*) BUT I WON'T ALLOW SUCH FILTH BROUGHT INTO MY HOUSE! No, no, no, no, no!

TOM. House, house! Who pays rent on it, who makes a slave of himself to—

AMANDA (*fairly screeching*). Don't you DARE to—

TOM. No, no, *I* musn't say things! *I've* got to just—

AMANDA. Let me tell you—

TOM. I don't want to hear any more! (*He tears the portieres open. The upstage area is lit with a turgid smoky red glow.*)

Amanda's hair is in metal curlers and she wears a very old bathrobe, much too large for her slight figure, a relic of the faithless Mr. Wingfield. An upright typewriter and a wild disarray of manuscripts are on the drop-leaf table. The quarrel was probably precipitated by Amanda's interruption of his creative labor. A chair lying overthrown on the floor. Their gesticulating shadows are cast on the ceiling by the fiery glow.

AMANDA. You *will* hear more, you—

TOM. No, I won't hear more, I'm going out!

AMANDA. You come right back in—

TOM. Out, out out! Because I'm—

AMANDA. Come back here, Tom Wingfield! I'm not through talking to you!

TOM. Oh, go—

LAURA (*desperately*). Tom!

AMANDA. You're going to listen, and no more insolence from you! I'm at the end of my patience! (*He comes back toward her.*)

TOM. What do you think I'm at? Aren't I supposed to have any patience to reach the end of, Mother? I know, I know. It seems unimportant to you, what I'm *doing*—what I *want* to do—having a little *difference* between them! You don't think that—

AMANDA. I think you've been doing things that you're ashamed of. That's why you act like this. I don't believe that you go every night to the movies. Nobody goes to the movies night after night. Nobody in their right minds goes to the movies as often as you pretend to. People don't go to the movies at nearly midnight, and movies don't let out at two A.M. Come in stumbling. Muttering to yourself like a maniac! You get three hours' sleep and then go to work. Oh, I can picture the way you're doing down there. Moping, doping, because you're in no condition.

TOM (*wildly*). No, I'm in no condition!

AMANDA. What right have you got to jeopardize your job? Jeopardize the security of us all? How do you think we'd manage if you were—

TOM. Listen! You think I'm crazy *about* the *warehouse?* (*He bends fiercely toward her slight figure.*) You think I'm in love with the Continental Shoemakers? You think I want to spend fifty-five *years* down there in that—*celotex interior! with*—*fluorescent*—*tubes!* Look! I'd rather somebody picked up a crowbar and battered out my brains than go back mornings! I *go!* Every time you come in yelling that God damn "*Rise and Shine!*" "*Rise and Shine!*" I say to myself "How *lucky dead* people are!" But I get up. I *go!* For sixty-five dollars a month I give up all that I dream of doing and being *ever!* And you say self—*self's* all I ever think of. Why, listen, if self is what I thought of, Mother, I'd be where he is—GONE! (*Pointing to father's picture.*) As far as the system of transportation reaches! (*He starts past her. She grabs his arm.*) Don't grab at me, Mother!

AMANDA. Where are you going?

TOM. I'm going to the *movies!*

AMANDA. I don't believe that lie!

TOM (*crouching toward her, overtowering her tiny figure. She backs away, gasping*). I'm going to opium dens! Yes, opium dens, dens of vice and criminals' hang-outs, Mother. I've joined the Hogan gang, I'm a hired assassin, I carry a tommy-gun in a violin case! I run a string of cat-houses in the Valley! They call me Killer, Killer Wingfield, I'm leading a double-life, a simple, honest warehouse worker by day, by night a dynamic *czar* of the *underworld, Mother.* I go to gambling casinos, I spin away fortunes on the roulette table! I wear a patch over one eye and a false mustache, sometimes I put on green whiskers. On those occasions they call me—*El Diablo!* Oh, I could tell you things to make you sleepless! My enemies plan to dynamite this place. They're going to blow us all sky-high some night! I'll be glad, very happy, and so will you! You'll go up, up on a broomstick, over Blue Mountain with seventeen gentlemen callers! You ugly—babbling old—*witch.* . . . (*He goes through a series of violent, clumsy movements, seizing his overcoat, lunging to the door, pulling it fiercely open. The women watch him, aghast. His arm catches in the sleeve of the coat as he struggles to pull it on. For a moment he is pinioned by the bulky garment. With an outraged groan he tears the coat off again, splitting the shoulders of it, and hurls it across the room. It strikes against the shelf of Laura's glass collection, there is a tinkle of shattering glass. Laura cries out as if wounded.*)

(**Music Legend: "The Glass Menagerie."**)

LAURA (*shrilly*). *My glass!*—menagerie. . . . (*She covers her face and turns away.*)

(*But Amanda is still stunned and stupefied by the "ugly witch" so that she barely notices this occurrence. Now she recovers her speech.*)

AMANDA (*in an awful voice*). I won't speak to you—until you apologize! (*She crosses through portieres and draws them together behind her. Tom is left with Laura. Laura clings weakly to the mantel with her face averted. Tom stares at her stupidly for a moment. Then he crosses to shelf. Drops awkwardly to his knees to collect the fallen glass, glancing at Laura as if he would speak but couldn't.*)

(**"The Glass Menagerie" steals in as the Scene Dims Out.**)

SCENE 4

The interior is dark. Faint light in the alley. A deep-voiced bell in a church is tolling the hour by five as the scene commences.

Tom appears at the top of the alley. After each solemn boom of the bell in the tower, he shakes a little noise-maker or rattle as if to express the tiny spasm of man in contrast to the sustained power and dignity of the Almighty. This and the unsteadiness of his advance make it evident that he has been drinking.

As he climbs the few steps to the fire-escape landing light steals up inside. Laura appears in night-dress, observing Tom's empty bed in the front room.

Tom fishes in his pockets for the door-key, removing a motley assortment of articles in the search, including a perfect shower of movie-ticket stubs and an empty bottle. At last he finds the key, but just as he is about to insert it, it slips from his fingers. He strikes a match and crouches below the door.

TOM (*bitterly*). One crack—and it falls through!

(*Laura opens the door.*)

LAURA. Tom! Tom, what are you doing?

TOM. Looking for a door-key.

LAURA. Where have you been all this time?

TOM. I have been to the movies.

LAURA. All this time at the movies?

TOM. There was a very long program. There was a Garbo picture and a Mickey Mouse and a travelogue and a newsreel and a preview of coming attractions. And there was an organ solo and a collection for the milk-fund—simultaneously—which ended up in a terrible fight between a fat lady and an usher!

LAURA (*innocently*). Did you have to stay through everything?

TOM. Of course! And, oh, I forgot! There was a big stage show! The headliner on this stage show was Malvolio the Magician. He performed wonderful tricks, many of them, such as pouring water back and forth between pitchers. First it turned to wine and then it turned to beer and then it turned to whiskey. I know it was whiskey it finally turned into because he needed somebody to come up out of the audience to help him, and I came up—both shows! It was Kentucky Straight Bourbon. A very generous fellow, he gave souvenirs. (*He pulls from his back pocket a shimmering rainbow-colored scarf.*) He gave me this. This is his magic scarf. You can have it, Laura. You wave it over a canary cage and you get a bowl of gold-fish. You wave it over the goldfish bowl and they fly away canaries. . . . But the wonderfulest trick of all was the coffin trick. We nailed him into a coffin and he got out of the coffin without removing one nail. (*He has come inside.*) There is a trick that would come in handy for me—get me out of this 2 by 4 situation! (*Flops onto bed and starts removing shoes.*)

LAURA. Tom—Shhh!

TOM. What you shushing me for?

LAURA. You'll wake up Mother.

TOM. Goody, goody! Pay 'er back for all those "Rise an' Shines." (*Lies down, groaning.*) You know it don't take much intelligence to get yourself into a nailed-up coffin, Laura. But who in hell ever got himself out of one without removing one nail?

(*As if in answer, the father's grinning photograph lights up.*)

(**Scene Dims Out.**)

Immediately following: The church bell is heard striking six. At the sixth stroke the alarm clock goes off in Amanda's room, and after a few moments we hear her calling: "Rise and Shine! Rise and Shine! Laura, go tell your brother to rise and shine!"

TOM (*sitting up slowly*). I'll rise—but I won't shine.

(*The light increases.*)

AMANDA. Laura, tell your brother his coffee is ready.

(*Laura slips into front room.*)

LAURA. Tom! it's nearly seven. Don't make Mother nervous. (*He stares at her stupidly. Beseechingly*) Tom, speak to Mother this morning. Make up with her, apologize, speak to her!

TOM. She won't to me. It's her that started not speaking.

LAURA. If you just say you're sorry she'll start speaking.

TOM. Her not speaking—is that such a tragedy?

LAURA. Please—please!

AMANDA (*calling from kitchenette*). Laura, are you going to do what I asked you to do, or do I have to get dressed and go out myself?

LAURA. Going, going—soon as I get on my coat! (*She pulls on a shapeless felt hat with nervous, jerky movement, pleadingly glancing at Tom. Rushes awkwardly for coat. The coat is one of Amanda's, inaccurately made-over, the sleeves too short for Laura.*) Butter and what else?

AMANDA (*entering upstage*). Just butter. Tell them to charge it.

LAURA. Mother, they make such faces when I do that.

AMANDA. Sticks and stones may break my bones, but the expression of Mr. Garfinkel's face won't harm me! Tell your brother his coffee is getting cold.

LAURA (*at door*). Do what I asked you, will you, will you, Tom?

(*He looks sullenly away.*)

AMANDA. Laura, go now or just don't go at all!

LAURA (*rushing out*). Going—going! (*A second later she cries out. Tom springs up and crosses to the door. Amanda rushes anxiously in. Tom opens the door.*)

TOM. Laura?

LAURA. I'm all right. I slipped, but I'm all right.

AMANDA (*peering anxiously after her*). If anyone breaks a leg on those fire-escape steps, the landlord ought to be sued for every cent he possesses! (*She shuts door. Remembers she isn't speaking and returns to other room.*)

(*As Tom enters listlessly for his coffee, she turns her back to him and stands rigidly facing the window on the gloomy gray vault of the areaway. Its light on her face with its aged but childish features is cruelly sharp, satirical as a Daumier print.*)

(**Music Under: "Ave Maria."**)

(*Tom glances sheepishly but sullenly at her averted figure and slumps at the table. The coffee is scalding hot; he sips it and gasps and spits it back in the cup. At his gasp, Amanda catches her breath and half turns. Then catches herself and turns back to window.*

Tom blows on his coffee, glancing sidewise at his mother. She clears her throat. Tom clears his. He starts to rise. Sinks back down again, scratches his head, clears his throat again. Amanda coughs. Tom raises his cup in both hands to blow on it, his eyes staring over the rim of it at his mother for several moments. Then he slowly sets the cup down and awkwardly and hesitantly rises from the chair.)

TOM (*hoarsely*). Mother. I—I apologize. Mother. (*Amanda draws a quick, shuddering breath. Her face works grotesquely. She breaks into childlike tears.*) I'm sorry for what I said, for everything that I said, I didn't mean it.

AMANDA (*sobbingly*). My devotion has made me a witch and so I make myself hateful to my children!

TOM. No, you *don't.*

AMANDA. I worry so much, don't sleep, it makes me nervous!

TOM (*gently*). I understand that.

AMANDA. I've had to put up a solitary battle all these years. But you're my right-hand bower! Don't fall down, don't fail!

TOM (*gently*). I try, Mother.

AMANDA (*with great enthusiasm*). Try and you will SUCCEED! (*The notion makes her breathless.*) Why, you—you're just *full* of natural endowments! Both of my children—they're *unusual* children! Don't you think I know it? I'm so—*proud!* Happy and—feel I've—so much to be thankful for but—Promise me one thing, son!

TOM. What, Mother?

AMANDA. Promise, son, you'll—never be a drunkard!

TOM (*turns to her grinning*). I will never be a drunkard, Mother.

AMANDA. That's what frightened me so, that you'd be drinking! Eat a bowl of Purina!

TOM. Just coffee, Mother.

AMANDA. Shredded wheat biscuit?

TOM. No. No, Mother, just coffee.

AMANDA. You can't put in a day's work on an empty stomach. You've got ten minutes—don't gulp! Drinking too-hot liquids makes cancer of the stomach.... Put cream in.

TOM. No, thank you.

AMANDA. To cool it.

TOM. No! No, thank you, I want it black.

AMANDA. I know, but it's not good for you. We have to do all that we can to build ourselves up. In these trying times we live in, all that we have to cling to is each other.... That's why it's so important to—Tom, I—I sent out your sister so I could discuss something with you. If you hadn't spoken I would have spoken to you. (*Sits down.*)

TOM (*gently*). What is it, Mother, that you want to discuss?

AMANDA. Laura!

(*Tom puts his cup down slowly.*)

(**Legend on Screen: "Laura."**)

(**Music: "The Glass Menagerie."**)

TOM. —Oh. —Laura . . .

AMANDA (*touching his sleeve*). You know how Laura is. So quiet but—still water runs deep! She notices things and

I think she—broods about them. (*Tom looks up.*) A few days ago I came in and she was crying.

TOM. What about?

AMANDA. You.

TOM. Me?

AMANDA. She has an idea that you're not happy here.

TOM. What gave her that idea?

AMANDA. What gives her any idea? However, you do act strangely. I—I'm not criticizing, understand *that!* I know your ambitions do not lie in the warehouse, that like everybody in the whole wide world—you've had to—make sacrifices, but—Tom—Tom—life's not easy, it calls for—Spartan endurance! There's so many things in my heart that I cannot describe to you! I've never told you but I—*loved* your father....

TOM (*gently*). I know that, Mother.

AMANDA. And you—when I see you taking after his ways! Staying out late—and—well, you *had* been drinking the night you were in that—terrifying condition! Laura says that you hate the apartment and that you go out nights to get away from it! Is that true, Tom?

TOM. No. You say there's so much in your heart that you can't describe to me. That's true of me, too. There's so much in my heart that I can t describe to *you!* So let's respect each other's—

AMANDA. But, why—*why,* Tom—are you always so *restless?* Where do you go to, nights?

TOM. I—go to the movies.

AMANDA. Why do you go to the movies so much, Tom?

TOM. I go to the movies because—I like adventure. Adventure is something I don't have much of at work, so I go to the movies.

AMANDA. But, Tom, you go to the movies *entirely too much!*

TOM. I like a lot of adventure.

(*Amanda looks baffled, then hurt. As the familiar inquisition resumes he becomes hard and impatient again. Amanda slips back into her querulous attitude toward him.*)

(**Image on Screen: Sailing Vessel with Jolly Roger.**)

AMANDA. Most young men find adventure in their careers.

TOM. Then most young men are not employed in a warehouse.

AMANDA. The world is full of young men employed in warehouses and offices and factories.

TOM. Do all of them find adventure in their careers?

AMANDA. They do or they do without it! Not everybody has a craze for adventure.

TOM. Man is by instinct a lover, a hunter, a fighter, and none of those instincts are given much play at the warehouse!

AMANDA. Man is by instinct! Don't quote instinct to me! Instinct is something that people have got away from! It belongs to animals! Christian adults don't want it!

TOM. What do Christian adults want, then, Mother?

AMANDA. Superior things! Things of the mind and the spirit! Only animals have to satisfy instincts! Surely your aims are somewhat higher than theirs! Than monkeys—pigs—

TOM. I reckon they're not.

AMANDA. You're joking. However, that isn't what I wanted to discuss.

TOM (*rising*). I haven't much time.

AMANDA (*pushing his shoulders*). Sit down.

TOM. You want me to punch in red at the warehouse, Mother?

AMANDA. You have five minutes. I want to talk about Laura.

(**Legend: "Plans and Provisions."**)

TOM. All right! What about Laura?

AMANDA. We have to be making plans and provisions for her. She's older than you, two years, and nothing has happened. She just drifts along doing nothing. It frightens me terribly how she just drifts along.

TOM. I guess she's the type that people call home girls.

AMANDA. There's no such type, and if there is, it's a pity! That is unless the home is hers, with a husband!

TOM. What?

AMANDA. Oh, I can see the handwriting on the wall as plain as I see the nose in front of my face! It's terrifying! More and more you remind me of your father! He was out all hours without explanation—Then *left! Good-bye!* And me with the bag to hold. I saw that letter you got from the Merchant Marine. I know what you're dreaming of. I'm not standing here blindfolded. Very well, then. Then *do* it! But not till there's somebody to take your place.

TOM. What do you mean?

AMANDA. I mean that as soon as Laura has got somebody to take care of her, married, a home of her own, independent—why, then you'll be free to go wherever you please, on land, on sea, whichever way the wind blows! But until that time you've got to look out for your sister. I don't say me because I'm old and don't matter! I say for your sister because she's young and dependent. I put her in business college—a dismal failure! Frightened her so it made her sick to her stomach. I took her over to the Young People's League at the church. Another fiasco. She spoke to nobody, nobody spoke to her. Now all she does is fool with those pieces of glass and play those worn-out records. What kind of a life is that for a girl to lead!

TOM. What can I do about it?

AMANDA. Overcome selfishness! Self, self, self is all that you ever think of! (*Tom springs up and crosses to get his coat. It is ugly and bulky. He pulls on a cap with earmuffs.*) Where is your muffler? Put your wool muffler on! (*He snatches it angrily from the closet and tosses it around his neck and pulls both ends tight.*) Tom! I haven't said what I had in mind to ask you.

TOM. I'm too late to—

AMANDA (*catching his arms very importunately. Then shyly.*) Down at the warehouse, aren't there some—nice young men?

TOM. No!

AMANDA. There *must* be—*some.*

TOM. Mother—

(*Gesture.*)

AMANDA. Find out one that's clean-living—doesn't drink and—ask him out for sister!

TOM. What?

AMANDA. For *sister!* To *meet!* Get acquainted!

TOM (*stamping to door*). Oh, my *go-osh!*

AMANDA. Will you? (*He opens door. Imploringly*) Will you? (*He starts down.*) Will you? *Will* you, dear?

TOM (*calling back*). YES!

(*Amanda closes the door hesitantly and with a troubled but faintly hopeful expression.*)

(**Screen Image: Glamor Magazine Cover.**)

(*Spot Amanda at phone.*)

AMANDA. Ella Cartwright? This is Amanda Wingfield! How are you, honey? How is that kidney condition? (*Count five.*) Horrors! (*Count five.*) You're a Christian martyr, yes, honey, that's what you are, a Christian martyr! Well, I just happened to notice in my little red book that your subscription to the *Companion* has just run out! I knew that you wouldn't want to miss out on the wonderful serial starting in this new issue. It's by Bessie Mae Hopper, the first thing she's written since *Honeymoon for Three.* Wasn't that a strange and interesting story? Well, this one is even lovelier, I believe. It has a sophisticated society background. It's all about the horsey set on Long Island!

(**Fade Out.**)

SCENE 5

(**Legend on Screen: "Annunciation."**) *Fade with music.*

It is early dusk of a spring evening. Supper has just been finished in the Wingfield apartment. Amanda and Laura in light-colored dresses are removing dishes from the table, in the upstage area, which is shadowy, their movements formalized almost as a dance or ritual, their moving forms as pale and silent as moths. Tom, in white shirt and trousers, rises from the table and crosses toward the fire-escape.

AMANDA (*as he passes her*). Son, will you do me a favor?

TOM. What?

AMANDA. Comb your hair! You look so pretty when your hair is combed! (*Tom slouches on sofa with evening paper. Enormous caption "Franco Triumphs."*) There is only one respect in which I would like you to emulate your father.

TOM. What respect is that?

AMANDA. The care he always took of his appearance. He never allowed himself to look untidy. (*He throws down the paper and crosses to fire-escape.*) Where are you going?

TOM. I'm going out to smoke.

AMANDA. You smoke too much. A pack a day at fifteen cents a pack. How much would that amount to in a month? Thirty times fifteen is how much, Tom? Figure it out and you will be astounded at what you could save. Enough to give you a night-school course in accounting at Washington U! Just think what a wonderful thing that would be for you, son!

(*Tom is unmoved by the thought.*)

TOM. I'd rather smoke. (*He steps out on landing, letting the screen door slam.*)

AMANDA (*sharply*). I know! That's the tragedy of it. . . . (*Alone, she turns to look at her husband's picture.*)

(**Dance Music: "All the World Is Waiting for the Sunrise!"**)

TOM (*to the audience*). Across the alley from us was the Paradise Dance Hall. On evenings in spring the windows and doors were open and the music came outdoors. Sometimes the lights were turned out except for a large glass sphere that hung from the ceiling. It would turn slowly about and filter the dusk with delicate rainbow colors. Then the orchestra played a waltz or a tango, something that had a slow and sensuous rhythm. Couples would come outside, to the relative privacy of the alley. You could see them kissing behind ashpits and telephone poles. This was the compensation for lives that passed like mine, without any change or adventure. Adventure and change were imminent in this year. They were waiting around the corner for all these kids. Suspended in the mist over Berchtesgaden, caught in the folds of Chamberlain's umbrella—In Spain there was Guernica! But here there was only hot swing music and liquor, dance halls, bars, and movies, and sex that hung in the gloom like a chandelier and flooded the world with brief, deceptive rainbows.... All the world was waiting for bombardments!

(*Amanda turns from the picture and comes outside.*)

AMANDA (*sighing*). A fire-escape landing's a poor excuse for a porch. (*She spreads a newspaper on a step and sits down, gracefully and demurely as if she were settling into a swing on a Mississippi veranda.*) What are you looking at?

TOM. The moon.

AMANDA. Is there a moon this evening?

TOM. It's rising over Garfinkel's Delicatessen.

AMANDA. So it is! A little silver slipper of a moon. Have you made a wish on it yet?

TOM. Um-hum.

AMANDA. What did you wish for?

TOM. That's a secret.

AMANDA. A secret, huh? Well, I won't tell mine either. I will be just as mysterious as you.

TOM. I bet I can guess what yours is.

AMANDA. Is my head so transparent?

TOM. You're not a sphinx.

AMANDA. No, I don't have secrets. I'll tell you what I wished for on the moon. Success and happiness for my precious children! I wish for that whenever there's a moon, and when there isn't a moon, I wish for it, too.

TOM. I thought perhaps you wished for a gentleman caller.

AMANDA. Why do you say that?

TOM. Don't you remember asking me to fetch one?

AMANDA. I remember suggesting that it would be nice for your sister if you brought home some nice young man from the warehouse. I think I've made that suggestion more than once.

TOM. Yes, you have made it repeatedly.

AMANDA. Well?

TOM. We are going to have one.

AMANDA. *What?*

TOM. A gentleman caller!

(**The Annunciation Is Celebrated with Music.**)

(*Amanda rises.*)

(**Image on Screen: Caller with Bouquet.**)

AMANDA. You mean you have asked some nice young man to come over?

TOM. Yep. I've asked him to dinner.

AMANDA. You really did?

TOM. I did!

AMANDA. You did, and did he—*accept?*

TOM. He did!

AMANDA. Well, well—well, well! That's—lovely!

TOM. I thought that you would be pleased.

AMANDA. It's definite, then?

TOM. Very definite.

AMANDA. Soon?

TOM. Very soon.

AMANDA. For heaven's sake, stop putting on and tell me some things, will you?

TOM. What things do you want me to tell you?

AMANDA. Naturally I would like to know when he's *coming!*

TOM. He's coming tomorrow.

AMANDA. *Tomorrow?*

TOM. Yep. Tomorrow.

AMANDA. But, Tom!

TOM. Yes, Mother?

AMANDA. Tomorrow gives me no time!

TOM. Time for what?

AMANDA. Preparations! Why didn't you phone me at once, as soon as you asked him, the minute that he accepted? Then, don't you see, I could have been getting ready!

TOM. You don't have to make any fuss.

AMANDA. Oh, Tom, Tom, Tom, of course I have to make a fuss! I want things nice, not sloppy! Not thrown together. I'll certainly have to do some fast thinking, won't I?

TOM. I don't see why you have to think at all.

AMANDA. You just don't know. We can't have a gentleman caller in a pig-sty! All my wedding silver has to be polished, the monogrammed table linen ought to be laundered! The windows have to be washed and fresh curtains put up. And how about clothes? We have to *wear* something, don't we?

TOM. Mother, this boy is no one to make a fuss over!

AMANDA. Do you realize he's the first young man we've had introduced to your sister? It's terrible, dreadful, disgraceful that poor little sister has never received a single gentleman caller! Tom, come inside! (*She opens the screen door.*)

TOM. What for?

AMANDA. I want to ask you some things.

TOM. If you're going to make such a fuss, I'll call it off, I'll tell him not to come.

AMANDA. You certainly won't do anything of the kind. Nothing offends people worse than broken engagements. It simply means I'll have to work like a Turk! We won't be brilliant, but we'll pass inspection. Come on inside. (*Tom follows, groaning.*) Sit down.

TOM. Any particular place you would like me to sit?

AMANDA. Thank heavens I've got that new sofa! I'm also making payments on a floor lamp I'll have sent out! And put the chintz covers on, they'll brighten things up! Of course I'd hoped to have these walls re-papered.... What is the young man's name?

TOM. His name is O'Connor.

AMANDA. That, of course, means fish—tomorrow is Friday! I'll have that salmon loaf—with Durkee's dressing! What does he do? He works at the warehouse?

TOM. Of course! How else would I—

AMANDA. Tom, he—doesn't drink?

TOM. Why do you ask me that?

AMANDA. Your father *did!*

TOM. Don't get started on that!

AMANDA. He *does* drink, then?

TOM. Not that I know of!

AMANDA. Make sure, be certain! The last thing I want for my daughter's a boy who drinks!

TOM. Aren't you being a little premature? Mr. O'Connor has not yet appeared on the scene!

AMANDA. But will tomorrow. To meet your sister, and what do I know about his character? Nothing! Old maids are better off than wives of drunkards!

TOM. Oh, my God!

AMANDA. Be still!

TOM (*leaning forward to whisper*). Lots of fellows meet girls whom they don't marry!

AMANDA. Oh, talk sensibly, Tom—and don't be sarcastic! (*She has gotten a hairbrush.*)

TOM. What are you doing?

AMANDA. I'm brushing that cow-lick down! What is this young man's position at the warehouse?

TOM (*submitting grimly to the brush and the interrogation*). This young man's position is that of a shipping clerk, Mother.

AMANDA. Sounds to me like a fairly responsible job, the sort of a job *you* would be in if you just had more *get-up.* What is his salary? Have you got any idea?

TOM. I would judge it to be approximately eighty-five dollars a month.

AMANDA. Well—not princely, but—

TOM. Twenty more than I make.

AMANDA. Yes, how well I know! But for a family man, eighty-five dollars a month is not much more than you can just get by on....

TOM. Yes, but Mr. O'Connor is not a family man.

AMANDA. He might be, mightn't he? Some time in the future?

TOM. I see. Plans and provisions.

AMANDA. You are the only young man that I know of who ignores the fact that the future becomes the present, the present the past, and the past turns into everlasting regret if you don't plan for it!

TOM. I will think that over and see what I can make of it.

AMANDA. Don't be supercilious with your mother! Tell me some more about this—what do you call him?

TOM. James D. O'Connor. The D. is for Delaney.

AMANDA. Irish on *both* sides! *Gracious!* And doesn't drink?

TOM. Shall I call him up and ask him right this minute?

AMANDA. The only way to find out about those things is to make discreet inquiries at the proper moment. When I was a girl in Blue Mountain and it was suspected that a young man drank, the girl whose attentions he had been receiving, if any girl *was,* would sometimes speak to the minister of his church, or rather her father would if her father was living, and sort of feel him out on the young man's character. That is the way such things are discreetly handled to keep a young woman from making a tragic mistake!

TOM. Then how did you happen to make a tragic mistake?

AMANDA. That innocent look of your father's had everyone fooled! He *smiled*—the world was *enchanted!* No girl can do worse than put herself at the mercy of a handsome appearance! I hope that Mr. O'Connor is not too good-looking.

TOM. No, he's not too good-looking. He's covered with freckles and hasn't too much of a nose.

AMANDA. He's not right-down homely, though?

TOM. Not right-down homely. Just medium homely, I'd say.

AMANDA. Character's what to look for in a man.

TOM. That's what I've always said, Mother.

AMANDA. You've never said anything of the kind and I suspect you would never give it a thought.

TOM. Don't be suspicious of me.

AMANDA. At least I hope he's the type that's up and coming.

TOM. I think he really goes in for self-improvement.

AMANDA. What reason have you to think so?

TOM. He goes to night school.

AMANDA (*beaming*). Splendid! What does he do, I mean study?

TOM. Radio engineering and public speaking!

AMANDA. Then he has visions of being advanced in the world! Any young man who studies public speaking is aiming to have an executive job some day! And radio engineering? A thing for the future! Both of these facts are very illuminating. Those are the sort of things that a mother should know concerning any young man who comes to call on her daughter. Seriously or—not.

TOM. One little warning. He doesn't know about Laura. I didn't let on that we had dark ulterior motives. I just said, why don't you come have dinner with us? He said okay and that was the whole conversation.

AMANDA. I bet it was! You're eloquent as an oyster. However, he'll know about Laura when he gets here. When he sees how lovely and sweet and pretty she is, he'll thank his lucky stars he was asked to dinner.

TOM. Mother, you mustn't expect too much of Laura.

AMANDA. What do you mean?

TOM. Laura seems all those things to you and me because she's ours and we love her. We don't even notice she's crippled any more.

AMANDA. Don't say crippled! You know that I never allow that word to be used!

TOM. But face facts, Mother. She is and—that's not all—

AMANDA. What do you mean "not all"?

TOM. Laura is very different from other girls.

AMANDA. I think the difference is all to her advantage.

TOM. Not quite all—in the eyes of others—strangers—she's terribly shy and lives in a world of her own and those things make her seem a little peculiar to people outside the house.

AMANDA. Don't say peculiar.

TOM. Face the facts. She is.

(**The Dance-Hall Music Changes to a Tango That Has a Minor and Somewhat Ominous Tone.**)

AMANDA. In what way is she peculiar—may I ask?

TOM (*gently*). She lives in a world of her own—a world of—little glass ornaments, Mother. . . . (*Gets up. Amanda remains holding brush, looking at him, troubled.*) She plays old phonograph records and—that's about all—(*He glances at himself in the mirror and crosses to door.*)

AMANDA (*sharply*). Where are you going?

TOM. I'm going to the movies. (*Out screen door.*)

AMANDA. Not to the movies, every night to the movies! (*Follows quickly to screen door.*) I don't believe you always go to the movies! (*He is gone. Amanda looks worriedly after him for a moment. Then vitality and optimism return and she turns from the door. Crossing to portieres.*) Laura! Laura! (*Laura answers from kitchenette.*)

LAURA. Yes, Mother.

AMANDA. Let those dishes go and come in front! (*Laura appears with dish towel. Gaily*) Laura, come here and make a wish on the moon!

LAURA (*entering*). Moon—moon?

AMANDA. A little silver slipper of a moon. Look over your left shoulder, Laura, and make a wish! (*Laura looks faintly puzzled as if called out of sleep. Amanda seizes her shoulders and turns her at angle by the door.*) Now! Now, darling, *wish!*

LAURA. What shall I wish for, Mother?

AMANDA (*her voice trembling and her eyes suddenly filling with tears*). Happiness! Good Fortune!

(*The violin rises and the stage dims out.*)

SCENE 6

(**Image: High School Hero.**)

TOM. And so the following evening I brought Jim home to dinner. I had known Jim slightly in high school. In high school Jim was a hero. He had tremendous Irish good nature and vitality with the scrubbed and polished look of white chinaware. He seemed to move in a continual spotlight. He was a star in basketball, captain of the debating club, president of the senior class and the glee club and he sang the male lead in the annual light operas. He was always running or bounding, never just walking. He seemed always at the point of defeating the law of gravity. He was shooting with such velocity through his adolescence that you would logically expect him to arrive at nothing short of the White House by the time he was thirty. But Jim apparently ran into more interference after his graduation from Soldan. His speed had definitely slowed. Six years after he left high school he was holding a job that wasn't much better than mine.

(**Image: Clerk.**)

He was the only one at the warehouse with whom I was on friendly terms. I was valuable to him as someone who could remember his former glory, who had seen him win basketball games and the silver cup in debating. He knew of my secret practice of retiring to a cabinet of the washroom to work on poems when business was slack in the warehouse. He called me Shakespeare. And while the other boys in the warehouse regarded me with suspicious hostility, Jim took a humorous attitude toward me. Gradually his attitude affected the others, their hostility wore off and they also began to smile at me as people smile at an oddly fashioned dog who trots across their path at some distance.

I knew that Jim and Laura had known each other at Soldan, and I had heard Laura speak admiringly of his voice. I didn't know if Jim remembered her or not. In high school Laura had been as unobtrusive as Jim had been astonishing. If he did remember Laura, it was not as my sister for when I asked him to dinner, he grinned and said, "You know, Shakespeare, I never thought of you as having folks!"

He was about to discover that I did. . . .

(**Light upstage.**)

(**Legend on Screen: "The Accent of a Coming Foot."**)

(*Friday evening. It is about five o'clock of a late spring evening which comes "scattering poems in the sky." A delicate lemony light is in the Wingfield apartment.*

Amanda has worked like a Turk in preparation for the gentleman caller. The results are astonishing. The new floor lamp with its rose-silk shade is in place, a colored paper lantern conceals the broken light fixture in the ceiling, new billowing white curtains are at the windows, chintz covers are on chairs and sofa, a pair of new sofa pillows make their initial appearance.

Open boxes and tissue paper are scattered on the floor.

Laura stands in the middle with lifted arms while Amanda crouches before her, adjusting the hem of the new dress, devout and ritualistic. The dress is colored and designed by memory. The arrangement of Laura's hair is changed; it is softer and more becoming. A fragile, unearthly prettiness has come out in Laura: she is like a piece of translucent glass touched by light, given a momentary radiance, not actual, not lasting.)

AMANDA (*impatiently*). Why are you trembling?

LAURA. Mother, you've made me so nervous!

AMANDA. How have I made you nervous?

LAURA. By all this fuss! You make it seem so important!

AMANDA. I don't understand you, Laura. You couldn't be satisfied with just sitting home, and yet whenever I try to arrange something for you, you seem to resist it. (*She gets up.*) Now take a look at yourself. No, wait! Wait just a moment—I have an idea!

LAURA. What is it now?

(*Amanda produces two powder puffs which she wraps in handkerchiefs and stuffs in Laura's bosom.*)

LAURA. Mother, what are you doing?

AMANDA. They call them "Gay Deceivers"!

LAURA. I won't wear them!

AMANDA. You will!

LAURA. Why should I?

AMANDA. Because, to be painfully honest, your chest is flat.

LAURA. You make it seem like we were setting a trap.

AMANDA. All pretty girls are a trap, a pretty trap, and men expect them to be. (**Legend: "A Pretty Trap."**) Now look at yourself, young lady. This is the prettiest you will ever be! I've got to fix myself now! You're going to be surprised by your mother's appearance! (*She crosses through portieres, humming gaily.*)

(*Laura moves slowly to the long mirror and stares solemnly at herself. A wind blows the white curtains inward in a slow, graceful motion and with a faint, sorrowful sighing.*)

AMANDA (*offstage*). It isn't dark enough yet. (*She turns slowly before the mirror with a troubled look.*)

(**Legend on Screen: "This Is My Sister: Celebrate Her with Strings!" Music.**)

AMANDA (*laughing, off*). I'm going to show you something. I'm going to make a spectacular appearance!

LAURA. What is it, Mother?

AMANDA. Possess your soul in patience—you will see! Something I've resurrected from that old trunk! Styles haven't changed so terribly much after all. . . . (*She parts the portieres.*) Now just look at your mother! (*She wears a girlish frock of yellowed voile with a blue silk sash. She carries a bunch of jonquils—the legend of her youth is nearly revived. Feverishly*) This is the dress in which I led the cotillion. Won the cakewalk twice at Sunset Hill, wore one spring to the Governor's ball in Jackson! See how I sashayed around the ballroom, Laura? (*She raises her skirt and does a mincing step around the room.*) I wore it on Sundays for my gentlemen callers! I had it on the day I met your father—I had malaria fever all that spring. The change of climate from East Tennessee to the Delta—weakened resistance—I had a little temperature all the time—not enough to be serious—just enough to make me restless and giddy! Invitations poured in parties all over the Delta!—"Stay in bed," said Mother, "you have fever!"—but I just wouldn't.—I took quinine but kept on going, going!—Evenings, dances!—Afternoons, long, long rides! Picnics—lovely!—So lovely, that country in May.—All lacy with dogwood, literally flooded with jonquils!—That was the spring I had the craze for jonquils. Jonquils became an absolute obsession. Mother said, "Honey, there's no more room for jonquils." And still I kept bringing in more jonquils. Whenever, wherever I saw them, I'd say, "Stop! Stop! I see jonquils!" I made the young men help me gather the jonquils! It was a joke, Amanda and her jonquils! Finally there were no more vases to hold them, every available space was filled with jonquils. No vases to hold them? All right, I'll hold them myself! And then I—(*She stops in front of the picture.*) (**Music.**) met your father! Malaria fever and jonquils and then—this—boy. . . . (*She switches on the rose-colored lamp.*) I hope they get here before it starts to rain. (*She crosses upstage and places the jonquils in bowl on table.*) I gave your brother a little extra change so he and Mr. O'Connor could take the service car home.

LAURA (*with altered look*). What did you say his name was?

AMANDA. O'Connor.

LAURA. What is his first name?

AMANDA. I don't remember. Oh, yes, I do. It was—Jim!

(*Laura sways slightly and catches hold of a chair.*)

(**Legend on Screen: "Not Jim!"**)

LAURA (*faintly*). Not—Jim!

AMANDA. Yes, that was it, it was Jim! I've never known a Jim that wasn't nice!

(**Music: Ominous.**)

LAURA. Are you sure his name is Jim O'Connor?

AMANDA. Yes. Why?

LAURA. Is he the one that Tom used to know in high school?

AMANDA. He didn't say so. I think he just got to know him at the warehouse.

LAURA. There was a Jim O'Connor we both knew in high school—(*Then, with effort.*) If that is the one that Tom is bringing to dinner—you'll have to excuse me, I won't come to the table.

AMANDA. What sort of nonsense is this?

LAURA. You asked me once if I'd ever liked a boy. Don't you remember I showed you this boy's picture?

AMANDA. You mean the boy you showed me in the year book?

LAURA. Yes, that boy.

AMANDA. Laura, Laura, were you in love with that boy?

LAURA. I don't know, Mother. All I know is I couldn't sit at the table if it was him!

AMANDA. It won't be him! It isn't the least bit likely. But whether it is or not, you will come to the table. You will not be excused.

LAURA. I'll have to be, Mother.

AMANDA. I don't intend to humor your silliness, Laura. I've had too much from you and your brother, both! So just sit down and compose yourself till they come. Tom has forgotten his key so you'll have to let them in, when they arrive.

LAURA (*panicky*). Oh, Mother—*you* answer the door!

AMANDA (*lightly*). I'll be in the kitchen—busy!

LAURA. Oh, Mother, please answer the door, don't make me do it!

AMANDA (*crossing into kitchenette*). I've got to fix the dressing for the salmon. Fuss, fuss—silliness!—over a gentleman caller!

(*Door swings shut. Laura is left alone.*)

(**Legend: "Terror!"**)

(*She utters a low moan and turns off the lamp—sits stiffly on the edge of the sofa, knotting her fingers together.*)

(**Legend on Screen: "The Opening of a Door!"**)

(*Tom and Jim appear on the fire-escape steps and climb to landing. Hearing their approach, Laura rises with a panicky gesture. She retreats to the portieres.*

The doorbell. Laura catches her breath and touches her throat. Low drums.)

AMANDA (*calling*). Laura, sweetheart! The door!

(*Laura stares at it without moving.*)

JIM. I think we just beat the rain.

TOM. Uh-huh. (*He rings again, nervously. Jim whistles and fishes for a cigarette.*)

AMANDA (*very, very gaily*). Laura, that is your brother and Mr. O'Connor! Will you let them in, darling?

(*Laura crosses toward kitchenette door.*)

LAURA (*breathlessly*). Mother—you go to the door!

(*Amanda steps out of the kitchenette and stares furiously at Laura. She points imperiously at the door.*)

LAURA. Please, please!

AMANDA (*in a fierce whisper*). What is the matter with you, you silly thing?

LAURA (*desperately*). Please, you answer it, *please!*

AMANDA. I told you I wasn't going to humor you, Laura. Why have you chosen this moment to lose your mind?

LAURA. Please, please, please, you go!

AMANDA. You'll have to go to the door because I can't!

LAURA (*despairingly*). I can't either!

AMANDA. Why?

LAURA. I'm *sick!*

AMANDA. I'm sick, too—of your nonsense! Why can't you and your brother be normal people? Fantastic whims and behavior! (*Tom gives a long ring.*) Preposterous goings on! Can you give me one reason—(*Calls out lyrically.*) COMING! JUST ONE SECOND!—why should you be afraid to open a door? Now you answer it, Laura!

LAURA. Oh, oh, oh . . . (*She returns through the portieres. Darts to the victrola and winds it frantically and turns it on.*)

AMANDA. Laura Wingfield, you march right to that door!

LAURA. Yes—yes, Mother!

(*A faraway, scratchy rendition of "Dardanella" softens the air and gives her strength to move through it. She slips to the door and draws it cautiously open. Tom enters with the caller, Jim O'Connor.*)

TOM. Laura, this is Jim. Jim, this is my sister, Laura.

JIM (*stepping inside*). I didn't know that Shakespeare had a sister!

LAURA (*retreating stiff and trembling from the door*). How—how do you do?

JIM (*heartily extending his hand*). Okay!

(*Laura touches it hesitantly with hers.*)

JIM. Your hand's *cold,* Laura!

LAURA. Yes, well—I've been playing the victrola....

JIM. Must have been playing classical music on it! You ought to play a little hot swing music to warm you up!

LAURA. Excuse me—I haven't finished playing the victrola....

(*She turns awkwardly and hurries into the front room. She pauses a second by the victrola. Then catches her breath and darts through the portieres like a frightened deer.*)

JIM (*grinning*). What was the matter?

TOM. Oh—with Laura? Laura is—terribly shy.

JIM. Shy, huh? It's unusual to meet a shy girl nowadays. I don't believe you ever mentioned you had a sister.

TOM. Well, now you know. I have one. Here is the *Post Dispatch*. You want a piece of it?

JIM. Uh-huh.

TOM. What piece? The comics?

JIM. Sports! (*Glances at it.*) Ole Dizzy Dean is on his bad behavior.

TOM (*disinterest*). Yeah? (*Lights cigarette and crosses back to fire-escape door.*)

JIM. Where are *you* going?

TOM. I'm going out on the terrace.

JIM (*goes after him*). You know, Shakespeare—I'm going to sell you a bill of goods!

TOM. What goods?

JIM. A course I'm taking.

TOM. Huh?

JIM. In public speaking! You and me, we're not the warehouse type.

TOM. Thanks—that's good news. But what has public speaking got to do with it?

JIM. It fits you for—executive positions!

TOM. Awww.

JIM. I tell you it's done a helluva lot for me.

(**Image: Executive at Desk.**)

TOM. In what respect?

JIM. In every! Ask yourself what is the difference between you an' me and men in the office down front? Brains?—No!—Ability?—No! Then what? Just one little thing—

TOM. What is that one little thing?

JIM. Primarily it amounts to—social poise! Being able to square up to people and hold your own on any social level!

AMANDA (*off stage*). Tom?

TOM. Yes, Mother?

AMANDA. Is that you and Mr. O'Connor?

TOM. Yes, Mother.

AMANDA. Well, you just make yourselves comfortable in there.

TOM. Yes, Mother.

AMANDA. Ask Mr. O'Connor if he would like to wash his hands.

JIM. Aw—no—no—thank you—I took care of that at the warehouse. Tom—

TOM. Yes?

JIM. Mr. Mendoza was speaking to me about you.

TOM. Favorably?

JIM. What do you think?

TOM. Well—

JIM. You're going to be out of a job if you don't wake up.

TOM. I am waking up—

JIM. You show no signs.

TOM. The signs are interior.

(**Image on Screen: The Sailing Vessel with Jolly Roger Again.**)

TOM. I'm planning to change. (*He leans over the rail speaking with quiet exhilaration. The incandescent marquees and signs of the first-run movie houses light his face from across the alley. He looks like a voyager.*) I'm right at the point of committing myself to a future that doesn't include the warehouse and Mr. Mendoza or even a night-school course in public speaking.

JIM. What are you gassing about?

TOM. I'm tired of the movies.

JIM. Movies!

TOM. Yes, movies! Look at them—(*A wave toward the marvels of Grand Avenue.*) All of those glamorous people—having adventures—hogging it all, gobbling the whole thing up! You know what happens? People go to the *movies* instead of *moving!* Hollywood characters are supposed to have all the adventures for everybody in America, while everybody in America sits in a dark room and watches them have them! Yes, until there's a war. That's when adventure becomes available to the masses! *Everyone's* dish, not only Gable's! Then the people in the dark room come out of the dark room to have some adventures themselves—Goody, goody—It's our turn now, to go to the South Sea Island—to make a safari—to be exotic, far-off—But I'm not patient. I don't want to wait till then. I'm tired of the *movies* and I am *about* to move!

JIM (*incredulously*). Move?

TOM. Yes.

JIM. When?

TOM. Soon!

JIM. Where? Where?

(**Theme Three: Music Seems to Answer the Question, While Tom Thinks It Over. He Searches Among His Pockets.**)

TOM. I'm starting to boil inside. I know I seem dreamy, but inside—well, I'm boiling! Whenever I pick up a shoe, I shudder a little thinking how short life is and what I am doing!—Whatever that means. I know it doesn't mean shoes—except as something to wear on a traveler's feet! (*Finds paper.*) Look—

JIM. What?

TOM. I'm a member.

JIM (*reading*). The Union of Merchant Seamen.

TOM. I paid my dues this month, instead of the light bill.

JIM. You will regret it when they turn the lights off.

TOM. I won't be here.

JIM. How about your mother?

TOM. I'm like my father. The bastard son of a bastard! See how he grins? And he's been absent going on sixteen years!

JIM. You're just talking, you drip. How does your mother feel about it?

TOM. Shhh—Here comes Mother! Mother is not acquainted with my plans!

AMANDA (*enters portieres*). Where are you all?

TOM. On the terrace, Mother.

(*They start inside. She advances to them. Tom is distinctly shocked at her appearance. Even Jim blinks a little. He is making his first contact with girlish Southern vivacity and in spite of the night-school course in public speaking is somewhat thrown off the beam by the unexpected outlay of social charm. Certain responses are attempted by Jim but are swept aside by Amanda's gay laughter and chatter. Tom is embarrassed but after the first shock Jim reacts very warmly. Grins and chuckles, is altogether won over.*

(**Image: Amanda as a Girl.**)

AMANDA (*coyly smiling, shaking her girlish ringlets*). Well, well, well, so this is Mr. O'Connor. Introductions entirely unnccessary. I've heard so much about you from my boy. I finally said to him, Tom—good gracious!—why don't you bring this paragon to supper? I'd like to meet this nice young man at the warehouse!—Instead of just hearing him sing your praises so much! I don't know why my son is so stand-offish—that's not Southern behavior! Let's sit down and—I think we could stand a little more air in here! Tom, leave the door open. I felt a nice fresh breeze a moment ago. Where has it gone? Mmm, so warm already! And not quite summer, even. We're going to burn up when summer really gets started. However, we're having—we're having a very light supper. I think light things are better fo' this time of year. The same as light clothes are. Light clothes an' light food are what warm weather calls fo'. You know our blood gets so thick during th' winter—it takes a while fo' us to *adjust* ou'selves!—when the season changes . . . It's come so quick this year. I wasn't prepared. All of a sudden—heavens! Already summer!—I ran to the trunk an' pulled out this light dress—Terribly old! Historical almost! But feels so good—so good an' co-ol, y'know. . . .

TOM. Mother—

AMANDA. Yes, honey?

TOM. How about—supper?

AMANDA. Honey, you go ask Sister if supper is ready! You know that Sister is in full charge of supper! Tell her you hungry boys are waiting for it. (*To Jim*) Have you met Laura?

JIM. She—

AMANDA. Let you in? Oh, good, you've met already! It's rare for a girl as sweet an' pretty as Laura to be domestic! But Laura is, thank heavens, not only pretty but also very domestic. I'm not at all. I never was a bit. I never could make a thing but angel-food cake. Well, in the South, we had so many servants. Gone, gone, gone. All vestiges of gracious living! Gone completely! I wasn't prepared for what the future brought me. All of my gentlemen callers were sons of planters and so of course I assumed that I would be married to one and raise my family on a large piece of land with plenty of servants. But man proposes—and woman accepts the proposal!—To vary that old, old saying a little bit—I married no planter! I married a man who worked for the telephone company!—that gallantly smiling gentleman over there! (*Points to the picture.*) A telephone man who—fell in love with long distance!—Now he travels and I don't even know where!—But what am I going on for about my—tribulations! Tell me yours—I hope you don't have any! Tom?

TOM (*returning*). Yes, Mother?

AMANDA. Is supper nearly ready?

TOM. It looks to me like supper is on the table.

AMANDA. Let me look—(*She rises prettily and looks through portieres.*) Oh, lovely—But where is Sister?

TOM. Laura is not feeling well and she says that she thinks she'd better not come to the table.

AMANDA. What?—Nonsense!—Laura? Oh, Laura!

LAURA (*off stage, faintly*). Yes, Mother.

AMANDA. You really must come to the table. We won't be seated until you come to the table! Come in, Mr. O'Connor. You sit over there and I'll—Laura? Laura Wingfield! You're keeping us waiting, honey! We can't say grace until you come to the table!

(*The back door is pushed weakly open and Laura comes in. She is obviously quite faint, her lips trembling, her eyes wide and staring. She moves unsteadily toward the table.*)

(**Legend: "Terror!"**)

(*Outside a summer storm is coming abruptly. The white curtains billow inward at the windows and there is a sorrowful murmur and deep blue dusk. Laura suddenly stumbles—She catches at a chair with a faint moan.*)

TOM. Laura!

AMANDA. Laura! (*There is a clap of thunder.*) (**Legend: "Ah!"**) (*Despairingly*) Why, Laura, you *are* sick, darling!

Tom, help your sister into the living room, dear! Sit in the living room, Laura—rest on the sofa. Well! (*To the gentleman caller*) Standing over the hot stove made her ill! I told her that it was just too warm this evening, but— (*Tom comes back in. Laura is on the sofa.*) Is Laura all right now?

TOM. Yes.

AMANDA. What *is* that? Rain? A nice cool rain has come up! (*She gives the gentleman caller a frightened look.*) I think we may—have grace—now . . . (*Tom looks at her stupidly.*) Tom, honey—you say grace!

TOM. Oh . . . "For these and all thy mercies—" (*They bow their heads, Amanda stealing a nervous glance at Jim. In the living room Laura, stretched on the sofa, clenches her hands to her lips, to hold back a shuddering sob.*) God's Holy Name be praised—

(**The Scene Dims Out.**)

SCENE 7

A SOUVENIR

Half an hour later. Dinner is just being finished in the upstage area which is concealed by the drawn portieres.

As the curtain rises Laura is still huddled upon the sofa, her feet drawn under her, her head resting on a pale blue pillow, her eyes wide and mysteriously watchful. The new floor lamp with its shade of rose-colored silk gives a soft, becoming light to her face, bringing out the fragile, unearthly prettiness which usually escapes attention. There is a steady murmur of rain, but it is slackening and stops soon after the scene begins; the air outside becomes pale and luminous as the moon breaks out.

A moment after the curtain rises, the lights in both rooms flicker and go out.

JIM. Hey, there, Mr. Light Bulb!

(*Amanda laughs nervously.*)

(**Legend: "Suspension of a Public Service."**)

AMANDA. Where was Moses when the lights went out? Ha-ha. Do you know the answer to that one, Mr. O'Connor?

JIM. No, Ma'am, what's the answer?

AMANDA. In the dark! (*Jim laughs appreciatively.*) Everybody sit still. I'll light the candles. Isn't it lucky we have them on the table? Where's a match? Which of you gentlemen can provide a match?

JIM. Here.

AMANDA. Thank you, sir.

JIM. Not at all, Ma'am!

AMANDA. I guess the fuse has burnt out. Mr. O'Connor, can you tell a burnt-out fuse? I know I can't and Tom is a total loss when it comes to mechanics. (**Sound: Getting Up: Voices Recede a Little to Kitchenette.**) Oh, be careful you don't bump into something. We don't want our gentleman caller to break his neck. Now wouldn't that be a fine howdy-do?

JIM. Ha-ha! Where is the fuse-box?

AMANDA. Right here next to the stove. Can you see anything?

JIM. Just a minute.

AMANDA. Isn't electricity a mysterious thing? Wasn't it Benjamin Franklin who tied a key to a kite? We live in such a mysterious universe, don't we? Some people say that science clears up all the mysteries for us. In my opinion it only creates more! Have you found it yet?

JIM. No, Ma'am. All these fuses look okay to me.

AMANDA. Tom!

TOM. Yes, Mother?

AMANDA. That light bill I gave you several days ago. The one I told you we got the notices about?

TOM. Oh.—Yeah.

(**Legend: "Ha!"**)

AMANDA. You didn't neglect to pay it by any chance?

TOM. Why, I—

AMANDA. Didn't! I might have known it!

JIM. Shakespeare probably wrote a poem on that light bill, Mrs. Wingfield.

AMANDA. I might have known better than to trust him with it! There's such a high price for negligence in this world!

JIM. Maybe the poem will win a ten-dollar prize.

AMANDA. We'll just have to spend the remainder of the evening in the nineteenth century, before Mr. Edison made the Mazda lamp!

JIM. Candlelight is my favorite kind of light.

AMANDA. That shows you're romantic! But that's no excuse for Tom. Well, we got through dinner. Very considerate of them to let us get through dinner before they plunged us into everlasting darkness, wasn't it, Mr. O'Connor?

JIM. Ha-ha!

AMANDA. Tom, as a penalty for your carelessness you can help me with the dishes.

JIM. Let me give you a hand.

AMANDA. Indeed you will not!

JIM. I ought to be good for something.

AMANDA. Good for something? (*Her tone is rhapsodic.*) *You?* Why, Mr. O'Connor, nobody, *nobody's* given me this much entertainment in years—as you have!

JIM. Aw, now, Mrs. Wingfield!

AMANDA. I'm not exaggerating, not one bit! But Sister

is all by her lonesome. You go keep her company in the parlor! I'll give you this lovely old candelabrum that used to be on the altar at the church of the Heavenly Rest. It was melted a little out of shape when the church burnt down. Lightning struck it one spring. Gypsy Jones was holding a revival at the time and he intimated that the church was destroyed because the Episcopalians gave card parties.

JIM. Ha-ha.

AMANDA. And how about coaxing Sister to drink a little wine? I think it would be good for her! Can you carry both at once?

JIM. Sure. I'm Superman!

AMANDA. Now, Thomas, get into this apron!

(*The door of kitchenette swings closed on Amanda's gay laughter; the flickering light approaches the portieres. Laura sits up nervously as he enters. Her speech at first is low and breathless from the almost intolerable strain of being alone with a stranger.*)

(**Legend: "I Don't Suppose You Remember Me at All!"**)

(*In her first speeches in this scene, before Jim's warmth overcomes her paralyzing shyness, Laura's voice is thin and breathless as though she has run up a steep flight of stairs. Jim's attitude is gently humorous. In playing this scene it should be stressed that while the incident is apparently unimportant, it is to Laura the climax of her secret life.*)

JIM. Hello, there, Laura.

LAURA (*faintly*). Hello. (*She clears her throat.*)

JIM. How are you feeling now? Better?

LAURA. Yes. Yes, thank you.

JIM. This is for you. A little dandelion wine. (*He extends it toward her with extravagant gallantry.*)

LAURA. Thank you.

JIM. Drink it—but don't get drunk! (*He laughs heartily. Laura takes the glass uncertainly; laughs shyly.*) Where shall I set the candles?

LAURA. Oh—oh, anywhere . . .

JIM. How about here on the floor? Any objections?

LAURA. No.

JIM. I'll spread a newspaper under to catch the drippings. I like to sit on the floor. Mind if I do?

LAURA. Oh, no.

JIM. Give me a pillow?

LAURA. What?

JIM. A pillow!

LAURA. Oh . . . (*Hands him one quickly.*)

JIM. How about you? Don't you like to sit on the floor?

LAURA. Oh—yes.

JIM. Why don't you, then?

LAURA: I—will.

JIM. Take a pillow! (*Laura does. Sits on the other side of the candelabrum. Jim crosses his legs and smiles engagingly at her.*) I can't hardly see you sitting way over there.

LAURA. I can—see you.

JIM. I know, but that's not fair, I'm in the limelight. (*Laura moves her pillow closer.*) Good! Now I can see you! Comfortable?

LAURA. Yes.

JIM. So am I. Comfortable as a cow. Will you have some gum?

LAURA. No, thank you.

JIM. I think that I will indulge, with your permission. (*Musingly unwraps it and holds it up.*) Think of the fortune made by the guy that invented the first piece of chewing gum. Amazing, huh? The Wrigley Building is one of the sights of Chicago.—I saw it summer before last when I went up to the Century of Progress. Did you take in the Century of Progress?

LAURA. No, I didn't.

JIM. Well, it was quite a wonderful exposition. What impressed me most was the Hall of Science. Gives you an idea of what the future will be in America, even more wonderful than the present time is! (*Pause. Smiling at her*) Your brother tells me you're shy. Is that right, Laura?

LAURA. I—don't know.

JIM. I judge you to be an old-fashioned type of girl. Well, I think that's a pretty good type to be. Hope you don't think I'm being too personal—do you?

LAURA (*hastily, out of embarrassment*). I believe I *will* take a piece of gum, if you—don't mind. (*Clearing her throat*) Mr. O'Connor, have you—kept up with your singing?

JIM. Singing? Me?

LAURA. Yes. I remember what a beautiful voice you had.

JIM. When did you bear me sing?

(**Voice Offstage in the Pause.**)

VOICE (*offstage*).

O blow, ye winds, heigh-ho,
A-roving I will go!
I'm off to my love
With a boxing glove—
Ten thousand miles away!

JIM. You say you've heard me sing?

LAURA. Oh, yes! Yes, very often . . . I—don't suppose you remember me—at all?

JIM (*smiling doubtfully*). You know I have an idea I've seen you before. I had that idea soon as you opened the door. It seemed almost like I was about to remember your name. But the name that I started to call you—wasn't a name! And so I stopped myself before I said it.

LAURA. Wasn't it—Blue Roses?

JIM (*springs up, grinning*). Blue Roses! My gosh, yes—Blue Roses! That's what I had on my tongue when you opened the door! Isn't it funny what tricks your memory plays? I didn't connect you with the high school somehow or other. But that's where it was; it was high school. I didn't even know you were Shakespeare's sister! Gosh, I'm sorry.

LAURA. I didn't expect you to. You—barely knew me!

JIM. But we did have a speaking acquaintance, huh?

LAURA. Yes, we—spoke to each other.

JIM. When did you recognize me?

LAURA. Oh, right away!

JIM. Soon as I came in the door?

LAURA. When I heard your name I thought it was probably you. I knew that Tom used to know you a little in high school. So when you came in the door—Well, then I was—sure.

JIM. Why didn't you *say* something, then?

LAURA (*breathlessly*). I didn't know what to say, I was—too surprised!

JIM. For goodness' sakes! You know, this sure is funny!

LAURA. Yes! Yes, isn't it, though . . .

JIM. Didn't we have a class in something together?

LAURA. Yes, we did.

JIM. What class was that?

LAURA. It was—singing—Chorus!

JIM. Aw!

LAURA. I sat across the aisle from you in the Aud.

JIM. Aw.

LAURA. Mondays, Wednesdays and Fridays.

JIM. Now I remember—you always came in late.

LAURA. Yes, it was so hard for me, getting upstairs. I had that brace on my leg—it clumped so loud!

JIM. I never heard any clumping.

LAURA (*wincing at the recollection*). To me it sounded like—thunder!

JIM. Well, well, well. I never even noticed.

LAURA. And everybody was seated before I came in. I had to walk in front of all those people. My seat was in the back row. I had to go clumping all the way up the aisle with everyone watching!

JIM. You shouldn't have been self-conscious.

LAURA. I know, but I was. It was always such a relief when the singing started.

JIM. Aw, yes, I've placed you now! I used to call you Blue Roses. How was it that I got started calling you that?

LAURA. I was out of school a little while with pleurosis. When I came back you asked me what was the matter. I said I had pleurosis—you thought I said Blue Roses. That's what you always called me after that!

JIM. I hope you didn't mind.

LAURA. Oh, no—I liked it. You see, I wasn't acquainted with many—people. . . .

JIM. As I remember you sort of stuck by yourself.

LAURA. I—I—never had much luck at—making friends.

JIM. I don't see why you wouldn't.

LAURA. Well, I—started out badly.

JIM. You mean being—

LAURA. Yes, it sort of—stood between me—

JIM. You shouldn't have let it!

LAURA. I know, but it did, and—

JIM. You were shy with people!

LAURA. I tried not to be but never could—

JIM. Overcome it?

LAURA. No, I—I never could!

JIM. I guess being shy is something you have to work out of kind of gradually.

LAURA (*sorrowfully*). Yes—I guess it—

JIM. Takes time!

LAURA. Yes

JIM. People are not so dreadful when you know them. That's what you have to remember! And everybody has problems, not just you, but practically everybody has got some problems. You think of yourself as having the only problems, as being the only one who is disappointed. But just look around you and you will see lots of people as disappointed as you are. For instance, I hoped when I was going to high school that I would be further along at this time, six years later, than I am now—You remember that wonderful write-up I had in *The Torch?*

LAURA. Yes! (*She rises and crosses to table.*)

JIM. It said I was bound to succeed in anything I went into! (*Laura returns with the annual.*) Holy Jeez! *The Torch!* (*He accepts it reverently. They smile across it with mutual wonder. Laura crouches beside him and they begin to turn through it. Laura's shyness is dissolving in his warmth.*)

LAURA. Here you are in *Pirates of Penzance!*

JIM (*wistfully*). I sang the baritone lead in that operetta.

LAURA (*rapidly*). So—*beautifully!*

JIM (*protesting*). Aw—

LAURA. Yes, yes—beautifully—beautifully!

JIM. You heard me?

LAURA. All three times!

JIM. No!

LAURA. Yes!

JIM. All three performances?

LAURA (*looking down*). Yes.

JIM. Why?

LAURA. I—wanted to ask you to—autograph my program.

JIM. Why didn't you ask me to?

LAURA. You were always surrounded by your own friends so much that I never had a chance to.

JIM. You should have just—

LAURA. Well, I—thought you might think I was—

JIM. Thought I might think you was—what?

LAURA. Oh—

JIM (*with reflective relish*). I was beleaguered by females in those days.

LAURA. You were terribly popular!

JIM. Yeah—

LAURA. You had such a—friendly way—

JIM. I was spoiled in high school.

LAURA. Everybody—liked you!

JIM. Including you?

LAURA. I—yes, I—I did, too—(*She gently closes the book in her lap.*)

JIM. Well, well, well!—Give me that program, Laura. (*She hands it to him. He signs it with a flourish.*) There you are—better late than never!

LAURA. Oh, I—what a—surprise!

JIM. My signature isn't worth very much right now. But some day—maybe—it will increase in value! Being disappointed is one thing and being discouraged is something else. I am disappointed but I'm not discouraged. I'm twenty-three years old. How old are you?

LAURA. I'll be twenty-four in June.

JIM. That's not old age!

LAURA. No, but—

JIM. You finished high school?

LAURA (*with difficulty*). I didn't go back.

JIM. You mean you dropped out?

LAURA. I made bad grades in my final examinations. (*She rises and replaces the book and the program. Her voice strained.*) How is—Emily Meisenbach getting along?

JIM. Oh, that kraut-head!

LAURA. Why do you call her that?

JIM. That's what she was.

LAURA. You're not still—going with her?

JIM. I never see her.

LAURA. It said in the Personal Section that you were—engaged!

JIM. I know, but I wasn't impressed by that—propaganda!

LAURA. It wasn't—the truth?

JIM. Only in Emily's optimistic opinion!

LAURA. Oh—

(**Legend: "What Have You Done Since High School?"**)

Jim lights a cigarette and leans indolently back on his elbows smiling at Laura with a warmth and charm which light her inwardly with altar candles. She remains by the table and turns in her hands a piece of glass to cover her tumult.

JIM (*after several reflective puffs on a cigarette*). What have you done since high school? (*She seems not to hear him.*) Huh? (*Laura looks up.*) I said what have you done since high school, Laura?

LAURA. Nothing much.

JIM. You must have been doing something these six long years.

LAURA. Yes.

JIM. Well, then, such as what?

LAURA. I took a business course at business college—

JIM. How did that work out?

LAURA. Well, not very—well—I had to drop out, it gave me—indigestion—

(*Jim laughs gently.*)

JIM. What are you doing now?

LAURA. I don't do anything—much. Oh, please don't think I sit around doing nothing! My glass collection takes up a good deal of my time. Glass is something you have to take good care of.

JIM. What did you say—about glass?

LAURA. Collection I said—I have one—(*She clears her throat and turns away again, acutely shy.*)

JIM (*abruptly*). You know what I judge to be the trouble with you? Inferiority complex! Know what that is? That's what they call it when someone low-rates himself! I understand it because I had it, too. Although my case was not so aggravated as yours seems to be. I had it until I took up public speaking, developed my voice, and learned that I had an aptitude for science. Before that time I never thought of myself as being outstanding in any way whatsoever! Now I've never made a regular study of it, but I have a friend who says I can analyze people better than doctors that make a profession of it. I don't claim that to be necessarily true, but I can sure guess a person's psychology, Laura! (*Takes out his gum.*) Excuse me, Laura. I always take it out when the flavor is gone. I'll use this scrap of paper to wrap it in. I know how it is to get it stuck on a shoe. Yep—that's what I judge to be your principal trouble. A lack of confidence in yourself as a person. You don't have the proper amount of faith in yourself. I'm basing that fact on a number of your remarks and also on certain observations I've made. For instance that clumping you thought was so awful in high school. You say that you even dreaded to walk into class. You see what you did? You dropped out of school, you gave up an education because of a clump, which as far as I know was practically nonexistent! A little physical defect is what you have. Hardly noticeable even! Magnified thousands of times by imagination! You know what my strong advice to you is? Think of yourself as *superior* in some way!

LAURA. In what way would I think?

JIM. Why, man alive, Laura! Just look about you a little. What do you see? A world full of common people! All of 'em born and all of 'em going to die! Which of them has one-tenth of your good points! Or mine! Or anyone else's, as far as that goes— Gosh! Everybody excels in some one thing. Some in many! (*Unconsciously glances at himself in the mirror.*) All you've got to do is discover in *what!* Take me, for instance. (*He adjusts his tie at the mirror.*) My interest happens to lie in electrodynamics. I'm taking a course in radio engineering at night school, Laura, on top of a fairly responsible job at the warehouse. I'm taking that course and studying public speaking.

LAURA. Ohhhh.

JIM. Because I believe in the future of television! (*Turning back to her.*) I wish to be ready to go up right along with it. Therefore I'm planning to get in on the ground floor. In fact, I've already made the right connections and all that remains is for the industry itself to get under way! Full steam—(*His eyes are starry.*) *Knowledge*—*Zzzzzp*! *Money*—*Zzzzzzp*! *Power!* That's the cycle democracy is built on! (*His attitude is convincingly dynamic. Laura stares at him, even her shyness eclipsed in her absolute wonder. He suddenly grins.*) I guess you think I think a lot of myself!

LAURA. No—o-o-o, I—

JIM. Now how about you? Isn't there something you take more interest in than anything else?

LAURA. Well, I do—as I said—have my—glass collection—

(*A peal of girlish laughter from the kitchen.*)

JIM. I'm not right sure I know what you're talking about. What kind of glass is it?

LAURA. Little articles of it, they're ornaments mostly! Most of them are little animals made out of glass, the tiniest little animals in the world. Mother calls them a glass menagerie! Here's an example of one, if you'd like to see it! This one is one of the oldest. It's nearly thirteen. (*He stretches out his hand.*) (**Music: "The Glass Menagerie."**) Oh, be careful—if you breathe, it breaks!

JIM. I'd better not take it. I'm pretty clumsy with things.

LAURA. Go on, I trust you with him! (*Places it in his palm.*) There now—you're holding him gently! Hold him over the light, he loves the light! You see how the light shines through him?

JIM. It sure does shine!

LAURA. I shouldn't be partial, but he is my favorite one.

JIM. What kind of a thing is this one supposed to be?

LAURA. Haven't you noticed the single horn on his forehead?

JIM. A unicorn, huh?

LAURA. Mmm-hmmm!

JIM. Unicorns, aren't they extinct in the modern world?

LAURA. I know!

JIM. Poor little fellow, he must feel sort of lonesome.

LAURA (*smiling*). Well, if he does he doesn't complain about it. He stays on a shelf with some horses that don't have horns and all of them seem to get along nicely together.

JIM. How do you know?

LAURA (*lightly*). I haven't heard any arguments among them!

JIM (*grinning*). No arguments, huh? Well, that's a pretty good sign! Where shall I set him?

LAURA. Put him on the table. They all like a change of scenery once in a while!

JIM (*stretching*). Well, well, well, well—Look how big my shadow is when I stretch!

LAURA. Oh, oh, yes—it stretches across the ceiling!

JIM (*crossing to door*). I think it's stopped raining. (*Opens fire-escape door.*) Where does the music come from?

LAURA. From the Paradise Dance Hall across the alley.

JIM. How about cutting the rug a little, Miss Wingfield?

LAURA. Oh, I—

JIM. Or is your program filled up? Let me have a look at it. (*Grasps imaginary card.*) Why, every dance is taken! I'll just have to scratch some out. (**Waltz Music: "La Golondrina."**) Ahhh, a waltz! (*He executes some sweeping turns by himself then holds his arms toward Laura.*)

LAURA (*breathlessly*). I—can't dance!

JIM. There you go, that inferiority stuff!

LAURA. I've never danced in my life!

JIM. Come on, try!

LAURA. Oh, but I'd step on you!

JIM. I'm not made out of glass.

LAURA. How—how—how do we start?

JIM. Just leave it to me. You hold your arms out a little.

LAURA. Like this?

JIM. A little bit higher. Right. Now don't tighten up, that's the main thing about it—relax.

LAURA (*laughing breathlessly*). It's hard not to.

JIM. Okay.

LAURA. I'm afraid you can't budge me.

JIM. What do you bet I can't? (*He swings her into motion.*)

LAURA. Goodness, yes, you can!

JIM. Let yourself go, now, Laura, just let yourself go.

LAURA. I'm—

JIM. Come on!

LAURA. Trying!

JIM. Not so stiff—Easy does it!

LAURA. I know but I'm—

JIM. Loosen th' backbone! There now, that's a lot better.
LAURA. Am I?
JIM. Lots, lots better! (*He moves her about the room in a clumsy waltz.*)
LAURA. Oh, my!
JIM. Ha-ha!
LAURA. Goodness, yes you can!
JIM. Ha-ha-ha! (*They suddenly bump into the table, Jim stops.*) What did we hit on?
LAURA. Table.
JIM. Did something fall off it? I think—
LAURA. Yes.
JIM. I hope that it wasn't the little glass horse with the horn!
LAURA. Yes.
JIM. Aw, aw, aw. Is it broken?
LAURA. Now it is just like all the other horses.
JIM. It's lost its—
LAURA. Horn! It doesn't matter. Maybe it's a blessing in disguise.
JIM. You'll never forgive me. I bet that that was your favorite piece of glass.
LAURA. I don't have favorites much. It's no tragedy, Freckles. Glass breaks so easily. No matter how careful you are. The traffic jars the shelves and things fall off them.
JIM. Still I'm awfully sorry that I was the cause.
LAURA (*smiling*). I'll just imagine he had an operation. The horn was removed to make him feel less—freakish! (*They both laugh.*) Now he will feel more at home with the other horses, the ones that don't have horns. . .
JIM. Ha-ha, that's very funny! (*Suddenly serious*) I'm glad to see that you have a sense of humor. You know—you're—well—very different! Surprisingly different from anyone else I know! (*His voice becomes soft and hesitant with a genuine feeling.*) Do you mind me telling you that? (*Laura is abashed beyond speech.*) You make me feel sort of—I don't know how to put it! I'm usually pretty good at expressing things, but—This is something that I don't know how to say! (*Laura touches her throat and clears it—turns the broken unicorn in her hands.*) (*Even softer*) Has anyone ever told you that you were pretty? (**Pause: Music.**) (*Laura looks up slowly, with wonder, and shakes her head.*) Well, you are! In a very different way from anyone else. And all the nicer because of the difference, too. (*His voice becomes low and husky. Laura turns away, nearly faint with the novelty of her emotions.*) I wish that you were my sister. I'd teach you to have some confidence in yourself. The different people are not like other people, but being different is nothing to be ashamed of. Because other people are not such wonderful people. They're one hundred times one thousand. You're one times one! They walk all over the earth. You just stay here. They're common as—weeds, but—you—well, you're—*Blue Roses!*

(**Image on Screen: Blue Roses.**)

(**Music Changes.**)

LAURA: But blue is wrong for—roses. . .
JIM. It's right for you—You're—pretty!
LAURA. In what respect am I pretty?
JIM. In all respects—believe me! Your eyes—your hair—are pretty! Your hands are pretty! (*He catches hold of her hand.*) You think I'm making this up because I'm invited to dinner and have to be nice. Oh, I could do that! I could put on an act for you, Laura, and say lots of things without being very sincere. But this time I am. I'm talking to you sincerely. I happened to notice you had this inferiority complex that keeps you from feeling comfortable with people. Somebody needs to build your confidence up and make you proud instead of shy and turning away and—blushing—Somebody ought to—ought to—*kiss* you, Laura! (*His hand slips slowly up her arm to her shoulder.*) (**Music Swells Tumultuously.**) (*He suddenly turns her about and kisses her on the lips. When he releases her Laura sinks on the sofa with a bright, dazed look. Jim backs away and fishes in his pocket for a cigarette.*) (**Legend on Screen: "Souvenir."**) Stumble-john! (*He lights the cigarette, avoiding her look. There is a peal of girlish laughter from Amanda in the kitchen. Laura slowly raises and opens her hand. It still contains the little broken glass animal. She looks at it with a tender, bewildered expression.*) Stumble-john! I shouldn't have done that—That was way off the beam. You don't smoke, do you? (*She looks up, smiling, not hearing the question. He sits beside her a little gingerly. She looks at him speechlessly—waiting. He coughs decorously and moves a little farther aside as he considers the situation and senses her feelings, dimly, with perturbation. Gently*) Would you—care for a—mint? (*She doesn't seem to hear him but her look grows brighter even.*) Peppermint—Life Saver? My pocket's a regular drug store—wherever I go . . . (*He pops a mint in his mouth. Then gulps and decides to make a clean breast of it. He speaks slowly and gingerly.*) Laura, you know, if I had a sister like you, I'd do the same thing as Tom. I'd bring out fellows—introduce her to them. The right type of boys of a type to—appreciate her. Only—well—he made a mistake about me. Maybe I've got no call to be saying this. That may not have been the idea in having me over. But what if it was? There's nothing wrong about that. The only trouble is that in my case—I'm not in a situation to—do the right thing. I can't take down your number and say I'll phone. I can't call up next week and—ask for a date. I thought I had better explain the situation in case you misunderstood it and—hurt your feelings. . . . (*Pause. Slowly, very slowly, Laura's look changes, her eyes returning slowly from his to the ornament in her palm.*)

(*Amanda utters another gay laugh in the kitchen.*)

LAURA (*faintly*). You—won't—call again?

JIM. No, Laura, I can't. (*He rises from the sofa.*) As I was just explaining, I've—got strings on me, Laura, I've—been going steady! I go out all the time with a girl named Betty. She's a home-girl like you, and Catholic, and Irish, and in a great many ways we—get along fine. I met her last summer on a moonlight boat trip up the river to Alton, on the *Majestic.* Well—right away from the start it was—love! (**Legend: Love!**) (*Laura sways slightly forward and grips the arm of the sofa. He fails to notice, now enrapt in his own comfortable being.*) Being in love has made a new man of me! (*Leaning stiffly forward, clutching the arm of the sofa, Laura struggles visibly with her storm. But Jim is oblivious, she is a long way off.*) The power of love is really pretty tremendous! Love is something that—changes the whole world, Laura! (*The storm abates a little and Laura leans back. He notices her again.*) It happened that Betty's aunt took sick, she got a wire and had to go to Centralia. So Tom—when he asked me to dinner—I naturally just accepted the invitation, not knowing that you—that he—that I—(*He stops awkwardly.*) Huh—I'm a stumble-john! (*He flops back on the sofa. The holy candles in the altar of Laura's face have been snuffed out! There is a look of almost infinite desolation. Jim glances at her uneasily.*) I wish that you would—say something. (*She bites her lip which was trembling and then bravely smiles. She opens her hand again on the broken glass ornament. Then she gently takes his hand and raises it level with her own. She carefully places the unicorn in the palm of his hand, then pushes his fingers closed upon it.*) What are you—doing that for? You want me to have him? —Laura? (*She nods.*) What for?

LAURA. A—souvenir . . .

(*She rises unsteadily and crouches beside the victrola to wind it up.*)

(**Legend on Screen: "Things Have a Way of Turning Out So Badly."**)

(**Or Image: "Gentleman Caller Waving Good-Bye—Gaily."**)

(*At this moment Amanda rushes brightly back in the front room. She bears a pitcher of fruit punch in an old-fashioned cut-glass pitcher and a plate of macaroons. The plate has a gold border and poppies painted on it.*)

AMANDA. Well, well, well! Isn't the air delightful after the shower? I've made you children a little liquid refreshment. (*Turns gaily to the gentleman caller.*) Jim, do you know that song about lemonade?

"Lemonade, lemonade
Made in the shade and stirred with a spade—
Good enough for any old maid!"

JIM (*uneasily*). Ha-ha! No—I never heard it.

AMANDA. Why, Laura! You look so serious!

JIM. We were having a serious conversation.

AMANDA. Good! Now you're better acquainted!

JIM (*uncertainly*). Ha-ha! Yes.

AMANDA. You modern young people are much more serious-minded than my generation. I was so gay as a girl!

JIM. You haven't changed, Mrs. Wingfield.

AMANDA. Tonight I'm rejuvenated! The gaiety of the occasion, Mr. O'Connor! (*She tosses her head with a peal of laughter. Spills lemonade.*) Oooo! I'm baptizing myself!

JIM. Here—let me—

AMANDA (*setting the pitcher down.*). There now. I discovered we had some maraschino cherries. I dumped them in, juice and all!

JIM. You shouldn't have gone to that trouble, Mrs. Wingfield.

AMANDA. Trouble, trouble? Why it was loads of fun! Didn't you hear me cutting up in the kitchen? I bet your ears were burning! I told Tom how outdone with him I was for keeping you to himself so long a time! He should have brought you over much, much sooner! Well, now that you've found your way, I want you to be a very frequent caller! Not just occasional but all the time. Oh, we're going to have a lot of gay times together! I see them coming! Mmm, just breathe that air! So fresh, and the moon's so pretty! I'll skip back out—I know where my place is when young folks are having a—serious conversation!

JIM. Oh, don't go out, Mrs. Wingfield. The fact of the matter is I've got to be going.

AMANDA. Going, now? You're joking! Why, it's only the shank of the evening, Mr. O'Connor!

JIM. Well, you know how it is.

AMANDA. You mean you're a young workingman and have to keep workingmen's hours. We'll let you off early tonight. But only on the condition that next time you stay later. What's the best night for you? Isn't Saturday night the best night for you workingmen?

JIM. I have a couple of time-clocks to punch, Mrs. Wingfield. One at morning, another one at night!

AMANDA. My, but you *are* ambitious! You work at night, too?

JIM. No, Ma'am, not work but—Betty! (*He crosses deliberately to pick up his hat. The band at the Paradise Dance Hall goes into a tender waltz.*)

AMANDA. Betty? Betty? Who's—Betty! (*There is an ominous cracking sound in the sky.*)

JIM. Oh, just a girl. The girl I go steady with! (*He smiles charmingly. The sky falls.*)

(**Legend: "The Sky Falls."**)

AMANDA (*a long-drawn exhalation*). Ohhhh . . . Is it a serious romance, Mr. O'Connor?

JIM. We're going to be married the second Sunday in June.

AMANDA. Ohhhh—how nice! Tom didn't mention that you were engaged to be married.

JIM. The cat's not out of the bag at the warehouse yet. You know how they are. They call you Romeo and stuff like that. (*He stops at the oval mirror to put on his hat. He carefully shapes the brim and the crown to give a discreetly dashing effect.*) It's been a wonderful evening, Mrs. Wingfield. I guess this is what they mean by Southern hospitality.

AMANDA. It really wasn't anything at all.

JIM. I hope it don't seem like I'm rushing off. But I promised Betty I'd pick her up at the Wabash depot, an' by the time I get my jalopy down there her train'll be in. Some women are pretty upset if you keep 'em waiting.

AMANDA. Yes, I know—The tyranny of women! (*Extends her hand.*) Goodbye, Mr. O'Connor. I wish you luck—and happiness—and success! All three of them, and so does Laura!—Don't you, Laura?

LAURA. Yes!

JIM (*taking her hand*). Goodbye, Laura. I'm certainly going to treasure that souvenir. And don't you forget the good advice I gave you. (*Raises his voice to a cheery shout.*) So long, Shakespeare! Thanks again, ladies—Good night!

(*He grins and ducks jauntily out. Still bravely grimacing, Amanda closes the door on the gentleman caller. Then she turns back to the room with a puzzled expression. She and Laura don't dare to face each other. Laura crouches beside the victrola to wind it.*)

AMANDA (*faintly*). Things have a way of turning out so badly. I don't believe that I would play the victrola. Well, well—well—Our gentleman caller was engaged to be married! Tom!

TOM (*from back*). Yes, Mother?

AMANDA. Come in here a minute. I want to tell you something awfully funny.

TOM (*enters with macaroon and a glass of the lemonade*). Has the gentleman caller gotten away already?

AMANDA. The gentleman caller has made an early departure. What a wonderful joke you played on us!

TOM. How do you mean?

AMANDA. You didn't mention that he was engaged to be married.

TOM. Jim? Engaged?

AMANDA. That's what he just informed us.

TOM. I'll be jiggered! I didn't know about that.

AMANDA. That seems very peculiar.

TOM. What's peculiar about it?

AMANDA. Didn't you call him your best friend down at the warehouse?

TOM. He is, but how did I know?

AMANDA. It seems extremely peculiar that you wouldn't know your best friend was going to be married!

TOM. The warehouse is where I work, not where I know things about people!

AMANDA. You don't know things anywhere! You live in a dream; you manufacture illusions! (*He crosses to door.*) Where are you going?

TOM. I'm going to the movies.

AMANDA. That's right, now that you've had us make such fools of ourselves. The effort, the preparations, all the expense! The new floor lamp, the rug, the clothes for Laura! All for what? To entertain some other girl's fiancé! Go to the movies, go! Don't think about us, a mother deserted, an unmarried sister who's crippled and has no job! Don't let anything interfere with your selfish pleasure! Just go, go, go—to the movies!

TOM. All right, I will! The more you shout about my selfishness to me the quicker I'll go, and I won't go to the movies!

AMANDA. Go, then! Then go to the moon—you selfish dreamer!

Tom smashes his glass on the floor. He plunges out on the fire-escape, slamming the door. Laura screams—cut by door.

Dance-hall music up. Tom goes to the rail and grips it desperately, lifting his face in the chill white moonlight penetrating the narrow abyss of the alley.

(Legend on Screen: "And So Good-Bye . . .")

(*Tom's closing speech is timed with the interior pantomime. The interior scene is played as though viewed through sound-proof glass. Amanda appears to be making a comforting speech to Laura who is huddled upon the sofa. Now that we cannot hear the mother's speech, her silliness is gone and she has dignity and tragic beauty. Laura's dark hair hides her face until at the end of the speech she lifts it to smile at her mother. Amanda's gestures are slow and graceful, almost dancelike, as she comforts the daughter. At the end of her speech she glances a moment at the father's picture—then withdraws through the portieres. At close of Tom's speech, Laura blows out the candles, ending the play.*)

TOM. I didn't go to the moon, I went much further—for time is the longest distance between two places—Not long after that I was fired for writing a poem on the lid of a shoe-box. I left Saint Louis. I descended the steps of this fire-escape for a last time and followed, from then on, in my father's footsteps, attempting to find in motion what was lost in space—I traveled around a great deal. The cities swept about me like dead leaves, leaves that were brightly colored but torn away from the branches. I would have stopped, but I was pursued by something. It always came upon me unawares, taking me altogether by surprise. Perhaps it was a familiar bit of music. Perhaps it was only a piece of transparent glass—Perhaps I am walking along a street at night, in some strange city, before I have found companions. I pass the lighted window of a shop where perfume is sold. The window is filled with pieces of colored glass, tiny transparent bottles in delicate colors, like bits of a shattered rainbow. Then all at once my sister touches my shoulder. I turn around and look into her eyes . . . Oh, Laura, Laura, I tried to leave you behind me, but I am more faithful than I intended to be! I reach for a cigarette, I cross the street, I run into the movies or a bar, I buy a drink, I speak to the nearest stranger—anything that can blow your candles out! (*Laura bends over the candles.*)—for nowadays the world is lit by lightning! Blow out your candles, Laura—and so goodbye . . .

(*She blows the candles out.*)

(**The Scene Dissolves.**)

TOPICS FOR DISCUSSION AND WRITING

1. In what ways, if any, is the setting relevant to the issues raised in the play?
2. What does the victrola offer to Laura? Why is the typewriter a better symbol (for the purposes of the play) than, say, a piano? After all, Laura could have been taking piano lessons.
3. What do you make out of Laura's glass menagerie? Why is it especially significant that the unicorn is Laura's favorite? How do you interpret the loss of the unicorn's horn? What is Laura saying to Jim in the gesture of giving him the unicorn?
4. Laura escapes to her glass menagerie. To what do Tom and Amanda escape? How complete do you think Tom's escape is at the end of the play?
5. Jim is described as "a nice, ordinary young man." To what extent can it be said that he, like the Wingfields, lives in a dream world? Tom says (speaking of the time of the play, 1939) that "The huge middle class was matriculating in a school for the blind." Does the play suggest that Jim, apparently a spokesman for the American dream, is one of the pupils in this school?
6. There is an implication that had Jim not been going steady he might have rescued Laura, but Jim also seems to represent (for example in his lines about money and power) the corrupt outside world that no longer values humanity. Is this a slip on Williams's part, or is it an interesting complexity?
7. What do you make out of the episode, at the end, when Laura blows out the candles? Is she blowing out illusions? Or her own life? Or both? Explain.
8. Some readers have seen great importance in the religious references in the play. To cite only a few examples: Scene 5 is called (on the screen) "Annunciation"; Amanda is associated with the music "Ave Maria"; Laura's candelabrum, from the altar of the Church of Heavenly Rest, was melted out of shape when the church burned down. Do you think these references add up to anything? If so, to what?
9. On page 545 Williams says, in a stage direction, "Now that we cannot hear the mother's speech, her silliness is gone and she has dignity and tragic beauty." Is Williams simply dragging in the word "tragic" because of its prestige, or is it legitimate? *Tragedy* is often distinguished from *pathos:* in the tragic, the suffering is experienced by persons who act and are in some measure responsible for their suffering; in the pathetic, the suffering is experienced by the passive and the innocent. For example, in discussing *The Suppliants,* a play by the ancient Greek dramatist Aeschylus, H. D. F. Kitto (in *Greek Tragedy*) says, "The Suppliants are not only pathetic, as the victims of outrage, but also tragic, as the victims of their own misconceptions." Given this distinction, to what extent are Amanda and Laura tragic? Pathetic? You might take into account the following quote from an interview with Williams, reprinted in *Conversations with Tennessee Williams* (ed. Albert J. Devlin): "The mother's valor is the *core* of *The Glass Menagerie.* . . . She's confused, pathetic, even stupid, but everything has *got* to be all right. She fights to make it that way in the only way she knows how."
10. Before writing *The Glass Menagerie,* Williams wrote a short story with the same plot, "Portrait of a Girl in Glass" (later published in his *Collected Stories*). You may want to compare the two works, noticing especially the ways in which Williams has turned a story into a play.

CONTEXTS FOR *THE GLASS MENAGERIE*

Production Notes

[by the Author]

Being a "memory play," *The Glass Menagerie* can be presented with unusual freedom of convention. Because of its considerably delicate or tenuous material, atmospheric touches and subtleties of direction play a particularly important part. Expressionism and all other unconventional techniques in drama have only one valid aim, and that is a closer approach to truth. When a play employs unconventional techniques, it is not, or certainly shouldn't be, trying to escape its responsibility of dealing with reality, or interpreting experience, but is actually or should be attempting to find a closer approach, a more penetrating and vivid expression of things as they are. The straight realistic play with its genuine frigidaire and authentic ice cubes, its characters that speak exactly as its audience speaks, corresponds to the academic landscape and has the same virtue of a photographic likeness. Everyone should know nowadays the unimportance of the photographic in art: that truth, life, or reality is an organic thing which the poetic imagination can represent or suggest, in essence, only through transformation, through changing into other forms than those which were merely present in appearance.

These remarks are not meant as comments only on this particular play. They have to do with a conception of a new, plastic theater which must take the place of the exhausted theater of realistic conventions if the theater is to resume vitality as a part of our culture.

The Screen Device

There is *only one important difference between the original and acting version of the play* and that is the *omission* in the latter of the device which I tentatively included in my *original* script. This device was the use of a screen on which were projected magic-lantern slides bearing images or titles: I do not regret the omission of this device from the . . . Broadway production. The extraordinary power of Miss Taylor's performance made it suitable to have the utmost simplicity in the physical production. But I think it may be interesting to some readers to see how this device was conceived. So I am putting it into the published manuscript. These images and legends, projected from behind, were cast on a section of wall between the front-room and dining-room areas, which should be indistinguishable from the rest when not in use.

The purpose of this will probably be apparent. It is to give accent to certain values in each scene. Each scene contains a particular point (or several) which is structurally the most important. In an episodic play, such as this, the basic structure or narrative line may be obscured from the audience; the effect may seem fragmentary rather than architectural. This may not be the fault of the play so much as a lack of attention in the audience. The legend or image upon the screen will strengthen the effect of what is merely allusion in the writing and allow the primary point to be made more simply and lightly than if the entire responsibility were on the spoken lines. Aside from this structural value, I think the screen will have a definite emotional appeal, less definable but just as important. An imaginative producer or director may invent many other uses for this device than those indicated in the present script. In fact the possibilities of the device seem much larger to me than the instance of this play can possibly utilize.

The Music

Another extra-literary accent in this play is provided by the use of music. A single recurring tune, "The Glass Menagerie," is used to give emotional emphasis to suitable passages. This tune is like circus music, not when you are on the grounds or in the immediate vicinity of the parade, but when you are at some distance and very likely thinking of something else. It seems under those circumstances to continue almost interminably and it weaves in and out of your preoccupied consciousness; then it is the lightest, most delicate music in the world and perhaps the saddest. It expresses the surface vivacity of life with the underlying strain of immutable and inexpressible sorrow. When you look at a piece of delicately spun glass you think of two things: how beautiful it is and how easily it can be broken. Both of those ideas should be woven into the recurring tune, which dips in and out of the play as if it were carried on a wind that changes. It serves as a thread of connection and allusion between the narrator with his separate point in time and space and the subject of his story. Between each episode it returns as reference to the emotion, nostalgia, which is the first condition of the play. It is primarily Laura's music and therefore comes out most clearly when the play focuses upon her and the lovely fragility of glass which is her image.

The Lighting

The lighting in the play is not realistic. In keeping with the atmosphere of memory, the stage is dim. Shafts of light are focused on selected areas or actors, sometimes in contradistinction to what is the apparent center. For instance, in the quarrel scene between Tom and Amanda, in which Laura has no active part, the clearest pool of light is on her figure. This is also true of the supper scene. The light upon Laura should be distinct from the others, having a peculiar pristine clarity such as light used in early religious portraits of female saints or madonnas. A certain correspondence to light in religious paintings, such as El Greco's, where the figures are radiant in atmosphere that is relatively dusky, could be effectively used throughout the play. (It will also permit a more effective use of the screen.) A free, imaginative use of light can be of enormous value in giving a mobile, plastic quality to plays of a more or less static nature.

The Timeless World of a Play

Tennessee Williams

Carson McCullers concludes one of her lyric poems with the line: "Time, the endless idiot, runs screaming 'round the world." It is this continual rush of time, so violent that it appears to be screaming, that deprives our actual lives of so much dignity and meaning, and it is, perhaps more than anything else, the *arrest of time* which has taken place in a completed work of art that gives to certain plays their feeling of depth and significance. In the London notices of *Death of a Salesman* a certain notoriously skeptical critic made the remark that Willy Loman was the sort of man that almost any member of the audience would have kicked out of an office had he applied for a job or detained one for conversation about his troubles. The remark itself possibly holds some truth. But the implication that Willy Loman is consequently a character with whom we have no reason to concern ourselves in drama, reveals a strikingly false conception of what plays are. Contemplation is something that exists outside of time, and so is the tragic sense. Even in the actual world of commerce, there exists in some persons a sensibility to the unfortunate situations of others, a capacity for concern and compassion, surviving from a more tender period of life outside the present whirling wire-cage of business activity. Facing Willy Loman across an office desk, meeting his nervous glance and hearing his querulous voice, we would be very likely to glance at our wrist watch and our schedule of other appointments. We would not kick him out of the office, no, but we would certainly *ease* him out with more expedition than Willy had feebly hoped for. But suppose there had been no wrist watch or office clock and suppose there had *not* been the schedule of pressing appointments, and suppose that we were not actually facing Willy across a desk—and facing a person is *not* the best way to *see* him!—suppose, in other words, that the meeting with Willy Loman had somehow occurred in a world *outside* of time. Then I think we would receive him with concern and kindness and even with respect. If the world of a play did not offer us this occasion to view its characters under that special condition of a *world without time,* then, indeed, the characters and occurrences of drama would become equally pointless, equally trivial, as corresponding meetings and happenings in life.

The classic tragedies of Greece had tremendous nobility. The actors wore great masks, movements were formal, dance-like, and the speeches had an epic quality which doubtless was as removed from the normal conversation of their contemporary society as they seem today. Yet they did not seem false to the Greek audiences: the magnitude of the events and the passions aroused by them did not seem ridiculously out of proportion to common experience. And I wonder if this was not because the Greek audiences knew, instinctively or by training, that the created world of a play is removed from that element which makes people *little* and their emotions fairly inconsequential.

Great sculpture often follows the lines of the human body: yet the repose of great sculpture suddenly transmutes those human lines to something that has an absoluteness, a purity, a beauty, which would not be possible in a living mobile form.

A play may be violent, full of motion: yet it has that special kind of repose which allows contemplation and produces the climate in which tragic importance is a possible thing, provided that certain modern conditions are met.

In actual existence the moments of love are succeeded by the moments of satiety and sleep. The sincere remark is followed by a cynical distrust. Truth is fragmentary, at best: we love and betray each other in not quite the same breath but in two breaths that occur in fairly close sequence. But the fact that passion occurred in *passing,* that it then declined into a more familiar sense of indifference, should not be regarded as proof of its inconsequence. And this is the very truth that drama wished to bring us. . . .

Whether or not we admit it to ourselves, we are all haunted by a truly awful sense of impermanence. I have always had a particularly keen sense of this at New York cocktail parties, and perhaps that is why I drink the martinis almost as fast as I can snatch them from the tray. This sense is the febrile thing that hangs in the air. Horror of insincerity, of *not meaning,* overhangs these affairs like the cloud of cigarette smoke and the hectic chatter. This horror is the only thing, almost, that is left unsaid at such functions. All social functions involving a group of people not intimately known to each other are always under this shadow. They are almost always (in an unconscious way) like that last dinner of the condemned: where steak or turkey, whatever the doomed man wants, is served in his cell as a mockingly cruel reminder of what the great-big-little-transitory world had to offer.

In a play, time is arrested in the sense of being confined. By a sort of legerdemain, events are made to remain *events,* rather than being reduced so quickly to mere *occurrences.* The audience can sit back in a comforting dusk to watch a world which is flooded with light and in which emotion and action have a dimension and dignity that they would likewise have in real existence, if only the shattering intrusion of time could be locked out.

About their lives, people ought to remember that when they are finished, everything in them will be contained in a marvelous state of repose which is the same as that which they unconsciously admired in drama. The rush is temporary. The great and only possible dignity of man lies in his power deliberately to choose certain moral values by which to live as steadfastly as if he, too, like a character in a play, were immured against the corrupting rush of time. Snatching the eternal out of the desperately fleeting is the great magic trick of human existence. As far as we know, as far as there exists any kind of empiric evidence, there is no way to beat the game of *being* against *non-being,* in which non-being is the predestined victor on realistic levels.

Yet plays in the tragic tradition offer us a view of certain moral values in violent juxtaposition. Because we do not participate, except as spectators, we can view them clearly, within the limits of our emotional equipment. These people on the stage do not return our looks. We do not have to answer their questions nor make any sign of being in company with them, nor do we have to compete with their virtues nor resist their offenses. All at once, for this reason, we are able to *see* them! Our hearts are wrung by recognition and pity, so that the dusky shell of the auditorium where we are gathered anonymously together is flooded with an almost liquid warmth of unchecked human sympathies, relieved of self-consciousness, allowed to function. . . .

Men pity and love each other more deeply than they permit themselves to know. The moment after the phone has been hung up, the hand reaches for a scratch pad and scrawls a notation: "Funeral Tuesday at five, Church of the Holy Redeemer, don't forget flowers." And the same hand is only a little shakier than usual as it reaches, some minutes later, for a highball glass that will pour a stupefaction over the kindled nerves. Fear and evasion are the two little beasts that chase each other's tails in the revolving wire-cage of our nervous world. They distract us from feeling too much about things. Time rushes toward us with its hospital tray of infinitely varied narcotics, even while it is preparing us for its inevitably fatal operation. . . .

So successfully have we disguised from ourselves the intensity of our own feelings, the sensibility of our own hearts, that plays in the tragic tradition have begun to seem untrue. For a couple of hours we may surrender ourselves to a world of fiercely illuminated values in conflict, but when the stage is covered and the auditorium lighted, almost immediately there is a recoil of disbelief. "Well, well!" we say as we shuffle back up the aisle, while the play dwindles behind us with the sudden perspective of an early Chirico painting. By the time we have arrived at Sardi's, if not as soon as we pass beneath the marquee, we have convinced ourselves once more that life has as little resemblance to the curiously stirring and meaningful occurrences on the stage as a jingle has to an elegy of Rilke.

This modern condition of his theater audience is something that an author must know in advance. The diminishing influence of life's destroyer, time, must be somehow worked into the context of his play. Perhaps it is a certain foolery, a certain distortion toward the grotesque, which will solve the problem for him. Perhaps it is only restraint, putting a mute on the strings that would like to break all bounds. But almost surely, unless he contrives in some way to relate the dimensions of his tragedy to the dimensions of a world in which time is *included*—he will be left among his magnificent debris on a dark stage, muttering to himself: "Those fools . . ."

And if they could hear him above the clatter of tongues, glasses, chinaware and silver, they would give him this answer: "But you have shown us a world not ravaged by time. We admire your innocence. But we have seen our photographs, past and present. Yesterday evening we passed our first wife on the street. We smiled as we spoke but we didn't really see her! It's too bad, but we know what is true and not true, and at 3 A.M. your disgrace will be in print!"

Top: Lee J. Cobb starred as Willy Loman in the 1949 original Broadway production of *Death of a Salesman.* (Photograph: Eileen Darby; reproduced courtesy of Hoblitzelle Theatre Arts, John Gassner Collection, Humanities Research Center, The University of Texas at Austin.) *Bottom:* Dustin Hoffman as Willy Loman and John Malkovich as Biff face each other in this scene from the 1984 production. (Photograph: Inge Morath; reproduced by permission of Magnum Photos, Inc.)

ARTHUR MILLER

Death of a Salesman

Certain private conversations in two acts and a requiem

Arthur Miller was born in New York in 1915. In 1938 he graduated from the University of Michigan, where he won several prizes for drama. Six years later he had his first Broadway production, *The Man Who Had All the Luck,* but the play was unlucky and closed after four days. By the time of his first commercial success, *All My Sons* (1947), he had already written eight or nine plays. In 1949 he won a Pulitzer prize with *Death of a Salesman* and achieved an international reputation. Among his other works are an adaptation (1950) of Ibsen's *Enemy of the People* and a play about the Salem witch trials, *The Crucible* (1953), both containing political implications, and *The Misfits* (1961, a screenplay), *After the Fall* (1964), and *Incident at Vichy* (1965).

COMMENTARY

For the ancient Greeks, at least for Aristotle, *pathos* was the destructive or painful act common in tragedy; but in English "pathos" refers to an element in art or life that evokes tenderness or sympathetic pity. Modern English critical usage distinguishes between tragic figures and pathetic figures by recognizing some element either of strength or of regeneration in the former that is not in the latter. The tragic protagonists perhaps act so that they bring their destruction upon themselves, or if their destruction comes from outside, they resist it, and in either case they come to at least a partial understanding of the causes of their suffering. Pathetic figures, however, are largely passive, unknowing, and unresisting innocents. In such a view, Macbeth is tragic, Duncan pathetic; Lear is tragic, Cordelia pathetic; Othello is tragic, Desdemona pathetic; Hamlet is tragic (the situation is not of his making, but he does what he can to alter it), Ophelia pathetic. (Note, by the way, that of the four pathetic figures named, the first is old and the remaining three are women. Pathos is more likely to be evoked by persons assumed to be relatively defenseless than by those who are able-bodied.)

That the spectators were not themselves heroic figures seems to have been assumed by the Greeks and by the Elizabethans; the lesser choral figures or nameless citizens interpret the action and call attention to the fact that even highly placed great heroes are not exempt from pain. Indeed, high place and strenuous activity invite pain: the lofty pine tree, or the mariner who ventures far from the coast, is more likely to meet destruction than the lowly shrub or the fair-weather sailor. For Greeks of the fifth century B.C., and for Elizabethans, high place was not a mere matter of rank, but of worth. In both ages, it was of course known that a king may be unkingly, but it was assumed that kingship required a special nature—though that nature was not always forthcoming. Put it this way: tragedy deals with kings not because they are men with a certain title (though of course the title does give them special power), but because they are men with a certain nature. This nature is an extraordinary capacity for action and for feeling; when they make an error its consequences are enormous, and they themselves feel it as lesser people would not. When Oedipus is polluted, all of Thebes feels it. Arthur Miller is somewhat misleading when he argues (p. 593) that because Oedipus has given his name to a complex that the common man may have, the common man is therefore "as apt a subject for tragedy." It is not Oedipus's "complex" but his unique importance that is the issue in the play. Moreover, even if one argues that a person of no public importance may suffer as much as one of public importance (and surely nobody doubts this), one may be faced with the fact that unimportant people by their ordinariness are not particularly good material for drama, and we are here concerned with drama rather than with life. In *Death of a Salesman* Willy Loman's wife says, rightly, "A small man can be just as exhausted as a great man." Yes, but is his exhaustion itself interesting, and do his activities (and this includes the words he utters) before his exhaustion have interesting dramatic possibilities? Isn't there a colorlessness that may weaken the play, an impoverishment of what John Milton called "gorgeous tragedy"?

Inevitably the rise of the bourgeoisie brought about the rise of bourgeois drama, and in the eighteenth century we get a fair number of tragedies with prologues that insist that characters like ourselves deserve our *pity:*

> No fustian hero rages here tonight,
> No armies fall, to fix a tyrant's right.
> From lower life we draw our scene's distress:
> —Let not your equals move your pity less.
>
> George Lillo, *Fatal Curiosity* (1733)

Note the deflation of older tragedy, the implication that its heroes were "fustian" (bombastic, pretentious) rather than genuinely heroic persons of deep feelings and high aspirations. Or, to put it differently, older tragedy in the bourgeois view dealt with persons of high rank, but rank (in this view) is not significant; therefore one may as well show persons of middle rank with whom the middle-class audience may readily identify. At the same time, the dismissal of heroic activities ("no fustian hero *rages,*" "no armies *fall*") and the substitution of "distress" indicates that we are well on the road to the Hero as Victim.

And we have kept on that road. As early as the sixteenth century Copernicus had shown that humanity and its planet were not the center of the universe, but the thought did not distress most people until much later. In 1859 Darwin published *The Origin of Species,* arguing that human beings are not a special creation but creatures that have evolved because "accidental variations" have aided them in the struggle for survival. At about the same time, Marx (who wished to dedicate *Capital* to Darwin) argued that economic forces guide our lives. Early in the twentieth century Freud seemed to argue that we are conditioned by infantile experiences and are enslaved by the dark forces of the id. All in all, by the time of the Depression of the 1930s, it was difficult to have much confidence in our ability to shape our destiny. The human condition was a sorry one; we were insignificant lust-ridden, soulless creatures in a terrifying materialistic universe. A human being was no Oedipus whose moral pollution infected a great city, no Brutus whose deed might bring civil war to Rome. A human being was really not much of anything, except perhaps to a few immediate dependents.

Arthur Miller accurately noted (*Theatre Arts,* October 1953) that American drama "has been a steady year by year documentation of the frustration of man," and it is evident that Miller has set out to restore a sense of importance if not greatness to the individual. In "Tragedy and the Common Man" (see p. 593), published in the same year that *Death of a Salesman* was produced and evidently a defense of the play, he argues on behalf of the common man as a tragic figure and he insists that tragedy and pathos are very different: "Pathos truly is the mode of the pessimist. . . . The plays we revere, century after century, are the tragedies. In them, and in them alone, lies the belief—optimistic, if you will—in the perfectibility of man."

Curiously, however, many spectators and readers find that by Miller's own terms Willy Loman fails to be a tragic figure; he seems to them pathetic rather than tragic, a victim rather than a man who acts and who wins our esteem. True, he is partly the victim of his own actions (although he could have chosen to be a carpenter, he chose to live by the bourgeois code that values a white collar), but he seems in larger part to be a victim of the system itself, a system of ruthless competition that has no place for the man who can no longer produce. (Here is an echo of the social-realist drama of the thirties.) Willy had believed in this system; and although his son Biff comes to the realization that Willy "had the wrong dreams," Willy himself seems not to achieve this insight. Of course he knows that he is out of a job, that the system does not value him any longer, but he still seems not to question the values he had subscribed to. Even in the last minutes of the play, when he is planning his suicide in order to provide money for his family—really for Biff—he says such things as "Can you imagine his magnificence with twenty thousand dollars in his pocket?" and "When the mail comes he'll be ahead of Bernard again." In the preface to his *Collected Plays,* Miller comments on the "exultation" with which Willy faces the end, but it is questionable whether an audience shares it. Many people find that despite the gulf in rank, they can share King Lear's feelings more easily than Willy's.

Perhaps, however, tradition has been too arbitrary in its use of the word *tragedy.* Perhaps we should be as liberal as the ancient Greeks were, who did not withhold it from any play that was serious and dignified.

ARTHUR MILLER *Death of a Salesman*

List of Characters

WILLY LOMAN
LINDA
BIFF
HAPPY
BERNARD
UNCLE BEN
HOWARD WAGNER
JENNY
STANLEY
MISS FORSYTHE
THE WOMAN
CHARLEY
LETTA

The action takes place in Willy Loman's house and yard and in various places he visits in the New York and Boston of today.

Throughout the play, in the stage directions, left and right mean stage left and stage right.

ACT 1

A melody is heard, played upon a flute. It is small and fine, telling of grass and trees and the horizon. The curtain rises.

Before us is the Salesman's house. We are aware of towering, angular shapes behind it, surrounding it on all sides. Only the blue light of the sky falls upon the house and forestage; the surrounding area shows an angry glow of orange. As more light appears, we see a solid vault of apartment houses around the small, fragile-seeming home. An air of the dream clings to the place, a dream rising out of reality. The kitchen at center seems actual enough, for there is a kitchen table with three chairs, and a refrigerator. But no other fixtures are seen. At the back of the kitchen there is a draped entrance, which leads to the living room. To the right of the kitchen, on a level raised two feet, is a bedroom furnished only with a brass bedstead and a straight chair. On a shelf over the bed a silver athletic trophy stands. A window opens onto the apartment house at the side.

Behind the kitchen, on a level raised six and a half feet, is the boy's bedroom, at present barely visible. Two beds are dimly seen, and at the back of the room a dormer window. (This bedroom is above the unseen living-room.) At the left a stairway curves up to it from the kitchen.

The entire setting is wholly or, in some places, partially transparent. The roof-line of the house is one-dimensional; under and over it we see the apartment buildings. Before the house lies an apron, curving beyond the forestage into the orchestra. This forward area serves as the back yard as well as the locale of all Willy's imaginings and of his city scenes. Whenever the action is in the present the actors observe the imaginary wall-lines, entering the house only through its door at the left. But in the scenes of the past these boundaries are broken, and characters enter or leave a room by stepping "through" a wall onto the forestage.

From the right, Willy Loman, the Salesman, enters, carrying two large sample cases. The flute plays on. He hears but is not aware of it. He is past sixty years of age, dressed quietly. Even as he crosses the stage to the doorway of the house, his exhaustion is apparent. He unlocks the door, comes into the kitchen, and thankfully lets his burden down, feeling the soreness of his palms. A word-sigh escapes his lips—it might be "Oh, boy, oh, boy." He closes the door, then carries his cases out into the living room, through the draped kitchen doorway.

Linda, his wife, has stirred in her bed at the right. She gets out and puts on a robe, listening. Most often jovial, she has developed an iron repression of her exceptions to Willy's behavior—she more than loves him, she admires him, as though his mercurial nature, his temper, his massive dreams and little cruelties, served her only as sharp reminders of the turbulent longings within him, longings which she shares but lacks the temperament to utter and follow to their end.

LINDA (*hearing Willy outside the bedroom, calls with some trepidation*). Willy!

WILLY. It's all right. I came back.

LINDA. Why? What happened? (*Slight pause.*) Did something happen, Willy?

WILLY. No, nothing happened.

LINDA. You didn't smash the car, did you?

WILLY (*with casual irritation*). I said nothing happened. Didn't you hear me?

LINDA. Don't you feel well?

WILLY. I am tired to the death. (*The flute has faded away. He sits on the bed beside her, a little numb.*) I couldn't make it. I just couldn't make it, Linda.

LINDA (*very carefully, delicately*). Where were you all day? You look terrible.

WILLY. I got as far as a little above Yonkers. I stopped for a cup of coffee. Maybe it was the coffee.

LINDA. What?

WILLY (*after a pause*). I suddenly couldn't drive any more. The car kept going off onto the shoulder, y'know?

LINDA (*helpfully*). Oh. Maybe it was the steering again. I don't think Angelo knows the Studebaker.

WILLY. No, it's me, it's me. Suddenly I realize I'm goin' sixty miles an hour and I don't remember the last five minutes. I'm—I can't seem to—keep my mind to it.

LINDA. Maybe it's your glasses. You never went for your new glasses.

WILLY. No, I see everything. I came back ten miles an hour. It took me nearly four hours from Yonkers.

LINDA (*resigned*). Well, you'll just have to take a rest, Willy, you can't continue this way.

WILLY. I just got back from Florida.

LINDA. But you didn't rest your mind. Your mind is overactive, and the mind is what counts, dear.

WILLY. I'll start out in the morning. Maybe I'll feel better in the morning. (*She is taking off his shoes.*) These goddam arch supports are killing me.

LINDA. Take an aspirin. Should I get you an aspirin? It'll soothe you.

WILLY (*with wonder*). I was driving along, you understand? And I was fine. I was even observing the scenery. You can imagine, me looking at scenery, on the road every week of my life. But it's so beautiful up there, Linda, the trees are so thick, and the sun is warm. I opened the windshield and just let the warm air bathe over me. And then all of a sudden I'm goin' off the road! I'm tellin' ya, I absolutely forgot I was driving. If I'd've gone the other way over the white line I might've killed somebody. So I went on again—and five minutes later I'm dreamin' again, and I nearly—(*He presses two fingers against his eyes.*) I have such thoughts, I have such strange thoughts.

LINDA. Willy, dear. Talk to them again. There's no reason why you can't work in New York.

WILLY. They don't need me in New York. I'm the New England man. I'm vital in New England.

LINDA. But you're sixty years old. They can't expect you to keep traveling every week.

WILLY. I'll have to send a wire to Portland. I'm supposed to see Brown and Morrison tomorrow morning at ten o'clock to show the line. Goddammit, I could sell them! (*He starts putting on his jacket.*)

LINDA (*taking the jacket from him*). Why don't you go down to the place tomorrow and tell Howard you've simply got to work in New York? You're too accommodating, dear.

WILLY. If old man Wagner was alive I'd a been in charge of New York now! That man was a prince, he was a masterful man. But that boy of his, that Howard, he don't appreciate. When I went north the first time, the Wagner Company didn't know where New England was!

LINDA. Why don't you tell those things to Howard, dear?

WILLY (*encouraged*). I will, I definitely will. Is there any cheese?

LINDA. I'll make you a sandwich.

WILLY. No, go to sleep. I'll take some milk. I'll be up right away. The boys in?

LINDA. They're sleeping. Happy took Biff on a date tonight.

WILLY (*interested*). That so?

LINDA. It was so nice to see them shaving together, one behind the other, in the bathroom. And going out together. You notice? The whole house smells of shaving lotion.

WILLY. Figure it out. Work a lifetime to pay off a house. You finally own it, and there's nobody to live in it.

LINDA. Well, dear, life is a casting off. It's always that way.

WILLY. No, no, some people—some people accomplish something. Did Biff say anything after I went this morning?

LINDA. You shouldn't have criticized him, Willy, especially after he just got off the train. You mustn't lose your temper with him.

WILLY. When the hell did I lose my temper? I simply asked him if he was making any money. Is that a criticism?

LINDA. But, dear, how could he make any money?

WILLY (*worried and angered*). There's such an undercurrent in him. He became a moody man. Did he apologize when I left this morning?

LINDA. He was crestfallen, Willy. You know how he admires you. I think if he finds himself, then you'll both be happier and not fight any more.

WILLY. How can he find himself on a farm? Is that a life? A farmhand? In the beginning, when he was young, I thought, well, a young man, it's good for him to tramp around, take a lot of different jobs. But it's more than ten years now and he has yet to make thirty-five dollars a week!

LINDA. He's finding himself, Willy.

WILLY. Not finding yourself at the age of thirty-four is a disgrace!

LINDA. Shh!

WILLY. The trouble is he's lazy, goddammit!

LINDA. Willy, please!

WILLY. Biff is a lazy bum!

LINDA. They're sleeping. Get something to eat. Go on down.

WILLY. Why did he come home? I would like to know what brought him home.

LINDA. I don't know. I think he's still lost, Willy. I think he's very lost.

WILLY. Biff Loman is lost. In the greatest country in the world a young man with such—personal attractiveness, gets lost. And such a hard worker. There's one thing about Biff—he's not lazy.

LINDA. Never.

WILLY (*with pity and resolve*). I'll see him in the morning; I'll have a nice talk with him. I'll get him a job selling. He could be big in no time. My God! Remember how they used to follow him around in high school? When he smiled at one of them their faces lit up. When he walked down the street . . . (*He loses himself in reminiscences.*)

LINDA (*trying to bring him out of it*). Willy, dear, I got a new kind of American-type cheese today. It's whipped.

WILLY. Why do you get American when I like Swiss?

LINDA. I just thought you'd like a change—

WILLY. I don't want a change! I want Swiss cheese. Why am I always being contradicted?

LINDA (*with a covering laugh*). I thought it would be a surprise.

WILLY. Why don't you open a window in here, for God's sake?

LINDA (*with infinite patience*). They're all open, dear.

WILLY. The way they boxed us in here. Bricks and windows, windows and bricks.

LINDA. We should've bought the land next door.

WILLY. The street is lined with cars. There's not a breath of fresh air in the neighborhood. The grass don't grow any more, you can't raise a carrot in the back yard. They should've had a law against apartment houses. Remember those two beautiful elm trees out there? When I and Biff hung the swing between them?

LINDA. Yeah, like being a million miles from the city.

WILLY. They should've arrested the builder for cutting those down. They massacred the neighborhood. (*Lost*)

More and more I think of those days, Linda. This time of year it was lilac and wisteria. And then the peonies would come out, and the daffodils. What fragrance in this room!

LINDA. Well, after all, people had to move somewhere.

WILLY. No, there's more people now.

LINDA. I don't think there's more people. I think—

WILLY. There's more people! That's what's ruining this country! Population is getting out of control. The competition is maddening! Smell the stink from that apartment house! And another one on the other side . . . How can they whip cheese?

(*On Willy's last line, Biff and Happy raise themselves up in their beds, listening.*)

LINDA. Go down, try it. And be quiet.

WILLY (*turning to Linda, guiltily*). You're not worried about me, are you, sweetheart?

BIFF. What's the matter?

HAPPY. Listen!

LINDA. You've got too much on the ball to worry about.

WILLY. You're my foundation and my support, Linda.

LINDA. Just try to relax, dear. You make mountains out of molehills.

WILLY. I won't fight with him any more. If he wants to go back to Texas, let him go.

LINDA. He'll find his way.

WILLY. Sure. Certain men just don't get started till later in life. Like Thomas Edison, I think. Or B. F. Goodrich. One of them was deaf. (*He starts for the bedroom doorway.*) I'll put my money on Biff.

LINDA. And Willy—if it's warm Sunday we'll drive in the country. And we'll open the windshield, and take lunch.

WILLY. No, the windshields don't open on the new cars.

LINDA. But you opened it today.

WILLY. Me? I didn't. (*He stops.*) Now isn't that peculiar! Isn't that a remarkable—(*He breaks off in amazement and fright as the flute is heard distantly.*)

LINDA. What, darling?

WILLY. That is the most remarkable thing.

LINDA. What, dear?

WILLY. I was thinking of the Chevvy. (*Slight pause.*) Nineteen twenty-eight . . . when I had that red Chevvy—(*Breaks off.*) That funny? I coulda sworn I was driving that Chevvy today.

LINDA. Well, that's nothing. Something must've reminded you.

WILLY. Remarkable. Ts. Remember those days? The way Biff used to simonize that car? The dealer refused to believe there was eighty thousand miles on it. (*He shakes his head.*) Heh! (*To Linda.*) Close your eyes, I'll be right up. (*He walks out of the bedroom.*)

HAPPY (*to Biff*). Jesus, maybe he smashed up the car again!

LINDA (*calling after Willy*). Be careful on the stairs, dear! The cheese is on the middle shelf! (*She turns, goes over to the bed, takes his jacket, and goes out of the bedroom.*)

(*Light has risen on the boys' room. Unseen, Willy is heard talking to himself, "Eighty thousand miles," and a little laugh. Biff gets out of bed, comes downstage a bit, and stands attentively. Biff is two years older than his brother Happy, well built, but in these days bears a worn air and seems less self-assured. He has succeeded less, and his dreams are stronger and less acceptable than Happy's. Happy is tall, powerfully made. Sexuality is like a visible color on him, or a scent that many women have discovered. He, like his brother, is lost, but in a different way, for he has never allowed himself to turn his face toward defeat and is thus more confused and hard-skinned, although seemingly more content.*)

HAPPY (*getting out of bed*). He's going to get his license taken away if he keeps that up. I'm getting nervous about him, y'know, Biff?

BIFF. His eyes are going.

HAPPY. No, I've driven with him. He sees all right. He just doesn't keep his mind on it. I drove into the city with him last week. He stops at a green light and then it turns red and he goes. (*He laughs.*)

BIFF. Maybe he's color-blind.

HAPPY. Pop? Why he's got the finest eye for color in the business. You know that.

BIFF (*sitting down on his bed*). I'm going to sleep.

HAPPY. You're not still sour on Dad, are you, Biff?

BIFF. He's all right, I guess.

WILLY (*underneath them, in the living room*). Yes, sir, eighty thousand miles—eighty-two thousand!

BIFF. You smoking?

HAPPY (*holding out a pack of cigarettes*). Want one?

BIFF (*taking a cigarette*). I can never sleep when I smell it.

WILLY. What a simonizing job, heh!

HAPPY (*with deep sentiment*). Funny, Biff, y'know? Us sleeping in here again? The old beds. (*He pats his bed affectionately.*) All the talk that went across those two beds, huh? Our whole lives.

BIFF. Yeah. Lotta dreams and plans.

HAPPY (*with a deep and masculine laugh*). About five hundred women would like to know what was said in this room.

(*They share a soft laugh.*)

BIFF. Remember that big Betsy something—what the hell was her name—over on Bushwick Avenue?

HAPPY (*combing his hair*). With the collie dog!

BIFF. That's the one. I got you in there, remember?

HAPPY. Yeah, that was my first time—I think. Boy, there was a pig! (*They laugh, almost crudely.*) You taught me everything I know about women. Don't forget that.

BIFF. I bet you forgot how bashful you used to be. Especially with girls.

HAPPY. Oh, I still am, Biff.

BIFF. Oh, go on.

HAPPY. I just control it, that's all. I think I got less bashful and you got more so. What happened, Biff? Where's the old humor, the old confidence? (*He shakes Biff's knee. Biff gets up and moves restlessly about the room.*) What's the matter?

BIFF. Why does Dad mock me all the time?

HAPPY. He's not mocking you, he—

BIFF. Everything I say there's a twist of mockery on his face. I can't get near him.

HAPPY. He just wants you to make good, that's all. I wanted to talk to you about Dad for a long time, Biff. Something's—happening to him. He—talks to himself.

BIFF. I noticed that this morning. But he always mumbled.

HAPPY. But not so noticeable. It got so embarrassing I sent him to Florida. And you know something? Most of the time he's talking to you.

BIFF. What's he say about me?

HAPPY. I can't make it out.

BIFF. What's he say about me?

HAPPY. I think the fact that you're not settled, that you're still kind of up in the air . . .

BIFF. There's one or two other things depressing him, Happy.

HAPPY. What do you mean?

BIFF. Never mind. Just don't lay it all to me.

HAPPY. But I think if you just got started—I mean—is there any future for you out there?

BIFF. I tell ya, Hap, I don't know what the future is. I don't know—what I'm supposed to want.

HAPPY. What do you mean?

BIFF. Well, I spent six or seven years after high school trying to work myself up. Shipping clerk, salesman, business of one kind or another. And it's a measly manner of existence. To get on that subway on the hot mornings in summer. To devote your whole life to keeping stock, or making phone calls, or selling or buying. To suffer fifty weeks of the year for the sake of a two-week vacation, when all you really desire is to be outdoors, with your shirt off. And always to have to get ahead of the next fella. And still—that's how you build a future.

HAPPY. Well, you really enjoy it on a farm? Are you content out there?

BIFF (*with rising agitation*). Hap, I've had twenty or thirty different kinds of jobs since I left home before the war, and it always turns out the same. I just realized it lately. In Nebraska when I herded cattle, and the Dakotas, and Arizona, and now in Texas. It's why I came home now, I guess, because I realized it. This farm I work on, it's spring there now, see? And they've got about fifteen new colts. There's nothing more inspiring or—beautiful than the sight of a mare and a new colt. And it's cool there now, see? Texas is cool now, and it's spring. And whenever spring comes to where I am, I suddenly get the feeling, my God, I'm not gettin' anywhere! What the hell am I doing, playing around with horses, twenty-eight dollars a week! I'm thirty-four years old, I oughta be makin' my future. That's when I come running home. And now, I get here, and I don't know what to do with myself. (*After a pause.*) I've always made a point of not wasting my life, and every time I come back here I know that all I've done is to waste my life.

HAPPY. You're a poet, you know that, Biff? You're a—you're an idealist!

BIFF. No, I'm mixed up very bad. Maybe I oughta get married. Maybe I oughta get stuck into something. Maybe that's my trouble. I'm like a boy. I'm not married, I'm not in business, I just—I'm like a boy. Are you content, Hap? You're a success, aren't you? Are you content?

HAPPY. Hell, no!

BIFF. Why? You're making money, aren't you?

HAPPY (*moving about with energy, expressiveness*). All I can do now is wait for the merchandise manager to die. And suppose I get to be merchandise manager? He's a good friend of mine, and he just built a terrific estate on Long Island. And he lived there about two months and sold it, and now he's building another one. He can't enjoy it once it's finished. And I know that's just what I would do. I don't know what the hell I'm workin' for. Sometimes I sit in my apartment—all alone. And I think of the rent I'm paying. And it's crazy. But then, it's what I always wanted. My own apartment, a car, and plenty of women. And still, goddammit, I'm lonely.

BIFF (*with enthusiasm*). Listen, why don't you come out West with me?

HAPPY. You and I, heh?

BIFF. Sure, maybe we could buy a ranch. Raise cattle, use our muscles. Men built like we are should be working out in the open.

HAPPY (*avidly*). The Loman Brothers, heh?

BIFF (*with vast affection*). Sure, we'd be known all over the counties!

HAPPY (*enthralled*). That's what I dream about, Biff. Sometimes I want to just rip my clothes off in the middle of the store and outbox that goddam merchandise manager.

I mean I can outbox, outrun, and outlift anybody in that store, and I have to take orders from those common, petty sons-of-bitches till I can't stand it any more.

BIFF. I'm tellin' you, kid, if you were with me I'd be happy out there.

HAPPY (*enthused*). See, Biff, everybody around me is so false that I'm constantly lowering my ideals . . .

BIFF. Baby, together we'd stand up for one another, we'd have someone to trust.

HAPPY. If I were around you—

BIFF. Hap, the trouble is we weren't brought up to grub for money. I don't know how to do it.

HAPPY. Neither can I!

BIFF. Then let's go!

HAPPY. The only thing is—what can you make out there?

BIFF. But look at your friend. Builds an estate and then hasn't the peace of mind to live in it.

HAPPY. Yeah, but when he walks into the store the waves part in front of him. That's fifty-two thousand dollars a year coming through the revolving door, and I got more in my pinky finger than he's got in his head.

BIFF. Yeah, but you just said—

HAPPY. I gotta show some of those pompous, self-important executives over there that Hap Loman can make the grade. I want to walk into the store the way he walks in. Then I'll go with you, Biff. We'll be together yet, I swear. But take those two we had tonight. Now weren't they gorgeous creatures?

BIFF. Yeah, yeah, most gorgeous I've had in years.

HAPPY. I get that any time I want, Biff. Whenever I feel disgusted. The only trouble is, it gets like bowling or something. I just keep knockin' them over and it doesn't mean anything. You still run around a lot?

BIFF. Naa. I'd like to find a girl—steady, somebody with substance.

HAPPY. That's what I long for.

BIFF. Go on! You'd never come home.

HAPPY. I would! Somebody with character, with resistance! Like Mom, y'know? You're gonna call me a bastard when I tell you this. That girl Charlotte I was with tonight is engaged to be married in five weeks. (*He tries on his new hat.*)

BIFF. No kiddin'!

HAPPY. Sure, the guy's in line for the vice-presidency of the store. I don't know what gets into me, maybe I just have an overdeveloped sense of competition or something, but I went and ruined her, and furthermore I can't get rid of her. And he's the third executive I've done that to. Isn't that a crummy characteristic? And to top it all, I go to their weddings! (*Indignantly, but laughing*) Like I'm not supposed to take bribes. Manufacturers offer me a hundred-dollar bill now and then to throw an order their way. You know how honest I am, but it's like this girl, see. I hate myself for it. Because I don't want the girl, and, still, I take it and—I love it!

BIFF. Let's go to sleep.

HAPPY. I guess we didn't settle anything, heh?

BIFF. I just got one idea that I think I'm going to try.

HAPPY. What's that?

BIFF. Remember Bill Oliver?

HAPPY. Sure, Oliver is very big now. You want to work for him again?

BIFF. No, but when I quit he said something to me. He put his arm on my shoulder, and he said, "Biff, if you ever need anything, come to me."

HAPPY. I remember that. That sounds good.

BIFF. I think I'll go to see him. If I could get ten thousand or even seven or eight thousand dollars I could buy a beautiful ranch.

HAPPY. I bet he'd back you. 'Cause he thought highly of you, Biff. I mean, they all do. You're well liked, Biff. That's why I say to come back here, and we both have the apartment. And I'm tellin' you, Biff, any babe you want . . .

BIFF. No, with a ranch I could do the work I like and still be something. I just wonder though. I wonder if Oliver still thinks I stole that carton of basketballs.

HAPPY. Oh, he probably forgot that long ago. It's almost ten years. You're too sensitive. Anyway, he didn't really fire you.

BIFF. Well, I think he was going to. I think that's why I quit. I was never sure whether he knew or not. I know he thought the world of me, though. I was the only one he'd let lock up the place.

WILLY (*below*). You gonna wash the engine, Biff?

HAPPY. Shh!

(*Biff looks at Happy, who is gazing down, listening. Willy is mumbling in the parlor.*)

HAPPY. You hear that?

(*They listen. Willy laughs warmly.*)

BIFF (*growing angry*). Doesn't he know Mom can hear that?

WILLY. Don't get your sweater dirty, Biff!

(*A look of pain crosses Biff's face.*)

HAPPY. Isn't that terrible? Don't leave again, will you? You'll find a job here. You gotta stick around. I don't know what to do about him, it's getting embarrassing.

WILLY. What a simonizing job!

BIFF. Mom's hearing that!

WILLY. No kiddin', Biff, you got a date? Wonderful!

HAPPY. Go on to sleep. But talk to him in the morning, will you?

BIFF (*reluctantly getting into bed*). With her in the house. Brother!

HAPPY (*getting into bed*). I wish you'd have a good talk with him.

(*The light on their room begins to fade.*)

BIFF (*to himself in bed*). That selfish, stupid . . .

HAPPY. Sh . . . Sleep, Biff.

(*Their light is out. Well before they have finished speaking, Willy's form is dimly seen below in the darkened kitchen. He opens the refrigerator, searches in there, and takes out a bottle of milk. The apartment houses are fading out, and the entire house and surroundings become covered with leaves. Music insinuates itself as the leaves appear.*)

WILLY. Just wanna be careful with those girls, Biff, that's all. Don't make any promises. No promises of any kind. Because a girl, y'know, they always believe what you tell 'em, and you're very young, Biff, you're too young to be talking seriously to girls.

(*Light rises on the kitchen. Willy, talking, shuts the refrigerator door and comes downstage to the kitchen table. He pours milk into a glass. He is totally immersed in himself, smiling faintly.*)

WILLY. Too young entirely, Biff. You want to watch your schooling first. Then when you're all set, there'll be plenty of girls for a boy like you. (*He smiles broadly at a kitchen chair.*) That so? The girls pay for you? (*He laughs.*) Boy, you must really be makin' a hit.

(*Willy is gradually addressing—physically—a point offstage, speaking through the wall of the kitchen, and his voice has been rising in volume to that of a normal conversation.*)

WILLY. I been wondering why you polish the car so careful. Ha! Don't leave the hubcaps, boys. Get the chamois to the hubcaps. Happy, use newspaper on the windows, it's the easiest thing. Show him how to do it, Biff! You see, Happy? Pad it up, use it like a pad. That's it, that's it, good work. You're doin' all right, Hap. (*He pauses, then nods in approbation for a few seconds, then looks upward.*) Biff, first thing we gotta do when we get time is clip that big branch over the house. Afraid it's gonna fall in a storm and hit the roof. Tell you what. We get a rope and sling her around, and then we climb up there with a couple of saws and take her down. Soon as you finish the car, boys, I wanna see ya. I got a surprise for you, boys.

BIFF (*offstage*). Whatta ya got, Dad?

WILLY. No, you finish first. Never leave a job till you're finished—remember that. (*Looking toward the "big trees"*) Biff, up in Albany I saw a beautiful hammock. I think I'll buy it next trip, and we'll hang it right between those two elms. Wouldn't that be something? Just swingin' there under those branches. Boy, that would be . . .

(*Young Biff and Young Happy appear from the direction Willy was addressing. Happy carries rags and a pail of water. Biff, wearing a sweater with a block "S," carries a football.*)

BIFF (*pointing in the direction of the car offstage*). How's that, Pop, professional?

WILLY. Terrific. Terrific job, boys. Good work, Biff.

HAPPY. Where's the surprise, Pop?

WILLY. In the back seat of the car.

HAPPY. Boy! (*He runs off.*)

BIFF. What is it, Dad? Tell me, what'd you buy?

WILLY (*laughing, cuffs him*). Never mind, something I want you to have.

BIFF (*turns and starts off*). What is it, Hap?

HAPPY (*offstage*). It's a punching bag!

BIFF. Oh, Pop!

WILLY. It's got Gene Tunney's signature on it!

(*Happy runs onstage with a punching bag.*)

BIFF. Gee, how'd you know we wanted a punching bag?

WILLY. Well, it's the finest thing for the timing.

HAPPY (*lies down on his back and pedals with his feet*). I'm losing weight, you notice, Pop?

WILLY (*to Happy*). Jumping rope is good too.

BIFF. Did you see the new football I got?

WILLY (*examining the ball*). Where'd you get a new ball?

BIFF. The coach told me to practice my passing.

WILLY. That so? And he gave you the ball, heh?

BIFF. Well, I borrowed it from the locker room. (*He laughs confidentially.*)

WILLY (*laughing with him at the theft*). I want you to return that.

HAPPY. I told you he wouldn't like it!

BIFF (*angrily*). Well, I'm bringing it back!

WILLY (*stopping the incipient argument, to Happy*). Sure, he's gotta practice with a regulation ball, doesn't he? (*To Biff*) Coach'll probably congratulate you on your intiative!

BIFF. Oh, he keeps congratulating my initiative all the time, Pop.

WILLY. That's because he likes you. If somebody else took that ball there'd be an uproar. So what's the report, boys, what's the report?

BIFF. Where'd you go this time, Dad? Gee we were lonesome for you.

WILLY (*pleased, puts an arm around each boy and they come down to the apron*). Lonesome, heh?

BIFF. Missed you every minute.

WILLY. Don't say? Tell you a secret, boys. Don't breathe

it to a soul. Someday I'll have my own business, and I'll never have to leave home any more.

HAPPY. Like Uncle Charley, heh?

WILLY. Bigger than Uncle Charley! Because Charley is not—liked. He's liked, but he's not—well liked.

BIFF. Where'd you go this time, Dad?

WILLY. Well, I got on the road, and I went north to Providence. Met the Mayor.

BIFF. The Mayor of Providence!

WILLY. He was sitting in the hotel lobby.

BIFF. What'd he say?

WILLY. He said, "Morning!" And I said, "You got a fine city here, Mayor." And then he had coffee with me. And then I went to Waterbury. Waterbury is a fine city. Big clock city, the famous Waterbury clock. Sold a nice bill there. And then Boston—Boston is the cradle of the Revolution. A fine city. And a couple of other towns in Mass., and on to Portland and Bangor and straight home!

BIFF. Gee, I'd love to go with you sometime, Dad.

WILLY. Soon as summer comes.

HAPPY. Promise?

WILLY. You and Hap and I, and I'll show you all the towns. America is full of beautiful towns and fine, upstanding people. And they know me, boys, they know me up and down New England. The finest people. And when I bring you fellas up, there'll be open sesame for all of us, 'cause one thing, boys: I have friends. I can park my car in any street in New England, and the cops protect it like their own. This summer, heh?

BIFF AND HAPPY (*together*). Yeah! You bet!

WILLY. We'll take our bathing suits.

HAPPY. We'll carry your bags, Pop!

WILLY. Oh, won't that be something! Me comin' into the Boston stores with you boys carryin' my bags. What a sensation!

(*Biff is prancing around, practicing passing the ball.*)

WILLY. You nervous, Biff, about the game?

BIFF. Not if you're gonna be there.

WILLY. What do they say about you in school, now that they made you captain?

HAPPY. There's a crowd of girls behind him every time the classes change.

BIFF (*taking Willy's hand*). This Saturday, Pop, this Saturday—just for you, I'm going to break through for a touchdown.

HAPPY. You're supposed to pass.

BIFF. I'm takin' one play for Pop. You watch me, Pop, and when I take off my helmet, that means I'm breakin' out. Then you watch me crash through that line!

WILLY (*kisses Biff*). Oh, wait'll I tell this in Boston!

(*Bernard enters in knickers. He is younger than Biff, earnest and loyal, a worried boy.*)

BERNARD. Biff, where are you? You're supposed to study with me today.

WILLY. Hey, looka Bernard. What're you lookin' so anemic about, Bernard?

BERNARD. He's gotta study, Uncle Willy. He's got Regents next week.

HAPPY (*tauntingly, spinning Bernard around*). Let's box, Bernard!

BERNARD. Biff! (*He gets away from Happy.*) Listen, Biff, I heard Mr. Birnbaum say that if you don't start studyin' math he's gonna flunk you, and you won't graduate. I heard him!

WILLY. You better study with him, Biff. Go ahead now.

BERNARD. I heard him!

BIFF. Oh, Pop, you didn't see my sneakers! (*He holds up a foot for Willy to look at.*)

WILLY. Hey, that's a beautiful job of printing!

BERNARD (*wiping his glasses*). Just because he printed University of Virginia on his sneakers doesn't mean they've got to graduate him, Uncle Willy!

WILLY (*angrily*). What're you talking about? With scholarships to three universities they're gonna flunk him?

BERNARD. But I heard Mr. Birnbaum say—

WILLY. Don't be a pest, Bernard! (*To his boys*) What an anemic!

BERNARD. Okay, I'm waiting for you in my house, Biff.

(*Bernard goes off. The Lomans laugh.*)

WILLY. Bernard is not well liked, is he?

BIFF. He's liked, but he's not well liked.

HAPPY. That's right, Pop.

WILLY. That's just what I mean. Bernard can get the best marks in school, y'understand, but when he gets out in the business world, y'understand, you are going to be five times ahead of him. That's why I thank Almighty God you're both built like Adonises. Because the man who makes an appearance in the business world, the man who creates personal interest, is the man who gets ahead. Be liked and you will never want. You take me, for instance. I never have to wait in line to see a buyer. "Willy Loman is here!" That's all they have to know, and I go right through.

BIFF. Did you knock them dead, Pop?

WILLY. Knocked 'em cold in Providence, slaughtered 'em in Boston.

HAPPY (*on his back, pedaling again*). I'm losing weight, you notice, Pop?

(*Linda enters, as of old, a ribbon in her hair, carrying a basket of washing.*)

LINDA (*with youthful energy*). Hello, dear!
WILLY. Sweetheart!
LINDA. How'd the Chevvy run?
WILLY. Chevrolet, Linda, is the greatest car ever built. (*To the boys*) Since when do you let your mother carry wash up the stairs?
BIFF. Grab hold there, boy!
HAPPY. Where to, Mom?
LINDA. Hang them up on the line. And you better go down to your friends, Biff. The cellar is full of boys. They don't know what to do with themselves.
BIFF. Ah, when Pop comes home they can wait!
WILLY (*laughs appreciatively*). You better go down and tell them what to do, Biff.
BIFF. I think I'll have them sweep out the furnace room.
WILLY. Good work, Biff.
BIFF (*goes through wall-line of kitchen to doorway at back and calls down*). Fellas! Everybody sweep out the furnace room! I'll be right down!
VOICES: All right! Okay, Biff.
BIFF. George and Sam and Frank, come out back! We're hangin' up the wash! Come on, Hap, on the double! (*He and Happy carry out the basket.*)
LINDA. The way they obey him!
WILLY. Well, that's training, the training. I'm tellin' you, I was sellin' thousands and thousands, but I had to come home.
LINDA. Oh, the whole block'll be at that game. Did you sell anything?
WILLY. I did five hundred gross in Providence and seven hundred gross in Boston.
LINDA. No! Wait a minute, I've got a pencil. (*She pulls pencil and paper out of her apron pocket.*) That makes your commission . . . Two hundred—my God! Two hundred and twelve dollars!
WILLY. Well, I didn't figure it yet, but . . .
LINDA. How much did you do?
WILLY. Well, I—I did—abouta hundred and eighty gross in Providence. Well, no—it came to—roughly two hundred gross on the whole trip.
LINDA (*without hesitation*). Two hundred gross. That's . . . (*She figures.*)
WILLY. The trouble was that three of the stores were half closed for inventory in Boston. Otherwise I woulda broke records.
LINDA. Well, it makes seventy dollars and some pennies. That's very good.
WILLY. What do we owe?
LINDA. Well, on the first there's sixteen dollars on the refrigerator—
WILLY. Why sixteen?
LINDA. Well, the fan belt broke, so it was a dollar eighty.
WILLY. But it's brand new.
LINDA. Well, the man said that's the way it is. Till they work themselves in, y'know.

(*They move through the wall-line into the kitchen.*)

WILLY. I hope we didn't get stuck on that machine.
LINDA. They got the biggest ads of any of them!
WILLY. I know, it's a fine machine. What else?
LINDA. Well, there's nine-sixty for the washing machine. And for the vacuum cleaner there's three and a half due on the fifteenth. Then the roof, you got twenty-one dollars remaining.
WILLY. It don't leak, does it?
LINDA. No, they did a wonderful job. Then you owe Frank for the carburetor.
WILLY. I'm not going to pay that man! That goddam Chevrolet, they ought to prohibit the manufacture of that car!
LINDA. Well, you owe him three and a half. And odds and ends, comes to around a hundred and twenty dollars by the fifteenth.
WILLY. A hundred and twenty dollars! My God, if business don't pick up I don't know what I'm gonna do!
LINDA. Well, next week you'll do better.
WILLY. Oh, I'll knock 'em dead next week. I'll go to Hartford. I'm very well liked in Hartford. You know, the trouble is, Linda, people don't seem to take to me.

(*They move onto the forestage.*)

LINDA. Oh, don't be foolish.
WILLY. I know it when I walk in. They seem to laugh at me.
LINDA. Why? Why would they laugh at you? Don't talk that way, Willy.

(*Willy moves to the edge of the stage. Linda goes into the kitchen and starts to darn stockings.*)

WILLY. I don't know the reason for it, but they just pass me by. I'm not noticed.
LINDA. But you're doing wonderful, dear. You're making seventy to a hundred dollars a week.
WILLY. But I gotta be at it ten, twelve hours a day. Other men—I don't know—they do it easier. I don't know why—I can't stop myself—I talk too much. A man oughta come in with a few words. One thing about Charley. He's a man of few words, and they respect him.
LINDA. You don't talk too much, you're just lively.
WILLY (*smiling*). Well, I figure, what the hell, life is short, a couple of jokes. (*To himself*) I joke too much! (*The smiles goes.*)

LINDA. Why? You're—

WILLY. I'm fat. I'm very—foolish to look at, Linda. I didn't tell you, but Christmas time I happened to be calling on F. H. Stewarts, and a salesman I know, as I was going in to see the buyer I heard him say something about—walrus. And I—I cracked him right across the face. I won't take that. I simply will not take that. But they do laugh at me. I know that.

LINDA. Darling . . .

WILLY. I gotta overcome it. I know I gotta overcome it. I'm not dressing to advantage, maybe.

LINDA. Willy, darling, you're the handsomest man in the world—

WILLY. Oh, no, Linda.

LINDA. To me you are. (*Slight pause.*) The handsomest.

(*From the darkness is heard the laughter of a woman. Willy doesn't turn to it, but it continues through Linda's lines.*)

LINDA. And the boys, Willy. Few men are idolized by their children the way you are.

(*Music is heard as behind a scrim, to the left of the house, The Woman, dimly seen, is dressing.*)

WILLY (*with great feeling*). You're the best there is, Linda, you're a pal, you know that? On the road—on the road I want to grab you sometimes and just kiss the life outa you.

(*The laughter is loud now, and he moves into a brightening area at the left, where The Woman has come from behind the scrim and is standing, putting on her hat, looking into a "mirror" and laughing.*)

WILLY. 'Cause I get so lonely—especially when business is bad and there's nobody to talk to. I get the feeling that I'll never sell anything again, that I won't make a living for you, or a business, business for the boys. (*He talks through The Woman's subsiding laughter; The Woman primps at the "mirror."*) There's so much I want to make for—

THE WOMAN. Me? You didn't make me, Willy. I picked you.

WILLY (*pleased*). You picked me?

THE WOMAN (*who is quite proper-looking, Willy's age*). I did. I've been sitting at that desk watching all the salesmen go by, day in, day out. But you've got such a sense of humor, and we do have such a good time together, don't we?

WILLY. Sure, sure. (*He takes her in his arms.*) Why do you have to go now?

THE WOMAN. It's two o'clock . . .

WILLY. No, come on in! (*He pulls her.*)

THE WOMAN. . . . my sisters'll be scandalized. When'll you be back?

WILLY. Oh, two weeks about. Will you come up again?

THE WOMAN. Sure thing. You do make me laugh. It's good for me. (*She squeezes his arm, kisses him.*) And I think you're a wonderful man.

WILLY. You picked me, heh?

THE WOMAN. Sure. Because you're so sweet. And such a kidder.

WILLY. Well, I'll see you next time I'm in Boston.

THE WOMAN. I'll put you right through to the buyers.

WILLY (*slapping her bottom*). Right. Well, bottoms up!

THE WOMAN (*slaps him gently and laughs*). You just kill me, Willy. (*He suddenly grabs her and kisses her roughly.*) You kill me. And thanks for the stockings. I love a lot of stockings. Well, good night.

WILLY. Good night. And keep your pores open!

THE WOMAN. Oh, Willy!

(*The Woman bursts out laughing, and Linda's laughter blends in. The Woman disappears into the dark. Now the area at the kitchen table brightens. Linda is sitting where she was at the kitchen table, but now is mending a pair of her silk stockings.*)

LINDA. You are, Willy. The handsomest man. You've got no reason to feel that—

WILLY (*coming out of The Woman's dimming area and going over to Linda*). I'll make it all up to you, Linda, I'll—

LINDA. There's nothing to make up, dear. You're doing fine, better than—

WILLY (*noticing her mending*). What's that?

LINDA. Just mending my stockings. They're so expensive—

WILLY (*angrily, taking them from her*). I won't have you mending stockings in this house! Now throw them out!

(*Linda puts the stockings in her pocket.*)

BERNARD (*entering on the run*). Where is he? If he doesn't study!

WILLY (*moving to the forestage, with great agitation*). You'll give him the answers!

BERNARD. I do, but I can't on a Regents! That's a state exam! They're liable to arrest me!

WILLY. Where is he? I'll whip him, I'll whip him!

LINDA. And he'd better give back that football, Willy, it's not nice.

WILLY. Biff! Where is he? Why is he taking everything?

LINDA. He's too rough with the girls, Willy. All the mothers are afraid of him!

WILLY. I'll whip him!

BERNARD. He's driving the car without a license!

(*The Woman's laugh is heard.*)

WILLY. Shut up!

LINDA. All the mothers—

WILLY. Shut up!

BERNARD (*backing quietly away and out*). Mr. Birnbaum says he's stuck up.

WILLY. Get outa here!

BERNARD. If he doesn't buckle down he'll flunk math! (*He goes off.*)

LINDA. He's right, Willy, you've gotta—

WILLY (*exploding at her*). There's nothing the matter with him! You want him to be a worm like Bernard? He's got spirit, personality . . .

(*As he speaks, Linda, almost in tears, exits into the living room. Willy is alone in the kitchen, wilting and staring. The leaves are gone. It is night again, and the apartment houses look down from behind.*)

WILLY. Loaded with it. Loaded! What is he stealing? He's giving it back, isn't he? Why is he stealing? What did I tell him? I never in my life told him anything but decent things.

(*Happy in pajamas has come down the stairs; Willy suddenly becomes aware of Happy's presence.*)

HAPPY. Let's go now, come on.

WILLY (*sitting down at the kitchen table*). Huh! Why did she have to wax the floors herself? Everytime she waxes the floors she keels over. She knows that!

HAPPY. Shh! Take it easy. What brought you back tonight?

WILLY. I got an awful scare. Nearly hit a kid in Yonkers. God! Why didn't I go to Alaska with my brother Ben that time! Ben! That man was a genius, that man was success incarnate! What a mistake! He begged me to go.

HAPPY. Well, there's no use in—

WILLY. You guys! There was a man started with the clothes on his back and ended up with diamond mines!

HAPPY. Boy, someday I'd like to know how he did it.

WILLY. What's the mystery? The man knew what he wanted and went out and got it! Walked into a jungle, and comes out, the age of twenty-one, and he's rich! The world is an oyster, but you don't crack it open on a mattress!

HAPPY. Pop, I told you I'm gonna retire you for life.

WILLY. You'll retire me for life on seventy goddam dollars a week? And your women and your car and your apartment, and you'll retire me for life! Christ's sake, I couldn't get past Yonkers today! Where are you guys, where are you? The woods are burning! I can't drive a car!

(*Charley has appeared in the doorway. He is a large man, slow of speech, laconic, immovable. In all he says, despite what he says, there is pity, and, now, trepidation. He has a robe over pajamas, slippers on his feet. He enters the kitchen.*)

CHARLEY. Everything all right?

HAPPY. Yeah, Charley, everything's . . .

WILLY. What's the matter?

CHARLEY. I heard some noise. I thought something happened. Can't we do something about the walls? You sneeze in here, and in my house hats blow off.

HAPPY. Let's go to bed, Dad. Come on.

(*Charley signals to Happy to go.*)

WILLY. You go ahead, I'm not tired at the moment.

HAPPY (*to Willy*). Take it easy, huh? (*He exits.*)

WILLY. What're you doin' up?

CHARLEY (*sitting down at the kitchen table opposite Willy*). Couldn't sleep good. I had a heartburn.

WILLY. Well, you don't know how to eat.

CHARLEY. I eat with my mouth.

WILLY. No, you're ignorant. You gotta know about vitamins and things like that.

CHARLEY. Come on, let's shoot. Tire you out a little.

WILLY (*hesitantly*). All right. You got cards?

CHARLEY (*taking a deck from his pocket*). Yeah, I got them. Someplace. What is it with those vitamins?

WILLY (*dealing*). They build up your bones. Chemistry.

CHARLEY. Yeah, but there's no bones in a heartburn.

WILLY. What are you talkin' about? Do you know the first thing about it?

CHARLEY. Don't get insulted.

WILLY. Don't talk about something you don't know anything about.

(*They are playing. Pause.*)

CHARLEY. What're you doin' home?

WILLY. A little trouble with the car.

CHARLEY. Oh. (*Pause.*) I'd like to take a trip to California.

WILLY. Don't say.

CHARLEY. You want a job?

WILLY. I got a job, I told you that. (*After a slight pause*) What the hell are you offering me a job for?

CHARLEY. Don't get insulted.

WILLY. Don't insult me.

CHARLEY. I don't see no sense in it. You don't have to go on this way.

WILLY. I got a good job. (*Slight pause.*) What do you keep comin' in here for?

CHARLEY. You want me to go?

WILLY (*after a pause, withering*). I can't understand it. He's going back to Texas again. What the hell is that?

CHARLEY. Let him go.

WILLY. I got nothin' to give him, Charley, I'm clean, I'm clean.

CHARLEY. He won't starve. None a them starve. Forget about him.

WILLY. Then what have I got to remember?

CHARLEY. You take it too hard. To hell with it. When a deposit bottle is broken you don't get your nickel back.

WILLY. That's easy enough for you to say.

CHARLEY. That ain't easy for me to say.

WILLY. Did you see the ceiling I put up in the living room?

CHARLEY. Yeah, that's a piece of work. To put up a ceiling is a mystery to me. How do you do it?

WILLY. What's the difference?

CHARLEY. Well, talk about it.

WILLY. You gonna put up a ceiling?

CHARLEY. How could I put up a ceiling?

WILLY. Then what the hell are you bothering me for?

CHARLEY. You're insulted again.

WILLY. A man who can't handle tools is not a man. You're disgusting.

CHARLEY. Don't call me disgusting, Willy.

(*Uncle Ben, carrying a valise and an umbrella, enters the forestage from around the right corner of the house. He is a stolid man, in his sixties, with a mustache and an authoritative air. He is utterly certain of his destiny, and there is an aura of far places about him. He enters exactly as Willy speaks.*)

WILLY. I'm getting awfully tired, Ben.

(*Ben's music is heard. Ben looks around at everything.*)

CHARLEY. Good, keep playing; you'll sleep better. Did you call me Ben?

(*Ben looks at his watch.*)

WILLY. That's funny. For a second there you reminded me of my brother Ben.

BEN. I only have a few minutes. (*He strolls, inspecting the place. Willy and Charley continue playing.*)

CHARLEY. You never heard from him again, heh? Since that time?

WILLY. Didn't Linda tell you? Couple of weeks ago we got a letter from his wife in Africa. He died.

CHARLEY. That so.

BEN (*chuckling*). So this is Brooklyn, eh?

CHARLEY. Maybe you're in for some of his money.

WILLY. Naa, he had seven sons. There's just one opportunity I had with that man . . .

BEN. I must make a train, William. There are several properties I'm looking at in Alaska.

WILLY. Sure, sure! If I'd gone with him to Alaska that time, everything would've been totally different.

CHARLEY. Go on, you'd froze to death up there.

WILLY. What're you talking about?

BEN. Opportunity is tremendous in Alaska, William. Surprised you're not up there.

WILLY. Sure, tremendous.

CHARLEY. Heh?

WILLY. There was the only man I ever met who knew the answers.

CHARLEY. Who?

BEN. How are you all?

WILLY (*taking a pot, smiling*). Fine, fine.

CHARLEY. Pretty sharp tonight.

BEN. Is Mother living with you?

WILLY. No, she died a long time ago.

CHARLEY. Who?

BEN. That's too bad. Fine specimen of a lady, Mother.

WILLY (*to Charley*). Heh?

BEN. I'd hoped to see the old girl.

CHARLEY. Who died?

BEN. Heard anything from Father, have you?

WILLY (*unnerved*). What do you mean, who died?

CHARLEY (*taking a pot*). What're you talkin' about?

BEN (*looking at his watch*). William, it's half-past eight!

WILLY (*as though to dispel his confusion he angrily stops Charley's hand*). That's my build!

CHARLEY. I put the ace—

WILLY. If you don't know how to play the game I'm not gonna throw my money away on you!

CHARLEY (*rising*). It was my ace, for God's sake!

WILLY. I'm through, I'm through!

BEN. When did Mother die?

WILLY. Long ago. Since the beginning you never knew how to play cards.

CHARLEY (*picks up the cards and goes to the door*). All right! Next time I'll bring a deck with five aces.

WILLY. I don't play that kind of game!

CHARLEY (*turning to him*). You ought to be ashamed of yourself!

WILLY. Yeah?

CHARLEY. Yeah! (*He goes out.*)

WILLY (*slamming the door after him*). Ignoramus!

BEN (*as Willy comes toward him through the wall-line of the kitchen*). So you're William.

WILLY (*shaking Ben's hand*). Ben! I've been waiting for you so long! What's the answer? How did you do it?

BEN. Oh, there's a story in that.

(*Linda enters the forestage, as of old, carrying the wash basket.*)

LINDA. Is this Ben?

BEN (*gallantly*). How do you do, my dear.

LINDA. Where've you been all these years? Willy's always wondered why you—

WILLY (*pulling Ben away from her impatiently*). Where is Dad? Didn't you follow him? How did you get started?

BEN. Well, I don't know how much you remember.

WILLY. Well, I was just a baby, of course, only three or four years old—

BEN. Three years and eleven months.

WILLY. What a memory, Ben!

BEN. I have many enterprises, William, and I have never kept books.

WILLY. I remember I was sitting under the wagon in—was it Nebraska?

BEN. It was South Dakota, and I gave you a bunch of wild flowers.

WILLY. I remember you walking away down some open road.

BEN (*laughing*). I was going to find Father in Alaska.

WILLY. Where is he?

BEN. At that age I had a very faulty view of geography, William. I discovered after a few days that I was heading due south, so instead of Alaska, I ended up in Africa.

LINDA. Africa!

WILLY. The Gold Coast!

BEN. Principally diamond mines.

LINDA. Diamond mines!

BEN. Yes, my dear. But I've only a few minutes—

WILLY. No! Boys! Boys! (*Young Biff and Happy appear.*) Listen to this. This is your Uncle Ben, a great man! Tell my boys, Ben!

BEN. Why, boys, when I was seventeen I walked into the jungle, and when I was twenty-one I walked out. (*He laughs.*) And by God I was rich.

WILLY (*to the boys*). You see what I been talking about? The greatest things can happen!

BEN (*glancing at his watch*). I have an appointment in Ketchikan Tuesday week.

WILLY. No, Ben! Please tell about Dad. I want my boys to hear. I want them to know the kind of stock they spring from. All I remember is a man with a big beard, and I was in Mamma's lap, sitting around a fire, and some kind of high music.

BEN. His flute. He played the flute.

WILLY. Sure, the flute, that's right!

(*New music is heard, a high, rollicking tune.*)

BEN. Father was a very great and a very wild-hearted man. We would start in Boston, and he'd toss the whole family into the wagon, and then he'd drive the team right across the country; through Ohio, and Indiana, Michigan, Illinois, and all the Western states. And we'd stop in the towns and sell the flutes that he'd made on the way. Great inventor, Father. With one gadget he made more in a week than a man like you could make in a lifetime.

WILLY. That's just the way I'm bringing them up, Ben—rugged, well liked, all-around.

BEN. Yeah? (*To Biff*). Hit that, boy—hard as you can. (*He pounds his stomach.*)

BIFF. Oh, no, sir!

BEN (*taking boxing stance*). Come on, get to me! (*He laughs.*)

WILLY. Go to it, Biff! Go ahead, show him!

BIFF. Okay! (*He cocks his fists and starts in.*)

LINDA (*to Willy*). Why must he fight, dear?

BEN (*sparring with Biff*). Good boy! Good boy!

WILLY. How's that, Ben, heh?

HAPPY. Give him the left, Biff!

LINDA. Why are you fighting?

BEN. Good boy! (*Suddenly comes in, trips Biff, and stands over him, the point of his umbrella poised over Biff's eye.*)

LINDA. Look out, Biff!

BIFF. Gee!

BEN (*patting Biff's knee*). Never fight fair with a stranger, boy. You'll never get out of the jungle that way. (*Taking Linda's hand and bowing*) It was an honor and a pleasure to meet you, Linda.

LINDA (*withdrawing her hand coldly, frightened*). Have a nice—trip.

BEN (*to Willy*). And good luck with your—what do you do?

WILLY. Selling.

BEN. Yes. Well . . . (*He raises his hand in farewell to all.*)

WILLY. No, Ben, I don't want you to think . . . (*He takes Ben's arm to show him.*) It's Brooklyn, I know, but we hunt too.

BEN. Really, now.

WILLY. Oh, sure, there's snakes and rabbits and—that's why I moved out here. Why, Biff can fell any one of these trees in no time! Boys! Go right over to where they're building the apartment house and get some sand. We're gonna rebuild the entire front stoop right now! Watch this, Ben!

BIFF. Yes, sir! On the double, Hap!

HAPPY (*as he and Biff run off*). I lost weight, Pop, you notice?

(*Charley enters in knickers, even before the boys are gone.*)

CHARLEY. Listen, if they steal any more from that building the watchman'll put the cops on them!

LINDA (*to Willy*). Don't let Biff . . .

(*Ben laughs lustily.*)

WILLY. You shoulda seen the lumber they brought home last week. At least a dozen six-by-tens worth all kinds a money.

CHARLEY. Listen, if that watchman—

WILLY. I gave them hell, understand. But I got a couple of fearless characters there.

CHARLEY. Willy, the jails are full of fearless characters.

BEN (*clapping Willy on the back, with a laugh at Charley*). And the stock exchange, friend!

WILLY (*joining in Ben's laughter*). Where are the rest of your pants?

CHARLEY. My wife bought them.

WILLY. Now all you need is a golf club and you can go upstairs and go to sleep. (*To Ben*) Great athlete! Between him and his son Bernard they can't hammer a nail!

BERNARD (*rushing in*). The watchman's chasing Biff!

WILLY (*angrily*). Shut up! He's not stealing anything!

LINDA (*alarmed, hurrying off left*). Where is he? Biff, dear! (*She exits.*)

WILLY (*moving toward the left, away from Ben*). There's nothing wrong. What's the matter with you?

BEN. Nervy boy. Good!

WILLY (*laughing*). Oh, nerves of iron, that Biff!

CHARLEY. Don't know what it is. My New England man comes back and he's bleedin', they murdered him up there.

WILLY. It's contacts, Charley, I got important contacts!

CHARLEY (*sarcastically*). Glad to hear it, Willy. Come in later, we'll shoot a little casino. I'll take some of your Portland money. (*He laughs at Willy and exits.*)

WILLY (*turning to Ben*). Business is bad, it's murderous. But not for me, of course.

BEN. I'll stop by on my way back to Africa.

WILLY (*longingly*). Can't you stay for a few days? You're just what I need, Ben, because I—I have a fine position here, but I—well, Dad left when I was such a baby and I never had a chance to talk to him and I still feel—kind of temporary about myself.

BEN. I'll be late for my train.

(*They are at opposite ends of the stage.*)

WILLY. Ben, my boys—can't we talk? They'd go into the jaws of hell for me, see, but I—

BEN. William, you're being first-rate with your boys. Outstanding, manly chaps!

WILLY (*hanging on to his words*). Oh, Ben, that's good to hear! Because sometimes I'm afraid that I'm not teaching them the right kind of—Ben, how should I teach them?

BEN (*giving great weight to each word, and with a certain vicious audacity*). William, when I walked into the jungle, I was seventeen. When I walked out I was twenty-one. And, by God, I was rich! (*He goes off into darkness around the right corner of the house.*)

WILLY. . . . was rich! That's just the spirit I want to imbue them with! To walk into a jungle! I was right! I was right! I was right!

(*Ben is gone, but Willy is still speaking to him as Linda, in nightgown and robe, enters the kitchen, glances around for Willy, then goes to the door of the house, looks out and sees him. Comes down to his left. He looks at her.*)

LINDA. Willy, dear? Willy?

WILLY. I was right!

LINDA. Did you have some cheese? (*He can't answer.*) It's very late, darling. Come to bed, heh?

WILLY (*looking straight up*). Gotta break your neck to see a star in this yard.

LINDA. You coming in?

WILLY. Whatever happened to that diamond watch fob? Remember? When Ben came from Africa that time? Didn't he give me a watch fob with a diamond in it?

LINDA. You pawned it, dear. Twelve, thirteen years ago. For Biff's radio correspondence course.

WILLY. Gee, that was a beautiful thing. I'll take a walk.

LINDA. But you're in your slippers.

WILLY (*starting to go around the house at the left*). I was right! I was! (*Half to Linda, as he goes, shaking his head*) What a man! There was a man worth talking to. I was right!

LINDA (*calling after Willy*). But in your slippers, Willy!

(*Willy is almost gone when Biff, in his pajamas, comes down the stairs and enters the kitchen.*)

BIFF. What is he doing out there?

LINDA. Sh!

BIFF. God Almighty, Mom, how long has he been doing this?

LINDA. Don't, he'll hear you.

BIFF. What the hell is the matter with him?

LINDA. It'll pass by morning.

BIFF. Shouldn't we do anything?

LINDA. Oh, my dear, you should do a lot of things, but there's nothing to do, so go to sleep.

(*Happy comes down the stairs and sits on the steps.*)

HAPPY. I never heard him so loud, Mom.

LINDA. Well, come around more often; you'll hear him. (*She sits down at the table and mends the lining of Willy's jacket.*)

BIFF. Why didn't you ever write me about this, Mom?

LINDA. How could I write to you? For over three months you had no address.

BIFF. I was on the move. But you know I thought of you all the time. You know that, don't you, pal?

LINDA. I know, dear, I know. But he likes to have a letter. Just to know that there's still a possibility for better things.

BIFF. He's not like this all the time, is he?

LINDA. It's when you come home he's always the worst.

BIFF. When I come home?

LINDA. When you write you're coming, he's all smiles,

and talks about the future, and—he's just wonderful. And then the closer you seem to come, the more shaky he gets, and then, by the time you get here, he's arguing, and he seems angry at you. I think it's just that maybe he can't bring himself to—to open up to you. Why are you so hateful to each other? Why is that?

BIFF (*evasively*). I'm not hateful, Mom.

LINDA. But you no sooner come in the door than you're fighting!

BIFF. I don't know why. I mean to change. I'm tryin', Mom, you understand?

LINDA. Are you home to stay now?

BIFF. I don't know. I want to look around, see what's doin'.

LINDA. Biff, you can't look around all your life, can you?

BIFF. I just can't take hold, Mom. I can't take hold of some kind of a life.

LINDA. Biff, a man is not a bird, to come and go with the springtime.

BIFF. Your hair . . . (*He touches her hair.*) Your hair got so gray.

LINDA. Oh, it's been gray since you were in high school. I just stopped dyeing it, that's all.

BIFF. Dye it again, will ya? I don't want my pal looking old. (*He smiles.*)

LINDA. You're such a boy! You think you can go away for a year and . . . You've got to get it into your head now that one day you'll knock on this door and there'll be strange people here—

BIFF. What are you talking about? You're not even sixty, Mom.

LINDA. But what about your father?

BIFF (*lamely*). Well, I meant him too.

HAPPY. He admires Pop.

LINDA. Biff, dear, if you don't have any feeling for him, then you can't have any feeling for me.

BIFF. Sure I can, Mom.

LINDA. No. You can't just come to see me, because I love him. (*With a threat, but only a threat, of tears*) He's the dearest man in the world to me, and I won't have anyone making him feel unwanted and low and blue. You've got to make up your mind now, darling, there's no leeway any more. Either he's your father and you pay him that respect, or else you're not to come here. I know he's not easy to get along with—nobody knows that better than me—but . . .

WILLY (*from the left, with a laugh*). Hey, hey, Biffo!

BIFF (*starting to go out after Willy*). What the hell is the matter with him? (*Happy stops him.*)

LINDA. Don't—don't go near him!

BIFF. Stop making excuses for him! He always, always wiped the floor with you. Never had an ounce of respect for you.

HAPPY. He's always had respect for—

BIFF. What the hell do you know about it?

HAPPY (*surlily*). Just don't call him crazy!

BIFF. He's got no character—Charley wouldn't do this. Not in his own house—spewing out that vomit from his mind.

HAPPY. Charley never had to cope with what he's got to.

BIFF. People are worse off than Willy Loman. Believe me, I've seen them!

LINDA. Then make Charley your father, Biff. You can't do that, can you? I don't say he's a great man. Willy Loman never made a lot of money. His name was never in the paper. He's not the finest character that ever lived. But he's a human being, and a terrible thing is happening to him. So attention must be paid. He's not to be allowed to fall into his grave like an old dog. Attention, attention must be finally paid to such a person. You called him crazy—

BIFF. I didn't mean—

LINDA. No, a lot of people think he's lost his—balance. But you don't have to be very smart to know what his trouble is. The man is exhausted.

HAPPY. Sure!

LINDA. A small man can be just as exhausted as a great man. He works for a company thirty-six years this March, opens up unheard-of territories to their trademark, and now in his old age they take his salary away.

HAPPY (*indignantly*). I didn't know that, Mom.

LINDA. You never asked, my dear! Now that you get your spending money someplace else you don't trouble your mind with him.

HAPPY. But I gave you money last—

LINDA. Christmas time, fifty dollars! To fix the hot water it cost ninety-seven fifty! For five weeks he's been on straight commission, like a beginner, an unknown!

BIFF. Those ungrateful bastards!

LINDA. Are they any worse than his sons? When he brought them business, when he was young, they were glad to see him. But now his old friends, the old buyers that loved him so and always found some order to hand him in a pinch—they're all dead, retired. He used to be able to make six, seven calls a day in Boston. Now he takes his valises out of the car and puts them back and takes them out again and he's exhausted. Instead of walking he talks now. He drives seven hundred miles, and when he gets there no one knows him any more, no one welcomes him. And what goes through a man's mind, driving seven hundred miles home without having earned a cent? Why shouldn't he talk to himself? Why? When he has to go to Charley and borrow fifty dollars a week and pretend to me that it's his pay? How long can that go on? How long? You see what I'm sitting here and waiting for? And you tell me he has no character?

The man who never worked a day but for your benefit? When does he get the medal for that? Is this his reward—to turn around at the age of sixty-three and find his sons, who he loved better than his life, one a philandering bum—

HAPPY. Mom!

LINDA. That's all you are, my baby! (*To Biff.*) And you! What happened to the love you had for him? You were such pals! How you used to talk to him on the phone every night! How lonely he was till he could come home to you!

BIFF. All right, Mom. I'll live here in my room, and I'll get a job. I'll keep away from him, that's all.

LINDA. No, Biff. You can't stay here and fight all the time.

BIFF. He threw me out of this house, remember that.

LINDA. Why did he do that? I never knew why.

BIFF. Because I know he's a fake and he doesn't like anybody around who knows!

LINDA. Why a fake? In what way? What do you mean?

BIFF. Just don't lay it all at my feet. It's between me and him—that's all I have to say. I'll chip in from now on. He'll settle for half my paycheck. He'll be all right. I'm going to bed. (*He starts for the stairs.*)

LINDA. He won't be all right.

BIFF (*turning on the stairs, furiously*). I hate this city and I'll stay here. Now what do you want?

LINDA. He's dying, Biff.

(*Happy turns quickly to her, shocked.*)

BIFF (*after a pause*). Why is he dying?

LINDA. He's been trying to kill himself.

BIFF (*with great horror*). How?

LINDA. I live from day to day.

BIFF. What're you talking about?

LINDA. Remember I wrote you that he smashed up the car again? in February?

BIFF. Well?

LINDA. The insurance inspector came. He said that they have evidence. That all these accidents in the last year—weren't—weren't—accidents.

HAPPY. How can they tell that? That's a lie.

LINDA. It seems there's a woman . . . (*She takes a breath as*—)

{ BIFF (*sharply but contained*). What woman?
{ LINDA (*simultaneously*). . . . and this woman . . .

LINDA. What?

BIFF. Nothing. Go ahead.

LINDA. What did you say?

BIFF. Nothing. I just said what woman?

HAPPY. What about her?

LINDA. Well, it seems she was walking down the road and saw his car. She says that he wasn't driving fast at all, and that he didn't skid. She says he came to that little bridge, and then deliberately smashed into the railing, and it was only the shallowness of the water that saved him.

BIFF. Oh, no, he probably just fell asleep again.

LINDA. I don't think he fell asleep.

BIFF. Why not?

LINDA. Last month . . . (*With great difficulty*) Oh, boys, it's so hard to say a thing like this! He's just a big stupid man to you, but I tell you there's more good in him than in many other people. (*She chokes, wipes her eyes.*) I was looking for a fuse. The lights blew out, and I went down the cellar. And behind the fuse box—it happened to fall out—was a length of rubber pipe—just short.

HAPPY. No kidding?

LINDA. There's a little attachment on the end of it. I knew right away. And sure enough, on the bottom of the water heater there's a new little nipple on the gas pipe.

HAPPY (*angrily*). That—jerk.

BIFF. Did you have it taken off?

LINDA. I'm—I'm ashamed to. How can I mention it to him? Every day I go down and take away that little rubber pipe. But, when he comes home, I put it back where it was. How can I insult him that way? I don't know what to do. I live from day to day, boys. I tell you, I know every thought in his mind. It sounds so old-fashioned and silly, but I tell you he put his whole life into you and you've turned your backs on him. (*She is bent over in the chair, weeping, her face in her hands.*) Biff, I swear to God! Biff, his life is in your hands!

HAPPY (*to Biff*). How do you like that damned fool!

BIFF (*kissing her*). All right, pal, all right. It's all settled now. I've been remiss. I know that, Mom. But now I'll stay, and I swear to you, I'll apply myself. (*Kneeling in front of her, in a fever of self-reproach*) It's just—you see, Mom, I don't fit in business. Not that I won't try. I'll try, and I'll make good.

HAPPY. Sure you will. The trouble with you in business was you never tried to please people.

BIFF. I know, I—

HAPPY. Like when you worked for Harrison's. Bob Harrison said you were tops, and then you go and do some damn fool thing like whistling whole songs in the elevator like a comedian.

BIFF (*against Happy*). So what? I like to whistle sometimes.

HAPPY. You don't raise a guy to a responsible job who whistles in the elevator!

LINDA. Well, don't argue about it now.

HAPPY. Like when you'd go off and swim in the middle of the day instead of taking the line around.

BIFF (*his resentment rising*). Well, don't you run off? You take off sometimes, don't you? On a nice summer day?

HAPPY. Yeah, but I cover myself!

LINDA. Boys!

HAPPY. If I'm going to take a fade the boss can call any number where I'm supposed to be and they'll swear to him that I just left. I'll tell you something that I hate to say, Biff, but in the business world some of them think you're crazy.

BIFF (*angered*). Screw the business world!

HAPPY. All right, screw it! Great, but cover yourself!

LINDA. Hap, Hap!

BIFF. I don't care what they think! They've laughed at Dad for years, and you know why? Because we don't belong in this nut-house of a city! We should be mixing cement on some open plain, or—or carpenters. A carpenter is allowed to whistle!

(*Willy walks in from the entrance of the house, at left.*)

WILLY. Even your grandfather was better than a carpenter. (*Pause. They watch him.*) You never grew up. Bernard does not whistle in the elevator, I assure you.

BIFF (*as though to laugh Willy out of it*). Yeah, but you do, Pop.

WILLY. I never in my life whistled in an elevator! And who in the business world thinks I'm crazy?

BIFF. I didn't mean it like that, Pop. Now don't make a whole thing out of it, will ya?

WILLY. Go back to the West! Be a carpenter, a cowboy, enjoy yourself!

LINDA. Willy, he was just saying—

WILLY. I heard what he said!

HAPPY (*trying to quiet Willy*). Hey, Pop, come on now . . .

WILLY (*continuing over Happy's line*). They laugh at me, heh? Go to Filene's, go to the Hub, go to Slattery's, Boston. Call out the name Willy Loman and see what happens! Big shot!

BIFF. All right, Pop.

WILLY. Big!

BIFF. All right!

WILLY. Why do you always insult me?

BIFF. I didn't say a word. (*To Linda*) Did I say a word?

LINDA. He didn't say anything, Willy.

WILLY (*going to the doorway of the living room*). All right, good night, good night.

LINDA. Willy, dear, he just decided . . .

WILLY (*to Biff*). If you get tired hanging around tomorrow, paint the ceiling I put up in the living room.

BIFF. I'm leaving early tomorrow.

HAPPY. He's going to see Bill Oliver, Pop.

WILLY (*interestedly*). Oliver? For what?

BIFF (*with reserve, but trying, trying*). He always said he'd stake me. I'd like to go into business, so maybe I can take him up on it.

LINDA. Isn't that wonderful?

WILLY. Don't interrupt. What's wonderful about it? There's fifty men in the City of New York who'd stake him. (*To Biff*) Sporting goods?

BIFF. I guess so. I know something about it and—

WILLY. He knows something about it! You know sporting goods better than Spalding, for God's sake! How much is he giving you?

BIFF. I don't know, I didn't even see him yet, but—

WILLY. Then what're you talkin' about?

BIFF (*getting angry*). Well, all I said was I'm gonna see him, that's all!

WILLY (*turning away*). Ah, you're counting your chickens again.

BIFF (*starting left for the stairs*). Oh, Jesus, I'm going to sleep!

WILLY (*calling after him*). Don't curse in this house!

BIFF (*turning*). Since when did you get so clean?

HAPPY (*trying to stop them*). Wait a . . .

WILLY. Don't use that language to me! I won't have it!

HAPPY (*grabbing Biff, shouts*). Wait a minute! I got an idea. I got a feasible idea. Come here, Biff, let's talk this over now, let's talk some sense here. When I was down in Florida last time, I thought of a great idea to sell sporting goods. It just came back to me. You and I, Biff—we have a line, the Loman Line. We train a couple of weeks, and put on a couple of exhibitions, see?

WILLY. That's an idea!

HAPPY. Wait! We form two basketball teams, see? Two water-polo teams. We play each other. It's a million dollars' worth of publicity. Two brothers, see? The Loman Brothers. Displays in the Royal Palms—all the hotels. And banners over the ring and the basketball court: "Loman Brothers." Baby, we could sell sporting goods!

WILLY. That is a one-million-dollar idea!

LINDA. Marvelous!

BIFF. I'm in great shape as far as that's concerned.

HAPPY. And the beauty of it is, Biff, it wouldn't be like a business. We'd be out playin' ball again.

BIFF (*enthused*). Yeah, that's . . .

WILLY. Million-dollar . . .

HAPPY. And you wouldn't get fed up with it, Biff. It'd be the family again. There'd be the old honor, and comradeship, and if you wanted to go off for a swim or somethin'—well, you'd do it! Without some smart cooky gettin' up ahead of you!

WILLY. Lick the world! You guys together could absolutely lick the civilized world.

BIFF. I'll see Oliver tomorrow. Hap, if we could work that out . . .

LINDA. Maybe things are beginning to—

WILLY (*wildly enthused, to Linda*). Stop interrupting! (*To Biff*) But don't wear sport jacket and slacks when you see Oliver.

BIFF. No, I'll—

WILLY. A business suit, and talk as little as possible, and don't crack any jokes.

BIFF. He did like me. Always liked me.

LINDA. He loved you!

WILLY (*to Linda*). Will you stop! (*To Biff*) Walk in very serious. You are not applying for a boy's job. Money is to pass. Be quiet, fine, and serious. Everybody likes a kidder, but nobody lends him money.

HAPPY. I'll try to get some myself, Biff. I'm sure I can.

WILLY. I see great things for you kids, I think your troubles are over. But remember, start big and you'll end big. Ask for fifteen. How much you gonna ask for?

BIFF. Gee, I don't know—

WILLY. And don't say "Gee." "Gee" is a boy's word. A man walking in for fifteen thousand dollars does not say "Gee!"

BIFF. Ten, I think, would be top though.

WILLY. Don't be so modest. You always started too low. Walk in with a big laugh. Don't look worried. Start off with a couple of your good stories to lighten things up. It's not what you say, it's how you say it—because personality always wins the day.

LINDA. Oliver always thought the highest of him—

WILLY. Will you let me talk?

BIFF. Don't yell at her, Pop, will ya?

WILLY (*angrily*). I was talking, wasn't I?

BIFF. I don't like you yelling at her all the time, and I'm tellin' you, that's all.

WILLY. What're you, takin' over this house?

LINDA. Willy—

WILLY (*turning on her*). Don't take his side all the time, goddammit!

BIFF (*furiously*). Stop yelling at her!

WILLY (*suddenly pulling on his cheek, beaten down, guilt ridden*). Give my best to Bill Oliver—he may remember me. (*He exits through the living room doorway.*)

LINDA (*her voice subdued*). What'd you have to start that for? (*Biff turns away*) You see how sweet he was as soon as you talked hopefully? (*She goes over to Biff*) Come up and say good night to him. Don't let him go to bed that way.

HAPPY. Come on, Biff let's buck him up.

LINDA. Please, dear. Just say good night. It takes so little to make him happy. Come. (*She goes through the living room doorway, calling upstairs from within the living room*) Your pajamas are hanging in the bathroom, Willy!

HAPPY (*looking toward where Linda went out*). What a woman! They broke the mold when they made her. You know that, Biff?

BIFF. He's off salary. My god, working on commission!

HAPPY. Well, let's face it: he's no hot-shot selling man. Except that sometimes, you have to admit, he's a sweet personality.

BIFF (*deciding*). Lend me ten bucks, will ya? I want to buy some new ties.

HAPPY. I'll take you to a place I know. Beautiful stuff. Wear one of my striped shirts tomorrow.

BIFF. She got gray. Mom got awful old. Gee, I'm gonna go in to Oliver tomorrow and knock him for a—

HAPPY. Come on up. Tell that to Dad. Let's give him a whirl. Come on.

BIFF (*steamed up*). You know, with ten thousand bucks, boy!

HAPPY (*as they go into the living room*). That's the talk, Biff, that's the first time I've heard the old confidence out of you! (*From within the living room, fading off*) You're gonna live with me, kid, and any babe you want just say the word . . . (*The last lines are hardly heard. They are mounting the stairs to their parents' bedroom.*)

LINDA (*entering her bedroom and addressing Willy, who is in the bathroom. She is straightening the bed for him*). Can you do anything about the shower? It drips.

WILLY (*from the bathroom*). All of a sudden everything falls to pieces! Goddam plumbing, oughta be sued, those people. I hardly finished putting it in and the thing . . . (*His words rumble off.*)

LINDA. I'm just wondering if Oliver will remember him. You think he might?

WILLY (*coming out of the bathroom in his pajamas*). Remember him? What's the matter with you, you crazy? If he'd've stayed with Oliver he'd be on top by now! Wait'll Oliver gets a look at him. You don't know the average caliber any more. The average young man today—(*he is getting into bed*)—is got a caliber of zero. Greatest thing in the world for him was to bum around.

(*Biff and Happy enter the bedroom. Slight pause.*)

WILLY (*stops short, looking at Biff*). Glad to hear it, boy.

HAPPY. He wanted to say good night to you, sport.

WILLY (*to Biff*). Yeah. Knock him dead, boy. What'd you want to tell me?

BIFF. Just take it easy, Pop. Good night. (*He turns to go.*)

WILLY (*unable to resist*). And if anything falls off the desk while you're talking to him—like a package or something—don't you pick it up. They have office boys for that.

LINDA. I'll make a big breakfast—

WILLY. Will you let me finish? (*To Biff*) Tell him you were in the business in the West. Not farm work.

BIFF. All right, Dad.

LINDA. I think everything—

WILLY (*going right through her speech*). And don't undersell yourself. No less than fifteen thousand dollars.

BIFF (*unable to bear him*). Okay. Good night, Mom. (*He starts moving.*)

WILLY. Because you got a greatness in you, Biff, remember that. You got all kinds a greatness . . .

(*He lies back, exhausted. Biff walks out.*)

LINDA (*calling after Biff*). Sleep well, darling!

HAPPY. I'm gonna get married, Mom. I wanted to tell you.

LINDA. Go to sleep, dear.

HAPPY (*going*). I just wanted to tell you.

WILLY. Keep up the good work. (*Happy exits.*) God . . . remember that Ebbets Field game? The championship of the city?

LINDA. Just rest. Should I sing to you?

WILLY. Yeah. Sing to me. (*Linda hums a soft lullaby.*) When that team came out—he was the tallest, remember?

LINDA. Oh, yes. And in gold.

(*Biff enters the darkened kitchen, takes a cigarette, and leaves the house. He comes downstage into a golden pool of light. He smokes, staring at the night.*)

WILLY. Like a young god. Hercules—something like that. And the sun, the sun all around him. Remember how he waved to me? Right up from the field, with the representatives of three colleges standing by? And the buyers I brought, and the cheers when he came out—Loman, Loman, Loman! God Almighty, he'll be great yet. A star like that, magnificent, can never really fade away!

(*The light on Willy is fading. The gas heater begins to glow through the kitchen wall, near the stairs, a blue flame beneath red coils.*)

LINDA (*timidly*). Willy dear, what has he got against you?

WILLY. I'm so tired. Don't talk any more.

(BIFF *slowly returns to the kitchen. He stops, stares toward the heater.*)

LINDA. Will you ask Howard to let you work in New York?

WILLY. First thing in the morning. Everything'll be all right.

(*Biff reaches behind the heater and draws out a length of rubber tubing. He is horrified and turns his head toward Willy's room, still dimly lit, from which the strains of Linda's desperate but monotonous humming rise.*)

WILLY (*staring through the window into the moonlight*). Gee, look at the moon moving between the buildings!

(*Biff wraps the tubing around his hand and quickly goes up the stairs.*)

CURTAIN

ACT 2

Music is heard, gay and bright. The curtain rises as the music fades away. Willy, in shirt sleeves, is sitting at the kitchen table, sipping coffee, his hat in his lap. Linda is filling his cup when she can.

WILLY. Wonderful coffee. Meal in itself.

LINDA. Can I make you some eggs?

WILLY. No. Take a breath.

LINDA. You look so rested, dear.

WILLY. I slept like a dead one. First time in months. Imagine, sleeping till ten on a Tuesday morning. Boys left nice and early, heh?

LINDA. They were out of here by eight o'clock.

WILLY. Good work!

LINDA. It was so thrilling to see them leaving together. I can't get over the shaving lotion in this house!

WILLY (*smiling*). Mmm—

LINDA. Biff was very changed this morning. His whole attitude seemed to be hopeful. He couldn't wait to get downtown to see Oliver.

WILLY. He's heading for a change. There's no question, there simply are certain men that take longer to get—solidified. How did he dress?

LINDA. His blue suit. He's so handsome in that suit. He could be a—anything in that suit!

(*Willy gets up from the table. Linda holds his jacket for him.*)

WILLY. There's no question, no question at all. Gee, on the way home tonight I'd like to buy some seeds.

LINDA (*laughing*). That'd be wonderful. But not enough sun gets back there. Nothing'll grow any more.

WILLY. You wait, kid, before it's all over we're gonna get a little place out in the country, and I'll raise some vegetables, a couple of chickens . . .

LINDA. You'll do it yet, dear.

(*Willy walks out of his jacket. Linda follows him.*)

WILLY. And they'll get married, and come for a weekend. I'd build a little guest house. 'Cause I got so many fine tools, all I'd need would be a little lumber and some peace of mind.

LINDA (*joyfully*). I sewed the lining . . .

WILLY. I could build two guest houses, so they'd both come. Did he decide how much he's going to ask Oliver for?

LINDA (*getting him into the jacket*). He didn't mention it, but I imagine ten or fifteen thousand. You going to talk to Howard today?

WILLY. Yeah. I'll put it to him straight and simple. He'll just have to take me off the road.

LINDA. And Willy, don't forget to ask for a little advance, because we've got the insurance premium. It's the grace period now.

WILLY. That's a hundred . . . ?

LINDA. A hundred and eight, sixty-eight. Because we're a little short again.

WILLY. Why are we short?

LINDA. Well, you had the motor job on the car . . .

WILLY. That goddam Studebaker!

LINDA. And you got one more payment on the refrigerator . . .

WILLY. But it just broke again!

LINDA. Well, it's old, dear.

WILLY. I told you we should've bought a well-advertised machine. Charley bought a General Electric and it's twenty years old and it's still good, that son-of-a-bitch.

LINDA. But, Willy—

WILLY. Whoever heard of a Hastings refrigerator? Once in my life I would like to own something outright before it's broken! I'm always in a race with the junkyard! I just finished paying for the car and it's on its last legs. The refrigerator consumes belts like a goddam maniac. They time those things. They time them so when you finally paid for them, they're used up.

LINDA (*buttoning up his jacket as he unbuttons it*). All told, about two hundred dollars would carry us, dear. But that includes the last payment on the mortgage. After this payment, Willy, the house belongs to us.

WILLY. It's twenty-five years!

LINDA. Biff was nine years old when we bought it.

WILLY. Well, that's a great thing. To weather a twenty-five year mortgage is—

LINDA. It's an accomplishment.

WILLY. All the cement, the lumber, the reconstruction I put in this house! There ain't a crack to be found in it any more.

LINDA. Well, it served its purpose.

WILLY. What purpose? Some stranger'll come along, move in, and that's that. If only Biff would take this house, and raise a family . . . (*He starts to go.*) Good-bye, I'm late.

LINDA (*suddenly remembering*). Oh, I forgot! You're supposed to meet them for dinner.

WILLY. Me?

LINDA. At Frank's Chop House on Forty-eighth near Sixth Avenue.

WILLY. Is that so! How about you?

LINDA. No, just the three of you. They're gonna blow you to a big meal!

WILLY. Don't say! Who thought of that?

LINDA. Biff came to me this morning, Willy, and he said, "Tell Dad, we want to blow him to a big meal." Be there six o'clock. You and your two boys are going to have dinner.

WILLY. Gee whiz! That's really somethin'. I'm gonna knock Howard for a loop, kid. I'll get an advance, and I'll come home with a New York job. Goddammit, now I'm gonna do it!

LINDA. Oh, that's the spirit, Willy!

WILLY. I will never get behind a wheel the rest of my life!

LINDA. It's changing, Willy, I can feel it changing!

WILLY. Beyond a question. G'by, I'm late. (*He starts to go again.*)

LINDA (*calling after him as she runs to the kitchen table for a handkerchief*). You got your glasses?

WILLY (*feels for them, then comes back in*). Yeah, yeah, got my glasses.

LINDA (*giving him the handkerchief*). And a handkerchief.

WILLY. Yeah, handkerchief.

LINDA. And your saccharine?

WILLY. Yeah, my saccharine.

LINDA. Be careful on the subway stairs.

(*She kisses him, and a silk stocking is seen hanging from her hand. Willy notices it.*)

WILLY. Will you stop mending stockings? At least while I'm in the house. It gets me nervous. I can't tell you. Please.

(*Linda hides the stocking in her hand as she follows Willy across the forestage in front of the house.*)

LINDA. Remember, Frank's Chop House.

WILLY (*passing the apron*). Maybe beets would grow out there.

LINDA (*laughing*). But you tried so many times.

WILLY. Yeah. Well, don't work hard today. (*He disappears around the right corner of the house.*)

LINDA. Be careful!

(*As Willy vanishes, Linda waves to him. Suddenly the phone rings. She runs across the stage and into the kitchen and lifts it.*)

LINDA. Hello? Oh, Biff! I'm so glad you called, I just . . . Yes, sure, I just told him. Yes, he'll be there for dinner at six o'clock, I didn't forget. Listen, I was just dying to tell you. You know that little rubber pipe I told you about? That he connected to the gas heater? I finally decided to go down the cellar this morning and take it away and destroy it. But it's gone! Imagine? He took it away himself, it isn't there! (*She listens.*) When? Oh, then you took it. Oh—nothing, it's just that I'd hoped he'd taken it away himself. Oh, I'm not worried, darling, because this morning he left in such high spirits, it was like the old days! I'm not afraid anymore. Did Mr. Oliver see you? . . . Well, you wait there then. And make a nice impression on him, darling. Just don't perspire too much before you see him. And have a nice time with Dad. He may have big news too! . . . That's right, a New York job. And be sweet to him tonight, dear. Be loving to him. Because he's only a little boat looking for a harbor. (*She is trembling with sorrow and joy.*) Oh, that's wonderful, Biff, you'll save his life. Thanks, darling. Just put your arm around him when he comes into the restaurant. Give him a smile. That's the boy . . . Goodbye, dear. . . . You got your comb? . . . That's fine. Good-bye, Biff dear.

(*In the middle of her speech, Howard Wagner, thirty-six, wheels in a small typewriter table on which is a wire-recording machine and proceeds to plug it in. This is on the left forestage. Light slowly fades on Linda as it rises on Howard. Howard is intent on threading the machine and only glances over his shoulder as Willy appears.*)

WILLY. Pst! Pst!

HOWARD. Hello, Willy, come in.

WILLY. Like to have a little talk with you, Howard.

HOWARD. Sorry to keep you waiting. I'll be with you in a minute.

WILLY. What's that, Howard?

HOWARD. Didn't you ever see one of these? Wire recorder.

WILLY. Oh. Can we talk a minute?

HOWARD. Records things. Just got delivery yesterday. Been driving me crazy, the most terrific machine I ever saw in my life. I was up all night with it.

WILLY. What do you do with it?

HOWARD. I bought it for dictation, but you can do anything with it. Listen to this. I had it home last night. Listen to what I picked up. The first one is my daughter. Get this. (*He flicks the switch and "Roll out the Barrel" is heard being whistled.*) Listen to that kid whistle.

WILLY. That is lifelike, isn't it?

HOWARD. Seven years old. Get that tone.

WILLY. Ts, ts. Like to ask a little favor of you . . .

(*The whistling breaks off, and the voice of Howard's Daughter is heard.*)

HIS DAUGHTER. "Now you, Daddy."

HOWARD. She's crazy for me! (*Again the same song is whistled.*) That's me! Ha! (*He winks.*)

WILLY. You're very good!

(*The whistling breaks off again. The machine runs silent for a moment.*)

HOWARD. Sh! Get this now, this is my son.

HIS SON. "The capital of Alabama is Montgomery; the capital of Arizona is Phoenix; the capital of Arkansas is Little Rock; the capital of California is Sacramento . . ." (*And on, and on.*)

HOWARD (*holding up five fingers*). Five years old, Willy!

WILLY. He'll make an announcer some day!

HIS SON (*continuing*). "The capital . . ."

HOWARD. Get that—alphabetical order! (*The machine breaks off suddenly.*) Wait a minute. The maid kicked the plug out.

WILLY. It certainly is a—

HOWARD. Sh, for God's sake!

HIS SON. "It's nine o'clock, Bulova watch time. So I have to go to sleep."

WILLY. That really is—

HOWARD. Wait a minute! The next is my wife.

(*They wait.*)

HOWARD'S VOICE. "Go on, say something." (*Pause.*) "Well, you gonna talk?"

HIS WIFE. "I can't think of anything."

HOWARD'S VOICE. "Well, talk—it's turning."

HIS WIFE (*shyly, beaten*). "Hello." (*Silence.*) "Oh, Howard, I can't talk into this . . ."

HOWARD (*snapping the machine off*). That was my wife.

WILLY. That is a wonderful machine. Can we—

HOWARD. I tell you, Willy, I'm gonna take my camera, and my bandsaw, and all my hobbies, and out they go. This is the most fascinating relaxation I ever found.

WILLY. I think I'll get one myself.

HOWARD. Sure, they're only a hundred and a half. You can't do without it. Supposing you wanna hear Jack Benny, see? But you can't be at home at that hour. So you tell the maid to turn the radio on when Jack Benny comes on, and this automatically goes on with the radio . . .

WILLY. And when you come home you . . .

HOWARD. You can come home twelve o'clock, one o'clock, any time you like, and you get yourself a Coke and sit yourself down, throw the switch, and there's Jack Benny's program in the middle of the night!

WILLY. I'm definitely going to get one. Because lots of time I'm on the road, and I think to myself, what I must be missing on the radio!

HOWARD. Don't you have a radio in the car?

WILLY. Well, yeah, but who ever thinks of turning it on?

HOWARD. Say, aren't you supposed to be in Boston?

WILLY. That's what I want to talk to you about, Howard. You got a minute? (*He draws a chair in from the wing.*)

HOWARD. What happened? What're you doing here?

WILLY. Well . . .

HOWARD. You didn't crack up again, did you?

WILLY. Oh, no. No . . .

HOWARD. Geez, you had me worried there for a minute. What's the trouble?

WILLY. Well, tell you the truth, Howard. I've come to the decision that I'd rather not travel any more.

HOWARD. Not travel! Well, what'll you do?

WILLY. Remember, Christmas time, when you had the party here? You said you'd try to think of some spot for me here in town.

HOWARD. With us?

WILLY. Well, sure.

HOWARD. Oh, yeah, yeah. I remember. Well, I couldn't think of anything for you, Willy.

WILLY. I tell ya, Howard. The kids are all grown up, y'know. I don't need much any more. If I could take home —well, sixty-five dollars a week, I could swing it.

HOWARD. Yeah, but Willy, see I—

WILLY. I tell ya why, Howard. Speaking frankly and between the two of us, y'know—I'm just a little tired.

HOWARD. Oh, I could understand that, Willy. But you're a road man, Willy, and we do a road business. We've only got a half-dozen salesmen on the floor here.

WILLY. God knows, Howard, I never asked a favor of any man. But I was with the firm when your father used to carry you in here in his arms.

HOWARD. I know that, Willy, but—

WILLY. Your father came to me the day you were born and asked me what I thought of the name of Howard, may he rest in peace.

HOWARD. I appreciate that, Willy, but there just is no spot here for you. If I had a spot I'd slam you right in, but I just don't have a single solitary spot.

(*He looks for his lighter. Willy has picked it up and gives it to him. Pause.*)

WILLY (*with increasing anger*). Howard, all I need to set my table is fifty dollars a week.

HOWARD. But where am I going to put you, kid?

WILLY. Look, it isn't a question of whether I can sell merchandise, is it?

HOWARD. No, but it's a business, kid, and everybody's gotta pull his own weight.

WILLY (*desperately*). Just let me tell you a story, Howard—

HOWARD. 'Cause you gotta admit, business is business.

WILLY (*angrily*). Business is definitely business, but just listen for a minute. You don't understand this. When I was a boy—eighteen, nineteen—I was already on the road. And there was a question in my mind as to whether selling had a future for me. Because in those days I had a yearning to go to Alaska. See, there were three gold strikes in one month in Alaska, and I felt like going out. Just for the ride, you might say.

HOWARD (*barely interested*). Don't say.

WILLY. Oh, yeah, my father lived many years in Alaska. He was an adventurous man. We've got quite a little streak of self-reliance in our family. I thought I'd go out with my older brother and try to locate him, and maybe settle in the North with the old man. And I was almost decided to go, when I met a salesman in the Parker House. His name was Dave Singleman. And he was eighty-four years old, and he'd drummed merchandise in thirty-one states. And old Dave, he'd go up to his room, y'understand, put on his green velvet slippers—I'll never forget—and pick up his phone and call the buyers, and without ever leaving his room, at the age of eighty-four, he made his living. And when I saw that, I realized that selling was the greatest career a man could want. 'Cause what could be more satisfying than to be able to go, at the age of eighty-four, into twenty or thirty different cities, and pick up a phone, and be remembered and loved and helped by so many different people? Do you know? when he died—and by the way he died the death of a salesman, in his green velvet slippers in the smoker of the New York, New Haven and Hartford, going into Boston—when he died, hundreds of salesmen and buyers were at his funeral. Things were sad on a lotta trains for months after that. (He stands up. *Howard* has not looked at him.) In those days there was personality in it, Howard. There was respect, and comradeship, and gratitude in it. Today, it's all cut and dried, and there's no chance for bringing friendship to bear—or personality. You see what I mean? They don't know me any more.

HOWARD (*moving away, to the right*). That's just the thing, Willy.

WILLY. If I had forty dollars a week—that's all I'd need. Forty dollars, Howard.

HOWARD. Kid, I can't take blood from a stone, I—

WILLY (*desperation is on him now*). Howard, the year Al Smith was nominated, your father came to me and—

HOWARD (*starting to go off*). I've got to see some people kid.

WILLY (*stopping him*). I'm talking about your father! There were promises made across this desk! You mustn't tell me you've got people to see—I put thirty-four years into this firm, Howard, and now I can't pay my insurance! You can't eat the orange and throw the peel away—a man is not a piece of fruit! (*After a pause*) Now pay attention. Your father—in 1928 I had a big year. I averaged a hundred and seventy dollars a week in commissions.

HOWARD (*impatiently*). Now, Willy, you never averaged—

WILLY (*banging his hand on the desk*). I averaged a hundred and seventy dollars a week in the year of 1928! And your father came to me—or rather, I was in the office here—it was right over this desk—and he put his hand on my shoulder—

HOWARD (*getting up*). You'll have to excuse me, Willy, I gotta see some people. Pull yourself together. (*Going out.*) I'll be back in a little while.

(*On Howard's exit, the light on his chair grows very bright and strange.*)

WILLY. Pull myself together! What the hell did I say to him? My God, I was yelling at him! How could I! (*Willy breaks off, staring at the light, which occupies the chair, standing across the desk from it.*) Frank, Frank, don't you remember what you told me that time? How you put your hand on my shoulder, and Frank . . . (*He leans on the desk and as he speaks the dead man's name he accidentally switches on the recorder, and instantly*—)

HOWARD'S SON. ". . . of New York is Albany. The capital of Ohio is Cincinnati, the capital of Rhode Island is . . ." (*The recitation continues.*)

WILLY (*leaping away with fright, shouting*). Ha! Howard! Howard! Howard!

HOWARD (*rushing in*). What happened?

WILLY (*pointing at the machine, which continues nasally, childishly, with the capital cities*). Shut it off! Shut it off!

HOWARD (*pulling the plug out*). Look, Willy . . .

WILLY (*pressing his hands to his eyes*). I gotta get myself some coffee. I'll get some coffee . . .

(*Willy starts to walk out. Howard stops him.*)

HOWARD (*rolling up the cord*). Willy, look . . .

WILLY. I'll go to Boston.

HOWARD. Willy, you can't go to Boston for us.

WILLY. Why can't I go?

HOWARD. I don't want you to represent us. I've been meaning to tell you for a long time now.

WILLY. Howard, are you firing me?

HOWARD. I think you need a good long rest, Willy.

WILLY. Howard—

HOWARD. And when you feel better, come back, and we'll see if we can work something out.

WILLY. But I gotta earn money, Howard. I'm in no position to—

HOWARD. Where are your sons? Why don't your sons give you a hand?

WILLY. They're working on a very big deal.

HOWARD. This is no time for false pride, Willy. You go to your sons and you tell them that you're tired. You've got two great boys, haven't you?

WILLY. Oh, no question, no question, but in the meantime . . .

HOWARD. Then that's that, heh?

WILLY. All right, I'll go to Boston tomorrow.

HOWARD. No, no.

WILLY. I can't throw myself on my sons. I'm not a cripple!

HOWARD. Look, kid, I'm busy this morning.

WILLY (*grasping Howard's arm*). Howard, you've got to let me go to Boston!

HOWARD (*hard, keeping himself under control*). I've got a line of people to see this morning. Sit down, take five minutes, and pull yourself together, and then go home, will ya? I need the office, Willy. (*He starts to go, turns, remembering the recorder, starts to push off the table holding the recorder.*) Oh, yeah. Whenever you can this week, stop by and drop off the samples. You'll feel better, Willy, and then come back and we'll talk. Pull yourself together, kid, there's people outside.

(*Howard exits, pushing the table off left. Willy stares into space, exhausted. Now the music is heard—Ben's music—first distantly, then closer, closer. As Willy speaks, Ben enters from the right. He carries valise and umbrella.*)

WILLY. Oh, Ben, how did you do it? What is the answer? Did you wind up the Alaska deal already?

BEN. Doesn't take much time if you know what you're doing. Just a short business trip. Boarding ship in an hour. Wanted to say good-bye.

WILLY. Ben, I've got to talk to you.

BEN (*glancing at his watch*). Haven't the time, William.

WILLY (*crossing the apron to Ben*). Ben, nothing's working out. I don't know what to do.

BEN. Now, look here, William. I've bought timberland in Alaska and I need a man to look after things for me.

WILLY. God, timberland! Me and my boys in those grand outdoors!

BEN. You've a new continent at your doorstep, William. Get out of these cities, they're full of talk and time payments and courts of law. Screw on your fists and you can fight for a fortune up there.

WILLY. Yes, yes! Linda, Linda!

(*Linda as of old, with the wash.*)

LINDA. Oh, you're back?

BEN. I haven't much time.

WILLY. No, wait! Linda, he's got a proposition for me in Alaska.

LINDA. But you've got—(*To Ben*) He's got a beautiful job here.

WILLY. But in Alaska, kid, I could—

LINDA. You're doing well enough, Willy!

BEN (*to Linda*). Enough for what, my dear?

LINDA (*frightened of Ben and angry at him*). Don't say those things to him! Enough to be happy right here, right now. (*To Willy, while Ben laughs*) Why must everybody conquer the world? You're well liked, and the boys love you, and someday—(*to Ben*)—why, old man Wagner told him just the other day that if he keeps it up he'll be a member of the firm, didn't he, Willy?

WILLY. Sure, sure. I am building something with this firm, Ben, and if a man is building something he must be on the right track, mustn't he?

BEN. What are you building? Lay your hand on it. Where is it?

WILLY (*hesitantly*). That's true, Linda, there's nothing.

LINDA. Why? (*To Ben*) There's a man eighty-four years old—

WILLY. That's right, Ben, that's right. When I look at that man I say, what is there to worry about?

BEN. Bah!

WILLY. It's true, Ben. All he has to do is go into any city, pick up the phone, and he's making his living and you know why?

BEN (*picking up his valise*). I've got to go.

WILLY (*holding Ben back*). Look at this boy!

(*Biff, in his high school sweater, enters carrying suitcase. Happy carries Biff's shoulder guards, gold helmet, and football pants.*)

WILLY. Without a penny to his name, three great universities are begging for him, and from there the sky's the limit, because it's not what you do, Ben. It's who you know and the smile on your face! It's contacts, Ben, contacts! The whole wealth of Alaska passes over the lunch table at the Commodore Hotel, and that's the wonder, the wonder of this country, that a man can end with diamonds here on the basis of being liked! (*He turns to Biff*) And that's why when you get out on that field today it's important. Because thousands of people will be rooting for you and loving you. (*To Ben, who has again begun to leave*) And Ben! when he walks into a business office his name will sound out like a bell and all the doors will open to him! I've seen it, Ben, I've seen it a thousand times! You can't feel it with your hand like timber, but it's there!

BEN. Good-bye, William.

WILLY. Ben, am I right? Don't you think I'm right? I value your advice.

BEN. There's a new continent at your doorstep, William. You could walk out rich. Rich! (*He is gone.*)

WILLY. We'll do it here, Ben! You hear me? We're gonna do it here!

(*Young Bernard rushes in. The gay music of the boys is heard.*)

BERNARD. Oh, gee, I was afraid you left already!

WILLY. Why? What time is it?

BERNARD. It's half-past one!

WILLY. Well, come on, everybody! Ebbets Field next stop! Where's the pennants? (*He rushes through the wall-line of the kitchen and out into the living room.*)

LINDA (*to Biff*). Did you pack fresh underwear?

BIFF (*who has been limbering up*). I want to go!

BERNARD. Biff, I'm carrying your helmet, ain't I?

HAPPY. No, I'm carrying the helmet.

BERNARD. Oh, Biff, you promised me.

HAPPY. I'm carrying the helmet.

BERNARD. How am I going to get in the locker room?

LINDA. Let him carry the shoulder guards. (*She puts her coat and hat on in the kitchen.*)

BERNARD. Can I, Biff? 'Cause I told everybody I'm going to be in the locker room.

HAPPY. In Ebbets Field it's the clubhouse.

BERNARD. I meant the clubhouse. Biff!

HAPPY. Biff!

BIFF (*grandly, after a slight pause*). Let him carry the shoulder guards.

HAPPY (*as he gives Bernard the shoulder guards*). Stay close to us now.

(*Willy rushes in with the pennants.*)

WILLY (*handing them out*). Everybody wave when Biff comes out on the field. (*Happy and Bernard run off.*) You set now, boy?

(*The music has died away.*)

BIFF. Ready to go, Pop. Every muscle is ready.

WILLY (*at the edge of the apron*). You realize what this means?

BIFF. That's right, Pop.

WILLY (*feeling Biff's muscles*). You're comin' home this afternoon captain of the All-Scholastic Championship Team of the City of New York.

BIFF. I got it, Pop. And remember, pal, when I take off my helmet, that touchdown is for you.

WILLY. Let's go! (*He is starting out, with his arm around Biff, when Charley enters, as of old, in knickers.*) I got no room for you, Charley.

CHARLEY. Room? For what?

WILLY. In the car.

CHARLEY. You goin' for a ride? I wanted to shoot some casino.

WILLY (*furiously*). Casino! (*Incredulously*) Don't you realize what today is?

LINDA. Oh, he knows, Willy. He's just kidding you.

WILLY. That's nothing to kid about!

CHARLEY. No, Linda, what's goin' on?

LINDA. He's playing in Ebbets Field.

CHARLEY. Baseball in this weather?

WILLY. Don't talk to him. Come on, come on! (*He is pushing them out.*)

CHARLEY. Wait a minute, didn't you hear the news?

WILLY. What?

CHARLEY. Don't you listen to the radio? Ebbets Field just blew up.

WILLY. You go to hell! (*Charley laughs. Pushing them out.*) Come on, come on! We're late.

CHARLEY (*as they go*). Knock a homer, Biff, knock a homer!

WILLY (*the last to leave, turning to Charley*). I don't think that was funny, Charley. This is the greatest day of his life.

CHARLEY. Willy, when are you going to grow up?

WILLY. Yeah, heh? When this game is over, Charley, you'll be laughing out of the other side of your face. They'll be calling him another Red Grange. Twenty-five thousand a year.

CHARLEY (*kidding*). Is that so?

WILLY. Yeah, that's so.

CHARLEY. Well, then, I'm sorry, Willy. But tell me something.

WILLY. What?

CHARLEY. Who is Red Grange?

WILLY. Put up your hands. Goddam you, put up your hands!

(*Charley, chuckling, shakes his head and walks away, around the left corner of the stage. Willy follows him. The music rises to a mocking frenzy.*)

WILLY. Who the hell do you think you are, better than everybody else? You don't know everything, you big, ignorant, stupid . . . Put up your hands!

(*Light rises, on the right side of the forestage, on a small table in the reception room of Charley's office. Traffic sounds are heard. Bernard, now mature, sits whistling to himself. A pair of tennis rackets and an overnight bag are on the floor beside him.*)

WILLY (*offstage*). What are you walking away for? Don't walk away! If you're going to say something say it to my face! I know you laugh at me behind my back. You'll laugh out of the other side of your goddam face after this game. Touchdown! Touchdown! Eighty thousand people! Touchdown! Right between the goal posts.

(*Bernard is a quiet, earnest, but self-assured young man. Willy's voice is coming from right upstage now. Bernard lowers his feet off the table and listens. Jenny, his father's secretary, enters.*)

JENNY (*distressed*). Say, Bernard, will you go out in the hall?

BERNARD. What is that noise? Who is it?

JENNY. Mr. Loman. He just got off the elevator.

BERNARD (*getting up*). Who's he arguing with?

JENNY. Nobody. There's nobody with him. I can't deal with him any more, and your father gets all upset every time he comes. I've got a lot of typing to do, and your father's waiting to sign it. Will you see him?

WILLY (*entering*). Touchdown! Touch—(*He sees Jenny*) Jenny, Jenny, good to see you. How're ya? Workin'? Or still honest?

JENNY. Fine. How've you been feeling?

WILLY. Not much any more, Jenny. Ha, ha! (*He is surprised to see the rackets.*)

BERNARD. Hello, Uncle Willy.

WILLY (*almost shocked*). Bernard! Well, look who's here! (*He comes quickly, guiltily, to Bernard and warmly shakes his hand.*)

BERNARD. How are you? Good to see you.

WILLY. What are you doing here?

BERNARD. Oh, just stopped by to see Pop. Get off my feet till my train leaves. I'm going to Washington in a few minutes.

WILLY. Is he in?

BERNARD. Yes, he's in his office with the accountant. Sit down.

WILLY (*sitting down*). What're you going to do in Washington?

BERNARD. Oh, just a case I've got there, Willy.

WILLY. That so? (*Indicating the rackets*) You going to play tennis there?

BERNARD. I'm staying with a friend who's got a court.

WILLY. Don't say. His own tennis court. Must be fine people, I bet.

BERNARD. They are, very nice. Dad tells me Biff's in town.

WILLY (*with a big smile*). Yeah, Biff's in. Working on a very big deal, Bernard.

BERNARD. What's Biff doing?

WILLY. Well, he's been doing very big things in the West. But he decided to establish himself here. Very big. We're having dinner. Did I hear your wife had a boy?

BERNARD. That's right. Our second.

WILLY. Two boys! What do you know!

BERNARD. What kind of a deal has Biff got?

WILLY. Well, Bill Oliver—very big sporting-goods man—he wants Biff very badly. Called him in from the West. Long distance, carte blanche, special deliveries. Your friends have their own private tennis court?

BERNARD. You still with the old firm, Willy?

WILLY (*after a pause*). I'm—I'm overjoyed to see how you made the grade, Bernard, overjoyed. It's an encouraging thing to see a young man really—really—Looks very good for Biff—very— (*He breaks off, then*) Bernard—(*He is so full of emotion, he breaks off again.*)

BERNARD. What is it, Willy?

WILLY (*small and alone*). What—what's the secret?

BERNARD. What secret?

WILLY. How—how did you? Why didn't he ever catch on?

BERNARD. I wouldn't know that, Willy.

WILLY (*confidentially, desperately*). You were his friend, his boyhood friend. There's something I don't understand about it. His life ended after that Ebbets Field game. From the age of seventeen nothing good ever happened to him.

BERNARD. He never trained himself for anything.

WILLY. But he did, he did. After high school he took so many correspondence courses. Radio mechanics; television; God knows what, and never made the slightest mark.

BERNARD (*taking off his glasses*). Willy, do you want to talk candidly?

WILLY (*rising, faces Bernard*). I regard you as a very brilliant man, Bernard. I value your advice.

BERNARD. Oh, the hell with the advice, Willy. I couldn't advise you. There's just one thing I've always wanted to ask you. When he was supposed to graduate, and the math teacher flunked him—

WILLY. Oh, that son-of-a-bitch ruined his life.

BERNARD. Yeah, but, Willy, all he had to do was go to summer school and make up that subject.

WILLY. That's right, that's right.

BERNARD. Did you tell him not to go to summer school?

WILLY. Me? I begged him to go. I ordered him to go!

BERNARD. Then why wouldn't he go?

WILLY. Why? Why! Bernard, that question has been trailing me like a ghost for the last fifteen years. He flunked the subject, and laid down and died like a hammer hit him!

BERNARD. Take it easy, kid.

WILLY. Let me talk to you—I got nobody to talk to. Bernard, Bernard, was it my fault? Y'see? It keeps going around in my mind, maybe I did something to him. I got nothing to give him.

BERNARD. Don't take it so hard.

WILLY. Why did he lay down? What is the story there? You were his friend!

BERNARD. Willy, I remember, it was June, and our grades came out. And he'd flunked math.

WILLY. That son-of-a-bitch!

BERNARD. No, it wasn't right then. Biff just got very angry, I remember, and he was ready to enroll in summer school.

WILLY (*surprised*). He was?

BERNARD. He wasn't beaten by it at all. But then, Willy, he disappeared from the block for almost a month. And I got the idea that he'd gone up to New England to see you. Did he have a talk with you then?

(*Willy stares in silence.*)

BERNARD. Willy?

WILLY (*with a strong edge of resentment in his voice*). Yeah, he came to Boston. What about it?

BERNARD. Well, just that when he came back—I'll never forget this, it always mystifies me. Because I'd thought so well of Biff, even though he'd always taken advantage of me. I loved him, Willy, y'know? And he came back after that month and took his sneakers—remember those sneakers with "University of Virginia" printed on them? He was so proud of those, wore them every day. And he took them down in the cellar, and burned them up in the furnace. We had a fist fight. It lasted at least half an hour. Just the two of us, punching each other down the cellar, and crying right through it. I've often thought of how strange it was that I knew he'd given up his life. What happened in Boston, Willy?

(*Willy looks at him as at an intruder.*)

BERNARD. I just bring it up because you asked me.

WILLY (*angrily*). Nothing. What do you mean, "What happened?" What's that got to do with anything?

BERNARD. Well, don't get sore.

WILLY. What are you trying to do, blame it on me? If a boy lays down is that my fault?

BERNARD. Now, Willy, don't get—

WILLY. Well, don't—don't talk to me that way! What does that mean, "What happened?"

(*Charley enters. He is in his vest, and he carries a bottle of bourbon.*)

CHARLEY. Hey, you're going to miss that train. (*He waves the bottle.*)

BERNARD. Yeah, I'm going. (*He takes the bottle.*) Thanks, Pop. (*He picks up his rackets and bag.*) Good-bye, Willy, and don't worry about it. You know, "If at first you don't succeed . . ."

WILLY. Yes, I believe in that.

BERNARD. But sometimes, Willy, it's better for a man just to walk away.

WILLY. Walk away?

BERNARD. That's right.

WILLY. But if you can't walk away?

BERNARD (*after a slight pause*). I guess that's when it's tough. (*Extending his hand*) Good-bye, Willy.

WILLY (*shaking Bernard's hand*). Good-bye, boy.

CHARLEY (*an arm on Bernard's shoulder*). How do you like this kid? Gonna argue a case in front of the Supreme Court.

BERNARD (*protesting*). Pop!

WILLY (*genuinely shocked, pained, and happy*). No! The Supreme Court!

BERNARD. I gotta run. 'Bye, Dad!

CHARLEY. Knock 'em dead, Bernard!

(*Bernard goes off.*)

WILLY (*as Charley takes out his wallet*). The Supreme Court! And he didn't even mention it!

CHARLEY (*counting out money on the desk*). He don't have to—he's gonna do it.

WILLY. And you never told him what to do, did you? You never took any interest in him.

CHARLEY. My salvation is that I never took any interest in anything. There's some money—fifty dollars. I got an accountant inside.

WILLY. Charley, look . . . (*With difficulty*) I got my insurance to pay. If you can manage it—I need a hundred and ten dollars.

(*Charley doesn't reply for a moment; merely stops moving.*)

WILLY. I'd draw it from my bank but Linda would know, and I . . .

CHARLEY. Sit down, Willy.

WILLY (*moving toward the chair*). I'm keeping an account of everything, remember. I'll pay every penny back. (*He sits.*)

CHARLEY. Now listen to me, Willy.

WILLY. I want you to know I appreciate . . .

CHARLEY (*sitting down on the table*). Willy, what're you doin'? What the hell is goin' on in your head?

WILLY. Why? I'm simply . . .

CHARLEY. I offered you a job. You can make fifty dollars a week. And I won't send you on the road.

WILLY. I've got a job.

CHARLEY. Without pay? What kind of a job is a job without pay? (*He rises.*) Now, look, kid, enough is enough. I'm no genius but I know when I'm being insulted.

WILLY. Insulted!

CHARLEY. Why don't you want to work for me?

WILLY. What's the matter with you? I've got a job.

CHARLEY. Then what're you walkin' in here every week for?

WILLY (*getting up*). Well, if you don't want me to walk in here—

CHARLEY. I am offering you a job.

WILLY. I don't want your goddam job!

CHARLEY. When the hell are you going to grow up?

WILLY (*furiously*). You big ignoramus, if you say that to me again I'll rap you one! I don't care how big you are! (*He's ready to fight.*)

(*Pause.*)

CHARLEY (*kindly, going to him*). How much do you need, Willy?

WILLY. Charley, I'm strapped. I'm strapped. I don't know what to do. I was just fired.

CHARLEY. Howard fired you?

WILLY. That snotnose. Imagine that? I named him. I named him Howard.

CHARLEY. Willy, when're you gonna realize that them things don't mean anything? You named him Howard, but you can't sell that. The only thing you got in this world is what you can sell. And the funny thing is that you're a salesman, and you don't know that.

WILLY. I've always tried to think otherwise, I guess. I always felt that if a man was impressive, and well liked, that nothing—

CHARLEY. Why must everybody like you? Who liked J. P. Morgan? Was he impressive? In a Turkish bath he'd look like a butcher. But with his pockets on he was very well liked. Now listen, Willy, I know you don't like me, and nobody can say I'm in love with you, but I'll give you a job because—just for the hell of it, put it that way. Now what do you say?

WILLY. I—I just can't work for you, Charley.

CHARLEY. What're you, jealous of me?

WILLY. I can't work for you, that's all, don't ask me why.

CHARLEY (*angered, takes out more bills*). You been jealous of me all your life, you damned fool! Here, pay your insurance. (*He puts the money in Willy's hand.*)

WILLY. I'm keeping strict accounts.

CHARLEY. I've got some work to do. Take care of yourself. And pay your insurance.

WILLY (*moving to the right*). Funny, y'know? After all the highways, and the trains, and the appointments, and the years, you end up worth more dead than alive.

CHARLEY. Willy, nobody's worth nothin' dead. (*After a slight pause.*) Did you hear what I said?

(*Willy stands still, dreaming.*)

CHARLEY. Willy!

WILLY. Apologize to Bernard for me when you see him. I didn't mean to argue with him. He's a fine boy. They're all fine boys, and they'll end up big—all of them. Someday they'll all play tennis together. Wish me luck, Charley. He saw Bill Oliver today.

CHARLEY. Good luck.

WILLY (*on the verge of tears*). Charley, you're the only friend I got. Isn't that a remarkable thing? (*He goes out.*)

CHARLEY. Jesus!

(*Charley stares after him a moment and follows. All light blacks out. Suddenly raucous music is heard, and a red glow rises behind the screen at right. Stanley, a young waiter, appears, carrying a table, followed by Happy, who is carrying two chairs.)*

STANLEY (*putting the table down*). That's all right, Mr. Loman, I can handle it myself. (*He turns and takes the chairs from Happy and places them at the table.*)

HAPPY (*glancing around*). Oh, this is better.

STANLEY. Sure, in the front there you're in the middle of all kinds a noise. Whenever you got a party, Mr. Loman, you just tell me and I'll put you back here. Y'know, there's a lotta people they don't like it private, because when they go out they like to see a lotta action around them because they're sick and tired to stay in the house by theirself. But I know you, you ain't from Hackensack. You know what I mean?

HAPPY (*sitting down*). So how's it coming, Stanley?

STANLEY. Ah, it's a dog's life. I only wish during the war they'd a took me in the Army. I coulda been dead by now.

HAPPY. My brother's back, Stanley.

STANLEY. Oh, he come back, heh? From the Far West.

HAPPY. Yeah, big cattle man, my brother, so treat him right. And my father's coming too.

STANLEY. Oh, your father too!

HAPPY. You got a couple of nice lobsters?

STANLEY. Hundred per cent, big.

HAPPY. I want them with the claws.

STANLEY. Don't worry, I don't give you no mice. (*Happy laughs.*) How about some wine? It'll put a head on the meal.

HAPPY. No. You remember, Stanley, that recipe I brought you from overseas? With the champagne in it?

STANLEY. Oh, yeah, sure. I still got it tacked up yet in the kitchen. But that'll have to cost a buck apiece anyways.

HAPPY. That's all right.

STANLEY. What'd you, hit a number or somethin'?

HAPPY. No, it's a little celebration. My brother is—I think he pulled off a big deal today. I think we're going into business together.

STANLEY. Great! That's the best for you. Because a family business, you know what I mean?—that's the best.

HAPPY. That's what I think.

STANLEY. 'Cause what's the difference? Somebody steals? It's in the family. Know what I mean? (*Sotto voce*) Like this bartender here. The boss is goin' crazy what kinda leak he's got in the cash register. You put it in but it don't come out.

HAPPY (*raising his head*). Sh!

STANLEY. What?

HAPPY. You notice I wasn't lookin' right or left, was I?

STANLEY. No.

HAPPY. And my eyes are closed.

STANLEY. So what's the—?

HAPPY. Strudel's comin'.

STANLEY (*catching on, looks around*). Ah, no, there's no—

(*He breaks off as a furred, lavishly dressed Girl enters and sits at the next table. Both follow her with their eyes.*)

STANLEY. Geez, how'd ya know?

HAPPY. I got radar or something. (*Staring directly at her profile*) Ooooooo . . . Stanley.

STANLEY. I think that's for you, Mr. Loman.

HAPPY. Look at that mouth. Oh, God. And the binoculars.

STANLEY. Geez, you got a life, Mr. Loman.

HAPPY. Wait on her.

STANLEY (*going to The Girl's table*). Would you like a menu, ma'am?

GIRL. I'm expecting someone, but I'd like a—

HAPPY. Why don't you bring her—excuse me, miss, do you mind? I sell champagne, and I'd like you to try my brand. Bring her a champagne, Stanley.

GIRL. That's awfully nice of you.

HAPPY. Don't mention it. It's all company money. (*He laughs.*)

GIRL. That's a charming product to be selling, isn't it?

HAPPY. Oh, gets to be like everything else. Selling is selling, y'know.

GIRL. I suppose.

HAPPY. You don't happen to sell, do you?

GIRL. No, I don't sell.

HAPPY. Would you object to a compliment from a stranger? You ought to be on a magazine cover.

GIRL (*looking at him a little archly*). I have been.

(*Stanley comes in with a glass of champagne.*)

HAPPY. What'd I say before, Stanley? You see? She's a cover girl.

STANLEY. Oh, I could see, I could see.

HAPPY (*to The Girl*). What magazine?

GIRL. Oh, a lot of them. (*She takes the drink.*) Thank you.

HAPPY. You know what they say in France, don't you? "Champagne is the drink of the complexion"—Hya, Biff!

(*Biff has entered and sits with Happy.*)

BIFF. Hello, kid. Sorry I'm late.

HAPPY. I just got here. Uh, Miss—?

GIRL. Forsythe.

HAPPY. Miss Forsythe, this is my brother.

BIFF. Is Dad here?

HAPPY. His name is Biff. You might've heard of him. Great football player.

GIRL. Really? What team?
HAPPY. Are you familiar with football?
GIRL. No, I'm afraid I'm not.
HAPPY. Biff is quarterback with the New York Giants.
GIRL. Well, that is nice, isn't it? (*She drinks.*)
HAPPY. Good health.
GIRL. I'm happy to meet you.
HAPPY. That's my name. Hap. It's really Harold, but at West Point they called me Happy.
GIRL (*now really impressed*). Oh, I see. How do you do? (*She turns her profile.*)
BIFF. Isn't Dad coming?
HAPPY. You want her?
BIFF. Oh, I could never make that.
HAPPY. I remember the time that idea would never come into your head. Where's the old confidence, Biff?
BIFF. I just saw Oliver—
HAPPY. Wait a minute. I've got to see that old confidence again. Do you want her? She's on call.
BIFF. Oh, no. (*He turns to look at The Girl.*)
HAPPY. I'm telling you. Watch this. (*Turning to The Girl*) Honey? (*She turns to him.*) Are you busy?
GIRL. Well, I am . . . but I could make a phone call.
HAPPY. Do that, will you, honey? And see if you can get a friend. We'll be here for a while. Biff is one of the greatest football players in the country.
GIRL (*standing up*). Well, I'm certainly happy to meet you.
HAPPY. Come back soon.
GIRL. I'll try.
HAPPY. Don't try, honey, try hard.

(*The Girl exits. Stanley follows, shaking his head in bewildered admiration.*)

HAPPY. Isn't that a shame now? A beautiful girl like that? That's why I can't get married. There's not a good woman in a thousand. New York is loaded with them, kid!
BIFF. Hap, look—
HAPPY. I told you she was on call!
BIFF (*strangely unnerved*). Cut it out, will ya? I want to say something to you.
HAPPY. Did you see Oliver?
BIFF. I saw him all right. Now look, I want to tell Dad a couple of things and I want you to help me.
HAPPY. What? Is he going to back you?
BIFF. Are you crazy? You're out of your goddam head, you know that?
HAPPY. Why? What happened?
BIFF (*breathlessly*). I did a terrible thing today, Hap. It's the strangest day I ever went through. I'm all numb, I swear.
HAPPY. You mean he wouldn't see you?
BIFF. Well, I waited six hours for him, see? All day. Kept sending my name in. Even tried to date his secretary so she'd get me to him, but no soap.
HAPPY. Because you're not showin' the old confidence, Biff. He remembered you, didn't he?
BIFF (*stopping Happy with a gesture*). Finally, about five o'clock, he comes out. Didn't remember who I was or anything. I felt like such an idiot, Hap.
HAPPY. Did you tell him my Florida idea?
BIFF. He walked away. I saw him for one minute. I got so mad I could've torn the walls down! How the hell did I ever get the idea I was a salesman there? I even believed myself that I'd been a salesman for him! And then he gave me one look and—I realized what a ridiculous lie my whole life has been! We've been talking in a dream for fifteen years. I was a shipping clerk.
HAPPY. What'd you do?
BIFF (*with great tension and wonder*). Well, he left, see. And the secretary went out. I was all alone in the waiting room. I don't know what came over me, Hap. The next thing I know I'm in his office—paneled walls, everything. I can't explain it. I—Hap, I took his fountain pen.
HAPPY. Geez, did he catch you?
BIFF. I ran out. I ran down all eleven flights. I ran and ran and ran.
HAPPY. That was an awful dumb—what'd you do that for?
BIFF (*agonized*). I don't know, I just—wanted to take something, I don't know. You gotta help me, Hap, I'm gonna tell Pop.
HAPPY. You crazy? What for?
BIFF. Hap, he's got to understand that I'm not the man somebody lends that kind of money to. He thinks I've been spiting him all these years and it's eating him up.
HAPPY. That's just it. You tell him something nice.
BIFF. I can't.
HAPPY. Say you got a lunch date with Oliver tomorrow.
BIFF. So what do I do tomorrow?
HAPPY. You leave the house tomorrow and come back at night and say Oliver is thinking it over. And he thinks it over for a couple of weeks, and gradually it fades away and nobody's the worse.
BIFF. But it'll go on forever!
HAPPY. Dad is never so happy as when he's looking forward to something!

(*Willy enters.*)

HAPPY. Hello, scout!
WILLY. Gee, I haven't been here in years!

(*Stanley has followed Willy in and sets a chair for him. Stanley starts off but Happy stops him.*)

HAPPY. Stanley!

(*Stanley stands by, waiting for an order.*)

BIFF (*going to Willy with guilt, as to an invalid*). Sit down, Pop. You want a drink?

WILLY. Sure, I don't mind.

BIFF. Let's get a load on.

WILLY. You look worried.

BIFF. N-no. (*To Stanley*) Scotch all around. Make it doubles.

STANLEY. Doubles, right. (*He goes.*)

WILLY. You had a couple already, didn't you?

BIFF. Just a couple, yeah.

WILLY. Well, what happened, boy? (*Nodding affirmatively, with a smile.*) Everything go all right?

BIFF (*takes a breath, then reaches out and grasps Willy's hand*). Pal . . . (*He is smiling bravely, and Willy is smiling too.*) I had an experience today.

HAPPY. Terrific, Pop.

WILLY. That so? What happened?

BIFF (*high, slightly alcoholic, above the earth*). I'm going to tell you everything from first to last. It's been a strange day. (*Silence. He looks around, composes himself as best he can, but his breath keeps breaking the rhythm of his voice.*) I had to wait quite a while for him, and—

WILLY. Oliver?

BIFF. Yeah, Oliver. All day, as a matter of cold fact. And a lot of—instances—facts, Pop, facts about my life came back to me. Who was it, Pop? Who ever said I was a salesman with Oliver?

WILLY. Well, you were.

BIFF. No, Dad, I was a shipping clerk.

WILLY. But you were practically—

BIFF (*with determination*). Dad, I don't know who said it first, but I was never a salesman for Bill Oliver.

WILLY. What're you talking about?

BIFF. Let's hold on to the facts tonight, Pop. We're not going to get anywhere bullin' around. I was a shipping clerk.

WILLY (*angrily*). All right, now listen to me—

BIFF. Why don't you let me finish?

WILLY. I'm not interested in stories about the past or any crap of that kind because the woods are burning, boys, you understand? There's a big blaze going on all around. I was fired today.

BIFF (*shocked*). How could you be?

WILLY. I was fired, and I'm looking for a little good news to tell your mother, because the woman has waited and the woman has suffered. The gist of it is that I haven't got a story left in my head, Biff. So don't give me a lecture about facts and aspects. I am not interested. Now what've you got to say to me?

(*Stanley enters with three drinks. They wait until he leaves.*)

WILLY. Did you see Oliver?

BIFF. Jesus, Dad!

WILLY. You mean you didn't go up there?

HAPPY. Sure he went up there.

BIFF. I did. I—saw him. How could they fire you?

WILLY (*on the edge of his chair*). What kind of a welcome did he give you?

BIFF. He won't even let you work on commission?

WILLY. I'm out! (*Driving*) So tell me, he gave you a warm welcome?

HAPPY. Sure, Pop, sure!

BIFF (*driven*). Well, it was kind of—

WILLY. I was wondering if he'd remember you. (*To Happy*) Imagine, man doesn't see him for ten, twelve years and gives him that kind of a welcome!

HAPPY. Damn right!

BIFF (*trying to return to the offensive*). Pop, look—

WILLY. You know why he remembered you, don't you? Because you impressed him in those days.

BIFF. Let's talk quietly and get this down to the facts, huh?

WILLY (*as though Biff had been interrupting*). Well, what happened? It's great news, Biff. Did he take you into his office or'd you talk in the waiting room?

BIFF. Well, he came in, see, and—

WILLY (*with a big smile*). What'd he say? Betcha he threw his arm around you.

BIFF. Well, he kinda—

WILLY. He's a fine man. (*To Happy*) Very hard man to see, y'know.

HAPPY (*agreeing*). Oh, I know.

WILLY (*to Biff*). Is that where you had the drinks?

BIFF. Yeah, he gave me a couple of—no, no!

HAPPY (*cutting in*). He told him my Florida idea.

WILLY. Don't interrupt. (*To Biff*) How'd he react to the Florida idea?

BIFF. Dad, will you give me a minute to explain?

WILLY. I've been waiting for you to explain since I sat down here! What happened? He took you into his office and what?

BIFF. Well—I talked. And—and he listened, see.

WILLY. Famous for the way he listens, y'know. What was his answer?

BIFF. His answer was—(*He breaks off, suddenly angry*) Dad, you're not letting me tell you what I want to tell you!

WILLY (*accusing, angered*). You didn't see him, did you?

BIFF. I did see him!

WILLY. What'd you insult him or something? You insulted him, didn't you?

BIFF. Listen, will you let me out of it, will you just let me out of it!

HAPPY. What the hell!

WILLY. Tell me what happened!
BIFF (*to Happy*). I can't talk to him!

(*A single trumpet note jars the ear. The light of green leaves stains the house, which holds the air of night and a dream. Young Bernard enters and knocks on the door of the house.*)

YOUNG BERNARD (*frantically*). Mrs. Loman, Mrs. Loman!
HAPPY. Tell him what happened!
BIFF (*to Happy*). Shut up and leave me alone!
WILLY. No, no! You had to go and flunk math!
BIFF. What math? What're you talking about?
YOUNG BERNARD. Mrs. Loman, Mrs. Loman!

(*Linda appears in the house, as of old.*)

WILLY (*wildly*). Math, math, math!
BIFF. Take it easy, Pop!
YOUNG BERNARD. Mrs. Loman!
WILLY (*furiously*). If you hadn't flunked you'd've been set by now!
BIFF. Now, look, I'm gonna tell you what happened, and you're going to listen to me.
YOUNG BERNARD. Mrs. Loman!
BIFF. I waited six hours—
HAPPY. What the hell are you saying?
BIFF. I kept sending in my name but he wouldn't see me. So finally he . . . (*He continues unheard as light fades low on the restaurant.*)
YOUNG BERNARD. Biff flunked math!
LINDA. No!
YOUNG BERNARD. Birnbaum flunked him! They won't graduate him!
LINDA. But they have to. He's gotta go to the university. Where is he? Biff! Biff!
YOUNG BERNARD. No, he left. He went to Grand Central.
LINDA. Grand—You mean he went to Boston!
YOUNG BERNARD. Is Uncle Willy in Boston?
LINDA. Oh, maybe Willy can talk to the teacher. Oh, the poor, poor boy!

(*Light on house area snaps out.*)

BIFF (*at the table, now audible, holding up a gold fountain pen*). . . . so I'm washed up with Oliver, you understand? Are you listening to me?
WILLY (*at a loss*). Yeah, sure. If you hadn't flunked—
BIFF. Flunked what? What're you talking about?
WILLY. Don't blame everything on me! I didn't flunk math—you did! What pen?
HAPPY. That was awful dumb, Biff, a pen like that is worth—
WILLY (*seeing the pen for the first time*). You took Oliver's pen?
BIFF (*weakening*). Dad, I just explained it to you.
WILLY. You stole Bill Oliver's fountain pen!
BIFF. I didn't exactly steal it! That's just what I've been explaining to you!
HAPPY. He had it in his hand and just then Oliver walked in, so he got nervous and stuck it in his pocket!
WILLY. My God, Biff!
BIFF. I never intended to do it, Dad!
OPERATOR'S VOICE. Standish Arms, good evening!
WILLY (*shouting*). I'm not in my room!
BIFF (*frightened*). Dad, what's the matter? (*He and Happy stand up.*)
OPERATOR. Ringing Mr. Loman for you!
WILLY. I'm not there, stop it!
BIFF (*horrified, gets down on one knee before Willy*). Dad, I'll make good, I'll make good. (*Willy tries to get to his feet. Biff holds him down.*) Sit down now.
WILLY. No, you're no good, you're no good for anything.
BIFF. I am, Dad, I'll find something else, you understand? Now don't worry about anything. (*He holds up Willy's face.*) Talk to me, Dad.
OPERATOR. Mr. Loman does not answer. Shall I page him?
WILLY (*attempting to stand, as though to rush and silence the Operator*). No, no, no!
HAPPY. He'll strike something, Pop.
WILLY. No, no . . .
BIFF (*desperately, standing over Willy*). Pop, listen! Listen to me! I'm telling you something good. Oliver talked to his partner about the Florida idea. You listening? He—he talked to his partner, and he came to me . . . I'm going to be all right, you hear? Dad, listen to me, he said it was just a question of the amount!
WILLY. Then you . . . got it?
HAPPY. He's gonna be terrific, Pop!
WILLY (*trying to stand*). Then you got it, haven't you? You got it! You got it!
BIFF (*agonized, holds Willy down*). No, no. Look, Pop. I'm supposed to have lunch with them tomorrow. I'm just telling you this so you'll know that I can still make an impression, Pop. And I'll make good somewhere, but I can't go tomorrow, see?
WILLY. Why not? You simply—
BIFF. But the pen, Pop!
WILLY. You give it to him and tell him it was an oversight!
HAPPY. Sure, have lunch tomorrow!
BIFF. I can't say that—
WILLY. You were doing a crossword puzzle and accidentally used his pen!

BIFF. Listen, kid, I took those balls years ago, now I walk in with his fountain pen? That clinches it, don't you see? I can't face him like that! I'll try elsewhere.

PAGE'S VOICE. Paging Mr. Loman!

WILLY. Don't you want to be anything?

BIFF. Pop, how can I go back?

WILLY. You don't want to be anything, is that what's behind it?

BIFF (*now angry at Willy for not crediting his sympathy*). Don't take it that way! You think it was easy walking into that office after what I'd done to him? A team of horses couldn't have dragged me back to Bill Oliver!

WILLY. Then why'd you go?

BIFF. Why did I go? Why did I go! Look at you! Look at what's become of you!

(*Off left, The Woman laughs.*)

WILLY. Biff, you're going to go to that lunch tomorrow, or—

BIFF. I can't go. I've got no appointment!

HAPPY. Biff, for . . . !

WILLY. Are you spiting me?

BIFF. Don't take it that way! Goddammit!

WILLY (*strikes Biff and falters away from the table*). You rotten little louse! Are you spiting me?

THE WOMAN. Someone's at the door, Willy!

BIFF. I'm no good, can't you see what I am?

HAPPY (*separating them*). Hey, you're in a restaurant! Now cut it out, both of you! (*The Girls enter.*) Hello, girls, sit down.

(*The Woman laughs, off left.*)

MISS FORSYTHE. I guess we might as well. This is Letta.

THE WOMAN. Willy, are you going to wake up?

BIFF (*ignoring Willy*). How'r ya, miss, sit down. What do you drink?

MISS FORSYTHE. Letta might not be able to stay long.

LETTA. I gotta get up very early tomorrow. I got jury duty. I'm so excited! Were you fellows ever on a jury?

BIFF. No, but I been in front of them! (*The Girls laugh.*) This is my father.

LETTA. Isn't he cute? Sit down with us, Pop.

HAPPY. Sit him down, Biff!

BIFF (*going to him*). Come on, slugger, drink us under the table. To hell with it! Come on, sit down, pal.

(*On Biff's insistence, Willy is about to sit.*)

THE WOMAN (*now urgently*). Willy, are you going to answer the door!

(*The Woman's call pulls Willy back. He starts right, befuddled.*)

BIFF. Hey, where are you going?

WILLY. Open the door.

BIFF. The door?

WILLY. The washroom . . . the door . . . where's the door?

BIFF (*leading Willy to the left*). Just go straight down.

(*Willy moves left.*)

THE WOMAN. Willy, Willy, are you going to get up, get up, get up, get up?

(*Willy exits left.*)

LETTA. I think it's sweet you bring your daddy along.

MISS FORSYTHE. Oh, he isn't really your father!

BIFF (*at left, turning to her resentfully*). Miss Forsythe, you've just seen a prince walk by. A fine, troubled prince. A hard-working, unappreciated prince. A pal, you understand? A good companion. Always for his boys.

LETTA. That's so sweet.

HAPPY. Well, girls, what's the program? We're wasting time. Come on, Biff. Gather round. Where would you like to go?

BIFF. Why don't you do something for him?

HAPPY. Me!

BIFF. Don't you give a damn for him, Hap?

HAPPY. What're you talking about? I'm the one who—

BIFF. I sense it, you don't give a good goddam about him. (*He takes the rolled-up hose from his pocket and puts it on the table in front of Happy.*) Look what I found in the cellar, for Christ's sake. How can you bear to let it go on?

HAPPY. Me? Who goes away? Who runs off and—

BIFF. Yeah, but he doesn't mean anything to you. You could help him—I can't! Don't you understand what I'm talking about? He's going to kill himself, don't you know that?

HAPPY. Don't I know it! Me!

BIFF. Hap, help him! Jesus . . . help him . . . Help me, help me, I can't bear to look at his face! (*Ready to weep, he hurries out, up right.*)

HAPPY (*starting after him*). Where are you going?

MISS FORSYTHE. What's he so mad about?

HAPPY. Come on, girls, we'll catch up with him.

MISS FORSYTHE (*as Happy pushes her out*). Say, I don't like that temper of his!

HAPPY. He's just a little overstrung, he'll be all right!

WILLY (*off left, as The Woman laughs*). Don't answer! Don't answer!

LETTA. Don't you want to tell your father—

HAPPY. No, that's not my father. He's just a guy. Come on, we'll catch Biff, and, honey, we're going to paint this town! Stanley, where's the check! Hey, Stanley!

(*They exit. Stanley looks toward left.*)

STANLEY (*calling to Happy indignantly*). Mr. Loman! Mr. Loman!

(*Stanley picks up a chair and follows them off. Knocking is heard off left. The Woman enters, laughing. Willy follows her. She is in a black slip; he is buttoning his shirt. Raw, sensuous music accompanies their speech.*)

WILLY. Will you stop laughing? Will you stop?

THE WOMAN. Aren't you going to answer the door? He'll wake the whole hotel.

WILLY. I'm not expecting anybody.

THE WOMAN. Whyn't you have another drink, honey, and stop being so damn self-centered?

WILLY. I'm so lonely.

THE WOMAN. You know you ruined me, Willy? From now on, whenever you come to the office, I'll see that you go right through to the buyers. No waiting at my desk any more, Willy. You ruined me.

WILLY. That's nice of you to say that.

THE WOMAN. Gee, you are self-centered! Why so sad? You are the saddest self-centeredest soul I ever did see-saw. (*She laughs. He kisses her.*) Come on inside, drummer boy. It's silly to be dressing in the middle of the night. (*As knocking is heard.*) Aren't you going to answer the door?

WILLY. They're knocking on the wrong door.

THE WOMAN. But I felt the knocking. And he heard us talking in here. Maybe the hotel's on fire!

WILLY (*his terror rising*). It's a mistake.

THE WOMAN. Then tell him to go away!

WILLY. There's nobody there.

THE WOMAN. It's getting on my nerves, Willy. There's somebody standing out there and it's getting on my nerves!

WILLY (*pushing her away from him*). All right, stay in the bathroom here, and don't come out. I think there's a law in Massachusetts about it, so don't come out. It may be that new room clerk. He looked very mean. So don't come out. It's a mistake, there's no fire.

(*The knocking is heard again. He takes a few steps away from her, and she vanishes into the wing. The light follows him, and now he is facing Young Biff, who carries a suitcase. Biff steps toward him. The music is gone.*)

BIFF. Why didn't you answer?

WILLY. Biff! What are you doing in Boston?

BIFF. Why didn't you answer? I've been knocking for five minutes, I called you on the phone—

WILLY. I just heard you. I was in the bathroom and had the door shut. Did anything happen home?

BIFF. Dad—I let you down.

WILLY. What do you mean?

BIFF. Dad . . .

WILLY. Biffo, what's this about? (*Putting his arm around Biff*) Come on, let's go downstairs and get you a malted.

BIFF. Dad, I flunked math.

WILLY. Not for the term?

BIFF. The term. I haven't got enough credits to graduate.

WILLY. You mean to say Bernard wouldn't give you the answers?

BIFF. He did, he tried, but I only got a sixty-one.

WILLY. And they wouldn't give you four points?

BIFF. Birnbaum refused absolutely. I begged him, Pop, to give me those points. You gotta talk to him before they close the school. Because if he saw the kind of man you are, and you just talked to him in your way, I'm sure he'd come through for me. The class came right before practice, see, and I didn't go enough. Would you talk to him? He'd like you, Pop. You know the way you could talk.

WILLY. You're on. We'll drive right back.

BIFF. Oh, Dad, good work! I'm sure he'll change it for you!

WILLY. Go downstairs and tell the clerk I'm checkin' out. Go right down.

BIFF. Yes, sir! See, the reason he hates me, Pop—one day he was late for class so I got up at the blackboard and imitated him. I crossed my eyes and talked with a lithp.

WILLY (*laughing*). You did? The kids like it?

BIFF. They nearly died laughing!

WILLY. Yeah? What'd you do?

BIFF. The thquare root of thixthy twee is . . . (*Willy bursts out laughing; Biff joins him.*) And in the middle of it he walked in!

(*Willy laughs and The Woman joins in offstage.*)

WILLY (*without hesitation*). Hurry downstairs and—

BIFF. Somebody in there?

WILLY. No, that was next door.

(*The Woman laughs offstage.*)

BIFF. Somebody got in your bathroom!

WILLY. No, it's the next room, there's a party—

THE WOMAN (*enters, laughing. She lisps this*). Can I come in? There's something in the bathtub, Willy, and it's moving!

(*Willy looks at Biff, who is staring open-mouthed and horrified at The Woman.*)

WILLY. Ah—you better go back to your room. They must be finished painting by now. They're painting her room so I let her take a shower here. Go back, go back . . . (*he pushes her.*)

THE WOMAN (*resisting*). But I've got to get dressed, Willy, I can't—

WILLY. Get out of here! Go back, go back . . . (*Suddenly striving for the ordinary*) This is Miss Francis, Biff, she's a buyer. They're painting her room. Go back, Miss Francis, go back . . .

THE WOMAN. But my clothes, I can't go out naked in the hall!

WILLY (*pushing her offstage*). Get outa here! Go back, go back!

(*Biff slowly sits down on his suitcase as the argument continues offstage.*)

THE WOMAN. Where's my stockings? You promised me stockings, Willy!

WILLY. I have no stockings here!

THE WOMAN. You had two boxes of size nine sheers for me, and I want them!

WILLY. Here, for God's sake, will you get outa here!

THE WOMAN (*enters holding a box of stockings*). I just hope there's nobody in the hall. That's all I hope. (*To Biff*). Are you football or baseball?

BIFF. Football.

THE WOMAN (*angry, humiliated*). That's me too. G'night. (*She snatches her clothes from Willy, and walks out.*)

WILLY (*after a pause*). Well, better get going. I want to get to the school first thing in the morning. Get my suits out of the closet. I'll get my valise. (*Biff doesn't move.*) What's the matter? (*Biff remains motionless, tears falling.*) She's a buyer. Buys for J. H. Simmons. She lives down the hall—they're painting. You don't imagine—(*He breaks off. After a pause.*) Now listen, pal, she's just a buyer. She sees merchandise in her room and they have to keep it looking just so . . . (*Pause. Assuming command*) All right, get my suits. (*Biff doesn't move.*) Now stop crying and do as I say. I gave you an order. Biff, I gave you an order! Is that what you do when I give you an order? How dare you cry! (*Putting his arm around Biff*) Now look, Biff, when you grow up you'll understand about these things. You mustn't—you mustn't overemphasize a thing like this. I'll see Birnbaum first thing in the morning.

BIFF. Never mind.

WILLY (*getting down beside Biff*). Never mind! He's going to give you those points. I'll see to it.

BIFF. He wouldn't listen to you.

WILLY. He certainly will listen to me. You need those points for the U. of Virginia.

BIFF. I'm not going there.

WILLY. Heh? If I can't get him to change that mark you'll make it up in summer school. You've got all summer to—

BIFF (*his weeping breaking from him*). Dad . . .

WILLY (*infected by it*). Oh, my boy .

BIFF. Dad . . .

WILLY. She's nothing to me, Biff. I was lonely, I was terribly lonely.

BIFF. You—you gave her Mama's stockings! (*His tears break through and he rises to go.*)

WILLY (*grabbing for Biff*). I gave you an order!

BIFF. Don't touch me, you—liar!

WILLY. Apologize for that!

BIFF. You fake! You phony little fake! You fake! (*Overcome, he turns quickly and weeping fully goes out with his suitcase. Willy is left on the floor on his knees.*)

WILLY. I gave you an order! Biff, come back here or I'll beat you! Come back here! I'll whip you!

(*Stanley comes quickly in from the right and stands in front of Willy.*)

WILLY (*shouts at Stanley*). I gave you an order . . .

STANLEY. Hey, let's pick it up, pick it up, Mr. Loman. (*He helps Willy to his feet.*) Your boys left with the chippies. They said they'll see you home.

(*A second waiter watches some distance away.*)

WILLY. But we were supposed to have dinner together.

(*Music is heard, Willy's theme.*)

STANLEY. Can you make it?

WILLY. I'll—sure, I can make it. (*Suddenly concerned about his clothes.*) Do I—I look all right?

STANLEY. Sure, you look all right. (*He flicks a speck off Willy's lapel.*)

WILLY. Here—here's a dollar.

STANLEY. Oh, your son paid me. It's all right.

WILLY (*putting it in Stanley's hand*). No, take it. You're a good boy.

STANLEY. Oh, no, you don't have to . . .

WILLY. Here—here's some more, I don't need it any more. (*After a slight pause.*) Tell me—is there a seed store in the neighborhood?

STANLEY. Seeds? You mean like to plant?

(*As Willy turns, Stanley slips the money back into his jacket pocket.*)

WILLY. Yes. Carrots, peas . . .

STANLEY. Well, there's hardware stores on Sixth Avenue, but it may be too late now.

WILLY (*anxiously*). Oh, I'd better hurry. I've got to get some seeds. (*He starts off to the right.*) I've got to get some seeds, right away. Nothing's planted. I don't have a thing in the ground.

(*Willy hurries out as the light goes down. Stanley moves

over to the right after him, watches him off. The other waiter has been staring at Willy.)

STANLEY (*to the waiter*). Well, whatta you looking at?

(*The waiter picks up the chairs and moves off right. Stanley takes the table and follows him. The light fades on this area. There is a long pause, the sound of the flute coming over. The light gradually rises on the kitchen, which is empty. Happy appears at the door of the house, followed by Biff. Happy is carrying a large bunch of long-stemmed roses. He enters the kitchen, looks around for Linda. Not seeing her, he turns to Biff, who is just outside the house door, and makes a gesture with his hands, indicating "Not here, I guess." He looks into the living room and freezes. Inside, Linda, unseen, is seated, Willy's coat on her lap. She rises ominously and quietly and moves toward Happy, who backs up into the kitchen, afraid.*)

HAPPY. Hey, what're you doing up? (*Linda says nothing but moves toward him implacably.*) Where's Pop? (*He keeps backing to the right, and now Linda is in full view in the doorway to the living room.*) Is he sleeping?

LINDA. Where were you?

HAPPY (*trying to laugh it off*). We met two girls, Mom, very fine types. Here, we brought you some flowers. (*Offering them to her*) Put them in your room, Ma.

(*She knocks them to the floor at Biff's feet. He has now come inside and closed the door behind him. She stares at Biff, silent.*)

HAPPY. Now what'd you do that for? Mom, I want you to have some flowers—

LINDA (*cutting Happy off, violently to Biff*). Don't you care whether he lives or dies?

HAPPY (*going to the stairs*). Come upstairs, Biff.

BIFF (*with a flare of disgust, to Happy*). Go away from me! (*To Linda*) What do you mean, lives or dies? Nobody's dying around here, pal.

LINDA. Get out of my sight! Get out of here!

BIFF. I wanna see the boss.

LINDA. You're not going near him!

BIFF. Where is he? (*He moves into the living room and Linda follows.*)

LINDA (*shouting after Biff*). You invite him for dinner. He looks forward to it all day—(*Biff appears in his parents' bedroom, looks around, and exits*)—and then you desert him there. There's no stranger you'd do that to!

HAPPY. Why? He had a swell time with us. Listen, when I—(*Linda comes back into the kitchen*)—desert him I hope I don't outlive the day!

LINDA. Get out of here!

HAPPY. Now look, Mom . . .

LINDA. Did you have to go to women tonight? You and your lousy rotten whores!

(*Biff re-enters the kitchen.*)

HAPPY. Mom, all we did was follow Biff around trying to cheer him up! (*To Biff*) Boy, what a night you gave me!

LINDA. Get out of here, both of you, and don't come back! I don't want you tormenting him any more. Go on now, get your things together! (*To Biff*) You can sleep in his apartment. (*She starts to pick up the flowers and stops herself.*) Pick up this stuff, I'm not your maid any more. Pick it up, you bum, you!

(*Happy turns his back to her in refusal. Biff slowly moves over and gets down on his knees, picking up the flowers.*)

LINDA. You're a pair of animals! Not one, not another living soul would have had the cruelty to walk out on that man in a restaurant!

BIFF (*not looking at her*). Is that what he said?

LINDA. He didn't have to say anything. He was so humiliated he nearly limped when he came in.

HAPPY. But, Mom, he had a great time with us—

BIFF (*cutting him off violently*). Shut up!

(*Without another word, Happy goes upstairs.*)

LINDA. You! You didn't even go in to see if he was all right!

BIFF (*still on the floor in front of Linda, the flowers in his hand; with self-loathing*). No. Didn't. Didn't do a damned thing. How do you like that, heh? Left him babbling in a toilet.

LINDA. You louse. You . . .

BIFF. Now you hit it on the nose! (*He gets up, throws the flowers in the wastebasket.*) The scum of the earth, and you're looking at him!

LINDA. Get out of here!

BIFF. I gotta talk to the boss, Mom. Where his he?

LINDA. You're not going near him. Get out of this house!

BIFF (*with absolute assurance, determination*). No. We're gonna have an abrupt conversation, him and me.

LINDA. You're not talking to him!

(*Hammering is heard from outside the house, off right. Biff turns toward the noise.*)

LINDA (*suddenly pleading*). Will you please leave him alone?

BIFF. What's he doing out there?

LINDA. He's planting the garden!

BIFF (*quietly*). Now? Oh, my God!

(*Biff moves outside, Linda following. The light dies down*

on them and comes up on the center of the apron as Willy walks into it. He is carrying a flashlight, a hoe, and a handful of seed packets. He raps the top of the hoe sharply to fix it firmly, and then moves to the left, measuring off the distance with his foot. He holds the flashlight to look at the seed packets, reading off the instructions. He is in the blue of night.)

WILLY. Carrots . . . quarter-inch apart. Rows . . . one-foot rows. (*He measures it off.*) One foot. (*He puts down a package and measures off.*) Beets. (*He puts down another package and measures again.*) Lettuce. (*He reads the package, puts it down.*) One foot—(*He breaks off as Ben appears at the right and moves slowly down to him.*) What a proposition, ts, ts. Terrific, terrific. 'Cause she's suffered, Ben, the woman has suffered. You understand me? A man can't go out the way he came in, Ben, a man has got to add up to something. You can't, you can't—(*Ben moves toward him as though to interrupt.*) You gotta consider, now. Don't answer so quick. Remember, it's a guaranteed twenty-thousand-dollar proposition. Now look, Ben, I want you to go through the ins and outs of this thing with me. I've got nobody to talk to, Ben, and the woman has suffered, you hear me?

BEN (*standing still, considering*). What's the proposition?

WILLY. It's twenty thousand dollars on the barrelhead. Guaranteed, gilt-edged, you understand?

BEN. You don't want to make a fool of yourself. They might not honor the policy.

WILLY. How can they dare refuse? Didn't I work like a coolie to meet every premium on the nose? And now they don't pay off? Impossible!

BEN. It's called a cowardly thing, William.

WILLY. Why? Does it take more guts to stand here the rest of my life ringing up a zero?

BEN (*yielding*). That's a point, William. (*He moves, thinking, turns.*) And twenty thousand—that *is* something one can feel with the hand, it is there.

WILLY (*now assured, with rising power*). Oh, Ben, that's the whole beauty of it! I see it like a diamond, shining in the dark, hard and rough, that I can pick up and touch in my hand. Not like—like an appointment! This would not be another damned-fool appointment, Ben, and it changes all the aspects. Because he thinks I'm nothing, see, and so he spites me. But the funeral—(*Straightening up*) Ben, that funeral will be massive! They'll come from Maine, Massachusetts, Vermont, New Hampshire! All the old-timers with the strange license plates—that boy will be thunderstruck, Ben, because he never realized—I am known! Rhode Island, New York, New Jersey—I am known, Ben, and he'll see it with his eyes once and for all. He'll see what I am, Ben! He's in for a shock, that boy!

BEN (*coming down to the edge of the garden*). He'll call you a coward.

WILLY (*suddenly fearful*). No, that would be terrible.

BEN. Yes. And a damned fool.

WILLY. No, no, he mustn't, I won't have that! (*He is broken and desperate.*)

BEN. He'll hate you, William.

(*The gay music of the boys is heard.*)

WILLY. Oh, Ben, how do we get back to all the great times? Used to be so full of light, and comradeship, the sleigh-riding in winter, and the ruddiness on his cheeks. And always some kind of good news coming up, always something nice coming up ahead. And never even let me carry the valises in the house, and simonizing, simonizing that little red car! Why, why can't I give him something and not have him hate me?

BEN. Let me think about it. (*He glances at his watch.*) I still have a little time. Remarkable proposition, but you've got to be sure you're not making a fool of yourself.

(*Ben drifts off upstage and goes out of sight. Biff comes down from the left.*)

WILLY (*suddenly conscious of Biff, turns and looks up at him, then begins picking up the packages of seeds in confusion*). Where the hell is that seed? (*Indignantly*) You can't see nothing out here! They boxed in the whole goddam neighborhood!

BIFF. There are people all around here. Don't you realize that?

WILLY. I'm busy. Don't bother me.

BIFF (*taking the hoe from Willy*). I'm saying good-bye to you, Pop. (*Willy looks at him, silent, unable to move.*) I'm not coming back any more.

WILLY. You're not going to see Oliver tomorrow?

BIFF. I've got no appointment, Dad.

WILLY. He put his arm around you, and you've got no appointment?

BIFF. Pop, get this now, will you? Every time I've left it's been a fight that sent me out of here. Today I realized something about myself and I tried to explain it to you and I—I think I'm just not smart enough to make any sense out of it for you. To hell with whose fault it is or anything like that. (*He takes Willy's arm.*) Let's just wrap it up, heh? Come on in, we'll tell Mom. (*He gently tries to pull Willy to left.*)

WILLY (*frozen, immobile, with guilt in his voice*). No, I don't want to see her.

BIFF. Come on! (*He pulls again, and Willy tries to pull away.*)

WILLY (*highly nervous*). No, no, I don't want to see her.

BIFF (*tries to look into Willy's face, as if to find the answer there*). Why don't you want to see her?

WILLY (*more harshly now*). Don't bother me, will you?
BIFF. What do you mean, you don't want to see her? You don't want them calling you yellow, do you? This isn't your fault; it's me, I'm a bum. Now come inside! (*Willy strains to get away.*) Did you hear what I said to you?

(*Willy pulls away and quickly goes by himself into the house. Biff follows.*)

LINDA (*to Willy*). Did you plant, dear?
BIFF (*at the door, to Linda*). All right, we had it out. I'm going and I'm not writing any more.
LINDA (*going to Willy in the kitchen*). I think that's the best way, dear. 'Cause there's no use drawing it out, you'll just never get along.

(*Willy doesn't respond.*)

BIFF. People ask where I am and what I'm doing, you don't know, and you don't care. That way it'll be off your mind and you can start brightening up again. All right? That clears it, doesn't it? (*Willy is silent, and Biff goes to him.*) You gonna wish me luck, scout? (*He extends his hand*) What do you say?
LINDA. Shake his hand, Willy.
WILLY (*turning to her, seething with hurt*). There's no necessity to mention the pen at all, y'know.
BIFF (*gently*). I've got no appointment, Dad.
WILLY (*erupting fiercely*). He put his arm around . . . ?
BIFF. Dad, you're never going to see what I am, so what's the use of arguing? If I strike oil I'll send you a check. Meantime forget I'm alive.
WILLY (*to Linda*). Spite, see?
BIFF. Shake hands, Dad.
WILLY. Not my hand.
BIFF. I was hoping not to go this way.
WILLY. Well, this is the way you're going. Good-bye.

(*Biff looks at him a moment, then turns sharply and goes to the stairs.*)

WILLY (*stops him with*). May you rot in hell if you leave this house!
BIFF (*turning*). Exactly what is it that you want from me?
WILLY. I want you to know, on the train, in the mountains, in the valleys, wherever you go, that you cut down your life for spite!
BIFF. No, no.
WILLY. Spite, spite, is the word of your undoing! And when you're down and out, remember what did it. When you're rotting somewhere beside the railroad tracks, remember, and don't you dare blame it on me!
BIFF. I'm not blaming it on you!
WILLY. I won't take the rap for this, you hear?

(*Happy comes down the stairs and stands on the bottom step, watching.*)

BIFF. That's just what I'm telling you!
WILLY (*sinking into a chair at the table, with full accusation*). You're trying to put a knife in me—don't think I don't know what you're doing!
BIFF. All right, phony! Then let's lay it on the line. (*He whips the rubber tube out of his pocket and puts it on the table.*)
HAPPY. You crazy—
LINDA. Biff! (*She moves to grab the hose, but Biff holds it down with his hand.*)
BIFF. Leave it there! Don't move it!
WILLY (*not looking at it*). What is that?
BIFF. You know goddam well what that is.
WILLY (*caged, wanting to escape*). I never saw that.
BIFF. You saw it. The mice didn't bring it into the cellar! What is this supposed to do, make a hero out of you? This supposed to make me sorry for you?
WILLY. Never heard of it.
BIFF. There'll be no pity for you, you hear it? No pity!
WILLY (*to Linda*). You hear the spite!
BIFF. No, you're going to hear the truth—what you are and what I am!
LINDA. Stop it!
WILLY. Spite!
HAPPY (*coming down toward Biff*). You cut it now!
BIFF (*to Happy*). The man don't know who we are! The man is gonna know! (*to Willy*) We never told the truth for ten minutes in this house!
HAPPY. We always told the truth!
BIFF (*turning on him*). You big blow, are you the assistant buyer? You're one of the two assistants to the assistant, aren't you?
HAPPY. Well, I'm practically—
BIFF. You're practically full of it! We all are! And I'm through with it. (*To Willy.*) Now hear this, Willy, this is me.
WILLY. I know you!
BIFF. You know why I had no address for three months? I stole a suit in Kansas City and I was in jail. (*To Linda, who is sobbing*) Stop crying. I'm through with it.

(*Linda turns away from them, her hands covering her face.*)

WILLY. I suppose that's my fault!
BIFF. I stole myself out of every good job since high school!
WILLY. And whose fault is that?
BIFF. And I never got anywhere because you blew me so full of hot air I could never stand taking orders from anybody! That's whose fault it is!

WILLY. I hear that!

LINDA. Don't, Biff!

BIFF. It's goddam time you heard that! I had to be boss big shot in two weeks, and I'm through with it!

WILLY. Then hang yourself! For spite, hang yourself!

BIFF. No! Nobody's hanging himself, Willy! I ran down eleven flights with a pen in my hand today. And suddenly I stopped, you hear me? And in the middle of that office building, do you hear this? I stopped in the middle of that building and I saw—the sky. I saw the things that I love in this world. The work and the food and time to sit and smoke. And I looked at the pen and said to myself, what the hell am I grabbing this for? Why am I trying to become what I don't want to be? What am I doing in an office, making a contemptuous, begging fool of myself, when all I want is out there, waiting for me the minute I say I know who I am! Why can't I say that, Willy? (*He tries to make Willy face him, but Willy pulls away and moves to the left.*)

WILLY (*with hatred, threateningly*). The door of your life is wide open!

BIFF. Pop! I'm a dime a dozen, and so are you!

WILLY (*turning on him now in an uncontrolled outburst*). I am not a dime a dozen! I am Willy Loman, and you are Biff Loman!

(*Biff starts for Willy, but is blocked by Happy. In his fury, Biff seems on the verge of attacking his father.*)

BIFF. I am not a leader of men, Willy, and neither are you. You were never anything but a hard-working drummer who landed in the ash can like all the rest of them! I'm one dollar an hour, Willy! I tried seven states and couldn't raise it. A buck an hour! Do you gather my meaning? I'm not bringing home any prizes any more, and you're going to stop waiting for me to bring them home!

WILLY (*directly to Biff*). You vengeful, spiteful mutt!

(*Biff breaks from Happy. Willy, in fright, starts up the stairs. Biff grabs him.*)

BIFF (*at the peak of his fury*). Pop, I'm nothing! I'm nothing, Pop. Can't you understand that? There's no spite in it any more. I'm just what I am, that's all.

(*Biff's fury has spent itself, and he breaks down, sobbing, holding on to Willy, who dumbly fumbles for Biff's face.*)

WILLY (*astonished*). What're you doing? What're you doing? (*To Linda*) Why is he crying?

BIFF (*crying, broken*). Will you let me go, for Christ's sake? Will you take that phony dream and burn it before something happens? (*Struggling to contain himself, he pulls away and moves to the stairs.*) I'll go in the morning. Put him—put him to bed. (*Exhausted, Biff moves up the stairs to his room.*)

WILLY (*after a long pause, astonished, elevated*). Isn't that—isn't that remarkable? Biff—he likes me!

LINDA. He loves you, Willy!

HAPPY (*deeply moved*). Always did, Pop.

WILLY. Oh, Biff! (*Staring wildly*) He cried! Cried to me. (*He is choking with his love, and now cries out his promise.*) That boy—that boy is going to be magnificent!

(*Ben appears in the light just outside the kitchen.*)

BEN. Yes, outstanding, with twenty thousand behind him.

LINDA (*sensing the racing of his mind, fearfully, carefully*). Now come to bed, Willy. It's all settled now.

WILLY (*finding it difficult not to rush out of the house*). Yes, we'll sleep. Come on. Go to sleep, Hap.

BEN. And it does take a great kind of a man to crack the jungle.

(*In accents of dread, Ben's idyllic music starts up.*)

HAPPY (*his arm around Linda*). I'm getting married, Pop, don't forget it. I'm changing everything. I'm gonna run that department before the year is up. You'll see, Mom. (*He kisses her.*)

BEN. The jungle is dark but full of diamonds, Willy.

(*Willy turns, moves, listening to Ben.*)

LINDA. Be good. You're both good boys, just act that way, that's all.

HAPPY. 'Night, Pop. (*He goes upstairs.*)

LINDA (*to Willy*). Come, dear.

BEN (*with greater force*). One must go in to fetch a diamond out.

WILLY (*to Linda, as he moves slowly along the edge of the kitchen, toward the door*). I just want to get settled down, Linda. Let me sit alone for a little.

LINDA (*almost uttering her fear*). I want you upstairs.

WILLY (*taking her in his arms*). In a few minutes, Linda. I couldn't sleep right now. Go on, you look awful tired. (*He kisses her.*)

BEN. Not like an appointment at all. A diamond is rough and hard to the touch.

WILLY. Go on now. I'll be right up.

LINDA. I think this is the only way, Willy.

WILLY. Sure, it's the best thing.

BEN. Best thing!

WILLY. The only way. Everything is gonna be—go on, kid, get to bed. You look so tired.

LINDA. Come right up.

WILLY. Two minutes.

(*Linda goes into the living room, then reappears in her bedroom. Willy moves just outside the kitchen door.*)

WILLY. Loves me. (*Wonderingly*) Always loved me. Isn't that a remarkable thing? Ben, he'll worship me for it!

BEN (*with promise*). It's dark there, but full of diamonds.

WILLY. Can you imagine that magnificence with twenty thousand dollars in his pocket?

LINDA (*calling from her room*). Willy! Come up!

WILLY (*calling into the kitchen*). Yes! Yes. Coming! It's very smart, you realize that, don't you, sweetheart? Even Ben sees it. I gotta go, baby. 'Bye! 'Bye! (*Going over to Ben, almost dancing*) Imagine? When the mail comes he'll be ahead of Bernard again!

BEN. A perfect proposition all around.

WILLY. Did you see how he cried to me? Oh, if I could kiss him, Ben!

BEN. Time, William, time!

WILLY. Oh, Ben, I always knew one way or another we were gonna make it, Biff and I!

BEN (*looking at his watch*). The boat. We'll be late. (*He moves slowly off into the darkness.*)

WILLY (*elegiacally, turning to the house*). Now when you kick off, boy, I want a seventy-yard boot, and get right down the field under the ball, and when you hit, hit low and hit hard, because it's important, boy. (*He swings around and faces the audience.*) There's all kinds of important people in the stands, and the first thing you know . . . (*Suddenly realizing he is alone.*) Ben! Ben, where do I . . . ? (*He makes a sudden movement of search.*) Ben, how do I . . . ?

LINDA (*calling*). Willy, you coming up?

WILLY (*uttering a gasp of fear, whirling about as if to quiet her*). Sh! (*He turns around as if to find his way; sounds, faces, voices, seem to be swarming in upon him and he flicks at them, crying*) Sh! Sh! (*Suddenly music, faint and high, stops him. It rises in intensity, almost to an unbearable scream. He goes up and down on his toes, and rushes off around the house.*) Shhh!

LINDA. Willy?

(*There is no answer. Linda waits. Biff gets up off his bed. He is still in his clothes. Happy sits up. Biff stands listening.*)

LINDA (*with real fear*). Willy, answer me! Willy!

(*There is the sound of a car starting and moving away at full speed.*)

LINDA. No!

BIFF (*rushing down the stairs*). Pop!

(*As the car speeds off, the music crashes down in a frenzy of sound, which becomes the soft pulsation of a single cello string. Biff slowly returns to his bedroom. He and Happy gravely don their jackets. Linda slowly walks out of her room. The music has developed into a dead march. The leaves of day are appearing over everything. Charley and Bernard, somberly dressed, appear and knock on the kitchen door. Biff and Happy slowly descend the stairs to the kitchen as Charley and Bernard enter. All stop a moment when Linda, in clothes of mourning, bearing a little bunch of roses, comes through the draped doorway into the kitchen. She goes to Charley and takes his arm. Now all move toward the audience, through the wall-line of the kitchen. At the limit of the apron, Linda lays down the flowers, kneels, and sits back on her heels. All stare down at the grave.*)

REQUIEM

CHARLEY. It's getting dark, Linda.

(*Linda doesn't react. She stares at the grave.*)

BIFF. How about it, Mom? Better get some rest, heh? They'll be closing the gate soon.

(*Linda makes no move. Pause.*)

HAPPY (*deeply angered*). He had no right to do that. There was no necessity for it. We would've helped him.

CHARLEY (*grunting*). Hmmm.

BIFF. Come along, Mom.

LINDA. Why didn't anybody come?

CHARLEY. It was a very nice funeral.

LINDA. But where are all the people he knew? Maybe they blame him.

CHARLEY. Naw. It's a rough world, Linda. They wouldn't blame him.

LINDA. I can't understand it. At this time especially. First time in thirty-five years we were just about free and clear. He only needed a little salary. He was even finished with the dentist.

CHARLEY. No man only needs a little salary.

LINDA. I can't understand it.

BIFF. There were a lot of nice days. When he'd come home from a trip; or on Sundays, making the stoop; finishing the cellar; putting on the new porch; when he built the extra bathroom; and put up the garage. You know something, Charley, there's more of him in that front stoop than in all the sales he ever made.

CHARLEY. Yeah. He was a happy man with a batch of cement.

LINDA. He was so wonderful with his hands.

BIFF. He had the wrong dreams. All, all, wrong.

HAPPY (*almost ready to fight Biff*). Don't say that!

BIFF. He never knew who he was.

CHARLEY (*stopping Happy's movement and reply. To Biff*). Nobody dast blame this man. You don't understand:

Willy was a salesman. And for a salesman, there is no rock bottom to the life. He don't put a bolt to a nut, he don't tell you the law or give you medicine. He's a man way out there in the blue, riding on a smile and a shoeshine. And when they start not smiling back—that's an earthquake. And then you get yourself a couple of spots on your hat, and you're finished. Nobody dast blame this man. A salesman is got to dream, boy. It comes with the territory.

BIFF. Charley, the man didn't know who he was.

HAPPY (*infuriated*). Don't say that!

BIFF. Why don't you come with me, Happy?

HAPPY. I'm not licked that easily. I'm staying right in this city, and I'm gonna beat this racket! (*He looks at Biff, his chin set.*) The Loman Brothers!

BIFF. I know who I am, kid.

HAPPY. All right, boy. I'm gonna show you and everybody else that Willy Loman did not die in vain. He had a good dream. It's the only dream you can have—to come out number-one man. He fought it out here, and this is where I'm gonna win it for him.

BIFF (*with a hopeless glance at Happy, bends toward his mother*). Let's go, Mom.

LINDA. I'll be with you in a minute. Go on, Charley. (*He hesitates.*) I want to, just for a minute. I never had a chance to say good-bye.

(*Charley moves away, followed by Happy. Biff remains a slight distance up and left of Linda. She sits there, summoning herself. The flute begins, not far away, playing behind her speech.*)

LINDA. Forgive me, dear. I can't cry. I don't know what it is, but I can't cry. I don't understand it. Why did you ever do that? Help me, Willy, I can't cry. It seems to me that you're just on another trip. I keep expecting you. Willy, dear, I can't cry. Why did you do it? I search and search and I search, and I can't understand it, Willy. I made the last payment on the house today. Today, dear. And there'll be nobody home. (*A sob rises in her throat.*) We're free and clear. (*Sobbing more fully, released.*) We're free. (*Biff comes slowly toward her.*) We're free . . . We're free . . .

(*Biff lifts her to her feet and moves out up right with her in his arms. Linda sobs quietly. Bernard and Charley come together and follow them, followed by Happy. Only the music of the flute is left on the darkening stage as over the house the hard towers of the apartment buildings rise into sharp focus, and—*)

THE CURTAIN FALLS

TOPICS FOR DISCUSSION AND WRITING

1. Miller says that tragedy shows man's struggle to secure "his sense of personal dignity" and that "his destruction in the attempt posits a wrong or an evil in his environment" (page 593). Do you think this makes sense when applied to some earlier tragedy (such as *Oedipus the King* or *Hamlet*), and does it apply convincingly to *Death of a Salesman*? Is this the tragedy of an individual's own making? Or is society at fault for corrupting and exploiting Willy? Or both?
2. Do you find Willy pathetic rather than tragic? If pathetic, does this imply that the play is less worthy than if he is tragic?
3. Do you feel that Miller is straining too hard to turn a play about a little man into a big, impressive play? For example, do the musical themes, the unrealistic setting, the appearances of Ben, and the speech at the grave seem out of keeping in a play about the death of a salesman?
4. We don't know what Willy sells, and we don't know whether or not the insurance will be paid after his death. Do you consider these uncertainties to be faults in the play?
5. Is Howard a villain?
6. Characterize Linda.
7. The critic Kenneth Tynan has written, in *Tynan Right and Left*: "*Death of a Salesman* . . . is not a tragedy. Its catastrophe depends entirely on the fact that the company Willy Loman works for has no pension scheme for its employees. What ultimately destroys Willy is economic injustice, which is curable, as the ills that plague Oedipus are not." What do you think of Tynan's view?

CONTEXTS FOR *DEATH OF A SALESMAN*

Tragedy and the Common Man

Arthur Miller

In this age few tragedies are written. It has often been held that the lack is due to a paucity of heroes among us, or else that modern man has had the blood drawn out of his organs of belief by the skepticism of science, and the heroic attack on life cannot feed on an attitude of reserve and circumspection. For one reason or another, we are often held to be below tragedy—or tragedy above us. The inevitable conclusion is, of course, that the tragic mode is archaic, fit only for the very highly placed, the kings or the kingly, and where this admission is not made in so many words it is most often implied.

I believe that the common man is as apt a subject for tragedy in its highest sense as kings were. On the face of it this ought to be obvious in the light of modern psychiatry, which bases its analysis upon classic formulations, such as the Oedipus and Orestes complexes, for instances, which were enacted by royal beings, but which apply to everyone in similar emotional situations.

More simply, when the question of tragedy in art is not at issue, we never hesitate to attribute to the well-placed and the exalted the very same mental processes as the lowly. And finally, if the exaltation of tragic action were truly a property of the high-bred character alone, it is inconceivable that the mass of mankind should cherish tragedy above all other forms, let alone be capable of understanding it.

As a general rule, to which there may be exceptions unknown to me, I think the tragic feeling is evoked in us when we are in the presence of a character who is ready to lay down his life, if need be, to secure one thing—his sense of personal dignity. From Orestes to Hamlet, Medea to Macbeth, the underlying struggle is that of the individual attempting to gain his "rightful" position in his society.

Sometimes he is one who has been displaced from it, sometimes one who seeks to attain it for the first time, but the fateful wound from which the inevitable events spiral is the wound of indignity, and its dominant force is indignation. Tragedy, then, is the consequence of a man's total compulsion to evaluate himself justly.

In the sense of having been initiated by the hero himself, the tale always reveals what has been called his "tragic flaw," a failing that is not peculiar to grand or elevated characters. Nor is it necessarily a weakness. The flaw, or crack in the character, is really nothing—and need be nothing, but his inherent unwillingness to remain passive in the face of what he conceives to be a challenge to his dignity, his image of his rightful status. Only the passive, only those who accept their lot without active retaliation, are "flawless." Most of us are in that category.

But there are among us today, as there always have been, those who act against the scheme of things that degrades them, and in the process of action everything we have accepted out of fear or insensitivity or ignorance is shaken before us and examined, and from this total onslaught by an individual against the seemingly stable cosmos surrounding us—from this total examination of the "unchangeable" environment—comes the terror and the fear that is classically associated with tragedy.

More important, from this total questioning of what has previously been unquestioned, we learn. And such a process is not beyond the common man. In revolutions around the world, these past thirty years, he has demonstrated again and again this inner dynamic of all tragedy.

Insistence upon the rank of the tragic hero, or the so-called nobility of his character, is really but a clinging to the outward forms of tragedy. If rank or nobility of character was indispensable, then it would follow that the problems of those with rank were the particular problems of tragedy. But surely the right of one monarch to capture the domain from another no longer raises our passions, nor are our concepts of justice what they were to the mind of an Elizabethan king.

The quality in such plays that does shake us, however, derives from the underlying fear of being displaced, the disaster inherent in being torn away from our chosen image of what and who we are in this world. Among us today this fear is as strong, and perhaps stronger, than it ever was. In fact, it is the common man who knows this fear best.

Now, if it is true that tragedy is the consequence of a man's total compulsion to evaluate himself justly, his destruction in the attempt posits a wrong or an evil in his environment. And this is precisely the morality of tragedy and its lesson. The discovery of the moral law, which is what the enlightenment of tragedy consists of, is not the discovery of some abstract or metaphysical quantity.

The tragic right is a condition of life, a condition in which the human personality is able to flower and realize itself. The wrong is the condition which suppresses man, perverts the flowing out of his love and creative instinct. Tragedy enlightens—and it must, in that it points the heroic finger at the enemy of man's freedom. The thrust for freedom is the quality in tragedy which exalts. The revolutionary questioning of the stable environment is what terrifies. In no way is the common man debarred from such thoughts or such actions.

Seen in this light, our lack of tragedy may be partially accounted for by the turn which modern literature has taken toward the purely psychiatric view of life, or the purely sociological. If all our miseries, our indignities, are born and bred within our minds, then all action, let alone the heroic action, is obviously impossible.

And if society alone is responsible for the cramping of our lives, then the protagonist must needs be so pure and faultless as to force us to deny his validity as a character. From neither of these views can tragedy derive, simply because neither represents a balanced concept of life. Above all else, tragedy requires the finest appreciation by the writer of cause and effect.

No tragedy can therefore come about when its author fears to question absolutely everything, when he regards any institution, habit or custom as being either everlasting, immutable or inevitable. In the tragic view the need of man to wholly realize himself is the only fixed star, and whatever it is that hedges his nature and lowers it is ripe for attack and examination. Which is not to say that tragedy must preach revolution.

The Greeks could probe the very heavenly origin of their ways and return to confirm the rightness of laws. And Job could face God in anger, demanding his right, and end in submission. But for a moment everything is in suspension, nothing is accepted, and in this stretching and tearing apart of the cosmos, in the very action of so doing, the character gains "size," the tragic stature which is spuriously attached to the royal or the high-born in our minds. The commonest of men may take on that stature to the extent of his willingness to throw all he has into the contest, the battle to secure his rightful place in his world.

There is a misconception of tragedy with which I have been struck in review after review, and in many conversations with writers and readers alike. It is the idea that tragedy is of necessity allied to pessimism. Even the dictionary says nothing more about the word than that it means a story with a sad or unhappy ending. This impression is so firmly fixed that I almost hesitate to claim that in truth tragedy implies more optimism in its author than does comedy, and that its final result ought to be the reinforcement of the onlooker's brightest opinions of the human animal.

For, if it is true to say that in essence the tragic hero is intent upon claiming his whole due as a personality, and if this struggle must be total and without reservation, then it automatically demonstrates the indestructible will of man to achieve his humanity.

The possibility of victory must be there in tragedy. Where pathos rules, where pathos is finally derived, a character has fought a battle he could not possibly have won. The pathetic is achieved when the protagonist is, by virtue of his witlessness, his insensitivity or the very air he gives off, incapable of grappling with a much superior force.

Pathos truly is the mode for the pessimist. But tragedy requires a nicer balance between what is possible and what is impossible. And it is curious, although edifying, that the plays we revere, century after century, are the tragedies. In them, and in them alone, lies the belief—optimistic, if you will, in the perfectibility of man.

It is time, I think, that we who are without kings, took up this bright thread of our history and followed it to the only place it can possibly lead in our time—the heart and spirit of the average man.

Willy Loman's Ideals

Arthur Miller

[In 1958 Arthur Miller made these comments during the course of a symposium on *Death of a Salesman.* The title is the editors'.]

Miller. The trouble with Willy Loman is that he has tremendously powerful ideals. We're not accustomed to speaking of ideals in his terms; but, if Willy Loman, for instance, had not had a very profound sense that his life as lived had left him hollow, he would have died contentedly polishing his car on some Sunday afternoon at a ripe old age. The fact is he has values. The fact that they cannot be realized is what is driving him mad—just as, unfortunately, it's driving a lot of other people mad. The truly valueless man, a man without ideals, is always perfectly at home anywhere . . . because there cannot be a conflict between nothing and something. Whatever negative qualities there are in the society or in the environment don't bother him, because they are not in conflict with what positive sense one may have. I think Willy Loman, on the other hand, is seeking for a kind of ecstasy in life, which the machine-civilization deprives people of. He's looking for his selfhood, for his immortal soul, so to speak. People who don't know the intensity of that quest, possibly, think he's odd. Now an extraordinarily large number of salesmen particularly, who are in a line of work where a large measure of ingenuity and individualism are required, have a very intimate understanding of this problem. More so, I think, than literary critics who probably need strive less after a certain point. A salesman is a kind of creative person (it's possibly idiotic to say so on a literary program, but they are), they have to get up in the morning and conceive a plan of attack and use all kinds of ingenuity all day long, just the way a writer does.

SAMUEL BECKETT

Happy Days

Samuel Beckett (1906–1989) was born in Dublin of middle-class Protestant parents. He was educated at Trinity College, Dublin, where he took his degree in modern languages, graduating in 1927. He went to Paris the next year where he met James Joyce, a fellow Irishman, and translated parts of *Finnegan's Wake* into French. He stayed in France until 1930, when he returned to Dublin to take up a lectureship in French at Trinity College. He soon decided against teaching and began a number of years of wandering, living in London, traveling about Germany and France, and then settling in Paris in 1937. During World War II, after narrowly escaping capture by the Gestapo for his work in the French Resistance, he fled to Roussillon in southwestern France, where he remained until the end of the war, when he returned to Paris. In 1961, the year he was writing *Happy Days,* he married a French woman, Suzanne Deschevaux-Dumesnil. In 1969 he was awarded the Nobel Prize for literature but refused to go to Stockholm for the ceremonies. Always a reclusive figure, he still lives in Paris with his wife. His best-known works include the novels *Molloy* (1951), *Malone Dies* (1951), and *The Unnamable* (1953), short stories collected as *More Pricks Than Kicks* (1934), and the plays *Waiting for Godot* (first published in French as *En attendant Godot* in 1952 but translated by Beckett into English and published in 1954), *Endgame* (1957), and *Happy Days* (1961). Numerous shorter works, including scripts for radio and television and even for a movie entitled *Film,* starring Buster Keaton, complete what John Updike called "a single holy book."

COMMENTARY

Aside from the background information on the development of modern tragicomedy given in "The Nature of Drama" at the beginning of this book, especially on pages 38–40, we need perhaps only mention that Beckett wrote *Happy Days* in English, in 1960–61. (He sometimes wrote his plays and novels in French, but in *Happy Days,* beyond describing the backdrop as *pompier trompe-l'oeil* ("ordinary illusionistic"), French is implied only in Winnie's uncertainty whether hair is "them" or "it," for in French "hair" is plural, *les cheveux.*)

List of Characters

WINNIE, *a woman about fifty*
WILLIE, *a man about sixty*

ACT 1

Expanse of scorched grass rising centre to low mound. Gentle slopes down to front and either side of stage. Back an abrupter fall to stage level. Maximum of simplicity and symmetry.

Blazing light.

Very pompier trompe-l'oeil[1] *backcloth to represent unbroken plain and sky receding to meet in far distance.*

Imbedded up to above her waist in exact centre of mound, Winnie. About fifty, well preserved, blond for preference, plump, arms and shoulders bare, low bodice, big bosom, pearl necklet. She is discovered sleeping, her arms on the ground before her, her head on her arms. Beside her on ground to her left a capacious black bag, shopping variety, and to her right a collapsible collapsed parasol, beak of handle emerging from sheath.

[1]***pompier trompe l'oeil*** ordinary illusionistic.

Dame Peggy Ashcroft in the National Theatre production of *Happy Days,* directed by Sir Peter Hall, 1975. (Photograph: Zoë Dominic F.R.P.S.)

To her right and rear, lying asleep on ground, hidden by mound, Willie.

Long pause. A bell rings piercingly, say ten seconds, stops. She does not move. Pause. Bell more piercingly, say five seconds. She wakes. Bell stops. She raises her head, gazes front. Long pause. She straightens up, lays her hands flat on ground, throws back her head and gazes at zenith. Long pause.

WINNIE (*gazing at zenith*). Another heavenly day. (*Pause. Head back level, eyes front, pause. She clasps hands to breast, closes eyes. Lips move in inaudible prayer, say ten seconds. Lips still. Hands remain clasped. Low*) For Jesus Christ sake Amen. (*Eyes open, hands unclasp, return to mound. Pause. She clasps hands to breast again, closes eyes, lips move again in inaudible addendum, say five seconds. Low*) World without end Amen. (*Eyes open, hands unclasp, return to mound. Pause.*) Begin, Winnie. (*Pause.*) Begin your day, Winnie. (*Pause. She turns to bag, rummages in it without moving it from its place, brings out toothbrush, rummages again, brings out flat tube of toothpaste, turns back front, unscrews cap of tube, lays cap on ground, squeezes with difficulty small blob of paste on brush, holds tube in one hand and brushes teeth with other. She turns modestly aside and back to her right to spit out behind mound. In this position her eyes rest on Willie. She spits out. She cranes a little further back and down. Loud*) Hoo-oo! (*Pause. Louder*) Hoo-oo! (*Pause. Tender smile as she turns back front, lays down brush.*) Poor Willie—(*examines tube, smile off*)—running out—(*looks for cap*)—ah well—(*finds cap*)—can't be helped—(*screws on cap*)—just one of those old things—(*lays down tube*)—another of those old things—(*turns towards bag*)—just can't be cured—(*brings out small mirror, turns back front*)—ah yes—(*inspects teeth in mirror*)—poor dear Willie—(*testing upper front teeth with thumb, indistinctly*)—good Lord!—(*pulling back upper lip to inspect gums, do*[2])—good God!—(*pulling back corner of mouth, mouth open, do*)—ah well—(*other corner, do*)—no worse—(*abandons inspection, normal speech*)—no better, no worse—(*lays down mirror*)—no change—(*wipes fingers on grass*)—no pain—(*looks for toothbrush*)—hardly any—(*takes up toothbrush*)—great thing that—(*examines handle of brush*)—nothing like it—(*examines handle, reads*)—pure . . . what?—(*pause*)—what?—(*lays down brush*)—ah yes—(*turns towards bag*)—poor Willie—(*rummages in bag*)—no zest—(*rummages*)—for anything (*brings out spectacles in case*)—no interest—(*turns back front*)—in life—(*takes spectacles from case*)—poor dear Willie—(*lays down case*)—sleep for ever—(*opens spectacles*)—marvellous gift—(*puts on spectacles*)—nothing to touch it—(*looks for toothbrush*)—in my opinion—(*takes up toothbrush*)—always said so—(*examines handle of brush*)—I wish I had it—(*examines handle, reads*)—genuine . . . pure . . . what?—(*lays down brush*)—blind next—(*takes off spectacles*)—ah well—(*lays down spectacles*)—seen enough—(*feels in bodice for handkerchief*)—I suppose—(*takes out folded handkerchief*)—by now—(*shakes out handkerchief*)—what are those wonderful lines—(*wipes one eye*)—woe woe is me—(*wipes the other*)—to see what I see—(*looks for spectacles*)—ah yes—(*takes up spectacles*)—wouldn't miss it—(*starts polishing spectacles, breathing on lenses*)—or would I?—(*polishes*)—holy light—(*polishes*)—bob up out of dark—(*polishes*)—blaze of hellish light. (*Stops polishing, raises face to sky, pause, head back level, resumes polishing, stops polishing, cranes back to her right and down.*) Hoo-oo! (*Pause. Tender smile as she turns back front and resumes polishing. Smile off.*) Marvellous gift—(*stops polishing, lays down spectacles*)—wish I had it—(*folds handkerchief*)—ah well—(*puts handkerchief back in bodice*)—can't complain—(*looks for spectacles*)—no no—(*takes up spectacles*)—mustn't complain—(*holds up spectacles, looks through lens*)—so much to be thankful for—(*looks through other lens*)—no pain—(*puts on spectacles*)—hardly any—(*looks for toothbrush*)—wonderful thing that—(*takes up toothbrush*)—nothing like it—(*examines handle of brush*)—slight headache sometimes—(*examines handle, reads*)—guaranteed . . . genuine . . . pure . . . what?—(*looks closer*)—genuine pure . . . —(*takes handkerchief from bodice*)—ah yes—(*shakes out handkerchief*)—occasional mild migraine—(*starts wiping handle of brush*)—it comes—(*wipes*)—then goes—(*wiping mechanically*)—ah yes—(*wiping*)—many mercies—(*wiping*)—great mercies—(*stops wiping, fixed lost gaze, brokenly*)—prayers perhaps not for naught—(*pause, do*)—first thing—(*pause, do*)—last thing—(*head down, resumes wiping, stops wiping, head up, calmed, wipes eyes, folds handkerchief, puts it back in bodice, examines handle of brush, reads*)—fully guaranteed . . . genuine pure . . . —(*looks closer*)—genuine pure . . . (*Takes off spectacles, lays them and brush down, gazes before her.*) Old things. (*Pause.*) Old eyes. (*Long pause.*) On, Winnie. (*She casts about her, sees parasol, considers it at length, takes it up and develops from sheath a handle of surprising length. Holding butt of parasol in right hand she cranes back and down to her right to hang over Willie.*) Hoo-oo! (*Pause.*) Willie! (*Pause.*) Wonderful gift. (*She strikes down at him with beak of parasol.*) Wish I had it. (*She strikes again. The parasol slips from her grasp and falls behind mound. It is immediately restored to her by Willie's invisible hand.*) Thank you, dear. (*She transfers parasol to left hand, turns back front and examines right palm.*) Damp. (*Returns parasol to right hand, examines left palm.*) Ah well, no worse. (*Head up, cheerfully*) No better, no worse, no change. (*Pause. Do*) No pain. (*Cranes back to look down at Willie, holding parasol by butt as before.*) Don't go off on me again now dear will you please, I may need you. (*Pause.*) No

[2] ***do*** ditto

hurry, no hurry, just don't curl up on me again. (*Turns back front, lays down parasol, examines palms together, wipes them on grass.*) Perhaps a shade off colour just the same. (*Turns to bag, rummages in it, brings out revolver, holds it up, kisses it rapidly, puts it back, rummages, brings out almost empty battle of red medicine, turns back front, looks for spectacles, puts them on, reads label.*) Loss of spirits . . . lack of keenness . . . want of appetite . . . infants . . . children . . . adults . . . six level . . . tablespoonfuls daily—(*head up, smile*)—the old style!—(*smile off, head down, reads*)—daily . . . before and after . . . meals . . . instantaneous . . . (*looks closer*) . . . improvement. (*Takes off spectacles, lays them down, holds up bottle at arm's length to see level, unscrews cap, swigs it off head well back, tosses cap and bottle away in Willie's direction. Sound of breaking glass.*) Ah that's better! (*Turns to bag, rummages in it, brings out lipstick, turns back front, examines lipstick.*) Running out. (*Looks for spectacles.*) Ah well. (*Puts on spectacles, looks for mirror.*) Mustn't complain. (*Takes up mirror, starts doing lips.*) What is that wonderful line? (*Lips.*) Oh fleeting joys—(*lips*)—oh something lasting woe. (*Lips. She is interrupted by disturbance from Willie. He is sitting up. She lowers lipstick and mirror and cranes back and down to look at him. Pause. Top back of Willie's bald head, trickling blood, rises to view above slope, comes to rest. Winnie pushes up her spectacles. Pause. His hand appears with handkerchief, spreads it on skull, disappears. Pause. The hand appears with boater, club ribbon, settles it on head, rakish angle, disappears. Pause. Winnie cranes a little further back and down.*) Slip on your drawers, dear, before you get singed. (*Pause.*) No? (*Pause.*) Oh I see, you still have some of that stuff left. (*Pause.*) Work it well in, dear. (*Pause.*) Now the other. (*Pause. She turns back front, gazes before her. Happy expression.*) Oh this is going to be another happy day! (*Pause. Happy expression off. She pulls down spectacles and resumes lips. Willie opens newspaper, hands invisible. Tops of yellow sheets appear on either side of his head. Winnie finishes lips, inspects them in mirror held a little further away.*) Ensign crimson. (*Willie turns page. Winnie lays down lipstick and mirror, turns towards bag.*) Pale flag.

(*Willie turns page. Winnie rummages in bag, brings out small ornate brimless hat with crumpled feather, turns back front, straightens hat, smooths feather, raises it towards head, arrests gesture as Willie reads.*)

WILLIE. His Grace and Most Reverend Father in God Dr. Carolus Hunter dead in tub.

(*Pause.*)

WINNIE (*gazing front, hat in hand, tone of fervent reminiscence*). Charlie Hunter! (*Pause.*) I close my eyes—(*she takes off spectacles and does so, hat in one hand, spectacles in other, Willie turns page*)—and am sitting on his knees again, in the back garden at Borough Green, under the horse-beech. (*Pause. She opens eyes, puts on spectacles, fiddles with hat.*) Oh the happy memories!

(*Pause. She raises hat towards head, arrests gesture as Willie reads.*)

WILLIE. Opening for smart youth.

(*Pause. She raises hat towards head, arrests gesture, takes off spectacles, gazes front, hat in one hand, spectacles in other.*)

WINNIE. My first ball! (*Long pause.*) My second ball! (*Long pause. Closes eyes.*) My first kiss! (*Pause. Willie turns page. Winnie opens eyes.*) A Mr. Johnson, or Johnston, or perhaps I should say John*stone*. Very bushy moustache, very tawny. (*Reverently*) Almost ginger! (*Pause.*) Within a toolshed, though whose I cannot conceive. We had no toolshed and he most certainly had no toolshed. (*Closes eyes.*) I see the piles of pots. (*Pause.*) The tangles of bast. (*Pause.*) The shadows deepening among the rafters.

(*Pause. She opens eyes, puts on spectacles, raises hat towards head, arrests gesture as Willie reads.*)

WILLIE. Wanted bright boy.

(*Pause. Winnie puts on hat hurriedly, looks for mirror. Willie turns page. Winnie takes up mirror, inspects hat, lays down mirror, turns toward bag. Paper disappears. Winnie rummages in bag, brings out magnifying-glass, turns back front, looks for toothbrush. Paper reappears, folded, and begins to fan Willie's face, hand invisible. Winnie takes up toothbrush and examines handle through glass.*)

WINNIE. Fully guaranteed . . . (*Willie stops fanning*) . . . genuine pure . . . (*Pause. Willie resumes fanning. Winnie looks closer, reads.*) Fully guaranteed . . . (*Willie stops fanning*) . . . genuine pure . . . (*Pause. Willie resumes fanning. Winnie lays down glass and brush, takes handkerchief from bodice, takes off and polishes spectacles, puts on spectacles, looks for glass, takes up and polishes glass, lays down glass, looks for brush, takes up brush and wipes handle, lays down brush, puts handkerchief back in bodice, looks for glass, takes up glass, looks for brush, takes up brush and examines handle through glass.*) Fully guaranteed . . . (*Willie stops fanning*) . . . genuine pure . . . (*pause, Willie resumes fanning*) . . . hog's (*Willie stops fanning, pause*) . . . setae. (*Pause. Winnie lays down glass and brush, paper disappears, Winnie takes off spectacles, lays them down, gazes front.*) Hog's setae. (*Pause.*) That is what I find so wonderful, that not a day goes by—(*smile*)—to speak in the old style—(*smile off*)—hardly a day, without some addition to one's knowledge however trifling, the addition I mean, provided one takes the pains. (*Willie's hand reappears with a postcard which he examines close to eyes.*) And if for some strange reason no further pains are possible, why then just close the eyes—(*she does so*)—and wait for the day to come—(*opens eyes*)—the happy day to come when flesh melts at so many degrees and the night of the moon has so many hundred hours. (*Pause.*) That is what I find so comforting when I lose heart and envy the brute beast. (*Turning towards Willie*) I hope you are taking in—(*She sees postcard, bends lower.*) What is that you have there, Willie, may I see? (*She reaches down with hand and Willie hands her card. The hairy forearm appears above slope, raised in gesture of giving, the hand open to take back, and remains in this position till card is returned. Winnie turns back front and examines card.*) Heavens what are they up to! (*She looks for spectacles, puts them on and examines card.*) No but this is just genuine pure filth! (*Examines card.*) Make any nice-minded person want to vomit! (*Impatience of Willie's fingers. She looks for glass, takes it up and examines card through glass. Long pause.*) What does that creature in the background think he's doing? (*Looks closer.*) Oh no really! (*Impatience of fingers. Last long look. She lays down glass, takes edge of card between right forefinger and thumb, averts head, takes nose between left forefinger and thumb.*) Pah! (*Drops card.*) Take it away! (*Willie's arm disappears. His hand reappears immediately, holding card. Winnie takes off spectacles, lays them down, gazes before her. During what follows Willie continues to relish card, varying angles and distance from his eyes.*) Hog's setae. (*Puzzled expression.*) What exactly is a hog? (*Pause. Do.*) A sow of course I know, but a hog . . . (*Puzzled expression off*) Oh well what does it matter, that is what I always say, it will come back, that is what I find so wonderful, all comes back. (*Pause.*) All? (*Pause.*) No, not all. (*Smile.*) No no. (*Smile off.*) Not quite. (*Pause.*) A part. (*Pause.*) Floats up, one fine day, out of the blue. (*Pause.*) That is what I find so wonderful. (*Pause. She turns towards bag. Hand and card disappear. She makes to rummage in bag, arrests gesture.*) No. (*She turns back front. Smile.*) No no. (*Smile off.*) Gently Winnie. (*She gazes front. Willie's hand reappears, takes off hat, disappears with hat.*) What then? (*Hand reappears, takes handkerchief from skull, disappears with handkerchief. Sharply, as to one not paying attention.*) Winnie! (*Willie bows head out of sight.*) What *is* the alternative? (*Pause.*) What *is* the al— (*Willie blows nose loud and long, head and hands invisible. She turns to look at him. Pause. Head reappears. Pause. Hand reappears with handkerchief, spreads it on skull, disappears. Pause. Hand reappears with boater, settles it on head, rakish angle, disappears. Pause.*) Would I had let you sleep on. (*She turns back front. Intermittent plucking at grass, head up and down, to animate following.*) Ah yes, if only I could bear to be alone, I mean prattle away with not a soul to hear. (*Pause.*) Not that I flatter myself you hear much, no Willie, God forbid. (*Pause.*) Days perhaps when you hear nothing. (*Pause.*) But days too when you answer. (*Pause.*) So that I may say at all times, even when you do not answer and perhaps hear nothing, something of this is being heard, I am not merely talking to myself, that is in the wilderness, a thing I could never bear to do—for any length of time. (*Pause.*) That is what enables me to go on, go on talking that is. (*Pause.*) Whereas if you were to die—(*smile*)—to speak in the old style—(*smile off*)—or go away and leave me, then what would I do, what *could* I do, all day long, I mean between the bell for waking and the bell for sleep? (*Pause.*) Simply gaze before me with compressed lips. (*Long pause while she does so. No more plucking.*) Not another word as long as I drew breath, nothing to break the silence of this place. (*Pause.*) Save possibly, now and then, every now and then, a sigh into my looking-glass. (*Pause.*) Or a brief . . . gale of laughter, should I happen to see the old joke again. (*Pause. Smile appears, broadens and seems about to culminate in laugh when suddenly replaced by expression of anxiety.*) My hair! (*Pause.*) Did I brush and comb my hair? (*Pause.*) I may have done. (*Pause.*) Normally I do. (*Pause.*) There is so little one *can* do. (*Pause.*) One does it all. (*Pause.*) All one can. (*Pause.*) Tis only human. (*Pause.*) Human nature. (*She begins to inspect mound, looks up.*) Human weakness. (*She resumes inspection of mound, looks up.*) Natural weakness. (*She resumes inspection of mound.*) I see no comb. (*Inspects.*) Nor any hairbrush. (*Looks up. Puzzled expression. She turns to bag, rummages in it.*) The comb is here. (*Back front. Puzzled expression. Back to bag. Rummages.*)The brush is here. (*Back front. Puzzled expression.*) Perhaps I put them back, after use. (*Pause. Do.*) But normally I do not put things back, after use, no, I leave them lying about and put them back all together, at the end of the day. (*Smile.*) To speak in the old style. (*Pause.*) The sweet old style. (*Smile off.*) And yet . . . I seem . . . to remember . . . (*Suddenly careless*) Oh well, what does it matter, that is what I always say, I shall simply brush and comb them later on, purely and simply, I have the whole—(*Pause. Puzzled*) Them? (*Pause.*) Or it? (*Pause.*) Brush and comb it? (*Pause.*) Sounds improper somehow. (*Pause. Turning a little towards Willie*) What would you say, Willie? (*Pause. Turning a little further*) What would you say, Willie, speaking of your hair, them or it? (*Pause.*) The hair on your head, I mean. (*Pause. Turning a little further.*) The hair on your head, Willie, what would you say speaking of the hair on your head, them or it?

(*Long pause.*)

WILLIE. It.

WINNIE (*turning back front, joyful*). Oh you are going to talk to me today, this is going to be a happy day! (*Pause. Joy off.*) Another happy day. (*Pause.*) Ah well, where was I, my hair, yes, later on, I shall be thankful for it later on. (*Pause.*) I have my—(*raises hands to hat*)—yes, on, my hat on—(*lowers hands*)—I cannot take it off now. (*Pause.*) To think there are times one cannot take off one's hat, not if one's life were at stake. Times one cannot put it on, times one cannot take it off. (*Pause.*) How often I have said, Put on your hat now, Winnie, there is nothing else for it, take off your hat now, Winnie, like a good girl, it will do you good, and did not. (*Pause.*) Could not. (*Pause. She raises hand, frees a strand of hair from under hat, draws it towards eye, squints at it, lets it go, hand down.*) Golden you called it, that day, when the last guest was gone—(*hand up in gesture of raising a glass*)—to your golden . . . may it never (*voice breaks*) . . . may it never . . . (*Hand down. Head down. Pause. Low*) That day. (*Pause. Do.*) What day? (*Pause. Head up. Normal voice*) What now? (*Pause.*) Words fail, there are times when even they fail. (*Turning a little towards Willie*) Is that not so, Willie? (*Pause. Turning a little further*) Is not that so, Willie, that even words fail, at times? (*Pause. Back front.*) What is one to do then, until they come again? Brush and comb the hair, if it has not been done, or if there is some doubt, trim the nails if they are in need of trimming, these things tide one over. (*Pause.*) That is what I mean. (*Pause.*) That is all I mean. (*Pause.*) That is what I find so wonderful, that not a day goes by—(*smile*)—to speak in the old style—(*smile off*)—without some blessing—(*Willie collapses behind slope, his head disappears, Winnie turns towards event*)—in disguise. (*She cranes back and down.*) Go back into your hole now, Willie, you've exposed yourself enough. (*Pause.*) Do as I say, Willie, don't lie sprawling there in this hellish sun, go back into your hole. (*Pause.*) Go on now, Willie. (*Willie invisible starts crawling left towards hole.*) That's the man. (*She follows his progress with her eyes.*) Not head first, stupid, how are you going to turn? (*Pause.*) That's it . . . right round . . . now . . . back in. (*Pause.*) Oh I know it is not easy, dear, crawling backwards, but it is rewarding in the end. (*Pause.*) You have left your vaseline behind. (*She watches as he crawls back for vaseline.*) The lid! (*She watches as he crawls back towards hole. Irritated*) Not head first, I tell you! (*Pause.*) More to the right. (*Pause.*) The *right,* I said. (*Pause. Irritated*) Keep your tail down, can't you! (*Pause.*) Now. (*Pause.*) There! (*All these directions loud. Now in her normal voice, still turned towards him*) Can you hear me? (*Pause.*) I beseech you, Willie, just yes or no, can you hear me, just yes or nothing.

(*Pause.*)

WILLIE. Yes.

WINNIE (*turning front, same voice*). And now?

WILLIE (*irritated*). Yes.

WINNIE (*less loud*). And now?

WILLIE (*more irritated*). Yes.

WINNIE (*still less loud*). And now? (*A little louder*) And now?

WILLIE (*violently*). Yes!

WINNIE (*same voice*). Fear no more the heat o' the sun. (*Pause.*) Did you hear that?

WILLIE (*irritated*). Yes.

WINNIE (*same voice*). What? (*Pause.*) What?

WILLIE (*more irritated*). Fear no more.

(*Pause.*)

WINNIE (*same voice*). No more what? (*Pause.*) Fear no more what?

WILLIE (*violently*). Fear no more!

WINNIE (*normal voice, garbled*). Bless you Willie I do appreciate your goodness I know what an effort it costs you, now you may relax I shall not trouble you again unless I am obliged to, by that I mean unless I come to the end of my own resources which is most unlikely, just to know that in theory you can hear me even though in fact you don't is all I need, just to feel you there within earshot and conceivably on the qui vive is all I ask, not to say anything I would not wish you to hear or liable to cause you pain, not to be babbling away on trust as it is were not knowing and something gnawing at me. (*Pause for breath.*) Doubt. (*Places index and second finger on heart area, moves them about, brings them to rest.*) Here. (*Moves them slightly.*) Abouts. (*Hand away.*) Oh no doubt the time will come when before I can utter a word I must make sure you heard the one that went before and then no doubt another come another time when I must learn to talk to myself a thing I could never bear to do such wilderness. (*Pause.*) Or gaze before me with compressed lips. (*She does so.*) All day long. (*Gaze and lips again.*) No. (*Smile.*) No no. (*Smile off.*) There is of course the bag. (*Turns towards it.*) There will always be the bag. (*Back front.*) Yes, I suppose so. (*Pause.*) Even when you are gone, Willie. (*She turns a little towards him.*) You *are* going, Willie, aren't you? (*Pause. Louder*) You *will* be going soon, Willie, won't you? (*Pause. Louder*) Willie! (*Pause. She cranes back and down to look at him.*) So you have taken off your straw, that is wise. (*Pause.*) You do look snug, I must say, with your chin on your hands and the old blue eyes like saucers in the shadows. (*Pause.*) Can you see me from there I wonder, I still wonder. (*Pause.*) No? (*Back front.*) Oh I know it does not follow when two are gathered together—(*faltering*)—in this way—(*normal*)—that because one sees the other the other sees the one, life has taught me that . . . too. (*Pause.*) Yes, life I suppose, there is no other word. (*She turns a little towards him.*) Could you see me, Willie, do you think, from where you are, if you were to raise your eyes in my direction? (*Turns a little further.*) Lift up your eyes to me, Willie, and tell me can you see me, do that for me, I'll lean back as far as I can. (*Does so. Pause.*) No? (*Pause.*) Well never mind. (*Turns back painfully front.*) The earth is very tight today, can it be I have put on flesh, I trust not. (*Pause. Absently, eyes*

eyes lowered) The great heat possibly. (*Starts to pat and stroke ground.*) All things expanding, some more than others. (*Pause. Patting and stroking*) Some less. (*Pause. Do.*) Oh I can well imagine what is passing through your mind, it is not enough to have to listen to the woman, now I must look at her as well. (*Pause. Do.*) Well it is very understandable. (*Pause. Do.*) Well it is very understandable. (*Pause. Do.*) Most understandable. (*Pause. Do.*) One does not appear to be asking a great deal, indeed at times it would seem hardly possible—(*voice breaks, falls to a murmur*)—to ask less—of a fellow-creature—to put it mildly—whereas actually—when you think about it—look into your heart—see the other—what he needs—peace—to be left in peace—then perhaps the moon—all this time—asking for the moon. (*Pause. Stroking hand suddenly still. Lively*) Oh I say, what have we here? (*Bending head to ground, incredulous*) Looks like life of some kind! (*Looks for spectacles, puts them on, bends closer. Pause.*) An emmet! (*Recoils. Shrill*) Willie, an emmet, a live emmet! (*Seizes magnifying-glass, bends to ground again, inspects through glass.*) Where's it gone? (*Inspects.*) Ah! (*Follows its progress through grass.*) Has like a little white ball in its arms. (*Follows progress. Hand still. Pause.*) It's gone in. (*Continues a moment to gaze at spot through glass, then slowly straightens up, lays down glass, takes off spectacles and gazes before her, spectacles in hand. Finally*) Like a little white ball.

(*Long pause. Gesture to lay down spectacles.*)

WILLIE. Eggs.

WINNIE (*arresting gesture*). What?

(*Pause.*)

WILLIE. Eggs. (*Pause. Gesture to lay down glasses.*) Formication.

WINNIE (*arresting gesture*). What?

(*Pause.*)

WILLIE. Formication.

(*Pause. She lays down spectacles, gazes before her. Finally.*)

WINNIE (*murmur*). God. (*Pause. Willie laughs quietly. After a moment she joins in. They laugh quietly together. Willie stops. She laughs on a moment alone. Willie joins in. They laugh together. She stops. Willie laughs on a moment alone. He stops. Pause. Normal voice.*) Ah well what a joy in any case to hear you laugh again, Willie, I was convinced I never would, you never would. (*Pause.*) I suppose some people might think us a trifle irreverent, but I doubt it. (*Pause.*) How can one better magnify the Almighty than by sniggering with him at his little jokes, particularly the poorer ones? (*Pause.*) I think you would back me up there, Willie. (*Pause.*) Or were we perhaps diverted by two quite different things? (*Pause.*) Oh well, what does it matter, that is what I always say, so long as one . . . you know . . . what is that wonderful line . . . laughing wild . . . something something laughing wild amid severest woe. (*Pause.*) And now? (*Long pause.*) Was I lovable once, Willie? (*Pause.*) Was I ever lovable? (*Pause.*) Do not misunderstand my question, I am not asking you if you loved me, we know all about that, I am asking you if you found me lovable—at one stage. (*Pause.*) No? (*Pause.*) You can't? (*Pause.*) Well I admit it is a teaser. And you have done more than your bit already, for the time being, just lie back now and relax, I shall not trouble you again unless I am compelled to, just to know you are there within hearing and conceivably on the semi-alert is . . . er . . . paradise enow. (*Pause.*) The day is now well advanced. (*Smile.*) To speak in the old style. (*Smile off.*) And yet it is perhaps a little soon for my song. (*Pause.*) To sing too soon is a great mistake, I find. (*Turning towards bag*) There is of course the bag. (*Looking at bag*) The bag. (*Back front.*) Could I enumerate its contents? (*Pause.*) No. (*Pause.*) Could I, if some kind person were to come along and ask, What all have you got in that big black bag, Winnie? give an exhaustive answer? (*Pause.*) No. (*Pause.*) The depths in particular, who knows what treasures. (*Pause.*) What comforts. (*Turns to look at bag.*) Yes, there is the bag. (*Back front.*) But something tells me, Do not overdo the bag, Winnie, make use of it of course, let it help you . . . along, when stuck, by all means, but cast your mind forward, something tells me, cast your mind forward, Winnie, to the time when words must fail—(*she closes eyes, pause, opens eyes*)—and do not overdo the bag. (*Pause. She turns to look at bag.*) Perhaps just one quick dip. (*She turns back front, closes eyes, throws out left arm, plunges hand in bag and brings out revolver. Disgusted.*) You again! (*She opens eyes, brings revolver front and contemplates it. She weighs it in her palm.*) You'd think the weight of this thing would bring it down among the . . . last rounds. But no. It doesn't. Ever uppermost, like Browning. (*Pause.*) Brownie . . . (*Turning a little towards Willie*) Remember Brownie, Willie? (*Pause.*) Remember how you used to keep on at me to take it away from you? Take it away, Winnie, take it away, before I put myself out of my misery. (*Back front. Derisive*) *Your* misery! (*To revolver*) Oh I suppose it's a comfort to know you're there, but I'm tired of you. (*Pause.*) I'll leave you out, that's what I'll do. (*She lays revolver on ground to her right.*) There, that's your home from this day out. (*Smile.*) The old style! (*Smile off.*) And now? (*Long pause.*) Is gravity what it was, Willie, I fancy not. (*Pause.*) Yes, the feeling more and more that if I were not held—(*gesture*)—in this way, I would simply float up into the blue. (*Pause.*) And that perhaps some day the earth will yield and let me go, the pull is so great, yes, crack all round me and let me out. (*Pause.*) Don't you ever have that feeling, Willie, of being sucked up? (*Pause.*) Don't you have to cling on sometimes, Willie? (*Pause. She turns a little towards him.*) Willie.

(*Pause.*)

WILLIE. *Sucked* up?

WINNIE. Yes, love, up into the blue, like gossamer. (*Pause.*) No? (*Pause.*) You don't? (*Pause.*) Ah well, natural laws, natural laws, I suppose it's like everything else, it all depends on the creature you happen to be. All I can say is for my part is that for me they are not what they were when I was young and . . . foolish and . . . (*faltering, head down*) . . . beautiful . . . possibly . . . lovely . . . in a way . . . to look at. (*Pause. Head up.*) Forgive me, Willie, sorrow keeps breaking in. (*Normal voice*) Ah well what a joy in any case to know you are there, as usual, and perhaps awake, and perhaps taking all this in, some of all this, what a happy day for me . . . it will have been. (*Pause.*) So far. (*Pause.*) What a blessing nothing grows, imagine if all this stuff were to start growing. (*Pause.*) Imagine. (*Pause.*) Ah yes, great mercies. (*Long pause.*) I can say no more. (*Pause.*) For the moment. (*Pause. Turns to look at bag. Back front. Smile.*) No no. (*Smile off. Looks at parasol.*) I suppose I might—(*takes up parasol*)—yes, I suppose I might . . . hoist this thing now. (*Begins to unfurl it. Following punctuated by mechanical difficulties overcome.*) One keeps putting off—putting up—for fear of putting up—too soon—and the day goes by—quite by—without one's having put up—at all. (*Parasol now fully open. Turned to her right she twirls it idly this way and that.*) Ah yes, so little to say, so little to do, and the fear so great, certain days, of finding oneself . . . left, with hours still to run, before the bell for sleep, and nothing more to say, nothing more to do, that the days go by, certain days go by, quite by, the bell goes, and little or nothing said, little or nothing done. (*Raising parasol*) That is the danger. (*Turning front*) To be guarded against. (*She gazes front, holding up parasol with right hand. Maximum pause.*) I used to perspire freely. (*Pause.*) Now hardly at all. (*Pause.*) The heat is much greater. (*Pause.*) The perspiration much less. (*Pause.*) That is what I find so wonderful. (*Pause.*) The way man adapts himself. (*Pause.*) To changing conditions. (*She transfers parasol to left hand. Long pause.*) Holding up wearies the arm. (*Pause.*) Not if one is going along. (*Pause.*) Only if one is at rest. (*Pause.*) That is a curious observation. (*Pause.*) I hope you heard that, Willie, I should be grieved to think you had not heard that. (*She takes parasol in both hands. Long pause.*) I am weary, holding it up, and I cannot put it down. (*Pause.*) I am worse off with it up than with it down, and I cannot put it down. (*Pause.*) Reason says, Put it down, Winnie, it is not helping you, put the thing down and get on with something else. (*Pause.*) I cannot. (*Pause.*) I cannot move. (*Pause.*) No, something must happen, in the world, take place, some change, I cannot, if I am to move again. (*Pause.*) Willie. (*Mildly*) Help. (*Pause.*) No? (*Pause.*) Bid me put this thing down, Willie, I would obey you instantly, as I have always done, honoured and obeyed. (*Pause.*) Please, Willie. (*Mildly*) For pity's sake. (*Pause.*) No? (*Pause.*) You can't? (*Pause.*) Well I don't blame you, no, it would ill become me, who cannot move, to blame my Willie because he cannot speak. (*Pause.*) Fortunately I am in tongue again. (*Pause.*) That is what I find so wonderful, my two lamps, when one goes out the other burns brighter. (*Pause.*) Oh yes, great mercies. (*Maximum pause. The parasol goes on fire. Smoke, flames if feasible. She sniffs, looks up, throws parasol to her right behind mound, cranes back to watch it burning. Pause.*) Ah earth you old extinguisher. (*Back front.*) I presume this has occurred before, though I cannot recall it. (*Pause.*) Can you, Willie? (*Turns a little towards him.*) Can you recall this having occurred before? (*Pause. Cranes back to look at him.*) Do you know what has occurred, Willie? (*Pause.*) Have you gone off on me again? (*Pause.*) I do not ask if you are alive to all that is going on, I merely ask if you have not gone off on me again. (*Pause.*) Your eyes appear to be closed, but that has no particular significance we know. (*Pause.*) Raise a finger, dear, will you please, if you are not quite senseless. (*Pause.*) Do that for me, Willie please, just the little finger, if you are still conscious. (*Pause. Joyful*) Oh all five, you are a darling today, now I may continue with an easy mind. (*Back front.*) Yes, what ever occurred that did not occur before and yet . . . I wonder, yes, I confess I wonder. (*Pause.*). With the sun blazing so much fiercer down, and hourly fiercer, is it not natural things should go on fire never known to do so, in this way I mean, spontaneous like. (*Pause.*) Shall I myself not melt perhaps in the end, or burn, oh I do not mean necessarily burst into flames, no, just little by little be charred to a black cinder, all this—(*ample gesture of arms*)—visible flesh. (*Pause.*) On the other hand, did I ever know a temperate time? (*Pause.*) No. (*Pause.*) I speak of temperate times and torrid times, they are empty words. (*Pause.*) I speak of when I was not yet caught—in this way—and had my legs and had the use of my legs, and could seek out a shady place, like you, when I was tired of the sun, or a sunny place when I was tired of the shade, like you, and they are all empty words. (*Pause.*) It is no hotter today than yesterday, it will be no hotter tomorrow than today, how could it, and so on back into the far past, forward into the far future. (*Pause.*) And should one day the earth cover my breasts, then I shall never have seen my breasts, no one ever seen my breasts. (*Pause.*) I hope you caught something of that, Willie, I should be sorry to think you had caught nothing of all that, it is not every day I rise to such heights. (*Pause.*) Yes, something seems to have occurred, something has seemed to occur, and nothing has occurred, nothing at all, you are quite right, Willie. (*Pause.*) The sunshade will be there again tomorrow, beside me on this mound, to help me through the day. (*Pause. She takes up mirror.*) I take up this little glass, I shiver it on a stone—(*does so*)—I throw it away—(*does so far behind her*)—it will be in the bag again tomorrow, without a scratch, to help me through the day. (*Pause.*) No, one can do nothing. (*Pause.*) That is what I find so wonderful, the way things . . . (*voice breaks, head down*) . . . things . . . so wonderful. (*Long pause, head down. Finally turns, still bowed, to bag, brings out unidentifiable odds and ends, stuffs them back, fumbles deeper, brings out finally musical-box, winds it up, turns it on, listens for a moment holding it in both hands, huddled over it, turns back front, straightens up and listens to tune, holding box to breast with both hands. It plays the Waltz Duet "I Love You So" from* The Merry Widow. *Gradually happy expression. She sways to the rhythm. Music stops. Pause. Brief burst of hoarse song without words—musical-box tune—from Willie. Increase of happy expression. She lays down box.*) Oh this will have been a happy day! (*She claps hands.*) Again, Willie, again! (*Claps.*) Encore, Willie, please! (*Pause. Happy expression off.*) No? You won't do that for me? (*Pause.*) Well it is very understandable, very understandable. One cannot sing just to please someone, however much one loves them, no, song must come from the heart, that is what I always say, pour out from the inmost, like a thrush. (*Pause.*) How often I have said, in evil hours, Sing now, Winnie, sing your song, there is nothing else for it, and did not. (*Pause.*) Could not. (*Pause.*) No, like the thrush, or the bird of dawning, with no thought of benefit, to oneself or anyone else. (*Pause.*) And now? (*Long pause. Low*) Strange feeling. (*Pause. Do.*) Strange feeling that someone is looking at me. I am clear, then dim, then gone, then dim again, then clear again, and so on, back and forth, in and out of someone's eye. (*Pause. Do.*) Strange? (*Pause. Do.*) No, here all is strange. (*Pause. Normal voice*) Something says, Stop talking now, Winnie, for a minute, don't squander all your words for the day, stop talking and do something for a change, will you? (*She raises hands and holds them open before her eyes. Apostrophic*) Do something! (*She closes hands.*) What claws! (*She turns to bag, rummages in it, brings out finally a nailfile, turns back front and begins to file nails. Files for a time in silence, then the following punctuated by filing.*) There floats up—into my thoughts—a Mr. Shower—a Mr. and perhaps a Mrs. Shower—no—they are holding hands—his fiancée then more likely—or just some—loved one. (*Looks closer at nails.*) Very brittle today. (*Resumes filing.*) Shower—Shower—does the name mean anything—to you, Willie—evoke any reality, I mean—for you, Willie—don't answer if you don't—feel up to it—you have done more—than your bit—already—Shower—Shower. (*Inspects filed nails.*) Bit more like it. (*Raises head, gazes front.*) Keep yourself nice, Winnie, that's what I always say, come what may, keep yourself nice. (*Pause. Resumes filing.*) Yes—Shower—Shower—(*stops filing, raises head, gazes front, pause*)—or Cooker, perhaps I should say Cooker. (*Turning a little towards Willie.*) Cooker, Willie, does Cooker strike a chord? (*Pause. Turns a little further. Louder*) Cooker, Willie, does Cooker ring a bell, the name Cooker? (*Pause. She cranes back to look at him. Pause.*) Oh really! (*Pause.*) Have you no handkerchief, darling? (*Pause.*) Have you no delicacy? (*Pause.*) Oh, Willie, you're not eating it! Spit it out, dear, spit it out! (*Pause. Back front.*) Ah well, I suppose it's only natural. (*Break in voice.*) Human. (*Pause. Do.*) What *is* one to do? (*Head down. Do.*) All day long. (*Pause. Do.*) Day after day. (*Pause. Head up. Smile. Calm*) The old style! (*Smile off. Resumes nails.*) No, done him. (*Passes on to next.*) Should have put on my glasses. (*Pause.*) Too late now. (*Finishes left hand, inspects it.*) Bit more human. (*Starts right hand. Following punctuated as before.*) Well anyway—this man Shower—or Cooker—no matter—and the woman—hand in hand—in the other hands bags—kind of big brown grips—standing there gaping at me—and at last this man Shower—or Cooker—ends in er anyway—stake my life on that—What's she doing? he says—What's the idea? he says—stuck up to her diddies in the bleeding ground—coarse fellow—What does it mean? he says—What's it meant to mean?—and so on—lot more stuff like that—usual drivel—Do you hear me? he says—I do, she says, God help me—What do you mean, he says, God help you? (*Stops filing, raises head, gazes front.*) And you, she says, what's the idea of you, she says, what are you meant to mean? It is because you're still on your two flat feet, with your old ditty full of tinned muck and changes of underwear, dragging me up and down this fornicating wilderness, coarse creature, fit mate—(*with sudden violence*)—let go of my hand and drop for God's sake, she says, drop! (*Pause. Resumes filing.*) Why doesn't he dig her out? he says—referring to you, my dear—What good is she to him like that?—What good is he to her like that?—and so on—usual tosh—Good! she says, have a heart for God's sake—Dig her out, he says, dig her out, no sense in her like that—Dig her out with what? she says—I'd dig her out with my bare hands, he says—must have been man and—wife. (*Files in silence.*) Next thing they're away—hand in hand—and the bags—dim—then gone—last human kind—to stray this way. (*Finishes right hand, inspects it, lays down file, gazes front.*) Strange thing, time like this, drift up into the mind. (*Pause.*) Strange? (*Pause.*) No, here all is strange. (*Pause.*) Thankful for it in any case. (*Voice breaks.*) Most thankful. (*Head down. Pause. Head up. Calm*) Bow and raise the head, bow and raise, always that. (*Pause.*) And now? (*Long pause. Starts putting things back in bag, toothbrush last. This operation, interrupted by pauses as indicated, punctuates following.*) It is perhaps a little soon—to make ready—for the night—(*stops tidying, head up, smile*)—the old style!—(*smile off, resumes tidying*)—and yet I do—make ready for the night—

feeling it at hand—the bell for sleep—saying to myself—Winnie—it will not be long now, Winnie—until the bell for sleep. (*Stops tidying, head up.*) Sometimes I am wrong. (*Smile.*) But not often. (*Smile off.*) Sometimes all is over, for the day, all done, all said, all ready for the night, and the day not over, far from over, the night not ready, far, far from ready. (*Smile.*) But not often. (*Smile off.*) Yes, the bell for sleep, when I feel it at hand, and so make ready for the night—(*gesture*)—in this way, sometimes I am wrong (*smile*)—but not often. (*Smile off. Resumes tidying.*) I used to think—I say I used to think—that all these things—put back into the bag—if too soon—put back too soon—could be taken out again—if necessary—if needed—and so on—indefinitely—back into the bag—back out of the bag—until the bell—went. (*Stops tidying, head up, smile.*) But no. (*Smile broader.*) No no. (*Smile off. Resumes tidying.*) I suppose this—might seem strange—this—what shall I say—this what I have said—yes—(*she takes up revolver*)—strange—(*she turns to put revolver in bag*)—were it not—(*about to put revolver in bag she arrests gesture and turns back front*)—were it not—(*she lays down revolver to her right, stops tidying, head up*)—that all seems strange. (*Pause.*) Most strange. (*Pause.*) Never any change. (*Pause.*) And more and more strange. (*Pause. She bends to mound again, takes up last object, i.e., toothbrush, and turns to put it in bag when her attention is drawn to disturbance from Willie. She cranes back and to her right to see. Pause.*) Weary of your hole, dear? (*Pause.*) Well I can understand that. (*Pause.*) Don't forget your straw. (*Pause.*) Not the crawler you were, poor darling. (*Pause.*) No, not the crawler I gave my heart to. (*Pause.*) The hands and knees, love, try the hands and knees. (*Pause.*) The knees! The knees! (*Pause.*) What a curse, mobility! (*She follows with eyes his progress towards her behind mound, i.e., towards place he occupied at beginning of act.*) Another foot, Willie, and you're home. (*Pause as she observes last foot.*) Ah! (*Turns back front laboriously, rubs neck.*) Crick in my neck admiring you. (*Rubs neck.*) But it's worth it, well worth it. (*Turning slightly towards him*) Do you know what I dream sometimes? (*Pause.*) What I dream sometimes, Willie. (*Pause.*) That you'll come round and live this side where I could see you. (*Pause. Back front.*) I'd be a different woman. (*Pause.*) Unrecognizable. (*Turning slightly towards him*) Or just now and then, come round this side just every now and then and let me feast on you. (*Back front.*) But you can't, I know. (*Head down.*) I know. (*Pause. Head up.*) Well anyway—(*looks at toothbrush in her hand*)—can't be long now—(*looks at brush*)—until the bell. (*Top back of Willie's head appears above slope. Winnie looks closer at brush.*) Fully guaranteed . . . (*head up*) . . . what's this it was? (*Willie's hand appears with handkerchief, spreads it on skull, disappears.*) Genuine pure . . . fully guaranteed . . . (*Willie's hand appears with boater, settles it on head, rakish angle, disappears*) . . . genuine pure . . . ah! hog's setae. (*Pause.*) What is a hog exactly? (*Pause. Turns slightly towards Willie*) What exactly is a hog, Willie, do you know, I can't remember. (*Pause. Turning a little further, pleading*) What *is* a hog, Willie, please!

(*Pause.*)

WILLIE. Castrated male swine. (*Happy expression appears on Winnie's face.*) Reared for slaughter.

(*Happy expression increases. Willie opens newspaper, hands invisible. Tops of yellow sheets appear on either side of his head. Winnie gazes before her with happy expression.*)

WINNIE. Oh this *is* a happy day! (*Pause.*) After all. (*Pause.*) So far.

(*Pause. Happy expression off. Willie turns page. Pause. He turns another page. Pause.*)

WILLIE. Opening for smart youth.

(*Pause. Winnie takes off hat, turns to put it in bag, arrests gesture, turns back front. Smile.*)

WINNIE. No. (*Smile broader.*) No no. (*Smile off. Puts on hat again, gazes front, pause.*) And now? (*Pause.*) Sing. (*Pause.*) Sing your song, Winnie. (*Pause.*) No? (*Pause.*) Then pray. (*Pause.*) Pray your prayer, Winnie.

(*Pause. Willie turns page. Pause.*)

WILLIE. Wanted bright boy.

(*Pause. Winnie gazes before her. Willie turns page. Pause. Newspaper disappears. Long pause.*)

WINNIE. Pray your old prayer, Winnie.

(*Long pause.*)

CURTAIN

ACT 2

Scene as before.

Winnie imbedded up to neck, hat on head, eyes closed. Her head, which she can no longer turn, nor bow, nor raise, faces front motionless throughout act. Movements of eyes as indicated.

Bag and parasol as before. Revolver conspicuous to her right on mound.

Long pause.

Bell rings loudly. She opens eyes at once. Bell stops. She gazes front. Long pause.

WINNIE. Hail, holy light. (*Long pause. She closes her eyes. Bell rings loudly. She opens eyes at once. Bell stops. She gazes front. Long smile. Smile off. Long pause.*) Someone is looking at me still. (*Pause.*) Caring for me still. (*Pause.*) That is what I find so wonderful. (*Pause.*) Eyes on my eyes. (*Pause.*) What is that unforgettable line? (*Pause. Eyes right.*) Willie. (*Pause. Louder*) Willie. (*Pause. Eyes front.*) May one still speak of time? (*Pause.*) Say it is a long time now, Willie, since I saw you. (*Pause.*) Since I heard you. (*Pause.*) May one? (*Pause.*) One does. (*Smile.*) The old style! (*Smile off.*) There is so little one can speak of. (*Pause.*) One speaks of it all. (*Pause.*) All one can. (*Pause.*) I used to think . . . (*pause*) . . . I say I used to think that I would learn to talk alone. (*Pause.*) By that I mean to myself, the wilderness. (*Smile.*) But no. (*Smile broader.*) No no. (*Smile off.*) Ergo you are there. (*Pause.*) Oh no doubt you are dead, like the others, no doubt you have died, or gone away and left me, like the others, it doesn't matter, you are there. (*Pause. Eyes left.*) The bag too is there, the same as ever, I can see it. (*Pause. Eyes right. Louder*) The bag is there, Willie, as good as ever, the one you gave me that day . . . to go to market. (*Pause. Eyes front.*) That day. (*Pause.*) What day? (*Pause.*) I used to pray. (*Pause.*) I say used to pray. (*Pause.*) Yes, I must confess I did. (*Smile.*) Not now. (*Smile broader.*) No no. (*Smile off. Pause.*) Then . . . now . . . what difficulties here, for the mind. (*Pause.*) To have been always what I am—and so changed from what I was. (*Pause.*) I am the one, I say the one, then the other. (*Pause.*) Now the one, then the other (*Pause.*) There is so little one can say, one says it all. (*Pause.*) All one can. (*Pause.*) And no truth in it anywhere. (*Pause.*) My arms. (*Pause.*) My breasts. (*Pause.*) What arms? (*Pause.*) What breasts? (*Pause.*) Willie. (*Pause.*) What Willie? (*Sudden vehement affirmation*) My Willie! (*Eyes right, calling*) Willie! (*Pause. Louder*) Willie! (*Pause. Eyes front.*) Ah well, not to know, not to know for sure, great mercy, all I ask. (*Pause.*) Ah yes . . . then . . . now . . . beechen green . . . this . . . Charlie . . . kisses . . . this . . . all that . . . deep trouble for the mind. (*Pause.*) But it does not trouble mine. (*Smile.*) Not now. (*Smile broader.*) No no. (*Smile off. Long pause. She closes eyes. Bell rings loudly. She opens eyes. Pause.*) Eyes float up that seem to close in peace . . . to see . . . in peace. (*Pause.*) Not mine. (*Smile.*) Not now. (*Smile broader.*) No no. (*Smile off. Long pause.*) Willie. (*Pause.*) Do you think the earth has lost its atmosphere, Willie? (*Pause.*) Do you, Willie? (*Pause.*) You have no opinion? (*Pause.*) Well that is like you, you never had any opinion about anything. (*Pause.*) It's understandable. (*Pause.*) Most. (*Pause.*) The earthball. (*Pause.*) I sometimes wonder. (*Pause.*) Perhaps not quite all. (*Pause.*) There always remains something. (*Pause.*) Of everything. (*Pause.*) Some remains. (*Pause.*) If the mind were to go. (*Pause.*) It won't of course. (*Pause.*) Not quite. (*Pause.*) Not mine. (*Smile.*) Not now. (*Smile broader.*) No no. (*Smile off. Long pause.*) It might be the eternal cold. (*Pause.*) Everlasting perishing cold. (*Pause.*) Just chance, I take it, happy chance. (*Pause.*) Oh yes, great mercies, great mercies. (*Pause.*) And now? (*Long pause.*) The face. (*Pause.*) The nose. (*She squints down.*) I can see it . . . (*squinting down*) . . . the tip . . . the nostrils . . . breath of life . . . that curve you so admired . . . (*pouts*) . . . a hint of lip . . . (*pouts again*) . . . if I pout them out . . . (*sticks out tongue*) . . . the tongue of course . . . you so admired . . . if I stick it out . . . (*sticks it out again*) . . . the tip . . . (*eyes up*) . . . suspicion of brow . . . eyebrow . . . imagination possibly . . . (*eyes left*) . . . cheek . . . no . . . (*eyes right*) . . . no . . . (*distends cheeks*) . . . even if I puff them out . . . (*eyes left, distends cheeks again*) . . . no . . . no damask. (*Eyes front.*) That is all. (*Pause.*) The bag of course . . . (*eyes left*) . . . a little blurred perhaps . . . but the bag. (*Eyes front. Offhand*) The earth of course and sky. (*Eyes right.*) The sunshade you gave me . . . that day . . . (*pause*) . . . that day . . . the lake . . . the reeds. (*Eyes front. Pause.*) What day? (*Pause.*) What reeds? (*Long pause. Eyes close. Bell rings loudly. Eyes open. Pause. Eyes right.*) Brownie of course. (*Pause.*) You remember Brownie, Willie, I can see him. (*Pause.*) Brownie is there, Willie, beside me. (*Pause. Loud*) Brownie is there, Willie. (*Pause. Eyes front.*) That is all. (*Pause.*) What would I do without them? (*Pause.*) What would I do without them, when words fail? (*Pause.*) Gaze before me, with compressed lips. (*Long pause while she does so.*) I cannot. (*Pause.*) Ah yes, great mercies, great mercies. (*Long pause. Low*) Sometimes I hear sounds. (*Listening expression. Normal voice*) But not often. (*Pause.*) They are a boon, sounds are a boon, they help me . . . through the day. (*Smile.*) The old style! (*Smile off.*) Yes, those are happy days, when there are sounds. (*Pause.*) When I hear sounds. (*Pause.*) I used to think . . . (*pause*) . . . I say I used to think they were in my head. (*Smile.*) But no. (*Smile broader.*) No no. (*Smile off.*) That was just logic. (*Pause.*) Reason. (*Pause.*) I have not lost my reason. (*Pause.*) Not yet. (*Pause.*) Not all. (*Pause.*) Some remains. (*Pause.*) Sounds. (*Pause.*) Like little . . . sunderings, little falls . . . apart. (*Pause. Low*) It's things, Willie. (*Pause. Normal voice*) In the bag, outside the bag. (*Pause.*) Ah yes, things have their life, that is what I always say, *things* have a life. (*Pause.*) Take my looking-glass, it doesn't need me. (*Pause.*) The bell. (*Pause.*) It hurts like a knife. (*Pause.*) A gouge. (*Pause.*) One cannot ignore it. (*Pause.*) How often . . . (*pause*) . . . I say how often I have said, Ignore it, Winnie, ignore the bell, pay no heed, just sleep and wake, sleep and wake, as you please, open and close the eyes, as you please, or in the way you find most helpful. (*Pause.*) Open and close the eyes, Winnie, open and close, always that. (*Pause.*) But no. (*Smile.*) Not now. (*Smile broader.*) No no. (*Smile off. Pause.*) What now? (*Pause.*) What now, Willie? (*Long pause.*) There is my story of course, when all else fails. (*Pause.*) A life. (*Smile.*) A long life. (*Smile off.*) Beginning in the womb, where life used to begin, Mildred has memories, she will have memories, of the womb, before she dies, the mother's womb. (*Pause.*) She is now four or five already and has recently been given a big waxen dolly. (*Pause.*) Fully clothed, complete outfit. (*Pause.*) Shoes, socks, undies, complete set, frilly frock, gloves. (*Pause.*) White mesh. (*Pause.*) A little white straw hat with a chin elastic. (*Pause.*) Pearly necklet. (*Pause.*) A little picture-book with legends in real print to go under her arm when she takes her walk. (*Pause.*) China blue eyes that open and shut. (*Pause. Narrative*) The sun was not well up when Milly rose, descended the steep . . . (*pause*) . . . slipped on her nightgown, descended all alone the steep wooden stairs, backwards on all fours, though she had been forbidden to do so, entered the . . . (*pause*) . . . tiptoed down the silent passage, entered the nursery and began to undress Dolly. (*Pause.*) Crept under the table and began to undress Dolly. (*Pause.*) Scolding her . . . the while. (*Pause.*) Suddenly a mouse—(*Long pause.*) Gently, Winnie. (*Long pause. Calling*) Willie! (*Pause. Louder*) Willie! (*Pause. Mild reproach*) I sometimes find your attitude a little strange, Willie, all this time, it is not like you to be wantonly cruel. (*Pause.*) Strange? (*Pause.*) No. (*Smile.*) Not here. (*Smile broader.*) Not now. (*Smile off.*) And yet . . . (*Suddenly anxious*) I do hope nothing is amiss. (*Eyes right, loud*) Is all well, dear? (*Pause. Eyes front. To herself*) God grant he did not go in head foremost! (*Eyes right, loud*) You're not stuck, Willie? (*Pause. Do.*) You're not jammed, Willie? (*Eyes front, distressed*) Perhaps he is crying out for help all this time and I do not hear him! (*Pause.*) I do of course hear cries. (*Pause.*) But they are in my head surely. (*Pause.*) Is it possible that . . . (*Pause. With finality*) No no, my head was always full of cries. (*Pause.*) Faint confused cries. (*Pause.*) They come. (*Pause.*) Then go. (*Pause.*) As on a wind. (*Pause.*) That is what I find so wonderful. (*Pause.*) They cease. (*Pause.*) Ah yes, great mercies, great mercies. (*Pause.*) The day is now well advanced. (*Smile. Smile off.*) And yet it is perhaps a little soon for my song. (*Pause.*) To sing too soon is fatal, I always find. (*Pause.*) On the other hand it is possible to leave it too late. (*Pause.*) The bell goes for sleep and one has not sung. (*Pause.*) The whole day has flown—(*smile, smile off*)—flown by, quite by, and no song of any class, kind or description. (*Pause.*) There is a problem here. (*Pause.*) One cannot sing . . . just like that, no. (*Pause.*) It bubbles up, for some unknown reason, the time is ill chosen, one chokes it back. (*Pause.*) One says, Now is the time, it is now or never, and one cannot. (*Pause.*) Simply cannot sing. (*Pause.*) Not a note. (*Pause.*) Another thing, Willie, while we are on this subject. (*Pause.*) The sadness after song. (*Pause.*) Have you run across that, Willie? (*Pause.*) In the course of your experience. (*Pause.*) No? (*Pause.*) Sadness after intimate sexual intercourse one is familiar with of course. (*Pause.*) You would concur with Aristotle there, Willie, I fancy. (*Pause.*) Yes, that one knows and is prepared to face. (*Pause.*) But after song . . . (*Pause.*) It does not last of course. (*Pause.*) That is what I find so wonderful. (*Pause.*) It wears away. (*Pause.*) What are those exquisite lines? (*Pause.*) Go forget me why should something o'er that something shadow fling . . . go forget me . . . why should sorrow . . . brightly smile . . . go forget me . . . never hear me . . . sweetly smile . . . brightly sing . . . (*Pause. With a sigh*) One loses one's classics. (*Pause.*) Oh not all. (*Pause.*) A part. (*Pause.*) A part remains. (*Pause.*) That is what I find so wonderful, a part remains, of one's classics, to help one through the day. (*Pause.*) Oh yes, many mercies, many mercies. (*Pause.*) And now? (*Pause.*) And now, Willie? (*Long pause.*) I call to the eye of the mind . . . Mr. Shower—or Cooker. (*She closes her eyes. Bell rings loudly. She opens her eyes. Pause.*) Hand in hand, in the other hands bags. (*Pause.*) Getting on . . . in life. (*Pause.*) No longer young, not yet old. (*Pause.*) Standing there gaping at me. (*Pause.*) Can't have been a bad bosom, he says, in its day. (*Pause.*) Seen worse shoulders, he says, in my time. (*Pause.*) Does she feel her legs? he says. (*Pause.*) Is there any life in her legs? he says. (*Pause.*) Has she anything on underneath? he says. (*Pause.*) Ask her, he says, I'm shy. (*Pause.*) Ask her what? she says. (*Pause.*) Is there any life in her legs. (*Pause.*) Has she anything on underneath. (*Pause.*) Ask her yourself, she says. (*Pause. With sudden violence*) Let go of me for Christ sake and drop! (*Pause. Do.*) Drop dead! (*Smile.*) But no. (*Smile broader.*) No no. (*Smile off.*) I watch them recede. (*Pause.*) Hand in hand—and the bags. (*Pause.*) Dim. (*Pause.*) Then gone. (*Pause.*) Last human kind—to stray this way. (*Pause.*) Up to date. (*Pause.*) And now? (*Pause. Low*) Help. (*Pause. Do.*) Help, Willie. (*Pause. Do.*) No? (*Long pause. Narrative*) Suddenly a mouse . . . (*Pause.*) Suddenly a mouse ran up her little thigh and Mildred, dropping Dolly in her fright, began to scream—(*Winnie gives a sudden piercing scream*)—and screamed and screamed—(*Winnie screams twice*)—screamed and screamed and screamed and screamed till all came running, in their night attire, papa, mamma, Bibby and . . . old Annie, to see what was the matter . . . (*pause*) . . . what on earth could possibly be the matter. (*Pause.*) Too late. (*Pause.*) Too late. (*Long pause. Just audible*) Willie. (*Pause. Normal voice*) Ah well, not long now, Winnie, can't be long now, until the bell for sleep. (*Pause.*) Then you may close your eyes, then you *must* close your eyes—and keep them closed. (*Pause.*) Why say that again? (*Pause.*) I used to think . . . (*pause*) . . . I say I used to think there was no difference between one fraction of a second and the next. (*Pause.*) I used to say . . . (*pause*) . . . I say I used to say, Winnie, you are changeless, there is never any difference between one fraction of a second and the next. (*Pause.*) Why bring that up again? (*Pause.*) There is so little one can bring up, one brings up all. (*Pause.*) All one can. (*Pause.*) My neck is hurting me. (*Pause. With sudden violence*) My neck is hurting me! (*Pause.*) Ah that's better. (*With mild irritation*) Everything within reason. (*Long pause.*) I can do no more. (*Pause.*) Say no more. (*Pause.*) But I must say more. (*Pause.*) Problem here. (*Pause.*) No, something must move, in the world, I can't any more. (*Pause.*) A zephyr. (*Pause.*) A breath. (*Pause.*) What are those immortal lines? (*Pause.*) It might be the eternal dark. (*Pause.*) Black night without end. (*Pause.*) Just chance, I take it, happy chance. (*Pause.*) Oh yes, abounding mercies. (*Long pause.*) And now? (*Pause.*) And now, Willie? (*Long pause.*) That day. (*Pause.*) The pink fizz. (*Pause.*) The flute glasses. (*Pause.*) The last guest gone. (*Pause.*) The last bumper with the bodies nearly touching. (*Pause.*) The look. (*Long pause.*) What day? (*Long pause.*) What look? (*Long pause.*) I hear cries. (*Pause.*) Sing. (*Pause.*) Sing your old song, Winnie.

(*Long pause. Suddenly alert expression. Eyes switch right. Willie's head appears to her right round corner of mound. He is on all fours, dressed to kill—top hat, morning coat, striped trousers, etc., white gloves in hand. Very long bushy white Battle of Britain moustache. He halts, gazes front, smoothes moustache. He emerges completely from behind mound, turns to his left, halts, looks up at Winnie. He advances on all fours towards centre, halts, turns head front, gazes front, strokes moustache, straightens tie, adjusts hat, advances a little further, halts, takes off hat and looks up at Winnie. He is now not far from centre and within her field of vision. Unable to sustain effort of looking up he sinks head to ground.*)

WINNIE (*mondaine*). Well this is an unexpected pleasure! (*Pause.*) Reminds me of the day you came whining for my hand. (*Pause.*) I worship you, Winnie, be mine. (*He looks up.*) Life a mockery without Win. (*She goes off into a giggle.*) What a get up, you do look a sight! (*Giggles.*) Where are the flowers? (*Pause.*) That smile today. (*Willie sinks head.*) What's that on your neck, an anthrax? (*Pause.*) Want to watch that, Willie, before it gets a hold on you. (*Pause.*) Where were you all this time? (*Pause.*) What were you doing all this time? (*Pause.*) Changing? (*Pause.*) Did you not hear me screaming for you? (*Pause.*) Did you get stuck in your hole? (*Pause. He looks up.*) That's right, Willie, look at me. (*Pause.*) Feast your old eyes, Willie. (*Pause.*) Does anything remain? (*Pause.*) Any remains? (*Pause.*) No? (*Pause.*) I haven't been able to look after it, you know. (*He sinks his head.*) You are still recognizable, in a way. (*Pause.*) Are you thinking of coming to live this side now . . . for a bit maybe? (*Pause.*) No? (*Pause.*) Just a brief call? (*Pause.*) Have you gone deaf, Willie? (*Pause.*) Dumb? (*Pause.*) Oh I know you were never one to talk, I worship you Winnie be mine and then nothing from that day forth only tidbits from Reynolds' News. (*Eyes front. Pause.*) Ah well, what matter, that's what I always say, it will have been a happy day, after all, another happy day. (*Pause.*) Not long now, Winnie. (*Pause.*) I hear cries. (*Pause.*) Do you ever hear cries, Willie? (*Pause.*) No? (*Eyes back on Willie.*) Willie. (*Pause.*) Look at me again, Willie. (*Pause.*) Once more, Willie. (*He looks up. Happily*) Ah! (*Pause. Shocked*) What ails you, Willie, I never saw such an expression! (*Pause.*) Put on your hat, dear, it's the sun, don't stand on ceremony, I won't mind. (*He drops hat and gloves and starts to crawl up mound towards her. Gleeful*) Oh I say, this is terrific! (*He halts, clinging to mound with one hand, reaching up with the other.*) Come on, dear, put a bit of jizz into it, I'll cheer you on. (*Pause.*) Is it me you're after, Willie . . . or is it something else? (*Pause.*) Do you want to touch my face . . . again? (*Pause.*) Is it a kiss you're after, Willie . . . or is it something else? (*Pause.*) There was a time when I could have given you a hand. (*Pause.*) And then a time before that again when I did give you a hand. (*Pause.*) You were always in dire need of a hand, Willie. (*He slithers back to foot of mound and lies with face to ground.*) Brrum! (*Pause. He rises to hands and knees, raises his face towards her.*) Have another go, Willie, I'll cheer you on. (*Pause.*) Don't look at me like that! (*Pause. Vehement*) Don't look at me like that! (*Pause. Low*) Have you gone off your head, Willie? (*Pause. Do.*) Out of your poor old wits, Willie?

(*Pause.*)

WILLIE (*just audible*). Win.

(*Pause. Winnie's eyes front. Happy expression appears, grows.*)

WINNIE. Win! (*Pause.*) Oh this *is* a happy day, this will have been another happy day! (*Pause.*) After all. (*Pause.*) So far.

(*Pause. She hums tentatively beginning of song, then sings softly, musical-box tune.*)

Though I say not
What I may not
Let you hear,
Yet the swaying
Dance is saying,
Love me dear!
Every touch of fingers
Tells me what I know,
Says for you,
It's true, it's true,
You love me so!

(*Pause. Happy expression off. She closes her eyes. Bell rings loudly. She opens her eyes. She smiles, gazing front. She turns her eyes, smiling, to Willie, still on his hands and knees looking up at her. Smile off. They look at each other. Long pause.*)

CURTAIN

TOPICS FOR DISCUSSION AND WRITING

Setting and Properties

1. In another of Beckett's plays, *Endgame,* two characters are in garbage cans. What do you think would be gained or lost if Winnie were in a garbage can instead of in a mound?
2. Is there some dramatic significance or advantage to burying Winnie in a mound, rather than at ground level?
3. Why is Winnie's bag black, rather than, say, brightly colored or patterned?
4. What do you imagine is the audience's reaction when the parasol goes on fire? How does this reaction compare to Winnie's and Willie's reaction?

Gestures and Movements

1. In the second act, when Winnie is buried up to the chin, gestures of course are fewer than in the first act. But what gestures or movements are there in Act 2?
2. When at the end Willie crawls up the mound and Winnie exclaims, "Don't look at me like that! Have you gone out of your head, Willie?" do you think Willie is expressing renewed love, or is he thinking of shooting her with the revolver? Is it relevant that Willie is said to be "dressed to kill"?

Sound Effects

1. The bell that wakes Winnie rings "piercingly." Why not, instead, a cheery cuckoo clock, or a musical sound? Winnie several times mentions "the bell for sleep," but we never hear it, even though it might easily have sounded at the end of Act 1. *Should* we have heard it?
2. In the first act the bell rings twice, at the beginning. In the second act it rings several times, interrupting Winnie's monologues. Is there any meaning to this? Does it perhaps mean that time is moving faster—and what does *that* mean?
3. Why the waltz duet, "I Love You So" from *The Merry Widow,* rather than some other song?

Dialogue

1. How does Beckett keep Winnie's talk from being dull jabbering? By what means does the dialogue hold our attention?
2. Take the first few lines, and imagine how each is spoken:

   "Another heavenly day."
   "Fer Jesus Christ sake Amen. . . . World without end Amen."
   "Begin, Winnie. . . . Begin your day, Winnie."

Character

1. The first director of *Happy Days,* Alan Schneider, said that Beckett originally conceived of Winnie's part as a male part but changed his mind because pockets wouldn't work as well as a handbag. Does the meaning of the present play depend to any degree on the fact that one character is male, the other female?
2. One critic (A. Alvarez, in *Samuel Beckett*) says the play offers "a sour view of a cozy marriage. . . . [Beckett] finds [Winnie] and her manic defenses ludicrous at best." How profitable do you find this line of thinking?

Structure

1. It has been said of Beckett's most widely known play, *Waiting for Godot,* that in it nothing happens, twice. How appropriate is this as a summary of *Happy Days*?

Meaning

1. On page 603 Winnie tells how a man and a woman came by, and she reproduces their conversation:

   What's she doing? he says—What's the idea? he says—stuck up to her diddies in the bleeding ground—coarse fellow—What does it mean? he says—What's it meant to mean?—and so on—lot more stuff like that—usual drivel—Do you hear me? he says—I do, she says, God help me—What do you mean, he says, God help you? . . . And you, she says, what's the idea of you, she says, what are you meant to mean?

   Do you think Beckett here is telling us that the play has no meaning?
2. The director Peter Brook has said of *Happy Days,* "The optimism of the lady buried in the ground is not a virtue, it is the element that blinds her to the truth of her situation." Evaluate.

EDWARD ALBEE

The Sandbox

Edward Albee (b. 1928) in infancy was adopted by the multimillionaires who owned the chain of Albee theaters. Though surrounded by material comfort, he was an unhappy child who disliked his adoptive parents. The only member of his family with whom he seems to have had an affectionate relationship was his grandmother. His work at school and in college was poor, but he wrote a good deal even as an adolescent; when in 1960 he achieved sudden fame with *Zoo Story* (written in 1958), he had already written plays for more than a decade. Among his other plays are *The Death of Bessie Smith* (1960), *The Sandbox* (1960), *The American Dream* (1961), *Who's Afraid of Virginia Woolf* (1962), *A Delicate Balance* (1966), and *The Man Who Had Three Arms* (1983).

COMMENTARY

In our discussion of tragicomedy (p. 37–38), and in the Glossary, we talk about the movement called the theater of the absurd—the theater of such writers as Beckett, Ionesco, Pinter, and Albee—but here we can briefly list the characteristics usually found in the works of these playwrights. We do not mean, of course, that all of these qualities are found in all of their works. In fact, we urge you, after reading this list, to think about the ways in which Albee's *The Sandbox* does *not* quite fit the list. (One of life's great truths is, in Bishop Butler's words, "Every thing is what it is, and not another thing.")

In the theater of the absurd:

1. The plays are "theatrical" rather than realistic, often setting forth obviously impossible situations with obviously unreal characters.
2. The plays are serious but often (or at least intermittently) comic, especially satiric.
3. The basic themes are (a) human loneliness in a world without God, (b) the inability to communicate, (c) the dehumanization and impotence of individuals in a bourgeois society, and (d) the meaninglessness of life.
4. Characters behave illogically, speak in clichés, rarely if ever communicate with each other, and seem to have no clearly defined coherent character.
5. The plays are relatively plotless (nothing much seems to happen).

In thinking about (and in rereading) *The Sandbox*, you may find that it does indeed embody some of these characteristics, but of course it may embody other qualities, too, and some of the points listed may not be relevant. In fact, the most useful function of this list may be that it will stimulate you to think about ways in which the play departs from it.

The 1962 Cherry Lane Theater production of *The Sandbox* starred John C. Becker and Jane Hoffman. (Photograph © 1962 Alix Jeffrey/Harvard Theatre Collection.)

EDWARD ALBEE *The Sandbox*

List of Characters

THE YOUNG MAN, *25, a good-looking, well-built boy in a bathing suit*

MOMMY, *55, a well-dressed, imposing woman*

DADDY, *60, a small man; gray, thin*

GRANDMA, *86, a tiny, wizened woman with bright eyes*

THE MUSICIAN, *no particular age, but young would be nice*

Note: When, in the course of the play, Mommy and Daddy call each other by these names, there should be no suggestion of regionalism. These names are of empty affection and point up the presenility and vacuity of their characters.

The Scene: A bare stage, with only the following: Near the footlights, far stage-right, two simple chairs set side by side, facing the audience; near the footlights, far stage-left, a chair facing stage-right with a music stand before it; farther back, and stage-center, slightly elevated and raked, a large child's sandbox with a toy pail and shovel; the background is the sky, which alters from brightest day to deepest night.

At the beginning, it is brightest day; the young man is alone on stage to the rear of the sandbox, and to one side. He is doing calisthenics; he does calisthenics until quite at the very end of the play. These calisthenics, employing the arms only, should suggest the beating and fluttering of wings. The young man is, after all, the Angel of Death.

Mommy and Daddy enter from stage-left, Mommy first.

MOMMY (*motioning to Daddy*). Well, here we are; this is the beach.

DADDY (*whining*). I'm cold.

MOMMY (*dismissing him with a little laugh*). Don't be silly; it's as warm as toast. Look at that nice young man over there; *he* doesn't think it's cold. (*Waves to the Young Man*) Hello.

YOUNG MAN (*with an endearing smile*). Hi!

MOMMY (*looking about*). This will do perfectly . . . don't you think so, Daddy? There's sand there . . . and the water beyond. What do you think, Daddy?

DADDY (*vaguely*). Whatever you say, Mommy.

MOMMY (*with the same little laugh*). Well, of course . . . whatever I say. Then, it's settled, is it?

DADDY (*shrugs*). She's *your* mother, not mine.

MOMMY. *I* know she's my mother. What do you take me for? (*A pause*) All right, now; let's get on with it. (*She shouts into the wings, stage-left*) You! Out there! You can come in now.

The Musician enters, seats himself in the chair, stage-left, places music on the music stand, is ready to play. Mommy nods approvingly.

MOMMY. Very nice; very nice. Are you ready, Daddy? Let's go get Grandma.

DADDY. Whatever you say, Mommy.

MOMMY (*leading the way out, stage-left*). Of course, whatever I say. (*To the Musician*) You can begin now.

The Musician begins playing; Mommy and Daddy re-enter, carrying Grandma. She is borne in by their hands under her armpits; she is quite rigid; her legs are drawn up; her feet do not touch the ground; the expression on her ancient face is that of puzzlement and fear.

DADDY. Where do we put her?

MOMMY (*the same little laugh*). Wherever I say, of course. Let me see . . . well . . . all right, over there . . . in the sandbox. (*Pause*) Well, what are you waiting for, Daddy? . . . The sandbox!

Together they carry Grandma over to the sand box and more or less dump her in.

GRANDMA (*righting herself to a sitting position, her voice a cross between a baby's laugh and cry*). Ahhhhhh! Graaaaa!

DADDY (*dusting himself*). What do we do now?

MOMMY (*to the Musician*). You can stop now. (*The Musician stops. Back to Daddy*) What do you mean, what do we do now? We go over there and sit down, of course. (*To the Young Man*) Hello there.

YOUNG MAN (*again smiling*). Hi!

Mommy and Daddy move to the chairs, stage-right, and sit down. A pause.

GRANDMA (*same as before*). Ahhhhhh! Ah-haaa-aaa! Graaaaaa!

DADDY. Do you think . . . do you think she's . . . comfortable?

MOMMY (*impatiently*). How would I know?

DADDY (*pause*). What do we do now?

MOMMY (*as if remembering*). We . . . wait. We . . . sit here . . . and we wait . . . that's what we do.

DADDY (*after a pause*). Shall we talk to each other?

MOMMY (*with that little laugh; picking something off her dress*). Well, *you* can talk, if you want to . . . if you can think of anything to *say* . . . if you can think of anything *new*.

DADDY (*thinks*). No . . . I suppose not.
MOMMY (*with a triumphant laugh*). Of course not!
GRANDMA (*banging the toy shovel against the pail*). Haaaaaa! Ah-haaaaaa!
MOMMY (*out over the audience*). Be quiet, Grandma . . . just be quiet, and wait.

Grandma throws a shovelful of sand at Mommy.

MOMMY (*still out over the audience*). She's throwing sand at me! You stop that, Grandma; you stop throwing sand at Mommy! (*To Daddy*) She's throwing sand at me.

Daddy looks around at Grandma, who screams at him.

GRANDMA. GRAAAAA!
MOMMY. Don't look at her. Just . . . sit here . . . be very still . . . and wait. (*To the Musician*) You . . . uh . . . you go ahead and do whatever it is you do.

The Musician plays. Mommy and Daddy are fixed, staring out beyond the audience. Grandma looks at them, looks at the Musician, looks at the sandbox, throws down the shovel.

GRANDMA. Ah-haaaaaa! Graaaaaa! (*Looks for reaction; gets none. Now . . . directly to the audience*) Honestly! What a way to treat an old woman! Drag her out of the house . . . stick her in a car . . . bring her out here from the city . . . dump her in a pile of sand . . . and leave her here to set. I'm eighty-six years old! I was married when I was seventeen. To a farmer. He died when I was thirty. (*To the Musician*) Will you stop that, please? (*The Musician stops playing*) I'm a feeble old woman . . . how do you expect anybody to hear me over that peep! peep! peep! (*To herself*) There's no respect around here. (*To the Young Man*) There's no respect around here!
YOUNG MAN (*same smile*). Hi!
GRANDMA (*after a pause, a mild double-take, continues, to the audience*). My husband died when I was thirty (*indicates Mommy*), and I had to raise that big cow over there all by my lonesome. You can imagine what *that* was *like*. Lordy! (*To the Young Man*) Where'd they get *you?*
YOUNG MAN. Oh . . . I've been around for a while.
GRANDMA. I'll bet you have! Heh, heh, heh. Will you look at you!
YOUNG MAN (*flexing his muscles*). Isn't that something? (*Continues his calisthenics*)
GRANDMA. Boy, oh boy; I'll say. Pretty good.
YOUNG MAN (*sweetly*). I'll say.
GRANDMA. Where ya from?
YOUNG MAN. Southern California.
GRANDMA (*nodding*). Figgers; figgers. What's your name, honey?
YOUNG MAN. I don't know . . .
GRANDMA (*to the audience*). Bright, too!
YOUNG MAN. I mean . . . I mean, they haven't given me one yet . . . the studio . . .
GRANDMA (*giving him the once-over*). You don't say . . . you don't say. Well . . . uh, I've got to talk some more . . . don't you go 'way.
YOUNG MAN. Oh, no.
GRANDMA (*turning her attention back to the audience*). Fine; fine. (*Then, once more, back to the Young Man*) You're . . . you're an actor, hunh?
YOUNG MAN (*beaming*). Yes. I am.
GRANDMA (*to the audience again; shrugs*). I'm smart that way. *Anyhow,* I had to raise . . . *that* over there all by my lonesome; and what's next to her there . . . that's what she married. Rich? I tell you . . . money, money, money. They took me off the *farm* . . . which was real decent of them . . . and they moved me into the big townhouse with *them* . . . fixed a nice place for me under the stove . . . gave me an army blanket . . . and my own dish . . . my very own dish! So, what have I got to complain about? Nothing, of course. I'm not complaining. (*She looks up at the sky, shouts to someone off stage*) Shouldn't it be getting dark now, dear?

The lights dim; night comes on. The Musician begins to play; it becomes deepest night. There are spots on all the players, including the Young Man, who is, of course, continuing his calisthenics.

DADDY (*stirring*). It's nighttime.
MOMMY. Shhhh. Be still . . . wait.
DADDY (*whining*). It's so hot.
MOMMY. Shhhhhh. Be still . . . wait.
GRANDMA (*to herself*). That's better. Night. (*To the Musician*) Honey, do you play all through this part? (*The Musician nods.*) Well, keep it nice and soft; that's a good boy. (*The Musician nods again; plays softly.*) That's nice.

There is an off-stage rumble.

DADDY (*starting*). What was that?
MOMMY (*beginning to weep*). It was nothing.
DADDY. It was . . . it was . . . thunder . . . or a wave breaking . . . or something.
MOMMY (*whispering, through her tears*). It was an off-stage rumble . . . and you know what *that* means . . .
DADDY. I forget . . .
MOMMY (*barely able to talk*). It means the time has come for poor Grandma . . . and I can't bear it!
DADDY (*vacantly*). I . . . suppose you've got to be brave.
GRANDMA (*mocking*). That's right, kid; be brave. You'll bear up; you'll get over it.

Another off-stage rumble . . . louder.

MOMMY. Ohhhhhhhhhh . . . poor Grandma . . . poor Grandma . . .

GRANDMA (*to Mommy*). I'm fine! I'm all right! It hasn't happened yet!

A violent off-stage rumble. All the lights go out, save the spot on the Young Man; the Musician stops playing.

MOMMY. Ohhhhhhhh ... Ohhhhhhhhh ...

Silence.

GRANDMA. Don't put the lights up yet ... I'm not ready; I'm not quite ready. (*Silence*) All right, dear ... I'm about done.

The lights come up again, to brightest day; the Musician begins to play. Grandma is discovered, still in the sandbox, lying on her side, propped up on an elbow, half covered, busily shoveling sand over herself.

GRANDMA (*muttering*). I don't know how I'm supposed to do anything with this goddam toy shovel ...

DADDY. Mommy! It's daylight!

MOMMY (*brightly*). So it is! Well! Our long night is over. We must put away our tears, take off our mourning ... and face the future. It's our duty.

GRANDMA (*still shoveling; mimicking*). ... take off our mourning ... face the future ... Lordy!

Mommy and Daddy rise, stretch. Mommy waves to the Young Man.

YOUNG MAN (*with that smile*). Hi!

Grandma plays dead. (!) *Mommy and Daddy go over to look at her; she is a little more than half buried in the sand; the toy shovel is in her hands, which are crossed on her breast.*

MOMMY (*before the sandbox; shaking her head*). Lovely! It's ... it's hard to be sad ... she looks ... so happy. (*With pride and conviction*) It pays to do things well. (*To the Musician*) All right, you can stop now, if you want to. I mean, stay around for a swim, or something, it's all right with us. (*She sighs heavily.*) Well, Daddy ... off we go.

DADDY. Brave Mommy!

MOMMY. Brave Daddy!

They exit, stage-left.

GRANDMA (*after they leave; lying quite still*). It pays to do things well ... Boy, oh boy! (*She tries to sit up*) ... well, kids ... (*but she finds she can't*) ... I ... I can't get up. I ... I can't move ...

The Young Man stops his calisthenics, nods to the Musician, walks over to Grandma, kneels down by the sandbox.

GRANDMA. I ... can't move ...

YOUNG MAN. Shhhhh ... be very still ...

GRANDMA. I ... I can't move ...

YOUNG MAN. Uh ... ma'am; I ... I have a line here.

GRANDMA. Oh, I'm sorry, sweetie; you go right ahead.

YOUNG MAN. I am ... uh ...

GRANDMA. Take your time, dear.

YOUNG MAN (*prepares; delivers the line like a real amateur*). I am the Angel of Death. I am ... uh ... I am come for you.

GRANDMA. What ... wha ... (*then, with resignation*) ... ohhhh ... ohhhh, I see.

The Young Man bends over, kisses Grandma gently on the forehead.

GRANDMA (*her eyes closed, her hands folded on her breast again, the shovel between her hands, a sweet smile on her face*). Well ... that was very nice, dear ...

YOUNG MAN (*still kneeling*). Shhhhh ... be still ...

GRANDMA. What I meant was ... you did that very well, dear ...

YOUNG MAN (*blushing*). ... oh ...

GRANDMA. No; I mean it. You've got that ... you've got a quality.

YOUNG MAN (*with his endearing smile*). Oh ... thank you; thank you very much ... ma'am.

GRANDMA (*slowly; softly—as the Young Man puts his hands on top of Grandma's*). You're ... you're welcome ... dear.

Tableau. The Musician continues to play as the curtain slowly comes down.

TOPICS FOR DISCUSSION AND WRITING

1. In a sentence, characterize Mommy, and in another sentence characterize Daddy. By the way, why doesn't Albee give them names?
2. Of the four characters in the play, which do you find the most sympathetic? Exactly why? Set forth your answer, with supporting evidence, in a paragraph, or perhaps in two paragraphs—the first devoted to the three less sympathetic characters, and the second devoted to the most sympathetic character.
3. Why, in your opinion, does Albee insist in the first stage

direction that the scene be "a bare stage"? Do you think a naturalistic setting would in some way diminish the play? Explain.

4. What do you make of the sandbox? Is it an image of the grave, with suggestions that life is meaningless and sterile? Or is it an image only of the sterility of life in the United States in the second half of the twentieth century? Does the fact that Grandma was married to a farmer suggest an alternative way of life? Explain.
5. In a longer play, *The American Dream,* Albee uses the same four characters that he uses in *The Sandbox.* Of *The American Dream* he wrote:

   > The play . . . is a condemnation of complacency, cruelty, emasculation and vacuity; it is a stand against the fiction that everything in this slipping land of ours is peachy-keen.

   To what extent does this statement help you to understand (and to enjoy) *The Sandbox*?
6. In *The New York Times Magazine* (February 25, 1962), Albee protested against the view that his plays, and others of the so-called theater of the absurd, are depressing. He includes a quotation from Martin Esslin's book *The Theatre of the Absurd:*

   > Ultimately . . . the Theatre of the Absurd does not reflect despair or a return to dark irrational forces but expresses modern man's endeavor to come to terms with the world in which he lives. It attempts to make him face up to the human condition as it really is, to free him from illusions that are bound to cause constant maladjustment and disappointment. . . . For the dignity of man lies in his reality in all its senselessness; to accept it freely, without fear, without illusions—and to laugh at it.

   In what what ways do you find this statement helpful? In what ways do you find it not helpful? Explain.
7. In an interview in 1979 Albee said:

   > I like to think people are forced to rethink some things as a result of the experience of seeing some of my plays, that they are not left exactly the way they came in.

   Has reading *The Sandbox* forced you to rethink anything? If so, what?

ATHOL FUGARD

"MASTER HAROLD" ... and the boys

Athol Fugard (his full name is Athol Harold Lannigan Fugard) was born in 1932 in Cape Province, South Africa. In 1958 he organized a multiracial theater, for which he wrote plays (*A Lesson of Aloes* won the New York Drama Critics' Circle Award as the best play of 1980) and also served as a director and an actor. In addition to writing plays, he has written a novel and an autobiographical volume entitled *Notebooks 1960–1977. "MASTER HAROLD"... and the boys* was first produced in 1982 at the Yale Repertory Theatre.

COMMENTARY

The origins of a play, like those of any other work of art, are ultimately mysterious. Perhaps the best that one can say is what Lady Murasaki said almost a thousand years ago, in a long Japanese book that is often called the first novel, *The Tale of Genji:*

> Again and again something in one's own life or in that around one will seem so important that one cannot bear to let it pass into oblivion. There must never come a time, the writer feels, when people do not know about this.

"Something in one's own life or in that around one" includes the reading and playgoing that an author does. For instance, before Shakespeare wrote his *King Lear* he must have seen the old play *King Leir*—which ends happily, with Leir restored to the throne—and felt, "Well, there is much of interest here, but the way it *really* ought to go, if it is to be true to life, is . . ." Similarly, the ancient Greek writers began with traditional myths, but each writer shaped the myth in a distinctive way, presumably in accordance with his insight into experience.

Some plays arise more obviously out of the life around the writer. Take Ibsen's *A Doll's House,* for example. Ibsen's wife was a vigorous champion of women's causes, and she must have influenced his thinking. More specifically, *A Doll's House* is partly based on the experience of a woman whom Ibsen knew—someone who had forged a check to pay for a vacation that her husband's health required. But Ibsen changed a good deal. For instance, Ibsen's Nora leaves her husband, whereas the woman whom Ibsen knew was thrust out of the house (and into an insane asylum, in fact) by her husband, though ultimately the couple was more or less reconciled for the sake of their children. Rather as Shakespeare must have felt that the anonymous author of *King Leir* didn't quite get the story right, so Ibsen must have felt that real life was a bit muddled, and that the story—to be enduring—should have gone this way: . . .

With Athol Fugard's *"MASTER HAROLD"... and the boys* (1982), however, we

Ramolao Makhene as Willie, Duart Sylwain as Hally, and John Kani as Sam in a 1983 Market Theatre Company production at Cottesloe. (Photograph by Donald Cooper © PHOTOSTAGE.)

are pretty close to real life, if an entry for 1961 in Fugard's *Notebooks* can be trusted. Fugard, whose full name is Athol Harold Lannigan Fugard, and who was called Hally, was ashamed of his father, a lame man with a drinking problem. The boy found a surrogate father in Sam Semela, a black man who worked in the café that the boy's parents operated. If after reading the play you read the account in the *Notebooks* (reprinted here on page 636), you will see how close the play is to certain of Fugard's experiences.

On the other hand, Fugard does not simply transcribe what really happened. For instance, Fugard was in fact fourteen at the time of the chief episode, but he makes his character Hally seventeen. Further, the episode in which Hally spits did not take place in the café but when Hally was bicycling. Similarly, Sam in fact was a skilled dancer, but so were Fugard and his sister, who were junior ballroom dancing champions during their teenage years. In writing the play, Fugard drew on his experience as a dancer and his consequent insight into the dance, but he does not endow Hally with his own passion, understanding, and skill.

Out of his own experience Fugard shaped a play that in many ways closely resembles his experience but that also departs from it. What has he done with this material? Fugard clearly has very strong views about South African society, particularly about the injustice of *apartheid* (racial segregation). It is significant, however, that the word *apartheid* never appears in the play. Nor, we think, do readers or viewers feel that they are receiving a lecture on politics or on human decency. The closest we come to hearing a lecture is perhaps when Sam explains that dancing "is like being in a dream about a world where accidents don't happen." What we are saying is that if *"MASTER HAROLD"* is a "problem play"—a play that calls attention to a social problem—it does not degenerate into a propaganda play, a play in which the author's passionate convictions overshadow everything else, including believable human beings. *"MASTER HAROLD"* seems to us to be rooted in what happened, rather than in the urge to make an abstract political point, though of course the "what happened" is for Fugard immensely important because it is a personal experience that goes far beyond the merely personal. In any case, one can say that for the most part Fugard allows his characters to remain characters; he does not turn them into spokespersons for opposing political points of view. If *"MASTER HAROLD"* were only a thesis play, it would already be obsolete now that the "Whites Only" signs are coming down in South Africa. But it remains a play about human relationships.

ATHOL FUGARD *"MASTER HAROLD"... and the boys*

The St. George's Park Tea Room on a wet and windy Port Elizabeth afternoon.

Tables and chairs have been cleared and are stacked on one side except for one which stands apart with a single chair. On this table a knife, fork, spoon and side plate in anticipation of a simple meal, together with a pile of comic books.

Other elements: a serving counter with a few stale cakes under glass and a not very impressive display of sweets, cigarettes and cool drinks, etc.; a few cardboard advertising handouts—Cadbury's Chocolate, Coca-Cola—and a blackboard on which an untrained hand has chalked up the prices of Tea, Coffee, Scones, Milkshakes—all flavors—and Cool Drinks; a few sad ferns in pots; a telephone; an old-style jukebox.

There is an entrance on one side and an exit into a kitchen on the other.

Leaning on the solitary table, his head cupped in one hand as he pages through one of the comic books, is SAM. *A black man in his mid-forties. He wears the white coat of a waiter. Behind him on his knees, mopping down the floor with a bucket of water and a rag, is* WILLIE. *Also black and about the same age as Sam. He has his sleeves and trousers rolled up.*

The year: 1950.

WILLIE (*singing as he works*).

"She was scandalizin' my name,
She took my money
She called me honey
But she was scandalizin' my name.
Called it love but was playin' a game . . ."

(*He gets up and moves the bucket. Stands thinking for a moment, then, raising his arms to hold an imaginary partner, he launches into an intricate ballroom dance step. Although a mildly comic figure, he reveals a reasonable degree of accomplishment.*)

Hey, Sam.

(*Sam, absorbed in the comic book, does not respond.*)

Hey, Boet[1] Sam!

(*Sam looks up.*)

I'm getting it. The quickstep. Look now and tell me. (*He repeats the step.*) Well?

SAM (*encouragingly*). Show me again.

WILLIE. Okay, count for me.

SAM. Ready?

WILLIE. Ready.

SAM. Five, six, seven, eight. . . . (*Willie starts to dance.*) A-n-d one two three four . . . and one two three four. . . . (*Ad libbing as Willie dances*) Your shoulders, Willie . . . your shoulders! Don't look down! Look happy, Willie! Relax, Willie!

WILLIE (*desperate but still dancing*). I am relax.

SAM. No, you're not.

WILLIE (*he falters*). Ag no man, Sam! Mustn't talk. You make me make mistakes.

SAM. But you're stiff.

WILLIE. Yesterday I'm not straight . . . today I'm too stiff!

SAM. Well, you are. You asked me and I'm telling you.

WILLIE. Where?

SAM. Everywhere. Try to glide through it.

WILLIE. Glide?

SAM. Ja, make it smooth. And give it more style. It must look like you're enjoying yourself.

WILLIE (*emphatically*). I wasn't.

[1] ***Boet*** Brother

SAM. Exactly.

WILLIE. How can I enjoy myself? Not straight, too stiff and now it's also glide, give it more style, make it smooth. . . . Haai! Is hard to remember all those things, Boet Sam.

SAM. That's your trouble. You're trying too hard.

WILLIE. I try hard because it is hard.

SAM. But don't let me see it. The secret is to make it look easy. Ballroom must look happy, Willie, not like hard work. It must . . . Ja! . . . it must look like romance.

WILLIE. Now another one! What's romance?

SAM. Love story with happy ending. A handsome man in tails, and in his arms, smiling at him, a beautiful lady in evening dress!

WILLIE. Fred Astaire, Ginger Rogers.

SAM. You got it. Tapdance or ballroom, it's the same. Romance. In two weeks' time when the judges look at you and Hilda, they must see a man and a woman who are dancing their way to a happy ending. What I saw was you holding her like you were frightened she was going to run away.

WILLIE. Ja! Because that is what she wants to do! I got no romance left for Hilda anymore, Boet Sam.

SAM. Then pretend. When you put your arms around Hilda, imagine she is Ginger Rogers.

WILLIE. With no teeth? You try.

SAM. Well, just remember, there's only two weeks left.

WILLIE. I know, I know! (*To the jukebox.*) I do it better with music. You got sixpence for Sarah Vaughan?

SAM. That's a slow foxtrot. You're practicing the quickstep.

WILLIE. I'll practice slow foxtrot.

SAM (*shaking his head*). It's your turn to put money in the jukebox.

WILLIE. I only got bus fare to go home. (*He returns disconsolately to his work.*) Love story and happy ending! She's doing it all right, Boet Sam, but is not me she's giving happy endings. Fuckin' whore! Three nights now she doesn't come practice. I wind up gramophone, I get record ready and I sit and wait. What happens? Nothing. Ten o'clock I start dancing with my pillow. You try and practice romance by yourself, Boet Sam. Struesgod, she doesn't come tonight I take back my dress and ballroom shoes and I find me new partner. Size twenty-six. Shoes size seven. And now she's also making trouble for me with the baby again. Reports me to Child Wellfed, that I'm not giving her money. She lies! Every week I am giving her money for milk. And how do I know is my baby? Only his hair looks like me. She's fucking around all the time I turn my back. Hilda Samuels is a bitch! (*Pause.*) Hey, Sam!

SAM. Ja.

WILLIE. You listening?

SAM. Ja.

WILLIE. So what you say?
SAM. About Hilda?
WILLIE. Ja.
SAM. When did you last give her a hiding?
WILLIE (*reluctantly*). Sunday night.
SAM. And today is Thursday.
WILLIE (*he knows what's coming*). Okay.
SAM. Hiding on Sunday night, then Monday, Tuesday and Wednesday she doesn't come to practice . . . and you are asking me why?
WILLIE. I said okay, Boet Sam!
SAM. You hit her too much. One day she's going to leave you for good.
WILLIE. So? She makes me the hell-in too much.
SAM (*emphasizing his point*). *Too* much and *too* hard. You had the same trouble with Eunice.
WILLIE. Because she also make the hell-in, Boet Sam. She never got the steps right. Even the waltz.
SAM. Beating her up every time she makes a mistake in the waltz? (*Shaking his head*) No, Willie! That takes the pleasure out of ballroom dancing.
WILLIE. Hilda is not too bad with the waltz, Boet Sam. Is the quickstep where the trouble starts.
SAM (*testing him gently*). How's your pillow with the quickstep?
WILLIE (*ignoring the tease*). Good! And why? Because it got no legs. That's her trouble. She can't move them quick enough, Boet Sam. I start the record and before halfway Count Basie is already winning. Only time we catch up with him is when gramophone runs down. (*Sam laughs.*) Haaikona, Boet Sam, is not funny.
SAM (*snapping his fingers*). I got it! Give her a handicap.
WILLIE. What's that?
SAM. Give her a ten-second start and then let Count Basie go. Then I put my money on her. Hot favorite in the Ballroom Stakes: Hilda Samuels ridden by Willie Malopo.
WILLIE (*turning away*). I'm not talking to you no more.
SAM (*relenting*). Sorry, Willie. . . .
WILLIE. It's finish between us.
SAM. Okay, okay . . . I'll stop.
WILLIE. You can also fuck off.
SAM. Willie, listen! I want to help you!
WILLIE. No more jokes?
SAM. I promise.
WILLIE. Okay. Help me.
SAM (*his turn to hold an imaginary partner*). Look and learn. Feet together. Back straight. Body relaxed. Right hand placed gently in the small of her back and wait for the music. Don't start worrying about making mistakes or the judges or the other competitors. It's just you, Hilda and the music, and you're going to have a good time. What Count Basie do you play?
WILLIE. "You the cream in my coffee, you the salt in my stew."
SAM. Right. Give it to me in strict tempo.
WILLIE. Ready?
SAM. Ready.
WILLIE. A-n-d . . . (*Singing*)

> "You the cream in my coffee.
> You the salt in my stew.
> You will always be
> my necessity.
> I'd be lost without you. . . ." (*etc.*)

(*Sam launches into the quickstep. He is obviously a much more accomplished dancer than Willie.* HALLY *enters. A seventeen-year-old white boy. Wet raincoat and school case. He stops and watches Sam. The demonstration comes to an end with a flourish. Applause from Hally and Willie.*)

HALLY. Bravo! No question about it. First place goes to Mr. Sam Semela.
WILLIE (*in total agreement*). You was gliding with style, Boet Sam.
HALLY (*cheerfully*). How's it, chaps?
SAM. Okay, Hally.
WILLIE (*springing to attention like a soldier and saluting*). At your service, Master Harold!
HALLY. Not long to the big event, hey!
SAM. Two weeks.
HALLY. You nervous?
SAM. No.
HALLY. Think you stand a chance?
SAM. Let's just say I'm ready to go out there and dance.
HALLY. It looked like it. What about you, Willie?

(*Willie groans.*)

What's the matter?
SAM. He's got leg trouble.
HALLY (*innocently*). Oh, sorry to hear that, Willie.
WILLIE. Boet Sam! You promised. (*Willie returns to his work.*)

(*Hally deposits his school case and takes off his raincoat. His clothes are a little neglected and untidy: black blazer with school badge, gray flannel trousers in need of an ironing, khaki shirt and tie, black shoes. Sam has fetched a towel for Hally to dry his hair.*)

HALLY. God, what a lousy bloody day. It's coming down cats and dogs out there. Bad for business, chaps . . . (*conspiratorial whisper*) . . . but it also means we're in for a nice quiet afternoon.
SAM. You can speak loud. Your Mom's not here.
HALLY. Out shopping?

SAM. No. The hospital.

HALLY. But it's Thursday. There's no visiting on Thursday afternoons. Is my Dad okay?

SAM. Sounds like it. In fact, I think he's going home.

HALLY (*stopped short by Sam's remark*). What do you mean?

SAM. The hospital phoned.

HALLY. To say what?

SAM. I don't know. I just heard your Mom talking.

HALLY. So what makes you say he's going home?

SAM. It sounded as if they were telling her to come and fetch him.

(*Hally thinks about what Sam has said for a few seconds.*)

HALLY. When did she leave?

SAM. About an hour ago. She said she would phone you. Want to eat?

(*Hally doesn't respond.*)

Hally, want your lunch?

HALLY. I suppose so. (*His mood has changed.*) What's on the menu? . . . as if I don't know.

SAM. Soup, followed by meat pie and gravy.

HALLY. Today's?

SAM. No.

HALLY. And the soup?

SAM. Nourishing pea soup.

HALLY. Just the soup. (*The pile of comic books on the table.*) And these?

SAM. For your Dad. Mr. Kempston brought them.

HALLY. You haven't been reading them, have you?

SAM. Just looking.

HALLY (*examining the comics*). *Jungle Jim . . . Batman and Robin . . . Tarzan . . .* God, what rubbish! Mental pollution. Take them away.

(*Sam exits waltzing into the kitchen. Hally turns to Willie.*)

HALLY. Did you hear my Mom talking on the telephone, Willie?

WILLIE. No, Master Hally. I was at the back.

HALLY. And she didn't say anything to you before she left?

WILLIE. She said I must clean the floors.

HALLY. I mean about my Dad.

WILLIE. She didn't say nothing to me about him, Master Hally.

HALLY (*with conviction*). No! It can't be. They said he needed at least another three weeks of treatment. Sam's definitely made a mistake. (*Rummages through his school case, finds a book and settles down at the table to read.*) So, Willie!

WILLIE. Yes, Master Hally! Schooling okay today?

HALLY. Yes, okay. . . . (*He thinks about it.*). . . . No, not really. Ag, what's the difference? I don't care. And Sam says you've got problems.

WILLIE. Big problems.

HALLY. Which leg is sore?

(*Willie groans.*)

Both legs.

WILLIE. There is nothing wrong with my legs. Sam is just making jokes.

HALLY. So then you *will* be in the competition.

WILLIE. Only if I can find a partner.

HALLY. But what about Hilda?

SAM (*returning with a bowl of soup*). She's the one who's got trouble with her legs.

HALLY. What sort of trouble, Willie?

SAM. From the way he describes it, I think the lady has gone a bit lame.

HALLY. Good God! Have you taken her to see a doctor?

SAM. I think a vet would be better.

HALLY. What do you mean?

SAM. What do you call it again when a racehorse goes very fast?

HALLY. Gallop?

SAM. That's it!

WILLIE. Boet Sam!

HALLY. "A gallop down the homestretch to the winning post." But what's that got to do with Hilda?

SAM. Count Basie always gets there first.

(*Willie lets fly with his slop rag. It misses Sam and hits Hally.*)

HALLY (*furious*). For Christ's sake, Willie! What the hell do you think you're doing!

WILLIE. Sorry, Master Hally, but it's him. . . .

HALLY. Act your bloody age! (*Hurls the rag back at Willie.*) Cut out the nonsense now and get on with your work. And you too, Sam. Stop fooling around.

(*Sam moves away.*)

No. Hang on. I haven't finished! Tell me exactly what my Mom said.

SAM. I have. "When Hally comes, tell him I've gone to the hospital and I'll phone him."

HALLY. She didn't say anything about taking my Dad home?

SAM. No. It's just that when she was talking on the phone. . . .

HALLY (*interrupting him*). No, Sam. They can't be discharging him. She would have said so if they were. In any case, we saw him last night and he wasn't in good shape at all. Staff nurse even said there was talk about taking more

X-rays. And now suddenly today he's better? If anything, it sounds more like a bad turn to me . . . which I sincerely hope it isn't. Hang on . . . how long ago did you say she left?

SAM. Just before two . . . (*his wrist watch*) . . . hour and a half.

HALLY. I know how to settle it. (*Behind the counter to the telephone. Talking as he dials*) Let's give her ten minutes to get to the hospital, ten minutes to load him up, another ten, at the most, to get home and another ten to get him inside. Forty minutes. They should have been home for at least half an hour already. (*Pause—he waits with the receiver to his ear.*) No reply, chaps. And you know why? Because she's at his bedside in hospital helping him pull through a bad turn. You definitely heard wrong.

SAM. Okay.

(*As far as Hally is concerned, the matter is settled. He returns to his table, sits down and divides his attention between the book and his soup. Sam is at his school case and picks up a textbook.*)

Modern Graded Mathematics for Standards Nine and Ten. (*Opens it at random and laughs at something he sees.*) Who is this supposed to be?

HALLY. Old fart-face Prentice.

SAM. Teacher?

ALLY: Thinks he is. And believe me, that is not a bad likeness.

SAM. Has he seen it?

HALLY. Yes.

SAM. What did he say?

HALLY. Tried to be clever, as usual. Said I was no Leonardo da Vinci and that bad art had to be punished. So, six of the best, and his are bloody good.

SAM. On your bum?

HALLY. Where else? The days when I got them on my hands are gone forever, Sam.

SAM. With your trousers down!

HALLY. No. He's not quite that barbaric.

SAM. That's the way they do it in jail.

HALLY (*flicker of morbid interest*). Really?

SAM. Ja. When the magistrate sentences you to "strokes with a light cane."

HALLY. Go on.

SAM. They make you lie down on a bench. One policeman pulls down your trousers and holds your ankles, another one pulls your shirt over your head and holds your arms. . .

HALLY. Thank you! That's enough.

SAM. . . . and the one that gives you the strokes talks to you gently and for a long time between each one. (*He laughs.*)

HALLY. I've heard enough, Sam! Jesus! It's a bloody awful world when you come to think of it. People can be real bastards.

SAM. That's the way it is, Hally.

HALLY. It doesn't have to be that way. There is something called progress, you know. We don't exactly burn people at the stake anymore.

SAM. Like Joan of Arc.

HALLY. Correct. If she was captured today, she'd be given a fair trial.

SAM. And then the death sentence.

HALLY (*a world-weary sigh*). I know, I know! I oscillate between hope and despair for this world as well, Sam. But things will change, you wait and see. One day somebody is going to get up and give history a kick up the backside and get it going again.

SAM. Like who?

HALLY (*after thought*). They're called social reformers. Every age, Sam, has got its social reformer. My history book is full of them.

SAM. So where's ours?

HALLY. Good question. And I hate to say it, but the answer is: I don't know. Maybe he hasn't even been born yet. Or is still only a babe in arms at his mother's breast. God, what a thought.

SAM. So we just go on waiting.

HALLY. Ja, looks like it. (*Back to his soup and the book.*)

SAM (*reading from the textbook*). "Introduction: In some mathematical problems only the magnitude . . ." (*He mispronounces the word "magnitude."*)

HALLY (*correcting him without looking up*). Magnitude.

SAM. What's it mean?

HALLY. How big it is. The size of the thing.

SAM. (*reading*). ". . . magnitude of the quantities is of no importance. In other problems we need to know whether these quantities are negative or positive. For example, whether there is a debit or credit bank balance . . ."

HALLY. Whether you're broke nor not.

SAM. ". . . whether the temperature is above or below Zero. . . ."

HALLY. Naught degrees. Cheerful state of affairs! No cash and you're freezing to death. Mathematics won't get you out of that one.

SAM. "All these quantities are called . . ." (*spelling the word*) . . . s-c-a-l . . .

HALLY. Scalars.

SAM. Scalars! (*Shaking his head with a laugh*) You understand all that?

HALLY (*turning a page*). No. And I don't intend to try.

SAM. So what happens when the exams come?

HALLY. Failing a maths exam isn't the end of the world, Sam. How many times have I told you that examination results don't measure intelligence?

SAM. I would say about as many times as you've failed one of them.

HALLY (*mirthlessly*). Ha, ha, ha.

SAM (*simultaneously*). Ha, ha, ha.

HALLY. Just remember Winston Churchill didn't do particularly well at school.

SAM. You've also told me that one many times.

HALLY. Well, it just so happens to be the truth.

SAM (*enjoying the word*). Magnitude! Magnitude! Show me how to use it.

HALLY (*after thought*). An intrepid social reformer will not be daunted by the magnitude of the task he has undertaken.

SAM (*impressed*). Couple of jaw-breakers in there!

HALLY. I gave you three for the price of one. Intrepid, daunted and magnitude. I did that once in an exam. Put five of the words I had to explain in one sentence. It was half a page long.

SAM. Well, I'll put my money on you in the English exam.

HALLY. Piece of cake. Eighty percent without even trying.

SAM (*another textbook from Hally's case*). And history?

HALLY. So-so. I'll scrape through. In the fifties if I'm lucky.

SAM. You didn't do too badly last year.

HALLY. Because we had World War One. That at least has some action. You try to find that in the South African Parliamentary system.

SAM (*reading from the history textbook*). "Napoleon and the principle of equality." Hey! This sounds interesting. "After concluding peace with Britain in 1802, Napoleon used a brief period of calm to in-sti-tute . . ."

HALLY. Introduce.

SAM. ". . . many reforms. Napoleon regarded all people as equal before the law and wanted them to have equal opportunities for advancement. All ves-ti-ges of the feu-dal system with its oppression of the poor were abolished." Vestiges, feudal system and abolished. I'm all right on oppression.

HALLY. I'm thinking. He swept away . . . abolished . . . the last remains . . . vestiges . . . of the bad old days . . . feudal system.

SAM. Ha! There's the social reformer we're waiting for. He sounds like a man of some magnitude.

HALLY. I'm not so sure about that. It's a damn good title for a book, though. A man of magnitude!

SAM. He sounds pretty big to me, Hally.

HALLY. Don't confuse historical significance with greatness. But maybe I'm being a bit prejudiced. Have a look in there and you'll see he's two chapters long. And hell! . . . has he only got dates, Sam, all of which you've got to remember! This campaign and that campaign, and then, because of all the fighting, the next thing is we get Peace Treaties all over the place. And what's the end of the story? Battle of Waterloo, which he loses. Wasn't worth it. No, I don't know about him as a man of magnitude.

SAM. Then who would you say was?

HALLY. To answer that, we need a definition of greatness, and I suppose that would be somebody who . . . somebody who benefited all mankind.

SAM. Right. But like who?

HALLY (*he speaks with total conviction*). Charles Darwin. Remember him? That big book from the library. *The Origin of the Species.*

SAM. Him?

HALLY. Yes. For his Theory of Evolution.

SAM. You didn't finish it.

HALLY. I ran out of time. I didn't finish it because my two weeks was up. But I'm going to take it out again after I've digested what I read. It's safe. I've hidden it away in the Theology section. Nobody ever goes in there. And anyway who are you to talk? You hardly even looked at it.

SAM. I tried. I looked at the chapters in the beginning and I saw one called "The Struggle for an Existence." Ah ha, I thought. At last! But what did I get? Something called the mistiltoe which needs the apple tree and there's too many seeds and all are going to die except one . . . ! No, Hally.

HALLY (*intellectually outraged*). What do you mean, No! The poor man had to start somewhere. For God's sake, Sam, he revolutionized science. Now we know.

SAM. What?

HALLY. Where we come from and what it all means.

SAM. And that's a benefit to mankind? Anyway, I still don't believe it.

HALLY. God, you're impossible. I showed it to you in black and white.

SAM. Doesn't mean I got to believe it.

HALLY. It's the likes of you that kept the Inquisition in business. It's called bigotry. Anyway, that's my man of magnitude. Charles Darwin! Who's yours?

SAM (*without hesitation*). Abraham Lincoln.

HALLY. I might have guessed as much. Don't get sentimental, Sam. You've never been a slave, you know. And anyway we freed your ancestors here in South Africa long before the Americans. But if you want to thank somebody on their behalf, do it to Mr. William Wilberforce. Come on. Try again. I want a real genius.

(*Now enjoying himself, and so is Sam. Hally goes behind the counter and helps himself to a chocolate.*)

SAM. William Shakespeare.

HALLY (*no enthusiasm*). Oh. So you're also one of them, are you? You're basing that opinion on only one play, you know. You've only read my *Julius Caesar* and even I don't understand half of what they're talking about. They should do what they did with the old Bible: bring the language up to date.

SAM. That's all you've got. It's also the only one you've read.

HALLY. I know. I admit it. That's why I suggest we reserve our judgment until we've checked up on a few others. I've got a feeling, though, that by the end of this year one is going to be enough for me, and I can give you the names of twenty-nine other chaps in the Standard Nine class of the Port Elizabeth Technical College who feel the same. But if you want him, you can have him. My turn now. (*Pacing*) This is a damned good exercise, you know! It started off looking like a simple question and here it's got us really probing into the intellectual heritage of our civilization.

SAM. So who is it going to be?

HALLY. My next man . . . and he gets the title on two scores: social reform and literary genius . . . Is Leo Nikolaevich Tolstoy.

SAM. That Russian.

HALLY. Correct. Remember the picture of him I showed you?

SAM. With the long beard.

HALLY (*trying to look like Tolstoy*). And those burning, visionary eyes. My God, the face of a social prophet if ever I saw one! And remember my words when I showed it to you? Here's a *man,* Sam!

SAM. Those were words, Hally.

HALLY. Not many intellectuals are prepared to shovel manure with the peasants and then go home and write a "little book" called *War and Peace.* Incidentally, Sam, he was somebody else who, to quote, ". . . did not distinguish himself scholastically."

SAM. Meaning?

HALLY. He was not good at school.

SAM. Like you and Winston Churchill.

HALLY (*mirthlessly*). Ha, ha, ha.

SAM (*simultaneously*). Ha, ha, ha.

HALLY. Don't get clever, Sam. That man freed his serfs of his own free will.

SAM. No argument. He was somebody, all right. I accept him.

HALLY. I'm sure Count Tolstoy will be very pleased to hear that. Your turn. Shoot. (*Another chocolate from behind the counter.*) I'm waiting, Sam.

SAM. I've got him.

HALLY. Good. Submit your candidate for examination.

SAM. Jesus.

HALLY (*stopped dead in his tracks*). Who?

SAM. Jesus Christ.

HALLY. Oh, come on, Sam!

SAM. The Messiah.

HALLY. Ja, but still . . . No, Sam. Don't let's get started on religion. We'll just spend the whole afternoon arguing again. Suppose I turn around and say Mohammed?

SAM. All right.

HALLY. You can't have them both on the same list!

SAM. Why not? You like Mohammed, I like Jesus.

HALLY. I *don't* like Mohammed. I never have. I was merely being hypothetical. As far as I'm concerned, the Koran is as bad as the Bible. No. Religion is out! I'm not going to waste my time again arguing with you about the existence of God. You know perfectly well I'm an atheist . . . and I've got homework to do.

SAM. Okay, I take him back.

HALLY. You've got time for one more name.

SAM (*after thought*). I've got one I know we'll agree on. A simple straightforward great Man of Magnitude . . . and no arguments. And *he* really *did* benefit all mankind.

HALLY. I wonder. After your last contribution I'm beginning to doubt whether anything in the way of an intellectual agreement is possible between the two of us. Who is he?

SAM. Guess.

HALLY. Socrates? Alexandre Dumas? Karl Marx, Dostoevsky? Nietzsche?

(*Sam shakes his head after each name.*)

Give me a clue.

SAM. The letter P is important. . . .

HALLY. Plato!

SAM. . . . and his name begins with an F.

HALLY. I've got it. Freud and Psychology.

SAM. No. I didn't understand him.

HALLY. That makes two of us.

SAM. Think of mouldy apricot jam.

HALLY (*after a delighted laugh*). Penicillin and Sir Alexander Fleming! And the title of the book: *The Microbe Hunters.* (*Delighted*) Splendid, Sam! Splendid. For once we are in total agreement. The major breakthrough in medical science in the Twentieth Century. If it wasn't for him, we might have lost the Second World War. It's deeply gratifying, Sam, to know that I haven't been wasting my time in talking to you. (*Strutting around proudly*) Tolstoy may have educated his peasants, but I've educated you.

SAM. Standard Four to Standard Nine.

HALLY. Have we been at it as long as that?

SAM. Yep. And my first lesson was geography.

HALLY (*intrigued*). Really? I don't remember.

SAM. My room there at the back of the old Jubilee Boarding House. I had just started working for your Mom. Little boy in short trousers walks in one afternoon and asks me seriously: "Sam, do you want to see South Africa?" Hey man! Sure I wanted to see South Africa!

HALLY. Was that me?

SAM. . . . So the next thing I'm looking at a map you had just done for homework. It was your first one and you were very proud of yourself.

HALLY. Go on.

SAM. Then came my first lesson. "Repeat after me, Sam: Gold in the Transvaal, mealies in the Free State, sugar in Natal and grapes in the Cape." I still know it!

HALLY. Well, I'll be buggered. So that's how it all started.

SAM. And your next map was one with all the rivers and the mountains they came from. The Orange, the Vaal, the Limpopo, the Zambezi. . . .

HALLY. You've got a phenomenal memory!

SAM. You should be grateful. That is why you started passing your exams. You tried to be better than me.

(*They laugh together. Willie is attracted by the laughter and joins them.*)

HALLY. The old Jubilee Boarding House. Sixteen rooms with board and lodging, rent in advance and one week's notice. I haven't thought about it for donkey's years . . . and I don't think that's an accident. God, was I glad when we sold it and moved out. Those years are not remembered as the happiest ones of an unhappy childhood.

WILLIE (*knocking on the table and trying to imitate a woman's voice*). "Hally, are you there?"

HALLY. Who's that supposed to be?

WILLIE. "What you doing in there, Hally? Come out at once!"

HALLY (*to Sam*). What's he talking about?

SAM. Don't you remember?

WILLIE. "Sam, Willie . . . is he in there with you boys?"

SAM. Hiding away in our room when your mother was looking for you.

HALLY (*another good laugh*). Of course! I used to crawl and hide under your bed! But finish the story, Willie. Then what used to happen? You chaps would give the game away by telling her I was in there with you. So much for friendship.

SAM. We couldn't lie to her. She knew.

HALLY. Which meant I got another rowing for hanging around the "servants' quarters." I think I spent more time in there with you chaps than anywhere else in that dump. And do you blame me? Nothing but bloody misery wherever you went. Somebody was always complaining about the food, or my mother was having a fight with Micky Nash because she'd caught her with a petty officer in her room. Maud Meiring was another one. Remember those two? They were prostitutes, you know. Soldiers and sailors from the troopships. Bottom fell out of the business when the war ended. God, the flotsam and jetsam that life washed up on our shores! No joking, if it wasn't for your room, I would have been the first certified ten-year-old in medical history. Ja, the memories are coming back now. Walking home from school and thinking: "What can I do this afternoon?" Try out a few ideas, but sooner or later I'd end up in there with you fellows. I bet you I could still find my way to your room with my eyes closed. (*He does exactly that.*) Down the corridor . . . telephone on the right, which my Mom keeps locked because somebody is using it on the sly and not paying . . . past the kitchen and unappetizing cooking smells . . . around the corner into the backyard, hold my breath again because there are more smells coming when I pass your lavatory, then into that little passageway, first door on the right and into your room. How's that?

SAM. Good. But, as usual, you forgot to knock.

HALLY. Like that time I barged in and caught you and Cynthia . . . at it. Remember? God, was I embarrassed! I didn't know what was going on at first.

SAM. Ja, that taught you a lesson.

HALLY. And about a lot more than knocking on doors, I'll have you know, and I don't mean geography either. Hell, Sam, couldn't you have waited until it was dark?

SAM. No.

HALLY. Was it that urgent?

SAM. Yes, and if you don't believe me, wait until your time comes.

HALLY. No, thank you. I am not interested in girls. (*Back to his memories. . . . Using a few chairs he re-creates the room as he lists the items.*) A gray little room with a cold cement floor. Your bed against that wall . . . and I now know why the mattress sags so much! . . . Willie's bed . . . it's propped up on bricks because one leg is broken . . . that wobbly little table with the washbasin and jug of water . . . Yes! . . . stuck to the wall above it are some pin-up pictures from magazines. Joe Louis . . .

WILLIE. Brown Bomber. World Title. (*Boxing pose.*) Three rounds and knockout.

HALLY. Against who?

SAM. Max Schmeling.

HALLY. Correct. I can also remember Fred Astaire and Ginger Rogers, and Rita Hayworth in a bathing costume which always made me hot and bothered when I looked at it. Under Willie's bed is an old suitcase with all his clothes in a mess, which is why I never hide there. Your things are neat and tidy in a trunk next to your bed, and on it there is a picture of you and Cynthia in your ballroom clothes, your first silver cup for third place in a competition and an old radio which doesn't work anymore. Have I left out anything?

SAM. No.

HALLY. Right, so much for the stage directions. Now

the characters. (*Sam and Willie move to their appropriate positions in the bedroom.*) Willie is in bed, under his blankets with his clothes on, complaining nonstop about something, but we can't make out a word of what he's saying because he's got his head under the blankets as well. You're on your bed trimming your toenails with a knife—not a very edifying sight—and as for me ... What am I doing?

SAM. You're sitting on the floor giving Willie a lecture about being a good loser while you get the checker board and pieces ready for a game. Then you go to Willie's bed, pull off the blankets and make him play with you first because you know you're going to win, and that gives you the second game with me.

HALLY. And you certainly were a bad loser, Willie!

WILLIE. Haai!

HALLY. Wasn't he, Sam? And so slow! A game with you almost took the whole afternoon. Thank God I gave up trying to teach you how to play chess.

WILLIE. You and Sam cheated.

HALLY. I never saw Sam cheat, and mine were mostly the mistakes of youth.

WILLIE. Then how is it you two was always winning?

HALLY. Have you ever considered the possibility, Willie, that it was because we were better than you?

WILLIE. Every time better?

HALLY. Not every time. There were occasions when we deliberately let you win a game so that you would stop sulking and go on playing with us. Sam used to wink at me when you weren't looking to show me it was time to let you win.

WILLIE. So then you two didn't play fair.

HALLY. It was for your benefit, Mr. Malopo, which is more than being fair. It was an act of self-sacrifice. (*To Sam*) But you know what my best memory is, don't you?

SAM. No.

HALLY. Come on, guess. If your memory is so good, you must remember it as well.

SAM. We got up to a lot of tricks in there, Hally.

HALLY. This one was special, Sam.

SAM. I'm listening.

HALLY. It started off looking like another of those useless nothing-to-do afternoons. I'd already been down to Main Street looking for adventure, but nothing had happened. I didn't feel like climbing trees in the Donkin Park or pretending I was a private eye and following a stranger ... so as usual: See what's cooking in Sam's room. This time it was you on the floor. You had two thin pieces of wood and you were smoothing them down with a knife. It didn't look particularly interesting, but when I asked you what you were doing, you just said, "Wait and see, Hally. Wait ... and see" ... in that secret sort of way of yours, so I knew there was a surprise coming. You teased me, you bugger, by being deliberately slow and not answering my questions!

(*Sam laughs.*)

And whistling while you worked away! God, it was infuriating! I could have brained you! It was only when you tied them together in a cross and put that down on the brown paper that I realized what you were doing. "Sam is making a kite?" And when I asked you and you said "Yes" ... ! (*Shaking his head with disbelief.*) The sheer audacity of it took my breath away! I mean, seriously, what the hell does a black man know about flying a kite? I'll be honest with you, Sam, I had no hopes for it. If you think I was excited and happy, you got another guess coming. In fact, I was shit-scared that we were going to make fools of ourselves. When we left the boarding house to go up onto the hill, I was praying quietly that there wouldn't be any other kids around to laugh at us.

SAM (*enjoying the memory as much as Hally*). Ja, I could see that.

HALLY. I made it obvious, did I?

SAM. Ja. You refused to carry it.

HALLY. Do you blame me? Can you remember what the poor thing looked like? Tomato-box wood and brown paper! Flour and water for glue! Two of my mother's old stockings for a tail, and then all those bits and pieces of string you made me tie together so that we could fly it! Hell, no, that was now only asking for a miracle to happen.

SAM. Then the big argument when I told you to hold the string and run with it when I let go.

HALLY. I was prepared to run, all right, but straight back to the boarding house.

SAM (*knowing what's coming*). So what happened?

HALLY. Come on, Sam, you remember as well as I do.

SAM. I want to hear it from you.

(*Hally pauses. He wants to be as accurate as possible.*)

HALLY. You went a little distance from me down the hill, you held it up ready to let it go. ... "This is it," I thought. "Like everything else in my life, here comes another fiasco." Then you shouted, "Go Hally!" and I started to run. (*Another pause.*) I don't know how to describe it, Sam. Ja! The miracle happened! I was running, waiting for it to crash to the ground, but instead suddenly there was something alive behind me at the end of the string, tugging at it as if it wanted to be free. I looked back ... (*Shakes his head.*) ... I still can't believe my eyes. It was flying! Looping around and trying to climb even higher into the sky. You shouted to me to let it have more string. I did, until there was none left and I was just holding that piece of wood we had tied it to. You came up and joined me. You were laughing.

SAM. So were you. And shouting, "It works, Sam! We've done it!"

HALLY. And we had! I was so proud of us! It was the most splendid thing I had ever seen. I wished there were hundreds of kids around to watch us. The part that scared me, though, was when you showed me how to make it dive down to the ground and then just when it was on the point of crashing, swoop up again!

SAM. You didn't want to try yourself.

HALLY. Of course not! I would have been suicidal if anything had happened to it. Watching you do it made me nervous enough. I was quite happy just to see it up there with its tail fluttering behind it. You left me after that, didn't you? You explained how to get it down, we tied it to the bench so that I could sit and watch it, and you went away. I wanted you to stay, you know. I was a little scared of having to look after it by myself.

SAM (*quietly*). I had work to do, Hally.

HALLY. It was sort of sad bringing it down, Sam. And it looked sad again when it was lying there on the ground. Like something that had lost its soul. Just tomato-box wood, brown paper and two of my mother's old stockings! But, hell, I'll never forget that first moment when I saw it up there. I had a stiff neck the next day from looking up so much.

(*Sam laughs. Hally turns to him with a question he never thought of asking before.*)

Why did you make that kite, Sam?

SAM (*evenly*). I can't remember.

HALLY. Truly?

SAM. Too long ago, Hally.

HALLY. Ja, I suppose it was. It's time for another one, you know.

SAM. Why do you say that?

HALLY. Because it feels like that. Wouldn't be a good day to fly it, though.

SAM. No. You can't fly kites on rainy days.

HALLY (*he studies Sam. Their memories have made him conscious of the man's presence in his life*). How old are you, Sam?

SAM. Two score and five.

HALLY. Strange, isn't it?

SAM. What?

HALLY. Me and you.

SAM. What's strange about it?

HALLY. Little white boy in short trousers and a black man old enough to be his father flying a kite. It's not every day you see that.

SAM. But why strange? Because the one is white and the other black?

HALLY. I don't know. Would have been just as strange, I suppose, if it had been me and my Dad ... cripple man and a little boy! Nope! There's no chance of me flying a kite without it being strange. (*Simple statement of fact—no self-pity.*) There's a nice little short story there. "The Kite-Flyers." But we'd have to find a twist in the ending.

SAM. Twist?

HALLY. Yes. Something unexpected. The way it ended with us was too straightforward ... me on the bench and you going back to work. There's no drama in that.

WILLIE. And me?

HALLY. You?

WILLIE. Yes me.

HALLY. You want to get into the story as well, do you? I got it! Change the title: "Afternoons in Sam's Room" ... expand it and tell all the stories. It's on its way to being a novel. Our days in the old Jubilee. Sad in a way that they're over. I almost wish we were still in that little room.

SAM. We're still together.

HALLY. That's true. It's just that life felt the right size in there ... not too big and not too small. Wasn't so hard to work up a bit of courage. It's got so bloody complicated since then.

(*The telephone rings. Sam answers it.*)

SAM. St. George's Park Tea Room ... Hello, Madam ... Yes, Madam, he's here. ... Hally, it's your mother.

HALLY. Where is she phoning from?

SAM. Sounds like the hospital. It's a public telephone.

HALLY (*relieved*). You see! I told you. (*The telephone.*) Hello, Mom ... Yes ... Yes no fine. Everything's under control here. How's things with poor old Dad? ... Has he had a bad turn? ... What? ... Oh, God! ... Yes, Sam told me, but I was sure he'd made a mistake. But what's this all about, Mom? He didn't look at all good last night. How can he get better so quickly? ... Then very obviously you must say no. Be firm with him. You're the boss. ... You know what it's going to be like if he comes home. ... Well then, don't blame me when I fail my exams at the end of the year. ... Yes! How am I expected to be fresh for school when I spend half the night massaging his gammy leg? ... So am I! ... So tell him a white lie. Say Dr. Colley wants more X-rays of his stump. Or bribe him. We'll sneak in double tots of brandy in future. ... What? ... Order him to get back into bed at once! If he's going to behave like a child, treat him like one. ... All right, Mom! I was just trying to ... I'm sorry. ... I said I'm sorry. ... Quick, give me your number. I'll phone you back. (*He hangs up and waits a few seconds.*) Here we go again! (*He dials.*) I'm sorry, Mom. ... Okay. ... But now listen to me carefully. All it needs is for you to put your foot down. Don't take no for an answer. ... Did you hear me? And whatever you do, don't discuss it with him. ... Because I'm frightened you'll give in to him. ... Yes, Sam gave me lunch. . . . I ate all of it! . . . No, Mom, not a soul. It's still raining here. . . . Right, I'll tell them. I'll just do some homework and then lock up. . . . But remember now, Mom. Don't listen to anything he says. And phone me back and let me know what happens. . . . Okay. Bye, Mom. (*He hangs up. The men are staring at him.*) My Mom says that when you're finished with the floors you must do the windows. (*Pause.*) Don't misunderstand me, chaps. All I want is for him to get better. And if he was, I'd be the first person to say: "Bring him home." But he's not, and we can't give him the medical care and attention he needs at home. That's what hospitals are there for. (*Brusquely*) So don't just stand there! Get on with it!

(*Sam clears Hally's table.*)

You heard right. My Dad wants to go home.

SAM. Is he better?

HALLY (*sharply*). No! How the hell can he be better when last night he was groaning with pain? This is not an age of miracles!

SAM. Then he should stay in hospital.

HALLY (*seething with irritation and frustration*). Tell me something I don't know, Sam. What the hell do you think I was saying to my Mom? All I can say is fuck-it-all.

SAM. I'm sure he'll listen to your Mom.

HALLY. You don't know what she's up against. He's already packed his shaving kit and pajamas and is sitting on his bed with his crutches, dressed and ready to go. I know him when he gets in that mood. If she tries to reason with him, we've had it. She's no match for him when it comes to a battle of words. He'll tie her up in knots. (*Trying to hide his true feelings.*)

SAM. I suppose it gets lonely for him in there.

HALLY. With all the patients and nurses around? Regular visits from the Salvation Army? Balls! It's ten times worse for him at home. I'm at school and my mother is here in the business all day.

SAM. He's at least got you at night.

HALLY (*before he can stop himself*). And we've got him! Please! I don't want to talk about it anymore. (*Unpacks his school case, slamming down books on the table.*) Life is just a plain bloody mess, that's all. And people are fools.

SAM. Come on, Hally.

HALLY. Yes, they are! They bloody well deserve what they get.

SAM. Then don't complain.

HALLY. Don't try to be clever, Sam. It doesn't suit you. Anybody who thinks there's nothing wrong with this world needs to have his head examined. Just when things are going along all right, without fail someone or something will come along and spoil everything. Somebody should write that down as a fundamental law of the Universe. The principle of perpetual disappointment. If there is a God who created this world, he should scrap it and try again.

SAM. All right, Hally, all right. What you got for homework?

HALLY. Bullshit, as usual. (*Opens an exercise book and reads*) "Write five hundred words describing an annual event of cultural or historical significance."

SAM. That should be easy enough for you.

HALLY. And also plain bloody boring. You know what he wants, don't you? One of their useless old ceremonies. The commemoration of the landing of the 1820 Settlers, or if it's going to be culture, Carols by Candlelight every Christmas.

SAM. It's an impressive sight. Make a good description, Hally. All those candles glowing in the dark and the people singing hymns.

HALLY. And it's called religious hysteria. (*Intense irritation*) Please, Sam! Just leave me alone and let me get on with it. I'm not in the mood for games this afternoon. And remember my Mom's orders . . . you're to help Willie with the windows. Come on now, I don't want any more nonsense in here.

SAM. Okay, Hally, okay.

(*Hally settles down to his homework; determined preparations . . . pen, ruler, exercise book, dictionary, another cake . . . all of which will lead to nothing.*)

(*Sam waltzes over to Willie and starts to replace tables and chairs. He practices a ballroom step while doing so. Willie watches. When Sam is finished, Willie tries.*)

Good! But just a little bit quicker on the turn and only move in to her after she's crossed over. What about this one?

(*Another step. When Sam is finished, Willie again has a go.*)

Much better. See what happens when you just relax and enjoy yourself? Remember that in two weeks' time and you'll be all right.

WILLIE. But I haven't got partner, Boet Sam.

SAM. Maybe Hilda will turn up tonight.

WILLIE. No, Boet Sam. (*Reluctantly*) I gave her a good hiding.

SAM. You mean a bad one.

WILLIE. Good bad one.

SAM. Then you mustn't complain either. Now you pay the price for losing your temper.

WILLIE. I also pay two pounds ten shilling entrance fee.

SAM. They'll refund you if you withdraw now.

WILLIE (*appalled*). You mean, don't dance?

SAM. Yes.

WILLIE. No! I wait too long and I practice too hard. If I

find me new partner, you think I can be ready in two weeks? I ask Madam for my leave now and we practice every day.

SAM. Quickstep nonstop for two weeks. World record, Willie, but you'll be mad at the end.

WILLIE. No jokes, Boet Sam.

SAM. I'm not joking.

WILLIE. So then what?

SAM. Find Hilda. Say you're sorry and promise you won't beat her again.

WILLIE. No.

SAM. Then withdraw. Try again next year.

WILLIE. No.

SAM. Then I give up.

WILLIE. Haaikona, Boet Sam, you can't.

SAM. What do you mean, I can't? I'm telling you: I give up.

WILLIE (*adamant*). No! (*Accusingly*) It was you who start me ballroom dancing.

SAM. So?

WILLIE. Before that I use to be happy. And is you and Miriam who bring me to Hilda and say here's partner for you.

SAM. What are you saying, Willie?

WILLIE. You!

SAM. But me what? To blame?

WILLIE. Yes.

SAM. Willie . . . ? (*Bursts into laughter.*)

WILLIE. And now all you do is make jokes at me. You wait. When Miriam leaves you is my turn to laugh. Ha! Ha! Ha!

SAM (*he can't take Willie seriously any longer*). She can leave me tonight! I know what to do. (*Bowing before an imaginary partner.*) May I have the pleasure? (*He dances and sings*)

> "Just a fellow with his pillow . . .
> Dancin' like a willow . . .
> In an autumn breeze . . ."

WILLIE. There you go again!

(*Sam goes on dancing and singing.*)

Boet Sam!

SAM. There's the answer to your problem! Judges' announcement in two weeks' time: "Ladies and gentlemen, the winner in the open section. Mr. Willie Malopo and his pillow!"

(*This is too much for a now really angry Willie. He goes for Sam, but the latter is too quick for him and puts Hally's table between the two of them.*)

HALLY (*exploding*). For Christ's sake, you two!

WILLIE (*still trying to get at Sam*). I donner you, Sam! Struesgod!

SAM (*still laughing*). Sorry, Willie . . . Sorry. . . .

HALLY. Sam! Willie! (*Grabs his ruler and gives Willie a vicious whack on the bum.*) How the hell am I supposed to concentrate with the two of you behaving like bloody children!

WILLIE. Hit him, too!

HALLY. Shut up, Willie.

WILLIE. He started jokes again.

HALLY. Get back to your work. You too, Sam. (*His ruler.*) Do you want another one, Willie?

(*Sam and Willie return to their work. Hally uses the opportunity to escape from his unsuccessful attempt at homework. He struts around like a little despot, ruler in hand, giving vent to his anger and frustration.*)

Suppose a customer had walked in then? Or the Park Superintendent. And seen the two of you behaving like a pair of hooligans. That would have been the end of my mother's license, you know. And your jobs? Well, this is the end of it. From now on there will be no more of your ballroom nonsense in here. This is a business establishment, not a bloody New Brighton dancing school. I've been far too lenient with the two of you. (*Behind the counter for a green cool drink and a dollop of ice cream. He keeps up his tirade as he prepares it.*) But what really makes me bitter is that I allow you chaps a little freedom in here when business is bad and what do you do with it? The foxtrot! Specially you, Sam. There's more to life than trotting around a dance floor and I thought at least you knew it.

SAM. It's a harmless pleasure, Hally. It doesn't hurt anybody.

HALLY. It's also a rather simple one, you know.

SAM. You reckon so? Have you ever tried?

HALLY. Of course not.

SAM. Why don't you? Now.

HALLY. What do you mean? Me dance?

SAM. Yes. I'll show you a simple step—the waltz—then you try it.

HALLY. What will that prove?

SAM. That it might not be as easy as you think.

HALLY. I didn't say it was easy. I said it was simple—like in simple-minded, meaning mentally retarded. You can't exactly say it challenges the intellect.

SAM. It does other things.

HALLY. Such as?

SAM. Make people happy.

HALLY (*the glass in his hand*). So do American cream sodas with ice cream. For God's sake, Sam, you're not asking me to take ballroom dancing serious, are you?

SAM. Yes.

HALLY (*sigh of defeat*). Oh, well, so much for trying to give you a decent education. I've obviously achieved nothing.

SAM. You still haven't told me what's wrong with admiring something that's beautiful and then trying to do it yourself.

HALLY. Nothing. But we happen to be talking about a foxtrot, not a thing of beauty.

SAM. But that is just what I'm saying. If you were to see two champions doing, two masters of the art ... !

HALLY. Oh God, I give up. So now it's also art!

SAM. Ja.

HALLY. There's a limit, Sam. Don't confuse art and entertainment.

SAM. So then what is art?

HALLY. You want a definition?

SAM. Ja.

HALLY (*He realizes he has got to be careful. He gives the matter a lot of thought before answering*). Philosophers have been trying to do that for centuries. What is Art? What is Life? But basically I suppose it's ... the giving of meaning to matter.

SAM. Nothing to do with beautiful?

HALLY. It goes beyond that. It's the giving of form to the formless.

SAM. Ja, well, maybe it's not art, then. But I still say it's beautiful.

HALLY. I'm sure the word you mean to use is entertaining.

SAM (*adamant*). No. Beautiful. And if you want proof come along to the Centenary Hall in New Brighton in two weeks' time.

(*The mention of the Centenary Hall draws Willie over to them.*)

HALLY. What for? I've seen the two of you prancing around in here often enough.

SAM (*he laughs*). This isn't the real thing, Hally. We're just playing around in here.

HALLY. So? I can use my imagination.

SAM. And what do you get?

HALLY. A lot of people dancing around and having a so-called good time.

SAM. That all?

HALLY. Well, basically it is that, surely.

SAM. No, it isn't. Your imagination hasn't helped you at all. There's a lot more to it than that. We're getting ready for the championships, Hally, not just another dance. There's going to be a lot of people, all right, and they're going to have a good time, but they'll only be spectators, sitting around and watching. It's just the competitors out there on the dance floor. Party decorations and fancy lights all around the walls! The ladies in beautiful evening dresses!

HALLY. My mother's got one of those, Sam, and, quite frankly, it's an embarrassment every time she wears it.

SAM (*undeterred*). Your imagination left out the excitement.

(*Hally scoffs.*)

Oh, yes. The finalists are not going to be out there just to have a good time. One of those couples will be the 1950 Eastern Province Champions. And your imagination left out the music.

WILLIE. Mr. Elijah Gladman Guzana and his Orchestral Jazzonions.

SAM. The sound of the big band, Hally. Trombone, trumpet, tenor and alto sax. And then, finally, your imagination also left out the climax of the evening when the dancing is finished, the judges have stopped whispering among themselves and the Master of Ceremonies collects their scorecards and goes up onto the stage to announce the winners.

HALLY. All right. So you make it sound like a bit of a do. It's an occasion. Satisfied?

SAM (*victory*). So you admit that!

HALLY. Emotionally yes, intellectually no.

SAM. Well, I don't know what you mean by that, all I'm telling you is that it is going to be *the* event of the year in New Brighton. It's been sold out for two weeks already. There's only standing room left. We've got competitors coming from Kingwilliamstown, East London, Port Alfred.

(*Hally starts pacing thoughtfully.*)

HALLY. Tell me a bit more.

SAM. I thought you weren't interested ... intellectually.

HALLY (*mysteriously*). I've got my reasons.

SAM. What do you want to know?

HALLY. It takes place every year?

SAM. Yes. But only every third year in New Brighton. It's East London's turn to have the championships next year.

HALLY. Which, I suppose, makes it an even more significant event.

SAM. Ah ha! We're getting somewhere. Our "occasion" is now a "significant event."

HALLY. I wonder.

SAM. What?

HALLY. I wonder if I would get away with it.

SAM. But what?

HALLY (*to the table and his exercise book*). "Write five hundred words describing an annual event of cultural or historical significance." Would I be stretching poetic license a little too far if I called your ballroom championships a cultural event?

SAM. You mean ... ?

HALLY. You think we could get five hundred words out of it, Sam?

SAM. Victor Sylvester has written a whole book on ballroom dancing.

WILLIE. You going to write about it, Master Hally?

HALLY. Yes, gentlemen, that is precisely what I am considering doing. Old Doc Bromely—he's my English teacher—is going to argue with me, of course. He doesn't like natives. But I'll point out to him that in strict anthropological terms the culture of a primitive black society includes its dancing and singing. To put my thesis into a nutshell: The war-dance has been replaced by the waltz. But it still amounts to the same thing: the release of primitive emotions through movement. Shall we give it a go?

SAM. I'm ready.

WILLIE. Me also.

HALLY. Ha! This will teach the old bugger a lesson. (*Decision taken.*) Right. Let's get ourselves organized (*This means another cake on the table. He sits.*) I think you've given me enough general atmosphere, Sam, but to build the tension and suspense I need facts. (*Pencil poised.*)

WILLIE. Give him facts, Boet Sam.

HALLY. What you called the climax . . . how many finalists?

SAM. Six couples.

HALLY (*making notes*). Go on. Give me the picture.

SAM. Spectators seated right around the hall. (*Willie becomes a spectator.*)

HALLY. . . . and it's a full house.

SAM. At one end, on the stage, Gladman and his Orchestral Jazzonions. At the other end is a long table with the three judges. The six finalists go onto the dance floor and take up their positions. When they are ready and the spectators have settled down, the Master of Ceremonies goes to the microphone. To start with, he makes some jokes to get people laughing. . . .

HALLY. Good touch (*as he writes*) ". . . creating a relaxed atmosphere which will change to one of tension and drama as the climax is approached."

SAM (*onto a chair to act out the M.C.*). "Ladies and gentlemen, we come now to the great moment you have all been waiting for this evening. . . . The finals of the 1950 Eastern Province Open Ballroom Dancing Championships. But first let me introduce the finalists! Mr. and Mrs. Welcome Tchabalala from Kingwilliamstown . . .

WILLIE (*he applauds after every name*). Is when the people clap their hands and whistle and make a lot of noise, Master Hally.

SAM. "Mr. Mulligan Njikelane and Miss Nomhle Nkonyeni of Grahamstown; Mr. and Mrs. Norman Nchinga from Point Alfred; Mr. Fats Bokolane and Miss Dina Plaatjies from East London; Mr. Sipho Dugu and Mrs. Mable Magada from Peddie; and from New Brighton our very own Mr. Willie Malopo and Miss Hilda Samuels."

(*Willie can't believe his ears. He abandons his role as spectator and scrambles into position as a finalist.*)

WILLIE. Relaxed and ready to romance!

SAM. The applause dies down. When everybody is silent, Gladman lifts up his sax, nods at the Orchestral Jazzonions. . . .

WILLIE. Play the jukebox please, Boet Sam!

SAM. I also only got bus fare, Willie.

HALLY. Hold it, everybody. (*Heads for the cash register behind the counter.*) How much is in the till, Sam?

SAM. Three shillings. Hally . . . Your Mom counted it before she left.

(*Hally hesitates.*)

HALLY. Sorry, Willie. You know how she carried on the last time I did it. We'll just have to pool our combined imaginations and hope for the best. (*Returns to the table.*) Back to work. How are the points scored, Sam?

SAM. Maximum of ten points each for individual style, deportment, rhythm and general appearance.

WILLIE. Must I start?

HALLY. Hold it for a second, Willie. And penalties?

SAM. For what?

HALLY. For doing something wrong. Say you stumble or bump into somebody . . . do they take off any points?

SAM (*aghast*). Hally . . . !

HALLY. When you're dancing. If you and your partner collide into another couple.

(*Hally can get no further. Sam has collapsed with laughter. He explains to Willie.*)

SAM. If me and Miriam bump into you and Hilda. . . .

(*Willie joins him in another good laugh.*)

Hally, Hally . . . !

HALLY (*perplexed*). Why? What did I say?

SAM. There's no collisions out there, Hally. Nobody trips or stumbles or bumps into anybody else. That's what that moment is all about. To be one of those finalists on that dance floor is like . . . like being in a dream about a world in which accidents don't happen.

HALLY (*genuinely moved by Sam's image*). Jesus, Sam! that's beautiful!

WILLIE (*can endure waiting no longer*). I'm starting!

(*Willie dances while Sam talks.*)

SAM. Of course it is. That's what I've been trying to say to you all afternoon. And it's beautiful because that is what we want life to be like. But instead, like you said, Hally, we're bumping into each other all the time. Look at the three of us this afternoon: I've bumped into Willie, the two of us have bumped into you, you've bumped into your mother, she bumping into your Dad.... None of us knows the steps and there's no music playing. And it doesn't stop with us. The whole world is doing it all the time. Open a newspaper and what do you read? America has bumped into Russia, England is bumping into India, rich man bumps into poor man. Those are big collisions, Hally. They make for a lot of bruises. People get hurt in all that bumping, and we're sick and tired of it now. It's been going on for too long. Are we never going to get it right? ... Learn to dance life like champions instead of always being just a bunch of beginners at it?

HALLY (*deep and sincere admiration of the man*). You've got a vision, Sam!

SAM. Not just me. What I'm saying to you is that everybody's got it. That's why there's only standing room left for the Centenary Hall in two week's time. For as long as the music lasts, we are going to see six couples get it right, the way we want life to be.

HALLY. But is that the best we can do, Sam ... watch six finalists dreaming about the way it should be?

SAM. I don't know. But it starts with that. Without the dream we won't know what we're going for. And anyway I reckon there are a few people who have got past just dreaming about it and are trying for something real. Remember that thing we read once in the paper about the Mahatma Gandhi? Going without food to stop those riots in India?

HALLY. You're right. He certainly was trying to teach people to get the steps right.

SAM. And the Pope.

HALLY. Yes, he's another one. Our old General Smuts as well, you know. He's also out there dancing. You know, Sam, when you come to think of it, that's what the United Nations boils down to ... a dancing school for politicians!

SAM. And let's hope they learn.

HALLY (*a little surge of hope*). You're right. We mustn't despair. Maybe there's some hope for mankind after all. Keep it up, Willie. (*Back to his table with determination.*) This is a lot bigger than I thought. So what have we got? Yes, our title: "A World Without Collisions."

SAM. That sounds good! "A World Without Collisions."

HALLY. Subtitle: "Global Politics on the Dance Floor." No. A bit too heavy, hey? What about "Ballroom Dancing as Political Vision"?

(*The telephone rings. Sam answers it.*)

SAM. St. George's Park Tea Room ... Yes, Madam ... Hally, it's your Mom.

HALLY (*back to reality*). Oh, God, yes! I'd forgotten all about that. Shit! remember my words, Sam? Just when you're enjoying yourself someone or something will come along and wreck everything.

SAM. You haven't heard what she's got to say yet.

HALLY. Public telephone?

SAM. No.

HALLY. Does she sound happy or unhappy?

SAM. I couldn't tell. (*Pause.*) She's waiting, Hally.

HALLY (*to the telephone*). Hello, Mom ... No, everything is okay here. Just doing my homework.... What's your news? ... You've what? ... (*Pause. He takes the receiver away from his ear for a few seconds. In the course of Hally's telephone conversation, Sam and Willie discreetly position the stacked tables and chairs. Hally places the receiver back to his ear.*) Yes, I'm still here. Oh, well, I give up now. Why did you do it, Mom? ... Well, I just hope you know what you've let us in for.... (*Loudly*) I said I hope you know what you've let us in for! It's the end of the peace and quiet we've been having. (*Softly*) Where is he? (*Normal voice*) He can't hear us from in there. But for God's sake, Mom, what happened? I told you to be firm with him.... Then you and the nurses should have held him down, taken his crutches away.... I know only too well he's my father! ... I'm not being disrespectful, but I'm sick and tired of emptying stinking chamber pots full of phlegm and piss.... Yes, I do! When you're not there, he asks me to do it.... If you really want to know the truth, that's why I've got no appetite for my food.... Yes! For your information, I still haven't got that science textbook I need. And you know why? He borrowed the money you gave me for it.... Because I didn't want to start another fight between you two.... He says that every time.... All right, Mom! (*Viciously*) Then just remember to start hiding your bag away again, because he'll be at your purse before long for money for booze. And when he's well enough to come down here, you better keep an eye on the till as well, because that is also going to develop a leak.... Then don't complain to me when he starts his old tricks.... Yes, you do. I get it from you on one side and from him on the other, and it makes life hell for me. I'm not going to be the peacemaker anymore. I'm warning you now: when the two of you start fighting again, I'm leaving home.... Mom, if you start crying, I'm going to put down the receiver.... Okay.... (*Lowering his voice to a vicious whisper*) Okay, Mom. I heard you. (*Desperate*) No.... Because I don't want to. I'll see him when I get home! Mom! ... (*Pause. When he speaks again, his tone changes completely. It is not simply pretense. We sense a genuine emotional conflict.*) Welcome home, chum! ... What's that? ... Don't be silly, Dad. You being home is just about the best news in the world.... I bet you are. Bloody depressing there with everybody going on about their ailments, hey! ... How you feeling? ... Good.... Here as well, pal. Coming down cats and dogs.... That's right. Just the day for a kip and a toss in your old Uncle Ned....

Everything's just hunky-dory on my side, Dad. . . . Well, to start with, there's a nice pile of comics for you on the counter. . . . Yes, old Kemple brought them in. *Batman and Robin, Supermariner* . . . just your cup of tea . . . I will. . . . Yes, we'll spin a few yarns tonight. . . . Okay, chum, see you in a little while. . . . No, I promise. I'll come straight home. . . . (*Pause—his mother comes back on the phone.*) Mom? Okay. I'll lock up now. . . . What? . . . Oh, the brandy . . . Yes, I'll remember! . . . I'll put it in my suitcase now, for God's sake. I know well enough what will happen if he doesn't get it. . . . (*Places a bottle of brandy on the counter.*) I *was* kind to him, Mom. I didn't say anything nasty! . . . All right. Bye. (*End of telephone conversation. A desolate Hally doesn't move. A strained silence.*)

SAM (*quietly*). That sounded like a bad bump, Hally.

HALLY (*having a hard time controlling his emotions. He speaks carefully*). Mind your own business, Sam.

SAM. Sorry. I wasn't trying to interfere. Shall we carry on? Hally? (*He indicates the exercise book. No response from Hally.*)

WILLIE (*also trying*). Tell him about when they give out the cups, Boet Sam.

SAM. Ja! That's another big moment. The presentation of the cups after the winners have been announced. You've got to put that in.

(*Still no response from Hally.*)

WILLIE. A big silver one, Master Hally, called floating trophy for the champions.

SAM. We always invite some big-shot personality to hand them over. Guest of honor this year is going to be His Holiness Bishop Jabulani of the All African Free Zionist Church.

(*Hally gets up abruptly, goes to his table and tears up the page he was writing on.*)

HALLY. So much for a bloody world without collisions.

SAM. Too bad. It was on its way to being a good composition.

HALLY. Let's stop bullshitting ourselves, Sam.

SAM. Have we been doing that?

HALLY. Yes! That's what all our talk about a decent world has been . . . just so much bullshit.

SAM. We did say it was still only a dream.

HALLY. And a bloody useless one at that. Life's a fuckup and it's never going to change.

SAM. Ja, maybe that's true.

HALLY. There's no maybe about it. It's a blunt and brutal fact. All we've done this afternoon is waste our time.

SAM. Not if we'd got your homework done.

HALLY. I don't give a shit about my homework, so for Christ's sake, just shut up about it. (*Slamming books viciously into his school case.*) Hurry up now and finish your work. I want to lock up and get out of here. (*Pause.*) And then go where? Home-sweet-fucking-home. Jesus, I hate that word.

(*Hally goes to the counter to put the brandy bottle and comics in his school case. After a moment's hesitation, he smashes the bottle of brandy. He abandons all further attempts to hide his feelings. Sam and Willie work away as unobtrusively as possible.*)

Do you want to know what is really wrong with your lovely little dream, Sam? It's not just that we are all bad dancers. That does happen to be perfectly true, but there's more to it than just that. You left out the cripples.

SAM. Hally!

HALLY (*now totally reckless*). Ja! Can't leave them out, Sam. That's why we always end up on our backsides on the dance floor. They're also out there dancing . . . like a bunch of broken spiders trying to do the quickstep! (*An ugly attempt at laughter.*) When you come to think of it, it's a bloody comical sight. I mean, it's bad enough on two legs . . . but one and a pair of crutches! Hell, no, Sam. That's guaranteed to turn that dance floor into a shambles. Why you shaking your head? Picture it, man. For once this afternoon let's use our imaginations sensibly.

SAM. Be careful, Hally.

HALLY. Of what? The truth? I seem to be the only one around here who is prepared to face it. We've had the pretty dream, it's time now to wake up and have a good long look at the way things really are. Nobody knows the steps, there's no music, the cripples are also out there tripping up everybody and trying to get into the act, and it's all called the All-Comers-How-to-Make-a-Fuckup-of-Life Championships. (*Another ugly laugh.*) Hang on, Sam! The best bit is still coming. Do you know what the winner's trophy is? A beautiful big chamber pot with roses on the side, and it's full to the brim with piss. And guess who I think is going to be this year's winner.

SAM (*almost shouting*). Stop now!

HALLY (*suddenly appalled by how far he has gone*). Why?

SAM. Hally? It's your father you're talking about.

HALLY. So?

SAM. Do you know what you've been saying?

(*Hally can't answer. He is rigid with shame. Sam speaks to him sternly.*)

No, Hally, you mustn't do it. Take back those words and ask for forgiveness! It's a terrible sin for a son to mock his father with jokes like that. You'll be punished if you carry on. Your father is your father, even if he is a . . . cripple man.

WILLIE. Yes, Master Hally. Is true what Sam say.

SAM. I understand how you are feeling, Hally, but even so. . . .

HALLY. No, you don't!

SAM. I think I do.

HALLY. And I'm telling you you don't. Nobody does. (*Speaking carefully as his shame turns to rage at Sam*) It's your turn to be careful, Sam. Very careful! You're treading on dangerous ground. Leave me and my father alone.

SAM. I'm not the one who's been saying things about him.

HALLY. What goes on between me and my Dad is none of your business!

SAM. Then don't tell me about it. If that's all you've got to say about him, I don't want to hear.

(*For a moment Hally is at loss for a response.*)

HALLY. Just get on with your bloody work and shut up.

SAM. Swearing at me won't help you.

HALLY. Yes, it does! Mind your own fucking business and shut up!

SAM. Okay. If that's the way you want it. I'll stop trying.

(*He turns away. This infuriates Hally even more.*)

HALLY. Good. Because what you've been trying to do is meddle in something you know nothing about. All that concerns you in here, Sam, is to try and do what you get paid for—keep the place clean and serve the customers. In plain words, just get on with your job. My mother is right. She's always warning me about allowing you to get too familiar. Well, this time you've gone too far. It's going to stop right now.

(*No response from Sam.*)

You're only a servant in here, and don't forget it.

(*Still no response. Hally is trying hard to get one.*)

And as far as my father is concerned, all you need to remember is that he is your boss.

SAM (*needled at last*). No, he isn't. I get paid by your mother.

HALLY. Don't argue with me, Sam!

SAM. Then don't say he's my boss.

HALLY. He's a white man and that's good enough for you.

SAM. I'll try to forget you said that.

HALLY. Don't! Because you won't be doing me a favor if you do. I'm telling you to remember it.

(*A pause. Sam pulls himself together and makes one last effort.*)

SAM. Hally, Hally . . . ! Come on now. Let's stop before it's too late. You're right. We *are* on dangerous ground. If we're not careful, somebody is going to get hurt.

HALLY. It won't be me.

SAM. Don't be so sure.

HALLY. I don't know what you're talking about, Sam.

SAM. Yes, you do.

HALLY (*furious*). Jesus, I wish you would stop trying to tell me what I do and what I don't know.

(*Sam gives up. He turns to Willie.*)

SAM. Let's finish up.

HALLY. Don't turn your back on me! I haven't finished talking.

(*He grabs Sam by the arm and tries to make him turn around. Sam reacts with a flash of anger.*)

SAM. Don't do that, Hally! (*Facing the boy*) All right, I'm listening. Well? What do you want to say to me?

HALLY (*pause as Hally looks for something to say*). To begin with, why don't you also start calling me Master Harold, like Willie.

SAM. Do you mean it?

HALLY. Why the hell do you think I said it?

SAM. And if I don't?

HALLY. You might just lose your job.

SAM (*quietly and very carefully*). If you make me say it once, I'll never call you anything else again.

HALLY. So? (*The boy confronts the man.*) Is that meant to be a threat?

SAM. Just telling you what will happen if you make me do that. You must decide what it means to you.

HALLY. Well, I have. It's good news. Because that is exactly what Master Harold wants from now on. Think of it as a little lesson in respect, Sam, that's long overdue, and I hope you remember it as well as you do your geography. I can tell you now that somebody who will be glad to hear I've finally given it to you will be my Dad. Yes! He agrees with my Mom. He's always going on about it as well. "You must teach the boys to show you more respect, my son."

SAM. So now you can stop complaining about going home. Everybody is going to be happy tonight.

HALLY. That's perfectly correct. You see, you mustn't get the wrong idea about me and my Dad, Sam. We also have our good times together. Some bloody good laughs. He's got a marvelous sense of humor. Want to know what our favorite joke is? He gives out a big groan, you see, and says: "It's not fair, is it, Hally?" Then I have to ask: "What, chum?" And then he says: "A nigger's arse" . . . and we both have a good laugh.

(*The men stare at him with disbelief.*)

What's the matter, Willie? Don't you catch the joke? You always were a bit slow on the uptake. It's what is called a pun. You, see, fair means both light in color and to be just and decent. (*He turns to Sam.*) I thought *you* would catch it, Sam.

SAM. Oh ja, I catch it all right.

HALLY. But it doesn't appeal to your sense of humor.

SAM. Do you really laugh?

HALLY. Of course.

SAM. To please him? Make him feel good?

HALLY. No, for heavens sake! I laugh because I think it's a bloody good joke.

SAM. You're really trying hard to be ugly, aren't you? And why drag poor old Willie into it? He's done nothing to you except show you the respect you want so badly. That's also not being fair, you know ... and *I* mean just or decent.

WILLIE. It's all right, Sam. Leave it now.

SAM. It's me you're after. You should just have said "Sam's arse" ... because that's the one you're trying to kick. Anyway, how do you know it's not fair? You've never seen it. Do you want to? (*He drops his trousers and underpants and presents his backside for Hally's inspection.*) Have a good look. A real Basuto arse ... which is about as nigger as they can come. Satisfied? (*Trousers up.*) Now you can make your Dad even happier when you go home tonight. Tell him I showed you my arse and he is quite right. It's not fair. And if it will give him an even better laugh next time, I'll also let him have a look. Come, Willie, let's finish up and go.

(*Sam and Willie start to tidy up the tea room. Hally doesn't move. He waits for a moment when Sam passes him.*)

HALLY (*quietly*). Sam ...

(*Sam stops and looks expectantly at the boy. Hally spits in his face. A long and heartfelt groan from Willie. For a few seconds Sam doesn't move.*)

SAM (*taking out a handkerchief and wiping his face.*). It's all right, Willie.

(*To Hally*)

Ja, well, you've done it ... Master Harold. Yes, I'll start calling you that from now on. It won't be difficult anymore. You've hurt yourself, Master Harold. I saw it coming. I warned you, but you wouldn't listen. You've just hurt yourself bad. And you're a coward, Master Harold. The face you should be spitting in is your father's ... but you used mine, because you think you're safe inside your fair skin ... and this time I don't mean just or decent. (*Pause, then moving violently towards Hally*) Should I hit him, Willie?

WILLIE (*stopping Sam*). No, Boet Sam.

SAM (*violently*). Why not?

WILLIE. It won't help, Boet Sam.

SAM. I don't want to help! I want to hurt him.

WILLIE. You also hurt yourself.

SAM. And if he had done it to you, Willie?

WILLIE. Me? Spit at me like I was a dog? (*A thought that had not occurred to him before. He looks at Hally.*) Ja. Then I want to hit him. I want to hit him hard!

(*A dangerous few seconds as the men stand staring at the boy. Willie turns away, shaking his head.*)

But maybe all I do is go cry at the back. He's little boy, Boet Sam. Little *white* boy. Long trousers now, but he's still little boy.

SAM (*his violence ebbing away into defeat as quickly as it flooded*). You're right. So go on, then: groan again, Willie. You do it better than me. (*To Hally*) You don't know all of what you've just done ... Master Harold. It's not just that you've made me feel dirtier than I've ever been in my life ... I mean, how do I wash off yours and your father's filth? ... I've also failed. A long time ago I promised myself I was going to try and do something, but you've just shown me ... Master Harold ... that I've failed. (*Pause.*) I've also got a memory of a little white boy when he was still wearing short trousers and a black man, and they're not flying a kite. It was the old Jubilee days, after dinner one night. I was in my room. You came in and just stood against the wall, looking down at the ground, and only after I'd asked you what you wanted, what was wrong, I don't know how many times, did you speak and even then so softly I almost didn't hear you. "Sam, please help me to go and fetch my Dad." Remember? He was dead drunk on the floor of the Central Hotel Bar. They'd phoned for your Mom, but you were the only one at home. And do you remember how we did it? You went in first by yourself to ask permission for me to go into the bar. Then I loaded him onto my back like a baby and carried him back to the boarding house with you following behind carrying his crutches. (*Shaking his head as he remembers*) A crowded Main Street with all the people watching a little white boy following his drunk father on a nigger's back! I felt for that little boy ... Master Harold. I felt for him. After that we still had to clean him up, remember? He'd messed in his trousers, so we had to clean him up and get him into bed.

HALLY (*great pain*). I love him, Sam.

SAM. I know you do. That's why I tried to stop you from saying these things about him. It would have been so simple if you could have just despised him for being a weak man. But he's your father. You love him and you're ashamed of him. You're ashamed of so much! ... And now that's going to include yourself. That was the promise I made to myself: to try and stop that happening. (*Pause.*) After we got him to bed you came back with me to my room and sat in a corner and carried on just looking down at the ground. And for days after that! You hadn't done anything wrong, but you went around as if you owed the world an apology for being alive. I didn't like seeing that! That's not the way a boy grows up to be a man! . . . But the one person who should have been teaching you what that means was the cause of your shame. If you really want to know, that's why I made you that kite. I wanted you to look up, be proud of something, of yourself . . . (*bitter smile at the memory*) . . . and you certainly were that when I left you with it up there on the hill. Oh, ja . . . something else! . . . If you ever do write it as a short story, there was a twist in our ending. I couldn't sit down there and stay with you. It was a "Whites Only" bench. You were too young, too excited to notice then. But not anymore. If you're not careful . . . Master Harold . . . you're going to be sitting up there by yourself for a long time to come, and there won't be a kite in the sky. (*Sam has got nothing more to say. He exits into the kitchen, taking off his waiter's jacket.*)

WILLIE. Is bad. Is all bad in here now.

HALLY (*books into his school case, raincoat on*). Willie . . . (*It is difficult to speak.*) Will you lock up for me and look after the keys?

WILLIE. Okay.

(*Sam returns. Hally goes behind the counter and collects the few coins in the cash register. As he starts to leave . . .*)

SAM. Don't forget the comic books.

(*Hally returns to the counter and puts them in his case. He starts to leave again.*)

SAM (*to the retreating back of the boy*). Stop . . . Hally. . . .

(*Hally stops, but doesn't turn to face him.*)

Hally . . . I've got no right to tell you what being a man means if I don't behave like one myself, and I'm not doing so well at that this afternoon. Should we try again, Hally?

HALLY. Try what?

SAM. Fly another kite, I suppose. It worked once, and this time I need it as much as you do.

HALLY. It's still raining, Sam. You can't fly kites on rainy days, remember.

SAM. So what do we do? Hope for better weather tomorrow?

HALLY (*helpless gesture*). I don't know. I don't know anything anymore.

SAM. You sure of that, Hally? Because it would be pretty hopeless if that was true. It would mean nothing has been learnt in here this afternoon, and there was a hell of a lot of teaching going on . . . one way or the other. But anyway, I don't believe you. I reckon there's one thing you know. You don't have to sit up there by yourself. You know what that bench means now, and you can leave it any time you choose. All you've got to do is stand up and walk away from it.

(*Hally leaves. Willie goes up quietly to Sam.*)

WILLIE. Is okay, Boet Sam. You see. Is . . . (*He can't find any better words.*) . . . is going to be okay tomorrow. (*Changing his tone*) Hey, Boet Sam! (*He is trying hard.*) You right. I think about it and you right. Tonight I find Hilda and say sorry. And make promise I won't beat her no more. You hear me, Boet Sam?

SAM. I hear you, Willie.

WILLIE. And when we practice I relax and romance with her from beginning to end. Nonstop! You watch! Two weeks' time: "First prize for promising newcomers: Mr. Willie Malopo and Miss Hilda Samuels." (*Sudden impulse.*) To hell with it! I walk home. (*He goes to the jukebox, puts in a coin and selects a record. The machine comes to life in the gray twilight, blushing its way through a spectrum of soft, romantic colors.*) How did you say it, Boet Sam? Let's dream. (*Willie sways with the music and gestures for Sam to dance.*)

(*Sarah Vaughan sings*)

"Little man you're crying,
I know why you're blue,
Someone took your kiddy car away;
Better go to sleep now,
Little man you've had a busy day."
(*etc., etc.*)

You lead. I'll follow.

(*The men dance together.*)

"Johnny won your marbles,
Tell you what we'll do;
Dad will get you new ones right away;
Better go to sleep now,
Little man you've had a busy day."

TOPICS FOR DISCUSSION AND WRITING

1. Exactly what do you think is implied in the title? Why is *"MASTER HAROLD"* in capital letters and in quotation marks, while *and the boys* (separated by three dots from Harold) is in lowercase letters? Why "Harold" rather than Hally, since he is called Hally in the play? Why "boys" for grown men?
2. Compare Sam and Willie, making specific references to the text in order to support your characterizations.

3. Characterize Hally, taking account of his relationships to his parents as well as to Sam and Willie. In his autobiographical volume, *Notebooks,* Fugard tells how as an adolescent he spat at Sam "out of a spasm of acute loneliness." In your characterization of Hally you may want to discuss the degree (if any) to which loneliness helps to explain the boy's behavior.
4. The play is set in Fugard's native country, South Africa, in the 1950s. How closely does that world resemble the United States of the 1950s?
5. Can it be argued that the relationship dramatized in this play is not limited to South Africa in the 1950s but is essentially rooted in the situation, that is, in the relationship of employees to the child of the employer?
6. Early in the play (page 621), when Sam describes policemen whipping a prisoner, Hally says "People can be real bastards," and Sam replies, "That's the way it is, Hally." Does the play as a whole suggest that hostility and cruelty are "the way it is," despite Hally's belief that "there is something called progress, you know"? Later (page 627), speaking of his father's plan to leave the hospital, Hally says "This is not an age of miracles!" Is it legitimate to connect these passages, and to relate them to the theme of the play?
7. Why does Fugard introduce (pages 625–26) the episode of the kite?
8. On page 632 Sam cautions Hally, "Be careful." Exactly what is he cautioning Hally against? And what is Hally cautioning Sam against when he says (page 633) "Very careful! You're treading on dangerous ground"?
9. "Reversal" (Aristotle's *peripeteia*) and "recognition" (Aristotle's *anagnorisis*) are discussed in Some Kinds of Drama (pages 30–31), in the Glossary, and in Aristotle's essay (pages 70–75). Consider the relevance of these terms to this play.
10. In Mary McCarthy's novel *A Charmed Life,* one of the characters says that tragedies depict "growing pains." How apt a characterization is this of other tragedies that you have read, and of this play?
11. In your opinion, why does Fugard end the play not with Hally's final exit but with three speeches and a song?

A CONTEXT FOR *"MASTER HAROLD"... and the boys*

Notebooks 1960–1977

Athol Fugard

[The following entry from Fugard' s notebook is dated March 1961]

Sam Semela—Basuto—with the family fifteen years. Meeting him again when he visited Mom set off string of memories.

The kite which he produced for me one day during those early years when Mom ran the Jubilee Hotel and he was a waiter there. He had made it himself: brown paper, its ribs fashioned from thin strips of tomato-box plank which he had smoothed down, a paste of flour and water for glue. I was surprised and bewildered that he had made it for me.

I vaguely recall shyly 'haunting' the servants' quarters in the well of the hotel—cold, cement-grey world—the pungent mystery of the dark little rooms—a world I didn't understand. Frightened to enter any of the rooms. Sam, broad-faced, broader based—he smelled of woodsmoke. The 'kaffir smell' of South Africa is the smell of poverty—woodsmoke and sweat.

Later, when he worked for her at the Park café, Mom gave him the sack: '... he became careless. He came late for work. His work went to hell. He didn't seem to care no more.' I was about thirteen and served behind the counter while he waited on table.

Realize now he was the most significant—the only—friend of my boyhood years. On terrible windy days when no-one came to swim or walk in the park, we would sit together and talk. Or I was reading—Introductions to Eastern Philosophy or Plato and Socrates—and when I had finished he would take the book back to New Brighton.

Can't remember now what precipitated it, but one day there was a rare quarrel between Sam and myself. In a truculent silence we closed the café, Sam set off home to New Brighton on foot and I followed a few minutes later on my bike. I saw him walking ahead of me and, coming out of a spasm of acute loneliness, as I rode up behind him I called his name, he turned in mid-stride to look back and, as I cycled past, I spat in his face. Don't suppose I will ever deal with the shame that overwhelmed me the second after I had done that.

Now he is thin. We had a long talk. He told about the old woman ('Ma') whom he and his wife have taken in to look after their house while he goes to work—he teaches ballroom dancing. 'Ma' insists on behaving like a domestic—making Sam feel guilty and embarrassed. She brings him an early morning cup of coffee. Sam: 'No, Ma, you mustn't, man.' Ma: 'I must.' Sam: 'Look, Ma, if I want it, I can make it.' Ma: 'No, I must.'

Occasionally, when she is doing something, Sam feels like a cup of tea but is too embarrassed to ask her, and daren't make one for himself. Similarly, with his washing. After three days or a week away in other towns, giving dancing lessons, he comes back with under-clothes that are very dirty. He is too shy to give them out to be washed so washes them himself. When Ma sees this she goes and complains to Sam's wife that he doesn't trust her, that it's all wrong for him to do the washing.

Of tsotsis, he said: 'They grab a old man, stick him with a knife and ransack him. And so he must go to hospital and his kids is starving with hungry.' Of others: 'He's got some little moneys. So he is facing starvation for the weekend.'

Of township snobs, he says there are the educational ones: 'If you haven't been to the big school, like Fort Hare, what you say isn't true.' And the money ones: 'If you aren't selling shops or got a business or a big car, man, you're nothing.'

Sam's incredible theory about the likeness of those 'with the true seed of love'. Starts with Plato and Socrates—they were round. 'Man is being shrinking all the time. An Abe Lincoln, him too, taller, but that's because man is shrinking.' Basically, those with the true seed of love look the same—'It's in the eyes.'

He spoke admiringly of one man, a black lawyer in East London, an educated man—university background—who was utterly without snobbery, looking down on no-one—any man, educated or ignorant, rich or poor, was another *man* to him, another human being, to be respected, taken seriously, to be talked to, listened to.

'They' won't allow Sam any longer to earn a living as a dancing teacher. 'You must get a job!' One of his fellow teachers was forced to work at Fraser's Quarries.

Scene from the TV adaptation, "El Theatro Campesino Special: Los Vendidos."
(KNBC, Los Angeles, 1972.)

LUIS VALDEZ

Los Vendidos

Luis Valdez was born into a family of migrant farm workers in Delano, California, in 1940. After completing high school he entered San José State College on a scholarship. He wrote his first plays while still an undergraduate, and after receiving his degree (in English and drama) from San José in 1964 he joined the San Francisco Mime Troupe, a left-wing group that performed in parks and streets. Revolutionary in technique as well as in political content, the Mime Troupe rejected the traditional forms of drama and instead drew on the circus and the carnival.

In 1965 Valdez returned to Delano, California, where Cesar Chavez had organized a strike of farm workers and a boycott against grape growers. Here he established El Teatro Campesino (the Farm Workers' Theater), which at first specialized in doing short, improvised, satirical skits called *actos.* When the *teatro* moved to Del Ray, California, it expanded its repertoire beyond farm issues. In time, Valdez moved from *actos* to *mitos* (myths)—plays that drew on Aztec mythology, Mexican folklore, and Christianity—and then to *Zoot Suit,* a play that ran for many months in California and that became the first Mexican-American play to be produced on Broadway. More recently he wrote and directed a hit movie, *La Bamba,* and in 1991 received an award from the A.T. and T. Foundation for his musical, *Bandido.*

Los Vendidos was written in 1967, when Ronald Reagan was governor of California.

COMMENTARY

As the preceding biographical note indicates, Valdez has not stood still as a dramatist, but one thread that runs through his career is his vision of drama as politics, a form of art that may be used to help shape society. Such a view is scarcely modern; it can be found as early as Aristophanes (c. 450 to c. 385 B.C.), who used comedy as a way of scolding Athens on a variety of matters, from its schools of philosophy to its destructive colonial politics. Closer to our own age, we find Bernard Shaw (1856–1950) and Bertolt Brecht (1898–1956) insisting that they seek not to please us by showing the surface of reality but to change our ways of thinking and, especially, to change the structure of our society.

One form of political theater, *agitprop,* developed in the Soviet Union in the 1920s by the Department of Agitation and Propaganda, consisted of short episodic plays—skits or sketches, we might call them—with a strong Marxist thrust. The playwrights were not interested in presenting rounded, plausible characters, and they were not interested in developing a complicated plot. In short, these works were not at all like the realistic drama of late nineteenth-century Europe, which is still the dominant form of drama in the commercial American theater. Rather, they used stereotypical characters—the worker (good), the boss (bad), the Marxist journalist (good), and so on—and they juxtaposed them in simple (and strong) conflicts. These skits were performed not in well-equipped theaters, but in bare halls and in the streets. In the United States agitprop influenced the work of some dramatists in the 1930s, for instance Clifford

Odets and Langston Hughes, but probably the closest thing to it in this country was the guerilla theater of the 1960s, which used theater as a working-class weapon in the workers' war against the bourgeoisie.

Valdez was deeply influenced by both the leftist politics and the improvisatory methods of guerilla theater. His *actos,* performed in streets, on flatbed trucks at the edges of vineyards, in meeting halls, and on campuses, were developed with and for the striking workers in the California vineyards. The plays are, he says, "collaborative work," sketches that took shape as he worked with his actors. These actors were not professionals, or even trained amateurs; rather, they were unemployed farm workers who were persuaded that they could help their cause by taking roles in the *actos.* Their lack of theatrical training, along with the audience's lack of theatrical experience, meant that the roles had to be drawn fairly broadly, but this was not necessarily a disadvantage, any more than the exaggeration of a caricature is a disadvantage. A caricature (in a newspaper, for instance) can offer us enjoyment, and it may even stimulate us to think and to act in a certain way—it may move us (at least in a tiny degree) to vote against a particular candidate. Such a picture is not to be judged by its realism or, for that matter, by its subtlety.

The stereotypes that Valdez often employed in the *actos* are, he has said, political realities. According to this view, in essence a person is, say, an exploited farm worker or an exploiting grower. Subtle distinctions are unimportant. Thus, a boss may be shown wearing a pig mask and (in pantomime) driving a big car. The facts that few bosses really look like pigs and that many do not drive big cars are said to be irrelevant. The pig-boss, the play implies, is the essence of bosses. It should be mentioned, too, that the plays were intended not only to instill political ideas but also to entertain and to keep up the spirits of his audience (chiefly striking workers).

In short, Valdez sought to produce a revolutionary theater for and by workers. A truly revolutionary theater, he believed, could be produced *without* the use of traditional theatrical methods and *with* the aid of workers. In 1966 he wrote:

> If you want unbourgeois theater, find unbourgeois people to do it. Your head could burst open at the simplicity of the *acto* . . . but that's the way it is in Delano. Real theater lies in the excited laughter (or silence) of recognition in the audience, not in all the paraphernalia on the stage. Minus actors, the entire Teatro can be packed into one trunk, and when the Teatro goes on tour, the spirit of the Delano grape strikers goes with it.

Although *Los Vendidos* ("The Sellouts") is no less political than the earlier *actos,* the focus is no longer on striking farm laborers. Here it is on the Chicano's relation to Anglo culture. Further, *Los Vendidos* departs from earlier *actos* in not offering a solution to a condition that it reveals. Earlier *actos* had in effect said "Strike" or "Join the union," but *Los Vendidos* seems less concerned with proposing a solution than with showing contrasting kinds of Chicanos, although it is clear where Valdez's sympathies lie.

Note: What can be called Spanish-American or Hispanic theater has had a long history; it ranges from religious drama in the sixteenth century to classic drama and to vaudeville skits. For a detailed study, see Nicolás Kanellos, *A History of Hispanic Theatre in the United States: The Origins to 1940* (1990).

LUIS VALDEZ *Los Vendidos*[1]

List of Characters

HONEST SANCHO
SECRETARY
FARM WORKER
JOHNNY
REVOLUCIONARIO
MEXICAN-AMERICAN

Scene: Honest Sancho's Used Mexican Lot and Mexican Curio Shop. Three models are on display in Honest Sancho's shop: to the right, there is a Revolucionario, complete with sombrero, carrilleras[2] and carabina 30-30. At center, on the floor, there is the Farm Worker, under a broad straw sombrero. At stage left is the Pachuco,[3] filero[4] in hand.

(*Honest Sancho is moving among his models, dusting them off and preparing for another day of business.*)

SANCHO. Bueno, bueno, mis monos, vamos a ver a quien vendemos ajora, ¿no?[5] (*To audience.*) ¡Quihubo! I'm Honest Sancho and this is my shop. Antes fui contratista pero ahora logré tener mi negocito.[6] All I need now is a customer. (*A bell rings offstage.*) Ay, a customer!

SECRETARY (*Entering*). Good morning, I'm Miss Jiménez from—

SANCHO. ¡Ah, una chicana! Welcome, welcome Señorita Jiménez.

SECRETARY (*Anglo pronunciation*). JIM-enez.

SANCHO. ¿Qué?

SECRETARY. My name is Miss JIM-enez. Don't you speak English? What's wrong with you?

SANCHO. Oh, nothing, Señorita JIM-enez. I'm here to help you.

SECRETARY. That's better. As I was starting to say, I'm a secretary from Governor Reagan's office, and we're looking for a Mexican type for the administration.

SANCHO. Well, you come to the right place, lady. This is Honest Sancho's Used Mexican lot, and we got all types here. Any particular type you want?

SECRETARY. Yes, we were looking for somebody suave—

SANCHO. Suave.

SECRETARY. Debonair.

SANCHO. De buen aire.

SECRETARY. Dark.

SANCHO. Prieto.

SECRETARY. But of course not too dark.

SANCHO. No muy prieto.

SECRETARY. Perhaps, beige.

SANCHO. Beige, just the tone. Así como cafecito con leche,[7] ¿no?

SECRETARY. One more thing. He must be hard-working.

SANCHO. That could only be one model. Step right over here to the center of the shop, lady. (*They cross to the Farm Worker.*) This is our standard farm worker model. As you can see, in the words of our beloved Senator George Murphy, he is "built close to the ground." Also take special notice of his four-ply Goodyear huaraches, made from the rain tire. This wide-brimmed sombrero is an extra added feature—keeps off the sun, rain, and dust.

SECRETARY. Yes, it does look durable.

SANCHO. And our farm worker model is friendly. Muy amable.[8] Watch. (*Snaps his fingers.*)

FARM WORKER (*Lifts up head*). Buenos días, señorita. (*His head drops.*)

SECRETARY. My, he's friendly.

SANCHO. Didn't I tell you? Loves his patrones! But his most attractive feature is that he's hard working. Let me show you. (*Snaps fingers. Farm Worker stands.*)

FARM WORKER. ¡El jale![9] (*He begins to work.*)

SANCHO. As you can see, he is cutting grapes.

SECRETARY. Oh, I wouldn't know.

SANCHO. He also picks cotton. (*Snap. Farm Worker begins to pick cotton.*)

SECRETARY. Versatile isn't he?

SANCHO. He also picks melons. (*Snap. Farm Worker picks melons.*) That's his slow speed for late in the season. Here's his fast speed. (*Snap. Farm Worker picks faster.*)

SECRETARY. ¡Chihuahua! . . . I mean, goodness, he sure is a hard worker.

SANCHO (*Pulls the Farm Worker to his feet*). And that isn't the half of it. Do you see these little holes on his arms that appear to be pores? During those hot sluggish days in the field, when the vines or the branches get so entangled, it's almost impossible to move; these holes emit a certain grease that allow our model to slip and slide right through the crop with no trouble at all.

SECRETARY. Wonderful. But is he economical?

[1]**Los Vendidos** The Sellouts [2]**carrilleras** cartridge belts [3]**Pachuco** an urban tough guy [4]**filero** blade [5]**Bueno . . . no?** Well, well, my darlings, let's see who we can sell now, O.K.? [6]**Antes . . . negocito** I used to be a contractor, but now I've succeeded in having my little business.

[7]**Así . . . leche** Like coffee with milk [8]**Muy amable** Very friendly [9]**¡El jale!** The job

SANCHO. Economical? Señorita, you are looking at the Volkswagen of Mexicans. Pennies a day is all it takes. One plate of beans and tortillas will keep him going all day. That, and chile. Plenty of chile. Chile jalapeños, chile verde, chile colorado. But, of course, if you do give him chile (*Snap. Farm Worker turns left face. Snap. Farm Worker bends over.*) then you have to change his oil filter once a week.

SECRETARY. What about storage?

SANCHO. No problem. You know these new farm labor camps our Honorable Governor Reagan has built out by Parlier or Raisin City? They were designed with our model in mind. Five, six, seven, even ten in one of those shacks will give you no trouble at all. You can also put him in old barns, old cars, river banks. You can even leave him out in the field overnight with no worry!

SECRETARY. Remarkable.

SANCHO. And here's an added feature. Every year at the end of the season, this model goes back to Mexico and doesn't return, automatically, until next Spring.

SECRETARY. How about that. But tell me: does he speak English?

SANCHO. Another outstanding feature is that last year this model was programmed to go out on STRIKE! (*Snap.*)

FARM WORKER. ¡HUELGA! ¡HUELGA! Hermanos, sálganse de esos files.[10] (*Snap. He stops.*)

SECRETARY. No! Oh no, we can't strike in the State Capitol.

SANCHO. Well, he also scabs. (*Snap.*)

FARM WORKER. Me vendo barato, ¿y qué?[11] (*Snap.*)

SECRETARY. That's much better, but you didn't answer my question. Does he speak English?

SANCHO. Bueno ... no, pero[12] he has other—

SECRETARY. No.

SANCHO. Other features.

SECRETARY. NO! He just won't do!

SANCHO. Okay, okay pues. We have other models.

SECRETARY. I hope so. What we need is something a little more sophisticated.

SANCHO. Sophisti—¿qué?

SECRETARY. An urban model.

SANCHO. Ah, from the city! Step right back. Over here in this corner of the shop is exactly what you're looking for. Introducing our new 1969 JOHNNY PACHUCO model! This is our fast-back model. Streamlined. Built for speed, low-riding, city life. Take a look at some of these features. Mag shoes, dual exhausts, green chartreuse paint-job, dark-tint windshield, a little poof on top. Let me just turn him on. (*Snap. Johnny walks to stage center with a pachuco bounce.*)

SECRETARY. What was that?

SANCHO. That, señorita, was the Chicano shuffle.

SECRETARY. Okay, what does he do?

SANCHO. Anything and everything necessary for city life. For instance, survival. He knife fights. (*Snap. Johnny pulls out switch blade and swings at Secretary.*)

(*Secretary screams.*)

SANCHO. He dances. (*Snap.*)

JOHNNY (*Singing*). "Angel Baby, my Angel Baby ..." (*Snap.*)

SANCHO. And here's a feature no city model can be without. He gets arrested, but not without resisting, of course. (*Snap.*)

JOHNNY. ¡En la madre, la placa![13] I didn't do it! I didn't do it! (*Johnny turns and stands up against an imaginary wall, legs spread out, arms behind his back.*)

SECRETARY. Oh no, we can't have arrests! We must maintain law and order.

SANCHO. But he's bilingual!

SECRETARY. Bilingual?

SANCHO. Simón que yes.[14] He speaks English! Johnny, give us some English. (*Snap.*)

JOHNNY (*Comes downstage*). Fuck-you!

SECRETARY (*Gasps*). Oh! I've never been so insulted in my whole life!

SANCHO. Well, he learned it in your school.

SECRETARY. I don't care where he learned it.

SANCHO. But he's economical!

SECRETARY. Economical?

SANCHO. Nickels and dimes. You can keep Johnny running on hamburgers, Taco Bell tacos, Lucky Lager beer, Thunderbird wine, yesca—

SECRETARY. Yesca?

SANCHO. Mota.

SECRETARY. Mota?

SANCHO. Leños[15] ... Marijuana. (*Snap; Johnny inhales on an imaginary joint.*)

SECRETARY. That's against the law!

JOHNNY (*Big smile, holding his breath*). Yeah.

SANCHO. He also sniffs glue. (*Snap. Johnny inhales glue, big smile.*)

JOHNNY. Tha's too much man, ése.

SECRETARY. No, Mr. Sancho, I don't think this—

SANCHO. Wait a minute, he has other qualities I know you'll love. For example, an inferiority complex. (*Snap.*)

[10]**¡HUELGA! ... files** Strike! Strike! Brothers, leave those rows. [11]**Me ... qué?** I come cheap. So what [12]**Bueno ... no, pero** Well, no, but

[13]**¡En ... la placa!** Wow, the cops. [14]**Simón que yes** Yeah, ... sure [15]**Leños** Joints (*marijuana*)

JOHNNY (*To Sancho*). You think you're better than me, huh ése?[16] (*Swings switch blade.*)

SANCHO. He can also be beaten and he bruises, cut him and he bleeds; kick him and he— (*He beats, bruises and kicks Pachuco.*) would you like to try it?

SECRETARY. Oh, I couldn't.

SANCHO. Be my guest. He's a great scapegoat.

SECRETARY. No, really.

SANCHO. Please.

SECRETARY. Well, all right. Just once. (*She kicks Pachuco.*) Oh, he's so soft.

SANCHO. Wasn't that good? Try again.

SECRETARY (*Kicks Pachuco*). Oh, he's so wonderful! (*She kicks him again.*)

SANCHO. Okay, that's enough, lady. You ruin the merchandise. Yes, our Johnny Pachuco model can give you many hours of pleasure. Why, the L.A.P.D. just bought twenty of these to train their rookie cops on. And talk about maintenance. Señorita, you are looking at an entirely self-supporting machine. You're never going to find our Johnny Pachuco model on the relief rolls. No, sir, this model knows how to liberate.

SECRETARY. Liberate?

SANCHO. He steals. (*Snap. Johnny rushes the Secretary and steals her purse.*)

JOHNNY. ¡Dame esa bolsa, vieja![17] (*He grabs the purse and runs. Snap by Sancho. He stops.*)

(*Secretary runs after Johnny and grabs purse away from him, kicking him as she goes.*)

SECRETARY. No, no, no! We can't have any *more* thieves in the State Administration. Put him back.

SANCHO. Okay, we still got other models. Come on, Johnny, we'll sell you to some old lady. (*Sancho takes Johnny back to his place.*)

SECRETARY. Mr. Sancho, I don't think you quite understand what we need. What we need is something that will attract the women voters. Something more traditional, more romantic.

SANCHO. Ah, a lover. (*He smiles meaningfully.*) Step right over here, señorita. Introducing our standard Revolucionario and/or Early California Bandit type. As you can see he is well-built, sturdy, durable. This is the International Harvester of Mexicans.

SECRETARY. What does he do?

SANCHO. You name it, he does it. He rides horses, stays in the mountains, crosses deserts, plains, rivers, leads revolutions, follows revolutions, kills, can be killed, serves as a martyr, hero, movie star—did I say movie star? Did you ever see *Viva Zapata*? *Viva Villa*? *Villa Rides*? *Pancho Villa Returns*? *Pancho Villa Goes Back*? *Pancho Villa Meets Abbott and Costello—*

SECRETARY. I've never seen any of those.

SANCHO. Well, he was in all of them. Listen to this. (*Snap.*)

REVOLUCIONARIO (*Scream*). ¡VIVA VILLAAAAA!

SECRETARY. That's awfully loud.

SANCHO. He has a volume control. (*He adjusts volume. Snap.*)

REVOLUCIONARIO (*Mousey voice*). ¡Viva Villa!

SECRETARY. That's better.

SANCHO. And even if you didn't see him in the movies, perhaps you saw him on TV. He makes commercials. (*Snap.*)

REVOLUCIONARIO. Is there a Frito Bandito in your house?

SECRETARY. Oh yes, I've seen that one!

SANCHO. Another feature about this one is that he is economical. He runs on raw horsemeat and tequila!

SECRETARY. Isn't that rather savage?

SANCHO. Al contrario,[18] it makes him a lover. (*Snap.*)

REVOLUCIONARIO (*To Secretary*). ¡Ay, mamasota, cochota, ven pa'ca![19] (*He grabs Secretary and folds her back—Latin-Lover style.*)

SANCHO (*Snap. Revolucionario goes back upright.*). Now wasn't that nice?

SECRETARY. Well, it was rather nice.

SANCHO. And finally, there is one outstanding feature about this model I KNOW the ladies are going to love. He's a GENUINE antique! He was made in Mexico in 1910!

SECRETARY. Made in Mexico?

SANCHO. That's right. Once in Tijuana, twice in Guadalajara, three times in Cuernavaca.

SECRETARY. Mr. Sancho, I thought he was an American product.

SANCHO. No, but—

SECRETARY. No, I'm sorry. We can't buy anything but American-made products. He just won't do.

SANCHO. But he's an antique!

SECRETARY. I don't care. You still don't understand what we need. It's true we need Mexican models such as these, but it's more important that he be American.

SANCHO. American?

SECRETARY. That's right. and judging from what you've shown me, I don't think you have what we want. Well, my lunch hour's almost over; I better—

SANCHO. Wait a minute! Mexican but American?

[16]**ése** fellow [17]**¡Dame . . . vieja!** Give me that bag, old lady!

[18]**Al contrario** On the contrary [19]**¡Ay . . . pa'ca!** get over here!

SECRETARY. That's correct.

SANCHO. Mexican but . . . (*A sudden flash.*) AMERICAN! Yeah, I think we've got exactly what you want. He just came in today! Give me a minute. (*He exits. Talks from backstage.*) Here he is in the shop. Let me just get some papers off. There. Introducing our new 1970 Mexican-American! Ta-ra-ra-ra-ra-ra-RA-RAAA!

(*Sancho brings out the Mexican-American model, a clean-shaven middle-class type in a business suit, with glasses.*)

SECRETARY (*Impressed*). Where have you been hiding this one?

SANCHO. He just came in this morning. Ain't he a beauty? Feast your eyes on him! Sturdy US STEEL frame, streamlined, modern. As a matter of fact, he is built exactly like our Anglo models except that he comes in a variety of darker shades: naugahyde, leather, or leatherette.

SECRETARY. Naugahyde.

SANCHO. Well, we'll just write that down. Yes, señorita, this model represents the apex of American engineering! He is bilingual, college educated, ambitious! Say the word "acculturate" and he accelerates. He is intelligent, well-mannered, clean—did I say clean? (*Snap. Mexican-American raises his arm.*) Smell.

SECRETARY (*Smells*). Old Sobaco, my favorite.

SANCHO (*Snap. Mexican-American turns toward Sancho.*). Eric! (*To Secretary.*) We call him Eric García. (*To Eric.*) I want you to meet Miss JIM-enez, Eric.

MEXICAN-AMERICAN. Miss JIM-enez, I am delighted to make your acquaintance. (*He kisses her hand.*)

SECRETARY. Oh, my, how charming!

SANCHO. Did you feel the suction? He has seven especially engineered suction cups right behind his lips. He's a charmer all right!

SECRETARY. How about boards? Does he function on boards?

SANCHO. You name them, he is on them. Parole boards, draft boards, school boards, taco quality control boards, surf boards, two-by-fours.

SECRETARY. Does he function in politics?

SANCHO. Señorita, you are looking at a political MACHINE. Have you ever heard of the OEO, EOC, COD, WAR ON POVERTY? That's our model! Not only that, he makes political speeches.

SECRETARY. May I hear one?

SANCHO. With pleasure. (*Snap.*) Eric, give us a speech.

MEXICAN-AMERICAN. Mr. Congressman, Mr. Chairman, members of the board, honored guests, ladies and gentlemen. (*Sancho and Secretary applaud.*) Please, please. I come before you as a Mexican-American to tell you about the problems of the Mexican. The problems of the Mexican stem from one thing and one thing alone. He's stupid. He's uneducated. He needs to stay in school. He needs to be ambitious, forward-looking, harder-working. He needs to think American, American, American, AMERICAN, AMERICAN, AMERICAN. GOD BLESS AMERICA! GOD BLESS AMERICA! GOD BLESS AMERICA!! (*He goes out of control.*)

(*Sancho snaps frantically and the Mexican-American finally slumps forward, bending at the waist.*)

SECRETARY. Oh my, he's patriotic too!

SANCHO. Sí, señorita, he loves his country. Let me just make a little adjustment here. (*Stands Mexican-American up.*)

SECRETARY. What about upkeep? Is he economical?

SANCHO. Well, no, I won't lie to you. The Mexican-American costs a little bit more, but you get what you pay for. He's worth every extra cent. You can keep him running on dry Martinis, Langendorf bread.

SECRETARY. Apple pie?

SANCHO. Only Mom's. Of course, he's also programmed to eat Mexican food on ceremonial functions, but I must warn you: an overdose of beans will plug up his exhaust.

SECRETARY. Fine! There's just one more question. HOW MUCH DO YOU WANT FOR HIM?

SANCHO. Well, I tell you what I'm gonna do. Today and today only, because you've been so sweet, I'm gonna let you steal this model from me! I'm gonna let you drive him off the lot for the simple price of—let's see taxes and license included—$15,000.

SECRETARY. Fifteen thousand DOLLARS? For a MEXICAN!

SANCHO. Mexican? What are you talking, lady? This is a Mexican-AMERICAN! We had to melt down two pachucos, a farm worker and three gabachos[20] to make this model! You want quality, but you gotta pay for it! This is no cheap run-about. He's got class!

SECRETARY. Okay, I'll take him.

SANCHO. You will?

SECRETARY. Here's your money.

SANCHO. You mind if I count it?

SECRETARY. Go right ahead.

SANCHO. Well, you'll get your pink slip in the mail. Oh, do you want me to wrap him up for you? We have a box in the back.

SECRETARY. No, thank you. The Governor is having a

[20]**gabachos** whites

luncheon this afternoon, and we need a brown face in the crowd. How do I drive him?

SANCHO. Just snap your fingers. He'll do anything you want.

(*Secretary snaps. Mexican-American steps forward.*)

MEXICAN-AMERICAN. RAZA QUERIDA, ¡VAMOS LEVANTANDO ARMAS PARA LIBERARNOS DE ESTOS DESGRACIADOS GABACHOS QUE NOS EXPLOTAN! VAMOS.[21]

SECRETARY. What did he say?

SANCHO. Something about lifting arms, killing white people, etc.

SECRETARY. But he's not supposed to say that!

SANCHO. Look, lady, don't blame me for bugs from the factory. He's your Mexican-American; you bought him, now drive him off the lot!

SECRETARY. But he's broken!

SANCHO. Try snapping another finger.

(*Secretary snaps. Mexican-American comes to life again.*)

MEXICAN-AMERICAN. ¡ESTA GRAN HUMANIDAD HA DICHO BASTA! Y SE HA PUESTO EN MARCHA! ¡BASTA! ¡BASTA! ¡VIVA LA RAZA! ¡VIVA LA CAUSA! ¡VIVA LA HUELGA! ¡VIVAN LOS BROWN BERETS! ¡VIVAN LOS ESTUDIANTES![22] ¡CHICANO POWER!

(*The Mexican-American turns toward the Secretary, who gasps and backs up. He keeps turning toward the Pachuco, Farm Worker, and Revolucionario, snapping his fingers and turning each of them on, one by one.*)

PACHUCO (*Snap. To Secretary*). I'm going to get you, baby! ¡Viva La Raza!

FARM WORKER (*Snap. To Secretary*). ¡Viva la huelga! ¡Viva la Huelga! ¡VIVA LA HUELGA!

REVOLUCIONARIO (*Snap. To Secretary*). ¡Viva la revolución! ¡VIVA LA REVOLUCIÓN!

(*The three models join together and advance toward the Secretary who backs up and runs out of the shop screaming. Sancho is at the other end of the shop holding his money in his hand. All freeze. After a few seconds of silence, the Pachuco moves and stretches, shaking his arms and loosening up. The Farm Worker and Revolucionario do the same. Sancho stays where he is, frozen to his spot.*)

JOHNNY. Man, that was a long one, ése.[23] (*Others agree with him.*)

FARM WORKER. How did we do?

JOHNNY. Perty good, look all that lana,[24] man! (*He goes over to Sancho and removes the money from his hand. Sancho stays where he is.*)

REVOLUCIONARIO. En la madre, look at all the money.

JOHNNY. We keep this up, we're going to be rich.

FARM WORKER. They think we're machines.

REVOLUCIONARIO. Burros.

JOHNNY. Puppets.

MEXICAN-AMERICAN. The only thing I don't like is—how come I always got to play the godamn Mexican-American?

JOHNNY. That's what you get for finishing high school.

FARM WORKER. How about our wages, ése?

JOHNNY. Here it comes right now. $3,000 for you, $3,000 for you, $3,000 for you, and $3,000 for me. The rest we put back into the business.

MEXICAN-AMERICAN. Too much, man. Heh, where you vatos[25] going tonight?

FARM WORKER. I'm going over to Concha's. There's a party.

JOHNNY. Wait a minute, vatos. What about our salesman? I think he needs an oil job.

REVOLUCIONARIO. Leave him to me.

(*The Pachuco, Farm Worker, and Mexican-American exit, talking loudly about their plans for the night. The Revolucionario goes over to Sancho, removes his derby hat and cigar, lifts him up and throws him over his shoulder. Sancho hangs loose, lifeless.*)

REVOLUCIONARIO (*To audience*). He's the best model we got! ¡Ajua![26]

(*Exit.*)

(*End.*)

[21] **RAZA . . . VAMOS.** Beloved Raza [persons of Mexican descent], let's take up arms to liberate ourselves from those damned whites who exploit us. Let's get going. [22] **¡ESTA . . . ESTUDIANTES!** This great mass of humanity has said enough! And it has begun to march. Enough! Enough! Long live La Raza! Long live the Cause! Long live the strike! Long live the Brown Berets! Long live the students! [23] **ése** man [24] **lana** money [25] **vatos** guys [26] **¡Ajua!** Wow!

TOPICS FOR DISCUSSION AND WRITING

1. If you are an Anglo (shorthand for a Caucasian with traditional Northern European values), do you find the play deeply offensive? Why, or why not? If you are a Mexican-American, do you find the play entertaining—or do you find parts of it offensive? What might Anglos enjoy in the play, and what might Mexican-Americans find offensive?
2. What stereotypes of Mexican-Americans are presented here? At the end of the play what image of the Mexican-American is presented? How does it compare with the stereotypes?
3. If you are a member of some other minority group, in a few sentences indicate how *Los Vendidos* might be adapted into a play about that group.
4. Putting aside the politics of the play (and your own politics), what do you think are the strengths of *Los Vendidos*? What do you think are the weaknesses?
5. The play was written in 1967. Putting aside a few specific references, for instance to Governor Reagan, do you find it dated? If not, why not?
6. When the play was videotaped by KNBC in Los Angeles for broadcast in 1973, Valdez changed the ending. In the revised version we discover that a scientist (played by Valdez) masterminds the operation, placing Mexican-American models wherever there are persons of Mexican descent. These models soon will become Chicanos (as opposed to persons with Anglo values) and will aid rather than work against their fellows. Evaluate this ending.
7. In 1971 when *Los Vendidos* was produced by El Teatro de la Esperanza, the group altered the ending by having the men decide to use the money to build a community center. Evaluate this ending.
8. In his short essay, "The Actos," Valdez says that *actos* "Inspire the audience to social action. Illuminate specific points about social problems. Satirize the opposition. Show or hint at a solution. Express what people are feeling." How much of this do you think *Los Vendidos* does?
9. Many people assume that politics gets in the way of serious art. That is, they assume that artists ought to be concerned with issues that transcend politics. Does this point make any sense to you? Why or why not?

A CONTEXT FOR *LOS VENDIDOS*

The Actos

Luis Valdez

Nothing represents the work of El Teatro Campesino (and other teatros Chicanos) better than the acto. In a sense, the acto is Chicano theatre, though we are now moving into a new, more mystical dramatic form we have begun to call the mito. The two forms are, in fact, cuates[1] that complement and balance each other as day goes into night, el sol la sombra, la vida la muerte, el pájaro la serpiente.[2] Our rejection of white western Europe (gabacho) proscenium theatre makes the birth of new Chicano forms necessary, thus, los actos y los mitos; one through the eyes of man, the other through the eyes of God.

The actos were born quite matter of factly in Delano. Nacieron hambrientos de la realidad. Anything and everything that pertained to the daily life, la vida cotidiana, of the huelguistas[3] became food for thought, material for actos. The reality of campesinos on strike had become dramatic, (and theatrical as reflected by newspapers, TV newscasts, films, etc.) and so the actos merely reflected the reality. Huelguistas portrayed huelguistas, drawing their improvised dialogue from real words they exchanged with the esquiroles (scabs) in the fields everyday.[4]

"Hermanos, compañeros, sálganse de esos files."
"Tenemos comida y trabajo para ustedes afuera de la huelga."
"Esquirol, ten verguenza."
"Unidos venceremos."
"¡Sal de ahi barrigón!"

The first huelguista to portray an esquirol in the teatro

[1] **cuates** twins [2] **el sol . . . serpiente** sun and shade, life and death, the bird and the serpent

[3] **huelguistas** strikers [4] The following five lines of dialogue can be translated thus: Brothers, friends, leave those rows. / We have food and work for you outside of the strike. / Scab, you ought to be ashamed. / United we will conquer. / Get out of here, fatso.

did it to settle a score with a particularly stubborn scab he had talked with in the fields that day. Satire became a weapon that was soon aimed at known and despised contractors, growers and mayordomos. The effect of those early actos on the huelguistas de Delano packed into Filipino Hall was immediate, intense and cathartic. The actos rang true to the reality of the huelga.

Looking back at those early, crude, vital, beautiful, powerful actos of 1965, certain things have now become clear about the dramatic form we were just beginning to develop. There was, of course, no conscious deliberate plan to develop the acto as such. Even the name we gave our small presentations reflects the hard pressing expediency under which we worked from day to day. We could have called them "skits," but we lived and talked in San Joaquin Valley Spanish (with a strong Tejano influence), so we needed a name that made sense to the raza. Cuadros, pasquines, autos, entremeses[5] all seemed too highly intellectualized. We began to call them actos for lack of a better word, lack of time and lack of interest in trying to sound like classical Spanish scholars. De todos modos éramos raza, ¿quién se iba a fijar?[6]

The acto, however, developed its own structure through five years of experimentation. It evolved into a short dramatic form now used primarily by los teatros de Aztlán, but utilized to some extent by other non-Chicano guerrilla theatre companies throughout the U.S., including the San Francisco Mime Troupe and the Bread and Puppet Theatre. (Considerable creative crossfeeding has occurred on other levels, I might add, between the Mime Troupe, the Bread and Puppet and the Campesino.) Each of these groups may have their own definition of the acto, but the following are some of the guidelines we have established for ourselves over the years:

Actos: Inspire the audience to social action. Illuminate specific points about social problems. Satirize the opposition. Show or hint at a solution. Express what people are feeling.

So what's new, right? Plays have been doing that for thousands of years. True, except that the major emphasis in the acto is the social vision, as opposed to the individual artist or playwright's vision. Actos are not written; they are created collectively, through improvisation by a group. The reality reflected in an acto is thus a social reality, whether it pertains to campesinos or to batos locos, not psychologically deranged self-projections, but rather, group archetypes. Don Sotaco, Don Coyote, Johnny Pachuco, Juan Raza, Jorge el Chingón, la Chicana, are all group archetypes that have appeared in actos.

The usefulness of the acto extended well beyond the huelga into the Chicano movement, because Chicanos in general want to identify themselves as a group. The teatro archtypes symbolize the desire for unity and group identity through Chicano heroes and heroines. One character can thus represent the entire Raza, and the Chicano audience will gladly respond to his triumphs or defeats. What to a non-Chicano audience may seem like oversimplification in an acto, is to the Chicano a true expression of his social state and therefore reality.

[5]**Cuadros . . . entremeses** various Spanish words for short plays [6]**De todos . . . fijar?** In all ways we are the Race (i.e., indigenous Americans mixed with European and African blood); who was going to pay attention?

Kathy Bates as Jessie and Anne Pitoniak as Mama in a scene from the American Repertory Theatre production of *'night, Mother.* (Photograph: Richard Feldman, courtesy of the American Repertory Theatre Company Inc., Cambridge, MA.)

MARSHA NORMAN

'night, Mother

Marsha Norman was born in Louisville, Kentucky, in 1947. After receiving a bachelor's degree from Agnes Scott College and a master of arts in teaching from the University of Louisville, she taught gifted children and disturbed children. Her reputation as a playwright was established with a two-act play, *Getting Out*, which was produced in Louisville (1977) and subsequently in New York (1978). *'night, Mother*, which had its world premiere in Cambridge, Massachusetts, in 1983, won the Pulitzer Prize for drama in that year.

COMMENTARY

First, a few words about women as playwrights. Although in England in the late seventeenth century a woman, Aphra Behn, was one of the most popular playwrights, and although in America in the mid-nineteenth century another woman, Anna Cora Mowatt, wrote *Fashion*, the best-known social comedy of the period, it is nevertheless true that very few women wrote for the theater until about 1915. And even when women did achieve some prominence as playwrights in the earlier twentieth century (for instance, Anne Nichols, author of the immensely popular *Abie's Irish Rose* [1922], and Lillian Hellman and Clare Boothe Luce in the 1930s), their plays usually did not reveal a distinctly feminist point of view. Nor were they (especially Hellman) noticeably sympathetic in their characterizations of women. In short, despite some important exceptions, women have not played a large role as writers for the theater, even though, of course, many women have made great contributions to the theater as actresses.

Honor Moore, in *The New Women's Theatre*, suggests an explanation: theater (unlike writing fiction or poetry) is a communal activity, and men have not welcomed women into this community. "Male exclusion of women," she says, "perhaps more than any other single factor, has been responsible for the lack of a female tradition in playwriting similar to that which exists in both fiction and poetry." Then, too, writing for the theater requires larger chunks of time—for instance, whole days at early rehearsals—than most women in the past, tied to households, were able to spare.

In any case, not until the late 1960s, as part of the women's movement, did a substantial number of women begin to set forth on the stage a drama of feminine sensibility—writing, for example, about the difficult business of surviving as a woman in a man's world. As Eve Merriam said in 1976, surveying playwrighting since 1960, "First you had to write an Arthur Miller play, then you had to write an absurd play. Now there is a new freedom—you can write empathetic women characters."

Now we'll look very briefly at Marsha Norman's play. In our introductory words to *Death of a Salesman* (p. 551), where we sketch the rise of the middle class, we mention that the ideas of Copernicus, Darwin, and Freud have contributed to the view that human beings are "lust-ridden, soulless creatures in a terrifying materialistic universe." In contrast to this somewhat despairing view, Marsha Norman gives us a figure whom she sees as very strong. In an interview published in *Interviews with Contemporary Women Playwrights* (eds. Kathleen Betsko and Rachel Koenig), Norman said that Jessie achieves a "nearly total triumph. Jessie is able to get what she feels she needs. It may look despairing from the outside, but it has cost her everything she has. If Jessie says it is worth it, it is."

In this quotation Norman is pretty much saying that Jessie is a traditional tragic hero, someone who ventures boldly and, in a way, turns apparent material defeat into some sort of spiritual triumph. Interestingly, the very success of Norman's play brought fairly widespread criticism from persons interested in the development of women's theater. The two chief objections are somewhat contradictory: (1) *'night, Mother* suggests that women are self-destructive neurotics; (2) *'night, Mother* is just another drama in the male tradition—that is, it emphasizes the heroism of the isolated individual and it ignores the strength, born out of communal action, a kind of action that many women today regard as necessary if they are to escape from the assigned roles of housewife and sexual object. (Many feminist theater groups reject the usual hierarchical structure—a director dominating actors, designers, and technicians—in favor of a leaderless group.)

MARSHA NORMAN *'night, Mother*

List of Characters

JESSIE CATES, *in her late thirties or early forties, is pale and vaguely unsteady physically. It is only in the last year that Jessie has gained control of her mind and body, and tonight she is determined to hold on to that control. She wears pants and a long black sweater with deep pockets, which contain scraps of paper, and there may be a pencil behind her ear or a pen clipped to one of the pockets of the sweater.*

As a rule, Jessie doesn't feel much like talking. Other people have rarely found her quirky sense of humor amusing. She has a peaceful energy on this night, a sense of purpose, but is clearly aware of the time passing moment by moment. Oddly enough, Jessie has never been as communicative or as enjoyable as she is on this evening, but we must know she has not always been this way. There is a familiarity between these two women that comes from having lived together for a long time. There is a shorthand to the talk and a sense of routine comfort in the way they relate to each other physically. Naturally, there are also routine aggravations.

THELMA CATES, "MAMA," *is Jessie's mother, in her late fifties or early sixties. She has begun to feel her age and so takes it easy when she can, or when it serves her purpose to let someone help her. But she speaks quickly and enjoys talking. She believes that things are what she says they are. Her sturdiness is more a mental quality than a physical one, finally. She is chatty and nosy, and this is* her *house.*

The play takes place in a relatively new house built way out on a country road, with a living room and connecting kitchen, and a center hall that leads off to the bedrooms. A pull cord in the hall ceiling releases a ladder which leads to the attic. One of these bedrooms opens directly onto the hall, and its entry should be visible to everyone in the audience. It should be, in fact, the focal point of the entire set, and the lighting should make it disappear completely at times and draw the entire set into it at others. It is a point of both threat and promise. It is an ordinary door that opens onto absolute nothingness. That door is the point of all the action, and the utmost care should be given to its design and construction.

The living room is cluttered with magazines and needlework catalogues, ashtrays and candy dishes. Examples of Mama's needlework are everywhere—pillows, afghans, and quilts, doilies and rugs, and they are quite nice examples. The house is more comfortable than messy, but there is quite a lot to keep in place here. It is more personal than charming. It is not quaint. Under no circumstances should the set and its dressing make a judgment about the intelligence or taste of Jessie and Mama. It should simply indicate that they are very specific real people who happen to live in a particular part of the country. Heavy accents, which would further distance the audience from Jessie and Mama, are also wrong.

The time is the present, with the action beginning about 8:15. Clocks onstage in the kitchen and on a table in the living room should run throughout the performance and be visible to the audience.

There will be no intermission.

Mama stretches to reach the cupcakes in a cabinet in the kitchen. She can't see them, but she can feel around for them, and she's eager to have one, so she's working pretty hard at it. This may be the most serious exercise Mama ever gets. She finds a cupcake, the coconut-covered, raspberry-and-marshmallow-filled kind known as a snowball, but sees that there's one missing from the package. She calls to Jessie, who is apparently somewhere else in the house.

MAMA (*unwrapping the cupcake*). Jessie, it's the last snowball, sugar. Put it on the list, O.K.? And we're out of Hershey bars, and where's that peanut brittle? I think maybe Dawson's been in it again. I ought to put a big mirror on the refrigerator door. That'll keep him out of my treats, won't it? You hear me, honey? (*Then more to herself*) I hate it when the coconut falls off. Why does the coconut fall off?

(*Jessie enters from her bedroom, carrying a stack of newspapers.*)

JESSIE. We got any old towels?

MAMA. There you are!

JESSIE (*holding a towel that was on the stack of newspapers*). Towels you don't want anymore. (*Picking up Mama's snowball wrapper*) How about this swimming towel Loretta gave us? Beach towel, that's the name of it. You want it? (*Mama shakes her head no.*)

MAMA. What have you been doing in there?

JESSIE. And a big piece of plastic, like a rubber sheet or something. Garbage bags would do if there's enough.

MAMA. Don't go making a big mess, Jessie. It's eight o'clock already.

JESSIE. Maybe an old blanket or towels we got in a soap box sometime?

MAMA. I said don't make a mess. Your hair is black enough, hon.

JESSIE (*continuing to search the kitchen cabinets, finding two or three more towels to add to her stack*). It's not for my hair, Mama. What about some old pillows anywhere, or a foam cushion out of a yard chair would be real good.

MAMA. You haven't forgot what night it is, have you? (*Holding up her fingernails*) They're all chipped, see? I've been waiting all week, Jess. It's Saturday night, sugar.

JESSIE. I know. I got it on the schedule.

MAMA (*crossing to the living room*). You want me to wash 'em now or are you making your mess first? (*Looking at the snowball*) We're out of these. Did I say that already?

JESSIE. There's more coming tomorrow. I ordered you a whole case.

MAMA (*checking the* TV Guide). A whole case will go stale, Jessie.

JESSIE. They can go in the freezer till you're ready for them. Where's Daddy's gun?

MAMA. In the attic.

JESSIE. Where in the attic? I looked your whole nap and couldn't find it anywhere.

MAMA. One of his shoeboxes, I think.

JESSIE. Full of shoes. I looked already.

MAMA. Well, you didn't look good enough, then. There's that box from the ones he wore to the hospital. When he died, they told me I could have them back, but I never did like those shoes.

JESSIE (*pulling them out of her pocket*). I found the bullets. They were in an old milk can.

MAMA (*as Jessie starts for the hall*). Dawson took the shotgun, didn't he? Hand me that basket, hon.

JESSIE (*getting the basket for her*). Dawson better not've taken that pistol.

MAMA (*stopping her again*). Now my glasses, please. (*Jessie returns to get the glasses.*) I told him to take those rubber boots, too, but he said they were for fishing. I told him to take up fishing.

(*Jessie reaches for the cleaning spray, and cleans Mama's glasses for her.*)

JESSIE. He's just too lazy to climb up there,

MAMA. Or maybe he's just being smart. That floor's not very steady.

MAMA (*getting out a piece of knitting*). It's not a floor at all, hon, it's a board now and then. Measure this for me. I need six inches.

JESSIE (*as she measures*). Dawson could probably use some of those clothes up there. Somebody should have them. You ought to call the Salvation Army before the whole thing falls in on you. Six inches exactly.

MAMA. It's plenty safe! As long as you don't go up there.

JESSIE (*turning to go again*). I'm careful.

MAMA. What do you want the gun for, Jess?

JESSIE (*not returning this time. Opening the ladder in the hall*). Protection. (*She steadies the ladder as Mama talks.*)

MAMA. You take the TV way too serious, hon. I've never seen a criminal in my life. This is way too far to come for what's out here to steal. Never seen a one.

JESSIE (*taking her first step up*). Except for Ricky.

MAMA. Ricky is mixed up. That's not a crime.

JESSIE. Get your hands washed. I'll be right back. And get 'em real dry. You dry your hands till I get back or it's no go, all right?

MAMA. I thought Dawson told you not to go up those stairs.

JESSIE (*going up*). He did.

MAMA. I don't like the idea of a gun, Jess.

JESSIE (*calling down from the attic*). Which shoebox, do you remember?

MAMA. Black.

JESSIE. The box was black?

MAMA. The shoes were black.

JESSIE. That doesn't help much, Mother.

MAMA. I'm not trying to help, sugar. (*No answer.*) We don't have anything anybody'd want, Jessie. I mean, I don't even want what we got, Jessie.

JESSIE. Neither do I. Wash your hands. (*Mama gets up and crosses to stand under the ladder.*)

MAMA. You come down from there before you have a fit. I can't come up and get you, you know.

JESSIE. I know.

MAMA. We'll just hand it over to them when they come, how's that? Whatever they want, the criminals.

JESSIE. That's a good idea, Mama.

MAMA. Ricky will grow out of this and be a real fine boy, Jess. But I have to tell you, I wouldn't want Ricky to know we had a gun in the house.

JESSIE. Here it is. I found it.

MAMA. It's just something Ricky's going through. Maybe he's in with some bad people. He just needs some time, sugar. He'll get back in school or get a job or one day you'll get a call and he'll say he's sorry for all the trouble he's caused and invite you out for supper someplace dress-up.

JESSIE (*coming back down the steps*). Don't worry. It's not for him, it's for me.

MAMA. I didn't think you would shoot your own boy, Jessie. I know you've felt like it, well, we've all felt like shooting somebody, but we don't do it. I just don't think we need . . .

JESSIE (*interrupting*). Your hands aren't washed. Do you want a manicure or not?

MAMA. Yes, I do, but . . .

JESSIE (*crossing to the chair*). Then wash your hands and don't talk to me any more about Ricky. Those two rings he took were the last valuable things *I* had, so now he's started in on other people, door to door. I hope they put him away sometime. I'd turn him in myself if I knew where he was.

MAMA. You don't mean that.

JESSIE. Every word. Wash your hands and that's the last time I'm telling you.

(*Jessie sits down with the gun and starts cleaning it, pushing the cylinder out, checking to see that the chambers and barrel are empty, then putting some oil on a small patch of cloth and pushing it through the barrel with the push rod that was in the box. Mama goes to the kitchen and washes her hands, as instructed, trying not to show her concern about the gun.*)

MAMA. I shoulda got you to bring down that milk can. Agnes Fletcher sold hers to somebody with a flea market for forty dollars apiece.

JESSIE. I'll go back and get it in a minute. There's a wagon wheel up there, too. There's even a churn. I'll get it all if you want.

MAMA (*coming over, now, taking over now*). What are you doing?

JESSIE. The barrel has to be clean, Mama. Old powder dust gets in it. . . .

MAMA. What for?

JESSIE. I told you.

MAMA (*reaching for the gun*). And I told you, we don't get criminals out here.

JESSIE (*quickly pulling it to her*). And I told you . . . (*Then trying to be calm*) The gun is for me.

MAMA. Well, you can have it if you want. When I die, you'll get it all, anyway.

JESSIE. I'm going to kill myself, Mama.

MAMA (*returning to the sofa*). Very funny. Very funny.

JESSIE. I am.

MAMA. You are not! Don't even say such a thing, Jessie.

JESSIE. How would you know if I didn't say it? You want it to be a surprise? You're lying there in your bed or maybe you're just brushing your teeth and you hear this . . . noise down the hall?

MAMA. Kill yourself.

JESSIE. Shoot myself. In a couple of hours.

MAMA. It must be time for your medicine.

JESSIE. Took it already.

MAMA. What's the matter with you?

JESSIE. Not a thing. Feel fine.

MAMA. You feel fine. You're just going to kill yourself.

JESSIE. Waited until I felt good enough, in fact.

MAMA. Don't make jokes, Jessie. I'm too old for jokes.

JESSIE. It's not a joke, Mama.

(*Mama watches for a moment in silence.*)

MAMA. That gun's no good, you know. He broke it right before he died. He dropped it in the mud one day.

JESSIE. Seems O.K. (*She spins the chamber, cocks the pistol, and pulls the trigger. The gun is not yet loaded, so all we hear is the click, but it will definitely work. It's also obvious that Jessie knows her way around a gun. Mama cannot speak.*) I had Cecil's all ready in there, just in case I couldn't find this one, but I'd rather use Daddy's.

MAMA. Those bullets are at least fifteen years old.

JESSIE (*pulling out another box*). These are from last week.

MAMA. Where did you get those?

JESSIE. Feed store Dawson told me about.

MAMA. Dawson!

JESSIE. I told him I was worried about prowlers. He said he thought it was a good idea. He told me what kind to ask for.

MAMA. If he had any idea . . .

JESSIE. He took it as a compliment. He thought I might be taking an interest in things. He got through telling me all about the bullets and then he said we ought to talk like this more often.

MAMA. And where was I while this was going on?

JESSIE. On the phone with Agnes. About the milk can, I guess. Anyway, I asked Dawson if he thought they'd send me some bullets and he said he'd just call for me, because he knew they'd send them if he told them to. And he was absolutely right. Here they are.

MAMA. How could he do that?

JESSIE. Just trying to help, Mama.

MAMA. And then I told you where the gun was.

JESSIE (*smiling, enjoying this joke*). See? Everybody's doing what they can.

MAMA. You told me it was for protection!

JESSIE. It is! I'm still doing your nails, though. Want to try that new Chinaberry color?

MAMA. Well, I'm calling Dawson right now. We'll just see what he had to say about this little stunt.

JESSIE. Dawson doesn't have any more to do with this.

MAMA. He's your brother.

JESSIE. And that's all.

MAMA (*stands up, moves toward the phone*). Dawson will put a stop to this. Yes be will. He'll take the gun away.

JESSIE. If you call him, I'll just have to do it before he gets here. Soon as you hang up the phone, I'll just walk in the bedroom and lock the door. Dawson will get here just in time to help you clean up. Go ahead, call him. Then call the police. Then call the funeral home. Then call Loretta and see if *she'll* do your nails.

MAMA. You will not! This is crazy talk, Jessie!

(*Mama goes directly to the telephone and starts to dial, but Jessie is fast, coming up behind her and taking the receiver out of her hand, putting it back down.*)

JESSIE (*firm and quiet*). I said no. This is private. Dawson is not invited.

MAMA. Just me.

JESSIE. I don't want anybody else over here. Just you and me. If Dawson comes over, it'll make me feel stupid for not doing it ten years ago.

MAMA. I think we better call the doctor. Or how about the ambulance. You like that one driver, I know. What's his name, Timmy? Get you somebody to talk to.

JESSIE (*going back to her chair*). I'm through talking, Mama. You're it. No more.

MAMA. We're just going to sit around like every other night in the world and then you're going to kill yourself? (*Jessie doesn't answer.*) You'll miss. (*Again there is no response.*) You'll just wind up a vegetable. How would you like that? Shoot your ear off? You know what the doctor said about getting excited. You'll cock the pistol and have a fit.

JESSIE. I think I can kill myself, Mama.

MAMA. You're not going to kill yourself Jessie. You're not even upset! (*Jessie smiles, or laughs quietly, and Mama tries a different approach.*) People don't really kill themselves, Jessie. No, mam, doesn't make sense, unless you're retarded or deranged, and you're as normal as they come, Jessie, for the most part. We're all *afraid* to die.

JESSIE. I'm not, Mama. I'm cold all the time, anyway.

MAMA. That's ridiculous.

JESSIE. It's exactly what I want. It's dark and quiet.

MAMA. So is the back yard, Jessie! Close your eyes. Stuff cotton in your ears. Take a nap! It's quiet in your room. I'll leave the TV off all night.

JESSIE. So quiet I don't know it's quiet. So nobody can get me.

MAMA. You don't know what dead is like. It might not be quiet at all. What if it's like an alarm clock and you can't wake up so you can't shut it off. Ever.

JESSIE. Dead is everybody and everything I ever knew, gone. Dead is dead quiet.

MAMA. It's a sin. You'll go to hell.

JESSIE. Uh-huh.

MAMA. You will!

JESSIE. Jesus was a suicide, if you ask me.

MAMA. You'll go to hell just for saying that. Jessie!

JESSIE (*with genuine surprise*). I didn't know I thought that.

MAMA. Jessie!

(*Jessie doesn't answer. She puts the now-loaded gun back in the box and crosses to the kitchen. But Mama is afraid she's headed for the bedroom.*)

MAMA (*in a panic*). You can't use my towels! They're my towels. I've had them for a long time. I like my towels.

JESSIE. I asked you if you wanted that swimming towel and you said you didn't.

MAMA. And you can't use your father's gun, either. It's mine now, too. And you can't do it in my house.

JESSIE. Oh, come on.

MAMA. No. You can't do it. I won't let you. The house is in my name.

JESSIE. I have to go in the bedroom and lock the door behind me so they won't arrest you for killing me. They'll probably test your hands for gunpowder, anyway, but you'll pass.

MAMA. Not in my house!

JESSIE. If I'd known you were going to act like this, I wouldn't have told you.

MAMA. How am I supposed to act? Tell you to go ahead? O.K. by me, sugar? Might try it myself. What took you so long?

JESSIE. There's just no point in fighting me over it, that's all. Want some coffee?

MAMA. Your birthday's coming up, Jessie. Don't you want to know what we got you?

JESSIE. You got me dusting powder, Loretta got me a new housecoat, pink probably, and Dawson got me new slippers, too small, but they go with the robe, he'll say. (*Mama cannot speak. Apparently Jessie is right.*) Be back in a minute.

(*Jessie takes the gun box, puts it on top of the stack of towels and garbage bags, and takes them into her bedroom. Mama, alone for a moment, goes to the phone, picks up the receiver, looks toward the bedroom, starts to dial, and then replaces the receiver in its cradle as Jessie walks back into the room. Jessie wonders, silently. They have lived together for so long there is very rarely any reason for one to ask what the other was about to do.*)

MAMA. I started to, but I didn't. I didn't call him.

JESSIE. Good. Thank you.

MAMA (*starting over, a new approach*). What's this all about, Jessie?

JESSIE. About?

(*Jessie now begins the next task she had "on the schedule" which is refilling all the candy jars, taking the empty papers out of the boxes of chocolates, etc. Mama generally snitches when Jessie does this. Not tonight, though. Nevertheless, Jessie offers.*)

MAMA. What did I do?

JESSIE. Nothing. Want a caramel?

MAMA (*ignoring the candy*). You're mad at me.

JESSIE. Not a bit. I am worried about you, but I'm going to do what I can before I go. We're not just going to sit around tonight. I made a list of things.

MAMA. What things?

JESSIE. How the washer works. Things like that.

MAMA. I know how the washer works. You put the clothes in. You put the soap in. You turn it on. You wait.

JESSIE. You do something else. You don't just wait.

MAMA. Whatever else you find to do, you're still mainly waiting. The waiting's the worst part of it. The waiting's what you pay somebody else to do, if you can.

JESSIE (*nodding*). O.K. Where do we keep the soap?

MAMA. I could find it.

JESSIE. See?

MAMA. If you're mad about doing the wash, we can get Loretta to do it.

JESSIE. Oh now, that might be worth staying to see.

MAMA. She'd never in her life, would she?

JESSIE. Nope.

MAMA. What's the matter with her?

JESSIE. She thinks she's better than we are. She's not.

MAMA. Maybe if she didn't wear that yellow all the time.

JESSIE. The washer repair number is on a little card taped to the side of the machine.

MAMA. Loretta doesn't ever have to come over here again. Dawson can just leave her at home when he comes. And we don't ever have to see Dawson either if he bothers you. Does he bother you?

JESSIE. Sure he does. Be sure you clean out the lint tray every time you use the dryer. But don't you ever put your house shoes in, it'll melt the shoes.

MAMA. What does Dawson do, that bothers you?

JESSIE. He just calls me Jess like he knows who he's talking to. He's always wondering what I do all day. I mean, I wonder that myself, but it's my day, so it's mine to wonder about, not his.

MAMA. Family is just accident, Jessie. It's nothing personal, hon. They don't mean to get on your nerves. They don't even mean to be your family, they just are.

JESSIE. They know too much.

MAMA. About what?

JESSIE. They know things about you, and they learned it before you had a chance to say whether you wanted them to know it or not. They were there when it happened and it don't belong to them, it belongs to you, only they got it. Like my mail-order bra got delivered to their house.

MAMA. By accident!

JESSIE. All the same . . . they opened it. They saw the little rosebuds on it. (*Offering her another candy*) Chewy mint?

MAMA (*shaking her head no*). What do they know about you? I'll tell them never to talk about it again. Is it Ricky or Cecil or your fits or your hair is falling out or you drink too much coffee or you never go out of the house or what?

JESSIE. I just don't like their talk. The account at the grocery is in Dawson's name when you call. The number's on a whole list of numbers on the back cover of the phone book.

MAMA. Well! Now we're getting somewhere. They're none of them ever setting foot in this house again.

JESSIE. It's not them, Mother. I wouldn't kill myself just to get away from them.

MAMA. You leave the room when they come over, anyway.

JESSIE. I stay as long as I can. Besides, it's you they come to see.

MAMA. That's because I stay in the room when they come.

JESSIE. It's not them.

MAMA. Then what is it?

JESSIE (*checking the list on her note pad*). The grocery won't deliver on Saturday anymore. And you want your order the same day, you have to call before ten. And they won't deliver less than fifteen dollars' worth. What I do is tell them what we need and tell them to add on cigarettes until it gets to fifteen dollars.

MAMA. It's Ricky. You're trying to get through to him.

JESSIE. If I thought I could do that, I would stay.

MAMA. Make him sorry he hurt you, then. That's it, isn't it?

JESSIE. He's hurt me, I've hurt him. We're about even.

MAMA. You'll be telling him killing is O.K. with you, you know. Want him to start killing next? Nothing wrong with it. Mom did it.

JESSIE. Only a matter of time, anyway, Mama. When the call comes, you let Dawson handle it.

MAMA. Honey, nothing says those calls are always going to be some new trouble he's into. You could get one that he's got a job, that he s getting married, or how about he's joined the army, wouldn't that be nice?

JESSIE. If you call the Sweet Tooth before you call the grocery, that Susie will take your fudge next door to the grocery and it'll all come out together. Be sure you talk to Susie, though. She won't let them put it in the bottom of a sack like that one time, remember?

MAMA. Ricky could come over, you know. What if he calls us?

JESSIE. It's not Ricky, Mama.

MAMA. Or anybody could call us, Jessie.

JESSIE. Not on Saturday night, Mama.

MAMA. Then what is it? Are you sick? If your gums are swelling again, we can get you to the dentist in the morning.

JESSIE. No. Can you order your medicine or do you want Dawson to? I've got a note to him. I'll add that to it if you want.

MAMA. Your eyes don't look right. I thought so yesterday.

JESSIE. That was just the ragweed. I'm not sick.

MAMA. Epilepsy is sick, Jessie.

JESSIE. It won't kill me. (*A pause.*) If it would, I wouldn't have to.

MAMA. You don't *have* to.

JESSIE. No, I don't. That's what I like about it.

MAMA. Well, I won't let you!

JESSIE. It's not up to you.

MAMA. Jessie!

JESSIE. I want to hang a big sign around my neck, like Daddy's on the barn. GONE FISHING.

MAMA. You don't like it here.

JESSIE (*smiling*). Exactly.

MAMA. I meant here in my house.

JESSIE. I know you did.

MAMA. You never should have moved back in here with me. If you'd kept your little house or found another place when Cecil left you, you'd have made some new friends at least. Had a life to lead. Had your own things around you. Give Ricky a place to come see you. You never should've come here.

JESSIE. Maybe.

MAMA. But I didn't force you, did I?

JESSIE. If it was a mistake, we made it together. You took me in. I appreciate that.

MAMA. You didn't have any business being by yourself right then, but I can see how you might want a place of your own. A grown woman should . . .

JESSIE. Mama . . . I'm just not having a very good time and I don't have any reason to think it'll get anything but worse. I'm tired. I'm hurt. I'm sad. I feel used.

MAMA. Tired of what?

JESSIE. It all.

MAMA. What does that mean?

JESSIE. I can't say it any better.

MAMA. Well, you'll have to say it better because I'm not letting you alone till you do. What were those other things? Hurt . . . (*Before Jessie can answer*) You had this all ready to say to me, didn't you? Did you write this down? How long have you been thinking about this?

JESSIE. Off and on, ten years. On all the time, since Christmas.

MAMA. What happened at Christmas?

JESSIE. Nothing.

MAMA. So why Christmas?

JESSIE. That's it. On the nose.

(*A pause. Mama knows exactly what Jessie means. She was there, too, after all.*)

JESSIE (*putting the candy sacks away*). See where all this

is? Red hots up front, sour balls and horehound mixed together in this one sack. New packages of toffee and licorice right in back there.

MAMA. Go back to your list. You're hurt by what?

JESSIE. (*Mama knows perfectly well*). Mama . . .

MAMA. O.K. Sad about what? There's nothing real sad going on right now. If it was after your divorce or something, that would make sense.

JESSIE (*looking at her list, then opening the drawer*). Now, this drawer has everything in it that there's no better place for. Extension cords, batteries for the radio, extra lighters, sandpaper, masking tape, Elmer's glue, thumbtacks, that kind of stuff. The mousetraps are under the sink, but you call Dawson if you've got one and let him do it.

MAMA. Sad about what?

JESSIE. The way things are.

MAMA. Not good enough. What things?

JESSIE. Oh, everything from you and me to Red China.

MAMA. I think we can leave the Chinese out of this.

JESSIE (*crosses back into the living room*). There's extra light bulbs in a box in the hall closet. And we've got a couple of packages of fuses in the fuse box. There's candles and matches in the top of the broom closet, but if the lights go out, just call Dawson and sit tight. But don't open the refrigerator door. Things will stay cool in there as long as you keep the door shut.

MAMA. I asked you a question.

JESSIE. I read the paper. I don't like how things are. And they're not any better out there than they are in here.

MAMA. If you're doing this because of the newspapers, I can sure fix that!

JESSIE. There's just more of it on TV.

MAMA (*kicking the television set*). Take it out, then!

JESSIE. You wouldn't do that.

MAMA. Watch me.

JESSIE. What would you do all day?

MAMA (*desperately*). Sing. (*Jessie laughs.*) I would, too. You want to watch? I'll sing till morning to keep you alive, Jessie, please!

JESSIE. No. (*Then affectionately*) It's a funny idea, though. What do you sing?

MAMA (*has no idea how to answer this*). We've got a good life here!

JESSIE (*going back into the kitchen*). I called this morning and canceled the papers, except for Sunday, for your puzzles; you'll still get that one.

MAMA. Let's get another dog, Jessie! You liked a big dog, now, didn't you? That King dog, didn't you?

JESSIE (*washing her hands*). I did like that King dog, yes.

MAMA. I'm so dumb. He's the one run under the tractor.

JESSIE. That makes him dumb, not you.

MAMA. For bringing it up.

JESSIE. It's O.K. Handi-Wipes and sponges under the sink.

MAMA. We could get a new dog and keep him in the house. Dogs are cheap!

JESSIE (*getting big pill jars out of the cabinet*). No.

MAMA. Something for you to take care of.

JESSIE. I've had you, Mama.

MAMA (*frantically starting to fill pill bottles*). You do too much for me. I can fill pill bottles all day, Jessie, and change the shelf paper and wash the floor when I get through. You just watch me. You don't have to do another thing in this house if you don't want to. You don't have to take care of me, Jessie.

JESSIE. I know that. You've just been letting me do it so I'll have something to do, haven't you?

MAMA (*realizing this was a mistake*). I don't do it as well as you. I just meant if it tires you out or makes you feel used . . .

JESSIE. Mama, I know you used to ride the bus. Riding the bus and it's hot and bumpy and crowded and too noisy and more than anything in the world you want to get off and the only reason in the world you don't get off is it's still fifty blocks from where you're going? Well, I can get off right now if I want to, because even if I ride fifty more years and get off then, it's the same place when I step down to it. Whenever I feel like it, I can get off. As soon as I've had enough, it's my stop. I've had enough.

MAMA. You're feeling sorry for yourself!

JESSIE. The plumber's helper is under the sink, too.

MAMA. You're not having a good time! Whoever promised you a good time? Do you think I've had a good time?

JESSIE. I think you're pretty happy, yeah. You have things you like to do.

MAMA. Like what?

JESSIE. Like crochet.

MAMA. I'll teach you to crochet.

JESSIE. I can't do any of that nice work, Mama.

MAMA. Good time don't come looking for you, Jessie. You could work some puzzles or put in a garden or go to the store. Let's call a taxi and go to the A&P!

JESSIE. I shopped you up for about two weeks already. You're not going to need toilet paper till Thanksgiving.

MAMA (*interrupting*). You're acting like some little brat, Jessie. You're mad and everybody's boring and you don't have anything to do and you don't like me and you don't like going out and you don't like staying in and you never talk on the phone and you don't watch TV and you're miserable and it's your own sweet fault.

JESSIE. And it's time I did something about it.

MAMA. Not something like killing yourself. Something

like . . . buying us all new dishes! I'd like that. Or maybe the doctor would let you get a driver's license now, or I know what let's do right this minute, let's rearrange the furniture.

JESSIE. I'll do that. If you want. I always thought if the TV was somewhere else, you wouldn't get such a glare on it during the day. I'll do whatever you want before I go.

MAMA (*badly frightened by those words*). You could get a job!

JESSIE. I took that telephone sales job and I didn't even make enough money to pay the phone bill, and I tried to work at the gift shop at the hospital and they said I made people real uncomfortable smiling the way I did.

MAMA. You could keep books. You kept your dad's books.

JESSIE. But nobody ever checked them.

MAMA. When he died, they checked them.

JESSIE. And that's when they took the books away from me.

MAMA. That's because without him there wasn't any business, Jessie!

JESSIE (*putting the pill bottles away*). You know I couldn't work. I can't do anything. I've never been around people my whole life except when I went to the hospital. I could have a seizure any time. What good would a job do? The kind of job I could get would make me feel worse.

MAMA. Jessie!

JESSIE. It's true!

MAMA. It's what you think is true!

JESSIE (*struck by the clarity of that*). That's right. It's what I think is true.

MAMA (*hysterically*). But I can't do anything about that!

JESSIE (*quietly*). No. You can't. (*Mama slumps, if not physically, at least emotionally.*) And I can't do anything either, about my life, to change it, make it better, make me feel better about it. Like it better, make it work. But I can stop it. Shut it down, turn it off like the radio when there's nothing on I want to listen to. It's all I really have that belongs to me and I'm going to say what happens to it. And it's going to stop. And I'm going to stop it. So. Let's just have a good time.

MAMA. Have a good time.

JESSIE. We can't go on fussing all night. I mean, I could ask you things I always wanted to know and you could make me some hot chocolate. The old way.

MAMA (*in despair*). It takes cocoa, Jessie.

JESSIE (*gets it out of the cabinet*). I bought cocoa, Mama. And I'd like to have a caramel apple and do your nails.

MAMA. You didn't eat a bit of supper.

JESSIE. Does that mean I can't have a caramel apple?

MAMA. Of course not. I mean. . . . (*Smiling a little*) Of course you can have a caramel apple.

JESSIE. I thought I could.

MAMA. I make the best caramel apples in the world.

JESSIE. I know you do.

MAMA. Or used to. And you don't get cocoa like mine anywhere anymore.

JESSIE. It takes time, I know, but . . .

MAMA. The salt is the trick.

JESSIE. Trouble and everything.

MAMA (*backing away toward the stove*). It's no trouble. What trouble? You put it in the pan and stir it up. All right. Fine. Caramel apples. Cocoa. O.K.

(*Jessie walks to the counter to retrieve her cigarettes as Mama looks for the right pan. There are brief near-smiles, and maybe Mama clears her throat. We have a truce, for the moment. A genuine but nevertheless uneasy one. Jessie, who has been in constant motion since the beginning, now seems content to sit.*

Mama starts looking for a pan to make the cocoa, getting out all the pans in the cabinets in the process. It looks like she's making a mess on purpose so Jessie will have to put them all away again. Mama is buying time, or trying to, and entertaining.)

JESSIE. You talk to Agnes today?

MAMA. She's calling me from a pay phone this week. God only knows why. She has a perfectly good Trimline at home.

JESSIE (*laughing*). Well, how is she?

MAMA. How is she every day, Jessie? Nuts.

JESSIE. Is she really crazy or just silly?

MAMA. No, she's really crazy. She was probably using the pay phone because she had another little fire problem at home.

JESSIE. Mother . . .

MAMA. I'm serious! Agnes Fletcher's burned down every house she ever lived in. Eight fires, and she's due for a new one any day now.

JESSIE (*laughing*). No!

MAMA. Wouldn't surprise me a bit.

JESSIE (*laughing*). Why didn't you tell me this before? Why isn't she locked up somewhere?

MAMA. 'Cause nobody ever got hurt, I guess. Agnes woke everybody up to watch the fires as soon as she set 'em. One time she set out porch chairs and served lemonade.

JESSIE (*shaking her head*). Real lemonade?

MAMA. The houses they lived in, you knew they were going to fall down anyway, so why wait for it, is all I could ever make out about it. Agnes likes a feeling of accomplishment.

JESSIE. Good for her.

MAMA (*finding the pan she wants*). Why are you asking about Agnes? One cup or two?

JESSIE. One. She's your friend. No marshmallows.

MAMA (*getting the milk, etc.*). You have to have marshmallows. That's the old way, Jess. Two or three? Three is better.

JESSIE. Three, then. Her whole house burns up? Her clothes and pillows and everything? I'm not sure I believe this.

MAMA. When she was a girl, Jess, not now. Long time ago. But she's still got it in her, I'm sure of it.

JESSIE. She wouldn't burn her house down now. Where would she go? She can't get Buster to build her a new one, he's dead. How could she burn it up?

MAMA. Be exciting, though, if she did. You never know.

JESSIE. You do too know, Mama. She wouldn't do it.

MAMA (*forced to admit, but reluctant*). I guess not.

JESSIE. What else? Why does she wear all those whistles around her neck?

MAMA. Why does she have a house full of birds?

JESSIE. I didn't know she had a house full of birds!

MAMA. Well, she does. And she says they just follow her home. Well, I know for a fact she's still paying on the last parrot she bought. You gotta keep your life filled up, she says. She says a lot of stupid things. (*Jessie laughs, Mama continues, convinced she's getting somewhere.*) It's all that okra she eats. You can't just willy-nilly eat okra two meals a day and expect to get away with it. Made her crazy.

JESSIE. She really eats okra twice a day? Where does she get it in the winter?

MAMA. Well, she eats it a lot. Maybe not two meals, but . . .

JESSIE. More than the average person.

MAMA (*beginning to get irritated*). I don't know how much okra the average person eats.

JESSIE. Do you know how much okra Agnes eats?

MAMA. No.

JESSIE. How many birds does she have?

MAMA. Two.

JESSIE. Then what are the whistles for?

MAMA. They're not real whistles. Just little plastic ones on a necklace she won playing Bingo, and I only told you about it because I thought I might get a laugh out of you for once even if it wasn't the truth, Jessie. Things don't have to be true to talk about 'em, you know.

JESSIE. Why won't she come over here?

(*Mama is suddenly quiet, but the cocoa and milk are in the pan now, so she lights the stove and starts stirring.*)

MAMA. Well now, what a good idea. We should've had more cocoa. Cocoa is perfect.

JESSIE. Except you don't like milk.

MAMA (*another attempt, but not as energetic*). I hate milk. Coats your throat as bad as okra. Something just downright disgusting about it.

JESSIE. It's because of me, isn't it?

MAMA. No, Jess.

JESSIE. Yes, Mama.

MAMA. O.K. Yes, then, but she's crazy. She's as crazy as they come. She's a lunatic.

JESSIE. What is it exactly? Did I say something, sometime? Or did she see me have a fit and's afraid I might have another one if she came over, or what?

MAMA. I guess.

JESSIE. You guess what? What's she ever said? She must've given you some reason.

MAMA. Your hands are cold.

JESSIE. What difference does that make?

MAMA. "Like a corpse," she says, "and I'm gonna be one soon enough as it is."

JESSIE. That's crazy.

MAMA. That's Agnes. "Jessie's shook the hand of death and I can't take the chance it's catching, Thelma, so I ain't comin' over, and you can understand or not, but I ain't comin'. I'll come up the driveway, but that's as far as I go."

JESSIE (*laughing, relieved*). I thought she didn't like me! She's scared of me! How about that! Scared of me.

MAMA. I could make her come over here, Jessie. I could call her up right now and she could bring the birds and come visit. I didn't know you ever thought about her at all. I'll tell her she just has to come and she'll come, all right. She owes me one.

JESSIE. No, that's all right. I just wondered about it. When I'm in the hospital, does she come over here?

MAMA. Her kitchen is just a tiny thing. When she comes over here, she feels like . . . (*Toning it down a little*) Well, we all like a change of scene, don't we?

JESSIE (*playing along*). Sure we do. Plus there's no birds diving around.

MAMA. I hate those birds. She says I don't understand them. What's there to understand about birds?

JESSIE. Why Agnes likes them, for one thing. Why they stay with her when they could be outside with the other birds. What their singing means. How they fly. What they think Agnes is.

MAMA. Why do you have to know so much about things, Jessie? There's just not that much *to* things that I could ever see.

JESSIE. That you could ever *tell*, you mean. You didn't have to lie to me about Agnes.

MAMA. I didn't lie. You never asked before!

JESSIE. You lied about setting fire to all those houses and about how many birds she has and how much okra she eats and why she won't come over here. If I have to keep dragging the truth out of you, this is going to take all night.

MAMA. That's fine with me. I'm not a bit sleepy.

JESSIE. Mama . . .

MAMA. All right. Ask me whatever you want. Here.

(*They come to an awkward stop, as the cocoa is ready and Mama pours it into the cups Jessie has set on the table.*)

JESSIE (*as Mama takes her first sip*). Did you love Daddy?

MAMA. No.

JESSIE (*pleased that Mama understands the rules better now*). I didn't think so. Were you really fifteen when you married him?

MAMA. The way he told it? I'm sitting in the mud, he comes along, drags me in the kitchen, "She's been there ever since"?

JESSIE. Yes.

MAMA. No. It was a big fat lie, the whole thing. He just thought it was funnier that way. God, this milk in here.

JESSIE. The cocoa helps.

MAMA (*pleased that they agree on this, at least*). Not enough, though, does it? You can still taste it, can't you?

JESSIE. Yeah, it's pretty bad. I thought it was my memory that was bad, but it's not. It's the milk, all right.

MAMA. It's a real waste of chocolate. You don't have to finish it.

JESSIE (*putting her cup down*). Thanks, though.

MAMA. I should've known not to make it. I knew you wouldn't like it. You never did like it.

JESSIE. You didn't ever love him, or he did something and you stopped loving him, or what?

MAMA. He felt sorry for me. He wanted a plain country woman and that's what he married, and then he held it against me the rest of my life like I was supposed to change and surprise him some how. Like I remember this one day he was standing on the porch and I told him to get a shirt on and he went in and got one and then he said, real peaceful, but to the point, "You're right, Thelma. If God had meant for people to go around without any clothes on, they'd have been born that way."

JESSIE (*sees Mama's hurt*). He didn't mean anything by that, Mama.

MAMA. He never said a word he didn't have to, Jessie. That was probably all he'd said to me all day, Jessie. So if he said it, there was something to it, but I never did figure that one out. What did that mean?

JESSIE. I don't know. I liked him better than you did, but I didn't know him any better.

MAMA. How could I love him, Jessie. I didn't have a thing he wanted. (*Jessie doesn't answer.*) He got his share, though. You loved him enough for both of us. You followed him around like some . . . Jessie, all the man ever did was farm and sit . . . and try to think of somebody to sell the farm to.

JESSIE. Or make me a boyfriend out of pipe cleaners and sit back and smile like the stick man was about to dance and wasn't I going to get a kick out of that. Or sit up with a sick cow all night and leave me a chain of sleepy stick elephants on my bed in the morning.

MAMA. Or just sit.

JESSIE. I liked him sitting. Big old faded blue man in the chair. Quiet.

MAMA. Agnes gets more talk out of her birds than I got from the two of you. He could've had that GONE FISHING sign around his neck in that chair. I saw him stare off at the water. I saw him look at the weather rolling in. I got where I could practically see the boat myself. But you, you knew what he was thinking about and you're going to tell me.

JESSIE. I don't know, Mama! His life, I guess. His corn. His boots. Us. Things. You know.

MAMA. No, I don't know, Jessie! You had those quiet little conversations after supper every night. What were you whispering about?

JESSIE. We weren't whispering, you were just across the room.

MAMA. What did you talk about?

JESSIE. We talked about why black socks are warmer than blue socks. Is that something to go tell Mother? You were just jealous because I'd rather talk to him than wash the dishes with you.

MAMA. I was jealous because you'd rather talk to him than anything! (*Jessie reaches across the table for the small clock and starts to wind it.*) If I had died instead of him, he wouldn't have taken you in like I did.

JESSIE. I wouldn't have expected him to.

MAMA. Then what would you have done?

JESSIE. Come visit.

MAMA. Oh, I see. He died and left you stuck with me and you're mad about it.

JESSIE (*getting up from the table*). Not anymore. He didn't mean to. I didn't have to come here. We've been through this.

MAMA. He felt sorry for you, too, Jessie, don't kid yourself about that. He said you were a runt and he said it from the day you were born and he said you didn't have a chance.

JESSIE (*getting the canister of sugar and starting to refill the sugar bowl*). I know he loved me.

MAMA. What if he did? It didn't change anything.

JESSIE. It didn't have to. I miss him.

MAMA. He never really went fishing, you know. Never once. His tackle box was full of chewing tobacco and all he ever did was drive out to the lake and sit in his car. Dawson told me. And Bennie at the bait shop, he told Dawson. They all laughed about it. And he'd come back from fishing and all he'd have to show for it was . . . a whole pipe-cleaner *family*—chickens, pigs, a dog with a bad leg—it was creepy strange. It made me sick to look at them and I hid his pipe cleaners a couple of times but he always had more somewhere.

JESSIE. I thought it might be better for you after he died. You'd get interested in things. Breathe better. Change somehow.

MAMA. Into what? The Queen? A clerk in a shoe store? Why should I? Because he said to? Because you said to? (*Jessie shakes her head.*) Well I wasn't here for his entertainment and I'm not here for yours either, Jessie. I don't know what I'm here for, but then I don't think about it. (*Realizing what all this means*) But I bet you wouldn't be killing yourself if he were still alive. That's a fine thing to figure out, isn't it?

JESSIE (*filling the honey jar now*). That's not true.

MAMA. Oh no? Then what were you asking about him for? Why did you want to know if I loved him?

JESSIE. I didn't think you did, that's all.

MAMA. Fine then. You were right. Do you feel better now?

JESSIE (*cleaning the honey jar carefully*). It feels good to be right about it.

MAMA. It didn't matter whether I loved him. It didn't matter to me and it didn't matter to him. And it didn't mean we didn't get along. It wasn't important. We didn't talk about it. (*Sweeping the pots off the cabinet*) Take all these pots out to the porch!

JESSIE. What for?

MAMA. Just leave me this one pan. (*She jerks the silverware drawer open.*) Get me one knife, one fork, one big spoon, and the can opener, and put them out where I can get them. (*Starts throwing knives and forks in one of the pans.*)

JESSIE. Don't do that! I just straightened that drawer!

MAMA (*throwing the pan in the sink*). And throw out all the plates and cups. I'll use paper. Loretta can have what she wants and Dawson can sell the rest.

JESSIE (*calmly*). What are you doing?

MAMA. I'm not going to cook. I never liked it, anyway. I like candy. Wrapped in plastic or coming in sacks. And tuna. I like tuna. I'll eat tuna, thank you.

JESSIE (*taking the pan out of the sink*). What if you want to make apple butter? You can't make apple butter in that little pan. What if you leave carrots on cooking and burn up that pan?

MAMA. I don't like carrots.

JESSIE. What if the strawberries are good this year and you want to go picking with Agnes.

MAMA. I'll tell her to bring a pan. You said you would do whatever I wanted! I don't want a bunch of pans cluttering up my cabinets I can't get down to, anyway. Throw them out. Every last one.

JESSIE (*gathering up the pots*). I'm putting them all back in. I'm not taking them to the porch. If you want them, they'll be here. You'll bend down and get them, like you got the one for the cocoa. And if somebody else comes over here to cook, they'll have something to cook in, and that's the end of it!

MAMA. Who's going to come cook here?

JESSIE. Agnes.

MAMA. In my pots? Not on your life.

JESSIE. There's no reason why the two of you couldn't just live here together. Be cheaper for both of you and somebody to talk to. And if the birds bothered you, well, one day when Agnes is out getting her hair done, you could take them all for a walk!

MAMA (*as Jessie straightens the silverware*). So that's why you're pestering me about Agnes. You think you can rest easy if you get me a new babysitter? Well, I don't want to live with Agnes. I barely want to talk with Agnes. She's just around. We go back, that's all. I'm not letting Agnes near this place. You don't get off as easy as that, child.

JESSIE. O.K., then. It's just something to think about.

MAMA. I don't like things to think about. I like things to go on.

JESSIE (*closing the silverware drawer*). I want to know what Daddy said to you the night he died. You came storming out of his room and said I could wait it out with him if I wanted to, but you were going to watch *Gunsmoke*. What did he say to you?

MAMA. He didn't have *anything* to say to me, Jessie. That's why I left. He didn't say a thing. It was his last chance not to talk to me and he took full advantage of it.

JESSIE (*after a moment*). I'm sorry you didn't love him. Sorry for you, I mean. He seemed like a nice man.

MAMA (*as Jessie walks to the refrigerator*). Ready for your apple now?

JESSIE. Soon as I'm through here, Mama.

MAMA. You won't like the apple, either. It'll be just like the cocoa. You never liked eating it all, did you? Any of it! What have you been living on all these years, toothpaste?

JESSIE (*as she starts to clean out the refrigerator*). Now, you know the milkman comes on Wednesdays and Saturdays, and he leaves the order blank in an egg box, and you give the bills to Dawson once a month.

MAMA. Do they still make that orangeade?

JESSIE. It's not orangeade, it's just orange.

MAMA. I'm going to get some. I thought they stopped making it. You just stopped ordering it.

JESSIE. You should drink milk.

MAMA. Not anymore, I'm not. That hot chocolate was the last. Hooray.

JESSIE (*getting the garbage can from under the sink*). I told them to keep delivering a quart a week no matter what you said. I told them you'd run out of Cokes and you'd have to drink it. I told them I knew you wouldn't pour it on the ground . . .

MAMA (*finishing her sentence*). And you told them you weren't going to be ordering anymore?

JESSIE. I told them I was taking a little holiday and to look after you.

MAMA. And they didn't think something was funny about that? You who doesn't go to the front steps? You, who only sees the driveway looking down from a stretcher passed out cold?

JESSIE (*enjoying this, but not laughing*). They said it was about time, but why didn't I take you with me? And I said I didn't think you'd want to go, and they said, "Yeah, everybody's got their own idea of vacation."

MAMA. I guess you think that's funny.

JESSIE (*pulling jars out of the refrigerator*). You know there never was any reason to call the ambulance for me. All they ever did for me in the emergency room was let me wake up. I could've done that here. Now, I'll just call them out and you say yes or no. I know you like pickles. Ketchup?

MAMA. Keep it.

JESSIE. We've had this since last Fourth of July.

MAMA. Keep the ketchup. Keep it all.

JESSIE. Are you going to drink ketchup from the bottle or what? How can you want your food and not want your pots to cook it in? This stuff will all spoil in here, Mother.

MAMA. Nothing I ever did was good enough for you and I want to know why.

JESSIE. That's not true.

MAMA. And I want to know why you've lived here this long feeling the way you do.

JESSIE. You have no earthly idea how I feel.

MAMA. Well, how could I? You're real far back there, Jessie.

JESSIE. Back where?

MAMA. What's it like over there, where you are? Do people always say the right thing or get whatever they want, or what?

JESSIE. What are you talking about?

MAMA. Why do you read the newspaper? Why don't you wear that sweater I made for you? Do you remember how I used to look, or am I just any old woman now? When you have a fit, do you see stars or what? How did you fall off the horse, really? Why did Cecil leave you? Where did you put my old glasses?

JESSIE (*stunned by Mama's intensity*). They're in the bottom drawer of your dresser in an old Milk of Magnesia box. Cecil left me because he made me choose between him and smoking.

MAMA. Jessie, I know he wasn't that dumb.

JESSIE. I never understood why he hated it so much when it's so good. Smoking is the only thing I know that's always just what you think it's going to be. Just like it was the last time, right there when you want it and real quiet.

MAMA. Your fits made him sick and you know it.

JESSIE. Say seizures, not fits. Seizures.

MAMA. It's the same thing. A seizure in the hospital is a fit at home.

JESSIE. They didn't bother him at all. Except he did feel responsible for it. It was his idea to go horseback riding that day. It was his idea I could do anything if I just made up my mind to. I fell off the horse because I didn't know how to hold on. Cecil left me for pretty much the same reason.

MAMA. He had a girl, Jessie. I walked right in on them in the toolshed.

JESSIE (*after a moment*). O.K. That's fair. (*Lighting another cigarette*) Was she very pretty?

MAMA. She was Agnes's girl, Carlene. Judge for yourself.

JESSIE (*as she walks to the living room*). I guess you and Agnes had a good talk about that, huh?

MAMA. I never thought he was good enough for you. They moved here from Tennessee, you know.

JESSIE. What are you talking about? You liked him better than I did. You flirted him out here to build your porch or I'd never even met him at all. You thought maybe he'd help you out around the place, come in and get some coffee and talk to you. God knows what you thought. All that curly hair.

MAMA. He's the best carpenter I ever saw. That little house of yours will still be standing at the end of the world, Jessie.

JESSIE. You didn't need a porch, Mama.

MAMA. All right! I wanted you to have a husband.

JESSIE. And I couldn't get one on my own, of course.

MAMA. How were you going to get a husband never opening your mouth to a living soul?

JESSIE. So I was quiet about it, so what?

MAMA. So I should have let you just sit here? Sit like your daddy? Sit here?

JESSIE. Maybe.

MAMA. Well, I didn't think so.

JESSIE. Well, what did you know?

MAMA. I never said I knew much. How was I supposed to learn anything living out here? I didn't know enough to do half the things I did in my life. Things happen. You do what you can about them and you see what happens next. I married you off to the wrong man, I admit that. So I took you in when he left. I'm sorry.

JESSIE. He wasn't the wrong man.

MAMA. He didn't love you, Jessie, or he wouldn't have left.

JESSIE. He wasn't the wrong man, Mama. I loved Cecil so much. And I tried to get more exercise and I tried to stay awake. I tried to learn to ride a horse. And I tried to stay outside with him, but he always knew I was trying, so it didn't work.

MAMA. He was a selfish man. He told me once he hated to see people move into his houses after he built them. He knew they'd mess them up.

JESSIE. I loved that bridge he built over the creek in back of the house. It didn't have to be anything special, a couple of boards would have been just fine, but he used that yellow pine and rubbed it so smooth . . .

MAMA. He had responsibilities here. He had a wife and son here and he failed you.

JESSIE. Or that baby bed he built for Ricky. I told him he didn't have to spend so much time on it, but he said it had to last, and the thing ended up weighing two hundred pounds and I couldn't move it. I said, "How long does a baby bed have to last, anyway?" But maybe he thought if it was strong enough, it might keep Ricky a baby.

MAMA. Ricky is too much like Cecil.

JESSIE. He is not. Ricky is as much like me as it's possible for any human to be. We even wear the same size pants. These are his, I think.

MAMA. That's just the same size. That's not you're the same person.

JESSIE. I see it on his face. I hear it when he talks. We look out at the world and we see the same thing: Not Fair. And the only difference between us is Ricky's out there trying to get even. And he knows not to trust anybody and he got it straight from me. And he knows not to try to get work, and guess where he got that. He walks around like there's loose boards in the floor, and you know who laid that floor, I did.

MAMA. Ricky isn't through yet. You don't know how he'll turn out!

JESSIE (*going back to the kitchen*). Yes I do and so did Cecil. Ricky is the two of us together for all time in too small a space. And we're tearing each other apart, like always, inside that boy, and if you don't see it, then you're just blind.

MAMA. Give him time, Jess.

JESSIE. Oh, he'll have plenty of that. Five years for forgery, ten years for armed assault. . . .

MAMA (*furious*). Stop that! (*Then pleading*) Jessie, Cecil might be ready to try it again, honey, that happens sometimes. Go downtown. Find him. Talk to him. He didn't know what he had in you. Maybe he sees things different now, but you're not going to know that till you go see him. Or call him up! Right now! He might be home.

JESSIE. And say what? Nothing's changed, Cecil, I'd just like to look at you, if you don't mind? No. He loved me, Mama. He just didn't know how things fall down around me like they do. I think he did the right thing. He gave himself another chance, that's all. But I did beg him to take me with him. I did tell him I would leave Ricky and you and everything I loved out here if only he would take me with him, but he couldn't and I understood that. (*Pause.*) I wrote that note I showed you. I wrote it. Not Cecil. I said, "I'm sorry, Jessie, I can't fix it all for you." I said I'd always love me, not Cecil. But that's how he felt.

MAMA. Then he should've taken you with him!

JESSIE (*picking up the garbage bag she has filled*). Mama, you don't pack your garbage when you move.

MAMA. You will not call yourself garbage, Jessie.

JESSIE (*taking the bag to the big garbage can near the back door*). Just a way of saying it, Mama. Thinking about my list, that's all. (*Opening the can, putting the garbage in, then securing the lid*) Well, a little more than that. I was trying to say it's all right that Cecil left. It was . . . a relief in a way. I never was what he wanted to see, so it was better when he wasn't looking at me all the time.

MAMA. I'll make your apple now.

JESSIE. No thanks. You get the manicure stuff and I'll be right there.

(*Jessie ties up the big garbage bag in the can and replaces the small garbage bag under the sink, all the time trying desperately to regain her calm. Mama watches, from a distance, her hand reaching unconsciously for the phone. Then she has a better idea. Or rather she thinks of the only other thing left and is willing to try it. Maybe she is even convinced it will work.*)

MAMA. Jessie, I think your daddy had little . . .

JESSIE (*interrupting her*). Garbage night is Tuesday. Put it out as late as you can. The Davis's dogs get in it if you don't. (*Replacing the garbage bag in the can under the sink*) And keep ordering the heavy black bags. It doesn't pay to buy the cheap ones. And I've got all the ties here with the hammers and all. Take them out of the box as soon as you open a new one and put them in this drawer. They'll get lost if you don't, and rubber bands or something else won't work.

MAMA. I think your daddy had fits, too. I think he sat in his chair and had little fits. I read this a long time ago in a magazine, how little fits go, just little blackouts where maybe their eyes don't even close and people just call them "thinking spells."

JESSIE (*getting the slipcover out of the laundry basket*). I don't think you want this manicure we've been looking forward to. I washed this cover for the sofa, but it'll take both of us to get it back on.

MAMA. I watched his eyes. I know that's what it was. The magazine said some people don't even know they've had one.

JESSIE. Daddy would've known if he'd had fits, Mama.

MAMA. The lady in this story had kept track of hers and she'd had eighty thousand of them in the last seven years.

JESSIE. Next time you wash this cover, it'll dry better if you put it on wet.

MAMA. Jessie, listen to what I'm telling you. This lady had anywhere between five and five hundred fits a day and they lasted maybe fifteen seconds apiece, so that out of her life, she'd only lost about two weeks altogether, and she had a full-time secretary job and an IQ of 120.

JESSIE (*amused by Mama's approach*). You want to talk about fits, is that it?

MAMA. Yes. I do. I want to say. . . .

JESSIE (*interrupting*). Most of the time I wouldn't even know I'd had one, except I wake up with different clothes on, feeling like I've been run over. Sometimes I feel my head start to turn around or hear myself scream. And sometimes there is this dizzy stupid feeling a little before it, but if the TV's on, well, it's easy to miss.

(*As Jessie and Mama replace the slipcover on the sofa and the afghan on the chair, the physical struggle somehow mirrors the emotional one in the conversation.*)

MAMA. I can tell when you're about to have one. Your eyes get this big! But, Jessie, you haven't . . .

JESSIE (*taking charge of this*). What do they look like? The seizures?

MAMA (*reluctant*). Different each time, Jess.

JESSIE. O.K. Pick one, then. A good one. I think I want to know now.

MAMA. There's not much to tell. You just . . . crumple, in a heap, like a puppet and somebody cut the strings all at once, or like the firing squad in some Mexican movie, you just slide down the wall, you know. You don't know what happens? How can you not know what happens?

JESSIE. I'm busy.

MAMA. That's not funny.

JESSIE. I'm not laughing. My head turns around and I fall down and then what?

MAMA. Well, your chest squeezes in and out, and you sound like you're gagging, sucking air in and out like you can't breathe.

JESSIE. Do it for me. Make the sound for me.

MAMA. I will not. It's awful-sounding.

JESSIE. Yeah. It felt like it might he. What's next?

MAMA. Your mouth bites down and I have to get your tongue out of the way fast, so you don't bite yourself.

JESSIE. Or you. I bite you, too, don't I?

MAMA. You got me once real good. I had to get a tetanus! But I know what to watch for now. And then you turn blue and the jerks start up. Like I'm standing there poking you with a cattle prod or you're sticking your finger in a light socket as fast as you can. . . .

JESSIE. Foaming like a mad dog the whole time.

MAMA. It's bubbling, Jess, not foam like the washer overflowed, for God's sake; it's bubbling like a baby spitting up. I go get a wet washcloth, that's all. And then the jerks slow down and you wet yourself and it's over. Two minutes tops.

JESSIE. How do I get to the bed?

MAMA. How do you think?

JESSIE. I'm too heavy for you now. How do you do it?

MAMA. I call Dawson. But I get you cleaned up before he gets here and I make him leave before you wake up.

JESSIE. You could just leave me on the floor.

MAMA. I want you to wake up someplace nice, O.K.? (*Then making a real effort*) But, Jessie, and this is the reason I even brought this up! You haven't had a seizure for a solid year. A whole year, do you realize that?

JESSIE. Yeah, the phenobarb's about right now, I guess.

MAMA. You bet it is. You might never have another one, ever! You might be through with it for all time!

JESSIE. Could be.

MAMA. You are. I know you are!

JESSIE. I sure am feeling good. I really am. The double vision's gone and my gums aren't swelling. No rashes or anything. I'm feeling as good as I ever felt in my life. I'm even feeling like worrying or getting mad and I'm not afraid it will start a fit if do, I just go ahead.

MAMA. Of course you do! You can even scream at me, if you want to. I can take it. You don't have to act like you're visiting here, Jessie. This is your house, too.

JESSIE. The best part is, my memory's back.

MAMA. Your memory's always been good. When couldn't you remember things? You're always reminding me what . . .

JESSIE. Because I've made lists for everything. But now I remember what things mean on my lists. I see "dish towels," and I used to wonder whether I was supposed to wash them, buy them, or look for them because I wouldn't remember where I put them after I washed them, and now I know it means wrap them up, they're a present for Loretta's birthday.

MAMA (*finished with the sofa now*). You used to go looking for your lists, too. I've noticed that. You always know where they are now! (*Then suddenly worried*) Loretta's birthday isn't coming up, is it?

JESSIE. I made a list of all the birthdays for you. I even put yours on it. (*A small smile.*) So you can call Loretta and remind her.

MAMA. Let's take Loretta to Howard Johnson's and have those fried clams. I *know* you love that clam roll.

JESSIE (*slight pause*). I won't be here, Mama.

MAMA. What have we just been talking about? You'll be here. You're well, Jessie. You're starting all over. You said it yourself. You're remembering things and . . .

JESSIE. I won't be here. If I'd ever had a year like this, to think straight and all, before now, I'd be gone already.

MAMA (*not pleading, commanding*). No, Jessie.

JESSIE (*folding the rest of the laundry*). Yes, Mama. Once I started remembering, I could see what it all added up to.

MAMA. The fits are over!

JESSIE. It's not the fits, Mama.

MAMA. Then it's me for giving them to you, but I didn't do it!

JESSIE. It's not the fits! You said it yourself, the medicine takes care of the fits.

MAMA (*interrupting*). Your daddy gave you those fits, Jessie. He passed it down to you like your green eyes, and your straight hair. It's not my fault!

JESSIE. So what if he had little fits? It's not inherited. I fell off the horse. It was an accident.

MAMA. The horse wasn't the first time, Jessie. You had a fit when you were five years old.

JESSIE. I did not.

MAMA. You did! You were eating a popsicle and down you went. He gave it to you. It's *his* fault, not mine.

JESSIE. Well, you took your time telling me.

MAMA. How do you tell that to a five-year-old?

JESSIE. What did the doctor say?

MAMA. He said kids have them all the time. He said there wasn't anything to do but wait for another one.

JESSIE. But I didn't have another one.

(*Now there is a real silence.*)

JESSIE. You mean to tell me I had fits all the time as a kid and you just told me I fell down or something and it wasn't till I had the fit when Cecil was looking that anybody bothered to find out what was the matter with me?

MAMA. It wasn't *all the time,* Jessie. And they changed when you started to school. More like your daddy's. Oh, that was some swell time, sitting here with the two of you turning off and on like light bulbs some nights.

JESSIE. How many fits did I have?

MAMA. You never hurt yourself. I never let you out of my sight. I caught you every time.

JESSIE. But you didn't tell anybody.

MAMA. It was none of their business.

JESSIE. You were ashamed.

MAMA. I didn't want anybody to know. Least of all you.

JESSIE. Least of all me. Oh, right. That was mine to know, Mama, not yours. Did Daddy know?

MAMA. He thought you were . . . you fell down a lot. That's what he thought. You were careless. Or maybe he thought I beat you. I don't know what he thought. He didn't think about it.

JESSIE. Because you didn't tell him!

MAMA. If I told him about you, I'd have to tell him about him!

JESSIE. I don't like this. I don't like this one bit.

MAMA. I didn't think you'd like it. That's why I didn't tell you.

JESSIE. If I'd known I was epileptic, Mama, I wouldn't have ridden any horses.

MAMA. Make you feel like a freak, is that what I should have done?

JESSIE. Just get the manicure tray and sit down!

MAMA (*throwing it to the floor*). I don't want a manicure!

JESSIE. Doesn't look like you do, no.

MAMA. Maybe I did drop you, you don't know.

JESSIE. If you say you didn't, you didn't.

MAMA (*beginning to break down*). Maybe I fed you the wrong thing. Maybe you had a fever sometime and I didn't know it soon enough. Maybe it's a punishment.

JESSIE. For what?

MAMA. I don't know. Because of how I felt about your father. Because I didn't want any more children. Because I smoked too much or didn't eat right when I was carrying you. It has to be something I did.

JESSIE. It does not. It's just a sickness, not a curse. Epilepsy doesn't mean anything. It just is.

MAMA. I'm not talking about the fits here, Jessie! I'm talking about this killing yourself. It has to be me that's the matter here. You wouldn't be doing this if it wasn't. I didn't tell you things or I married you off to the wrong man or I took you in and let your life get away from you or all of it put together. I don't know what I did, but I did it, I know.This is all my fault, Jessie, but I don't know what to do about it now!

JESSIE (*exasperated at having to say this again*). It doesn't have anything to do with you!

MAMA. Everything you do has to do with me, Jessie. You can't do *anything,* wash your face or cut your finger, without doing it to me. That's right! You might as well kill me as you, Jessie, it's the same thing. This has to do with me, Jessie.

JESSIE. Then what if it does! What if it has everything to do with you! What if you are all I have and you're not enough? What if I could take all the rest of it if only I didn't have you here? What if the only way I can get away from you for good is to kill myself? What if it is? I can *still* do it!

MAMA (*in desperate tears*). Don't leave me, Jessie! (*Jessie stands for a moment, then turns for the bedroom.*) No! (*She grabs Jessie's arm.*)

JESSIE (*carefully taking her arm away*). I have a box of things I want people to have. I'm just going to go get it for you. You . . . just rest a minute.

(*Jessie is gone. Mama heads for the telephone, but she can't even pick up the receiver this time and, instead, stoops to clean up the bottles that have spilled out of the manicure tray.*

Jessie returns, carrying a box that groceries were delivered in. It probably says Hershey Kisses or Starkist Tuna. Mama is still down on the floor cleaning up, hoping that maybe if she just makes it look nice enough, Jessie will stay.)

MAMA. Jessie, how can I live here without you? I need you! You're supposed to tell me to stand up straight and say how nice I look in my pink dress, and drink my milk. You're supposed to go around and lock up so I know we're safe for the night, and when I wake up, you're supposed to be out there making the coffee and watching me get older every day, and you're supposed to help me die when the time comes. I can't do that by myself, Jessie. I'm not like you, Jessie. I hate the quiet and I don t want to die and I don't want you to go, Jessie. How can I . . . (*Has to stop a moment.*) How can I get up every day knowing you had to kill yourself to make it stop hurting and I was here all the time and I never even saw it. And then you gave me this chance to make it better, convince you to stay alive, and I couldn't do it. How can I live with myself after this, Jessie?

JESSIE. I only told you so I could explain it, so you wouldn't blame yourself, so you wouldn't feel bad. There wasn't anything you could say to change my mind. I didn't want you to save me. I just wanted you to know.

MAMA. Stay with me just a little longer. Just a few more years. I don't have that many more to go, Jessie. And as soon as I'm dead, you can do whatever you want. Maybe with me gone, you'll have all the quiet you want, right here in the house. And maybe one day you'll put in some begonias up the walk and get just the right rain for them all summer. And Ricky will be married by then and he'll bring your grandbabies over and you can sneak them a piece of candy when their daddy's not looking and then be real glad when they've gone home and left you to your quiet again.

JESSIE. Don't you see, Mama, everything I do winds up like this. How could I think you would understand? How could I think you would want a manicure? We could hold hands for an hour and then I could go shoot myself? I'm sorry about tonight, Mama, but it's exactly why I'm doing it.

MAMA. If you've got the guts to kill yourself, Jessie, you've got the guts to stay alive.

JESSIE. I know that. So it's really just a matter of where I'd rather be.

MAMA. Look, maybe I can't think of what you should do, but that doesn't mean there isn't something that would help. You find it. You think of it. You can keep trying. You can get brave and try some more. You don't have to give up!

JESSIE. I'm not giving up! This *is* the other thing I'm trying. And I'm sure there are some other things that might work, but *might* work isn't good enough anymore. I need something that *will* work. *This* will work. That's why I picked it.

MAMA. But something might happen. Something that could change everything. Who knows what it might be, but it might be worth waiting for! (*Jessie doesn't respond.*) Try it for two more weeks. We could have more talks like tonight.

JESSIE. No, Mama.

MAMA. I'll pay more attention to you. Tell the truth when you ask me. Let you have your say.

JESSIE. No, Mama! We wouldn't have more talks like tonight, because it's this next part that's made this last part so good, Mama. No, Mama. This is how I have my say. *This* is how I say what I thought about it *all* and I say no. To Dawson and Loretta and the Red Chinese and epilepsy and Ricky and Cecil and you. And me. And hope. I say no! (*Then going to Mama on the sofa*) Just let me go easy, Mama.

MAMA. How can I let you go?

JESSIE: You can because you have to. It's what you've always done.

MAMA. You are my child!

JESSIE. I am what became of your child. (*Mama cannot answer.*) I found an old baby picture of me. And it was somebody else, not me. It was somebody pink and fat who never heard of sick or lonely, somebody who cried and got fed, and reached up and got held and kicked but didn't hurt anybody, and slept whenever she wanted to, just by closing her eyes. Somebody who mainly just laid there and laughed at the colors waving around over her head and chewed on a polka-dot whale and woke up knowing some new trick nearly every day, and rolled over and drooled on the sheet and felt your hand pulling my quilt back up over me. That's who I started out and this is who is left. (*There is no self-pity here.*) That's what this is about. It's somebody I lost, all right, it's my own self. Who I never was. Or who I tried to be and never got there. Somebody I waited for who never came. And never will. So, see, it doesn't much matter what else happens in the world or in this house, even. I'm what was worth waiting for and I didn't make it. Me . . . who might have made a difference to me . . . I'm not going to show up, so there's no reason to stay, except to keep you company, and that's . . . not reason enough because I'm not . . . very good company. (*Pause.*) Am I.

MAMA (*knowing she must tell the truth*). No. And neither am I.

JESSIE. I had this strange little thought, well, maybe it's not so strange. Anyway, after Christmas, after I decided to do this, I would wonder, sometimes, what might keep me here, what might be worth staying for, and you know what it was? It was maybe if there was something I really liked, like maybe if I really liked rice pudding or corn-flakes for breakfast or something, that might be enough.

MAMA. Rice pudding is good.

JESSIE. Not for me.

MAMA. And you're not afraid?

JESSIE. Afraid of what?

MAMA. I'm afraid of it, for me, I mean. When my time comes. I know it's coming, but . . .

JESSIE. You don't know when. Like in a scary movie.

MAMA. Yeah, sneaking up on me like some killer on the loose, hiding out in the back yard just waiting for me to have my hands full someday and how am I supposed to protect myself anyhow when I don't know what he looks like and I don't know how he sounds coming up behind me like that or if it will hurt or take very long or what I don't get done before it happens.

JESSIE. You've got plenty of time left.

MAMA. I forget what for, right now.

JESSIE. For whatever happens, I don't know. For the rest of your life. For Agnes burning down one more house or Dawson losing his hair or . . .

MAMA (*quickly*). Jessie. I can't just sit here and say O.K., kill yourself if you want to.

JESSIE. Sure you can. You just did. Say it again.

MAMA. (*really startled*). Jessie! (*Quiet horror*) How dare you! (*Furious*) How dare you! You think you can just leave whenever you want, like you're watching television here? No, you can't, Jessie. You make me feel like a fool for being alive, child, and you are so wrong! I like it here, and I will stay here until they make me go, until they drag me screaming and I mean screeching into my grave, and you're real smart to get away before then because, I mean, honey, you've never heard noise like that in your life. (*Jessie turns away.*) Who am I talking to? You're gone already, aren't you? I'm looking right through you! I can't stop you because you're already gone! I guess you think they'll all have to talk about you now! I guess you think this will really confuse them. Oh, yes, ever since Christmas you've been laughing to yourself and thinking, "Boy, are they all in for a surprise." Well, nobody's going to be a bit surprised, sweetheart. This is just like you. Do it the hard way, that's my girl, all right. (*Jessie gets up and goes into the kitchen, but Mama follows her.*) You know who they're going to feel sorry for? Me! How about that! Not you, me! They're going to be ashamed of you. Yes. Ashamed! If somebody asks Dawson about it, he'll change the subject as fast as he can. He'll talk about how much he has to pay to park his car these days.

JESSIE. Leave me alone.

MAMA. It's the truth!

JESSIE. I should've just left you a note!

MAMA (*screaming*). Yes! (*Then suddenly understanding what she has said, nearly paralyzed by the thought of it, she turns slowly to face Jessie, nearly whispering.*) No. No. I . . . might not have thought of all the things you've said.

JESSIE. It's O.K., Mama.

(*Mama is nearly unconscious from the emotional devastation of these last few moments. She sits down at the kitchen table, hurt and angry and desperately afraid. But she looks almost numb. She is so far beyond what is known as pain that she is virtually unreachable and Jessie knows this, and talks quietly, watching for signs of recovery.*)

JESSIE (*washes her hands in the sink*). I remember you liked that preacher who did Daddy's, so if you want to ask him to do the service, that's O.K. with me.

MAMA (*not an answer, just a word*). What.

JESSIE (*putting on hand lotion as she talks*). And pick some songs you like or let Agnes pick, she'll know exactly which ones. Oh, and I had your dress cleaned that you wore to Daddy's. You looked real good in that.

MAMA. I don't remember, hon.

JESSIE. And it won't be so bad once your friends start coming to the funeral home. You'll probably see people you haven't seen for years, but I thought about what you should say to get you over that nervous part when they first come in.

MAMA (*simply repeating*). Come in.

JESSIE. Take them up to see their flowers, they'd like that. And when they say, "I'm so sorry, Thelma," you just say, "I appreciate your coming, Connie." And then ask how their garden was this summer or what they're doing for Thanksgiving or how their children . . .

MAMA. I don't think I should ask about their children. I'll talk about what they have on, that's always good. And I'll have some crochet work with me.

JESSIE. And Agnes will be there, so you might not have to talk at all.

MAMA. Maybe if Connie Richards does come, I can get her to tell me where she gets that Irish yarn, she calls it. I know it doesn't come from Ireland. I think it just comes with a green wrapper.

JESSIE. And be sure to invite enough people home afterward so you get enough food to feed them all and have some left for you. But don't let anybody take anything home, especially Loretta.

MAMA. Loretta will get all the food set up, honey. It's only fair to let her have some macaroni or something.

JESSIE. No, Mama. You have to be more selfish from now on. (*Sitting at the table with Mama.*) Now, somebody's bound to ask you why I did it and you just say you don't know. That you loved me and you know I loved you and we just sat around tonight like every other night of our lives, and then I came over and kissed you and said, "'night, Mother," and you heard me close my bedroom door and the next thing you heard was the shot. And whatever reasons I had, well, you guess I just took them with me.

MAMA (*quietly*). It was something personal.

JESSIE. Good. That's good, Mama.

MAMA. That's what I'll say, then.

JESSIE. Personal. Yeah.

MAMA. Is that what I tell Dawson and Loretta, too? We sat around, you kissed me, "'night, Mother"? They'll want to know more, Jessie. They won't believe it.

JESSIE. Well, then, tell them what we did. I filled up the candy jars. I cleaned out the refrigerator. We made some hot chocolate and put the cover back on the sofa. You had no idea. All right? I really think it's better that way. If they know we talked about it, they really won't understand how you let me go.

MAMA. I guess not.

JESSIE. It's private. Tonight is private, yours and mine, and I don't want anybody else to have any of it.

MAMA. O.K., then.

JESSIE (*standing behind Mama now, holding her shoulders*). Now, when you hear the shot, I don't want you to come in. First of all, you won't be able to get in by yourself but I don't want you trying. Call Dawson, then call the police, and then call Agnes. And then you'll need something to do till somebody gets here, so wash the hot-chocolate pan. You wash that pan till you hear the doorbell ring and I don't care if it's an hour, you keep washing that pan.

MAMA. I'll make my calls and then I'll just sit. I won't need something to do. What will the police say?

JESSIE. They'll do that gunpowder test, I guess, and ask you what happened, and by that time, the ambulance will be here and they'll come in and get me and you know how that goes. You stay out here with Dawson and Loretta. You keep Dawson out here. I want the police in the room first, not Dawson, O.K.?

MAMA. What if Dawson and Loretta want me to go home with them?

JESSIE (*returning to the living room*). That's up to you.

MAMA. I think I'll stay here. All they've got is Sanka.

JESSIE. Maybe Agnes could come stay with you for a few days.

MAMA (*standing up, looking into the living room*). I'd rather be by myself I think. (*Walking toward the box Jessie brought in earlier*) You want me to give people those things?

JESSIE (*they sit down on the sofa, Jessie holding the box on her lap*). I want Loretta to have my little calculator. Dawson bought it for himself, you know, but then he saw one he liked better and he couldn't bring both of them home with Loretta counting every penny the way she does, so he gave the first one to me. Be funny for her to have it now, don't you think? And all my house slippers are in a sack for her in my closet. Tell her I know they'll fit and I've never worn any of them, and make sure Dawson hears you tell her that. I'm glad he loves Loretta so much, but I wish he knew not everybody has her size feet.

MAMA (*taking the calculator*). O.K.

JESSIE (*reaching into the box again*). This letter is for Dawson, but it's mostly about you, so read it if you want. There's a list of presents for you for at least twenty more Christmases and birthdays, so if you want anything special you better add it to this list before you give it to him. Or if you want to be surprised, just don't read that page. This Christmas, you're getting mostly stuff for the house, like a new rug in your bathroom and needlework, but next Christmas, you're really going to cost him next Christmas. I think you'll like it a lot and you'd never think of it.

MAMA. And you think he'll go for it?

JESSIE. I think he'll feel like a real jerk if he doesn't. Me telling him to, like this and all. Now, this number's where you call Cecil. I called it last week and he answered, so I know he still lives there.

MAMA. What do you want me to tell him?

JESSIE. Tell him we talked about him and I only had good things to say about him, but mainly tell him to find Ricky and tell him what I did, and tell Ricky you have something for him, out here, from me, and to come get it. (*Pulls a sack out of the box.*)

MAMA (*the sack feels empty*). What is it?

JESSIE (*taking it off*). My watch. (*Putting it in the sack and taking a ribbon out of the sack to tie around the top of it.*)

MAMA. He'll sell it!

JESSIE. That's the idea. I appreciate him not stealing it already. I'd like to buy him a good meal.

MAMA. He'll buy dope with it!

JESSIE. Well, then, I hope he gets some good dope with it, Mama. And the rest of this is for you. (*Handing Mama the box now. Mama picks up the things and looks at them.*)

MAMA (*surprised and pleased*). When did you do all this? During my naps, I guess.

JESSIE. I guess. I tried to be quiet about it. (*As Mama is puzzled by the presents.*) Those are just little presents. For whenever you need one. They're not bought presents, just things I thought you might like to look at, pictures or things you think you've lost. Things you didn't know you had, even. You'll see.

MAMA. I'm not sure I want them. They'll make me think of you.

JESSIE. No they won't. They're just things, like a free tube of toothpaste I found hanging on the door one day.

MAMA. Oh. All right, then.

JESSIE. Well, maybe there's one nice present in there somewhere. It's Granny's ring she gave me and I thought you might like to have it, but I didn't think you'd wear it if I gave it to you right now.

MAMA (*taking the box to a table nearby*). No. Probably not. (*Turning back to face her*) I'm ready for my manicure, I guess. Want me to wash my hands again?

JESSIE (*standing up*). It's time for me to go, Mama.

MAMA (*starting for her*). No, Jessie, you've got all night!

JESSIE (*as Mama grabs her*). No, Mama.

MAMA. It's not even ten o'clock.

JESSIE (*very calm*). Let me go, Mama.

MAMA. I can't. You can't go. You can't do this. You didn't say it would be so soon, Jessie. I'm scared. I love you.

JESSIE (*takes her hands away*). Let go of me, Mama. I've said everything I had to say.

MAMA (*standing still a minute*). You said you wanted to do my nails.

JESSIE (*taking a small step backward*). I can't. It's too late.

MAMA. It's not too late!

JESSIE. I don't want you to wake Dawson and Loretta when you call. I want them to still be up and dressed so they can get right over.

MAMA (*as Jessie backs up, Mama moves in on her, but carefully*). They wake up fast, Jessie, if they have to. They don't matter here, Jessie. You do. I do. We're not through yet. We've got a lot of things to take care of here. I don't know where my prescriptions are and you didn't tell me what to tell Dr. Davis when he calls or how much you want me to tell Ricky or who I call to rake the leaves or . . .

JESSIE. Don't try to stop me, Mama, you can't do it.

MAMA (*grabbing her again, this time hard*). I can too! I'll stand in front of this hall and you can't get past me. (*They struggle.*) You'll have to knock me down to get away from me, Jessie. I'm not about to let you . . .

(*Mama struggles with Jessie at the door and in the struggle Jessie gets away from her and—*

JESSIE (*almost a whisper*). 'night, Mother. (*She vanishes into her bedroom and we hear the door lock just as Mama gets to it.*)

MAMA (*screams*). Jessie! (*Pounding on the door*) Jessie, you let me in there. Don't you do this, Jessie. I'm not going to stop screaming until you open this door, Jessie. Jessie! Jessie! What if I don't do any of the things you told me to do! I'll tell Cecil what a miserable man he was to make you feel the way he did and I'll give Ricky's watch to Dawson if I feel like it and the only way you can make sure I do what you want is you come out here and make me. Jessie! (*Pounding again*) Jessie! Stop this! I didn't know! I was here with you all the time. How could I know you were so alone?

(*And Mama stops for a moment, breathless and frantic, putting her ear to the door, and when she doesn't hear anything, she stands up straight again and screams once more.*)

Jessie! Please!

(*And we hear the shot, and it sounds like an answer, it sounds like No.*

Mama collapses against the door, tears streaming down her face, but not screaming anymore. In shock now).

Jessie, Jessie, child . . . Forgive me. (*Pause.*) I thought you were mine.

(*And she leaves the door and makes her way through the living room, around the furniture, as though she didn't know where it was, not knowing what to do. Finally, she goes to the stove in the kitchen and picks up the hot-chocolate pan and carries it with her to the telephone, and holds on to it while she dials the number. She looks down at the pan, holding it tight like her life depended on it. She hears Loretta answer.*)

MAMA. Loretta, let me talk to Dawson, honey.

TOPICS FOR DISCUSSION AND WRITING

1. Early in the play, on page 652, Jessie says she wants the gun for "protection." In the context of the entire play, what does this mean?
2. On page 653 Jessie says she would rather use her father's gun than her husband's. Why?
3. The playwright specifies that "The time is the present, with the action beginning about 8:15. Clocks on stage in the kitchen and on a table in the living room should run throughout the performance and be visible to the audience." Why?
4. Jessie insists (page 662) that Ricky is like her and not like his father Cecil. Exactly what do you think she is getting at?
5. On page 653 Mama says, "People don't really kill themselves, Jessie. No, mam, doesn't make sense, unless you're retarded or deranged." Specify the various reasons that Mama assumes are the motives for Jessie's suicide.
6. Most theories of suicide can be classified into one of two groups, psychoanalytical and sociological. Psychoanalytical theories (usually rooted in Freud) assume that human beings have dual impulses, *eros* (life instinct) and *thanatos* (death instinct). When the death instinct, expressed as hostility and aggression, is turned against others, it takes the form of homicide; but when it is turned against the self, it takes the form of suicide. Most sociological theories assume that suicide occurs among three types of peo-

ple: egoistic suicides, people who are excessively individualistic (i.e., who are not integrated into society); altruistic suicides, people who have an excessive sense of duty to society and who die willingly to serve society; and anomic suicides, people who find their usual lifestyles disrupted by sudden social changes such as the loss of a job during an economic depression. Do any of these theories strike you as helpful in explaining Jessie's suicide? Exactly why does Jessie kill herself? (You may want to do some research on suicide, for instance by consulting Freud's *Civilization and Its Discontents,* or Andrew F. Henry and James F. Short, *Homicide and Suicide,* or Edwin S. Scheidman, ed., *Essays in Self-Destruction,* or A. Alvarez, *The Savage God.*)

7. The greatest tragedies somehow suggest that the tragic figures are not only particular individuals—Oedipus, Lear, and so forth—but also are universal figures who somehow embody our own hopes and fears. Another way of putting it is to say that the greatest plays are not case histories but are visions of a central aspect of life. To what extent do you think *'night, Mother* meets this criterion?

A CONTEXT FOR *'NIGHT, MOTHER*

Interview with Marsha Norman

Norman. . . . I'm also always exploring the rules. I want to know which ones are breakable and which ones are not. I'm convinced that there are absolutely unbreakable rules in the theater, and that it doesn't matter how good you are, you can't break them.

Interviewer. Do you care to list them?

Norman. Sure. It's real easy, you could put this on the back of a cereal box! You must state the issue at the beginning of the play. The audience must know what is at stake; they must know when they will be able to go home: "This is a story of a little boy who lost his marbles." They must know, when the little boy either gets his marbles back or finds something that is better than his marbles, or kills himself because he can't live without his marbles, that the play will end and they can applaud and go home. He can't *not* care about the marbles. He has to want them with such a passion that you are interested, that you connect to that passion. The theater is all about wanting things that you can or can't have or you do or do not get. Now, the boy himself has to be likable. It has to matter to you whether he gets his marbles or not. The other things—language, structure, et cetera,—are variables. One other thing: You can't stop the action for detours. On the way to finding his marbles, the boy can't stop and go swimming. He might do that in a novel, but not in a play.

I like to talk about plays as pieces of machinery. A ski lift. When you get in it, you must feel absolutely secure; you must know that this thing can hold you up. And the first movement of it must be so smooth that whatever residual fears you had about the machine or the mountain are allayed. The journey up the mountain on the ski lift must be continuous. You can't stop and just dangle. If you do, people will realize how far down it is, and they will suddenly get afraid and start grasping the corners of their chairs, which you don't want them to do.

Interviewer. You've said the main character must want something. Is *'night, Mother,* then, Thelma's play? It seems that Jessie, the suicidal daughter, has lost all desire.

Norman. Well, Jessie certainly doesn't want to have anything more to do with *her* life, but she does want Mama to be able to go on, and that's a very strong desire on Jessie's part. She *wants* Mama to be able to do the wash and know where everything is. She wants Mama to live, and to live free of the guilt that Mama might have felt had Jessie just left her a note. Jessie's desires are so strong in the piece. The play exists because Jessie wants something for Mama. Then, of course, Mama wants Jessie to stay. So you have two conflicting goals. And at that point it is a real struggle. It might as well be armed warfare. Only very late in the piece do they realize that both goals are achievable given some moderation. What Mama does understand, finally, is that there wasn't anything she could do. And so Jessie does win. Mama certainly loses in the battle to keep her alive, but Mama does gain other things in the course of the evening.

Interviewer. For instance?

Norman. They have never been so close as they are on this evening. It is calling the question that produces the closeness.

Interviewer. What happens to a woman like Thelma Cates after her daughter has committed suicide?

Norman. Well, what's very clear about Thelma from the beginning is that she lives in an intense network of both things and people. Her friend Agnes says, "You have to keep your life filled up." That's what Thelma has done. She is devoted to her candy and her *TV Guide* and her handwork; she loves talking on the phone to her friends. After Jessie's suicide, Thelma's physical life continues pretty much the way it always was. Thelma is not weak and sick and old. She has only seemed weak and sick and old so that Jessie would feel useful. Jessie, of course, saw right through that. One of the things I think is new in Thelma's life is the experience of this evening, which will belong only to her forever. Probably for the first time, Thelma has something that is securely hers, that she does not need for anybody else to understand and would not dare tell anybody. She has a holy object: this evening that they spent together. And that probably makes for some change in Thelma. But it's probably not a change any of her friends would notice.

Interviewer. Is the holy object The Truth?

Norman. It's the moment of connection between them. Basically, it is a moment when two people are willing to go as far as they can with each other. That doesn't happen very often, and we are lucky if we have two or three moments in our lives when we know that, with this person, we have gone as far as it is possible to go. After a lifetime of missing this daughter, of somehow just living in the same space, they finally had a moment when they actually lived together, when the issues of their lives were standing there with them, in silent witness of their meeting. This is exactly the kind of meeting the theater can document, can present and preserve. In an odd way, writing for the theater is like nominating people for the archives of human history. As playwright, I select a person to nominate for permanent memory by the race. The audience, the worldwide audience, does the voting. Some of my nominations make it and some of them don't. But it seems that Jessie and Thelma are going to make it. They are going to be remembered for what they did that night.

Interviewer. Writing for the theater is an attempt to immortalize your characters?

Norman. Preserve is more like it. We preserve valuable things because they will be needed, because they are the heritage of the people who come after us. We have benefited from that preservation effort up till now—I am grateful that King Lear was preserved, that he is here for me, and I can look at his life and know what he did. We all have a responsibility to preserve those people from our own time who deserve to be remembered or must be remembered for some reason. It's the struggle that makes them memorable. Because on that night, Thelma does as good a job as anybody could do. It's that effort that gives her a place.

Interviewer. Why doesn't Thelma go a bit further? Why doesn't she attack her daughter physically to prevent the suicide?

Norman. Well, there is that final moment at the door, and it posed an interesting dilemma. At that moment in the script, Thelma is reaching for something to hit Jessie with. In the early versions of the script, there was a line that said, "I'll knock you out cold before I'll let you . . ." In my mind I saw Thelma reaching for the frying pan. Like, "I am going to hurt you now. And we will straighten this out when you wake up." [Laughter] Then Tom Moore, the director, pointed out that while it may be tragedy to pick up a frying pan, it is farce when you put it down.

Interviewer. You weren't willing then to risk humor at that point?

Norman. Right. And you can't leave Thelma standing there at the door holding the frying pan.

Interviewer. But did you try it that way during rehearsal?

Norman. We tried to make the fight as violent as we could. Thelma only has one thing left to try and that is physical harm. But I don't know if the audience ever understands that effort.

Interviewer. Did the fact that you could not demonstrate Thelma's passion in a physical way put more weight on her final verbal plea to Jessie?

Norman. The struggle at the door is one of the most difficult moments for both of them. The actress, Anne Pitoniak, as a human being inside that character, realizes she must fight and she must lose.

Interviewer. Does she let go of Jessie in that moment?

Norman. Thelma's crucial letting go has occurred earlier in the piece. This fight is pure instinct. This has nothing to do with thinking or feeling, this is just physical. This is that last moment when you realize you're cornered, and you're not going to try to talk to the grizzly bear anymore. . . . She *does* know that she has lost. Jessie is simply too powerful. But that doesn't mean that Thelma is just going to stand there.

Interviewer. You've said it's important to you to confront life and death issues. Many writers have done it through metaphor, while you confronted it literally. Not that the play is without metaphor—but the central issue is very concrete. How did you come to that decision?

Norman. Suicide is not a new issue on stage. I had seen a couple of pieces that treated it obliquely. Pieces that did not have, for example, the person that loved you most standing there across the room saying *No* to you. I felt that if you were going to talk about suicide, there was really no way to talk about it without having someone argue back. It wasn't that I wanted to work in such a naturalistic way, it was that the issue required it. We're talking about a real gun, a real fight, a real death. One of the interesting attempts that I had seen was a play that a friend of mine, Vaughan McBride, had written. Vaughan and I both had seen a newspaper article about a man who knew that he had terminal cancer and was going to commit suicide. This man went to stay with his friend over a weekend, the idea being that they would spend this weekend talking and being together; then on Sunday morning the friend would go off to get milk and the paper, he would come back, and the other man would have had his opportunity to kill himself. Vaughan showed the evening of talking, the going to bed, and the friend going off to get the newspaper in the morning. Then the man who was going to kill himself walked back up the stairs and the play was over. There was never a mention of the suicide or the friend's agreement to this plan. There was a note in the program that said the man killed himself the next morning, and this had all been arranged. I found it unsatisfying, because I wanted them to deal with it. I didn't want to read it in the program. What I came to with *'night, Mother* was a kind of final submission to the naturalistic form. I simply felt that the subject required that it be treated in a naturalistic manner.

Interviewer. The play is due to go to Japan soon, where I believe that suicide is considered a civil right. I should think the audiences there will experience your story very differently than a Western audience.

Norman. It's going to be fascinating, isn't it? I thought the same thing. I have no idea. Americans have a life-at-all-costs attitude. It's a very privileged point of view, actually.

Interviewer. Where else is *'night, Mother* playing now?

Norman. Australia, Germany, South Africa, New Guinea . . . all over the world. The only trouble we've had is that all the translators—literally all of them—called me and said, "I don't understand. This person who once owned a farm is a peasant, yes? But how can a peasant have a dishwasher?" It is an interesting problem.

. . .

Actually, I'm only writing today because I'm not good enough to have a life as a musician! That is what I'd love to be doing. Making music with people is a lot better than talking. I am a better than average amateur musician. But that's just not good enough.

Interviewer. Would you like to compose?

Norman. Well, you know, it's very funny. I almost enrolled at Juilliard in composition, but, instead, I sat down and wrote *'night Mother.* That is the literal truth. I was so angry then. And I thought, well, all right. I'm going to do one of these two things. It doesn't even matter which one. To be able to compose would be the greatest joy in the world. And yet . . . composers certainly have a difficult life. I was privileged to meet Ellen Zwillich, who's a composer, and listening to her talk about what she has to do to make money . . . of course now she's doing well. But can you imagine? That "starving composer" business is no joke. It's like poets. How do poets and composers live? I have no idea.

Interviewer. Is musical composition a more emotional art form than dramatic writing?

Norman. Well, there are things that music can do that language could never do, that painting can never do, or sculpture: Music is capable of going directly to the source of the mystery. It doesn't have to explain it. It can simply celebrate it. If I'm listening to music, that's all I want to do. It's a great joy to have studied the piano for so long, and so seriously, as a kid. There are pieces of music that I go back to play, that I understand so much more about now. I certainly can't play them as well as I did when I was a kid. But the adult mind is better at some things. Such as understanding the structure of a piece.

Interviewer. Were you aware of the musical structure of *'night, Mother* as you were working on it?

Norman. Oh, yes.

Interviewer. Which came first, the structure or the content?

Norman. When I realized that the piece had basically three parts, suddenly I recognized the musical equivalent was right there and ready. That's an instant occurrence. In each of the three movements of *'night, Mother,* you'll see that it builds and then settles down and stops, there's a moment of silence, and then that second movement picks up. Instruments could do that; better, I'm sorry to say.

. . .

My sense of *'night, Mother* is that it is, by my own definitions of these words, a play of nearly total triumph. Jessie is able to get what she feels she needs. That is not a despairing act. It may look despairing from the outside, but it has cost her everything she has. If Jessie says it's worth it, then it is.

Interviewer. But suicide is not survival. That's what I'm questioning.

Norman. But see, by Jessie's definition of survival, it is. As Jessie says, "My life is all I really have that belongs to me, and I'm going to say what happens to it." . . . Jessie has taken an action on her own behalf that for her is the final test of all that she has been. That's how I see it. Now you don't have to see it that way; nor does anybody else have to see it that way.

Interviewer. Better death with honor than a life of humiliation?

Norman. Right. I think that the question the play asks is, "What does it take to survive? What does it take to save your life?" Now Jessie's answer is "It takes killing myself." Mama's answer is "It takes cocoa and marshmallows and doilies and the *TV Guide* and Agnes and the birds and trips to the grocery." Jessie feels, "No, I'm sorry. That's not enough."

Seattle Repertory Theatre production with (left to right) Francis Foster as Rose Maxon, Keith Amos as Cory Maxon, William Jay as Gabriel, and Gilbert Lewis as Troy Maxon. (Photograph © Chris Bennion.)

AUGUST WILSON

Fences

for Lloyd Richards,
who adds to whatever he touches

When the sins of our fathers visit us
We do not have to play host.
We can banish them with forgiveness
As God, in His Largeness and Laws.
—August Wilson

August Wilson was born in Pittsburgh in 1945, the son of a black woman and a white man. After dropping out of school at the age of fifteen, Wilson took various odd jobs, such as stock clerk and short-order cook, in his spare time educating himself in the public library, chiefly by reading works by such black writers as Richard Wright, Ralph Ellison, Langston Hughes, and Amiri Baraka (LeRoi Jones). In 1978 the director of a black theater in St. Paul, Minnesota, who had known Wilson in Pittsburgh, invited him to write a play for the theater. Six months later Wilson moved permanently to St. Paul.

The winner of the Pulitzer Prize for drama in 1987, Wilson's *Fences* was first presented as a staged reading in 1983 and was later performed in Chicago, Seattle, Rochester (New York), and New Haven (Connecticut) before reaching New York City in 1987. An earlier play, *Ma Rainey's Black Bottom,* was voted Best Play of the Year 1984–85 by the New York Drama Critics' Circle. In 1981 when *Ma Rainey* was first read at the O'Neill Center in Waterford, Connecticut, Wilson met Lloyd Richards, a black director with whom he has continued to work closely.

COMMENTARY

In a very limited sense, African-American theater in the United States has a long history. At least as early as 1821 a semiprofessional black company performed in New York: and in the middle of the nineteenth century the black actor Ira Aldridge achieved international fame. But both of these facts are misleading: the early nineteenth-century company chiefly performed plays by Shakespeare, and Aldridge—not welcome in the white companies of the United States—had to go to Europe to achieve his fame. At the end of the nineteenth century, and in the first decades of the twentieth, things were not much different, though a few black playwrights were emerging, and some black companies performed original plays, chiefly musicals. Still, it was not until the 1920s that black companies did much in the way of performing serious plays written by blacks, about blacks, and even then black actors chiefly found employment as performers in plays about black life written by white playwrights. But in 1926 William E. DuBois, a black leader, organized a black theater in Harlem and enunciated his vision of a new black drama:

The plays of a real Negro theatre must be: 1. About us. That is, they must have plots that

> reveal Negro life as it is. 2. By us; they must be written by Negro authors who understand from birth and continued association just what it means to be a Negro today. 3. For us; that is, the Negro theatre must cater primarily to Negro audiences and be supported by their entertainment and approval. 4. Near us. The theatre must be in a neighborhood near the mass of Negro people.

But when it came to putting ink on paper, not every black writer was quite sure about how to proceed. In 1928, in an article titled "The Dilemma of the Negro Artist," James Weldon Johnson wrote:

> The moment a Negro writer picks up his pen and sits down to his typewriter he is immediately called upon to solve, consciously or unconsciously. this problem of the double audience. To whom shall he address himself, to his own black group or to white America?

Johnson in fact went on to assert that the black writer's audience "is always both white America and black America," but as we shall see in a moment, in the 1960s—the period when "black" displaced "Negro"—not all black writers agreed.

The plays written by blacks from, say, 1920 to the early 1960s fit rather comfortably into the mainstream of American drama. Two plays by and about blacks, Langston Hughes's *Mulatto* (1938) and Lorraine Hansberry's *A Raisin in the Sun* (1959), enjoyed long runs on Broadway, which is to say that much of their support came from whites. These plays are not fundamentally different from, say, Philip Yordan's *Anna Lucasta,* which is by a white playwright and originally dealt with a working-class Polish family in Philadelphia but was altered for a black cast and then became a Broadway hit. With the growth of the Civil Rights Movement in the 1960s, however, black theater changed decisively, helping to form the black power movement.

The most talented black dramatists, including LeRoi Jones (Imamu Amiri Baraka) and Ed Bullins, largely turned their backs on white audiences and in effect wrote plays aimed at showing blacks that *they*—not their white oppressors—must change, must cease to accept the myths that whites had created. Today, however, strongly revolutionary plays by and about blacks have difficulty getting a hearing. Instead, the newest black writers seem to be concerned less with raising the consciousness of blacks than with depicting black life and with letting both blacks and whites respond aesthetically rather than politically. Baraka has attributed the change to a desire by many blacks to become assimilated in today's society, and surely there is much to his view. One might also say, however, that black dramatists may for other reasons have come to assume that the business of drama is not to preach but to show, and that a profound, honest depiction—in a traditional, realistic dramatic form—of things as they are, or in Wilson's play, things as they were in the 1950s—will touch audiences whatever their color. "Part of the reason I wrote *Fences,*" Wilson has said, "was to illuminate that generation, which shielded its children from all of the indignities they went through."

This is not to say, of course, that *Fences* is a play about people who just happen to be black. The Polish family of *Anna Lucasta* could easily be converted to a black family (though perhaps blacks may feel that there is something unconvincing about this family), but Troy Maxson's family cannot be whitewashed. The play is very much about persons who are what they are because they are blacks living in an unjust society run by whites. We are not allowed to forget this. Troy is a baseball player who was too old to join a white team when the major leagues began to hire blacks. For Troy's friend, Bono, "Troy just came along too early"; but Troy pungently replies, "There ought not never have been no time called too early." Blacks of Troy's day were expected to subscribe to American ideals—for instance, to serve in the army in time of war—but they were also expected to sit in the back of the bus and to accept the fact that they were barred from decent jobs. Wilson shows us the scars that such treatment left. Troy is no paragon. Although he has a deep sense of responsibility to his family, his behavior toward them is deeply flawed: he oppresses his son Cory, he is unfaithful to his wife, Rose, and he exploits his brother Gabriel.

Wilson, as we have seen, calls attention to racism in baseball, and he indicates that Troy turned to crime because he could not earn money. But Wilson does not allow *Fences,* to become a prolonged protest against white oppression—though one can never quite forget that Troy insists on a high personal ideal in a world that has cheated him. The interest in the play is in Troy as a human being, or, rather, in all of the characters as human beings rather than as representatives of white victimization. As Troy sees it, by preventing Cory from engaging in athletics—the career that frustrated Troy—he is helping rather than oppressing Cory: "I don't want him to be like me. I want him to move as far from me as he can." But Wilson also makes it clear that Troy has other (very human) motives, of which Troy perhaps is unaware.

AUGUST WILSON *Fences*

List of Characters

TROY MAXSON
JIM BONO, *Troy's friend*
ROSE, *Troy's wife*
LYONS, *Troy's oldest son by previous marriage*
GABRIEL, *Troy's brother*
CORY, *Troy and Rose's son*
RAYNELL, *Troy's daughter*

Setting

The setting is the yard which fronts the only entrance to the Maxson household, an ancient two-story brick house set back off a small alley in a big-city neighborhood. The entrance to the house is gained by two or three steps leading to a wooden porch badly in need of paint.

A relatively recent addition to the house and running its full width, the porch lacks congruence. It is a sturdy porch with a flat roof. One or two chairs of dubious value sit at one end where the kitchen window opens onto the porch. An old-fashioned icebox stands silent guard at the opposite end.

The yard is a small dirt yard, partially fenced, except for the last scene, with a wooden sawhorse, a pile of lumber, and other fence-building equipment set off to the side. Opposite is a tree from which hangs a ball made of rags. A baseball bat leans against the tree. Two oil drums serve as garbage receptacles and sit near the house at right to complete the setting.

The Play

Near the turn of the century, the destitute of Europe sprang on the city with tenacious claws and an honest and solid dream. The city devoured them. They swelled its belly until it burst into a thousand furnaces and sewing machines, a thousand butcher shops and bakers' ovens, a thousand churches and hospitals and funeral parlors and moneylenders. The city grew. It nourished itself and offered each man a partnership limited only by his talent, his guile, and his willingness and capacity for hard work. For the immigrants of Europe, a dream dared and won true.

The descendants of African slaves were offered no such welcome or participation. They came from places called the Carolinas and the Virginias, Georgia, Alabama, Mississippi, and Tennessee. They came strong, eager, searching. The city rejected them and they fled and settled along the riverbanks and under bridges in shallow, ramshackle houses made of sticks and tar-paper. They collected rags and wood. They sold the use of their muscles and their bodies. They cleaned houses and washed clothes, they shined shoes, and in quiet desperation and vengeful pride, they stole, and lived in pursuit of their own dream. That they could breathe free, finally, and stand to meet life with the force of dignity and whatever eloquence the heart could call upon.

By 1957, the hard-won victories of the European immigrants had solidified the industrial might of America. War had been confronted and won with new energies that used loyalty and patriotism as its fuel. Life was rich, full, and flourishing. The Milwaukee Braves won the World Series, and the hot winds of change that would make the sixties a turbulent, racing, dangerous, and provocative decade had not yet begun to blow full.

ACT 1

SCENE 1

It is 1957. Troy and Bono enter the yard, engaged in conversation. Troy is fifty-three years old, a large man with thick, heavy hands; it is this largeness that he strives to fill out and make an accommodation with. Together with his blackness, his largeness informs his sensibilities and the choices he has made in his life.

Of the two men, Bono is obviously the follower. His commitment to their friendship of thirty-odd years is rooted in his admiration of Troy's honesty, capacity for hard work, and his strength, which Bono seeks to emulate.

It is Friday night, payday, and the one night of the week the two men engage in a ritual of talk and drink. Troy is usually the most talkative and at times he can be crude and almost vulgar, though he is capable of rising to profound heights of expression. The men carry lunch buckets and wear or carry burlap aprons and are dressed in clothes suitable to their jobs as garbage collectors.

BONO. Troy, you ought to stop that lying!

TROY. I ain't lying! The nigger had a watermelon this big. (*He indicates with his hands.*) Talking about . . . "What watermelon, Mr. Rand?" I liked to fell out! "What watermelon, Mr. Rand?" . . . And it sitting there big as life.

BONO. What did Mr. Rand say?

TROY. Ain't said nothing. Figure if the nigger too dumb to know he carrying a watermelon, he wasn't gonna get much sense out of him. Trying to hide that great big old watermelon under his coat. Afraid to let the white man see him carry it home.

BONO. I'm like you . . . I ain't got no time for them kind of people.

TROY. Now what he look like getting mad cause he see the man from the union talking to Mr. Rand?

BONO. He come to me talking about . . . "Maxson gonna get us fired." I told him to get away from me with that. He walked away from me calling you a troublemaker. What Mr. Rand say?

TROY. Ain't said nothing. He told me to go down the Commissioner's office next Friday. They called me down there to see them.

BONO. Well, as long as you got your complaint filed, they can't fire you. That's what one of them white fellows tell me.

TROY. I ain't worried about them firing me. They gonna fire me cause I asked a question? That's all I did. I went to Mr. Rand and asked him, "Why? Why you got the white mens driving and the colored lifting?" Told him, "what's the matter, don't I count? You think only white fellows got sense enough to drive a truck. That ain't no paper job! Hell, anybody can drive a truck. How come you got all whites driving and the colored lifting?" He told me "take it to the union." Well, hell, that's what I done! Now they wanna come up with this pack of lies.

BONO. I told Brownie if the man come and ask him any questions . . . just tell the truth! It ain't nothing but something they done trumped up on you cause you filed a complaint on them.

TROY. Brownie don't understand nothing. All I want them to do is change the job description. Give everybody a chance to drive the truck. Brownie can't see that. He ain't got that much sense.

BONO. How you figure he be making out with that gal be up at Taylors' all the time . . . that Alberta gal?

TROY. Same as you and me. Getting just as much as we is. Which is to say nothing.

BONO. It is, huh? I figure you doing a little better than me . . . and I ain't saying what I'm doing.

TROY. Aw, nigger, look here . . . I know you. If you had got anywhere near that gal, twenty minutes later you be looking to tell somebody. And the first one you gonna tell . . . that you gonna want to brag to . . . is gonna be me.

BONO. I ain't saying that. I see where you be eyeing her.

TROY. I eye all the women. I don't miss nothing. Don't never let nobody tell you Troy Maxson don't eye the women.

BONO. You been doing more than eyeing her. You done bought her a drink or two.

TROY. Hell yeah, I bought her a drink! What that mean? I bought you one, too. What that mean cause I buy her a drink? I'm just being polite.

BONO. It's all right to buy her one drink. That's what you call being polite. But when you wanna be buying two or three . . . that's what you call eyeing her.

TROY. Look here, as long as you known me . . . you ever known me to chase after women?

BONO. Hell yeah! Long as I done known you. You forgetting I knew you when.

TROY. Naw, I'm talking about since I been married to Rose?

BONO. Oh, not since you been married to Rose. Now, that's the truth, there. I can say that.

TROY. All right then! Case closed.

BONO. I see you be walking up around Alberta's house. You supposed to be at Taylors' and you be walking up around there.

TROY. What you watching where I'm walking for? I ain't watching after you.

BONO. I seen you walking around there more than once.

TROY. Hell, you liable to see me walking anywhere! That don't mean nothing cause you see me walking around there.

BONO. Where she come from anyway? She just kinda showed up one day.

TROY. Tallahassee. You can look at her and tell she one of them Florida gals. They got some big healthy women down there. Grow them right up out the ground. Got a little bit of Indian in her. Most of them niggers down in Florida got some Indian in them.

BONO. I don't know about that Indian part. But she damn sure big and healthy. Woman wear some big stockings. Got them great big old legs and hips as wide as the Mississippi River.

TROY. Legs don't mean nothing. You don't do nothing but push them out of the way. But them hips cushion the ride!

BONO. Troy, you ain't got no sense.

TROY. It's the truth! Like you riding on Goodyears!

(*Rose enters from the house. She is ten years younger than Troy, her devotion to him stems from her recognition of the possibilities of her life without him: a succession of abusive men and their babies, a life of partying and running the streets, the Church, or aloneness with its attendant pain and frustration. She recognizes Troy's spirit as a fine and illuminating one and she either ignores or forgives his faults, only some of which she recognizes. Though she doesn't drink, her presence is an integral part of the Friday night rituals. She alternates between the porch and the kitchen, where supper preparations are under way.*)

ROSE. What you all out here getting into?

TROY. What you worried about what we getting into for? This is men talk, woman.

ROSE. What I care what you all talking about? Bono, you gonna stay for supper?

BONO. No, I thank you, Rose. But Lucille say she cooking up a pot of pigfeet.

TROY. Pigfeet! Hell, I'm going home with you! Might even stay the night if you got some pigfeet. You got something in there to top them pigfeet, Rose?

ROSE. I'm cooking up some chicken. I got some chicken and collard greens.

TROY. Well, go on back in the house and let me and Bono finish what we was talking about. This is men talk. I got some talk for you later. You know what kind of talk I mean. You go on and powder it up.

ROSE. Troy Maxson, don't you start that now!

TROY (*puts his arm around her*). Aw, woman . . . come here. Look here, Bono . . . when I met this woman . . . I got out that place, say, "Hitch up my pony, saddle up my mare . . . there's a woman out there for me somewhere. I looked here. Looked there. Saw Rose and latched on to her." I latched on to her and told her—I'm gonna tell you the truth—I told her, "Baby, I don't wanna marry, I just wanna be your man." Rose told me . . . tell him what you told me, Rose.

ROSE. I told him if he wasn't the marrying kind, then move out the way so the marrying kind could find me.

TROY. That's what she told me. "Nigger, you in my way. You blocking the view! Move out the way so I can find me a husband." I thought it over two or three days. Come back—

ROSE. Ain't no two or three days nothing. You was back the same night.

TROY. Come back, told her . . . "Okay, baby . . . but I'm gonna buy me a banty rooster and put him out there in the backyard . . . and when he sees a stranger come, he'll flap his wings and crow . . ." Look here, Bono, I could watch the front door by myself . . . it was that back door I was worried about.

ROSE. Troy, you ought not talk like that. Troy ain't doing nothing but telling a lie.

TROY. Only thing is . . . when we first got married . . . forget the rooster . . . we ain't had no yard!

BONO. I hear you tell it. Me and Lucille was staying down there on Logan Street. Had two rooms with the outhouse in the back. I ain't mind the outhouse none. But when that goddamn wind blow through there in the winter . . . that's what I'm talking about! To this day I wonder why in the hell I ever stayed down there for six long years. But see, I didn't know I could do no better. I thought only white folks had inside toilets and things.

ROSE. There's a lot of people don't know they can do no better than they doing now. That's just something you got to learn. A lot of folks still shop at Bella's.

TROY. Ain't nothing wrong with shopping at Bella's. She got fresh food.

ROSE. I ain't said nothing about if she got fresh food. I'm talking about what she charge. She charge ten cents more than the A&P.

TROY. The A&P ain't never done nothing for me. I spends my money where I'm treated right. I go down to Bella, say, "I need a loaf of bread, I'll pay you Friday." She give it to me. What sense that make when I got money to go and spend it somewhere else and ignore the person who done right by me? That ain't in the Bible.

ROSE. We ain't talking about what's in the Bible. What sense it make to shop there when she overcharge?

TROY. You shop where you want to. I'll do my shopping where the people been good to me.

ROSE. Well, I don't think it's right for her to overcharge. That's all I was saying.

BONO. Look here . . . I got to get on. Lucille going be raising all kind of hell.

TROY. Where you going, nigger? We ain't finished this pint. Come here, finish this pint.

BONO. Well, hell, I am . . . if you ever turn the bottle loose.

TROY (*hands him the bottle*). The only thing I say about the A&P is I'm glad Cory got that job down there. Help him take care of his school clothes and things. Gabe done moved out and things getting tight around here. He got that job. . . . He can start to look out for himself.

ROSE. Cory done went and got recruited by a college football team.

TROY. I told that boy about that football stuff. The white man ain't gonna let him get nowhere with that football. I told him when he first come to me with it. Now you come telling me he done went and got more tied up in it. He ought to go and get recruited in how to fix cars or something where he can make a living.

ROSE. He ain't talking about making no living playing football. It's just something the boys in school do. They gonna send a recruiter by to talk to you. He'll tell you he ain't talking about making no living playing football. It's a honor to be recruited.

TROY. It ain't gonna get him nowhere. Bono'll tell you that.

BONO. If he be like you in the sports . . . he's gonna be all right. Ain't but two men ever played baseball as good as you. That's Babe Ruth and Josh Gibson. Them's the only two men ever hit more home runs than you.

TROY. What it ever get me? Ain't got a pot to piss in or a window to throw it out of.

ROSE. Times have changed since you was playing baseball, Troy. That was before the war. Times have changed a lot since then.

TROY. How in hell they done changed?

ROSE. They got lots of colored boys playing ball now. Baseball and football.

BONO. You right about that, Rose. Times have changed, Troy. You just come along too early.

TROY. There ought not never have been no time called too early! Now you take that fellow . . . what's that fellow they had playing right field for the Yankees back then? You know who I'm talking about, Bono. Used to play right field for the Yankees.

ROSE. Selkirk?

TROY. Selkirk! That's it! Man batting .269, understand? .269. What kind of sense that make? I was hitting .432 with thirty-seven home runs! Man batting .269 and playing right field for the Yankees! I saw Josh Gibson's daughter yesterday. She walking around with raggedy shoes on her feet. Now I bet you Selkirk's daughter ain't walking around with raggedy shoes on her feet! I bet you that!

ROSE. They got a lot of colored baseball players now. Jackie Robinson was the first. Folks had to wait for Jackie Robinson.

TROY. I done seen a hundred niggers play baseball better than Jackie Robinson. Hell, I know some teams Jackie Robinson couldn't even make! What you talking about Jackie Robinson. Jackie Robinson wasn't nobody. I'm talking about if you could play ball then they ought to have let you play. Don't care what color you were. Come telling me I come along too early. If you could play . . . then they ought to have let you play.

(*Troy takes a long drink from the bottle.*)

ROSE. You gonna drink yourself to death. You don't need to be drinking like that.

TROY. Death ain't nothing. I done seen him. Done wrassled with him. You can't tell me nothing about death. Death ain't nothing but a fastball on the outside corner. And you know what I'll do to that! Lookee here, Bono . . . am I lying? You get one of them fastballs, about waist high, over the outside corner of the plate where you can get the meat of the bat on it . . . and good god! You can kiss it goodbye. Now, am I lying?

BONO. Naw, you telling the truth there. I seen you do it.

TROY. If I'm lying . . . that 450 feet worth of lying! (*Pause.*) That's all death is to me. A fastball on the outside corner.

ROSE. I don't know why you want to get on talking about death.

TROY. Ain't nothing wrong with talking about death. That's part of life. Everybody gonna die. You gonna die, I'm gonna die. Bono's gonna die. Hell, we all gonna die.

ROSE. But you ain't got to talk about it. I don't like to talk about it.

TROY. You the one brought it up. Me and Bono was talking about baseball . . . you tell me I'm gonna drink myself to death. Ain't that right, Bono? You know I don't drink this but one night out of the week. That's Friday night. I'm gonna drink just enough to where I can handle it. Then I cuts it loose. I leave it alone. So don't you worry about me drinking myself to death. 'Cause I ain't worried about Death. I done seen him. I done wrestled with him.

Look here, Bono . . . I looked up one day and Death was marching straight at me. Like Soldiers on Parade! The Army of Death was marching straight at me. The middle of July, 1941. It got real cold just like it be winter. It seem like Death himself reached out and touched me on the shoulder. He touch me just like I touch you. I got cold as ice and Death standing there grinning at me.

ROSE. Troy, why don't you hush that talk.

TROY. I say . . . What you want, Mr. Death? You be wanting me? You done brought your army to be getting me? I looked him dead in the eye. I wasn't fearing nothing. I was ready to tangle. Just like I'm ready to tangle now. The Bible say be ever vigilant. That's why I don't get but so drunk. I got to keep watch.

ROSE. Troy was right down there in Mercy Hospital. You remember he had pneumonia? Laying there with a fever talking plumb out of his head.

TROY. Death standing there staring at me . . . carrying that sickle in his hand. Finally he say, "You want bound over for another year?" See, just like that . . . "You want bound over for another year?" I told him, "Bound over hell! Let's settle this now!"

It seem like he kinda fell back when I said that, and all the cold went out of me. I reached down and grabbed that sickle and threw it just as far as I could throw it . . . and me and him commenced to wrestling.

We wrestled for three days and three nights. I can't say where I found the strength from. Every time it seemed like he was gonna get the best of me, I'd reach way down deep inside myself and find the strength to do him one better.

ROSE. Every time Troy tell that story he find different ways to tell it. Different things to make up about it.

TROY. I ain't making up nothing. I'm telling you the facts of what happened. I wrestled with Death for three days and three nights and I'm standing here to tell you about it. (*Pause.*) All right. At the end of the third night we done weakened each other to where we can't hardly move. Death stood up, throwed on his robe . . . had him a white robe with a hood on it. He throwed on that robe and went off to look for his sickle. Say, "I'll be back." Just like that. "I'll be back." I told him, say, "Yeah, but . . . you gonna have to find me!" I wasn't no fool. I wasn't going looking for him. Death ain't nothing to play with. And I know he's gonna get me. I know I got to join his army . . . his camp followers. But as long as I keep my strength and see him coming . . . as long as I keep up my vigilance . . . he's gonna have to fight to get me. I ain't going easy.

BONO. Well, look here, since you got to keep up your vigilance . . . let me have the bottle.

TROY. Aw hell, I shouldn't have told you that part. I should have left out that part.

ROSE. Troy be talking that stuff and half the time don't even know what he be talking about.

TROY. Bono know me better than that.

BONO. That's right. I know you. I know you got some Uncle Remus in your blood. You got more stories than the devil got sinners.

TROY. Aw hell, I done seen him too! Done talked with the devil.

ROSE. Troy, don't nobody wanna be hearing all that stuff.

(*Lyons enters the yard from the street. Thirty-four years old, Troy's son by a previous marriage, he sports a neatly trimmed goatee, sport coat, white shirt, tieless and buttoned at the collar. Though he fancies himself a musician, he is more caught up in the rituals and "idea" of being a musician than in the actual practice of the music. He has came to borrow money from Troy, and while he knows he will be successful, he is uncertain as to what extent his lifestyle will be held up to scrutiny and ridicule.*)

LYONS. Hey, Pop.

TROY. What you come "Hey, Popping" me for?

LYONS. How you doing, Rose? (*He kisses her.*) Mr. Bono. How you doing?

BONO. Hey, Lyons . . . how you been?

TROY. He must have been doing all right. I ain't seen him around here last week.

ROSE. Troy, leave your boy alone. He come by to see you and you wanna start all that nonsense.

TROY. I ain't bothering Lyons. (*Offers him the bottle.*) Here . . . get you a drink. We got an understanding. I know why he come by to see me and he know I know.

LYONS. Come on, Pop . . . I just stopped by to say hi . . . see how you was doing.

TROY. You ain't stopped by yesterday.

ROSE. You gonna stay for supper, Lyons? I got some chicken cooking in the oven.

LYONS. No, Rose . . . thanks. I was just in the neighborhood and thought I'd stop by for a minute.

TROY. You was in the neighborhood alright, nigger. You

telling the truth there. You was in the neighborhood cause it's my payday.

LYONS. Well, hell, since you mentioned it . . . let me have ten dollars.

TROY. I'll be damned! I'll die and go to hell and play blackjack with the devil before I give you ten dollars.

BONO. That's what I wanna know about . . . that devil you done seen.

LYONS. What . . . Pop done seen the devil? You too much, Pops.

TROY. Yeah, I done seen him. Talked to him too!

ROSE. You ain't seen no devil. I done told you that man ain't had nothing to do with the devil. Anything you can't understand, you want to call it the devil.

TROY. Look here, Bono . . . I went down to see Hertzberger about some furniture. Got three rooms for two-ninety-eight. That what it say on the radio. "Three rooms . . . two-ninety-eight." Even made up a little song about it. Go down there . . . man tell me I can't get no credit. I'm working every day and can't get no credit. What to do? I got an empty house with some raggedy furniture in it. Cory ain't got no bed. He's sleeping on a pile of rags on the floor. Working every day and can't get no credit. Come back here—Rose'll tell you—madder than hell. Sit down . . . try to figure what I'm gonna do. Come a knock on the door. Ain't been living here but three days. Who know I'm here? Open the door . . . devil standing there bigger than life. White fellow . . . got on good clothes and everything. Standing there with a clipboard in his hand. I ain't had to say nothing. First words come out of his mouth was . . . "I understand you need some furniture and can't get no credit." I liked to fell over. He say, "I'll give you all the credit you want, but you got to pay the interest on it." I told him, "Give me three rooms worth and charge whatever you want." Next day a truck pulled up here and two men unloaded them three rooms. Man what drove the truck give me a book. Say send ten dollars, first of every month to the address in the book and everything will be alright. Say if I miss a payment the devil was coming back and it'll be hell to pay. That was fifteen years ago. To this day . . . the first of the month I send my ten dollars, Rose'll tell you.

ROSE. Troy lying.

TROY. I ain't never seen that man since. Now you tell me who else that could have been but the devil? I ain't sold my soul or nothing like that, you understand. Naw, I wouldn't have truck with the devil about nothing like that. I got my furniture and pays my ten dollars the first of the month just like clockwork.

BONO. How long you say you been paying this ten dollars a month?

TROY. Fifteen years!

BONO. Hell, ain't you finished paying for it yet? How much the man done charged you.

TROY. Aw hell, I done paid for it. I done paid for it ten times over! The fact is I'm scared to stop paying it.

ROSE. Troy lying. We got that furniture from Mr. Glickman. He ain't paying no ten dollars a month to nobody.

TROY. Aw hell, woman. Bono know I ain't that big a fool.

LYONS. I was just getting ready to say . . . I know where there's a bridge for sale.

TROY. Look here, I'll tell you this . . . it don't matter to me if he was the devil. It don't matter if the devil give credit. Somebody has got to give it.

ROSE. It ought to matter. You going around talking about having truck with the devil . . . God's the one you gonna have to answer to. He's the one gonna be at the Judgment.

LYONS. Yeah, well, look here, Pop . . . let me have that ten dollars. I'll give it back to you. Bonnie got a job working at the hospital.

TROY. What I tell you, Bono? The only time I see this nigger is when he wants something. That's the only time I see him.

LYONS. Come on, Pop, Mr. Bono don't want to hear all that. Let me have the ten dollars. I told you Bonnie working.

TROY. What that mean to me? "Bonnie working." I don't care if she working. Go ask her for the ten dollars if she working. Talking about "Bonnie working." Why ain't you working?

LYONS. Aw, Pop, you know I can't find no decent job. Where am I gonna get a job at? You know I can't get no job.

TROY. I told you I know some people down there. I can get you on the rubbish if you want to work. I told you that the last time you came by here asking me for something.

LYONS. Naw, Pop . . . thanks. That ain't for me. I don't wanna be carrying nobody's rubbish. I don't wanna be punching nobody's time clock.

TROY. What's the matter, you too good to carry people's rubbish? Where you think that ten dollars you talking about come from? I'm just supposed to haul people's rubbish and give my money to you cause you too lazy to work. You too lazy to work and wanna know why you ain't got what I got.

ROSE. What hospital Bonnie working at? Mercy?

LYONS. She's down at Passavant working in the laundry.

TROY. I ain't got nothing as it is. I give you that ten dollars and I got to eat beans the rest of the week. Naw . . . you ain't getting no ten dollars here.

LYONS. You ain't got to be eating no beans. I don't know why you wanna say that.

TROY. I ain't got no extra money. Gabe done moved

over to Miss Pearl's paying her the rent and things done got tight around here. I can't afford to be giving you every payday.

LYONS. I ain't asked you to give me nothing. I asked you to loan me ten dollars. I know you got ten dollars.

TROY. Yeah. I got it. You know why I got it? Cause I don't throw my money away out there in the streets. You living the fast life . . . wanna be a musician . . . running around in them clubs and things . . . then, you learn to take care of yourself. You ain't gonna find me going and asking nobody for nothing. I done spent too many years without.

LYONS. You and me is two different people. Pop.

TROY. I done learned my mistake and learned to do what's right by it. You still trying to get something for nothing. Life don't owe you nothing. You owe it to yourself. Ask Bono. He'll tell you I'm right.

LYONS. You got your way of dealing with the world . . . I got mine. The only thing that matters to me is the music.

TROY. Yeah, I can see that! It don't matter how you gonna eat . . . where your next dollar is coming from. You telling the truth there.

LYONS. I know I got to eat. But I got to live too. I need something that gonna help me to get out of the bed in the morning. Make me feel like I belong in the world. I don't bother nobody. Just stay with my music cause that's the only way I can find to live in the world. Otherwise there ain't no telling what I might do. Now I don't come criticizing you and how you live. I just come by to ask you for ten dollars. I don't wanna hear all that about how I live.

TROY. Boy, your mama did a hell of a job raising you.

LYONS. You can't change me, Pop. I'm thirty-four years old. If you wanted to change me, you should have been there when I was growing up. I come by to see you . . . ask for ten dollars and you want to talk about how I was raised. You don't know nothing about how I was raised.

ROSE. Let the boy have ten dollars, Troy.

TROY (*To Lyons*). What the hell you looking at me for? I ain't got no ten dollars. You know what I do with my money. (*To Rose*) Give him ten dollars if you want him to have it.

ROSE. I will. Just as soon as you turn it loose.

TROY (*handing Rose the money*). There it is. Seventy-six dollars and forty-two cents. You see this, Bono? Now, I ain't gonna get but six of that back.

ROSE. You ought to stop telling that lie. Here, Lyons. (*She hands him the money.*)

LYONS. Thanks, Rose. Look . . . I got to run . . . I'll see you later.

TROY. Wait a minute. You gonna say, "thanks, Rose" and ain't gonna look to see where she got that ten dollars from? See how they do me, Bono?

LYONS. I know she got it from you, Pop. Thanks. I'll give it back to you.

TROY. There he go telling another lie. Time I see that ten dollars . . . he'll be owing me thirty more.

LYONS. See you. Mr. Bono.

BONO. Take care, Lyons!

LYONS. Thanks, Pop. I'll see you again.

(*Lyons exits the yard.*)

TROY. I don't know why he don't go and get him a decent job and take care of that woman he got.

BONO. He'll be alright, Troy. The boy is still young.

TROY. The *boy* is thirty-four years old.

BONO. Let's not get off into all that.

BONO. Look here . . . I got to be going. I got to be getting on. Lucille gonna be waiting.

TROY (*puts his arm around Rose*). See this woman, Bono? I love this woman. I love this woman so much it hurts. I love her so much . . . I done run out of ways of loving her. So I got to go back to basics. Don't you come by my house Monday morning talking about time to go to work . . . 'cause I'm still gonna be stroking!

ROSE. Troy! Stop it now!

BONO. I ain't paying him no mind, Rose. That ain't nothing but gin-talk. Go on, Troy. I'll see you Monday.

TROY. Don't you come by my house, nigger! I done told you what I'm gonna be doing.

(*The lights go down to black.*)

SCENE 2

The lights come up on Rose hanging up clothes. She hums and sings softly to herself. It is the following morning.

ROSE (*Sings*).

Jesus, be a fence all around me every day
Jesus, I want you to protect me as I travel on my
way
Jesus, be a fence all around me every day.

(*Troy enters from the house.*)

ROSE (*continues*).

Jesus, I want you to protect me
As I travel on my way.

(*To Troy*) 'Morning. You ready for breakfast? I can fix it soon as I finish hanging up these clothes?

TROY. I got the coffee on. That'll be all right. I'll just drink some of that this morning.

ROSE. That 651 hit yesterday. That's the second time this month. Miss Pearl hit for a dollar . . . seem like those that need the least always get lucky. Poor folks can't get nothing.

TROY. Them numbers don't know nobody. I don't know why you fool with them. You and Lyons both.

ROSE. It's something to do.

TROY. You ain't doing nothing but throwing your money away.

ROSE. Troy, you know I don't play foolishly. I just play a nickel here and a nickel there.

TROY. That's two nickels you done thrown away.

ROSE. Now I hit sometimes . . . that makes up for it. It always comes in handy when I do hit. I don't hear you complaining then.

TROY. I ain't complaining now. I just say it's foolish. Trying to guess out of six hundred ways which way the number gonna come. If I had all the money niggers, these Negroes, throw away on numbers for one week—just one week—I'd be a rich man.

ROSE. Well, you wishing and calling it foolish ain't gonna stop folks from playing numbers. That's one thing for sure. Besides . . . some good things come from playing numbers. Look where Pope done bought him that restaurant off of numbers.

TROY. I can't stand niggers like that. Man ain't had two dimes to rub together. He walking around with his shoes all run over bumming money for cigarettes. All right. Got lucky there and hit the numbers . . .

ROSE. Troy, I know all about it.

TROY. Had good sense, I'll say that for him. He ain't throwed his money away. I seen niggers hit the numbers and go through two thousand dollars in four days. Man bought him that restaurant down there . . . fixed it up real nice . . . and then didn't want nobody to come in it! A Negro go in there and can't get no kind of service. I seen a white fellow come in there and order a bowl of stew. Pope picked all the meat out the pot for him. Man ain't had nothing but a bowl of meat! Negro come behind him and ain't got nothing but the potatoes and carrots. Talking about what numbers do for people, you picked a wrong example. Ain't done nothing but make a worser fool out of him than he was before.

ROSE. Troy, you ought to stop worrying about what happened at work yesterday.

TROY. I ain't worried. Just told me to be down there at the Commissioner's office on Friday. Everybody think they gonna fire me. I ain't worried about them firing me. You ain't got to worry about that. (*Pause.*) Where's Cory? Cory in the house? (*Calls*) Cory?

ROSE. He gone out.

TROY. Out, huh? He gone out 'cause he know I want him to help me with this fence. I know how he is. That boy scared of work.

(*Gabriel enters. He comes halfway down the alley and, hearing Troy's voice, stops.*)

TROY (*continues*). He ain't done a lick of work in his life.

ROSE. He had to go to football practice. Coach wanted them to get in a little extra practice before the season start.

TROY. I got his practice . . . running out of here before he get his chores done.

ROSE. Troy, what is wrong with you this morning? Don't nothing set right with you. Go on back in there and go to bed . . . get up on the other side.

TROY. Why something got to be wrong with me? I ain't said nothing wrong with me.

ROSE. You got something to say about everything. First it's the numbers . . . then it's the way the man runs his restaurant . . . then you done got on Cory. What's it gonna be next? Take a look up there and see if the weather suits you . . . or is it gonna be how you gonna put up the fence with the clothes hanging in the yard.

TROY. You hit the nail on the head then.

ROSE. I know you like I know the back of my hand. Go on in there and get you some coffee . . . see if that straighten you up. 'Cause you ain't right this morning.

(*Troy starts into the house and sees Gabriel. Gabriel starts singing. Troy's brother, he is seven years younger than Troy. Injured in World War II, he has a metal plate in his head. He carries an old trumpet tied around his waist and believes with every fiber of his being that he is the Archangel Gabriel. He carries a chipped basket with an assortment of discarded fruits and vegetables he has picked up in the strip district and which he attempts to sell.*)

GABRIEL (*singing*).
Yes, ma'am, I got plums
You ask me how I sell them
Oh ten cents apiece
Three for a quarter
Come and buy now
'Cause I'm here today
And tomorrow I'll be gone

(*Gabriel enters.*)

Hey, Rose!

ROSE. How you doing, Gabe?

GABRIEL. There's Troy . . . Hey, Troy!

TROY. Hey, Gabe. (*Exits into kitchen.*)

ROSE (*to Gabriel*). What you got there?

GABRIEL. You know what I got, Rose. I got fruits and vegetables.

ROSE (*looking in basket*). Where's all these plums you talking about?

GABRIEL. I ain't got no plums today, Rose. I was just

singing that. Have some tomorrow. Put me in a big order for plums. Have enough plums tomorrow for St. Peter and everybody.

(*Troy re-enters from kitchen, crosses to steps.*)

(*To Rose*) Troy's mad at me.

TROY. I ain't mad at you. What I got to be mad at you about? You ain't done nothing to me.

GABRIEL. I just moved over to Miss Pearl's to keep out from in your way. I ain't mean no harm by it.

TROY. Who said anything about that? I ain't said anything about that.

GABRIEL. You ain't mad at me, is you?

TROY. Naw . . . I ain't mad at you, Gabe. If I was mad at you I'd tell you about it.

GABRIEL. Got me two rooms. In the basement. Got my own door, too. Wanna see my key? (*He holds up a key.*) That's my own key! Ain't nobody else got a key like that. That's my key! My two rooms!

TROY. Well, that's good, Gabe. You got your own key . . . that's good.

ROSE. You hungry, Gabe? I was just fixing to cook Troy his breakfast.

GABRIEL. I'll take some biscuits. You got some biscuits? Did you know when I was in heaven . . . every morning me and St. Peter would sit down by the gate and eat some big fat biscuits? Oh, yeah! We had us a good time. We'd sit there and eat us them biscuits and then St. Peter would go off to sleep and tell me to wake him up when it's time to open the gates for the judgment.

ROSE. Well, come on . . . I'll make up a batch of biscuits.

(*Rose exits into the house.*)

GABRIEL. Troy . . . St. Peter got your name in the book. I seen it. It say . . . Troy Maxson. I say . . . I know him! He got the same name like what I got. That's my brother!

TROY. How many times you gonna tell me that, Gabe?

GABRIEL. Ain't got my name in the book. Don't have to have my name. I done died and went to heaven. He got your name though. One morning St. Peter was looking at his book . . . marking it up for the judgment . . . and he let me see your name. Got it in there under M. Got Rose's name . . . I ain't seen it like I seen yours . . . but I know it's in there. He got a great big book. Got everybody's name what was ever been born. That's what he told me. But I seen your name. Seen it with my own eyes.

TROY. Go on in the house there. Rose going to fix you something to eat.

GABRIEL. Oh, I ain't hungry. I done had breakfast with Aunt Jemimah. She come by and cooked me up a whole mess of flapjacks. Remember how we used to eat them flapjacks?

TROY. Go on in the house and get you something to eat now.

GABRIEL. I got to go sell my plums. I done sold some tomatoes. Got me two quarters. Wanna see? (*He shows Troy his quarters.*) I'm gonna save them and buy me a new horn so St. Peter can hear me when it's time to open the gates. (*Gabriel stops suddenly. Listens.*) Hear that? That's the hellhounds. I got to chase them out of here . . . Go on get out of here! Get out! (*Gabriel exits singing.*)

Better get ready for the judgment
Better get ready for the judgment
My Lord is coming down

(*Rose enters from the house.*)

TROY. He gone off somewhere.

GABRIEL (*offstage*).
Better get ready for the judgment
Better get ready for the judgment morning
Better get ready for the judgment
My God is coming down

ROSE. He ain't eating right. Miss Pearl say she can't get him to eat nothing.

TROY. What you want me to do about it, Rose? I done did everything I can for the man. I can't make him get well. Man got half his head blown away . . . what you expect?

ROSE. Seem like something ought to be done to help him.

TROY. Man don't bother nobody. He just mixed up from that metal plate he got in his head. Ain't no sense for him to go back into the hospital.

ROSE. Least he be eating right. They can help him take care of himself.

TROY. Don't nobody wanna be locked up, Rose. What you wanna lock him up for? Man go over there and fight the war . . . messin' around with them Japs . . . get half his head blown off . . . and they give him a lousy three thousand dollars. And I had to swoop down on that.

ROSE. Is you fixing to go into that again?

TROY. That's the only way I got a roof over my head . . . cause of that metal plate.

ROSE. Ain't no sense you blaming yourself for nothing. Gabe wasn't in no condition to manage that money. You done what was right by him. Can't nobody say you ain't done what was right by him. Look how long you took care of him . . . till he wanted to have his own place and moved over there with Miss Pearl.

TROY. That ain't what I'm saying, woman! I'm just stating the facts. If my brother didn't have that metal plate in his head . . . I wouldn't have a pot to piss in or a window to throw it out of. And I'm fifty-three years old. Now see if you can understand that!

(*Troy gets up from the porch and starts to exit the yard.*)

ROSE. Where you going off to? You been running out of here every Saturday for weeks. I thought you was gonna work on this fence?

TROY. I'm gonna walk down to Taylors'. Listen to the ball game. I'll be back in a bit. I'll work on it when I get back.

(*He exits the yard. The lights go to black.*)

SCENE 3

The lights come up on the yard. It is four hours later. Rose is taking down the clothes from the line. Cory enters carrying his football equipment.

ROSE. Your daddy like to had a fit with you running out of here without doing your chores.

CORY. I told you I had to go to practice.

ROSE. He say you were supposed to help him with this fence.

CORY. He been saying that the last four or five Saturdays, and then he don't never do nothing, but go down to Taylors'. Did you tell him about the recruiter?

ROSE. Yeah, I told him.

CORY. What he say?

ROSE. He ain't said nothing too much. You get in there and get started on your chores before he gets back. Go on and scrub down them steps before he gets back here hollering and carrying on.

CORY. I'm hungry. What you got to eat, Mama?

ROSE. Go on and get started on your chores. I got some meat loaf in there. Go on and make you a sandwich . . . and don't leave no mess in there. (*Cory exits into the house. Rose continues to take down the clothes. Troy enters the yard and sneaks up and grabs her from behind.*) Troy! Go on, now. You liked to scared me to death. What was the score of the game? Lucille had me on the phone and I couldn't keep up with it.

TROY. What I care about the game? Come here, woman. (*He tries to kiss her.*)

ROSE. I thought you went down Taylors' to listen to the game. Go on, Troy! You supposed to be putting up this fence.

TROY (*attempting to kiss her again*). I'll put it up when I finish with what is at hand.

ROSE. Go on, Troy. I ain't studying you.

TROY (*chasing after her*). I'm studying you . . . fixing to do my homework!

ROSE. Troy, you better leave me alone.

TROY. Where's Cory? That boy brought his butt home yet?

ROSE. He's in the house doing his chores.

TROY (*calling*). Cory! Get your butt out here, boy!

(*Rose exits into the house with the laundry. Troy goes over to the pile of wood, picks up a board, and starts sawing. Cory enters from the house.*)

TROY. You just now coming in here from leaving this morning?

CORY. Yeah, I had to go to football practice.

TROY. Yeah, what?

CORY. Yessir.

TROY. I ain't but two seconds off you noway. The garbage sitting in there overflowing . . . you ain't done none of your chores . . . and you come in here talking about "Yeah."

CORY. I was just getting ready to do my chores now, Pop . . .

TROY. Your first chore is to help me with this fence on Saturday. Everything else come after that. Now get that saw and cut them boards.

(*Cory takes the saw and begins cutting the boards. Troy continues working. There is a long pause.*)

CORY. Hey, Pop . . . why don't you buy a TV?

TROY. What I want with a TV? What I want one of them for?

CORY. Everybody got one. Earl, Ba Bra . . . Jesse!

TROY. I ain't asked you who had one. I say what I want with one?

CORY. So you can watch it. They got lots of things on TV. Baseball games and everything. We could watch the World Series.

TROY. Yeah . . . and how much this TV cost?

CORY. I don't know. They got them on sale for around two hundred dollars.

TROY. Two hundred dollars, huh?

CORY. That ain't that much, Pop.

TROY. Naw, it's just two hundred dollars. See that roof you got over your head at night? Let me tell you something about that roof. It's been over ten years since that roof was last tarred. See now . . . the snow come this winter and sit up there on that roof like it is . . . and it's gonna seep inside. It's just gonna be a little bit . . . ain't gonna hardly notice it. Then the next thing you know, it's gonna be leaking all over the house. Then the wood rot from all that water and you gonna need a whole new roof. Now, how much you think it cost to get that roof tarred?

CORY. I don't know.

TROY. Two hundred and sixty-four dollars . . . cash

money. While you thinking about a TV, I got to be thinking about the roof . . . and whatever else go wrong around here. Now if you had two hundred dollars, what would you do . . . fix the roof or buy a TV?

CORY. I'd buy a TV. Then when the roof started to leak . . . when it needed fixing . . . I'd fix it.

TROY. Where you gonna get the money from? You done spent it for a TV. You gonna sit up and watch the water run all over your brand new TV.

CORY. Aw, Pop. You got money. I know you do.

TROY. Where I got it at, huh?

CORY. You got it in the bank.

TROY. You wanna see my bankbook? You wanna see that seventy-three dollars and twenty-two cents I got sitting up in there?

CORY. You ain't got to pay for it all at one time. You can put a down payment on it and carry it on home with you.

TROY. Not me. I ain't gonna owe nobody nothing if I can help it. Miss a payment and they come and snatch it right out your house. Then what you got? Now, soon as I get two hundred dollars clear, then I'll buy a TV. Right now, as soon as I get two hundred and sixty-four dollars, I'm gonna have this roof tarred.

CORY. Aw . . . Pop!

TROY. You go on and get you two hundred dollars and buy one if ya want it. I got better things to do with my money.

CORY. I can't get no two hundred dollars. I ain't never seen two hundred dollars.

TROY. I'll tell you what . . . you get you a hundred dollars and I'll put the other hundred with it.

CORY. All right, I'm gonna show you.

TROY. You gonna show me how you can cut them boards right now.

(*Cory begins to cut the boards. There is a long pause.*)

CORY. The Pirates won today. That make five in a row.

TROY. I ain't thinking about the Pirates. Got an all-white team. Got that boy . . . that Puerto Rican boy . . . Clemente. Don't even half-play him. That boy could be something if they give him a chance. Play him one day and sit him on the bench the next.

CORY. He gets a lot of chances to play.

TROY. I'm talking about playing regular. Playing every day so you can get your timing. That's what I'm talking about.

CORY. They got some white guys on the team that don't play every day. You can't play everybody at the same time.

TROY. If they got a white fellow sitting on the bench . . . you can bet your last dollar he can't play! The colored guy got to be twice as good before he get on the team. That's why I don't want you to get all tied up in them sports. Man on the team and what it get him? They got colored on the team and don't use them. Same as not having them. All them teams the same.

CORY. The Braves got Hank Aaron and Wes Covington. Hank Aaron hit two home runs today. That makes forty-three.

TROY. Hank Aaron ain't nobody. That's what you supposed to do. That's how you supposed to play the game. Ain't nothing to it. It's just a matter of timing . . . getting the right follow-through. Hell, I can hit forty-three home runs right now!

CORY. Not off no major-league pitching, you couldn't.

TROY. We had better pitching in the Negro leagues. I hit seven home runs off of Satchel Paige. You can't get no better than that!

CORY. Sandy Koufax. He's leading the league in strikeouts.

TROY. I ain't thinking of no Sandy Koufax.

CORY. You got Warren Spahn and Lew Burdette. I bet you couldn't hit no home runs off of Warren Spahn.

TROY. I'm through with it now. You go on and cut them boards. (*Pause.*) Your mama tell me you done got recruited by a college football team? Is that right?

CORY. Yeah. Coach Zellman say the recruiter gonna be coming by to talk to you. Get you to sign the permission papers.

TROY. I thought you supposed to be working down there at the A&P. Ain't you suppose to be working down there after school?

CORY. Mr. Stawicki say he gonna hold my job for me until after the football season. Say starting next week I can work weekends.

TROY. I thought we had an understanding about this football stuff? You suppose to keep up with your chores and hold that job down at the A&P. Ain't been around here all day on a Saturday. Ain't none of your chores done . . . and now you telling me you done quit your job.

CORY. I'm gonna be working weekends.

TROY. You damn right you are! And ain't no need for nobody coming around here to talk to me about signing nothing.

CORY. Hey, Pop . . . you can't do that. He's coming all the way from North Carolina.

TROY. I don't care where he coming from. The white man ain't gonna let you get nowhere with that football noway. You go on and get your book-learning so you can work yourself up in that A&P or learn how to fix cars or build houses or something, get you a trade. That way you have something can't nobody take away from you. You go on and learn how to put your hands to some good use. Besides hauling people's garbage.

CORY. I get good grades, Pop. That's why the recruiter

wants to talk with you. You got to keep up your grades to get recruited. This way I'll be going to college. I'll get a chance . . .

TROY. First you gonna get your butt down there to the A&P and get your job back.

CORY. Mr. Stawicki done already hired somebody else 'cause I told him I was playing football.

TROY. You a bigger fool than I thought . . . to let somebody take away your job so you can play some football. Where you gonna get your money to take out your girlfriend and whatnot? What kind of foolishness is that to let somebody take away your job?

CORY. I'm still gonna be working weekends.

TROY. Naw . . . naw. You getting your butt out of here and finding you another job.

CORY. Come on, Pop! I got to practice. I can't work after school and play football, too. The team needs me. That's what Coach Zellman say . . .

TROY. I don't care what nobody else say. I'm the boss . . . you understand? I'm the boss around here. I do the only saying what counts.

CORY. Come on, Pop!

TROY. I asked you . . . did you understand?

CORY. Yeah . . .

TROY. What?!

CORY. Yessir.

TROY. You go on down there to that A&P and see if you can get your job back. If you can't do both . . . then you quit the football team. You've got to take the crookeds with the straights.

CORY Yessir. (*Pause.*) Can I ask you a question?

TROY. What the hell you wanna ask me? Mr. Stawicki the one you got the questions for.

CORY. How come you ain't never liked me?

TROY. Liked you? Who the hell say I got to like you? What law is there say I got to like you? Wanna stand up in my face and ask a damn fool-ass question like that. Talking about liking somebody. Come here, boy, when I talk to you.

(*Cory comes over to where Troy is working. He stands slouched over and Troy shoves him on his shoulder.*)

Straighten up, goddammit! I asked you a question . . . what law is there say I got to like you?

CORY. None.

TROY. Well, all right then! Don't you eat every day? (*Pause.*) Answer me when I talk to you! Don't you eat every day?

CORY. Yeah.

TROY. Nigger, as long as you in my house, you put that sir on the end of it when you talk to me!

CORY. Yes . . . sir.

TROY. You eat every day.

CORY. Yessir!

TROY. Got a roof over your head.

CORY. Yessir!

TROY. Got clothes on your back.

CORY. Yessir.

TROY. Why you think that is?

CORY. Cause of you.

TROY. Aw, hell I know it's 'cause of me . . . but why do you think that is?

CORY (*hesitant*). Cause you like me.

TROY. Like you? I go out of here every morning . . . bust my butt . . . putting up with them crackers every day . . . cause I like you? You about the biggest fool I ever saw. (*Pause.*) It's my job. It's my responsibility! You understand that? A man got to take care of his family. You live in my house . . . sleep you behind on my bedclothes . . . fill you belly up with my food . . . cause you my son. You my flesh and blood. Not 'cause I like you! Cause it's my duty to take care of you. I owe a responsibility to you!

Let's get this straight right here . . . before it go along any further . . . I ain't got to like you. Mr. Rand don't give me my money come payday cause he likes me. He gives me cause he owe me. I done give you everything I had to give you. I gave you your life! Me and your mama worked that out between us. And liking your black ass wasn't part of the bargain. Don't you try and go through life worrying about if somebody like you or not. You best be making sure they doing right by you. You understand what I'm saying, boy?

CORY. Yessir.

TROY. Then get the hell out of my face, and get on down to that A&P.

(*Rose has been standing behind the screen door for much of the scene. She enters as Cory exits.*)

ROSE. Why don't you let the boy go ahead and play football, Troy? Ain't no harm in that. He's just trying to be like you with the sports.

TROY. I don't want him to be like me! I want him to move as far away from my life as he can get. You the only decent thing that ever happened to me. I wish him that. But I don't wish him a thing else from my life. I decided seventeen years ago that boy wasn't getting involved in no sports. Not after what they did to me in the sports.

ROSE. Troy, why don't you admit you was too old to play in the major leagues? For once . . . why don't you admit that?

TROY. What do you mean too old? Don't come telling me I was too old. I just wasn't the right color. Hell, I'm fifty-three years old and can do better than Selkirk's .269 right now!

ROSE. How's was you gonna play ball when you were over forty? Sometimes I can't get no sense out of you.

TROY. I got good sense, woman. I got sense enough not

to let my boy get hurt over playing no sports. You been mothering that boy too much. Worried about if people like him.

ROSE. Everything that boy do . . . he do for you. He wants you to say "Good job, son." That's all.

TROY. Rose, I ain't got time for that. He's alive. He's healthy. He's got to make his own way. I made mine. Ain't nobody gonna hold his hand when he get out there in that world.

ROSE. Times have changed from when you was young, Troy. People change. The world's changing around you and you can't even see it.

TROY (*slow, methodical*). Woman . . . I do the best I can do. I come in here every Friday. I carry a sack of potatoes and a bucket of lard. You all line up at the door with your hands out. I give you the lint from my pockets. I give you my sweat and my blood. I ain't got no tears. I done spent them. We go upstairs in that room at night . . . and I fall down on you and try to blast a hole into forever. I get up Monday morning . . . find my lunch on the table. I go out. Make my way. Find my strength to carry me through to the next Friday. (*Pause.*) That's all I got, Rose. That's all I got to give. I can't give nothing else.

(*Troy exits into the house. The lights go down to black.*)

SCENE 4

It is Friday. Two weeks later. Cory starts out of the house with his football equipment. The phone rings.

CORY (*calling*). I got it!

(*He answers the phone and stands in the screen door talking.*)

Hello? Hey, Jesse. Naw . . . I was just getting ready to leave now.

ROSE (*calling*). Cory!

CORY. I told you, man, them spikes is all tore up. You can use them if you want, but they ain't no good. Earl got some spikes.

ROSE (*calling*). Cory!

CORY (*calling to Rose*). Mam? I'm talking to Jesse. (*Into phone*) When she say that? (*Pause.*) Aw, you lying, man. I'm gonna tell her you said that.

ROSE (*calling*). Cory, don't you go nowhere!

CORY. I got to go to the game, Ma! (*Into the phone*) Yeah, hey, look, I'll talk to you later. Yeah, I'll meet you over Earl's house. Later. Bye, Ma.

(*Cory exits the house and starts out the yard.*)

ROSE. Cory, where you going off to? You got that stuff all pulled out and thrown all over your room.

CORY (*in the yard*). I was looking for my spikes. Jesse wanted to borrow my spikes.

ROSE. Get up there and get that cleaned up before your daddy get back in here.

CORY. I got to go to the game! I'll clean it up when I get back.

(*Cory exits.*)

ROSE. That's all he need to do is see that room all messed up.

(*Rose exits into the house. Troy and Bono enter the yard. Troy is dressed in clothes other than his work clothes.*)

BONO. He told him the same thing he told you. Take it to the union.

TROY. Brownie ain't got that much sense. Man wasn't thinking about nothing. He wait until I confront them on it . . . then he wanna come crying seniority. (*Calls*) Hey Rose!

BONO. I wish I could have seen Mr. Rand's face when he told you.

TROY. He couldn't get it out of his mouth! Liked to bit his tongue! When they called me down there to the Commissioner's office . . . he thought they was gonna fire me. Like everybody else.

BONO. I didn't think they was gonna fire you. I thought they was gonna put you on the warning paper.

TROY. Hey, Rose! (*To Bono*). Yeah, Mr. Rand like to bit his tongue.

(*Troy breaks the seal on the bottle, takes a drink, and hands it to Bono.*)

BONO. I see you run right down to Taylors' and told that Alberta gal.

TROY (*calling*). Hey Rose! (*To Bono*) I told everybody. Hey, Rose! I went down there to cash my check.

ROSE (*entering from the house*). Hush all that hollering, man! I know you out here. What they say down there at the Commissioner's office?

TROY. You supposed to come when I call you, woman. Bono'll tell you that. (*To Bono*). Don't Lucille come when you call her?

ROSE. Man, hush your mouth. I ain't no dog . . . talk about "come when you call me."

TROY (*puts his arm around Rose*). You hear this Bono? I had me an old dog used to get uppity like that. You say, "C'mere, Blue!" . . . and he just lay there and look at you. End up getting a stick and chasing him away trying to make him come.

ROSE. I ain't studying you and your dog. I remember you used to sing that old song.

TROY (*he sings*).
Hear it ring! Hear it ring!
I had a dog and his name was Blue.

ROSE. Don't nobody wanna hear you sing that old song.

TROY (*sings*).
You know Blue was mighty true.

ROSE. Used to have Cory running around here singing that song.

BONO. Hell, I remember that song myself.

TROY (*sings*).
You know Blue was a good old dog
Blue treed a possum in a hollow log.

That was my daddy's song. My daddy made up that song.

ROSE. I don't care who made it up. Don't nobody wanna hear you sing it.

TROY (*makes a song like calling a dog*). Come here, woman.

ROSE. You come in here carrying on, I reckon they ain't fired you. What they say down there at the Commissioner's office?

TROY. Look here, Rose . . . Mr. Rand called me into his office today when I got back from talking to them people down there . . . it come from up top . . . he called me in and told me they was making me a driver.

ROSE. Troy, you kidding!

TROY. No I ain't. Ask Bono.

ROSE. Well, that's great, Troy. Now you don't have to hassle them people no more.

(*Lyons enters from the street.*)

TROY. Aw hell, I wasn't looking to see you today. I thought you was in jail. Got it all over the front page of the *Courier* about them raiding Sefus' place . . . where you be hanging out with all them thugs.

LYONS. Hey, Pop . . . that ain't got nothing to do with me. I don't go down there gambling. I go down there to sit in with the band. I ain't got nothing to do with the gambling part. They got some good music down there.

TROY. They got some rogues . . . is what they got.

LYONS. How you been, Mr. Bono? Hi, Rose.

BONO. I see where you playing down at the Crawford Grill tonight.

ROSE. How come you ain't brought Bonnie like I told you. You should have brought Bonnie with you, she ain't been over in a month of Sundays.

LYONS. I was just in the neighborhood . . . thought I'd stop by.

TROY. Here he come . . .

BONO. Your daddy got a promotion on the rubbish. He's gonna be the first colored driver. Ain't got to do nothing but sit up there and read the paper like them white fellows.

LYONS. Hey, Pop . . . if you knew how to read you'd be all right.

BONO. Naw . . . naw . . . you mean if the nigger knew how to drive he'd be all right. Been fighting with them people about driving and ain't even got a license. Mr. Rand know you ain't got no driver's license?

TROY. Driving ain't nothing. All you do is point the truck where you want it to go. Driving ain't nothing.

BONO. Do Mr. Rand know you ain't got no driver's license? That's what I'm talking about. I ain't asked if driving was easy. I asked if Mr. Rand know you ain't got no driver's license.

TROY. He ain't got to know. The man ain't got to know my business. Time he find out, I have two or three driver's licenses.

LYONS (*going into his pocket*). Say, look here, Pop . . .

TROY. I knew it was coming. Didn't I tell you, Bono? I know what kind of "Look here, Pop" that was. The nigger fixing to ask me for some money. It's Friday night. It's my payday. All them rogues down there on the avenue . . . the ones that ain't in jail . . . and Lyons is hopping in his shoes to get down there with them.

LYONS. See, Pop . . . if you give somebody else a chance to talk sometime, you'd see that I was fixing to pay you back your ten dollars like I told you. Here . . . I told you I'd pay you when Bonnie got paid.

TROY. Naw . . . you go ahead and keep that ten dollars. Put it in the bank. The next time you feel like you wanna come by here and ask me for something . . . you go on down there and get that.

LYONS.: Here's your ten dollars, Pop. I told you I don't want you to give me nothing. I just wanted to borrow ten dollars.

TROY. Naw . . . you go on and keep that for the next time you want to ask me.

LYONS. Come on, Pop . . . here go your ten dollars.

ROSE. Why don't you go on and let the boy pay you back, Troy?

LYONS. Here you go, Rose. If you don't take it I'm gonna have to hear about it for the next six months. (*He hands her the money.*)

ROSE. You can hand yours over here too, Troy.

TROY. You see this, Bono. You see how they do me.

BONO. Yeah, Lucille do me the same way.

(*Gabriel is heard singing offstage. He enters.*)

GABRIEL. Better get ready for the Judgment! Better get ready for . . . Hey! . . . Hey! . . . There's Troy's boy!

LYONS. How you doing, Uncle Gabe?

GABRIEL. Lyons . . . The King of the Jungle! Rose . . . hey, Rose. Got a flower for you. (*He takes a rose from his pocket.*) Picked it myself. That's the same rose like you is!

ROSE. That's right nice of you, Gabe.

LYONS. What you been doing, Uncle Gabe?

GABRIEL. Oh, I been chasing hellhounds and waiting on the time to tell St. Peter to open the gates.

LYONS. You been chasing hellhounds, huh? Well . . . you doing the right thing, Uncle Gabe. Somebody got to chase them.

GABRIEL. Oh, yeah . . . I know it. The devil's strong. The devil ain't no pushover. Hellhounds snipping at everybody's heels. But I got my trumpet waiting on the judgment time.

LYONS. Waiting on the Battle of Armageddon, huh?

GABRIEL. Ain't gonna be too much of a battle when God get to waving that Judgment sword. But the people's gonna have a hell of a time trying to get into heaven if them gates ain't open.

LYONS (*putting his arm around Gabriel*). You hear this, Pop. Uncle Gabe, you all right!

GABRIEL (*laughing with Lyons*). Lyons! King of the Jungle.

ROSE. You gonna stay for supper, Gabe. Want me to fix you a plate?

GABRIEL. I'll take a sandwich, Rose. Don't want no plate. Just wanna eat with my hands. I'll take a sandwich.

ROSE. How about you, Lyons? You staying? Got some short ribs cooking.

LYONS. Naw, I won't eat nothing till after we finished playing. (*Pause.*) You ought to come down and listen to me play, Pop.

TROY. I don't like that Chinese music. All that noise.

ROSE. Go on in the house and wash up, Gabe . . . I'll fix you a sandwich.

GABRIEL (*to Lyons, as he exits*). Troy's mad at me.

LYONS. What you mad at Uncle Gabe for, Pop?

ROSE. He thinks Troy's mad at him cause he moved over to Miss Pearl's.

TROY. I ain't mad at the man. He can live where he want to live at.

LYONS. What he move over there for? Miss Pearl don't like nobody.

ROSE. She don't mind him none. She treats him real nice. She just don't allow all that singing.

TROY. She don't mind that rent he be paying . . . that's what she don't mind.

ROSE. Troy, I ain't going through that with you no more. He's over there cause he want to have his own place. He can come and go as he please.

TROY. Hell, he could come and go as he please here. I wasn't stopping him. I ain't put no rules on him.

ROSE. It ain't the same thing, Troy. And you know it. (*Gabriel comes to the door*). Now, that's the last I wanna hear about that. I don't wanna hear nothing else about Gabe and Miss Pearl. And next week . . .

GABRIEL. I'm ready for my sandwich, Rose.

ROSE. And next week when that recruiter come from that school . . . I want you to sign that paper and go on and let Cory play football. Then that'll be the last I have to hear about that.

TROY (*to Rose as she exits into the house*). I ain't thinking about Cory nothing.

LYONS. What . . . Cory got recruited? What school he going to?

TROY. That boy walking around here smelling his piss . . . thinking he's grown. Thinking he's gonna do what he want, irrespective of what I say. Look here, Bono . . . I left the Commissioner's office and went down to the A&P . . . that boy ain't working down there. He lying to me. Telling me be got his job back . . . telling me he working weekends . . . telling me he working after school . . . Mr. Stawicki tell me he ain't working down there at all!

LYONS. Cory just growing up. He's just busting at the seams trying to fill out your shoes.

TROY. I don't care what he's doing. When he get to the point where he wanna disobey me . . . then it's time for him to move on. Bono'll tell you that. I bet he ain't never disobeyed his daddy without paying the consequences.

BONO. I ain't never had a chance. My daddy came on through . . . but I ain't never knew him to see him . . . or what he had on his mind or where he went. Just moving on through. Searching out the New Land. That's what the old folks used to call it. See a fellow moving around from place to place . . . woman to woman . . . called it searching out the New Land. I can't say if he ever found it. I come along, didn't want no kids. Didn't know if I was gonna be in one place long enough to fix on them right as their daddy. I figured I was going searching, too. As it turned out I been hooked up with Lucille near about as long as your daddy been with Rose. Going on sixteen years.

TROY. Sometimes I wish I hadn't known my daddy. He ain't cared nothing about no kids. A kid to him wasn't nothing. All he wanted was for you to learn how to walk so he could start you to working. When it come time for eating . . . he ate first. If there was anything left over, that's what you got. Man would sit down and eat two chickens and give you the wing.

LYONS. You ought to stop that, Pop. Everybody feed their kids. No matter how hard times is . . . everybody care about their kids. Make sure they have something to eat.

TROY. The only thing my daddy cared about was getting them bales of cotton in to Mr. Lubin. That's the only thing that mattered to him. Sometimes I used to wonder why he was living. Wonder why the devil hadn't come and got him. "Get them bales of cotton in to Mr. Lubin" and find out he owe him money . . .

LYONS. He should have just went on and left when he saw he couldn't get nowhere. That's what I would have done.

TROY. How he gonna leave with eleven kids? And where he gonna go? He ain't knew how to do nothing but farm. No, he was trapped and I think he knew it. But I'll say this for him . . . he felt a responsibility toward us. Maybe he ain't treated us the way I felt he should have . . . but without that responsibility he could have walked off and left us . . . made his own way.

BONO. A lot of them did. Back in those days what you talking about . . . they walk out their front door and just take on down one road or another and keep on walking.

LYONS. There you go! That's what I'm talking about.

BONO. Just keep on walking till you come to something else. Ain't you never heard of nobody having the walking blues? Well, that's what you call it when you just take off like that.

TROY. My daddy ain't had them walking blues! What you talking about? He stayed right there with his family. But he was just as evil as he could be. My mama couldn't stand him. Couldn't stand that evilness. She run off when I was about eight. She sneaked off one night after he had gone to sleep. Told me she was coming back for me. I ain't never seen her no more. All his women run off and left him. He wasn't good for nobody.

When my turn come to head out, I was fourteen and got to sniffing around Joe Canewell's daughter. Had us an old mule we called Greyboy. My daddy sent me out to do some plowing and I tied up Greyboy and went to fooling around with Joe Canewell's daughter. We done found us a nice little spot, got real cozy with each other. She about thirteen and we done figured we was grown anyway . . . so we down there enjoying ourselves . . . ain't thinking about nothing. We didn't know Greyboy had got loose and wandered back to the house and my daddy was looking for me. We down there by the creek enjoying ourselves when my daddy come up on us. Surprised us. He had them leather straps off the mule and commenced to whupping me like there was no tomorrow. I jumped up, mad and embarrassed. I was scared of my daddy. When he commenced to whupping on me . . . quite naturally I run to get out of the way. (*Pause.*)

Now I thought he was mad cause I ain't done my work. But I see where he was chasing me off so he could have the gal for himself. When I see what the matter of it was, I lost all fear of my daddy. Right there is where I become a man . . . at fourteen years of age. (*Pause.*)

Now it was my turn to run him off. I picked up them same reins that he had used on me. I picked up them reins and commenced to whupping on him. The gal jumped up and run off . . . and when my daddy turned to face me, I could see why the devil had never come to get him . . . cause he was the devil himself. I don't know what happened. When I woke up, I was laying right there by the creek, and Blue . . . this old dog we had . . . was licking my face. I thought I was blind. I couldn't see nothing. Both my eyes were swollen shut. I layed there and cried. I didn't know what I was gonna do. The only thing I knew was the time had come for me to leave my daddy's house. And right there the world suddenly got big. And it was a long time before I could cut it down to where I could handle it.

Part of that cutting down was when I got to the place where I could feel him kicking in my blood and knew that the only thing that separated us was the matter of a few years.

(*Gabriel enters from the house with a sandwich.*)

LYONS. What you got there, Uncle Gabe?

GABRIEL. Got me a ham sandwich. Rose gave me a ham sandwich.

TROY. I don't know what happened to him. I done lost touch with everybody except Gabriel. But I hope he's dead. I hope he found some peace.

LYONS. That's a heavy story, Pop. I didn't know you left home when you was fourteen.

TROY. And didn't know nothing. The only part of the world I knew was the forty-two acres of Mr. Lubin's land. That's all I knew about life.

LYONS. Fourteen's kinda young to be out on your own. (*Phone rings.*) I don't even think I was ready to be out on my own at fourteen. I don't know what I would have done.

TROY. I got up from the creek and walked on down to Mobile. I was through with farming. Figured I could do better in the city. So I walked the two hundred miles to Mobile.

LYONS. Wait a minute . . . you ain't walked no two hundred miles, Pop. Ain't nobody gonna walk no two hundred miles. You talking about some walking there.

BONO. That's the only way you got anywhere back in them days.

LYONS. Shhh. Damn if I wouldn't have hitched a ride with somebody!

TROY. Who you gonna hitch it with? They ain't had no cars and things like they got now. We talking about 1918.

ROSE (*entering*). What you all out here getting into?

TROY (*to Rose*). I'm telling Lyons how good he got it. He don't know nothing about this I'm talking.

ROSE. Lyons, that was Bonnie on the phone. She say you supposed to pick her up.

LYONS. Yeah, okay, Rose.

TROY. I walked on down to Mobile and hitched up with some of them fellows that was heading this way. Got up here and found out . . . not only couldn't you get a job . . . you couldn't find no place to live. I thought I was in freedom. Shhh. Colored folks living down there on the riverbanks in whatever kind of shelter they could find for themselves. Right down there under the Brady Street Bridge. Living in shacks made of sticks and tarpaper. Messed around there and went from bad to worse. Started stealing. First it was food. Then I figure, hell, if I steal money I can buy me some food. Buy me some shoes, too! One thing led to another. Met your mama. I was young and anxious to be a man. Met your mama and had you. What I do that for? Now I got to worry about feeding you and her. Got to steal three times as much. Went out one day looking for somebody to rob . . . that's what I was, a robber. I'll tell you the truth. I'm ashamed of it today. But it's the truth. Went to rob this fellow . . . pulled out my knife . . . and he pulled out a gun. Shot me in the chest. It felt just like somebody had taken a hot branding iron and laid it on me. When he shot me I jumped at him with my knife. They told me I killed him and they put me in the penitentiary and locked me up for fifteen years. That's where I met Bono. That's where I learned how to play baseball. Got out that place and your mama had taken you and went on to make life without me. Fifteen years was a long time for her to wait. But that fifteen years cured me of that robbing stuff. Rose'll tell you. She asked me when I met her if I had gotten all that foolishness out of my system. And I told her "Baby, it's you and baseball all what count with me." You hear me, Bono? I meant it, too. She say, "Which one comes first?" I told her, "Baby, ain't no doubt it's baseball . . . but you stick and get old with me and we'll both outlive this baseball." Am I right, Rose? And it's true.

ROSE. Man, hush your mouth. You ain't said no such thing. Talking about "Baby, you know you'll always be number one with me." That's what you was talking.

TROY. You hear that, Bono. That's why I love her.

BONO. Rose'll keep you straight. You get off the track, she'll straighten you up.

ROSE. Lyons, you better get on up and get Bonnie. She waiting on you.

LYONS (*gets up to go*). Hey, Pop, why don't you come on down to the Grill and hear me play?

TROY. I ain't going down there. I'm too old to be sitting around in them clubs.

BONO. You got to be good to play down at the Grill.

LYONS. Come on, Pop . . .

TROY. I got to get up in the morning.

LYONS. You ain't got to stay long.

TROY. Naw, I'm gonna get my supper and go on to bed.

LYONS. Well, I got to go. I'll see you again.

TROY. Don't you come around my house on my payday.

ROSE. Pick up the phone and let somebody know you coming. And bring Bonnie with you. You know I'm always glad to see her.

LYONS. Yeah, I'll do that, Rose. You take care now. See you, Pop. See you, Mr. Bono. See you, Uncle Gabe.

GABRIEL. Lyons! King of the Jungle!

(*Lyons exits.*)

TROY. Is supper ready, woman? Me and you got some business to take care of. I'm gonna tear it up, too.

ROSE. Troy, I done told you now!

TROY (*puts his arm around Bono*). Aw hell, woman . . . this is Bono. Bono like family. I done known this nigger since . . . how long I done know you?

BONO. It's been a long time.

TROY. I done known this nigger since Skippy was a pup. Me and him done been through some times.

BONO. You sure right about that.

TROY. Hell, I done know him longer than I known you. And we still standing shoulder to shoulder. Hey, look here, Bono . . . a man can't ask for no more than that. (*Drinks to him.*) I love you, nigger.

BONO. Hell, I love you too . . . but I got to get home see my woman. You got yours in hand. I got to go get mine.

(*Bono starts to exit as Cory enters the yard, dressed in his football uniform. He gives Troy a hard, uncompromising look.*)

CORY. What you do that for, Pop? (*He throws his helmet down in the direction of Troy.*)

ROSE. What's the matter? Cory . . . what's the matter?

CORY. Papa done went up to the school and told Coach Zellman I can't play football no more. Wouldn't even let me play the game. Told him to tell the recruiter not to come.

ROSE. Troy . . .

TROY. What you Troying me for. Yeah, I did it. And the boy know why I did it.

CORY. Why you wanna do that to me? That was the one chance I had.

ROSE. Ain't nothing wrong with Cory playing football, Troy.

TROY. The boy lied to me. I told the nigger if he wanna play football . . . to keep up his chores and hold down that job at the A&P. That was the conditions. Stopped down there to see Mr. Stawicki . . .

CORY. I can't work after school during the football season, Pop! I tried to tell you that Mr. Stawicki's holding my job for me. You don't never want to listen to nobody. And then you wanna go and do this to me!

TROY. I ain't done nothing to you. You done it to yourself.

CORY. Just cause you didn't have a chance! You just scared I'm gonna be better than you, that's all.

TROY. Come here.

ROSE. Troy . . .

(*Cory reluctantly crosses over to Troy.*)

TROY. All right! See. You done made a mistake

CORY. I didn't even do nothing!

TROY. I'm gonna tell you what your mistake was. See . . . you swung at the ball and didn't hit it. That's strike one. See, you in the batter's box now. You swung and you missed. That's strike one. Don't you strike out!

(*Lights fade to black.*)

ACT 2

SCENE 1

The following morning. Cory is at the tree hitting the ball with the bat. He tries to mimic Troy, but his swing is awkward, less sure. Rose enters from the house.

ROSE. Cory, I want you to help me with this cupboard.

CORY. I ain't quitting the team. I don't care what Poppa say.

ROSE. I'll talk to him when he gets back. He had to go see about your Uncle Gabe. The police done arrested him. Say he was disturbing the peace. He'll be back directly. Come on in here and help me clean out the top of this cupboard.

(*Cory exits into the house. Rose sees Troy and Bono coming down the alley.*)

Troy . . . what they say down there?

TROY. Ain't said nothing. I give them fifty dollars and they let him go. I'll talk to you about it. Where's Cory?

ROSE. He's in there helping me clean out these cupboards.

TROY. Tell him to get his butt out here.

(*Troy and Bono go over to the pile of wood. Bono picks up the saw and begins sawing.*)

TROY (*to Bono*). All they want is the money. That makes six or seven times I done went down there and got him. See me coming they stick out their *hands.*

BONO. Yeah. I know what you mean. That's all they care about . . . that money. They don't care about what's right. (*Pause.*) Nigger, why you got to go and get some hard wood? You ain't doing nothing but building a little old fence. Get you some soft pine wood. That's all you need.

TROY. I know what I'm doing. This is outside wood. You put pine wood inside the house. Pine wood is inside wood. This here is outside wood. Now you tell me where the fence is gonna be?

BONO. You don't need this wood. You can put it up with pine wood and it'll stand as long as you gonna be here looking at it.

TROY. How you know how long I'm gonna be here, nigger? Hell, I might just live forever. Live longer than old man Horsely.

BONO. That's what Magee used to say.

TROY. Magee's a damn fool. Now you tell me who you ever heard of gonna pull their own teeth with a pair of rusty pliers.

BONO. The old folks . . . my granddaddy used to pull his teeth with pliers. They ain't had no dentists for the colored folks back then.

TROY. Get clean pliers! You understand? Clean pliers! Sterilize them! Besides we ain't living back then. All Magee had to do was walk over to Doc Goldblum's.

BONO. I see where you and that Tallahassee gal . . . that Alberta . . . I see where you all done got tight.

TROY. What do you mean "got tight?"

BONO. I see where you be laughing and joking with her all the time.

TROY. I laughs and jokes with all of them, Bono. You know me.

BONO. That ain't the kind of laughing and joking I'm talking about.

(*Cory enters from the house.*)

CORY. How you doing, Mr. Bono?

TROY. Cory? Get that saw from Bono and cut some wood. He talking about the wood's too hard to cut. Stand back there, Jim, and let that young boy show you how it's done.

BONO. He's sure welcome to it.

(*Cory takes the saw and begins to cut the wood.*)

Whew-e-e! Look at that. Big old strong boy. Look like Joe Louis. Hell, must be getting old the way I'm watching that boy whip through that wood.

CORY. I don't see why Mama want a fence around the yard noways.

TROY. Damn if I know either. What the hell she keeping out with it? She ain't got nothing nobody want.

BONO. Some people build fences to keep people out . . . and other people build fences to keep people in. Rose wants to hold on to you all. She loves you.

TROY. Hell, nigger, I don't need nobody to tell me my wife loves me. Cory . . . go on in the house and see if you can find that other saw.

CORY. Where's it at?

TROY. I said find it! Look for it till you find it!

(*Cory exits into the house.*)

What's that supposed to mean? Wanna keep us in?

BONO. Troy . . . I done known you seem like damn near my whole life. You and Rose both. I done know both of you all for a long time. I remember when you met Rose. When you was hitting them baseball out the park. A lot of them old gals was after you then. You had the pick of the litter. When you picked Rose, I was happy for you. That was the first time I knew you had any sense. I said . . . My man Troy knows what he's doing . . . I'm gonna follow this nigger . . . he might take me somewhere. I been following you, too. I done learned a whole heap of things about life watching you. I done learned how to tell where the shit lies. How to tell it from the alfalfa. You done learned me a lot of things. You showed me how to not make the same mistakes . . . to take life as it comes along and keep putting one foot in front of the other. (*Pause.*) Rose a good woman, Troy.

TROY. Hell, nigger, I know she a good woman. I been married to her for eighteen years. What you got on your mind, Bono?

BONO. I just say she a good woman. Just like I say anything. I ain't got to have nothing on my mind.

TROY. You just gonna say she a good woman and leave it hanging out there like that? Why you telling me she a good woman?

BONO. She loves you, Troy. Rose loves you.

TROY. You saying I don't measure up. That's what you trying to say. I don't measure up cause I'm seeing this other gal. I know what you trying to say.

BONO. I know what Rose means to you, Troy. I'm just trying to say I don't want to see you mess up.

TROY. Yeah, I appreciate that, Bono. If you was messing around on Lucille I'd be telling you the same thing.

BONO. Well that's all I got to say. I just say that because I love you both.

TROY. Hell, you know me . . . I wasn't out there looking for nothing. You can't find a better woman than Rose. I know that. But seems like this woman just stuck onto me where I can't shake her loose. I done wrestled with it, tried to throw her off me . . . but she just stuck on tighter. Now she's stuck on for good.

BONO. You's in control . . . that's what you tell me all the time. You responsible for what you do.

TROY. I ain't ducking the responsibility of it. As long as it sets right in my heart . . . then I'm okay. Cause that's all I listen to. It'll tell me right from wrong every time. And I ain't talking about doing Rose no bad turn. I love Rose. She done carried me a long ways and I love and respect her for that.

BONO. I know you do. That's why I don't want to see you hurt her. But what you gonna do when she find out? What you got then? If you try to juggle both of them . . . sooner or later you gonna drop one of them. That's common sense.

TROY. Yeah, I hear what you saying, Bono. I been trying to figure a way to work it out.

BONO. Work it out right, Troy. I don't want to be getting all up between you and Rose's business . . . but work it so it come out right.

TROY. Aw hell, I get all up between you and Lucille's business. When you gonna get that woman that refrigerator she been wanting? Don't tell me you ain't got no money now. I know who your banker is. Mellon don't need that money bad as Lucille want that refrigerator. I'll tell you that.

BONO. Tell you what I'll do . . . when you finish building this fence for Rose . . . I'll buy Lucille that refrigerator.

TROY. You done stuck your foot in your mouth now! (*Troy grabs up a board and begins to saw. Bono starts to walk out the yard.*) Hey, nigger . . . where you going?

BONO. I'm going home. I know you don't expect me to help you now. I'm protecting my money. I wanna see you put that fence up by yourself. That's what I want to see. You'll be here another six months without me.

TROY. Nigger, you ain't right.

BONO. When it comes to my money . . . I'm right as fireworks on the Fourth of July.

TROY. All right, we gonna see now. You better get out your bankbook.

(*Bono exits, and Troy continues to work. Rose enters from the house.*)

ROSE. What they say down there? What's happening with Gabe?

TROY. I went down there and got him out. Cost me fifty dollars. Say he was disturbing the peace. Judge set up a hearing for him in three weeks. Say to show cause why he shouldn't be recommitted.

ROSE. What was he doing that cause them to arrest him?

TROY. Some kids was teasing him and he run them off home. Say he was howling and carrying on. Some folks seen him and called the police. That's all it was.

ROSE. Well, what's you say? What'd you tell the judge?

TROY. Told him I'd look after him. It didn't make no sense to recommit the man. He stuck out his big greasy palm and told me to give him fifty dollars and take him on home.

ROSE. Where's he at now? Where'd he go off to?

TROY. He's gone on about his business. He don't need nobody to hold his hand.

ROSE. Well, I don't know. Seem like that would be the

best place for him if they did put him into the hospital. I know what you're gonna say. But that's what I think would be best.

TROY. The man done had his life ruined fighting for what? And they wanna take and lock him up. Let him be free. He don't bother nobody.

ROSE. Well, everybody got their own way of looking at it I guess. Come on and get your lunch. I got a bowl of lima beans and some cornbread in the oven. Come on get something to eat. Ain't no sense you fretting over Gabe.

(*Rose turns to go into the house.*)

TROY. Rose . . . got something to tell you.

ROSE. Well, come on . . . wait till I get this food on the table.

TROY. Rose! (*She stops and turns around.*) I don't know how to say this. (*Pause.*) I can't explain it none. It just sort of grows on you till it gets out of hand. It starts out like a little bush . . . and the next thing you know it's a whole forest.

ROSE. Troy . . . what is you talking about?

TROY. I'm talking, woman, let me talk. I'm trying to find a way to tell you . . . I'm gonna be a daddy. I'm gonna be somebody's daddy.

ROSE. Troy . . . you're not telling me this? You're gonna be . . . what?

TROY. Rose . . . now . . . see . . .

ROSE. You telling me you gonna be somebody's daddy? You telling your *wife* this?

(*Gabriel enters from the street. He carries a rose in his hand.*)

GABRIEL. Hey, Troy! Hey, Rose!

ROSE. I have to wait eighteen years to hear something like this.

GABRIEL. Hey, Rose . . . I got a flower for you. (*He hands it to her.*) That's a rose. Same rose like you is.

ROSE. Thanks, Gabe.

GABRIEL. Troy, you ain't mad at me is you? Them bad mens come and put me away. You ain't mad at me is you?

TROY. Naw, Gabe, I ain't mad at you.

ROSE. Eighteen years and you wanna come with this.

GABRIEL (*takes a quarter out of his pocket*). See what I got? Got a brand new quarter.

TROY. Rose . . . it's just . . .

ROSE. Ain't nothing you can say, Troy. Ain't no way of explaining that.

GABRIEL. Fellow that give me this quarter had a whole mess of them. I'm gonna keep this quarter till it stop shining.

ROSE. Gabe, go on in the house there. I got some watermelon in the frigidaire. Go on and get you a piece.

GABRIEL. Say, Rose . . . you know I was chasing hellhounds and them bad mens come and get me and take me away. Troy helped me. He come down there and told them they better let me go before he beat them up. Yeah, he did!

ROSE. You go on and get you a piece of watermelon, Gabe. Them bad mens is gone now.

GABRIEL. Okay, Rose . . . gonna get me some watermelon. The kind with the stripes on it.

(*Gabriel exits into the house.*)

ROSE. Why, Troy? Why? After all these years to come dragging this in to me now. It don't make no sense at your age. I could have expected this ten or fifteen years ago, but not now.

TROY. Age ain't got nothing to do with it, Rose.

ROSE. I done tried to be everything a wife should be. Everything a wife could be. Been married eighteen years and I got to live to see the day you tell me you been seeing another woman and done fathered a child by her. And you know I ain't never wanted no half nothing in my family. My whole family is half. Everybody got different fathers and mothers . . . my two sisters and my brother. Can't hardly tell who's who. Can't never sit down and talk about Papa and Mama. It's your papa and your mama and my papa and my mama . . .

TROY. Rose . . . stop it now.

ROSE. I ain't never wanted that for none of my children. And now you wanna drag your behind in here and tell me something like this.

TROY. You ought to know. It's time for you to know.

ROSE. Well, I don't want to know, goddamn it!

TROY. I can't just make it go away. It's done now. I can't wish the circumstance of the thing away.

ROSE. And you don't want to either. Maybe you want to wish me and my boy away. Maybe that's what you want? Well, you can't wish us away. I've got eighteen years of my life invested in you. You ought to have stayed upstairs in my bed where you belong.

TROY. Rose . . . now listen to me . . . we can get a handle on this thing. We call talk this out . . . come to an understanding.

ROSE. All of a sudden it's "we." Where was "we" at when you was down there rolling around with some god-forsaken woman? "We" should have come to an understanding before you started making a damn fool of yourself. You're a day late and a dollar short when it comes to an understanding with me.

TROY. It's just . . . She gives me a different idea . . . a different understanding about myself. I can step out of this house and get away from the pressures and problems . . . be a different man. I ain't got to wonder how I'm gonna pay the bills or get the roof fixed. I can just be a part of myself that ain't never been.

ROSE. What I want to know . . . is do you plan to continue seeing her. That's all you can say to me.

TROY. I can sit up in her house and laugh. Do you understand what I'm saying. I can laugh out loud . . . and it feels good. It reaches all the way down to the bottom of my shoes. (*Pause.*) Rose, I can't give that up.

ROSE. Maybe you ought to go on and stay down there with her . . . if she a better woman than me.

TROY. It ain't about nobody being a better woman or nothing. Rose, you ain't the blame. A man couldn't ask for no woman to be a better wife than you've been. I'm responsible for it. I done locked myself into a pattern trying to take care of you all that I forgot about myself.

ROSE. What the hell was I there for? That was my job, not somebody else's.

TROY. Rose, I done tried all my life to live decent . . . to live a clean . . . hard . . . useful life. I tried to be a good husband to you. In every way I knew how. Maybe I come into the world backwards, I don't know. But . . . you born with two strikes on you before you come to the plate. You got to guard it closely . . . always looking for the curve-ball on the inside corner. You can't afford to let none get past you. You can't afford a call strike. If you going down . . . you going down swinging. Everything lined up against you. What you gonna do. I fooled them, Rose. I bunted. When I found you and Cory and a halfway decent job . . . I was safe. Couldn't nothing touch me. I wasn't gonna strike out no more. I wasn't going back to the penitentiary. I wasn't gonna lay in the streets with a bottle of wine. I was safe. I had me a family. A job. I wasn't gonna get that last strike. I was on first looking for one of them boys to knock me in. To get me home.

ROSE. You should have stayed in my bed, Troy.

TROY. Then when I saw that gal . . . she firmed up my backbone. And I got to thinking that if I tried . . . I just might he able to steal second. Do you understand after eighteen years I wanted to steal second.

ROSE. You should have held me tight. You should have grabbed me and held on.

TROY. I stood on first base for eighteen years and I thought . . . well, goddamn it . . . go on for it!

ROSE. We're not talking about baseball! We're talking about you going off to lay in bed with another woman . . . and then bring it home to me. That's what we're talking about. We ain't talking about no baseball.

TROY. Rose, you're not listening to me. I'm trying the best I can to explain it to you. It's not easy for me to admit that I been standing in the same place for eighteen years.

ROSE. I been standing with you! I been right here with you, Troy. I got a life too. I gave eighteen years of my life to stand in the same spot with you. Don't you think I ever wanted other things? Don't you think I had dreams and hopes? What about my life? What about me? Don't you think it ever crossed my mind to want to know other men? That I wanted to lay up somewhere and forget about my responsibilities? That I wanted someone to make me laugh so I could feel good? You not the only one who's got wants and needs. But I held on to you, Troy. I took all my feelings, my wants and needs, my dreams . . . and I buried them inside you. I planted a seed and watched and prayed over it. I planted myself inside you and waited to bloom. And it didn't take me no eighteen years to find out the soil was hard and rocky and it wasn't never gonna bloom.

But I held on to you, Troy. I held on tighter. You was my husband. I owed you everything I had. Every part of me I could find to give you. And upstairs in that room . . . with the darkness falling in on me . . . I gave everything I had to try and erase the doubt that you wasn't the finest man in the world. And wherever you was going . . . I wanted to be there with you. Cause you was my husband. Cause that's the only way I was gonna survive as your wife. You always talking about what you give . . . and what you don't have to give. But you take, too. You take . . . and don't even know nobody's giving!

(*Rose turns to exit into the house; Troy grabs her arm.*)

TROY. You say I take and don't give!

ROSE. Troy! You're hurting me!

TROY. You say I take and don't give.

ROSE. Troy . . . you're hurting my arm! Let go!

TROY. I done give you everything I got. Don't you tell that lie on me.

ROSE. Troy!

TROY. Don't you tell that lie on me!

(*Cory enters from the house.*)

CORY. Mama!

ROSE. Troy. You're hurting me.

TROY. Don't you tell me about no taking and giving.

(*Cory comes up behind Troy and grabs him. Troy, surprised, is thrown off balance just as Cory throws a glancing blow that catches him on the chest and knocks him down. Troy is stunned, as is Cory.*)

ROSE. Troy. Troy. No!

(*Troy gets to his feet and starts at Cory.*)

Troy . . . no. Please! Troy!

(*Rose pulls on Troy to hold him back. Troy stops himself.*)

TROY (*to Cory*). All right. That's strike two. You stay away from around me, boy. Don't you strike out. You living with a full count. Don't you strike out.

(*Troy exits out the yard as the lights go down.*)

SCENE 2

It is six months later, early afternoon. Troy enters from the house and starts to exit the yard. Rose enters from the house.

ROSE. Troy, I want to talk to you.

TROY. All of a sudden, after all this time, you want to talk to me, huh? You ain't wanted to talk to me for months. You ain't wanted to talk to me last night. You ain't wanted no part of me then. What you wanna talk to me about now?

ROSE. Tomorrow's Friday.

TROY. I know what day tomorrow is. You think I don't know tomorrow's Friday? My whole life I ain't done nothing but look to see Friday coming and you got to tell me it's Friday.

ROSE. I want to know if you're coming home.

TROY. I always come home, Rose. You know that. There ain't never been a night I ain't come home.

ROSE. That ain't what I mean . . . and you know it. I want to know if you're coming straight home after work.

TROY. I figure I'd cash my check . . . hang out at Taylors' with the boys . . . maybe play a game of checkers . . .

ROSE. Troy, I can't live like this. I won't live like this.You livin' on borrowed time with me. It's been going on six months now you ain't been coming home.

TROY. I be here every night. Every night of the year. That's 365 days.

ROSE. I want you to come home tomorrow after work.

TROY. Rose . . . I don't mess up my pay. You know that now. I take my pay and I give it to you. I don't have no money but what you give me back. I just want to have a little time to myself . . . a little time to enjoy life.

ROSE. What about me? When's my time to enjoy life?

TROY. I don't know what to tell you, Rose. I'm doing the best I can.

ROSE. You ain't been home from work but time enough to change your clothes and run out . . . and you wanna call that the best you can do?

TROY. I'm going over to the hospital to see Alberta. She went into the hospital this afternoon. Look like she might have the baby early. I won't be gone long.

ROSE. Well, you ought to know. They went over to Miss Pearl's and got Gabe today. She said you told them to go ahead and lock him up.

TROY. I ain't said no such thing. Whoever told you that is telling a lie. Pearl ain't doing nothing but telling a big fat lie.

ROSE. She ain't had to tell me. I read it on the papers.

TROY. I ain't told them nothing of the kind.

ROSE. I saw it right there on the papers.

TROY. What it say, huh?

ROSE. It said you told them to take him.

TROY. Then they screwed that up, just the way they screw up everything. I ain't worried about what they got on the paper.

ROSE. Say the government send part of his check to the hospital and the other part to you.

TROY. I ain't got nothing to do with that if that's the way it works. I ain't made up the rules about how it work.

ROSE. You did Gabe just like you did Cory. You wouldn't sign the paper for Cory . . . but you signed for Gabe. You signed that paper.

(*The telephone is heard ringing inside the house.*)

TROY. I told you I ain't signed nothing, woman! The only thing I signed was the release form. Hell, I can't read, I don't know what they had on that paper! I ain't signed nothing about sending Gabe away.

ROSE. I said send him to the hospital . . . you said let him be free . . . now you done went down there and signed him to the hospital for half his money. You went back on yourself, Troy. You gonna have to answer for that.

TROY. See now . . . you been over there talking to Miss Pearl. She done got mad cause she ain't getting Gabe's rent money. That's all it is. She's liable to say anything.

ROSE. Troy, I seen where you signed the paper.

TROY. You ain't seen nothing I signed. What she doing got papers on my brother anyway? Miss Pearl telling a big fat lie. And I'm gonna tell her about it too! You ain't seen nothing I signed. Say . . . you ain't seen nothing I signed.

(*Rose exits into the house to answer the telephone. Presently she returns.*)

ROSE. Troy . . . that was the hospital. Alberta had the baby.

TROY. What she have? What is it?

ROSE. It's a girl.

TROY. I better get on down to the hospital to see her.

ROSE. Troy.

TROY. Rose . . . I got to go see her now. That's only right . . . what's the matter . . . the baby's all right, ain't it?

ROSE. Alberta died having the baby.

TROY. Died . . . you say she's dead? Alberta's dead?

ROSE. They said they done all they could. They couldn't do nothing for her.

TROY. The baby? How's the baby?

ROSE. They say it's healthy. I wonder who's gonna bury her.

TROY. She had family, Rose. She wasn't living in the world by herself.

ROSE. I know she wasn't living in the world by herself.

TROY. Next thing you gonna want to know if she had any insurance.

ROSE. Troy, you ain't got to talk like that.

TROY. That's the first thing that jumped out your mouth. "Who's gonna bury her?" Like I'm fixing to take on that task for myself.

ROSE. I am your wife. Don't push me away.

TROY. I ain't pushing nobody away. Just give me some space. That's all. Just give me some room to breathe.

(*Rose exits into the house. Troy walks about the yard.*)

TROY (*with a quiet rage that threatens to consume him*). All right . . . Mr. Death. See now . . . I'm gonna tell you what I'm gonna do. I'm gonna take and build me a fence around this yard. See? I'm gonna build me a fence around what belongs to me. And then I want you to stay on the other side. See? You stay over there until you're ready for me. Then you come on. Bring your army. Bring your sickle. Bring your wrestling clothes. I ain't gonna fall down on my vigilance this time. You ain't gonna sneak up on me no more. When you ready for me . . . when the top of your list say Troy Maxson . . . that's when you come around here. You come up and knock on the front door. Ain't nobody else got nothing to do with this. This is between you and me. Man to man. You stay on the other side of that fence until you ready for me. Then you come up and knock on the front door. Anytime you want. I'll be ready for you.

(*The lights go down to black.*)

SCENE 3

The lights come up on the porch. It is late evening three days later. Rose sits listening to the ball game waiting for Troy. The final out of the game is made and Rose switches off the radio. Troy enters the yard carrying an infant wrapped in blankets. He stands back from the house and calls.

Rose enters and stands on the porch. There is a long, awkward silence, the weight of which grows heavier with each passing second.

TROY. Rose . . . I'm standing here with my daughter in my arms. She ain't but a wee bittie little old thing. She don't know nothing about grownups' business. She innocent . . . and she ain't got no mama.

ROSE. What you telling me for, Troy?

(*She turns and exits into the house.*)

TROY. Well . . . I guess we'll just sit out here on the porch.

(*He sits down on the porch. There is an awkward indelicateness about the way he handles the baby. His largeness engulfs and seems to swallow it. He speaks loud enough for Rose to hear.*)

A man's got to do what's right for him. I ain't sorry for nothing I done. It felt right in my heart. (*To the baby*) What you smiling at? Your daddy's a big man. Got these great big old hands. But sometimes he's scared. And right now your daddy's scared cause we sitting out here and ain't got no home. Oh, I been homeless before. I ain't had no little baby with me. But I been homeless. You just be out on the road by your lonesome and you see one of them trains coming and you just kinda go like this . . . (*He sings as a lullaby*)

Please, Mr. Engineer let a man ride the line
Please, Mr. Engineer let a man ride the line
I ain't got no ticket please let me ride the blinds

(*Rose enters from the house. Troy hearing her steps behind him, stands and faces her.*)

She's my daughter, Rose. My own flesh and blood. I can't deny her no more than I can deny them boys. (*Pause.*) You and them boys is my family. You and them and this child is all I got in the world. So I guess what I'm saying is . . . I'd appreciate it if you'd help me take care of her.

ROSE. Okay, Troy . . . you're right. I'll take care of your baby for you . . . cause . . . like you say . . . she's innocent . . . and you can't visit the sins of the father upon the child. A motherless child has got a hard time. (*She takes the baby from him.*) From right now . . . this child got a mother. But you a womanless man.

(*Rose turns and exits into the house with the baby. Lights go down to black.*)

SCENE 4

It is two months later. Lyons enters from the street. He knocks on the door and calls.

LYONS. Hey, Rose! (*Pause.*) Rose!

ROSE (*from inside the house*). Stop that yelling. You gonna wake up Raynell. I just got her to sleep.

LYONS. I just stopped by to pay Papa this twenty dollars I owe him. Where's Papa at?

ROSE. He should be here in a minute. I'm getting ready to go down to the church. Sit down and wait on him.

LYONS. I got to go pick up Bonnie over her mother's house.

ROSE. Well, sit it down there on the table. He'll get it.

LYONS (*enters the house and sets the money on the table*). Tell Papa I said thanks. I'll see you again.

ROSE. All right, Lyons. We'll see you.

(*Lyons starts to exit as Cory enters.*)

CORY. Hey, Lyons.

LYONS. What's happening, Cory. Say man, I'm sorry I missed your graduation. You know I had a gig and couldn't get away. Otherwise, I would have been there, man. So what you doing?

CORY. I'm trying to find a job.

LYONS. Yeah I know how that go, man. It's rough out here. Jobs are scarce.

CORY. Yeah, I know.

LYONS. Look here, I got to run. Talk to Papa . . . he know some people. He'll he able to help get you a job. Talk to him . . . see what he say.

CORY. Yeah . . . all right, Lyons.

LYONS. You take care. I'll talk to you soon. We'll find some time to talk.

(Lyons exits the yard. Cory wanders over to the tree, picks up the bat and assumes a batting stance. He studies an imaginary pitcher and swings. Dissatisfied with the result, he tries again. Troy enters. They eye each other for a beat. Cory puts the bat down and exits the yard. Troy starts into the house as Rose exits with Raynell. She is carrying a cake.)

TROY. I'm coming in and everybody's going out.

ROSE. I'm taking this cake down to the church for the bake sale. Lyons was by to see you. He stopped by to pay you your twenty dollars. It's laying in there on the table.

TROY *(going into his pocket)*. Well . . . here go this money.

ROSE. Put it in there on the table, Troy. I'll get it.

TROY. What time you coming back?

ROSE. Ain't no use you studying me. It don't matter what time I come back.

TROY. I just asked you a question, woman. What's the matter . . . can't I ask you a question?

ROSE. Troy, I don't want to go into it. Your dinner's in there on the stove. All you got to do is heat it up. And don't you be eating the rest of them cakes in there. I'm coming back for them. We having a bake sale at the church tomorrow.

(Rose exits the yard. Troy sits down on the steps, takes a pint bottle from his pocket, opens it and drinks. He begins to sing.)

TROY.

Hear it ring! Hear it ring!
Had an old dog his name was Blue
You know Blue was mighty true
You know Blue was a good old dog
Blue trees a possum in a hollow log
You know from that he was a good old dog

(Bono enters the yard.)

BONO. Hey, Troy.

TROY. Hey, what's happening, Bono?

BONO. I just thought I'd stop by to see you.

TROY. What you stop by and see me for? You ain't stopped by in a month of Sundays. Hell, I must owe you money or something.

BONO. Since you got your promotion I can't keep up with you. Used to see you every day. Now I don't even know what route you working.

TROY. They keep switching me around. Got me out in Greentree now . . . hauling white folks' garbage.

BONO. Greentree, huh? You lucky, at least you ain't got to be lifting them barrels. Damn if they ain't getting heavier. I'm gonna put in my two years and call it quits.

TROY. I'm thinking about retiring myself.

BONO. You got it easy. You can *drive* for another five years.

TROY. It ain't the same, Bono. It ain't like working the back of the truck. Ain't got nobody to talk to . . . feel like you working by yourself. Naw, I'm thinking about retiring. How's Lucille?

BONO. She all right. Her arthritis get to acting up on her sometime. Saw Rose on my way in. She going down to the church, huh?

TROY. Yeah, she took up going down there. All them preachers looking for somebody to fatten their pockets. *(Pause.)* Got some gin here.

BONO. Naw, thanks. I just stopped by to say hello.

TROY Hell, nigger . . . you can take a drink. I ain't never known you to say no to a drink. You ain't got to work tomorrow.

BONO. I just stopped by. I'm fixing to go over to Skinner's. We got us a domino game going over his house every Friday.

TROY. Nigger, you can't play no dominoes. I used to whup you four games out of five.

BONO. Well, that learned me. I'm getting better.

TROY. Yeah? Well, that's all right.

BONO. Look here . . . I got to be getting on. Stop by sometime, huh?

TROY. Yeah, I'll do that, Bono. Lucille told Rose you bought her a new refrigerator.

BONO. Yeah, Rose told Lucille you had finally built your fence . . . so I figured we'd call it even.

TROY. I knew you would.

BONO. Yeah . . . okay. I'll be talking to you.

TROY. Yeah, take care, Bono. Good to see you. I'm gonna stop over.

BONO. Yeah. Okay, Troy.

(Bono exits. Troy drinks from the bottle.)

TROY.
Old Blue died and I dig his grave
Let him down with a golden chain
Every night when I hear old Blue bark
I know Blue treed a possum in Noah's Ark.
Hear it ring! Hear it ring!

(*Cory enters the yard. They eye each other for a beat. Troy is sitting in the middle of the steps. Cory walks over.*)

CORY. I got to get by.

TROY. Say what? What's you say?

CORY. You in my way. I got to get by.

TROY. You got to get by where? This is my house. Bought and paid for. In full. Took me fifteen years. And if you wanna go in my house and I'm sitting on the steps . . . you say excuse me. Like your mama taught you.

CORY. Come on, Pop . . . I got to get by.

(*Cory starts to maneuver his way past Troy. Troy grabs his leg and shoves him back.*)

TROY. You just gonna walk over top of me?

CORY. I live here, too!

TROY (*advancing toward him*). You just gonna walk over top of me in my own house?

CORY. I ain't scared of you.

TROY. I ain't asked if you was scared of me. I asked you if you was fixing to walk over top of me in my own house? That's the question. You ain't gonna say excuse me? You just gonna walk over top of me?

CORY. If you wanna put it like that.

TROY. How else am I gonna put it?

CORY. I was walking by you to go into the house cause you sitting on the steps drunk, singing to yourself. You can put it like that.

TROY. Without saying excuse me???

(*Cory doesn't respond.*)

I asked you a question. Without saying excuse me???

CORY. I ain't got to say excuse me to you. You don't count around here no more.

TROY. Oh, I see . . . I don't count around here no more. You ain't got to say excuse me to your daddy. All of a sudden you done got so grown that your daddy don't count around here no more . . . Around here in his own house and yard that he done paid for with the sweat of his brow. You done got so grown to where you gonna take over. You gonna take over my house. Is that right? You gonna wear my pants. You gonna go in there and stretch out on my bed. You ain't got to say excuse me cause I don't count around here no more. Is that right?

CORY. That's right. You always talking this dumb stuff. Now, why don't you just get out my way.

TROY. I guess you got someplace to sleep and something to put in your belly. You got that, huh? You got that? That's what you need. You got that, huh?

CORY. You don't know what I got. You ain't got to worry about what I got.

TROY. You right! You one hundred percent right! I done spent the last seventeen years worrying about what you got. Now it's your turn, see? I'll tell you what to do. You grown . . . we done established that. You a man. Now, let's see you act like one. Turn your behind around and walk out this yard. And when you get out there in the alley . . . you can forget about this house. See? 'Cause this is my house. You go on and be a man and get your own house. You can forget about this. 'Cause this is mine. You go on and get yours 'cause I'm through with doing for you.

CORY. You talking about what you did for me . . . what'd you ever give me?

TROY. Them feet and bones! That pumping heart, nigger! I give you more than anybody else is ever gonna give you.

CORY. You ain't never gave me nothing! You ain't never done nothing but hold me back. Afraid I was gonna be better than you. All you ever did was try and make me scared of you. I used to tremble every time you called my name. Every time I heard your footsteps in the house. Wondering all the time . . . what's Papa gonna say if I do this? . . . What's he gonna say if I do that? . . . What's Papa gonna say if I turn on the radio? And Mama, too . . . she tries . . . but she's scared of you.

TROY. You leave your mama out of this. She ain't got nothing to do with this.

CORY. I don't know how she stands you . . . after what you did to her.

TROY. I told you to leave your mama out of this!

(*He advances toward Cory.*)

CORY. What you gonna do . . . give me a whupping? You can't whup me no more. You're too old. You just an old man.

TROY (*shoves him on his shoulder*). Nigger! That's what you are. You just another nigger on the street to me!

CORY. You crazy! You know that?

TROY. Go on now! You got the devil in you. Get on away from me!

CORY. You just a crazy old man . . . talking about I got the devil in me.

TROY. Yeah, I'm crazy! If you don't get on the other side of that yard . . . I'm gonna show you how crazy I am! Go on . . . get the hell out of my yard.

CORY. It ain't your yard. You took Uncle Gabe's money he got from the army to buy this house and then you put him out.

TROY (*advances on Cory*). Get your black ass out of my yard!

(*Troy's advance backs Cory up against the tree. Cory grabs up the bat.*)

CORY. I ain't going nowhere! Come on . . . put me out! I ain't scared of you.
TROY. That's my bat!
CORY. Come on!
TROY. Put my bat down!
CORY. Come on, put me out.

(*Cory swings at Troy, who backs across the yard.*)

What's the matter? You so bad . . . put me out!

(*Troy advances toward Cory.*)

CORY (*backing up*). Come on! Come on!
TROY. You're gonna have to use it! You wanna draw that bat back on me . . . you're gonna have to use it.
CORY. Come on! . . . Come on!

(*Cory swings the bat at Troy a second time. He misses. Troy continues to advance toward him.*)

TROY. You're gonna have to kill me! You wanna draw that bat back on me. You're gonna have to kill me.

(*Cory, backed up against the tree, can go no farther. Troy taunts him. He sticks out his head and offers him a target.*)

Come on! Come on!

(*Cory is unable to swing the bat. Troy grabs it.*)

TROY. Then I'll show you.

(*Cory and Troy struggle over the bat. The struggle is fierce and fully engaged. Troy ultimately is the stronger, and takes the bat from Cory and stands over him ready to swing. He stops himself.*)

Go on and get away from around my house.

(*Cory, stung by his defeat, picks himself up, walks slowly out of the yard and up the alley.*)

CORY. Tell Mama I'll be back for my things.
TROY. They'll be on the other side of that fence.

(*Cory exits.*)

TROY. I can't taste nothing. Helluljah! I can't taste nothing no more. (*Troy assumes a batting posture and begins to taunt Death, the fastball in the outside corner.*) Come on! It's between you and me now! Come on! Anytime you want! Come on! I be ready for you . . . but I ain't gonna he easy.

(*The lights go down on the scene.*)

SCENE 5

The time is 1965. The lights come up in the yard. It is the morning of Troy's funeral. A funeral plaque with a light hangs beside the door. There is a small garden plot off to the side. There is noise and activity in the house as Rose, Lyons, and Bono have gathered. The door opens and Raynell, seven years old, enters dressed in a flannel nightgown. She crosses to the garden and pokes around with a stick. Rose calls from the house.

ROSE. Raynell!
RAYNELL. Mam?
ROSE. What you doing out there?
RAYNELL. Nothing.

(*Rose comes to the door.*)

ROSE. Girl, get in here and get dressed. What you doing?
RAYNELL. Seeing if my garden growed.
ROSE. I told you it ain't gonna grow overnight. You got to wait.
RAYNELL. It don't look like it never gonna grow. Dag!
ROSE. I told you a watched pot never boils. Get in here and get dressed.
RAYNELL. This ain't even no pot, Mama.
ROSE. You just have to give it a chance. It'll grow. Now you come on and do what I told you. We got to be getting ready. This ain't no morning to be playing around. You hear me?
RAYNELL. Yes, mam.

(*Rose exits into the house. Raynell continues to poke at her garden with a stick. Cory enters. He is dressed in a Marine corporal's uniform, and carries a duffel bag. His posture is that of a military man, and his speech has a clipped sternness.*)

CORY (*to Raynell*). Hi. (*Pause.*) I bet your name is Raynell.
RAYNELL. Uh huh.
CORY. Is your mama home?

(*Raynell runs up on the porch and calls through the screen door.*)

RAYNELL. Mama . . . there's some man out here. Mama?

(*Rose comes to the door.*)

ROSE. Cory? Lord have mercy! Look here, you all!

(*Rose and Cory embrace in a tearful reunion as Bono and Lyons enter from the house dressed in funeral clothes.*)

BONO. Aw, looka here . . .
ROSE. Done got all grown up!

CORY. Don't cry, Mama. What you crying about?
ROSE. I'm just so glad you made it.
CORY. Hey Lyons. How you doing, Mr. Bono.

(*Lyons goes to embrace Cory.*)

LYONS. Look at you, man. Look at you. Don't he look good, Rose? Got them Corporal stripes.
ROSE. What took you so long?
CORY. You know how the Marines are, Mama. They got to get all their paperwork straight before they let you do anything.
ROSE. Well, I'm sure glad you made it. They let Lyons come. Your Uncle Gabe's still in the hospital. They don't know if they gonna let him out or not. I just talked to them a little while ago.
LYONS. A Corporal in the United States Marines.
BONO. Your daddy knew you had it in you. He used to tell me all the time.
LYONS. Don't he look good, Mr. Bono?
BONO. Yeah, he remind me of Troy when I first met him. (*Pause.*) Say, Rose, Lucille's down at the church with the choir. I'm gonna go down and get the pallbearers lined up. I'll be back to get you all.
ROSE. Thanks, Jim.
CORY. See you, Mr. Bono.
LYONS (*with his arm around Raynell*). Cory . . . look at Raynell. Ain't she precious? She gonna break a whole lot of hearts.
ROSE. Raynell, come and say hello to your brother. This is your brother, Cory. You remember Cory.
RAYNELL. No, Mam.
CORY. She don't remember me, Mama.
ROSE. Well, we talk about you. She heard us talk about you. (*To Raynell*) This is your brother, Cory. Come on and say hello.
RAYNELL. Hi.
CORY. Hi. So you're Raynell. Mama told me a lot about you.
ROSE. You all come on into the house and let me fix you some breakfast. Keep up your strength.
CORY. I ain't hungry, Mama.
LYONS. You can fix me something, Rose. I'll be in there in a minute.
ROSE. Cory, you sure you don't want nothing? I know they ain't feeding you right.
CORY. No, Mama . . . thanks. I don't feel like eating. I'll get something later.
ROSE. Raynell . . . get on upstairs and get that dress on like I told you.

(*Rose and Raynell exit into the house.*)

LYONS. So . . . I hear you thinking about getting married.
CORY. Yeah, I done found the right one, Lyons. It's about time.
LYONS. Me and Bonnie been split up about four years now. About the time Papa retired. I guess she just got tired of all them changes I was putting her through. (*Pause.*) I always knew you was gonna make something out yourself. Your head was always in the right direction. So . . . you gonna stay in . . . make it a career . . . put in your twenty years?
CORY. I don't know. I got six already, I think that's enough.
LYONS. Stick with Uncle Sam and retire early. Ain't nothing out here. I guess Rose told you what happened with me. They got me down the workhouse. I thought I was being slick cashing other people's checks.
CORY. How much time you doing?
LYONS. They give me three years. I got that beat now. I ain't got but nine more months. It ain't so bad. You learn to deal with it like anything else. You got to take the crookeds with the straights. That's what Papa used to say. He used to say that when he struck out. I seen him strike out three times in a row . . . and the next time up he hit the ball over the grandstand. Right out there in Homestead Field. He wasn't satisfied hitting in the seats . . . he want to hit it over everything! After the game he had two hundred people standing around waiting to shake his hand. You got to take the crookeds with the straights. Yeah, Papa was something else.
CORY. You still playing?
LYONS. Cory . . . you know I'm gonna do that. There's some fellows down there we got us a band . . . we gonna try and stay together when we get out . . . but yeah, I'm still playing. It still helps me to get out of bed in the morning. As long as it do that I'm gonna be right there playing and trying to make some sense out of it.
ROSE (*calling*). Lyons, I got these eggs in the pan.
LYONS. Let me go on and get these eggs, man. Get ready to go bury Papa. (*Pause.*) How you doing? You doing all right?

(*Cory nods. Lyons touches him on the shoulder and they share a moment of silent grief. Lyons exits into the house. Cory wanders about the yard. Raynell enters.*)

RAYNELL. Hi.
CORY. Hi.
RAYNELL. Did you used to sleep in my room?
CORY. Yeah . . . that used to be my room.
RAYNELL. That's what Papa call it. "Cory's room." It got your football in the closet.

(*Rose comes to the door.*)

ROSE. Raynell, get in there and get them good shoes on.
RAYNELL. Mama, can't I wear these? Them other one hurt my feet.

ROSE. Well, they just gonna have to hurt your feet for a while. You ain't said they hurt your feet when you went down to the store and got them.

RAYNELL. They didn't hurt then. My feet done got bigger.

ROSE. Don't you give me no backtalk now. You get in there and get them shoes on. (*Raynell exits into the house.*) Ain't too much changed. He still got that piece of rag tied to that tree. He was out here swinging that bat. I was just ready to go back in the house. He swung that bat and then he just fell over. Seem like he swung it and stood there with this grin on his face . . . and then he just fell over. They carried him on down to the hospital, but I knew there wasn't no need . . . why don't you come on in the house?

CORY. Mama . . . I got something to tell you. I don't know how to tell you this . . . but I've got to tell you . . . I'm not going to Papa's funeral.

ROSE. Boy, hush your mouth. That's your daddy you talking about. I don't want hear that kind of talk this morning. I done raised you to come to this? You standing there all healthy and grown talking about you ain't going to your daddy's funeral?

CORY. Mama . . . listen . . .

ROSE. I don't want to hear it, Cory. You just get that thought out of your head.

CORY. I can't drag Papa with me everywhere I go. I've got to say no to him. One time in my life I've got to say no.

ROSE. Don't nobody have to listen to nothing like that. I know you and your daddy ain't seen eye to eye, but I ain't got to listen to that kind of talk this morning. Whatever was between you and your daddy . . . the time has come to put it aside. Just take it and set it over there on the shelf and forget about it. Disrespecting your daddy ain't gonna make you a man, Cory. You got to find a way to come to that on your own. Not going to your daddy's funeral ain't gonna make you a man.

CORY. The whole time I was growing up . . . living in his house . . . Papa was like a shadow that followed you everywhere. It weighed on you and sunk into your flesh. It would wrap around you and lay there until you couldn't tell which one was you anymore. That shadow digging in your flesh. Trying to crawl in. Trying to live through you. Everywhere I looked, Troy Maxson was staring back at me . . . hiding under the bed . . . in the closet. I'm just saying I've got to find a way to get rid of that shadow, Mama.

ROSE. You just like him. You got him in you good.

CORY. Don't tell me that, Mama.

ROSE. You Troy Maxson all over again.

CORY. I don't want to be Troy Maxson. I want to be me.

ROSE. You can't be nobody but who you are, Cory. That shadow wasn't nothing but you growing into yourself. You either got to grow into it or cut it down to fit you. But that's all you got to make life with. That's all you got to measure yourself against that world out there. Your daddy wanted you to be everything he wasn't . . . and at the same time he tried to make you into everything he was. I don't know if he was right or wrong . . . but I do know he meant to do more good than he meant to do harm. He wasn't always right. Sometimes when he touched he bruised. And sometimes when he took me in his arms he cut.

When I first met your daddy I thought . . . Here is a man I can lay down with and make a baby. That's the first thing I thought when I seen him. I was thirty years old and had done seen my share of men. But when he walked up to me and said, "I can dance a waltz that'll make you dizzy," I thought, Rose Lee, here is a man that you can open yourself up to and be filled to bursting. Here is a man that can fill all them empty spaces you been tipping around the edges of. One of them empty spaces was being somebody's mother.

I married your daddy and settled down to cooking his supper and keeping clean sheets on the bed. When your daddy walked through the house he was so big he filled it up. That was my first mistake. Not to make him leave some room for me. For my part in the matter. But at that time I wanted that. I wanted a house that I could sing in. And that's what your daddy gave me. I didn't know to keep up his strength I had to give up little pieces of mine. I did that. I took on his life as mine and mixed up the pieces so that you couldn't hardly tell which was which anymore. It was my choice. It was my life and I didn't have to live it like that. But that's what life offered me in the way of being a woman and I took it. I grabbed hold of it with both hands.

By the time Raynell came into the house, me and your daddy had done lost touch with one another. I didn't want to make my blessing off of nobody's misfortune . . . but I took on to Raynell like she was all them babies I had wanted and never had. (*The phone rings.*) Like I'd been blessed to relive a part of my life. And if the Lord see fit to keep up my strength . . . I'm gonna do her just like your daddy did you . . . I'm gonna give her the best of what's in me.

RAYNELL (*entering, still with her old shoes*). Mama . . . Reverend Tollivier on the phone.

(*Rose exits into the house.*)

RAYNELL. Hi.

CORY. Hi.

RAYNELL. You in the Army or the Marines?

CORY. Marines.

RAYNELL. Papa said it was the Army. Did you know Blue?

CORY. Blue? Who's Blue?

RAYNELL. Papa's dog what he sing about all the time.

CORY (*singing*).

Hear it ring! Hear it ring!

I had a dog his name was Blue
You know Blue was mighty true
You know Blue was a good old dog
Blue treed a possum in a hollow log
You know from that he was a good old dog.
Hear it ring! Hear it ring!

(*Raynell joins in singing*)

CORY AND RAYNELL.
Blue treed a possum out on a limb
Blue looked at me and I looked at him
Grabbed that possum and put him in a sack
Blue stayed there till I came back
Old Blue's feets was big and round

Never allowed a possum to touch the ground.
Old Blue died and I dug his grave
I dug his grave with a silver spade
Let him down with a golden chain
And every night I call his name
Go on Blue, you good dog you
Go on Blue, you good dog you.

RAYNELL.
Blue laid down and died like a man
Blue laid down and died . . .

BOTH.
Blue laid down and died like a man
Now he's treeing possums in the Promised Land
I'm gonna tell you this to let you know
Blue's gone where the good dogs go
When I hear old Blue bark
When I hear old Blue bark
Blue treed a possum in Noah's Ark
Blue treed a possum in Noah's Ark.

(*Rose comes to the screendoor.*)

ROSE. Cory, we gonna be ready to go in a minute.

CORY (*to Raynell*). You go on in the house and change them shoes like Mama told you so we can go to Papa's funeral.

RAYNELL. Okay, I'll be back.

(*Raynell exits into the house. Cory gets up and crosses over to the tree. Rose stands in the screendoor watching him. Gabriel enters from the alley.*)

GABRIEL (*calling*). Hey, Rose!
ROSE. Gabe?
GABRIEL. I'm here, Rose. Hey Rose, I'm here!

(*Rose enters from the house.*)

ROSE. Lord . . . Look here, Lyons!

LYONS. See, I told you, Rose . . . I told you they'd let him come.

CORY. How you doing, Uncle Gabe?

LYONS. How you doing, Uncle Gabe?

GABRIEL. Hey, Rose. It's time. It's time to tell St. Peter to open the gates. Troy, you ready? You ready, Troy. I'm gonna tell St. Peter to open the gates. You get ready now.

(*Gabriel, with great fanfare, braces himself to blow. The trumpet is without a mouthpiece. He puts the end of it into his mouth and blows with great force, like a man who has been waiting some twenty-odd years for this single moment. No sound comes out of the trumpet. He braces himself and blows again with the same result. A third time he blows. There is a weight of impossible description that falls away and leaves him bare and exposed to a frightful realization. It is a trauma that a sane and normal mind would be unable to withstand. He begins to dance. A slow, strange dance, eerie and life-giving. A dance of atavistic signature and ritual. Lyons attempts to embrace him. Gabriel pushes Lyons away. He begins to howl in what is an attempt at song, or perhaps a song turning back into itself in an attempt at speech. He finishes his dance and the gates of heaven stand open as wide as God's closet.*)

That's the way that go!

BLACKOUT

TOPICS FOR DISCUSSION AND WRITING

1. What do you think Bono means when he says, early in Act 2, "Some people build fences to keep people out . . . and some people build fences to keep people in"? Why is the play called *Fences*? What has fenced Troy in? What is Troy fencing in? (Take account of Troy's last speech in Act 2, Scene 2, but do not limit your discussion to this speech.)
2. What do you think Troy's reasons are—conscious and unconscious—for not wanting Cory to play football at college?
3. Compare and contrast Cory and Lyons. Consider, too, in what ways they resemble Troy, and in what ways they differ from him.
4. In what ways is Troy like his father, and in what ways unlike?

5. What do you make out of the prominence given to the song about Blue?
6. There is a good deal of anger in the play, but there is also humor. Which passages do you find humorous, and why?
7. Characterize Rose Maxson.
8. Some scenes begin by specifying that "the lights come up." Others do not, presumably beginning with an illuminated stage. All scenes except the last one end with the lights going down to blackness. Explain Wilson's use of lighting.

A CONTEXT FOR *FENCES*

Talking about Fences

August Wilson

[Part of an interview conducted with David Savran, on March 13, 1987]

In reading Fences, *I came to view Troy more and more critically as the play progressed, sharing Rose's point of view. We see that Troy has been crippled by his father. That's being replayed in Troy's relationship with Cory. Do you think there's a way out of that cycle?*

Surely. First of all, we're all like our parents. The things we are taught early in life, how to respond to the world, our sense of morality—everything, we get from them. Now you can take that legacy and do with it anything you want to do. It's in your hands. Cory is Troy's son. How can he be Troy's son without sharing Troy's values? I was trying to get at why Troy made the choices he made, how they have influenced his values and how he attempts to pass those along to his son. Each generation gives the succeeding generation what they think they need. One question in the play is, "Are the tools we are given sufficient to compete in a world that is different from the one our parents knew?" I think they are—it's just that we have to do different things with the tools. That's all Troy has to give. Troy's flaw is that he does not recognize that the world was changing. That's because he spent fifteen years in a penitentiary.

As African-Americans, we should demand to participate in society as Africans. That's the way out of the vicious cycle of poverty and neglect that exists in 1987 in America, where you have a huge percentage of blacks living in the equivalent of South African townships, in housing projects. No one is inviting these people to participate in society. Look at the poverty levels—$8,500 for a family of four, if you have $8,501 you're not counted. Those statistics would go up enormously if we had an honest assessment of the cost of living in America. I don't know how anybody can support a family of four on $8,500. What I'm saying is that 85 or 90 percent of blacks in America are living in abject poverty and, for the most part, are crowded into what amount to concentration camps. The situation for blacks in America is worse than it was forty years ago. Some sociologists will tell you about the tremendous progress we've made. They didn't put me out when I walked in the door. And you can always point to someone who works on Wall Street, or is a doctor. But they don't count in the larger scheme of things.

Do you have any idea how these political changes could take place?

I'm not sure. I know that blacks must be allowed their cultural differences. I think the process of assimilation to white American society was a big mistake. We don't want to be like you. Blacks living in housing projects are isolated from the society, for the most part—living as they choose, as Africans. Only they don't realize the value in what they're doing because they have accepted their victimization. They've marked themselves as victims. Once they recognize that, they can begin to move through society in a different manner, from a stronger position, and claim what is theirs.

A project of yours is to point up what happens when oppression is internalized.

Yes, transfer of aggression to the wrong target. I think it's interesting that the two roads open to blacks for "full participation" are entertainment and sports. *Ma Rainey* and *Fences,* and I didn't plan it that way. I don't think that they're the correct roads. I think Troy's right. Now with the benefit of historical perspective, I can say that the athletic scholarship was actually a way of exploiting. Now you've got two million kids who think they're going to play in the NBA. In the sixties the universities made a lot of money off of athletics. You had kids playing for free who, by and large, were not getting educated, were taking courses in basketweaving. Some of them could barely read.

Troy may be right about that issue, but it seems that he has passed on certain destructive traits in spite of himself. Take the hostility between father and son.

I think every generation says to the previous generation: you're in my way, I've got to get by. The father-son conflict is actually a normal generational conflict that happens all the time.

So it's a healthy and a good thing?

Oh, sure. Troy is seeing this boy walk around, smelling his piss. Two men cannot live in the same household. Troy would have been tremendously disappointed if Cory had not challenged him. Troy knows that this boy has to go out and do battle with that world: "So I had best prepare him because I know that's a harsh, cruel place out there. But that's going to be easy compared to what he's getting here. Ain't nobody gonna whip your ass like I'm gonna whip it." He has a tremendous love for the kid. But he's not going to say, "I love you," he's going to demonstrate it. He's carrying garbage for seventeen years just for the kid. The only world Troy knows is the one that he made. Cory's going to go on to find another one, he's going to arrive at the same place as Troy. I think one of the most important lines in the play is when Troy is talking about his father: "I got to the place where I could feel him kicking in my blood and knew that the only thing that separated us was the matter of a few years."

Hopefully, Cory will do things a bit differently with his son. For Troy, sports was not the way to go, the white man wouldn't let him get away with that. "Get you a job, with your hands, something that nobody can take away from you." The idea of school—he doesn't know what that is. That's for white folks. Very few blacks had paperwork jobs. But if you knew how to fix cars—you could always make some money. That's what Troy wants for Cory. There aren't many people who ever jumped up in Troy's face. So he's proud of the kid at the same time that he expresses a hurt that all men feel. You got to cut your kid loose at some point. There's that sense of loss and separation. You find out how Troy left his father's house and you see how Cory leaves his house. I suspect with Cory it will repeat with some differences and maybe, after five or six generations, they'll find a different way to do it.

Where Cory ends up is very ambiguous, as a marine in 1965.

Yes. For the average black kid on the street, that was an alternative. You went into the army because you could learn how to do something. I can remember my parents talking about the son of some friends: "He's in the navy. He *did* something"—as opposed to standing on the street corner, shooting drugs, drinking wine and robbing stores. Lyons says to Cory, "I always knew you were going to make something out of yourself." It really wounds me. He's a corporal in the marines. For blacks, that is a sense of accomplishment. Therein lies one of the tragedies of blacks in America. Cory says, "I don't know. I put in six years. That's enough." Anyone who goes into the army and makes a career out of it is a loser. They sit there and are nurtured by the army and they don't have to confront life. Then they get out of the army and find there's nothing to do. They didn't learn any skills. And if they did, they can't find a job. Four months later, they're shooting dope. In the sixties a whole bunch of blacks went over, fought and died in the Vietnam War. The survivors came back to the same street corners and found out nothing had changed. They still couldn't get a job.

At the end of *Fences* every person, with the exception of Raynell, is institutionalized. Rose is in a church. Lyons is in a penitentiary. Gabriel's in a mental hospital and Cory's in the marines. The only free person is the girl, Troy's daughter, the hope for the future. That was conscious on my part because in '57 that's what I saw. Blacks have relied on institutions which are really foreign—except for the black church, which has been our saving grace. I have some problems with it but I recognize it as a central social organization and sometimes an economic organization for the black community. I would like to see blacks develop their own institutions that respond to their needs.

The Man in a Case. (Photograph © Diane Gorodnitzki.)

WENDY WASSERSTEIN

The Man in a Case

Wendy Wasserstein was born in Brooklyn, New York, in 1950, daughter of immigrants from central Europe. After graduating from Mt. Holyoke College she took creative writing courses at the City College of New York and then completed a degree program at the Yale School of Drama. Wasserstein has had a highly successful career as a playwright (*The Heidi Chronicles* won a Pulitzer Prize in 1989), and she has also achieved recognition for her television screenplays and a book of essays.

The Man in a Case is based on a short story by Anton Chekhov, one of her favorite writers.

COMMENTARY

In our introductory comments about comedy we suggest that comedy often shows the absurdity of ideals. The miser, the puritan, the health-faddist, and so on, are people of ideals, but their ideals are suffocating. In his famous essay on comedy (1884) Henri Bergson suggested that an organism is comic when it behaves like a mechanism, i.e., when instead of responding freely, flexibly, resourcefully—one might almost say intuitively and also intelligently—to the vicissitudes of life, it responds in a predictable, mechanical (and, given life's infinite variety, often inappropriate) way. It is not surprising that the first line in Wasserstein's comedy, spoken by a pedant to his betrothed, is "You are ten minutes late." This is not the way that Demetrius and Lysander speak in *A Midsummer Night's Dream.* True, a Shakespearean lover may fret about time when he is not in the presence of his mistress, but when he sees her, all thoughts of the clock disappear and he is nothing but lover. The Shakespearean lover is, in his way, mechanical too, but the audience feels a degree of sympathy for him that it does not feel for the pedantic clock-watcher.

The very title, *The Man in a Case,* alerts us to a man who is imprisoned—a man, it turns out, who lives in a prison of his own making. Byelinkov says, "I don't like change very much." His words could be said by many other butts of satire—jealous husbands or misers, for example. And of course the comic writer takes such figures and places them where they will be subjected to maximum change. The dramatist puts the jealous husband or the miser, for instance, into a plot in which a stream of men visit the house, and every new visitor is (in the eyes of the comic figure) a potential seducer or a potential thief. In *The Man in a Case,* we meet a man of highly disciplined habits who is confronted by an uninhibited woman. The inevitable result of this juxtaposition is comic.

In this play, then, we have a pedant who unaccountably has fallen in love with a vivacious young woman. (In Chekhov's story, Byelinkov's acquaintances have decided that it is time for him to get married, so they conspire to persuade him that he is in love.) The pedant is a stock comic character who can be traced back to the "doctor" (*il dottore,* not a medical doctor but a pedant) of Renaissance Italian comedy. Such a figure values Latin more than life. True, Byelinkov is in love, but (as his first line shows) he remains the precise schoolmaster. Later, when Varinka says, "It is time for tea," he replies, "It is too early for tea. Tea is at half past the hour." Perhaps tea regularly is served at half past the hour, but again, a lover does not talk this way; a true lover will take every opportunity to have tea with his mistress.

We are not surprised to hear that Byelinkov describes his career as the teaching of "the discipline and contained beauty of the classics." "Discipline" and containment are exactly what we expect from this sort of comic figure, a man who tells us that he smiles three times every day and that in twenty years of teaching he has never been late to school. The speech that begins "I don't like change very much," goes on thus: "If one works out the arithmetic, the final fraction of improvement is at best less than an eighth of value over the total damage caused by disruption."

Why, then, is this man talking to Varinka? Because he has fallen in love. Love conquers all, even mathematicians and classicists. For the most part, when such monomaniacs fall in love they are, as we have said, comic, objects of satire, but since audiences approve of love, these figures—if young and genuinely in love—also can generate some sympathy from the audience. Thus, when Byelinkov says he will put a lilac in Varinka's hair, he almost becomes sympathetic—but when he makes an entry in his notebook, reminding him to do this again next year, he reverts to the pedant whom we find ridiculous.

Is Byelinkov only a comic figure, or does he sometimes evoke at least a little pathos? In seeing the play in your mind's eye, when you get to the end of the play try to envision his final action. You might think about how, if you were directing a production of *The Man in a Case,* you would have him perform the action specified in the last stage direction. In fact, you might from the very start of this short play set yourself the pleasant task of mentally directing the actors. The first stage direction tells us that "Byelinkov is pacing," but exactly how does he pace? Does he have his arms behind his back? Does he pace regularly, or does he occasionally stop, perhaps to look at his watch? His first line of dialogue, when Varinka enters, is, "You are ten minutes late." Does he take out a pocket watch when he first sees her, or when she is close to him? Does he replace it before speaking? The choices are yours.

WENDY WASSERSTEIN *The Man in a Case*

List of Characters

BYELINKOV

VARINKA

A small garden in the village of Mironitski. 1898.

Byelinkov is pacing. Enter Varinka out of breath.

BYELINKOV. You are ten minutes late.

VARINKA. The most amazing thing happened on my way over here. You know the woman who runs the grocery store down the road. She wears a black wig during the week, and a blond wig on Saturday nights. And she has the daughter who married an engineer in Moscow who is doing very well thank you and is living, God bless them, in a three-room apartment. But he really is the most boring man in the world. All he talks about is his future and his station in life. Well, she heard we were to be married and she gave me this basket of apricots to give to you.

BYELINKOV. That is a most amazing thing!

VARINKA. She said to me, Varinka, you are marrying the most honorable man in the entire village. In this village he is the only man fit to speak with my son-in-law.

BYELINKOV. I don't care for apricots. They give me hives.

VARINKA. I can return them. I'm sure if I told her they give you hives she would give me a basket of raisins or a cake.

BYELINKOV. I don't know this woman or her pompous son-in-law. Why would she give me her cakes?

VARINKA. She adores you!

BYELINKOV. She is emotionally loose.

VARINKA. She adores you by reputation. Everyone adores you by reputation. I tell everyone I am to marry Byelinkov, the finest teacher in the county.

BYELINKOV. You tell them this?

VARINKA. If they don't tell me first.

BYELINKOV. Pride can be an imperfect value.

VARINKA. It isn't pride. It is the truth. You are a great man!

BYELINKOV. I am the master of Greek and Latin at a local school at the end of the village of Mironitski.

(*Varinka kisses him*)

VARINKA. And I am to be the master of Greek and Latin's wife!

BYELINKOV. Being married requires a great deal of responsibility. I hope I am able to provide you with all that a married man must properly provide a wife.

VARINKA. We will be very happy.

BYELINKOV. Happiness is for children. We are entering into a social contract, an amicable agreement to provide us with a secure and satisfying future.

VARINKA. You are so sweet! You are the sweetest man in the world!

BYELINKOV. I'm a man set in his ways who saw a chance to provide himself with a small challenge.

VARINKA. Look at you! Look at you! Your sweet round spectacles, your dear collar always starched, always raised, your perfectly pressed pants always creasing at right angles perpendicular to the floor, and my most favorite part, the sweet little galoshes, rain or shine, just in case. My Byelinkov, never taken by surprise. Except by me.

BYELINKOV. You speak about me as if I were your pet.

VARINKA. You are my pet! My little school mouse.

BYELINKOV. A mouse?

VARINKA. My sweetest dancing bear with galoshes, my little stale babka![1]

[1]**babka** cake with almonds and raisins

BYELINKOV. A stale babka?

VARINKA. I am not Pushkin.[2]

BYELINKOV (*Laughs*). That depends what you think of Pushkin.

VARINKA. You're smiling. I knew I could make you smile today.

BYELINKOV. I am a responsible man. Every day I have for breakfast black bread, fruit, hot tea, and every day I smile three times. I am halfway into my translation of the *Aeneid*[3] from classical Greek hexameter into Russian alexandrines. In twenty years I have never been late to school. I am a responsible man, but no dancing bear.

VARINKA. Dance with me.

BYELINKOV. Now? It is nearly four weeks before the wedding!

VARINKA. It's a beautiful afternoon. We are in your garden. The roses are in full bloom.

BYELINKOV. The roses have beetles.

VARINKA. Dance with me!

BYELINKOV. You are a demanding woman.

VARINKA. You chose me. And right. And left. And turn. And right. And left.

BYELINKOV. And turn. Give me your hand. You dance like a school mouse. It's a beautiful afternoon! We are in my garden. The roses are in full bloom! And turn. And turn. (*Twirls Varinka around*)

VARINKA. I am the luckiest woman!

(*Byelinkov stops dancing*)

Why are you stopping?

BYELINKOV. To place a lilac in your hair. Every year on this day I will place a lilac in your hair.

VARINKA. Will you remember?

BYELINKOV. I will write it down. (*Takes a notebook from his pocket*) Dear Byelinkov, don't forget the day a young lady, your bride, entered your garden, your peace, and danced on the roses. On that day every year you are to place a lilac in her hair.

VARINKA. I love you.

BYELINKOV. It is convenient we met.

VARINKA. I love you.

BYELINKOV. You are a girl.

VARINKA. I am thirty.

BYELINKOV. But you think like a girl. That is an attractive attribute.

VARINKA. Do you love me?

BYELINKOV. We've never spoken about housekeeping.

VARINKA. I am an excellent housekeeper. I kept house

[2]**Pushkin** Alexander Pushkin (1799–1837), Russian poet
[3]***Aeneid*** Latin epic poem by the Roman poet Virgil (70–19 B.C.)

for my family on the farm in Gadyatchsky. I can make a beetroot soup with tomatoes and aubergines which is so nice. Awfully awfully nice.

BYELINKOV. You are fond of expletives.

VARINKA. My beet soup, sir, is excellent!

BYELINKOV. Please don't be cross. I too am an excellent housekeeper. I have a place for everything in the house. A shelf for each pot, a cubby for every spoon, a folder for favorite recipes. I have cooked for myself for twenty years. Though my beet soup is not outstanding, it is sufficient.

VARINKA. I'm sure it's very good.

BYELINKOV. No. It is awfully, awfully not. What I am outstanding in, however, what gives me greatest pleasure, is preserving those things which are left over. I wrap each tomato slice I haven't used in a wet cloth and place it in the coolest corner of the house. I have had my shoes for seven years because I wrap them in the galoshes you are so fond of. And every night before I go to sleep I wrap my bed in quilts and curtains so I never catch a draft.

VARINKA. You sleep with curtains on your bed?

BYELINKOV. I like to keep warm.

VARINKA. I will make you a new quilt.

BYELINKOV. No. No new quilt. That would be hazardous.

VARINKA. It is hazardous to sleep under curtains.

BYELINKOV. Varinka, I don't like change very much. If one works out the arithmetic the final fraction of improvement is at best less than an eighth of value over the total damage caused by disruption. I never thought of marrying till I saw your eyes dancing among the familiar faces at the headmaster's tea. I assumed I would grow old preserved like those which are left over, wrapped suitably in my case of curtains and quilts.

VARINKA. Byelinkov, I want us to have dinners with friends and summer country visits. I want people to say, "Have you spent time with Varinka and Byelinkov? He is so happy now that they are married. She is just what he needed."

BYELINKOV. You have already brought me some happiness. But I never was a sad man. Don't ever think I thought I was a sad man.

VARINKA. My sweetest darling, you can be whatever you want! If you are sad, they'll say she talks all the time, and he is soft-spoken and kind.

BYELINKOV. And if I am difficult?

VARINKA. Oh, they'll say he is difficult because he is highly intelligent. All great men are difficult. Look at Lermontov, Tchaikovsky, Peter the Great.

BYELINKOV. Ivan the Terrible.[4]

VARINKA. Yes, him too.

BYELINKOV. Why are you marrying me? I am none of these things.

VARINKA. To me you are.

BYELINKOV. You have imagined this. You have constructed an elaborate romance for yourself. Perhaps you are the great one. You are the one with the great imagination.

VARINKA. Byelinkov, I am a pretty girl of thirty. You're right, I am not a woman. I have not made myself into a woman because I do not deserve that honor. Until I came to this town to visit my brother I lived on my family's farm. As the years passed I became younger and younger in fear that I would never marry. And it wasn't that I wasn't pretty enough or sweet enough, it was just that no man ever looked at me and saw a wife. I was not the woman who would be there when he came home. Until I met you I thought I would lie all my life and say I never married because I never met a man I loved. I will love you, Byelinkov. And I will help you to love me. We deserve the life everyone else has. We deserve not to be different.

BYELINKOV. Yes. We are the same as everyone else.

VARINKA. Tell me you love me.

BYELINKOV. I love you.

VARINKA (*Takes his hands*). We will be very happy. I am very strong. (*Pauses*) It is time for tea.

BYELINKOV. It is too early for tea. Tea is at half past the hour.

VARINKA. Do you have heavy cream? It will be awfully nice with apricots.

BYELINKOV. Heavy cream is too rich for teatime.

VARINKA. But today is special. Today you placed a lilac in my hair. Write in your note pad. Every year we will celebrate with apricots and heavy cream. I will go to my brother's house and get some.

BYELINKOV. But your brother's house is a mile from here.

VARINKA. Today it is much shorter. Today my brother gave me his bicycle to ride. I will be back very soon.

BYELINKOV. You rode to my house by bicycle! Did anyone see you?

VARINKA. Of course. I had such fun. I told you I saw the grocery store lady with the son-in-law who is doing very well thank you in Moscow, and the headmaster's wife.

BYELINKOV. You saw the headmaster's wife!

VARINKA. She smiled at me.

BYELINKOV. Did she laugh or smile?

VARINKA. She laughed a little. She said, "My dear, you are very progressive to ride a bicycle." She said you and your fiancé Byelinkov must ride together sometime. I wonder if he'll take off his galoshes when he rides a bicycle.

[4]**Lermontov . . . Ivan the Terrible** Mikhail Lermontov (1814–41), poet and novelist; Peter Ilich Tchaikovsky (1840–93) composer; Peter the Great (1672–1725) and Ivan the Terrible (1530–84), czars credited with making Russia a great European power

BYELINKOV. She said that?

VARINKA. She adores you. We had a good giggle.

BYELINKOV. A woman can be arrested for riding a bicycle. That is not progressive, it is a premeditated revolutionary act. Your brother must be awfully, awfully careful on behalf of your behavior. He has been careless—oh so careless—in giving you the bicycle.

VARINKA. Dearest Byelinkov, you are wrapping yourself under curtains and quilts! I made friends on the bicycle.

BYELINKOV. You saw more than the headmaster's wife and the idiot grocery woman.

VARINKA. She is not an idiot.

BYELINKOV. She is a potato-vending, sausage-armed fool!

VARINKA. Shhhh! My school mouse. Shhh!

BYELINKOV. What other friends did you make on this bicycle?

VARINKA. I saw students from my brother's classes. They waved and shouted, "Anthropos in love! Anthropos in love!!"

BYELINKOV. Where is that bicycle?

VARINKA. I left it outside the gate. Where are you going?

BYELINKOV (*Muttering as he exits*). Anthropos in love, anthropos in love.

VARINKA. They were cheering me on. Careful, you'll trample the roses.

BYELINKOV (*Returning with the bicycle*). Anthropos is the Greek singular for man. Anthropos in love translates as the Greek and Latin master in love. Of course they cheered you. Their instructor, who teaches them the discipline and contained beauty of the classics, is in love with a sprite on a bicycle. It is a good giggle, isn't it? A very good giggle! I am returning this bicycle to your brother.

VARINKA. But it is teatime.

BYELINKOV. Today we will not have tea.

VARINKA. But you will have to walk back a mile.

BYELINKOV. I have my galoshes on. (*Gets on the bicycle*) Varinka, we deserve not to be different. (*Begins to pedal. The bicycle doesn't move*)

VARINKA. Put the kickstand up.

BYELINKOV. I beg your pardon.

VARINKA (*Giggling*). Byelinkov, to make the bicycle move, you must put the kickstand up.

(*Byelinkov puts it up and awkwardly falls off the bicycle as it moves*)

(*Laughing*) Ha ha ha. My little school mouse. You look so funny! You are the sweetest dearest man in the world. Ha ha ha!

(*Pause*)

BYELINKOV. Please help me up. I'm afraid my galosh is caught.

VARINKA (*Trying not to laugh*). Your galosh is caught! (*Explodes in laughter again*) Oh, you are so funny! I do love you so. (*Helps Byelinkov up*) You were right, my pet, as always. We don't need heavy cream for tea. The fraction of improvement isn't worth the damage caused by the disruption.

BYELINKOV. Varinka, it is still too early for tea. I must complete two stanzas of my translation before late afternoon. That is my regular schedule.

VARINKA. Then I will watch while you work.

BYELINKOV. No. You had a good giggle. That is enough.

VARINKA. Then while you work I will work too. I will make lists of guests for our wedding.

BYELINKOV. I can concentrate only when I am alone in my house. Please take your bicycle home to your brother.

VARINKA. But I don't want to leave you. You look so sad.

BYELINKOV. I never was a sad man. Don't ever think I was a sad man.

VARINKA. Byelinkov, it's a beautiful day, we are in your garden. The roses are in bloom.

BYELINKOV. Allow me to help you on to your bicycle. (*Takes Varinka's hand as she gets on the bike.*)

VARINKA. You are such a gentleman. We will be very happy.

BYELINKOV. You are very strong. Good day, Varinka.

(*Varinka pedals off. Byelinkov, alone in the garden, takes out his pad and rips up the note about the lilac, strews it over the garden, then carefully picks up each piece of paper and places them all in a small envelope as lights fade to black*)

TOPICS FOR DISCUSSION AND WRITING

1. You will probably agree that the scene where Byelinkov gets on the bicycle and pedals but goes nowhere is funny. But *why* is it funny? Can you formulate some sort of theory of comedy based on this episode?
2. At the end of the play Byelinkov tears up the note but then collects the pieces. What do you interpret these actions to mean?

Left to right: Harvey Fierstein, Ricky Addison Reed, and Anne de Salvo in the 1987 production of *On Tidy Endings* at the Lyceum Theater in New York City. (Photograph: Peter Cunningham.)

HARVEY FIERSTEIN

On Tidy Endings

Harvey Fierstein was born in Brooklyn, New York, the son of parents who had emigrated from Eastern Europe. While studying painting at Pratt Institute he acted in plays and revues, and one of his plays was produced in 1973, but he did not achieve fame until his *Torch Song Trilogy* (1976–79) moved from Off Broadway to Broadway in 1982. *Torch Song Trilogy* won the Theatre World Award, the Tony Award, and the Drama Desk Award. In addition, Fierstein won the Best Actor Tony Award and the Best Actor Drama Desk Award. He later received a third Tony Award for the book for the musical version of *La Cage aux Folles* (1983).

COMMENTARY

Beginning with the 1970s, plays about homosexuality became fairly common, but before that the topic was hardly mentioned in drama. For instance, in all of Greek and Elizabethan drama there are only a few brief gibes at the homosexual proclivities of some people, and certainly there were no sympathetic portraits of homosexuals, nor was homosexuality the chief or central subject matter of any play.

The first play in English that was seen widely on the stage and that was built on a homosexual relationship was Mordaunt Shairp's *The Green Bay Tree* (1933). The wealthy, witty, sinister Mr. Dulcimer—whom we first see arranging flowers—has adopted Julian (played by the young Laurence Olivier), a handsome working-class youth, and brought him up in a life of idle luxury. Julian's girl friend tries to free Julian from the influence of Dulcimer, but she fails. Julian's father resorts to a desperate measure: he kills Dulcimer, thus freeing Julian to marry his girl friend. But even in death Dulcimer triumphs, for at the end of the play, the wealthy young man rejects the girl and (like Dulcimer in the first scene) sets about arranging flowers. The interesting thing is that, so far as we can find, none of the contemporary reviewers mentioned homosexuality, although they did talk about "corruption" and about "abominable people." In a period when homosexuality was for most people unmentionable and even unthinkable, the play *could* be taken, and apparently *was* widely taken, as a play about the triumph of materialism over love.

In the following year, 1934, Lillian Hellman's *The Children's Hour* was produced. Here, homosexuality—lesbianism—was clearly part of the subject. For most of the play the audience sympathizes with women who, it believes, are falsely accused of lesbianism. Late in the play we learn that one of the women is in fact a lesbian, and so the play at the last minute shifts from a condemnation of a society that harasses the innocent to a condemnation of a society that harasses lesbians (the lesbian commits suicide). The thrust of the play, in any case, is about society's treatment of the individual, not about sexuality. Somewhat similarly, Robert Anderson's *Tea and Sympathy* (1953) can be said to deal with homosexuality but doesn't really, since the play is about a boy who fears he may be gay but who in fact is straight. ("Thank God," most people in the audience must have thought.)

In 1958 Shelagh Delaney's *A Taste of Honey* appeared, a comedy in which the unmarried pregnant heroine sets up house with her mother, the mother's drunken husband, and a homosexual art student. Homosexuality is not central to the play, but it is conspicuously there, treated comically but sympathetically. (The pregnant woman, who shares a bedroom with the painter, is curious: "What d'you do? Go on—what d'you do?").

Thus far we have omitted mention of the plays of Noel Coward, who from the late 1920s to the early 1940s almost always had a comedy on Broadway. The plays dealt ostensibly with witty heterosexual couples, but reviewers usually described these plays with such words as "frothy," "witty," "brittle," "bohemian," "frivolous"—words that, in fact, called up the stock image of the irresponsible male homosexual. Probably most members of the audience regarded the plays as sophisticated comedies of heterosexual love and marriage, but those who knew that Coward was gay could easily see the plays' characters as gay.

The 1960s brought Vietnam, anti-war demonstrations, and the Civil Rights Movement, and, on the stage, a theater of political commitment. The extension of interest to previously marginalized groups, which produced the Women's Theater, Black Theater, and Chicano Theater, also produced Gay Theater. Many of the early gay plays, i.e., those of the 1960s, were campy, out-of-the-closet self-parodies that were political in their assertion of a life-style that previously had been concealed. Ronald Tavel's *Gorilla Queen* (1967), for instance, consisted of musical skits about a gay King Kong, called Queen Kong; most of the female parts were played by men in drag. Since the 1980s, however, most gay plays have been more evidently serious, though they usually include a good deal of wit. Usually they are tragicomedies, witty (gay?) but bitter plays about AIDS.

Harvey Fierstein seems to have been the first writer of gay plays to have achieved the respectability implied by public awards. (Other gay playwrights, such as Tennessee Williams and Edward Albee, had been honored long before Fierstein, but their works were about the straight world.) In 1982 Fierstein's *Torch Song Trilogy* played on Broadway (it had appeared off-Broadway in 1978), won a Tony Award, was voted best play of the year by the Dramatists' Guild, and was made into a film. One might say that *On Tidy Endings* (part of a later trilogy) is, in large measure, about AIDS, but to say so might make it sound like an Ibsen-derived problem play or discussion play. It is not, and that is one of the things that makes it remarkable. It does not raise such issues as whether AIDS is a divine punishment, or whether the government is spending enough on medical research, or whether health workers should undergo mandatory testing. Rather, although AIDS is central to the play, the play is not really *about* AIDS. It is about people, about personal relationships that keep shifting as the play proceeds. As Fierstein said in an interview, "This is not a play about disease, it's a play about life."

These people—four characters appear in the play, but two do most of the talking—engage in action in the sense that, as Elizabeth Bowen has said, dialogue is action: "Dialogue is what the characters *do* to each other." And one aspect of the dialogue—the comedy—perhaps requires special mention. Consider dialogue in the the following exchange. Arthur has just said that he has gained a lot of weight since the death of his lover. The deceased lover's ex-wife, Marion, says "You'd never know," and Arthur replies:

> Marion, *you'd* never know, but ask my belt. Ask my pants. Ask my underwear. Even my stretch socks have stretch marks.

AIDS and all of the grief associated with it are scarcely laughing matters, and indeed one writer has said, "If art is to confront AIDS more honestly than the media have done, it must begin in fact, avoid humor, and end in anger." The point (in this view) is that humor must be avoided because it "domesticates terror." But of course we are all familiar with the fact that laughter may be defensive, a way of dealing with extreme grief. In Byron's words, "And if I laugh at any mortal thing, / 'Tis that I may not weep." One might reply that it is for this very reason—that humor makes us put up with the intolerable—that anyone writing about AIDS must avoid humor. We leave it to readers of *On Tidy Endings* to decide for themselves.

HARVEY FIERSTEIN *On Tidy Endings*

The curtain rises on a deserted, modern Upper West Side apartment. In the bright daylight that pours in through the windows we can see the living room of the apartment. Far Stage Right is the galley kitchen, next to it the multilocked front door with intercom. Stage Left reveals a hallway that leads to the two bedrooms and baths.

Though the room is still fully furnished (couch, coffee table, etc.), there are boxes stacked against the wall and several photographs and paintings are on the floor leaving shadows on the wall where they once hung. Obviously someone is moving out. From the way the boxes are neatly labeled and stacked, we know that this is an organized person.

From the hallway just outside the door we hear the rattling of keys and two arguing voices:

JIM (*Offstage*). I've got to be home by four. I've got practice.

MARION (*Offstage*). I'll get you to practice, don't worry.

JIM (*Offstage*). I don't want to go in there.

MARION (*Offstage*). Jimmy, don't make Mommy crazy, alright? We'll go inside, I'll call Aunt Helen and see if you can go down and play with Robbie. (*The door opens. Marion is a handsome woman of forty. Dressed in a business suit, her hair conservatively combed, she appears to be going to a business meeting. Jim is a boy of eleven. His playclothes are typical, but someone has obviously just combed his hair. Marion recovers the key from the lock.*)

JIM. Why can't I just go down and ring the bell?

MARION. Because I said so.

(*As Marion steps into the room she is struck by some unexpected emotion. She freezes in her path and stares at the empty apartment. Jim lingers by the door.*)

JIM. I'm going downstairs.

MARION. Jimmy, please.

JIM. This place gives me the creeps.

MARION. This was your father's apartment. There's nothing creepy about it.

JIM. Says you.

MARION. You want to close the door, please?

(*Jim reluctantly obeys.*)

MARION. Now, why don't you go check your room and make sure you didn't leave anything.

JIM. It's empty.

MARION. Go look.

JIM. I looked last time.

MARION (*Trying to be patient*). Honey, we sold the apartment. We're never going to be here again. Go make sure you have everything you want.

JIM. But Uncle Arthur packed everything.

MARION. (*Less patiently*). Go make sure.

JIM. There's nothing in there.

MARION (*Exploding*). I said make sure!

(*Jim jumps, then realizing that she's not kidding, obeys.*)

MARION. Everything's an argument with that one. (*She looks around the room and breathes deeply. There is sadness here. Under her breath:*) I can still smell you. (*Suddenly not wanting to be alone*) Jimmy? Are you okay?

JIM (*Returning*). Nothing. Told you so.

MARION. Uncle Arthur must have worked very hard. Make sure you thank him.

JIM. What for? Robbie says (*Fey mannerisms*) "They love to clean up things!"

MARION. Sometimes you can be a real joy.

JIM. Did you call Aunt Helen?

MARION. Do I get a break here? (*Approaching the boy understandingly*) Wouldn't you like to say goodbye?

JIM. To who?

MARION. To the apartment. You and your daddy spent a lot of time here together. Don't you want to take one last look around?

JIM. Ma, get a real life.

MARION. "Get a real life!" (*Going for the phone*) Nice. Very nice.

JIM. Could you call already?

MARION (*Dialing*). Jimmy, what does this look like I'm doing?

(*Jim kicks at the floor impatiently. Someone answers the phone at the other end*)

MARION (*Into the phone*). Helen? Hi, we're upstairs. . . . No, we just walked in the door. Jimmy wants to know if he can come down. . . . Oh, thanks.

(*Hearing that, Jim breaks for the door*)

MARION (*Yelling after him*). Don't run in the halls! And don't play with the elevator buttons!

(*The door slams shut behind him*)

MARION (*Back to the phone*). Hi. . . . No, I'm okay. It's a little weird being here. . . . No. Not since the funeral, and then there were so many people. Jimmy told me to get "a real life." I don't think I could handle anything realer. . . . No, please. Stay where you are. I'm fine. The doorman said Arthur would be right back and my lawyer should have been here already. . . . Well, we've got the papers to sign and a few other odds and ends to clean up. Shouldn't take long.

(*The intercom buzzer rings*)

MARION. Hang on, that must be her. (*Marion goes to the intercom and speaks*) Yes? . . . Thank you. (*Back to the phone*) Helen? Yeah, it's the lawyer. I'd better go. . . . Well, I could use a stiff drink, but I drove down. Listen, I'll stop by on my way out. Okay? Okay. 'Bye.

(*She hangs up the phone, looks around the room. That uncomfortable feeling returns to her quickly. She gets up and goes to the front door, opens it and looks out. No one there yet. She closes the door, shakes her head knowing that she's being silly and starts back into the room. She looks around, can't make it and retreats to the door. She opens it, looks out, closes it, but stays right there, her hand on the doorknob. The bell rings. She throws open the door*)

MARION. That was quick.

(*June Lowell still has her finger on the bell. Her arms are loaded with contracts. Marion's contemporary, June is less formal in appearance and more hyper in her manner*)

JUNE. *That* was quicker. What, were you waiting by the door?

MARION (*Embarrassed*). No. I was just passing it. Come on in.

JUNE. Have you got your notary seal?

MARION. I think so.

JUNE. Great. Then you can witness. I left mine at the office and thanks to gentrification I'm double-parked downstairs. (*Looking for a place to dump her load*) Where?

MARION (*Definitely pointing to the coffee table*). Anywhere. You mean you're not staying?

JUNE. If you really think you need me I can go down and find a parking lot. I think there's one over on Columbus. So, I can go down, park the car in the lot and take a cab back if you really think you need me.

MARION. Well . . . ?

JUNE. But you shouldn't have any problems. The papers are about a straightforward as papers get. Arthur is giving you power of attorney to sell the apartment and you're giving him a check for half the purchase price. Everything else is just signing papers that state that you know that you signed the other papers. Anyway, he knows the deal, his lawyers have been over it all with him, it's just a matter of signatures.

MARION (*Not fine*). Oh, fine.

JUNE. Unless you just don't want to be alone with him . . . ?

MARION. With Arthur? Don't be silly.

JUNE (*Laying out the papers*). Then you'll handle it solo? Great. My car thanks you, the parking lot thanks you, and the cab driver that wouldn't have gotten a tip thanks you. Come have a quick look-see.

MARION (*Joining her on the couch*). There are a lot of papers here.

JUNE. Copies. Not to worry. Start here.

(*Marion starts to read*)

JUNE. I ran into Jimmy playing Elevator Operator.

(*Marion jumps*)

JUNE. I got him off at the sixth floor. Read on.

MARION. This is definitely not my day for dealing with him. (*June gets up and has a look around*)

JUNE. I don't believe what's happening to this neighborhood. You made quite an investment when you bought this place.

MARION. Collin was always very good at figuring out those things.

JUNE. Well, he sure figured this place right. What, have you tripled your money in ten years?

MARION. More.

JUNE. It's a shame to let it go.

MARION. We're not ready to be a two-dwelling family.

JUNE. So, sublet it again.

MARION. Arthur needs the money from the sale.

JUNE. Arthur got plenty already. I'm not crying for Arthur.

MARION. I don't hear you starting in again, do I?

JUNE. Your interests and your wishes are my only concern.

MARION. Fine.

JUNE. I still say we should contest Collin's will.

MARION. June . . . !

JUNE. You've got a child to support.

MARION. And a great job, and a husband with a great job. Tell me what Arthur's got.

JUNE. To my thinking, half of everything that should have gone to you. And more. All of Collin's personal effects, his record collection . . .

MARION. And I suppose their three years together meant nothing.

JUNE. When you compare them to your sixteen-year marriage? Not nothing, but not half of everything.

MARION (*Trying to change the subject*). June, who gets which copies?

JUNE. Two of each to Arthur. One you keep.The originals and everything else come back to me. (*Looking around*) I still say you should've sublet the apartment for a year and then sold it. You would've gotten an even better price. Who wants to buy a apartment when they know someone died in it. No one. And certainly no one wants to buy a apartment when they know the person died of AIDS.

MARION (*Snapping*). June. Enough!

JUNE (*Catching herself*). Sorry. That was out of line. Sometimes my mouth does that to me. Hey, that's why I'm a lawyer. If my brain worked as fast as my mouth I would have gotten a real job.

MARION (*Holding out a stray paper*). What's this?

JUNE. I forgot. Arthur's lawyer sent that over yesterday. He found it in Collin's safety-deposit box. It's a insurance policy that came along with some consulting job he did in Japan. He either forgot about it when he made out his will or else he wanted you to get the full payment. Either way, it's yours.

MARION. Are you sure we don't split this?

JUNE. Positive.

MARION. But everything else . . . ?

JUNE. Hey, Arthur found it, his lawyer sent it to me. Relax, it's all yours. Minus my commission, of course. Go out and buy yourself something. Anything else before I have to use my cut to pay the towing bill?

MARION. I guess not.

JUNE (*Starting to leave*). Great. Call me when you get home. (*Stopping at the door and looking back*) Look, I know that I'm attacking this a little coldly. I am aware that someone you loved has just died. But there's a time and place for everything. This is about tidying up loose ends, not holding hands. I hope you'll remember that when Arthur gets here. Call me.

(*And she's gone*)

(*Marion looks ill at ease to be alone again. She nervously straightens the papers into neat little piles, looks at them and then remembers:*)

MARION. Pens. We're going to need pens.

(*As a last chore to be done. She looks in her purse and finds only one. She goes to the kitchen and opens a drawer where she finds two more. She starts back to the table with them but suddenly remembers something else. She returns to the kitchen and begins going through the cabinets until she finds what she's looking for: a blue Art Deco teapot. Excited to find it, she takes it back to the couch. Guilt strikes. She stops, considers putting it back, wavers, then:*)

MARION (*To herself*). Oh, he won't care. One less thing to pack.

(*She takes the teapot and places it on the couch next to her purse. She is happier. Now she searches the room with her eyes for any other treasures she may have overlooked. Nothing here. She wanders off into the bedroom.*

We hear keys outside the front door. Arthur lets himself into the apartment carrying a load of empty cartons and a large shopping bag.

Arthur is in his mid-thirties, pleasant looking though sloppily dressed in work clothes and slightly overweight.

Arthur enters the apartment just as Marion comes out of the bedroom carrying a framed watercolor painting. They jump at the sight of each other.)

MARION. Oh, hi, Arthur. I didn't hear the door.

ARTHUR (*Staring at the painting*). Well hello, Marion.

MARION (*Guiltily*). I was going to ask you if you were

thinking of taking this painting because if you're not going to then I'll take it. Unless, of course, you want it.

ARTHUR. No. You can have it.

MARION. I never really liked it, actually. I hate cats. I didn't even like the show. I needed something for my college dorm room. I was never the rock star poster type. I kept it in the back of a closet for years till Collin moved in here and took it. He said he liked it.

ARTHUR. I do too.

MARION. Well, then you keep it.

ARTHUR. No. Take it.

MARION. I've really got no room for it. You keep it.

ARTHUR. I don't want it.

MARION. Well, if you're sure.

ARTHUR (*Seeing the teapot*) You want the teapot?

MARION. If you don't mind.

ARTHUR. One less thing to pack.

MARION. Funny, but that's exactly what I thought. One less thing to pack. You know, my mother gave it to Collin and me when we moved in to our first apartment. Silly sentimental piece of junk, but you know.

ARTHUR. That's not the one.

MARION. Sure it is. Hall used to make them for Westinghouse back in the thirties. I see them all the time at antiques shows and I always wanted to buy another, but they ask such a fortune for them.

ARTHUR. We broke the one your mother gave you a couple of years ago. That's a reproduction. You can get them almost anywhere in the Village for eighteen bucks.

MARION. Really? I'll have to pick one up.

ARTHUR. Take this one. I'll get another.

MARION. No, it's yours. You bought it.

ARTHUR. One less thing to pack.

MARION. Don't be silly. I didn't come here to raid the place.

ARTHUR. Well, was there anything else of Collin's that you thought you might like to have?

MARION. Now I feel so stupid, but actually I made a list. Not for me. But I started thinking about different people; friends, relatives, you know, that might want to have something of Collin's to remember him by. I wasn't sure just what you were taking and what you were throwing out. Anyway, I brought the list. (*Gets it from her purse*) Of course these are only suggestions. You probably thought of a few of these people yourself. But I figured it couldn't hurt to write it all down. Like I said, I don't know what you are planning on keeping.

ARTHUR (*Taking the list*). I was planning on keeping it all.

MARION. Oh, I know. But most of these things are silly. Like his high school yearbooks. What would you want with them?

ARTHUR. Sure. I'm only interested in his Gay period.

MARION. I didn't mean it that way. Anyway, you look it over. They're only suggestions. Whatever you decide to do is fine with me.

ARTHUR (*Folding the list*). It would have to be, wouldn't it. I mean, it's all mine now. He did leave this all to me.

(*Marion is becoming increasingly nervous, but tries to keep a light approach as she takes a small bundle of papers from her bag*)

MARION. While we're on the subject of what's yours. I brought a batch of condolence cards that were sent to you care of me. Relatives mostly.

ARTHUR (*Taking them*). More cards? I'm going to have to have another printing of thank-you notes done.

MARION. I answered these last week, so you don't have to bother. Unless you want to.

ARTHUR. Forge my signature?

MARION. Of course not. They were addressed to both of us and they're mostly distant relatives or friends we haven't seen in years. No one important.

ARTHUR. If they've got my name on them, then I'll answer them myself.

MARION. I wasn't telling you not to, I was only saying that you don't have to.

ARTHUR. I understand.

(*Marion picks up the teapot and brings it to the kitchen*)

MARION. Let me put this back.

ARTHUR. I ran into Jimmy in the lobby.

MARION. Tell me you're joking.

ARTHUR. I got him to Helen's.

MARION. He's really racking up the points today.

ARTHUR. You know, he still can't look me in the face.

MARION. He's reacting to all of this in strange ways. Give him time. He'll come around. He's really very fond of you.

ARTHUR. I know. But he's at that awkward age: under thirty. I'm sure in twenty years we'll be the best of friends.

MARION. It's not what you think.

ARTHUR. What do you mean?

MARION. Well, you know.

ARTHUR. No I don't know. Tell me.

MARION. I thought that you were intimating something about his blaming you for Collin's illness and I was just letting you know that it's not true. (*Foot in mouth, she braves on*) We discussed it a lot and . . . uh . . . he understands that his father was sick before you two ever met.

ARTHUR. I don't believe this.

MARION. I'm just trying to say that he doesn't blame you.

ARTHUR. First of all, who asked you? Second of all,

that's between him and me. And third and most importantly, of course he blames me. Marion, he's eleven years old. You can discuss all you want, but the fact is that his father died of a "fag" disease and I'm the only fag around to finger.

MARION. My son doesn't use that kind of language.

ARTHUR. Forget the language. I'm talking about what he's been through. Can you imagine the kind of crap he's taken from his friends? That poor kid's been chased and chastised from one end of town to the other. He's got to have someone to blame just to survive. He can't blame you, you're all he's got. He can't blame his father; he's dead. So, Uncle Arthur gets the shaft. Fine, I can handle it.

MARION. You are so wrong, Arthur. I know my son and that is not the way his mind works.

ARTHUR. I don't know what you know. I only know what I know. And all I know is what I hear and see. The snide remarks, the little smirks . . . And it's not just the illness. He's been looking for a scapegoat since the day you and Collin first split up. Finally he has one.

MARION (*Getting very angry now*). Wait. Are you saying that if he's going to blame someone it should be me?

ARTHUR. I think you should try to see things from his point of view.

MARION. Where do you get off thinking you're privy to my son's point of view?

ARTHUR. It's not that hard to imagine. Life's rolling right along, he's having a happy little childhood, when suddenly one day his father's moving out. No explanations, no reasons, none of the fights that usually accompany such things. Divorce is hard enough for a kid to understand when he's listened to years of battles, but yours?

MARION. So what should we have done? Faked a few months' worth of fights before Collin moved out?

ARTHUR. You could have told him the truth, plain and simple.

MARION. He was seven years old at the time. How the hell do you tell a seven-year-old that his father is leaving his mother to go sleep with other men?

ARTHUR. Well, not like that.

MARION. You know, Arthur, I'm going to say this as nicely as I can: Butt out. You're not his mother and you're not his father.

ARTHUR. Thank you. I wasn't acutely aware of that fact. I will certainly keep that in mind from now on.

MARION. There's only so much information a child that age can handle.

ARTHUR. So it's best that he reach his capacity on the street.

MARION. He knew about the two of you. We talked about it.

ARTHUR. Believe me, he knew before you talked about it. He's young, not stupid.

MARION. It's very easy for you to stand here and criticize, but there are aspects that you will just never be able to understand. You weren't there. You have no idea what it was like for me. You're talking to someone who thought that a girl went to college to meet a husband. I went to protest rallies because I liked the music. I bought a guitar because I thought it looked good on the bed! This lifestyle, this knowledge that you take for granted, was all a little out of left field for me.

ARTHUR. I can imagine.

MARION. No, I don't think you can. I met Collin in college, married him right after graduation and settled down for a nice quiet life of Kids and Careers. You think I had any idea about this? Talk about life's little surprises. You live with someone for sixteen years, you share your life, your bed, you have a child together, and then you wake up one day and he tells you that to him it's all been a lie. A lie. Try that on for size. Here you are the happiest couple you know, fulfilling your every life fantasy and he tells you he's living a lie.

ARTHUR. I'm sure he never said that.

MARION. Don't be so sure. There was a lot of new ground being broken back then and plenty of it was muddy.

ARTHUR. You know that he loved you.

MARION. What's that supposed to do, make things easier? It doesn't. I was brought up to believe, among other things, that if you had love that was enough. So what if I wasn't everything he wanted. Maybe he wasn't exactly everything I wanted either. So, you know what? You count your blessings and you settle.

ARTHUR. No one has to settle. Not him. Not you.

MARION. Of course not. You can say, "Up yours!" to everything and everyone who depends and needs you, and go off to make yourself happy.

ARTHUR. It's not that simple.

MARION. No. This is simpler. Death is simpler. (*Yelling, out*) Happy now?

(*They stare at each other. Marion calms the rage and catches her breath. Arthur holds his emotions in check*)

ARTHUR. How about a nice hot cup of coffee? Tea with lemon? Hot cocoa with a marshmallow floating in it?

MARION (*laughs*). I was wrong. You *are* a mother.

(*Arthur goes into the kitchen and starts preparing things. Marion loafs by the doorway.*)

MARION. I lied before. He *was* everything I ever wanted.

(*Arthur stops, looks at her, and then changes the subject as he goes on with his work.*)

ARTHUR. When I came into the building and saw

Jimmy in the lobby I absolutely freaked for a second. It's amazing how much they look alike. It was like seeing a little miniature Collin standing there.

MARION. I know. He's like Collin's clone. There's nothing of me in him.

ARTHUR. I always kinda hoped that when he grew up he'd take after me. Not much chance, I guess.

MARION. Don't do anything fancy in there.

ARTHUR. Please. Anything we can consume is one less thing to pack.

MARION. So you've said.

ARTHUR. So *we've* said.

MARION. I want to keep seeing you and I want you to see Jim. You're still part of this family. No one's looking to cut you out.

ARTHUR. Ah, who'd want a kid to grow up looking like me anyway. I had enough trouble looking like this. Why pass on the misery?

MARION. You're adorable.

ARTHUR. Is that like saying I have a good personality?

MARION. I think you are one of the most naturally handsome men I know.

ARTHUR. Natural is right, and the bloom is fading.

MARION. All you need is a few good nights' sleep to kill those rings under your eyes.

ARTHUR. Forget the rings under my eyes, (*Grabbing his middle*) . . . how about the rings around my moon?

MARION. I like you like this.

ARTHUR. From the time that Collin started using the wheelchair until he died, about six months, I lost twenty-three pounds. No gym, no diet. In the last seven weeks I've gained close to fifty.

MARION. You're exaggerating.

ARTHUR. I'd prove it on the bathroom scale, but I sold it in working order.

MARION. You'd never know.

ARTHUR. Marion, *you'd* never know, but ask my belt. Ask my pants. Ask my underwear. Even my stretch socks have stretch marks. I called the ambulance at five A.M., he was gone at nine and by nine-thirty, I was on a first-name basis with Sara Lee. I can quote the business hours of every ice-cream parlor, pizzeria and bakery on the island of Manhattan. I know the location of every twenty-four-hour grocery in the greater New York area, and I have memorized the phone numbers of every Mandarin, Szechuan and Hunan restaurant with free delivery.

MARION. At least you haven't wasted your time on useless hobbies.

ARTHUR. Are you kidding? I'm opening my own Overeater's Hotline. We'll have to start small, but expansion is guaranteed.

MARION. You're the best, you know that? If I couldn't be everything that Collin wanted then I'm grateful that he found someone like you.

ARTHUR (*Turning on her without missing a beat*). Keep your goddamned gratitude to yourself. I didn't go through any of this for you. So your thanks are out of line. And he didn't find "someone like" me. It was me.

MARION (*Frightened*). I didn't mean . . .

ARTHUR. And I wish you'd remember one thing more: He died in my arms, not yours.

(*Marion is totally caught off guard. She stares disbelieving, openmouthed. Arthur walks past her as he leaves the kitchen with place mats. He puts them on the coffee table. As he arranges the papers, and place mats, he speaks, never looking at her.*)

ARTHUR. Look, I know you were trying to say something supportive. Don't waste your breath. There's nothing you can say that will make any of this easier for me. There's no way for you to help me get through this. And that's your fault. After three years you still have no idea or understanding of who I am. Or maybe you do know but refuse to accept it. I don't know and I don't care. But at least understand, from my point of view, who you are: You are my husband' *ex*-wife. If you like, the mother of *my* stepson. Don't flatter yourself into thinking you were any more than that. And whatever you are, you're certainly not my friend.

(*He stops, looks up at her, then passes her again as he goes back to the kitchen. Marion is shaken, working hard to control herself. She moves toward the couch.*)

MARION. Why don't we just sign these papers and I'll be out of your way.

ARTHUR. Shouldn't you say *I'll* be out of *your* way? After all, I'm not just signing papers. I'm signing away my home.

MARION (*Resolved not to fight, she gets her purse*). I'll leave the papers here. Please have them notarized and returned to my lawyer.

ARTHUR. Don't forget my painting.

MARION (*Exploding*). What do you want from me, Arthur?

ARTHUR (*Yelling back*). I want you the hell out of my apartment! I want you out of my life! And I want you to leave Collin alone!

MARION. The man's dead. I don't know how much more alone I can leave him.

(*Arthur laughs at the irony, but behind the laughter is something much more desperate.*)

ARTHUR. Lots more, Marion. You've got to let him go.

MARION. For the life of me, I don't know what I did or what you think I did, for you to treat me like this. But you're not going to get away with it. You will not take your anger out on me. I will not stand here and be badgered and insulted by you. I know you've been hurt and I know you're hurting but you're not the only one who lost someone here.

ARTHUR (*Topping her*). Yes I am! You didn't just lose him. I did! You lost him five years ago when he divorced you. This is not your moment of grief and loss, it's mine! (*Picking up the bundle of cards and throwing it toward her*) These condolences do not belong to you, they're mine. (*Tossing her list back to her*) His things are not yours to give away, they're mine! This death does not belong to you, it's mine! Bought and paid for outright. I suffered for it, I bled for it.

I was the one who cooked his meals. I was the one who spoon-fed them. I pushed his wheelchair. I carried and bathed him. I wiped his backside and changed his diapers. I breathed life into and wrestled fear out of his heart. I kept him alive for two years longer than any doctor thought possible and when it was time I was the one who prepared him for death.

I paid in full for my place in his life and I will *not* share it with you. We are not the two widows of Collin Redding. Your life was not here. Your husband didn't just die. You've got a son and a life somewhere else. Your husband's sitting, waiting for you at home, wondering, as I am, what the hell you're doing here and why you can't let go.

(*Marion leans back against the couch. She's blown away. Arthur stands staring at her*)

ARTHUR (*Quietly*). Let him go, Marion. He's mine. Dead or alive; mine.

(*The teakettle whistles. Arthur leaves the room, goes to the kitchen and pours the water as Marion pulls herself together. Arthur carries the loaded tray back into the living room and sets it down on the coffee table. He sits and pours a cup*)

ARTHUR. One marshmallow or two?

(*Marion stares, unsure as to whether the attack is really over or not*)

ARTHUR (*Placing them in her cup*). Take three, they're small.

(*Marion smiles and takes the offered cup*)

ARTHUR (*Campily*). Now let me tell you how I *really* feel.

(*Marion jumps slightly, then they share a small laugh. Silence as they each gather themselves and sip their refreshments*)

MARION (*Calmly*). Do you think that I sold the apartment just to throw you out?

ARTHUR. I don't care about the apartment . . .

MARION. . . . Because I really didn't. Believe me.

ARTHUR. I know.

MARION. I knew the expenses here were too much for you, and I knew you couldn't afford to buy out my half . . . I figured if we sold it, that you'd at least have a nice chunk of money to start over with.

ARTHUR. You could've given me a little more time.

MARION. Maybe. But I thought the sooner you were out of here, the sooner you could go on with your life.

ARTHUR. Or the sooner you could go on with yours.

MARION. Maybe. (*Pause to gather her thoughts*) Anyway, I'm not going to tell you that I have no idea what you're talking about. I'd have to be worse than deaf and blind not to have seen the way you've been treated. Or mistreated. When I read Collin's obituary in the newspaper and saw my name and Jimmy's name and no mention of you . . . (*Shakes her head, not knowing what to say*) You know that his secretary was the one who wrote that up and sent it in. Not me. But I should have done something about it and I didn't. I know.

ARTHUR. Wouldn't have made a difference. I wrote my own obituary for him and sent it to the smaller papers. They edited me out.

MARION. I'm sorry. I remember, at the funeral, I was surrounded by all of Collin's family and business associates while you were left with your friends. I knew it was wrong. I knew I should have said something but it felt good to have them around me and you looked like you were holding up . . . Wrong. But saying that it's all my fault for not letting go . . . ? There were other people involved.

ARTHUR. Who took their cue from you.

MARION. Arthur, you don't understand. Most people that we knew as a couple had no idea that Collin was gay right up to his death. And even those that did know only found out when he got sick and the word leaked out that it was AIDS. I don't think I have to tell you how stupid and ill-informed most people are about homosexuality. And AIDS . . . ? The kinds of insane behavior that word inspires . . . ?

Those people at the funeral, how many times did they call to see how he was doing over these years? How many of them ever went to see him in the hospital? Did any of them even come here? So, why would you expect them to act any differently after his death?

So, maybe that helps to explain their behavior, but what about mine, right? Well, maybe there is no explanation. Only excuses. And excuse number one is that you're right, I have never really let go of him. And I am jealous of you. Hell, I was jealous of anyone that Collin ever talked to, let alone slept with . . . let alone loved.

The first year, after he moved out, we talked all the time

about the different men he was seeing. And I always listened and advised. It was kind of fun. It kept us close. It kept me a part of his intimate life. And the bottom line was always that he wasn't happy with the men he was meeting. So, I was always allowed to hang on to the hope that one day he'd give it all up and come home. Then he got sick.

He called me, told me he was in the hospital and asked if I'd come see him. I ran. When I got to his door there was a sign, INSTRUCTIONS FOR VISITORS OF AN AIDS PATIENT. I nearly died.

ARTHUR. He hadn't told you?

MARION. No. And believe me, a sign is not the way to find these things out. I was so angry . . . And he was so sick . . . I was sure that he'd die right then. If not from the illness then from the hospital staff's neglect. No one wanted to go near him and I didn't bother fighting with them because I understood that they were scared. I was scared. That whole month in the hospital I didn't let Jimmy visit him once.

You learn.

Well, as you know, he didn't die. And he asked if he could come stay with me until he was well. And I said yes. Of course, yes. Now, here's something I never thought I'd ever admit to anyone: had he asked to stay with me for a few weeks I would have said no. But he asked to stay with me until he was well and knowing there was no cure I said yes. In my craziness I said yes because to me that meant forever. That he was coming back to me forever. Not that I wanted him to die, but I assumed from everything I'd read . . . And we'd be back together for whatever time he had left. Can you understand that?

(*Arthur nods.*)

MARION (*Gathers her thoughts again*).Two weeks later he left. He moved in here. Into this apartment that we had bought as an investment. Never to live in. Certainly never to live apart in. Next thing I knew, the name Arthur starts appearing in every phone call, every dinner conversation.

"Did you see the doctor?"

"Yes. Arthur made sure I kept the appointment."

"Are you going to your folks for Thanksgiving?"

"No. Arthur and I are having some friends over."

I don't know which one of us was more of a coward, he for not telling or me for not asking about you. But eventually you became a given. Then, of course,we met and became what I had always thought of as friends.

(*Arthur winces in guilt*)

MARION. I don't care what you say, how could we not be friends with someone so great in common: love for one of the most special human beings there ever was. And don't try and tell me there weren't times when you enjoyed me being around as an ally. I can think of a dozen occasions when we ganged up on him, teasing him with our intimate knowledge of his personal habits.

(*Arthur has to laugh*)

MARION. Blanket stealing? Snoring? Excess gas, no less? (*Takes a moment to enjoy this truce*) I don't think that my loving him threatened your relationship. Maybe I'm not being truthful with myself. But I don't. I never tried to step between you. Not that I ever had the opportunity. Talk about being joined at the hip! And that's not to say I wasn't jealous. I was. Terribly. Hatefully. But always lovingly. I was happy for Collin because there was no way to deny that he was happy. With everything he was facing, he was happy. Love did that. You did that.

He lit up with you. He came to life. I envied that and all the time you spent together, but more, I watched you care for him (sometimes *overcare* for him), and I was in awe. I could never have done what you did. I never would have survived. I really don't know how you did.

ARTHUR. Who said I survived?

MARION. Don't tease. You did an absolutely incredible thing. It's not as if you met him before he got sick. You entered a relationship that you knew in all probability would end this way and you never wavered.

ARTHUR. Of course I did. Don't have me sainted, Marion. But sometimes you have no choice. Believe me, if I could've gotten away from him I would've. But I was a prisoner of love.

(*He makes a campy gesture and pose*)

MARION. Stop.

ARTHUR. And there were lots of pluses. I got to quit a job I hated, stay home all day and watch game shows. I met a lot of doctors and learned a lot of big words. (*Arthur jumps up and goes to the pile of boxes where he extracts one and brings it back to the couch.*)

And then there was all the exciting traveling I got to do. This box has a souvenir from each one of our trips. Wanna see? (*Marion nods. He opens the box and pulls things out one by one. Holding up an old bottle*)

This is from the house we rented in Reno when we went to clear out his lungs. (*Holding handmade potholders*)

This is from the hospital in Reno. Collin made them. They had a great arts and crafts program. (*Copper bracelets*)

These are from a faith healer in Philly. They don't do much for a fever, but they look great with a green sweater. (*Glass ashtrays*)

These are from our first visit to the clinic in France. Such lovely people. (*A Bible*)

This is from our second visit to the clinic in France. (*A lead necklace*)

A Voodoo doctor in New Orleans. Next time we'll have to get there earlier in the year. I think he sold all the pretty ones at Mardi Gras. (*A tiny piñata*)

Then there was Mexico. Black market drugs and empty wallets. (*Now pulling things out at random*)

L.A., San Francisco, Houston, Boston . . . We traveled everywhere they offered hope for sale and came home with souvenirs. (*Arthur quietly pulls a few more things out and then begins to put them all back into the box slowly. Softly as he works:*) Marion, I would have done anything, traveled anywhere to avoid . . . or delay . . . Not just because I loved him so desperately, but when you've lived the way we did for three years . . . the battle becomes your life. (*He looks at her and then away*) His last few hours were beyond any scenario I had imagined. He hadn't walked in nearly six months. He was totally incontinent. If he spoke two words in a week I was thankful. Days went by without his eyes ever focusing on me. He just stared out at I don't know what. Not the meals as I fed him. Not the TV I played constantly for company. Just out. Or maybe in.

It was the middle of the night when I heard his breathing become labored. His lungs were filling with fluid again. I knew the sound. I'd heard it a hundred times before. So, I called the ambulance and got him to the hospital.

They hooked him up to the machines, the oxygen, shot him with morphine and told me that they would do what they could to keep him alive.

But, Marion, it wasn't the machines that kept him breathing. He did it himself. It was that incredible will and strength inside him. Whether it came from his love of life or fear of death, who knows. But he'd been counted out a hundred times and a hundred times he fought his way back.

I got a magazine to read him, pulled a chair up to the side of his bed and holding his hand, I wondered whether I should call Helen to let the cleaning lady in or if he'd fall asleep and I could sneak home for an hour. I looked up from the page and he was looking at me. Really looking right into my eyes. I patted his cheek and said, "Don't worry, honey, you're going to be fine."

But there was something else in his eyes. He wasn't satisfied with that. And I don't know why, I have no idea where it came from, I just heard the words coming out of my mouth, "Collin, do you want to die?"

His eyes filled and closed, he nodded his head.

I can't tell you what I was thinking, I'm not sure I was. I slipped off my shoes, lifted his blanket and climbed into bed next to him. I helped him to put his arms around me, and mine around him, and whispered as gently as I could into his ear, "It's alright to let go now. It's time to go on." And he did.

Marion, you've got your life and your son. All I have is a intangible place in a man's history. Leave me that. Respect that.

MARION. I understand.

(*Arthur suddenly comes to life, running to get the shopping bag that he'd left at the front door*)

ARTHUR. Jeez! With all the screamin' and sad storytelling I forgot something. (*He extracts a bouquet of flowers from the bag*) I brung you flowers and everything.

MARION. You brought me flowers?

ARTHUR. Well, I knew you'd never think to bring me flowers and I felt that on an occasion such as this somebody oughta get flowers from somebody.

MARION. You know, Arthur, you're really making me feel like a worthless piece of garbage.

ARTHUR. So what else is new? (*He presents the flowers*) Just promise me one thing. Don't press one in a book. Just stick them in a vase and when they fade just throw them out. No more memorabilia.

MARION. Arthur, I want to do something for you and I don't know what. Tell me what you want.

ARTHUR. I want little things. Not much. I want to be remembered. If you get a Christmas card from Collin's mother make sure she sent me one too. If his friends call to see how you are, ask if they've called me. Have me to dinner so I can see Jimmy. Let me take him out now and then. Invite me to his wedding. (*They both laugh*)

MARION. You've got it.

ARTHUR (*Clearing the table*). Let me get all this cold cocoa out of the way. You still have the deed to do.

MARION (*Checking her watch*). And I've got to get Jimmy home in time for practice.

ARTHUR. Band practice?

MARION. Baseball. (*Picking her list off the floor*) About this list, you do what you want.

ARTHUR. Believe me, I will. But I promise to consider your suggestions. Just don't rush me. I'm not ready to give it all away. (*Arthur is off to the kitchen with his tray and the phone rings. He answers in the kitchen*) "Hello? . . . Just a minute. (*Calling out*) It's your eager Little Leaguer.

(*Marion picks up the living room extension and Arthur hangs his up*)

MARION (*Into phone*). Hello, honey . . . I'll be down in five minutes. No. You know what? You come up here and get me. . . . No, I said you should come up here. . . . I said I want you to come up here. . . . Because I said so. . . . Thank you. (*She hangs the receiver*)

ARTHUR (*Rushing to the papers*). Alright, where do we start on these?

MARION (*Getting out her seal*). I guess you should just start signing everything and I'll stamp along with you. Keep one of everything on the side for you.

ARTHUR. Now I feel so rushed. What am I signing?

MARION. You want to do this another time?

ARTHUR. No. Let's get it over with. I wouldn't survive another session like this.

(*He starts to sign and she starts her job*)

MARION. I keep meaning to ask you; how are you?

ARTHUR (*At first puzzled and then:*) Oh, you mean my health? Fine. No. I'm fine. I've been tested, and nothing. We were very careful. We took many precautions. Collin used to make jokes about how we should invest in rubber futures.

MARION. I'll bet.

ARTHUR (*Stops what he's doing*). It never occurred to me until now. How about you?

MARION (*Not stopping*). Well, we never had sex after he got sick.

ARTHUR. But before?

MARION (*Stopping but not looking up*). I have the antibodies in my blood. No signs that it will ever develop into anything else. And it's been five yours so my chances are pretty good that I'm just a carrier.

ARTHUR. I'm so sorry. Collin never told me.

MARION. He didn't know. In fact, other than my husband and the doctors, you're the only one I've told.

ARTHUR. You and your husband . . . ?

MARION. Have invested in rubber futures. There'd only be a problem if we wanted to have a child. Which we do. But we'll wait. Miracles happen every day.

ARTHUR. I don't know what to say.

MARION. Tell me you'll be there if I ever need you.

(*Arthur gets up, goes to her and puts his arm around her. They hold each other. He gently pushes her away to make a joke.*)

ARTHUR. Sure! Take something else that should have been mine.

MARION. Don't even joke about things like that.

(*The doorbell rings. They pull themselves together*)

ARTHUR. You know we'll never get these done today.

MARION. So, tomorrow.

(*Arthur goes to open the door as Marion gathers her things. He opens the doors and Jimmy is standing in the hall*)

JIM. C'mon, Ma. I'm gonna be late.

ARTHUR. Would you like to come inside?

JIM. We've gotta go.

MARION. Jimmy, come on.

JIM. Ma!

(*She glares. He comes in. Arthur closes the door*)

MARION (*Holding out the flowers*). Take these for Mommy.

JIM (*Taking them*). Can we go?

MARION (*Picking up the painting*). Say good-bye to your Uncle Arthur.

JIM. 'Bye, Arthur. Come on.

MARION. Give him a kiss.

ARTHUR. Marion, don't.

MARION. Give your uncle a kiss good-bye.

JIM. He's not my uncle.

MARION. No. He's a hell of a lot more than your uncle.

ARTHUR (*Offering his hand*). A handshake will do.

MARION. Tell Uncle Arthur what your daddy told you.

JIM. About what?

MARION. Stop playing dumb. You know.

ARTHUR. Don't embarrass him.

MARION. Jimmy, please.

JIM (*He regards his mother's softer tone and then speaks*). He said that after me and Mommy he loved you the most.

MARION (*Standing behind him*). Go on.

JIM. And that I should love you too. And make sure that you're not lonely or very sad.

ARTHUR. Thank you.

(*Arthur reaches down to the boy and they hug. Jim gives him a little peck on the cheek and then breaks away*)

MARION (*Going to open the door*). Alright, kid, you done good. Now let's blow this joint before you muck it up.

(*Jim rushes out the door. Marion turns to Arthur*)

MARION. A child's kiss is magic. Why else would they be so stingy with them. I'll call you.

(*Arthur nods understanding. Marion pulls the door closed behind her. Arthur stands quietly as the lights fade to black*)

THE END

Note: If being performed on film, the final image should be of Arthur leaning his back against the closed door on the inside of the apartment and Marion leaning on the outside of the door. A moment of thought and then they both move on.

TOPICS FOR DISCUSSION AND WRITING

1. We first hear about AIDS on page 717. Were you completely surprised, or did you think the play might introduce the subject? That is, did the author in any way prepare you for the subject? If so, how?
2. So far as the basic story goes, June (the lawyer) is not necessary. Marion could have brought the papers with her. Why do you suppose Fierstein introduces June? What function(s) does she serve? How would you characterize her?
3. On page 717 Marion says of the teapot, "One less thing to pack." Arthur says the same words a moment later, and then he repeats them yet again. A little later, while drinking cocoa, he repeats the words, and Marion says, "So you've said," to which Arthur replies, "So *we've* said." Exactly what tone do you think should be used when Marion first says these words? When Arthur says them? And what significance, if any, do you attach to the fact that both characters speak these words?
4. A reviewer of the play said that Arthur is "bitchy" in many of his responses to Marion. What do you suppose the reviewer meant by this? Does the term imply that Fierstein presents a stereotype of the homosexual? If so, what is this stereotype? If you think that the term applies (even though you might not use such a word yourself), do you think that Fierstein's portrayal of Arthur is stereotypical? If it is stereotypical, is this a weakness in the play?
5. Arthur says that Jimmy blames him for Collin's death, but Marion denies it. Who do you think is right? Can a reader be sure? Why, or why not?
6. When Arthur tells Marion that she should have told Jimmy why Collin left her, Marion says, "How the hell do you tell a seven-year-old that his father is leaving his mother to go sleep with other men?" Arthur replies, "well, not like that." What does Arthur mean? How might Marion have told Jimmy? Do you think she should have told Jimmy?
7. Do you agree with a reader who found Marion an unconvincing character because she is "so passive and unquestioningly loving in her regard for her ex-husband"? If you disagree, how would you argue your case?
8. During the course of the play, what (if anything) does Marion learn? What (if anything) does Arthur learn? What (if anything) does Jimmy learn? What (if anything) does the reader or viewer learn from the play?
9. One reader characterized the play as "propaganda." Do you agree? Why, or why not? And if you think *On Tidy Endings* is propaganda, are you implying that it is therefore deficient as a work of art?

In Darkest America (*Tone Clusters*) by Joyce Carol Oates. 1990 Humana Festival of New American Plays. (Photograph: Richard Trigg/Actors' Theatre of Louisville.)

JOYCE CAROL OATES

Tone Clusters

A Play in Nine Scenes

Joyce Carol Oates was born in 1938 in Millerport, New York. She won a scholarship to Syracuse University, from which she graduated (Phi Beta Kappa and valedictorian) in 1960. She then did graduate work in English, first at the University of Wisconsin and then at Rice University, but she withdrew from Rice in order to be able to devote more time to writing. Her first collection of stories, *By the North Gate,* was published in 1963; since then she has published at least 40 books—stories, poems, essays, and (in 20 years) 16 novels. Recently she has become especially interested in writing plays. She has received many awards, has been elected to the American Academy and Institute of Arts and Letters, and now teaches creative writing at Princeton University.

COMMENTARY

Oates begins *Tone Clusters* by telling the reader that her play

> is not intended to be a realistic work; thus, any inclination toward the establishment of character should be resisted. . . . The mood is one of fragmentation, confusion, yet, at times, strong emotion. A fractured narrative emerges that the audience will have no difficulty piecing together even as—and this is the tragicomedy of the piece—the characters Mr. and Mrs. Gulick deny it.

We won't tell you what the "fractured narrative" is, but we think that you will agree, when you read *Tone Clusters,* that a story emerges that is both astounding and at the same time not at all unbelievable, given the fact that we know that almost anybody seems capable of almost anything. (The play was inspired by the case of Robert Golub, a young man who in 1990 was convicted of murdering a thirteen-year-old girl.)

Early in this book, in our comments about tragedy, comedy, and tragicomedy, we mentioned that in the late nineteenth century one notices in dramatic literature a decided dissolution in character, and we quoted the dramatist August Strindberg, who in 1888 wrote, "Since the persons in my play are modern characters, living in a transitional era more hurried and hysterical than the previous one at least, I have depicted them as more unstable, as torn and divided, a mixture of the old and the new."

In her introductory stage direction, from which we have already quoted, Oates says that her play "is not intended to be a realistic work." A little later she says that "in structure, *Tone Clusters* suggests an interview, but a stylized interview in which questions and answers are frequently askew."

Can we account for the renewed turning away from realism and for the presentation of a world in which things are "askew"? First, we should mention that it is sometimes said that just as one of the results of the invention of photography was to turn painters away from realism—because they couldn't compete with the camera, they produced different sorts of pictures—so also one of the results of the invention of television was to move short-story writers and novelists away from realism toward allegory, fantasy, and dream-like works. After all, if television gives us an image of life as it is lived, writers will have to find something else to do.

In fact, television does not give us much sense of reality, or at least it does not give us much sense of a coherent reality. It gives us, instead, astounding events that seem utterly implausible, such as a walk on the moon or the assassination of a leader or coverage of a Supreme Court nominee who is accused of talking obscenely to a young woman who worked for him. Moreover, it is not simply that certain events that receive lots of coverage are hard to believe. What we hear from individuals on television, whatever their status, is also hard to believe, or, to put the matter slightly differently, it is hard for us to make sense out of some of the characters whom we see. We are not speaking only of politicians who before the election promise not to raise taxes and later, after the election, raise them, but of people who we might at first think are ordinary people. Let's begin with television interviewers. They pry into the sex lives of their subjects and then profess shock that these people have done these things. (Such programs of course allow us, as spectators, to become virtuous voyeurs: we enjoy hearing the scandal, and we also enjoy clucking our tongues in moral disapproval of such goings-on.) But beyond the interviewers are the subjects, sometimes ordinary-seeming people who turn out to be rapists or mass-murderers. Or, if the subject is not an ordinary person, perhaps he is a millionaire philanthropist who turns out to have engaged in illegal business practices. In short, an hour in front of the television set, listening to the news and to interviews, is enough to convince the viewer that he or she lives in an incoherent and utterly unpredictable world.

Traditional plays and works of fiction show the viewer a coherent world. It might be, and in fact usually is, a world of violence and even of mystery, but by the end of the work the viewer sees that the characters are coherent: King Lear, for instance, though capable of terrible mistakes, is at bottom not a villain, whereas Edmund is always a thorough villain even though he fools some people for a while. Similarly, Ibsen's Nora is mistaken about her husband and even about herself, but she is fundamentally smart and resourceful. Moreover, the people in older fiction and drama live in a world where actions have consequences. King Oedipus and King Lear act, and whatever their intentions, their actions have disastrous consequences; thus the doers of deeds learn that they must pay the price, since the world is, at bottom, an orderly world, a world of cause and effect.

Oates's play takes us into a different world, the baffling, fragmented world that we get nightly on television, when thirty seconds with a murderer (a very nice young man, according to his teachers) is immediately followed by thirty seconds of shots of starving Ethiopians, which in turn is followed by thirty seconds of advertising devoted to cute toddlers who are wearing a new kind of diaper.

The effect is heightened if one flips through the TV channels, a tiny action that brings about all sorts of grotesque juxtapositions—today's football games yield to old cowboy movies, which in turn yield to ads for the newest models of cars. No wonder Oates says, in "On Writing Drama," that when she began writing plays she "wanted the play's dialogue to be random, with no lines assigned to either speaker; a kind of aleatory music." (Aleatory music—so called because in Latin *alea* means dice—is music resulting from the purely random succession of tones and noises.) In fact, when you have finished *Tone Clusters* you might spend a moment thinking about the degree to which the work is structured and the characters are coherent.

JOYCE CAROL OATES *Tone Clusters*

List of Characters

FRANK GULICK, *fifty-three years old*

EMILY GULICK, *fifty-one years old*

VOICE, *male, indeterminate age*

These are white Americans of no unusual distinction, nor are they in any self-evident way "representative."

Tone Clusters is not intended to be a realistic work, thus any inclination toward the establishment of character should be resisted. Its primary effect should be visual (the dominance of the screen at center stage, the play of lights of sharply contrasting degrees of intensity) and audio (the Voice, the employment of music—"tone clusters" of Henry Cowell and/or Charles Ives, and electronic music, etc.). The mood is one of fragmentation, confusion, yet, at times, strong emotion. A fractured narrative emerges which the audience will have no difficulty piecing together even as—and this is the tragicomedy of the piece—the characters Mr. and Mrs. Gulick deny it.

In structure, *Tone Clusters* suggests an interview, but a stylized interview in which questions and answers are frequently askew. Voices trail off into silence or may be mocked or extended by strands of music. The Voice is sometimes overamplified and booming; sometimes marred by static; sometimes clear, in an ebullient tone, like that of a talk-show host. The Voice has no identity but must be male. It should not be represented by any actual presence on the stage or within view of the audience. At all times, the Voice is in control: the principals on the stage are dominated by their interrogator and by the screen, which is seemingly floating in the air above them, at center stage. Indeed the screen emerges as a character.

The piece is divided into nine uneven segments. When one ends, the lights dim, then come up again immediately. (After the ninth segment the lights go out completely and darkness is extended for some seconds to indicate that the piece is ended: it ends on an abrupt cutoff of lights and images on the screen and the monitors.)

By degree the Gulicks become somewhat accustomed to the experience of being interviewed and filmed, but never wholly accustomed: they are always slightly disoriented, awkward, confused, inclined to speak slowly and methodically or too quickly, "unprofessionally," often with inappropriate emotion (fervor, enthusiasm, hope, sudden rage) or no emotion at all (like "computer voices"). The Gulicks may at times speak in unison (as if one were an echo of the other); they may mimic the qualities of tone-cluster music or electronic music (I conceive of their voices, and that of the Voice, as music of a kind); should the director wish, there may be some clear-cut relationship between subject and emotion or emphasis—but the piece should do no more than approach "realism," and then withdraw. The actors must conceive of themselves as elements in a dramatic structure, not as "human characters" wishing to establish rapport with an audience.

Tone Clusters is about the absolute mystery—the *not knowing*—at the core of our human experience. That the mystery is being exploited by a television documentary underscores its tragicomic nature.

SCENE 1

Lights up. Initially very strong, near-blinding. On a bare stage, middle-aged Frank and Emily Gulick sit ill-at-ease in "comfortable" modish cushioned swivel chairs, trying not to squint or grimace in the lights (which may be represented as the lights of a camera crew provided the human figures involved can be kept shadowy, even indistinct). They wear clip-on microphones, to which they are unaccustomed. they are "dressed up" for the occasion, and clearly nervous: they continually touch their faces, or clasp their hands firmly in their laps, or fuss with fingernails, buttons, the microphone cords, their hair. The nervous mannerisms continue throughout the piece but should never be too distracting and never comic.

Surrounding the Gulicks, dominating their human presence, are the central screen and the TV monitors and/or slide screens upon which, during the course of the play, disparate images, words, formless flashes of light are projected. Even when the Gulicks' own images appear on the screens they are upstaged by it: they glance at it furtively, with a kind of awe.

The rest of the time, the monitors always show the stage as we see it: the Gulicks seated, glancing uneasily up at the large screen. Thus there is a "screen within a screen."

The employment of music is entirely at the director's discretion. The opening might be accompanied by classical tone cluster piano pieces—Henry Cowell's "Advertisement," for instance. The music should never be intrusive. The ninth scene might well be completely empty of music. There should certainly be no "film-music" effect. (The Gulicks do not hear the music.)

The Voice too in its modulations is at the discretion of the director. Certainly at the start the Voice is booming and commanding. There should be intermittent audio trouble (whistling, static, etc.); the Voice, wholly in control, can exude any number of effects throughout the play—pomposity, charity, condescension, bemusement, false chattiness, false pedantry, false sympathy, mild incredulity (like that of a television emcee), affectless "computer talk." The Gulicks are entirely intimidated by the Voice and try very hard to answer its questions.

Screen shifts from its initial image to words: IN A CASE OF MURDER—*large black letters on white.*

VOICE. In a case of murder (taking murder as an abstraction) there is
always a sense of the Inevitable once the identity of the murderer
is established. Beforehand there is a sense of
disharmony.
And humankind fears and loathes disharmony,
Mr. and Mrs. Gulick of Lakepointe, New Jersey, would you comment?

FRANK. . . . Yes I would say. I think that

EMILY. What is that again, exactly? I . . .

FRANK. My wife and I, we . . .

EMILY. Disharmony . . . ?

FRANK. I don't like disharmony. I mean, all the family,
we are a law-abiding family.

VOICE. A religious family I believe?

FRANK. Oh yes. Yes,
We go to church every

EMILY. We almost never miss a, a Sunday
For a while, I helped with Sunday School classes
The children, the children don't always go but they believe,
our daughter Judith for instance she and Carl

FRANK. oh yes yessir

EMILY. and Dennis. they do believe they were raised to
believe in God and, and Jesus Christ

FRANK. We raised them that way because we were raised that way,

EMILY. there *is* a God whether you agree with Him or not.

VOICE. "Religion" may be defined as a sort of adhesive matter invisibly
holding together nation-states, nationalities, tribes, families
for the good of those so
held together,
would you comment?

FRANK. Oh, oh yes.

EMILY. For the good of . . .

FRANK. Yes I would say so, I think so.

EMILY. My husband and I, we were married in church, in

FRANK. In the Lutheran Church.

EMILY. In Penns Neck.

FRANK. In New Jersey.

EMILY. All our children,

BOTH. they believe.

EMILY. God sees into the human heart.

VOICE. Mr. and Mrs. Gulick from your experience would you theorize for
our audience: is the Universe "predestined" in every particular
or is man capable of acts of "freedom"?

BOTH. . . .

EMILY. . . . I would say, that is hard to say.

FRANK. Yes. I believe that man is free.

EMILY. If you mean like, I guess choosing good and evil? Yes

FRANK. I would have to say yes. You would have to say
mankind is free.

FRANK. Like moving my hand. (*moves hand*)

EMILY. If nobody is free it wouldn't be right would it
to punish anybody?

FRANK. There is always Hell.
I believe in Hell.

EMILY. Anybody at all

FRANK. Though I am not free to, to fly up in the air am I? (*laughs*)
because Well I'm not built right for that am I? (*laughs*)

VOICE. Man is free. Thus man is responsible for his acts.

EMILY. Except, oh sometime if, maybe for instance if
A baby born without

FRANK. Oh one of those "AIDS" babies

EMILY. poor thing

FRANK. "crack" babies
Or if you were captured by some enemy, y'know and tortured
Some people never have a chance.

EMILY. But God sees into the human heart,
God knows who to forgive   and who not.

Lights down.

SCENE 2

Lights up. Screen shows a suburban street of lower-income homes; the Gulicks stare at the screen and their answers are initially distracted.

VOICE. Here we have Cedar Street   in Lakepointe, New Jersey   neatly kept homes (as you can see)   American suburb   low crime rate, single-family homes   suburb of Newark, New Jersey
population twelve thousand   the neighborhood of
Mr. and Mrs. Frank Gulick the parents of   Carl Gulick
Will you introduce yourselves to our audience please?

(*House lights come up.*)

FRANK. . . . Go on, you first

EMILY. I, I don't know what to say

FRANK. My name is   Frank Gulick, I   I am fifty-three years old
that's our house there   2368 Cedar Street

EMILY. My name is Emily Gulick, fifty-one years old,

VOICE. How employed,   would you care to say?   Mr. Gulick?

FRANK. I work for the post office.   I'm a supervisor for

EMILY. He has worked for the post office for twenty-five years

FRANK. . . . The Terhune Avenue branch.

VOICE. And how long have you resided   in your attractive home   on Cedar Street?

(*House lights begin to fade down.*)

FRANK. . . . Oh I guess, how long   if this is
this is 1990?

EMILY. (oh just think: 1990!)

FRANK. We moved there in, uh   Judith wasn't born yet so

EMILY. Oh there was our thirtieth anniversary a year ago,

FRANK. wedding
no that was two years ago

EMILY. was it?

FRANK. or three, I   twenty-seven years, this is 1990

EMILY. Yes: Judith is twenty-six,   now I'm a grandmother

FRANK. Carl is twenty-two

EMILY. Denny is seventeen, he's a senior in high school
No none of them are living at home now

FRANK. not now

EMILY. Right now poor Denny is staying with my sister in

VOICE. Frank and Emily Gulick you have been happy here   in Lakepointe
raising your family like any   American couple   with your hopes and aspirations
until recently?

FRANK. . . . Yes, oh yes.

EMILY. Oh for a long time we *were*

FRANK. oh yes.

EMILY. It's so strange to,   to think of
The years go by so

VOICE. You have led a   happy family life   like so many millions
of Americans

EMILY. Until this,   this terrible thing

FRANK. *Innocent until proven guilty*—that's a laugh!

EMILY. Oh it's a, a terrible thing

FRANK. Never any hint beforehand of   the meanness of people's hearts.
I mean the neighbors.

EMILY. Oh now don't start that,   this isn't the

FRANK. Oh God you just try to   comprehend

EMILY. this isn't the place, I

FRANK. Like last night: this carload of kids
drunk, beer-drinking   foul language in the night

EMILY. oh don't, my hands are

FRANK. Yes but you know it's the parents   set them going
And telephone calls   our number is changed now, but

EMILY. my hands are shaking so
we are both on medication   the doctor says,

FRANK. oh you would not believe, you would not   believe   the hatred
like Nazi Germany

EMILY. Denny had to drop out of school,   he loved school he is
an honor student

FRANK. everybody turned against us

EMILY. My sister in Yonkers, he's staying with

FRANK. Oh he'll never be the same   boy again.
none of us will.

VOICE. In the development of   human identity   there's the element
of chance,   and there is genetic determinism.
Would you comment please?

FRANK. The thing is,   you try your best.

EMILY. oh dear God yes.

FRANK. Your best.

EMILY. You give all that's in your heart

FRANK. you
can't do more than that can you?

EMILY. Yes but there is certain to be   justice.
There *is* a, a sense of things.

FRANK. Sometimes there is a chance, the way they   turn out
but also   what they *are.*

EMILY. Your own babies

VOICE. Frank Gulick   and Mary   what is your assessment of

American civilization today?

EMILY. . . . it's Emily.

FRANK. My wife's name is,

EMILY. it's
Emily.

VOICE. Frank and EMILY Gulick.

FRANK. . . . The state of the civilization?

EMILY. It's so big,

FRANK. We are here to tell our side of,

EMILY. . . . I don't know: it's a, a Democracy

FRANK. the truth is, do you want the truth?
the truth is where we live
Lakepointe
it's changing too

EMILY. it has changed

FRANK. Yes but it's all over, it's
terrible, just terrible

EMILY. Now we are grandparents we fear for

FRANK. Yes what you read and see on TV

EMILY. You don't know what to think,

FRANK. Look: in this country half the crimes
are committed by the, by half the population against
the other half. (*laughs*)
You have your law-abiding citizens,

EMILY. taxpayers

FRANK. and you have the rest of them
Say you went downtown into a city like Newark, some night

EMILY. you'd be crazy if you got out of your car

FRANK. you'd be dead. That's what.

VOICE. Is it possible, probable or in your assessment *im*probable
that the slaying of fourteen-year-old Edith Kaminsky
on February 12, 1990 is related to
the social malaise
of which you speak?

FRANK. . . . "ma-lezz"?

EMILY. . . . oh it's hard to. I would say yes

FRANK. . . . whoever did it, he

EMILY. Oh it's terrible the things that
keep happening

FRANK. If only the police would arrest the right person,

VOICE. Frank and Emily Gulick you remain adamant in your belief
in your faith in your twenty-two-year-old son Carl
that he is innocent in the death of
fourteen-year-old Edith Kaminsky
on February 12, 1990?

EMILY. Oh yes.

FRANK. oh yes that is
the single thing we are convinced of.

EMILY. On this earth.

BOTH. With God as our witness,

FRANK. yes

EMILY. Yes.

FRANK. The single thing.

Lights down.

SCENE 3

Lights up. Screen shows violent movement: urban scenes, police patrol cars, a fire burning out of control, men being arrested and herded into vans; a body lying in the street. The Gulicks stare at the screen.

VOICE. Of today's pressing political issues the rise in violent crime
most concerns American citizens Number-one political issue of
Mr. and Mrs. Gulick tell our viewers your opinion?

FRANK. In this state,
the state of New Jersey

EMILY. Oh it's everywhere

FRANK. there's capital punishment supposedly

EMILY. But the lawyers the lawyers get them off,

FRANK. you bet
There's public defenders the taxpayer pays

EMILY. Oh, it's it's out of control
(like that, what is it "acid rain"

FRANK. it can fall on you anywhere,

EMILY. the sun is too hot too:

BOTH. the "greenhouse effect")

FRANK. It's a welfare state by any other name

EMILY. Y'know who pays:

BOTH. the taxpayer

FRANK. The same God damn criminal, you pay for him then he
That's the joke of it (*laughs*)
the same criminal who slits your throat (*laughs*)
He's the one you pay bail for, to get out.
But it sure isn't funny. (*laughs*)

EMILY. Oh God.

FRANK. It sure isn't funny.

VOICE. Many Americans have come to believe this past decade that
capital punishment is one of the answers: would you
comment please?

FRANK. Oh in cases of actual, proven murder

EMILY. Those drug dealers

FRANK. Yes *I* would have to say, definitely yes

EMILY. I would say so yes

FRANK. You always hear them say opponents of the death penalty
"The death penalty doesn't stop crime"

EMILY. Oh that's what they say!

FRANK. Yes but *I* say, once a man is dead he sure ain't gonna commit any more crimes, is he. (*laughs*)

VOICE. The death penalty is a deterrent to crime in those cases when the criminal has been executed

FRANK. But you have to find the right,
the actual murderer.

EMILY. Not some poor innocent* some poor innocent*

Lights down.

SCENE 4

Lights up. Screen shows a grainy magnified snapshot of a boy about ten. Quick jump to a snapshot of the same boy a few years older. Throughout this scene images of "Carl Gulick" appear and disappear on the screen though not in strict relationship to what is being said, nor in chronological order. "Carl Gulick" in his late teens and early twenties is muscular but need not have any other outstanding characteristics: he may look like any American boy at all.

VOICE. Carl Gulick, twenty-two years old the second-born child of Frank and Emily Gulick of Lakepointe, New Jersey How would you describe your son. Frank and Emily

FRANK. D'you mean how he looks or . . . ?

EMILY. He's a shy boy, he's shy Not backward just

FRANK. He's about my height I guess brown hair, eyes

EMILY. Oh! no I think no he's much taller Frank
he's been taller than you for years

FRANK. Well that depends on how we're both standing.
How we're both standing
Well in one newspaper it said six feet one inch, in the other six feet three inches, that's the kind of

EMILY. accuracy

FRANK. reliability of the news media
you can expect!

EMILY. And oh that terrible picture of,
in the paper
that face he was making the police carrying him
against his will laying their hands on him

FRANK. handcuffs

EMILY. Oh that isn't *him*

BOTH. that isn't our son

(*Gulicks respond dazedly to snapshots flashed on screen.*)

*"innocent" is an adjective here, not a noun [Author's note]

EMILY. Oh! that's Carl age I guess about

FRANK. four?

EMILY. that's at the beach one summer

FRANK. only nine or ten, he was big for

FRANK. that's my brother George

EMILY. That's

EMILY. With his sister Judith

FRANK. He loved Boy Scouts,

EMILY. but
Oh when you are the actual parents it's
a different

FRANK. Oh it is so different!
from something just on TV.

VOICE. In times of disruption of fracture it is believed that
human behavior moves in unchartable leaps History is a formal
record of such leaps but in large-scale demographical terms
in which the individual is lost
Frank and Emily Gulick it's said your son Carl charged
in the savage slaying of fourteen-year-old shows no sign of
remorse that is to say, *awareness* of the act:
thus the question we pose to you Can guilt reside in those
without conscience.
or is memory conscience, and conscience memory?
can "the human" reside in those
devoid of "memory"

EMILY. . . . Oh the main thing is,
he is innocent.

FRANK. . . . Stake my life on it.

EMILY. He has always been cheerful, optimistic

FRANK. a good boy, of course he has not
forgotten

BOTH. He is innocent.

EMILY. How could our son "forget" when he has nothing to

BOTH. "forget"

FRANK. He took that lie detector test voluntarily didn't he

EMILY. Oh there he is weight-lifting, I don't remember
who took that picture?

FRANK. When you are the actual parents you see them every day,
you don't form judgments.

VOICE. And how is your son employed, Mr. and Mrs. Kaminsky?
Excuse me: GULICK.

FRANK. Up until Christmas he was working in
This butcher shop in East Orange

FRANK. . . . it isn't easy, at that age

FRANK. Before that, loading and unloading

EMILY. at Sears' at the mall

FRANK. No: that was before, that was before the other

EMILY. No: the job at Sears' was

FRANK. . . . Carl was working for that Italian, y'know that

EMILY. the lawn service

FRANK. Was that before?   or after
Oh in this butcher shop   his employer

EMILY. yes there were hard feelings, on both sides

FRANK. Look: you can't believe a single thing   in the newspaper or TV

EMILY. it's not that they lie

FRANK. Oh yes they lie

EMILY. not that they lie, they just   get everything wrong

FRANK. Oh they do lie!   and it's printed and you can't stop them.

EMILY. In this meat shop, I never wanted him to work there

FRANK. In this shop there was pressure on him
to join the union.

EMILY. Then the other side, his employer
did not want him to join.
He's a sensitive boy.   his stomach and nerves
He lost his appetite for weeks. he'd say "oh, if you could see
some of the things I see"   "the insides of things"
and so much blood

VOICE. There was always a loving   relationship   in the household?

EMILY. . . . When they took him away he said,   he was so brave
he said Momma I'll be back soon
I'll be right back,   I am innocent he said
I don't know how she came to be in   our house
I don't know.   I don't know he said
I looked into my son's eyes and saw   truth shining
His eyes have always been   dark green,
like mine.

VOICE. On the afternoon of   February 12 you have told police that
no one was home   in your house?

EMILY. I, I was . . . I had a doctor's appointment,
My husband was working, he doesn't get home until

FRANK. Whoever did it,   and brought her body in

EMILY. No: they say she was   they say it,   it happened there

FRANK. No I don't buy that,   he brought her in   carried her
whoever that was,
I believe he tried   other houses
seeing who was home and who   wasn't
and then he

EMILY. Oh it was like lightning striking

VOICE. Your son Dennis   was at Lakepointe High School attending a meeting
of the yearbook staff.   your son Carl has told police he
was   riding   his   motor scooter
in the park,

FRANK. They dragged him like an animal
put their hands on him like
Like Nazi Germany,

EMILY. it couldn't be any worse

FRANK. And that judge
it's a misuse of power, it's

EMILY. I just don't understand

VOICE. Your son Carl on and after February 12 did not exhibit
(in your presence) any unusual sign of emotion?
agitation? guilt?

EMILY. Every day in a house, a household
is like the other days. Oh you never step back, never *see.*
Like I told them, the police, everybody. *He did not.*

Lights down.

SCENE 5

Lights up. Screen shows snapshots, photographs, of the murdered girl Kaminsky. Like Carl Gulick, she is anyone at all of that age: white, neither strikingly beautiful nor unattractive.

VOICE. Sometime in the evening of February 12 of this year forensic reports
say fourteen-year-old Edith Kaminsky daughter of neighbors
2361 Cedar Street, Lakepointe, New Jersey multiple stab wounds,
sexual assault strangulation
An arrest has been made but legally or otherwise, the absolute
identity of the murderer has yet to be

EMILY. Oh it's so unjust,

FRANK. the power of a single man
That judge

EMILY. Carl's birthday is next week
Oh God he'll be in that terrible cold place

FRANK. "segregated" they call it
How can a judge refuse to set bail

EMILY. oh I would borrow a million dollars
if I could

FRANK. Is this America or Russia?

EMILY. I can't stop crying

FRANK. . . . we are both under medication you see but

EMILY. Oh it's true he wasn't himself sometimes.

FRANK. But that day when it happened, that wasn't one of the times.

VOICE. You hold out for the possibility that the true murderer
carried Edith Kaminsky into your house, into your basement
thus meaning to throw suspicion on your son?

FRANK. Our boy is guiltless that's the main thing, I will never doubt that.

EMILY. Our body is innocent . . . What did I say?

FRANK. Why the hell do they make so much of

Carl lifting weights, his   muscles
he is not a freak.

EMILY. There's lots of them   and women too, today   like that,

FRANK. He has other interests he used to collect stamps   play baseball

EMILY. Oh there's so much misunderstanding

FRANK. actual lies
Because the police do not know who the murderer *is*
of course they will blame   anyone they can.

Lights down.

SCENE 6

Lights up. Screen shows the exterior of the Gulick house seen from various angles: then the interior (the basement, evidently, and the "storage area" where the young girl's body was found).

VOICE. If, as is believed, "premeditated" acts arise   out of a
mysterious sequence of neuron discharges   (in the brain)
out of what source   do
"unpremeditated"   acts   arise?

EMILY. Nobody was down in,   in the basement
until the police came.   The storage space is behind the
water heater.   but

FRANK. My God if my son is   so shiftless   like people are saying
just look: he helped me paint the house last summer

EMILY. Yes Carl and Denny both,

FRANK. Why are they telling such   lies, our neighbors?   We have never
wished them harm,

EMILY. I believed a certain neighbor was my friend,   her and I, we
we'd go shopping together   took my car
Oh my heart is broken

FRANK. It's robin's-egg blue,   the paint turned out brighter than
when it dried, a little brighter than we'd   expected

EMILY. *I* think it's pretty

FRANK. Well.   We'll have to sell the house,   there's no choice
the legal costs   Mr. Filco our attorney has said

EMILY. He told us

FRANK. he's going to fight all the way, he believes Carl is   innocent

EMILY. My heart is broken.

FRANK. *My* heart isn't,
I'm going to fight this all the way

EMILY. A tragedy like this,   you learn fast who is your friend and who
is your enemy

FRANK. Nobody's your friend.

VOICE. The Gulicks and Kaminskys were   well acquainted?

EMILY. We lived on Cedar first,   when they moved in I don't remember:
my mind isn't right these days

FRANK. Oh yes we knew them

EMILY. I'd have said Mrs. Kaminsky was my friend, but
that's how people are

FRANK. Yes

EMILY. Carl knew her, Edith
I mean, we all did

FRANK. but not well.

EMILY. just neighbors
Now they're our declared enemies, the Kaminskys

FRANK. well, so be it.

EMILY. Oh! that poor girl if only she hadn't,
I mean, there's no telling who she was with, walking home
walking home from school I guess

FRANK. Well she'd been missing overnight,

EMILY. yes overnight

FRANK. of course we were aware

FRANK. The Kaminskys came around ringing doorbells,

EMILY. then the police,

FRANK. then
they got a search party going, Carl helped them out

EMILY. Everybody said how much he helped

FRANK. he kept at it for hours
They walked miles and miles,
he's been out of work for a while,

EMILY. he'd been looking
in the *help wanted* ads but

FRANK. . . . He doesn't like to use the telephone.

EMILY. People laugh at him he says,

FRANK. I told him no he was imagining it.

EMILY. This neighborhood:

FRANK. you would not believe it.

EMILY. Call themselves Christians

FRANK. Well some are Jews.

EMILY. Well it's still white isn't it a white neighborhood, you expect
better.

VOICE. The murder weapon has yet to be found?

FRANK. One of the neighbors had to offer an opinion, something sarcastic
I guess

EMILY. Oh don't go into *that*

FRANK. the color of the paint on our house
So Carl said, You don't like it, wear sunglasses.

EMILY. But,
he was smiling.

VOICE. A young man with a sense of humor.

FRANK. Whoever hid that poor girl's
body
in the storage space of our
basement well clearly it
obviously it was   to deceive
to cast blame on our son.

EMILY. Yes   if there were fingerprints down there,

BOTH. that handprint they found on the wall

EMILY. well for God's sake it was from when Carl
was down there

BOTH. helping them

FRANK. He cooperated with them,

EMILY. Frank wasn't home,

FRANK. Carl led them downstairs

EMILY. Why they came to our house, I don't know.
Who was saying things   I don't know,
it was like everybody had gone   crazy
casting blame on all sides.

VOICE. Mr. and Mrs. Gulick   it's said that from your son's room
Lakepointe police officers confiscated   comic books, military
magazines, pornographic magazines   a cache of more than one dozen
knives including   switchblades   plus
a U.S. Army bayonet (World War II)   Nazi memorabilia
including a "souvenir" SS helmet   (manufactured in Taiwan)
a pink plastic skull   with lightbulbs in eyes
a naked Barbie doll, badly scratched   bitten
numerous pictures of naked women
and women in fashion magazines,   their eyes
breasts   crotches   cut out with a scissors

(*pause*)

Do you have any comment   Mr. and Mrs. Gulick

FRANK. . . .
Mainly they were hobbies,

EMILY. I guess I don't,

FRANK. we didn't know about

EMILY. Well   he wouldn't allow me in his room,   to vacuum, or

FRANK. You know how boys are

EMILY. Didn't want his mother

FRANK. poking her nose in

EMILY. So . . .

(*Emily upsets a glass of water on the floor.*)

VOICE. Police forensic findings   bloodstains, hairs, semen
and DNA 'fingerprinting'   constitute a tissue of
circumstance   linking your son to

EMILY. (*interrupting*) Mr. Filco says   it's all pieced together

'Circumstantial evidence,' he says not proof

FRANK. *I* call it bullshit (*laughs*)

EMILY. Oh Frank

FRANK. I call it bullshit (*laughs*)

VOICE. Eyewitness accounts disagree. two parties report
having seen Carl Gulick and Edith Kaminsky walking together
in the afternoon, in the alley behind Cedar Street
a third party a neighbor claims to have seen
the girl in the company of a stranger at approximately
4:15 PM And Carl Gulick insists
he was 'riding his motor scooter' all afternoon

FRANK. He is a boy

EMILY. not capable of lying

FRANK. Look: I would have to discipline him sometimes,

EMILY. You have to, with boys

FRANK. Oh yes you have to, otherwise

EMILY. He was always a good eater didn't fuss

FRANK. He's a quiet boy

EMILY. You can't guess his thoughts

FRANK. But he loved his mother and father respected

EMILY. Always well behaved at home
That ugly picture in the paper, oh

FRANK. THAT WASN'T HIM

EMILY. You can't believe the cruelty in the human heart

FRANK. Giving interviews! his own teachers from the school

EMILY. Telling lies cruel nasty

FRANK. His own teachers from the school

VOICE. Mr. and Mrs. Gulick you had no suspicion
no awareness
you had no sense of the fact
that the battered raped mutilated body of
fourteen-year-old Edith Kaminsky
was hidden in your basement in a storage space
wrapped in plastic garbage bags
for approximately forty hours

GULICKS. . . . .

VOICE. No consciousness of disharmony
in your household?

FRANK. It was a day like

EMILY. It *was,* I mean, it wasn't

FRANK. I keep the cellar clean, I There's leakage

EMILY. Oh
Last week at my sister's where we were staying,
we had to leave this terrible place
in Yonkers I was crying, I could not stop crying

downstairs in the kitchen three in the morning
I was standing by a window and there was suddenly it looked like snow!
it was moonlight moving in the window and there came a shadow I guess
like an eclipse? was there an eclipse?
Oh I felt so, I felt my heart stopped Oh but I, I wasn't scared
I was thinking I was seeing how the world is
how the universe *is*
it's so hard to say, I feel like a a fool
I was gifted by this, by seeing how the world *is* not
how you see it with your eyes, or talk talk about it
I mean names you give to, parts of it No I mean how it *is*
when there is nobody there.

VOICE. A subliminal conviction of disharmony may be nullified by a transcendental leap of consciousness: to a "higher plane" of celestial harmony,
would you comment Mr. and Mrs. Gulick?

EMILY. Then Sunday night it was.

FRANK. this last week

EMILY. they came again

FRANK. threw trash on our lawn

EMILY. screamed
Murderers! they were drunk, yelling in the night *Murderers!*

FRANK. There was the false report that Carl was released on bail
that he was home with us,

EMILY. Oh dear God if only that was true

FRANK. I've lost fifteen pounds since February

EMILY. Oh Frank has worked so hard on that lawn,
it's his pride and joy and in the neighborhood everybody knows,
they compliment him, and now
Yes he squats right out there, he pulls out crabgrass by hand
Dumping such such ugly nasty disgusting things
Then in the A&P a woman followed me up and down the aisles
I could hear people *That's her, that's the mother of the murderer* I could hear them everywhere in the store
Is that her, is that the mother of the murderer? they were saying
Lived in this neighborhood, in this town for so many years
we thought we were welcome here and now
Aren't you ashamed to show your face! a voice screamed
What can I do with my face. can I hide it forever?

FRANK. And all this when, our boy is innocent.

VOICE. Perceiving the inviolate nature of the Universe apart from human suffering rendered you happy, Mrs. Gulick is this so?
for some precious moments?

EMILY. Oh yes, I was crying but
not because of
no I was crying because

I was happy I think.

Lights down.

SCENE 7

Lights up. Screen shows neurological X-rays, medical diagrams, charts as of EEG and CAT-scan tests.

VOICE. Is it possible that in times of fracture, of evolutionary
unease or, perhaps, at any time human behavior mimics that
of minute particles of light? The atom is primarily emptiness
the neutron dense-packed
The circuitry of the human brain circadian rhythms can be tracked
but never, it's said comprehended. And then in descent
from "identity"—(memory?) to tissue to cells to cell-particles
electrical impulses axon-synapse-dendrite
and beyond, be-
neath
to subatomic bits
Where is "Carl Gulick"?

(*Gulicks turn to each other in bewilderment. Screen flashes images: kitchen interior; weightlifting paraphernalia; a shelf of trophies; photographs; domestic scenes, etc.*)

VOICE. Mr. and Mrs. Gulick you did not notice anything unusual in
your son's behavior on the night of February 12 or the following
day, to the best of your recollection?

EMILY. . . . Oh we've told the police this so many many times

FRANK. Oh you forget what you remember,

EMILY. That night, before we knew there was anyone missing I mean, in
the neighborhood anyone we knew

FRANK. I can't remember.

EMILY. Yes but Carl had supper with us like always

FRANK. No I think, he was napping up in his room

EMILY. he was at the table with us:

FRANK. I remember he came down around nine o'clock, but he did eat.

EMILY. Him and Denny, they were at the table with us—

FRANK. We've told the police this so many times, it's
I don't know any longer

EMILY. I'm sure it was Denny too. Both our sons.
We had meatloaf ketchup baked on top, it's the boys'
favorite dish just about isn't it?

FRANK. Oh anything with hamburger and ketchup!

EMILY. Of course he was at the table with us, he had his usual appetite.

FRANK. . . . he was upstairs, said he had a touch of flu

EMILY. Oh no he was there.

FRANK. It's hard to speak of your own flesh and blood, as if
they are other people
it's hard without giving false testimony against your will.

VOICE. Is the intrusion of the "extra-ordinary" into the dimension of the "ordinary" an indication that such Aristotelian categories are invalid? If one day fails to resemble the preceding what does it resemble?

FRANK. . . . He has sworn to us, we are his parents
He did not touch a hair of that poor child's head let alone the rest.
Anybody who knew him, they'd know

EMILY. Oh those trophies! he was so proud
one of them is from the, I guess the Lakepointe YMCA
there's some from the New Jersey competition at Atlantic City
two years ago?

FRANK. no, he was in high school
the first was, Carl was only fifteen years old

EMILY. Our little muscleman!

VOICE. Considering the evidence of thousands of years of human culture
of language art religion the judicial system "The family unit" athletics hobbies fraternal organizations
charitable impulses gods of all species
is it possible that humankind desires
not to know
its place in
the
food cycle?

EMILY. One day he said
he wasn't going back to school,
my heart was broken.

FRANK. Only half his senior year ahead
but you can't argue. not with

EMILY. oh his temper! he takes after,
oh I don't know who

FRANK. we always have gotten along together
in this household haven't we

EMILY. yes but the teachers would laugh at him he said
girls laughed at him he said stared and pointed at him he said
and there was this pack of oh we're not prejudiced
against Negros, it's just that
the edge of the Lakepointe school district
well

FRANK. Carl got in fights sometimes
in the school cafeteria and I guess the park?

EMILY. the park isn't safe for law-abiding people these days
they see the color of your skin, they'll attack
some of them are just like animals yes they *are*

FRANK. Actually our son was attacked first it isn't like he got
into fights by himself

EMILY. Who his friends are now, I don't remember

FRANK. He is a quiet boy, keeps to himself

EMILY. he wanted to work

he was looking for work

FRANK. Well: our daughter Judith was misquoted about that

EMILY. also about Carl having a bad temper   she never said that
the reporter for the paper twisted her words
Mr. Filco says   we might sue

FRANK. Look: our son never raised a hand against anybody let alone against

EMILY. He loves his mother and father,   he respects us

FRANK. He is a religious boy at heart

EMILY. He looked me in the eyes he said   Momma you believe me don't you?   and I said Oh yes   Oh yes   he's just my baby

FRANK. nobody knows him

EMILY. nobody knows him the way we do

FRANK. who would it be, if they did?
I ask you.

SCENE 8

House lights come up. TV screen shows video rewind. Sounds of audio rewind. Screen shows Gulicks onstage.

VOICE. Frank and Mary Gulick we're very sorry   something happened to the tape we're going to have to re-shoot   Let's go back just to, we're showing an interior   Carl's room   the trophies
I will say,   I'll be repeating
Are you ready?

(*House lights out, all tech returns to normal.*)

Well Mr. and Mrs. Gulick your son has
quite a collection of trophies!

FRANK. . . . I,   I don't remember what I

EMILY. . . . yes he,

FRANK. Carl was proud of   he had other hobbies though

EMILY. Oh he was so funny, didn't want his mother   poking in his room he said

FRANK. Yes but that's   how boys are

EMILY. That judge refuses to set bail, which I don't   understand

FRANK. Is this the United States or   is this the Soviet Union?

EMILY. we are willing to sell our house to stand up for what is

VOICE. You were speaking of your son Carl   having quit school.
his senior year?   and then?

EMILY. . . . He had a hard time, the teachers   were down on him.

FRANK. I don't know why,

EMILY. we were never told
And now in the newspapers

FRANK. the kinds of lies they are saying

EMILY. that he got into fights, that he was

FRANK. that kind of thing is all a distortion

EMILY. He was always a quiet boy

FRANK. but he had his own friends

EMILY. they came over to the house sometime, I don't remember who

FRANK. there was that one boy what was his name

EMILY. Oh Frank Carl hasn't seen him in years
he had friends in grade school

FRANK. Look: in the newspaper there were false statements

EMILY. Mr. Filco says we might sue

FRANK. Oh no: he says we can't, we have to prove "malice"

EMILY. Newspapers and TV are filled with lies

FRANK. Look: our son Carl never raised a hand against anybody let alone against

EMILY. He loves his mother and father,

FRANK. he respects us

VOICE. Frank and, it's Emily isn't it Frank and Emily Gulick
that is very moving.

Lights down.

SCENE 9

Lights up. Screen shows Gulicks in theater.

VOICE. The discovery of radioactive elements in the late nineteenth century enabled scientists to set back the estimated age of the Earth to several billion years, and the discovery in more recent decades that the Universe is expanding thus that there is a point in Time when the Universe was tightly compressed smaller than your tiniest fingernail!
thus that the age of the Universe is many billions
of years
uncountable.
Yet humankind resides in Time, God bless us.
Frank and Emily Gulick as we wind clown *our* time together
What are your plans for the future?

FRANK. . . . Oh that is, that's hard to that's hard to answer.

EMILY. It depends I guess on

FRANK. Mr. Filco has advised

EMILY. I guess it's,
next is the grand jury

FRANK. Yes: the grand jury.
Mr. Filco cannot be present for the session to protect our boy
I don't understand the law, just the prosecutor is there
swaying the jurors' minds
Oh I try to understand but I can't,

EMILY. he says we should be prepared
we should be prepared for a trial

VOICE. You are ready for the trial to clear your son's name?

FRANK. Oh yes . . .

EMILY. yes that is a way of, of putting it
Yes. To clear Carl's name.

FRANK. . . . Oh yes you have to be realistic.

EMILY. Yes but before that the true murderer of Edith Kaminsky
might come forward.
If the true murderer is watching this *Please come forward.*

FRANK. . . . Well we both believe Carl is protecting, someone, some
friend another boy

EMILY. the one who really committed that terrible crime

FRANK. So all we can do is pray. Pray Carl will come
to his senses give police the other boy's name, or
I believe this: if it's a friend of Carl's
he must have some decency in his heart

VOICE. Your faith in your son remains unshaken?

EMILY. You would have had to see his toes,
his tiny baby toes in his bath.
His curly hair, splashing in the bath.
His yellow rompers or no: I guess that was Denny

FRANK. If your own flesh and blood looks you in the eye,
you believe

EMILY. Oh yes.

VOICE. Human personality, it might be theorized, is a phenomenon of memory
yet memory built up from cells, and atoms does not "exist":
thus memory like mind like personality
is but a fiction?

EMILY. Oh remembering backward is so hard!
oh it's,

FRANK. it pulls your brain in two.

EMILY. This medication the doctor gave me, my mouth my mouth is so
dry
In the middle of the night I wake up drenched in

FRANK. You don't know who you are until a thing like this happens,
then you don't know.

EMILY. It tears your brain in two, trying to remember,
like even looking at the pictures
Oh you are lost

FRANK. in Time you are lost

EMILY. You fall and fall,
. . . ever since the, the butcher shop
he wasn't always himself but
who he was then, I don't know. But
it's so hard, remembering why.

FRANK. Yes my wife means thinking backward the way the way the police
make you. so many questions you start forgetting right away
it comes out crazy.
Like now, right here, I don't remember anything up to now
I mean, I can't swear to it: the first time, you see, we just

lived. We lived in our house. I am a, I am a post office employee
I guess I said that? well, we live in our, our house.
I mean, it was the first time through. Just living.
Like the TV, the picture's always on if nobody's watching it
you know? So, the people we were then,
I guess I'm trying to say
those actual people, me and her the ones you see *here*
aren't them. (*laughs*)
I guess that sounds crazy,

VOICE. We have here the heartbeat of parental love and faith, it's
a beautiful thing Frank and Emily Gulick, please comment?

FRANK. We are that boy's father and mother.
We know that our son is not a murderer and a, a rapist

EMILY. We know, if that girl came to harm, there is some reason
for it to be revealed, but
they never found the knife, for one thing

FRANK. or whatever it was

EMILY. They never found the knife, the murderer could tell them where
it's buried, or whatever it was.
Oh he could help us so if he just would.

VOICE. And your plans for the future, Mr. and Mrs. Gulick of Lakepointe,
New Jersey?

FRANK. . . . Well,
I guess, I guess we don't have any.

(*Long silence, to the point of awkwardness.*)

VOICE. . . . Plans for the future, Mr. and Mrs. Gulick of Lakepointe, New Jersey?

FRANK. The thing is, you discover you need to be protected
from your own thoughts sometimes, but
who is there to do it?

EMILY. God didn't make any of us strong enough I guess.

FRANK. Look: one day in a family like this, it's like the next day
and the day before.

EMILY. You could say it *is* the next day, I mean the same the same day.

FRANK. Until one day it isn't

Lights slowly down, then out.

(THE END)

TOPICS FOR DISCUSSION AND WRITING

1. In her introductory note Oates says that in *Tone Clusters* "A fractured narrative emerges which the audience will have no difficulty piecing together even as—and this is the tragicomedy of the piece—the characters Mr. and Mrs. Gulick deny it." In a few sentences set forth the narrative, and then evaluate Oates's view that the piece is a "tragicomedy."
2. The first stage direction begins, "Lights up. Initially very strong, near-blinding." Why do you suppose Oates begins this way? Later in the first stage direction we are told

that the Gulicks "are 'dressed up' for the occasion." If you were the director, exactly how might you dress them?

3. On the basis of the Voice's first speech (two sentences), how would you characterize the Voice? (Incidentally, Oates in her initial stage direction says that the Voice "has no identity but must be male.") Do you think that if the Voice were female the play would be substantially changed? Why?

4. In "On Writing Drama" Oates says (page 752):

   [The play] which exists in my imagination as a purely experimental work about the fracturing of reality in an electronic era, is always, for others, "about" a crime.

   What do you take Oates to mean when she speaks of "the fracturing of reality in an electronic era"?

A CONTEXT FOR *TONE CLUSTERS*

On Writing Drama

Joyce Carol Oates

Writing for the stage when one has written primarily for publication, to be read, is an extremely challenging task, though it's difficult to say why. The written word and the spoken word are both *words*—aren't they?

Yet, as the fiction writer begins the task of writing drama, he or she discovers that the techniques of prose fiction simply do not apply to the stage. Still more, the task of "adapting" fiction for the stage is problematic, for one quickly discovers that it is not "adapting" so much as "transposing" that must be done. How much easier, how much more expedient, simply to set aside the fiction and begin anew, from a new angle of vision!

The essential difference between prose fiction and drama is that in prose fiction, it is the narrative voice, the writerly voice, that tells the story; in drama, of course, characters' voices are usually unmediated, direct. In a memory play, the central character may speak to the audience as a narrator, but only to introduce the action in which, then, he or she will participate. The prose writer's sheltering cocoon of language dissolves in the theater, and what is exposed is the bare skeleton of dialogue—action—subterranean/subtextual movement. Suddenly, everything must be dramatized for the eye and the ear; nothing can be summarized. Description simply *is*. Does that sound easy?

Many a gifted prose writer has failed at writing plays for lack of, not talent exactly, but an elusive quality that might just be humility. In itself, humility won't make a fiction writer or a poet into a playwright, but it is a helpful starting place.

Drama, unlike prose fiction, is not an interior esthetic phenomenon. It is communal; its meeting ground is the juncture at which the sheerly imaginary (the playwright's creation) is brought into being by the incontestably real (the living stage). Unlike prose fiction, with its many strategies of advance and retreat, flashbacks, flashforwards, digressions, analyses, interruptions, drama depends upon immediately establishing and sustaining visceral tension; in powerful plays, force fields of emotion are virtually visible on stage. When tension is resolved, it must be in purely emotional terms.

Drama remains our highest communal celebration of the mystery of being, and of our being together, in relationships we struggle to define, and which define us. It makes the point, ceaselessly, that our lives are *now;* there is no history that is not *now.*

When I write poetry and prose fiction, every punctuation mark is debated over in my head; my poetry is a formalist's obsession, in which even margins and blank spaces function as part of the poem. (Not that anyone else would notice, or that I would expect anyone else to notice. Poets quickly learn, and come to be content in, the loneliness of their obsessions.) When I write for the stage, however, I write for others; especially in the hope of striking an imaginative chord in a director whose sensibility is as quirky as my own. Which is not to imply that I am without a deep, abiding, and frequently stubborn sense of what a play of mine is, or an interior vision with which it is inextricably bound. It's simply that, to me, a text is a text—inviolable, yet without life. A play is something else entirely, and so is a film. It is this mysterious "something else"—the something that is others' imaginations in collaboration with my own—that arouses my interest.

Well-intentioned, print-oriented people are forever asking, "Doesn't it upset you to see your characters taken over by other people, out of your control?" My reply is generally a mild one: "But isn't that the point of writing for the theater?"

As soon ask of a novelist, "Doesn't it upset you if strangers read your books, and impose their own interpretations on them?"

In 1985 I attended the West Coast premiere of my play *The Triumph of the Spider Monkey* at the Los Angeles Theatre Center. As directed by Al Rossi and featuring the popular young actor Shaun Cassidy, my grimly satirical posthumous-confessional play about a youthful mass murderer who becomes a fleeting media celebrity in Southern California had been transformed into a fluid succession of brief scenes, with a rock music score and arresting stage devices—a sort of showcase for Cassidy, whose energetic presence in this unknown work by a little-known playwright assured sellout performances for the play's limited run, and some enthusiastic reviews by critics who might otherwise have been skeptical about the credentials of a prose writer turned playwright. My collaboration with Mr. Rossi had been by way of telephone and through the mail, and my pleasure in the production was enormous, both because it was very well done and because it was in the nature of a surprise. *The Triumph of the Spider Monkey,* reimagined by another, was no longer my play; "my" play, published in book form (in *Three Plays,* Ontario Review Press, 1980), consists of words, a text. This was something else. And it may have been that my fascination with it was in direct proportion to the degree to which I was surprised by it.

Of course, over the years, since I first began writing plays (in 1967, at the invitation of Frank Corsaro, who directed my first play, *The Sweet Enemy,* for the Actors Studio), I have had a few stunning surprises too. Yet, in fact, very few—and even these have been instructive.

In the spring of 1990 I learned with much gratitude what can work—and what can't—on the stage. At the invitation of Jon Jory and Michael Dixon, I accepted a commission to write two linked one-act plays for the Humana Festival of New Plays at the Actors' Theatre of Louisville, *Tone Clusters* and *The Eclipse.* The first began as a purely conceptual piece, devoid of story: an idea, a mood, a sequence of jarring and discordant sounds. "Tone clusters" refers to the eerie, haunting, dissonant music, primarily for piano, composed by Charles Ives and Henry Cowell in the early twentieth century. The music is unsettling and abrades the nerves, suggesting as it does a radical disjuncture of perception; a sense that the universe is not after all harmonious or logical. In conjunction with these tone clusters of sound I envisioned philosophical inquiries of the kind humankind has posed since the pre-Socratic philosophers, but rarely answered—"Is the universe predetermined in every particular, or is mankind 'free'?"; "Where does identity reside?"—being put to an ordinary American couple of middle age, as in a hallucinatory television interview. The horror of the piece arises from its revelation that we reside in ignorance, not only of most of the information available to us, but of our own lives, our own motives: *Death wrapped in plastic garbage bags! in the basement! and we never knew, never had a premonition!* Only later, by degrees, in the writing of the play, did the nightmare interview become linked with a crime, thus with the specific, the timebound and finite. It is subsequently ironic to me that *Tone Clusters,* which exists in my imagination as a purely experimental work about the fracturing of reality in an electronic era, is always, for others, "about" a crime.

When rehearsals were begun in Louisville, however, under the direction of Steve Albreezi, and I saw actors inhabiting the roles (Adale O'Brien and Peter Michael Goetz), I soon realized the impracticability of my original vision. Why, I thought, there the Gulicks are, and they're *real.*

In my original idealism, or naiveté, I had even wanted the play's dialogue to be random, with no lines assigned to either speaker; a kind of aleatory music. What madness!

Equally impractical was my notion, for the second play, *The Eclipse,* that an actual eclipse—a "blade of darkness"—move from left to right across the stage, in mimicry of an older woman's relentless gravitation toward death. As soon as the gifted actresses Beth Dixon and Madeleine Sherwood inhabited their roles, this purely symbolic device became unnecessary. (I have left the direction in the play, however. My impractical idealism remains—maybe, somehow, it might be made to work?)

In my writing for the theater I always have in mind, as an undercurrent shaping and guiding the surface action, the ancient structure of drama as sacrificial rite. Stories are being told not by us but by way of us—"drama" is our formal acknowledgment of this paradox, which underscores our common humanity. Obviously, this phenomenon involves not only performers on a stage but an audience as well, for there is no ritual without community, and, perhaps, no community without ritual. To experience the play, the playwright must become a part of the audience, and this can occur only when there is an actual stage, living actors, voices other than one's own.

The question of how a writer knows when a work is fully realized is rather more of a riddle than a question. In terms of prose fiction and poetry, one writes, and rewrites, until there seems quite literally nothing more to say, or to feel; the mysterious inner integrity of the work has been expressed, and that phase of the writer's life is over. (Which is why writers so frequently occupy melancholy zones—always, we are being expelled from phases of our lives that, for sheer intensity and drama, can rarely be replicated in the real world.) Theater is the same, yet different: for the living work is communal, and there can be no final, fully realized performance.

I sense that my work is done when I feel, as I sit in the audience, that I am, not the playwright, nor even a quivering network of nerves invisibly linked to what is happening on the stage, but a member of the audience. In the theater, such distance, and such expulsion, is the point.

PART THREE

Writing

Writing about Drama

WHY WRITE?

People write about plays in order to clarify and to account for their responses to works that interest or excite or frustrate them. In order to put words on paper we have to take a second and a third look at what is in front of us and at what is within us. And so writing is a way of learning. The last word is never said about complex thoughts and feelings, but when we write we hope to make at least a little progress in the difficult but rewarding job of talking about our responses. We learn, and then we hope to interest our reader because we are communicating our responses to something that for one reason or another is worth talking about.

This communication is, in effect, teaching. You may think that you are writing for the teacher, but such a belief is a misconception; when you write, *you* are the teacher. An essay on a play is an attempt to help someone to see the play as you see it. If this chapter had to be boiled down to a single sentence of advice, that sentence would be: Because you are teaching, your essay should embody those qualities that you value in teachers—probably intelligence, open-mindedness, and effort; certainly a desire to offer what help you can.

ANALYSIS

Analysis is, literally, a separation into parts in order to understand. An analysis commonly considers one part and the relation of this part to the whole. For example, it may consider only the functions of the setting in *The Sandbox,* of the Fool in *King Lear,* or of the music in *Happy Days.*

Analysis, of course, is not a process used only in talking about literature. It is commonly applied in thinking about almost any complex matter. Boris Becker plays a deadly game of tennis; what makes it so good? How does his backhand contribute to his game? What does his serve do to the opponent? Because a play is usually long and complicated, in a paper written for a college course you probably do not have enough space to analyze all aspects of the play, and so you will probably choose one aspect and relate it to the whole. Of course all of the parts are related; a study of one character, for example, will have to take some account of other characters and of plot and perhaps even of setting; but, still, an analysis may legitimately devote most of its space to one part, taking account of other parts only insofar as they are relevant to the topic.

FINDING A TOPIC

If a work is fairly long and complex, and you are writing only a few pages, almost surely you will write an analysis of some part. Unless you have an enormous amount of time for reflection and revision, you cannot write a meaningful essay of five hundred or even a thousand words on *Oedipus* or *The Cherry Orchard.* You cannot even write on "Character in *Oedipus*" or "Symbolism in *The Cherry Orchard.*" And probably you won't really want to write on such topics anyway. Probably *one* character or *one* symbol has caught your interest. Trust your feelings; you are probably on to something interesting, and it will be best to think about this smaller topic for the relatively few hours that you have. A "smaller" topic need not be dull or trivial; treated properly, it may illuminate the entire work, or, to change the metaphor, it may serve as a mine shaft that gives entry to the work. "The Dramatic Function of the Gloucester Subplot in *King Lear,*" carefully thought about, will in five hundred or a thousand words tell a reader more (and will have taught its author more) than will "*King Lear* as a Tragedy." Similarly, "Imagery of Blindness in *King Lear*" is a better topic than "Imagery in *King Lear,*" and "The Meanings of 'Nature' in *King Lear*" is a better topic than "The Meaning of *King Lear.*"

Every play affords its own topics for analysis, and every essayist must set forth his or her own thesis, but a few useful generalizations may be made. You can often find a thesis by asking one of two questions:

1. *What is this doing?* That is, why is this scene in the play? Why is the Fool in *King Lear*? Why the music in *Happy Days*? Why are these lines verse and those lines prose? Why is a certain action reported to us rather than represented on the stage? What is the significance of the parts of the work? (Titles are often highly significant parts of the work: Ibsen's *A Doll's House* and Chekhov's *The Cherry Orchard* would be slightly different if they had other titles.)
2. *Why do I have this response?* Why do I find this scene clever, or moving, or puzzling? How did the author make this character funny or dignified or pathetic? How did he or she communicate the idea that this character is a bore without boring me?

The first of these questions, "What is this doing?" requires that you identify yourself with the dramatist, wondering, for example, whether this opening scene is the best possible for this story. The second question, "Why do I have this response?" requires that you trust your feelings. If you are amused or bored or puzzled or annoyed, assume that these responses are appropriate and follow them up, at least until a rereading of the play provides other responses.

Later, on page 774, we will suggest a good many questions that you can ask yourself in order to stimulate ideas for an essay, but here we will briefly suggest a few topics:

1. Compare two somewhat similar characters;
2. Discuss the function of a relatively minor character:
3. Compare a play with a film version of the play (what has been added, and what omitted, and why?);
4. Write the director's notes for one scene.

FROM TOPIC TO THESIS

How do you find a topic and how do you turn it into a thesis, that is, a point you want to make? An idea may hit you suddenly; as you are reading you find yourself jotting it in the margin, "Contrast with Nora's earlier response," or "Note the change of costume," or "too heavy irony," or "ugh." Or an idea may come slowly on rereading. Perhaps you gradually become aware that in *Antigone* the chorus may not be a static character but changes its views as the play progresses. At this point, then, you have a thesis—an angle—as well as a topic.

Think of it this way: a topic is a subject, and a thesis is a subject with a predicate: "Imagery in *King Lear*" is a topic, but it can be turned into a thesis thus: "Imagery helps to distinguish the characters in *King Lear.*" Once you can formulate a thesis, you are well on the way to writing a good paper. But note that the more precise the formulation of the thesis, the better the paper will probably be. After all, "Imagery in *King Lear* is interesting" is a thesis, but such a vague formulation gives you little to go on. Not until you can turn it into something like "Imagery in *King Lear* serves three important purposes" are you anywhere near to being able to draft your essay.

Following is a short essay written by a student. The student told us privately that when she began work on the paper she was planning to write on the irrationality of the fairies in *A Midsummer Night's Dream* as a sort of mirror of the irrationality of the young lovers, but when she searched the play for supporting detail she found, to her surprise, that she had to revise her thesis.

Her earliest jottings—a sort of preliminary outline and guide to rereading the play—looked like this:

fairies—like lovers, irrational?
  Puck
    mischievous
  Titania and Oberon
      equally quarrelsome?
        quarrel disturbs human world
      Titania wants Indian boy
        isn't she right?
          if so, she's not irrational
      Oberon
        jealous
        cruel to Titania?
        unfaithful?
  Other fairies
    do they do anything?
    T's different from O's?

In rereading the play, and in jotting down notes, she came to see that the supernatural characters were not as malicious and irrational as she had thought, and so she changed the focus of her thesis.

A SAMPLE ANALYSIS

Fairy Mischief and Morality and

A Midsummer Night's Dream

Title is informative.

If we read A Midsummer Night's Dream casually, or come away from a delightful performance, we may have the vague impression that the fairies are wild, mischievous, willful

Opening paragraph leads into the subject.

creatures who perhaps represent the irrational qualities of mankind. But in fact the text lends only a little support to this view. The irrationality of mankind is really represented chiefly by the human beings in the play--we are told in the first scene, for example, that Demetrius used to love Helena, but now loves Hermia--and the fairies are really largely responsible for the happy ending finally achieved.

It is, of course, easy to see why we may think of the fairies as wild and mischievous. Titania and Oberon have quarreled over a little Indian boy, and their quarrel had led to fogs, floods, and other disorders in nature. Moreover, Titania accuses Oberon of infidelity, and Oberon returns the charge:

Short quotation provides evidence.

> How canst thou thus for shame, Titania
> Glance at my credit with Hippolyta,
> Knowing I know thy love to Theseus?
> (2.1.74–76)[1]

Titania rejects this countercharge, saying "These are the forgeries of jealousy" (2.1.81), but we are not convinced of her innocence. It would be easy to give additional examples of speeches in which the king and queen of fairyland present unflattering pictures of each other, but probably one of the strongest pieces of evidence of their alleged irrationality is the fact that Oberon causes Titania to fall in love with the asinine Bottom. We should not forget, however, that later Oberon will take pity on her: "Her dotage now I do begin to pity" (4.1.46).

Citation in parentheses to reduce the number of footnotes.

In fact, it is largely through Oberon's sense of pity--this time for the quarreling young lovers in the forest--that the lovers finally are successfully paired off. And we should

Footnote gives source, and explains that other footnotes will not be necessary.

[1] All quotations from this play are from the text reprinted in Sylvan Barnet, Morton Berman, and William Burto, <u>Types of Drama,</u> 6th ed. (New York: HarperCollins, 1993). Further references to the play will be given parenthetically, within the text of the essay.

remember, too, before we claim that the fairies are consistently quarrelsome and mischievous, that at the very end of the play Oberon and Titania join in a song and dance blessing the newlyweds and promising healthy offspring. The fairies, though quarrelsome, are fundamentally benevolent spirits.

The main point having been set forth, essayist now turns to an apparent exception.

But what of Robin Goodfellow, the Puck of this play? Is he not mischievous? One of the fairies says Robin is a "shrewd and knavish sprite" (2.1.33) who frightens maids and plays tricks on housewives; Robin admits the charge, saying "Thou speakest aright" (2.1.42), and two lines later he says "I jest to Oberon, and make him smile," and then he goes on to describe some of his practical jokes, including his fondness for neighing to tease a horse, and pulling a stool from under an old lady. But this is not quite the whole story. The fact is, despite this speech, that we do <u>not</u> see Robin engage in any mischievous pranks. After all, he does not deliberately anoint the eyes of the wrong Athenian lover. Oberon tells Robin that he will recognize the young man by his Athenian clothing, and when Puck encounters a young man in Athenian clothing he anoints the youth's eyes. The fault is really Oberon's, though of course Oberon meant well when he instructed Robin:

Essayist concedes a point, but then goes on in the rest of the paragraph to argue that the main point nevertheless still holds.

> A sweet Athenian lady is in love
> With a disdainful youth. Anoint his eyes;
> But do it when the next thing he espies
> May be the lady.
>
> (2.1.260–263)

So Robin's error is innocent. He is speaking honestly when he says, "Believe me, king of shadows, I mistook" (3.2.347). Of course he does enjoy the confusion he mistakenly causes, but we can hardly blame him severely for that. After all, we enjoy it, too.

Concluding paragraph summarizes, but it does not merely repeat what has come before; it offers a few brief new quotations. The paragraph ends by setting the conclusion (fairies are decent) in a fresh context (it's the mortals who are irrational).

The fairies, by their very nature, of course suggest a mysterious, irrational world, but--even though, as we have just seen, Oberon is called the "king of shadows"--they are not to be confused with "ghosts, wand'ring here and there," "damnèd spirits" who "willfully themselves exile from light/ And must for aye consort with black-browed night" (3.2.381–387). Oberon explicitly says, after this speech, "But we are spirits of another sort," and his speech is filled with references not to darkness but to light: "morning," "eastern gate," "blessèd beams." The closer we observe them in the play, then, the closer their behavior is to that of normal, decent human beings. There is plenty of irrationality in the play, but it is found for the most part in the mortals.

Notice that this first-rate essay

1. has a thesis, and
2. develops the thesis effectively.

Notice also that

3. the title gives the reader some idea of what is coming, and
4. the first paragraph pretty clearly sets forth the thesis.
5. The essay next takes up the evidence that might seem to contradict the thesis—Oberon and Titania, and Robin Goodfellow—and it shows that this evidence is not decisive.
6. All the while, then, the essay is moving forward, substantiating the thesis,
7. especially by using well-chosen quotations.
8. The last paragraph slightly restates the thesis, in light of what the essay has demonstrated.

WRITING A REVIEW

Your instructor may ask you to write a review of a local production. A review requires analytic skill but it is not identical with an analysis. First of all, a reviewer normally assumes that the reader is unfamiliar with the production being reviewed, and unfamiliar with the play if the play is not a classic. Thus, the first paragraph usually provides a helpful introduction, along these lines:

> Marsha Norman's new play, *'night, Mother,* a tragedy with only two actors and one set, shows us a woman's preparation for suicide. Jessie has concluded that she no longer wishes to live, and so she tries to put her affairs into order, which chiefly means preparing her rather uncomprehending mother to get along without her.

Inevitably some retelling of the plot is necessary if the play is new, and a summary of a sentence or two is acceptable even for a familiar play, but the review will chiefly be concerned with

1. describing,
2. analyzing, and, especially,
3. evaluating.

(By the way, don't confuse description with analysis. Description tells what something—for instance, the set or the costumes—looks like; analysis tells us how they work, what they add up to, what they contribute to the total effect.) If the play is new, much of the evaluation may center on the play itself, but if the play is a classic, the evaluation probably will be devoted chiefly to the acting, the set, and the direction.

Other points:

1. **Save the playbill;** it will give you the names of the actors, and perhaps a brief biography of the author, a synopsis of the plot, and a photograph of the set, all of which may be helpful.
2. **Draft your review as soon as possible,** while the performance is still fresh in your mind. If you can't draft it immediately after seeing the play, at least jot down some notes about the setting and the staging, the acting, and the audience's response.
3. If possible, **read the play**—ideally, before the performance and again after it.
4. **In your first draft, don't worry about limitations of space;** write as long a review as you can, putting down everything that comes to mind. Later you can cut it to the required length, retaining only the chief points and the necessary supporting details. But in your first draft try to produce a fairly full record of the performance and your response to it, so that a day or two later, when you revise, you won't have to trust a fading memory for details.

If you read reviews of plays in *Time, Newsweek,* or a newspaper, you will soon develop a sense of what reviews normally do.

The following example, an undergraduate's review of a college production of *Macbeth,* is typical except in one respect: reviews of new plays customarily include a few sentences summarizing the plot and classifying the play (a tragedy, a farce, a rock musical, or whatever), perhaps briefly putting it into the context of the author's other works, but because *Macbeth* is so widely known the reviewer has chosen not to risk offending her readers by telling them that *Macbeth* is a tragedy by Shakespeare.

A SAMPLE REVIEW

An Effective Macbeth

Title implies thesis.

Macbeth at the University Theater is a thoughtful and occasionally exciting production, partly because the director, Mark Urice, has trusted Shakespeare and has not imposed a gimmick on the play. The characters do not wear cowboy costumes as they did in last year's production of A Midsummer Night's Dream.

Opening paragraph is informative, letting the reader know the reviewer's overall attitude.

Probably the chief problem confronting a director of Macbeth is how to present the witches so that they are powerful supernatural forces and not silly things that look

Reviewer promptly turns to a major issue.

as though they came from a Halloween party. Urice gives us ugly but not absurdly grotesque witches, and he introduces them most effectively. The stage seems to be a bombed-out battlefield littered with rocks and great chunks of earth, but some of these begin to stir--the earth seems to come alive--and the clods move, unfold, and become the witches, dressed in brown and dark gray rags. The suggestion is that the witches are a part of nature, elemental forces that can hardly be escaped. This effect is increased by the moans and creaking noises that they make, all of which could be comic but which in this production are impressive.

First sentence of this paragraph provides an effective transition.

The witches' power over Macbeth is further emphasized by their actions. When the witches first meet Macbeth, they encircle him, touch him, caress him, even embrace him, and he seems helpless, almost their plaything. Moreover, in the scene in which he imagines that he sees a dagger, the director has arranged for one of the witches to appear, stand near Macbeth, and guide his hand toward the invisible dagger. This is, of course, not in the text, but the interpretation is reasonable rather than intrusive. Finally, near the end of the play, just before Macduff kills Macbeth, a witch appears and laughs at Macbeth as Macduff explains that he was not "born of woman." There is no doubt that throughout the tragedy Macbeth has been a puppet of the witches.

Paragraph begins with a broad assertion and then offers supporting details.

Stephen Beers (Macbeth) and Tina Peters (Lady Macbeth) are excellent. Beers is sufficiently brawny to be convincing as a battlefield hero, but he also speaks the lines sensitively, so the audience feels that in addition to being a hero, he is a man of gentleness. One can believe Lady Macbeth when she says that she fears he is "too full o' the milk of human kindness" to murder Duncan. Lady Macbeth is especially effective in the scene in which she asks the spirits to "unsex her." During this speech she is reclining on a bed and as she delivers the lines she becomes increasingly sexual in her

Reference to a particular scene.

bodily motions, deriving excitement from her own stimulating words. Her attachment to Macbeth is strongly sexual, and so is his attraction to her. The scene when she persuades him to kill Duncan ends with them passionately embracing. The strong attraction of each for the other, so evident in the early part of the play, disappears after the murder, when Macbeth keeps his distance from Lady Macbeth and does not allow her to touch him. The acting of the other performers is effective, except for John Berens (Duncan), who recites the lines mechanically and seems not to take much account of their meaning.

The set consists of a barren plot at the rear of which stands a spidery framework of piping of the sort used by construction companies, supporting a catwalk. This framework fits with the costumes (lots of armor, leather, heavy boots), suggesting a sort of elemental, primitive, and somewhat sadistic world. The catwalk, though effectively used when Macbeth goes off to murder Duncan (whose room is presumably upstairs and offstage) is not much used in later scenes. For the most part it is an interesting piece of scenery but it is not otherwise helpful. For instance, there is no reason why the scene with Macduff's wife and children is staged on it. The costumes are not in any way Scottish--no plaids--but in several scenes the sound of a bagpipe is heard, adding another weird or primitive tone to the production.

Description, but also analysis.

Concrete details to support evaluation.

This Macbeth appeals to the eye, the ear, and the mind. The director has given us a unified production that makes sense and that is faithful to the spirit of Shakespeare's play.

Summary.

Much of what we want to say about this review we have already said in our marginal notes, but three additional points should be made:

1. The reviewer's feelings and evaluations are clearly expressed, not in such expressions as "furthermore I feel," and "it is also my opinion," but in such expressions as "a thoughtful and occasionally exciting production," "excellent," and "appeals to the eye, the ear, and the mind."

2. The evaluations are supported by details. For instance, the evaluation that the witches are effectively presented is supported by a brief description of their appearance.
3. The reviewer is courteous, even when (as in the discussion of the catwalk, in the next-to-last paragraph) she is talking about aspects of the production she doesn't care for.

WRITING A COMPARISON Something should be said about an essay organized around a comparison or a contrast between, say, two characters—in one play or even in two plays. Probably the student's first thought, after making some jottings, is to discuss half of the comparison and then go on to the second half. Instructors and textbooks usually condemn such an organization, arguing that the essay breaks into two parts and that the second part involves a good deal of repetition of categories set up in the first part. Usually they recommend that the student organize his or her thoughts differently, somewhat along the lines:

1. First similarity
   a. first work (or character, or characteristic)
   b. second work
2. Secondary similarity
   a. first work
   b. second work
3. First difference
   a. first work
   b. second work
4. Second difference
   a. first work
   b. second work

and so on, for as many additional differences as seen relevant. For example, if one wishes to compare King Lear with King Oedipus, one may organize the material thus:

1. First similarity: Each figure is a person of great authority
   a. Lear
   b. Oedipus
2. Second similarity: Each figure is ignorant
   a. Lear's ignorance of his daughters
   b. Oedipus's ignorance of his birth
3. First difference: Stage at which the character attains self-knowledge
   a. Lear's early recognition
   b. Oedipus's continuing ignorance until late in the play

Here is another way of organizing a comparison and contrast:

1. First point: Lack of self-knowledge
   a. similarities between Lear and Oedipus
   b. differences between Lear and Oedipus

2. Second point: The corrupt world
   a. similarities between the worlds in *King Lear* and *Oedipus*
   b. differences between the worlds in *King Lear* and *Oedipus*
3. Third point: Degree of attainment of self-knowledge
   a. similarities between Lear and Oedipus
   b. differences between Lear and Oedipus

A SIMPLE, EFFECTIVE ORGANIZATION FOR A COMPARISON

But a comparison need not employ either of these structures. There is even the danger that an essay employing either of them may not come into focus until the essayist stands back from the seven-layer cake and announces, in the concluding paragraph, that the odd layers taste better. In one's preparatory thinking, one may want to make comparisons in pairs (Faults: Lear and Oedipus; Children: Lear's daughters, Oedipus's sons; Comments by others: the Fool on Lear, the Chorus on Oedipus . . .), but one must come to some conclusions about what these add up to before writing the final version. This final version should not duplicate one's thought processes; rather, it should be organized so as to make the point clearly and effectively. After reflection, one may believe that although there are superficial similarities between Lear and Oedipus, there are essential differences; then in the finished essay one probably will not wish to obscure the main point by jumping back and forth from play to play, working through a series of similarities and differences. It may be better to discuss King Lear and then point out that, although Oedipus resembles him in *A, B,* and *C,* Oedipus in *D, E,* and *F* does *not* resemble Lear. Some repetition in the second half of the essay (for example, "Oedipus comes very late to the deep self-knowledge that we see Lear achieve by the middle of the play") will serve to bind the two halves into a meaningful whole, making clear the degree of similarity or difference.

The point of the essay presumably is not to list pairs of similarities or differences but to illuminate a work, or works, by making thoughtful comparison. Although in a long essay one cannot postpone until page 30 a discussion of the second half of the comparison, in an essay of, say, fewer than ten pages nothing is wrong with setting forth first one half of the comparison and then, in light of it, the second half. The essay will break into two unrelated parts if the second half makes no use of the first, or if it fails to modify the first half, but not if the second half looks back to the first half and calls attention to differences that the new material reveals. Students ought to learn how to write an essay with interwoven comparisons, but they ought also to know that there is another, simpler and clearer way to write a comparison.

COMMUNICATING JUDGMENTS

Because a critical essay on a play is a judicious attempt to help a reader see what is going on in a work or in a part of a work, the voice of the critic sounds, on first hearing, impartial; but good criticism includes—at least implicitly—evaluation. You can say not only that the setting changes (a neutral expression) but also that "the playwright aptly shifts the setting" or "unconvincingly introduces a new character," or "effectively juxtaposes . . ." These evaluations you support with evidence. You have feelings about the work under discussion, and you reveal them, as we have already pointed out in our discussion of the review of *Macbeth,* not by continually saying "I feel" and "this moves me," but by calling attention to the degree of success or failure you perceive. Nothing is wrong with occasionally using "I," and noticeable avoidances of it—passives, "this writer," "we," and the like—suggest an offensive sham modesty; but too much talk of "I" makes a writer sound like an egomaniac.

ASKING QUESTIONS TO GET ANSWERS

On page 756 we set forth a few topics for essays, such as the function of a relatively minor character. We have already suggested that you can often find a thesis by asking two questions: *What is this doing?* and *Why do I have this response?* In a moment we will suggest many additional questions, but first we want to mention that the editorial apparatus throughout this book is intended to help you to read, enjoy, and discuss drama as fully as possible. When you are sitting down to write about a play, you may want to reread some parts of this apparatus for guidance on your topic, perhaps paying special attention to the Glossary entries on **character, convention, dialogue, diction, foil, irony, motivation, plot, suspense,** and **unity.** You may also want to reread some of the earlier material in the book, especially "The Language of Drama."

Now for additional questions that may help you to find topics and to sharpen them into theses.

Plot and Conflict

1. Does the exposition introduce elements that will be ironically fulfilled? During the exposition do you perceive things differently from the way the characters perceive them?
2. Are certain happenings or situations recurrent? If so, what significance do you attach to them?
3. If the play has more than one plot, do the plots seem to be related? Is one plot clearly the main plot, and another plot a sort of subplot, a minor variation on the theme?
4. Do any scenes strike you as irrelevant?
5. Are certain scenes so strongly foreshadowed that you anticipated them? If so, did the happenings in these scenes merely fulfill your expectations, or did they also surprise you?
6. What kinds of conflict are presented? One character against another, one group against another, one part of a personality against another part in the same person?
7. How is the conflict resolved? By an unambiguous triumph of one side, or by a triumph that is also in some degree a loss for the triumphant side? Do you find the resolution satisfying, or unsettling, or what? Why?

Character

1. A dramatic character is not likely to be thoroughly realistic, a copy of someone we might know. Still, we may ask if the character is consistent and coherent. If not, why not? We may also ask whether the character is complex or is a rather simple representative of some human type.
2. How is the character defined? Consider what the character says and does and what others say about him or her and do to him or her. Also consider other characters who more or less resemble the character in question, because the similarities—and the differences—may be significantly revealing.

3. How trustworthy are the characters when they characterize themselves? When they characterize others?
4. Do characters change as the play goes on, or do we simply know them better at the end?
5. What do you make of the minor characters? Are they merely necessary to the plot, or are they foils to other characters? Or do they serve some other functions?
6. If a character is tragic, does the tragedy seem to proceed from a moral flaw, from an intellectual error, from the malice of others, from sheer chance, or from some combination of these?
7. What are the character's goals? To what degree do you sympathize with them? If a character is comic, do you laugh *with* or *at* the character?
8. Do you think the characters are adequately motivated?
9. Is a given character so meditative that you feel he or she is engaged less in a dialogue with others than in a dialogue with the self? If so, do you feel that this character is in large degree a spokesperson for the author, commenting not only on the world of the play but also on the outside world?

Nonverbal Language

1. If the playwright does not provide full stage directions, try to imagine for at least one scene what gestures and tones might accompany each speech. (The first scene is usually a good one to try your hand at.)
2. What do you make of the setting? Does it help reveal character? Do changes of scene strike you as symbolic? If so, symbolic of what?
3. Do certain costumes (dark suits, flowery shawls, stiff collars, etc.) or certain properties (books, pictures, toys, candlesticks, etc.) strike you as symbolic? If so, symbolic of what?

The Play on Film

1. If the play has been turned into a film, what has been added? What has been omitted? Why?
2. Has the film medium been used to advantage—for example, in focusing attention through close-ups or reaction shots (shots showing not the speaker but a person reacting to the speaker)? Or do some of the inventions, such as outdoor scenes that were not possible in the play, seem mere busy work, distracting from the urgency or the unity of the play?

ORGANIZING AN ESSAY

Like a play, an essay on a play should be organized, and one can hardly go wrong in saying (as Aristotle said of plays) that an essay should have a beginning, a middle, and an end.

In the *beginning,* probably in the first paragraph, it's usually a good idea to state your thesis. You don't have to state it in the first sentence (you may, for example, want to open with a quotation from the play), but state it early and clearly. In the *middle,* support your thesis with evidence, probably including some brief quotations from the play.

The middle, like the essay as a whole, should be organized. For example, if you are discussing the development of a character, you will probably want to move through the play act by act; if you are discussing symbolism—maybe blindness in *King Lear*—you may first want to discuss literal blindness (Gloucester's eyes are put out), and then figurative blindness (Lear doesn't "see" what he is doing). Probably you'll move from the obvious to the less obvious, or from the less important to the more important, in order to avoid a sense of anticlimax.

In the *end,* or conclusion, you will briefly recapitulate, but try also (lest your conclusion strike the reader as nothing more than an unnecessary restatement of what you said a moment ago) to set your findings in a larger context, the context of the entire play.

SUMMARY: HOW TO WRITE AN EFFECTIVE ESSAY

All writers must work out their own procedures and rituals (John C. Calhoun liked to plough his farm before writing), but the following suggestions provide some help.

1. **Read the play carefully.**

2. **Choose a worthwhile and manageable subject,** something that interests you and is not so big that your handling of it must be superficial. As you work, shape your topic into a thesis, moving, for example, from "The Character of King Lear" to "Change in King Lear."

3. **Reread the play, jotting down notes** of all relevant matters. As you read, reflect on your reading and record your reflections. If you have a feeling or an idea, jot it down; don't assume that you will remember it when you get around to writing your essay. The margins of this book are a good place for initial jottings, but many people find that in the long run it is easier to transfer these notes to 3×5 cards, writing on one side only.

4. **Sort out your cards** into some kind of reasonable division, and reject cards irrelevant to your topic. If you have adequately formulated your thesis (let's say, "Tom, not Laura, is the central character in *The Glass Menagerie*") you ought to be able to work out a tentative organization. As you work you may discover a better way to group your notes. If so, start reorganizing. Speaking generally, it is a good idea to organize your essay from the lesser material to the greater (to avoid anticlimax) or from the simple to the complex (to ensure intelligibility). If, for example, you are discussing the roles of three characters, it may be best to build up to the one of the three that you think the most important. If you are comparing two characters, it may be best to move from the most obvious contrasts to the least obvious. (In your opening paragraph, which will probably be almost the last thing you will write, you should of course give the reader an idea of the scope of the paper, but at this stage you are organizing the material chiefly for yourself and so you need not yet worry about an introductory paragraph.) When you have arranged your notes into a meaningful sequence of packets, you have approximately divided your material into paragraphs.

5. **Get it down on paper.** Most essayists find it useful to jot down some sort of outline, indicating the main idea of each paragraph and, under each main idea, supporting details that give it substance. An outline—not necessarily anything highly formal with capital and lowercase letters and roman and arabic numerals but merely key phrases in

some sort of order—will help you to overcome the paralysis called "writer's block" that commonly afflicts professionals as well as students. A page of paper with ideas in some sort of sequence, however rough, ought to encourage you that you do have something to say. And so, despite the temptation to sharpen another pencil or to put a new ribbon into the typewriter, the best thing to do at this point is to sit down and start writing.

If you don't feel that you can work from note cards and a rough outline, try another method: get something down on paper, writing freely, sloppily, automatically, or whatever, but allow your ideas about what the work means to you and how it conveys its meaning—rough as they may be—to begin to take visible form. If you are like most people, you can't do much precise thinking until you have committed to paper at least a rough sketch of your initial ideas. Later you can push and polish your ideas into shape, perhaps even deleting all of them and starting over, but it's a lot easier to improve your ideas once you see them in front of you than it is to do the job in your head. On paper (or on a computer screen) one word leads to another; in your head one word often blocks another.

Just keep going; you may realize, as you near the end of a sentence, that you no longer believe it. O.K.; be glad that your first idea led you to a better one, and pick up your better one and keep going with it. What you are doing is, in a sense, by trial and error pushing your way not only toward clear expression but toward sharper ideas and richer responses.

6. If there is time, **reread the play,** looking for additional material that strengthens or weakens your main point; take account of it in your outline or draft.

7. **With your outline or draft in front of you, write a more lucid version,** checking your notes for fuller details, such as supporting quotations. If, as you work, you find that some of the points in your earlier jottings are no longer relevant, eliminate them; but make sure that the argument flows from one point to the next. As you write, your ideas will doubtless become clearer; some may prove to be poor ideas. (We rarely know exactly what our ideas are until we have them set down on paper. As the little girl said, replying to the suggestion that she should think before she spoke, "How do I know what I think until I say it?") Not until you have written a draft do you really have a strong sense of how good your essay may be.

8. After a suitable interval, preferably a few days, **read the draft with a view toward revising it,** not with a view toward congratulating yourself. A revision, after all, is a re-vision, a second (and presumably sharper) view. When you revise, you will be in the company of Picasso, who said that in painting a picture he advanced by a series of destructions. A revision—say, the addition of an example, or the reorganization of the sequence of examples, or even the substitution of a precise word for an imprecise one—is not a matter of prettifying but of thinking. As you read, correct things that disturb you (for example, awkward repetitions that bore, inflated utterances that grate), add supporting detail where the argument is undeveloped (a paragraph of only one or two sentences is usually an undeveloped paragraph), and ruthlessly delete irrelevancies however well written they may be. But remember that a deletion probably requires some adjustment in the preceding and subsequent material. Make sure that the opening

paragraph gives the readers some sense of where they will be going, and that between the opening and the closing paragraphs the argument, aided by transitions (such as "furthermore," "on the other hand," "in the next scene"), runs smoothly. The details should be relevant, the organization reasonable, the argument clear. Check all quotations for accuracy. Quotations are evidence, usually intended to support your assertions, and it is not nice to alter the evidence, even unintentionally. If there is time (there almost never is), put the revision aside, reread it in a day or two, and revise it again, especially with a view toward shortening it.

9. **Type or write a clean copy,** following the principles concerning margins, pagination, footnotes, and so on set forth in the next section of this discussion. If you have borrowed any ideas, be sure to give credit, usually in footnotes, to your sources. Remember that plagiarism is not limited to the unacknowledged borrowing of words; a borrowed idea, even when put into your own words, requires acknowledgment.

10. **Proofread and make corrections.**

BASIC MANUSCRIPT FORM

Much of what follows regarding basic manuscript form is nothing more than common sense.

1. Use 8½ × 11 paper of good weight. Keep as lightweight a carbon copy as you wish, or make a photocopy, but hand in a sturdy original.
2. If you typewrite or use a word processor, be sure to use a reasonably fresh ribbon, double-space, and type on one side of the page only. If you submit a handwritten copy, use lined paper and write on one side of the page only, in ink, on every other line. Most instructors do *not* want papers to be enclosed in any sort of binder; and most instructors want papers to be stapled in the upper left corner; do not crimp or crease corners and expect them to hold together.
3. Leave an adequate margin—an inch or an inch and a half—at top, bottom, and sides.
4. Number the pages consecutively, using arabic numerals in the upper right-hand corner.
5. Put your name and class or course number in the upper left-hand corner of the first page. It is a good idea to put your name in the upper right corner of each later page so that your essay can be easily reassembled if a page gets separated.
6. Create your own title—one that reflects your topic or thesis. For example, a paper on *The Glass Menagerie* should not be called "*The Glass Menagerie*" but might be called "Tom's Romanticization of Laura: A View of *The Glass Menagerie*."
7. Center the title of your essay below the top margin of the first page. Begin the first word of the title with a capital, and capitalize each subsequent word except articles (*the, a, an*) and prepositions (*in, on, or, with,* and so forth), thus:

The Truth of Dreams in A Midsummer Night's Dream

8. Begin the essay an inch or two below the title.

9. Your extensive revisions should have been made in your drafts, but minor last-minute revisions may be made—neatly—on the finished copy. Proofreading may catch some typographical errors, and you may notice some small weaknesses. Additions should be made *above* the line, with a caret (^) *below* the line to indicate placement of the correction. Mark deletions by drawing a horizontal line through the word or words you wish to delete. Delete a single letter by drawing a vertical line through it. Use a vertical line, too, to separate words that should not have been run together.

QUOTATIONS AND QUOTATION MARKS

Excerpts from the plays you are writing about are indispensable. Such quotations not only let the reader know what you are talking about, they present the material you are responding to, thus letting the reader share your responses.

Here are some mechanical matters:

1. Identify the speaker or writer of the quotation, so that the reader is not left with a sense of uncertainty. Usually this identification precedes the quoted material (for example, "Smith says . . .") in accordance with the principle of letting readers know where they are going, but occasionally it may follow the quotation, especially if it will provide something of a pleasant surprise. For instance, in a discussion of Williams's *The Glass Menagerie,* you might quote a comment that seems to belittle the play and then reveal that Williams himself was the speaker.

2. The quotation must fit grammatically into your sentence. Suppose you want to use Lear's line, addressed to the Fool, "In boy; go first." Do *not* say:

> In 3.4, in response to Lear's command, the Fool "go first."

You'll have to say something like this:

> In 3.4, in response to Lear's command to "go first," the Fool enters the hovel.

Or, of course, you can say,

> In 3.4, Lear says to the Fool, "In boy; go first," and the Fool obeys.

3. The quotation must be exact. Any material that you add—even one or two words—must be in square brackets, thus:

> When Lear says, "In boy; go [into the hovel] first," he shows a touch of humility.

If you wish to omit material from within a quotation, indicate the ellipsis by three spaced periods. If a sentence ends in an omission, add a closed-up period and then three spaced periods to indicate the omission. The following example is based on a quotation from the sentences immediately above this one:

> The instructions say that "if you . . . omit material from within a quotation, [you must] indicate the ellipsis. . . . If a sentence ends in an omission, add a closed-up period and then three spaced periods. . . ."

Notice that although material preceded "If you," periods are not needed to indicate the omission because "If you" began a sentence in the original. Customarily, initial and terminal omissions are indicated only when they are part of the sentence you are quoting. Even such omissions need not be indicated when the quoted material is obviously incomplete—when, for instance, it is a word or phrase. Notice, too, that although quotations must be given word for word, the initial capitalization can be adapted, as here where "If" is reduced to "if."

When a line or more of verse is omitted from a passage that is set off, the three spaced periods are printed on a separate line:

> If we shadows have offended,
> Think but this, and all is mended;
>
> . . .
>
> Give me your hands, if we be friends,
> And Robin shall restore amends.

4. Distinguish between short and long quotations, and treat each appropriately. Short quotations (usually defined as fewer than three lines of verse or five lines of prose) are enclosed within quotation marks and run into the text (rather than set off, without quotation marks). Examples:

> Near the end of Oedipus Rex the Chorus reminds the audience that Oedipus "solved the famous riddle," but it does not tell us what the riddle was.

> King Lear's first long speech begins authoritatively: "Meantime we shall express our darker purpose. / Give me the map there. Know that we have divided / In three our kingdom." His authoritative manner is evident throughout the act.

Notice in the first passage that although four words only are being quoted, quotation marks are used, indicating that these are Sophocles's words, not the essayist's. Notice that in the second example a slash (diagonal line, virgule) is used to indicate the end of a line of verse other than the last line quoted. The slash is, of course, not used for prose, and it is not used if poetry is set off, indented, and printed as verse, thus:

> King Lear's first long speech begins authoritatively:
>
> > Meantime we shall express our darker purpose.
> > Give me the map there. Know that we have divided

In three our kingdom; and 'tis our fast intent
To shake all cares and business from our age,
Conferring them on younger strengths, while we
Unburthened crawl toward death.

Material that is set off (usually three or more lines of verse, five or more lines of prose) is *not* enclosed within quotation marks. To set it off, triple-space before and after the quotation and single-space the quotation. Poetry should be centered; prose quotations should be flush with both right and left margins. (Note: Some manuals of style call for double-spacing, some for indenting prose quotations; but whichever procedure you adopt, be consistent. Be sparing in your use of long quotations.) Use quotations as evidence, not as padding. Do not bore the reader with material that can be effectively reduced either by paraphrase or by cutting. If you cut, indicate ellipses as explained above under 3.

5. Commas and periods go inside the quotation marks. (Exception: if the quotation is immediately followed by material in parentheses or in square brackets, close the quotation, then give the parenthetic or bracketed material, and then—after the closing parenthesis or bracket, put the comma or period.)

Semicolons, colons, and dashes go outside quotation marks. Question marks and exclamation points go inside if they are part of the quotation, outside if they are your own. In the following example, the first two question marks are Shakespeare's, so they go *inside* the quotation marks. The third question mark, however, is the essayist's, so it goes *outside* the quotation marks.

Lear asks the beggar, "Dids't thou give all to thy daughters?" The beggar's reply is, "Who gives anything to Poor Tom?" Are we surprised when he goes on to say, "Do Poor Tom some charity, whom the foul fiend vexes"?

6. Use *single* quotation marks for material contained within a quotation that itself is within quotation marks, thus:

The editors of Types of Drama say, "With Puck we look at the antics in the forest, smile tolerantly, and say with a godlike perspective, 'Lord, what fools these mortals be!'"

7. Use quotation marks around titles of short works, that is, for titles of chapters in books and for essays that might not be published by themselves. Unpublished works, even book-length dissertations, are also enclosed in quotation marks. Use italics (indicated by underlining) for books, that is, for plays, periodicals, and collections of essays.

A NOTE ON FOOTNOTES AND ENDNOTES

You may wish to use a footnote or endnote, telling the reader that the passage you are quoting is found in this book on such-and-such a page. Let us assume that you have already mentioned the author and the title of the play and have just quoted a passage. At the end of the sentence that includes the quotation, or at the end of the quotation if you are offering it as an independent sentence, following the period type or write the number 1, elevating it slightly above the line. Do not put a period after the digit. Near the bottom of the paper, indent five spaces and type or write the number 1, elevated and without a period. Then write (giving the appropriate page number):

> [1]Reprinted in Sylvan Barnet, Morton Berman, and William Burto, Types of Drama, 6th ed. (New York: HarperCollins, 1993), p. 236.

Notice that the abbreviation for *page* is p., not pg.; the abbreviation for *pages* is pp., thus: pp. 236–237. For verse plays whose lines are numbered, the usual procedure is not to cite a page but to cite act, scene, and line numbers in parentheses after the quotation. The old method was to give the act in capital roman numerals, the scene in small roman numerals, and the line in arabic numerals, with periods following the act and scene (V.i.7–11), but the preferred method today is to give the act, scene, and line (if numbered in the text) in arabic numerals, with periods but no extra spaces.

> The lunatic, the lover and the poet
> Are of imagination all compact.
> One sees more devils than vast hell can hold,
> That is the madman. The lover, all as frantic,
> Sees Helen's beauty in a brow of Egypt.
> (5.1.7-11)[1]

The footnote will then read:

> [1]All quotations from A Midsummer Night's Dream are from the text reprinted in Sylvan Barnet, Morton Berman, and William Burto, Types of Drama, 6th ed. (New York: HarperCollins, 1993).

If you have not mentioned the author or title of the work quoted, you need to give that information in the note, thus:

> [1]William Shakespeare, A Midsummer Night's Dream, reprinted in Sylvan Barnet, Morton Berman, and William Burto, Types of Drama, 6th ed. (New York: HarperCollins, 1993).

If you have mentioned the author, but not the work, the note will go thus:

> [1]A Midsummer Night's Dream, reprinted in Sylvan Barnet, Morton Berman, and William Burto, Types of Drama, 6th ed. (New York: HarperCollins, 1993).

In short, you need not give information in the note that is already given in the main body of the essay.

In order to eliminate writing many footnotes, each one merely citing the page of a quotation, you can say, in the first footnote, after giving the bibliographical information as above, something like this:

> All further references to this work will be given parenthetically, within the text of the essay.

Thus, when you quote the next passage from the play, at the end of the sentence—just before the period—you need only insert a pair of parentheses enclosing the page number or the act, scene, and line number. Here is an example:

> At this point Lear goes out, saying, "O Fool, I shall go mad!" (p. 208).

or

> At this point Lear goes out, saying, "O Fool, I shall go mad!" (II.iv.282).

Notice that in the sample analysis on pp. 757–60 the author used only one footnote and then cited all of the other quotations parenthetically.

A NOTE ON INTERNAL CITATIONS

If you use secondary sources, your instructor may want you to cite your source—usually an authority you are quoting or summarizing—parenthetically, within the body of your paper. Here is an example, citing page 29 of a book:

> In Comic Women, Tragic Men, Linda Bamber says that in Shakespeare's plays, "The natural order, the status quo, is for men to rule women" (29).

Or:

> In Shakespeare's plays "the natural order," Bamber says, "is for men to rule women" (29), but she goes on to modify this statement.

At the end of your paper, on a separate page, give a list headed "Works Cited," listing all of your sources, alphabetically by author, with last name first, then the title (underlined, to indicate italics), then the place of publication, the publisher, and the date. After the date, type a period.

> Bamber, Linda. Comic Women, Tragic Men. Stanford. Stanford UP, 1982.

For details on how to cite journals, books published in more than one volume, translations, and dozens of other troublesome works, see Joseph Gibaldi and Walter S. Achtert, *MLA Handbook for Writers of Research Papers,* 2nd ed. (New York: MLA, 1984). (By the way, MLA stands for Modern Language Association.)

Writing Drama

Your instructor may ask you to write some dialogue, such as might constitute one scene in a realistic play; or you may be asked to turn some classic short story into a one-act play, or even to write an original one-act play.

WRITING A SCENE

If you are asked to write a scene that might be part of a longer work, once you have settled on the situation, try to get your characters fairly clearly in mind even before you begin writing—though of course once you start writing you will doubtless revise your view of them.

Where do you start? Where do you find your characters? All writers are asked where they get their ideas, and the answers vary greatly. Some writers draw on their family and friends, others begin with something they may have glimpsed on the street (a well-dressed woman accompanied by a disheveled man) or with a scrap of conversation they have overheard on the bus ("So I told him I'd do what I could, but I wouldn't do *that*"), and from this they imagine a relationship and invent dialogue.

Whether you start with some such sight or sound, or whether you begin by imagining characters, think hard about who these people are. Let's say that your scene concerns a college student who tells her parents that she is dropping out of college:

What is their race and ethnic background?
What do they wear?
What sort of furnishings surround them?
What kinds of food do they eat?
How old are they?
How much money do they have?
What are their attitudes toward education? Why?
Is the student immature, mature, troubled, timid, adventurous, or what?
What gestures do the characters use?
How do they stand or sit?
How do they speak (thoughtfully, hesitantly, vigorously)?
What sort of vocabulary do they use? What are their speech rhythms?
What sorts of people are the parents? Is the father intolerant but the mother sympathetic, or the father baffled and the mother hostile, or what?

Further, if (for instance) you conceive of the mother as intolerant of the daughter's goals, *why* is she intolerant? Because she is afraid that the daughter will excel her? Or because, on the contrary, she strongly feels her own limitations and is so eager for her daughter to transcend them that she cannot understand the daughter's choice of what seems to the mother to be a very limited goal. To overstate a bit, a viewer ought to be able to imagine the entire history of this family from the dialogue that you create for this scene. Difficult? Yes, but exciting, too.

Following is a list of encounters you might want to set forth in a scene of two or three pages. But first we want to add three points.

1. We leave to you the challenging job of creating the particular personalities who are in these situations. In your introductory stage directions you can describe and briefly characterize the speakers and the setting, but remember that an audience will not be aware of these comments. The audience will understand the characters only through the language, gestures (stage business), and setting.
2. Your characters should be believable individuals, not mere stereotypes, though of course even a highly individualized character is in some degree representative of some aspect of a culture—let's say the bourgeois parent (or the neglectful father) or the rebellious adolescent (or the dutiful son). That is, each character will be a coherent personality, and at the same time each will in some degree stand for something. Each will be a concrete embodiment (but not a flat or abstract vision) of a point of view and also of a type of person in a given culture.
3. Among the most interesting confrontations in drama are those of one right against another rather than of right against wrong.

Now for the sample encounters.

1. A female college student tells her drama instructor (a male) that she wants to stage Wendy Wasserstein's *The Man in a Case.* (How does he respond, and why?)
2. A person responding to an ad offering to sell a car comes to talk to the owner. (Your dialogue should give the reader a strong sense of what sort of person each one is.)
3. A young woman, seeking a job as a driver, is interviewed by the male owner of a taxi cab company.
4. A Chicano or Asian American is telling a friend (of similar ethnic background) about a job interview that he or she has just had with an Anglo employer.
5. A young white man tells his parents (or some friends) that he intends to marry a young black woman.
6. A young black woman tells her parents (or some black friends) that she plans to marry a white man.
7. A middle-aged married woman, assuming that her older unmarried sister must be unhappy, tells her that marriage isn't so great.
8. A character wants something (perhaps money, a job, or approval) that another character does not want to give.
9. A member of some minority group is talking with a friend who makes what is supposed to be an amusing ethnic slur.
10. Take two characters from some play—perhaps from Molière's *The Misanthrope,* Ibsen's *A Doll's House,* or Wilson's *Fences*—and let them continue the issue, in today's terms. Or write a monologue, for instance by Linda Loman five years after the death of Willy Loman.

Two additional points:

1. Before you set to work, please read the rest of this discussion; it concerns the importance of giving a shape or pattern to a scene.
2. After you have drafted and revised your scene, ask some friends to take the roles and to read the dialogue aloud. Listen as impartially as possible, and then revise

your work where necessary, making the dialogue more convincing and the dramatic conflict more effective.

Your instructor may want not just a scene but a play, perhaps your dramatized version of a short story, say by Poe or Updike or Sandra Cisneros. If so, your plot and characters (and some of your lines) are already established for you, but you will still have to invent much of the dialogue and the gestures. Almost surely you will have to arrange the dialogue to include exposition that a storyteller may simply tell the reader directly, and probably you will have to omit some episodes and combine some others into one episode. The author of the original story will doubtless have given it a significant structure, but you may have to reshape it at least slightly, since you are converting a story into a play.

CONSTRUCTION IN DRAMA

At this point we'll digress for a moment, and talk about construction in drama. A playwright (not "playwrite") is a *wright,* that is, a maker—a maker of plays, just as a shipwright is a maker of ships. And a play is made with characters engaged in a plot. The word *plot* itself suggests the importance of "making" or "building" or "constructing," since the original meaning of the word was a parcel of land (as in "a plot of ground"); the plot originally was the area staked out, on which one might then build. When one looks closely at a good play, one always sees that it has been designed carefully and built well. Consider, for instance, the basic pattern or groundplan of *A Midsummer Night's Dream.*

a) The play begins (1.1) and ends (5.1) in Athens.
b) Just after the first scene, and then again just before the last scene, Shakespeare gives us scenes of the comic workmen (1.2 and 4.2).
c) And in between these scenes we are in the forest (2.1–4.1).

A close analysis will reveal numerous contrasts and similarities between scenes. Few if any viewers are conscious of the pattern—of the architecture, we might say—but the pattern probably makes its effect nevertheless. In the words of the dramatist Friedrich Hebbel,

> A genuine drama is comparable to one of those big buildings which have almost as many rooms and corridors below ground as above ground. People in general are aware only of the latter; the master builder is aware of the former as well.

Or take the structure not of an entire play but of a single scene, the first in *King Lear,* where Lear makes the enormous mistake of giving his kingdom to two of his daughters and of banishing the third. If (so to speak) we stand back from the scene, we notice that it falls into three parts, which we can characterize as

a prologue (lines 1–32, in prose),
a central portion (Lear's decisions), and
an epilogue (lines 264–303, the latter part of it in prose).

The prologue is rather intimate; Gloucester and Kent begin the play by chatting about public affairs, and then their conversation turns to talk about Gloucester's sons. The epilogue, too (which is about the same length as the prologue), is relatively intimate or private; it begins with the banished sister taking her farewell of her two wicked sisters, and it ends with the two wicked sisters, speaking prose, plotting against Lear. Between these two passages, beginning with Lear's entrance at line 33 and ending with Lear's exit at line 263, is, of course, the highly ceremonial scene of Lear inviting his three daughters to speak, their speeches, and his responses. Further, within this central part of the scene the speeches of the three daughters fall into patterns, but here we need not go into that.

THE ONE-ACT PLAY

Your instructor may ask you to write a one-act play of your own invention. A distinction is often made between the one-act play and the full-length play, but the terms are a bit misleading. A one-act play, like a three-act play or a five-act play, is "full-length" in the sense that it treats its material as fully as is appropriate. Usually, of course, the material of the one-act play is more limited than that of a longer play. For instance, it usually covers less time and deals with fewer characters. Thus, if the piece really is a one-act play and not just a short play with two or more scenes, the time covered by the play usually corresponds closely to real time; that is, the play covers something like from twenty to perhaps forty minutes. And, again, the action probably involves only a few characters; indeed, some one-act plays are monologues, although most use two or three characters.

Generally only a single incident is dramatized: two strangers exchange words on a park bench, and one ends up dead (Albee, *The Zoo Story*); an angry man goes to a woman to collect an overdue payment and ends up courting her (Chekhov, *The Boor*); sailors on a ship during war suspect a fellow sailor of being a spy, break into his locker, and find not incriminating documents but a letter concerning a failed love affair (O'Neill, *In the Zone*). None of these plays has the scope of, say, *King Lear,* which covers several months and which is rich in parallels and contrasts. For instance, in *Lear* the stories of Cordelia, Kent, and Edgar all involve persons whose love is so deep that they can forgive actions that others might think intolerable.

A one-act play cannot have the complexity of a three- or five-act play; still, we will see something of the subtlety that even a one-act play can convey if we think about Susan Glaspell's *Trifles* (page 10). To take perhaps the two most obvious examples: (1) the men form a contrast to the women (though the two women are by no means interchangeable), and (2) the broken hinge of the bird cage, the broken neck of the bird, the broken neck of the man, and the broken spirit of the wife are all part of a pattern.

Most writers of one-act plays do not try to pack a three-act play into one act; rather, as we have already said, they severely limit the time covered and the number of characters, usually concentrating on one or two figures involved in a single episode. What sort of structure does a one-act play have? In the late nineteenth century, and in the first half of the twentieth, it was commonplace to say that a play, whether in three acts or in one, has a pyramidal structure; that is, it rises to a climax, and it then descends or unknots. A variation was to say that the structure of a play is like an arch, with the turning point in the plot resembling the keystone. Or, to go back more than two thousand years, in Aristotle's terms a play has a beginning, a middle, and an end. Although some plays since the 1950s have seemed to use a different structure (a wit has said that in Beckett's *Waiting for Godot*—a play in two acts—nothing happens, twice), the old pattern is still often used effectively, and indeed it may be found even in many works that, at first glance, seem not to use it.

There are other ways of expressing the idea: one ancient formula (speaking of the three-act play, but applicable also to the structure of a one-act play) goes thus: In the first act, get your people up a tree, in the second act throw stones at them, and in the third act get them down. In romantic comedy this formula often takes the shape of "Boy meets girl, boy loses girl, boy gets girl." With a little thought it is evident that such formulas are versions of Aristotle's beginning, middle, and end—or, as Peter De Vries cleverly put it, "beginning, muddle, and end." That is, a stable situation (the beginning) is disrupted (the middle) and then resolved (the end).

Almost every scene or act in a long play has something of this structure, at least to the extent that a scene or act develops. Line by line it may seem to be simply adding a unit to a unit, but in retrospect the whole has a unity, a definite shape. Even a scene that consists of a single speech is likely to move from (in effect), "What am I to do?" to "I'll do X," to "Now I feel better (or worse)"; that is, the scene builds to a climax in complexity or tension and then settles toward a resolution or relaxation.

Almost surely your first few drafts of a scene or an act will not have an effective pattern—but then comes the job of rewriting the material so that it becomes not mere dialogue but drama. You can test your scene by rewriting it in a few sentences as a scenario, that is, without any dialogue. Does the summary of the encounter have a shape —a beginning, a middle, and an end?

LAST WORDS

And this gets us to our final point. An effective scene, or an effective one-act play, of course gives us characters in whom we are interested—characters whose ideas or passions hold our attention—but it also gives a shape to the presentation of those ideas or passions. Aristotle said that the arts arise from two impulses, *the impulse to imitate,* and *the impulse toward harmony.* The first of these (except in certain forms, such as farce) requires fairly realistic dialogue and convincing characterization; we listen to the characters speak and we say, "Yes, that is how people sound, that's the way they behave." But obviously works of art do not simply offer language that imitates the language we can hear on the campus or in a bus. Works of art—songs are the most obvious example—put language into a harmonious shape. They impose a pattern (songs use meter, melody, and rhyme), and here we get to Aristotle's second point, that works of art arise partly from the human instinct for harmony. The impulse toward harmony requires a shapely "plot," a territory staked out, and then a blueprint or plan that is converted into a well-ordered construction.

APPENDIX A *The Script and the Stage*

PETER ARNOTT

Peter Arnott was born and educated in Great Britain, where he received degrees from the University of Wales and Oxford University. He taught drama at Tufts University, wrote numerous books on the theater and on ancient civilizations. Arnott was also an actor, director, and the creator of the Marionette Theater of Peter Arnott, which specialized in performing Greek drama for audiences throughout the continent.

The dramatic author writing his play is engaged in the same one-to-one relationship as the artist with his canvas or the sculptor with his block of stone. He shapes his material as his particular genius dictates, and is responsive only to those imperatives that he decides to set himself. The production of a play, however, is a much more complex process involving a variety of factors, and a number of professional skills, each of which may influence the way in which the work is finally presented to the public. Theater is community, and the author must resign himself to being merely one, and not necessarily the most important member, of the group.

Of whom does this group consist? In the modern theater, the production of a play normally involves, besides the author, the director and his assistants; the actors; the set and costume designer (who may not be the same person); the lighting designer; and a stage staff responsible for the mechanical execution of the project. Although these elements have always been present, in some degree, in the theater, their relative importance has changed over the centuries, and it is necessary to consider which held first place when the play was originally conceived.

The Author

For those accustomed to think of a play primarily as a work of literature, it comes as a shock to learn that, at some of the most productive periods of the theater, the author was by no means the most important figure. In Elizabethan London, for example, the playwright was often no more than a hack, turning out material on demand as the company's needs and the public taste dictated. As well as writing his own material, he was expected to collaborate with others, to be able to work up a scenario suggested by someone else, or to write new scenes to freshen an old play. Once his work had been sold to the company, he had no further financial interest in it, and no artistic control. Several plays which enjoyed a long life in the Elizabethan public playhouse have come down to us as patchwork pieces, continually revised or added to by different hands over the years. For a long time plays, however distinguished, were not considered as literature. It was not until Ben Jonson had the effrontery to publish his dramatic with his nondramatic works that the playwright's status began to show a change. French playwrights of the seventeenth century were the first who found themselves able to charge substantial sums for their works, and the first, tentative beginnings of the modern system of author's royalties appeared at the same time.

The Actors

In the modern commercial theater, actors are normally cast for each new production on an *ad hoc* basis. When the play closes they go their separate ways, and though their paths may sometimes recross, it may well be that they never meet on the stage again. There are, of course, important exceptions to this. The national theaters of various countries—the United States still does not have one—try to retain at least the nucleus of a permanent company for a period of years. In France, once an actor has been admitted to full membership of the Comédie Française, he may remain, if he wishes, for life. Theaters with a particular aim or identity, such as the Stratford, Ontario, Shakespeare Festival, recruit a large company for a number of plays and then stage the works in repertory. What is the exception now, however, was common practice until the present century. For most of the history of the theater, actors formed themselves into companies that worked together for years, so that the members grew to know one another's work intimately. This gave dramatists of earlier periods an advantage that they rarely enjoy today. They were writing for a known group, and could tailor the roles to particular abilities and talents. Shakespeare wrote *Hamlet* and *Othello* with Richard Burbage in mind. Molière's comedies made the best of his company's physical characteristics. Congreve and Sheridan, similarly, knew who was going to play each part before they wrote them. In this kind of company, actors tended to fall into what were called "lines of business": that is, they would specialize in playing the same kind of character, whatever the play. Certain members of the King's Men would always play the fools and clowns. Sheridan had a gallery of comic types around which to build a new work. Dickens, in *Nicholas Nickleby,* gives a delightful description of a nineteenth-century touring company in which the members are identified, not by their names, but by the roles they customarily play on stage: the swaggering hero, the angry old father, the ingenue, and so forth. You will often find, therefore, that this kind of company organization induces certain sorts of dramatic formulae in playwrights. As early as Sophocles, dramatists were returning to the same types of character, and similar kinds of dramatic situation, because they could rely on actors who were able to exploit them powerfully. The modern author usually lacks this resource. He creates his characters out of the blue. It is up to the producing agency, and the casting director, to find actors capable of bringing them to life.

The Director

The director is the most recent member of the producing group, and still one of the most controversial. Throughout the history of the theater, obviously, someone always had to be in charge. In the Greek theater it was usually the playwright. Aeschylus played his own leading parts and supervised his assistant actors; as well as providing the script, he was his own composer, choreographer, and designer. The medieval theater provided a *maître de jeu,* who had general responsibility for seeing that his actors knew their lines, rehearsed their moves, and stood more or less in the right places. Shakespeare's playhouse had its "bookholder," who combined the functions of prompter and stage manager. In the eighteenth and nineteenth centuries we see the emergence of the actor-manager, a paternalistic figure who played the leading roles himself and imposed some cohesion on the company—sometimes a difficult task, for many actors were individualists, intent on drawing attention to their own performance at the expense of the ensemble effect. In the late nineteenth century the growing complexity of the theater's technical resources, and dissatisfaction with certain haphazard methods of the past, combined to create the need for a master mind who would stand apart from the production, see it as a whole, and harness its various resources to a common end. This figure emerges, in the twentieth century, as the American director, the British producer, or the European *régisseur,* and there are still widely different views as to what his function should be. Some directors have established themselves as autocrats, allowing nothing to happen on the stage that has not evolved from their minds or, at least, won their considered approval. In many cases, it has been possible to identify a given directorial style as easily as a writing style. A production by Tyrone Guthrie, or by Roger Planchon, was unmistakably his, and could be no one else's. Other directors have considered their function to be to allow the actor's initiative to predominate; they merely shape and control his creative imagination, offering suggestions, not directives. As the theater is constantly in a state of flux, so the director's role is still changing. Twenty years ago, the director expected to walk into his first rehearsal with every move of the play blocked out on paper, or at least in his mind. Now, he hopes to come to the same result after long working sessions with his actors, in the course of which a number of different approaches may be tried and discarded. Particular directors and actors may achieve a long and mutually fruitful working relationship over a number of productions, each helping and inspiring the other. The same may happen between directors and playwrights. Elia Kazan has had a long partnership with Tennessee Williams, contributing materially to the final shaping of the plays. Alan Schneider has done the same for Edward Albee.

The Designers

Designers, too, represent a fairly recent innovation in theater practice. For most eras of the past, design as we now know it did not exist. The theater provided a conventional background for its actors. Sometimes, as in the Greek and Elizabethan theaters, this was simply the permanent architectural structure of the stage building, with the audience left to imagine the settings suggested by the language of the author. Even when the theater began to develop painted, illusionistic scenery the same stock settings were used for play after play; each playhouse owned a basic collection which could be used, with minimal adaptation, for the entire repertoire. Costumes, similarly, were drawn from stock, with the actors most of the time wearing the same sorts of clothes that they, and the audience, wore for everyday usage. The role of the designer begins to emerge in the early nineteenth century, out of the same dissatisfactions that eventually created the director. There was a growing desire for greater consistency, and greater appropriateness, in the stage picture, coupled with an increased concern for historical accuracy. The first "designed" production is usually said, with some justice, to be Shakespeare's *King John* as presented on the London stage in 1823, with every character dressed in the historical period indicated by the play, and the settings inspired by authentic medieval records. Since then, of course, the designer has developed into far more than a historical researcher, though that kind of study may still represent the basis of his design. He is expected, first, to lay out the playing space in a way that will be usable by actors, and at the same time say something about the play's intent; in other words, he must provide a visual metaphor of the play's action. In the same way, the costumes must be related to the dramatic intent, as seen by the director either alone or in combination with the author. Each costume must make a statement about the character who wears it, and be related to the others as part of a unified concept. The stage lighting, usually in different hands, must also contribute to the total effect, illuminating selectively and significantly the crucial moments of the action and suggesting mood and contrast.

All these things have to be kept in mind when taking a play from the printed page and translating it into stage action. As we have stated, many of the above are functions of the modern theater only. Selective stage lighting was impossible before the appearance of gas; seventeenth-century audiences would have been astonished at the suggestion that they should sit in the dark, while only the stage was lit. But even when considering the plays of the past, it is essential to consider what practical facilities were available to the playwright, and how these influenced the form in which he wrote. Plays are rarely written in a vacuum. When they are, they tend not to be good plays. Normally, an author writes with a particular kind of theater in mind, a particular acting style, a particular audience with reasonably predictable responses. The final shape of his play will be determined by all these things.

The Playhouse

Particularly important is the shape of the playhouse at any given period, for this largely determines not what the author says, but how he says it. Was it large or small? Spectacular or intimate? Designed to provide elaborate scenic illusion, or working largely through the active complicity of the audience's imagination? Greek plays, for instance, were written for open-air theaters which were enormous by today's standards (see photo on page 45). They held upwards of 15,000 spectators, and the actor was dwarfed by his environment. In such a theater there was little place for subtle visual effect, or for the intricate physical business that a modern dramatist now writes into his stage directions. As a compensating factor, the acoustics of these theaters, by reason of their bowl-shaped structure, were superb. Audiences could hear every word, even at so great a remove from the action. Thus, by necessity, the dramatist worked largely in terms of language. In Greek plays, characters tell you everything: who and what they are, what they are doing and going to do, what they feel about it all. In the smaller, more intimate modern theater, Greek plays often seem unnecessarily wordy because the actors now have other resources. A modern actor may show in a look what his ancient counterpart had to express in a sentence. Directors who revive Greek plays have to keep these problems of transposition in mind.

In the Elizabethan theater, as most scholars now assume, actors worked on a deep thrust stage which could carry them into the center of their audience (see illustrations on pages 144–45). Thus, a characteristic feature of the theater building encouraged the use of the stage soliloquy. Also, Elizabethan theaters seem to have relied very little on illusionistic, representational scenery. They offered, instead, a neutral space defined largely by the words of the actors. Shakespeare's characters tell you where they are, if it matters; if they do not, then the precise location is unimportant. In these circumstances the theater could develop a fast-moving pattern of action in which one scene followed rapidly on the heels of another with no necessity to drop the curtain for a change of setting. Victorian actor-managers, mounting Shakespeare on their own heavily pictorial stages, found this to be a major problem, for their productions stretched out to an inordinate length as one elaborately painted set was replaced by another. Once again, the factors governing the original production have to be taken into account, even if one intends to depart from them.

Interpreting a Play for the Stage

Let us now trace the progress of a production through its various stages. First, it is the task of the director to consider his interpretation of the play, and how this may be realized in practical terms. He must determine what he thinks the play means, for on this everything else will hang. If the author is living and accessible, the director will almost certainly consult him. This may be a mixed blessing, for the author will usually have his private vision of the play, shaped by his own proximity to it. The director, standing apart from the work, is able to be more objective. Authors are, notoriously, fallible directors of their own work, though a number have refused to recognize this and tried to impose their will on actors and director alike. George Bernard Shaw is a case in point; his plays contain inordinately lengthy stage directions, dictating the appearance of the stage setting, the properties, costumes and movements in such explicit detail that, if followed to the letter, they would leave the director nothing to do.

In the case of a dead, particularly a long-dead, author the director has different problems. He must arrive at the best interpretation that he can, aided only by the second-hand resources of scholarship. This is not to denigrate the scholar. Any intelligent director will read all the editions and commentaries that he can. But it is in the matter of bringing the play to the stage that the practitioner and the scholar conspicuously part company. Scholarship has space and leisure to be expansive. It can discuss alternative explanations, point to ambiguities, and illuminate textual problems with footnotes suggesting various ways in which they may be resolved. A good scholar is more inclined to discuss a range of interpretations than to commit himself to one. The theater, on the other hand, has to be decisive. It offers no footnotes. It cannot ask the spectator to go back and reconsider. In performance, if something is not clear at first hearing, it is not clear at all. Therefore the director, for better or worse, has to commit himself to one interpretation, to one vision of the play; and inevitably, there will be those who disagree with him. Laurence Olivier prefaced his film of *Hamlet* with the statement that this is a play about a man who could not

Top: Engraving of Benjamin Wilson's painting of David Garrick (1717–1770) as King Lear, Act III. (Photograph: Raymond Mander and Joe Mitchenson Theatre Collection.)
Bottom: John Gielgud as Lear in the Royal Shakespeare Theatre production, Stratford-upon-Avon, England, 1955. (Photograph: Royal Shakespeare Theatre.)

make up his mind. An immediate response rang out from a segment of the audience: "Wrong!" It is ever thus. The theater, unfortunately, cannot offer a variety of interpretations and ask the audience to choose. It has to settle for one; and what this is will vary with the director and his times. Part of the measure of greatness of a play is the number of different interpretations it can bear without forfeiting its dramatic viability.

The initial decision, once arrived at, carries others in its train. A directorial interpretation involves matters of setting and costume, and these are usually worked out well in advance with the appropriate people. Let us take, as an example, the case of *King Lear.* The same play may assume a number of stage shapes, depending on what the director assumes its meaning and purpose to be. Does he see it, for instance, on the most rudimentary level, as a chronicle play about certain events in remote British history? (Unlikely, perhaps; but it has been done.) The name of Lear, after all, appears in early British records, and a rough date may be assigned to him. In this case we will have a *Lear* dressed in furs and skins, and set against a background of rocks and monoliths. Alternatively, does the director see the play, as some scholars have suggested, as closely related to political events of Shakespeare's own time? Does Lear's division of his kingdom give stage form to the fears of those who looked uneasily into the future of an England whose queen would die unmarried and childless? This gives another line for sets and costumes to take. Does the director envisage the work as having a particular meaning for now, for the present generation? He may therefore decide to stage it in modern dress, against settings evoking the audience's present. As noted above, "modern-dress" Shakespeare was the regular practice before the nineteenth century; it became modish again in the 1920s and 30s, and still occasionally reappears with value today, though perhaps *Lear* is not the ideal play for such treatment. Is it a cosmic drama, located in no particular time and place, but expressive only of man's constant inhumanity to man, and his subservience to forces beyond his control? Sets and costumes may display this too, by choosing forms linked to no specific style or period but creating their own theatrical logic. Thus the stage has shown us all manner of Lears. One has been Ancient British, another Elizabethan. Olivier's production suggested an almost prehistoric world without actually depicting it, a world of towering crags and swirling mists. Gielgud chose a timeless *Lear,* dressed in costumes of stylized shape and set among abstract sculptural forms. Yet another production looked to the future and set the play in a blackened, smouldering landscape, the neo-primitive world that had survived the atomic war.

The director's basic interpretation must also decide the placement and movement of his characters. It is his task to illuminate what he considers to be the underlying pattern of the play through significant action. To this end he will create a subtext, working with his actors to build up a mental background and justification for the lines they speak. In *Lear* again, the play begins with the King's announcement that he proposes to divide his kingdom, and his challenge to his daughters to proclaim their love for him. Why does he do this? Is it simply the datum, the formal beginning to the play, which neither asks nor needs explanation? In this case, the director may stage the opening scenes almost as a prologue, quite simply and formally, a bare proclamation. Or is there a more complex human explanation? Olivier saw Lear in this scene as a man on the verge of senility, making his momentous decision almost as a whim; and he worked up to this from his first appearance on stage, having Lear stop as if to address a remark to a soldier, then changing his mind and going on. Why does Cordelia refuse to answer? Is she simply revolted by her sisters' protestations, or is there some other reason? Nahum Tate, the Restoration playwright, was so obsessed by this problem that he postulated a love affair between Cordelia and Edgar dividing her loyalty so that she was unable to answer her father as he wished; and he carried this idea to such lengths that he rewrote the play. So far may interpretation go.

A further example. What relationship exists between Lear and the Fool? Is the latter intended to be the King's conscience? His *alter ego*? A daughter-substitute? Or an objective commentator on his master's folly? Once again, whatever interpretation is decided upon can be emphasized by the relative placing of the characters and their contact, or lack of it. Gloucester is blinded. Is the director concerned with the physical violence of the act, or its symbolic performance? If the former, the deed can be portrayed most graphically on the stage. If the latter, it can be merely suggested, not shown. All these are things which must be worked out by the director with his actors, and they must ultimately agree on the meaning of what is being done. Discrepancies of interpretation show up with painful clarity in performance. An actor may sometimes disagree totally with his director's interpretation. He will usually follow it, nonetheless. In the long rehearsal process, the interpretation may change. Alec Guinness has recorded that he went through several interpretations of Shakespeare's *Richard II* before he found a view of the character that satisfied him as being logical and self-consistent.

Amid all these interpretations, then, where is the play? The answer must be that it is in none of them, and all of them. The play's values change as the theaters, the actors, and the audiences change. The *Lear* we see is not the *Lear* that Burbage performed, and the Elizabethan playgoers saw, though the text is the same. The *Lear* of Garrick (1717–79) was totally different from that of Edmund Kean (1787–

Top: King Lear, the final scene of the 1986 production, The National Theatre, London. *Bottom:* Paul Scofield as Lear in Peter Brook's production by the Royal Shakespeare Company in London, 1962. (Photograph: Angus McBean/Harvard Theatre Collection.)

1833). In the same way, Lincoln Center bears small resemblance to the Globe Playhouse, Drury Lane, or the Lyceum. Each generation finds a new meaning in the script, illuminating it with contemporary concerns and preoccupations. It is the theater's continual task to bring about a rapprochement between the play and its successive audiences, finding a new frame of reference in which it will be meaningful. The actor, who works in the ephemeral, who sculpts, as has been said, in snow, accepts this as a condition of his art. The text remains, but its illumination changes.

The Mechanics of Production

However ornate the director's conception, the commercial theater imposes strict limitations on time and cost. A Broadway production may expect a minimum of three weeks' rehearsal; the cost, regulated by strict union standards for actors and stage crew, may be upwards of $1,000,000 for a nonmusical play, vastly more for a musical. In university theaters, which have tended to become more and more the home of the classics, conditions are somewhat happier. Campus productions usually work with five or six weeks of rehearsal time, uninhibited by union hours, and the budget is far smaller when salaries do not have to be paid: perhaps as little as $2,500 for a *King Lear.* Given these differences, rehearsals in both situations tend to follow the same pattern. They will begin with a general reading of the play, during which the director explains his conception; the cast may also see preliminary designs of sets and costumes, so that they know the environment in which they will be working. Early rehearsals are conducted book-in-hand, with normally only the barest indication of a set. The principal acting areas, steps and levels are marked out on the floor with tape. Any furniture that is to hand may be used; a chair may stand in for a throne, a bench for a bed. During this period cuts and changes may still be made, imposed sometimes by such commercial considerations as the length and expense of the performance, sometimes by changes in the director's conception as he absorbs what his actors bring to their parts. Gradually, the actors memorize. It is the director's hope that parts will be learnt as rapidly as possible, as only then can serious work begin. Once they have discarded their scripts, actors can relate to one another and to their surroundings.

During the course of rehearsals the other production elements are added. Actors start to work with the actual props, instead of rehearsal equivalents. In a university theater, the setting begins to grow around the actors as they rehearse. Actual steps replace the lines on the floor and walls appear where there was only empty space. In the commercial theater, again because of expense, the company may never know the actual set until the last stages of rehearsal; they do most of their work in an empty hall lit by a single bulb. In either case, the last days are spent in integrating the total production. The full set appears, and actors have to adjust to its intricacies. The full lighting plot is put into action. Sound effects and music are added. The actors are introduced to their costumes, and have to master, very rapidly, the difficulties of wearing them. There is usually one technical rehearsal, during which the actors are subordinated to the other demands of the performance; they usually move from one lighting or scene cue to the next, so that the technical staff may become accustomed to the changes. Finally, full dress rehearsals, run like a full performance, with the director no longer intervening, but confining himself to notes at the end.

In the commercial theater, even this may not be the end of the process. Most Broadway productions go through a series of tryouts out-of-town, before paying public audiences. Depending on the reaction, important changes may be made in the production, or even in the script itself. It is not unknown for actors to be handed new material every day. Thus the production is established; it opens; and even then, over a long commercial run, it may change, as new actors replace the original cast or as those who were with the play from the beginning make new discoveries about it and about each other. A script, once it has been published, achieves a certain permanency. A production is always changing, and no two audiences ever see exactly the same dramatic event.

APPENDIX B *A Glossary of Dramatic Terms*

absurd, theater of the. Drama of such writers as Eugene Ionesco and Samuel Beckett in France and Harold Pinter in England that imitates the absurdity of our existence. "Everything, as I see it, is an aberration," Ionesco has said. Among the basic themes are: loneliness in a world without God; inability to communicate; dehumanization at the hands of mass media; and impotence in the face of society and of death. Though the plays are serious, they may contain extravagantly comic scenes in depicting a reality that is absurd, illogical, senseless, a world of futility and meaningless clichés. In Ionesco's *The Chairs* (1951) an elderly couple rush about, filling a room with chairs for nonexistent visitors. Old age is a fact, but an absurdity, too, and old people are incomprehensible. At the end of *The Chairs,* an orator who is to deliver a solemn talk about the truths of life turns out to be deaf and dumb and merely makes unintelligible noises and gestures to the invisible crowd. Ionesco summarizes the theme of *The Chairs* (*The New York Times,* June 1, 1958): "I have tried to deal . . . with emptiness, with frustration, with this world, at once fleeting and crushing. The characters I have used are not fully conscious of their spiritual rootlessness, but they feel it instinctively and emotionally." One basis of the inability to communicate, and one that the "Absurd" dramatists seize upon, is the corruption of language. The absurdity of trying to communicate by means of a debased language is dramatized by Ionesco in *The Bald Soprano* (1948), where the characters speak in clichés. Because the characters are incomprehensible and the happenings illogical and baffling, the spectators cannot simply sit back in ease but are continually challenged to grasp the play's meaning. The theater of the absurd can be said to be a descendent of expressionism (see p. 794). Consult M. Esslin, *The Theatre of the Absurd.*

act. A main division in drama or opera. Act divisions probably arose in Roman theory and derive ultimately from the Greek practice of separating episodes in a play by choral interludes, but Greek (and probably Roman) plays were performed without interruption, for the choral interludes were part of the plays themselves. The division of Elizabethan plays into five acts is often the work of editors rather than authors. No play of Shakespeare's was published in his lifetime with divisions into five acts. Today an act division is commonly indicated by lowering the curtain and turning up the houselights. A **scene** is a smaller unit, either (1) a division with no change of locale or abrupt shift of time, or (2) a division consisting of an actor or a group of actors on the stage. According to the second definition, the departure or entrance of an actor changes the composition of the group and thus produces a new scene. In an entirely different sense, the scene is the locale where a work is set. The first speech in *Romeo and Juliet* informs the audience of the play's locale: "In fair Verona, where we lay our scene." Often the décor lets the spectator know where the play is set, but during the last hundred years playwrights have tended, for the convenience of readers, to write long stage directions describing the scene. Here is the beginning of the first stage direction in Shaw's *Candida:* "A fine morning in October 1894 in the north east quarter of London, a vast district miles away from the London of Mayfair and St. James's, and much less narrow, squalid, fetid and airless in its slums."

acting. The imitation by one person of another. The two extreme views of the actor's methods are, on the one hand, that acting is a craft, a matter of developing the technical skill to arouse certain feelings in an audience by means of gesture and voice, and, on the other hand, that acting is a matter of psychologically exploring the character, playing (so to speak) from the heart rather than the head. The first view is especially identified with Denis Diderot, who in *The Paradox of Acting* (1773–88) said, "Actors impress the public not when they are impassioned but when they effectively imitate passion." The second view is especially associated with Constantin Stanislavski (1863–1938), who insisted that the actor must "sense" the "inner state" of the role. In America in the 1930s and '40s a school of acting called *The Method* was greatly influenced by Stanislavski.

action. (1) The physical movement of an actor, whether he is leaping into Ophelia's grave or speaking softly to himself. That talk is action is easily seen in the Bastard's remark (*King John,* 2.1.466): "Zounds! I was never so bethumped with words / Since I first called my brother's father dad." (2) An incident in the plot, an episode. Aristotle's statement that a drama is an "imitation of an action" (*praxis*) has provoked considerable controversy; recently there has been a tendency to regard this action as the motive underlying the outward deeds of the plot. Francis Fergusson says (in *The Human Image in Dramatic Literature,* p. 116), for example, that the action of *Oedipus the King* "is the quest for Laius's slayer, . . . which persists through the changing circumstances of the play."

acto. A short dramatic sketch, written in a mixture of Spanish and English, often with stereotyped characters satirizing the anglo establishment. The form, developed by Luis Valdez in 1965 during a strike by farm workers in California, aims at stimulating Chicanos to value their culture and to unite against exploitation (see p. 646). Consult *The Drama Review* 11:4 (1967).

aesthetic distance, or **psychical distance.** The detachment between the receptor and the work of art. The concept is chiefly associated with Edward Bullough (see the essay in his *Aesthetics,* reprinted in Melvin Rader, *A Modern Book of Aesthetics*). Bullough explains that there must be some sort of psychical "distance" (gap) between our practical self (our personal needs) and the work of art. Thus, an old man who has been treated harshly by his children may be unable to divorce his personal feelings from *King Lear.* He may be too involved with the piece as life to see it as art. But "distance" does not mean that the receptor is totally detached or objective. Rather, he is detached from his usual personal involvements, and because of this detachment he can look with a new vigorous interest—he can look with a new sort of passion born of his new personality—at the work of art as art. Persons who do not understand the need for distance between themselves and a work, Bullough explains, commonly say that they do not wish to see a tragedy because there is enough suffering in real life. But the more sophisticated spectator at a tragedy realizes that as a picture is distanced by the frame, a play is distanced from the audience (the characters may speak verse, they perform behind footlights, and their deeds cohere to make a unified harmonious pattern); the feelings it evokes are not the feelings evoked by a roughly similar event in real life. In the theater we feel "rapturous awe" at what in life would be depressing. See also *dramatic illusion, empathy, epic drama.*

agit-prop. Propaganda theater. The term is derived from the Department of Agitation and Propaganda, formed in the Soviet Union in 1920.

agon (Greek: *contest*). A debate in a Greek comedy. See page 100. In the last few decades the term has been used (e.g., by Francis Fergusson, *The Idea of a Theater*) to designate a scene of conflict in tragedy, such as the agonizing struggle between Oedipus and Teiresias.

agroikos. See *character.*

alazon. See *character.*

alienation effect. See *epic drama.*

allegory. Often a narrative wherein abstractions (e.g., virtue, fear) are made concrete (Mr. Virtue, Giant Fear), for the purpose of effectively communicating a moral. But in essence an allegory is merely a system of equivalents. Though allegory need not personify abstractions, allegoric drama almost always does. *Everyman* (c. 1500), an allegoric morality play, includes among its dramatis personae Death, Good Deeds, Beauty, and of course, Everyman. But morality plays may also include allegoric castles (standing for strength or chastity), roses (standing for love or virtue), and so on. Consult Bernard Spivack, *Shakespeare and the Allegory of Evil.* (See also *symbolism.*)

alternative theater. The theater that sees itself in opposition to the established bourgeois theater. For example, The Living Theatre, an experimental company founded in New York in 1951 and influential in the 1960s, held anarchist and pacifist goals and often sought to arouse the hostility of the audience. Another example: the Teatro Campesino of Luis Valdez, on which see pages 639 and 646. See T. Shank, *American Alternative Theatre.*

anagnorisis, or **disclosure, disovery, recognition.** For Aristotle the "recognition," or "disclosure," seemed to be merely a recognition of who is who, by such tokens as birthmarks, clothes, and so on, but the term has been extended to include the tragic hero's recognition of himself and/or the essence of life. Thus Othello, having murdered his faithful wife, learns he was beguiled into thinking her dishonest and finally recognizes himself as "one not easily jealous, but being wrought / Perplexed in the extreme"; and he exacts justice from himself by suicide. For examples from *King Lear, Hamlet,* and *Macbeth* see pages 30–31.

antagonist. See *plot, protagonist.*

antecedent action. See *plot.*

anticlimax. A descent, the lines or happenings being markedly less important or less impressive than their predecessors. In melodrama, a decrease in tension may cause disappointment and loss of interest; in comedy, a sharp descent (the beautiful princess opens her mouth and sounds like a burlesque queen) may get a desirable laugh. On the desirability of a gradual decrease in tension in tragedy (i.e., a "quiet ending"), consult Max Beerbohm, "Last Acts," in *Around Theatres.*

anti-hero. A central character who, reversing the conventional idea of a hero (attractive, brave, high-minded), forces the audience to examine its conception of heroism and indeed of society. Examples: Samuel Beckett's tramps.

antimasque. See *masque.*

Apollonian. See *Dionysus.*

arena stage. (1) In British usage, a stage with a back wall and with an audience on three sides. (2) In American usage, a playing space surrounded by spectators, **theater-in-the-round.** Proponents of arena staging (in the American sense) stress the intimacy afforded by having actors in the midst of the audience, but opponents suggest that at least for some plays the intimacy ought not to be very great. (See *aesthetic distance.*) It has been noted, too, that even in arena staging the audience normally feels set apart from the actors, for the audience is in the dark while the actors are in an illuminated playing area. Critics of arena staging cite the following difficulties: soliloquies, asides, and direct addresses are hard to deliver in such a theater; directors, aware that the back of an actor's head is not very expressive, tend to have the actors gyrate disturbingly and meaninglessly; entrances and exits are cumbersome; little use can be made of elevation and of groupings of actors.

arras. See page 143.

aside. See *convention, soliloquy.*

atmosphere. The mood created by setting, language, and happenings.

blocking. The director's organization of the movement on the stage in order to form effective stage positions and groupings.

bombast. Rant, speech that is too inflated for the occasion; from a word meaning "cotton stuffing." In Marlowe's *Tamburlaine* (c. 1587) Tamburlaine brags thus:

> Our quivering lances, shaking in the air,
> And bullets, like Jove's dreadful thunderbolts,
> Enrolled in flames and fiery smoldering mists,
> Shall threat the gods more than Cyclopian wars:
> And with our sun-bright armor as we march,
> Will chase the stars from Heaven and dim their eyes
> That stand and muse at our admirèd arms.

bomolochos. See *character.*

bourgeois drama. A serious play with middle-class dramatis personae. There are a few Elizabethan tragedies of middle-class life, but bourgeois drama, with its emphasis on pathos, is more or less an eighteenth-century invention. Bourgeois dramas were written in the eighteenth and nineteenth centuries, apparently in response to the middle class's desire to see itself on the stage; the bourgeoisie by the eighteenth century regarded themselves as a suitable replacement for the noblemen of earlier tragedy. Speaking generally, the characteristics of these plays are middle-class dramatis personae, virtue in distress, sentimentality, and an unreasonably high moral tone. Eighteenth-century critics, not sure what to do with pathetic plays on middle-class life, used the terms ***drame, drame bourgeois, comédie larmoyante*** (tearful comedy), ***tragédie bourgeoise,*** and ***bürgerliches Trauerspiel*** (bourgeois tragedy) interchangeably. (Note that a *comédie larmoyante* need not end happily, nor a *tragédie bourgeoise* end sadly.) In England, George Lillo's *The London Merchant* (1731), "a tale of private woe. A London 'prentice ruined," depicted an apprentice who murdered his benefactor. Bourgeois drama in the nineteenth century became melodrama in many hands and tragedy in Ibsen's hands. Consult Fred O. Nolte, *Early Middle Class Drama;* and Eric Auerbach, *Mimesis,* Ch. 17. On Ibsen as a bourgeois dramatist consult Eric Bentley, *The Playwright as Thinker.* See *domestic tragedy, sentimental,* and pages 37–38, 551–53.

box set. Flats connected to form three walls with movable doors and windows. The box set, developed in the mid-nineteenth century, replaced sliding wings and canvas backdrops on which windows, doors, and even pieces of furniture were painted. See *realism.*

burla. See *commedia dell'arte.*

burlesque. Any imitation that, by distortion, aims to amuse. Its subject matter is sometimes said to be faults rather than vices, and its tone is neither shrill nor savage. Thus, in distinction from satire it can be defined as a comic imitation of a mannerism or a minor fault (either in style or subject matter), contrived to arouse amusement rather than indignation. In the theater, a burlesque may be a play that amusingly criticizes another play by grotesquely imitating aspects of it, as Gay's *The Beggar's Opera* (1728) mimicked serious operas. In England, a burlesque may be a musical extravaganza in which fantasy has almost entirely ousted criticism. In America, burlesque (especially popular in the late nineteenth and first half of the twentieth century) is usually a sort of vaudeville or variety show stressing bawdy humor and sex. The sexual theme is most fully revealed in the striptease, introduced about 1920. See *comedy, satire.*

catastrophe. See *plot.*

catharsis. Aristotle and countless followers said that tragedy evokes pity and fear and that it produces in the spectator a catharsis (purgation, or, some scholars hold, purification) of these emotions: it drains or perhaps refines or modifies these emotions, and thus tragedy is socially useful. (Aristotle's *Poetics* is the subject of much controversy; one cannot with security assert that Aristotle said anything without a counter-argument being offered. For various views of catharsis, consult F. L. Lucas, *Tragedy,* and Gerald F. Else's monumental *Aristotle's Poetics.*)

character. (1) One of the dramatis personae, e.g., King Lear. (2) The personality of such a figure. Characters are sometimes divided into **flat** and **round characters.** The former have only one "side," representing a single trait (e.g., the faithful wife, the genial drunkard); the latter have many traits and are seen, as it were, from all sides, in the round. The behavior of flat characters is thoroughly predictable; that of round characters is sometimes unexpected though credible. A **stock character** is a type that recurs in many works. For example, from Greek comedy to the present there have been numerous braggart soldiers, stubborn fathers, jealous husbands. Northrop Frye finds four chief types of comic figures: (1) the ***alazon,*** the imposter, boaster, hypocrite; (2) the ***eiron*** (see irony), the man who deprecates himself and exposes the boaster; (3) the ***bomolochos,*** the buffoon, or more generally, the man who entertains by his mannerisms and talk; and (4) the ***agroikos,*** the straight man who is the unwitting butt of humor. Each of these types appears in many dresses; the *alazon,* for example, is most commonly the braggart soldier (*miles gloriosus*), but he is also the pedant, the crank, or anyone who is full of ideas that have no relation to reality. (See *commedia dell'arte;* consult Northrop Frye, *Anatomy of Criticism,* pp. 171–76, and R. L. Hunter, *The New Comedy of Greece and Rome.*) Stock characters are not limited to comedy: the proud tragic hero is a stock character, as are, for example, the cruel stepmother and the son who wishes to avenge his father. See also *motivation, plot.* Consult J. L. Styan, *The Elements of Drama,* Ch. 8.

chorus. In Greek drama, a group of singers and dancers (*khoros* in Greek means "dancer") who play a role, e.g., Old Men of Corinth. (The chorus leader is the ***koryphaios.***) In Aeschylus's *The Suppliants* (c. 490 B.C.), perhaps the earliest extant play, the chorus consists of the heroines, but in most Greek plays the chorus consists of subsidiary figures who comment rather helplessly on what is happening to the important people. Aeschylus reduced the chorus of fifty to twelve; Sophocles increased it to fifteen, where it remained. The Greek chorus, it is often said, is a sort of middleman between the unusual main figures and the humdrum spectators. Elizabethan dramas occasionally had a chorus of one actor who, not a participant in the story, commented on it. The Chorus (or prologue) in Shakespeare's *Henry V* urges the audience to

> Think when we talk of horses that you see them
> Printing their proud hoofs i' the receiving earth;
> For 'tis your thoughts that now must deck our kings.
> Carry them here and there, jumping o'er times,
> Turning the accomplishment of many years
> Into an hour-glass: for the which supply,
> Admit me Chorus to this history:
> Who prologue-like your humble patience pray,
> Gently to hear, kindly to judge, our play.

A **chorus character,** or ***raisonneur,*** however, such as Enobarbus in *Antony and Cleopatra,* is a character who participates in the story yet seems to be the author's mouthpiece, intelligently commenting (often with irony) on the actions of the other characters. But Alfred Harbage, in *As They Liked It,* skeptically and aptly calls such a figure "The Unreliable Spokesman." The use of the chorus, in one form or another, continues into our times, for example in T. S. Eliot's *Murder in the Cathedral,* whose "Chorus of Women of Canterbury," like a Greek chorus and like the audience, "are forced to bear witness"; and in Tennessee Williams's *The Glass Menagerie,* whose Tom Wingfield tells the audience he is "the narrator of the play, and also a character in it." See also *plot.*

climax. See *plot.*

closet drama. A play suited only for reading, not for acting. Most nineteenth-century English poetic dramas (e.g., Coleridge's, Shelley's, Tennyson's) fit into this category, although Byron's plays have recently been moving out of the closet. Consult Moody Prior, *The Language of Tragedy.*

comedy. Most broadly, anything amusing, whether a literary work or a situation. More specifically, comedy is (in Dr. Johnson's words) "such a dramatic representation of human life, as may excite mirth." Dramatic comedies generally depict a movement from unhappiness to happiness, from (for example) young lovers frustrated by their parents to young lovers happily married. The unhappy situation is so presented that it entertains rather than distresses the spectator; it is ridiculous or diverting rather than painful.

Comic drama seems related to fertility rituals; it celebrates generation, renewal, variety (laughing away any narrow-minded persons who seek to limit life's abundance), and it celebrates human triumphs over the chances of life. Irate parents and shipwrecks cannot prevent journeys from ending with lovers meeting. For the kinds of Greek comedy (Old, Middle, and New) see pages 99–102. For the stock characters in Greek comedy see *character.* Consult C. Hoy, *The Hyacinth Room; Theories of Comedy,* ed. P. Lauter; L. J. Potts, *Comedy.*

comedy of humors. A term sometimes applied to plays—notably those of Ben Jonson—wherein the characters, though somewhat individualized, obviously represent types or moods (the jealous husband, the witless pedant). A humor was a bodily liquid (blood [Latin: *sanguis*], phlegm, yellow bile, black bile) thought to control one's behavior. Allegedly, a proper mixture produced a well-adjusted person, but a preponderance of any one humor produced a distorted personality. The old sense of the word survives in the phrase, "He is in a bad humor"; *sanguine, phlegmatic,* and *bilious* are also modern survivals of the old psychology of humors. **Humor characters** are common in **situational comedy;** they are engineered by a clever plot into a situation that displays their absurdity: the man who craves silence is confronted with a talkative woman; the coward is confronted by the braggart.

comedy of manners, comedy of wit. See *high comedy.*

comic relief. Humorous episodes in tragedy, alleged to alleviate or lighten the tragic effect. Some comic scenes in tragedy, however, not only provide "relief" but enlarge the canvas of tragedy, showing us a fuller picture of life. The clown who brings Cleopatra the poisonous asp sets her tragedy against the daily world. Critics have increasingly noted that the comic scenes (such as the macabre comments of the gravediggers in *Hamlet*) often deepen rather than alleviate the tragic effect. See *tragicomedy.* Consult A. P. Rossiter, *Angel with Horns,* Ch. 14.

commedia dell'arte. Italian drama, more or less improvised, performed by professionals in Italy and abroad, mostly in the sixteenth century but still alive in the early eighteenth century. In contrast to the classically inspired written drama (***commedia erudita***) performed by actors who memorized their lines, *commedia dell'arte* (perhaps best translated "professional drama") employed sketches of plots (***scenario;*** plural: ***scenarii***) specifying entrances and exits and the gist of the dialogue; in performance these *scenarii* were fleshed out with stock bits of comic stage business (***lazzi***) or larger pieces of business (***burle***) such as practical jokes. (The singulars are ***lazzo*** and ***burla.***) Thus a *scenario* may call for the *lazzo* of anger, or the *burla* of chasing a fly, and leave it to the actor to work out the swats and the smile when at last he munches the fly. Though these plays are said to have been improvised, the stock characters, stock situations, and stock stage business make them something more —or less—than improvised. The chief characters—most of whom wore masks—are Pantolone, an elderly Venetian merchant wearing a little cap, a red jacket, loose trousers (hence our word "pants"), and slippers; his age, amours, and avarice make him ridiculous; Dottore, a Bolognese doctor wearing a black academic gown; his age and his pedantry make him ridiculous; Capitano, a soldier, ridiculous because a braggart and a coward; several servants called *zanne* (singular: *zanni,* from *Gianni,* "Johnny"), including Arlecchino (later Harlequin), who in the sixteenth century wore patches that in the next century were represented by triangles or diamonds; Brighella, a rather cruel and crafty rogue; Pulcinella, noted for his resourcefulness and his disguises; Pedrolino, a naive valet who becomes the melancholy Pagliacci and Pierrot; Colombina, who later becomes Columbine and loves Harlequin. Further, there are usually four lovers, children of the two Old Men. Consult Allardyce Nicoll, *Masks, Mimes and Miracles,* and *The World of Harliquin;* and K. M. Lea, *Italian Popular Comedy.*

complication. See *plot.*

confidant (feminine: **confidante**). A character in whom a principal character confides, revealing his state of mind and often furthering the exposition. Horatio is Hamlet's confidant; Oenone is Phèdre's. Although Horatio and Oenone are memorable, the confidant is sometimes absurdly vapid; though the French defended the device as more plausible than the soliloquy, the confidant may be more trouble than he is worth. In *The Critic* (1779), Sheridan ridiculed it thus: "Enter Tilburina stark mad in white satin, and her confidante stark mad in white linen."

conflict. See *plot.*

convention. An unrealistic device that the public agrees to tolerate. Thus, a character in a drama may express her thoughts aloud and not be heard by other characters (the **aside**), or she may speak her thoughts aloud on the empty stage (the **soliloquy**). Italian characters (e.g., Desdemona and Iago) speak English, yet are understood to be speaking Italian. In motion pictures, one image fades out, another fades in, and through this convention the audience knows that there is a shift in time or place. More generally any character-type, any theme or motif (e.g., the suspected butler), widely used in literature or drama is a convention. Similarly, **realism,** though apparently opposed to conventions, has its own conventions. For instance, a realistic set showing a room is, when one thinks about it, highly conventional since the room lacks a fourth wall. Consult Harry Levin, *Refractions;* M. C. Bradbrook, *Themes and Conventions of Elizabethan Tragedy.*

cosmic irony. See *irony.*

cothurnus. See *sock and buskin.*

coup de théatre. A surprise, especially a striking turn of events in the plot. Consult Alan R. Thompson, *The Anatomy of Drama.*

crisis. See *plot.*

cruelty, theater of. Antonin Artaud (1896–1948) used the term in 1933 to refer to a drama that, working rather like a plague, would shock people out of the bonds of their "logical" or "civilized" conceptions and would release the suppressed primitive or prelogical powers within them, such as criminal instincts and erotic obsessions, revealing the "cruelty" or terrible mystery of existence. This drama, relying more on gestures, shapes, music, and light than on words (Artaud was immensely impressed by Balinese drama although he did not understand Indonesian), would bypass mere realism (i.e., psychology) and would make manifest the truly real supernatural, creating in the spectator a "kind of terror" or a purifying delirium. Artaud, a poet, actor, and director, published relatively little, but his metaphysics and his emphasis on an antirealistic theater in various ways have influenced Sartre, Camus, Beckett, Ionesco, Genet (consult the preface to *The Maids*) and others: language sometimes becomes gibberish, and madness and violence are presented in order to jolt spectators out of their comfortable false view of humankind and of the universe—or, in less metaphysical plays, in order to reflect on the stage the cruelty of the modern world. Consult Artaud's *The Theater and Its Double;* several articles in *Tulane Drama Review,* 8 (Winter 1963); and the "Conclusion" in Jacques Guicharnaud and June Beckelman, *Modern French Theatre.*

denouement. See *plot.*

deus ex machina. Literally, a god out of a machine. (1) In Greek drama a god who descends by a cranelike arrangement and solves a problem in the story, thus allowing the play to end. It was much used by Euripides; Sophocles in his old age borrowed the idea and introduced Heracles at the end of *Philoctetes* to induce the title character to go to Troy. (2) Any unexpected and improbable device (e.g., an unexpected inheritance from a long-lost uncle in Australia) used to unknot a problem and thus conclude the work.

deuteragonist. See *protagonist.*

dialogue. The speech exchanged between characters or, loosely, even the speech of a single character. Dialogue is sometimes contrasted to action, but Elizabeth Bowen aptly says that dialogue is what the characters *do* to each other, and Shaw aptly says that his plays are all talk just as Beethoven's symphonies are all music. *Stichomythia* is a special form of dialogue, wherein two speakers in a verbal duel thrust and parry in alternating lines or fragments of lines. Example:

QUEEN.
Hamlet, thou hast thy father much offended.
HAMLET.
Mother, you have my father much offended.
QUEEN.
Come, come, you answer with an idle tongue.
HAMLET.
Go, go, you question with a wicked tongue.

See *action, soliloquy.* Consult J. L. Styan, *The Elements of Drama,* Chs. 1–2, and Eric Bentley, *The Life of the Drama.*

diction. (1) Choice of words, wording. Dr. Johnson objected to the "knife" ("an instrument used by butchers and cooks," he said) that Lady Macbeth says she will use to murder the King. "Words too familiar, or too remote," Johnson said, "defeat the purpose of a poet." Consult Moody Prior, *The Language of Tragedy.* (2) A performer's manner or style of speaking, including pronunciation and phrasing.

Dionysus. Greek god of wine, the phallus, the surge of growth, and (to join all these) irrational impulse. It is commonly held that Greek tragedy grew from choral celebrations in his honor; in any case, from the sixth century B.C. tragedies were performed in Athens at the **Great** (or **Greater,** or **City**) **Dionysia,** a festival in Dionysus's honor. (For a survey of theories of the origin of tragedy, see A. W. Pickard-Cambridge, *Dithyramb, Tragedy and Comedy,* 2nd ed., revised by T. B. L. Webster. For a brief rejection of the theory that drama originated in Dionysian festivals, see H. D. F. Kitto, in *Theatre Survey,* 1 [1960], 3–17.) Friedrich Nietzsche suggested in *The Birth of Tragedy* (1872) that Greek tragedy, usually considered calm and poised, was not the product of quiet minds. If tragedy, Nietzsche said, showed light and beauty (over which the god Apollo presided), it was nevertheless also indebted to Dionysus, who represented the frenzied, buried self-assertions of the mind. That is, Greek tragedy was the product of **Dionysian** ecstatic and violent self-assertion tamed by (or fused with) the **Apollonian** sense of reason, of moderation, and of external order. "Apollonian" is often associated with classicism, and "Dionysian" with romanticism.

direct address. See *soliloquy.*

disclosure, discovery. See *anagnorisis.*

disguising. See *masque.*

domestic tragedy. A serious play showing the misfortunes (especially within the family) of a private citizen rather than of a person of high rank who is involved in events that shake a realm. See *bourgeois drama.* Consult Henry H. Adams, *English Domestic or Homiletic Tragedy 1575 to 1642.*

double plot. See *plot.*

downstage. The front half of the stage, or any part of the stage considered in relation to someone or something further from the audience.

drama (from Greek *dran:* to do). (1) A play, a work that tells a story by means of impersonators. (2) The whole body of work written for the theater. (3) A serious but untragic play (see *drame*). (4) Events containing conflict, tension, surprise ("life is full of drama"; "the first act lacks drama"). See *closet drama, comedy, melodrama, tragedy.* A play is written by a **dramatist;** the art of writing plays is **dramaturgy.** A person who writes plays is also a **playwright.** (Note that the last syllable is not "-write" but "-wright," denoting a maker, as a shipwright is a maker of ships.) Consult Kenneth T. Rowe, *Write That Play;* Walter Kerr, *How Not to Write a Play;* Bernard Grebanier, *Playwriting.*

drama of ideas. See *pièce à thèse.*

dramatic illusion. The state between delusion (the spectators think the world on the stage is real) and full awareness (the spectators never forget they are looking at scenery and actors). In *A Midsummer Night's Dream,* Bottom fears that delusion will occur unless the audience is carefully warned: "Write me a prologue, and let the prologue seem to say we will do no harm with our swords, and that Pyramus is not killed indeed. And, for the more better assurance, tell them that I Pyramus am not Pyramus, but Bottom the Weaver. This will put them out of fear." See *aesthetic distance.*

George Henry Lewes (1817–78) introduced into English dramatic criticism the term ***optique du théâtre,*** taken from the French actor François René Molé (1734–1802). Spectators must have this "theater view," this understanding of "scenic illusion," if they are to enjoy the theater; if they lack it, they will complain that Hamlet ought to be speaking Danish (see *convention*). *Optique du théâtre* requires that we be given not reality but a symbolic representation of it. A stage miser should finger his gold differently from a real miser; a stage character must be heard, even though in real life the character might speak inaudibly.

Staging that aims at delusion or a high degree of illusion is **representational** staging. Here the stage characters eat real food on stage, speak with their backs to the audience, and so on. (See *naturalism, realism.*) When David Belasco staged *The Governor's Lady* in 1912, he was representational, placing on the stage an exact duplicate of a particular (Child's) restaurant. On the other hand, **presentational** staging is antirealistic; in Thornton Wilder's *Our Town* (1938), a drugstore counter, for example, consisted of a board across the backs of two chairs. The staging in musical comedies, ballets, and puppet shows is, of course, presentational. Presentational staging is sometimes called **theatrical** staging. **Theatricalism,** by its unreality, continually reminds us that we are in the theater, not in the street. On theatricalism, see *style.* A derogatory way of saying a work is theatrical is to say it is "**stagy.**"

dramatic irony. See *irony.*

dramatist. See *drama.*

dramaturgy. See *drama.*

drame. A solemn but untragic play, especially an eighteenth-century play that, quietly glorifying the bourgeois virtues, preaches and appeals to the audience's emotions. See *bourgeois drama.* Consult Alan R. Thompson, *The Anatomy of Drama,* which classifies most naturalistic and realistic plays (e.g., Ibsen's and Chekhov's) as *drames.*

eiron. See *character.*

Elizabethan playhouse. See pages 143–45.

empathy. The projection of one's feelings into a perceived object. The Germans call it *Einfühling*—"a feeling into." Vernon Lee, one of the formulators of the idea, claimed that when we say "the mountain rises" we do so not because the mountain rises (it doesn't) but because we have often raised our eyes, head, and total muscular structure to look at mountains or other tall objects. In perceiving a mountain, we merge (unawares) its image with the previously accumulated idea of rising. We are said to empathize with a character if we flinch at a blow directed at him, or if we feel bowed with his grief—if, in short, we *experience* as well as *see* his behavior. Empathy is often distinguished from **sympathy:** we empathize if we feel *with* the character; we sympathize if we feel *for* the character. See *aesthetic distance.* Consult Vernon Lee's essay in *A Modern Book of Aesthetics,* ed. Melvin Rader; and Herbert S. Langfield, *The Aesthetic Attitude.*

epic drama. Bertolt Brecht (1898–1956) labeled "Aristotelian" most drama before his own. He held that it aimed at enthralling the spectators by building up to a climax, thus arousing and then purging their emotions. In contrast, Brecht said, epic drama (he borrowed the phrase from Erwin Piscator) aims at arousing the audience's detached thought; it teaches, keeping the spectators alert by preventing any emotional involvement. The epic drama (probably so-called because it resembles the epic in its abundance of loosely connected scenes and its tendency to deal with a society rather than merely with a few individuals) achieves this estrangement, or **alienation effect** (German: ***Verfremdungseffekt***), by many means: the epic play (e.g., Brecht's *The Good Woman of Setzuan,* or his *Mother Courage*) commonly consists of a series of loosely connected scenes rather than a tightly organized plot with a climax; the settings are not realistic but merely suggest the locale, and they are often changed in full view of the audience, preventing any entrancing illusion (a night scene may be done on an illuminated stage, again to prevent the audience from emotionally entering into the play); the actor may address the audience directly, sometimes in song, aiming not at becoming the character but to present the character, or, to put it differently, to make a comment on the character, as we might do when we put aside a cigarette and say, "He said to me, ' . . . ' "; loudspeakers, films, and placards may be used; and the whole is something of a lecture-demonstration, aimed not at arousing and then quieting the audience's emotions but at making things somewhat strange to the audience so that the audience will look sharply and will think (see page 459). Consult Bertolt Brecht, "A Short Organum," in *Playwrights on Playwriting,* ed. Toby Cole; *Brecht on Theatre,* trans. John Willett; R. Gray "Brecht," *The Tulane Drama Review,* 6 (Sept. 1961).

epilogue. (1) An appendix (usually a concluding address) to a play; (2) the actor who recites such an appendix (e.g., Puck, at the close of Shakespeare's *A Midsummer Night's Dream*).

exposition. See *plot.*

expressionism. An antinaturalistic movement chiefly associated with Germany just after World War I. It was foreshadowed by Strindberg, notably in his trilogy *To Damascus* (1898–1904) and in his *A Dream Play* (1902). Expressionism does not seek to "hold the mirror up to nature" (Hamlet's words) or to present reality dispassionately; rather, it seeks to show the world as we feel (rather than literally see) it. Thus, when Mr. Zero shakes his employer (in Elmer Rice's *The Adding Machine* [1923]), the office spins; when he is on trial, the walls of the courtroom veer crazily. In other words, the dramatist makes visible the symbolic, subjective experience of the characters (or of the dramatist) by distorting objective or literal reality. Speaking broadly, expressionist plays (in addition to being unrealistic) usually (1) depict types or classes (Rice's Mr. Zero; the Man, the Woman, the Nameless One in Ernst Toller's *Man and Masses* [1921]), (2) employ dream sequences and (3) assume that society is responsible for our troubles. Though Arthur Miller's *Death of a Salesman* (see p. 550) is in many ways "realistic," it also is indebted to expressionism, especially in the scenes involving Willy's memories. (Miller originally planned to call the play *The Inside of His Head.*) Note, too, the name of Miller's hero—Loman, i.e., low man. Tennessee Williams's *The Glass Menagerie* (see p. 517) similarly reveals a modified—one might say Americanized—expressionism. Consult John Willett, *Expressionism.*

falling action. See *plot.*

farce. A sort of comedy based not on clever language or subtleties of character but on broadly humorous situations (a man mistakenly enters the ladies' locker room). Farce is lucidly defended by Eric Bentley in his introduction to *"Let's Get a Divorce" and Other Plays,* where he suggests that farce, like dreams, shows "the disguised fulfillment of repressed wishes." Farce is usually filled with surprise, with swift physical action, and with assault. The characters are physically and intellectually insensitive, and characterization is subordinated to plot. See also Bentley's *The Life of the Drama.* **Slapstick,** named for an implement made of two slats that resound when slapped against a posterior, is farce that relies on physical assault. Farce and slapstick are **low comedy,** as is comedy that depends on obscenity.

feminist theater. A movement that seeks to expand the opportunities for women in the theater and to heighten the public's awareness of women, especially by concentrating on female experience. See H. Keysaar, *Feminist Theatre.*

foil. A character who sets off another, as Laertes and Fortinbras—young men who, like Hamlet, have lost a father—help to set off Hamlet, or as a braggart soldier helps to set off a courageous one.

foreshadowing. See *suspense.*

Great Dionysia. See *Dionysus.*

Greek theater. See A Note on the Greek Theater, page 44.

groundlings. See A Note on the Elizabethan Theater, page 143.

guerilla theater. Dramatic performances, especially in the 1960s, seeking to help the populace to throw off what was said to be an oppressive bourgeois government. Theater was viewed not as a means of producing beauty or of exploring ideas but as a weapon in a class war. Performances were given in such places as streets, fields, and gymnasiums rather than in conventional theaters. Thus, the traditional separation of players from audience was broken down; moreover, the audience itself might be in some degree assaulted, for instance by obscenities or by the spectacle of nudity, offered in an effort to shock the spectators into an awareness of new ideals. Further, "performance" and "drama" were loosely interpreted. For example, Luis Valdez, founder of El Teatro Campesino (1965) in *Actos* wrote, "A demonstration with a thousand Chicanos, all carrying flags and picket signs, shouting 'Chicano Power!' is . . . theater." Consult Henry Lesnik, ed., *Guerilla Street Theatre,* and (especially for El Teatro Campesino) C. W. E. Bigsby, *A Critical Introduction to Twentieth-Century American Drama,* vol. 3.

hamartia. A Greek word variously translated as "tragic flaw" or "error" or "shortcoming" or "weakness." In many plays it is a flaw or even a vice such as ***hybris*** (also ***hubris***) —a word that in classical Greek meant bullying, or even assault and battery, but that in discussions of tragedy means overweening pride, arrogance, excessive confidence. But in other plays it is merely a misstep, such as a choice that turns out badly. Indeed, the tragic hero may be undone by his virtue—his courage, for example, when others are not merely prudent but cowardly. See pages 29–30. On *hamartia* and *hybris* see Richmond Lattimore, *Story Patterns in Greek Tragedy.*

Hellenistic theater. Theaters of, say, the third and second centuries B.C. erected in towns to which Greek culture had been spread by Alexander's conquests seem to have been much like the Greek theater, though the *proskenion* was apparently more highly decorated, having pillars a few feet in front of it and being fitted with painted panels called *pinakes.* And the *skene,* now of stone rather than of wood, may have had projections at the sides (*paraskenia*) and an upper story (*episkenion*). The playing area on this upper level is the *logeion.* Consult Margarete Bieber *The History of the Greek and Roman Theater.*

hero, heroine. The protagonist in a drama. Until the rise of middle-class drama in the late eighteenth century, heroes were usually persons of high rank (King Oedipus, King Lear) and therefore of political power. Heroines too were sometimes politically powerful (Clytemnestra, in Aeschylus's *Agamemnon*) but more often their power was moral (Desdemona, in Shakespeare's *Othello*). When heroines have exerted physical power they have often been regarded—at least by men—as wicked. See T. H. Henn, "The Woman's Part," in Henn's *The Harvest of Tragedy.*

high comedy. Intellectual rather than physical, a type of comedy that requires the close attention of a sophisticated audience, flourishing (says George Meredith in his *Essay on Comedy* [1877]) in a "society of cultivated men and women . . . wherein ideas are current, and the perceptions quick." Etherege, Wycherley, Congreve, and other playwrights of the decades following the Restoration of Charles II to the throne of England (1660) wrote **Restoration comedy,** high comedy of a particular sort, often called **comedy of manners** or **comedy of wit.** Their plays abound in witty **repartee** (what Dr. Johnson called "gay remarks and unexpected answers") and often strike modern audiences as cynical. Restoration comedy has no precise terminal date, but can be said to have ended about 1700, with the development of sentimental comedy, plays of venerable parents and middle-class dutiful sons who love pure young things. Example: Richard Steele's *The Conscious Lovers* (1722). Consult Thomas H. Fujimura, *The Restoration Comedy of Wit;* Louis Kronenberger, *The Thread of Laughter;* Norman N. Holland, *The First Modern Comedies.*

humor character. See *comedy of humors.*

hubris (***hybris***). See *hamartia.*

imitation (Greek: *mimesis*). Not a pejorative term in much criticism, for it often implies a "making" or "re-creating" or "representing" of a form in a substance not natural to it. Thus Michelangelo reproduced or imitated the form of Moses, in stone. For Aristotle, tragedy was the imitation (i.e., representation, re-creation) by means of words, gesture, music, and scenery, of an important action.

irony. Irony is of several sorts. **Socratic irony,** named for Socrates, who commonly feigned more ignorance than he possessed, denotes understatement. The ***eiron*** (see *character*) is the cunning fellow who plays the underdog. **Dramatic irony,** or **Sophoclean irony,** or **tragic irony** refers to a condition of affairs that is the tragic reverse of what the participants think. Thus, it is ironic that Macbeth kills Duncan, thinking he will achieve happiness; he later finds he loses all that makes life worth living. Oedipus accuses the blind prophet of corruption, but by the end of the play Oedipus learns (as the audience knew at the outset) that he himself is corrupt, that he has been mentally blind (ignorant) and that the prophet has had vision (knowledge). Oedipus meant what he said, but his words have proved to be ironic. (Aristotle's word for reversal is *peripeteia.*) We have dramatic irony, it can be said, when a speech or action is more fully understood by the spectators than by the characters. This sort of irony, based on misunderstanding, or partial knowledge, is common in tragedy, but comedy too has its misunderstandings; comic speeches or actions are ironic if they bring about the opposite of what is intended. More generally, the contrast implied in irony need be neither tragic nor comic; it is ironic that the strong man is overthrown by the weak man and that the liar unknowingly tells the truth. **Irony of fate** (a phrase that H. W. Fowler's *Modern English Usage* aptly says is hackneyed), or **cosmic irony,** denotes the view that God, or fate, or some sort of supernatural figure, is amused to manipulate human beings as a puppeteer manipulates his puppets. Thus, by an irony of fate the messenger delivers the prisoner's pardon an instant too late. Consult Garnett G. Sedgewick, *Of Irony,* and Alan R. Thompson, *The Dry Mock.*

koryphaios. See *chorus.*

kothurnus. See *sock and buskin.*

lazzo. See *commedia dell'arte.*

Lenaea. See A Note on the Greek Theater, page 44.

liturgical drama. A play that is part of the church service or liturgy. In the tenth century the churchmen put on a playlet of a few lines as part of the Easter liturgy. The text was based on Mark 16:1–7: clerics dressed as the Three Marys approached the "tomb" of Christ (the altar) and were asked by a cleric, disguised as an angel, whom they sought. When they replied that they sought Christ, he told them that Christ had risen and showed them the empty "tomb." The performers were all male, and the dialogue (in Latin) was chanted or sung; probably the gestures were stylized.

low comedy. See *farce.*

masque, mask, disguising. An entertainment (apparently derived from an ancient ritual) in the Renaissance court, wherein noblemen performed a dignified playlet, usually allegorical and mythological. The masque was lavishly produced, but its basic structure was generally simple: the masquers (costumed and masked noble performers) entered, supposedly having come from afar, they danced with the ladies of the court, and then they departed. Because the masquers were of the same rank as the ladies, and because performers and audience joined in a dance, the masque was very close to the masked ball. Ben Jonson (1572–1637) popularized what he called the **antimasque** (a grotesque dance of monsters or clowns), performed by professionals representing chaos, who were dispelled by the courtly performers. (*Anti,* from *antic,* meaning "a grotesque caper" or "a fool," is sometimes written *ante* because the antimasque precedes the masque.) Consult Enid Welsford, *The Court Masque,* and E. K. Chambers, *The Mediaeval Stage* and *The Elizabethan Stage.*

melodrama. Originally, in Renaissance Italy, an opera; later, a drama with occasional songs, or with music (*melos* is Greek for "song") expressing a character's thoughts, much as in films today. In the early nineteenth century plays with musical accompaniment became so stereotyped that the word acquired a second (and now dominant) meaning: a play wherein characters clearly virtuous or vicious are pitted against each other in sensational situations filled with suspense, until justice triumphs. The situations, not the characters, are exciting. The exotic horror (castles and dungeons) dominant in early nineteenth-century melodramas was often replaced later in the century by local horror (the cruel landlord), but whether exotic or local, melodrama is improbable. and virtue—unsullied by any touch of guilt—triumphs over unlikely circumstances. Melodrama is sometimes said to be tragedy with character left out (i.e., it contains serious happenings), but by virtue of its happy ending and its one-sided characters it can better be described as comedy with good-humor left out. Some critics use *melodrama* without any pejorative connotation to describe such serious, often sensational, plays as Emlyn Williams's *Night Must Fall* (1935). Robert Ardrey's *Thunder Rock* (1939), and Arthur Miller's *All My Sons.* Consult Robert B. Heilman, *Tragedy and Melodrama.*

miracle play, mystery play. Interchangeable terms for a medieval play on a biblical episode or a saint's life. The term *mystery play* derives from the French *métier* ("work," "occupation," "ministry") from the Latin *ministerium* ("attendant," "servant"). The plays were sponsored by *mysteries,* i.e., trades or guilds. Consult Arnold Williams, *The Drama of Medieval England.*

monologue. See *soliloquy.*

morality play. A late medieval development, popular well into the sixteenth century, allegorically dramatizing some aspect of the moral life, including such characters as Everyman, Good Deeds, and Avarice. It usually showed the conflict between good and evil, or the way in which the Christian faces death. Consult Arnold Williams, *The Drama of Medieval England;* Bernard Spivack, *Shakespeare and the Allegory of Evil;* and R. Potter, *The English Morality Play.*

motivation. Grounds in character and situation that make behavior plausible. Such grounds are not always present, even in great drama: when Othello asks why Iago "hath thus ensnared my soul," Iago replies, "Demand me nothing: what you know, you know." See *character.* Consult J. I. M. Stewart, *Character and Motive in Shakespeare.*

naturalism. Sometimes defined, like realism, as the portrayal of "a scientifically accurate, detached picture of life, including everything and selecting nothing." The spectators looking through the peephole of the proscenium, as a scientist looks through the eyepiece of a microscope, are to feel they are witnessing life rather than a symbolic representation of life. More commonly, however, naturalism alludes neither to a panoramic view nor to the detailed presentation of a narrow **slice of life** (French: *tranche de vie*) but to a particular attitude held by some writers since the middle of the nineteenth century. Though claiming to be dispassionate observers, they were influenced by evolutionary thought and regarded humans not as possessed of a soul and of free will but as creatures determined by their heredity and environment. The movement in drama can be said to have begun with the Goncourt Brothers' unsuccessful *Henriette Maréchal* (1865), but it is usual to say that the opening gun in the battle for naturalism was fired in Émile Zola's dramatization (1873) of his novel *Thérèse Raquin.* Thérèse and her lover drown her husband but are then so guilt-ridden that they poison themselves. In his preface Zola urged that the theater be brought "into closer relation with the great movement toward truth and experimental science which has since the last century been on the increase. . . . I have chosen characters who were completely dominated by their nerves and blood." In Paris, André Antoine opened his Théâtre Libre in 1887, devoting it mostly to plays showing the power of instincts and the influence of heredity and environment. These plays were staged as untheatrically as possible; for example, the actors turned their backs to the audience. In Germany, Otto Brahm opened the Freie Bühne in 1889, and in England J. T. Grein opened the Independent Theatre in 1891, both with Ibsen's *Ghosts* (1881), a play showing the destruction of a young man by inherited syphilis. Ibsen's greatness does not allow him to be pinned down by the label "naturalist," but he can be said to be naturalistic (among other things) by virtue of his serious interests in the effects of heredity and environment. Other dramatists who wrote naturalistic plays include August Strindberg (e.g., his *Miss Julie* [1888]) and Gerhart Hauptmann (early in his career, say, through *The Weavers* [1892]), and Eugene O'Neill (again, the early plays such as *The Rope,* [1918] and *Diff'rent* [1920]). Note, however, that the major naturalistic writers usually are more than naturalistic; Strindberg's *Miss Julie,* for example, has a preface that talks about the influence of heredity and environment, and it deals with sordid aspects of reality, but it also has symbolic overtones, notably in Julie's and Jean's dreams. Consult Mordecai Gorelik, *New Theatres for Old; TDR: The Drama Review* 13 (Winter 1968); and (for Strindberg, O'Neill, and the sources of their ideas) Oscar Cargill, *Intellectual America.*

nuntius. See *Senecan tragedy.*

obligatory scene. See *scène à faire.*

optique du théâtre. See *dramatic illusion.*

orchestra. See A Note on the Greek Theater, page 44.

pathos. The quality that evokes pity. The pathetic is often distinguished from the tragic; in the former, the suffering is experienced by the passive and the innocent (especially women and children), while in the latter it is experienced by persons who act, struggle, and are in some measure responsible for their sufferings. Discussing Aeschylus's *The Suppliants,* H. D. F. Kitto says in *Greek Tragedy* (2nd ed.): "The Suppliants are not only pathetic, as the victims of outrage, but also tragic, as the victims of their own misconceptions." See *bourgeois drama.*

performance theater. A movement in the 1960s and early 1970s especially associated with Julian Beck, a cofounder of the Living Theatre. Influenced by Antonin Artaud's **theater of cruelty,** performance theater rejected the gap between performers and spectators (performers moving on stage, spectators impassively sitting in the dark); it therefore necessarily minimized the role of the playwright and gave the actors freedom to improvise. Verbal and visual assaults (for instance nudity) on the audience, as well as physical contact with it, supposedly gave actor and spectator freedom to celebrate bodily and spiritual unity and liberation. Consult Julian Beck, *The Life of the Theatre,* and for a critical and historical survey, see part 2 of the third volume of C. W. E. Bigsby, *A Critical Introduction to Twentieth-Century American Drama.*

peripeteia (anglicized to **peripety,** meaning reversal). The reversal occurs when an action produces the opposite of what was intended or expected, and it is therefore a kind of irony. In *Julius Caesar,* Brutus kills Caesar in order to free Rome from tyranny, but the deed introduces tyranny into Rome. See *irony, plot.*

picture-frame stage. See *proscenium stage.*

pièce à thèse. A play with a thesis, a play in which the dramatist argues a point. Commonly the thesis is not about, say, the benevolence of God, but about the merits or defects of some social institution; a play dealing with a social institution may also be called a **problem play** or a **drama of ideas.** Some critics distinguish between the terms, saying that a problem play merely poses a social problem, as Galsworthy does in *Strife* (1909), while a thesis play propounds a solution. Shaw says that "the material of the dramatist is always some conflict of human feeling with circumstances"; when the circumstances are "human institutions" (e.g., divorce laws, penal codes) rather than unchanging facts of life (e.g., death) and the audience is forced to meditate on the value of the institutions, we have a problem play. Shaw's essay, "The Problem Play," is reprinted in *Shaw on Theatre,* ed. E. J. West, a volume that also contains Shaw's "The Play of Ideas." Consult also Walter Kerr, *How Not to Write a Play,* Ch. 5.

pièce bien faite, or **well-made play.** Of course all good plays are "well-made," but the term has come to mean a play with much suspense and with little depth of characterization, that relies on a cleverly constructed plot, first developing a situation, then building the crisis to a climax, and then resolving the business. The type, which perhaps can be described as melodrama with the fisticuffs left out, is chiefly associated with Victorien Sardou (1831–1908), but Sardou was indebted to Eugène Scribe (1791–1861), who indeed coined the term *pièce bien faite* in describing his farces and melodramas. Shaw called their plays clockwork mice, and Sardoodledom, but the influence of Sardou on Shaw's hero, Ibsen, is undeniable. See *plot,* and consult Walter Kerr, *How Not to Write a Play,* Ch. 10; Eric Bentley, "Homage to Scribe," *What Is Theatre?;* C. E. Montague, *Dramatic Values,* pp. 63–74; *Camille and Other Plays,* ed. Stephen S. Stanton.

plot and **character.** The plot is sometimes the "story," the "narrative," but usually it is the happenings *as the author arranges them.* In *Hamlet,* for example, the story involves the poisoning of Hamlet's father, but Shakespeare omits this scene from his plot. Aristotle, in Chapter 6 of the *Poetics,* calls plot "the whole structure of the incidents," and he speaks of plot as the "soul of tragedy," thus making it more important than character. By *character* he means the personalities of the figures in the story. Menander (a Greek comic dramatist) is said to have told a friend that he had finished a comedy, though he had not yet written a line of dialogue; the anecdote implies that Menander had completed his idea of *what happens* (action) and in *what order* (plot), and he would find it easy then to write the lines of the characters necessary to his plot. The separation, however, between plot and character is misleading, for the two usually interplay. Although it is true that there may be much plot and little character (as in a thriller), in most great plays there is such a fusion between what is done and the personality of the doer that we feel the truth of Henry James's questions: "What is character but the determination of incident? What is incident but the illustration of character?" (See *also character.*)

Most plots entail a **conflict,** wherein the protagonist is somehow opposed. If the protagonist is opposed chiefly by another person rather than by a force such as Fate or God or by an aspect of himself or herself, the opposing figure is the **antagonist.** The German critic Gustav Freytag, in *Technique of the Drama* (1863), held that a play dramatizes "the rushing forth of will power from the depths of man's soul toward the external world" and "the coming into being of a deed and its consequences on the human soul." The five-act play, he said, commonly arranged such an action into a **pyramidal structure,** consisting of a **rising action,** a **climax,** and **falling action** (In Peter de Vries's witty formulation, a plot has a beginning, a muddle, and an end.) The rising action begins with the **exposition,** in which is given essential information, especially about the **antecedent action** (what has occurred before this piece of action begins). The two gossiping servants who tell each other that after a year away in Paris the young master is coming home today with his new wife are giving the audience the exposition. The action rises through a **complication** (the protagonist is opposed) to a high point or **crisis** or **climax** (a moment at which tension is high, and which is a decisive turning point). The falling action goes through a **reversal** (if a tragedy, the protagonist loses power), and then into a **catastrophe,** also called a **denouement** (unknotting) or resolution. (Aristotle's word for the reversal is ***peripeteia,*** anglicized to **peripety,** and, translated as "irony of events," would in a comedy be a change from bad fortune to good, and the catastrophe would thus be happy.) The denouement frequently involves what Aristotle called an ***anagnorisis*** (**recognition, disclosure, discovery**). This recognition may be as simple as the identification of a long-lost brother by a birth mark, or it may involve a character's recognition of his own true condition. Shakespeare sometimes used a pyramidal structure, placing his climax neatly in the middle of what seems to us to be the third of five acts. In *Julius Caesar,* Brutus rises in the first half of the play, reaching his height in 3.1, with the death of Caesar; but later in this scene he gives Marc Antony permission to speak at Caesar's funeral and thus sets in motion his own fall, which occupies the second half of the play. In *Macbeth,* the protagonist attains his height in 3.1 ("Thou hast it now: King"), but he soon perceives that he is going downhill:

> I am in blood
> Stepped in so far that, should I wade no more,
> Returning were as tedious as go o'er.

Some works have a **double plot,** that is, two plots, usually with some sort of relation. For example, the **subplot** or **underplot** (the secondary narrative) might be a grotesque version of the serious main plot. In Shakespeare's *The Tempest,* the main plot and subplot both deal with usurpation. In *King Lear,* the main plot concerns Lear's relation to his daughters, while the parallel subplot concerns Gloucester's relation to his sons. For another aspect of the subplot see *comic relief.* Consult William Empson, *Some Versions of Pastoral,* Ch. 2. On plotting see *pièce bien faite* and *scène à faire.*

poetic justice. A term coined by Thomas Rymer in 1678, denoting the reward of the virtuous and the punishment of the vicious. Aristotle had said or implied that the tragic hero is undone partly by some sort of personal flaw—i.e., he is at least partly responsible for the suffering he later encounters. (See *hamartia* and pp. 29–30). Poetic justice, with its idea that all characters reap the harvest of their just deserts, is a hardening of Aristotle's suggestion. Consult M. A. Quinlan, *Poetic Justice in the Drama.*

poor theater. A term associated with the Polish director Jerzy Grotowski (b. 1933). Unlike the "rich" theater, which uses elaborate lighting, scenery, and costumes, the poor theater rejects technology and concentrates on the involvement of actor and audience in "a living collaboration." The actors' faces are the only "masks," and their voices are the only "sound effects." Gestures, at least in moments of strong emotion, tend to be stylized rather than naturalistic. See J. Grotowski, *Towards a Poor Theatre.*

presentational theater. A type of theater in which there is little or no illusionism in the acting and staging (as opposed to realistic or naturalistic or representational theater). Communication is achieved by means of evident conventions, such as direct address to the audience (which acknowledges the existence of the audience), the soliloquy, and the aside. Similarly, a voyage in a boat may be indicated by pantomiming the motion of rowing. Virtually all drama before the middle of the nineteenth century was highly presentational, if only because of the inability to produce illusionistic lighting effects. But a largely presentational theater, such as Shakespeare's (where, on the open-air stage, a night scene might be indicated in daylight by the presence of characters holding torches), also might aim at realism. For instance, in Shakespeare's *The Tempest* a stage direction specifies that the sailors are "wet." On the other hand, even highly illusionistic sets of the later nineteenth century also employ conventions; for instance, the audience agrees to pretend that there is a fourth wall for the living room it sees exposed on the stage. On one form of twentieth-century presentational theater, see *expressionism.*

problem play. See *pièce à thèse.*

prologue. (1) A preface or introduction. For the Greeks the *prologos* was the first scene, which gave the exposition. Elizabethan prologues commonly summarize the plot, as the Chorus does in the prologue to *Romeo and Juliet,* but in the English theater of the late seventeenth century, the prologue was almost an independent verse essay spoken before the play began. (2) The actor who speaks a piece of the sort described above.

properties, props. Objects used on the stage, other than scenery and costumes. Examples: umbrellas, books, food.

proscenium stage, or **picture-frame stage.** A playing-area framed in the front, and thus separated from the audience. This frame is the *proscenium arch* or the *proscenium;* the empty space it contains, sometimes filled with a curtain, is the *proscenium opening.* Basically a proscenium theater has two rooms, one for the audience and another (with a hole in the mutual wall) for the performers. Such a theater is at least as old as the early seventeenth century, when the Farnese Theater was built in Parma. Consult Allardyce Nicoll, *The Development of the Theatre.*

protagonist. The chief figure in a play. In Greek, the word means literally the "first contender," i.e., the chief actor (*protos:* first). The second role was given to the **deuteragonist,** the third to the **tritagonist.** The protagonist is commonly opposed by the **antagonist**, played by the deuteragonist. For the relationship between the protagonist and the antagonist, see *plot.*

psychical distance. See *aesthetic distance.*

pyramidal structure. See *plot.*

raisonneur. See *chorus.*

realism. The reproduction of life, especially as it appears to the eye and ear; the illusion of nature. Usually it deals with ordinary people in ordinary situations, moving in scenery that closely imitates reality. In England, T. W. Robertson (1829–71) insisted, for example, that doorknobs not be painted on the doors but be three-dimensional. Wings and a backcloth (i.e., projecting flats at the sides and a painted cloth at the rear) were increasingly replaced by the box set (a room with the front wall missing, containing real furniture) for interior scenes. Gas lighting, introduced to the stage about 1820, soon became capable of producing effects of sunlight, moonlight, and so on. The dialogue, as well as the sets, came closer to what the senses perceive. Realistic plays (in prose, of course) avoid soliloquies, asides, and declamation. (On the other hand, realism makes use of its conventions. See the entry on *convention.*) The great playwrights of the movement are Ibsen and Chekhov. As Mary McCarthy says of American realistic drama (*On the Contrary*), "realism is a depreciation of the real," for in "its resolve to tell the whole truth" it tends to deflate, to reveal human littleness. (It doesn't believe in exceptional, heroic people; when it treats the upper classes, it usually tends toward satire.) The oppressive box set of realistic plays, Miss McCarthy points out, "is the box or 'coffin' of average middle-class life opened at one end to reveal the corpse within." That realism shades into naturalism is clear; that in Ibsen it shades into symbolism is less obvious but is well demonstrated by John Northam, *Ibsen's Dramatic Method.* A simple example of Ibsen's symbolism: In *Hedda Gabler,* Hedda's hair is "not particularly ample," but Thea's is "unusually rich and wavy," suggesting Hedda's barrenness and Thea's fertility. Consult Mordecai Gorelik, *New Theatres for Old;* A. Nicholas Vardac, *Stage to Screen,* Chs. 4, 9; and Ernest B. Watson, *Sheridan to Robertson.* In **selective realism,** some of the scenery (e.g., a window and a door) closely reproduce reality, but some (e.g., a framework *suggesting* a roof) does not.

recognition. See *anagnorisis.*

repartee. See *high comedy.*

Restoration comedy. See *high comedy.*

revenge play. See *Senecan tragedy.*

reversal. See *peripeteia.*

rising action. See *plot.*

Roman theater. A permanent theater was not built at Rome until the first century B.C. The plays of Plautus (254?–184 B.C.) and Terence (190?–159? B.C.) were performed on temporary stages erected in the Circus Maximus and the Forum during holidays. In the permanent Roman theater, the enormous audience (40,000 or more) sat in a semicircle around a level space that was a vestige of what had been called the *orchestra* ("dancing place") of the Greek theater. Behind this vestige was the stage, running through what would have been the diameter of the circle. The long, slightly elevated stage was backed by a façade (painted to resemble two or three houses) with several doors through which actors made some of their exits and entrances, the others being made at the ends of the stage. Behind the façade was the dressing-room. The Roman theater, unlike the Greek and Hellenistic theaters, was a self-enclosed structure, built on level ground, not against a hillside. Consult Margarete Bieber, *The History of the Greek and Roman Theater.*

satire. A work ridiculing aspects of human behavior and seeking to arouse in the audience contempt for its object. Satirists almost always justify their attacks by claiming that satire is therapeutic. Shaw says, in the preface to his *Complete Plays,* "If I make you laugh at yourself remember that my business as a classic writer of comedies is to 'chasten morals with ridicule'; and if I sometimes make you feel like a fool, remember that I have by the same action cured your folly." Satire, however, is sometimes distinguished from comedy on the grounds that satire aims to correct by ridiculing, while comedy aims simply to evoke amusement. Among notable satires are the plays of Aristophanes; Gay's *The Beggar's Opera* (1728); Brecht's *The Threepenny Opera* (1928); and Kaufman, Ryskind, and Gershwin's *Of Thee I Sing* (1931)—though Kaufman himself has defined satire as "that which closes on Saturday night." See *burlesque, comedy.* Consult Northrop Frye, *Anatomy of Criticism.*

satyr-play. A piece in which there is a chorus of lewd satyrs (creatures half-man, the other half either horse or goat). The Greek tragic playwrights of the fifth century B.C. presented three tragedies and a satyr-play for the dramatic festival. Apparently the satyr-play often burlesqued a hero, showing him in a ludicrous situation. Only one complete satyr-play (Euripides' *The Cyclops*) is extant; it travesties the legend of Odysseus's encounter with Polyphemus. Consult Philip W. Harsh, *A Handbook of Classical Drama.*

scenario. See *commedia dell'arte.*

scene. See *act.*

scène à faire, or (in William Archer's translation of Francisque Sarcey's term) **obligatory scene.** "An obligatory scene [Archer says] is one which the audience (more or less clearly and consciously) foresees and desires, and the absence of which it may with reason resent." For example, a familiar legend may make a scene obligatory, or a dramatist may cause the audience to expect a certain scene. In Hamlet the play-within-the-play (3.2) has been called such a scene: Hamlet has doubted the ghost, and we must see the ghost's words verified. But most often an obligatory scene is an expected critical confrontation in which information previously hidden from a character or from the audience is revealed. Consult William Archer, *Play-making.*

scenery. The carpentry and painted cloths (and projected images) used on a stage. Scenery may be used to conceal parts of the stage, to decorate, to imitate or suggest locales, to establish time, or to evoke mood. For comments on early scenery, see A Note on the Greek Theater, page 44, and A Note on the Elizabethan Theater, page 143. The Elizabethan public theater did not use much scenery. In *Twelfth Night,* when Viola asks, "What country, friends, is this?" she is told, "This is Illyria, lady," and the audience knows all that carpenters and painters can tell them. But even before Shakespeare's birth, Renaissance Italians had placed buildings, probably of lath and cloth, at the right and left of the stage. Behind the buildings, which were three-dimensional and embellished with moldings, projected flat pieces cut and painted to look like other buildings at a distance, and behind these flat pieces were yet other flats, still smaller.

selective realism. See *realism.*

Senecan tragedy. Any of the serious plays by the Roman author Seneca (4 B.C.–65 A.D.), or imitations of them. Of the ten extant Roman tragedies, nine are attributed to Seneca, and these were probably written not for the stage but for private readings. The heroes seem to us to be almost madmen, but perhaps they are to be regarded sympathetically as people overwhelmed by passion. Seneca's influence on the Elizabethan dramatists was considerable; the **revenge play,** with its ghosts and its deranged hero who seeks vengeance, doubtless would have been different had Seneca not existed. Among the signs of Seneca's influence are ghosts, revenge, deeds of horror (e.g., children stewed and served to their parents), occasional stoical speeches but a predominance of passionate speeches, use of *stichomythia* (see *dialogue*), and a ***nuntius*** (messenger) who recites in a heightened style an off-stage happening (e.g., the wounded soldier in *Macbeth,* 1.1). But, of course, not every use of any of these characteristics is necessarily attributable to Seneca's influence. And there are differences; for example, the horrors in Seneca are narrated, but in *King Lear* Gloucester is blinded on the stage. Consult F. L. Lucas, *Seneca and Elizabethan Tragedy*; Madeleine Doran, *Endeavors of Art;* and Willard Farnham, *The Medieval Heritage of Elizabethan Tragedy.* Howard Baker, *Introduction to Tragedy,* minimizes Seneca's influence.

sensibility. See sentimental.

sentimental. Generally a pejorative word in criticism, indicating a superabundance of tender emotion, a disproportionate amount of sentiment (feeling). It is sentimental to be intensely distressed because one has stepped on a flower. A character, say Hamlet, may display deep emotions, but they are sentimental only if they are in excess of what the situation warrants. More specifically, "sentimental" writing refers to writing wherein evil is facilely conquered, denied, overlooked, or bathed in a glow of forgiving tenderness. In the eighteenth century the ability to respond emotionally (usually tearfully) to acts of benevolence or malevolence was called **sensibility.** In its **sentimental drama** there is at the expense of reason an emphasis on tearful situations; people's benevolent emotions are overestimated, for they are assumed to be innately good, and villains reform, usually in bursts of repenting tears. There is little wit, the characters are usually of the middle class, and they demonstrate their virtue by weeping at the sight of distress. In his "Comparison between Sentimental and Laughing Comedy" (1772), Oliver Goldsmith attacked sentimental comedy, saying that in it

> the virtues of private life are exhibited, rather than the vices exposed; and the distresses rather than the faults of mankind make our interest in the piece.... Almost all the characters are good, ... and though they want humor, have abundance of sentiment and feeling. If they happen to have faults or foibles, the spectator is taught, not only to pardon, but to applaud them, in consideration of the goodness of their hearts; so that folly, instead of being ridiculed, is commended, and the comedy aims at touching our passions, without the power of being truly pathetic.

See *bourgeois drama.* Consult Ernest Bernbaum, *The Drama of Sensibility,* and Arthur Sherbo, *English Sentimental Drama.*

set. The scenery constructed for a theatrical performance, especially the three-dimensional environment (as opposed to two-dimensional wings) in which the characters move.

situational comedy. See *comedy of humors.*

slapstick. See *farce.*

slice of life. See *naturalism.*

sock and **buskin.** Performers of Latin comedy wore a light slipper or sandal called the *soccus.* The sock is either this piece of footwear or comedy itself. The high boot worn by Greek tragic actors was the *cothurnus* or *kothurnus.* In Hellenistic times it acquired a very thick sole, giving the performer the height appropriate to a great man. In English this footgear (or tragic drama in general) is called the buskin, apparently from Old French *broissequin,* from Middle Dutch *brosekin,* a small leather boot. Consult Margarete Bieber, *The History of the Greek and Roman Theater.*

Socratic irony. See *irony.*

soliloquy. A monologue wherein a character utters his or her thoughts aloud while alone. An **aside** is a speech wherein a character expresses his or her thoughts in words audible to the spectators but supposedly unheard by the other stage characters present. Both were important conventions in Elizabethan drama and, later, in melodrama, but the late nineteenth century sought so vigorously to present on the stage the illusion of real life that both techniques were banished. They have, however, been revived in the twentieth century, as in Eugene O'Neill's *Strange Interlude,* where the asides represent the characters' thoughts and unspoken desires. In **direct address,** a character turns from the world on the stage and speaks directly to the audience, telling it, for instance, to watch closely. Consult Una Ellis-Fermor, *The Frontiers of Drama,* Ch. 6; George E. Duckworth, *The Nature of Roman Comedy;* and Max Beerbohm, "Soliloquies in Drama," *Around Theatres.* The soliloquy, the aside, and direct address are all monologues, but more often a **monologue** is either a long speech delivered by one character, which may be heard but not interrupted by others in his presence, or a performance by a single actor.

Sophoclean irony. See *irony.*

sound effect. An imitative noise, usually produced by simple machinery. Though a sound effect may be a mere imitation of nature, it may also be a richly symbolic suggestion. Chekhov's *The Cherry Orchard* (1904) concludes: "There is a far-off sound as if out of the sky, the sound of a snapped string, dying away, sad. A stillness falls, and there is only the thud of an ax on a tree, far away in the orchard." Consult Frank Napier, *Noises Off.*

spectacle. The last of Aristotle's six elements of drama, spectacle denotes what appeals to the eye, such as costume and scenery. Greek drama was splendidly costumed and made some use of scenery. Aeschylus especially seems to have contrived moments that caught the eye, such as Agamemnon's entrance in a chariot. The Elizabethan stage, though sparse in scenery, apparently was architecturally impressive, and doubtless military scenes were embellished with waving banners. In the Restoration, spectacle sometimes got the upper hand. Alexander Pope complained:

> The play stands still; damn action and discourse,
> Back fly the scenes, and enter foot and horse;
> Pageants on pageants, in long order drawn,
> Peers, heralds, bishops, ermine, gold, and lawn.

In the nineteenth century the development of gas light and then electric light made possible elaborate sunrises and twilights, and at the end of the century (especially in Russia) there was an emphasis on ensemble acting that gave a tableau effect. Pictorial effects in late-nineteenth-century productions of Shakespeare were often achieved at the cost of Shakespeare's lines. At the very end of the century William Poel rejected spectacle and helped establish a trend to stage Shakespeare in what was thought to be an Elizabethan manner: an uncluttered stage, allowing the action to proceed rapidly. Consult James Laver, *Drama,* and A. Nicholas Vardac, *Stage to Screen,* Chs. 3-4.

stage. A platform or space for theatrical performances. See *arena stage, Hellenistic theater, proscenium stage,* and *thrust stage.* See also A Note on the Elizabethan Theater, page 143, and A Note on the Greek Theater, page 44.

stage business. Minor physical action—including posture and facial expression—by a performer. Business ranges from head scratching to an addition Henry Irving made to *The Merchant of Venice,* 2.4: in Shakespeare's scene, Jessica and Lorenzo elope and the scene ends quietly; Irving added business in which Shylock entered and knocked on the door of his empty house while the curtain fell. Irving's successors amplified his business: Shylock entered the house, cried out, reappeared, and so on. Consult Arthur C. Sprague, *Shakespeare and the Actors.*

stichomythia. See *dialogue.*

stock character. See *character.*

structure. The arrangement of episodes.

style. The mode of expression. Newman, talking of the writer's style, called it "a thinking out into language." This idea of "a thinking out" (but not into language) is applicable also to the style of the scene designer, the costume designer, and so on. Kenneth Tynan in *Curtains* defines good style as "a happy consonance of manner with matter, of means with end, of tools with job." To **stylize** a play commonly means to present it with a noticeable artful manner rather than to present it realistically, though in fact realism itself is a style. A **stylized production** usually is presentational or anti-illusionistic rather than representational (see *dramatic illusion*). Consult George R. Kernodle, "Style, Stylization, and styles of Acting," *Educational Theatre Journal,* 12 (1960), 251–61.

subplot. See *plot.*

sub-text. Constantin Stanislavski's term for a text assumed to be hidden beneath the surface. Thus, Stanislavski wanted his actors to discover and communicate the character's unspoken but felt life.

surprise. See *suspense.*

surrealism. A literary movement, especially vigorous in France in the 1920s and 1930s, that insisted that reality is grasped by the unconscious, the irrational, rather than by the conscious. The best art, it is held, is the dream. Among the forerunners were Alfred Jarry, whose *Ubu Roi* (1896) combined grotesque farce with antibourgeois satire; August Strindberg, whose *To Damascus* (three parts, 1898–1904) and *The Dream Play* (1902) had presented dreamlike worlds; and Guillaume Apollinaire, whose *Breasts of Tiresias* (1917) was called a "*drame surréaliste*" (the first use of the word) by the author. Perhaps the chief surrealist dramatist is Jean Cocteau, notably in his *Orpheus* (1926), in which a glazier is an angel and a horse dictates prophetic words. Consult Georges E. Lemaître, *From Cubism to Surrealism in French Literature.*

suspense. Uncertainty, often characterized by anxiety. Suspense is usually a curious mixture of pain and pleasure, as Gwendolen, in Oscar Wilde's *The Importance of Being Earnest,* implies: "This suspense is terrible. I hope it will last." Most great art relies more heavily on suspense than on **surprise** (the unexpected). One can rarely sit twice through a play depending on surprise; the surprise gone, the interest is gone. Suspense is usually achieved in part by **foreshadowing**—hints of what is to come. Dumas *fils* put it this way: "The art of the theater is the art of preparations." Coleridge, who held that Shakespeare gives us not surprise but expectation and then the satisfaction of perfect knowledge, once wrote: "As the feeling with which we startle at a shooting star, compared with that of watching the sunrise at the pre-established moment, such and so low is surprise compared with expectation." Thus, in *Hamlet,* the ghost does not pop up surprisingly, but satisfies the eager expectations that have been aroused by references to "this thing," "this dreaded sight," and "this apparition." Often, in fact, Shakespeare—like the Greek dramatists—used traditional stories; the audience presumably was not surprised by the deaths of Caesar and Brutus, and it enjoyed the suspense of anticipating them. Suspense is thus related to tragic irony. The tragic character moves closer and closer to his doom, and though he may be surprised by it, we are not; we are held by suspense. On surprise, consult David L. Grossvogel, *The Self-Conscious Stage in Modern French Drama* (reprinted in paperback as *Twentieth-Century French Drama*).

symbolism. Derived from Greek *symballein,* "to throw together," which thus suggests the essential quality of symbolism, the drawing together of two worlds; it presents the concrete material world of roses, toads, caves, stars, and so on and through them reveals an otherwise invisible world. Thus, the storm in *King Lear* symbolizes both the disorder in Lear's kingdom (brother against brother, etc.) and also the disorder in Lear's mind. The strangled canary in Glaspell's *Trifles* symbolizes the maltreatment that Minnie Wright experienced from her husband.

Symbolism is often distinguished from **allegory.** Where the allegorist commonly invents a world (the author of *Ev-*

eryman, [c. 1500] invents a figure called Everyman, who seeks aid from figures called Goods, Kindred, etc.) in order to talk about the real world, the symbolist commonly presents the phenomena of what we usually call the real world in order to reveal a "higher," eternal world of which the symbol is a part. The allegorist is free to invent any number of imaginary worlds to talk about the real world, but the symbolist feels that there is only one way by which he or she can present the "higher" real world he or she envisions. The everyday world is often considered by symbolists as a concrete but transient version of a more important realm, and the symbolist who presents, say, a rose, is (he might hold) speaking about a rose and also about the eternal beauty of womanhood in the only possible way.

In the second half of the nineteenth century there arose in France the so-called **Symbolist Movement,** but it must be emphasized that symbolism of a sort is probably as old as literature. An author's insistence on some object may cause us to regard it as more than its apparent nature. For example, the forest or greenwood in *As You Like It* suggests a benevolent nature that restores humans to their best part. But on the whole Shakespeare's plays do not leave the world of sensible reality. The plays of the Symbolists do. The Symbolic writer presents a world that seems to be a dream world, a world that is not the usual world enriched, but a new world. In his preface to *The Dream Play* (1902), Strindberg says he "has tried to imitate the disconnected but seemingly logical form of the dream. Anything may happen.... The characters split, double, multiply, vanish, solidify, blur, clarify." A play is the expression of a "soul-state" (Stéphane Mallarmé's term) rather than an imitation of an external action. See *surrealism.*

The best naturalists (Ibsen, Chekhov, Strindberg, and Hauptmann) at times wrote symbolic works, but the chief Symbolic dramatists are the French (if we include the Belgian Maurice Maeterlinck) and William Butler Yeats. In Maeterlinck's *The Intruder* (1890) a blind old man sees with his soul the approach of Death. In *The Blind* (1896) a group of blind men are lost in a forest; their leader was a priest, but he has died. Maeterlinck occasionally said some of his plays were for marionettes, and though his statement is sometimes held to be a mildly self-deprecating joke, in fact there is much in the plays that belongs to the realm of impassive, other-worldly dolls, not surprising in the work of a writer who said he wished to study man . . . in the presence of eternity and mystery." Paul Claudel's *Tidings Brought to Mary* (written in 1892, revised in 1899 and 1912) was acted in 1912. Claudel, who said he had gained from Arthur Rimbaud (one of the leading Symbolists) "an almost physical impression of the supernatural," in this play envelops his medieval characters in a divine world, and dramatizes salvation. In Ireland, Yeats, who compared an artistic work to a magic talisman ("it entangles . . . a part of the Divine essence") wrote verse plays of Irish supernatural creatures and heroes. In *On Baile's Strand* (1903), for instance, Cuchulain, the protagonist, is said to have been sired by a hawk. The bird imagery is insisted on; Cuchalain's associates are chicks and nestlings, and the Fool (who represents Cuchulain on another level) is delighted with feathers. Near the conclusion of the play, Cuchulain rushes out to fight the waves, literally doing what Hamlet spoke metaphorically of doing.

In Russia, Meyerhold in 1906 staged Ibsen's *Hedda Gabler* (1890) as symbolically as possible, turning what had been a naturalistic play into a vision suggestive of another world, something (in the words of a hostile critic) "halfway between metaphysics and ballet." (Consult Nikolai Gorchakov, *The Theater in Soviet Russia.*) For symbolism in the sense of richly suggestive images, consult Alan S. Downer, "The Life of Our Design: the Function of Imagery in the Poetic Drama," *The Hudson Review,* 2 (Summer 1949), 242–60. On the Symbolist Movement, consult William Butler Yeats, *Essays and Introductions;* Arthur Symons, *The Symbolist Movement in Literature; Yale French Studies,* No. 9; Eric Bentley, *The Playwright as Thinker;* and John Gassner, *Form and Idea in the Modern Theatre.*

sympathy. See *empathy.*

theater-in-the-round. See *arena stage.*

theater of the absurd. See *absurd, theater of the.*

theatrical. Literally, characteristic of the theater, but often (unfortunately) used pejoratively, to suggest artificially contrived, melodramatic, implausible.

theme. The underlying idea, such as the triumph of love or the failure of idealism. A *theme* can thus be distinguished from a *thesis,* which is a message, such as "Love ought to triumph" or "Idealism is short-sighted."

three unities. See *unity.*

thrust stage. A stage that projects into the auditorium. It encourages direct address to the spectators because even a large audience can be fairly close to the actors. On the other hand, since some members of the audience will be to the side of, or even behind, the performers, there may be acoustical problems.

total theater. The idea that the theater should not try to imitate realistically an aspect of life but should embody a synthesis of all of the expressive arts—music, movement, speech, lighting, and so on. The expression total theater is probably derived from Richard Wagner's *Gesamtkunstwerk,* "united" or "total artwork. " Consult *Total Theatre,* ed. E. T. Kirby.

tragedy. For Aristotle, tragedy was a dramatic imitation (representation) of an "action of high importance." A Greek tragedy was serious, but it did not necessarily end unhappily. Aeschylus's *Eumenides,* for example, ends on a note of solemn joy. For us a tragedy is generally a play that faces evil, depicts suffering, and ends with death or (especially in the naturalistic tragedies since the latter part of the nineteenth century) ends with the hero alive but spiritually crushed. Tragedy's essence, Alfred North Whitehead says (*Science and the Modern World,* Ch. 1) resides not in unhappiness but "in the solemnity of the remorseless working of things." H. D. F. Kitto says (*The Greeks,* Ch. 4) that Greek tragedy—and perhaps one might add the great tragedy of other countries—was in part the product of intellectualism and humanism. Intellectualism let the Greeks see that human life must be lived within a great framework of what might be called the will of the gods, or Necessity: "Actions must have their consequences; ill-judged actions must have uncomfortable results." Humanism denied the Greeks an easy view of a heavenly life and gave them an "almost fierce joy in life, the exultation in human achievement and in human personality." The tragic note, Kitto suggests, is produced by a tension between this unalterable framework and this passionate delight in life. Consult R. Sewall, *The Vision of Tragedy;* T. R. Henn, *The Harvest of Tragedy;* and H. J. Muller, *The Spirit of Tragedy.*

tragic irony. See *irony.*

tragicomedy. Renaissance critical theorists, embroidering on Aristotle's *Poetics,* assumed that tragedy dealt with noble (important) figures and ended with a death; comedy dealt with trivial (laughable) figures and ended with a celebration. A tragicomedy was some sort of mixture: high characters in a play ending happily, or a mingling of deaths and feasts, or, most often (as in many American films) threats of death that are happily—and unconvincingly—evaded. John Fletcher (1579–1625), who with his collaborator Francis Beaumont wrote graceful dramas relying heavily on passionate outbursts and surprising turns of plot, defined a tragicomedy as a play that lacks deaths (and thus is no tragedy) but "brings some near it, which is enough to make it no comedy." One of the speakers in John Dryden's *Essay of Dramatick Poesie* (1668) says: "There is no theater in the world has anything so absurd as the English tragicomedy; ... here a course of mirth, there another of sadness and passion, and a third of honor and a duel: thus, in two hours and a half, we run through all the fits of Bedlam." Consult Eugene Waith, *The Pattern of Tragi-Comedy.* On what can roughly be called the bitter or ironic comedy of the nineteenth and twentieth centuries, consult K. S. Guthke, *Modern Tragicomedy;* C. Hoy, *The Hyacinth Room;* and Eric Bentley, *The Life of the Drama.*

trilogy. A unit of three works. Though Greek tragic dramatists submitted three tragedies at a time, the plays are only a trilogy if they have an internal unity. Aeschylus's *Oresteia* (458 B.C.) is the only extant complete Greek trilogy; Sophocles's three plays on the Oedipus legend—*Antigone* (c. 422 B.C.), *Oedipus the King* (c. 425), and *Oedipus at Colonus* (c. 406) are not properly a trilogy because they were written at widely separated times and do not cohere into a consistent, unified whole. A modern trilogy: O'Neill's *Mourning Becomes Electra* (1931).

tritagonist. See *protagonist.*

underplot. See *plot.*

unity. Generally means something like "coherence," "congruence"; in a unified piece the parts work together and jointly contribute to the whole. The subplot of a play may parallel the main plot, or one character may be a foil to another. In any case, unity suggests "completeness" or "pattern" resulting from a controlling intelligence. In the *Poetics,* Aristotle said that a tragedy should have a unified action, and he mentioned that most tragedies cover a period of twenty-four hours. Italian critics, making his comments rigid, in the late sixteenth century established the **Three Unities** of Time, Place, and Action: a play (1) must not cover more than twenty-four hours, (2) must be set in one locale only or, at worst, in various parts of a single city, and (3) must be either entirely tragic or entirely comic, rather than a mixture of (as Sir Philip Sidney said) "hornpipes and funerals." (Consult H. B. Charlton, *Castelvetro's Theory of Poetry.*) Actually, the time covered by Greek tragedies is vague; characters come from distant places in the space of relatively few lines. For example, in *Oedipus the King,* a shepherd who lives in the "farthest" fields from Corinth is sent for in line 863 and arrives in line 1108. Nor is unity of place invariable in Greek tragedy; there are violations of it in, for example, Aeschylus's *The Eumenides* and Sophocles's *Ajax.*

upstage. The back half of the acting area, or any part of the stage considered in relation to someone or something nearer the audience.

well-made play. See *pièce bien faite.*

ACKNOWLEDGMENTS

Edward Albee, *The Sandbox,* reprinted by permission of the Putnam Publishing Group from *The Sandbox* by Edward Albee. Copyright © 1960 by Edward Albee. *The Sandbox* is sole property of the author and is fully protected by copyright. It may not be acted either by professionals or amateurs without written consent. Public readings, radio and television broadcasts likewise are forbidden. All inquiries concerning the rights should be addressed to the William Morris Agency, 1350 Avenue of the Americas, New York, N.Y. 10019.

Aristophanes, *Lysistrata: An English Version* by Dudley Fitts, copyright 1954 by Harcourt Brace Jovanovich, Inc. and renewed 1982 by Cornelia Fitts, Daniel H. Fitts, and Deborah W. Fitts, reprinted by permission of the publisher. *CAUTION:* All rights, including professional, amateur, motion picture, recitation, lecturing, performance, public reading, radio broadcasting, and television are strictly reserved. Inquiries on all rights should be addressed to Harcourt Brace Jovanovich, Inc., Orlando, Florida 32887.

Aristotle, *The Poetics,* from *Aristotle on the Art of Fiction* by L. J. Potts, ed. Copyright © 1953 by Cambridge University Press. Reprinted with the permission of Cambridge University Press.

Peter Arnott, "The Script and the Stage" copyright © 1977 by Scott, Foresman and Company. Reprinted by permission.

Anton Chekhov, *The Cherry Orchard.* Revised translation copyright © 1985 by Laurence Senelick. Used by permission.

Samuel Beckett, *Happy Days,* copyright © 1961, 1989 by Samuel Beckett. Used by permission of Grove Press, Inc.

Bertolt Brecht, *The Good Woman of Szechuan* in *Parables for Theatre: Two Plays by Bertolt Brecht,* translated and revised by Eric Bentley. © 1947, 1948, 1956, 1961, Epilogue © 1965 by Eric Bentley.

Harvey Fierstein, *On Tidy Endings.* Reprinted with the permission of Atheneum Publishers from *Safe Sex* by Harvey Fierstein. Copyright © 1987 by Harvey Fierstein. This play may not be reprinted in whole or in part without written permission of the publishers. No performance of any kind may be given without permission in writing from the author's agent, William Morris Agency, 1350 Avenue of the Americas, New York, NY 10019.

Athol Fugard, *"MASTER HAROLD" . . . and the boys* by Athol Fugard. Copyright © 1982 by Athol Fugard. Excerpts from *Notebooks 1960–1977* by Athol Fugard. Copyright © 1983 by Athol Fugard. Play and excerpts reprinted by permission of Alfred A. Knopf, Inc.

Susan Glaspell, *Trifles,* copyright 1951 by Walter H. Baker Company. *Trifles* is the sole property of the author and is fully protected under the copyright laws of the United States, the British Empire including the Dominion of Canada, and all other countries of the Copyright Union, and are subject to royalty. The play may not be acted by professionals or amateurs without formal permission in writing and the payment of royalty. All rights, including professional, amateur, stock, radio and television broadcasting, motion picture, recitation, lecturing, public reading and the rights of translation in foreign languages are reserved. All inquiries should be directed to Baker's Plays, 100 Chauncy Street, Boston, Massachusetts 02111.

Henrik Ibsen, *A Doll's House,* in *Ghosts and Other Plays* by Henrik Ibsen, translated by Michael Meyer. Reprinted by permission of Harold Ober Associates Incorporated. Copyright © 1966 by Michael Meyer. *CAUTION:* These plays are fully protected in whole, in part, or in any form under the copyright laws of the United States of America, the British Empire including the Dominion of Canada, and all other countries of the Copyright Union, and are subject to royalty. All rights including motion picture, radio, television, recitation, public reading, are strictly reserved. For professional rights and amateur rights all inquiries should be addressed to the Author's Agent: Robert A. Freedman Dramatic Agency Inc., 1501 Broadway, New York, NY 10036. "Notes for the Tragedy of Modern Times" and "Alternate Ending for *A Doll's House*" reprinted from *Oxford Ibsen,* Volume 5, edited by J. W. Macfarlane with the permission of Oxford University Press. "Speech at the Banquet of the Norwegian League for Women's Rights" from *Ibsen: Letters and Speeches* edited by Evert Sprinchorn. Copyright © 1964 by Evert Sprinchorn. Reprinted by permission of Hill and Wang, a division of Farrar, Straus & Giroux, Inc.

Arthur Miller, *Death of a Salesman,* from *Death of a Salesman* by Arthur Miller. Copyright 1949, renewed © 1977 by Arthur Miller. Used by permission of Viking Penguin, a division of Penguin Books USA Inc. "Tragedy and the Common Man" copyright 1949 by Arthur Miller; copyright renewed © 1977 by Arthur Miller, from *The Theatre Essays of Arthur Miller* by Arthur Miller, edited by Robert A. Martin. Used by permission of Viking Penguin, a division of Penguin Books USA Inc. "Willy Loman's Ideals" [editor's title] from *Conversations with Arthur Miller,* edited by Matthew C. Roudane 1987. Reprinted by permission of the University Press of Mississippi.

Molière, *The Misanthrope,* translated by Richard Wilbur, copyright © 1955 and renewed 1983 by Richard Wilbur, reprinted by permission of Harcourt Brace Jovanovich, Inc. *CAUTION:* Professionals and amateurs are hereby warned that this translation, being fully protected under the copyright laws of the United States, the British Commonwealth, including Canada, and all other countries which are signatories to the Universal Copyright Convention, is subject to royalty. All rights, including professional, amateur, motion picture, recitation, lecturing, public reading, radio broadcasting, and television are strictly reserved. Particular emphasis is laid on the question of readings, permission for which must be secured from the author's agent in writing. Inquiries on professional rights (except for amateur rights) should be addressed to Mr. Gilbert Parker, Curtis Brown, Ltd., Ten Astor Place, New York, NY 10003. The amateur acting rights of *The Misanthrope* are controlled exclusively by the Dramatists Play Service, Inc., 440 Park Avenue South, New York, NY 10016. No amateur performance of the play may be given without obtaining in advance the written permission of the Dramatists Play Service, Inc. and paying the requisite fee. Translation rights should be addressed to Harcourt Brace Jovanovich, Inc., Permissions Department, Orlando, Florida 32887.

Marsha Norman, *'night Mother.* Copyright © 1983 by Marsha Norman. Reprinted by permission of Hill and Wang, a division of Farrar, Straus & Giroux, Inc. *CAUTION:* Professionals and amateurs are hereby warned that *'night Mother,* being fully protected under the Copyright Laws of the United States of America and all other countries of the Berne and Universal Copyright Conventions, is subject to a royalty. All rights including, but not limited to professional, amateur, motion picture, recitation, lecturing, public reading, radio and television broadcasting, video or sound taping, photocopying, all other forms of mechanical or electronic reproduction, and the rights of translation into foreign languages are expressly reserved. All inquiries concerning rights (other than stock and amateur rights) should be addressed to author's agent, William Morris Agency, attention: Samuel Liff, 1350 Avenue of the Americas, New York, NY 10019. Stock and amateur production rights are controlled exclusively by the Dramatists Play Service Inc., 440 Park Avenue South, New York, NY 10016. No amateur performance of the play may be given without obtaining in advance the written permission of the Dramatists Play Service, Inc. and paying the requisite fee. Interview with Marsha Norman from *Interviews with Contemporary Women Playwrights* by Kathleen Betsko and Rachel Koenig. Copyright © 1987 by Kathleen Betsko and Rachel Koenig. Reprinted by permission of William Morrow & Company, Inc.

Eugene O'Neill, *Desire under the Elms* from *The Plays of Eugene O'Neill* by Eugene O'Neill. Copyright © 1924 and renewed 1952 by Eugene O'Neill. Reprinted by permission of Random House, Inc. Letters written by Eugene O'Neill to George Jean Nathan, Grace Dupre Hills, Sophus Keith Winter, and Arthur Hobson Quinn are reprinted by permission of the Yale Committee on Literary Property, Yale University.

Joyce Carol Oates, *Tone Clusters,* copyright © 1991 by The Ontario Review, Inc. "Afterword" copyright © 1990, 1991 by The Ontario Review, Inc., from *Twelve Plays* by Joyce Carol Oates. Used by permission of New American Library, a division of Penguin Books USA Inc.

Luigi Pirandello, *Six Characters in Search of an Author,* copyright 1922 by E.P. Dutton. Renewed 1950 in the names of Stefano, Fausto, and Lietta Pirandello. From *Naked Masks: Five Plays* by Luigi Pirandello, edited by Eric Bentley. Translation copyright 1922, 1952 by E.P. Dutton. Renewed 1950 in the names of Stefano, Fausto, and Lietta Pirandello. Introduction copyright 1952 © renewed 1980 by Eric Bentley. Used by permission of the publisher, Dutton, an imprint of New American Library, a division of Penguin Books USA Inc.

William Shakespeare, *A Midsummer Night's Dream* by William Shakespeare from *A Midsummer Night's Dream* by William Shakespeare. Copyright © 1963, 1986 by Wolfgang Clemen. Used by permission of New American Library, a division of Penguin Books USA Inc. *The Tragedy of King Lear* by William Shakespeare from *The Tragedy of King Lear* by William Shakespeare. Copyright © 1963, renewed 1991 by Russell Fraser, introduction, annotation, compilation. Used by permission of New American Library, a division of Penguin Books USA Inc.

Bernard Shaw, *Arms and the Man,* Copyright 1898, 1913, 1926, 1931, 1933, 1941 George Bernard Shaw. Copyright 1905, Brentanos. Copyright © 1958 The Public Trustees as Executors of the Estate of George Bernard Shaw. Reprinted by permission of the Society of Authors on behalf of the Estate of Bernard Shaw.

Sophocles, *Oedipus the King* and *Antigone* from *Sophocles: Three Tragedies* translated by H. D. F. Kitto. Copyright © 1962 by Oxford University Press. Reprinted by permission of Oxford University Press.

Gertrude Stein, *The Mother of Us All,* reprinted by permission of the Estate of Gertrude Stein.

Virgil Thomson, excerpt from *Virgil Thomson* by Virgil Thomson. Copyright © 1966 by Virgil Thomson. Reprinted by permission of Alfred A. Knopf, Inc. Three letters by Virgil Thomson are reprinted from *Selected Letters of Virgil Thomson* by Virgil Thomson. Copyright © 1988 by Virgil Thomson. Reprinted by permission of Summit, a division of Simon & Schuster, Inc. "How *The Mother of Us All* Was Created" by Virgil Thomson in *The New York Times,* April 15, 1956. Copyright © 1956 by The New York Times Company. Reprinted by permission.

Luis Valdez, *Los Vendidos* and "The Actos" from *Actos.* Reprinted by permission of Arte Publico Press.

Wendy Wasserstein, "The Man in a Case" from *Orchards* by Anton Chekhov, et. al. Copyright © 1986 by Wendy Wasserstein. Reprinted by permission of Alfred A. Knopf, Inc.

Tennessee Williams, *The Glass Menagerie* from *The Glass Menagerie* by Tennessee Williams. Copyright 1945 by Tennessee Williams and Edwina D. Williams and renewed 1973 by Tennessee Williams. Reprinted by permission of Random House, Inc. "The Timeless World of the Play" from *Tennessee Williams: Where I Live.* Copyright © 1951 by Tennessee Williams. Reprinted by permission of New Directions Publishing Corporation.

August Wilson, *Fences* from *Fences* by August Wilson. Copyright © 1986 by August Wilson. Used by permission of New American Library, a division of Penguin Books USA Inc. Excerpt from August Wilson interview in *In Their Own Words: Contemporary American Playwrights* by David Savran, copyright © 1988 by David Savran. Reprinted by permission of Theatre Communications Group.